MasteringBiology®

Optimizes Learning and Maximizes Study Time for Students by

- Showing how concepts across various chapters connect to each other

- Aiding with test prep through practice quizzes, coaching with feedback specific to your needs, and providing hints when you get stuck

Chlorophyll is found in the _____ of chloroplasts.

- ☐ stroma
- ☑ thylakoid membranes
- ☐ outer membrane
- ☐ thylakoid space

Submit   Hints My Answers Give Up Review Part

Correct

This is where light absorption occurs during photosynthesis and therefore is the place where chlorophyll molecules are located.

Connecting the Concepts Activities

Link the concepts you learned and see how they work together.

MasteringBiology®

Optimizes Teaching and Maximizes Lecture Time for Educators by

- Offering a wealth of customizable, easy-to-assign activities and assessments

- **Add** your own questions and **easily edit** any of the existing questions or answers to match the language used in the course

Grading assignments

- **Shades of red highlight** vulnerable students and challenging assignments

- **Export grades** to Microsoft® Excel or other course management systems readily

Providing insight into student performance

- **Student performance data** reveals how individual and class achievement compares to a national average

- **Wrong answer summaries** give unique insight into students' misconceptions and support just-in-time teaching

Gradebook
Get easy-to-interpret insights into student performance using the **Gradebook**.
- Every assignment is **automatically graded.**
- At a glance, **shades of red** highlight vulnerable students and challenging assignments.

Student Performance Data
reveals how students are doing compared to a national average and which topics they're struggling with.

Wrong answer summaries
give unique insight into your students' misconceptions and support just-in-time teaching.

CAMPBELL
BIOLOGY
CONCEPTS & CONNECTIONS

CAMPBELL
BIOLOGY
CONCEPTS & CONNECTIONS

CANADIAN EDITION

Jane B. Reece
Berkeley, California

Martha R. Taylor
Cornell University

Eric J. Simon
New England College

Jean L. Dickey
Clemson University

Kevin G-E. Scott
University of Manitoba

PEARSON

Toronto

Vice-President, Editorial Director: Gary Bennett
Senior Acquisitions Editor: Lisa Rahn
Marketing Managers: Kim Ukrainec and Jenna Wulff
Supervising Developmental Editor: Maurice Esses
Lead Project Manager: Avinash Chandra
Project Manager: Sarah Gallagher
Program Manager: Darryl Kamo
Manufacturing Coordinator: Jane Schell
Production Editor: Roxanne Klaas
Copy Editor: Deborah Cooper-Bullock
Proofreader: Julie Lewis
Compositor: S4Carlisle Publishing Services
Photo and Permissions Researcher: Terri Rothman
Cover and Interior Designer: Anthony Leung
Cover Image: © Breene Yuen

Credits and acknowledgments for material borrowed from other sources and reproduced, with permission, in this textbook appear on pages C1–C9.

Original edition published by Pearson Education, Inc., Upper Saddle River, New Jersey, USA. Copyright © 2012 Pearson Education, Inc. This edition is authorized for sale only in Canada.

If you purchased this book outside the United States or Canada, you should be aware that it has been imported without the approval of the publisher or the author.

10 9 8 7 6 5 4 3 2 1 [CKV]

Library and Archives Canada Cataloguing in Publication

Campbell biology : concepts & connections / Jane B. Reece ... [et al.]. -- Canadian ed.
  Includes index.
  ISBN 978-0-321-77448-4
  1. Biology--Textbooks.   I. Reece, Jane B.
QH308.2.C343 2013
570
                              C2012-908453-0

PEARSON

ISBN: 978-0-32-177448-4

About the Authors

Jane B. Reece has worked in biology publishing since 1978, when she joined the editorial staff of Benjamin Cummings. Her education includes an A.B. in biology from Harvard University (where she was initially a philosophy major), an M.S. in microbiology from Rutgers University, and a Ph.D. in bacteriology from the University of California, Berkeley. At UC Berkeley and later as a postdoctoral fellow in genetics at Stanford University, her research focused on genetic recombination in bacteria. Dr. Reece taught biology at Middlesex County College (New Jersey) and Queensborough Community College (New York). During her 12 years as an editor at Benjamin Cummings, she played a major role in a number of successful textbooks. She is lead author of *Campbell Biology*, Ninth Edition, and coauthor of *Campbell Essential Biology*, Fourth Edition, and *Campbell Essential Biology with Physiology*, Third Edition.

Martha R. Taylor has been teaching biology for more than 35 years. She earned her B.A. in biology from Gettysburg College and her M.S. and Ph.D. in science education from Cornell University. She was assistant director of the Office of Instructional Support at Cornell for 7 years. Dr. Taylor has taught introductory biology for both majors and nonmajors at Cornell University and is currently a lecturer in the Learning Strategies Center teaching supplemental biology courses. Her experience working with students in classrooms, in laboratories, and with tutorials has increased her commitment to helping students create their own knowledge of and appreciation for biology. She has been the author of the *Student Study Guide* for all nine editions of *Campbell Biology*.

Eric J. Simon is an associate professor in the Department of Biology and Health Science at New England College, in Henniker, New Hampshire. He teaches introductory biology to science majors and nonscience majors, as well as upper-level courses in genetics, microbiology, tropical marine biology, and molecular biology. Dr. Simon received a B.A. in biology and computer science and an M.A. in biology from Wesleyan University and a Ph.D. in biochemistry from Harvard University. His research focuses on innovative ways to use technology to improve teaching and learning in the science classroom, particularly for nonscience majors. Dr. Simon is the lead author of *Campbell Essential Biology*, Fourth Edition, and *Campbell Essential Biology with Physiology*, Third Edition.

Jean L. Dickey is a professor of biology at Clemson University. She had no idea that science was interesting until her senior year in high school, when a scheduling problem landed her in an advanced biology course. Abandoning plans to study English or foreign languages, she enrolled in Kent State University as a biology major. After receiving her B.S. in biology, she went on to earn a Ph.D. in ecology and evolution from Purdue University. Since joining the faculty at Clemson in 1984, Dr. Dickey has specialized in teaching nonscience majors, including a course designed for preservice elementary teachers and workshops for in-service teachers. She also developed an investigative laboratory curriculum for general biology. Dr. Dickey is author of *Laboratory Investigations for Biology*, Second Edition, and coauthor of *Campbell Essential Biology*, Fourth Edition, and *Campbell Essential Biology with Physiology*, Third Edition.

Neil A. Campbell (1946–2004) combined the inquiring nature of a research scientist with the soul of a caring teacher. Over his 30 years of teaching introductory biology to both science majors and nonscience majors, many thousands of students had the opportunity to learn from him and be stimulated by his enthusiasm for the study of life. While he is greatly missed by his many friends in the biology community, his coauthors remain inspired by his visionary dedication to education and are committed to searching for ever better ways to engage students in the wonders of biology.

Kevin G-E. Scott is a senior instructor at the University of Manitoba where he teaches introductory biology for science majors and nonscience majors; ecology for nonbiology majors; and upper-level animal physiology laboratories. In the past, he has also taught courses in immunology, parasitology, human anatomy and physiology, and microbiology. Dr. Scott received a B.Sc. in zoology and a Ph.D. in zoology and cellular, molecular, and microbial biology at the University of Calgary. As an instructor, Dr. Scott has centred his career on teaching and the classroom, where he shares his excitement for biology. This is the first time Dr. Scott has authored a biology textbook.

Brief Contents

Table of Contents

UNIT I
The Living Cell

UNIT II

Cellular Reproduction and Genetics

9 Patterns of Inheritance 168

10 Molecular Genetics 199

11 Gene Expression 224

UNIT III

Concepts of Evolution

UNIT IV

The Evolution of Biodiversity

17 Bacteria and Other Prokaryotes 359

18 Biodiversity of Protists and Fungi 376

19 Biodiversity of Plants 396

UNIT V

Plants: Structure and Function

22 Plant Structure, Growth, and Reproduction 466

UNIT VI

Structure and Function of Animals

Preface

Inspired by thousands of students in our own classes over the years and the enthusiastic feedback from many professors who used earlier U.S. Editions, we are delighted to present the Canadian Edition of *Campbell Biology: Concepts and Connections*. We worked hard to reflect the evolving needs of today's courses and students, as well as current progress in biology. This book's title continues to honour Neil Campbell's founding role and his many contributions to biology education. The Canadian Edition maintains the dual purposes of prior versions: to engage students from a wide variety of majors in the wonders of the living world and to show them how biology relates to their own existence and the world they inhabit. Most of these students will not become biologists themselves, but their lives will be touched by biology every day. Understanding the concepts of biology and their connections to our lives is more important than ever. Whether we are concerned with our own health or the health of our planet, a familiarity with biology is essential. This basic knowledge plus an appreciation for how science works are elements of good citizenship in an era when informed evaluations of health issues, environmental problems, and applications of new technology are critical.

The Canadian Edition

In creating a Canadian Edition of *Campbell Biology: Concepts and Connections*, our primary goal is to expose students to biology that they will encounter in Canada. Relating content to local experiences provides a powerful teaching strategy and makes learning more meaningful. The focus on Canadians and Canadian issues, examples, statistics, policies and regulations, flora, fauna, and species allows students to form deeper connections with the material. Canadians have made significant contributions to our current understanding of biology, and accordingly this text features their discoveries as well as research conducted in Canada. When students read about a scientist from their own institution, the subject matter comes to life.

Concepts and Connections

Concepts Biology is a vast subject that gets bigger every year, but an introductory biology course is still only one or two semesters long. This introductory biology textbook is the first to use concept modules to help students recognize and focus on the main ideas of each chapter. Each module's heading is a carefully crafted statement of a key concept. For example, "Two photosystems connected by an electron transport chain generate ATP and NADPH" announces a key concept about the light reactions of photosynthesis (Module 7.8). Such a concept heading serves as a focal point, and the module's text and illustrations converge on that concept with explanation and, often, analogies. The module text walks the student through the illustrations, just as an educator might do in class. And in teaching a sequential process, such as the one diagrammed in Figure 7.8A, we number the steps in

the text to correspond to numbered steps in the figure. The synergy between a module's verbal and graphic components transforms the concept heading into an idea with meaning to the student. The checkpoint question at the end of each module encourages students to test themselves as they proceed through a chapter. Finally, the chapter review lists all the concept statements under the overarching section titles, explicitly reminding students of what they have just studied.

Connections Students are more motivated to study biology when they can connect it to their own lives and interests—for example, to health issues, economic problems, environmental quality, ethical controversies, and social responsibility. In this edition, red tabs labelled *Everyday Biology* indicate the numerous application modules that go beyond core biological concepts. The chapter-opening essays and other sections in the text make connections for readers. Moreover, we connect the content of each chapter to the grand unifying theme of evolution, without which the study of life has no coherence. This book remains the only nonmajors biology text to connect every single chapter to evolution, with highlights featured in the green-tabbed *Evolution Connection* modules.

Special Features

- **See where the chapter takes you:** *Big Ideas* provide a road map to overarching concepts with a visual list at the beginning of each chapter, and subheadings throughout to orient students.

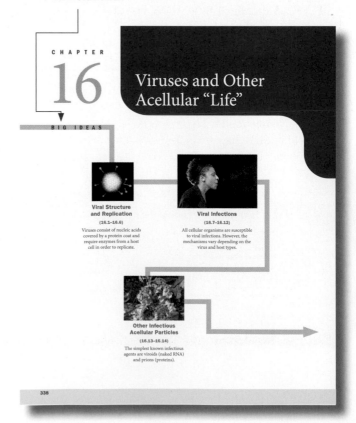

- **Discover and explore:** The **opening essays** of each chapter introduce the topic through stories written to pique interest.

Oh Deer! North America's Prion Disease

"Outbreak of Mad Cow Disease Feared!" is a headline that you have probably seen or heard at least once. The technical name for this disease in cattle is bovine spongiform encephalopathy (BSE) because of the spongy appearance of damaged brain tissue in affected areas. BSE leads to abnormal behaviours and ultimately death in cattle. Of even greater concern is the ability of this disease to also affect humans.

What makes this disease different from other infections is that it is not caused by a living cell (such as a parasite or bacterium) or even a virus, but by a simple infectious protein. Prion proteins have a primary structure (that is, an amino acid sequence) similar to healthy proteins found in the body. However, prion proteins are folded differently. Their different shape lowers their solubility in cytoplasm causing the formation of protein crystals.

What causes an outbreak of BSE? The answer is still being debated. Many believe that it is related to the practice of feeding cattle infected animal by-products, including nervous tissue and bone marrow. Once infected, prions cause normal proteins to refold into the prion shape, making the damaging crystals even larger. Cellular damage in the brain leads to a spongy appearance and neurological symptoms, which progresses to a loss of sensory and motor function, and eventually death.

Prion diseases came into the spotlight in the mid-1990s when several people living in or having visited Great Britain were diagnosed with variant Creutzfeldt-Jakob disease (vCJD), a degenerative neurological condition caused by the same prion as BSE. As of 2012, only two cases of vCJD have been confirmed in Canada. Many of those infected had come into direct contact with the BSE prion. How did this happen? Improper handling of infected animal tissues may have contaminated meat. The subsequent ingestion of contaminated meat by humans probably accounts for the majority of these vCJD cases.

Although cases of BSE have been identified in Canada, there is another lesser-known prion disease in our deer, moose, and elk populations that is of rising concern. Chronic wasting disease (CWD) is a prion disease similar to BSE, characterized by dramatic weight loss. CWD was first identified from an emaciated mule deer in Colorado. Since then, this disease has spread to Southern Alberta, Saskatchewan, and many U.S. states. In endemic areas the incidence of infection in the wild population is 10% to 12% and rising annually. In some captive deer populations the incidence can be as high as 80%. This poses a particular risk to wild deer populations in these regions, and their numbers may drastically decline in the coming decades.

The symptoms of CWD are similar to those of BSE. Initially the animal will exhibit psychological disturbances. At about three to four years after infection, the animal will display unusual behaviours. Physical or motor disturbances follow, including a lack of coordination, excessive urination, weight loss, and finally death.

Unlike the BSE prion, which is transmitted directly by the ingestion of contaminated tissues, the CWD prion can be transmitted indirectly when an animal ingests material contaminated by excretions (such as saliva, feces, and urine). Thus, normal grazing behaviours in endemic areas can place animals at risk for infection. This indirect method of transmission leads to its high incidence and makes it very difficult to contain.

Like other prion diseases, CWD has no treatment. The current method of control is the quarantine of herds and euthanization of infected animals. While these containment methods work well in captive herds, it is difficult to control the disease in the wild populations. The Alberta and Saskatchewan governments, working with the Canadian Food Inspection Agency (CFIA) and the Canadian Cooperative Wildlife Health Centre, have established a surveillance program where local hunters submit heads of

339

- **Integrate text and visuals:** The **figures** illustrate important concepts in the text while the **surrounding text** explains the figures, which helps students access information easily while promoting a deeper understanding of the subject matter.
- **Test yourself:** Get immediate feedback with a **checkpoint question** at the end of each module.
- **Question what you hear and read:** *Rumour Has It* modules within each chapter challenge common misconceptions about biology, thereby encouraging critical thinking.

RUMOUR HAS IT 3.6 Is high-fructose corn syrup to blame for obesity?

If you want to sweeten your coffee or tea, you probably reach for sugar—the disaccharide sucrose. If you drink soft drinks or fruit cocktails, you're probably consuming the monosaccharides of sucrose in the form of high-fructose corn syrup (HFCS; also called glucose-fructose on some Canadian food labels). In fact, if you look at the label of almost any processed food, you will see HFCS on the list of ingredients **(Figure 3.6A)**. You have probably heard rumours linking HFCS to the "obesity epidemic."

What is glucose-fructose? Industrial processing breaks down cornstarch into monomers of glucose, producing what is called corn syrup. Glucose, however, does not taste as sweet to us as sucrose. Fructose, on the other hand, tastes much sweeter than both

▲ Figure 3.6A Glucose-fructose (HFCS) is a main ingredient of many processed foods

44   UNIT I   The Living Cell

- **Make connections:** *Everyday Biology* modules relate biology to everyday life and interests, making the subject matter relevant and more meaningful.

EVERYDAY BIOLOGY 19.12 Angiosperms sustain us—and add spice to our diets

We depend on the fruits and seeds of angiosperms for much of our food. Corn, rice, wheat, and other grains, the main food sources for most of the world's people and their domesticated animals, are dry fruits. Many food crops are fleshy fruits, including apples, cherries, oranges, tomatoes, squash, and cucumbers. (In scientific terms, a fruit is an angiosperm structure containing seeds, so some of what many people consider vegetables are actually fruits.) While most people can easily recognize grains and fleshy fruits as plant products, fewer realize that spices such as nutmeg, cinnamon, cumin, cloves, ginger, and licorice come from angiosperms. Figure 19.12 shows the source of a condiment found on most Canadian dinner tables: black pepper. The pepper fruits are harvested before ripening, and then dried and ground into powder or sold whole as "peppercorns." In medieval Europe, peppercorns were so valuable that they were used

as currency. Rent and taxes could be paid in peppercorns; as a form of wealth, peppercorns were included in dowries and left in wills. The search for a sea route to obtain pepper and other precious spices from India and Southeast Asia led to the Age of Exploration and had a lasting impact on European history.

? Suppose you found a cluster of pepper berries like the ones in Figure 19.12. How would you know that they are fruits?

Each berry has seeds inside it.
▲ Figure 19.12 Berries (fruits) of *Piper nigrum*

410   UNIT IV   The Evolution of Biodiversity

- **Practice good citizenship:** *Biology and Society* modules highlight the role of biology in various aspects of society and what students can do to help.

BIOLOGY AND SOCIETY 41.4 Human activities are responsible for rising concentrations of greenhouse gases

Without its blanket of natural greenhouse gases such as CO_2 and water vapour to trap heat, Earth would be too cold to support most life. However, increasing the insulation that the blanket provides is making the planet uncomfortably warm, and that increase is occurring rapidly. For 650 000 years, the atmospheric concentration of CO_2 did not exceed 300 parts per million (ppm); the preindustrial concentration was 280 ppm. Today, atmospheric CO_2 is approximately 385 ppm. The levels of nitrous oxide (N_2O) and methane (CH_4), which also trap heat in the atmosphere, have increased dramatically, too (Figure 41.4A). CO_2 and N_2O are released when fossil fuels—oil, coal, and natural gas—are burned. N_2O is also released when nitrogen fertilizers are used in agriculture. Landfills are a factor responsible for increases of atmospheric CH_4. The consensus of scientists, as reported by the IPCC, is that rising concentrations of greenhouse gases—and thus, climate change—are the result of human activities.

Let's take a closer look at CO_2, the dominant greenhouse gas. Recall from Module 40.7 that atmospheric CO_2 is a major reservoir for carbon. (CH_4 is also part of that reservoir.) CO_2 is removed from the atmosphere by the process of photosynthesis and stored in organic molecules such as carbohydrates (Figure 41.4B). Thus, biomass, the organic molecules in an ecosystem, is a biotic carbon reservoir. The carbon-containing molecules in living organisms may be used in the process of cellular respiration, which releases carbon in the form of CO_2. Nonliving biomass may be decomposed by microorganisms or fungi that also release CO_2. Overall, uptake of CO_2 by photosynthesis roughly equals the release of CO_2 by cellular respiration. CO_2 is also exchanged between the atmosphere and the surface waters of the oceans.

Fossil fuels consist of biomass that was buried under sediments without being completely decomposed (see Module 19.7). The burning of fossil fuels and wood, which is also an organic material, can be thought of as a rapid form of decomposition. While cellular respiration releases energy from organic molecules slowly and harnesses it to make ATP, combustion liberates the energy rapidly as heat and light. In both processes, the carbon atoms that make up the organic fuel are released in CO_2.

The CO_2 flooding into the atmosphere from combustion of fossil fuels may be absorbed by photosynthetic organisms and incorporated into biomass. But deforestation has significantly decreased the number of CO_2 molecules that can be accommodated by this pathway. CO_2 may also be absorbed into the ocean. For decades, the oceans have been absorbing considerably more CO_2 than they have released, and they will continue to do so; but, the excess CO_2 is beginning to affect ocean chemistry. When CO_2 dissolves in water, it becomes carbonic acid. Recently, measurable decreases in ocean pH have raised concern among biologists. Organisms that construct shells or exoskeletons out of calcium carbonate ($CaCO_3$), including corals and many plankton, are most likely to be affected as decreasing pH reduces the concentration of the carbonate ions (see Module 2.16).

Greenhouse gas emissions are accelerating. From 2000 to 2009, global CO_2 emissions increased four times faster than in the preceding 10-year span. At this rate, further climate change is inevitable.

In the next module, we will take a closer look at the rumour about the impact bovine flatulence has on the climate.

? The amount of CO_2 you are responsible for releasing every year is called your *carbon footprint*. Search for an online calculator that estimates your carbon footprint. What are the primary sources of the CO_2 you generate?

▲ Figure 41.4A Atmospheric concentrations of CO_2 and N_2O (y-axis, left), and CH_4 (y-axis, right), as of 2009

Legend: Carbon Dioxide (CO_2); Nitrous Oxide (N_2O); Methane (CH_4)

▲ Figure 41.4B Carbon cycling

CHAPTER 41   Conservation and Sustainability   865

- **Learn about the mechanisms underlying evolution:** *Evolution Connection* modules in every chapter relate evolution to a wide spectrum of biology topics and help to explain the mechanisms underlying evolution and the evidence for it.
- **Review the main points:** The *Reviewing the Concepts* section provides a helpful summary of the chapter along with key diagrams.
- **Link the chapter's key concepts:** *Connecting the Concepts* activities test students' ability to relate topics from the different modules and include concept mapping, labelling, and categorizing exercises.
- **Prepare for assessment:** Questions in the *Testing Your Knowledge* section help students to prepare for upcoming tests.
- **Learn the Language of Biology: Appendix D** presents an etymology of biological terminology. Breaking down words into their prefixes, roots, and suffixes assists with learning new terms.

This Book's Flexibility

Though a biology textbook's table of contents must be linear, biology itself is more like a web of related concepts without a single starting point or prescribed path. Courses can navigate this network starting with molecules, with ecology, or somewhere in between. The Canadian Edition of *Campbell Biology: Concepts and Connections* provides flexibility as the seven units of the book are largely self-contained, and in a number of the units, chapters can be assigned in a different order without much loss of coherence. The numbered modules make it easy to omit modules or to relocate modules within a syllabus.

Organizational and Content Highlights of the Canadian Edition

Chapter 1   Designed to engage Canadian students' interest in the discipline from the start, the chapter-opening essay features our cover subject, the Kermode bear. This topic is revisited throughout the chapter and elsewhere in the book. Chapter 1 sets the stage for what is to come by introducing several themes central to the field. Evolution is presented as the unifying concept that explains the unity and diversity of life on Earth. This introductory chapter introduces the scientific method as a means to understand the world around us, with a focus on observations and hypotheses. The chapter ends with an examination of connections between biology, technology, and society, which shows how biology can be linked to our everyday lives.

Unit I – The Living Cell   The first unit delves into the lives of living cells.

Chapter 2 begins with an examination of the basic chemistry necessary to understanding biology, such as atoms and compounds, chemical bonding, and the properties of water. This chapter incorporates an engaging discussion about acid precipitation in Eastern Canada.

Chapter 3 moves into the chemistry of the major biological molecules, including carbohydrates, proteins, nucleic acids, and lipids. Students will learn about the membrane composition of an Arctic animal of interest.

Chapter 4 tackles cellular structure—that is, cell and cellular components including the nucleus, endomembrane system, mitochondria and chloroplasts, and the cytoskeleton. This chapter features the production of silk proteins by Montreal-based Nexia Biotechnologies.

Opening with an essay on bioluminescence, Chapter 5 examines cellular components with a focus on the structure and function of cell membranes. The exploration of cell function progresses into biochemical reactions, including the flow of energy and how enzymes function. This chapter showcases the research of Dr. Berghuis at McGill University on enzyme inhibitors.

The last two chapters of this unit explain how cells obtain energy to perform work. Chapter 6 begins with an overview of cellular respiration, followed by a more detailed explanation of each of the major steps. An alternative metabolic pathway, fermentation, is introduced, and highlights research on fermentation during beer production by Dr. Speers at Dalhousie University. The chapter concludes with a discussion connecting the major metabolic pathways.

Photosynthesis is the topic of Chapter 7. Following an overview of the entire pathway, this chapter presents a detailed explanation of the light-dependent reactions and light-independent reactions. Chapter 7 showcases Canadian biomass energy plantations growing switchgrass, a C_4 plant.

Unit II – Cellular Reproduction and Genetics   Unit II explains the relationship between DNA, chromosomes, and organisms. Students learn that genetics is not purely hypothetical, but connects in many important and interesting ways to their lives, human society, and other life on Earth. This edition provides a basic understanding of genetics to some of the latest discoveries in epigenetics.

Chapter 8 talks about the two major mechanisms of cell division in the eukaryotes, mitosis and meiosis. After explaining the various roles of mitosis, a detailed discussion on the eukaryotic cell cycle follows. Inheritance and genetic recombination are introduced as we look at meiosis and crossing over. A module in this chapter explores the research of University of Calgary's Dr. Buret on the benefits of epidermal growth factor.

Launching with a chapter-opening essay on the phylogeny of show dogs, the discussion of inheritance continues in Chapter 9 with an examination of the patterns of inheritance, including Mendel's laws and their variations. After an interesting discussion on genetic screening as well as the incidence of cystic fibrosis in the small, isolated population of Saguenay–Lac-Saint-Jean, Quebec, this chapter concludes by developing the link between meiosis, Mendelian inheritance, and chromosomal behaviour in an exploration of the chromosomal basis of inheritance.

Fans of the TV series *Breaking Bad* will find Chapter 10's opening essay on the effects of ricin, a toxin, interesting. The flow of information from gene to protein is the topic of this chapter. This discussion includes examinations of DNA structure, DNA replication, transcription, and translation.

Chapter 11 explains how gene expression is controlled. We end this chapter with discussions on two practical examples of controlling gene expression: cloning and cancer.

The final chapter of this unit, Chapter 12, identifies DNA technologies such as gene cloning, genetically modified organisms, DNA profiling, and the study of whole genomes in the field of genomics. Module 12.8 features the environmentally transgenic "Enviropig" developed at the University of Guelph.

Unit III – Concepts of Evolution

A main goal of this book is to present the basic principles of evolution and natural selection, the evidence that support these theories, as well as their relevance to all of biology and to the lives of students.

Chapter 13 explains theories regarding the origins of life on Earth and major evolutionary events. Students will learn more about the Burgess Shale, one of the world's most celebrated fossil fields found in the Rocky Mountains of British Columbia.

Chapter 14 covers the mechanisms of evolution. This chapter begins by explaining that populations are the unit of evolution and goes on to describe both microevolution and macroevolution.

Chapter 15 concludes the evolution unit with an examination of speciation and phylogeny. We introduce students first to different concepts of what a species is and then to how new species can form after barriers to reproduction are established. Module 15.2 explores the hybridization of grizzly and polar bears in the Canadian Arctic. A discussion of phylogeny and the tree of life provides an excellent link between evolution and the next unit on the diversity of life.

Unit IV – The Evolution of Biodiversity

The diversity unit surveys all life on Earth in less than 125 pages! Descriptions and illustrations of the unifying characteristics of each major group of organisms, along with a small sample of its diversity, make up much of the content. Two recurring elements are interwoven with these descriptions: evolutionary history and examples of relevance to our everyday lives and society at large.

Opening with an essay on the chronic wasting disease in Alberta deer populations, Chapter 16's discussion of the vast diversity of organisms on the planet starts with organisms that many consider not living: viruses and other acellular, molecular organisms. This chapter compares various viral structures and replicative cycles and several viral infections in bacteria, animals, and plants. The chapter discusses the replicative West Nile virus, a concern of many who live in Canada. Chapter 16 ends with a brief discussion on viroids and prions.

Starting with an essay that details antibiotic resistant bacteria, Chapter 17 explores the diversity and genetics of bacteria. This chapter ends by exposing students to how bacteria can affect their daily lives.

Chapter 18 surveys the diversity of the eukaryotic microorganisms, including the protists and fungi.

Chapter 19 considers the diversity of plants, including a brief exploration of their evolutionary patterns. As the major group of land plants, the final Big Idea focuses on the diversity of the flowering plants.

Invertebrate animal diversity is the topic of Chapter 20. We discuss what an animal is and survey nine of the major animal phyla. This chapter details the impact of invasive earthworms on the soil in Canadian forests. It ends with a brief discussion on the evolution of our understanding of the relationships between the major phyla.

Chapter 21 features vertebrate diversity. In this chapter, we cover the major events in the evolution of the vertebrates, including the evolution of jaws and limbs, and adaptations for life on land. The chapter concludes with a focus on the evolution of primates and humans.

Unit V – Plants: Structure and Function

To help students gain an appreciation of the importance of plants, this unit presents the anatomy and physiology of angiosperms with frequent connections to the importance of plants to society.

Focusing on the flowering plants, Chapter 22's opening essay describes Cathedral Grove on Vancouver Island and then the chapter shifts into an overview of plant structure, comparing monocots with eudicots. The chapter next describes three basic organs and three tissue systems of angiosperms as well as primary and secondary growth patterns. A discussion of the mechanisms of plant reproduction and development follows this content. This chapter showcases the work by Dr. Fowler at the University of Saskatchewan on the benefits of planting winter wheat.

The text devotes Chapter 23 to plant nutrition. Covering the uptake of nutrients from the soil and their transport throughout the organism, the chapter highlights common fertilization regimes for Canadian crops.

Chapter 24 discusses how plants can regulate their growth through several plant hormones, and how plants can respond to stimuli such as light and herbivores.

Unit VI – Structure and Function of Animals

Unit VI outlines unifying concepts of animal form and function, introducing students to the major organ systems of vertebrates. Most chapters start with an overview of a general problem that animals face followed by a comparison of how different animals address this problem, within an evolutionary context. The early modules of each chapter discuss the diversity of form and function seen in the animal kingdom. The last part of every chapter devotes a detailed presentation of human body systems, enhanced by an exploration of the health consequences of disorders in those systems.

Chapter 25 starts with an overview of the basic tissue types and organ systems seen among animals. This chapter ends with a discussion on how animals exchange matter and energy with their external environment while they regulate their internal environment.

Chapter 26 addresses animal nutrition, starting with the various ways by which animals acquire their meals. Subsequently, the human digestive system and human nutrition are explored.

The mechanisms of gas exchange seen within the animal kingdom open Chapter 27. Module 27.8 features the fascinating work by Dr. Yauk at Carleton University on the relationship between second-hand smoke and inheritable cancers; consequently, this chapter is very relevant for students. The discussion on the human respiratory system and the transport of oxygen and carbon dioxide within the human body at the end of this chapter links Chapter 27 to the circulatory system covered in Chapter 28.

Chapter 28 covers both the circulatory and urinary systems, which—given their close interactions—creates a natural flow and progression for the coverage of systems. This chapter offers an overview of animal circulatory systems, including that of the diving sperm whale, and then delves into the human condition.

Chapter 29 focuses on the endocrine system, a third system that relies on circulation. Students can read about the nature of chemical regulation, including how hormones work, and the vertebrate endocrine system, with emphasis on the human animal. An investigation of hormone-based performance enhancing drugs will pique students' interest given the recent media attention of athletes who take those substances to improve results.

Dr. Vance Trudeau's work at the University of Ottawa on the captive breeding of endangered frog species provides an appropriate opening to Chapter 30, which is devoted to animal reproduction and development. Covering the principles of sexual reproduction and embryonic development, the chapter investigates human reproductive systems and the developing human.

Chapter 31 examines the organization and evolution of nervous systems in animals and the function of neurons and the transmission of electrical signals. This chapter highlights the research of Dr. Norman Doidge on retraining the adult brain and the work of the Rick Hansen Foundation on spinal cord injuries. The chapter concludes with an exploration of the human brain.

The examination of the nervous system continues in Chapter 32 by delving into the senses. First covering sensory reception, the chapter then focuses on hearing and balance, vision, taste, and smell.

Highlighting the University of Calgary's Dr. Cy Frank and his knee surgery techniques in the chapter-opening essay sets the tone for Chapter 33's coverage of the skeletal and muscular systems and animal locomotion. First, the chapter introduces the requirements for locomotion. This is followed by a deeper investigation of skeletons and muscle contraction. This chapter includes the research of Drs. Rudnicki (University of Ottawa), Rossi (University of British Columbia), and Tremblay (Université Laval) on satellite cells and muscle repair in Duchenne muscular dystrophy (Module 33.13).

Finally, Chapter 34 explores animal defences and their immune systems. In this chapter, we talk about innate and acquired immunities, and end with the conditions that may result from specific examples of inappropriate immune responses.

Unit VII – Ecology   The final unit of this book explores the basic principles of ecology and how these principles apply to environmental challenges.

Chapter 35 explores the physical and chemical factors that influence life on Earth. Opening with an essay on Arctic sea ice, this chapter offers an overview of the major aquatic and terrestrial biomes. The chapter closes with the water cycle, which connects the biomes.

Chapter 36 revisits animals, this time focusing on behavioural ecology and the forms of learning and reproductive and social behaviours. This chapter profiles work by Dr. Wilson at the Bamfield Marine Sciences Centre on Pacific herring communication.

Chapter 37 covers population ecology by exploring population structure and dynamics, and applies these principles to the human population. This chapter includes a discussion of the Atlantic cod moratorium.

Beginning with details of the devastating effects of the mountain pine beetle, Chapter 38 covers concepts of community ecology with an exploration of aspects of community structure (that is, species interactions) as well as community dynamics (that is, disturbances). Landscape ecology, a new topic for this edition, includes a module on structural changes in communities across a landscape and a module on transition zones between adjacent communities.

A new chapter to *Campbell Biology: Concepts and Connections*, Chapter 39 on symbioses explores some of the more intimate interactions between species. It examines symbiotic relationships such as mutualism, parasitism, commensalism, altruism, and mimicry. A discussion of the co-evolution of symbioses ends this new chapter.

Chapter 40's focus is ecosystem ecology. Beginning with an examination of ecosystem structure, the chapter offers a detailed look at ecosystem dynamics, including energy flow and chemical cycling within ecosystems. Module 40.10 offers insight into the eutrophication of Lake Winnipeg.

The final chapter of Unit VII and the book features conservation and sustainability, returning to the importance of good citizenship by examining the impact of human actions. While this chapter reviews human activities that lead to a loss in biodiversity, we convey a message of hope and optimism by showcasing the restoration of aquatic ecosystems in La Mauricie National Park in Quebec and by focusing on how we can contribute to sustainability and conservation.

Appendices   The appendices to this book include: the periodic table of the elements, now with electronegativity values (Appendix A); amino acids found in proteins (Appendix B); major organic functional groups and their properties (Appendix C); a new appendix on the etymology of the terminology of biology (Appendix D); and answers to the end-of-chapter review questions (Appendix E).

Instructor Ancillaries

MasteringBiology®   www.masteringbiology.com

MasteringBiology® is a instructor-assigned homework system that makes it easy to organize your class, personalize your students' educational experience, and push their learning to the next level.

Designed to help maximize class time, MasteringBiology offers customizable, easy-to-assign, and automatically graded assessments and pedagogical tools that motivate students to learn outside of class and to arrive prepared for lecture.

Developed by science educators for science students and professors, the Mastering platform has over one million active users, and a proven history with over nine years of student use in 30 countries.

With MasteringBiology® professors can assign pre-lecture quizzes, coaching activities, test bank questions, and more. Educators can import their own questions, and edit any of our questions or answers to match the precise language used in the course. The system automatically grades every assignment that features machine-graded questions, and students' results appear in the gradebook.

MasteringBiology® features activities that assist with vocabulary building, extend the text's emphasis on visual learning, demonstrate connections among key concepts, and provide coaching on difficult concepts. Additionally, adaptive Follow-Up Assignments within MasteringBiology provide coaching and practise that continually adapt to each student's needs, making efficient use of study time.

LearningCatalytics™, available through MasteringBiology, is an interactive classroom solution and response system that leads to just-in-time teaching opportunities. Educators can create multiple-choice questions, or open-ended questions that require graphical, textual, or numerical answers, and students can use their smartphones, tablets, or laptops to respond.

Testbank   A testbank offering over 2000 questions is available either in Word (Test Item File) or in a computerized format (Pearson TestGen). Pearson TestGen is a powerful program that enables instructors to view and edit existing questions, create new questions, and generate quizzes, tests, exams, or homework. With Pearson TestGen educators can also administer tests on a local area network, have tests graded electronically, and then have the results prepared in electronic or printed reports.

PowerPoint Slides   Every chapter features a Microsoft PowerPoint® slide deck that highlights, illuminates, and builds on key concepts for your lecture or online delivery. Think-pair-share questions appear after major topics to help with the integration of active learning opportunities. You can tailor each deck to your specifications.

Image Libraries   Image libraries of labelled and unlabelled art help with the creation of vibrant lecture presentations. Most figures, tables, charts, and photos from the text are provided in electronic format and are organized by chapter for convenience. These images can be imported easily into Microsoft PowerPoint®.

Clicker Questions   Clicker questions—multiple choice and true/false—give you in-the-moment opportunities to engage and to assess students' understanding during lecture.

CourseSmart for Instructors   CourseSmart goes beyond traditional expectations—providing instant, online access to the textbooks and course materials. You can save time with a digital eTextbook that allows you to search for the most relevant content at the very moment you need it. Whether it's evaluating textbooks or creating lecture notes to help students with difficult concepts, CourseSmart can make life a little easier. See how when you visit www.coursesmart.com/instructors.

Student Supplements

MasteringBiology® Study Area   The Study Area in MasteringBiology® offers a plethora of resources that allow students to assess their knowledge of the material and their progress.

eText   MasteringBiology® features an interactive eText of *Campbell Biology: Concepts and Connections* that allows for easy highlighting, annotating, and searching with a Google®-based search function.

Students can also access their text via a tablet by downloading the free Pearson eText app and using their MasteringBiology® login credentials.

Study on the Go

At the end of every chapter, students will find a QR code that provides access to Study on the Go, an unprecedented mobile integration between text and online content. Students can access text-specific resources, including quizzes and flashcards, by using their smartphones to scan the code.

Students can visit one of the sites below to download a free app to their smartphone. Once installed, the phone can scan the QR code and link to a website that leads to Pearson's Study on the Go and resources for *Campbell Biology: Concepts and Connections*.

ScanLife
http://getscanlife.com
NeoReader
http://get.neoreader.com
QuickMark
www.quickmark.com.tw

Customizable Text Options

Pearson Custom Library (PCL)   For enrollments of at least 25 students, you can create your own textbook by choosing the chapters that best suit your own course needs. To begin building your custom text, visit www.pearsoncustomlibrary.com. You may also work with a dedicated Pearson Custom editor to create your ideal text—publishing your own original content or mixing and matching Pearson content. Contact your local Pearson Representative to get started.

Acknowledgements

This Canadian Edition of *Campbell Biology: Concepts and Connections* is the result of the combined efforts of many talented and hardworking people. I wish to extend my heartfelt appreciation to all those who contributed, especially the authors of the U.S. Editions. The final version of this book was shaped by input from the dedicated reviewers listed in the next column, who have shared their experiences and ideas to improve the book.

Keith Bruce (*St. Clair College*)
Lisa Carter (*Athabasca University*)
Michael Durrant (*Champlain Regional College*)
Carol Evans (*Algonquin College*)
Tracy Fawcett (*SAIT Polytechnic*)
Gary Grothman (*St. Mary's University College*)
Stephen B. Heard (*University of New Brunswick*)
Tanya Jessup (*Durham College*)
Zafar Khan (*Centennial College*)
Wilfred Langmaid (*University of New Brunswick*)
Jennifer Matecki (*Algonquin College*)
Tammy McMullan (*Simon Fraser University*)
Ivona Mladenovic (*Simon Fraser University*)
Mario Moniz de Sa (*Langara College*)
Alison Moran (*Camosun College*)
E. Blythe Nilson (*University of British Columbia, Okanagan*)

Gavin Park *(Nipissing University)*
Nagina Parmar *(Ryerson University)*
Lily Peters *(Nicola Valley Institute of Technology)*
Naman Sharma *(University of Ottawa)*
Michael Silvergieter *(Fraser International College)*
Joanne Simala-Grant *(University of Alberta)*
Julie Smit *(University of Windsor)*
Sharla Stolhandske *(Fraser International College)*
Jeff Stuart *(Brock University)*
David Thomas *(Fanshawe College)*
Tamara Western *(McGill University)*
Catherine A. Young *(Heritage College)*

■ ■ ■

For many students, introductory biology is the only science course that they will take during their college or university years. Long after today's students have forgotten most of the specific content of their biology course, they will be left with general impressions and attitudes about science and scientists. We hope that this Canadian Edition of *Campbell Biology: Concepts and Connections* helps to make those impressions positive and supports instructors' goals for sharing the fun of biology. In our continuing efforts to improve the book and its supporting materials, we benefit tremendously from instructor feedback, not only in formal reviews but also via informal communication. Please let us know how we are doing and how we can improve the next edition of the book.

Kevin Scott, kevin.scott@ad.umanitoba.ca

Exploring Biology

BIG IDEAS

Themes in the Study of Biology

(1.1–1.4)

Common themes help to organize the study of life.

Evolution, the Core Theme of Biology

(1.5–1.7)

Evolution accounts for the unity and diversity of life and the evolutionary adaptations of organisms to their environment.

The Scientific Method

(1.8–1.9)

In studying nature, scientists make observations, form hypotheses, and test predictions with experiments.

Biology and Everyday Life

(1.10–1.12)

Learning about biology helps us understand many issues involving science, technology, and society.

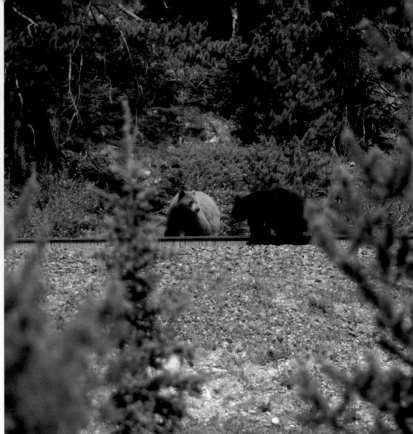

Canada's Other Iconic White Bear

The white bear depicted here is not a polar bear, nor an albino. This bear is a rare white colour phase of the North American black bear (*Ursus americanus*) from an isolated population in Great Bear Rainforest on Vancouver Island. Alternative colour phases (varieties) of North American black bears are not uncommon. The photograph on the right shows the black and cinnamon colour phases in Banff National Park. Other colour phases found among black bears include brown and slate blue-grey.

The Great Bear Rainforest population of black bears is a subspecies called Kermode bears (*Ursus americanus kermodei*), named after Francis Kermode, curator of the Royal BC Museum from 1904 to 1940, and one of the first biologists to study the white black bears. Although the white-coloured bears are often referred to as Kermode bears, this name technically refers to all bears in the population regardless of fur colour. The First Nations peoples of the area (as well as this textbook) specifically refer to the white bears as spirit bears. The **spirit bear** became a Canadian icon when it was used as a mascot for the 2010 Winter Olympics in Vancouver.

The white colour, a phenomenon called kermodism, comes from a recessive genetic mutation that prevents pigment formation in the skin and hair. How is kermodism different from albinism, another genetic disorder that causes an abnormally white coloration? The most prominent difference is that spirit bears have black noses and dark eyes. Only their fur colour is affected. Albinism affects pigment production in all cells, making the noses and eyes of albinos pink (although some albinos have pale blue eyes). A less obvious difference is in the frequency of occurrence. Albinism is very rare, occurring once in every 10 000 mammalian births. In the Great Bear National Forest, however, 10% of the bears are white.

A similar phenomenon has been observed in other animals as well. Several white-phase Eastern grey squirrels inhabit Exeter, Ontario. The Assiniboine Park Zoo in Winnipeg is home to two white-phase North American bison. Many other non-albino white animals have been reported, including lions, peafowl, and crocodiles. Although the exact genetic cause in each species may be different, the outcome is similar: abnormally white animals with pigmented eyes.

For many animals, conspicuous white coloration may be detrimental, as predators can easily see them. The spirit bear, however, has no natural predators, and therefore its coloration is not a disadvantage. In fact, Dr. Thomas Reimchen at the University of Victoria has shown that the white-colour phase may actually be advantageous. Part of the Kermode bears' diet consists of salmon, which the bears catch as the fish return to their spawning grounds. From the salmon's point of view looking up, black-coloured bears stand out against the bright sky and are easier to see and avoid. The spirit bears, however, blend into the light background and, as a result, catch up to 30% more fish than their darker counterparts. This advantage fades with the evening light, however, as all bears have similar success when the sky is dark.

These bears highlight many aspects of biology that we will discuss throughout this book, including Mendelian and population genetics, natural selection, and conservation. In this chapter, we begin our exploration of biology—the scientific study of life, its evolution, and its amazing diversity.

Themes in the Study of Biology

1.1 All forms of life share common properties

Defining **biology** as the scientific study of life raises the obvious question: What is *life*? How would you describe what distinguishes living things from nonliving things? Even a small child realizes that a bug or a flower is alive, while a rock or water is not. They, like all of us, recognize life mainly by what living things do. **Figure 1.1** highlights seven of the properties and processes that we associate with life.

(1) *Order*. This close-up of a sunflower illustrates the highly ordered structure that typifies life. Living cells are the basis of this complex organization.

(2) *Reproduction*. Organisms reproduce their own kind. Here an emperor penguin protects its baby.

(3) *Growth and development*. Inherited information in the form of DNA controls the pattern of growth and development of all organisms, including this hatching crocodile.

(4) *Energy processing*. When this bear eats its catch, it will use the chemical energy stored in the fish to power its own activities and chemical reactions.

(5) *Response to the environment*. All organisms respond to environmental stimuli. This Venus flytrap closed its trap rapidly in response to the stimulus of a damselfly landing on it.

(6) *Regulation*. Many types of mechanisms regulate an organism's internal environment, keeping it within limits that sustain life. Pictured here is a typical lemur behaviour with a regulatory function—"sunbathing"—which helps raise the animal's body temperature on cold mornings.

(7) *Evolutionary adaptation*. The leaflike appearance of this katydid camouflages it in its environment. Such adaptations evolve over many generations as individuals with traits best suited to their environment have greater reproductive success and pass their traits to offspring.

Figure 1.1 reminds us that the living world is wondrously varied. How do biologists make sense of this diversity and complexity, and how can you? Indeed, biology is a subject of enormous scope that gets bigger every year. One of the ways to help you organize all this information is to connect what you learn to a set of themes that you will encounter throughout your study of life. The next few modules introduce several of these themes: novel properties emerging at each level of biological organization, the cell as the fundamental unit of life, the correlation of structure and function, and the exchange of matter and energy as organisms interact with the environment. We then focus on the core theme of biology—evolution, the theme that makes sense of both the unity and diversity of life. And in the final two sections of the chapter, we look at the scientific method and the relationship of biology to our everyday lives.

Let's begin our journey with a tour through the levels of the biological hierarchy.

? **How would you define life?**

● Life can be defined by a set of common properties such as those described in this module.

▲ **Figure 1.1** Some important properties of life

(1) Order
(2) Reproduction
(3) Growth and development
(4) Energy processing
(5) Response to the environment
(6) Regulation
(7) Evolutionary adaptation

1.2 In life's hierarchy of organization, new properties emerge at each level

As **Figure 1.2** illustrates, the study of life extends from the global scale of the biosphere to the microscopic scale of molecules. At the upper left we take a distant view of the **biosphere**, all the environments on Earth that support life. These include most regions of land, bodies of water, and the lower atmosphere. A closer look at one of these environments brings us to the level of an **ecosystem**, which consists of all the organisms living in a particular area, as well as the physical components with which the organisms interact, such as air, soil, water, and sunlight.

The entire array of organisms in an ecosystem is called a **community**. The community in this forest ecosystem in British Columbia includes the bears and the salmon that they eat, as well as the birds, trees, and ferns; a huge diversity of insects; many kinds of trees and other plants; fungi; and enormous numbers of microscopic protists and bacteria. Each unique form of life is called a species.

A **population** includes all the individuals of a particular species living in an area, such as all the Kermode bears in the forest community. Next in the hierarchy is the **organism**, an individual living thing.

Within a complex organism such as a bear, life's hierarchy continues to unfold. An **organ system**, such as the circulatory system or nervous system, consists of several organs that cooperate in a specific function. For instance, the organs of the nervous system are the brain, the spinal cord, and the nerves. A bear's nervous system controls its actions, such as fishing for salmon.

An **organ** is made up of several different **tissues**, each made up of a group of similar cells that perform a specific function. A **cell** is the fundamental unit of life. In the nerve cell shown here, you can see several organelles, such as the nucleus. An **organelle** is a membrane-enclosed structure that performs a specific function in a cell.

Finally, we reach the level of molecules in the hierarchy. A **molecule** is a cluster of small chemical units called atoms held together by chemical bonds. Our example in Figure 1.2 is a computer graphic of a section of DNA (deoxyribonucleic acid)—the molecule of inheritance.

Now let's work our way in the opposite direction in Figure 1.2, moving up life's hierarchy from molecules to the biosphere. It takes many molecules to build organelles, numerous organelles to make a cell, many cells to make a tissue, and so on. At each new level, novel properties arise, properties that were not present at the preceding level. For example, life emerges at the level of the cell—a test tube full of organelles is not alive. Such **emergent properties** represent an important theme of biology. The familiar saying that "the whole is greater than the sum of its parts" captures this idea. The emergent properties of each level result from the specific arrangement and interactions of its parts.

? Which of these levels of biological organization includes all others in the list: cell, molecule, organ, and tissue?

Organ ●

Biosphere

Vancouver Island

Ecosystem
Forest on Vancouver Island

Community
All organisms in the forest

Population
Group of Kermode black bears

Organism
Kermode Spirit bear

Organ system
Nervous system

Spinal

Brain

Nerve

Organ
Brain

Tissue
Nervous tissue

Cell
Nerve cell

Nucleus

Organelle
Nucleus

Molecule
DNA

Atom

▲ **Figure 1.2** Life's hierarchy of organization

1.3 Cells are the structural and functional units of life

The cell has a special place in the hierarchy of biological organization. It is the level at which the properties of life emerge— the lowest level of structure that can perform all activities required for life. A cell can regulate its internal environment, take in and use energy, respond to its environment, and develop and maintain its complex organization. The ability of cells to give rise to new cells is the basis for all reproduction and for the growth and repair of multicellular organisms.

All organisms are composed of cells. They occur singly as a great variety of unicellular (single-celled) organisms, such as amoebas and most bacteria. And cells are the subunits that make up multicellular organisms, such as bears and trees. Your body consists of trillions of cells of many different kinds.

All cells share many characteristics. For example, every cell is enclosed by a membrane that regulates the passage of materials between the cell and its surroundings. And every cell uses DNA as its genetic information. There are two basic types of cells. **Prokaryotic cells** were the first to evolve and were Earth's sole inhabitants for about the first 1.5 billion years of life on Earth. Fossil evidence indicates that **eukaryotic cells** evolved about 2.1 billion years ago.

Figure 1.3 shows these two types of cells as artificially coloured photographs taken with an electron microscope. A prokaryotic cell is much simpler and usually much smaller than a eukaryotic cell. The cells of the microorganisms we call bacteria are prokaryotic. Plants, animals, fungi, and protists are all composed of eukaryotic cells. As you can see in Figure 1.3, a eukaryotic cell is subdivided by membranes into many functional compartments, called organelles. These include a nucleus, which houses the cell's DNA.

The properties of life emerge from the ordered arrangement and interactions of the structures of a cell. Such a combination of components forms a more complex organization that we can call a *system*. Cells are examples of biological systems, as are organisms and ecosystems. Systems and their emergent properties are not unique to life. Consider a box of bicycle parts. When all the individual parts are properly assembled, the result is a mechanical system you can use for exercise or transportation.

The emergent properties of life, however, are particularly challenging to study because of the unrivalled complexity of biological systems. At the cutting edge of large-scale research today is an approach called **systems biology**. The goal of systems biology is to construct models for the dynamic behaviour of whole systems based on studying the interactions among the parts. Biological systems can range from the functioning of the biosphere to the molecular machinery of an organelle.

Cells illustrate another theme of biology: the correlation of structure and function. Experience shows you that form

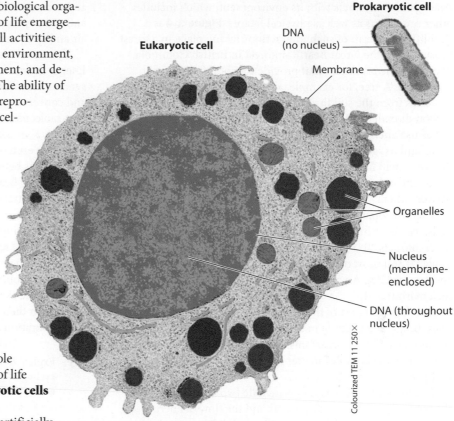

▲ Figure 1.3 Contrasting the size and complexity of prokaryotic and eukaryotic cells (shown here approximately 11 250 times their real size)

generally fits function. A screwdriver tightens or loosens screws; a hammer pounds nails. Because of their form, these tools can't do each other's jobs. Applied to biology, this theme of form fitting function is a guide to the structure of life at all its organizational levels. For example, the long extension of the nerve cell shown in Figure 1.2 enables it to transmit impulses across long distances in the body. Often, analyzing a biological structure gives us clues about what it does and how it works.

The activities of organisms are all based on cells. For example, your every thought is based on the actions of nerve cells, and your movements depend on muscle cells. Even a global process such as the cycling of carbon is the result of cellular activities, including the photosynthesis of plant cells and the cellular respiration of nearly all cells, a process that uses oxygen to break down sugar for energy and releases carbon dioxide. In the next module, we explore these processes and how they relate to the theme of organisms interacting with their environments.

 Why are cells considered the basic units of life?

● They are the lowest level in the hierarchy of biological organization at which the properties of life emerge.

1.4 Organisms interact with their environment, exchanging matter and energy

An organism interacts with its environment, which includes other organisms as well as physical factors. **Figure 1.4** is a simplified diagram of such interactions taking place in a forest ecosystem in the Great Bear Rainforest in British Columbia. Plants are the *producers* that provide the food for a typical ecosystem. A tree, for example, absorbs water (H_2O) and minerals from the soil through its roots, and its leaves take in carbon dioxide (CO_2) from the air. In photosynthesis, a tree's leaves use energy from sunlight to convert CO_2 and H_2O to sugar and oxygen (O_2). The leaves release O_2 to the air, and the roots help form soil by breaking up rocks. Thus, both organism and environment are affected by the interactions between them.

The *consumers* of the ecosystem eat plants and other animals. The bear in Figure 1.4 eats berries, nuts, grasses, and other animals. To release the energy in food, animals (as well as plants and most other organisms) take in O_2 from the air and release CO_2. An animal's wastes return other chemicals to the environment.

Another vital part of the ecosystem includes the small animals, fungi, and bacteria in the soil that decompose wastes and the remains of dead organisms. These *decomposers* act as recyclers, changing complex matter into simpler mineral nutrients that plants can absorb and use.

The dynamics of ecosystems include two major processes—the recycling of chemical nutrients and the flow of energy. These processes are illustrated in Figure 1.4. The most basic chemicals necessary for life—carbon dioxide, oxygen, water,

and various minerals—cycle within an ecosystem from the air and soil to plants, to animals and decomposers, and back to the air and soil (blue arrows in the figure).

By contrast, an ecosystem gains and loses energy constantly. Energy flows into the ecosystem when plants and other photosynthesizers absorb light energy from the sun (yellow arrow) and convert it to the chemical energy of sugars and other complex molecules. Chemical energy (orange arrow) is then passed through a series of consumers and, eventually, decomposers, powering each organism in turn. In the process of these energy conversions between and within organisms, some energy is converted to heat, which is then lost from the system (red arrow). In contrast to chemical nutrients, which recycle within an ecosystem, energy flows through an ecosystem, entering as light and exiting as heat.

In this first section, we have touched on several themes of biology, from emergent properties in the biological hierarchy of organization, to cells as the structural and functional units of life, to the exchange of matter and energy as organisms interact with their environment. In the next section, we begin our exploration of evolution, the core theme of biology.

? **Explain how the photosynthesis of plants functions in both cycling of chemical nutrients and the flow of energy in an ecosystem.**

● Photosynthesis uses light energy to convert carbon dioxide and water to energy-rich food, making it the pathway by which both chemical nutrients and energy become available to most organisms.

Ecosystem

Sunlight

O_2 O_2

Producers (such as plants)

Chemical energy (food)

Consumers (such as animals)

Heat

CO_2 CO_2

Water and minerals taken up by plants

Cycling of chemical nutrients

Decomposers (in soil)

▲ **Figure 1.4** The cycling of nutrients and flow of energy in an ecosystem

Evolution, the Core Theme of Biology

1.5 The unity of life is based on DNA and a common genetic code

All cells have DNA, and the continuity of life depends on this universal genetic material. DNA is the chemical substance of **genes**, the units of inheritance that transmit information from parents to offspring. Genes, which are grouped into very long DNA molecules called chromosomes, also control all the activities of a cell. The molecular structure of DNA accounts for these functions. Let us explain: Each DNA molecule is made up of two long chains coiled together into what is called a double helix. The chains are made up of four kinds of chemical building blocks. **Figure 1.5** illustrates these four building blocks, called nucleotides, with different colours and letter abbreviations of their names. The right side of the figure shows a short section of a DNA double helix.

▲ **Figure 1.5** The four building blocks of DNA (left); part of a DNA double helix (right)

The way DNA encodes a cell's information is analogous to the way we arrange letters of the alphabet into precise sequences with specific meanings. The word *rat*, for example, conjures up an image of a rodent; *tar* and *art*, which contain the same letters, mean very different things. We can think of the four building blocks as the alphabet of inheritance. Specific sequential arrangements of these four chemical letters encode precise information in genes, which are typically hundreds or thousands of "letters" long.

The DNA of genes provides the blueprints for making proteins, and proteins serve as the tools that actually build and maintain the cell and carry out its activities. A bacterial gene may direct the cell to "Make a yellow pigment." A particular human gene may mean "Make the hormone insulin." All forms of life use essentially the same genetic code to translate the information stored in DNA into proteins. This makes it possible to engineer cells to produce proteins normally found only in some other organism. Thus, bacteria can be used to produce insulin for the treatment of diabetes by inserting a gene for human insulin into bacterial cells.

The diversity of life arises from differences in DNA sequences—in other words, from variations on the common theme of storing genetic information in DNA. Bacteria and humans are different because they have different genes. But both sets of instructions are written in the same language.

In the next module, we see how biologists attempt to organize the diversity of life.

 What is the chemical basis for all of life's kinship?

● DNA as the genetic material

1.6 The diversity of life can be arranged into three domains

We can think of biology's enormous scope as having two dimensions. The "vertical" dimension, which we examined in Module 1.2, is the size scale that stretches from molecules to the biosphere. But biology also has a "horizontal" dimension, spanning across the great diversity of organisms existing now and over the long history of life on Earth.

Grouping Species   Diversity is a hallmark of life. Biologists have so far identified and named about 1.8 million species, and thousands more are identified each year. Estimates of the total number of species range from 10 million to more than 100 million. Whatever the actual number, biologists face a major challenge in attempting to make sense of this enormous variety of life.

There seems to be a human tendency to group diverse items according to similarities. We may speak of bears or butterflies, though we recognize that each group includes many different species. We may even sort groups into broader categories, such

as mammals and insects. Taxonomy, the branch of biology that names and classifies species, arranges species into a hierarchy of broader and broader groups, from genus, family, order, class, and phylum, to kingdom.

The Three Domains of Life   Until the 1990s, most biologists used a taxonomic scheme that divided all of life into five kingdoms. But new methods for assessing evolutionary relationships, such as comparison of DNA sequences, have led to an ongoing reevaluation of the number and boundaries of kingdoms. As that debate continues, however, there is consensus that life can be organized into three higher levels called **domains**. **Figure 1.6** shows representatives of the three domains: Bacteria, Archaea, and Eukarya.

Domains **Bacteria** and **Archaea** both consist of prokaryotes, organisms with prokaryotic cells. Most prokaryotes are single-celled and microscopic. The photos of the prokaryotes

Domain Bacteria

Colourized SEM 6 000×

Bacteria

Domain Archaea

Colourized SEM 7 700×

Archaea

Domain Eukarya

LM 275×

Protists (multiple kingdoms)   Kingdom Plantae

Kingdom Fungi   Kingdom Animalia

▲ **Figure 1.6** The three domains of life

in Figure 1.6 were made with an electron microscope, and the number along the side indicates the magnification of the image. (We will discuss microscopy in Chapter 4.) Bacteria and archaea were once combined in a single kingdom. But much evidence indicates that they represent two very distinct branches of life, each of which includes multiple kingdoms.

Bacteria are the most diverse and widespread prokaryotes. In the photo of bacteria in Figure 1.6, each of the rod-shaped structures is a bacterial cell.

Many of the prokaryotes known as archaea live in Earth's extreme environments, such as salty lakes and boiling hot springs. Each round structure in the photo of archaea in Figure 1.6 is an archaeal cell.

All the eukaryotes, organisms with eukaryotic cells, are grouped in domain **Eukarya**. As we discussed in Module 1.3, eukaryotic cells have a nucleus and other internal structures called organelles.

Protists are a diverse collection of mostly single-celled organisms and some relatively simple multicellular relatives. Pictured in Figure 1.6 is an assortment of protists in a drop of pond water. Although protists were once placed in a single kingdom, it is now clear that they do not form a single natural group of species. Biologists are currently debating how to split the protists into groups that accurately reflect their evolutionary relationships.

The three remaining groups within Eukarya contain multicellular eukaryotes. These kingdoms are distinguished partly by their modes of nutrition. Kingdom Plantae consists of plants, which produce their own food by photosynthesis. The representative of kingdom Plantae in Figure 1.6 is a tropical bromeliad, a plant native to the Americas.

Kingdom Fungi, represented by the mushrooms in Figure 1.6, is a diverse group, whose members mostly decompose the remains of dead organisms and organic wastes and absorb the nutrients into their cells.

Animals obtain food by ingestion, which means they eat other organisms. Representing kingdom Animalia, the sloth in Figure 1.6 resides in the trees of Central and South American rainforests. There are actually members of two other groups in the sloth photo. The sloth is clinging to a tree (kingdom Plantae), and the greenish tinge in the animal's hair is a luxuriant growth of photosynthetic prokaryotes (domain Bacteria). This photograph exemplifies a theme reflected in our book's title: connections between living things. The sloth depends on trees for food and shelter; the tree uses nutrients from the decomposition of the sloth's feces; the prokaryotes gain access to the sunlight necessary for photosynthesis by living on the sloth; and the sloth is camouflaged from predators by its green coat.

The diversity of life and its interconnectedness are evident almost everywhere. Earlier we looked at life's unity in its shared properties, two basic types of cell structure, and common genetic code. And now we have briefly surveyed its diversity. In the next module, we explore how evolution explains both the unity and the diversity of life.

? **To which of the three domains of life do we belong?**

Eukarya ●

1.7 Evolution explains the unity and diversity of life

The history of life, as documented by fossils, is a saga of a changing Earth billions of years old, inhabited by an evolving cast of living forms (Figure 1.7A). And yet, there is relatedness among these diverse forms, and patterns of ancestry can be traced through the fossil record and other evidence. Evolution accounts for life's dual nature of kinship and diversity.

In November 1859, the English naturalist Charles Darwin (Figure 1.7B) published one of the most important and influential books ever written. Titled *On the Origin of Species by Means of Natural Selection*, Darwin's book was an immediate bestseller and soon made his name almost synonymous with the concept of evolution. Darwin stands out in history with people such as Newton and Einstein, scientists who synthesized comprehensive theories with great explanatory power.

The Origin of Species articulated two main points. First, Darwin presented a large amount of evidence to support the idea of **evolution**—that species living today are descendants of ancestral species. Darwin called his evolutionary theory "descent with modification." It was an insightful phrase, as it captured both the unity of life (descent from a common ancestor) and the diversity of life (modification as species diverged from their ancestors).

Darwin's second point was to propose a mechanism for evolution, which he called **natural selection**. Darwin synthesized this idea from observations that by themselves were neither profound nor original. Others had the pieces of the puzzle, but Darwin saw how they fit together. He started with the following two observations: (1) Individuals in a population vary in their traits, many of which are passed on from parents to offspring. (2) A population can produce far more offspring than the environment can support. From these two observations, Darwin inferred that those individuals with heritable traits best suited to the environment are more likely to survive and reproduce than are less well-suited individuals. As a result of this unequal reproductive success over many generations, a higher and higher proportion of individuals will have the advantageous traits. The result

▲ Figure 1.7B Charles Darwin in 1859

of natural selection is evolutionary adaptation, the accumulation of favourable traits in a population over time.

Figure 1.7C uses a simple example to show how natural selection works. ❶ An imaginary beetle population has colonized an area where the soil has been blackened by a recent brush fire. Initially, the population varies extensively in the inherited coloration of individuals, from very light grey to charcoal. ❷ A bird eats the beetles it sees most easily, the light-coloured ones. This selective predation reduces the number of light-coloured beetles and favours the survival and reproductive success of the darker beetles. ❸ The surviving beetles reproduce. After several generations, the population is quite different from the original one. As a result of natural selection, the frequencies of the darker-coloured beetles in the population have increased.

Darwin realized that numerous small changes in populations caused by natural selection could eventually lead to major alterations of species. He proposed that new species could evolve as a result of the gradual accumulation of changes

❶ Population with varied inherited traits

❷ Elimination of individuals with certain traits

▲ Figure 1.7A Fossil of *Dimetrodon*. This 3-metre-long carnivore was more closely related to mammals than to reptiles.

❸ Reproduction of survivors

▲ Figure 1.7C An example of natural selection in action

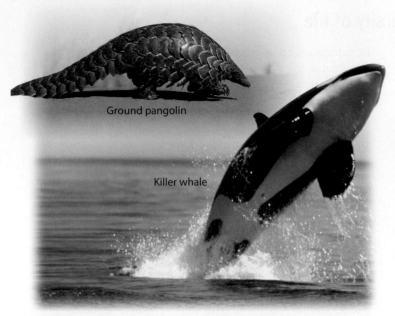

Ground pangolin

Killer whale

▲ **Figure 1.7D** Examples of adaptations to different environments

We see the exquisite results of natural selection in every kind of organism. Each species has its own set of evolutionary adaptations that have evolved over time. Consider the two very different mammals shown in **Figure 1.7D**. The ground pangolin, found in southern and eastern Africa, has a tough body armour of overlapping scales, protecting it from most predators. The pangolin uses its unusually long tongue to prod ants out of their nests. The killer whale is a mammal adapted for life at sea. It breathes air through nostrils on the top of its head and communicates with its companions by emitting clicking sounds that carry in water. Killer whales use sound echoes to detect schools of fish or other prey. The pangolin's armour and the killer whale's echolocating ability arose over many, many generations as individuals with heritable traits that made them better adapted to the environment had greater reproductive success. Evolution—descent with modification—explains both how these two mammals are related and how they differ. Evolution is the core theme that makes sense of everything we know and learn about life.

 How does natural selection adapt a population of organisms to its environment?

over long periods of time. (We'll explore evolution and natural selection in more detail in Chapters 14 and 15.)

● On average, those individuals with heritable traits best suited to the local environment produce the greatest number of offspring. This unequal reproductive success increases the frequency of those traits in the population.

The Scientific Method

1.8 Scientific inquiry is used to ask and answer questions about nature

The word *science* is derived from a Latin verb meaning "to know." Science is an attempt to obtain knowledge through the process of inquiry—a search for information, explanations, and answers to specific questions. The process attempts to eliminate human bias and observe biology in its truest sense. It stems from our curiosity about ourselves and the world around us. Scientific inquiry involves making observations, forming hypotheses, and testing predictions. It is important to note that science does not arrive at certain knowledge with absolute proofs, only theories that get progressively stronger as they are supported by more evidence.

Recorded observations and measurements are the data of science. Some data are *quantitative*, such as numerical measurements. Other data may be descriptive, or *qualitative*. For example, primatologist Alison Jolly has spent more than 40 years making observations of lemur behaviour during field research in Madagascar, amassing data that is mostly qualitative **(Figure 1.8)**.

Collecting and analyzing observations can lead to conclusions based on a type of logic called **inductive reasoning**. This kind of reasoning derives generalizations from a large number of specific observations. "All organisms are made of cells" is an inductive conclusion based on the discovery of cells in every biological specimen observed over two centuries of time. Careful observations and the inductive conclusions they lead to are fundamental to understanding nature.

Observations often stimulate us to seek natural causes and explanations. Such inquiry usually involves the forming and testing of hypotheses. A **hypothesis** is a proposed explanation for a set of observations that must be testable and falsifiable. A good hypothesis leads to predictions that scientists can test by recording additional observations or by designing experiments.

Deduction is the type of logic used to come up with ways to test hypotheses. In **deductive reasoning**, the logic flows from general premises to the specific results we should expect if the premises are true. If all organisms are made of cells (premise 1), and humans are organisms (premise 2), then humans are composed of cells (deduction). This deduction is a prediction that can be tested by examining human tissues.

▲ **Figure 1.8** Alison Jolly with her research subjects, ring-tailed lemurs

Theories in Science How is a theory different from a hypothesis? A scientific **theory** is also predictive but is much broader in scope than a hypothesis. It is usually general enough to generate many new, specific hypotheses that can then be tested. And a theory is supported by a large and usually growing body of evidence. Theories that become widely adopted (such as the theory of evolution) explain a great diversity of observations and are supported by a vast accumulation of evidence.

 Contrast inductive reasoning with deductive reasoning.

⦿ Inductive reasoning derives a generalization from many observations; deductive reasoning predicts specific outcomes from a general premise.

1.9 Scientists form and test hypotheses and share their results

Let's explore the elements of scientific inquiry with two case studies, one from everyday life and one from a research project.

A Case Study from Everyday Life We all use hypotheses in solving everyday problems. Let's say, for example, that you have three identical houseplants, all with yellowing leaves, sitting on your bedroom dresser far away from the window. That's an observation. An obvious question would be this:

Why are the leaves not as green as they were when you bought the plants? Two reasonable hypotheses based on past experience are that either the plants are not getting enough sunlight or they are not getting enough nutrients from the soil. Each of these hypotheses leads to predictions you can test with experiments or further observations. For example, the low-sunlight hypothesis predicts that placing a plant closer to the window will fix the problem. **Figure 1.9A** diagrams this botanical inquiry.

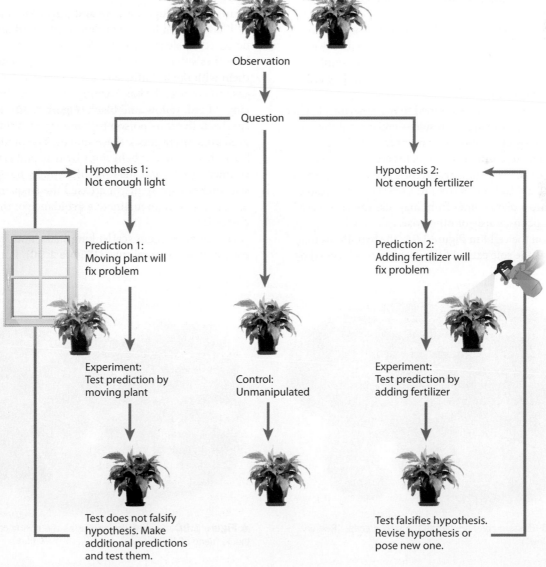

▲ **Figure 1.9A** An example of hypothesis-based science

The houseplant example illustrates two important points. First, a hypothesis must be testable: There must be some way to check its validity. Second, a hypothesis must be falsifiable: There must be some observation or experiment that could show that it is not true. To effectively test a hypothesis, a good experimental design is essential. A properly planned experiment reduces the role of chance in determining the results and makes them more informative. A properly designed experiment should use a large number of samples and be **controlled**, **randomized**, and **blinded**.

The houseplant example contains only one plant or sample in each group (for simplicity); however, the observed results would become stronger with multiple plants in each group. A control group is included for comparative purposes. Ideally, the experimental and control groups differ only in the one factor the experiment is designed to test. In this example, one plant is moved to the windowsill, a second plant receives fertilizer (testing a second hypothesis), and a third plant is treated the same as it always has been. This third plant serves as a control, allowing the observer to compare whether a treatment had any effect. Specimens should be randomly assigned to the experimental and control groups.

Randomization prevents any bias that may arise from assigning specific plants—for example, those with fewer yellow leaves—into the same group. So in our example all plants are given a random designation when they are assigned to their group.

Lastly, observers should be blinded to the experiment. That is, when they are measuring the results—greening of the leaves in this example—they should be unaware as to which group the plant is from. To ensure this, all plants are moved to a new location before the observer assesses each plant in random order. Blinding an experiment removes observer bias. Knowing which group a plant comes from may bias the observer's assessment, subconsciously or otherwise.

As shown on the right in Figure 1.9A, the hypothesis that low nutrients is the sole cause of the problem was falsified by adding fertilizer to one of the plants. As shown on the left, the low-sunlight hypothesis is the more likely explanation of the yellow leaves. Notice that testing supports a hypothesis not by proving that it is correct but by not eliminating it through falsification. Testing cannot prove a hypothesis beyond a shadow of doubt, because it is impossible to exhaust all alternative hypotheses. A hypothesis gains credibility by surviving multiple attempts to falsify it, while testing eliminates alternative hypotheses.

A Case Study from Science   To learn more about how science works, let's examine some actual scientific research.

The story begins with a set of observations and generalizations. Many poisonous animals are brightly coloured, often with distinctive patterns. This so-called warning coloration apparently says "dangerous species" to potential predators. But there are also mimics. These imposters resemble poisonous species but are actually harmless. A question that follows from these observations is this: What is the function of mimicry? A reasonable hypothesis is that mimicry is an evolutionary adaptation that reduces the harmless animal's risk of being eaten.

In 2001, biologists David and Karin Pfennig, along with William Harcombe, one of their undergraduate students, designed an elegant set of field experiments to test the hypothesis that mimics benefit because predators confuse them with the harmful species. A venomous snake called the eastern coral snake has warning coloration: bold, alternating rings of red, yellow, and black **(Figure 1.9B)**. (A *venomous* species delivers its poison by stinging, stabbing, or biting.) Predators rarely attack these snakes. The predators do not learn this avoidance behaviour by trial and error; a first encounter with a coral snake would usually be deadly. Natural selection has apparently increased the frequency of predators that inherit an instinctive avoidance of the coral snake's coloration.

The nonvenomous scarlet king snake mimics the ringed coloration of the coral snake **(Figure 1.9C)**. Both types of

▲ **Figure 1.9B** Eastern coral snake (as the saying goes, "Red on yellow, kill a fellow")

▲ **Figure 1.9C** Scarlet king snake (as the saying continues, "Red on black, friend of Jack")

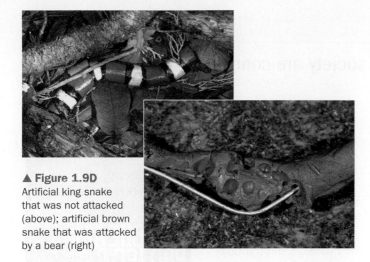

▲ Figure 1.9D
Artificial king snake that was not attacked (above); artificial brown snake that was attacked by a bear (right)

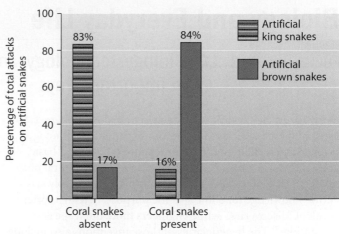

▲ Figure 1.9E Results of mimicry experiment

snakes can be found living in the same areas, but king snakes are also found in regions that have no coral snakes.

The geographic distribution of these snakes made it possible for the researchers to test a key prediction of the mimicry hypothesis: Mimicry should help to protect king snakes from predators, but only in regions where coral snakes also live. Avoiding snakes with warning coloration is an adaptation of predator populations that evolved in areas where coral snakes are present. Therefore, predators adapted to the warning coloration of coral snakes will attack king snakes less frequently than will predators in areas where coral snakes are absent.

To test this prediction, Harcombe made hundreds of artificial snakes out of wire covered with a claylike substance called Plasticine. He made two versions of fake snakes: an *experimental group* with the colour pattern of king snakes and a *control group* of plain brown snakes as a basis of comparison.

The researchers placed equal numbers of the two types of artificial snakes in field sites throughout North and South Carolina, including the region where coral snakes are absent. After four weeks, they retrieved the snakes and recorded how many had been attacked by looking for bite or claw marks. The most common predators were foxes, coyotes, and raccoons, but black bears also attacked some of the snakes (**Figure 1.9D**).

The data fit the key prediction of the mimicry hypothesis. The artificial king snakes were attacked less frequently than the artificial brown snakes only in field sites within the geographic range of the venomous coral snakes. The bar graph in **Figure 1.9E** summarizes the results.

This case study is another example of a **controlled experiment**. The artificial king snakes are the experimental group and the artificial brown snakes are the control. These groups test the effect of the snakes' coloration on the behaviour of predators. Without the control group, the researchers would not have been able to rule out other

variables, such as the number of predators in the different test areas. The experimental design left coloration as the only factor that could account for the low predation rate on the artificial king snakes placed within the range of coral snakes. An important control in the houseplant example would be ensuring that both plants receive the same watering regimen, so the amount of water is not a factor in the results.

The Culture of Science Science is a social activity, with most scientists working in teams, which often include graduate and undergraduate students. Scientists share information through publications, seminars, meetings, and personal communication. The Internet has added a new medium for this exchange of ideas and data. Scientists build on what has been learned from earlier research and often check one another's claims by attempting to confirm observations or repeat experiments.

Science seeks natural causes for natural phenomena. Thus, the scope of science is limited to the study of structures and processes that we can directly observe and measure. Science can neither support nor falsify hypotheses about supernatural forces or explanations, for such questions are outside the bounds of science.

The scientific method is necessarily repetitive: In testing a hypothesis, researchers may make observations that call for rejection of the hypothesis or at least revision and further testing. This process allows biologists to circle closer and closer to their best estimation of how nature works. As in all quests, science includes elements of challenge, adventure, and luck, along with careful planning, reasoning, creativity, cooperation, competition, patience, and persistence.

 ? Why is it difficult to draw a conclusion from an experiment that does not include a control group?

● Without a control group, you don't know if the experimental outcome is due to the variable you are trying to test or to some other variable.

Biology and Everyday Life

1.10 Biology, technology, and society are connected in important ways

Many issues facing society are related to biology (**Figure 1.10**). Most of these issues also involve our expanding technology. Science and technology are interdependent, but their basic goals differ. The goal of science is to understand natural phenomena. In contrast, the goal of **technology** is to apply scientific knowledge for some specific purpose. Scientists often speak of "discoveries," while engineers more often speak of "inventions." The beneficiaries of those inventions also include scientists, who use new technology in their research. And scientific discoveries often lead to the development of new technologies.

Technology depends less on the curiosity that drives basic science than on the needs and wants of people and on the social environment of the times. Debates about technology centre more on "Should we do it?" than "Can we do it?" Should insurance companies have access to individuals' DNA information? Should we permit research with embryonic stem cells? The line becomes blurred when we consider the application of scientific discoveries in a technological setting. For example, the question "Should we apply DNA testing to all newborn babies?" concerns both science and technology.

Technology has improved our standard of living in many ways, but not without adverse consequences. Technology that keeps people healthier has enabled Earth's population to grow 10-fold in the past three centuries and to more than double to 7 billion in just the past 40 years. The environmental effects of this growth can be devastating. Global climate change, toxic wastes, deforestation, nuclear accidents, and extinction

of species are just some of the repercussions of more and more people wielding more and more technology. Science can help us identify such problems and provide insight into what course of action may prevent further damage. But solutions to these problems have as much to do with politics, economics, and cultural values as with science and technology. Now that science and technology have become such powerful aspects of society, every citizen has a responsibility to develop a reasonable amount of scientific literacy. Scientific literacy is very important for politicians who are creating policy to deal with today's challenges. The crucial science-technology-society relationship is a theme that adds to the significance of any biology course. We will highlight some important connections between biology and society in the so-named modules throughout this book.

▲ **Figure 1.10** Biology and technology in the media

 How do science and technology interact?

New scientific discoveries may lead to new technologies; new technologies may increase the ability of scientists to search for new knowledge.

1.11 Evolution is connected to our everyday lives

Evolution is the core theme of biology. To emphasize the centrality of evolution to biology, we include an Evolution Connection module in each chapter in this book. But is evolution connected to your everyday life? And if so, in what ways?

Biologists now recognize that differences in DNA among individuals, populations, and species reflect the patterns of evolutionary change. The new technology of automatic DNA-sequencing machines has enabled scientists to determine the order of the billions of DNA bases in the human genome and in the genomes of other species. Comparisons of those sequences allow us to identify genes shared across many species, to study the actions of such genes in other species, and, in some cases, to search for new medical treatments. Identifying beneficial genes in relatives of our crop plants has permitted the breeding or genetic engineering of enhanced crops.

The recognition that DNA differs between people has led to the use of DNA tests to identify individuals. DNA profiling is now used to help convict or exonerate the accused, determine paternity, and identify remains.

Evolution teaches us that the environment is a powerful selective force for traits that best adapt populations to their environment. We are major agents of environmental change when we take drugs to combat infection or grow crops in pesticide-dependent monocultures or alter Earth's habitats. We have seen the effects of such environmental changes in antibiotic-resistant bacteria, pesticide-resistant pests, endangered species, and increasing rates of extinction.

How can evolutionary theory help? It can help us be more judicious in our use of antibiotics and pesticides and help us develop strategies for conservation efforts. It can help us create flu vaccines and HIV drugs by tracking the rapid evolution of these viruses. It can identify new sources of drugs. For example, by tracing the evolutionary history of the endangered Pacific yew tree, once the only source of the cancer drug Taxol, scientists have discovered similar compounds in more common trees.

We hope this book will help you develop an appreciation for evolution and biology and help you apply your new knowledge to evaluating issues ranging from your personal health to the well-being of the whole world. Biology offers us a deeper understanding of ourselves and our planet and a chance to more fully appreciate life in all of its diversity.

 How might an understanding of evolution contribute to the development of new drugs?

As one example, we can find organisms that share our genes and similar cellular processes and test the actions of potential drugs in these organisms.

RUMOUR HAS IT ## 1.12 Do malicious rumours spread like diseases?

Within each of the chapters of this book, we have highlighted one rumour or misconception about a related topic in biology. These special modules are intended to encourage critical thinking. The world is full of misinformation. With easy access to the Internet, rumours can spread at extraordinary speeds, making critical thinking even more essential than it has been in the past.

Malicious rumours are social contagions: stories based on misinformation and hearsay, spread among individuals through various social interactions **(Figure 1.12)**. Many psychologists have compared the transmission of a rumour to that of an infectious disease. Do malicious rumours actually spread like diseases?

In the science of spreading malicious rumours, there are three kinds of people: An *ignorant person* is an individual who has not heard the rumour; a *spreader* has heard the rumour and repeats it to others; and a *stifler* has heard the rumour but chooses not to tell others. Scientists who track disease transmission also refer to three analogous categories of individuals. Respectively, a *susceptible person* has not been infected, an *infectious person* has the disease and is capable of transmitting it to others, and an *immune person* has been cured of the disease and cannot contract it again.

Malicious rumour transmission does in fact have several similarities to disease transmission. With many infectious diseases, such as bacterial and viral infections, the pathogen (i.e., the disease-causing agent) can change as the disease spreads. Most infectious organisms replicate very rapidly. An infection that begins with a few bacteria can quickly grow to one with billions. Within these vast numbers, genetic mutations are not uncommon. For instance, some mutations may give bacteria resistance to antibiotics (see Module 17.10). As mutations accumulate, the pathogen evolves. Just as diseases can change through mutation, rumours also evolve as their details are twisted or altered when they are told and retold.

An infectious person who has contact with more susceptible people in their daily life may transmit a disease faster than someone with fewer in-person contacts. Likewise, not all spreaders tell malicious rumours with the same efficiency. Some influential spreaders are capable of perpetuating a malicious rumour much faster and further than others. With today's social media, rumours can travel along the information

▲ **Figure 1.12** Rumours spread quickly through social networks

superhighway quickly. People who have more followers have a greater potential to disseminate the rumour.

After a disease runs its course, individuals often develop some immunity to the disease (see Chapter 34). Upon exposure to a previously encountered disease, it is often quickly cured by the individual's immune system. If a spreader decides to become a stifler and stop transmitting the malicious rumour, they become resistant to "reinfection" by the same story.

Although there are definite similarities between the transmission of rumours and diseases, there are some important differences. As a rumour spreads from a spreader to an ignorant person, the ignorant person becomes transformed into either a spreader or a stifler. However, unlike an ignorant person, a susceptible person cannot choose to become immune.

Another difference is that a spreader generally stops rumour transmission when they have told all of their friends. In contrast, infectious people can transmit the disease to random susceptible people outside of their circle of followers and only stop transmission of the pathogen after the course of infection. Most spreaders do not share malicious rumours with people they do not know.

 How is an infectious person similar to a spreader?

Both are agents of transmission. An infectious person spreads disease, whereas a spreader transmits rumours.

MasteringBiology® For Practice Quizzes, BioFlix, MP3 Tutors, and Activities, go to masteringbiology.com.

Reviewing the Concepts

Themes in the Study of Biology (1.1–1.4)

1.1 All forms of life share common properties. Biology is the scientific study of life. Properties of life include order, reproduction, growth and development, energy processing, response to the environment, regulation, and evolutionary adaptation.

1.2 In life's hierarchy of organization, new properties emerge at each level. Biological organization unfolds as follows: biosphere > ecosystem > community > population > organism > organ system > organ > tissue > cell > organelle > molecule. Emergent properties result from the interactions among component parts.

1.3 Cells are the structural and functional units of life. Eukaryotic cells contain membrane-enclosed organelles, including a nucleus containing DNA. Prokaryotic cells are smaller and lack such organelles. Structure is related to function at all levels of biological organization. Systems biology models the complex interactions of biological systems, such as the molecular interactions within a cell.

1.4 Organisms interact with their environment, exchanging matter and energy. Ecosystems are characterized by the cycling of chemical nutrients from the atmosphere and soil through producers, consumers, decomposers, and back to the environment. Energy flows one way through an ecosystem—entering as sunlight, converted to chemical energy by producers, passed on to consumers, and exiting as heat.

Ecosystem

Evolution, the Core Theme of Biology (1.5–1.7)

1.5 The unity of life is based on DNA and a common genetic code. DNA is responsible for heredity and for programming the activities of a cell. A species' genes are coded in the sequences of the four building blocks making up DNA's double helix.

1.6 The diversity of life can be arranged into three domains. Taxonomy names species and classifies them into a system of broader groups. Domains Bacteria and Archaea consist of prokaryotes. The eukaryotic domain, Eukarya, includes various protists and the kingdoms Fungi, Plantae, and Animalia.

1.7 Evolution explains the unity and diversity of life. Darwin synthesized the theory of evolution by natural selection.

The Scientific Method (1.8–1.9)

1.8 Scientific inquiry is used to ask and answer questions about nature. Scientists use inductive reasoning to draw general conclusions from many observations. They form hypotheses and use deductive reasoning to make predictions. Data may be qualitative or quantitative. A scientific theory is broad in scope, generates new hypotheses, and is supported by a large body of evidence.

1.9 Scientists form and test hypotheses and share their results. Predictions can be tested with experiments, and results can either falsify or support the hypothesis. In a controlled experiment, the use of control and experimental groups helps to demonstrate the effect of a single variable. Science is a social process: scientists share information and review one another's results.

Biology and Everyday Life (1.10–1.12)

1.10 Biology, technology, and society are connected in important ways. Technological advances stem from scientific research, and research benefits from new technologies.

1.11 Evolution is connected to our everyday lives. Evolutionary theory is useful in medicine, agriculture, forensics, and conservation. Human-caused environmental changes are powerful selective forces that affect the evolution of many species.

1.12 Do malicious rumours spread like diseases? Although the transmission of a rumour resembles that of a disease, there are some important differences.

Connecting the Concepts

1. Biology can be described as having both a vertical scale and a horizontal scale. Explain what that means.

2. Complete the following map organizing some of biology's major concepts.

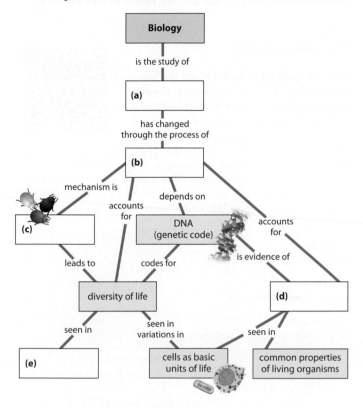

Testing Your Knowledge

Multiple Choice

3. Which of the following best describes the logic of the scientific method?
   a. If I generate a testable hypothesis, tests and observations will support it.
   b. If my prediction is correct, it will lead to a testable hypothesis.
   c. If my observations are accurate, they will not falsify my hypothesis.
   d. If my hypothesis is correct, I can make predictions and my results will not falsify my hypothesis.
   e. If my predictions are good and my tests are right, they will prove my hypothesis.

4. Single-celled amoebas and bacteria are grouped into different domains because
   a. amoebas eat bacteria.
   b. bacteria are not made of cells.
   c. bacterial cells lack a membrane-enclosed nucleus.
   d. bacteria decompose amoebas.
   e. amoebas are motile; bacteria are not.

5. A biologist studying interactions among the protists in an ecosystem could *not* be working at which level in life's hierarchy? *(Choose carefully and explain your answer.)*
   a. the population level
   b. the molecular level
   c. the community level
   d. the organism level
   e. the organ level

6. Which of the following questions is outside the realm of science?
   a. Which organisms play the most important role in energy input to a forest?
   b. What percentage of music majors take a biology course?
   c. What is the physical nature of the universe?
   d. What is the influence of the supernatural on current events?
   e. What is the dominance hierarchy in a population of Kermode bears?

7. Which of the following statements best distinguishes hypotheses from theories in science?
   a. Theories are hypotheses that have been proved.
   b. Hypotheses are tentative guesses; theories are correct answers to questions about nature.
   c. Hypotheses usually are narrow in scope; theories have broad explanatory power.
   d. Hypotheses and theories are different terms for essentially the same thing in science.
   e. Theories cannot be falsified; hypotheses can be falsified.

8. Which of the following best demonstrates the unity among all living organisms?
   a. descent with modification
   b. common genetic code
   c. emergent properties
   d. natural selection
   e. the three domains

9. The core idea that makes sense of all of biology is
   a. the scientific method.
   b. the correlation of function with structure.
   c. systems biology.
   d. evolution.
   e. the emergence of life at the level of the cell.

Describing, Comparing, and Explaining

10. In an ecosystem, how is the movement of energy similar to that of chemical nutrients, and how is it different?

11. Explain the role of heritable variations in Darwin's theory of natural selection.

12. Explain what is meant by this statement: The scientific method is not rigid.

13. Contrast technology with science. Give an example of each to illustrate the difference.

14. Explain what is meant by this statement: Natural selection is an editing mechanism rather than a creative process.

Applying the Concepts

15. The graph below shows the results of an experiment in which mice learned to run through a maze.

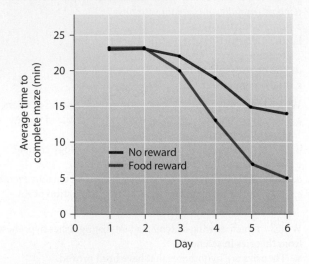

a. State the hypothesis and prediction that you think this experiment tested.
b. Which was the control group and which the experimental group? Why was a control group needed?
c. List some variables that must have been controlled so as not to affect the results.
d. Do the data support the hypothesis? Explain.

16. In an experiment similar to the mimicry experiment described in Module 1.9, a researcher counted more predator attacks on artificial king snakes in areas with coral snakes than in areas outside the range of coral snakes. From those numbers, the researcher concluded that the mimicry hypothesis is false. Do you think this conclusion is justified? Why or why not?

17. The fruits of wild species of tomato are tiny compared to the giant beefsteak tomatoes available today. This difference in fruit size is almost entirely because of the larger number of cells in the domesticated fruits. Plant biologists have recently discovered genes that are responsible for controlling cell division in tomatoes. Why would such a discovery be important to producers of other kinds of fruits and vegetables? To the study of human development and disease? To our basic understanding of biology?

18. The news media and popular magazines frequently report stories that are connected to biology. In the next 24 hours, record the ones you hear or read about in three different sources and briefly describe the biological connections in each story.

Answers to all questions can be found in Appendix E.

 Study on the Go

This QR code leads to Study on the Go— mobile study resources, including practice quizzes, videos, and glossary flashcards.

You can access Study on the Go content via your smartphone, allowing you to study whenever and wherever you want. Note: Your login information for MasteringBiology is required.

Go to one of the sites below to download a free app. Once installed, the phone will scan the code and link to a website with *Campbell Biology: Concepts and Connections'* Study on the Go resources.

ScanLife
http://getscanlife.com

NeoReader
http://get.neoreader.com

QuickMark
http://www.quickmark.com.tw/

The Living Cell

2

The Essential Chemistry of Life

BIG IDEAS

Elements, Atoms, and Compounds

(2.1–2.4)

Living organisms are made of atoms of certain elements, mostly combined into compounds.

Chemical Bonds

(2.5–2.10)

The structure of an atom determines what types of bonds it can form with other atoms.

Water's Life-Supporting Properties

(2.11–2.17)

The unique properties of water derive from the polarity of water molecules.

Androstadienone

Testosterone

Scents and Sensibility

Biology is the study of life. Because living organisms are made of atoms, molecules, and compounds, biology must also involve chemistry. Your cells, tissues, and organs are all made of chemical compounds. And the activities of your body—from reading these words to running a race—are all based on chemical reactions. So understanding and appreciating life begins with a basic understanding of chemistry: the elements that make up living matter and the ways in which the atoms of those elements interact.

Chemicals may also have a role in aspects of your life you may not have thought about. For example, when two people share romantic "chemistry," they may actually be sharing chemical signals called pheromones. A pheromone is a substance released by one organism to elicit an effect on a neighbouring organism. Pheromones are commonly used in the reproductive behaviours of animals. Many organisms communicate through the release of pheromones into the air. For example, male sheep (rams) release a pheromone into the air, which stimulates ovulation in nearby females (ewes) in what is called the ram effect.

Some plants release chemical signals—not only to communicate with their own species, but also to elicit responses in other species. For instance, floral scents are used to attract animal pollinators. In fact, many of the chemicals released by plants actually mimic insect pheromones. Orchids do not produce nectar, which repays would-be pollinators by providing a meal. Instead, by releasing chemicals like those produced by females, some orchids—including Canada's yellow bee orchid (*Ophrys lutea*), pictured here—attract male pollinators without having to spend energy feeding them.

Do humans use pheromones? The answer to this question is a topic of great debate. Many biologists feel that humans have evolved to become a visual species, one that relies less on olfaction than our ancestors. Others believe that humans may still subconsciously use chemical signals. Very few controlled scientific studies have supported the existence of chemical signals in humans. One report suggested a role for pheromones in the menstrual synchronization of women living together. However, the production of synchronizing pheromones by human females remains a topic of debate.

If human pheromones are produced, your response to them is likely not a conscious one. Indeed, you may simply find someone attractive without knowing why. Some fragrance companies add putative (potential but unproven) human pheromones to their products. One such additive in male fragrances is androstadienone, which is released in sweat. Androstadienone is a metabolite of the male sex hormone testosterone, both of which are shown here. Although not proven, this chemical is purported to increase a man's attractiveness to heterosexual women and homosexual men. Interestingly, studies have shown that androstadienone can affect the mood of heterosexual women when tested by a male, but not female, experimenter.

This chapter will discuss the basic components of chemistry and also make connections to the themes introduced in Chapter 1. One of these themes is the organization of life into a hierarchy of structural levels, with new properties emerging at each successive level. The intricate structures and complex functions of all living organisms arise from these interactions. We begin our story of biology with the basic concepts of chemistry that will apply throughout our study of life.

Elements, Atoms, and Compounds

2.1 Organisms are composed of elements, in combinations called compounds

Living organisms and everything around them are composed of **matter**, which is defined as anything that occupies space and has mass. Matter is found on Earth in three physical states: solid, liquid, and gas.

Types of matter as diverse as rocks, water, air, and biology students are all composed of chemical elements. An **element** is a substance that cannot be broken down to other substances by ordinary chemical means. Today, chemists recognize 112 unique chemical elements, which are organized in the form of the periodic table of elements (see Appendix A). Of these elements, 92 are found naturally on Earth, while the remaining ones have been synthesized by chemists in the laboratory. Each element has a symbol, the first letter or two of its English, Latin, or German name. For instance, the symbol for sodium, *Na*, is from the Latin word *natrium*; the symbol *O* comes from the English word *oxygen*.

A **molecule** is formed when two or more atoms are joined chemically. For example, a molecule of oxygen that we breathe contains two oxygen atoms. A **compound** is a substance consisting of two or more different elements combined in a fixed ratio. Compounds are much more common than pure elements. In fact, few elements exist in a pure state in nature.

Many compounds consist of only two elements; for instance, table salt (sodium chloride, NaCl) has equal parts of the elements sodium (Na) and chlorine (Cl). Pure sodium is a metal, and pure chlorine is a poisonous gas. Chemically combined, however, they form an edible compound **(Figure 2.1)**. The elements hydrogen (H) and oxygen (O) exist as gases. Combined in a ratio of 2:1, they form the most abundant compound on Earth—water (H_2O). These are simple examples of organized matter having emergent properties: A compound has characteristics different from those of its elements.

Most of the compounds in living organisms contain at least three or four elements. Sugar, for example, is formed of carbon (C), hydrogen, and oxygen. Proteins are compounds containing carbon, hydrogen, oxygen, nitrogen (N), and a small amount of sulphur (S). Different arrangements of the atoms of these elements give rise to the unique properties of each compound. Compounds that consist of carbon and hydrogen or carbon and hydrogen together with a few other elements (such as oxygen and nitrogen) are called *organic compounds*.

TABLE 2.1 | ELEMENTS IN THE HUMAN BODY

Element	Symbol	Percentage of Body Weight (Including Water)	
Oxygen	O	65.0%	
Carbon	C	18.5%	96.3%
Hydrogen	H	9.5%	
Nitrogen	N	3.3%	
Calcium	Ca	1.5%	
Phosphorus	P	1.0%	
Potassium	K	0.4%	3.7%
Sulphur	S	0.3%	
Sodium	Na	0.2%	
Chlorine	Cl	0.2%	
Magnesium	Mg	0.1%	

Trace elements, less than 0.01% of human body weight: Boron (B), chromium (Cr), cobalt (Co), copper (Cu), fluorine (F), iodine (I), iron (Fe), manganese (Mn), molybdenum (Mo), selenium (Se), silicon (Si), tin (Sn), vanadium (V), zinc (Zn)

About 25 elements are essential to life. As you can see in **Table 2.1**, four of these—oxygen, carbon, hydrogen, and nitrogen—make up about 96% of the weight of the human body, as well as that of most other living organisms. These four elements are the main ingredients of organic compounds such as proteins, sugars, and fats. Calcium (Ca), phosphorus (P), potassium (K), sulphur, sodium, chlorine, and magnesium (Mg) account for most of the remaining 4% of the human body. These elements are involved in such important functions as bone formation (calcium and phosphorus) and nerve signaling (potassium, sodium, calcium, and chlorine).

The **trace elements** listed at the bottom of the table are essential, but only in minute quantities. We explore the importance of trace elements to your health next.

 Explain how table salt illustrates the theme of emergent properties.

● The elements that make up the edible crystals of table salt, sodium and chlorine, are in pure form a metal and a poisonous gas.

Sodium   Chlorine   Sodium chloride

▲ **Figure 2.1** The emergent properties of the edible compound sodium chloride

2.2 Trace elements are common additives to food and water

Some trace elements, such as iron (Fe), are needed by nearly all forms of life. The bacterium that causes Lyme disease, *Borrelia burgdorferi*, can survive in the complete absence of iron, using manganese in its place. Iron makes up only about 0.004% of your body weight but is vital for energy processing and for transporting oxygen in your blood. Other trace elements, such as iodine (I), are required only by certain species. You need to ingest only a tiny amount of iodine each day, about 0.15 milligram (mg). Iodine is an essential ingredient of a hormone produced by the thyroid gland, which is located in the neck. An iodine deficiency in the diet causes the thyroid gland to grow to abnormal size, a condition called goiter **(Figure 2.2A)**. Iodine deficiency impairs brain development in children. Adding iodine to table salt has reduced the incidence of iodine deficiency in many countries. Unfortunately, iodized salt is not available everywhere, and an estimated 2 billion people worldwide have insufficient iodine intake. Seafood, kelp, strawberries, and dark, leafy greens are good natural sources. Thus, deficiencies are often found in inland regions, especially in areas where the soil is lacking in iodine. Although most common in developing nations, iodine deficiencies may also result from excessive consumption of highly processed foods (which often use non-iodized salt) and low-salt diets intended to lower the risk of cardiovascular disease.

Iodine is just one example of a trace element added to food or water to improve health. The Canadian Dental Association supports fluoridation of community drinking water as a public health measure. Fluoride is a form of fluorine (F), an element in Earth's crust that is found in small amounts in all water sources. In many areas, fluoride is added during the municipal water treatment process to raise levels to a concentration that can reduce tooth decay. If you mostly drink bottled water, your fluoride intake may be reduced, although some bottled water now contains added fluoride. Fluoride is also frequently added to dental products, such as toothpaste and mouthwash **(Figure 2.2B)**.

Chemicals are added to food to help preserve it, make it more nutritious, or simply make it look better. Look at the nutrition facts label from the side of the cereal box in **Figure 2.2C** to see a familiar example of how foods are fortified with mineral elements. Iron, for example, is a trace element commonly added to foods. (You can actually

▲ **Figure 2.2A** Goiter, a symptom of iodine deficiency, in a Burmese woman

◀ **Figure 2.2B** Mouthwash and toothpaste with added fluoride

see that iron has been added to a fortified cereal by crushing the cereal and then stirring a magnet through it.)

In the next module, we explore the structure of an atom and how this structure determines the chemical properties of elements.

 In addition to iron, what other trace element is found in the cereal in Figure 2.2C? How much of these elements does the cereal provide?

● Zinc: This cereal (with milk) provides 50% of the iron and 20% of the zinc needed in a day.

Nutrition Facts		
Per 1 cup (55 g)		
Amount	Cereal	With 1/2 cup skim milk
Calories	200	240
		% Daily Value
Fat 1 g*	2 %	2 %
Saturated 0.2 g + Trans 0 g	1 %	2 %
Cholesterol 0 mg	0 %	1 %
Sodium 200 mg	8 %	10 %
Carbohydrate 45 g	15 %	17 %
Fibre 6 g	24 %	24 %
Sugars 9 g		
Protein 6 g		
Vitamin A	0 %	8 %
Vitamin C	0 %	0 %
Calcium	2 %	15 %
Iron	50 %	50 %
Vitamin D	0 %	25 %
Thiamin	80 %	90 %
Riboflavin	4 %	20 %
Niacin	15 %	25 %
Vitamin B6	20 %	20 %
Folate	15 %	20 %
Vitamin B12	0 %	35 %
Pantothenate	15 %	20 %
Phosphorus	15 %	30 %
Magnesium	30 %	35 %
Zinc	15 %	20 %
* Amount in 55 g cereal		

▲ **Figure 2.2C** Nutrition facts from a breakfast cereal

2.3 Atoms consist of protons, neutrons, and electrons

Each element consists of one kind of atom, which is different from the atoms of other elements. An **atom**, named from a Greek word meaning "indivisible," is the smallest unit of matter that still retains the properties of an element. Atoms are so small that it would take about a million of them to stretch across the period printed at the end of this sentence.

Subatomic Particles Physicists have split the atom into more than a hundred types of subatomic particles. However, only three kinds of particles are relevant here. A **proton** is a subatomic particle with a single positive electrical charge (+). An **electron** is a subatomic particle with a single negative charge (−). A **neutron**, as its name implies, is electrically neutral (has no charge).

Figure 2.3A shows two very simple models of an atom of the element helium (He), the "lighter-than-air" gas that makes balloons rise. Notice that two protons (⊕) and two neutrons (⬤) are tightly packed in the atom's central core, or **nucleus**. Two electrons (⊖) move around the nucleus at nearly the speed of light. The attraction between the negatively charged electrons and the positively charged protons holds the electrons near the nucleus. The left-hand model shows the number of electrons in the atom. The right-hand model, slightly more realistic, shows a spherical cloud of negative charge created by the rapidly moving electrons. Neither model is drawn to scale. In real atoms, the electrons are much smaller than the protons and neutrons, and the electron cloud is much bigger compared to the nucleus. Imagine that this atom was the size of a football stadium: The nucleus would be the size of a fly on the 55-yard line, and the electrons would be like two tiny gnats buzzing around the stadium.

Atomic Number and Atomic Mass All atoms of a particular element have the same unique number of protons. This number is the element's **atomic number**. Thus, an atom of helium, with 2 protons, has an atomic number of 2. Carbon, with 6 protons, has an atomic number of 6 **(Figure 2.3B)**. Note

that in these atoms, the atomic number is also the number of electrons. Unless otherwise indicated, an atom has an equal number of protons and electrons, and thus its net electrical charge is 0 (zero).

An atom's **mass number** is the sum of the number of protons and neutrons in its nucleus. For helium, the mass number is 4; for carbon, it is 12 (Figures 2.3A and 2.3B). The mass of a proton and the mass of a neutron are almost identical and are expressed in a unit of measurement called the dalton. Protons and neutrons each have masses close to 1 dalton. An electron has only about 1/2000 the mass of a proton, so it contributes very little to an atom's mass. Thus, an atom's **atomic mass** (or weight) is approximately equal to its mass number—the sum of its protons and neutrons.

Isotopes All atoms of an element have the same atomic number, but some atoms of that element may differ in mass number. The different **isotopes** of an element have the same number of protons and behave identically in chemical reactions, but they have different numbers of neutrons. Table 2.3 shows the numbers of subatomic particles in the three isotopes of carbon. Carbon-12 (also written ^{12}C), with 6 neutrons, accounts for about 99% of the carbon in nature. Most of the remaining 1% consists of carbon-13 (^{13}C), with 7 neutrons. A third isotope, carbon-14 (^{14}C), with 8 neutrons, occurs in minute quantities. Notice that all three isotopes have 6 protons; otherwise, they would not be carbon.

Both ^{12}C and ^{13}C are stable isotopes, meaning their nuclei remain intact more or less forever. The isotope ^{14}C, on the other hand, is unstable, or radioactive. A **radioactive isotope** (or **radioisotope**) is one in which the nucleus decays spontaneously, giving off particles and energy. Radiation from decaying isotopes can damage cellular molecules and thus can pose serious risks to living organisms. But radioisotopes can be helpful, as in their use in dating fossils (see Module 13.12). They are also used in biological research and medicine, as we see next.

? A nitrogen atom has 7 protons, and its most common isotope has 7 neutrons. A radioactive isotope of nitrogen has 9 neutrons. What is the atomic number and mass number of this radioactive nitrogen?

TABLE 2.3 | ISOTOPES OF CARBON

		Carbon-12		Carbon-13		Carbon-14
Protons	6	Mass number 12	6	Mass number 13	6	Mass number 14
Neutrons	6		7		8	
Electrons	6		6		6	

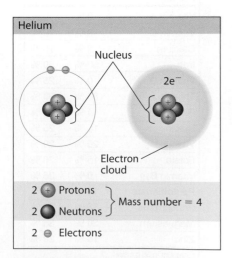

▲ Figure 2.3A Two models of a helium atom

Helium

Nucleus

Electron cloud

2e⁻

2 ⊕ Protons
2 ⬤ Neutrons } Mass number = 4
2 ⊖ Electrons

▲ Figure 2.3B Model of a carbon atom

Carbon

Electron cloud

6e⁻

Nucleus

6 ⊕ Protons
6 ⬤ Neutrons } Mass number = 12
6 ⊖ Electrons

Atomic number = 7; mass number = 16

2.4 Radioisotopes can help or harm us

Living cells cannot distinguish between isotopes of the same element. Consequently, organisms take up and use compounds containing radioisotopes in the usual way. Because radioactivity is easily detected by instruments, radioisotopes are useful as tracers—biological spies, in effect—for monitoring the fate of atoms in living organisms.

Basic Research   Biologists often use radioactive tracers to follow molecules as they undergo chemical changes in an organism. For example, researchers have used carbon dioxide (CO_2) containing the radioisotope ^{14}C to study photosynthesis. Using sunlight to power the conversion, plants take in CO_2 from the air and use it to make sugar molecules. Radioactively labelled CO_2 has enabled researchers to trace the sequence of molecules made by plants in the chemical route from CO_2 to sugar.

Medical Diagnosis and Treatment   Radioisotopes may also be used to tag chemicals that accumulate in specific areas of the body, such as phosphorus in bones. After injection of such a tracer, a special camera produces an image of where the radiation collects. In most diagnostic uses, the patient receives only a tiny amount of an isotope.

Sometimes radioisotopes are used for treatment. As we discussed in Module 2.2, the body uses iodine to make a thyroid hormone. Because radioactive iodine (^{131}I) accumulates in the thyroid, it can be used to kill cancer cells there.

It is important to note that not all isotopes emit radiation that harms living cells. Thus, there are some safe radioisotopes that can be used as tracers in biological studies or medical tests or as treatments for some diseases. Canada is a leading supplier of medical isotopes used worldwide. Substances that the body metabolizes, such as glucose or oxygen, may also be labelled with a radioactive isotope. **Figure 2.4A** shows a patient being examined by a PET (positron-emission tomography) scanner, which can produce three-dimensional images of areas of the body with high metabolic activity. PET is useful for diagnosing certain heart disorders and cancers and for basic research on the brain.

The early detection of Alzheimer's disease may be a new use for such techniques. This devastating illness gradually destroys a person's memory and ability to think. As the disease progresses, the brain becomes riddled with deposits (plaques) of a protein

Healthy person   **Alzheimer's patient**

▲ **Figure 2.4B** PET images of brains of a healthy person (left) and a person with Alzheimer's disease (right). Red and yellow colours indicate high levels of PIB bound to beta-amyloid plaques.

called beta-amyloid. Researchers have identified a protein molecule called PIB that binds to beta-amyloid. PIB contains a radioactive isotope that can be detected on a PET scan. **Figure 2.4B** shows PET images of the brains of a healthy person (left) and a person with Alzheimer's (right) injected with PIB. Notice that the brain of the Alzheimer's patient has high levels of PIB (red and yellow areas), whereas the unaffected person's brain has lower levels (blue). New therapies are focused on limiting the production of beta-amyloid or clearing it from the brain. A diagnostic test using PIB would allow researchers to monitor the effectiveness of new drugs in people living with the disease.

Dangers   Although radioisotopes have many beneficial uses, uncontrolled exposure to them can harm living organisms by damaging molecules, especially DNA. The particles and energy thrown off by radioactive atoms can break chemical bonds and also cause abnormal bonds to form. The explosion of a nuclear reactor at Chernobyl, Ukraine, in 1986 released large amounts of radioisotopes into the environment, which drifted over large areas of Russia, Belarus, and Europe. A few dozen people died from acute radiation poisoning, and more than 100 000 people were evacuated from the immediate area. Increased rates of thyroid cancer in children exposed to the radiation have been reported, and many thousands may be at increased risk of future cancers. Time will tell if similar effects will develop in the years after the accident at the Fukushima Daiichi nuclear power plant in Japan, which was caused by an earthquake and tsunami in March 2011. Already, higher mutation rates and more abnormalities have been reported in butterflies collected in Fukushima since the accident.

Natural sources of radiation can also pose a threat. Radon, a radioactive gas, may be a cause of lung cancer. Radon can contaminate buildings in regions where underlying rocks naturally contain uranium, a radioactive element. Homeowners can buy a radon detector or hire a company to test their home to ensure that radon levels are safe. If levels are found to be unsafe, technology exists to remove radon from homes.

? **Why are radioisotopes useful as tracers in research on the chemistry of life?**

▲ **Figure 2.4A** Technician monitoring the output of a PET scanner

● Organisms incorporate radioisotopes of an element into their molecules, and researchers can use special scanning devices to detect the presence of these isotopes in biological pathways or locations in the body.

Chemical Bonds

2.5 The distribution of electrons determines an atom's chemical properties

To understand how atoms interact with one another—the main subject of this section—we need to explore atomic structure further. Of the three subatomic particles—protons, neutrons, and electrons—only electrons are directly involved in the chemical activity of an atom. Electrons vary in the amount of energy they possess. The farther an electron is from the positively charged nucleus, the greater its energy. Electrons move around the nucleus only at certain energy levels, called **electron shells**. Depending on an element's atomic number, an atom may have one, two, or more electron shells surrounding the nucleus.

Figure 2.5 is an abbreviated version of the periodic table of the elements (see Appendix A). It shows the distribution of electrons for the first 18 elements, arranged in rows according to the number of electron shells (one, two, or three). Within each shell, electrons travel in different *orbitals*, which are discrete volumes of space in which electrons are most likely to be found.

Each orbital can hold a maximum of 2 electrons. The first electron shell has only one orbital and can hold only 2 electrons. Thus, hydrogen and helium are the only elements in the first row. For the second and third rows, the outer shell has four orbitals and can hold up to 8 electrons (four pairs). Note that the number of electrons increases by one as you read from left to right across each row in the table and that the electrons don't pair up until all orbitals have at least one electron.

It is the number of electrons in the outermost shell, called the **valence shell**, that determines the chemical properties of an atom. Atoms whose outer shells are not full (have unpaired electrons) tend to interact with other atoms—that is, to participate in chemical reactions.

Look at the electron shells of the atoms of the four elements that are the main components of biological molecules (highlighted in green in Figure 2.5). Because their outer shells are incomplete, all these atoms react readily with other atoms. The hydrogen atom has only 1 electron in its single electron shell, which can accommodate 2 electrons. Atoms of carbon, nitrogen, and oxygen also are reactive because their valence shells, which can hold 8 electrons, are also incomplete. In contrast, the helium atom has a first-level shell that is full with 2 electrons. Neon and argon also have full outer electron shells. As a result, these elements are chemically inert (unreactive).

How do chemical interactions between atoms enable them to fill their outer electron shells? When two atoms with incomplete outer shells react, each atom will share, donate, or receive electrons, so that both partners end up with completed outer shells. These interactions usually result in atoms staying close together, held by attractions known as **chemical bonds**. In the next two modules, we look at two important types of chemical bonds.

? How many electrons and electron shells does a sodium atom have? How many electrons are in its valence shell?

11 electrons, 3 electron shells, 1 electron in the outer shell

▲ **Figure 2.5** The electron distribution diagrams of the first 18 elements in the periodic table

2.6 Covalent bonds join atoms into molecules through electron sharing

The strongest kind of chemical bond is the **covalent bond**, in which two atoms *share* one or more pairs of outer-shell electrons. Two or more atoms held together by covalent bonds form a **molecule**. For example, a covalent bond connects two hydrogen atoms in a molecule of the gas H_2.

Table 2.6 shows four ways to represent this molecule. The symbol H_2, called the molecular formula, tells you that a hydrogen molecule consists of two atoms of hydrogen. The electron distribution diagram shows that the atoms share two electrons; as a result, both atoms fill their outer (and only)

26 | UNIT I | The Living Cell

TABLE 2.6 | ALTERNATIVE WAYS TO REPRESENT FOUR COMMON MOLECULES

Molecular Formula	Electron Distribution Diagram	Structural Formula	Space-Filling Model
H_2 Hydrogen		H—H Single bond	
O_2 Oxygen		O=O Double bond	
H_2O Water		H O H	
CH_4 Methane		H—C—H (with H above and H below)	

for shared electrons is called its **electronegativity**. The more electronegative an atom, the more strongly it pulls shared electrons toward its nucleus. In molecules of only one element, such as O_2 and H_2, the two identical atoms exert an equal pull on the electrons. The bonds in such molecules are said to be **nonpolar covalent bonds** because the electrons are shared equally between the atoms. Compounds such as methane also have nonpolar bonds, because the atoms of carbon and hydrogen are not substantially different in electronegativity.

In contrast to O_2, H_2, and CH_4, water is composed of atoms with different electronegativities. Oxygen is one of the most electronegative of the elements. (Nitrogen is also highly electronegative.) As indicated by the arrows in **Figure 2.6**, oxygen attracts the shared electrons in H_2O much more strongly than does hydrogen, so that the electrons spend more time near the oxygen atom than near the hydrogen atoms. This unequal sharing of electrons produces a **polar covalent bond**. In a polar covalent bond, the pulling of shared, negatively charged electrons closer to the more electronegative atom makes that atom partially negative and the other atom partially positive. Thus, in H_2O, the oxygen atom actually has a slight negative charge and each hydrogen atom a slight positive charge. Because of its polar covalent bonds and the wide V shape of the molecule, water is a **polar molecule**—that is, it has an unequal distribution of charges. It is slightly negative at the oxygen end of the molecule (point of the V) and slightly positive at each of the two hydrogen ends.

In some cases, two atoms are so unequal in their attraction for electrons that the more electronegative atom strips an electron completely away from its partner, as we see next.

? **What is chemically nonsensical about this structure?**

$$H—C=C—H$$

• Each carbon atom has only three covalent bonds instead of the four required by its valence.

shells. The third column shows a structural formula. The line between the hydrogen atoms represents the single covalent bond formed by the sharing of a pair of electrons (1 electron from each atom). A space-filling model, shown in the fourth column, uses colour-coded balls to symbolize atoms and comes closest to showing a molecule's shape.

How many covalent bonds can an atom form? It depends on the number of additional electrons needed to fill its outer, or valence, shell. This number is called the *valence*, or bonding capacity, of an atom. Looking back at the electron distribution diagrams in Figure 2.5, we see that H can form one bond; O can form two; N, three; and C, four.

In an oxygen molecule (O_2), shown in Table 2.6, the two oxygen atoms share two pairs of electrons, forming a double bond. A double bond is indicated by a pair of lines.

H_2 and O_2 are molecules composed of only one element. The third example in the table is a compound. Water (H_2O) is a molecule in which two hydrogen atoms are joined to oxygen by single bonds. And as shown at the bottom of Table 2.6, it takes four hydrogen atoms, each with a valence of 1, to satisfy carbon's valence of 4. This compound, methane (CH_4), is a major component of natural gas.

Atoms in a molecule are in a constant tug-of-war for the shared electrons of their covalent bonds. An atom's attraction

(slightly −)

(slightly +)   (slightly +)

▲ **Figure 2.6** A water molecule, with polar covalent bonds

2.7 Ionic bonds are attractions between ions of opposite charge

Table salt (NaCl) is an example of how the transfer of electrons can bond atoms together. **Figure 2.7A** shows how a sodium atom and a chlorine atom can form the compound sodium chloride (NaCl). Notice that sodium has only 1 electron in its outer shell, whereas chlorine has 7. When these atoms interact, the sodium atom donates its single outer electron to chlorine. Sodium now has only two shells, the outer shell having a full set of 8 electrons. When chlorine accepts sodium's electron, its own outer shell is now full with 8 electrons.

Remember that electrons are negatively charged particles. The transfer of an electron between the two atoms moves one unit of negative charge from one atom to the other. As you can see on the right in Figure 2.7A, sodium, with 11 protons but now only 10 electrons, has a net electrical charge of 1+. Chlorine, having gained an extra electron, now has 18 electrons but only 17 protons, giving it a net electrical charge of 1−. In each case, an atom has become what is called an ion. An **ion** is an atom or molecule with an electrical charge resulting from a gain or loss of one or more electrons. (As shown in the figure, the ion formed from chlorine is called a chloride ion.) Two ions with opposite charges attract each other. When the attraction holds them together, it is called an **ionic bond**. The resulting compound, in this case NaCl, is electrically neutral.

Sodium chloride is a familiar type of **salt**, a synonym for an ionic compound. Salts often exist as crystals in nature. **Figure 2.7B** shows the ions Na⁺ and Cl⁻ in a crystal of sodium chloride. An NaCl crystal can be of any size (there is no fixed number of ions), but sodium and chloride ions are always present in a 1:1 ratio. The ratio of ions can differ in the various kinds of salts.

The environment affects the strength of ionic bonds. In a dry salt crystal, the bonds are so strong that it takes a hammer and chisel to break enough of them to crack the crystal. If the same salt crystal is placed in water, however, the ionic bonds break when the ions interact with water molecules and the salt dissolves, as we'll discuss in Module 2.13. As a result, in an aqueous setting such as the cytoplasm of a cell, ionic bonds are much weaker than covalent bonds. Most drugs are manufactured as salts because they are quite stable when dry but can dissolve easily in water.

? **Explain what holds together the atoms in a crystal of table salt (NaCl).**

● Opposite charges attract. The positively charged sodium ions (Na⁺) and the negatively charged chloride ions (Cl⁻) are held together by ionic bonds, attractions between oppositely charged ions.

▲ **Figure 2.7A** Formation of an ionic bond, producing sodium chloride

▲ **Figure 2.7B** A crystal of sodium chloride

2.8 Hydrogen bonds are weak bonds important in the chemistry of life

In living organisms, most of the strong chemical bonds are covalent, intramolecular (*intra* means "inside", see Appendix D) linkages between atoms within a cell's molecules. But crucial to the functioning of a cell are weaker bonds within and between molecules (intermolecular bonds), such as the ionic bonds we just discussed. Most large molecules are held in their three-dimensional shape by weak bonds, as you will read in the next chapter. In addition, molecules in a cell may be held together briefly by weak bonds, respond to one another in some way, and then separate.

As you saw in Module 2.6, a hydrogen atom that has formed a polar covalent bond with an electronegative atom

(such as oxygen or nitrogen) has a partial positive charge. This partial positive charge allows it to be attracted to a nearby partially negative atom (often an oxygen or nitrogen) of another molecule. These weak but important bonds are best illustrated with water molecules, as shown in **Figure 2.8**. The charged regions on each water molecule are electrically attracted to oppositely charged regions on neighbouring molecules. Because the positively charged region in this special type of bond is always a hydrogen atom, the bond is called a **hydrogen bond**. As Figure 2.8 shows, the negative (oxygen) pole of a water molecule can form hydrogen bonds (dotted lines) to two hydrogen atoms. And each hydrogen atom of

Hydrogen bond {

▶ **Figure 2.8** Hydrogen bonds between water molecules

a water molecule can form a hydrogen bond with a nearby partial negative oxygen atom of another water molecule. Thus, each H_2O molecule can hydrogen-bond to as many as four partners.

You will learn in Chapter 3 how hydrogen bonds help to create a protein's shape (and thus its function) and hold the two strands of a DNA molecule together. Later in this chapter, we explore how water's polarity and hydrogen bonds give it unique, life-supporting properties. But first we discuss how the making and breaking of bonds change the composition of matter.

? **What enables neighbouring water molecules to hydrogen-bond to one another?**

● The molecules are polar, with the negative end (oxygen end) of one molecule attracted to a positive end (hydrogen end) of its neighbour.

2.9 Chemical reactions make and break chemical bonds

The basic chemistry of life has an overarching theme: The structure of atoms and molecules determines the way they behave. As we have seen, the chemical behaviour of an atom is determined by the number and arrangement of its subatomic particles, particularly its electrons. Other properties emerge when atoms combine to form molecules and when molecules interact. Water is a good example, because its emergent properties sustain all life on Earth.

Hydrogen and oxygen gases can react to form water:

$$2 H_2 + O_2 \rightarrow 2 H_2O$$

This is a **chemical reaction**, the breaking and making of chemical bonds, leading to changes in the composition of matter. In this case, two molecules of hydrogen ($2 H_{2 \, (gas)}$) react with one molecule of oxygen ($O_{2 \, (gas)}$) to produce two molecules of water ($2 H_2O_{(liquid)}$). The arrow indicates the conversion of the starting materials, called the **reactants**, to the **product**, the material resulting from the chemical reaction. Notice that the same *numbers* of hydrogen and oxygen atoms appear on the left and right sides of the arrow, although they are grouped differently. Chemical reactions do not create or destroy matter; they only rearrange it in various ways. As shown in **Figure 2.9**, the covalent bonds (represented here as white

"sticks" between atoms) holding hydrogen atoms together in H_2 and holding oxygen atoms together in O_2 are broken, and new bonds are formed to yield the H_2O product molecules.

Organisms cannot make water from H_2 and O_2, but they do carry out a great number of chemical reactions that rearrange matter in significant ways. Let's examine a chemical reaction that is essential to life on Earth: photosynthesis. The raw materials of photosynthesis are carbon dioxide ($CO_{2 \, (gas)}$), which is taken from the air, and water (H_2O), which plants absorb from the soil. Within green plant cells, sunlight powers the conversion of these reactants to the sugar product glucose ($C_6H_{12}O_{6 \, (aqueous \, solution)}$) and oxygen ($O_2$), a by-product that the plant releases into the air. The following chemical shorthand summarizes the process:

$$6 CO_2 + 6 H_2O \rightarrow C_6H_{12}O_6 + 6 O_2$$

Although photosynthesis is actually a sequence of many chemical reactions, we see that we end up with the same number and kinds of atoms we started with. Matter has simply been rearranged, with an input of energy provided by sunlight.

The chemistry of life is dynamic. Living cells routinely carry out thousands of chemical reactions. These reactions take place in the watery environment of a cell, and we look at the life-supporting properties of water in the next Big Idea. But first, let's examine a rumour you may have heard about a specific chemical reaction in swimming pools.

? **Fill in the blanks with the correct numbers in the following chemical process:**

$$C_6H_{12}O_6 + \_O_2 \rightarrow \_CO_2 + \_H_2O$$

What process do you think this reaction represents? (*Hint:* Think about how your cells use these reactants to produce energy.)

2 H₂   +   O₂   ⟶   2 H₂O

Reactants   **Products**

▲ **Figure 2.9** Breaking and making of bonds in a chemical reaction

● $C_6H_{12}O_6 + 6 O_2 \rightarrow 6 CO_2 + 6 H_2O$; the breakdown of sugar in the presence of oxygen to carbon dioxide and water, with the release of energy that the cell can use

2.10 Is there a chemical indicator in swimming pools that detects urine?

Whether in your backyard, at the local public pool, or at a resort during spring break, a quick dip on a hot day has been a refreshing pastime for generations (**Figure 2.10A**). For the past few generations, children have been warned that if they urinated in the pool, a chemical dye would turn the water an embarrassing shade of red. Furthermore, this rumour has been propagated through popular culture, appearing in movies. Is the rumour about this chemical tattletale true? Or is it simply a little white lie parents tell to prevent a socially unacceptable behaviour?

In the previous module, you read how chemical reactions rearrange matter as they change reactants into products. The products can have very different properties than the reactants, including colour. **Figure 2.10B** shows a series of test tubes in which a chemical reaction has occurred. In this reaction, a yellow reactant is converted into a green product when it reacts with ammonia. The amount of green product produced is proportional to the amount of ammonia in the solution. Therefore, by quantifying the amount of green colour, the concentration of ammonia can be determined. Similar colour-changing reactions are commonly used in a variety of scientific applications. Indeed, the proper maintenance of a swimming pool requires several such reactions. Technicians frequently measure the concentrations of chlorine in water samples as well as its acidity (i.e., its pH, a concept discussed in Module 2.15) using colours as indicators.

What is it in urine that could possibly be detected? Urine is a complex solution that contains the nitrogenous waste urea as one of its main solutes (see Modules 28.15 and 28.18). This makes urea the most likely reactant for the urine-indicator dye; although the rumour has never mentioned this specifically. Scientists can use colour-changing reactions to measure urea concentration in solutions. However, these reactions usually require several steps and some of the chemicals involved, such as thio-semicarbazide, are known to cause cancer and birth defects. Clearly, these reagents could never be used as urine indicators in a public pool.

Pool staff and parents alike have allowed this story to survive to encourage children to leave the pool to use the facilities. If a harmless chemical existed that turned red when urea is present, you probably would not want it in your swimming pool. Some things are best left unknown; after all, kids will be kids. Although the rumour about the urine indicator in pools is untrue, it still carries a useful message.

▲ **Figure 2.10A** Swimmers cooling off

Ammonia (NH$_3$) + Bleach (HOCl) ⟶ Monochloramine (NH$_2$Cl) + H$_2$O

NH$_2$Cl + ⬡—OH ⟶ H$_2$N—⬡—OH + Cl$^-$
          |COO$^-$ |COO$^-$

Salicylate   5-Aminosalicylate
(Yellow colour)   (Green colour)

▲ **Figure 2.10B** Colour reactions testing for ammonia

 Which tube in Figure 2.10B has the highest concentration of ammonia? Explain.

● Tube 9 has the highest ammonia concentration. The greener result means more product was produced meaning there was more ammonia in solution to react.

Water's Life-Supporting Properties

2.11 Hydrogen bonds make liquid water cohesive

We can trace water's life-supporting properties to the structure and interactions of its molecules—their polarity and resulting hydrogen bonding between molecules (review Figure 2.8).

Hydrogen bonds between molecules of liquid water last for only a few trillionths of a second, yet at any instant, many molecules are hydrogen-bonded to others. This tendency of molecules of the same kind to stick together, called **cohesion**, is much stronger for water than for most other liquids. The cohesion of water is important in the living world. Trees, for example, depend on cohesion to help transport water and nutrients from their roots to their leaves. The evaporation of water from a leaf exerts a pulling force on water within the veins of the leaf. Because of cohesion, the force is relayed all the way down to the roots. **Adhesion**, the clinging of one substance to another, also plays a role. The adhesion of water to the cell walls of a plant's thin veins helps counter the downward pull of gravity.

Related to cohesion is **surface tension**, a measure of how difficult it is to stretch or break the surface of a liquid.

◀ **Figure 2.11** Surface tension allows a water strider to walk on water

Hydrogen bonds give water unusually high surface tension, making it behave as though it were coated with an invisible film. You can observe the surface tension of water by slightly overfilling a glass; the water will stand above the rim. The water strider in **Figure 2.11** takes advantage of the high surface tension of water to "stride" across ponds without breaking the surface.

 After a hard workout, you may see "beads" of sweat on your face. Can you explain what holds the sweat in droplet form?

● The cohesion of water molecules and its high surface tension hold water in droplets. The adhesion of water to your skin helps hold the beads in place.

2.12 Water's hydrogen bonds moderate temperature

If you have ever burned your finger on a metal pot while waiting for the water in it to boil, you know that water heats up much more slowly than metal. In fact, because of hydrogen bonding, water has a stronger resistance to temperature change than most other substances.

Temperature and heat are related but different. A swimmer in the Great Lakes has a higher temperature than the water, but the lake contains far more heat because of its immense volume. **Heat** is the amount of energy associated with the movement of atoms and molecules in a body of matter. **Temperature** measures the intensity of heat—that is, the *average* speed of molecules rather than the *total* amount of heat energy in a body of matter.

Heat must be absorbed in order to break hydrogen bonds, and heat is released when hydrogen bonds form. To raise the temperature of water, heat energy must first disrupt hydrogen bonds before water molecules can move faster. Thus, water absorbs a large amount of heat while warming up only a few degrees. Conversely, when water cools, more hydrogen bonds form, and a considerable amount of heat is released.

Earth's giant water supply moderates temperatures, helping to keep them within limits that permit life. Oceans, lakes, and rivers store a huge amount of heat from the sun during warm periods. Heat given off from gradually cooling water warms the air. That's why coastal areas generally have milder climates than inland regions. Water's resistance to temperature change also stabilizes ocean temperatures, creating a favourable environment for marine life. Since water accounts for approximately 66% of your body weight, it also helps moderate your temperature.

◀ **Figure 2.12** Evaporative cooling occurs as sweat dries

When a substance evaporates (changes physical state from a liquid to a gas), the surface of the liquid that remains behind cools down. This **evaporative cooling** occurs because the molecules with the greatest energy (the "hottest" ones) leave. It's as if the 10 fastest runners on the track team left school, lowering the average speed of the remaining team. Evaporative cooling helps prevent some land-dwelling organisms from overheating. Evaporation from a plant's leaves keeps them from becoming too warm in the sun, just as sweating helps dissipate our excess body heat (**Figure 2.12**). On a much larger scale, the evaporation of surface waters cools tropical seas.

 Explain the popular adage "It's not the heat; it's the humidity."

● High humidity hampers cooling by slowing the evaporation of sweat.

2.13 Ice is less dense than liquid water

Water exists on Earth in the form of a gas (water vapour), liquid, and solid. Unlike most substances, water is less dense as a solid than as a liquid. And as you might guess, this unusual property is due to hydrogen bonds.

As water freezes, each molecule forms stable hydrogen bonds with its neighbours, holding them at "arm's length" and creating a three-dimensional crystal. In **Figure 2.13**, compare the spaciously arranged molecules in the ice crystal with the more tightly packed molecules in the liquid water. The ice crystal has fewer molecules than an equal volume of liquid water. Therefore, ice is less dense and floats on top of liquid water.

If ice sank, then eventually ponds, lakes, and even oceans would freeze solid. Instead, when a deep body of water cools, the floating ice insulates the water below from colder air above. This "blanket" prevents the water below from freezing and allows fish and many other aquatic forms of life to survive under the frozen surface. We'll return to how these fish survive below the sea ice in Module 35.7.

In the Arctic, the sea ice is melting earlier and earlier in the spring. Because of warmer average winter temperatures, the ice does not have time to become as thick as it was previously. Therefore, after hibernating in dens with their new cubs, female polar bears have less pack ice on which to hunt for seals. In short, the shrinking of this ice cover as a result of global climate change may doom these bears.

Ice
Hydrogen bonds are stable.

Hydrogen bond

Liquid water
Hydrogen bonds constantly break and re-form.

▲ **Figure 2.13** Hydrogen bonds between water molecules in ice and water

? Explain how the freezing of water can crack boulders.

● Water in the crevices of a boulder expands as it freezes because the water molecules become spaced farther apart in forming ice crystals, cracking the rock.

2.14 Water is the solvent of life

If you add a teaspoon of table salt to a glass of water, the salt will dissolve and eventually become evenly mixed with the water, forming a solution. A **solution** is a liquid consisting of a uniform mixture of two or more substances. The dissolving agent (in this case, water) is the **solvent**, and a substance that is dissolved (salt) is a **solute**. An **aqueous solution** (from the Latin *aqua*, water) is one in which water is the solvent.

Water's versatility as a solvent results from the polarity of its molecules. **Figure 2.14** shows how a teaspoon of salt dissolves in water. At the surface of each grain, or crystal, the sodium and chloride ions are exposed to water. These ions and the water molecules are attracted to each other because of their opposite charges. The oxygen ends (red) of the water molecules have a partial negative charge and cling to the positive sodium ions (Na^+). The hydrogens of the water molecules, with their partial positive charge, are attracted to the negative chloride ions (Cl^-). Working inward from the surface of each salt crystal, water molecules eventually surround and separate all the ions. Water dissolves other ionic compounds as well. Seawater, for instance, contains a great variety of dissolved ions, as do your cells.

A compound doesn't need to be ionic to dissolve in water. A spoonful of sugar will also dissolve in a glass of water. Polar molecules such as sugar dissolve as water molecules surround them and form hydrogen bonds with their polar regions. It is important to note that unlike ionic bonds, the covalent bonds holding the atoms of a compound together do not dissociate. Even large molecules, such as proteins, can dissolve if they have ionic or polar regions on their surface. As the solvent inside all cells, in blood, and in plant sap, water dissolves an enormous variety of solutes necessary for life.

? Why are blood and most other biological fluids classified as aqueous solutions?

Ion in solution

Cl^- Na^+

Na^+ Cl^-

Salt crystal

▲ **Figure 2.14** A crystal of salt (NaCl) dissolving in water

● The solvent is water.

2.15 The chemistry of life is sensitive to acidic and basic conditions

In aqueous solutions, a very small percentage of the water molecules actually break apart (dissociate) into ions. The ions formed are called hydrogen ions (H^+) and hydroxide ions (OH^-). Hydrogen and hydroxide ions are very reactive. The proper balance of these ions is critical for the chemical processes that occur within an organism.

Some chemical compounds contribute additional H^+ to an aqueous solution, whereas others remove H^+ from it. A compound that donates hydrogen ions to solutions is called an **acid**. One example of a strong acid is hydrochloric acid (HCl), the acid in the gastric juice in your stomach. In solution, HCl dissociates completely into H^+ and Cl^-. An acidic solution has a higher concentration of H^+ than OH^-.

A **base** is a compound that accepts hydrogen ions and removes them from solution. Some bases, such as sodium hydroxide (NaOH), do this by donating OH^-; the OH^- combines with H^+ to form H_2O, thus reducing the H^+ concentration. Sodium hydroxide, also called lye, is a common ingredient in oven cleaners. The more basic a solution, the higher its OH^- concentration and the lower its H^+ concentration. Basic solutions are sometimes called alkaline solutions, although the two terms should not be used interchangeably.

We use the **pH scale** to describe how acidic or basic a solution is (pH stands for "potential of hydrogen"). As shown in **Figure 2.15**, the scale ranges from 0 (most acidic) to 14 (most basic). Each pH unit represents a 10-fold change in the concentration of H^+ in a solution. For example, lemon juice at pH 2 has 10 times more H^+ than an equal amount of a cola at pH 3 and 100 times more H^+ than tomato juice at pH 4.

Pure water and aqueous solutions that are neither acidic nor basic are said to be neutral; they have a pH of 7. They do contain some hydrogen and hydroxide ions, but the concentrations of the two kinds of ions are equal. The pH of the solution inside most living cells is close to 7. Even a slight change in pH can be harmful because the proteins and other complex molecules in cells are extremely sensitive to the concentrations of H^+ and OH^-.

The pH of human blood plasma (the fluid portion of the blood) is very close to 7.4. A person cannot survive for more than a few minutes if the blood pH drops to 7.0 or rises to 7.8. If you add a small amount of a strong acid to a litre of pure water, the pH drops from 7.0 to 2.0. If the same amount of acid is added to a litre of blood, however, the pH decrease is only from 7.4 to 7.3. How can the acid have so much less effect on the pH of blood? A **buffer** is a substance that minimizes changes in pH. It does so by accepting H^+ when in excess and donating H^+ when depleted. Several types of buffers contribute to the pH stability in blood and many other biological fluids.

pH scale

Increasingly ACIDIC
(Higher H^+ concentration)

- 0
- 1 — Battery acid
- 2 — Lemon juice, gastric juice
- 3 — Vinegar, cola
- 4 — Tomato juice
- 5 —
- — Rainwater
- 6 — Human urine
- — Saliva
- NEUTRAL
$[H^+]=[OH^-]$
- 7 — **Pure water**
- — Human blood, tears
- 8 — Seawater
- 9 —

Increasingly BASIC
(Higher OH^- concentration)

- 10 —
- — Milk of magnesia
- 11 —
- — Household ammonia
- 12 —
- — Household bleach
- 13 —
- — Oven cleaner
- 14 —

Acidic solution

Neutral solution

Basic solution

▲ **Figure 2.15** The pH scale reflects the relative concentrations of H^+ and OH^-

In the next module, we explore how changes in acidity can have environmental consequences.

? Compared to a basic solution at pH 9, the same volume of an acidic solution at pH 4 has _____ times more hydrogen ions (H^+).

000 001 ●

2.16 Acid precipitation and ocean acidification threaten the environment

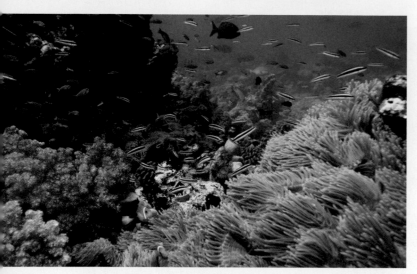

▲ **Figure 2.16** Coral reefs are threatened by ocean acidification

Considering the dependence of all life on water, contamination of rivers, lakes, seas, and precipitation poses serious environmental problems. The burning of fossil fuels (coal, oil, and gas), which release air-polluting compounds and large amounts of CO_2 into the atmosphere, is among the many threats to water quality posed by human activities. Chemical reactions of these compounds with water increase acidity and alter the delicate balance of conditions for life on Earth.

Sulphur oxides and nitrogen oxides released by burning fossil fuels react with water in the air to form strong acids, which fall to Earth with rain or snow. **Acid precipitation** refers to rain, snow, or fog with a pH lower than 5.2 (the pH of uncontaminated rain is 5.6). Acid precipitation has damaged life in lakes and streams and adversely affected plants through changes in soil chemistry. In Canada and the United States, amendments made in 1990 to the *Clean Air Act* have reduced acid precipitation and improved the health of most North American lakes and forests.

Carbon dioxide is the main product of fossil fuel combustion, and its steadily increasing release into the atmosphere is linked to global climate change (see Module 41.7). About 25% of human-generated CO_2 is absorbed by the oceans. An increase in CO_2 absorption is changing ocean chemistry and harming marine life and ecosystems.

In **ocean acidification**, CO_2 dissolving in seawater lowers ocean pH. That's because CO_2 reacts with water to produce carbonic acid (H_2CO_3). The change in acidity decreases the concentration of carbonate ions, which are required by corals and other organisms to produce their skeletons or shells, a process called calcification. Coral reef ecosystems act as havens for a great diversity of organisms **(Figure 2.16)**. Other calcifying organisms are important food sources for salmon, herring, and other ocean fishes. Decreased calcification is affecting marine food webs and is substantially altering the productivity and biodiversity of Earth's oceans.

Acid precipitation can also have significant impact on both freshwater and terrestrial environments. Ecosystems established on limestone bedrock—for example, in Southern Alberta and Southeastern Ontario—have naturally alkaline soils and water systems. The higher pH of these ecosystems quickly neutralizes or buffers (raises the pH nearer to 7) the acid precipitation. However, areas in much of Eastern Canada lay on top of granite bedrock. Unlike limestone, granite cannot buffer the low pH of the precipitation and protect the environment. In fact, nearly half of Canada's area sits above granite bedrock. In these areas, acid precipitation can lower the pH of the water systems and soil, negatively affecting life in these habitats.

? **What is the relationship between fossil fuel consumption and coral reefs?**

 Some of the increased CO_2 released by burning fossil fuels dissolves in and lowers the pH of the oceans. A lower pH reduces levels of carbonate ions, which then lowers the rate of calcification by coral animals.

2.17 The search for extraterrestrial life centres on the search for water

When astrobiologists search for signs of extraterrestrial life on distant planets, they look for evidence of water. Why? As we've seen in this chapter, the emergent properties of water (its cohesion, its ability to moderate temperature and insulate, and its versatility as a solvent) support life on Earth in many ways. Is it possible that some form of life has evolved on other planets that have water in their environment?

Researchers with the National Aeronautics and Space Administration (NASA) in the United States have found evidence that water was once abundant on Mars. In

January 2004, NASA succeeded in landing two golf-cart-sized rovers, named *Spirit* and *Opportunity*, on Mars. These robotic geologists, using sophisticated instruments to determine the composition of rocks, detected a mineral that is formed only in the presence of water. And pictures sent back from the rovers and various orbiting Mars spacecraft have revealed physical evidence of past water.

In 2008, an analysis of Martian soil by the *Phoenix Mars Lander* provided evidence that components of the soil had at one time been dissolved in water.

Figure 2.17 shows a robotic arm of *Phoenix* that has gathered samples and scraped trenches that exposed ice just below the surface on Mars.

More recently, in August 2012, NASA landed the car-sized rover named *Curiosity* on Mars in the search for evidence of life. The alpha particle X-ray spectrometer designed by the Canadian Space Agency is an essential tool for *Curiosity's* mission.

No evidence for life on Mars has yet been found. But is it possible that life is not unique to planet Earth? Chapter 13 presents evidence that life could originate in the environment of early Earth. Finding evidence of life elsewhere would support the hypothesis that the chemical evolution of life is possible.

? Why is the presence of water important in the search for extraterrestrial life?

Water plays important roles in life as we know it, from moderating temperatures on the planet to functioning as the solvent of life.

▲ **Figure 2.17** Robotic arm of the *Phoenix Mars Lander* probing for evidence of water

REVIEW

MasteringBiology® **For Practice Quizzes, BioFlix, MP3 Tutors, and Activities, go to masteringbiology.com.**

Reviewing the Concepts

Elements, Atoms, and Compounds (2.1–2.4)

2.1 Organisms are composed of elements, in combinations called compounds. Oxygen, carbon, hydrogen, and nitrogen make up about 96% of living matter.

2.2 Trace elements are common additives to food and water. Some additives are useful preservatives and others are required in small amounts to promote health.

2.3 Atoms consist of protons, neutrons, and electrons.

Protons (+ charge) determine element

Neutrons (no charge) determine isotope

Atom

Nucleus

Electrons (– charge) form negative cloud and determine chemical behaviour

2.4 Radioisotopes can help or harm us. Radioactive isotopes (radioisotopes) are valuable in basic research and medicine.

Chemical Bonds (2.5–2.10)

2.5 The distribution of electrons determines an atom's chemical properties. An atom whose outer electron shell is not full tends to interact with other atoms and share, gain, or lose electrons, resulting in attractions called chemical bonds.

2.6 Covalent bonds join atoms into molecules through electron sharing. In a nonpolar covalent bond, electrons are shared equally. In polar covalent bonds, such as those found in water, electrons are pulled closer to the more electronegative atom.

2.7 Ionic bonds are attractions between ions of opposite charge. Electron gain and loss create charged atoms, called ions.

2.8 Hydrogen bonds are weak bonds important in the chemistry of life. The slightly positively charged H atoms in one polar molecule may be attracted to the partial negative charge of an O or N atom in a neighbouring molecule.

2.9 Chemical reactions make and break chemical bonds. The composition of matter is changed as bonds are broken and formed to convert reactants to products.

2.10 Is there a chemical indicator in swimming pools that detects urine? The rumour that a chemical dye will turn red if urine is present in a pool is untrue.

Water's Life-Supporting Properties (2.11–2.17)

2.11 Hydrogen bonds make liquid water cohesive. Cohesion creates surface tension and allows water to move from plant roots to leaves.

2.12 Water's hydrogen bonds moderate temperature. Heat is absorbed when hydrogen bonds break and released when hydrogen bonds form. This helps keep temperatures relatively steady. As the most energetic water molecules evaporate, the surface of a substance cools.

2.13 Ice is less dense than liquid water. Floating ice protects lakes and oceans from freezing solid.

Liquid water: Hydrogen bonds form and break

Ice: Stable hydrogen bonds

2.14 Water is the solvent of life. Polar or charged solutes dissolve when water molecules surround them, forming aqueous solutions.

2.15 The chemistry of life is sensitive to acidic and basic conditions. A compound that releases H^+ in solution is an acid, and one that accepts H^+ is a base. The pH scale ranges from 0 (most acidic) to 14 (most basic). The pH of most cells is close to 7 (neutral) and kept that way by buffers.

2.16 Acid precipitation and ocean acidification threaten the environment. The burning of fossil fuels increases the amount of CO_2 in the atmosphere and dissolved in the oceans. The acidification of the ocean threatens coral reefs and other marine organisms.

2.17 The search for extraterrestrial life centres on the search for water. The emergent properties of water support life on Earth and may contribute to the potential for life to have evolved on other planets.

Connecting the Concepts

1. Fill in the blanks in this concept map to help you tie together the key concepts concerning elements, atoms, and molecules.

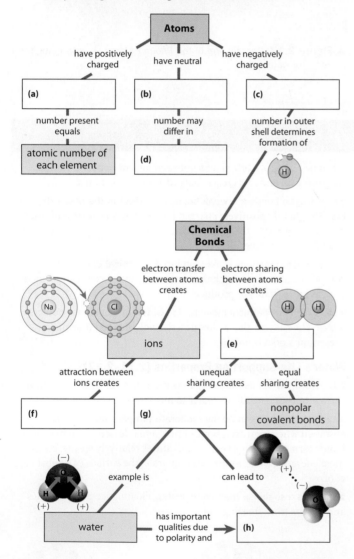

2. Create a concept map to organize your understanding of the life-supporting properties of water. A sample map is in the answer section, but the value of this exercise is in the thinking and integrating you must do to create your own map.

Testing Your Knowledge

Multiple Choice

3. Changing the _____ would change it into an atom of a different element.
   a. number of electrons surrounding the nucleus of an atom
   b. number of bonds formed by an atom
   c. number of protons in the nucleus of an atom
   d. electrical charge of an atom
   e. number of neutrons in the nucleus of an atom

4. Your body contains the smallest amount of which of the following elements?
   a. nitrogen   b. phosphorus
   c. carbon   d. oxygen
   e. hydrogen

5. A solution at pH 6 contains _____ than the same amount of a solution at pH 8.
   a. 2 times more H^+
   b. 4 times more H^+
   c. 100 times more H^+
   d. 4 times less H^+
   e. 100 times less H^+

6. Most of the unique properties of water result from the fact that water molecules
   a. are very small.
   b. are held together by covalent bonds.
   c. easily separate from one another.
   d. are constantly in motion.
   e. are polar and form hydrogen bonds.

7. A sulphur atom has 6 electrons in its outer shell. As a result, it forms _____ covalent bonds with other atoms. (*Explain your answer.*)
   a. two   b. three
   c. four   d. six
   e. eight

8. What does the word *trace* mean when you're talking about a trace element?
   a. The element is required in very small amounts.
   b. The element can be used as a label to trace atoms through an organism's body.
   c. The element is very rare on Earth.
   d. The element enhances health but is not essential for the organism's long-term survival.
   e. The element passes rapidly through the organism.

9. A can of cola consists mostly of sugar dissolved in water, with some carbon dioxide gas that makes it fizzy and makes the pH less than 7. In chemical terms, you could say that cola is an aqueous solution where water is the _____, sugar is a _____, and carbon dioxide makes the solution _____.
   a. solvent, solute, basic
   b. solute, solvent, basic
   c. solvent, solute, acidic
   d. solute, solvent, acidic
   e. not enough information to say

10. Radioisotopes can be used in medical studies because
    a. they allow researchers to time how long processes take.
    b. they are more reactive than nonradioisotopes.
    c. the cell does not recognize the extra protons in the nucleus, so isotopes are readily used in cellular processes.
    d. their location or quantity can be determined because of their radioactivity.
    e. their extra neutrons produce different colours that can be traced through the body.

True/False (Change false statements to make them true.)

11. Table salt, water, and carbon are compounds.

12. The smallest unit of an element is a molecule.

13. A bathtub full of lukewarm water may hold more heat than a teakettle full of boiling water.

14. If the atoms in a molecule share electrons equally, the molecule is said to be nonpolar.

15. Ice floats because water molecules in ice are more tightly packed than in liquid water.

16. Atoms in a water molecule are held together by the sharing of electrons.

17. Most acid precipitation results from the presence of pollutants from aerosol cans and air conditioners.

18. An atom that has gained or lost electrons is called an ion.

Describing, Comparing, and Explaining

19. Make a sketch that shows how water molecules hydrogen-bond with one another. Why do water molecules form hydrogen bonds? What unique properties of water result from water's tendency to form hydrogen bonds?

20. Describe two ways in which the water in your body helps stabilize your body temperature.

21. Compare covalent and ionic bonds.

22. What is an acid? A base? How is the acidity of a solution described?

Applying the Concepts

23. The diagram below shows the arrangement of electrons around the nucleus of a fluorine atom (left) and a potassium atom (right). What kind of bond do you think would form between these two atoms?

Fluorine atom   Potassium atom

24. Look back at the abbreviated periodic table of the elements in Figure 2.5. If two or more elements are in the same row, what do they have in common? If two elements are in the same column, what do they have in common?

25. This chapter explains how the emergent properties of water contribute to the suitability of the environment for life. Until fairly recently, scientists assumed that other physical requirements for life included a moderate range of temperature, pH, and atmospheric pressure, as well as low levels of toxic chemicals. That view has changed with the discovery of organisms known as extremophiles, which have been found flourishing in hot, acidic sulphur springs, around hydrothermal vents deep in the ocean, and in soils with high levels of toxic metals. Why would astrobiologists be interested in studying extremophiles? What does the existence of life in such extreme environments say about the possibility of life on other planets?

Answers to all questions can be found in Appendix E.

 Study on the Go

This QR code leads to Study on the Go—mobile study resources, including practice quizzes, videos, and glossary flashcards.

You can access Study on the Go content via your smartphone, allowing you to study whenever and wherever you want. Note: Your login information for MasteringBiology is required.

Go to one of the sites below to download a free app. Once installed, the phone will scan the code and link to a website with *Campbell Biology: Concepts and Connections'* Study on the Go resources.

ScanLife
http://getscanlife.com

NeoReader
http://get.neoreader.com

QuickMark
http://www.quickmark.com.tw/

CHAPTER

3

The Compounds of Cells

BIG IDEAS

Introduction to Organic Compounds

(3.1–3.3)

Carbon-containing compounds are the chemical building blocks of life.

Maltose

Carbohydrates

(3.4–3.7)

Carbohydrates serve as a cell's fuel and building material.

Proteins

(3.8–3.10)

Proteins are essential to the structures and functions of life.

Nucleic Acids

(3.11–3.13)

Nucleic acids store, transmit, and help express hereditary information.

Lipids

(3.14–3.16)

Lipids are hydrophobic molecules with diverse functions.

trans-Oleic acid

cis-Oleic acid

To Eat or Not to Eat, Fat Is the Question

We are continually inundated with advertisements for healthy food choices. Whether you are riding the bus, watching television, or listening to the radio, messages of "Eat this" or "Don't eat that" have been given a prominent spot. And fats are at the centre of many advertising campaigns. We are told to avoid some fats, such as *trans* fats, and encouraged to eat others, those containing omega fatty acids. Why is one type of fat praised, while another shunned?

Although *trans* fats exist naturally in small amounts in animal tissues, the majority of those found in our diets come from artificial sources. When you see "hydrogenated vegetable oils" on a margarine label, it means that unsaturated fats have been converted to saturated fats by breaking their double bonds and adding hydrogen. This process is used to transform liquid canola oil into margarine, a solid fat. Unfortunately, hydrogenation also creates *trans* fats, a form of fat that recent research associates with health risks. A *trans* fat is an unsaturated fat with a double bond in the hydrocarbon chain that has its hydrogen atoms on opposite sides. As shown in the figure, a *trans* fat is an isomer (compounds with the same chemical composition, but with different structures) of the original molecule (which chemists refer to as a *cis* fat, which has its hydrogen atoms on the same side of the double bond).

Diets rich in *trans* fats may contribute to cardiovascular disease by promoting atherosclerosis. In this condition, lipid-containing deposits called plaques build up within the walls of blood vessels, reducing blood flow. *Trans* fats also raise levels of the "bad" cholesterol in the blood while reducing blood

levels of "good" cholesterol. Both changes further increase the risk of heart disease.

Trans fats may put more than your heart at risk. Several studies have demonstrated that *trans* fats may also have detrimental effects on your brain. In combination with other factors, *trans* fats have recently been linked to dementia and Alzheimer's disease. Even ingestion of moderate amounts of *trans* fats increases the risk of Alzheimer's disease by up to three times.

Canada is one of the highest consumers of *trans* fats in the world, with an average of 8.4 g (10% of total fat intake) eaten daily. This statistic has raised concerns among medical professionals as well as politicians. In 2003, Canada was the first country to mandate that *trans* fats be included in nutritional labels. Health Canada has called upon the food industry to limit the levels of *trans* fat to less than 2% of the total fat content for margarines and 5% for other foods. Using a technique developed by Health Canada scientist Dr. Nimal Ratnayake, these levels are carefully monitored with the results posted on Health Canada's website.

But not all fats are suspect in such severe health concerns. In fact, some fats are actually protective and promote good health. Certain essential unsaturated fatty acids called omega-3 and omega-6 fatty acids appear to protect against cardiovascular disease and Alzheimer's disease. These fatty acids are essential as we are unable to synthesize them and must obtain them through our diet. Sources of the good omega fatty acids include certain nuts, plant oils, and fatty fish. Studies have shown that fish oil reduces the risk of developing heart disease and reduces the severity of pre-existing conditions. The omega-3 fatty acid referred to as DHA is required for proper brain development during childhood. Eating fish such as salmon is a very good dietary source of DHA. Several food companies supplement foods children crave with DHA to help them obtain this good fat. However, the quantities are usually so small that they are actually insignificant. For example, to acquire the amount of

DHA in a single serving of salmon (75 g), you would have to eat more than 20 omega-3 enriched eggs.

In this chapter, we explore the structure and function of sugars, proteins, nucleic acids, and fats—the biological molecules that are essential to life. We end the chapter with a brief look at lipids, but first, let's look at carbon, the versatile atom at the centre of life's molecules.

Introduction to Organic Compounds

3.1 Life's molecular diversity is based on the properties of carbon

When it comes to making molecules, carbon usually takes centre stage. Almost all the molecules a cell makes are composed of carbon atoms bonded to one another and to atoms of other elements. Carbon is unparalleled in its ability to form large and complex molecules, which build the structures and carry out the functions required for life.

Carbon-based molecules are called **organic compounds**. Why are carbon atoms the lead players in the chemistry of life? As we discussed in Chapter 2, the number of electrons in the outermost shell of its atoms determines an element's chemical properties. A carbon atom has 4 electrons in a valence shell that holds 8. Carbon completes its outer shell by sharing electrons with other atoms in four covalent bonds (see Module 2.6). Thus, each carbon atom is a connecting point from which a molecule can branch in up to four directions.

Figure 3.1A illustrates three representations of methane (CH_4), one of the simplest organic molecules. The structural formula shows that covalent bonds link four hydrogen atoms to the carbon atom. Each of the four lines in the formula represents a pair of shared electrons. The two models help you see that methane is three-dimensional, with the space-filling model on the right better portraying its overall shape. The ball-and-stick model shows that carbon's four bonds (the grey "sticks") angle out toward the corners of an imaginary tetrahedron (an object with four triangular sides). The red lines trace this shape, which occurs wherever a carbon atom participates in four single bonds. Different bond angles and shapes occur when carbon atoms form double bonds. Large organic molecules can have very elaborate shapes. And as we will see many times, a molecule's shape often determines its function.

Compounds composed of only carbon and hydrogen are called **hydrocarbons**. Methane and propane are examples of

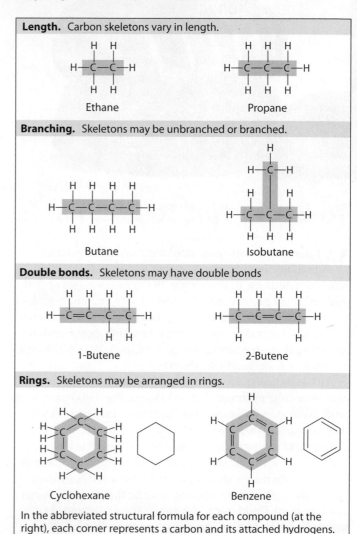

Length. Carbon skeletons vary in length.

Ethane

Propane

Branching. Skeletons may be unbranched or branched.

Butane

Isobutane

Double bonds. Skeletons may have double bonds

1-Butene

2-Butene

Rings. Skeletons may be arranged in rings.

Cyclohexane

Benzene

In the abbreviated structural formula for each compound (at the right), each corner represents a carbon and its attached hydrogens.

▲ **Figure 3.1B** Four ways that carbon skeletons can vary

hydrocarbon fuels. As components of fats, longer hydrocarbons provide fuel to your body cells. **Figure 3.1B** illustrates some of the variety of hydrocarbon structures. The chain of carbon atoms in an organic molecule is called a **carbon skeleton** (shaded in grey in the figure). Carbon skeletons can vary in length and can be unbranched or branched. Carbon skeletons may also include double bonds, which can vary in number and location. Some carbon skeletons are arranged in rings.

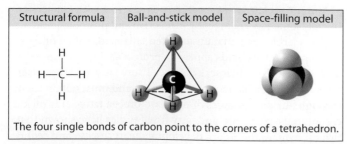

Structural formula	Ball-and-stick model	Space-filling model

The four single bonds of carbon point to the corners of a tetrahedron.

▲ **Figure 3.1A** Three representations of methane (CH_4)

The two compounds in the second row of Figure 3.1B, butane and isobutane, have the same molecular formula, C_4H_{10}, but differ in the bonding pattern of their carbon skeleton. The two molecules in the third row also have the same numbers of atoms, but they have different three-dimensional shapes because of the location of the double bond. Compounds with the same formula but different structural arrangements are called **isomers**. Isomers can also result from different spatial arrangements of the four partners bonded to a carbon atom. This type of isomer is important in the pharmaceutical industry, because the two isomers of a drug may not be equally effective or may have different (and sometimes harmful) effects. The different shapes of isomers result in unique properties and add greatly to the diversity of organic molecules.

 One isomer of methamphetamine is the addictive illegal drug known as crank. The other is a medicine for sinus congestion. How can you explain the differing effects of the two isomers?

● Isomers have different structures, or shapes, and the shape of a molecule usually helps to determine the way it functions in the body.

3.2 A few chemical groups are key to the functioning of biological molecules

The unique properties of an organic compound depend not only on the size and shape of its carbon skeleton but also on the groups of atoms that are attached to that skeleton.

Table 3.2 illustrates six chemical groups important in the chemistry of life. The first five are called **functional groups**. They affect a molecule's function by participating in chemical reactions in characteristic ways. These particular five groups are polar, because oxygen or nitrogen atoms exert a strong pull on shared electrons. This polarity tends to make compounds containing these groups **hydrophilic** (water-loving, see Appendix D) and therefore soluble in water—a necessary condition for their roles in water-based life. The sixth group, a methyl group, is nonpolar and not reactive, but it affects molecular shape and thus function.

A **hydroxyl group** consists of a hydrogen atom bonded to an oxygen atom, which in turn is bonded to the carbon skeleton. Ethanol, shown in the table, and other organic compounds containing hydroxyl groups are called alcohols.

In a **carbonyl group**, a carbon atom is linked by a double bond to an oxygen atom. If the carbonyl group is at the end of a carbon skeleton, the compound is called an aldehyde; if it is within the chain, the compound is called a ketone. Sugars contain a carbonyl group and several hydroxyl groups.

A **carboxyl group** consists of a carbon double-bonded to an oxygen atom and also bonded to a hydroxyl group. The carboxyl group acts as an acid by contributing an H^+ to a solution (see Module 2.15) and thus becoming ionized. Compounds with carboxyl groups are called carboxylic acids. Acetic acid, shown in the table, gives vinegar its sour taste.

An **amino group** has a nitrogen bonded to two hydrogens and the carbon skeleton. It acts as a base by picking up an H^+ from a solution. Organic compounds with an amino group are called amines. The building blocks of proteins are called amino acids because they contain an amino and a carboxyl group.

A **phosphate group** consists of a phosphorus atom bonded to four oxygen atoms. It is usually ionized and attached to the carbon skeleton by one of its oxygen atoms. This structure is abbreviated as ⓟ in this text. Compounds with phosphate groups are called organic phosphates and are often involved in energy transfers, as is the energy-rich compound ATP, shown in the table.

Chemical Group	Examples
Hydroxyl group —OH	Alcohol
Carbonyl group C=O	Aldehyde Ketone
Carboxyl group —COOH	Carboxylic acid Ionized
Amino group —NH₂	Amine Ionized
Phosphate group —OPO₃²⁻	Organic phosphate
Methyl group —CH₃	Methylated compound

TABLE 3.2 | IMPORTANT CHEMICAL GROUPS OF ORGANIC COMPOUNDS

A **methyl group** consists of a carbon bonded to three hydrogens. Compounds with methyl groups are called methylated compounds. The addition of a methyl group to the component of DNA shown in the table affects the expression of genes.

Figure 3.2 shows how a small difference in chemical groups can lead to a big difference in body form and behaviour. The male and female sex hormones shown here differ only in the groups highlighted with coloured boxes. These subtle differences result in the different actions of these molecules, which help produce the contrasting features of males and females in lions and other vertebrates. Keeping in mind this basic scheme—carbon skeletons with chemical groups—we are now ready to see how our cells make large molecules out of smaller ones.

Testosterone   **Estradiol**

? **Identify the chemical groups that do *not* contain carbon.**

● The hydroxyl, amino, and phosphate groups

▲ **Figure 3.2** Differences in the chemical groups of sex hormones

3.3 Cells make a huge number of large molecules from a limited set of small molecules

Given the rich complexity of life on Earth, we might expect there to be an enormous diversity of types of molecules. Remarkably, however, the important molecules of all living things—from bacteria to elephants—fall into just four main classes: carbohydrates, proteins, nucleic acids, and lipids. On a molecular scale, molecules of three of these classes—carbohydrates, proteins, and nucleic acids—may be gigantic; in fact, biologists call them **macromolecules**. For example, a protein may consist of thousands of atoms. How does a cell make such a huge molecule?

Cells make most of their macromolecules by joining smaller molecules into chains called **polymers** (from the Greek *polys*, many, and *meros*, part). A polymer is a large molecule consisting of many identical or similar building blocks strung together, much as a train consists of a chain of cars. The building blocks of polymers are called **monomers**.

Making Polymers   Cells link monomers together to form polymers by a **dehydration reaction**, a reaction that removes a molecule of water. As you can see in **Figure 3.3A**, an unlinked monomer has a hydrogen atom (—H) at one end and

a hydroxyl group (—OH) at the other. For each monomer added to a chain, a water molecule (H_2O) is released. Notice in Figure 3.3A that one monomer (the one at the right end of the short polymer in this example) loses a hydroxyl group and the other monomer loses a hydrogen atom to form H_2O. As this occurs, a new covalent bond forms, linking the two monomers. Dehydration reactions are the same regardless of the specific monomers and the type of polymer the cell is producing.

Breaking Polymers   Cells not only make macromolecules but also have to break them down. For example, most of the organic molecules in your food are in the form of polymers that are much too large to enter your cells. You must digest these polymers to make their monomers available to your cells. This digestion process is called **hydrolysis**. Essentially the reverse of a dehydration reaction, hydrolysis means to break (*lyse*) with water (*hydro-*). As **Figure 3.3B** shows, the bond between monomers is broken by the addition of a water molecule, with the hydroxyl group from the water attaching to one monomer and a hydrogen attaching to the adjacent monomer.

▲ **Figure 3.3A** Dehydration reaction building a polymer chain

▲ **Figure 3.3B** Hydrolysis breaking down a polymer

Lactose-intolerant individuals are unable to hydrolyze such a bond in the sugar lactose because they lack the enzyme lactase. Both dehydration reactions and hydrolysis require the help of enzymes to make and break bonds. **Enzymes** are specialized macromolecules that speed up chemical reactions in cells.

The Diversity of Polymers   The diversity of macromolecules in the living world is vast. Remarkably, a cell makes all of its thousands of different macromolecules from a small list of ingredients—about 40 to 50 common components and a few others that are rare. Proteins, for example, are built from only 20 kinds of amino acids. Your DNA is built from just four kinds of monomers called nucleotides. The key to the great diversity of polymers is arrangement—variation in the sequence in which monomers are strung together.

The variety in polymers accounts for the uniqueness of each organism. The monomers themselves, however, are essentially universal. Your proteins and those of a tree or an ant are assembled from the same 20 amino acids. Life has a simple yet elegant molecular logic: Small molecules common to all organisms are ordered into large molecules, which vary from species to species and even from individual to individual in the same species.

In the remainder of the chapter, we explore each of the four classes of large biological molecules. Like water and simple organic molecules, large biological molecules have unique emergent properties arising from the orderly arrangement of their atoms. As you will see, for these molecules of life, structure and function are inseparable.

 Suppose you eat some cheese. What reactions must occur for the protein of the cheese to be broken down into its amino acid monomers and then for these monomers to be converted to proteins in your body?

● In digestion, the proteins are broken down into amino acids by hydrolysis. New proteins are formed in your body cells from these monomers in dehydration reactions.

Carbohydrates

3.4 Monosaccharides are the simplest carbohydrates

The name **carbohydrate** refers to a class of molecules ranging from the small sugar molecules dissolved in soft drinks to large polysaccharides, such as the starch molecules we consume in pasta and potatoes.

The carbohydrate monomers (single-unit sugars) are **monosaccharides** (from the Greek *monos*, single, and *sacchar*, sugar). The honey shown in **Figure 3.4A** consists mainly of monosaccharides called glucose and fructose. These and other single-unit sugars can be hooked together by dehydration reactions to form more complex sugars and polysaccharides.

Monosaccharides generally have molecular formulas that are some multiple of CH_2O. For example, the formula for glucose, a common monosaccharide of central importance in the chemistry of life, is $C_6H_{12}O_6$. **Figure 3.4B** illustrates the molecular structure of glucose, with its carbons numbered 1 to 6. This structure also shows the two trademarks of a sugar: a number of hydroxyl groups (—OH) and a carbonyl group ($>C=O$, highlighted in blue). The hydroxyl groups make a sugar an alcohol, and the carbonyl group, depending on its location, makes it either an aldose (an aldehyde sugar) or a ketose (a ketone sugar). As you see in Figure 3.4B, glucose is an aldose and fructose is a ketose. (Note that most names for sugars end in *-ose* and the names for most enzymes end in *-ase*. For example, the enzyme lactase digests the disaccharide lactose.)

If you count the numbers of different atoms in the fructose molecule in Figure 3.4B, you will find that its molecular formula is $C_6H_{12}O_6$, identical to that of glucose. Thus, glucose and fructose are isomers; they differ only in the arrangement of their atoms (in this case, the positions of the carbonyl groups). Seemingly minor differences like this give isomers different properties, such as how they react with other molecules. These differences also make fructose taste considerably sweeter than glucose.

The carbon skeletons of both glucose and fructose are six carbon atoms long. Other monosaccharides may have three to seven carbons. Five-carbon sugars, called pentoses,

▲ **Figure 3.4B** Structures of glucose and fructose

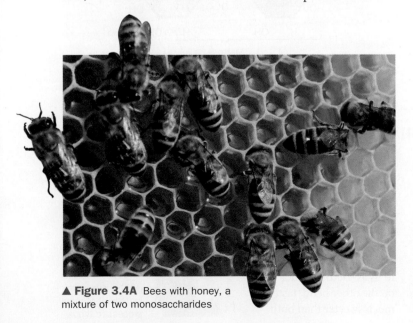

▲ **Figure 3.4A** Bees with honey, a mixture of two monosaccharides

Structural formula — Abbreviated structure — Simplified structure

▲ **Figure 3.4C** Three representations of the ring form of glucose

and six-carbon sugars, called hexoses, are among the most common.

It is convenient to draw sugars as if their carbon skeletons were linear, but in aqueous solutions, many monosaccharides form rings, as shown for glucose in **Figure 3.4C**. To form the glucose ring, carbon 1 bonds to the oxygen attached to carbon 5. As shown in the middle representation, the ring diagram of glucose and other sugars may be abbreviated by not

showing the carbon atoms at the corners of the ring. Also, the bonds in the ring are often drawn with varied thickness, indicating that the ring is a relatively flat structure with attached atoms extending above and below it. The simplified ring symbol on the right is often used in this book to represent glucose.

Monosaccharides, particularly glucose, are the main fuel molecules for cellular work. Because cells release energy from glucose when they break it down, an aqueous solution of glucose (often called dextrose) may be injected into the bloodstream of sick or injured patients; the glucose provides an immediate energy source to tissues in need of repair. Cells also use the carbon skeletons of monosaccharides as raw material for making other kinds of organic molecules, such as amino acids and fatty acids. Sugars not used in these ways may be incorporated into disaccharides and polysaccharides, as we see next.

? Write the formula for a monosaccharide that has three carbons.

● $C_3H_6O_3$

3.5 Two monosaccharides are linked to form a disaccharide

Cells construct a **disaccharide** from two monosaccharide monomers by a dehydration reaction. **Figure 3.5** shows how maltose, also called malt sugar, is formed from two glucose monomers. One monomer gives up a hydroxyl group and the other gives up a hydrogen atom from a hydroxyl group. As H_2O is released, an oxygen atom is left, linking the two monomers. Maltose, which is common in germinating seeds, is used in making beer, malted milkshakes, and malted milk candy.

The most common disaccharide is sucrose, which is made of a glucose monomer linked to a fructose monomer. Transported in plant sap, sucrose provides a source of energy and raw materials to all the parts of the plant. We extract it from the stems of sugarcane or the roots of sugar beets to use as table sugar.

? Lactose is the disaccharide sugar in milk. It is formed from glucose and galactose. The formula for both these monosaccharides is $C_6H_{12}O_6$. What is the formula for lactose?

● $C_{12}H_{22}O_{11}$

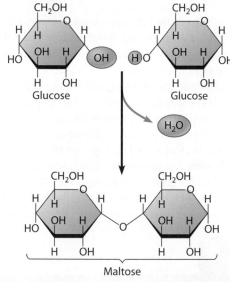

▲ **Figure 3.5** Disaccharide formation by a dehydration reaction

3.6 Is high-fructose corn syrup to blame for obesity?

If you want to sweeten your coffee or tea, you probably reach for sugar—the disaccharide sucrose. If you drink soft drinks or fruit cocktails, you're probably consuming the monosaccharides of sucrose in the form of high-fructose corn syrup (HFCS; also called glucose-fructose on some Canadian food labels). In fact, if you look at the label of almost any processed food, you will see HFCS on the list of ingredients **(Figure 3.6A)**. You have probably heard rumours linking HFCS to the "obesity epidemic."

What is glucose-fructose? Industrial processing breaks down cornstarch into monomers of glucose, producing what is called corn syrup. Glucose, however, does not taste as sweet to us as sucrose. Fructose, on the other hand, tastes much sweeter than both

◀ **Figure 3.6A** Glucose-fructose (HFCS) is a main ingredient of many processed foods

glucose and sucrose. A process developed in the 1970s uses an enzyme to rearrange the atoms of glucose into the sweeter isomer fructose (see Figure 3.4B). This newly processed fructose is combined with regular corn syrup to produce a mixture of monosaccharides as a ratio of 55% fructose and 45% glucose, not much different from the 50-50 ratio found in sucrose (a disaccharide). This clear, goopy liquid is cheaper than sucrose and easier to mix into drinks and processed food. And it contains the same monosaccharides as sucrose, the disaccharide it is replacing.

The rate of obesity in Canada is increasing at an alarming rate. The national obesity rate increased from 12% to 18% between 1994 and 2010 (**Figure 3.6B**). Moreover, childhood obesity has tripled in Canada over the last 25 years. But is HFCS to blame for these disturbing trends? Scientific studies are ongoing, and the jury is still out. Some reports, which were based on circumstantial evidence, have claimed a link between obesity and HFCS consumption. Individuals who ingest a lot of fructose may increase lipogenesis, the production of fats. However, the newly created fats are generally stored within the liver (a serious condition with its own concerns) and may not contribute significantly to overall obesity. The nutritional value of sucrose and HFCS are essentially identical, having the same caloric content. So how can it contribute to obesity more than sucrose? Some people claim that the higher sweetness of HFCS increases cravings and consequently the amount consumed. However, Statistics Canada reports that the amount of HFCS consumed by Canadians has actually decreased over the same time (see Figure 3.6B). These opposite trends do not support the hypothesis that HFCS consumption is responsible for obesity.

Diet is only one factor that leads to weight gain. Another major contributor is not enough physical activity. The

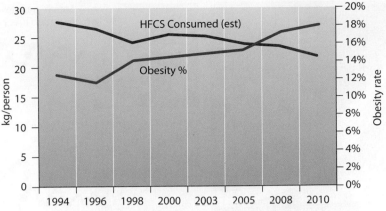

▲ **Figure 3.6B** Obesity rate and HFCS consumption in Canada, 1994–2010

consensus is that overconsumption of calories—in sugar, HFCS, or dietary fat—in combination with decreased physical activity is contributing to the weight gain epidemic. Perhaps Canadians are consuming excess calories from sources other than HFCS and not getting enough physical exercise.

No scientific evidence supports the rumour that HFCS is responsible for the obesity problem in Canada. In fact, Canadians are consuming less HFCS but are still gaining weight. To combat the obesity epidemic, Canadians must become more active and eat healthier. A healthy diet consists of a balance of proteins, fats, vitamins, and minerals, as well as complex carbohydrates, the topic of the next module.

 How is glucose-fructose made from corn?

● Cornstarch is hydrolyzed to glucose; then enzymes convert glucose to fructose. This fructose is combined with corn syrup to produce glucose-fructose.

3.7 Polysaccharides are long chains of sugar units

Polysaccharides are macromolecules, polymers of hundreds to thousands of monosaccharides linked together by dehydration reactions. Polysaccharides may function as storage molecules or as structural compounds. **Figure 3.7** illustrates three common types of polysaccharides: starch, glycogen, and cellulose.

Starch, a storage polysaccharide in plants, consists entirely of glucose monomers. Starch molecules coil into a helical shape and may be unbranched (as shown in the figure) or branched. Starch granules serve as carbohydrate "banks" from which plant cells can withdraw glucose for energy or building materials. Humans and most other animals have enzymes that can hydrolyze plant starch to glucose. Potatoes and grains, such as wheat, corn, and rice, are the major sources of starch in the human diet.

Animals store glucose in a different form of polysaccharide, called **glycogen**. Glycogen is more highly branched than starch, as shown in the figure. Most of your glycogen is stored as granules in your liver and muscle cells, which hydrolyze the glycogen to release glucose when it is needed.

Cellulose, the most abundant organic compound on Earth, is a major component of the tough walls that enclose plant cells. Cellulose is also a polymer of glucose, but its monomers are linked together in a different orientation. (Carefully compare the oxygen "bridges" highlighted in yellow between glucose monomers in starch, glycogen, and cellulose in the figure.) Arranged parallel to each other, cellulose molecules are joined by hydrogen bonds, forming cablelike microfibrils. Layers of microfibrils combine with other polymers including lignin, producing strong support for trees and structures we build with lumber.

Most animals including humans do not have enzymes that can hydrolyze the glucose linkages in cellulose. Therefore, cellulose is not a nutrient for humans, although it does contribute to digestive system health. The cellulose that passes unchanged through your digestive tract is referred to as "insoluble fibre." Fresh fruits, vegetables, and grains are rich in fibre.

Some microorganisms have cellulase, an enzyme that hydrolyzes cellulose. Cows and termites house such microorganisms in their digestive tracts and are thus able to derive energy from

Starch granules in potato tuber cells

Starch

Glucose monomer

Glycogen granules in muscle tissue

Glycogen

Cellulose microfibrils in a plant cell wall

Cellulose

Cellulose molecules

Hydrogen bonds

▲ **Figure 3.7** Polysaccharides

cellulose. It was recently discovered that some termites actually produce their own cellulase. Decomposing fungi also digest cellulose, helping to recycle its chemical elements within ecosystems.

Another structural polysaccharide, **chitin**, is used by insects and crustaceans to build their exoskeleton, the hard case enclosing the animal. Chitin is also found in the cell walls of fungi. Humans use chitin to make a strong and flexible surgical thread that decomposes after a wound or incision heals.

Almost all carbohydrates are hydrophilic owing to the many hydroxyl groups attached to their sugar monomers

(see Figure 3.4B). Thus, cotton bath towels, which are mostly cellulose, are quite water absorbent because of the water-loving nature of cellulose. The next class of macromolecules that we will look at are proteins.

? Compare and contrast starch and cellulose, two plant polysaccharides.

● Both are polymers of glucose, but the bonds between glucose monomers have different shapes. Starch functions mainly for sugar storage. Cellulose is a structural polysaccharide that is the main material of plant cell walls.

Proteins

3.8 Proteins are made from amino acids linked by peptide bonds

Nearly every dynamic function in your body depends on proteins. You have tens of thousands of different proteins, each with a specific structure and function. Of all of life's molecules, proteins are structurally the most elaborate and diverse. A **protein** is a polymer of amino acids. Protein diversity is based on differing arrangements of a common set of just 20 amino acid monomers.

Amino acids all have an amino group and a carboxyl group (which makes it an acid, hence the name amino *acid*). As you can see in the general structure shown in **Figure 3.8A**,

Amino group

Carboxyl group

▲ **Figure 3.8A**
General structure of an amino acid

both of these functional groups are covalently bonded to a central carbon atom, called the alpha carbon. Also bonded to the alpha carbon is a hydrogen atom and a chemical group symbolized by the letter *R*. The R group, also called the side chain, differs with each amino acid. In the simplest amino acid (glycine), the R group is just a hydrogen atom. In all others, such as those shown in **Figure 3.8B**, the R group consists of one or more carbon atoms with various chemical groups attached. The composition and structure of the R group determines the specific properties of each of the 20 amino acids that are found in proteins (see Appendix B).

The amino acids in Figure 3.8B represent two main types, hydrophobic and hydrophilic. Leucine (abbreviated Leu) is

Hydrophobic	Hydrophilic	
Leucine (Leu)	Serine (Ser)	Aspartic acid (Asp)

▲ **Figure 3.8B** Examples of amino acids with hydrophobic and hydrophilic R groups

an example of an amino acid in which the R group is non-polar and hydrophobic. Serine (Ser), with a hydroxyl group in its R group, is an example of an amino acid with a polar, hydrophilic R group. Aspartic acid (Asp) is acidic and nega-tively charged at the pH of a cell. (Indeed, all the amino and carboxyl groups of amino acids are usually ionized at cellular pH, as shown in Table 3.2.) Other amino acids have basic R groups and are positively charged. Amino acids with polar and charged R groups help proteins dissolve in the aqueous solutions inside cells.

Now that we have examined amino acids, let's see how they are linked to form polymers. Can you guess? Cells join amino acids together in a dehydration reaction that links the carboxyl group of one amino acid to the amino group of the next amino acid as a water molecule is removed (**Figure 3.8C**). The result-ing covalent linkage is called a **peptide bond**. The product of the reaction shown in the figure is called a *di*peptide, because it was made from *two* amino acids. Additional amino acids can be added by the same process to form a chain of amino acids, a **polypeptide**. To release amino acids from the polypeptide by hydrolysis, a molecule of H_2O must be added back to break each peptide bond.

How is it possible to make thousands of different kinds of proteins from just 20 amino acids? The answer has to do with sequence. You know that thousands of English words can be made by varying the sequence of letters and word length. Although the protein "alphabet" is slightly smaller (just 20 "letters," rather than 26), the "words" are much longer. Most polypeptides are at least 100 amino acids in length; some are 1000 or more. Each polypeptide has a unique sequence of amino acids. But a long polypeptide chain of specific sequence is not the same as a protein, any more than a long strand of yarn is the same as a sweater that can be knit from that yarn. A function-ing protein is one or more polypeptide chains precisely coiled, twisted, and folded into a unique three-dimensional shape.

 In what way is the production of a dipeptide similar to the production of a disaccharide?

● In both cases, the monomers are joined by a dehydration reaction.

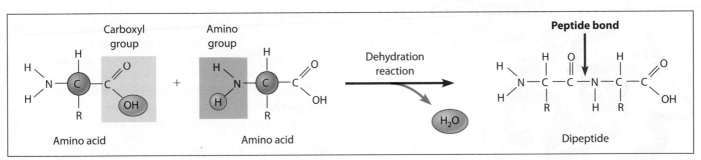

▲ **Figure 3.8C** Peptide bond formation

3.9 A protein's specific shape determines its function

What do the tens of thousands of different proteins in your body do? Probably their most important role is as *enzymes*, the chemical catalysts that speed and regulate virtually all chemical reactions in cells.

In **Figure 3.9A**, you can see examples of two types of pro-teins. *Structural proteins* are found in hair and the fibres that make up connective tissues such as tendons and ligaments. Muscle cells are packed with *contractile proteins*.

Other types of proteins include *defensive proteins*, such as the antibodies of the immune system, and *signal proteins*, such as many of the hormones and other chemical messengers that help coordinate body activities by facilitating communi-cation between cells. *Receptor proteins* may be built into cell membranes and transmit signals into cells. Hemoglobin in red blood cells is a *transport protein* that delivers O_2 to work-ing muscles and tissues throughout the body. Other transport proteins move sugar molecules into cells for energy. Some pro-teins are *storage proteins*, such as ovalbumin, the protein of egg white, which serves as a source of amino acids for developing embryos. Milk proteins provide amino acids for baby mam-mals, and plant seeds contain storage proteins that nourish developing plant embryos.

The functions of all these different types of proteins depend on their specific shape. **Figure 3.9B** shows a ribbon model of lysozyme, an enzyme found in your sweat, tears, and saliva. Lysozyme consists of one long polypeptide, represented by the

▲ **Figure 3.9A** Structural proteins make up hair, tendons, and ligaments; contractile proteins are found in muscles

purple ribbon. Lysozyme's general shape is called **globular**. This overall shape is more apparent in **Figure 3.9C**, a space-filling model of lysozyme. In that model, the colours represent the different atoms of carbon, oxygen, nitrogen, and hydrogen. The barely visible yellow balls are sulphur atoms that form the stabilizing bonds shown as yellow lines in the ribbon model. Most enzymes and other proteins are globular. Structural

proteins, such as those making up hair, tendons, and ligaments, are typically long and thin and are called **fibrous proteins**.

Descriptions such as globular and fibrous refer to a protein's general shape. Each protein also has a much more specific shape. The coils and twists of lysozyme's polypeptide ribbon appear haphazard, but they represent the molecule's specific, three-dimensional shape, and this shape is what determines its specific function. Nearly all proteins must recognize and bind to some other molecule to function. Lysozyme, for example, can destroy bacterial cells, but first it must bind to specific molecules on the bacterial cell surface. Lysozyme's specific shape enables it to recognize and attach to its molecular target, which fits into the groove you see on the right in the figures.

The dependence of protein function on a protein's specific shape becomes clear when proteins are altered. In a process called **denaturation**, polypeptide chains unravel, losing their specific shape and, as a result, their function. Changes in salt concentration and pH can denature many proteins, as can excessive heat. For example, visualize what happens when you fry an egg. Heat quickly denatures the clear proteins surrounding the yolk, making them solid, white, and opaque. One of the reasons why extremely high fevers are so dangerous is that some proteins in the body become denatured and cannot function.

Groove

▲ **Figure 3.9C** Space-filling model of the protein lysozyme

Given the proper cellular environment, a newly synthesized polypeptide chain spontaneously folds into its functional shape. We examine the four levels of a protein's structure next.

? Why does a denatured protein no longer function normally?

● The function of each protein is a consequence of its specific shape, which is lost when a protein denatures.

Groove

▲ **Figure 3.9B** Ribbon model of the protein lysozyme

3.10 A protein's shape depends on four levels of structure

Primary Structure The **primary structure** of a protein is its unique sequence of amino acids. As an example, let's consider transthyretin, an important transport protein found in your blood. Its specific shape enables it to transport vitamin A and one of the thyroid hormones throughout your body. A complete molecule of transthyretin has four identical polypeptide chains, each made up of 127 amino acids. **Figure 3.10A**, on the next page, shows part of one of these chains unravelled for a closer look at its primary structure. The three-letter abbreviations represent the specific amino acids that make up the chain.

In order for transthyretin or any other protein to perform its specific function, it must have the correct amino acids

arranged in a precise order. The primary structure of a protein is determined by inherited genetic information. Even a slight change in primary structure may affect a protein's overall shape and thus its ability to function. For instance, a single amino acid change in hemoglobin, the oxygen-carrying blood protein, causes sickle-cell disease, a serious blood disorder.

Secondary Structure In the second level of protein structure, parts of the polypeptide coil or fold into local patterns called **secondary structure**. Coiling of a polypeptide chain results in a secondary structure called an alpha helix; a certain kind of folding leads to a secondary structure called a beta

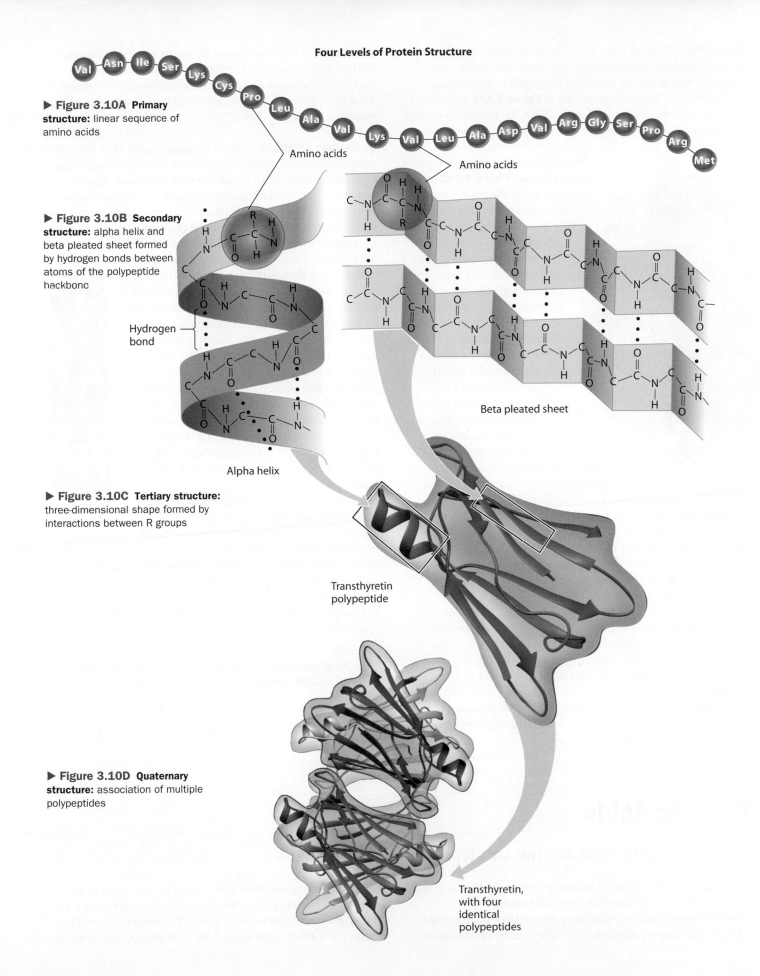

Four Levels of Protein Structure

▶ **Figure 3.10A Primary structure:** linear sequence of amino acids

Amino acids

Amino acids

▶ **Figure 3.10B Secondary structure:** alpha helix and beta pleated sheet formed by hydrogen bonds between atoms of the polypeptide backbone

Hydrogen bond

Alpha helix

Beta pleated sheet

▶ **Figure 3.10C Tertiary structure:** three-dimensional shape formed by interactions between R groups

Transthyretin polypeptide

▶ **Figure 3.10D Quaternary structure:** association of multiple polypeptides

Transthyretin, with four identical polypeptides

pleated sheet. Both of these patterns are maintained by regularly spaced hydrogen bonds between hydrogen atoms and oxygen atoms along the backbone of the polypeptide chain. Each hydrogen bond is represented in **Figure 3.10B** by a row of dots. Because the R groups of the amino acids are not involved in forming these secondary structures, they are omitted from the diagrams.

Transthyretin has only one alpha helix region (see **Figure 3.10C**). In contrast, some fibrous proteins, such as the structural protein of hair, have the alpha helix structure over most of their length.

Beta pleated sheets make up the core of many globular proteins, as is the case for transthyretin. Pleated sheets also dominate some fibrous proteins, including the silk protein of a spider's web, shown to the left. The combined strength of so many hydrogen bonds makes each silk fibre stronger than a steel strand of the same weight. Potential uses of spider silk proteins include surgical thread, fishing line, and bulletproof vests.

Tertiary Structure   The term **tertiary structure** refers to the overall three-dimensional shape of a polypeptide, which, as we've said, determines the function of a protein. As shown in Figure 3.10C, a transthyretin polypeptide has a globular shape, which results from the compact arrangement of its alpha helix region and beta pleated sheet regions.

Here the R groups of the amino acids making up the polypeptide get involved in creating a protein's shape. Tertiary structure results from interactions between these R groups. For example, transthyretin and other proteins found in aqueous solutions are folded so that the hydrophobic R groups are on the inside of the molecule and the hydrophilic R groups on the outside, exposed to water. In addition to the clustering of hydrophobic groups, hydrogen bonding between polar side chains and ionic bonding of

some of the charged (ionized) R groups help maintain the tertiary structure. A protein's shape may be reinforced further by covalent bonds called disulphide bridges. You saw disulphide bridges as the yellow lines in the ribbon model of lysozyme in Figure 3.9B.

Quaternary Structure   Many proteins consist of two or more polypeptide chains aggregated into one functional macromolecule. Such proteins have a **quaternary structure**, resulting from the association of these polypeptides, which are known as subunits. **Figure 3.10D** shows a complete transthyretin molecule with its four identical globular subunits.

Another example of a protein with quaternary structure is collagen, shown to the right. Collagen is a fibrous protein with three helical polypeptides intertwined into a larger triple helix. This arrangement gives the long fibres great strength, suited to their function as the girders of connective tissue in skin, bone, tendons, and ligaments. Collagen accounts for 40% of the protein in your body.

Many other proteins have subunits that are different from one another. For example, the oxygen-transporting molecule hemoglobin has four polypeptides of two distinct types (see Figure 27.12). Each polypeptide has a nonprotein attachment, called a heme, with an iron atom that binds oxygen.

What happens if a protein folds incorrectly? Many diseases, such as Alzheimer's and Parkinson's, involve an accumulation of misfolded proteins. Prions are infectious misshapen proteins that are associated with serious degenerative brain diseases such as mad cow disease (see Module 16.14). Such diseases reinforce the theme that structure fits function: A protein's unique three-dimensional shape determines its proper functioning.

Polypeptide chain

Collagen

 If a genetic mutation changes the primary structure of a protein, how might this destroy the protein's function?

● Primary structure, the amino acid sequence, affects the secondary structure, which affects the tertiary structure, which affects the quaternary structure (if any). Thus, primary structure determines the shape of a protein, and the function of a protein depends on its shape. A shape change could eliminate function.

Nucleic Acids

3.11 DNA and RNA are the two types of nucleic acids

As we just saw, the primary structure of a polypeptide determines the shape of a protein. But what determines the primary structure? The amino acid sequence of a polypeptide is programmed by a discrete unit of inheritance known as a **gene**. Genes consist

of **DNA** (**d**eoxyrib**o**nucleic **acid**), one of the two types of polymers called **nucleic acids**. The name *nucleic* comes from their location in the nuclei of eukaryotic cells. The genetic material that humans and other organisms inherit from their parents consists of DNA. Unique among molecules, DNA provides directions for its own replication. Thus, as a cell divides, its genetic instructions are passed to each daughter cell. These instructions program all of a cell's activities by directing the synthesis of proteins.

The genes present in DNA do not build proteins directly. They work through an intermediary—the second type of nucleic acid, known as **ribonucleic acid** (**RNA**). **Figure 3.11** illustrates the main roles of these two types of nucleic acids in the production of proteins. In the nucleus of a eukaryotic cell, a gene directs the synthesis of an RNA molecule. We say that DNA is transcribed into RNA. The RNA molecule moves out of the nucleus and interacts with the protein-building machinery of the cell. There, the gene's instructions, written in "nucleic acid language," are translated into "protein language," the amino acid sequence of a polypeptide. (In prokaryotic cells, which lack nuclei, both transcription and translation take place within the cytoplasm of the cell.)

Recent research has found previously unknown types of RNA molecules that play many other roles in the cell. We return to the functions of DNA and RNA later in the book.

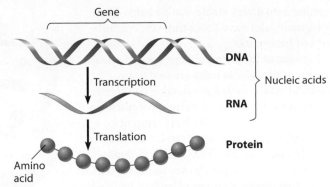

▲ **Figure 3.11** The flow of genetic information in the building of a protein

? How are the two types of nucleic acids functionally related?

● The hereditary material of DNA contains the instructions for the primary structure of polypeptides. RNA is the intermediary that conveys those instructions to the protein-making machinery that assembles amino acids in the designated order.

3.12 Nucleic acids are polymers of nucleotides

The monomers that make up nucleic acids are **nucleotides**. As indicated in **Figure 3.12A**, each nucleotide contains three parts. At the centre of a nucleotide is a five-carbon sugar (blue); the sugar in DNA is deoxyribose (shown in Figure 3.12A), whereas RNA has a slightly different sugar called ribose. Linked to one side of the sugar in both types of nucleotides is a negatively charged phosphate group (yellow). Linked to the sugar's other side is a nitrogenous base (green), a molecular structure containing nitrogen and carbon. (The nitrogen atoms tend to take up H^+ in aqueous solutions, which explains why it is called a nitrogenous *base*.) Each DNA nucleotide has one of four different nitrogenous bases: adenine (A), thymine (T), cytosine (C), and guanine (G). Thus, all genetic information is written in a four-letter alphabet.

RNA nucleotides also contain the bases A, C, and G; but the base uracil (U) is found instead of thymine.

Like polysaccharides and polypeptides, a nucleic acid polymer—a polynucleotide—is built from its monomers by dehydration reactions. In this process, the sugar of one nucleotide bonds to the phosphate group of the next monomer. The result is a repeating sugar-phosphate backbone in the polymer, as represented by the blue and yellow ribbon in **Figure 3.12B**. (Note that the nitrogenous bases are not part of the backbone.)

RNA usually consists of a single polynucleotide strand, but DNA is a **double helix**, in which two polynucleotides wrap around each other **(Figure 3.12C)**. The nitrogenous bases protrude from the two sugar-phosphate backbones and pair in the centre of the helix. As shown by their diagrammatic shapes in the figure, A always pairs with T, and C always pairs with G. The two DNA chains are held together by hydrogen bonds (indicated by the dotted lines) between their paired bases. These bonds are individually weak, but collectively they zip the two strands

▲ **Figure 3.12A** A nucleotide, consisting of a phosphate group, a sugar, and a nitrogenous base

Phosphate group

Sugar

Nitrogenous base (adenine)

Nucleotide

Sugar-phosphate backbone

▲ **Figure 3.12B** Part of a polynucleotide

together into a very stable double helix. Most DNA molecules have thousands or even millions of base pairs.

Because of the base-pairing rules, the two strands of the double helix are said to be *complementary*, each a predictable counterpart of the other. Thus, if a stretch of nucleotides on one strand has the base sequence –AGCACT–, then the same stretch on the other strand must be –TCGTGA–. Complementary base pairing is the key to how a cell makes two identical copies of each of its DNA molecules every time it divides. Thus, the structure of DNA accounts for its function of transmitting genetic information whenever a cell reproduces. The same base-pairing rules (with the exception that U nucleotides of RNA pair with A nucleotides of DNA) also

account for the precise transcription of information from DNA to RNA. Gene transcription and translation are covered in detail in Chapter 10.

An organism's genes determine the proteins and thus the structures and functions of its body. We'll look at a specific example of this relationship in the next module. In the next chapter, we move up in the biological hierarchy to the level of the cell.

Base pair

▲ **Figure 3.12C** DNA double helix

? **What roles do complementary base pairing play in the functioning of nucleic acids?**

● Complementary base pairing makes possible the precise replication of DNA, ensuring that genetic information is faithfully transmitted every time a cell divides. It also ensures that RNA molecules carry accurate instructions for the synthesis of proteins.

3.13 Lactose tolerance is a recent event in human evolution

Normally, mammals consume only milk, and therefore the milk sugar lactose, when they are nursing. After weaning, lactase (the enzyme that digests lactose) production ceases. The majority of people stop producing lactase in early childhood and thus do not easily digest lactose. Researchers were curious about the genetic and evolutionary basis for the regional distribution of lactose tolerance and intolerance. In 2002, a group of scientists completed a study of the genes of 196 lactose-intolerant adults of African, Asian, and European descent. They determined that lactose intolerance is actually the human norm. It is "lactose tolerance" that represents a relatively recent mutation in the human genome.

The ability to make lactase into adulthood is concentrated in people of northern European descent, and the researchers speculated that lactose tolerance became widespread among this group because it offered a survival advantage. In northern Europe's relatively cold climate, only one harvest a year is possible. Therefore, animals were a main source of food for early humans in that region. Cattle were first domesticated in northern Europe about 9000 years ago (**Figure 3.13**). With milk and other dairy products at hand year-round, natural selection would have favoured anyone with a mutation that kept the lactase gene switched on.

Researchers wondered whether the lactose tolerance mutation found in Europeans might be present in other cultures who kept dairy herds. Indeed, a 2006 study compared the genetic makeup and lactose tolerance of 43 ethnic groups in East Africa. The researchers identified three mutations, all different from each other and from the European mutation, that keep the lactase gene permanently turned on. The mutations appear

▲ **Figure 3.13** A prehistoric European cave painting of cattle

to have occurred beginning about 7000 years ago, around the time that archaeological evidence shows the domestication of cattle in these African regions.

Mutations that conferred a selective advantage, such as surviving cold winters or withstanding drought by drinking milk, spread rapidly in these early pastoral peoples. Their evolutionary and cultural history is thus recorded in their genes and in their continuing ability to digest milk.

? **Explain how lactose tolerance involves three of the four major classes of biological macromolecules.**

● Lactose, milk sugar, is a carbohydrate that is hydrolyzed by the enzyme lactase, a protein. The ability to make this enzyme and the regulation of when it is made is coded for in DNA, a nucleic acid.

Lipids

3.14 Fats are lipids that are mostly energy-storage molecules

Lipids are diverse compounds that are grouped together because they share one trait: They do not mix well with water. Lipids consist mainly of carbon and hydrogen atoms linked by nonpolar covalent bonds. In contrast to most other biological molecules, lipids are **hydrophobic** (water-fearing). You can see this chemical behaviour in an unshaken bottle of salad dressing: The oil (a type of lipid) separates from the vinegar (which is mostly water). The oils that ducks spread on their feathers make the feathers repel water **(Figure 3.14A)**, which helps such waterfowl stay afloat.

Lipids also differ from carbohydrates, proteins, and nucleic acids in that they are neither huge macromolecules nor polymers built from similar monomers. You will see that lipids vary a great deal in structure and function. In this and the next module, we will consider three types of lipids: fats, phospholipids, and steroids.

A **fat** is a large lipid made from two kinds of smaller molecules: glycerol and fatty acids. Shown at the top in **Figure 3.14B**, glycerol is an alcohol with three carbons, each bearing a hydroxyl group (—OH). A fatty acid consists of a carboxyl group (the functional group that gives these molecules the name fatty *acid*, —COOH) and a hydrocarbon chain, usually 16 or 18 carbon atoms in length. The nonpolar hydrocarbon chains are the reason fats are hydrophobic.

Figure 3.14B shows how one fatty acid molecule can link to a glycerol molecule by a dehydration reaction. Linking three fatty acids to glycerol produces a fat, as illustrated in **Figure 3.14C**. A synonym for fat is *triglyceride*, a term you may see on food labels or on medical tests for fat in the blood.

Fatty acids with no double bonds in their hydrocarbon chain have the maximum number of hydrogen atoms (are "saturated" with hydrogens) and are called **saturated fatty acids**. Most animal fats are saturated. The unkinked fatty acid chains of saturated fats can pack closely together, making butter and beef fat solid at room temperature. Some fatty acids contain one or more double bonds, which cause kinks (or bends) in the carbon chain. See the third fatty acid in Figure 3.14C. Such an unsaturated fatty acid has one fewer hydrogen atom on each carbon of the double bond. The kinks in

◀ **Figure 3.14A** Water beading on the oily coating of feathers

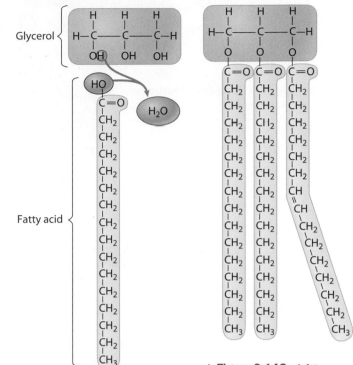

▲ **Figure 3.14B** A dehydration reaction linking a fatty acid molecule to a glycerol molecule

▲ **Figure 3.14C** A fat molecule (triglyceride) consisting of three fatty acids linked to glycerol

unsaturated fatty acids prevent fats containing them from packing together tightly and solidifying at room temperature. Olive oil and other vegetable oils are unsaturated fats and are liquid at room temperature.

The main function of fats is long-term energy storage. A gram of fat stores more than twice as much energy as a gram of polysaccharide. For immobile plants, the bulky energy storage form of starch is not a problem. (Vegetable oils are generally obtained from seeds, where more compact energy storage is a benefit.) A mobile animal, such as a duck or a human, can get around much more easily carrying its energy stores in the form of fat. Of course, the downside of this energy-packed storage form is that it takes more effort for a person to "burn off" excess fat. In addition to storing energy, fatty tissue cushions vital organs and insulates the body.

? How do you think the structure of a monounsaturated fat differs from a polyunsaturated fat?

● A monounsaturated fat has a fatty acid with a single double bond in its carbon chain. A polyunsaturated fat has a fatty acid with several double bonds.

3.15 Phospholipids and steroids are important lipids with a variety of functions

Cells could not exist without **phospholipids**, the major component of cell membranes. Phospholipids are structurally similar to fats, but they contain only two fatty acids attached to glycerol instead of three. As shown in **Figure 3.15A**, a negatively charged phosphate group (shown as a yellow circle in the figure and linked to another small molecule) is attached to

▲ **Figure 3.15A** Chemical structure of a phospholipid molecule

▲ **Figure 3.15B** Section of a phospholipid membrane

properties—fluidity. Temperature greatly affects membrane fluidity. Compare the hardness of butter stored in the refrigerator to some at room temperature. The cold butter is more solid. Animals that live in cold climates must protect their cell membranes from becoming too solid. A cold phospholipid membrane containing more saturated fatty acids will also be more solid (less fluid). To prevent this, animals—including the caribou in the Canadian Arctic—have cells with membranes that contain more unsaturated fatty acids. As a result, their membranes retain more fluidity even when the temperature of the tissues drops to near freezing. We will explore the structure and function of biological membranes further in Chapters 4 and 5.

Steroids are lipids in which the carbon skeleton contains four fused rings, as shown in the structural formula of cholesterol in **Figure 3.15C**. (The diagram omits the carbons making up the rings and most of the chain and also their attached hydrogens.) **Cholesterol** is a common component in animal cell membranes, and animal cells also use it as a starting material for making other steroids, including sex hormones. Different steroids vary in the chemical groups attached to the rings, as you saw in Figure 3.2. Too much cholesterol in the blood may contribute to atherosclerosis. We'll discuss good and bad cholesterol further in the next module.

▲ **Figure 3.15C** Cholesterol, a steroid

glycerol's third carbon. (Note that glycerol is shown in orange.) The structure of phospholipids provides a classic example of how form fits function. The hydrophilic and hydrophobic ends of multiple molecules assemble in a bilayer of phospholipids to form a membrane **(Figure 3.15B)**. The hydrophobic tails of the fatty acids cluster in the centre, and the hydrophilic phosphate heads face the watery environment on either side of the membrane. Each grey-headed, yellow-tailed structure in the membrane shown here represents a phospholipid; this symbol is used throughout this book.

The type of fatty acids within a membrane's phospholipid membrane can influence one of its important

? **Compare and contrast the structure of a phospholipid with that of a fat (triglyceride).**

● A phospholipid has two fatty acids and a phosphate group attached to glycerol. Three fatty acids are attached to the glycerol of a fat molecule.

3.16 Cholesterol must be specially packaged for transport in the blood

Accounting for nearly one-third of all deaths in 2008, cardiovascular disease (diseases of the heart and blood vessels) is a major killer of Canadians. From 2002 to 2012, however, the rate of cardiovascular disease declined 25%. The decline was due in part to improved treatments and greater public awareness about risk factors, including atherosclerosis caused by high cholesterol. But not all cholesterol is bad for you. The cells of your body require cholesterol to regulate the fluidity of their plasma membranes. And "good" cholesterol can help lower the amount of "bad" cholesterol in your blood and help prevent atherosclerosis. What makes some cholesterol good for you and other cholesterol bad for you? It depends on the manner in which cholesterol is packaged for travel through your bloodstream.

Cholesterol, like other lipids, is a hydrophobic compound and insoluble in aqueous solutions such as blood. Therefore,

to be transported throughout your body, cholesterol has to be packaged in a way that makes it soluble. In your intestines, dietary fats and cholesterol are packaged into **lipoproteins** for transport in your blood **(Figure 3.16A)**. Lipoproteins are complex structures composed of proteins, triglycerides, phospholipids, and cholesterol. However, the percentage of each component varies among the different forms of lipoproteins, affecting their relative densities. Those with higher protein content are denser than lipoproteins containing more triglycerides and cholesterol.

As shown in Figure 3.16A, the centre of the lipoprotein contains triglycerides and cholesterol. The hydrophobic core is surrounded by a single leaflet of phospholipids, with embedded proteins and additional cholesterol. The structure of this leaflet resembles half of the phospholipid membrane (bilayer)

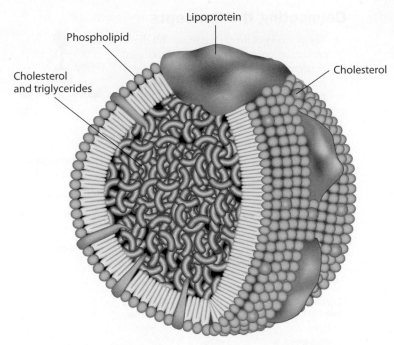

Phospholipid

Lipoprotein

Cholesterol and triglycerides

Cholesterol

▲ **Figure 3.16A** A lipoprotein

Artery wall

Cholesterol deposition

LDL

Plaque

HDL

HDL with excess cholesterol

Cholesterol removal

▲ **Figure 3.16B** LDLs contribute to plaque formation while HDLs inhibit it

shown in Figure 3.15A. The hydrophobic fatty acid tails are directed inward and the outwardly directed hydrophilic heads allow the lipoprotein to be suspended in the aqueous solvent of your blood.

When physicians talk about good and bad cholesterol, they are actually speaking about different types of lipoproteins and not specifically about the compound itself. So-called bad cholesterol refers to low-density lipoproteins (LDLs), which contain few proteins and large amounts of cholesterol. When too many LDLs circulate in the blood, they can stick to the artery walls where they slowly build up, contributing to plaque formation **(Figure 3.16B)**. Plaque narrows the arteries, restricting blood flow (atherosclerosis). If the vessel becomes blocked, an individual becomes at risk of a heart attack or stroke. On the contrary, good cholesterol or high-density lipoproteins (HDLs) are lipoproteins with more proteins and lower cholesterol. Circulating HDLs actually reduce the risk of heart attack and stroke. By removing excess cholesterol from plaque buildup, HDL can slow its accumulation.

Because plaque slowly accumulates throughout life, blood cholesterol levels become an important health concern as we age. Having your cholesterol monitored becomes part of a routine health checkup. If your LDL level is found to be too high, reducing it typically requires a regulated diet. Reducing your consumption of foods containing saturated fats and cholesterol can lower circulating LDL levels. However, some people are genetically predisposed to produce high levels of LDLs (see Module 9.10), regardless of their diets. These individuals may have to rely on medications to lower their LDLs and increase their HDLs.

 How is good cholesterol different from bad cholesterol?

● The good cholesterol is high-density lipoprotein with high protein and lower lipid content than bad cholesterol or low-density lipoprotein.

REVIEW

MasteringBiology® **For Practice Quizzes, BioFlix, MP3 Tutors, and Activities, go to masteringbiology.com.**

Reviewing the Concepts

Introduction to Organic Compounds (3.1–3.3)

3.1 Life's molecular diversity is based on the properties of carbon. Carbon's ability to bond with four other atoms is the basis for building large and diverse organic compounds. Hydrocarbons are composed of only carbon and hydrogen. Isomers have the same molecular formula but different structures.

3.2 A few chemical groups are key to the functioning of biological molecules. Hydrophilic functional groups give organic molecules specific chemical properties.

3.3 Cells make a huge number of large molecules from a limited set of small molecules. Dehydration reactions combine monomers into polymers. Hydrolysis reactions break polymers into smaller pieces.

H_2O

Short polymer — OH + H — Monomer — H

Dehydration ⇌ Hydrolysis

Longer polymer — H

H_2O

Carbohydrates (3.4–3.7)

3.4 Monosaccharides are the simplest carbohydrates. A monosaccharide has a formula that is a multiple of CH_2O and contains hydroxyl groups and a carbonyl group.

3.5 Two monosaccharides are linked to form a disaccharide. Sucrose, or table sugar, is the most common disaccharide.

3.6 Is high-fructose corn syrup to blame for obesity? Glucose-fructose, a mixture of glucose and fructose derived from corn, is commonly added to drinks and processed foods.

3.7 Polysaccharides are long chains of sugar units. Starch and glycogen are storage polysaccharides; cellulose is structural, found in plant cell walls. Chitin is a component of insect exoskeletons and fungal cell walls.

Proteins (3.8–3.10)

3.8 Proteins are made from amino acids linked by peptide bonds. Protein diversity is based on different sequences of amino acids, monomers that contain an amino group, a carboxyl group, an H, and an R group, all attached to a central carbon. The R groups distinguish 20 amino acids, each with specific properties.

3.9 A protein's specific shape determines its function. Proteins are involved in almost all of a cell's activities; as enzymes, they regulate chemical reactions.

3.10 A protein's shape depends on four levels of structure. A protein's primary structure is the sequence of amino acids in its polypeptide chain. Its secondary structure is the coiling or folding of the chain, stabilized by hydrogen bonds. Tertiary structure is the overall three-dimensional shape of a polypeptide, resulting from interactions among R groups. Proteins made of more than one polypeptide have quaternary structure.

Nucleic Acids (3.11–3.13)

3.11 DNA and RNA are the two types of nucleic acids. DNA and RNA serve as the blueprints for proteins and thus control the life of a cell.

3.12 Nucleic acids are polymers of nucleotides. Nucleotides, nucleic acid monomers, are composed of a sugar, a phosphate group, and a nitrogenous base. DNA is a double helix; RNA is a single polynucleotide chain.

3.13 Lactose tolerance is a recent event in human evolution. Mutations in DNA have led to lactose tolerance in several human groups whose ancestors raised dairy cattle.

Lipids (3.14–3.16)

3.14 Fats are lipids that are mostly energy-storage molecules. Lipids are diverse, hydrophobic compounds composed largely of carbon and hydrogen. Fats (triglycerides) consist of glycerol linked to three fatty acids. Saturated fatty acids are found in animal fats; unsaturated fatty acids are typical of plant oils.

3.15 Phospholipids and steroids are important lipids with a variety of functions. Phospholipids are components of cell membranes. Steroids include cholesterol and some hormones.

3.16 Cholesterol must be specially packaged for transport in the blood. Hydrophobic cholesterol molecules are packaged in various lipoproteins in order to increase their solubility in the blood. Too many low-density lipoproteins contribute to heart disease whereas high-density lipoproteins reduce the risk.

Connecting the Concepts

1. The diversity of life is staggering. Yet the molecular logic of life is simple and elegant: Small molecules common to all organisms are ordered into unique macromolecules. Explain why carbon is central to this diversity of organic molecules. How do carbon skeletons, chemical groups, monomers, and polymers relate to this molecular logic of life?

2. Complete the table to help review the structures and functions of the four classes of organic molecules.

Carbohydrates Monosaccharide	Energy for cell, raw material	a. _____	
	b. _____	Starch, glycogen	
	Plant cell support	c. _____	
Lipids (don't form polymers) Glycerol / Fatty acid Components of a fat molecule	Energy storage	d. _____	
	e. _____	Phospholipids	
	Hormones	f. _____	
Proteins g. _____ h. _____ i. _____ Amino acid	j. _____	Lactase	
	k. _____	Hair, tendons	
	l. _____	Muscles	
	Transport	m. _____	
	Communication	Signal proteins	
	n. _____	Antibodies	
	Storage	Egg albumin	
	Receive signals	Receptor protein	
Nucleic Acids o. _____ p. _____ Nucleotide q. _____	Heredity	r. _____	
	s. _____	DNA and RNA	

Testing Your Knowledge
Multiple Choice

3. A glucose molecule is to starch as *(Explain your answer.)*
   a. a steroid is to a lipid.
   b. a protein is to an amino acid.
   c. a nucleic acid is to a polypeptide.
   d. a nucleotide is to a nucleic acid.
   e. an amino acid is to a nucleic acid.

4. What makes a fatty acid an acid?
   a. It does not dissolve in water.
   b. It is capable of bonding with other molecules to form a fat.
   c. It has a carboxyl group that donates an H^+ to a solution.
   d. It contains only two oxygen atoms.
   e. It is a polymer made of many smaller subunits.

5. Where in the tertiary structure of a water-soluble protein would you most likely find an amino acid with a hydrophobic R group?
   a. at both ends of the polypeptide chain
   b. on the outside, next to the water
   c. covalently bonded to another R group
   d. on the inside, away from water
   e. hydrogen-bonded to nearby amino acids

6. Cows can derive nutrients from cellulose because
   a. they produce enzymes that recognize the shape of the glucose-glucose bonds and hydrolyze them.
   b. they rechew their cud to break down cellulose fibres.
   c. one of their stomachs contains prokaryotes that can hydrolyze the bonds of cellulose.
   d. their intestinal tract contains termites, which produce enzymes to hydrolyze cellulose.
   e. they convert cellulose to starch and can digest starch.

7. A shortage of phosphorus in the soil would make it especially difficult for a plant to manufacture
   a. DNA.   b. proteins.
   c. cellulose.   d. fatty acids.
   e. sucrose.

8. Lipids differ from other large biological molecules in that they
   a. are much larger.
   b. are not polymers.
   c. do not have specific shapes.
   d. are nonpolar and therefore hydrophilic.
   e. contain nitrogen atoms.

9. Of the following functional groups, which is/are polar, tending to make organic compounds hydrophilic?
   a. carbonyl   b. amino
   c. hydroxyl   d. carboxyl
   e. all of the above

10. Unsaturated fats
    a. are more common in animals than in plants.
    b. have fewer fatty acid molecules per fat molecule.
    c. are associated with greater health risks than are saturated fats.
    d. have double bonds in their fatty acid chains.
    e. are usually solid at room temperature.

Describing, Comparing, and Explaining

11. List three different kinds of lipids and describe their functions.

12. Explain why heat, pH changes, and other environmental changes can interfere with a protein's function.

13. How can a cell make many different kinds of protein out of only 20 amino acids? Of the myriad possibilities, how does the cell "know" which proteins to make?

14. Briefly describe the various functions performed by proteins in a cell.

15. Explain how DNA controls the functions of a cell.

16. Sucrose is broken down in your intestine to the monosaccharides glucose and fructose, which are then absorbed into your blood. What is the name of this type of reaction? Using this diagram of sucrose, show how this would occur.

Sucrose

17. Circle and name the functional groups in this organic molecule. What type of compound is this? For which class of macromolecules is it a monomer?

Applying the Concepts

18. Enzymes usually function best at an optimal pH and temperature. The following graph shows the effectiveness of two enzymes at various temperatures.

    a. At which temperature does enzyme A perform best? Enzyme B?
    b. One of these enzymes is found in humans and the other in thermophilic (heat-loving) bacteria. Which enzyme would you predict comes from which organism?
    c. From what you know about enzyme structure, explain why the rate of the reaction catalyzed by enzyme A slows down at temperatures above 40°C.

19. Some scientists hypothesize that life elsewhere in the universe might be based on the element silicon (atomic number 14) rather than on carbon (atomic number 6). Look at the electron shell diagrams in Figure 2.6. What properties does silicon share with carbon that would make silicon-based life more likely than, for example, neon-based or sulphur-based life? The atomic numbers of neon and sulphur are 10 and 16, respectively.

Answers to all questions can be found in Appendix E.

Cellular Structure

BIG IDEAS

Introduction to the Cell

(4.1–4.4)

Microscopes reveal the structures of cells—the fundamental units of life.

The Nucleus and Ribosomes

(4.5–4.6)

A cell's genetic instructions are housed in the nucleus and carried out by ribosomes.

The Endomembrane System

(4.7–4.12)

The endomembrane system participates in the manufacture, distribution, and breakdown of materials.

Energy-Converting Organelles

(4.13–4.15)

Mitochondria in all cells and chloroplasts in plant cells function in energy processing.

The Cytoskeleton and Cell Surfaces

(4.16–4.22)

The cytoskeleton and extracellular components provide support, motility, and functional connections.

Cells on the Move

Movement might seem like a characteristic of life—at least animal life and the lives of some single-celled organisms. Indeed, any biology student who has tried to chase a *Paramecium* under a microscope knows that some protists move quite fast. When you think about cells of the human body, you probably know that sperm cells swim and white blood cells creep about, engulfing bacteria and debris from injury sites. You may also realize that, unfortunately, cancer cells move, letting go of connections with neighbouring cells and moving to other tissues, where they establish secondary tumours. The micrograph (photo taken through a microscope) shown here (left) is of beautifully stained but deadly cancer cells in the process of dividing. But what about plant cells? Or bacteria? Do they move? In 1665, Robert Hooke used a crude microscope to examine a piece of bark (cork). Hooke compared these structures to *cellulae* (meaning "little rooms" in Latin) and the term *cells* stuck. These cells certainly did not move, because they were merely the outer cell walls of former plant cells.

But some of the cells viewed by Hooke's contemporary Anton van Leeuwenhoek, did move. Working in the late 1600s with refined lenses that he crafted, Leeuwenhoek examined numerous samples, from human blood and sperm to pond water. Leeuwenhoek identified the parasite *Giardia* (centre), the organism that causes the disease "beaver fever," from his own diarrheal stool. His reports to the Royal Society of London included drawings and descriptions of his discoveries. Of his stool examination he wrote, "Wherein I have sometimes also seen animalcules a-moving very prettily; some of them bit bigger than a blood globule [a red blood cell]. Their bodies were somewhat longer than broad, and their belly, which was flatlike, furnisht with sundry little paws [flagella], wherewith they made such a stir in the medium."

Leeuwenhoek was the first to observe and describe bacteria and establish that some bacterial cells move. In fact, we now know that some move at incredible speeds. For example, *Bdellovibrio bacteriophorus* is a bacterium that attacks other bacteria. It can charge its prey at speeds of up to 100 micrometres per second, comparable to a human running 600 kilometres per hour. It then bores into its hapless victim by spinning at 100 revolutions per second. Most bacteria aren't quite that fast, but they can locomote with whipping flagella or by spiralling through their environment.

Can plant cells move as well? If you look through a microscope at a thin piece of the common aquarium plant *Elodea* (right), you may see green chloroplasts marching in an orderly procession around the perimeter of the cells. The micrograph pictured above shows what such plant cells would look like, minus the movement. The fact is that all living cells have movement inside, even if they are anchored within a leaf or attached to other cells in your body. Whereas some cells are motile and move from place to place, all cells have internal structures that move about and interact.

Since the days of Leeuwenhoek and Hooke, improved microscopes have vastly expanded our view of the intricate structures within a cell. Photography and electronic imaging now enable biologists to capture microscope images directly. Just as Hooke and Leeuwenhoek illustrated what they saw, drawings and diagrams are still important in helping us understand the microscopic world. You will see in this chapter, for example, that the use of different colours in drawings makes it easier to distinguish between the various cellular structures, most of which are actually colourless. You will also notice that drawings are often paired with micrographs of cell structures. This pairing provides the best of both worlds: The micrograph shows a structure as a biologist sees it, and the drawing helps you understand the micrograph by emphasizing specific details.

Neither drawings nor micrographs allow you to see the movement that is characteristic of all living cells. For that you need to look for yourself through a microscope or view videos in lecture or on websites, such as the one associated with this book. As you study the still images in this textbook, remind yourself that these cellular parts aren't static—they move. This chapter focuses on the cellular structures that microscopes have revealed and describes their functions in a living cell. Cells are dynamic, moving, living systems. As we discuss their parts, remember that the phenomenon we call life emerges from the arrangement and interactions of the components of a cell.

Introduction to the Cell

4.1 Microscopes reveal the world of the cell

Our understanding of nature often goes hand in hand with the invention and refinement of instruments that extend human senses. Before microscopes were first used in the 17th century, no one knew that living organisms were composed of cells. The first microscopes were light microscopes. Although they worked using the same principles, they looked very different from the ones you may use in a biology laboratory. In a **light microscope (LM)**, visible light is passed through a specimen, such as a microorganism or a thin slice of animal or plant tissue, and then through glass lenses. The lenses bend the light in such a way that the image of the specimen is magnified as it is projected into your eye or a camera.

Magnification is the increase in the apparent size of an object. **Figure 4.1A** shows a single-celled protist called *Paramecium*. The notation *LM 230×* printed along the right edge of this **micrograph** tells you that the photograph was taken through a light microscope and that this image is 230 times the actual size of the organism.

The actual size of this *Paramecium* is about 0.33 millimetre (mm) in length. **Figure 4.1B** shows the size range of cells compared with objects both larger and smaller. The most common units of length that biologists use are listed at the bottom of the figure. Notice that the scale along the left side of the figure is logarithmic to accommodate the range of sizes shown. Starting at the top of the scale with 10 metres (m) and going down,

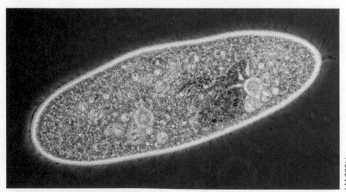

▲ **Figure 4.1A** Light micrograph of a protist, *Paramecium*

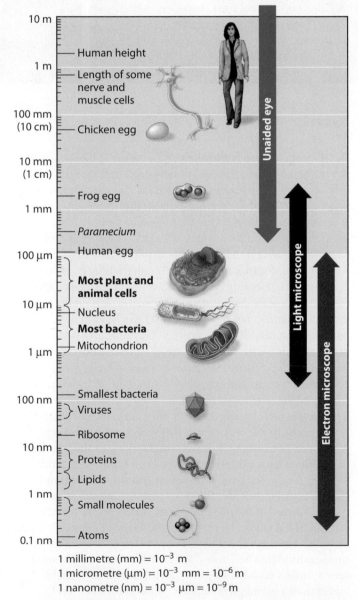

Scale	Object
10 m	
1 m	Human height
100 mm (10 cm)	Length of some nerve and muscle cells / Chicken egg
10 mm (1 cm)	
1 mm	Frog egg
100 µm	*Paramecium* / Human egg
10 µm	Most plant and animal cells / Nucleus
1 µm	Most bacteria / Mitochondrion
100 nm	Smallest bacteria / Viruses
10 nm	Ribosome / Proteins
1 nm	Lipids / Small molecules
0.1 nm	Atoms

1 millimetre (mm) = 10^{-3} m
1 micrometre (µm) = 10^{-3} mm = 10^{-6} m
1 nanometre (nm) = 10^{-3} µm = 10^{-9} m

▲ **Figure 4.1B** The size range of cells and related objects each reference measurement marks a 10-fold decrease in length. Most cells are between 1 and 100 micrometres (µm) in diameter (yellow region of the figure) and are therefore visible only with a microscope. Certain bacteria are as small as 0.2 µm in diameter and can barely be seen with a light microscope, whereas bird eggs are large enough to be seen with the unaided eye. What we refer to as the yolk of an egg is actually one very large cell. A single nerve cell running from the base of your spinal cord to your big toe may be 1 m in length, although it is so thin you would still need a microscope to see it.

Light microscopes can effectively magnify objects about 1000 times. Greater magnification does not show more details clearly; indeed, the image becomes blurry. Thus, another important factor in microscopy is *resolution*, a measure of the clarity of an image. Resolution is the ability of an optical instrument to show two nearby objects as separate. For example, if you took a photograph with a high-resolution camera, you could zoom in to see fine details clearly, unlike a low-resolution camera where the image becomes pixelated. Just as the resolution of the human eye is limited, the light microscope cannot resolve detail finer than about 0.2 µm, about the size of the smallest bacterium. No matter how many times its image of such a bacterium is magnified, the light microscope cannot show the details of this small cell's structure.

From the time that Hooke discovered cells in 1665 until the middle of the 20th century, biologists had only light microscopes for viewing cells. With these microscopes and various staining techniques to increase contrast and highlight parts of the sample, these early biologists discovered a great deal—microorganisms, animal and plant cells, and even some of the structures within cells. By the mid-1800s, these discoveries led to the **cell theory**, which states that all living things are composed of cells and that all cells come from other cells.

Our knowledge of cell structure took a giant leap forward as biologists began using the electron microscope in the 1950s. Instead of using light, an **electron microscope (EM)** focuses a beam of electrons through a specimen or onto its surface. Electron microscopes can distinguish biological structures as small as about 2 nanometres (nm), a 100-fold improvement over the light microscope. This high resolution has enabled biologists to explore cell ultrastructure, the complex internal anatomy of a cell.

Figures 4.1C and 4.1D show images produced by two kinds of electron microscopes. Biologists use the **scanning electron microscope (SEM)** to study the detailed architecture of cell surfaces. The SEM uses an electron beam to scan the surface of a cell or other sample, which is usually coated with a thin film of gold. The beam excites electrons on the surface, and these electrons are then detected by a device that translates their pattern into an image projected onto a video screen. The scanning electron micrograph in Figure 4.1C highlights the numerous cilia on *Paramecium*, projections it uses for movement. Notice the indentation, called the oral groove, through which food enters the cell. As you can see, the SEM produces images that look three-dimensional.

The **transmission electron microscope (TEM)** is used to study the details of internal cell structure. The TEM aims an electron beam through a very thin section of a specimen, just as a light microscope aims a beam of light through a specimen. The section is stained with atoms of heavy metals, which attach to certain cellular structures more than others. Electrons are scattered by these more dense parts, and the image is created by the pattern of transmitted electrons. Instead of using glass lenses, the TEM uses electromagnets as lenses to bend the paths of the electrons, magnifying and focusing an image onto a viewing screen or photographic film. The transmission electron micrograph in **Figure 4.1D** shows internal details of a protist called *Toxoplasma*. SEMs and TEMs are initially black and white but are often artificially colourized, as they are in these figures, to highlight or clarify structural features.

Electron microscopes have truly revolutionized the study of cells and their structures. Nonetheless, they have not replaced the light microscope. For a biologist studying a living process, such as the movement of *Paramecium*, a light microscope equipped with a video camera is more suitable than either an SEM or a TEM. When an organism is viewed under magnification, its velocity also appears to be magnified, making high magnification techniques impractical for viewing these swimming cells.

Colourized SEM 580×

▲ **Figure 4.1C** Scanning electron micrograph of *Paramecium*

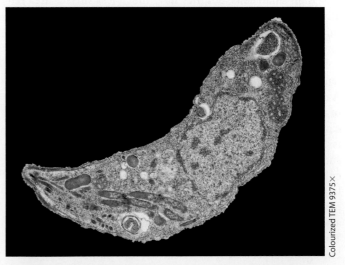

Colourized TEM 9375×

▲ **Figures 4.1D** Transmission electron micrograph of *Toxoplasma*

There are different types of light microscopy. **Figure 4.1E** shows *Paramecium* as seen using differential interference contrast microscopy. This optical technique amplifies differences in density so that the structures in living cells appear almost three-dimensional. Other techniques use fluorescent stains that selectively bind to various cellular molecules. In the last decade or two, light microscopy has seen significant and exciting technical advances that have increased magnification, resolution, and contrast. You will see many beautiful and illuminating examples of microscopy in this textbook.

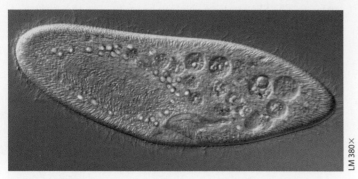

LM 380×

▲ **Figure 4.1E** Differential interference contrast micrograph of *Paramecium*

 ? Which type of microscope would you use to study (a) the changes in shape of a living human white blood cell; (b) the finest details of surface texture of a human hair; (c) the detailed structure of an organelle in a liver cell?

● (a) Light microscope; (b) scanning electron microscope; (c) transmission electron microscope

4.2 The small size of cells relates to the need to exchange materials across the plasma membrane

As you saw in Figure 4.1B, most cells are microscopic—that is, unable to be seen without a microscope. Are there advantages to being so small? The logistics of carrying out a cell's functions appear to set both lower and upper limits on cell size. At minimum, a cell must be large enough to house enough DNA, protein molecules, and structures to survive and reproduce. But why aren't most cells as large as chicken eggs? The maximum size of a cell is influenced by geometry—the need to have a surface area large enough to service the volume of a cell. Active cells have a huge amount of traffic across their outer surface. A chicken's egg cell isn't very active, but once a chick embryo starts to develop, the egg is divided into many microscopic cells, each bounded by a membrane that allows the essential flow of oxygen, nutrients, and wastes across its surface.

Surface-to-Volume Ratio   Large cells have more surface area than small cells, but they have much less surface area relative to their volume than small cells. **Figure 4.2A** illustrates this relationship by comparing one large cube to 27 small ones. Using arbitrary units of measurement, the total volume is the same in both cases: 27 units³ (height × width × length). The total surface areas, however, are quite different. A cube has six sides; thus, its surface area is six times the area of each side (height × width). The surface area of the large cube is 54 units², while the total surface area of all 27 cubes is 162 units² (27 × 6 × 1 × 1), three times greater than the surface area of the large cube. Thus, we see that the smaller cubes have a much greater surface-to-volume ratio than the large cube. How about those neurons that extend from the base of your spine to your toes? Very thin, elongated shapes also provide a large surface area relative to a cell's volume. The surface-to-volume ratio of a cell can affect its function. For example, cells with larger surface-to-volume ratios, such

Total volume	27 units³	27 units³
Total surface area	54 units²	162 units²
Surface-to-volume ratio	2	6

▲ **Figure 4.2A** Effect of cell size on surface area

as the cells lining your intestines, have more membrane across which they absorb nutrients.

The Plasma Membrane   So what is a cell's surface like? And how does it control the traffic of molecules across it? The **plasma membrane** forms a flexible boundary between the living cell and its surroundings. For a structure that separates life from nonlife, this membrane is amazingly thin. It would take a stack of more than 8000 of them to equal the thickness of this page. And, as you have come to expect with all things biological, the structure of the plasma membrane correlates with its function.

As you learned in Module 3.15, the structure of phospholipid molecules is well suited to their role as the main components of biological membranes. Composed of two distinct regions—a head with a negatively charged phosphate

Hydrophilic heads
Hydrophobic tails
Phospholipid
Outside cell
Inside cell
Hydrophobic region of a protein
Hydrophilic region of a protein
Channel protein
Proteins

▲ **Figure 4.2B** A plasma membrane: a phospholipid bilayer with associated proteins

group and two nonpolar fatty acid tails—phospholipids form a two-layer sheet called a phospholipid bilayer. As you can see in **Figure 4.2B**, the phospholipids' hydrophilic (water-loving) heads face outward, exposed to the aqueous solutions on both sides of a membrane. Their hydrophobic (water-fearing) tails point inward, mingling together and shielded from water. Embedded in this lipid bilayer are diverse proteins, floating like icebergs in a phospholipid sea. The regions of the proteins within the centre of the membrane are hydrophobic; the exterior sections exposed to water are hydrophilic.

Now let's see how the properties of the phospholipid bilayer and the proteins embedded in it relate to the plasma membrane's job as a traffic cop, regulating the flow of material into and out of the cell. Nonpolar molecules, such as O_2 and CO_2, can easily move across the membrane's hydrophobic interior. Some of the membrane's proteins form channels (tunnels) that shield ions and polar molecules as they pass through the hydrophobic centre of the membrane. Still other proteins serve as pumps, using energy to actively transport molecules into or out of the cell.

We will return to a more detailed look at the structure and function of biological membranes in Chapter 5. In the next module, we consider other features common to all cells and take a closer look at the prokaryotic cells of the domains Bacteria and Archaea.

 To convince yourself that a small cell has more surface area relative to volume than a large cell, compare the surface-to-volume ratios of the large cube and the small cubes in Figure 4.2A.

● Large cube: 54/27 = 2; small cube: 6/1 = 6 (surface area is 1 × 1 × 6 sides = 6 units²; volume is 1 × 1 × 1 unit³)

4.3 Prokaryotic cells are structurally simpler than eukaryotic cells

Two kinds of cells, which differ in size and structure, have evolved over time. Bacteria and archaea consist of **prokaryotic cells**, whereas all other forms of life (protists, fungi, plants, and animals) are composed of **eukaryotic cells**. Eukaryotic cells are distinguished by having a membrane-enclosed nucleus, which houses most of their DNA. The word *eukaryote* means "true nucleus" (from the Greek *eu*, true, and *karyon*, kernel, referring to the nucleus). The word *prokaryote* means "before nucleus" (from the Greek *pro*, before), reflecting the fact that prokaryotic cells evolved before eukaryotic cells. They are also, as you will see, structurally much simpler than eukaryotic cells while sharing some common characteristics.

All cells have several basic features in common. In addition to being bounded by a plasma membrane, all cells have one or more **chromosomes** carrying genes made of DNA. And all cells contain **ribosomes**, tiny structures that make proteins according to instructions from the genes. The interior of both types of cell is called the **cytoplasm**. However, in eukaryotic cells, this term refers only to the region between the nucleus and the plasma membrane. The cytoplasm of a eukaryotic cell contains many membrane-enclosed organelles that perform specific functions.

The cutaway diagram in **Figure 4.3** reveals the structure of a generalized prokaryotic cell. Notice that the DNA is coiled into a region called the **nucleoid** (nucleus-like) but,

in contrast to the nucleus of eukaryotic cells, no membrane surrounds the DNA. The ribosomes of prokaryotes (shown here in brown) are smaller and differ somewhat from those of eukaryotes. These molecular differences are the basis for the action of some antibiotics, such as tetracycline and streptomycin, which target prokaryotic ribosomes. Thus, protein synthesis can be blocked for the bacterium that's invaded you, but not for you, the eukaryote who is taking the drug.

Outside the plasma membrane (shown here in grey) of most prokaryotes is a fairly rigid, chemically complex cell wall (orange). The wall protects the cell and helps to maintain its shape. Some antibiotics, such as penicillin, prevent the formation of these protective walls. Again, since your cells don't have such walls, these antibiotics can kill invading bacteria without harming your cells. Certain prokaryotes have a sticky outer coat called a capsule (yellow) around the cell wall, helping to glue the cells to surfaces, such as sticks and rocks in fast-flowing streams or tissues within the human body. In addition to capsules, some prokaryotes have surface projections. Short projections help to attach prokaryotes to each other or their substrate. Longer projections called **flagella** (singular, *flagellum*) propel a prokaryotic cell through its liquid environment.

It takes an electron microscope to see the details of any cell, and this is especially true of prokaryotic cells

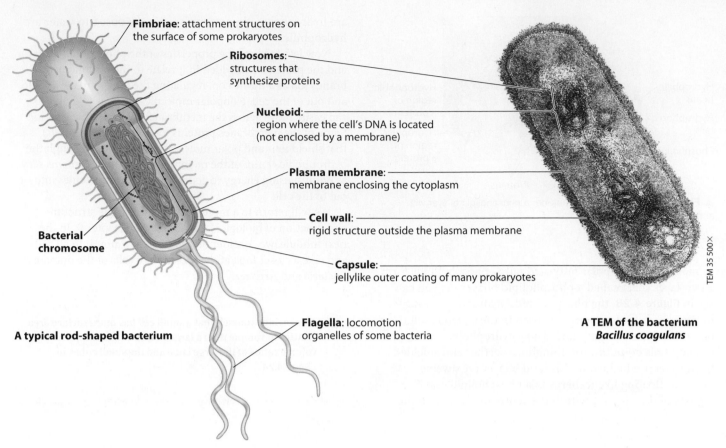

Fimbriae: attachment structures on the surface of some prokaryotes

Ribosomes: structures that synthesize proteins

Nucleoid: region where the cell's DNA is located (not enclosed by a membrane)

Plasma membrane: membrane enclosing the cytoplasm

Cell wall: rigid structure outside the plasma membrane

Capsule: jellylike outer coating of many prokaryotes

Bacterial chromosome

Flagella: locomotion organelles of some bacteria

A typical rod-shaped bacterium

A TEM of the bacterium *Bacillus coagulans*

TEM 35 500×

▲ **Figure 4.3** A diagram (left) and electron micrograph (right) of a typical prokaryotic cell

(Figure 4.3, right side). Most prokaryotic cells are about one-tenth the diameter of a typical eukaryotic cell (see Figure 1.3). Prokaryotes will be described in more detail in Chapter 17. Eukaryotic cells are the main focus of this chapter, so we turn to these next.

 List three features that are common to prokaryotic and eukaryotic cells. List three features that differ.

● Both types of cells have plasma membranes, chromosomes containing DNA, and ribosomes. Prokaryotic cells are smaller, do not have a nucleus that houses their DNA or other membrane-enclosed organelles, and have smaller, somewhat different ribosomes.

4.4 Eukaryotic cells are partitioned into functional compartments

All eukaryotic cells—whether from animals, plants, protists, or fungi—are fundamentally similar to one another and profoundly different from prokaryotic cells. Let's look at an animal cell and a plant cell as representatives of the eukaryotes.

Figure 4.4A is a diagram of an idealized animal cell. No cell would look exactly like this. We colour-coded the various organelles and other structures in the diagrams for easier identification. And recall from the chapter introduction that in living cells many of these structures are moving and interacting.

The nucleus is the most obvious difference between a prokaryotic and eukaryotic cell. A eukaryotic cell also contains various other organelles ("little organs"), which perform specific functions in the cell. Just as the cell itself is wrapped in a membrane made of phospholipids and proteins that perform

various functions, each organelle is bounded by a membrane with a lipid and protein composition that suits its function.

The organelles and other structures of eukaryotic cells can be organized into four basic functional groups as follows: (1) The nucleus and ribosomes carry out the genetic control of the cell. (2) Organelles involved in the manufacture, distribution, and breakdown of molecules include the endoplasmic reticulum, Golgi apparatus, lysosomes, vacuoles, and peroxisomes. (3) Mitochondria in all cells and chloroplasts in plant cells function in energy processing. (4) Structural support, movement, and communication between cells are the functions of the cytoskeleton, plasma membrane, and plant cell wall. These cellular components are identified in the figures on pages 65 and 66 and will be examined in greater detail in the remaining modules of this chapter.

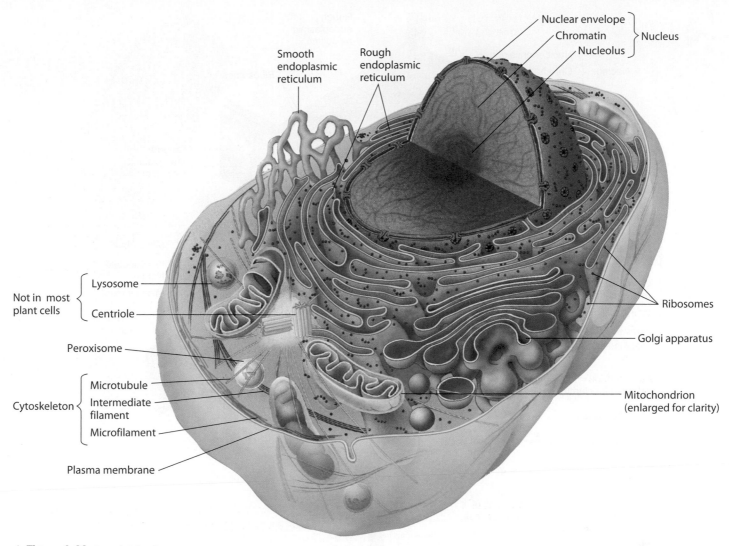

Smooth endoplasmic reticulum

Rough endoplasmic reticulum

Nuclear envelope
Chromatin
Nucleolus
} Nucleus

Not in most plant cells { Lysosome
Centriole

Ribosomes

Peroxisome

Golgi apparatus

Cytoskeleton { Microtubule
Intermediate filament
Microfilament

Mitochondrion (enlarged for clarity)

Plasma membrane

▲ **Figure 4.4A** An animal cell

In essence, the internal membranes of a eukaryotic cell partition it into compartments. Many of the chemical activities of cells—activities known collectively as **cellular metabolism**—occur within organelles. In fact, many enzymatic proteins essential for metabolic processes are built into the membranes of organelles. The fluid-filled spaces within organelles are important as sites where specific chemical conditions are maintained. These conditions vary from one organelle to another and favour the metabolic processes occurring in each kind of organelle. For example, while a part of the endoplasmic reticulum is engaged in making steroid hormones, neighbouring peroxisomes may be detoxifying harmful compounds and making hydrogen peroxide (H_2O_2) as a poisonous by-product of their activities. But because the H_2O_2 is confined within peroxisomes, where it is quickly converted to H_2O by resident enzymes, the rest of the cell is protected from destruction.

Almost all the organelles and other structures of animal cells are also present in plant cells. As you can see in Figure 4.4A, however, there are a few exceptions:

Lysosomes and centrioles are not found in plant cells. Also, although some animal cells have flagella or cilia (not shown in Figure 4.4A), among plants, only the sperm cells of a few species have flagella. As you will learn in Chapter 17, the flagella of prokaryotic cells differ in both structure and function from eukaryotic flagella.

A plant cell **(Figure 4.4B)** also has some structures that an animal cell lacks. For example, a plant cell has a rigid, rather thick cell wall (as do the cells of fungi and many protists). Cell walls protect cells and help to maintain their shape. Chemically different from prokaryotic cell walls, plant cell walls contain the polysaccharide cellulose. Plasmodesmata (singular, *plasmodesma*) are cytoplasmic channels through cell walls that connect adjacent cells. An important organelle found in plant cells is the chloroplast, where photosynthesis occurs. (Chloroplasts are also found in algae and some other protists.) Unique to plant cells is a large central vacuole, a compartment that stores water and a variety of chemicals.

Although we have emphasized organelles, eukaryotic cells contain nonmembranous structures as well. The cytoskeleton

Rough
endoplasmic
reticulum

Nucleus
Nuclear envelope
Chromatin
Nucleolus

Ribosomes

Smooth
endoplasmic
reticulum

Golgi
apparatus

Microtubule

Intermediate
filament

Cytoskeleton

Microfilament

Not in
animal
cells
Central
vacuole
Chloroplast
(enlarged for clarity)
Cell wall
Plasmodesma

Mitochondrion
(enlarged for clarity)

Peroxisome

Plasma membrane

Cell wall of
adjacent cell

▲ **Figure 4.4B** A plant cell

is composed of different types of protein fibres that extend throughout the cell. These networks provide for support and movement. As you can see by the many brown dots in both figures, ribosomes occur throughout the cytoplasm, as they do in prokaryotic cells. In addition, eukaryotic cells have many ribosomes attached to parts of the endoplasmic reticulum (making it appear rough) and to the outer membrane of the nucleus.

Let's begin our in-depth tour of the eukaryotic cell, starting with the nucleus.

? **Which of the following cellular structures differs from the others in the list: mitochondrion, chloroplast, ribosome, lysosome, or vacuole? How does it differ?**

● Ribosome, because it is the only structure in the list that is not bounded by a membrane.

The Nucleus and Ribosomes

4.5 The nucleus is the cell's genetic control centre

You just saw a preview of the many intricate structures that can be found in a eukaryotic cell. A cell must build and maintain these structures and process energy for the work of transport, import, export, movement, and communication. But who is in charge of this bustling factory? Who stores the master plans, gives the orders, changes course in response to environmental

input, and, when called upon, makes another factory just like itself? The cell's nucleus is this command centre.

The **nucleus** contains most of the cell's DNA—its master plans—and controls the cell's activities by directing protein synthesis. The DNA is associated with many proteins in the structures called chromosomes. The proteins help to organize

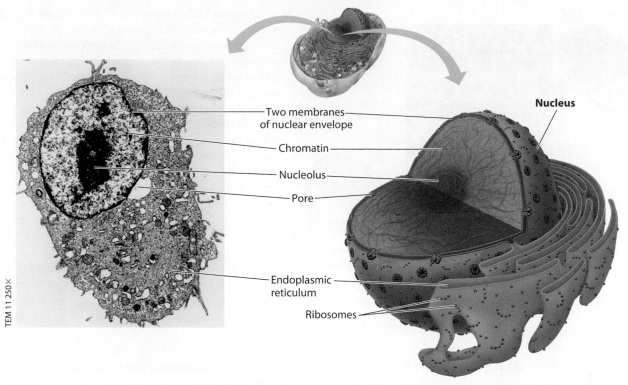

▲ **Figure 4.5** Transmission electron micrograph (left) and diagram (right) of the nucleus

Labels on figure:
Two membranes of nuclear envelope
Chromatin
Nucleolus
Pore
Endoplasmic reticulum
Ribosomes
Nucleus
TEM 11 250×

and coil the long DNA molecule. Indeed, the DNA of the 46 chromosomes in one of your cells laid end to end would stretch to a length of over 2 m, but it must coil up to fit into a nucleus only 5 μm in diameter. When a cell is not dividing, this complex of proteins and DNA, called **chromatin**, appears as a diffuse mass, as shown in the TEM (left) and diagram (right) of a nucleus in **Figure 4.5**.

As a cell prepares to divide, the DNA is copied so that each daughter cell can later receive an identical set of genetic instructions. Just prior to cell division, the thin chromatin fibres coil up further, becoming thick enough to be visible with a light microscope as the familiar separate structures you would probably recognize as chromosomes.

Enclosing the nucleus is a double membrane called the **nuclear envelope**. Each of the membranes is a separate phospholipid bilayer with associated proteins. Similar in function to the plasma membrane, the nuclear envelope controls the flow of materials into and out of the nucleus. As you can see in the diagram in Figure 4.5, the nuclear envelope is perforated with protein-lined pores that regulate the movement of large molecules and also connects with the cell's network of membranes called the endoplasmic reticulum.

The **nucleolus**, a prominent structure in the nucleus, is the site where a special type of RNA called *ribosomal RNA* (rRNA) is synthesized according to instructions in the DNA. Proteins brought in through the nuclear pores from the cytoplasm are assembled with this rRNA to form the subunits of ribosomes. These subunits then exit through the pores to the cytoplasm, where they will join to form functional ribosomes.

The nucleus directs protein synthesis by making another type of RNA, *messenger RNA* (mRNA). Essentially, mRNA is a transcription of protein-synthesizing instructions written in a gene's DNA (see Figure 3.11). The mRNA moves through the pores in the nuclear envelope to the cytoplasm. There it is translated by ribosomes into the amino acid sequences of proteins. Let's look at ribosomes next.

? What are the main functions of the nucleus?

 To house and copy DNA and pass it on to daughter cells in cell division; to build ribosomal subunits; to transcribe DNA instructions into RNA and thereby control the cell's functions

4.6 Ribosomes make proteins for use in the cell and for export

If the nucleus is the command centre, then ribosomes are the machines that make the proteins that will carry out the commands. Ribosomes are the cellular components that use instructions sent from the nucleus to carry out protein synthesis. Cells that make a lot of proteins have a large number of ribosomes. For example, a human pancreas cell producing

Ribosomes   ER

Cytoplasm

Endoplasmic reticulum (ER)

Free ribosomes

Bound ribosomes

Colourized TEM 73 000×

Colourized TEM showing ER and ribosomes

mRNA

Protein

Diagram of a ribosome

▲ **Figure 4.6** The locations and structure of ribosomes

As shown in the colourized TEM in **Figure 4.6**, ribosomes are found in two locations in the cell. *Free ribosomes* are suspended in the fluid of the cytoplasm, while *bound ribosomes* are attached to the outside of the endoplasmic reticulum or nuclear envelope. Free and bound ribosomes are structurally identical, and ribosomes can alternate between the two locations.

Most of the proteins made on free ribosomes function within the cytoplasm; examples are enzymes that catalyze the first steps of sugar breakdown. In Module 4.8, you will see how bound ribosomes make proteins that will be inserted into membranes, packaged in certain organelles, or exported from the cell.

At the bottom right in Figure 4.6, you see how ribosomes interact with messenger RNA (carrying the instructions from a gene) to build a protein. The nucleotide sequence of an mRNA molecule is translated into the amino acid sequence of a polypeptide. Protein synthesis is explored in more detail in Chapter 10. Next let's look at more of the manufacturing equipment of the cell.

digestive enzymes may contain a few million ribosomes. What other structure would you expect to be prominent in cells that are active in protein synthesis? As you just learned, nucleoli assemble the subunits of ribosomes out of ribosomal RNA and protein.

? **What role do ribosomes play in carrying out the genetic instructions of a cell?**

● Ribosomes synthesize proteins according to the instructions carried by messenger RNA from the DNA in the nucleus.

The Endomembrane System

4.7 Overview: Many cell organelles are connected through the endomembrane system

Ribosomes may be a cell's protein-making machines, but running a factory as complex as a cell requires infrastructure and many different departments that perform separate but related functions. Internal membranes, a distinguishing feature of eukaryotic cells, are involved in most of a cell's functions. Many of the membranes of the eukaryotic cell are part of an **endomembrane system**. Some of these membranes are physically connected and some are related by the transfer of membrane segments by tiny **vesicles**, sacs made of membrane.

The endomembrane system includes the nuclear envelope, endoplasmic reticulum, Golgi apparatus, lysosomes, vacuoles, and the plasma membrane. (The plasma membrane is not exactly an *endo*membrane in physical location, but it is related to the other membranes by the transfer of vesicles). Many of these organelles work together in the synthesis, distribution, storage, and export of molecules. We focus on these interrelated membranes in Modules 4.8–4.11.

The extensive network of flattened sacs and tubules called the **endoplasmic reticulum (ER)** is a prime example of the direct interrelatedness of parts of the endomembrane system. (The term *endoplasmic* means "within the cytoplasm," and *reticulum* is Latin for "little net.") As shown in Figure 4.5, membranes of the ER are continuous with the nuclear envelope. As we discuss next, there are two regions of ER—smooth ER and rough ER—that differ both in structure and in function. The membranes that form them, however, are connected.

The tubules and sacs of the ER enclose an interior space that is separate from the cytoplasmic fluid. Dividing the cell into separate functional compartments is an important aspect of the endomembrane system.

? **Which structure includes all others in the list: rough ER, smooth ER, endomembrane system, or nuclear envelope?**

● Endomembrane system

4.8 The endoplasmic reticulum is a biosynthetic factory

One of the major manufacturing sites in a cell is the endoplasmic reticulum (ER). The diagram in **Figure 4.8A** shows a cutaway view of the interconnecting membranes of the smooth and rough ER. These two types of ER can be distinguished in the electron micrograph. **Smooth endoplasmic reticulum** is called *smooth* because it lacks attached ribosomes. **Rough endoplasmic reticulum** has ribosomes that stud the outer surface of the membrane; thus, it appears *rough* in the electron micrograph.

Smooth ER   The smooth ER of various cell types functions in a variety of metabolic processes. Enzymes of the smooth ER are important in the synthesis of lipids, including oils, phospholipids, and steroids. In vertebrates, for example, cells of the ovaries and testes synthesize the steroid sex hormones. These cells are rich in smooth ER, a structural feature that fits their function by providing ample machinery for steroid synthesis.

Our liver cells also have large amounts of smooth ER, with other important functions. Certain enzymes in the smooth ER of liver cells help process drugs, alcohol, and other potentially harmful substances. The sedative phenobarbital and other barbiturates are examples of drugs detoxified by these enzymes. As liver cells are exposed to such chemicals, the amount of smooth ER and its detoxifying enzymes increases, thereby increasing the rate of detoxification and thus the body's tolerance to the drugs. The result is a need for higher and higher doses of a drug to achieve a particular effect, such as sedation. Also, because detoxifying enzymes often cannot distinguish among related chemicals, the growth of smooth ER in response to one drug can increase tolerance to other drugs. Barbiturate abuse, for example, can decrease the effectiveness of certain antibiotics and other useful drugs.

Smooth ER has yet another function, the storage of calcium ions. In muscle cells, for example, a specialized smooth ER membrane pumps calcium ions into the interior of the ER. When a nerve signal stimulates a muscle cell, calcium ions rush from the smooth ER into the cytoplasmic fluid and trigger contraction of the cell.

Rough ER   One of the functions of ER is to make more membrane. Phospholipids made by enzymes of the smooth ER, along with proteins synthesized within the rough ER are inserted into the ER membrane. Thus, the ER membrane grows, and portions of it are transferred to other components of the endomembrane system as vesicles.

The bound ribosomes attached to rough ER produce proteins that will be inserted into the growing ER membrane, transported to other organelles, or secreted by the cell. The rough ER also contains enzymes that help fold the proteins after they are produced by the ribosomes. An example of a secretory protein is insulin, a hormone secreted by specialized cells in the pancreas. Type 1 diabetes results when these cells are destroyed and a lack of insulin disrupts glucose metabolism in the body.

Figure 4.8B follows the synthesis, modification, and packaging of a secretory protein. ❶ As the polypeptide is

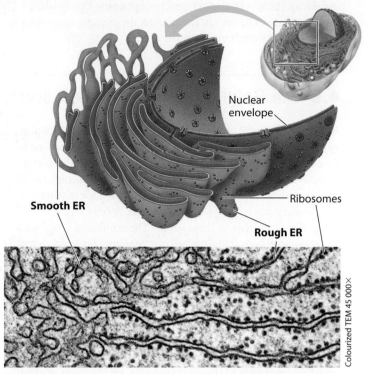

Nuclear envelope

Smooth ER

Ribosomes

Rough ER

Colourized TEM 45 000×

▲ **Figure 4.8A** Smooth and rough endoplasmic reticulum

Transport vesicle buds off

❹

mRNA

Ribosome

Secretory protein inside transport vesicle

❸

Sugar chain

Polypeptide

❶

❷

Glycoprotein

Rough ER

▲ **Figure 4.8B** Synthesis and packaging of a secretory protein by the rough ER

synthesized by a bound ribosome following the instructions of an mRNA, it is threaded into the cavity of the rough ER. As it enters, the new protein folds into its three-dimensional shape. ❷ Short chains of sugars are often linked to the polypeptide, making the molecule a **glycoprotein** (*glyco* means "sugar"). ❸ When the molecule is ready for export from the ER, it is packaged in a **transport vesicle**, a vesicle that moves from one part of the cell to another. ➍ This vesicle buds off from the ER membrane. The vesicle now carries the protein to the Golgi apparatus (described in the next module) for further processing. From there, a transport vesicle containing the finished molecule makes its way to the plasma membrane, fuses with it, and releases its contents from the cell.

? Explain why we say that the endoplasmic reticulum is a biosynthetic factory.

● The ER produces a huge variety of molecules—including phospholipids for cell membranes, steroid hormones, and proteins (synthesized by bound ribosomes)—for membranes and other organelles, and for secretion by the cell.

4.9 The Golgi apparatus finishes, sorts, and ships cell products

After leaving the ER, many transport vesicles travel to the **Golgi apparatus**. Using a light microscope and a staining technique he developed, Italian scientist Camillo Golgi discovered this membranous organelle in 1898. The electron microscope confirmed his discovery more than 50 years later, revealing a stack of flattened sacs, looking much like a pile of pita bread. A cell may contain many, even hundreds, of these stacks. The number of Golgi stacks correlates with how active the cell is in secreting proteins—a multistep process that, as we have just seen, is initiated in the rough ER.

The Golgi apparatus serves as a molecular warehouse and finishing factory for products manufactured by the ER. You can follow this process in **Figure 4.9**. Note that the flattened Golgi sacs are not connected, as are ER sacs. ➊ One side of a Golgi stack serves as a receiving dock for transport vesicles produced by the ER. ➋ A vesicle fuses with a Golgi sac, adding its membrane and contents to the receiving side. ➌ Products of the ER are modified during their transit through the Golgi. ➍ The other side of the Golgi, the shipping side, gives rise to vesicles, which bud off and travel to other sites.

How might ER products be processed during their transit through the Golgi? Various Golgi enzymes modify the carbohydrate portions of the glycoproteins made in the ER, removing some sugars and substituting others. Molecular identification tags, such as phosphate groups, may be added that help the Golgi sort molecules into different

batches for different destinations. In eukaryotic cells, processing by the Golgi is essential for proper protein function. Transferring genes into bacteria (see Chapter 12) will not yield a functional product because these organisms lack the endomembrane system. Thus, in order for technology companies such as Nexia Biotechnologies in Montreal, Quebec, to synthesize artificial spider silk proteins, they must do so in living eukaryotic cells—in Nexia's case, those of goats.

Until recently, the Golgi was viewed as a static structure, with products in various stages of processing moved from sac to sac by transport vesicles. Recent research has given rise to a new *maturation model* in which entire sacs "mature" as they move from the receiving to the shipping side, carrying and modifying their cargo as they go. The shipping side of the Golgi stack serves as a depot from which finished secretory products, packaged in transport vesicles, move to the plasma membrane for export from the cell. Alternatively, finished products may become part of the plasma membrane itself or part of another organelle, such as a lysosome, which we discuss next.

? What is the relationship of the Golgi apparatus to the ER in a protein-secreting cell?

● The Golgi receives transport vesicles that bud from the ER and that contain proteins synthesized by ribosomes attached to the ER. The Golgi finishes processing the proteins and then dispatches transport vesicles that secrete the proteins to the outside of the cell.

Golgi apparatus

"Receiving" side of Golgi apparatus

➊ Transport vesicle from ER

➋

➌

Transport vesicle from the Golgi

➍

"Shipping" side of Golgi apparatus

➍

Golgi apparatus

Colourized TEM 120 000×

▲ **Figure 4.9** The Golgi apparatus

4.10 Lysosomes are digestive compartments within a cell

A **lysosome** (meaning "breakdown body") is a membranous sac of digestive enzymes. The enzymes and membranes of lysosomes are made by rough ER and processed in the Golgi apparatus. Illustrating a main theme of eukaryotic cell structure—compartmentalization—a lysosome provides an acidic environment for its enzymes, while safely isolating them from the rest of the cell.

Lysosomes have several types of digestive functions. Many protists engulf food particles into membranous sacs called food vacuoles. As **Figure 4.10A** shows, lysosomes fuse with food vacuoles and digest the food. The nutrients are then released into the cell fluid. Our white blood cells engulf and destroy bacteria by using lysosomal enzymes. Lysosomes also serve as recycling centres for animal cells. Damaged organelles or small amounts of cell fluid become surrounded by a membrane. A lysosome fuses with such a vesicle **(Figure 4.10B)** and dismantles its contents, making organic molecules available for reuse. With the help of lysosomes, a cell continually renews itself.

The cells of people with inherited lysosomal storage diseases lack one or more lysosomal enzymes. The lysosomes become engorged with undigested material, eventually interfering with cellular function. In Tay-Sachs disease, for example, a lipid-digesting enzyme is missing, and brain cells become impaired by an accumulation of lipids. Lysosomal storage diseases are often fatal in early childhood.

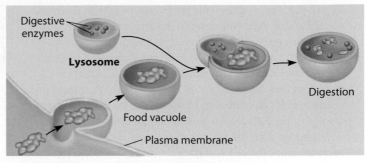

▲ **Figure 4.10A** Lysosome fusing with a food vacuole and digesting food

▲ **Figure 4.10B** Lysosome fusing with a vesicle containing a damaged organelle and digesting and recycling its contents

? How is a lysosome like a recycling centre?

 It breaks down damaged organelles and recycles their molecules.

4.11 Vacuoles function in the general maintenance of the cell

Vacuoles are large vesicles that have a variety of functions. In Figure 4.10A, you saw how a food vacuole forms as a cell ingests food. **Figure 4.11A** shows two contractile vacuoles in the protist *Paramecium*, looking somewhat like wheel hubs with radiating spokes. The "spokes" collect water from the cell, and the hub expels it to the outside. Freshwater protists constantly take in water from their environment by osmosis (see Module 5.4). Without a way to get rid of the excess water, the cell would swell and burst. In plants, some vacuoles have a digestive function similar to that of lysosomes in animal cells. Vacuoles in flower petals contain pigments that attract pollinating insects. Vacuoles

Central vacuole

Chloroplast

Nucleus

Colourized TEM 9 840×

▲ **Figure 4.11B** Central vacuole in a plant cell

may also contain poisons or unpalatable compounds that protect the plant against herbivores; examples include nicotine, caffeine, and various chemicals we use as pharmaceutical drugs. **Figure 4.11B** shows a plant cell's large **central vacuole**, which helps the cell grow in size by absorbing water and enlarging. It also stockpiles vital chemicals and acts as a trash can, safely storing toxic waste products.

? Is a food vacuole part of the endomembrane system?

 Yes; it forms by pinching in from the plasma membrane, which is part of the endomembrane system.

Contractile vacuoles

Nucleus

LM 650×

▲ **Figure 4.11A** Contractile vacuoles in *Paramecium*, a single-celled organism

4.12 A review of the structures involved in manufacturing and breakdown

Figure 4.12 summarizes the relationships within the endomembrane system. You can see the direct *structural* connections between the nuclear envelope, rough ER, and smooth ER. The red arrows show the *functional* connections, as membranes and proteins produced by the ER travel in transport vesicles to the Golgi and on to other destinations. Some vesicles develop into lysosomes or vacuoles. Others transport products to the outside of the cell. When these vesicles fuse with the plasma membrane, their contents are secreted from the cell and their membrane is added to the plasma membrane.

Peroxisomes (see Figures 4.4A and 4B) are metabolic compartments that do not originate from the endomembrane system. In fact, how they are related to other organelles is still unknown. Some peroxisomes break down fatty acids to be used as cellular fuel. In your liver, peroxisomes detoxify harmful compounds, including alcohol. In these processes, enzymes transfer hydrogen from various compounds to oxygen, producing hydrogen peroxide (H_2O_2). Other enzymes in the peroxisome quickly convert this toxic product to water—another example of the importance of a cell's compartmental structure.

A cell requires a continuous supply of energy to perform the work of life. Next we consider two organelles that act as cellular power stations—mitochondria and chloroplasts.

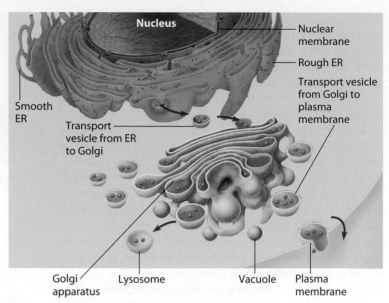

▲ **Figure 4.12** Connections among the organelles of the endomembrane system

? How do transport vesicles help tie together the endomembrane system?

● Transport vesicles move membranes and substances they enclose between components of the endomembrane system.

Energy-Converting Organelles

4.13 Mitochondria harvest chemical energy from food

Mitochondria (singular, *mitochondrion*) are organelles that carry out cellular respiration in nearly all eukaryotic cells, converting the chemical energy of foods such as sugars to the chemical energy of the molecule called ATP (adenosine triphosphate). ATP is the main energy source for cellular work.

As you have come to expect, a mitochondrion's structure suits its function. It is enclosed by two membranes, each a phospholipid bilayer with a unique collection of embedded proteins (**Figure 4.13**). The mitochondrion has two internal compartments. The first is the intermembrane space, the narrow region between the inner and outer membranes. The inner membrane encloses the second compartment, the **mitochondrial matrix**, which contains mitochondrial DNA and ribosomes, as well as many enzymes that catalyze some of the reactions of cellular respiration. The inner membrane is highly folded and contains many embedded protein molecules that function in ATP synthesis. The folds, called **cristae**, increase the membrane's surface area, enhancing the mitochondrion's ability to produce ATP. We discuss the role of mitochondria in cellular respiration in more detail in Chapter 6.

? What is cellular respiration?

● A process that converts the chemical energy of sugars and other food molecules to the chemical energy of ATP

▲ **Figure 4.13** The mitochondrion

4.14 Chloroplasts convert solar energy to chemical energy

Most of the living world runs on the energy provided by photosynthesis, the conversion of light energy from the sun to the chemical energy of sugar molecules. **Chloroplasts** are the photosynthesizing organelles of all photosynthetic eukaryotes. The chloroplast's solar power system is much more efficient than anything yet produced by human ingenuity.

Befitting an organelle that carries out complex, multistep processes, internal membranes partition the chloroplast into compartments (**Figure 4.14**). The chloroplast is enclosed by an inner and outer membrane separated by a thin intermembrane space. The compartment inside the inner membrane holds a thick fluid called **stroma**, which contains chloroplast DNA and ribosomes as well as many enzymes. A network of interconnected sacs called thylakoids is inside the chloroplast. The compartment inside these sacs is called the thylakoid space. In some regions, **thylakoids** are stacked like poker chips; each stack is called a **granum** (plural, *grana*). The grana are the chloroplast's solar power packs—the sites where the green chlorophyll molecules embedded in thylakoid membranes trap solar energy. In Chapter 7, you will learn how this compartmental organization enables the chloroplast to convert solar energy to chemical energy. In the next module, we explore the origin of mitochondria and chloroplasts.

TEM 10 350×

Inner and outer membranes — Granum — Stroma — **Chloroplast** — Thylakoid

▲ **Figure 4.14** The chloroplast

 Which membrane in a chloroplast appears to be the most extensive? Why might this be so?

● The thylakoid membranes are most extensive, providing a large area of membrane that contains chlorophyll for photosynthesis.

4.15 Mitochondria and chloroplasts evolved by endosymbiosis

Does it seem odd to you that mitochondria and chloroplasts contain DNA and ribosomes? Indeed, they have a single circular DNA molecule, similar in structure to the chromosome of prokaryotes. And their ribosomes are more similar to prokaryotic ribosomes than to eukaryotic ribosomes. Another interesting observation is that mitochondria and chloroplasts reproduce by a splitting process that is similar to that of certain prokaryotes.

The widely accepted **endosymbiont theory** states that mitochondria and chloroplasts were formerly small prokaryotes that began living within larger cells. The term *endosymbiont* refers to an organism that lives within another organism, called the host. More examples of this type of relationship are discussed in Chapter 39. These small prokaryotes may have gained entry to the larger cell as undigested prey or internal parasites (**Figure 4.15**). The endosymbiont theory explains the double-membrane of both mitochondria and chloroplasts as well as the presence of organelle-specific DNA within these structures.

By whatever means the relationship began, we can hypothesize how the symbiosis could have become beneficial. In a world that was becoming increasingly aerobic from the oxygen-generating photosynthesis of prokaryotes, a host would have benefited from an endosymbiont that was able to use oxygen to release large amounts of energy from organic molecules by cellular respiration. And a host cell could derive nourishment from a photosynthetic endosymbiont. Over time,

Mitochondrion — Nucleus — Endoplasmic reticulum — Ancestral algal cells — Engulfing of photosynthetic prokaryote — Chloroplast — Engulfing of oxygen-using prokaryote — Host cell — Mitochondrion — Host cell

▲ **Figure 4.15** Endosymbiotic origin of mitochondria and chloroplasts

the host and endosymbionts would have become increasingly interdependent, eventually becoming a single organism.

 All eukaryotes have mitochondria, but not all eukaryotes have chloroplasts. Can you propose an evolutionary explanation for this observation?

● The first endosymbiotic event would have given rise to eukaryotic cells containing mitochondria. At least one of these cells may have then taken up a photosynthetic prokaryote, giving rise to eukaryotic cells that contain chloroplasts in addition to mitochondria.

The Cytoskeleton and Cell Surfaces

4.16 Are the organelles of a cell free-floating in a cytoplasm soup?

The previous modules have described the organelles that can be found in eukaryotic cells. But how are these organelles grouped together within the cell? There is a common misconception that the organelles are simply floating around the watery cytoplasm like vegetables in a soup. In fact, biologists used to have this same belief about cellular structure. If organelles are not floating freely in the cell, then what are they doing? Another question you may have is how they move within the cell (as we alluded to in the chapter-opening essay).

With improvements in both light microscopy and electron microscopy, scientists have uncovered a network of protein fibres, collectively called the **cytoskeleton**, extending throughout the cytoplasm of a cell. These fibres function like a skeleton, providing for both structural support and cell motility. Cell motility includes both the internal movement of cell parts and the locomotion of a cell. These movements generally require the interaction of the cytoskeleton with proteins called motor proteins.

Three main kinds of fibres make up the cytoskeleton: microfilaments, the thinnest fibre; microtubules, the thickest; and intermediate filaments, in between in thickness. **Figure 4.16A** shows three micrographs of cells of the same type, each stained with a different fluorescent dye that selectively highlights one of these types of fibres.

Microfilaments, also called actin filaments, are solid rods composed mainly of globular proteins called actin, arranged in a twisted double chain (bottom left of Figure 4.16A). Microfilaments form a three-dimensional network just inside the plasma membrane that helps to support the cell's shape. This is especially important for animal cells, which lack cell walls.

Microfilaments are also involved in cell movements. As we will see in Chapter 33, actin filaments and thicker filaments made of the motor protein myosin interact to cause contraction of muscle cells. Localized contractions brought about by actin and myosin are involved in the amoeboid (crawling) movement of the protist *Amoeba* and some of our white blood cells.

Intermediate filaments may be made of various fibrous proteins that coil together into thicker cables. Intermediate filaments serve mainly to reinforce cell shape and anchor certain organelles. **Figure 4.16B** shows a small section of a cell with some of the interactions between the organelles and cytoskeleton. For simplicity, these associations are not shown in the other diagrams of this textbook. The nucleus is held in place by a cage of intermediate filaments. While microfilaments may be disassembled and reassembled elsewhere, intermediate filaments are often more permanent fixtures in the cell. The outer layer of your skin consists of dead skin cells full of intermediate filaments made of keratin proteins.

Microtubules are straight, hollow tubes composed of globular proteins called tubulins. As indicated in the bottom right of Figure 4.16A, microtubules elongate by the addition of tubulin proteins, which consist of two subunits. Microtubules are readily disassembled in a reverse manner, and the tubulin proteins can be reused elsewhere in the cell. In many animal cells, microtubules grow out from a "microtubule-organizing centre" near the nucleus. Within this region is a pair of **centrioles** (see Figure 4.4A). We will return to centrioles when we discuss cell division in Chapter 8.

▲ **Figure 4.16A** Three types of fibres of the cytoskeleton: microfilaments are stained red (left), intermediate filaments yellow-green (centre), and microtubules green (right)

Nuclear envelope
Endoplasmic reticulum
Ribosome
Microtubule
Mitochondrion
Microfilament

▲ **Figure 4.16B** Interactions between organelles and the cytoskeleton

Microtubules shape and support the cell and also act as tracks along which organelles equipped with motor proteins move. For example, a lysosome might "walk" along a microtubule to reach a food vacuole. Microtubules also guide the movement of chromosomes when cells divide, and as we see next, they are the main components of cilia and flagella—the locomotive appendages of cells.

The misconception that organelles are free floating in the cytoplasm has now been laid to rest. The cytoplasm contains several protein filaments, which make up the cytoskeleton. Organelles are closely associated with both intermediate

filaments and microtubules. Other structures associated with these protein filaments will be discussed in the following modules.

 Which component of the cytoskeleton is most important in (a) holding the nucleus in place within the cell; (b) guiding transport vesicles from the Golgi to the plasma membrane; and (c) contracting muscle cells?

● (a) Intermediate filaments; (b) microtubules; (c) microfilaments

4.17 Cilia and flagella move when microtubules bend

The role of the cytoskeleton in movement is clearly seen in the motile appendages that protrude from certain cells. The short, numerous appendages that propel protists such as *Paramecium* (see Figure 4.1C) are called **cilia** (singular, *cilium*). Other protists may move using flagella, which are longer than cilia and usually limited to one or a few per cell.

Some cells of multicellular organisms also have cilia or flagella. For example, **Figure 4.17A** shows cilia on cells lining the human windpipe. In this case, the cilia sweep mucus containing trapped debris out of your lungs. (This cleaning function is impaired by cigarette smoke, which paralyzes the cilia.) Most animals and some plants have flagellated sperm. A flagellum, shown in **Figure 4.17B**, propels the cell by an undulating whiplike motion. In contrast, cilia work more like the coordinated oars of a rowing team.

Cilia

Colourized SEM 3000×

▲ **Figure 4.17A** Cilia on cells lining the respiratory tract

Though different in length and beating pattern, cilia and flagella have a common structure and mechanism of movement (**Figure 4.17C**). Both are composed of microtubules wrapped in an extension of the plasma membrane. In nearly all eukaryotic cilia and flagella, a ring of nine microtubule doublets surrounds a central pair of microtubules. This arrangement is called the 9 + 2 pattern. The microtubule assembly extends into an anchoring structure called a basal body (not shown in the figure), which consists of a ring of nine microtubule triplets. Basal bodies are very similar in structure to centrioles, which are found in the microtubule-organizing centre of animal cells.

How does this microtubule assembly produce the bending movement of cilia and flagella? Bending involves large motor proteins called dyneins (red in the figure) that are attached along each outer microtubule doublet. A dynein protein has two "feet" that "walk" along an adjacent doublet, one foot maintaining contact while the other releases and reattaches one step farther along its neighbouring microtubule. The outer doublets and two central microtubules are held together by flexible cross-linking proteins and radial spokes (blue in the diagram). If the doublets were not held in place, the walking action would make them slide past each other. Instead, the movements of the dynein feet cause the microtubules—and consequently the cilium or flagellum—to bend.

A cilium may also serve as a signal-receiving "antenna" for the cell. Cilia with this function are generally nonmotile (they lack the central pair of microtubules) and there is only one per cell. In fact, in vertebrate

TEM 254 000×

Colourized SEM 1400×

Flagellum

▲ **Figure 4.17B** Undulating flagellum on a human sperm cell

Outer microtubule doublet

Central microtubules

Radial spoke

Dynein proteins

Plasma membrane

▲ **Figure 4.17C** Structure of a eukaryotic flagellum or cilium

animals, it appears that almost all cells have what is called a *primary cilium*. Although the primary cilium was discovered over a century ago, its importance to embryonic development, sensory reception, and cell function is only now being recognized. Defective primary cilia have been linked to polycystic kidney disease and other human disorders.

? **Compare and contrast cilia and flagella.**

● Both cilia and flagella have the same 9 + 2 pattern of microtubules and mechanism for bending. Cilia are shorter, are more numerous, and beat in a coordinated oarlike pattern. The longer flagella, which are limited to one or a few per cell, undulate like a whip.

4.18 Problems with sperm motility may be environmental or genetic

Human sperm quality varies among men and in different geographic areas. In developed countries over the last 50 years, there has been an apparent decline in sperm quality—lower sperm counts, higher proportions of malformed sperm, and reduced motility. Various environmental factors are being studied as possible causes. One hypothesis links this trend to an increase in hormonally active chemicals in the environment. See Module 36.16 for more on the effects of hormonally active chemicals in the environment.

One common group of chemicals that may be implicated is phthalates. These chemicals are used to soften plastics, making them more pliable. Phthalates have been used in cosmetics, medical tubing, and children's toys. New regulations imposed by Health Canada limit the quantities of phthalates in soft vinyl toys and childcare articles to no more than 0.1%. Scientific evidence suggests that this level is well below what is considered a health risk. However, Health Canada recommends removing soft vinyl toys if your child chews or sucks on them for extended periods of time. Research has indicated that phthalates interfere with sex hormones and adversely affect sperm quality in rodents. Critics of these studies have claimed that the environmental exposures of people are beneath the levels causing effects in rodents. Several new studies, however, have indicated that normal levels of human exposure to these chemicals may result in impaired sperm quality.

Results of a five-year study of 463 men who had come to a hospital for infertility treatment found that the men with higher concentrations of breakdown products of phthalates in their urine had lower sperm counts and motility. But does a statistical correlation indicate cause and effect? Research continues on the potential reproductive health risks of hormone-disrupting chemicals in the environment.

Other problems with sperm motility are clearly genetic. Primary ciliary dyskinesia (PCD), also known as immotile cilia syndrome, is a fairly rare disease characterized by recurrent infections of the respiratory tract and immotile sperm. Compare the cross-section of the flagellum of a sperm of a male with PCD in **Figure 4.18** with the TEM in Figure 4.17C. Do you notice the absence of the dynein proteins? How does that explain the seemingly unrelated symptoms of PCD? If microtubules cannot bend (see Module 4.17), then cilia cannot help to cleanse the respiratory tract and sperm cannot swim.

▲ **Figure 4.18** Cross-section of immotile sperm flagellum

? Why does a lack of dynein proteins affect the action of both cilia and flagella?

● Both cilia and flagella have the same arrangement of microtubule doublets with attached dynein motor proteins that cause them to bend.

4.19 The extracellular matrix of animal cells functions in support and regulation

The plasma membrane is usually regarded as the boundary of the living cell, but most cells synthesize and secrete materials that remain outside the plasma membrane. These extracellular structures are essential to many cell functions.

Animal cells produce an elaborate **extracellular matrix (ECM) (Figure 4.19)**. This layer helps hold cells together in tissues and protects and supports the plasma membrane. The main components of the ECM are glycoproteins, proteins bonded with carbohydrates. In animals, the most abundant glycoprotein is collagen, which forms strong fibres outside the cell. In fact, collagen accounts for about 40% of the protein in your body. The collagen fibres are embedded in a network woven from other types of glycoproteins. Large complexes form when hundreds of small glycoproteins connect to a central long polysaccharide molecule (green in the figure). The ECM may attach to the cell through other glycoproteins that then bind to membrane proteins called integrins. **Integrins** span the membrane, attaching on the other side to proteins connected to microfilaments of the cytoskeleton.

As their name implies, integrins have the function of integration: They transmit signals between the ECM and the cytoskeleton. Thus, the cytoskeleton can influence the organization of the ECM and vice versa. For example, research shows that the ECM can regulate a cell's behaviour, directing the path along which embryonic cells move and even influencing the activity of genes through the signals it relays. Genetic changes in cancer cells may result in a

▲ **Figure 4.19** The extracellular matrix (ECM) of an animal cell

change in the composition of the ECM they produce, causing such cells to lose their connections and spread to other tissues.

? Referring to Figure 4.19, describe the structures that provide support to the plasma membrane.

● The membrane is attached through membrane proteins (integrins) to the microfilaments in the cytoskeleton and the glycoproteins and collagen fibres of the ECM.

4.20 Three types of cell junctions are found in animal tissues

Neighbouring cells in animal tissues often adhere, interact, and communicate through specialized junctions between them. **Figure 4.20** uses cells lining the digestive tract to illustrate three types of cell junctions. (The projections at the top of the cells increase the surface area for absorption of nutrients.)

At *tight junctions*, the plasma membranes of neighbouring cells are tightly pressed against each other and knit together by proteins. Forming continuous seals around cells, tight junctions prevent leakage of fluid across a layer of cells. The green arrows in the figure show how tight junctions prevent the contents of the digestive tract from leaking into surrounding tissues. Originally thought to be impermeable barriers, we now know that the "tightness" of these junctions is highly regulated by the cell.

Anchoring junctions (also called desmosomes) function like rivets, fastening cells together into strong sheets. Intermediate filaments made of sturdy keratin proteins anchor these junctions in the cytoplasm. Anchoring junctions are common in tissues subject to stretching or mechanical stress, such as skin and heart muscle.

Gap junctions, also called communicating junctions, are channels that allow small molecules to flow through protein-lined pores between cells. The flow of ions through gap junctions in the cells of heart muscle coordinates their contraction. Gap junctions are common in embryos, where communication between cells is essential for development.

▲ **Figure 4.20** Three types of cell junctions in animal tissues

 A muscle tear injury would probably involve the rupture of which type of cell junction?

Anchoring junction ●

4.21 Cell walls enclose and support plant cells

The **cell wall** is one feature that distinguishes plant cells from animal cells. This rigid extracellular structure not only protects the cells but provides the skeletal support that keeps plants upright on land. Plant cell walls consist of fibres of cellulose (see Figure 3.7) embedded in a matrix of other polysaccharides and proteins. This fibres-in-a-matrix construction resembles that of fibreglass, a manufactured product also noted for its strength.

Figure 4.21 shows the layered structure of plant cell walls. Cells initially lay down a relatively thin and flexible primary wall, which allows the growing cell to continue to enlarge. Some cells then add a secondary wall deposited in laminated layers. Wood consists mainly of secondary walls, which are strengthened with rigid molecules called lignin. Between adjacent cells is a layer of sticky polysaccharides called pectins (shown here in dark brown), which glue the cells together. (Pectin is used to thicken jams and jellies.)

Despite their thickness, plant cell walls do not totally isolate the cells from each other. To function in a coordinated way as part of a tissue, the cells must have cell junctions, structures that connect them to one another. Figure 4.21 shows the numerous channels between adjacent plant cells, called plasmodesmata (singular, *plasmodesma*). Notice that the plasma membrane and the cytoplasm of the cells extend through the plasmodesmata,

▲ **Figure 4.21** Plant cell walls and plasmodesmata

so that water and other small molecules can readily pass from cell to cell. Through plasmodesmata, the cells of a plant tissue share water, nourishment, and chemical messages.

 Which animal cell junction is analogous to a plasmodesma?

A gap junction ●

4.22 Review: Eukaryotic cell structures can be grouped on the basis of four main functions

Congratulations, you have completed the grand tour of the cell. In the process, you have been introduced to many important cell structures. To provide a framework for this information and reinforce the theme that structure is correlated with function, we have grouped the eukaryotic cell structures into four categories by general function, as reviewed in **Table 4.22**.

The first category is genetic control. Here we include the nucleus that houses a cell's genetic instructions and the ribosomes that produce the proteins coded for in those instructions. The second category includes organelles of the endomembrane system that are involved in the manufacture, distribution, and breakdown of materials. (Vacuoles have other functions as well.) The third category includes the two energy-processing organelles. The fourth category is structural support, movement, and intercellular communication. These functions are related because there must be rigid support against which force can be applied for movement to occur. In addition, a supporting structure that forms the cell's outer boundary is necessarily involved in communication with neighbouring cells.

Within most of these categories, a structural similarity underlies the general function of each component. Manufacturing depends heavily on a network of structurally and functionally connected membranes. All the organelles involved in the breakdown or recycling of materials are membranous sacs, inside of which enzymatic digestion can safely occur. In the energy-processing category, expanses of metabolically active membranes and intermembrane compartments within the organelles enable chloroplasts and mitochondria to perform the complex energy conversions that power the cell. Even in the diverse fourth category, there is a common structural theme in the various protein fibres of these cellular systems.

We can summarize further by emphasizing that these cellular structures form an integrated team—with the property of life emerging at the level of the cell from the coordinated functions of the team members. And finally we note that

TABLE 4.22 | EUKARYOTIC CELL STRUCTURES AND FUNCTIONS

1. Genetic Control	
Nucleus	DNA replication, RNA synthesis; assembly of ribosomal subunits (in nucleoli)
Ribosomes	Polypeptide (protein) synthesis
2. Manufacturing, Distribution, and Breakdown	
Rough ER	Synthesis of membrane lipids and proteins, secretory proteins, and hydrolytic enzymes; formation of transport vesicles
Smooth ER	Lipid synthesis; detoxification in liver cells; calcium ion storage
Golgi apparatus	Modification and sorting of macromolecules; formation of lysosomes and transport vesicles
Lysosomes (in animal cells and some protists)	Digestion of ingested food, bacteria, and a cell's damaged organelles and macromolecules for recycling
Vacuoles	Digestion (food vacuole); storage of chemicals and cell enlargement (central vacuole); water balance (contractile vacuole)
Peroxisomes (not part of endomembrane system)	Diverse metabolic processes, with breakdown of toxic hydrogen peroxide by-product
3. Energy Processing	
Mitochondria	Conversion of chemical energy in food to chemical energy of ATP
Chloroplasts (in plants and some protists)	Conversion of light energy to chemical energy of sugars
4. Structural Support, Movement, and Communication Between Cells	
Cytoskeleton (microfilaments, intermediate filaments, and microtubules)	Maintenance of cell shape; anchorage for organelles; movement of organelles within cells; cell movement (crawling, muscle contraction, bending of cilia and flagella)
Extracellular matrix (in animals)	Support; regulation of cellular activities
Cell junctions	Communication between cells; binding of cells in tissues
Cell walls (in plants, fungi, and some protists)	Support and protection; binding of cells in tissues

the overall structure of a cell is closely related to its specific function. Thus, cells that produce proteins for export contain a large quantity of ribosomes and rough ER, while muscle cells are packed with microfilaments, myosin motor proteins, and mitochondria.

All organisms share the fundamental feature of consisting of cells, each enclosed by a membrane that maintains internal conditions different from the surroundings and each carrying out metabolism, which involves the interconversion of different forms of energy and of chemical compounds. We expand on the subjects of membranes and metabolism in Chapter 5.

 How do mitochondria, smooth ER, and the cytoskeleton all contribute to the contraction of a muscle cell?

● Mitochondria supply energy in the form of ATP. The smooth ER helps to regulate contraction by the uptake and release of calcium ions. Microfilaments function in the actual contractile apparatus.

Reviewing the Concepts

Introduction to the Cell (4.1–4.4)

4.1 Microscopes reveal the world of the cell. The light microscope can magnify up to 1000 times. The greater magnification and resolution of the scanning and transmission electron microscopes reveal the ultrastructure of cells.

4.2 The small size of cells relates to the need to exchange materials across the plasma membrane. The microscopic size of most cells provides a large surface-to-volume ratio. The plasma membrane is a phospholipid bilayer with embedded proteins.

4.3 Prokaryotic cells are structurally simpler than eukaryotic cells. All cells have a plasma membrane, DNA, ribosomes, and cytoplasm. Prokaryotic cells are smaller than eukaryotic cells and lack a membrane-enclosed nucleus.

4.4 Eukaryotic cells are partitioned into functional compartments. Membranes form the boundaries of organelles, compartmentalizing a cell's activities.

The Nucleus and Ribosomes (4.5–4.6)

4.5 The nucleus is the cell's genetic control centre. The nucleus houses the cell's DNA and directs protein synthesis by making messenger RNA. The nucleolus makes the subunits of ribosomes.

4.6 Ribosomes make proteins for use in the cell and for export. Composed of ribosomal RNA and proteins, ribosomes synthesize proteins according to directions from DNA.

The Endomembrane System (4.7–4.12)

4.7 Overview: Many cell organelles are connected through the endomembrane system. The endomembrane system consists of the endoplasmic reticulum, Golgi apparatus, lysosomes, vacuoles, as well as the nuclear envelope and plasma membrane.

4.8 The endoplasmic reticulum is a biosynthetic factory. The ER is a membranous network of tubes and sacs. Smooth ER synthesizes lipids and processes toxins. Rough ER manufactures membranes, and ribosomes on its surface produce membrane and secretory proteins.

4.9 The Golgi apparatus finishes, sorts, and ships cell products. The Golgi apparatus consists of stacks of sacs that modify ER products and then ship them to other organelles or the cell surface.

4.10 Lysosomes are digestive compartments within a cell. Lysosomes house enzymes that function in digestion and recycling within the cell.

4.11 Vacuoles function in the general maintenance of the cell. Some protists have contractile vacuoles. Plant cells contain a large central vacuole that stores molecules and wastes and facilitates growth.

4.12 A review of the structures involved in manufacturing and breakdown. The organelles of the endomembrane system are interconnected structurally and functionally.

Energy-Converting Organelles (4.13–4.15)

4.13 Mitochondria harvest chemical energy from food. Mitochondria, found in nearly all eukaryotic cells, are self-replicating and a major site of ATP synthesis.

4.14 Chloroplasts convert solar energy to chemical energy. Chloroplasts are found in plants and some protists. These organelles capture light energy and convert it into chemical energy.

4.15 Mitochondria and chloroplasts evolved by endosymbiosis. These organelles originated from prokaryotic cells that became residents in a host cell.

The Cytoskeleton and Cell Surfaces (4.16–4.22)

4.16 Are the organelles of a cell free-floating in a cytoplasm soup? Organelles are not free-floating but are associated with the cytoskeletal network of protein fibres. Microfilaments of actin enable cells to change shape and move. Intermediate filaments reinforce the cell and anchor certain organelles. Microtubules give the cell rigidity and act as tracks for organelle movement.

4.17 Cilia and flagella move when microtubules bend. Eukaryotic cilia and flagella are locomotor appendages made of microtubules in a 9 + 2 arrangement.

4.18 Problems with sperm motility may be environmental or genetic. Environmental chemicals or genetic disorders may interfere with the movement of sperm or cilia.

4.19 The extracellular matrix of animal cells functions in support and regulation. The ECM consists mainly of glycoproteins, which bind tissue cells together, support the membrane, and communicate with the cytoskeleton.

4.20 Three types of cell junctions are found in animal tissues. Tight junctions bind cells to form leakproof sheets. Anchoring junctions rivet cells into strong tissues. Gap junctions allow substances to flow from cell to cell.

4.21 Cell walls enclose and support plant cells. Plant cell walls are made largely of cellulose. Plasmodesmata are connecting channels between cells.

4.22 Review: Eukaryotic cell structures can be grouped on the basis of four main functions. These functions are (1) genetic control; (2) manufacturing, distribution, and breakdown; (3) energy processing; and (4) structural support, movement, and communication between cells.

Connecting the Concepts

1. Label the structures in this diagram of an animal cell. Review the functions of each of these organelles.

a. _____

b. _____

c. _____

d. _____

e. _____

f. _____

g. _____

h. _____

i. _____

j. _____

k. _____

l. _____

2. List some structures found in animal cells but not in plant cells.

3. List some structures found in plant cells but not in animal cells.

Testing Your Knowledge

Multiple Choice

4. The ultrastructure of a chloroplast is best studied using a
   a. light microscope.
   b. telescope.
   c. scanning electron microscope.
   d. transmission electron microscope.
   e. light microscope and fluorescent dyes.

5. The cells of an ant and a horse are, on average, the same small size; a horse just has more of them. What is the main advantage of small cell size? (*Explain your answer.*)
   a. Small cells are less likely to burst than large cells.
   b. A small cell has a larger plasma membrane surface area than does a large cell.
   c. Small cells can better take up sufficient nutrients and oxygen to service their cell volume.
   d. It takes less energy to make an organism out of small cells.
   e. Small cells require less oxygen than do large cells.

6. Which of the following clues would tell you whether a cell is prokaryotic or eukaryotic?
   a. the presence or absence of a rigid cell wall
   b. whether or not the cell is partitioned by internal membranes
   c. the presence or absence of ribosomes
   d. whether or not the cell carries out cellular metabolism
   e. whether or not the cell contains DNA

7. Which statement correctly describes bound ribosomes?
   a. Bound ribosomes are enclosed in a membrane.
   b. Bound and free ribosomes are structurally different.
   c. Bound ribosomes are most commonly found on the surface of the plasma membrane.
   d. Bound ribosomes generally synthesize membrane proteins and secretory proteins.
   e. Bound ribosomes produce the subunits of microtubules, microfilaments, and intermediate filaments.

Choose from the following cells for questions 8–12:
   a. muscle cell in thigh of long-distance runner
   b. pancreatic cell that secretes digestive enzymes
   c. ovarian cell that produces the steroid hormone estrogen
   d. cell in tissue layer lining digestive tract
   e. white blood cell that engulfs bacteria

8. In which cell would you find the most lysosomes?

9. In which cell would you find the most mitochondria?

10. In which cell would you find the most smooth ER?

11. In which cell would you find the most rough ER?

12. In which cell would you find the most tight junctions?

13. A type of cell called a lymphocyte makes proteins that are exported from the cell. Which of the following traces the path of a protein from the site where its polypeptides are made to its export?
    a. chloroplast; Golgi; lysosomes; plasma membrane
    b. Golgi; rough ER; smooth ER; transport vesicle
    c. rough ER; Golgi; transport vesicle; plasma membrane
    d. smooth ER; Golgi; lysosome; plasma membrane
    e. nucleus; rough ER; Golgi; plasma membrane

Describing, Comparing, and Explaining

14. What four cellular components are shared by prokaryotic and eukaryotic cells?

15. Briefly describe the three kinds of junctions that can connect animal cells, and compare their functions.

16. What general function do the chloroplast and mitochondrion have in common? How are their functions different?

17. In what ways do the internal membranes of a eukaryotic cell contribute to the functioning of the cell?

18. Describe two different ways in which the motion of cilia can function in organisms.

19. Explain how a protein inside the ER can be exported from the cell without ever crossing a membrane.

20. Is this statement true or false? "Animal cells have mitochondria; plant cells have chloroplasts." *Explain your answer.*

21. Describe the structure of the plasma membrane of an animal cell. What would be found directly inside and outside the membrane?

Applying the Concepts

22. Imagine a spherical cell with a radius of 10 μm. What is the cell's surface area in μm^2? Its volume in μm^3? What is the ratio of surface area to volume for this cell? Now do the same calculations for a second cell, this one with a radius of 20 μm. Compare the surface-to-volume ratios of the two cells. How is this comparison significant to the functioning of cells? (*Note:* For a sphere of radius r, surface area $= 4\pi r^2$ and volume $= \frac{1}{3}\pi r^3$. Remember that the value of π is 3.14.)

23. Cilia are found on cells in almost every organ of the human body, and the malfunction of cilia is involved in several human disorders. During embryological development, for example, cilia generate a leftward flow of fluid that initiates the left-right organization of the body organs. Some individuals with primary ciliary dyskinesia (PCD; see Module 4.18) exhibit *situs inversus*, in which internal organs such as the heart are on the wrong side of the body. Explain why this reversed arrangement may be a symptom of PCD.

24. The cells of plant seeds store oils in the form of droplets enclosed by membranes. Unlike typical biological membranes, this oil droplet membrane consists of a single layer of phospholipids rather than a bilayer. Draw a model for a membrane around such an oil droplet. Explain why this arrangement is more stable than a bilayer of phospholipids.

Answers to all questions can be found in Appendix E.

Cellular Function

Membrane Structure and Function

(5.1–5.8)

The phospholipid and protein structure of cell membranes enables their many important functions.

Energy and the Cell

(5.9–5.11)

A cell's metabolic reactions transform energy, producing ATP, which drives cellular work.

How Enzymes Function

(5.12–5.16)

Enzymes speed up a cell's chemical reactions and provide precise control of metabolism.

Bioluminescence: The Light of Life

How does one hide in the open ocean? Animals on land can crouch behind trees or rocks, and many use amazing camouflage disguises. There are insects that look like sticks, toads that resemble rocks, rabbits that blend in with the snow. But would camouflage work when there is nothing around but water?

Ocean predators often hunt by looking up, searching for a silhouette of their prey above them. Can an animal hide its silhouette? The answer is yes, if it can use light. The deep-sea firefly squid (*Watasenia scintillans*) shown here has light-producing organs called photophores dotting its ventral (lower) surface. These organs emit a soft glow that matches the light filtering down from above. During the day, the squid remain in deep, cold water, and their photophores glow blue, matching the blue wavelengths of light that penetrate into deeper water. As night approaches, the squid come closer to the warmer surface, and their glow turns to green, again matching the ambient light.

These squid aren't the only ones to use this mechanism, called counter-illumination. Many marine invertebrates and fishes avoid their predators by producing light to hide their silhouettes. The cookiecutter shark (*Isistius brasiliensis*), shown in the figure, uses a variation on this theme to help it hunt. This small shark has densely packed photophores on its ventral surface, except on a small patch in an area close to its head. This dark band may appear as a small fish to large predators such as tuna and mackerel. When they approach from below to prey on this "small fish," the cookiecutter shark snags a cookie-sized bite from the potential predator's side and darts off.

The light these animals produce, referred to as bioluminescence, comes from a chemical reaction that converts chemical energy into visible light. These reactions involve enzymes located within membranes in special light-producing cells. In the presence of oxygen (O_2), an enzyme called luciferase catalyzes the conversion of a molecule called luciferin to a molecule that emits light. (Both are named for the Latin word *lucifer*, meaning "light bearer.") You may be familiar with bioluminescence in the familiar fireflies that use particular patterns of flashes of yellow or green light to attract mates. Such light production is fairly rare on land, but it is actually the norm in the ocean, where an estimated 90% of deep-sea marine life can produce bioluminescence.

Life and death stories involving bioluminescence abound in the ocean. Some microorganisms light up when attacked, drawing the attention of larger predators that may come to feed on their attackers. Certain squid expel a cloud of bioluminescence instead of ink to escape. Whether for camouflage, attraction of mates or prey, repulsion of predators, or communication, the production of light by living organisms is a widespread phenomenon. It has evolved in certain bacteria, algae, mushrooms, many marine invertebrates, and fishes. Different versions of light-emitting luciferin and catalyzing luciferase have evolved in these various groups. Bioluminescence demonstrates how living cells put energy to work by means of enzyme-controlled chemical reactions. Light is a form of energy, and the ability of bioluminescent organisms to convert chemical energy to light energy is just one example of the myriad of energy conversions central to life.

Many of these energy-converting reactions of cells take place in organelles, such as those in the light-producing cells in a squid. The enzymes that control these reactions are often embedded in membranes of the organelle. Indeed, everything that happens when a squid turns on the lights to hide has some relation to the topics of this chapter: how working cells use membranes, energy, and enzymes.

Membrane Structure and Function

5.1 Membranes are fluid mosaics of lipids and proteins with many functions

The plasma membrane is the edge of life, the boundary that encloses a living cell. In eukaryotic cells, internal membranes partition the cell into specialized compartments. Recall from Modules 4.2 and 4.19 that membranes are composed of a bilayer of phospholipids with embedded and attached proteins. Biologists describe such a structure as a **fluid mosaic**.

In the cell, a membrane remains about as fluid as salad oil, with most of its components able to drift about like partygoers moving through a crowded room. Double bonds in the unsaturated fatty acid tails of some phospholipids produce kinks that prevent phospholipids from packing too tightly and help to control the level of fluidity of the membrane (see Module 3.15). In animal cell membranes, the steroid cholesterol helps stabilize the membrane at warm temperatures but also helps to keep the membrane fluid at lower temperatures.

A membrane is a "mosaic" in that it has diverse protein molecules embedded in its fluid framework. The word *mosaic* can also refer to the varied functions of these proteins. Different types of cells have different membrane proteins, and the various membranes of cellular organelles contain unique collections of proteins.

Figure 5.1, which diagrams the plasma membranes of two adjacent cells, illustrates six major functions performed by membrane proteins, represented by the purple oval structures. Some proteins help to maintain cell shape and coordinate changes inside and outside the cell through their attachment to the cytoskeleton and extracellular matrix (ECM). Other proteins function as receptors for chemical messengers (signalling molecules) from other cells. The binding of a signalling molecule triggers a change in the protein, which relays the message into the cell, activating molecules that perform specific functions. This message-transfer process, called signal transduction, will be described in more detail in Module 11.10.

Some membrane proteins are enzymes, which may be grouped in a membrane to carry out sequential steps of a metabolic pathway. Membrane glycoproteins may be involved in cell-cell recognition. Their attached carbohydrates function as identification tags that are recognized by membrane proteins of other cells. This recognition allows cells in an embryo to sort into tissues and enables cells of the immune system to recognize and reject foreign cells, such as infectious bacteria. Membrane proteins also participate in the intercellular junctions that attach adjacent cells (see Module 4.20).

A final critical function is the transport of substances across the membrane. Membranes exhibit **selective permeability**; that is, they allow some substances to cross more easily than others. Many essential ions and molecules, such as glucose, require transport proteins to enter or leave the cell.

? Review the six different types of functions that proteins in a plasma membrane can perform.

● Attachment to the cytoskeleton and ECM, signal transduction, enzymatic activity, cell-cell recognition, intercellular joining, and transport

▲ **Figure 5.1** Some functions of membrane proteins

5.2 Membranes form spontaneously, a critical step in the origin of life

Phospholipids, the key ingredients of biological membranes, were probably among the first organic molecules that formed from chemical reactions on early Earth (see Module 13.9). These lipids could spontaneously self-assemble into simple membranes, as we can demonstrate in a test tube. When a mixture of phospholipids and water is shaken, the phospholipids organize into bilayers surrounding water-filled bubbles (**Figure 5.2**). This

assembly requires neither genes nor other information beyond the properties of the phospholipids themselves.

The formation of membrane-enclosed collections of molecules was probably a critical step in the evolution of the first cells. A membrane can enclose a solution that is different in composition from its surroundings. A plasma membrane that allows cells to regulate their chemical exchanges with the environment is a basic requirement for life. Indeed, all cells are enclosed by a plasma membrane that is similar in structure and function—illustrating the evolutionary unity of life.

Water-filled bubble made of phospholipids

▲ **Figure 5.2** Artificial membrane-bounded sacs

? This is a diagram of a section of one of the membrane sacs shown in Figure 5.2. Describe its structure.

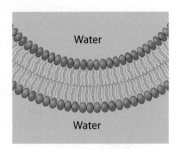

Water

Water

● The phospholipids form a bilayer. The hydrophobic fatty acid tails cluster in the centre, and the hydrophilic phosphate heads face the water on both sides.

5.3 Passive transport is diffusion across a membrane with no energy investment

Molecules vibrate and move randomly as a result of a type of energy called thermal motion (heat). One result of this motion is **diffusion**, the tendency for particles of any kind to spread out evenly in an available space. How might diffusion affect the movement of substances into or out of a cell?

The figures to the right will help you visualize diffusion across a membrane. **Figure 5.3A** shows a solution of green dye separated from pure water by a membrane. Assume that this membrane has microscopic pores through which dye molecules can move. Thus, we say it is *permeable* to the dye. If there are more dye molecules on one side of the membrane than the other, there is said to be a **concentration gradient**. Although each molecule moves randomly, there will be a *net* movement of dye molecules down the concentration gradient by diffusion. Eventually, the solutions on both sides will have equal concentrations of dye. At this dynamic equilibrium, molecules still move back and forth, but there is no *net* change in concentration on either side of the membrane.

Figure 5.3B illustrates the important point that two or more substances diffuse independently of each other; that is, each diffuses down its own concentration gradient.

Because a cell does not have to expend energy or do work when molecules diffuse across its membrane, such movement across a membrane is called **passive transport**. Much of the traffic across cell membranes occurs by diffusion. For example, diffusion down concentration gradients is the sole means by which oxygen (O_2), essential for metabolism, enters your cells and carbon dioxide (CO_2), a metabolic waste, passes out of them.

O_2 is a small, nonpolar molecule that diffuses easily across the phospholipid bilayer of a membrane. But can ions and

Molecules of dye   Membrane

Pores

Net diffusion   Net diffusion   Equilibrium

▲ **Figure 5.3A** Passive transport of one type of molecule

Net diffusion   Net diffusion   Equilibrium

Net diffusion   Net diffusion   Equilibrium

▲ **Figure 5.3B** Passive transport of two types of molecules

polar molecules also diffuse across the hydrophobic interior of a membrane? Although they cannot easily cross a membrane down their concentration gradient on their own, they can if they have transport proteins to help them cross.

? Why is diffusion across a membrane called passive transport?

● The cell does not expend energy to transport substances that are diffusing down their concentration gradients.

5.4 Osmosis is the diffusion of water across a membrane

One of the most important substances that crosses membranes by passive transport is water. In the next module, we consider the critical balance of water between a cell and its environment. But first let's explore a physical model of the diffusion of water across a selectively permeable membrane, a process called **osmosis**. Remember that a selectively permeable membrane allows some substances to cross more easily than others.

The top of **Figure 5.4** shows what happens if a membrane permeable to water but not to a solute (such as glucose) separates two solutions with different concentrations of solute. (A solute is a substance that dissolves in a liquid solvent, producing a solution.) The solution on the right side initially has a higher concentration of solute than that on the left. As you can see, water crosses the membrane until the solute concentrations are equal on both sides.

In the close-up view at the bottom of Figure 5.4, you can see what happens at the molecular level. Polar water molecules cluster around hydrophilic (water-loving) solute molecules. The effect is that on the right side, there are fewer water molecules available to cross the membrane. The less concentrated solution on the left, with fewer solute molecules, has more water molecules *free* to move. There is a net movement of water down its own concentration gradient, from the solution with more free water molecules (and lower solute concentration) to that with fewer free water molecules (and higher solute concentration). The result of this water movement is the difference in water levels you see at the top right of Figure 5.4.

Let's now apply to living cells what we have learned about osmosis in artificial systems.

▲ **Figure 5.4** Osmosis, the diffusion of water across a membrane

? Indicate the direction of net water movement between two solutions—a 0.5% sucrose solution and a 2% sucrose solution—separated by a membrane not permeable to sucrose.

● From the 0.5% sucrose solution (lower solute concentration) to the 2% sucrose solution (higher solute concentration).

5.5 Water balance between cells and their surroundings is crucial to organisms

Biologists use a special vocabulary to describe the relationship between a cell and its surroundings with regard to the movement of water. In this context, the term **tonicity** refers to the ability of a surrounding solution to cause a cell to gain or lose water. The tonicity of a solution mainly depends on its concentration of solutes that cannot cross the plasma membrane relative to the concentration of solutes inside the cell.

Figure 5.5 illustrates how the principles of osmosis and tonicity apply to cells. The effects of placing an animal cell in solutions of various tonicities are shown in the top row of the illustration; the effects of the same solutions on a plant cell are shown in the bottom row.

As shown in the top centre of the figure, when an animal cell is immersed in a solution that is **isotonic** to the cell (*iso*, same, and *tonos*, tension), the cell's volume remains constant. The solute concentration of a cell and its isotonic environment are essentially equal, and the cell gains water at the same rate that it loses it. In your body, red blood cells are transported in the isotonic plasma of the blood. Intravenous (IV) fluids administered in hospitals must also be isotonic to blood cells. The body cells of most animals are bathed in an extracellular

fluid that is isotonic to the cells. And seawater is isotonic to the cells of many marine animals, such as sea stars and crabs.

The upper left of the figure shows what happens when an animal cell is placed in a **hypotonic** solution (*hypo*, below), a solution with a solute concentration lower than that of the cell. (Can you figure out in which direction osmosis will occur? Where are there more free water molecules available to move?) The cell gains water, swells, and may burst (lyse) like an overfilled balloon. The upper right shows the opposite case—an animal cell placed in a **hypertonic** solution (*hyper*, above), a solution with a higher solute concentration. The cell shrivels and can die from water loss.

For an animal to survive in a hypotonic or hypertonic environment, it must have a way to prevent excessive uptake or excessive loss of water. The control of water balance is called **osmoregulation**. For example, a freshwater fish, which lives in a hypotonic environment, has kidneys and gills that work constantly to prevent an excessive buildup of water in the body. (We will discuss osmoregulation further in Module 25.19.)

Water balance issues are somewhat different for the cells of plants, prokaryotes, and fungi because of their cell walls.

As shown in the bottom centre of Figure 5.5, a plant cell immersed in an isotonic solution is flaccid (limp). In contrast, a plant cell is turgid (very firm), which is the healthy state for most plant cells, in a hypotonic environment (bottom left). To become turgid, a plant cell needs a net inflow of water. Although the somewhat elastic cell wall expands a bit, the pressure it exerts prevents the cell from taking in too much water and bursting, as an animal cell would in a hypotonic environment. Plants that are not woody, such as most houseplants, depend on their turgid cells for mechanical support.

In a hypertonic environment (bottom right), a plant cell is no better off than an animal cell. As a plant cell loses water, it shrivels, and its plasma membrane pulls away from the cell wall. This process, called plasmolysis, causes the plant to wilt and can be lethal to the cell and the plant. The walled cells of bacteria and fungi also plasmolyze in hypertonic environments. Thus, meats and other foods can be preserved with concentrated salt solutions because the cells of food-spoiling bacteria or fungi become plasmolyzed and eventually die.

Hypotonic solution **Isotonic solution** **Hypertonic solution**

Animal cell: H_2O — Lysed / H_2O H_2O — Normal / H_2O — Shrivelled

Plant cell: H_2O — Turgid (normal) / H_2O — Flaccid / Plasma membrane — H_2O — Shrivelled (plasmolyzed)

▲ **Figure 5.5** How animal and plant cells react to changes in tonicity. (Deepening shades of blue reflect increasing concentrations of solutes in the surrounding solutions.)

In the next module, we explore how water and other polar solutes move across cell membranes.

? Explain the function of the contractile vacuoles in the freshwater *Paramecium* shown in Figure 4.11A in terms of what you have just learned about water balance in cells.

● The pond water in which *Paramecium* lives is hypotonic to the cell. The contractile vacuoles expel the water that constantly enters the cell by osmosis.

5.6 Transport proteins can facilitate diffusion across membranes

Recall that nonpolar, hydrophobic molecules can dissolve in the lipid bilayer of a membrane and cross it with ease. Polar or charged substances, meanwhile, can move across a membrane with the help of specific transport proteins in a process called **facilitated diffusion**. Without the transport protein, the substance cannot cross the membrane or it diffuses across it too slowly to be useful to the cell. Facilitated diffusion is a type of passive transport because it does not require energy input. As in all passive transport, the driving force is the concentration gradient.

Figure 5.6A shows a common type of transport protein, which provides a hydrophilic channel that some molecules or ions use as a tunnel through the membrane. Another type of transport protein binds its passenger, changes shape, and releases its passenger on the other side. In both cases, the transport protein is specific for the substance it helps to move across the membrane. The greater the number of transport proteins for a particular solute in a membrane, the faster the solute's rate of diffusion across the membrane.

Solute molecule

Transport protein

▲ **Figure 5.6A** Transport protein providing a channel for the diffusion of a specific solute across a membrane

Substances that use facilitated diffusion for crossing cell membranes include a number of sugars, amino acids, ions—and even water. The water molecule is very small, but because it is polar (see Module 2.6), its diffusion through a membrane's hydrophobic interior is relatively slow. The very rapid diffusion of water into and out of certain cells, such as plant cells, kidney cells, and red blood cells, is made possible by a protein channel called an **aquaporin**. A single aquaporin allows the entry or exit of up to 3 billion water molecules per second—a tremendous increase in water transport over simple diffusion without requiring transport proteins.

Figure 5.6B is an image taken from a simulation produced by computational biophysicists. This model includes four aquaporin

▲ **Figure 5.6B** Aquaporin in action

channels spanning a membrane. You can see a line of blue water molecules flipping their way single file through the gold aquaporin. The simulation of this flipping movement allowed researchers to discover how aquaporins selectively let only water molecules pass through them.

? **How do transport proteins contribute to a membrane's selective permeability?**

● Because they are specific for the solutes they transport, the numbers and kinds of transport proteins affect a membrane's permeability to various solutes.

5.7 Cells expend energy in the active transport of a solute

In **active transport**, a cell must expend energy to move a solute *against* its concentration gradient—that is, across a membrane toward the side where the solute is more concentrated. The energy molecule ATP (described in more detail in Module 5.11) directly or indirectly supplies the energy for most active transport.

Figure 5.7 shows a simple model of an active transport system that pumps a solute out of the cell against its concentration gradient. ❶ The process begins when solute molecules on the cytoplasmic side of the plasma membrane attach to specific binding sites on the transport protein. ❷ ATP then transfers a phosphate group to the transport protein, ❸ causing the protein to change shape in such a way that the solute is released on the other side of the membrane. ❹ The phosphate group detaches, and the transport protein returns to its original shape.

Active transport allows a cell to maintain internal concentrations of small molecules and ions that are different from concentrations in its surroundings. For example, the inside of an animal cell has a higher concentration of potassium ions (K^+) and a lower concentration of sodium ions (Na^+) than the solution outside the cell. The

generation of nerve signals depends on these concentration differences, which a transport protein called the sodium-potassium pump helps to maintain by shuttling Na^+ and K^+ against their concentration gradients. The ATP used during continual operation of the sodium-potassium pumps in the cells of the brain accounts for more than 70% of the organ's total energy consumption.

? **Cells actively transport Ca^{2+} out of the cell. Is calcium more concentrated inside or outside of the cell? Explain.**

● Outside: Active transport moves calcium against its concentration gradient.

❶ Solute binding ❷ Phosphate attaching ❸ Transport ❹ Protein reversion

▲ **Figure 5.7** Active transport of a solute across a membrane

5.8 Exocytosis and endocytosis transport large molecules across membranes

So far, we've focused on how water and small solutes enter and leave cells. The story is different for large molecules.

A cell uses the process of **exocytosis** (from the Greek *exo*, outside, and *kytos*, cell) to export bulky materials such

as proteins or polysaccharides. As you saw in Figure 4.12, a transport vesicle filled with macromolecules buds from the Golgi apparatus and moves to the plasma membrane. Once there, the vesicle fuses with the plasma membrane, and the vesicle's contents spill out of the cell when the vesicle membrane becomes part of the plasma membrane. When we weep, for instance, cells in our tear glands use exocytosis to export a salty solution containing proteins. In another example, certain cells in the pancreas manufacture the hormone insulin and secrete it into the bloodstream by exocytosis.

Endocytosis (*endo*, inside) is a transport process that is the opposite of exocytosis. In endocytosis, a cell takes in large molecules. A depression in the plasma membrane pinches in and forms a vesicle enclosing material that had been outside the cell.

Figure 5.8 shows three kinds of endocytosis. The top diagram illustrates **phagocytosis**, or "cellular eating." A cell engulfs a particle by wrapping extensions called pseudopodia around it and packaging it within a membrane-enclosed sac large enough to be called a vacuole. As described in Module 4.10, the vacuole then fuses with a lysosome, whose hydrolytic enzymes digest the contents of the vacuole. The micrograph on the top right shows an amoeba taking in a food particle via phagocytosis.

The centre diagram shows **pinocytosis**, or "cellular drinking." The cell "gulps" droplets of fluid into tiny vesicles. Pinocytosis is not specific; it takes in any and all solutes dissolved in the droplets. The micrograph in the middle shows pinocytosis vesicles forming (arrows) in a cell lining a small blood vessel.

In contrast to pinocytosis, **receptor-mediated endocytosis** is highly selective. Receptor proteins for specific molecules are embedded in regions of the membrane that are lined by a layer of coat proteins. The bottom diagram shows that the plasma membrane has indented to form a coated pit, whose receptor proteins have picked up particular molecules from the surroundings. The coated pit then pinches closed to form a vesicle that carries the molecules into the cytoplasm. The micrograph shows material bound to receptor proteins inside a coated pit. Your cells use receptor-mediated endocytosis to take in cholesterol from the blood for synthesis of membranes and as a precursor for other steroids. Cholesterol circulates in the blood in particles called low-density lipoproteins (LDLs). LDLs bind to receptor proteins and then enter

cells by endocytosis. In humans with the inherited disease familial hypercholesterolemia, LDL receptor proteins are defective and cholesterol accumulates to high levels in the blood, leading to atherosclerosis (see Modules 3.16 and 9.10).

? As a cell grows, its plasma membrane expands. Does this involve endocytosis or exocytosis? Explain.

● Exocytosis: When a transport vesicle fuses with the plasma membrane, its contents are released and the vesicle membrane adds to the plasma membrane.

Phagocytosis

EXTRACELLULAR FLUID   CYTOPLASM

Pseudopodium

"Food" or other particle

Food vacuole

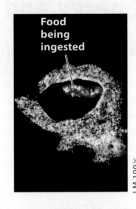

Food being ingested

LM 100×

Pinocytosis

Plasma membrane

Vesicle

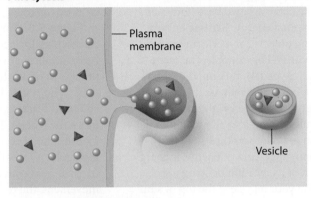

TEM 62 000×

Plasma membrane

Receptor-mediated endocytosis

Coat protein

Receptor

Coated vesicle

Specific molecule

Coated pit

Coated pit

Material bound to receptor proteins

TEM109 000×

▲ **Figure 5.8** Three kinds of endocytosis

Energy and the Cell

5.9 Cells transform energy as they perform work

What type of work does a cell do? You just learned that a cell actively transports substances across membranes. The cell also builds those membranes and the proteins embedded in them. A cell is a miniature chemical factory in which thousands of reactions occur within a microscopic space. Some of these reactions release energy; others require energy. To understand how the cell works, you must have a basic knowledge of energy.

Forms of Energy   We can define **energy** as the capacity to cause change or perform work. There are two basic forms of energy: kinetic energy and potential energy. **Kinetic energy** is the energy of motion. Moving objects can perform work by transferring motion to other matter. For example, the movement of your legs can push bicycle pedals, turning the wheels and moving you and your bike up a hill. **Heat**, or thermal energy, is a type of kinetic energy associated with the random movement of atoms or molecules. Light, also a type of kinetic energy, can be harnessed to power photosynthesis.

Potential energy, the second main form of energy, is energy that matter possesses as a result of its location or structure. Water behind a dam and you on your bicycle at the top of a hill possess potential energy. Similarly, a solute concentration gradient across a plasma membrane is a source of potential energy. Molecules possess potential energy because of the arrangement of electrons in the bonds between their atoms. **Chemical energy** is the potential energy available for release in a chemical reaction. Chemical energy is the most important type of energy for living organisms; it is the energy that can be transformed to power the work of the cell.

Energy Transformations   Scientists use the word *system* for the matter under study and refer to the rest of the universe—everything outside the system—as the *surroundings*. A system can be an electric power plant, a single cell, or the entire planet. An organism is an open system; that is, it exchanges both energy and matter with its surroundings. **Thermodynamics** is the study of energy transformations that occur in a collection of matter.

The **first law of thermodynamics**, also known as the law of energy conservation, states that the energy in the universe is constant. Energy can be transferred and transformed, but it cannot be created or destroyed. A power plant does not create energy; it merely converts it from one form (such as the kinetic energy of moving water) to a more convenient form of electricity. A plant cell converts light energy to chemical energy; it, too, is an energy transformer, not an energy producer.

If energy cannot be destroyed, then why can't organisms simply recycle their energy? It turns out that during every transfer or transformation, some energy becomes unusable—unavailable to do work. In most energy transformations, some energy is converted to heat, a disordered form of energy. Scientists use a quantity called **entropy** as a measure of disorder, or randomness. The more randomly arranged a collection of matter is, the greater its entropy. According to the **second law of thermodynamics**, energy conversions increase the entropy (disorder) of the universe.

Figure 5.9 compares a car and a cell to show how energy can be transformed and how entropy increases as a result. Automobile engines and living cells use the same basic process to make the chemical energy of their fuel available for work. The engine mixes oxygen with gasoline in an explosive chemical reaction that pushes the pistons, which eventually move the wheels. The waste products emitted from the exhaust pipe are mostly carbon dioxide and water, energy-poor, simple molecules. Only about 25% of the chemical energy stored in gasoline is converted to the kinetic energy of the car's movement; the rest is lost as heat.

Cells also use oxygen in reactions that release energy from fuel molecules. In the process called **cellular respiration**, the

▲ **Figure 5.9** Energy transformations (with an increase in entropy) in a car and a cell

chemical energy stored in organic molecules is converted to a form that the cell can use to perform work. Just like for the car, the waste products are mostly carbon dioxide and water. Cells are more efficient than car engines, however, converting about 34% of the chemical energy in their fuel to energy for cellular work. The other 66% generates heat, which explains why vigorous exercise makes you so warm.

According to the second law of thermodynamics, energy transformations result in the universe becoming more disordered. How, then, can we account for biological order? A cell creates intricate structures from less organized materials. Although this increase in order corresponds to a decrease in entropy, it is accomplished at the expense of ordered forms of matter and energy taken in from the surroundings. As shown in Figure 5.9, cells extract the chemical energy of glucose and return disordered heat and lower-energy carbon dioxide and water to the surroundings. In a thermodynamic sense, a cell is an island of low entropy in an increasingly random universe.

 How does the second law of thermodynamics explain the diffusion of a solute across a membrane?

● Diffusion across a membrane results in equal concentrations of solute, which is a more disordered arrangement (higher entropy) than a high concentration on one side and a low concentration on the other.

5.10 Chemical reactions either release or store energy

Chemical reactions are of two types: Either they release energy or they require an input of energy and store energy.

An **exergonic reaction** is a chemical reaction that releases energy (*exergonic* means "energy outward"). As shown in Figure 5.10A, an exergonic reaction begins with reactants whose covalent bonds contain more energy than those in the products. The reaction releases to the surroundings an amount of energy equal to the difference in potential energy between the reactants and the products.

As an example of an exergonic reaction, consider what happens when wood burns. One of the major components of wood is cellulose, a large energy-rich carbohydrate composed of many glucose monomers. The burning of wood releases the energy of glucose as heat and light. Carbon dioxide and water are the products of the reaction.

As you learned in Module 5.9, cells release energy from fuel molecules in the process called cellular respiration. Burning and cellular respiration are alike in being exergonic. They differ in that burning is essentially a one-step process that releases all of a substance's energy at once. Cellular respiration, however, involves many steps, each a separate chemical reaction; you can think of it as a "slow burn." Some of the energy released from glucose by cellular respiration escapes as heat, but a substantial amount is converted to the chemical energy of ATP. Cells use ATP as an immediate source of energy.

The other type of chemical reaction requires a net input of energy. **Endergonic reactions** yield products that are rich in potential energy (*endergonic* means "energy inward"). As shown in Figure 5.10B, an endergonic reaction starts out with reactant molecules that contain relatively little potential energy. Energy is absorbed from the surroundings as the reaction occurs, so the products of an endergonic reaction contain more chemical energy than the reactants did. And as the graph shows, the amount of additional energy stored in the products equals the difference in potential energy between the reactants and the products.

Photosynthesis, the process by which plant cells make sugar, is an example of an endergonic process. Photosynthesis starts with energy-poor reactants (carbon dioxide and water molecules) and, using energy absorbed from sunlight, produces energy-rich sugar molecules.

Every working cell in every organism carries out thousands of exergonic and endergonic reactions. The total of an

◄ **Figure 5.10A**
Exergonic reaction, energy released

◄ **Figure 5.10B**
Endergonic reaction, energy required

organism's chemical reactions is called **metabolism** (from the Greek *metabole*, change). We can picture a cell's metabolism as a road map of thousands of chemical reactions arranged as intersecting metabolic pathways. A **metabolic pathway** is a series of chemical reactions that either builds a complex molecule or breaks down a complex molecule into simpler compounds. The "slow burn" of cellular respiration is an example of a metabolic pathway in which a sequence of reactions slowly releases the potential energy stored in sugar.

All of an organism's activities require energy, which is obtained from sugar and other molecules by the exergonic reactions of cellular respiration. Cells then use that energy in endergonic reactions to make molecules and do the work of the cell. **Energy coupling**—the use of energy released from exergonic reactions to drive essential endergonic reactions—is a crucial ability of all cells. ATP molecules are the key to energy coupling. In the next module, we explore the structure and function of ATP.

 Cellular respiration is an exergonic process. Remembering that energy must be conserved, what becomes of the energy extracted from food during cellular respiration?

● Some of it is stored in ATP molecules; the rest is released as heat.

5.11 ATP drives cellular work by coupling exergonic and endergonic reactions

ATP powers nearly all forms of cellular work. The structure of ATP, or adenosine triphosphate, is shown below in **Figure 5.11A**. The adenosine part of ATP consists of adenine, a nitrogenous base (see Module 3.12), and ribose, a five-carbon sugar. The triphosphate part is a chain of three phosphate groups (each symbolized by ⓟ). All three phosphate groups are negatively charged (see Table 3.2). These like charges are crowded together, and their mutual repulsion makes the triphosphate chain of ATP the chemical equivalent of a compressed spring.

As a result, the bonds connecting the phosphate groups are unstable and can readily be broken by hydrolysis, the addition of water. Notice in Figure 5.11A that when the bond to the third group breaks, a phosphate group leaves ATP—which becomes ADP (adenosine diphosphate)—and energy is released.

Thus, the hydrolysis of ATP is exergonic—it releases energy. How does the cell couple this reaction to an endergonic one? It usually does so by transferring a phosphate group from ATP to some other molecule. This phosphate transfer is called **phosphorylation**, and most cellular work depends on ATP energizing molecules by phosphorylating them.

There are three main types of cellular work: chemical, mechanical, and transport. As **Figure 5.11B** shows, ATP drives all three types of work. In chemical work, the phosphorylation of reactants provides energy to drive the endergonic synthesis of products. In an example of mechanical work, the transfer of phosphate groups to special motor proteins in muscle cells causes the proteins to change shape and pull on protein filaments, in turn causing the cells to contract. In transport work, as discussed in Module 5.7, ATP drives the active transport of solutes across a membrane against their concentration gradient by phosphorylating transport proteins.

▲ **Figure 5.11B** How ATP powers cellular work

Work can be sustained because ATP is a renewable resource that cells regenerate. **Figure 5.11C**, below, shows the ATP cycle. Each side of this cycle illustrates energy coupling. Energy released in exergonic reactions, such as the breakdown of glucose during cellular respiration, is used to regenerate ATP from ADP. In this endergonic (energy-storing) process, a phosphate group is bonded to ADP. The hydrolysis of ATP releases energy that drives endergonic reactions. A cell at work uses ATP continuously, and the ATP cycle runs at an astonishing pace. In fact, a working muscle cell may consume and regenerate 10 million ATP molecules each second.

But even with a constant supply of energy, few metabolic reactions would occur without the assistance of enzymes. We explore these biological catalysts next.

? Explain how ATP transfers energy from exergonic to endergonic processes in the cell.

● Exergonic processes phosphorylate ADP to form ATP. ATP transfers energy to endergonic processes by phosphorylating other molecules.

▲ **Figure 5.11A** The structure and hydrolysis of ATP. The reaction of ATP and water yields ADP, a phosphate group, and energy.

▲ **Figure 5.11C** The ATP cycle

How Enzymes Function

5.12 Enzymes speed up the cell's chemical reactions by lowering energy barriers

Your room gets messier; water flows downhill; sugar crystals dissolve in your coffee. Ordered structures tend toward disorder, and high-energy systems tend to change toward a more stable state of low energy. Proteins, DNA, carbohydrates, lipids—most of the complex molecules of your cells are rich in potential energy. Why don't these high-energy, ordered molecules spontaneously break down into less ordered, lower-energy molecules? They remain intact for the same reason that wood doesn't normally burst into flames and the gas in an automobile's gas tank doesn't spontaneously explode.

There is an energy barrier that must be overcome before a chemical reaction can begin. Energy must be absorbed to contort or weaken bonds in reactant molecules so that they can break and new bonds can form. We call this the **activation energy** (abbreviated E_A for energy of activation). We can think of E_A as the amount of energy needed for reactant molecules to move "uphill" to a higher-energy, unstable state so that the "downhill" part of a reaction can begin.

The energy barrier of E_A protects the highly ordered molecules of your cells from spontaneously breaking down. But now we have a dilemma. Life depends on countless chemical reactions that constantly change a cell's molecular makeup. Most of the essential reactions of metabolism must occur quickly and precisely for a cell to survive. How can the specific reactions that a cell requires get over that energy barrier?

One way to speed reactions is to add heat. Heat speeds up molecules and agitates atoms so that bonds break more easily and reactions can proceed. Certainly, adding a match to kindling will start a fire, and the firing of a spark plug ignites gasoline in an engine. But heating a cell would speed up all chemical reactions, not just the necessary ones, and too much heat would kill the cell.

The answer to our dilemma lies in **enzymes**—molecules that function as biological catalysts, increasing the rate of a reaction without being consumed by the reaction. Almost all enzymes are proteins, although some RNA molecules can also function as enzymes. An enzyme speeds up a reaction by lowering the E_A needed for a reaction to begin. **Figure 5.12** compares a reaction without (left) and with (right) an enzyme. Notice how much easier it is for the reactant to get over the activation energy barrier when an enzyme is involved. In the next module, we explore how the structure of an enzyme enables it to lower the activation energy, allowing a reaction to proceed.

 The graph below illustrates the course of a reaction with and without an enzyme. Which curve represents the enzyme-catalyzed reaction? What energy changes are represented by the lines labelled a, b, and c?

● The red (lower) curve is the enzyme-catalyzed reaction. Line a is E_A without enzyme; b is E_A with enzyme; and c is the change in energy between reactants and products, which is the same for both the catalyzed and uncatalyzed reactions.

▲ **Figure 5.12** The effect of an enzyme in lowering E_A

5.13 A specific enzyme catalyzes each cellular reaction

You just learned that an enzyme catalyzes a reaction by lowering the E_A barrier. How does it do that? With the aid of an enzyme, the bonds in a reactant are contorted into the higher-energy, unstable state from which the reaction can proceed. Without an enzyme, the energy of activation might never be reached. For example, a solution of sucrose (table sugar) can sit for years at room temperature with no appreciable hydrolysis into its components glucose and fructose. But if we add a small amount of an enzyme to the solution, all the sucrose will be hydrolyzed within seconds.

An enzyme is very selective in the reaction it catalyzes. As a protein, an enzyme has a unique three-dimensional shape, and that shape determines, in part, the enzyme's specificity. The specific reactant that an enzyme acts on is called the enzyme's **substrate**. A substrate fits into a region of the enzyme called an **active site**. An active site is typically a pocket or groove on the surface of the enzyme formed by only a few of the enzyme's amino acids. The rest of the protein maintains the shape of the active site. Enzymes are specific because their active sites fit only specific substrate molecules.

The properties of the amino acid R groups (see Module 3.8) within the active site also contribute to enzyme specificity (see Appendix B). For example, negatively charged R groups would attract positively charged substrates and repel negatively charged molecules. In addition to these ionic interactions between an enzyme and its substrate, hydrogen bonds can also form between specific R groups in the active site and the substrate.

The Catalytic Cycle   **Figure 5.13A** illustrates the catalytic cycle of an enzyme. Our example is the enzyme sucrase, which catalyzes the hydrolysis of sucrose to glucose and fructose. (Most enzymes have names that end in -ase, and many are named for their substrate.) ❶ The enzyme starts with an empty active site. ❷ Sucrose enters the active site, attaching by hydrogen bonds. The active site changes shape slightly, embracing the substrate more snugly, like a firm handshake. This **induced fit** may contort substrate bonds or place R groups of the amino acids making up the active site in position to catalyze the reaction. (In reactions involving two or more reactants, the active site holds the substrates in the proper orientation for a reaction to occur.) ❸ The strained bond of sucrose reacts with water, and the substrate is converted (hydrolyzed) to the products glucose and fructose. ❹ The enzyme releases the products and emerges unchanged from the reaction. Its active site is now available for another substrate molecule, and another round of the cycle can begin. It is important to note that a single enzyme molecule may act on thousands or even millions of substrate molecules per second.

Optimal Conditions for Enzymes   As with all proteins, an enzyme's shape is central to its function, and this three-dimensional shape is affected by the environment. For every enzyme, there are optimal conditions under which it is most effective, for example, temperature as shown in **Figure 5.13B**. Temperature, affects molecular motion, and an enzyme's optimal temperature produces the highest rate of contact between reactant molecules and the enzyme's active site. Higher temperatures denature the enzyme, altering its specific shape and destroying its function. Most human enzymes work best at 35–40°C, close to our normal body temperature of 37°C (Figure 5.13B). Thermophilic (*heat-loving*) bacteria that live in hot springs, however, contain enzymes with optimal temperatures of 77°C or higher. You will learn in Module 12.12 how the enzymes of these bacteria are used in a technique that rapidly replicates DNA sequences from small samples.

The optimal pH for most enzymes is near neutrality, in the range of 6–8. There are exceptions, however. Pepsin, a digestive enzyme in the stomach, works best at pH 2. Such an environment would denature most enzymes, but the structure of

❶ Enzyme available with empty active site

Active site

Enzyme (sucrase)

Glucose

Fructose

❹ Products are released

Substrate (sucrose)

❷ Substrate binds to enzyme with induced fit

H_2O

❸ Substrate is converted to products

▲ **Figure 5.13A** The catalytic cycle of an enzyme

▲ **Figure 5.13B** Optimal temperatures for two enzymes

pepsin is most stable and active in the acidic environment of the stomach.

Cofactors Many enzymes require nonprotein helpers called **cofactors**, which bind to the active site and function in catalysis. The cofactors of some enzymes are inorganic, such as the ions of zinc, iron, and copper. If the cofactor is an organic molecule, it is called a **coenzyme**. Most vitamins are important in nutrition because they function as coenzymes or raw materials from which coenzymes are made. For example, folic acid is a coenzyme for a number of enzymes involved in the synthesis of nucleic acids. And in Chapter 6, you will learn about the roles of riboflavin and niacin as coenzymes of important enzymes involved in cellular respiration.

Chemical chaos would result if all of a cell's metabolic pathways were operating simultaneously. A cell must tightly control when and where its various enzymes are active. It does this either by switching on or off the genes that encode specific enzymes (as you will learn in Chapter 11) or by regulating the activity of enzymes once they are made. We explore this second mechanism in the next module.

? Explain how an enzyme speeds up a specific reaction.

● An enzyme lowers the activation energy needed for a reaction when its specific substrate enters its active site. With an induced fit, the enzyme strains bonds that need to break or positions substrates in an orientation that aids the conversion of reactants to products.

5.14 Enzyme inhibitors can regulate enzyme activity in a cell

A chemical that interferes with an enzyme's activity is called an inhibitor. Scientists have learned a great deal about enzyme function by studying the effects of these chemicals. Dr. Albert Berghuis at McGill University in Montreal uses X-ray protein crystallography to obtain three-dimensional images of enzyme active sites in order to develop novel inhibitors as potential drug therapies. Some inhibitors resemble the enzyme's normal substrate and compete for entry into the active site. As shown in the lower left of **Figure 5.14A**, such a **competitive inhibitor** reduces an enzyme's productivity by blocking substrate molecules from entering the active site. Competitive inhibition can be overcome by increasing the concentration of the substrate, making it more likely that a substrate molecule rather than an inhibitor will be nearby when an active site becomes vacant.

In contrast, a **noncompetitive inhibitor** does not enter the active site. Instead, it binds to the enzyme somewhere else, a place called an allosteric site, and its binding changes the shape of the enzyme so that the active site no longer fits the substrate (lower right of Figure 5.14A).

Although enzyme inhibition sounds harmful, cells use inhibitors as important regulators of cellular metabolism. Many of a cell's chemical reactions are organized into metabolic pathways in which a molecule is altered in a series of steps, each catalyzed by a specific enzyme, to form a final product. If a cell is producing more of that product than it needs, the product may act as an inhibitor of one of the enzymes early in the pathway. **Figure 5.14B** illustrates this sort of inhibition, called **feedback inhibition**. Because only weak interactions bind inhibitor and enzyme, this inhibition is reversible. When the product is used up by the cell, the enzyme is no longer inhibited and the pathway functions again.

Certain enzymes in the body are produced in inactive forms called **proenzymes**. For example, pepsin, the enzyme that digests protein in your stomach, is inactive when produced. This prevents pepsin from digesting the proteins of the cells that make it. The pepsin proenzyme is activated only after being exposed to the conditions inside the stomach where it digests dietary proteins.

? Explain an advantage of feedback inhibition to a cell.

● It prevents the cell from wasting valuable resources by synthesizing more of a particular product than is needed.

Normal binding of substrate

Enzyme inhibition

▲ **Figure 5.14A** How inhibitors interfere with substrate binding

▲ **Figure 5.14B** Feedback inhibition of a biosynthetic pathway in which product D acts as an inhibitor of enzyme 1

5.15 Does eating raw vegetables provide valuable enzymes for digestion?

The raw food diet has been around for decades and has gained momentum in recent years. While on this diet, participants are encouraged to eat most of their food uncooked. Proponents claim that some enzymes in plants assist in the digestion of our food and therefore are beneficial to our health. They explain by saying that cooking destroys these digestive enzymes. Is there any truth behind this rumour? Can enzymes in our food actually assist in its digestion?

Raw food is anything that has not been altered by cooking or other processing that involves heat. Cooking at high temperatures also denatures proteins (see Module 5.13). Therefore, the enzymes within the plants we cook are also denatured. It is well known that cooking can destroy organic nutrients in food. For example, simmering turkey liver at 100°C for 20 minutes destroys approximately 70% of its vitamin C. Cooking can also increase nutrient-binding molecules referred to as antinutrients. These molecules reduce the nutritional value of food by preventing the absorption of nutrients that they bind. Despite these numbers, cooking vegetables does offer some health benefits. Cooking tomatoes, for example, actually increases the amounts of the cancer-fighting antioxidant lycopene. Cooking also softens the fibre of plant tissue and allows for the release of more nutrients. Because of improper cleaning, people who eat large amounts of raw vegetables are more likely to get food poisoning. Proper cooking can kill most of bacteria that washing may leave behind and reduces this risk. The important choice is how the vegetables are cooked. Steaming, boiling, and even microwaving vegetables retains much of their original nutritional value, while frying does not.

Our digestive system has evolved to break down our foods very efficiently (see Chapter 26). The digestive enzymes we produce readily break down the macromolecules in our diets, including proteins. Protein digestion begins in our stomachs where the acid environment denatures them and enzymes start cleaving their peptide bonds. There is little evidence to suggest that plant enzymes escape the natural digestive process within our intestinal tracts. If by chance, some plant enzymes did escape degradation, any digestive gain would be insignificant compared to the efficiency of our own enzymes. Furthermore, if the plant enzymes supposedly aid in digestion after we eat the plant material, what would prevent these enzymes from digesting the plant tissue before we eat it?

Although it is unlikely that plant enzymes aid significantly in digestion, some may offer other health benefits. Many plant molecules, including sulphoraphane, have been identified as cancer-fighting molecules. This organic sulphur-containing molecule can inhibit the growth of antibiotic-resistant bacteria, making their treatment easier. In the laboratory, sulphoraphane kills cancer cells as well as prevents healthy cells from becoming cancerous. Whether this benefit extends to humans eating broccoli remains to be determined.

Sources of sulphoraphane include broccoli, Brussels sprouts, and cabbage (**Figure 5.15**). An enzyme within these plants produces sulphoraphane only after tissue damage. On the one hand, cooking denatures the enzyme and prevents further accumulation of sulphoraphane. On the other hand, if you chew raw broccoli, the enzyme remains active long enough to produce large amounts of sulphoraphane. The enzymes in raw broccoli provide 10 times the amount of this cancer-fighting molecule than the same amount of cooked broccoli. Chopping your broccoli a few minutes before cooking it increases the time in which sulphoraphane production can take place and the subsequent health benefit also increases.

A diet filled with vegetables has proven health benefits. However, to claim that raw vegetables are better for you than cooked vegetables may be an oversimplification. Certainly some vitamins may be destroyed, but the other benefits of properly cooked vegetables likely outweigh this. It is also unlikely that any digestive enzymes within raw vegetables help digestion to any significant degree. Thus, this rumour is unfounded.

 Why is eating raw broccoli healthier than eating cooked broccoli?

● The enzyme that produces sulphoraphane remains active longer in raw broccoli, producing more of this cancer-fighting molecule.

▲ **Figure 5.15** Raw vegetables with health promoting enzymes

5.16 Many drugs, pesticides, and poisons are enzyme inhibitors

Many beneficial drugs act as enzyme inhibitors. Ibuprofen (Figure 5.16) is a common drug that inhibits an enzyme involved in the production of prostaglandins—messenger molecules that increase the sensation of pain and inflammation. Other drugs that function as enzyme inhibitors include some blood pressure medicines and antidepressants. Many antibiotics work by inhibiting enzymes of disease-causing bacteria. Penicillin, for example, blocks the active site of an enzyme that many bacteria use in making cell walls. Protease inhibitors are HIV drugs that target a key viral enzyme. And many cancer drugs are inhibitors of enzymes that promote cell division.

▲ **Figure 5.16** Ibuprofen, an enzyme inhibitor

Humans have developed enzyme inhibitors as pesticides, and occasionally as deadly poisons for use in warfare. Poisons often attach to an enzyme by covalent bonds, making the inhibition irreversible. Poisons called nerve gases bind in the active site of an enzyme vital to the transmission of nerve impulses. The inhibition of this enzyme leads to rapid paralysis of vital functions and death. Pesticides such as malathion and parathion are toxic to insects (and dangerous to the people who apply them) because they also irreversibly inhibit this enzyme. Interestingly, some drugs reversibly inhibit this same enzyme and are used in anaesthesia and the treatment of certain diseases.

 What determines whether enzyme inhibition is reversible or irreversible?

● If the inhibitor binds to the enzyme with covalent bonds, the inhibition is usually irreversible. When weak chemical interactions bind the inhibitor and the enzyme, the inhibition is reversible.

R E V I E W

MasteringBiology® **For Practice Quizzes, BioFlix, MP3 Tutors, and Activities, go to masteringbiology.com.**

Reviewing the Concepts

Membrane Structure and Function (5.1–5.8)

5.1 Membranes are fluid mosaics of lipids and proteins with many functions. The proteins embedded in a membrane's phospholipid bilayer perform various functions.

5.2 Membranes form spontaneously, a critical step in the origin of life. The chemical properties of phospholipids allow them to self-assemble into lipid bilayers.

5.3 Passive transport is diffusion across a membrane with no energy investment. Solutes diffuse across membranes down their concentration gradients.

5.4 Osmosis is the diffusion of water across a membrane. When solutes cannot diffuse across a membrane, water molecules will move by osmosis instead.

5.5 Water balance between cells and their surroundings is crucial to organisms. Cells shrink in a hypertonic solution and swell in a hypotonic solution. In isotonic solutions, animal cells are normal, but plant cells are flaccid.

5.6 Transport proteins can facilitate diffusion across membranes. Solutes can cross a membrane through specific channels in facilitated diffusion. Aquaporins are water channels in cells with high water transport needs.

5.7 Cells expend energy in the active transport of a solute.

5.8 Exocytosis and endocytosis transport large molecules across membranes. A vesicle may fuse with the membrane and expel its contents (exocytosis), or the membrane may fold inward, enclosing material from the outside (endocytosis).

Energy and the Cell (5.9–5.11)

5.9 Cells transform energy as they perform work. Kinetic energy is the energy of motion. Potential energy is energy stored in the location or structure of matter. Chemical energy is potential energy available for release in a chemical reaction. According to the laws of thermodynamics, energy can change form but cannot be created or destroyed, and energy transformations increase disorder, or entropy, with some energy being lost as heat.

5.10 Chemical reactions either release or store energy. Exergonic reactions release energy. Endergonic reactions require energy and yield products rich in potential energy. Metabolism encompasses all of a cell's chemical reactions.

5.11 ATP drives cellular work by coupling exergonic and endergonic reactions. The transfer of a phosphate group from ATP is involved in chemical, mechanical, and transport work.

ATP cycle

ATP

Energy from exergonic reactions

ADP + P

Energy for endergonic reactions

How Enzymes Function (5.12–5.16)

5.12 Enzymes speed up the cell's chemical reactions by lowering energy barriers. Enzymes are protein catalysts that decrease the activation energy (E_A) needed to begin a reaction.

5.13 A specific enzyme catalyzes each cellular reaction. An enzyme's substrate binds specifically to its active site.

5.14 Enzyme inhibitors can regulate enzyme activity in a cell. A competitive inhibitor competes with the substrate for the active site. A noncompetitive inhibitor alters an enzyme's function by changing its shape. Feedback inhibition helps to regulate metabolism.

5.15 Does eating raw vegetables provide valuable enzymes for digestion? Some plant enzymes produce beneficial products, but it is unlikely that they aid digestion.

5.16 Many drugs, pesticides, and poisons are enzyme inhibitors. Enzymes are common targets for pharmaceutical agents.

Connecting the Concepts

1. Fill in the following concept map to review the processes by which molecules move across membranes.

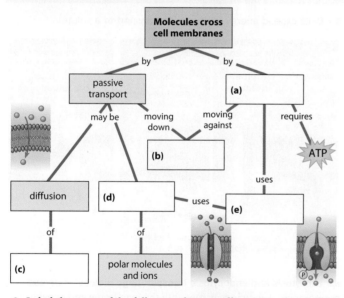

Molecules cross cell membranes

by — passive transport

by — (a)

may be — moving down

moving against — (b)

requires

ATP

diffusion

(d)

uses

uses — (e)

of — (c)

of — polar molecules and ions

2. Label the parts of the following diagram illustrating the catalytic cycle of an enzyme.

a. _____
b. _____
c. _____
d. _____
e. _____
f. _____

Testing Your Knowledge

Multiple Choice

3. Which best describes the structure of a cell membrane?
   a. proteins between two bilayers of phospholipids
   b. proteins embedded in a bilayer of phospholipids
   c. a bilayer of protein coating a layer of phospholipids
   d. phospholipids between two layers of protein
   e. cholesterol embedded in a bilayer of phospholipids

4. Consider the following: chemical bonds in the gasoline in a car's gas tank and the movement of the car along the road; a biker at the top of a hill and the ride he took to get there. The first parts of these situations illustrate _____, and the second parts illustrate _____.
   a. the first law of thermodynamics; the second law
   b. kinetic energy; potential energy
   c. an exergonic reaction; an endergonic reaction
   d. potential energy; kinetic energy
   e. the second law of thermodynamics; the first law

5. A plant cell placed in distilled water will _____; an animal cell placed in distilled water will _____.
   a. burst; burst
   b. become flaccid; shrivel
   c. become flaccid; be normal in shape
   d. become turgid; be normal in shape
   e. become turgid; burst

6. The sodium concentration in a cell is 10 times less than the concentration in the surrounding fluid. How can the cell move sodium out of the cell? (*Explain your answer.*)
   a. passive transport   b. diffusion
   c. active transport   d. osmosis
   e. any of these processes

7. The synthesis of ATP from ADP and P
   a. is an exergonic process.
   b. involves the hydrolysis of a phosphate bond.
   c. transfers a phosphate, priming a protein to do work.
   d. stores energy in a form that can drive cellular work.
   e. releases energy.

8. Facilitated diffusion across a membrane requires _____ and moves a solute _____ its concentration gradient.
   a. transport proteins; up (against)
   b. transport proteins; down
   c. energy; up
   d. energy and transport proteins; up
   e. energy and transport proteins; down

9. Which of the following statements comparing an uncatalyzed reaction to the same reaction with an enzyme catalyst is *true*?
   a. The catalyzed reaction will be slower.
   b. The catalyzed reaction will produce different products.
   c. The catalyzed reaction will have a different amount of energy between products and reactants.
   d. The catalyzed reaction will have lower activation energy.
   e. The catalyzed reaction will require more heat for the reaction to occur.

10. Proenzymes are
    a. substances that increase the activity of an enzyme.
    b. an inactive form of enzymes.
    c. compounds that bind to and inhibit the function of enzymes.
    d. inorganic cofactors that bind to enzymes to activate them.
    e. organic cofactors that bind to enzymes to activate them.

Describing, Comparing, and Explaining

11. What are aquaporins? Where would you expect to find them?

12. How do the two laws of thermodynamics apply to living organisms?

13. What are the main types of cellular work? How does ATP provide the energy for this work?

14. Why is the barrier of the activation energy beneficial for organic molecules? Explain how enzymes lower E_A.

15. How do the components and structure of cell membranes relate to the functions of membranes?

16. Sometimes inhibitors can be harmful to a cell; often they are beneficial. Explain.

Applying the Concepts

17. Explain how each of the following food preservation methods would interfere with a microbe's enzyme activity and ability to break down food: canning (heating), freezing, pickling (soaking in acetic acid), and salting.

18. A biologist performed two series of experiments on lactase, the enzyme that hydrolyzes lactose to glucose and galactose. First, she made up 10% lactose solutions containing different concentrations of enzyme and measured the rate at which galactose was produced (grams of galactose per minute). Results of these experiments are shown in Table A below. In the second series of experiments (Table B), she prepared 2% enzyme solutions containing different concentrations of lactose and again measured the rate of galactose production.

Table A Rate and Enzyme Concentration

Lactose concentration	10%	10%	10%	10%	10%
Enzyme concentration	0%	1%	2%	4%	8%
Reaction rate	0	25	50	100	200

Table B Rate and Substrate Concentration

Lactose concentration	0%	5%	10%	20%	30%
Enzyme concentration	2%	2%	2%	2%	2%
Reaction rate	0	25	50	65	65

a. Graph and explain the relationship between the reaction rate and the enzyme concentration.

b. Graph and explain the relationship between the reaction rate and the substrate concentration. How and why did the results of the two experiments differ?

19. The following graph shows the rate of reaction for two different enzymes: One is pepsin, a digestive enzyme found in the stomach; the other is trypsin, a digestive enzyme found in the intestine. As you may know, gastric juice in the stomach contains hydrochloric acid. Which curve belongs to which enzyme?

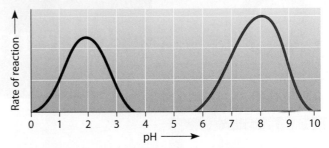

A lysosome, a digestive organelle in a cell, has an internal pH of around 4.5. Draw a curve on the graph that you would predict for a lysosomal enzyme, labelling its optimal pH.

20. Organophosphates (organic compounds containing phosphate groups) are commonly used as insecticides to improve crop yield. Organophosphates typically interfere with nerve signal transmission by inhibiting the enzymes that degrade transmitter molecules. They affect humans and other vertebrates as well as insects. Thus, on the one hand, the use of organophosphate pesticides poses some health risks. On the other hand, these molecules break down rapidly upon exposure to air and sunlight. As a consumer, what level of risk are you willing to accept in exchange for an abundant and affordable food supply?

Answers to all questions can be found in Appendix E.

How Cells Harvest Chemical Energy

BIG IDEAS

Cellular Respiration: Aerobic Harvesting of Energy

(6.1–6.5)

Glycolysis is a universal pathway of living organisms and the first step in obtaining energy from glucose.

Stages of Cellular Respiration

(6.6–6.12)

Cellular respiration, involving the citric acid cycle and oxidative phosphorylation, oxidizes fuel molecules and generates ATP for cellular work.

Fermentation: Anaerobic Harvesting of Energy

(6.13–6.14)

Fermentation regenerates NAD^+, allowing glycolysis and ATP production to continue without oxygen.

Connections Between Metabolic Pathways

(6.15–6.17)

The breakdown pathways of cellular respiration intersect with biosynthetic pathways.

Biotechnology by Ancient Humans

Ancient humans were nomadic, moving from place to place, hunting and gathering food as they went. It was necessary to kill and gather only enough food to be eaten within a few days. Food spoiled quickly, making it risky to store it for more than a couple days before consuming it. The constant need to travel to where food was readily accessible prevented humans from settling down. But sometime between 10 000 and 15 000 years ago, ancient humans began to transition from the hunter-gatherer lifestyle to a more stationary agricultural existence. What happened that allowed for this fundamental shift in lifestyle?

The change, believe it or not, largely occurred because of biotechnology. Of course, the first agricultural peoples did not call it that. Biotechnology is generally defined as the application of living organisms and biological processes in any technology, such as manufacturing. Today, the term is heavily used in industries such as pharmaceuticals, genetic engineering, and even bioremediation. Ten thousand years ago, however, biotechnology meant one thing—fermentation. Anthropological evidence shows that wine and beer have been made for more than 8000 years. Large clay pots called *qvevri*, similar to those shown in the photograph, have been used to brew wine for millennia. Also, the smaller photograph is of an ancient Egyptian sculpture depicting beer making. Some anthropologists claim that the first cultivated grains were used for beer production, rather than consumption.

As you will learn in this chapter, fermentation is an anaerobic metabolic process (i.e., one that occurs in the absence of oxygen) that utilizes the products of the energy-yielding process called glycolysis. Bacteria and yeast, which can grow without O_2, have been commonly used in the fermentation of food products for millennia. The end products of fermentation vary depending on the organisms and the food involved but are typically organic acids (such as vinegar) and/or ethanol and CO_2.

Fermentation was likely discovered by accident. You are probably aware that fruit sitting on a counter, untouched for a week or two starts to rot. Under such conditions, food quickly spoils as it becomes contaminated with bacteria and fungi, which consume all of the food's valuable nutrients. However, when the early agriculturalists stored foods in enclosed containers, O_2 may have been excluded and fermentation, rather than spoiling, would have occurred. The fermentation process was found to preserve food for longer. This meant ancient humans did not have to move as much in search of food.

But how does fermentation preserve food? Under anaerobic conditions, organisms that require O_2 cannot grow, preventing them from spoiling the food. Furthermore, the acids or ethanol produced during fermentation accumulate to levels that become toxic for most microorganisms. Growth of microorganisms—including the fermenting bacteria or yeast within the fermented product—is inhibited, extending the shelf life of the food for a period of time. By using the biotechnology of microorganisms and fermentation reactions to preserve food, ancient humans were able to start living a more stationary life, an important first step in the civilization of *Homo sapiens*.

In this chapter, we will discuss other common uses of fermentation in the food industries. But first, we'll present some basic concepts about cellular respiration and then focus on the key stages of the process: glycolysis, the citric acid cycle, and oxidative phosphorylation. We'll also consider fermentation, an extended version of glycolysis that has deep evolutionary roots. We complete the chapter with a look at how the metabolic pathways that break down organic molecules connect to those that build such molecules. But first let's take a step back and consider the original source of the energy for most cellular work on Earth today.

Cellular Respiration: Aerobic Harvesting of Energy

6.1 Photosynthesis and cellular respiration provide energy for life

Life requires energy. In almost all ecosystems, that energy ultimately comes from the sun. Photosynthesis, the process by which the sun's energy is captured, is the topic of Chapter 7. But a brief overview here of the relationship between photosynthesis and cellular respiration will illustrate how these two processes provide energy for life (**Figure 6.1**). In photosynthesis, which takes place in a plant cell's chloroplasts, the energy of sunlight is used to rearrange the atoms of carbon dioxide (CO_2) and water (H_2O) to produce glucose and oxygen (O_2). The spirit bear in Figure 6.1 obtains energy for its daily activities by feeding on salmon and fruit. In **cellular respiration**, O_2 is consumed as glucose is broken down to CO_2 and H_2O; the cell captures the energy released in ATP. Cellular respiration takes place in the mitochondria of almost all eukaryotic cells.

This figure also shows that in these energy conversions, some energy is lost as heat. Life on Earth is solar powered, and energy makes a one-way trip through an ecosystem. Chemicals, however, are recycled. The CO_2 and H_2O released by cellular respiration are converted through photosynthesis to glucose and O_2, which are then used in respiration.

? What is misleading about the following statement? "Plant cells perform photosynthesis, and animal cells perform cellular respiration."

● The statement implies that cellular respiration does not occur in plant cells. In fact, almost all eukaryotic cells use cellular respiration to obtain energy for their cellular work.

▲ **Figure 6.1** The connection between photosynthesis and cellular respiration

6.2 Breathing supplies O_2 for use in cellular respiration and removes CO_2

We often use the word *respiration* as a synonym for "breathing," the meaning of its Latin root. In that sense of the word, respiration refers to an exchange of gases: An animal obtains O_2 from its environment and releases CO_2 as a waste product. You will learn more about gas exchange in Chapter 27. Biologists also define respiration as the aerobic (oxygen-requiring) harvesting of energy from food molecules by cells. This process is called cellular respiration to distinguish it from breathing.

Breathing and cellular respiration are closely related and it is important not to confuse them. As the soccer player in **Figure 6.2** breathes in air, her lungs take up O_2 and pass it to her bloodstream. The bloodstream carries the O_2 to her muscle cells. Mitochondria in the muscle cells use the O_2 in cellular respiration to harvest energy from glucose and other organic molecules and to generate ATP. Muscle cells use ATP to contract. The soccer player's bloodstream and lungs also perform the vital function of disposing of the CO_2 waste, which, as you can see by the equation at the bottom of the figure, is produced in cellular respiration.

? How is your breathing related to your cellular respiration?

● In breathing, CO_2 and O_2 are exchanged between your lungs and the air. In cellular respiration, cells use the O_2 obtained through breathing to break down fuel, releasing CO_2 as a waste product.

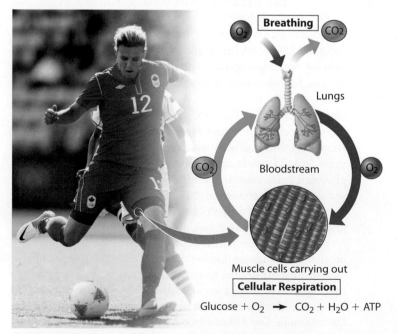

$$Glucose + O_2 \rightarrow CO_2 + H_2O + ATP$$

▲ **Figure 6.2** The connection between breathing and cellular respiration in an animal

6.3 Cellular respiration banks energy in ATP molecules

As the athlete example in Figure 6.2 implies, oxygen usage is only a means to an end. Generating ATP for cellular work is the fundamental function of cellular respiration.

The balanced chemical equation in **Figure 6.3** summarizes cellular respiration as carried out by cells that use O_2 in harvesting energy from glucose. The simple sugar glucose ($C_6H_{12}O_6$) is the fuel that cells use most often, although other organic molecules can also be "burned" in cellular respiration. The equation tells us that the atoms of the reactant molecules $C_6H_{12}O_6$ and O_2 are rearranged to form the products CO_2 and H_2O. In this exergonic process, the chemical energy of the bonds in glucose is released and stored (or "banked") in the chemical bonds of ATP (see Modules 5.9 to 5.11). The series of arrows in Figure 6.3 indicates that cellular respiration consists of many steps, not just a single reaction.

Cellular respiration can produce up to 32 ATP molecules for each glucose molecule, a capture of about 34% of the energy originally stored in glucose. The rest of the energy is released as heat (see Module 5.9). This may seem inefficient,

▲ **Figure 6.3** Summary equation for cellular respiration:
$C_6H_{12}O_6 + 6\ O_2 \rightarrow 6\ CO_2 + 6\ H_2O + $ Energy (ATP + Heat)

but it compares very well with the efficiency of most energy-conversion systems. For instance, the average automobile engine is able to convert only about 25% of the energy in gasoline to the kinetic energy of movement.

How great are the energy needs of a cell? If ATP could not be regenerated through cellular respiration, you would use up nearly your body weight in ATP each day. Let's consider the energy requirements for various human activities next.

 Why are sweating and other body-cooling mechanisms necessary during vigorous exercise?

● The demand for ATP is supported by an increased rate of cellular respiration, but about 66% of the energy from food produces heat instead of ATP.

EVERYDAY BIOLOGY ## 6.4 The human body uses energy from ATP for all its activities

Your body requires a continuous supply of energy just to stay alive—to keep the heart pumping, breathe, and maintain body temperature. Your brain requires a huge amount of energy; its cells burn about 120 grams (g)—about half of a cup—of glucose a day, accounting for about 15% of total oxygen consumption. Maintaining brain cells and other life-sustaining activities uses as much as 75% of the energy a person takes in as food during a typical day.

Above and beyond the energy you need for body maintenance, cellular respiration provides energy for voluntary activities. **Figure 6.4** shows the amount of energy it takes to perform some of these activities. The energy units are **kilocalories (kcal)**, the quantity of heat required to raise the temperature of 1 kilogram (kg) of water by 1°C. (The "Calories" listed on food packages are actually kilocalories, usually signified by a capital *C*.) The values shown do not include the energy the body consumes for its basic life-sustaining activities. Even sleeping or lying quietly requires energy for metabolism.

Canada's Food Guide estimates that the average adult (ages 19–30) needs to take in food that provides about 2700 kcal of energy per day for men and about 2100 kcal per day for women. This includes the energy expended in both maintenance and voluntary activity. We will explore nutritional needs (and the maintenance of a healthy weight) in Chapter 26. But now we begin the study of how cells liberate the energy stored in fuel molecules to produce the ATP used to power the work of cells and thus the activities of the body.

Activity	kcal consumed per hour by a 67.5–kg (150–lb) person*
Running (13–14 km/h)	979
Dancing (fast)	510
Bicycling (16 km/h)	490
Swimming (3.2 km/h)	408
Walking (6.4 km/h)	341
Walking (4.8 km/h)	245
Dancing (slow)	204
Driving a car	61
Sitting (writing)	28

*Not including kcal needed for body maintenance

▲ **Figure 6.4** Energy consumed by various activities

 Walking at 4.8 kilometres per hour (km/h), how far would you have to travel to "burn off" the equivalent of an extra slice of pizza, which has about 475 kcal? How long would that take?

● You would have to walk about 9.3 km, which would take you about 2 hours. (Now you understand why the most effective exercise for losing weight is pushing away from the table!)

6.5 Cells tap energy from electrons "falling" from organic fuels to oxygen

How do your cells extract energy from glucose? The answer involves the transfer of electrons during chemical reactions.

Redox Reactions   During cellular respiration, electrons are transferred from glucose to oxygen, releasing energy. Oxygen attracts electrons very strongly, and an electron loses potential energy when it "falls" to oxygen. If you burn a cube of sugar, this electron fall happens very rapidly, releasing energy in the form of heat and light. Cellular respiration is a more controlled descent of electrons—more like stepping down an energy staircase, with energy released in small amounts that can be stored in the chemical bonds of ATP.

The movement of electrons from one molecule to another is an oxidation-reduction reaction, or **redox reaction** for short. In a redox reaction, the loss of electrons from one substance is called **oxidation**, and the addition of electrons to another substance is called **reduction**. A molecule is said to become oxidized when it loses one or more electrons and reduced when it gains one or more electrons. Because an electron transfer requires both a donor and an acceptor, oxidation and reduction always go together.

In the cellular respiration equation in **Figure 6.5A**, you cannot see any electron transfers. What you do see are changes in the location of hydrogen atoms. These hydrogen movements represent electron transfers because each hydrogen atom consists of an electron (e^-) and a proton (hydrogen ion, or H^+). Glucose ($C_6H_{12}O_6$) loses hydrogen atoms (electrons) as it becomes oxidized to CO_2; simultaneously, O_2 gains hydrogen atoms (electrons) as it becomes reduced to H_2O. As they pass from glucose to oxygen, the electrons lose potential energy.

NADH and Electron Transport Chains   An important player in the process of oxidizing glucose is a coenzyme called **NAD⁺**, which accepts electrons and becomes reduced to NADH. NAD^+ (nicotinamide adenine dinucleotide) is an organic molecule that cells make from the vitamin niacin and use to shuttle electrons in redox reactions. The top equation in **Figure 6.5B** depicts the oxidation of an organic molecule. We show only its three carbons (⚫) and a few of its other atoms. An enzyme called dehydrogenase strips two hydrogen atoms from this molecule. Simultaneously, as shown in the lower equation, NAD^+ picks up the two electrons (⊖) and becomes reduced to NADH. One hydrogen ion (H⁺) is released. (NADH is represented throughout this chapter as a light brown box carrying two blue electrons.)

▲ **Figure 6.5B** A pair of redox reactions occurring simultaneously

Using the energy staircase analogy for electrons falling from glucose to oxygen, the transfer of electrons from an organic molecule to NAD^+ represents the first step. **Figure 6.5C** shows NADH delivering these electrons to the rest of the staircase—an **electron transport chain**. The steps in the chain are electron carrier molecules, shown here as purple ovals, built into the inner membrane of a mitochondrion. At the bottom of the staircase is O_2, the final electron acceptor.

The electron transport chain undergoes a series of redox reactions in which electrons pass from carrier to carrier down to oxygen. The redox steps in the staircase release energy stored as a chemical gradient that powers the synthesis of ATP.

With an understanding of this basic mechanism of electron transfer and energy release, we can now explore cellular respiration in more detail.

? **What chemical characteristic of the element oxygen accounts for its function in cellular respiration?**

● Oxygen is very electronegative (see Module 2.6), making it very powerful in pulling electrons down the electron transport chain.

▲ **Figure 6.5C** In cellular respiration, electrons fall down an energy staircase and finally reduce O_2

Loss of hydrogen atoms (becomes oxidized)

Gain of hydrogen atoms (becomes reduced)

Glucose   + Heat

▲ **Figure 6.5A** Rearrangement of hydrogen atoms (with their electrons) in the redox reactions of cellular respiration

Stages of Cellular Respiration

6.6 Overview: Cellular respiration occurs in three main stages

Cellular respiration consists of a sequence of steps that can be divided into three main stages. **Figure 6.6** gives an overview of the three stages and shows where they occur in a eukaryotic cell. (In prokaryotic cells that use aerobic respiration, these steps occur in the cytoplasm, and the electron transport chain is built into the plasma membrane.)

Stage 1: Glycolysis (shown with an aqua background throughout this chapter) occurs in the cytoplasmic fluid of the cell. Glycolysis begins cellular respiration by breaking glucose into two molecules of a three-carbon compound called pyruvate.

Stage 2: Pyruvate oxidation and the citric acid cycle (shown in a salmon colour) take place within the mitochondria. Pyruvate is oxidized to a two-carbon compound. The citric acid cycle then completes the breakdown of glucose to carbon dioxide. As suggested by the smaller ATP symbols in the diagram, the cell makes a small amount of ATP during glycolysis and the citric acid cycle. The main function of these first two stages, however, is to supply the third stage of respiration with electrons (shown with gold arrows).

Stage 3: Oxidative phosphorylation (purple background) requires an electron transport chain and a process known as chemiosmosis. NADH and a related electron carrier, $FADH_2$ (flavin adenine dinucleotide), shuttle electrons to an electron transport chain embedded in the inner mitochondrial membrane. Most of the ATP produced by cellular respiration is generated by oxidative phosphorylation, which uses the energy released by the downhill fall of electrons from NADH and $FADH_2$ to O_2 to phosphorylate ADP.

(Recall from Module 5.11 that cells generate ATP by adding a phosphate group to ADP.)

What couples the electron transport chain to ATP synthesis? As the electron transport chain passes electrons down the energy staircase, it also pumps hydrogen ions (H^+) across the inner mitochondrial membrane into the narrow intermembrane space (see Figure 4.13). The result is a concentration gradient of H^+ across the membrane. In **chemiosmosis**, the potential energy of this concentration gradient is used to make ATP. The details of this process are explored in Module 6.10. In 1978, British biochemist Peter Mitchell was awarded the Nobel Prize for developing the theory of chemiosmosis.

The small amount of ATP produced in glycolysis and the citric acid cycle is made by substrate-level phosphorylation, a process we discuss in the next module. In the next several modules, we look more closely at the three stages of cellular respiration and the two mechanisms of ATP synthesis.

? Of the three main stages of cellular respiration represented in Figure 6.6, which one uses oxygen to extract chemical energy from organic compounds?

● Oxidative phosphorylation, using the electron transport chain, which eventually transfers electrons to oxygen

CYTOPLASM

NADH

Electrons carried by NADH

NADH + $FADH_2$

Glycolysis

Glucose ⟹ Pyruvate

Pyruvate Oxidation

Citric Acid Cycle

Oxidative Phosphorylation (electron transport and chemiosmosis)

Mitochondrion

ATP — Substrate-level phosphorylation

ATP — Substrate-level phosphorylation

ATP — Oxidative phosphorylation

◀ **Figure 6.6** An overview of cellular respiration

6.7 Glycolysis harvests chemical energy by oxidizing glucose to pyruvate

Now that you have been introduced to the major players and processes, it's time to focus on the individual stages of cellular respiration. The term for the first stage, *glycolysis*, means "splitting of sugar" (*glyco*, sweet, and *lysis*, split), and that's exactly what happens during this phase.

Figure 6.7A below gives an overview of glycolysis in terms of input and output. Glycolysis begins with a single molecule of glucose and concludes with two molecules of pyruvate. (Pyruvate is the ionized form of pyruvic acid.) The grey balls represent the carbon atoms in each molecule; glucose has six carbons, and these same six carbons end up in the two molecules of pyruvate (three carbons in each). The straight arrow from glucose to pyruvate actually represents nine chemical steps, each catalyzed by its own enzyme. As these reactions occur, two molecules of NAD^+ are reduced to two molecules of NADH, and a net gain of two molecules of ATP is produced.

Figure 6.7B illustrates how ATP is formed in glycolysis by the process called **substrate-level phosphorylation**. In this process, an enzyme transfers a phosphate group from a substrate molecule directly to ADP, forming ATP. You will meet substrate-level phosphorylation again in the citric acid cycle, where a small amount of ATP is generated by this process.

The energy extracted from glucose during glycolysis is banked in a combination of ATP and NADH. The cell can use the energy in ATP immediately, but for it to use the energy in NADH, electrons from NADH must pass down an electron transport chain located in the inner mitochondrial membrane. And the pyruvate molecules still hold most of the energy of glucose; these molecules will be oxidized in the citric acid cycle.

Let's take a closer look at glycolysis. **Figure 6.7C**, on the next page, shows all the organic compounds that form in the nine chemical reactions of glycolysis. Commentary on the left highlights the main features of these reactions. The grey balls

▲ **Figure 6.7B** Substrate-level phosphorylation: transfer of a phosphate group ⓟ from a substrate to ADP, producing ATP

represent the carbon atoms in each of the compounds named on the right side of the figure.

The compounds that form between the initial reactant, glucose, and the final product, pyruvate, are known as **intermediates**. Glycolysis is an example of a *metabolic pathway*, in which each chemical step leads to the next one. For instance, the intermediate glucose 6-phosphate is the product of step 1 and the reactant for step 2. Similarly, fructose 6-phosphate is the product of step 2 and the reactant for step 3. Also essential are the specific enzymes that catalyze each chemical step; however, to help to simplify the figure, we have not included the enzymes.

As indicated in Figure 6.7C, the steps of glycolysis can be grouped into two main phases. Steps ❶–❹, the energy investment phase, actually *consume* energy. In this phase, ATP is used to energize a glucose molecule, which is then split into two small sugars that are now primed to release energy. The figure follows both of these three-carbon sugars through the second phase.

Steps ❺–❾, the energy payoff phase, *yield* energy for the cell. In this phase, two NADH molecules are produced for each initial glucose molecule, and four ATP molecules are generated. Remember that the first phase used two molecules of ATP, so the net gain to the cell is two ATP molecules for each glucose molecule that enters glycolysis.

These two ATP molecules from glycolysis account for only about 6% of the energy that a cell can harvest from a glucose molecule. The two NADH molecules generated during step 5 represent about another 16%, but their stored energy is not available for use in the absence of O_2. Some organisms—yeasts and certain bacteria, for instance—can satisfy their energy needs with the ATP produced by glycolysis alone. And some cells, such as muscle cells, may use this anaerobic production of ATP for short periods. Most cells and organisms, however, have far greater energy demands. The stages of cellular respiration that follow glycolysis release much more energy. In the next modules, we see what happens in most organisms after glycolysis oxidizes glucose to pyruvate.

 For each glucose molecule processed, what are the net molecular products of glycolysis?

▶ **Figure 6.7A** An overview of glycolysis

● Two molecules of pyruvate, two molecules of ATP, and two molecules of NADH

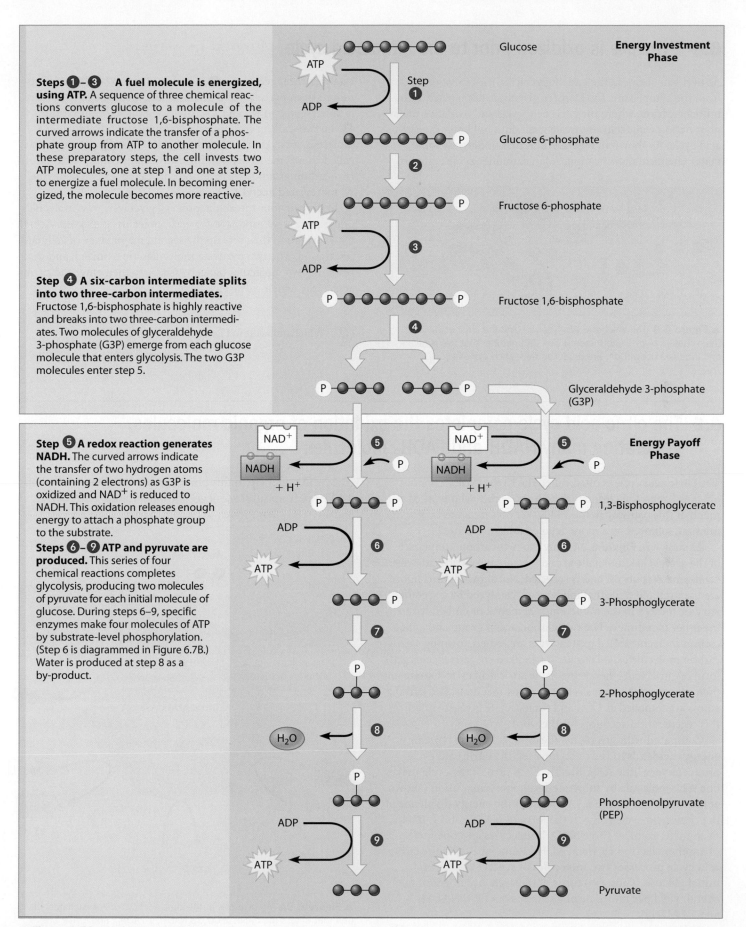

Steps ❶–❸   A fuel molecule is energized, using ATP. A sequence of three chemical reactions converts glucose to a molecule of the intermediate fructose 1,6-bisphosphate. The curved arrows indicate the transfer of a phosphate group from ATP to another molecule. In these preparatory steps, the cell invests two ATP molecules, one at step 1 and one at step 3, to energize a fuel molecule. In becoming energized, the molecule becomes more reactive.

Step ❹ A six-carbon intermediate splits into two three-carbon intermediates. Fructose 1,6-bisphosphate is highly reactive and breaks into two three-carbon intermediates. Two molecules of glyceraldehyde 3-phosphate (G3P) emerge from each glucose molecule that enters glycolysis. The two G3P molecules enter step 5.

Step ❺ A redox reaction generates NADH. The curved arrows indicate the transfer of two hydrogen atoms (containing 2 electrons) as G3P is oxidized and NAD$^+$ is reduced to NADH. This oxidation releases enough energy to attach a phosphate group to the substrate.

Steps ❻–❾ ATP and pyruvate are produced. This series of four chemical reactions completes glycolysis, producing two molecules of pyruvate for each initial molecule of glucose. During steps 6–9, specific enzymes make four molecules of ATP by substrate-level phosphorylation. (Step 6 is diagrammed in Figure 6.7B.) Water is produced at step 8 as a by-product.

Glucose — **Energy Investment Phase**

ATP → ADP, Step ❶

Glucose 6-phosphate

❷

Fructose 6-phosphate

ATP → ADP, ❸

Fructose 1,6-bisphosphate

❹

Glyceraldehyde 3-phosphate (G3P)

NAD$^+$ → NADH + H$^+$, ❺ — **Energy Payoff Phase**

1,3-Bisphosphoglycerate

ADP → ATP, ❻

3-Phosphoglycerate

❼

2-Phosphoglycerate

H$_2$O, ❽

Phosphoenolpyruvate (PEP)

ADP → ATP, ❾

Pyruvate

▲ **Figure 6.7C** Details of glycolysis

6.8 Pyruvate is oxidized prior to the citric acid cycle

As pyruvate forms at the end of glycolysis, it is transported from the cytoplasmic fluid, where glycolysis takes place, into a mitochondrion, where the citric acid cycle and oxidative phosphorylation will occur. Pyruvate itself does not enter the citric acid cycle. As shown in **Figure 6.8**, it first undergoes some major chemical modification. A large, multienzyme complex

catalyzes three reactions: ❶ A carboxyl group (—COO⁻) is removed from pyruvate and given off as a molecule of CO_2 (this is the first step in which CO_2 is released during respiration); ❷ the two-carbon compound remaining is oxidized while a molecule of NAD^+ is reduced to NADH; and ❸ a compound called coenzyme A, derived from a B vitamin, joins with the two-carbon group to form a molecule called acetyl coenzyme A, abbreviated **acetyl CoA**.

In the previous metabolic process, glycolysis, two molecules of pyruvate were produced for each molecule of glucose. Acetyl CoA formation then sets up the second major stage of cellular respiration. The two pyruvate molecules are oxidized, and the resulting two molecules of acetyl CoA can then enter the citric acid cycle, which we discuss next.

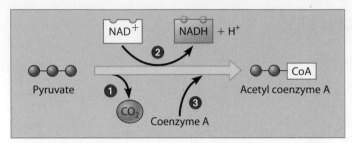

▲ **Figure 6.8** The link between glycolysis and the citric acid cycle: the oxidation of pyruvate to acetyl CoA. (Remember that two pyruvate, and thus two acetyl CoA, are produced from each glucose.)

? Which molecule in Figure 6.8 has been reduced?

● NAD^+ has been reduced to NADH.

6.9 The citric acid cycle completes the oxidation of organic molecules, generating many NADH and FADH₂ molecules

The citric acid cycle is often called the Krebs cycle in honour of Hans Krebs, the German-British researcher who worked out much of this pathway in the 1930s. We present an overview figure first, followed by a more detailed look at this cycle.

As shown in **Figure 6.9A**, only the two-carbon acetyl part of the acetyl CoA molecule actually enters the citric acid cycle; coenzyme A splits off and is recycled. Not shown in this figure are the multiple steps that follow, each catalyzed by a specific enzyme located in the mitochondrial matrix or embedded in the inner membrane. The two-carbon acetyl group and a four-carbon molecule called oxaloacetate are joined, forming a six-carbon molecule called citrate, the ionized (negatively charged) form of citric acid—hence the name *citric acid cycle*. Citrate is then processed through a series of redox reactions, two carbon atoms are removed as CO_2, and oxaloacetate is regenerated; this regeneration accounts for the word *cycle*.

Compared with glycolysis, the citric acid cycle pays big energy dividends to the cell. However, the citric acid cycle produces very little ATP directly. Each turn of the cycle makes one ATP molecule by substrate-level phosphorylation (shown at the bottom of Figure 6.9A). Most of the energy dividends of the citric acid cycle come in the form of NADH and FADH₂. Each turn produces three NADH molecules and one molecule of another electron carrier, FADH₂. Remember that the citric acid cycle processes two molecules of acetyl CoA for each initial glucose. Thus, two turns of the cycle occur, and the overall yield per molecule of glucose is 2 ATP, 6 NADH, and 2 FADH₂.

So how many energy-rich molecules have been produced by processing one molecule of glucose through glycolysis and the

citric acid cycle? Up to this point, the cell has gained a total of 4 ATP (all from substrate-level phosphorylation), 10 NADH, and 2 FADH₂. For the cell to be able to harvest the energy

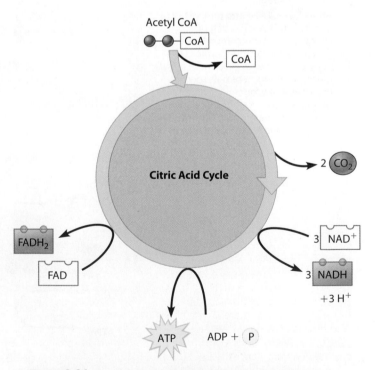

▲ **Figure 6.9A** An overview of the citric acid cycle: For each acetyl CoA that enters the cycle, 2 CO_2, 3 NADH, 1 FADH₂, and 1 ATP are produced. (Remember that 2 acetyl CoA are produced from glucose, so multiply by 2 to calculate a per-glucose return.)

banked in NADH and FADH$_2$, these molecules must shuttle their high-energy electrons to an electron transport chain. There the energy from the *oxidation* of organic molecules is used to *phosphorylate* ADP to ATP—hence the name *oxidative phosphorylation*. Before we look at how oxidative phosphorylation works, you may want to examine the inner workings of the citric acid cycle in **Figure 6.9B**.

? What is the total number of NADH molecules generated during the complete breakdown of one glucose molecule to six molecules of CO$_2$? (*Hint:* Combine the outputs of Modules 6.7–6.9.)

● **10 NADH:** 2 from glycolysis; 2 from the oxidation of pyruvate; 6 from the citric acid cycle. (Did you remember to double the output because of the sugar-splitting step of glycolysis?)

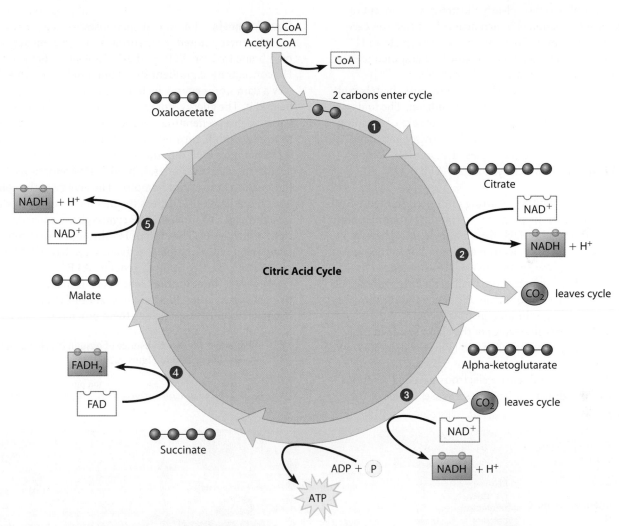

Step ❶
Acetyl CoA stokes the furnace.

A turn of the citric acid cycle begins (top centre) as enzymes strip the CoA portion from acetyl CoA and combine the remaining two-carbon acetyl group with the four-carbon molecule oxaloacetate (top left) already present in the mitochondrion. The product of this reaction is the six-carbon molecule citrate. Citrate is the ionized form of citric acid. All the acid compounds in this cycle exist in the cell in their ionized form, hence the suffix *-ate*.

Steps ❷ – ❸
NADH, ATP, and CO$_2$ are generated during redox reactions.

Successive redox reactions harvest some of the energy of the acetyl group by stripping hydrogen atoms from organic acid intermediates (such as alpha-ketoglutarate) and producing energy-laden NADH molecules. In two places, an intermediate compound loses a CO$_2$ molecule. Energy is harvested by substrate-level phosphorylation of ADP to produce ATP. A four-carbon compound called succinate emerges at the end of step 3.

Steps ❹ – ❺
Further redox reactions generate FADH$_2$ and more NADH.

Enzymes rearrange chemical bonds, eventually completing the citric acid cycle by regenerating oxaloacetate. Redox reactions reduce the electron carriers FAD and NAD$^+$ to FADH$_2$ and NADH, respectively. One turn of the citric acid cycle is completed with the conversion of a molecule of malate to oxaloacetate. This compound is then ready to start the next turn of the cycle by accepting another acetyl group from acetyl CoA.

▲ **Figure 6.9B** A closer look at the citric acid cycle. (Each glucose molecule yields two molecules of acetyl CoA, so the cycle runs two times for each glucose molecule oxidized.)

6.10 Most ATP production occurs by oxidative phosphorylation

Your main objective in this chapter is to learn how cells harvest the energy of glucose to make ATP. But so far, you've seen the production of only 4 ATP per glucose molecule. Now it's time for the big energy payoff. The final stage of cellular respiration is oxidative phosphorylation, which uses the electron transport chain and chemiosmosis—a process introduced in Module 6.6. Oxidative phosphorylation clearly illustrates the concept of structure fitting function: The arrangement of electron carriers built into a membrane makes it possible to create an H^+ concentration gradient across the membrane and then use the energy of that gradient to drive ATP synthesis.

Figure 6.10 shows how an electron transport chain is built into the inner membrane of the mitochondrion. The folds (cristae) of this membrane enlarge its surface area, providing space for thousands of copies of the chain. Also embedded in the membrane are multiple copies of an enzyme complex called **ATP synthase**, which synthesizes ATP.

Electron Transport Chain   Starting on the left in Figure 6.10, the gold arrow traces the path of electron flow from the shuttle molecules NADH and $FADH_2$ through the electron transport chain to oxygen, the final electron acceptor. It is in this end stage of cellular respiration that oxygen finally steps in to play its critical role. Each oxygen atom (half of an oxygen molecule or $1/2$ O_2) accepts 2 electrons from the chain and picks up 2 H^+ from the surrounding solution, forming H_2O.

Most of the carrier molecules of the chain reside in four main protein complexes (labelled I to IV in the diagram), while two mobile carriers transport electrons between the complexes. All the carriers bind and release electrons in redox reactions, passing electrons down the "energy staircase." Three of the

protein complexes use the energy released from these electron transfers to actively transport H^+ across the membrane, from where H^+ is less concentrated to where it is more concentrated. The green vertical arrows show H^+ being transported from the matrix of the mitochondrion (its innermost compartment) into the narrow intermembrane space.

Chemiosmosis   Recall that chemiosmosis is a process that uses the energy stored in a hydrogen ion gradient across a membrane to drive ATP synthesis. How does that work? The H^+ concentration gradient stores potential energy, much the way a dam stores energy by holding back the elevated water behind it. The energy stored by a dam can be harnessed to do work (such as generating electricity) when the water is allowed to rush downhill, turning giant wheels called turbines. The ATP synthases built into the inner mitochondrial membrane act like miniature turbines. Indeed, ATP synthase is considered the smallest known rotary motor. The energy of the concentration gradient of H^+ across the membrane drives hydrogen ions through a channel in ATP synthase, as shown on the far right of the figure. The rush of H^+ through the channel spins a component of the complex, activating catalytic sites that attach phosphate groups to ADP to generate ATP.

We will account for how much ATP is made by oxidative phosphorylation in Module 6.12. But first, let's see what happens if something disrupts these processes.

?   **What effect would an absence of oxygen (O_2) have on the process illustrated in Figure 6.10?**

● Without oxygen to "pull" electrons down the electron transport chain, the energy stored in NADH could not be harnessed for ATP synthesis.

▲ **Figure 6.10** Oxidative phosphorylation: electron transport and chemiosmosis in a mitochondrion

6.11 Interrupting cellular respiration can have both harmful and beneficial effects

A number of poisons produce their deadly effects by interfering with some of the events of cellular respiration that we have just discussed. **Figure 6.11** shows the places where three different categories of poisons obstruct the process of oxidative phosphorylation.

Poisons in one category block the electron transport chain. A substance called rotenone, for instance, binds tightly with one of the electron carrier molecules in the first protein complex, preventing electrons from passing to the next carrier molecule. By blocking the electron transport chain near its start and thus preventing ATP synthesis, rotenone literally starves an organism's cells of energy. Rotenone is often used to kill pest insects and fish.

Two other poisons in this category, cyanide and carbon monoxide, bind to an electron carrier in the fourth protein complex, where they block the passage of electrons to oxygen. This blockage is like turning off a faucet; electrons can no longer flow through the "pipe." The result is the same as with rotenone: No H^+ gradient is generated, and no ATP can be made. Cyanide was the lethal agent in an infamous case of product tampering: the Tylenol murders of 1982. Seven people in the Chicago area died after ingesting Tylenol capsules that had been laced with cyanide.

A second category of respiratory poison inhibits ATP synthase. An example of this type of poison is the antibiotic oligomycin, a compound used on the skin to combat fungal infections there. The right side of the figure shows that oligomycin blocks the passage of H^+ through the channel in ATP synthase, preventing fungal cells from making ATP and thereby killing them. The drug does not harm human cells because it cannot get through our outer layer of dead skin cells.

Poisons in a third category, called uncouplers, make the membrane of the mitochondrion leaky to hydrogen ions. Electron transport continues normally, but ATP cannot be made because leakage of H^+ through the membrane destroys the H^+ gradient. Cells continue to burn fuel and consume oxygen, often at a higher than normal rate, but to no avail, for they cannot make any ATP through chemiosmosis because no H^+ gradient exists.

A highly toxic uncoupler called dinitrophenol (DNP) is shown in the figure. When DNP is present, all steps of cellular respiration except chemiosmosis continue to run, even though almost all the energy is lost as heat. DNP poisoning produces an enormous increase in metabolic rate, profuse sweating as

▲ **Figure 6.11** How some poisons affect the electron transport chain and chemiosmosis

the body attempts to dissipate excess heat, and finally death. For a short time in the 1930s, some physicians prescribed DNP in low doses as weight loss pills, but fatalities soon made it clear that there were far safer ways to lose weight.

Under certain conditions, however, an uncoupler that generates heat by abolishing the H^+ gradient in a mitochondrion may be beneficial. A remarkable adaptation is found in hibernating mammals and newborn infants in a tissue called brown fat. The cells of brown fat are packed full of mitochondria. The inner mitochondrial membrane contains an uncoupling protein, which allows H^+ to flow back down its concentration gradient without generating ATP. Activation of these uncouplers results in ongoing oxidation of stored fuel (fats) and the generation of heat, which protects hibernating mammals and newborns from dangerous drops in body temperature. In 2009, scientists discovered that adults retain deposits of brown fat. These tissues were found to be more active in colder weather, not surprisingly, and also in individuals who were thinner. This second finding suggests that brown fat may cause lean individuals to burn calories faster than other people do, and prompted some researchers to propose that these tissues could be a target for obesity-fighting drugs.

In the next module, we take a final look at the stages of cellular respiration and calculate the total amount of ATP harvested as a cell oxidizes glucose in the presence of oxygen to carbon dioxide and water.

 Looking at Figure 6.11, explain where uncoupling proteins would be found in the mitochondria of brown fat cells.

● They would span the inner mitochondrial membrane, providing a channel through which H^+ would diffuse down its concentration gradient back into the matrix.

6.12 Review: Each molecule of glucose yields many molecules of ATP

Let's review what the cell accomplishes by oxidizing a molecule of glucose. **Figure 6.12** shows where each stage of cellular respiration occurs in a eukaryotic cell and how much ATP it produces. Starting on the left, glycolysis, which occurs in the cytoplasmic fluid, and the citric acid cycle, which occurs in the mitochondrial matrix, contribute a net total of 4 ATP per glucose molecule by substrate-level phosphorylation. The cell harvests much more energy than this via the carrier molecules NADH and FADH$_2$, which are produced in glycolysis and the citric acid cycle. The energy of the electrons they carry is used to make (according to current estimates) about 28 molecules of ATP by oxidative phosphorylation. Thus, the total yield of ATP molecules per glucose is about 32.

The number of ATP molecules produced cannot be stated exactly for several reasons. As shown in the figure, the NADH produced in glycolysis passes its electrons across the mitochondrial membrane to either NAD$^+$ or FAD, depending on the type of shuttle system used. Because FADH$_2$ adds its electrons later in the electron transport chain (see Figure 6.10),

it contributes less to the H$^+$ gradient and thus generates less ATP. In addition, some of the energy of the H$^+$ gradient may be used for work other than ATP production, such as the active transport of pyruvate into the mitochondrion.

More important than the actual number of ATP molecules is the point that a cell can harvest a great deal of energy from glucose—up to about 34% of the molecule's potential energy. Because most of the ATP generated by cellular respiration results from oxidative phosphorylation, the ATP yield depends on an adequate supply of oxygen to the cell. Without oxygen to function as the final electron acceptor, electron transport and ATP production stop. But as we see next, some cells can oxidize organic fuel and generate ATP *without* oxygen.

 What would a cell's net ATP yield per glucose be in the presence of the poison DNP? (See Module 6.11.)

4 ATP, all from substrate-level phosphorylation. The uncoupler would destroy the H$^+$ concentration gradient necessary for chemiosmosis.

▶ **Figure 6.12** An estimated tally of the ATP produced by substrate-level and oxidative phosphorylation in cellular respiration

Fermentation: Anaerobic Harvesting of Energy

6.13 Fermentation enables cells to produce ATP without oxygen

The prokaryotes that first harvested energy through glycolysis did so in environments devoid of oxygen and before the evolution of the electron transport chain. To oxidize glucose in glycolysis, NAD$^+$ must be present as an electron acceptor. In order for glycolysis to continue under such anaerobic conditions, NAD$^+$ must be regenerated by the oxidation of NADH. Fermentation recycles NADH back into NAD$^+$ and

allows glycolysis to continue. As we have discussed in previous modules, under aerobic conditions NAD$^+$ is regenerated when NADH donates its electrons to the electron transport chain within the mitochondria.

The metabolic pathway that generates ATP during fermentation is glycolysis, the same pathway that functions in the first stage of cellular respiration. Remember that glycolysis uses no oxygen; it simply generates a net gain of 2 ATP while oxidizing glucose to two molecules of pyruvate and reducing NAD^+ to NADH. The yield of 2 ATP is certainly a lot less than the possible 32 ATP per glucose generated during aerobic respiration; but, it is enough to meet the energy requirements for many anaerobic microorganisms (those that live in environments with little to no O_2). Your muscles also use fermentation so they can continue to contract for a short period of time when oxygen is scarce.

During fermentation, NAD^+ is regenerated when NADH reduces organic molecules within the cell. Pyruvate, another product of glycolysis, is a common electron acceptor in some fermentation reactions. However, other molecules may become reduced in other fermentation pathways. The various fermentation reactions are named for their different products.

Lactic Acid Fermentation One common type of fermentation is called **lactic acid fermentation**. Your muscle cells and certain bacteria can regenerate NAD^+ by this process, as illustrated in **Figure 6.13A**. You can see that NADH is oxidized to NAD^+ as pyruvate is reduced to lactate (the ionized form of lactic acid). Muscle cells can switch to lactic acid fermentation when the need for ATP outpaces the delivery of O_2 via the bloodstream. The lactate is carried in the blood to the liver, where it is converted back to pyruvate and oxidized in the mitochondria of liver cells.

The dairy industry uses lactic acid fermentation by bacteria to make cheese and yogourt. Other types of microbial fermentation turn soybeans into soy sauce and cabbage into sauerkraut.

Alcohol Fermentation For thousands of years, people have used **alcohol fermentation** in brewing, winemaking, and baking. Yeasts are single-celled fungi that normally use aerobic respiration to process their food. But they are also able to survive in anaerobic environments. Yeasts and certain bacteria recycle their NADH back to NAD^+ while converting pyruvate to CO_2 and ethanol (**Figure 6.13B**). The CO_2 provides the bubbles in beer and champagne. Bubbles of CO_2 generated by baker's yeast cause bread dough to rise. Ethanol (ethyl alcohol), the two-carbon end product, is toxic to the organisms that produce it. Yeasts release their alcohol wastes to their surroundings, where it usually diffuses away. When yeasts are confined in a wine vat, they die when the alcohol concentration reaches 14%.

In any brewery, alcohol fermentation must be carefully monitored to ensure the desired results. Small changes in the barley, the main ingredient of most beers, can alter the quality of the final product. For example, if the barley has been infected with a fungus before being used in beer making, it prevents the yeast from finishing the fermentation process and produces a beer with high sugar levels. Dr. Alex Speers at Dalhousie University studies brewing and fermentation to better understand how differences in the barley can affect the taste of the beer. Speers hopes that the development of a fungus-resistant strain of barley will significantly help the Canadian economy. Canada produces nearly 10 million tonnes of barley every year, 30% of which is used in the brewing industry.

Types of Anaerobes Unlike muscle cells and yeasts, many bacteria that live in stagnant ponds and deep in the soil are *obligate anaerobes*, meaning they require anaerobic conditions

▲ **Figure 6.13A** Lactic acid fermentation: NAD^+ is regenerated as pyruvate is reduced to lactate

▲ **Figure 6.13B** Alcohol fermentation: NAD^+ is regenerated as pyruvate is broken down to CO_2 and ethanol

▲ **Figure 6.13C** Wine barrels and beer fermentation vats

and are poisoned by oxygen. Yeasts and many other bacteria are facultative anaerobes. A *facultative anaerobe* can make ATP either by fermentation or by oxidative phosphorylation, depending on whether O_2 is available. On the cellular level, our muscle cells behave as facultative anaerobes.

For a facultative anaerobe, pyruvate is a fork in the metabolic road. If oxygen is available, the organism will always use the more productive aerobic respiration. Thus, to make wine and beer, yeasts must be grown anaerobically so that they will ferment sugars and produce ethanol. For this reason, the

wine barrels and beer fermentation vats in **Figure 6.13C** are designed to keep out air.

 A glucose-fed yeast cell is moved from an aerobic environment to an anaerobic one. For the cell to continue generating ATP at the same rate, how would its rate of glucose consumption need to change?

● The cell would have to consume glucose at a rate about 16 times the consumption rate in the aerobic environment (2 ATP per glucose molecule is made by fermentation versus 32 ATP by cellular respiration).

6.14 Do African elephants get drunk from fermented marula fruit and wreak havoc?

For many, a drink at the local pub is a weekend tradition. Occasionally, some people have a few drinks too many and become inebriated. In this drunken state, emotions may be overexpressed, words may be slurred, and walking may be uncoordinated. But are humans the only animals to voluntarily partake in such libations? Rumour has it that African elephants (*Loxodonta africana*) become inebriated after consuming fermented marula fruit. Is there any truth behind these stories? Or are they simply public house folklore?

Each marula tree (*Sclerocarya birrea*) of Southern and Western Africa can produce up to 8000 golf ball–sized marula fruit (**Figure 6.14**). In such large numbers, many of the fruit become overripe and fall to the ground before they are consumed. When overripe, bacteria and yeast from the environment start fermenting the sugars into ethanol. Although the average ethanol content of the fruit is only 3%, ethanol concentrations can reach as high as 7%. Therefore, it is possible for animals to become intoxicated from eating the fermented marula fruit.

Once consumed, ethanol circulates in the blood until it is broken down in the liver by the enzyme alcohol dehydrogenase. This enzyme oxidizes ethanol into acetaldehyde. At the same time, NAD^+ is reduced, forming NADH. Both products of this reaction are subsequently used in energy-generating reactions. Another enzyme converts acetaldehyde into acetyl CoA, which can enter the citric acid cycle. This reaction also

involves the reduction of a second molecule of NAD^+ into NADH. The two NADH molecules donate their electrons to the electron transport chain. After the citric acid cycle, one molecule of ethanol can produce about 18 molecules of ATP.

It is, however, unlikely that an African elephant would become intoxicated from eating fermented marula fruit. The biggest obstacle to inebriation is body size. Female African elephants can reach 3000 kg and males can grow twice as large. For a 70 kg (150 pound) human, it takes 90 mL of pure ethanol to yield a blood alcohol concentration of 0.15 (g/100 mL). Extrapolating from this value and accounting for metabolic differences, a 3000 kg elephant would have to ingest 1900 mL of pure ethanol to obtain an equivalent blood alcohol concentration. This would require the ingestion of more than 1200 fruit that had fermented to 7% ethanol.

Elephants eat about 1% to 2% of their body weight daily. Thus, a 3000 kg animal can eat 30 kg of food every day. If an elephant ate only marula fruit, that would be just over 700 fruit—much less than the required 1200. Making intoxication even more unlikely is that the elephant would have to consume all the fruit in a very short period of time, before their alcohol dehydrogenase enzymes remove the ethanol from the blood. Otherwise the ethanol from earlier fruit would be metabolized before the required 1900 mL could be reached. Furthermore, eating rotten fruit is not a typical behaviour for African elephants. They would rather work harder to get fresh fruit off of a tree than easily obtain rotting fruit that is abundant on the ground.

Animal behaviour can be very complex. It is common for people to apply human characteristics to animals—called anthropomorphism—to explain curious observations. Abnormal behaviours by elephants after eating marula fruit are easily but erroneously attributed to intoxication. Biologists, however, avoid anthropomorphizing the elephants' behaviour and remain objective. British scientist Dr. Steve Morris has provided other explanations for the intoxication-like behaviour of elephants. A poisonous beetle often resides within the bark of the marula tree. It is plausible that the behavioural changes in the elephants come from this beetle, rather than the alcohol.

 Why is it unlikely that an elephant can get intoxicated on marula fruit?

● An elephant cannot eat enough fruit in a short enough period of time to reach an intoxicating blood alcohol concentration.

▲ **Figure 6.14** The fruit of the marula tree

Connections Between Metabolic Pathways

6.15 Glycolysis evolved early in the history of life on Earth

Glycolysis is the universal energy-harvesting process of life. If you looked inside a bacterial cell, inside one of your body cells, or inside virtually any other living cell, you would find the metabolic machinery of glycolysis.

The role of glycolysis as the first step in harvesting energy in both fermentation and respiration has an evolutionary basis. Ancient prokaryotes are thought to have used glycolysis to make ATP long before oxygen was present in Earth's atmosphere. The oldest known fossils of bacteria date back over 3.5 billion years, and they resemble some types of photosynthetic bacteria still found today. The evidence indicates, however, that significant levels of O_2, formed as a by-product of bacterial photosynthesis, did not accumulate in the atmosphere until about 2.7 billion years ago. Thus, for almost a billion years, prokaryotes most likely generated ATP exclusively from glycolysis, a process that does not require oxygen.

The fact that glycolysis is the most widespread metabolic pathway found in Earth's organisms today suggests that it evolved very early in the history of life. The location of glycolysis within the cell also implies great antiquity; the pathway does not require any of the membrane-bound organelles of the eukaryotic cell, which evolved more than a billion years after the prokaryotic cell. Glycolysis is a metabolic heirloom from early cells that continues to function in fermentation and as the first stage in the breakdown of organic molecules by cellular respiration.

 List some of the characteristics of glycolysis that indicate that it is an ancient metabolic pathway.

Glycolysis occurs universally (functioning in both fermentation and respiration), does not require oxygen, and does not occur in a membrane-bound organelle.

6.16 Cells use many kinds of organic molecules as fuel for cellular respiration

Throughout this chapter, we have spoken of glucose as the fuel for cellular respiration. But free glucose molecules are not common in your diet. You obtain most of your calories as carbohydrates (such as sucrose and other disaccharide sugars and starch, a polysaccharide), fats, and proteins. You consume all three of these classes of organic molecules when you eat a handful of peanuts, for instance.

Figure 6.16 illustrates how a cell can use these three types of molecules to make ATP. A wide range of carbohydrates can be funnelled into glycolysis, as indicated by the arrows on the far left of the diagram. For example, enzymes in your digestive tract hydrolyze starch to glucose, which is then broken down by glycolysis and the citric acid cycle. Similarly, glycogen, the polysaccharide stored in your liver and muscle cells, can be hydrolyzed to glucose to serve as fuel between meals.

Fats make excellent cellular fuel because they contain many hydrogen atoms and thus many energy-rich electrons. As the diagram shows (tan arrows), a cell first hydrolyzes fats to glycerol and fatty acids. It then converts the glycerol to glyceraldehyde 3-phosphate (G3P), one of the intermediates in glycolysis. The fatty acids are broken into two-carbon fragments that enter the citric acid cycle as acetyl CoA. A gram of fat yields more than twice as much ATP as a gram of carbohydrate. Because so many calories are stockpiled in each gram of fat, you must expend a large amount of energy to burn fat stored in your body. This helps to explain why it is so difficult for a dieter to lose excess fat.

▲ **Figure 6.16** Pathways that break down various food molecules

Proteins (purple arrows in Figure 6.16) can also be used for fuel, although your body preferentially burns sugars and fats first. To be oxidized as fuel, proteins must first be digested to their constituent amino acids. Typically, a cell will use most of these amino acids to make its own proteins. Enzymes can convert excess amino acids to intermediates of glycolysis or the citric acid cycle, and their energy is then harvested by cellular respiration. During the conversion, the amino groups are stripped off and later disposed of in urine.

 Animals store most of their energy reserves as fats, not as polysaccharides. What is the advantage of this mode of storage for an animal?

● Most animals are mobile and benefit from a compact and concentrated form of energy storage. Also, because fats are hydrophobic, they can be stored without extra water associated with them (see Module 3.14).

6.17 Food molecules provide raw materials for biosynthesis

Not all food molecules are destined to be oxidized as fuel for making ATP. Food also provides the raw materials your cells use for biosynthesis—the production of organic molecules using energy-requiring metabolic pathways. A cell must be able to make its own molecules to build its structures and perform its functions. Some raw materials, such as amino acids, can be incorporated directly into your macromolecules. However, your cells also need to make molecules that are not present in your food. Indeed, glycolysis and the citric acid cycle function as metabolic interchanges that enable your cells to convert some kinds of molecules to others as you need them.

Figure 6.17 outlines the pathways by which your cells can make three classes of organic molecules using some of the intermediate molecules of glycolysis and the citric acid cycle. By comparing Figures 6.16 and 6.17, you can see clear connections between the energy-harvesting processes of cellular respiration and the biosynthetic pathways used to construct the organic molecules of the cell.

Basic principles of supply and demand regulate these pathways. If there is an excess of a certain amino acid, for example, the pathway that synthesizes it is switched off. The most common mechanism for this control is feedback inhibition: The end product inhibits an enzyme that catalyzes an early step in the pathway (see Module 5.14). Feedback inhibition also controls cellular respiration. If ATP accumulates in a cell, it inhibits an early enzyme in glycolysis, slowing down respiration and conserving resources. On the other hand, the same enzyme is activated by a buildup of ADP in the cell, signalling the need for more energy.

The cells of all living organisms—including those of the bear shown in Figure 6.17 and the plants it eats—have the ability to harvest energy from the breakdown of organic molecules. When the process is cellular respiration, the atoms of the starting materials end up in carbon dioxide and water. In contrast, the ability to make organic molecules from carbon dioxide and water is not universal. Animal cells lack this ability, but plant cells can actually produce organic molecules from inorganic ones by using the energy of sunlight. This process, photosynthesis, is the subject of Chapter 7.

 Explain how someone can gain weight and store fat even when on a low-fat diet. (Hint: Look for G3P and acetyl CoA in Figures 6.16 and 6.17.)

● If caloric intake is excessive, body cells use metabolic pathways to convert the excess to fat. The glycerol and fatty acids of fats are made from G3P and acetyl CoA, respectively, both produced from the oxidation of carbohydrates.

▲ **Figure 6.17** Biosynthesis of large organic molecules from intermediates of cellular respiration

ATP needed to drive biosynthesis

ATP

Citric Acid Cycle

Pyruvate Oxidation Acetyl CoA

Glucose Synthesis
Pyruvate → G3P → Glucose

Amino groups

Amino acids   Fatty acids Glycerol   Sugars

Proteins   **Fats**   **Carbohydrates**

Cells, tissues, organisms

Reviewing the Concepts

Cellular Respiration: Aerobic Harvesting of Energy (6.1–6.5)

6.1 Photosynthesis and cellular respiration provide energy for life. Photosynthesis uses solar energy to produce glucose and O_2 from CO_2 and H_2O. In cellular respiration, O_2 is consumed during the breakdown of glucose to CO_2 and H_2O, and energy is released.

6.2 Breathing supplies O_2 for use in cellular respiration and removes CO_2. Breathing, sometimes called respiration, supplies the O_2 for cellular respiration and removes the CO_2 waste product.

6.3 Cellular respiration banks energy in ATP molecules. The summary equation for cellular respiration is $C_6H_{12}O_6 + 6\ O_2 \rightarrow 6\ CO_2 + 6\ H_2O + $ Energy (ATP + Heat).

6.4 The human body uses energy from ATP for all its activities. Everything you do, from sitting to running requires energy. Your cells use energy in the form of ATP.

6.5 Cells tap energy from electrons "falling" from organic fuels to oxygen. Electrons removed from fuel molecules (oxidation) are transferred to NAD+ (reduction). NADH passes electrons to an electron transport chain. As electrons "fall" from carrier to carrier and finally to O_2, energy is released.

Stages of Cellular Respiration (6.6–6.12)

6.6 Overview: Cellular respiration occurs in three main stages.

6.7 Glycolysis harvests chemical energy by oxidizing glucose to pyruvate. ATP is used to prime a glucose molecule, which is split in two. These three-carbon intermediates are oxidized to two molecules of pyruvate, yielding a net of 2 ATP and 2 NADH. ATP is formed by substrate-level phosphorylation, in which a phosphate group is transferred from an organic molecule to ADP.

6.8 Pyruvate is oxidized prior to the citric acid cycle. In the oxidation of pyruvate to acetyl CoA, CO_2 and NADH are produced.

6.9 The citric acid cycle completes the oxidation of organic molecules, generating many NADH and $FADH_2$ molecules. For each turn of the cycle, two carbons from acetyl CoA are added and 2 CO_2 are released; the energy yield is 1 ATP, 3 NADH, and 1 $FADH_2$.

6.10 Most ATP production occurs by oxidative phosphorylation. In mitochondria, electrons from NADH and $FADH_2$ travel down the electron transport chain to O_2, which picks up H^+ to form water.

Energy released by these redox reactions is used to pump H^+ from the mitochondrial matrix into the intermembrane space. In chemiosmosis, the H^+ diffuses back across the inner membrane through ATP synthase complexes, driving the synthesis of ATP.

6.11 Interrupting cellular respiration can have both harmful and beneficial effects. Poisons can block electron flow, block the movement of H^+ through ATP synthase, or allow H^+ to leak through the membrane. Uncouplers in brown fat produce body heat.

6.12 Review: Each molecule of glucose yields many molecules of ATP. Substrate-level phosphorylation and oxidative phosphorylation produce up to 32 ATP molecules for every glucose molecule oxidized in cellular respiration.

Fermentation: Anaerobic Harvesting of Energy (6.13–6.14)

6.13 Fermentation enables cells to produce ATP without oxygen. Under anaerobic conditions, muscle cells, yeasts, and certain bacteria produce ATP by glycolysis. NAD^+ is recycled from NADH as pyruvate is reduced to lactate (lactic acid fermentation) or, in microbes, alcohol and CO_2 (alcohol fermentation).

6.14 Do African elephants get drunk from fermented marula fruit and wreak havoc? It is unlikely that an animal as large as an elephant can consume enough fermented marula fruit to become intoxicated.

Connections Between Metabolic Pathways (6.15–6.17)

6.15 Glycolysis evolved early in the history of life on Earth. Glycolysis occurs in the cytoplasm of nearly all organisms and is thought to have evolved in ancient prokaryotes.

6.16 Cells use many kinds of organic molecules as fuel for cellular respiration. Carbohydrates, fats, and proteins can all fuel cellular respiration.

6.17 Food molecules provide raw materials for biosynthesis. Cells use intermediates from cellular respiration and ATP for biosynthesis of other organic molecules. Metabolic pathways are often regulated by feedback inhibition.

Connecting the Concepts

1. Fill in the blanks in this summary map to help you review the key concepts of cellular respiration.

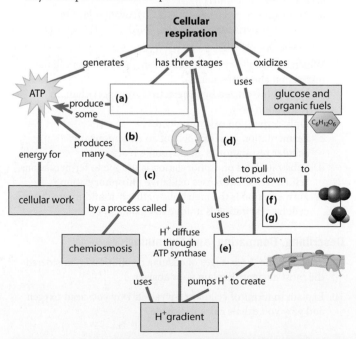

Testing Your Knowledge

Multiple Choice

2. What is the role of oxygen in cellular respiration?
   a. It is reduced in glycolysis as glucose is oxidized.
   b. It provides electrons to the electron transport chain.
   c. It combines with the carbon removed during the citric acid cycle to form CO_2.
   d. It is required for the production of heat and light.
   e. It accepts electrons from the electron transport chain.

3. When the poison cyanide blocks the electron transport chain, glycolysis and the citric acid cycle soon grind to a halt as well. Why do they stop? (*Explain your answer.*)
   a. They both run out of ATP.
   b. Unused O_2 interferes with cellular respiration.
   c. They run out of NAD^+ and FAD.
   d. Electrons are no longer available.
   e. They run out of ADP.

4. A biochemist wanted to study how various substances were used in cellular respiration. In one experiment, he allowed a mouse to breathe air containing O_2 "labelled" by a particular isotope. In the mouse, the labelled oxygen first showed up in
   a. ATP.
   b. glucose ($C_6H_{12}O_6$).
   c. NADH.
   d. CO_2.
   e. H_2O.

5. In glycolysis, _____ is oxidized and _____ is reduced.
   a. NAD^+; glucose
   b. glucose; oxygen
   c. ATP; ADP
   d. glucose; NAD^+
   e. ADP; ATP

6. Which of the following is the immediate source of energy for making most of the ATP in your cells?
   a. the reduction of oxygen
   b. the transfer of ⓟ from intermediate substrates to ADP
   c. the movement of H^+ across a membrane down its concentration gradient
   d. the splitting of glucose into two molecules of pyruvate
   e. electrons moving through the electron transport chain

7. In which of the following is the first molecule becoming reduced to the second molecule? (*Explain the oxidation reaction that occurs at the same time.*)
   a. pyruvate → acetyl CoA
   b. pyruvate → lactate
   c. glucose → pyruvate
   d. $NADH + H^+ → NAD^+ + 2\,H$
   e. $C_6H_{12}O_6 → 6\,CO_2$

8. Which of the following is a *true* distinction between cellular respiration and fermentation?
   a. NADH is oxidized by the electron transport chain in respiration only.
   b. Only respiration oxidizes glucose.
   c. Fermentation is an example of an endergonic reaction; cellular respiration is an exergonic reaction.
   d. Substrate-level phosphorylation is unique to fermentation; cellular respiration uses oxidative phosphorylation.
   e. Fermentation is the metabolic pathway found in prokaryotes; cellular respiration is unique to eukaryotes.

Describing, Comparing, and Explaining

9. Which of the three stages of cellular respiration is considered the most ancient? Explain your answer.

10. Explain in terms of cellular respiration why you need oxygen and why you exhale carbon dioxide.

11. Compare and contrast fermentation as it occurs in your muscle cells and as it occurs in yeast cells.

12. Explain how your body can convert excess carbohydrates in the diet to fats. Can excess carbohydrates be converted to protein? What else must be supplied?

13. How many molecules of ATP are produced from the complete metabolism of 4 molecules of glucose? In your answer, outline the products of glycolysis, acetyl CoA formation, the citric acid cycle, and the electron transport chain. Also, indicate whether the ATP is produced by substrate-level phosphorylation or oxidative phosphorylation.

Applying the Concepts

14. An average adult human requires 2200 kcal of energy per day. Suppose your diet provides an average of 2300 kcal per day. How many hours per week would you have to walk to burn off the extra calories? Swim? Run? (See Figure 6.4.)

15. Your body makes NAD^+ and FAD from two B vitamins, niacin and riboflavin. The Recommended Dietary Allowance for niacin is 15 milligrams (mg) and for riboflavin, 1.2 mg. These amounts are thousands of times less than the amount of glucose your body needs each day to fuel its energy needs. Why is the daily requirement for these vitamins so small?

16. In a detail of the citric acid cycle not shown in Figure 6.9B, an enzyme converts succinate to a compound called fumarate, with the release of H^+. You are studying this reaction using a suspension of bean cell mitochondria and a blue dye that loses its colour as it takes up H^+. You know that the higher the concentration of succinate, the more rapid the decolorization of the dye. You set up reaction mixtures with mitochondria, dye, and three different concentrations of succinate (0.1 mg/L, 0.2 mg/L, and 0.3 mg/L). Which of the following graphs represents the results you would expect, and why?

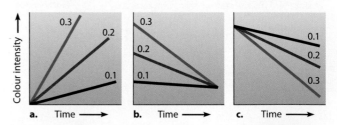

17. ATP synthase enzymes are found in the prokaryotic plasma membrane and in the inner membrane of a mitochondrion. What does this suggest about the evolutionary relationship of this eukaryotic organelle to prokaryotes?

18. Excess consumption of alcohol by a pregnant woman can cause a complex of birth defects called fetal alcohol syndrome (FAS). Symptoms of FAS include head and facial irregularities, heart defects, mental retardation, and behavioural problems. Health Canada recommends that pregnant women abstain from drinking alcohol, and the government has mandated a warning label on liquor bottles: "Drinking alcohol during pregnancy can seriously harm an unborn baby." Imagine you are a server in a restaurant. An obviously pregnant woman orders several alcoholic drinks. How would you respond? Is it the woman's right to make those decisions about her unborn child's health? Do you bear any responsibility in the matter? Is a restaurant responsible for monitoring the health habits of its customers?

Answers to all questions can be found in Appendix E.

CHAPTER

7

Photosynthesis

BIG IDEAS

An Overview of Photosynthesis

(7.1–7.5)

Plants and other photoautotrophs use the energy of sunlight to convert CO_2 and H_2O to sugar and O_2.

The Light-Dependent Reactions: Converting Solar Energy to Chemical Energy

(7.6–7.9)

In the thylakoids of a chloroplast, the light-dependent reactions generate ATP and NADPH.

CO_2, ATP, NADPH

Calvin Cycle

G3P

The Calvin Cycle: Reducing CO_2 to Sugar

(7.10–7.11)

The Calvin cycle, which takes place in the stroma of the chloroplast, uses ATP and NADPH to reduce CO_2 to sugar.

Photosynthesis Reviewed and Extended

(7.12–7.14)

Photosynthesis provides the energy and building material for ecosystems. It also affects global climate and the ozone layer.

Plant Power

With every new car, MP3 player, and smartphone, the world's demand for energy grows. In an era when most energy is generated from pollution-laden fossil fuels, more power often means more air pollution, more acid precipitation, and more of the greenhouse gases that contribute to global warming. Is there a better energy solution, one that could somehow produce power without harming our atmosphere? Some scientists believe they've found such a solution; and if you can see green through a nearby window, their answer might literally be in sight.

Energy researchers across Canada and North America have seized on the potential of plant power. They are turning to trees and other green vegetation to create "energy plantations" as a promising fuel source. In many ways, this solution draws from an ancient one; it relies on one of the oldest energy pathways on the planet—photosynthesis. In this process, green plants, algae, and certain bacteria transform light energy to chemical energy stored in the bonds of the sugar they make from carbon dioxide and water. During the process, they also produce the oxygen we and all other aerobic organisms (including the plants themselves) need for cellular respiration. In addition, the plants store an energy source that could help to solve the human power problem.

Photosynthesis happens on a microscopic level; but, carried out repeatedly in plants around the world, it is responsible for an enormous amount of product. Earth's plants and other photosynthetic organisms make about 160 billion tonnes of carbohydrate each year, which humans use in various ways. For example, almost all food can be traced back to plants, which are either eaten directly or fed to animals that are then consumed. And, for most of human history, burning plant material has been a major source of heat, light, and cooking fuel. It is only relatively recently that the developed world has replaced plant material with fossil fuels.

Now, as fossil fuel supplies dwindle and pollution accumulates, scientists are once again looking to plants and researching ways to make them a more efficient energy source. Some fast-growing trees or grasses have shown promise as fuel that can be both grown and burned in power generation facilities. Willows, for example, grow quickly and resprout once they are cut, limiting the amount of new planting, herbicides, and pesticides required to produce each generation of trees. They also grow much faster than most trees: Willow crops in Newfoundland and Labrador produce up to 12 dry tonnes of wood per hectare each year. In comparison, natural forests produce only one-fifth as much wood per hectare. Other fast-growing tree species are used for biomass energy in Canada, including the silver maple, alder, and poplar in Eastern Ontario.

Fuel from energy plantations is not only a renewable energy source; it can also be environmentally safer than fossil fuels. The products of burned wood do not include the sulphur contaminants released by fossil fuels that contribute to acid rain. To be sure, burning wood fuel releases CO_2 into the air. But as energy plantation crops are quickly regrown, their photosynthesizing removes CO_2 from the atmosphere—even as recently harvested trees release the gas through a power plant's smokestack. In contrast, when fossil fuels, which come from the remains of ancient organisms, are burned, they release CO_2 into the atmosphere that was removed from it through photosynthesis hundreds of millions of years ago.

Today, this "biomass energy" accounts for only 4.7% of all energy consumed in Canada. But the idea has enough support that it is being studied or tried in many countries. It may play a role in meeting future energy needs.

In this chapter, you will learn how photosynthesis works. Because photosynthesis is a complex process, we begin with some basic concepts. Then we look more closely at the two stages of photosynthesis: the light-dependent reactions, in which solar energy is transformed into chemical energy, and the Calvin cycle, in which that chemical energy is used to make organic molecules. Finally, we explore ways in which photosynthesis affects our global environment.

An Overview of Photosynthesis

7.1 Autotrophs are the producers of the biosphere

Plants are **autotrophs** (meaning "self-feeders" in Greek) in that they make their own food and thus sustain themselves without consuming organic molecules derived from any other organisms. Plant cells capture light energy that has travelled 150 million kilometres from the sun and convert it to chemical energy. Because they use the energy of light, plants are specifically called *photoautotrophs*. Through the process of **photosynthesis**, plants convert CO_2 and H_2O to their own organic molecules and release O_2 as a by-product. Photoautotrophs are the ultimate source of organic molecules for almost all other organisms. They are often referred to as the producers of the biosphere because they produce its food supply. (In Chapter 17, you will learn about chemoautotrophs—prokaryotes that use inorganic chemicals as their energy source.) Producers feed the consumers of the biosphere—the **heterotrophs** that consume other plants or animals or decompose organic material (*hetero* means "other").

Plants are not the only photoautotrophic organisms. The photographs on this page illustrate some of the diversity among photoautotrophs. On land, plants, such as those in the forest scene in **Figure 7.1A**, are the predominant producers. In aquatic environments, there are several types of photoautotrophs. **Figure 7.1B** is a micrograph of unicellular photosynthetic protists. **Figure 7.1C** shows kelp, a large alga that forms extensive underwater "forests" off the coast of British Columbia. **Figure 7.1D** is a micrograph of cyanobacteria, abundant and important producers in freshwater and marine ecosystems.

In this chapter, we focus on photosynthesis in plants, which takes place in chloroplasts. The remarkable ability to harness light energy and use it to drive the synthesis of organic compounds emerges from the structural organization of these organelles: Photosynthetic pigments, enzymes, and other molecules are grouped together in membranes, allowing the sequences of reactions to be carried out efficiently. The process of photosynthesis most likely originated in a group of bacteria that had infolded regions of the plasma membrane containing such clusters of enzymes and other molecules. In fact, according to the widely accepted theory of endosymbiosis, chloroplasts originated from a photosynthetic prokaryote that took up residence inside a eukaryotic cell (see Module 4.15).

Let's begin our study of photosynthesis with an overview of the location and structure of plant chloroplasts.

 What do "self-feeding" photoautotrophs require from the environment in order to make their own food?

● Light, carbon dioxide, and water (Minerals are also required; you'll learn about the needs of plants in Chapter 23.)

▲ **Figure 7.1A** Forest plants

LM 1400×

▲ **Figure 7.1B** Photosynthetic protists

▲ **Figure 7.1C** Kelp, a multicellular alga

LM 368×

▲ **Figure 7.1D** Cyanobacteria (photosynthetic prokaryotes)

7.2 Photosynthesis occurs in chloroplasts in plant cells

All green parts of a plant have chloroplasts in their cells and can carry out photosynthesis. In most plants, however, the leaves have the most chloroplasts (about half a million in a square millimetre surface area of a leaf) and are the major sites of photosynthesis. Their green colour comes from **chlorophyll**, a light-absorbing pigment in the chloroplasts that plays a central role in converting solar energy to chemical energy.

Figure 7.2 zooms in on a leaf to show the actual sites of photosynthesis. The leaf cross-section shows a slice through a leaf. Chloroplasts are concentrated in the cells of the **mesophyll**, the green tissue in the interior of the leaf. Carbon dioxide enters the leaf, and oxygen exits, by way of tiny pores called **stomata** (singular, *stoma*, meaning "mouth"). Water absorbed by the roots is delivered to the leaves in veins. Leaves also use veins to export sugar to roots and other parts of the plant.

As you can see in the light micrograph of a single mesophyll cell, each cell has numerous chloroplasts. A typical mesophyll cell has about 30 to 40 chloroplasts. The bottom drawing and electron micrograph show the structures in a single chloroplast. Membranes in the chloroplast form the framework where many of the reactions of photosynthesis occur, just as mitochondrial membranes are the site for much of the energy-harvesting machinery we discussed in Chapter 6. In the chloroplast, an envelope of two membranes encloses an inner compartment, which is filled with a thick fluid called **stroma**. Suspended in the stroma is a system of interconnected membranous sacs, called **thylakoids**, which enclose another internal compartment, called the thylakoid space. (As you will see later, this thylakoid space plays a role analogous to the intermembrane space of a mitochondrion in the generation of ATP.) In many places, thylakoids are concentrated in stacks called **grana** (singular, *granum*). Built into the thylakoid membranes are the chlorophyll molecules that capture light energy. The thylakoid membranes also house much of the machinery that converts light energy to chemical energy, which is used in the stroma to make sugar.

Later in the chapter, we examine the function of these structures in more detail. But first, let's look more closely at the general process of photosynthesis.

? **How do the reactant molecules of photosynthesis reach the chloroplasts in leaves?**

CO_2 enters leaves through stomata, and H_2O enters the roots and is carried to leaves through veins.

▲ **Figure 7.2** Zooming in on the location and structure of chloroplasts

Leaf

Leaf Cross-Section

Mesophyll

Vein

CO_2

O_2

Stoma

Mesophyll Cell

LM 2600×

Chloroplast

Inner and outer membranes

Granum

Thylakoid

Thylakoid space

Stroma

Colourized TEM 1000×

7.3 Scientists traced the process of photosynthesis by using isotopes

The leaves of plants that live in lakes and ponds are often covered with bubbles like the ones shown in **Figure 7.3A**. The bubbles are oxygen gas (O_2) produced during photosynthesis. But where does this O_2 come from?

The overall process of photosynthesis has been known since the 1800s: In the presence of light, green plants produce sugar and oxygen from carbon dioxide and water. Consider the basic equation for photosynthesis:

$$6 CO_2 + 6 H_2O \rightarrow C_6H_{12}O_6 + 6 O_2$$

Looking at this equation, you can understand why scientists hypothesized that photosynthesis first splits carbon dioxide ($CO_2 \rightarrow C + O_2$), releasing oxygen gas, and then adds water (H_2O) to the carbon to produce sugar. In the 1930s, this idea was challenged by C. B. van Niel, who was working with photosynthesizing bacteria that produce sugar from CO_2 but do not release O_2. He hypothesized that in plants H_2O is split, with the hydrogen becoming incorporated into sugar and the O_2 released as gas.

▲ **Figure 7.3A** Oxygen bubbles on the leaves of an aquatic plant

In the 1950s, scientists confirmed van Niel's hypothesis by using a heavy isotope of oxygen, ^{18}O, to follow the fate of oxygen atoms during photosynthesis. (This was one of the first uses of isotopes as tracers in biological research. Remember from Module 2.3 that isotopes are atoms with differing numbers of neutrons.) The photosynthesis equation you will see in the description of these experiments is slightly more detailed than the summary equation written above. It shows that water is actually both a reactant and a product in the reaction. (As is often done, glucose is shown as a product, although the direct product of photosynthesis is a three-carbon sugar that can be

used to make glucose.) In these equations, the red type denotes the labelled oxygen—^{18}O.

Experiment 1: $6 CO_2 + 12 H_2O \rightarrow C_6H_{12}O_6 + 6 H_2O + 6 O_2$

Experiment 2: $6 CO_2 + 12 H_2O \rightarrow C_6H_{12}O_6 + 6 H_2O + 6 O_2$

In experiment 1, a plant given CO_2 containing ^{18}O gave off no labelled (^{18}O-containing) oxygen gas. But in experiment 2, a plant given H_2O containing ^{18}O did produce labelled O_2. These experiments show that the O_2 produced during photosynthesis comes from water and not from CO_2.

Additional experiments have revealed that the oxygen atoms in CO_2 and the hydrogen atoms in the reactant H_2O molecules end up in the sugar molecule and in water that is formed as a product. **Figure 7.3B** summarizes the fates of all the atoms that start out in the reactant molecules of photosynthesis.

The synthesis of sugar in photosynthesis involves numerous chemical reactions. Working out the details of these reactions also involved the use of isotopes, in this case, radioactive isotopes. In the mid-1940s, American biochemist Melvin Calvin and his colleagues began using radioactive ^{14}C to trace the sequence of intermediates formed in the cyclic pathway that produces sugar from CO_2. They worked for 10 years to elucidate this cycle, which is now called the Calvin cycle. Calvin received the Nobel Prize in 1961 for this work.

 Photosynthesis produces billions of tons of carbohydrate a year. Where does most of the mass of this huge amount of organic matter come from?

● Mostly from CO_2 in the air, which provides both the carbon and oxygen in carbohydrate. Water supplies only the hydrogen.

▲ **Figure 7.3B** Fates of all the atoms in photosynthesis

7.4 Photosynthesis is a redox process, as is cellular respiration

What actually happens when CO_2 and water are converted to sugar and O_2? Photosynthesis is a redox (oxidation-reduction) process, just as cellular respiration is (see Module 6.5). As indicated in the summary equation for photosynthesis (**Figure 7.4A**), CO_2 becomes reduced to sugar as electrons, along with hydrogen ions (H^+) from water, are added to it. Meanwhile, water molecules are oxidized; that is, they lose electrons, along with hydrogen ions. Recall that oxidation and reduction always go hand in hand.

Now compare the food-producing equation for photosynthesis with the energy-releasing equation for cellular respiration that you learned about in Chapter 6 (**Figure 7.4B**).

▲ **Figure 7.4A** Photosynthesis (uses light energy)

▲ **Figure 7.4B** Cellular respiration (releases chemical energy)

Overall, cellular respiration harvests energy stored in a glucose molecule by oxidizing the sugar and reducing O_2 to H_2O. This process involves a number of energy-releasing redox reactions, with electrons losing potential energy as they "fall" down an electron transport chain to O_2. Along the way, the mitochondrion uses some of the energy to synthesize ATP.

In contrast, the food-producing redox reactions of photosynthesis require energy. The potential energy of electrons increases as they move from H_2O to CO_2 during photosynthesis.

The light energy captured by chlorophyll molecules in the chloroplast provides this energy boost. Photosynthesis converts light energy to chemical energy and stores it in the chemical bonds of sugar molecules, which can provide energy for later use or raw materials for biosynthesis.

? Which redox process, photosynthesis or cellular respiration, is endergonic, requiring energy input? (*Hint:* See Module 5.11.)

● Photosynthesis

7.5 Overview: The two stages of photosynthesis are linked by ATP and NADPH

The equation for photosynthesis is a simple summary of a very complex process. Actually, photosynthesis occurs in two stages, each with multiple steps. **Figure 7.5** shows the inputs and outputs of the two stages and how the stages are related.

The **light-dependent reactions** include the steps that convert light energy to chemical energy and release O_2. As shown in the figure, the light-dependent reactions occur in the thylakoid membranes. Water is split, providing a source of electrons and giving off O_2 as a by-product. Light energy absorbed by chlorophyll molecules built into the membranes is used to drive the transfer of electrons and H^+ from water to the electron acceptor **NADP+**, reducing it to NADPH. This electron carrier is very similar to NADH, which transports electrons in cellular respiration. The two differ only in the extra phosphate group in NADPH. NADPH temporarily stores electrons and hydrogen ions and provides "reducing power" to the Calvin cycle. The light-dependent reactions also generate ATP from ADP and a phosphate group.

In summary, the light-dependent reactions absorb solar energy and convert it to chemical energy stored in both ATP and NADPH. Notice that these reactions produce no sugar; sugar is not made until the Calvin cycle, which is the second stage of photosynthesis.

The **Calvin cycle** occurs in the stroma of the chloroplast (see Figure 7.5). It is a cyclic series of reactions that assembles sugar molecules by using CO_2 and the energy-rich products of the light-dependent reactions. The incorporation of carbon from CO_2 into organic compounds, shown in the figure as CO_2 entering the Calvin cycle, is called **carbon fixation**. After carbon fixation, enzymes of the cycle make sugars by further reducing the carbon compounds.

As the figure suggests, it is NADPH produced by the light-dependent reactions that provides the electrons for reducing carbon in the Calvin cycle. And ATP from the light-dependent reactions provides chemical energy that powers several of the

▲ **Figure 7.5** An overview of the two stages of photosynthesis in a chloroplast

steps of the Calvin cycle. The Calvin cycle is sometimes referred to as the light-independent reactions because none of the steps requires light directly. However, in most plants, the Calvin cycle occurs during daylight, when the light-dependent reactions power the cycle's sugar assembly line by supplying it with NADPH and ATP.

The word *photosynthesis* encapsulates the two stages. *Photo*, from the Greek word for "light," refers to the light-dependent reactions; *synthesis*, meaning "putting together," refers to sugar construction by the Calvin cycle. In the next several modules, we look at these two stages in more detail. But first, let's consider some of the properties of light, the energy source that powers photosynthesis.

? For chloroplasts to produce sugar from carbon dioxide in the dark, they would need to be supplied with _____ and _____.

● ATP, NADPH

The Light-Dependent Reactions: Converting Solar Energy to Chemical Energy

7.6 Do plants absorb all light during photosynthesis?

What do we mean when we say that photosynthesis is powered by light energy from the sun? There is a common misconception among students that plants can absorb all light and convert it to sugars. But can plants actually use all the light that reaches them during photosynthesis?

The Nature of Sunlight Sunlight is a type of energy called electromagnetic energy or electromagnetic radiation.

Electromagnetic energy travels in space as rhythmic waves analogous to those made by a pebble dropped in a puddle of water. **Figure 7.6A** shows the **electromagnetic spectrum**, the full range of electromagnetic wavelengths from the very short gamma rays to the very long wavelength radio waves. The distance between the crests of two adjacent waves is called a **wavelength** (illustrated at the bottom right of the figure). As you can see in the centre of the figure, visible light—the radiation your eyes see as different colours—is only a small fraction of the spectrum. It consists of wavelengths from about 380 nm to about 750 nm.

The model of light as waves explains many of light's properties. However, light also behaves as discrete packets of energy called photons. A **photon** has a fixed quantity of energy, and the shorter the wavelength of light, the greater the energy of its photons. In fact, the photons of wavelengths that are shorter than those of visible light have enough energy to damage molecules such as proteins and nucleic acids. This is why ultraviolet (UV) radiation can cause sunburns and skin cancer.

Photosynthetic Pigments **Figure 7.6B** shows what happens to visible light in the chloroplast. Light-absorbing molecules called **pigments** are built into the thylakoid membranes. A pigment can absorb only some wavelengths of light. Wavelengths that are not absorbed are either reflected off the chloroplast or transmitted through the chloroplast. We do not see the

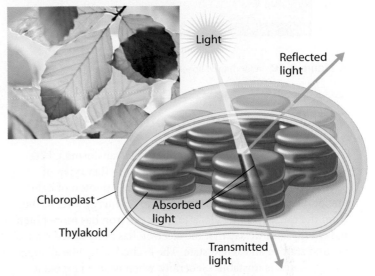

▲ **Figure 7.6B** The interaction of light with a chloroplast

absorbed wavelengths; pigment molecules have absorbed their energy. What we see when we look at a leaf are the green wavelengths that the pigments transmit and reflect.

Different pigments absorb light of different wavelengths, and chloroplasts contain more than one type of pigment. **Figure 7.6C** shows the ability of three chloroplast pigments to absorb different wavelengths of light (each line represents what is called an absorbance spectrum for the given pigment). **Chlorophyll _a_**, which participates directly in the light-dependent reactions, absorbs mainly blue-violet and red light. It looks blue-green because it reflects mainly green light. A very similar molecule, chlorophyll _b_, absorbs mainly blue and orange light and reflects (and appears) yellow-green. Chlorophyll _b_ broadens the range of light that a plant can use by conveying absorbed energy to chlorophyll _a_, which then puts the energy to work in the light-dependent reactions.

Chloroplasts also contain pigments called carotenoids, which are various shades of yellow and orange. The spectacular colours of fall foliage in, for example, Eastern Canada are due partly to the yellow-orange hues of longer-lasting carotenoids that show through once the green chlorophyll breaks down. Carotenoids may broaden the spectrum of colours that can drive photosynthesis (see Figure 7.6C). However, a more important function seems to be _photoprotection_: Some carotenoids absorb and dissipate excessive light energy that would otherwise damage chlorophyll or interact with oxygen to form reactive oxidative molecules that can damage cell molecules. Similar carotenoids, which we obtain from carrots and some other plants, have a photoprotective role in our eyes.

Each type of pigment absorbs certain wavelengths of light because it is able to absorb the specific amounts of energy in those photons. Even with a variety of pigments in its thylakoid

▲ **Figure 7.6A** The electromagnetic spectrum and the wavelengths of visible light. (A wavelength of 650 nm is illustrated.)

▲ **Figure 7.6C** Absorbance spectra for three pigments

Absorption of light by chloroplast pigments (y-axis)

Chlorophyll *a*
Chlorophyll *b*
Carotenoids

400   500   600   700
Wavelength of light (nm)

membrane, a plant cannot absorb all wavelengths of light. As you can see in Figure 7.6C, the green wavelengths (those between 510 nm and 550 nm) are poorly absorbed, resulting in the green colour of most plants. Now that any misconception regarding light absorption have been laid to rest, we will see in the next module what happens when a pigment molecule such as chlorophyll absorbs a photon of light.

? What colour would a plant appear if it could absorb all wavelengths of visible light?

● Black, because if all colours of light were absorbed, none would be reflected or transmitted.

7.7 Photosystems capture solar energy

Energy cannot be destroyed, but it can be transformed. Let's see how light energy can be transformed to other types of energy. When a pigment molecule absorbs a photon of light, one of the pigment's electrons jumps to an energy level farther from the nucleus. In this location, the electron has more potential energy, and we say that the electron has been raised from a ground state to an excited state. The excited state, like all high-energy states, is unstable. Generally, when isolated pigment molecules absorb light, their excited electrons drop back down to the ground state in a billionth of a second, releasing their excess energy as heat. This conversion of light energy to heat is what makes a black car so hot on a sunny day (black pigments absorb all wavelengths of light).

Some isolated pigments, including chlorophyll, emit light as well as heat after absorbing photons. We can demonstrate this phenomenon in the laboratory with a chlorophyll solution, as shown on the left in **Figure 7.7A**. When illuminated, the chlorophyll emits photons of light that produce a reddish glow called fluorescence. The right side of Figure 7.7A illustrates what happens in fluorescence: An absorbed photon boosts an electron of chlorophyll to an excited state, from which it falls back to the ground state, emitting its energy as heat and light.

But chlorophyll behaves very differently in isolation than it does in an intact chloroplast. In their native habitat of the thylakoid membrane, chlorophyll and other pigment molecules that absorb photons transfer the energy to other pigment molecules and eventually to a special pair of chlorophyll molecules. This pair passes off an excited electron to a neighbouring molecule before it has a chance to drop back to the ground state.

In the thylakoid membrane, chlorophyll molecules are organized along with other pigments and proteins into clusters called photosystems **(Figure 7.7B)**. A **photosystem** consists of a number of light-harvesting complexes surrounding a reaction-centre complex. A *light-harvesting complex* contains various pigment molecules bound to proteins. Collectively, the light-harvesting complexes function as a light-gathering antenna. The pigments absorb photons and pass the energy from molecule to molecule (thin yellow arrows) until it reaches the reaction centre. The *reaction-centre complex* contains the pair of special chlorophyll *a* molecules and a molecule called the

▲ **Figure 7.7A** A solution of chlorophyll glowing red when illuminated (left); a diagram of an isolated, light-excited chlorophyll molecule that releases a photon of red light (right)

Excited state
Photon of light
Heat
Photon (fluorescence)
Ground state
Chlorophyll molecule

Photosystem

Light
Light-harvesting complexes
Reaction-centre complex
Primary electron acceptor
Thylakoid membrane
Transfer of energy
Pair of chlorophyll *a* molecules
Pigment molecules

▲ **Figure 7.7B** A light-excited pair of chlorophyll molecules in the reaction centre of a photosystem passing an excited electron to a primary electron acceptor *primary electron acceptor*, which is capable of accepting electrons and becoming reduced. The solar-powered transfer of an electron from the reaction-centre chlorophyll *a* to the primary electron acceptor is the first step in the transformation of light energy to chemical energy in the light-dependent reactions.

Two types of photosystems have been identified, and they cooperate in the light-dependent reactions. They are referred to as photosystem I and photosystem II, in order of their discovery, although photosystem II actually functions first in the sequence of steps that make up the light-dependent reactions. Each photosystem has a characteristic reaction-centre complex. In photosystem II, the chlorophyll *a* of the reaction-centre complex is called P680 because the light it absorbs best is red light

with a wavelength of 680 nm. The reaction-centre chlorophyll of photosystem I is called P700 because the wavelength of light it absorbs best is 700 nm (in the far-red part of the spectrum). Now let's see how the two photosystems work together in the light-dependent reactions to generate ATP and NADPH.

? **Compared with a solution of isolated chlorophyll, why do intact chloroplasts release less heat and fluorescence when illuminated?**

● In the chloroplasts, energy is passed from pigment molecule to pigment molecule, and eventually the light-excited electrons of reaction-centre chlorophyll molecules are trapped by a primary electron acceptor rather than giving up their energy as heat and light.

7.8 Two photosystems connected by an electron transport chain generate ATP and NADPH

In the light-dependent reactions, light energy is transformed into the chemical energy of ATP and NADPH. In this process, electrons removed from H_2O pass from photosystem II to photosystem I to NADP$^+$. Between the two photosystems, the electrons move down an electron transport chain (similar to the one in cellular respiration) and provide energy for the synthesis of ATP. All the ATP produced in the light-dependent reactions is used during the next stage of photosynthesis (see Module 7.10). For everyday functions, plant cells use ATP generated from cellular respiration as discussed in the previous chapter.

Let's follow the flow of electrons (represented by gold arrows) in **Figure 7.8A**, which shows the two photosystems embedded in a thylakoid membrane. ❶ A pigment molecule in a light-harvesting complex absorbs a photon of light. The energy is passed to other pigment molecules and finally to the reaction centre of photosystem II, where it excites an electron of chlorophyll

P680 to a higher energy state. ❷ This electron is captured by the primary electron acceptor. ❸ Water is split, and its electrons are supplied one by one to P680, each replacing an electron lost to the primary electron acceptor. The oxygen atom combines with a second oxygen from another split water molecule, forming O_2.

❹ Each photoexcited electron passes from photosystem II to photosystem I via an electron transport chain. The exergonic "fall" of electrons provides energy for the synthesis of ATP by pumping H$^+$ across the membrane (not shown here). ❺ Meanwhile, light energy excites an electron of chlorophyll P700 in the reaction centre of photosystem I. An adjacent primary electron acceptor captures the electron, and an electron that reaches the bottom of the electron transport chain from photosystem II replaces the lost electron in P700. ❻ Photoexcited electrons of photosystem I are passed through a short electron transport chain to NADP$^+$, reducing it to NADPH.

▲ **Figure 7.8A** Electron flow in the light-dependent reactions: light energy driving electrons from water to NADPH

Figure 7.8A shows how the two photosystems cooperate in generating ATP and NADPH. To help you grasp this point, we have provided a mechanical analogy in **Figure 7.8B**. The input of light energy, represented by the large yellow mallets, boosts electrons in the reaction-centre complexes of both photosystems up to the excited state. The electrons are caught by the primary electron acceptor on top of the platform in each photosystem. Photosystem II passes the electrons through an ATP mill. Photosystem I hands its electrons off to reduce NADP$^+$ to NADPH.

NADPH, ATP, and O$_2$ are the products of the light-dependent reactions. Next we look in more detail at how ATP is formed.

? Tracing the light-dependent reactions in Figure 7.8A, there is a flow of electrons from _____ to _____, which is reduced to _____, the source of electrons for sugar synthesis in the _____ cycle.

● water; NADP$^+$; NADPH; Calvin

▲ **Figure 7.8B** A mechanical analogy of the light-dependent reactions

7.9 Chemiosmosis powers ATP synthesis in the light-dependent reactions

You first encountered chemiosmosis in Modules 6.6 and 6.10 as the mechanism of oxidative phosphorylation (ATP formation) in cellular respiration in a mitochondrion. Chemiosmosis is also the mechanism that generates ATP in a chloroplast. Recall that in chemiosmosis, the potential energy of a concentration gradient of hydrogen ions (H$^+$) across a membrane powers ATP synthesis. This gradient is created when an electron transport chain uses the energy released as it passes electrons down the chain to pump H$^+$ across a membrane.

Figure 7.9 illustrates the relationship between chloroplast structure and function in the light-dependent reactions. As in Figure 7.8A, we show the two photosystems and electron transport chains, all located within the thylakoid membrane of a chloroplast. Here you can see that as photoexcited electrons are passed down the electron transport chain connecting the two photosystems, hydrogen ions are pumped across the membrane from the stroma into the thylakoid space (inside the thylakoid sacs). This generates a concentration gradient across the membrane.

The flask-shaped structure in the figure represents an ATP synthase complex, which is very similar to the ones found in a mitochondrion. The energy of the concentration gradient drives H$^+$ back across the membrane through ATP synthase, which

Chloroplast

▲ **Figure 7.9** The production of ATP by chemiosmosis (numerous copies of these components present in each thylakoid)

couples the flow of H⁺ to the phosphorylation of ADP. Because the initial energy input is light, this chemiosmotic production of ATP in photosynthesis is called **photophosphorylation**.

How does photophosphorylation compare with oxidative phosphorylation? In cellular respiration, the high-energy electrons passed down the electron transport chain come from the oxidation of organic molecules. In photosynthesis, light energy is used to drive electrons that originally came from water to the top of the transport chain. Mitochondria transfer chemical energy from food to ATP; chloroplasts transform light energy into the chemical energy of ATP.

Notice that in the light-driven flow of electrons through the two photosystems, the final electron acceptor is NADP⁺, not O_2 as in cellular respiration. Electrons do not end up at a low energy level in H_2O, as they do in respiration. Instead, they are stored at a high state of potential energy in NADPH.

In summary, the light-dependent reactions provide the chemical energy (ATP) and reducing power (NADPH) for the next stage of photosynthesis, the Calvin cycle. In the next module we see how that cycle makes sugar.

? **What is the advantage of the light-dependent reactions producing NADPH and ATP on the stroma side of the thylakoid membrane?**

● The Calvin cycle, which uses the NADPH and ATP, occurs in the stroma.

The Calvin Cycle: Reducing CO₂ to Sugar

7.10 ATP and NADPH power sugar synthesis in the Calvin cycle

Input { CO₂ ATP NADPH

Output: G3P

▲ **Figure 7.10A** An overview of the Calvin cycle

The Calvin cycle functions like a sugar factory within a chloroplast. As **Figure 7.10A** shows, inputs to this all-important food-making process are CO₂ (from the air) and ATP and NADPH (both generated by the light-dependent reactions). Using CO₂, energy from ATP, and high-energy electrons from NADPH, the Calvin cycle constructs an energy-rich, three-carbon sugar, glyceraldehyde 3-phosphate (G3P). A plant cell can use G3P to make glucose and other organic molecules as needed. (You already met G3P in glycolysis: It is the three-carbon sugar formed by the splitting of glucose.)

Figure 7.10B presents the details of the Calvin cycle. It is called a cycle because, like the citric acid cycle in cellular respiration, the starting material is regenerated with each turn of the cycle. In this case, the starting material is a five-carbon sugar named ribulose bisphosphate (RuBP). **❶** In the carbon fixation step, the enzyme rubisco attaches CO₂ to RuBP. (Rubisco is thought to be the most abundant protein on Earth.) **❷** In the next step, a reduction reaction, NADPH reduces the organic acid 3-PGA to G3P by using the energy of ATP.

Step ❶ Carbon fixation. An enzyme called rubisco combines CO₂ with a five-carbon sugar called ribulose bisphosphate (abbreviated RuBP). The unstable product splits into two molecules of the three-carbon organic acid, 3-phosphoglyceric acid (3-PGA). For three CO₂ entering, six 3-PGA result.

Step ❷ Reduction. Two chemical reactions (indicated by the two blue arrows) consume energy from six molecules of ATP and oxidize six molecules of NADPH. Six molecules of 3-PGA are reduced, producing six molecules of the energy-rich three-carbon sugar, G3P.

Step ❸ Release of one molecule of G3P. Five of the G3Ps from step 2 remain in the cycle. The single molecule of G3P you see leaving the cycle is the net product of photosynthesis. A plant cell uses G3P to make glucose and other organic compounds.

Step ❹ Regeneration of RuBP. A series of chemical reactions uses energy from ATP to rearrange the atoms in the five G3P molecules (15 carbons total), forming three RuBP molecules (15 carbons). These can start another turn of the cycle.

▲ **Figure 7.10B** Details of the Calvin cycle, which takes place in the stroma of a chloroplast

To make a molecule of G3P, the cycle must incorporate the carbon atoms from three molecules of CO_2. The cycle actually incorporates one carbon at a time, but we show it starting with three CO_2 molecules so that we end up with a complete G3P molecule.

For this to be a cycle, RuBP must be regenerated. ❸ For every three CO_2 molecules fixed, one G3P molecule leaves the cycle as product, and the remaining five G3P molecules are rearranged, ❹ using energy from ATP to regenerate three molecules of RuBP.

Note that for the net synthesis of one G3P molecule, the Calvin cycle consumes nine ATP and six NADPH molecules, which were provided by the light-dependent reactions. The large amount of energy required to synthesize one molecule of glucose should reinforce for you why glucose is such a good source of energy for cells.

> **?** To synthesize one glucose molecule, the Calvin cycle uses _____ CO_2, _____ ATP, and _____ NADPH. Explain why this high number of ATP and NADPH molecules is consistent with the value of glucose as an energy source.

● 6; 18; 12. Glucose is a valuable energy source because it is highly reduced, storing lots of potential energy in its electrons. The more energy a molecule stores, the more energy and reducing power required to produce that molecule.

7.11 Other methods of carbon fixation have evolved in hot, dry climates

As you just learned in the previous module, the first step of the Calvin cycle is carbon fixation. Most plants use CO_2 directly from the air, and carbon fixation occurs when the enzyme rubisco adds CO_2 to RuBP (see step 1 of Figure 7.10B). Such plants are called **C_3 plants** because the first product of carbon fixation is the three-carbon compound 3-PGA. C_3 plants are widely distributed; they include such important agricultural crops as soybeans, oats, wheat, and rice. One problem that farmers face in growing C_3 plants is that hot, dry weather can decrease crop yield. In response to such conditions, plants close their stomata, the pores in their leaves. This adaptation reduces water loss and helps to prevent dehydration, but it also prevents CO_2 from entering the leaf and O_2 from leaving. As a result, CO_2 levels get very low in the leaf and photosynthesis slows. And the O_2 released from the light-dependent reactions begins to accumulate, creating another problem.

As O_2 builds up in a leaf, rubisco adds O_2 instead of CO_2 to RuBP. A two-carbon product of this reaction is then broken down in the cell. This process is called **photorespiration** because it occurs in the light and, like respiration, it consumes O_2 and releases CO_2. But unlike cellular respiration, it uses ATP instead of producing it; and unlike photosynthesis, it yields no sugar. Photorespiration can, however, drain away as much as 50% of the carbon fixed by the Calvin cycle.

According to one hypothesis, photorespiration is an evolutionary relic from when the atmosphere had less O_2 than it does today. In the ancient atmosphere that prevailed when rubisco first evolved, the inability of the enzyme's active site to exclude O_2 would have made little difference. It is only after O_2 became so concentrated in the atmosphere that the "sloppiness" of rubisco presented a problem. New evidence also indicates that photorespiration may play a protective role when the products of the light-dependent reactions build up in a cell (as occurs when the Calvin cycle slows because of a lack of CO_2).

C_4 Plants   In some plant species found in hot, dry climates, alternative modes of carbon fixation have evolved that minimize photorespiration and optimize the Calvin cycle. **C_4 plants** are so named because they first fix CO_2 into a four-carbon compound. When the weather is hot and dry, a C_4 plant keeps

▲ **Figure 7.11** Comparison of C_4 and CAM photosynthesis: The fixing of CO_2 into a four-carbon compound and the Calvin cycle occur in different cells in C_4 plants and at different times of day in CAM plants.

its stomata mostly closed, thus conserving water. It continues making sugars via photosynthesis by using the pathway and the two types of cells shown on the left side of **Figure 7.11**. An enzyme in the mesophyll cells has a high affinity for CO_2 and can fix carbon even when the CO_2 concentration in the leaf is low. The resulting four-carbon compound then acts as a carbon shuttle; it moves into bundle-sheath cells, which are packed around the veins of the leaf, and releases CO_2. Thus, the CO_2 concentration in these cells remains high enough for the Calvin cycle to make sugars and avoid photorespiration. Corn and sugarcane are examples of agriculturally important C_4 plants. In addition to the plants discussed in this chapter's opening essay, some biomass energy plantations in the warmer, drier regions of Canada grow switchgrass, a C_4 plant.

CAM Plants A second photosynthetic adaptation has evolved in pineapples, many cacti, and other succulent (water-storing) plants, such as aloe and jade plants. Called **CAM plants**, these species are adapted to very dry climates. A CAM plant (right side of Figure 7.11) conserves water by opening its stomata and admitting CO_2 only at night. CO_2 is fixed into a four-carbon compound, which banks CO_2 at night and releases it during the day. Thus, the Calvin cycle can operate, even with the leaf's stomata closed during the day.

In C_4 plants, carbon fixation and the Calvin cycle occur in different types of cells. In CAM plants, these processes occur in the same cells, but at different times of the day. Keep in mind that CAM, C_4, and C_3 plants all eventually use the Calvin cycle to make sugar from CO_2. The C_4 and CAM pathways are two evolutionary adaptations that minimize photorespiration and maximize photosynthesis in hot, dry climates.

> **?** Why would you expect photorespiration on a hot, dry day to occur less in C_4 and CAM plants than in C_3 plants?

● Because of their initial fixing of carbon, both C_4 and CAM plants can supply rubisco with CO_2. When a C_3 plant closes its stomata, CO_2 levels drop and O_2 rises, making it more likely that rubisco will add O_2 to RuBP.

Photosynthesis Reviewed and Extended

7.12 Review: Photosynthesis uses light energy, carbon dioxide, and water to make organic molecules

Life on Earth is solar powered. As we have discussed, most of the living world depends on the food-making machinery of photosynthesis. **Figure 7.12** summarizes this vital process. The production of sugar from CO_2 is an emergent property that arises from the structure of a chloroplast—a structural arrangement that integrates the two stages of photosynthesis.

Starting on the left in the diagram, you see a summary of the light-dependent reactions, which occur in the thylakoid membranes. Two photosystems in the membranes capture solar energy, energizing electrons in chlorophyll molecules. Simultaneously, water is split, and O_2 is released. The photoexcited electrons are transferred through an electron transport chain,

where energy is harvested to make ATP, and finally to $NADP^+$, reducing it to the high-energy compound NADPH.

The chloroplast's sugar factory is the Calvin cycle, the second stage of photosynthesis. In the stroma, the enzyme rubisco combines CO_2 with RuBP. ATP and NADPH are used to reduce 3-PGA to G3P. Sugar molecules made from G3P serve as a plant's own food supply.

About 50% of the carbohydrate made by photosynthesis is consumed as fuel for cellular respiration in the mitochondria of plant cells. Sugars also serve as starting material for making other organic molecules, such as a plant's proteins and lipids. Many glucose molecules are linked together to make cellulose,

◀ **Figure 7.12** A summary of photosynthesis

the main component of cell walls. Cellulose is the most abundant organic molecule in a plant—and probably on the surface of the planet. Most plants make much more food each day than they need. They store the excess in roots, tubers, seeds, and fruits.

Plants (and other photosynthesizers) not only feed themselves, but also are the ultimate source of food for virtually all other organisms. Humans and other animals are dependent on the organic matter made by photosynthesizers. Even the energy we acquire when we eat meat was originally captured by photosynthesis. The energy in a hamburger, for instance, came from sunlight that was originally converted to a chemical form in the grasses eaten by cattle.

The collective productivity of the tiny chloroplasts is truly amazing: Photosynthesis makes an estimated 160 billion tonnes of carbohydrate per year. That's equivalent in mass to a stack of about 100 trillion copies of this textbook. No other chemical process on Earth can match the output of photosynthesis.

This review of photosynthesis is an appropriate place to reflect on the metabolic ground we have covered in this chapter and the previous one. In Chapter 6, we saw that virtually all organisms, plants included, use cellular respiration to obtain the energy they need from fuel molecules such as glucose. We followed the chemical pathways of glycolysis and the citric acid cycle, which oxidize glucose and release energy from it. We have now come full circle, seeing how plants trap sunlight energy and use it to reduce carbon dioxide to make glucose.

In tracing glucose synthesis and its breakdown, we have also seen that cells use several of the same mechanisms—electron transport, redox reactions, and chemiosmosis—in energy storage (photosynthesis) and energy harvest (cellular respiration).

 Explain this statement: No process is more important than photosynthesis to the welfare of life on Earth.

● Photosynthesis is the ultimate source of the food for almost all organisms and the oxygen they need for cellular respiration.

7.13 Photosynthesis may moderate global climate change

The greenhouse in **Figure 7.13A** is used to grow plants when the weather outside is too cold. The glass or plastic walls of a greenhouse allow solar radiation to pass through. The sunlight heats the soil, which in turn warms the air. The walls trap the warm air, raising the temperature inside.

An analogous process, called the **greenhouse effect**, operates on a global scale (**Figure 7.13B**). Solar radiation reaching Earth's atmosphere includes ultraviolet radiation and visible light. As we discuss in the next module, the ozone layer filters out most of the damaging UV radiation. Visible light passes through and is absorbed by the planet's surface, warming it. Heat radiating from the warmed planet is absorbed by gases in the atmosphere, which then reflect some of the heat back to Earth. This natural heating effect is highly beneficial. Without it, Earth would be much colder, and most life as we know it could not exist.

The gases in the atmosphere that absorb heat radiation are called greenhouse gases. Some occur naturally, such as water vapour, carbon dioxide, and methane, while others are synthetic, such as the chlorofluorocarbons we discuss in the next module. Human activities add to the levels of these greenhouse gases.

Carbon dioxide is one of the most important greenhouse gases. You have just learned that CO_2 is a raw material for photosynthesis and a waste product of cellular respiration. These two processes, taking place in microscopic chloroplasts and mitochondria, keep carbon cycling between CO_2 and more complex organic compounds on a global scale. Photosynthetic organisms absorb billions of tonnes of CO_2 each year. Most of that fixed carbon returns to the atmosphere via cellular respiration, the action of decomposers, and

fires. But much of it remains locked in large tracts of forests and undecomposed organisms. And large amounts of carbon are in long-term storage in fossil fuels buried deep under Earth's surface.

Since 1850, the start of the Industrial Revolution, the atmospheric concentration of CO_2 has increased about 40%, mostly because of the combustion of fossil fuels, such as coal, oil, and gasoline. Increasing concentrations of greenhouse gases have been linked to **global climate change**, of which the major aspect is *global warming*. The predicted consequences of this slow but steady increase in average global temperature include melting of polar ice, rising sea levels, extreme weather patterns, droughts, increased extinction rates, and the spread of tropical diseases. Indeed, many of these effects are already being documented.

Unfortunately, the rise in atmospheric CO_2 levels during the last century coincided with widespread deforestation, which

▲ **Figure 7.13A** Plants growing in a greenhouse

▲ **Figure 7.13B** CO_2 in the atmosphere and the greenhouse effect

CO₂ levels will continue to rise. We discuss global climate change in more detail in Chapter 41.

Can photosynthesis offset this increase in atmospheric CO_2? Certainly, slowing the destruction of our forests will sustain their photosynthetic and carbon-storing contributions. Taking a lesson from plants, we can explore technologies that utilize solar energy for some of our energy needs. Biofuels hold out the promise of a renewable fuel source (see Module 18.4). As the plants or algae used for biofuels grow, their photosynthesis removes CO_2 from the atmosphere. Growing and using alternative fuels could keep the cycle of CO_2 removal in photosynthesis balanced with CO_2 release in fuel burning. However, it is unlikely that photosynthesis alone will offset the rising atmospheric CO_2 concentrations, and other changes, such as lowering CO_2 emissions, will need to occur in conjunction.

aggravated the global warming problem by reducing an effective CO_2 sink. As forests are cleared for lumber or agriculture, and as population growth increases the demand for fossil fuels,

 Explain the greenhouse effect.

● Sunlight warms Earth's surface, which radiates heat to the atmosphere. CO_2 and other greenhouse gases absorb and radiate some heat back to Earth.

7.14 Scientific study of Earth's ozone layer has global significance

The process and importance of scientific discovery are illustrated by the story of how synthetic chemicals were destroying Earth's protective ozone layer and how the work of many scientists led to changes in worldwide environmental policies. As you now know, photosynthesis produces the O_2 on which almost all organisms depend for cellular respiration. This O_2 has another benefit: High in the atmosphere, high-energy solar radiation converts it to ozone (O_3). Acting as sunscreen for the planet, the ozone layer shields Earth from ultraviolet radiation. The balance between ozone formation and its natural destruction in the atmosphere, however, has been upset by human actions.

Chlorofluorocarbons (CFCs) are chemicals developed in the 1930s that became widely used in aerosol sprays, refrigerators, and Styrofoam production. In 1970, a scientist wondered whether CFCs were accumulating in the environment and sent a homemade detector on a boat trip to Antarctica. He found CFCs in the air all along the journey. When he reported his findings at a scientific meeting in 1972, two chemists, Sherwood Rowland and Mario Molina, wondered what happened to CFCs once they entered the atmosphere. A search of the literature found that these chemicals were not broken down in the lower atmosphere.

But the intense solar radiation in the upper atmosphere could break down CFCs, releasing chlorine atoms. Molina learned that chlorine reacts with ozone, reducing it to O_2. Other reactions liberate the chlorine, allowing it to destroy more ozone. In 1974, Molina and Rowland published their

Southern tip of South America

Antarctica

▲ **Figure 7.14** The ozone hole in the Southern Hemisphere, September 2006

work predicting that the release of CFCs would damage the ozone layer.

As other researchers tested the CFC-ozone depletion hypothesis, the evidence accumulated, and more people became concerned about ozone depletion. Others worried about the economic impact of banning CFCs, and CFC manufacturers mounted a campaign to cast doubt on the Molina–Rowland hypothesis in any way they could.

Then, in 1982, a researcher noted a dramatic dip in the ozone layer over Antarctica. At first he suspected an instrument malfunction. After recording this decline for two more years, he published his observations. A reanalysis of data collected by the American organization NASA over that period confirmed a gigantic hole in the ozone layer. This hole has appeared every spring over Antarctica since the late 1970s and continues today. **Figure 7.14** shows an image produced from atmospheric data from 2006. Blue and purple colours show where there is the least ozone. The ozone depletion was much greater than had been predicted by Molina and Rowland. How could it be explained?

Research showed that unusual ice clouds that appear during early spring in Antarctica could speed up the reactions that destroy ozone. The icy particles made CFCs hundreds of times more damaging than they normally are.

In response to these scientific findings, the first treaty to address Earth's environment was signed in 1987. In the Montreal Protocol on Substances that Deplete the Ozone Layer, many nations—Canada included—agreed to phase out CFCs. As research continued to establish the extent and danger of ozone depletion, these agreements were strengthened in 1990. Since 1996, the import and export of CFCs has been prohibited in Canada, except for a few essential uses. In 1995, Molina and Rowland shared a Nobel Prize for their work on how CFCs were damaging the atmosphere.

Today, global emissions of CFCs are near zero; but, because these compounds are so stable, recovery of the ozone layer is not expected until around 2060. Meanwhile, unblocked UV radiation is predicted to increase skin cancer and cataracts, as well as damage crops and phytoplankton in the oceans.

In addition to being ozone destroyers, CFCs are also potent greenhouse gases. The phase-out of CFCs has avoided what would have been the equivalent of adding 10 gigatons of CO_2 to the atmosphere. (For comparison, the Kyoto Protocol of 1997 set a 2012 target of a reduction of 2 gigatons of CO_2 emissions.)

Whether an environmental problem involves CFCs or CO_2, the scientific research is often complicated and the solutions complex. The connections between science, technology, and society, so clearly exemplified by the work of the scientists studying the ozone layer, are a major theme of this book.

 Where does the ozone layer come from, and why is it so important to life on Earth?

High in the atmosphere, radiation from the sun converts O_2 to ozone. The ozone layer absorbs potentially damaging UV radiation.

REVIEW

Reviewing the Concepts

An Overview of Photosynthesis (7.1–7.5)

7.1 Autotrophs are the producers of the biosphere. Plants, algae, and some protists and bacteria are photoautotrophs, the producers of food consumed by virtually all heterotrophic organisms.

7.2 Photosynthesis occurs in chloroplasts in plant cells. Chloroplasts are surrounded by a double membrane and contain stacks of thylakoids and a thick fluid called stroma.

7.3 Scientists traced the process of photosynthesis by using isotopes. Experiments using both heavy and radioactive isotopes helped to determine the details of the process of photosynthesis.

7.4 Photosynthesis is a redox process, as is cellular respiration. In photosynthesis, H_2O is oxidized and CO_2 is reduced.

7.5 Overview: The two stages of photosynthesis are linked by ATP and NADPH. The light-dependent reactions occur in the thylakoids, producing ATP and NADPH for the Calvin cycle, which takes place in the stroma.

The Light-Dependent Reactions: Converting Solar Energy to Chemical Energy (7.6–7.9)

7.6 Do plants absorb all light during photosynthesis? Certain wavelengths of visible light are absorbed by chlorophyll and other pigments. Carotenoids also function in photoprotection from excessive light.

7.7 Photosystems capture solar energy. Thylakoid membranes contain photosystems, each consisting of light-harvesting complexes and a reaction-centre complex. A primary electron acceptor receives photoexcited electrons from chlorophyll.

7.8 Two photosystems connected by an electron transport chain generate ATP and NADPH. Electrons shuttle from photosystem II to photosystem I, providing energy to make ATP, and then reduce $NADP^+$ to NADPH. Photosystem II regains electrons as water is split and O_2 released.

7.9 Chemiosmosis powers ATP synthesis in the light-dependent reactions. In photophosphorylation, the electron transport chain pumps H^+ into the thylakoid space. The concentration gradient drives H^+ back through ATP synthase, driving the synthesis of ATP.

The Calvin Cycle: Reducing CO_2 to Sugar (7.10–7.11)

7.10 ATP and NADPH power sugar synthesis in the Calvin cycle. The steps of the Calvin cycle include carbon fixation, reduction, release of G3P, and regeneration of RuBP. Using carbon from CO_2, electrons from NADPH, and energy from ATP, the cycle constructs G3P, which is used to build glucose and other organic molecules.

7.11 Other methods of carbon fixation have evolved in hot, dry climates. In C_3 plants, a drop in CO_2 and rise in O_2 when stomata close divert the Calvin cycle to photorespiration. C_4 plants and CAM plants first fix CO_2 into a four-carbon compound that provides CO_2 to the Calvin cycle even when stomata close on hot, dry days.

Photosynthesis Reviewed and Extended (7.12–7.14)

7.12 Review: Photosynthesis uses light energy, carbon dioxide, and water to make organic molecules.

7.13 Photosynthesis may moderate global climate change. Reducing deforestation and fossil fuel use and growing biofuel crops, which remove CO_2 from the atmosphere, may help to moderate the global warming caused by increasing CO_2 levels.

7.14 Scientific study of Earth's ozone layer has global significance. Solar radiation converts O_2 high in the atmosphere to ozone (O_3), which shields organisms from damaging UV radiation. Industrial chemicals called CFCs have caused dangerous thinning of the ozone layer, but international restrictions on CFC use are allowing a slow recovery.

Connecting the Concepts

1. The following diagram compares the chemiosmotic synthesis of ATP in mitochondria and chloroplasts. Fill in the blanks, which label the molecules shared by both processes and the regions in the chloroplast. Then, for both organelles, indicate which side of the membrane has the higher H^+ concentration.

2. Continue your comparison of chemiosmosis and electron transport in mitochondria and chloroplasts. In each case,
   a. where do the electrons come from?
   b. how do the electrons get their high potential energy?
   c. what picks up the electrons at the end of the chain?
   d. how is the energy given up by the electrons used?

3. Complete this summary map of photosynthesis.

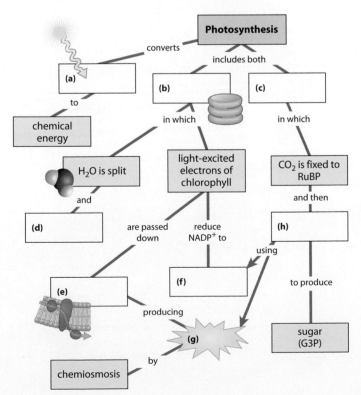

Testing Your Knowledge

Multiple Choice

4. In photosynthesis, _____ is oxidized and _____ is reduced.
   a. glucose; oxygen
   b. carbon dioxide; water
   c. water; carbon dioxide
   d. glucose; carbon dioxide
   e. water; oxygen

5. Which of the following are produced by reactions that take place in the thylakoids and consumed by reactions in the stroma?
   a. CO_2 and H_2O
   b. $NADP^+$ and ADP
   c. ATP and NADPH
   d. ATP, NADPH, and CO_2
   e. O_2 and ATP

6. When light strikes chlorophyll molecules in the reaction-centre complex, they lose electrons, which are ultimately replaced by
   a. splitting water.
   b. breaking down ATP.
   c. oxidizing NADPH.
   d. fixing carbon.
   e. oxidizing glucose.

7. The reactions of the Calvin cycle are not directly dependent on light, but they usually do not occur at night. Why? *(Explain.)*
   a. It is often too cold at night for these reactions to take place.
   b. Carbon dioxide concentrations decrease at night.
   c. The Calvin cycle depends on products of the light-dependent reactions.
   d. Plants usually close their stomata at night.
   e. Most plants do not make four-carbon compounds, which they would need for the Calvin cycle at night.

8. How many "turns" of the Calvin cycle are required to produce one molecule of glucose? (Assume one CO_2 is fixed in each turn of the cycle.)
   a. 1   b. 2
   c. 3   d. 6
   e. 12

9. Which of the following does *not* occur during the Calvin cycle?
   a. carbon fixation
   b. oxidation of NADPH
   c. consumption of ATP
   d. regeneration of RuBP, the CO_2 acceptor
   e. release of oxygen

10. Why is it difficult for most plants to carry out photosynthesis in very hot, dry environments such as deserts?
    a. The light is too intense and destroys the pigment molecules.
    b. The closing of stomata keeps CO_2 from entering and O_2 from leaving the plant.
    c. They must rely on photorespiration to make ATP.
    d. Global warming is intensified in a desert environment.
    e. CO_2 builds up in the leaves, blocking carbon fixation.

11. How is photosynthesis similar in C_4 plants and CAM plants?
    a. In both cases, the light-dependent reactions and the Calvin cycle are separated in both time and location.
    b. Both types of plants make sugar without the Calvin cycle.
    c. In both cases, rubisco is not used to fix carbon initially.
    d. Both types of plants make most of their sugar in the dark.
    e. In both cases, thylakoids are not involved in photosynthesis.

Describing, Comparing, and Explaining

12. What are the major inputs and outputs of the two stages of photosynthesis?

13. Explain why a poison that inhibits an enzyme of the Calvin cycle will also inhibit the light-dependent reactions.

14. What do plants do with the sugar they produce in photosynthesis?

Applying the Concepts

15. Most experts agree that global climate change is already occurring and will increase rapidly in this century. Many countries have made a commitment to reduce CO_2 emissions. Recent international negotiations, however, including a 2012 meeting in Doha, Qatar, have yet to reach a consensus on a global strategy to reduce greenhouse gas emissions. Some countries have resisted taking action because a few scientists and policymakers think that the warming trend may be just a random fluctuation in temperature that is not related to human activities or that cutting CO_2 emissions would sacrifice economic growth. Do you think we need more evidence before taking action? Or is it better to act now to reduce CO_2 emissions? What are the possible costs and benefits of each of these two strategies?

16. The use of biofuels avoids many of the problems associated with gathering, refining, transporting, and burning fossil fuels. Yet biofuels are not without their own set of problems. What challenges do you think would arise from a large-scale conversion to biofuels? How do these challenges compare with those encountered with fossil fuels? Do you think any other types of energy sources have more benefits and fewer costs than the others? Which ones, and why?

Answers to all questions can be found in Appendix E.

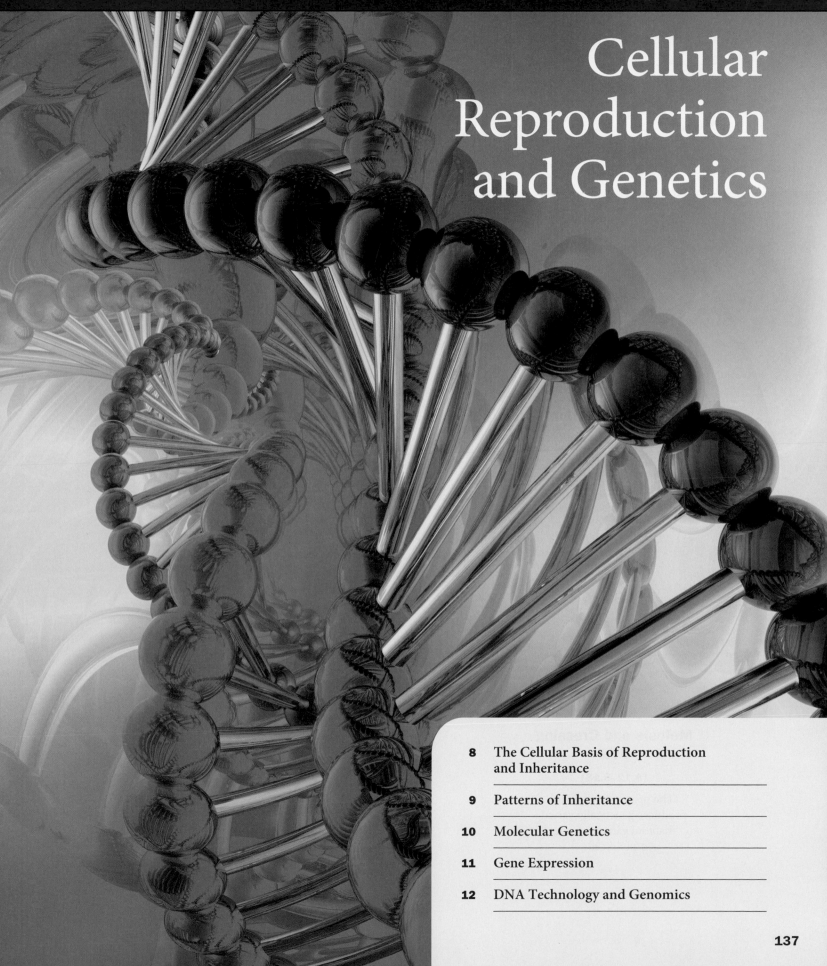

Cellular Reproduction and Genetics

The Cellular Basis of Reproduction and Inheritance

BIG IDEAS

Cell Division and Reproduction

(8.1–8.2)

Cell division underlies many of life's important processes.

The Eukaryotic Cell Cycle and Mitosis

(8.3–8.11)

Cells produce genetic duplicates through an ordered, tightly controlled series of steps.

Meiosis and Crossing Over

(8.12–8.18)

The process of meiosis produces genetically varied haploid gametes from diploid cells.

Alterations of Chromosome Number and Structure

(8.19–8.24)

Errors in cell division can produce organisms with abnormal numbers of chromosomes.

Rainforest Rescue

Deep in a Hawaiian rainforest, the thrumming of a helicopter cuts through the dense tropical air. After the helicopter touches down in a clearing, a pair of rescuers jump out, one of them carrying a precious bundle. A 20-minute hike through dense foliage brings them to their "patient": the last known wild *Cyanea kuhihewa* (*C. kuhihewa*) plant, a member of the bellflower family (pictured here). The rescuers, armed with the pollen of a species on the very brink of extinction, are part of a life-or-death battle.

Despite its tiny size, the Hawaiian rainforest is home to more than 300 endangered or threatened species. Of these, 11 plant species have fewer than five representatives growing anywhere in the wild. In 2002, the time of the rescue attempt described above, the small bellflower was one of the rarest.

So when this lone wild bellflower bloomed, scientists from the National Tropical Botanical Garden on Kauai recognized an opportunity. Their goal was to promote the sexual reproduction of the plant (the process that involves fertilization: the union of a sperm and an egg). Using a fine brush, the botanical rescuers transferred sperm-carrying pollen from a garden-grown plant to the egg-containing wild bloom. If sperm and egg join, the resulting fertilized egg can divide and eventually form an embryo and then a seed. Upon germination of the seed, the embryo may further develop into a juvenile and later into an adult plant.

Development from a fertilized egg to a new adult organism is one phase of a multicellular organism's life cycle, the sequence of stages leading from the adults of one generation to the adults of the next. The other phase of the life cycle is reproduction, the formation of new individuals from pre-existing ones. The reproductive phase of the life cycle entails the creation of offspring carrying the genetic information, DNA, of their parents. Sperm and egg each carry one set of genetic information—that is, one copy of the organism's genome. Thus, the offspring of sexual reproduction inherit traits from two parents. In the case of *C. kuhihewa*, sexual reproduction could provide desperately needed genetic diversity.

Unfortunately, the bellflower fertilization attempt failed. Even worse, the last remaining wild specimen died in 2003. But hope remains for *C. kuhihewa*. The garden's botanists are now trying asexual reproduction, the production of offspring by a single parent. Many plants that normally reproduce sexually can be induced to reproduce asexually in laboratories. Indeed, by using stem tissue snipped from wild plants in the 1990s, botanists at Kauai's botanical garden have produced several new bellflower plants through asexual reproduction.

This example illustrates the main point of this chapter: The perpetuation of life, including all aspects of reproduction and inheritance, is based on the reproduction of cells, or cell division. In this chapter, we discuss the two main types of cell division—mitosis and meiosis—and how they function within organisms.

Cell Division and Reproduction

8.1 Cell division plays many important roles in the lives of organisms

The ability of organisms to reproduce their own kind is the one characteristic that best distinguishes living things from nonliving matter (see Module 1.1 to review the characteristics of life). Only amoebas produce more amoebas, only people make more people, and only maple trees produce more maple trees. These simple facts of life have been recognized for thousands of years and are summarized by the age-old saying "Like begets like."

However, the biological concept of reproduction includes more than just the birth of new organisms: Reproduction actually occurs much more often at the cellular level. When a cell undergoes reproduction, or **cell division**, the two "daughter" cells that result are genetically identical to each other and to the original "parent" cell. (Biologists traditionally use the word *daughter* in this context, but it does not imply gender.) Before the parent cell splits into two, it duplicates its **chromosomes**, the structures that contain most of the cell's DNA. Then, during the division process, one set of chromosomes is distributed to each daughter cell. As a rule, the daughter cells receive identical sets of chromosomes from the lone original parent cell. Each offspring cell will thus be genetically identical to the other and to the original parent cell.

Sometimes, cell division results in the reproduction of a whole organism. Many single-celled organisms, such as prokaryotes or the eukaryotic yeast cell in **Figure 8.1A**, reproduce by dividing in half, and the offspring are genetic replicas. This is an example of **asexual reproduction**, the creation of genetically identical offspring by a single parent, without the participation of sperm and egg.

Many multicellular organisms can reproduce asexually as well. For example, some sea star species have the ability to grow new individuals from fragmented pieces (**Figure 8.1B**). And if you've ever grown a houseplant from a clipping, you've observed asexual reproduction in plants (**Figure 8.1C**). In asexual reproduction, there is one simple principle of inheritance: The lone parent and each of its offspring have identical genes.

Sexual reproduction is different; it requires fertilization of an egg by a sperm. The production of gametes—egg and sperm—involves a special type of cell division that occurs only in reproductive organs (such as testes and ovaries in humans). As you'll learn later in the chapter, a gamete has only half as many chromosomes as the parent cell that gave rise to it, and these chromosomes contain unique combinations of genes. Therefore, in sexually reproducing species, like does not precisely beget like (**Figure 8.1D**). Offspring produced by sexual reproduction generally resemble their parents more closely than they resemble unrelated individuals of the same species, but they are not identical to their parents or to each other. Each offspring inherits a unique combination of genes from its two parents, and this one-and-only set

▲ **Figure 8.1B** A sea star reproducing asexually

▲ **Figure 8.1A**
A yeast cell producing a genetically identical daughter cell by asexual reproduction

▲ **Figure 8.1C** An African violet reproducing asexually from a cutting (the large leaf on the left)

▼ **Figure 8.1D** Sexual reproduction produces offspring with unique combinations of genes

Colourized TEM 5000×

▲ **Figure 8.1E** Dividing cells in an early human embryo

of genes programs a unique combination of traits. As a result, sexual reproduction can produce great variation among offspring.

In multicellular organisms, cell division plays other important roles, in addition to the production of gametes. Cell division enables sexually reproducing organisms to develop from a single cell—the fertilized egg, or zygote—into an adult organism (**Figure 8.1E**). All the trillions of cells in your body arose via repeated cell divisions that began in your mother's body with a single fertilized egg cell. After an organism is fully grown, cell division continues to function in renewal and repair, replacing cells that die from normal wear and tear or accidents. Within your body, millions of cells must divide every second to replace damaged or lost cells (**Figure 8.1F**).

▲ **Figure 8.1F** A human kidney cell dividing

The type of cell division responsible for asexual reproduction and for the growth and maintenance of multicellular organisms involves a process called mitosis. The production of egg and sperm cells involves a special type of cell division called meiosis. In the remainder of this chapter, you will learn the details of both types of cell division. To start, we'll look briefly at prokaryotic cell division in the next module.

? What function does cell division play in an amoeba? What functions does it play in your body?

● *Amoeba: reproduction; Humans: development, growth, and repair*

8.2 Prokaryotes reproduce by binary fission

Prokaryotes (bacteria and archaea) reproduce by a type of cell division called **binary fission** (which means "dividing in half"). In typical prokaryotes, the majority of genes are carried on a single circular DNA molecule that, with associated proteins,

constitutes the organism's chromosome. Although prokaryotic chromosomes are much smaller than those of eukaryotes, duplicating them in an orderly fashion and distributing the copies equally to two daughter bacteria is still a formidable task. Consider, for example, that when stretched out, the chromosome of the bacterium *Escherichia coli* (*E. coli*) is about 500 times longer than the cell itself. Accurately replicating this molecule when it is coiled and packed inside the cell is no small achievement.

Figure 8.2A illustrates binary fission in a prokaryote. **1** As the chromosome is duplicating, the copies move toward the opposite ends of the cell. **2** Meanwhile, the cell elongates. **3** When chromosome duplication is complete and the cell has reached about twice its initial size, the plasma membrane grows inward and more cell wall is made, dividing the parent cell into two daughter cells. **Figure 8.2B** is an electron micrograph of a dividing bacterium (this cell is at a stage similar to the third illustration in Figure 8.2A).

? Why is binary fission classified as asexual reproduction?

● *Because the genetically identical offspring inherit their DNA from a single parent*

Plasma membrane

Cell wall

Prokaryotic chromosome

1 Duplication of the chromosome and separation of the copies

2 Continued elongation of the cell and movement of the copies

3 Division into two daughter cells

▲ **Figure 8.2A** Binary fission of a prokaryotic cell

Prokaryotic chromosomes

▲ **Figure 8.2B** An electron micrograph of a dividing bacterium

The Eukaryotic Cell Cycle and Mitosis

8.3 The large, complex chromosomes of eukaryotes duplicate with each cell division

Eukaryotic cells, in general, are more complex and much larger than prokaryotic cells, and they have many more genes. Human cells, for example, carry around 21 000 genes, versus a typical bacterium that has about 3000. Almost all the genes in the cells of humans, and in all other eukaryotes, are found in the cell nucleus, grouped into multiple chromosomes. (The exceptions include genes on the small DNA molecules of mitochondria and, in plants, chloroplasts.)

Most of the time, chromosomes exist as a diffuse mass of long, thin fibres that, if stretched out, would be far too long to fit in a cell's nucleus. In fact, the total length of DNA in just one of your cells would exceed your total height! In this loose state called **chromatin**, the fibres are composed of roughly equal amounts of DNA and protein molecules. Chromatin is too thin to be seen even with a light microscope.

As a cell prepares to divide, its chromatin coils up, forming tight, distinct chromosomes that are visible under a light microscope. Why is it necessary for a cell's chromosomes to be compacted in this way? Imagine a situation from your own life: Your belongings are spread out over a considerable area of your home, but as you prepare to move to a new home, you need to gather them all up and pack them into small containers. Similarly, before a cell can undergo division, it must compact all of its DNA into manageable packages. **Figure 8.3A** is a micrograph of a plant cell that is about to divide; each thick purple thread is a tightly packed individual chromosome.

Like a prokaryotic chromosome, each eukaryotic chromosome contains one long DNA molecule bearing hundreds or thousands of genes and, attached to the DNA, a number of protein molecules. However, the eukaryotic chromosome has a much more complex structure than the prokaryotic chromosome. The eukaryotic chromosome includes many more protein molecules, which help to maintain the chromosome's structure and control the activity of its genes. The number of chromosomes in a eukaryotic cell depends on the species. For example,

Chromosomes   **DNA molecules**

Sister chromatids

Chromosome duplication

Centromere — Sister chromatids

Chromosome distribution to the daughter cells

SEM 38 065×

▲ **Figure 8.3B** Chromosome duplication and distribution

human body cells generally have 46 chromosomes, while the body cells of a dog have 78. The adder's tongue fern has the highest number of chromosomes, with more than 1200 in every cell.

The chromosomes of a eukaryotic cell are duplicated before they condense and the cell divides. The DNA molecule of each chromosome is replicated (as you'll learn in Chapter 10), and new protein molecules attach as needed. Each chromosome now consists of two copies called **sister chromatids**, which contain identical copies of the DNA molecule **(Figure 8.3B)**. The two sister chromatids are joined together especially tightly at a narrow "waist" called the **centromere** (visible near the centre of each chromosome shown in the figure).

When the cell divides, the sister chromatids of a duplicated chromosome separate from each other. Once separated from its sister, each chromatid is called a chromosome, and it is identical to the chromosome the cell started with. One of the new chromosomes goes to one daughter cell, and the other goes to the other daughter cell. In this way, each daughter cell receives a complete and identical set of chromosomes. In humans, for example, a typical dividing cell has 46 duplicated chromosomes (or 92 chromatids), and each of the two daughter cells that results from it has 46 single chromosomes.

▶ **Figure 8.3A**
A plant cell (from an African blood lily) just before cell division

LM 565×

? **When does a chromosome consist of two identical chromatids?**

● When the cell is preparing to divide and has duplicated its chromosomes, but before the duplicates actually separate

8.4 The cell cycle multiplies cells

How do chromosome duplication and cell division fit into the life of a cell—and the life of an organism? As discussed in Module 8.1, cell division is essential to all life. Cell division is the basis of reproduction for every organism. It enables a multicellular organism to grow to adult size. It also replaces worn-out or damaged cells, keeping the total cell number in a mature individual relatively constant. In your own body, for example, millions of cells must divide every second to maintain the total number of about 10 trillion cells. Some cells divide once a day, others less often, and highly specialized cells, such as our mature muscle cells, not at all. The fact that some mature cells never divide explains why some kinds of damage—such as the death of cardiac muscle cells during a heart attack or the death of brain cells during a stroke—can never be reversed.

The process of cell division is a key component of the **cell cycle**, an ordered sequence of events that extends from the time a cell is first formed from a dividing parent cell until its own division into two cells. The cell cycle consists of two main stages: a growing stage (called interphase), during which the cell roughly doubles everything in its cytoplasm and precisely replicates its chromosomal DNA, and the actual cell division (called the mitotic phase).

As **Figure 8.4** indicates, most of the cell cycle is spent in **interphase**. This is a time when a cell's metabolic activity is very high and the cell performs its various functions within the organism. For example, a cell in your intestine might release digestive enzymes and absorb nutrients, while a white blood cell might circulate in your bloodstream, interacting with invading microbes. During interphase, a cell makes more cytoplasm. It increases its supply of proteins, creates more cytoplasmic organelles (such as mitochondria and ribosomes), and grows in size. Additionally, the chromosomes duplicate during this period. Typically, interphase lasts for at least 90% of the total time required for the cell cycle.

Interphase can be divided into three subphases: the G_1 phase ("first gap"), the S phase, and the G_2 phase ("second gap"). During all three subphases, the cell grows. However, chromosomes are duplicated only during the S phase. S stands for *synthesis* of DNA—also known as DNA replication. At the beginning of the S phase, each chromosome is single. At the end of this phase, after DNA replication, the chromosomes are double, each consisting of two sister chromatids. To summarize interphase: A cell grows (G_1), continues to grow as it copies its chromosomes (S), and then grows more as it completes preparations for cell division (G_2).

The **mitotic phase** (**M phase**; the blue area of the figure), the part of the cell cycle when the cell actually divides, accounts for only about 10% of the total time required for the cell cycle. The mitotic phase is itself divided into two overlapping stages, called mitosis and cytokinesis. In **mitosis**, the nucleus and its contents—most importantly the duplicated chromosomes—divide and are evenly distributed, forming two daughter nuclei. During **cytokinesis**, which usually begins before mitosis ends, the cytoplasm is divided in two.

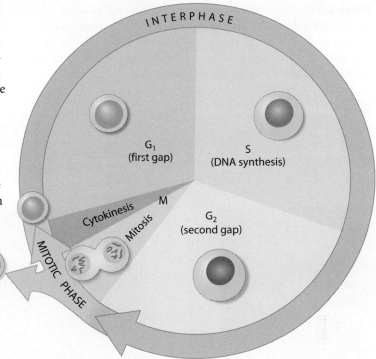

▲ **Figure 8.4** The eukaryotic cell cycle

The combination of mitosis and cytokinesis produces two genetically identical daughter cells, each with a single nucleus, surrounding cytoplasm stocked with organelles, and a plasma membrane. Each newly produced daughter cell may then proceed through G_1 and repeat the cycle.

Mitosis is unique to eukaryotes and is the evolutionary solution to the problem of allocating identical copies of all the separate chromosomes to two daughter cells. Mitosis is a remarkably accurate mechanism. Experiments with yeast, for example, indicate that an error in chromosome distribution occurs only once in about 100 000 cell divisions.

The extreme accuracy of mitosis is essential to the development of your own body. All of us began as a single cell. Mitotic cell division ensures that all your body cells receive copies of the 46 chromosomes that were found in this original cell. Thus, every one of the trillions of cells in your body today can trace its ancestry back through mitotic divisions to that first cell produced when your father's sperm and mother's egg fused about nine months before your birth.

During the mitotic phase, the appearance of a living cell's chromosomes and other structures undergoes dramatic changes that can be viewed through a light microscope. In the next module, we'll use these visible changes as a guide to the stages of mitosis.

? **A researcher treats cells with a chemical that prevents DNA synthesis from starting. This treatment would trap the cells in which part of the cell cycle?**

G_1

8.5 Cell division is a continuum of dynamic changes

Figure 8.5 illustrates the cell cycle for an animal cell by using micrographs, drawings (simplified to include just four chromosomes), and text. The micrographs show cells from a newt, with chromosomes in blue and the mitotic spindle in green. Interphase is included, but the emphasis is on the dramatic changes that occur during cell division, the mitotic phase. Mitosis is a continuum, but biologists distinguish five main stages: **prophase**, **prometaphase**, **metaphase**, **anaphase**, and **telophase**. These stages are usually, but not always, followed by cell division or **cytokinesis** which is the topic of the next module.

Interphase Interphase is the period of cell growth, when the cell synthesizes new molecules and organelles. At the point shown here, during late interphase (G$_2$), the cell has doubled much of its earlier contents and the cytoplasm contains two centrosomes. Each centrosome has a pair of centrioles, can-shaped structures made of microtubules. Within the nucleus, the chromosomes are duplicated, but they cannot be distinguished individually because they are still in the form of loosely packed chromatin.

Prophase During prophase, changes occur in both the nucleus and the cytoplasm. Within the nucleus, the chromatin fibres become more tightly coiled and folded, forming discrete chromosomes that can be seen with the light microscope. Each duplicated chromosome appears as two identical sister chromatids joined together, with a narrow "waist" at the centromere. In the cytoplasm, the mitotic spindle begins to form as microtubules rapidly grow out from the centrosomes, which begin to move away from each other.

Prometaphase The nuclear envelope breaks into fragments and disappears. Microtubules emerging from the centrosomes at the poles (ends) of the mitotic spindle reach the chromosomes, now highly condensed. At the centromere region, each sister chromatid has a protein structure called a kinetochore (shown as a black dot). Some of the spindle microtubules attach to the kinetochores, throwing the chromosomes into agitated motion. Other spindle microtubules make contact with microtubules coming from the opposite pole. Forces exerted by protein "motors" associated with spindle microtubules move the chromosomes toward the centre of the cell.

▲ **Figure 8.5** The stages of cell division by mitosis

The chromosomes are the stars of the mitotic drama. Their movements depend on the **mitotic spindle**, a football-shaped structure of microtubules that guides the separation of the two sets of daughter chromosomes. The spindle microtubules emerge from two **centrosomes**, clouds of cytoplasmic material that in animal cells contain pairs of centrioles (see Module 4.16 for more information on microtubules and centrioles). Centrosomes are also known as *microtubule-organizing centres*, a term describing their function.

? You view an animal cell through a microscope and observe dense, duplicated chromosomes scattered throughout the cell. Which state of mitosis are you looking at?

● Prophase (since the chromosomes are condensed but not yet aligned)

Metaphase

Anaphase

Telophase and Cytokinesis

Telophase and cytokinesis
Anaphase
Metaphase

Metaphase plate

Mitotic spindle

Daughter chromosomes

Cleavage furrow

Nuclear envelope forming

Metaphase At metaphase, the mitotic spindle is fully formed, with its poles at opposite ends of the cell. The chromosomes convene on the metaphase plate, an imaginary plane equidistant between the two poles of the spindle. The centromeres of all the chromosomes are lined up on the metaphase plate. For each chromosome, the kinetochores of the two sister chromatids face opposite poles of the spindle. The microtubules attached to a particular chromatid all come from one pole of the spindle, and those attached to its sister chromatid come from the opposite pole.

Anaphase Anaphase begins when the two centromeres of each chromosome come apart, separating the sister chromatids. Once separate, each sister chromatid is considered a full-fledged (daughter) chromosome. Motor proteins of the kinetochores, powered by ATP, "walk" the daughter chromosomes centromere-first along the microtubules toward opposite poles of the cell. As this happens, the spindle microtubules attached to the kinetochores shorten. However, the spindle microtubules not attached to chromosomes lengthen. The poles are moved farther apart, elongating the cell. Anaphase is over when the chromosomes have reached the two poles of the cell.

Telophase The cell elongation that started in anaphase continues. Daughter nuclei appear at the two poles of the cell as nuclear envelopes form around the chromosomes. In terms of chromosome and spindle structure, telophase is roughly the reverse of prophase. By the end of telophase, the chromatin fibre of each chromosome uncoils, and the mitotic spindle disappears. Mitosis, the equal division of one nucleus into two genetically identical daughter nuclei, is now finished.

Cytokinesis Cytokinesis, the division of the cytoplasm, usually occurs along with telophase, with two daughter cells completely separating soon after the end of mitosis. In animal cells, a cleavage furrow forms and the cell pinches into two.

8.6 Cytokinesis differs for plant and animal cells

Cytokinesis, the division of the cytoplasm into two cells, typically begins during telophase. Given the differences between animal and plant cells (particularly the presence of a stiff cell wall in plant cells), it isn't surprising that cytokinesis proceeds differently for these two types of eukaryotic cells.

In animal cells, cytokinesis occurs by a process known as cleavage. As shown in **Figure 8.6A**, the first sign of cleavage is the appearance of a **cleavage furrow**, a shallow indentation in the cell surface. At the site of the furrow, the cytoplasm has a ring of microfilaments made of actin, which is associated with molecules of myosin. (Actin and myosin are the same proteins responsible for muscle contraction; see Module 33.8.) When the actin microfilaments interact with the myosin, the ring contracts. Contraction of the myosin ring is much like the pulling of a drawstring on a hooded sweatshirt: As the drawstring is pulled, the ring of the hood contracts inward, eventually

pinching shut. Similarly, the cleavage furrow deepens and eventually pinches the parent cell in two, producing two completely separate daughter cells, each with its own nucleus and share of cytoplasm.

Cytokinesis is markedly different in plant cells, which possess cell walls **(Figure 8.6B)**. During telophase, membranous vesicles containing cell wall material collect at the middle of the parent cell. The vesicles fuse, forming a membranous disc called the **cell plate**. The cell plate grows outward, accumulating more cell wall materials as more vesicles fuse with it. Eventually, the membrane of the cell plate fuses with the plasma membrane, and the cell plate's contents join the parental cell wall. The result is two daughter cells, each bounded by its own plasma membrane and cell wall.

In some cells, cytokinesis does not occur at the end of telophase. These cells grow as expected during interphase and replicate their DNA during S phase. The stages of

Cytokinesis

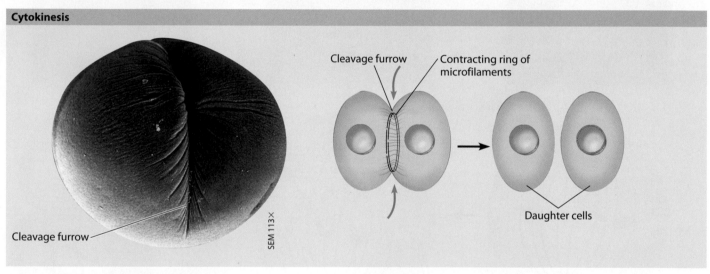

▲ **Figure 8.6A** Cleavage of an animal cell

Cytokinesis

▲ **Figure 8.6B** Cell plate formation in a plant cell

▲ Figure 8.6C A slime mould syncytium

mitosis progress normally until after the daughter nuclei appear when the cell does not divide. The result is a bigger cell with two identical nuclei. For example, mitosis in yellow slime mould is not culminated by cytokinesis **(Figure 8.6C)**. For part of its complex life cycle, this organism exists as a very large cell containing multiple nuclei called a **syncytium** (plural, *syncytia*). The cells of your muscles developed in the same way and are also large, multinucleated syncytia.

? Contrast cytokinesis in animals with cytokinesis in plants.

● In animals, cytokinesis involves a cleavage furrow in which contracting microfilaments pinch the cell in two. In plants, it involves formation of a cell plate, a fusion of vesicles that forms new plasma membranes and new cell walls between the cells.

8.7 Anchorage, cell density, and chemical growth factors affect cell division

For a plant or an animal to grow and develop normally and maintain its tissues once fully grown, it must be able to control the timing of cell division in different parts of its body. For example, in the adult human, skin cells and the cells lining the digestive tract divide frequently throughout life, replacing cells that are constantly being abraded and sloughed off. In contrast, cells in the human liver usually do not divide unless the liver is damaged.

By growing animal cells in culture, researchers have been able to identify many factors, both physical and chemical, that can influence cell division. For example, cells fail to divide if an essential nutrient is left out of the culture medium. And most types of mammalian cells divide in culture only if certain specific growth factors are included. A **growth factor** is a protein secreted by certain body cells that stimulates other cells to divide **(Figure 8.7A)**. Researchers have discovered at least 50 different growth factors that can trigger cell division. Different cell types respond specifically to certain growth factors or a combination of growth factors. For example, injury to the skin causes blood platelets to release a protein called platelet-derived growth factor. This protein promotes the rapid growth of connective tissue cells that help to seal the wound. Another example is epidermal growth factor (EGF), a protein secreted by salivary and mammary glands that promotes rapid growth of the intestinal epithelium. Dr. André Buret at the University of Calgary has shown that EGF also makes the intestine more resistant to bacterial infections. Buret has also demonstrated that EGF improves the prognosis of premature infants with necrotizing enterocolitis, an often fatal intestinal disease with no effective treatments. This disease may require surgical removal of segments of intestine. EGF can promote the rapid growth of the remaining intestine to compensate for the loss.

The effect of a physical factor on cell division is clearly seen in **density-dependent inhibition**, a phenomenon in

Cultured cells suspended in liquid

The addition of growth factor

▲ Figure 8.7A An experiment demonstrating the effect of growth factors on the division of cultured animal cells

which crowded cells stop dividing. For example, animal cells growing on the surface of a dish multiply to form a single layer and usually stop dividing when they fill the space and touch one another **(Figure 8.7B)**. If some cells are removed, those bordering the open space begin dividing again and continue until the vacancy is filled. What actually causes the cessation of growth? Studies of cultured cells suggest that

Cells anchor to the dish surface and divide.

When the cells have formed a complete single layer, they stop dividing (density-dependent inhibition).

If some cells are scraped away, the remaining cells divide to fill the dish with a single layer and then stop (density-dependent inhibition).

▲ **Figure 8.7B** An experiment demonstrating density-dependent inhibition, using animal cells grown in culture

physical contact of cell-surface proteins between adjacent cells is responsible for inhibiting cell division, which is associated with a depletion of growth factors. One of the characteristics that distinguishes cancerous cells from normal body cells is their failure to exhibit density-dependent inhibition; cancer cells continue to divide even at high densities, piling up on one another.

Most animal cells also exhibit **anchorage dependence**; they must be in contact with a solid surface—such as the inside of a culture dish or the extracellular matrix of a tissue—to divide. Anchorage dependence, density-dependent inhibition, and the availability of growth factors are all important regulatory mechanisms controlling the division of the body's cells. How exactly do growth factors work? We pursue answers to this question in the next module.

? Compared to a control culture, the cells in an experimental culture are fewer but much larger in size when they cover the dish surface and stop growing. What is a reasonable hypothesis for this difference?

● The experimental culture is deficient in one or more growth factors.

8.8 Growth factors signal the cell cycle control system

In a living animal, most cells are anchored in a fixed position and bathed in a solution of nutrients supplied by the blood, yet they usually do not divide unless they are signalled by other cells to do so. Growth factors are the main signals, and their role in promoting cell division leads us back to our earlier discussion of the cell cycle.

The sequential events of the cell cycle, represented by the circle of flat blocks in **Figure 8.8A**, are directed by a distinct cell cycle control system, represented by the knob in the figure's centre. The grey bar extending from the centre represents the current position in the cell cycle. The **cell cycle control system** is a cyclically operating set of molecules in the cell that both triggers and coordinates key events in the cell cycle. The cell cycle is *not* like a row of falling dominoes, with each event causing the next one in line. Within the M phase, for example, metaphase does not automatically lead to anaphase. Instead, proteins of the cell cycle control system must trigger the separation of sister chromatids that marks the start of anaphase.

A checkpoint in the cell cycle is a critical control point where stop and go-ahead signals (represented by stop/go lights in the figure) can regulate the cycle. The default state in most animal cells is to halt the cell cycle at these checkpoints unless overridden by specific go-ahead signals.

The red and white gates in Figure 8.8A represent three major checkpoints in the cell cycle: during the G_1 and G_2

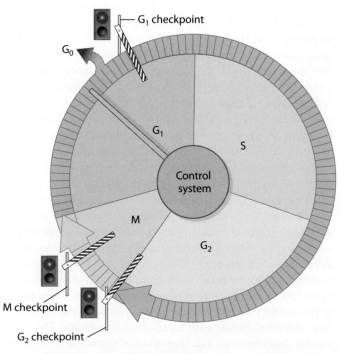

G_1 checkpoint

G_0

G_1

S

Control system

M

G_2

M checkpoint

G_2 checkpoint

▲ **Figure 8.8A** A schematic model for the cell cycle control system subphases of interphase and in the M phase. Intra-cellular signals detected by the control system tell it whether key cellular processes up to each point have been completed and thus whether or not the cell cycle should proceed past that point. The control system also receives messages from outside the cell, indicating both general environmental conditions and the presence of specific signal molecules from other cells. For many cells, the G_1 checkpoint seems to be the most important. If a cell receives a go-ahead signal—for example, from a growth factor—at the G_1 checkpoint, it will usually enter the S phase, eventually going on to complete its cycle and divide. If such a signal never arrives, the cell will switch to a permanently nondividing state called the G_0 phase. Many cells in the human body, such as mature nerve cells and muscle cells, are in the G_0 phase.

Figure 8.8B shows a simplified model for how a growth factor might affect the cell cycle control system at the G_1 checkpoint. A cell that responds to a growth factor (▽) has molecules of a specific receptor protein in its plasma membrane. Binding of the growth factor to the receptor triggers a signal transduction pathway in the cell. A signal transduction pathway is a series of protein molecules that conveys a message (see Modules 5.1 and 11.10). In this case, that message leads to cell division. The "signals" are changes that each protein molecule induces in the next molecule in the pathway. Via a series of relay proteins, a signal finally reaches the cell cycle control system and overrides the brakes that otherwise prevent progress of the cell cycle. In Figure 8.8B, the cell cycle is set off from the cell in a separate diagram because the proteins making up the

▲ **Figure 8.8B** How a growth factor signals the cell cycle control system

control system in the cell are not actually located together in one place.

Research on the control of the cell cycle is one of the hottest areas in biology today. This research is leading to a better understanding of cancer, which we discuss next.

 At which of the three checkpoints described in this module do the chromosomes exist as duplicated sister chromatids?

● G_2 and M checkpoints

8.9 Growing out of control, cancer cells produce malignant tumours

Cancer, which claims the lives of one out of every five people in Canada and other industrialized nations, is a disease of the cell cycle. Cancer cells do not heed the normal signals that regulate the cell cycle; they divide excessively and may invade other tissues of the body. If unchecked, cancer cells may continue to grow until they kill the organism.

The abnormal behaviour of cancer cells begins when a single cell undergoes transformation, a process that converts a normal cell to a cancer cell. Transformation occurs following a mutation in one or more genes that encode for proteins in the cell cycle control system. Because a transformed cell grows abnormally, the immune system usually recognizes it and destroys it. However, if the cell evades destruction, it may proliferate to form a **tumour**, an abnormally growing mass of body cells. If the abnormal cells remain at the original site, the lump is called a **benign tumour**. Benign tumours can cause problems if they grow in and disrupt certain organs, such as the brain, but often they can be completely removed by surgery.

In contrast, a **malignant tumour** can spread into neighbouring tissues and other parts of the body, displacing normal

tissue and interrupting organ function as it goes (**Figure 8.9**). An individual with a malignant tumour is said to have **cancer**. Cancer cells may separate from the original tumour or secrete signal molecules that cause blood vessels to grow toward the tumour. A few tumour cells may then enter the blood and lymph vessels and move to other parts of the body, where they may proliferate and form new tumours. The spread of cancer cells beyond their original site is called **metastasis**.

Cancers are named according to the organ or tissue in which they originate. Liver cancer, for example, starts in liver tissue and may or may not spread from there. Based on their site of origin, cancers are grouped into four categories. **Carcinomas** are cancers that originate in the external or internal coverings of the body, such as the skin or the lining of the intestine. **Sarcomas** arise in tissues that support the body, such as bone and muscle. Cancers of blood-forming tissues, such as bone marrow, spleen, and lymph nodes, are called **leukemias** and **lymphomas**.

From studying cancer cells in culture, researchers have learned that these cells do not heed the normal signals that regulate the cell cycle. For example, many cancer cells have defective cell cycle control systems that proceed past checkpoints even in the absence of growth factors. Other cancer cells synthesize growth factors themselves, making them divide continuously. If cancer cells do stop dividing, they seem to do so at random points in the cell cycle, rather than at the normal cell cycle checkpoints. Moreover, in culture, cancer cells are "immortal"; they can go on dividing indefinitely, as long as they have a supply of nutrients (whereas normal mammalian cells divide only about 20 to 50 times before they stop).

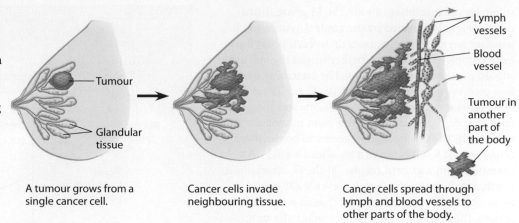

A tumour grows from a single cancer cell.

Cancer cells invade neighbouring tissue.

Cancer cells spread through lymph and blood vessels to other parts of the body.

▲ **Figure 8.9** Growth and metastasis of a malignant (cancerous) tumour of the breast

Luckily, many tumours can be successfully treated. A tumour that appears to be localized may be removed surgically. Alternatively, it can be treated with concentrated beams of high-energy radiation, which usually damages DNA in cancer cells more than it does in normal cells, perhaps because cancer cells have lost the ability to repair such damage. However, there is sometimes enough damage to normal body cells to produce harmful side effects. For example, radiation damage to cells of the ovaries or testes can lead to sterility.

To treat widespread or metastatic tumours, chemotherapy is used. During periodic chemotherapy treatments, drugs are administered that disrupt specific steps in the cell cycle. For instance, the drug paclitaxel (trade name Taxol) freezes the mitotic spindle after it forms, which stops actively dividing cells from proceeding past metaphase. (Interestingly, Taxol was originally discovered in the bark of the Pacific yew tree,

found along the Pacific coast of Canada and the United States.) Vinblastine, a chemotherapeutic drug first obtained from the periwinkle plant (found in the rainforests of Madagascar), prevents the mitotic spindle from forming.

The side effects of chemotherapy are due to the drugs' effects on normal cells that rapidly divide. Nausea results from chemotherapy's effects on intestinal cells, hair loss from effects on hair follicle cells, and susceptibility to infection from effects on immune cell production.

We will return to the topic of cancer in Chapter 11, after studying the structure and function of genes. You will see that cancer results from changes in genes that code for proteins that control cell division.

? **What is metastasis?**

Metastasis is the spread of cancer cells from their original site of formation to other sites in the body.

RUMOUR HAS IT | **8.10 Are sharks immune to cancer?**

Unfortunately, because of cancer's prominent place in our lives, many rumours circulate about this disease. One rumour in particular—that sharks do not get cancer—has put several species at risk. The rumour encourages people to believe that the consumption of shark cartilage is a potential anticancer treatment. Every year, millions of sharks are killed so tablets containing their cartilage can be made. But is it true that sharks are immune to cancer? Is there scientific evidence that shark cartilage is an effective cancer treatment?

Sharks are ancient fishes whose skeletons are made entirely of cartilage, and these intriguing creatures have changed little in the last 300 million years **(Figure 8.10)**. Many people have taken this longevity as anecdotal evidence that suggests sharks are resistant to many diseases, including cancer. Sharks caught and sold commercially and those dissected in biology teaching labs seldom have abnormal growths or tumours. The media has exaggerated these subjective observations by stating that sharks do not get cancer.

▲ **Figure 8.10** A cancer-free shark, a cancer cure, or neither?

Although rarely seen, cancerous tumours, both benign and malignant, have been documented in many shark species. Furthermore, dozens of scientific publications state that sharks have been found with numerous types of cancer, including tumours of the skin, liver, brain, and blood. Although the actual rates of these cancers in sharks are unknown, the rumour that sharks are immune to cancer is clearly untrue.

But even though sharks do get cancer, can shark cartilage prevent the development of cancer in humans? Rapid cell division in a tumour requires large amounts of nutrients. To accommodate their increased need, cancerous tumours release factors that stimulate the formation of new blood vessels in a process called angiogenesis. Metastasis of tumours is also dependent on these newly formed blood vessels. A great deal of research has been performed to find agents that can prevent angiogenesis and, therefore, the growth and spread of tumour cells. Apparently, cartilage contains something that can do this. Extract of rat, bovine, and even shark cartilage have been shown to prevent tumour angiogenesis under experimental conditions.

Although experimental models may show promise for a given treatment, there is no guarantee that the therapy will work in humans. Many promising drugs for a wide array of diseases may work very well in experimental trials but have little to no effect in human trials. Shark cartilage is one such treatment. No scientific evidence supports the claim that shark cartilage prevents the growth and metastasis of human cancers. In controlled clinical trials, patients who received shark cartilage saw no more improvement in their condition than those who were given placebos.

Both rumours regarding sharks and cancer are untrue. Unfortunately, many people still believe them, leading to two significant and negative effects: First, many shark species have been overharvested for their cartilage skeletons, and many of these species are now at risk of extinction. Second, people have been lured away from effective cancer treatments, choosing instead to take shark cartilage capsules. Because these pills have no proven benefit, patients who switch to the nonconventional cartilage treatment are taking an unjustifiable risk.

? How does angiogenesis make cancerous tumours worse?

● It allows for increased tumour growth by supplying more nutrients and encouraging metastasis.

8.11 Review: Mitosis provides for growth, cell replacement, and asexual reproduction

The three micrographs in Figures 8.11A, 8.11B, and 8.11C summarize the roles that mitotic cell division plays in the lives of multicellular organisms. **Figure 8.11A** shows some of the cells from the tip of a rapidly growing onion plant root. Notice the two cells in the middle row, whose nuclei are in the process of mitosis, as evidenced by the visibly compact chromosomes. Cell division in the root tip produces new cells, which elongate and bring about growth of the root.

Figure 8.11B shows a dividing bone marrow cell. Mitotic cell division within the red marrow of your body's bones—particularly within your ribs, vertebrae, breastbone, and hip—continuously creates new blood cells that replace older ones. Similar processes replace cells throughout your body. For example, dividing cells within your epidermis continuously replace dead cells that slough off the surface of your skin.

Figure 8.11C is a micrograph of a hydra, a cnidarian (relative of a sea jelly) that is a common inhabitant of freshwater lakes. A hydra is a tiny multicellular animal that

▲ **Figure 8.11B** Cell replacement (in bone marrow)

LM 1030×

LM 700×

▲ **Figure 8.11A** Growth (in an onion root)

reproduces by either sexual or asexual means. This individual is reproducing asexually by budding. A bud starts out as a mass of mitotically dividing cells growing on the side of the parent. Eventually, the offspring detaches from the parent and takes up life on its own. The offspring is literally a "chip off the old block," being genetically identical to (a clone of) its parent.

In all the examples described here, the new cells have exactly the same number and types of chromosomes as the parent cells because of the way duplicated chromosomes divide during mitosis. Mitosis makes it possible for organisms to grow, regenerate and repair tissues, and

▲ **Figure 8.11C** Asexual reproduction (of a hydra)

reproduce asexually by producing cells that carry the same genes as the parent cells.

If we examine the cells of any individual organism or those from individuals of any one species, we see that almost all of them contain the same number and types of chromosomes. In the next module, we take a look at how genetic material is organized in chromosomes.

 The body cells of elephants have 56 chromosomes. If an elephant skin cell with 56 chromosomes divides by mitosis, each daughter cell will have ____ chromosomes.

56 ●

Meiosis and Crossing Over

8.12 Chromosomes are matched in homologous pairs

In humans, a typical body cell, called a **somatic cell**, has 46 chromosomes. If we use a microscope to examine human chromosomes in metaphase of mitosis, we see that the chromosomes, each consisting of two sister chromatids, can be arranged into matching pairs; **Figure 8.12** illustrates one pair of metaphase chromosomes. A human cell at metaphase contains 23 sets of duplicated chromosomes. Other species have different numbers of chromosomes, but these, too, usually occur in matched pairs. Moreover, when treated with special dyes, the chromosomes of a pair display matching staining patterns (represented by coloured stripes in Figure 8.12).

Notice that each chromosome is duplicated, consisting of two sister chromatids joined at the centromere. Every (or almost every) chromosome has a twin that resembles it in length and centromere position. The two chromosomes of such a matching pair are called **homologous chromosomes** (or homologues) because they both carry genes controlling the same inherited characteristics. For example, if a gene that determines whether a person has freckles is located at a particular place, or **locus** (plural, *loci*), on one chromosome—within the narrow orange band in our drawing, for instance—then the homologous chromosome has that same gene at that same locus. However, the two chromosomes of a homologous pair may have different versions of the same gene.

In human females, the 46 chromosomes fall neatly into 23 homologous pairs. For a male, however, the chromosomes in one pair do not look alike. The nonidentical pair, only partly homologous, is the male's sex chromosomes. These **sex chromosomes** determine an individual's sex (male versus female), although these chromosomes carry genes that perform other functions as well. In mammals, males have one X chromosome and one Y chromosome. Females have two X chromosomes. The 22 remaining pairs of chromosomes, found in both males and females, are called **autosomes**. In the next module, we discuss how chromosomes are inherited.

Pair of homologous chromosomes

Locus

Centromere

Sister chromatids

One duplicated chromosome

▲ **Figure 8.12** A pair of homologous chromosomes

 Are all of *your* chromosomes fully homologous?

● If you are female, then yes. If you are male, then no (your X and Y are only partly homologous).

8.13 Gametes have a single set of chromosomes

The development of a fertilized egg into a new adult organism is one phase of a multicellular organism's **life cycle**, the sequence of stages leading from the adults of one generation to the adults

of the next **(Figure 8.13A)**. Having two sets of chromosomes, one inherited from each parent, is a key factor in the life cycle of humans and all other species that reproduce sexually.

Humans, as well as most other animals and many plants, are said to be **diploid** organisms because all body cells contain pairs of homologous chromosomes. The total number of

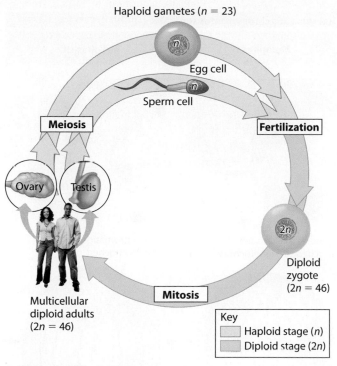

Haploid gametes ($n = 23$)

Egg cell

Sperm cell

Meiosis

Fertilization

Ovary   Testis

Multicellular diploid adults ($2n = 46$)

Mitosis

Diploid zygote ($2n = 46$)

Key
☐ Haploid stage (n)
☐ Diploid stage ($2n$)

▲ **Figure 8.13A** The human life cycle

chromosomes is called the diploid number (abbreviated $2n$). For humans, the diploid number is 46; that is, $2n = 46$. The exceptions are the egg and sperm cells, collectively known as **gametes**. Each gamete has a single set of chromosomes: 22 autosomes plus a sex chromosome, either X or Y. A cell with a single chromosome set is called a **haploid** cell; it has only one member of each homologous pair. For humans, the haploid number (abbreviated n) is 23; that is, $n = 23$.

In the human life cycle, a haploid sperm cell from the father fuses with a haploid egg cell from the mother in the process of **fertilization**. The resulting fertilized egg, called a **zygote**, has two sets of homologous chromosomes and so is diploid. One set of homologous chromosomes comes from each parent. The life cycle is completed as a sexually mature adult develops from the zygote.

All sexual life cycles, including our own, involve an alternation of diploid and haploid stages. Producing haploid gametes prevents the chromosome number from doubling in every generation. Gametes are made by a special sort of cell division called meiosis, which occurs only in reproductive organs (ovaries and testes in animals). Whereas mitosis produces daughter cells with the same number of chromosomes as the parent cell, meiosis reduces the chromosome number by half. **Figure 8.13B** tracks one pair of homologous chromosomes. ❶ Each of the chromosomes is duplicated during interphase (before meiosis). ❷ The first division, meiosis I, segregates the two chromosomes of the homologous pair, packaging them in separate (haploid) daughter cells.

But each chromosome is still doubled. ❸ Meiosis II separates the sister chromatids. Each of the four daughter cells is haploid and contains only a single chromosome from the homologous pair. We turn to meiosis next.

| INTERPHASE | MEIOSIS I | MEIOSIS II |

Sister chromatids

A pair of homologous chromosomes in a diploid parent cell

A pair of duplicated homologous chromosomes

▲ **Figure 8.13B** How meiosis halves chromosome number

? Imagine you stain a human cell and view it under a microscope. You observe 23 chromosomes, including a Y chromosome. You could conclude that this must be a _____ cell taken from the organ called the _____.

● sperm (since it is haploid); testis (since it is from a male)

8.14 Meiosis reduces the chromosome number from diploid to haploid

Meiosis is a type of cell division that produces haploid cells (gametes or spores) in diploid organisms. Two haploid gametes may combine via fertilization to restore the diploid state in the zygote. Were it not for meiosis, each generation would have twice as much genetic material as the generation before! Spores of fungi and plants divide by mitosis to produce haploid organisms (see Chapters 18 and 19).

Many of the stages of meiosis closely resemble corresponding stages in mitosis. Meiosis, like mitosis, is preceded by the

duplication of chromosomes. However, this single duplication is followed by two consecutive cell divisions, called meiosis I and meiosis II. Because one duplication of the chromosomes is followed by two divisions, each of the four daughter cells resulting from meiosis has a haploid set of chromosomes—half as many chromosomes as the parent cell. The photographs and drawings in **Figure 8.14** show the two meiotic divisions for an animal cell with a diploid number of 6. The members of a pair of homologous chromosomes in Figure 8.14

(and later figures) are coloured red and blue to help you distinguish them. (Imagine that the red chromosomes were inherited from the mother and the blue chromosomes from the father.)

One of the most important events in meiosis occurs during prophase I. At this stage, four chromatids (two sets of sister chromatids) are aligned and physically touching each other.

INTERPHASE: Chromosomes duplicate

MEIOSIS I: Homologous chromosomes separate

Prophase I | **Metaphase I** | **Anaphase I**

Centrosomes (with centriole pairs)
Centrioles
Nuclear envelope
Chromatin

Sites of crossing over
Spindle
Sister chromatids
Fragments of the nuclear envelope
Tetrad

Spindle microtubules attached to a kinetochore
Centromere (with a kinetochore)
Metaphase plate

Sister chromatids remain attached
Homologous chromosomes separate

Interphase
Like mitosis, meiosis is preceded by an interphase, during which the chromosomes duplicate. At the end of interphase, each chromosome consists of two genetically identical sister chromatids attached together. The cell's centrosome has also duplicated by the end of this interphase.

Prophase I
Early in this phase, the chromatin coils up, so that individual chromosomes become visible with the microscope. In a process called **synapsis**, homologous chromosomes, each composed of two sister chromatids, come together as pairs. The resulting structure, consisting of four chromatids, is called a tetrad.

During synapsis, chromatids of homologous chromosomes exchange segments in a process called crossing over. Because the versions of some genes on a chromosome differ from those on its homologue, crossing over rearranges genetic information. As we will discuss in Module 8.18, the genetic shuffling produced by crossing over can make an important contribution to the genetic variability resulting from sexual reproduction.

As prophase I continues, the chromosomes condense further. The centrosomes move away from each other, and a spindle forms between them. The nuclear envelope breaks into fragments, and the chromosome tetrads, captured by spindle microtubules, are moved toward the centre of the cell.

Metaphase I
At metaphase I, the chromosome tetrads are aligned on the metaphase plate, midway between the two poles of the spindle. Each chromosome is condensed and thick, with its sister chromatids still attached at their centromeres. Spindle microtubules are attached to kinetochores at the centromeres. In each tetrad, the homologous chromosomes are held together at sites of crossing over. Notice that, for each tetrad, the spindle microtubules attached to one of the homologous chromosomes come from one pole of the cell, and the microtubules attached to the other homologous chromosome come from the opposite pole. With this arrangement, the homologous chromosomes of each tetrad are poised to move toward opposite poles of the cell.

Anaphase I
Like anaphase of mitosis, anaphase I of meiosis is marked by the migration of chromosomes toward the two poles of the cell. In contrast to mitosis, however, the sister chromatids making up each doubled chromosome remain attached at their centromeres. Only the tetrads (pairs of homologous chromosomes) split up. Thus, in the drawing you see three still-doubled chromosomes (the haploid number of three in this case) moving toward each spindle pole. If this were anaphase of mitosis, you would see six daughter chromosomes moving toward each pole.

▲ **Figure 8.14** The stages of meiosis

When in this configuration, nonsister chromatids may trade segments. As you will learn in Module 8.18, this exchange of chromosome segments—called crossing over—is a key step in the generation of genetic diversity that occurs during sexual reproduction.

? A cell has the haploid number of chromosomes, but each chromosome has two chromatids. The chromosomes are arranged singly at the centre of the spindle. What is the meiotic stage?

● Metaphase II (since the chromosomes line up two by two in metaphase I)

MEIOSIS II: Sister chromatids separate

| Telophase I and Cytokinesis | Prophase II | Metaphase II | Anaphase II | Telophase II and Cytokinesis |

Cleavage furrow

Sister chromatids separate

Haploid daughter cells forming

Telophase I and Cytokinesis

In telophase I, the chromosomes have arrived at the poles of the cell. When the chromosomes finish their journey, each pole of the cell has a haploid chromosome set, although each chromosome is still in duplicate form at this point. In other words, each chromosome still consists of two sister chromatids. Usually, cytokinesis occurs along with telophase I, and two haploid daughter cells are formed.

Following telophase I in some organisms, the chromosomes uncoil and the nuclear envelope re-forms, and there is an interphase before meiosis II begins. In other species, daughter cells produced in the first meiotic division immediately begin preparation for the second meiotic division. In either case, no chromosome duplication occurs between telophase I and the onset of meiosis II.

Meiosis II

Meiosis II is essentially the same as mitosis. The important difference is that meiosis II starts with a haploid cell.

During prophase II, a spindle forms and moves the chromosomes toward the middle of the cell. During metaphase II, the chromosomes are aligned on the metaphase plate as they are in mitosis, with the kinetochores of the sister chromatids of each chromosome pointing toward opposite poles. In anaphase II, the centromeres of sister chromatids finally separate, and the sister chromatids of each pair, now individual daughter chromosomes, move toward opposite poles of the cell. In telophase II, nuclei form at the cell poles, and cytokinesis occurs at the same time. There are now four daughter cells, each with the haploid number of (single) chromosomes.

8.15 Mitosis and meiosis have important similarities and differences

You have now learned the two ways that cells of eukaryotic organisms divide. Mitosis, which provides for growth, tissue repair, and asexual reproduction, produces daughter cells that are genetically identical to the parent cell. Meiosis, needed for sexual reproduction, yields genetically unique haploid daughter cells—cells with only one member of each homologous chromosome pair.

For both mitosis and meiosis, the chromosomes duplicate only once, during the S phase of the preceding interphase. Mitosis involves one division of the nucleus, and it is usually accompanied by cytokinesis, producing two identical diploid cells. Meiosis entails two nuclear and cytoplasmic divisions, yielding four haploid cells.

Figure 8.15 compares mitosis and meiosis, tracing these two processes for a diploid parent cell with four chromosomes. Homologous chromosomes are those matching in size.

Notice that all the events unique to meiosis occur during meiosis I. In prophase I, duplicated homologous chromosomes

pair to form **tetrads**, sets of four chromatids, with each pair of sister chromatids joined at their centromeres. In metaphase I, tetrads (not individual chromosomes) are aligned at the metaphase plate. During anaphase I, pairs of homologous chromosomes separate, but the sister chromatids of each chromosome stay together. At the end of meiosis I, there are two haploid cells, but each chromosome still has two sister chromatids.

Meiosis II is virtually identical to mitosis in that it separates sister chromatids. But unlike mitosis, each daughter cell produced by meiosis II has only a *haploid* set of chromosomes.

? Explain how mitosis conserves chromosome number while meiosis reduces the number from diploid to haploid.

● In mitosis, the duplication of chromosomes is followed by one division of the cell. In meiosis, homologous chromosomes separate in the first of two cell divisions; after the second division, each new cell ends up with just a single haploid set.

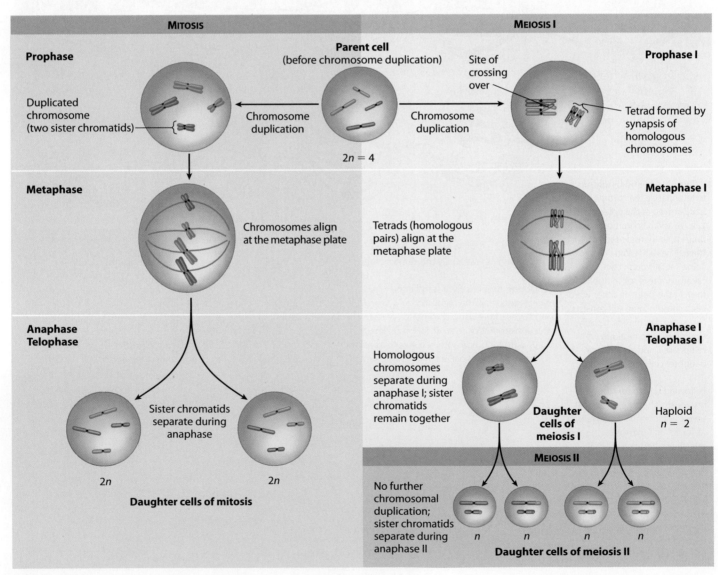

MITOSIS	MEIOSIS I

Prophase

Duplicated chromosome (two sister chromatids)

Parent cell (before chromosome duplication)

Chromosome duplication

Chromosome duplication

$2n = 4$

Site of crossing over

Prophase I

Tetrad formed by synapsis of homologous chromosomes

Metaphase

Chromosomes align at the metaphase plate

Tetrads (homologous pairs) align at the metaphase plate

Metaphase I

Anaphase
Telophase

Sister chromatids separate during anaphase

$2n$ $2n$

Daughter cells of mitosis

Homologous chromosomes separate during anaphase I; sister chromatids remain together

Daughter cells of meiosis I

Anaphase I
Telophase I

Haploid $n = 2$

MEIOSIS II

No further chromosomal duplication; sister chromatids separate during anaphase II

n n n n

Daughter cells of meiosis II

▲ **Figure 8.15** Comparison of mitosis and meiosis

8.16 Independent orientation of chromosomes in meiosis and random fertilization lead to varied offspring

As we discussed in Module 8.1, offspring that result from sexual reproduction are highly varied; they are genetically different from their parents and from one another. How does this genetic variation result from meiosis?

Figure 8.16 illustrates one way in which the process of meiosis contributes to genetic differences in gametes. The figure shows how the arrangement of homologous chromosome pairs at metaphase of meiosis I affects the resulting gametes. Once again, our example is from a diploid organism with four chromosomes (two homologous pairs), with colours used to differentiate homologous chromosomes (red for chromosomes inherited from the mother and blue for those from the father).

The orientation of the pairs of homologous chromosomes (tetrads) at metaphase I—whether the maternal (red) or paternal (blue) chromosome is closer to a given pole—is as random as the flip of a coin. Thus, there is a 50% chance that a particular daughter cell will get the maternal chromosome of a certain homologous pair and a 50% chance that it will receive the paternal chromosome. In this example, there are two possible ways that the two tetrads can align during metaphase I. In possibility A, the tetrads are oriented with both red chromosomes on the same side of the metaphase plate. Therefore, the gametes produced in possibility A can each have either two red *or* two blue chromosomes (bottom row, combinations 1 and 2).

In possibility B, the tetrads are oriented differently (blue/red and red/blue). This arrangement produces gametes that each have one red and one blue chromosome. Furthermore, half the gametes have a big blue chromosome and a small red one (combination 3), and half have a big red chromosome and a small blue one (combination 4).

So we see that for this example, four chromosome combinations are possible in the gametes, and in fact the organism will produce gametes of all four types in equal quantities. For a species with more than two pairs of chromosomes, such as humans, *all* the chromosome pairs orient independently at metaphase I. (Chromosomes X and Y behave as a homologous pair in meiosis.)

For any species, the total number of combinations of chromosomes that meiosis can package into gametes is 2^n, where n is the haploid number. For the organism in this figure, $n = 2$, so the number of chromosome combinations is 2^2, or 4. For a human ($n = 23$), there are 2^{23}, or about 8 million possible chromosome combinations! This means that each gamete you produce contains one of roughly 8 million possible combinations of chromosomes inherited from your mother and father.

How many possibilities are there when a gamete from one individual unites with a gamete from another individual in fertilization? In humans, the random fusion of a single sperm with a single ovum during fertilization will produce a zygote with any of about 64 trillion (8 million $\times$ 8 million) combinations of chromosomes! While the random nature of fertilization adds a huge amount of potential variability to the offspring of sexual reproduction, there is in fact even more variety created during meiosis, as we see in the next two modules.

? A particular species of worm has a diploid number of 10. How many chromosomal combinations are possible for gametes formed by meiosis?

● 32; $2n = 10$, so $n = 5$ and $2^n = 32$

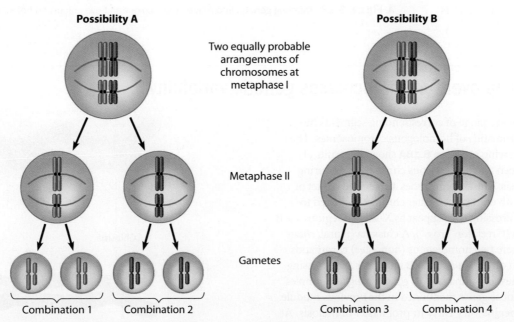

Possibility A | Possibility B

Two equally probable arrangements of chromosomes at metaphase I

Metaphase II

Gametes

Combination 1   Combination 2   Combination 3   Combination 4

▲ **Figure 8.16**   Results of the independent orientation of chromosomes at metaphase I

8.17 Homologous chromosomes may carry different versions of genes

So far, we have focused on genetic variability in gametes and zygotes at the whole-chromosome level. We have yet to discuss the actual genetic information—the genes—contained in the chromosomes. The question we need to answer now is this: What is the significance of the independent orientation of metaphase chromosomes at the level of genes?

Let's take a simple example, the single tetrad in **Figure 8.17**. The letters on the homologous chromosomes represent genes. Recall that homologous chromosomes have genes for the same characteristic at corresponding loci. Our example involves hypothetical genes controlling the appearance of mice. *C* and *c* are different versions of a gene for one characteristic, coat colour; *E* and *e* are different versions of a gene for another characteristic, eye colour. (As you'll learn in later chapters, different versions of a gene contain slightly different nucleotide sequences in the chromosomal DNA.)

Let's say that *C* represents the gene for a brown coat and that *c* represents the gene for a white coat. In the chromosome diagram, notice that *C* is at the same locus on the red homologue as *c* is on the blue one. Likewise, gene *E* (for black eyes) is at the same locus as *e* (pink eyes).

The fact that homologous chromosomes can bear two different kinds of genetic information for the same characteristic (for instance, coat colour) is what really makes gametes—and therefore offspring—different from one another. In our example, a gamete carrying a red chromosome would have genes specifying brown coat colour and black eye colour, while a gamete with the homologous

blue chromosome would have genes for white coat and pink eyes. Thus, we see how a tetrad with genes shown for only two characteristics can yield two genetically different kinds of gametes. In the next module, we go a step further and see how this same tetrad can actually yield *four* different kinds of gametes.

? In the tetrad of Figure 8.17, use labels to distinguish the pair of homologous chromosomes from sister chromatids.

▲ Figure 8.17 Differing genetic information (coat colour and eye colour) on homologous chromosomes

8.18 Crossing over further increases genetic variability

Crossing over is an exchange of corresponding segments between nonsister chromatids of homologous chromosomes. The micrograph and drawing in **Figure 8.18A** show the results of crossing over between two homologous chromosomes during prophase I of meiosis. The chromosomes are a tetrad—a set of four chromatids, with each pair of sister chromatids joined together. The sites of crossing over appear as X-shaped regions; each is called a **chiasma** (Greek for "cross"). A chiasma (plural, *chiasmata*) is a place where two homologous (nonsister) chromatids are attached to each other. **Figure 8.18B** illustrates how crossing over can produce new combinations of genes, using as examples the hypothetical mouse genes mentioned in the previous module.

Crossing over begins very early in prophase I of meiosis. At that time, homologous chromosomes are paired all along their

▲ Figure 8.18A Chiasmata, the sites of crossing over

Tetrad
(pair of homologous chromosomes in synapsis)

1 Breakage of homologous chromatids

2 Joining of homologous chromatids

Chiasma

3 Separation of homologous chromosomes at anaphase I

4 Separation of chromatids at anaphase II and completion of meiosis

Parental type of chromosome

Recombinant chromosome

Recombinant chromosome

Parental type of chromosome

Gametes of four genetic types

▲ **Figure 8.18B** How crossing over leads to genetic recombination

lengths, with a precise gene-by-gene alignment. At the top of the figure is a tetrad with coat-colour (*C, c*) and eye-colour (*E, e*) genes labelled. **1** The DNA molecules of two nonsister chromatids—one maternal (red) and one paternal (blue)—break at the same place. **2** Immediately, the two broken chromatids join together in a new way (red to blue and blue to red). In effect, the two homologous segments trade places, or cross over, producing hybrid chromosomes (red/blue and blue/red) with new combinations of maternal and paternal genes. **3** When the homologous chromosomes separate in anaphase I, each contains a new segment originating from its homologue. **4** Finally, in meiosis II, the sister chromatids separate, each going to a different gamete.

In this example, if there were no crossing over, meiosis could produce only two genetic types of gametes. These would be the ones ending up with the "parental" types of chromosomes (either all blue or all red), carrying either genes *C* and *E* or genes *c* and *e*. These are the same two kinds of gametes we saw in Figure 8.17. With crossing over, two other types of gametes can result, those that are part blue and part red. One of these carries genes *C* and *e*, and the other carries genes *c* and *E*. Chromosomes with these combinations of genes would not exist if not for crossing over. They are called recombinant because they result from **genetic recombination**, the production of gene combinations different from those carried by the original parental chromosomes.

In meiosis in humans, an average of one to three crossover events occur per chromosome pair. Thus, if you were to examine a chromosome from one of your gametes, you would most likely find that it is not exactly like any one of your own chromosomes. Rather, it is probably a patchwork of segments derived from a pair of homologous chromosomes, cut and pasted together to form a chromosome with a unique combination of genes.

We have now examined three sources of genetic variability in sexually reproducing organisms: independent orientation of chromosomes at metaphase I, random fertilization, and crossing over during prophase I of meiosis. When we study molecular genetics in Chapter 10, we will see yet another source of variability: mutations, or rare changes in the DNA of genes. The different versions of genes that homologous chromosomes may have at each locus originally arise from mutations, so mutations are ultimately responsible for genetic diversity in living organisms. Once these differences arise, reshuffling of the different versions during sexual reproduction increases genetic variation. When we discuss natural selection and evolution in Unit III, we will see that this genetic variety in offspring is the raw material for natural selection.

Our discussion of meiosis to this point has focused on the process as it normally occurs. In the next, and last, major section of the chapter, we consider some of the consequences of errors in the process.

? Describe how crossing over and the random alignment of homologous chromosomes on the metaphase I plate account for the genetic variation among gametes formed by meiosis.

● Crossing over creates recombinant chromosomes having a combination of genes that were originally on different, though homologous, chromosomes. Homologous chromosome pairs are oriented randomly at metaphase of meiosis I.

Alterations of Chromosome Number and Structure

8.19 A karyotype is a photographic inventory of an individual's chromosomes

Errors in meiosis can lead to daughter cells, such as gametes, containing chromosomes in abnormal numbers or with major alterations in their structure. Fertilization involving such abnormal gametes results in offspring with chromosomal abnormalities. Such conditions can be readily detected in a **karyotype**, an ordered display of magnified images of an individual's chromosomes arranged in pairs. A karyotype shows the chromosomes condensed and doubled, as they appear in metaphase of mitosis.

To prepare a karyotype, medical scientists often use lymphocytes, a type of white blood cell. A blood sample is treated with a chemical that stimulates mitosis. After growing in culture

for several days, the cells are treated with another chemical to arrest mitosis at metaphase, when the chromosomes, each consisting of two joined sister chromatids, are most highly condensed. **Figure 8.19** outlines the steps in one method for the preparation of a karyotype from a blood sample.

The photograph in step 5 shows the karyotype of a normal human male. Images of the 46 chromosomes from a single diploid cell are arranged in 23 homologous pairs: autosomes numbered from 1 to 22 (starting with the largest) and one pair of sex chromosomes (X and Y in this case). The chromosomes had been stained to reveal band patterns, which are helpful in

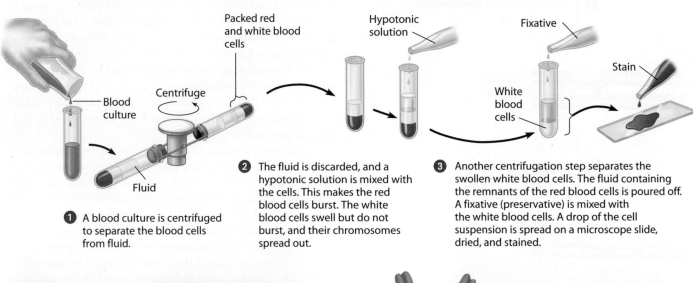

❶ A blood culture is centrifuged to separate the blood cells from fluid.

❷ The fluid is discarded, and a hypotonic solution is mixed with the cells. This makes the red blood cells burst. The white blood cells swell but do not burst, and their chromosomes spread out.

❸ Another centrifugation step separates the swollen white blood cells. The fluid containing the remnants of the red blood cells is poured off. A fixative (preservative) is mixed with the white blood cells. A drop of the cell suspension is spread on a microscope slide, dried, and stained.

❹ The slide is viewed with a microscope equipped with a digital camera. A photograph of the chromosomes is entered into a computer, which electronically arranges them by size and shape.

❺ The resulting display is the karyotype. The 46 chromosomes here include 22 pairs of autosomes and two sex chromosomes, X and Y. Although difficult to discern in the karyotype, each of the chromosomes consists of two sister chromatids lying very close together (as shown in the diagram).

▲ Figure 8.19 Preparation of a karyotype from a blood sample differentiating the chromosomes and in detecting structural abnormalities. Among the alterations that can be detected by karyotyping is trisomy 21, the basis of Down syndrome, which we discuss next.

? How would the karyotype of a human female differ from the male karyotype in Figure 8.19?

Instead of an XY combination for the sex chromosomes, there would be a homologous pair of X chromosomes (XX).

8.20 An extra copy of chromosome 21 causes Down syndrome

The karyotype in Figure 8.19 shows the normal human complement of 23 pairs of chromosomes. Contrast it with **Figure 8.20A**. Besides having two X chromosomes (because it is from a female), the karyotype shows three number 21 chromosomes, making 47 chromosomes in total. This chromosomal arrangement is called **trisomy 21**.

In most cases, a human embryo with an abnormal number of chromosomes is spontaneously aborted (miscarried) long before birth. But some alterations in chromosome number, including trisomy 21, appear to be less drastic, and individuals carrying them can survive. These people display a common set of characteristics called a syndrome **(Figure 8.20B)**. A person with trisomy 21, for instance, has Down syndrome, named after John Langdon Down, who first described the syndrome in 1866.

Trisomy 21 is the most common chromosome number abnormality. Down syndrome occurs in about 1 out of every 500 children born in Canada. Chromosome 21 is one of our smallest chromosomes, but an extra copy produces a number of effects. Down syndrome includes characteristic facial features—frequently a round face, a skin fold at the inner corner of the eye, a flattened nose bridge, and small, irregular teeth—as well as short stature, correctable heart defects, and susceptibility to respiratory infections, childhood leukemia, and early onset Alzheimer's disease. Individuals with Down syndrome also have lower risk of high blood pressure, lower rates of many solid tumour cancers and almost no atherosclerosis. They

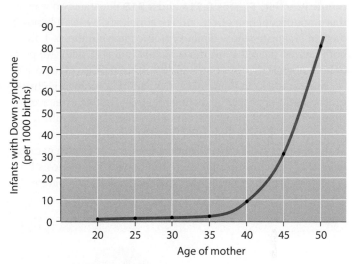

▲ **Figure 8.20C** Maternal age and incidence of Down syndrome

usually have a lifespan shorter than normal, but with proper medical care many are living into their sixties. They exhibit varying degrees of developmental delay, and many have jobs, live independently, and get married. A few women with Down syndrome have had children, though most people with the syndrome are infertile. Half the eggs produced by a woman with Down syndrome will have the extra chromosome 21, so there is a 50% chance that she will transmit the syndrome to her child.

As indicated in **Figure 8.20C**, the incidence of Down syndrome in the offspring of normal karyotype parents increases markedly with the age of the mother. Down syndrome affects less than 0.05% of children (fewer than 1 in 2000) born to women under age 30. The probability is 1% (10 in 1000) for mothers at age 40 and is higher for older mothers. All women in Canada are now offered prenatal testing for Down syndrome as well as other genetic differences. These increased screening efforts make the primary health professional's job of ensuring accurate and value-neutral information about Down syndrome even more important. A great deal of information is available to prospective parents through parent support groups such as the Canadian Down Syndrome Society.

What causes trisomy 21? We address that question in the next module.

▼ **Figure 8.20B** Two teens with Down syndrome

Trisomy 21

▲ **Figure 8.20A** A karyotype showing trisomy 21

? For 47-year-old women, the risk of having a baby with Down syndrome is about _____ per 1000 births, or _____ %.

● 40; 4

8.21 Accidents during meiosis can alter chromosome number

Within the human body, meiosis occurs repeatedly as the testes or ovaries produce gametes. Almost always, the meiotic spindle distributes chromosomes to daughter cells without error. But there is an occasional mishap in which the members of a chromosome pair fail to separate. Such an error is called a **nondisjunction**. **Figures 8.21A** and **8.21B** illustrate two ways that a nondisjunction can occur. For simplicity, we use a hypothetical organism whose diploid chromosome number is 4. In both figures, the cell at the top is diploid ($2n = 4$), with two pairs of homologous chromosomes undergoing anaphase of meiosis I.

Sometimes, as in Figure 8.21A, a pair of homologous chromosomes do not separate during meiosis I. In this case, even though the rest of meiosis occurs normally, all the resulting gametes end up with abnormal numbers of chromosomes. Two of the gametes have three chromosomes; the other two gametes have only one chromosome each. In Figure 8.21B, meiosis I is normal, but one pair of sister chromatids fails to separate

during meiosis II. In this case, two of the resulting gametes are abnormal; the other two gametes are normal.

If an abnormal gamete produced by nondisjunction unites with a normal gamete during fertilization, the result is a zygote with an abnormal number of chromosomes. Mitosis will then transmit the mistake to all embryonic cells. If this were a real organism and it survived, it would have an abnormal karyotype and probably a syndrome of disorders caused by the abnormal number of genes. For example, if there is nondisjunction affecting human chromosome 21, some resulting gametes will carry an extra chromosome 21. If one of these gametes unites with a normal gamete, trisomy 21 (Down syndrome) will result. Nondisjunction can also affect chromosomes other than 21, as we see next.

? Explain how nondisjunction could result in a diploid gamete.

A diploid gamete would result if the nondisjunction affected all the chromosomes during one of the meiotic divisions.

Number of chromosomes

▲ **Figure 8.21A** Nondisjunction in meiosis I

▲ **Figure 8.21B** Nondisjunction in meiosis II

8.22 Abnormal numbers of sex chromosomes do not usually affect survival

Nondisjunction can result in abnormal numbers of sex chromosomes, X and Y. Unusual numbers of sex chromosomes seem to upset the genetic balance less than unusual numbers of autosomes. This may be because the Y chromosome is very small and carries relatively few genes. Furthermore, mammalian cells usually operate with only one functioning

X chromosome because other copies of the chromosome become inactivated in each cell (as you'll learn in Module 11.2).

Table 8.22 lists the most common human sex chromosome abnormalities. An extra X chromosome in a male, making him XXY, occurs approximately once in every 2000 live births (once in every 1000 male births). Men with this disorder,

TABLE 8.22 | ABNORMALITIES OF SEX CHROMOSOME NUMBER IN HUMANS

Sex Chromosomes	Syndrome	Origin of Nondisjunction	Frequency in Population
XXY	Klinefelter syndrome (male)	Meiosis in egg or sperm formation	$\frac{1}{2000}$
XYY	None (normal male)	Meiosis in sperm formation	$\frac{1}{2000}$
XXX	None (normal female)	Meiosis in egg or sperm formation	$\frac{1}{1000}$
XO	Turner syndrome (female)	Meiosis in egg or sperm formation	$\frac{1}{5000}$

called Klinefelter syndrome, have male sex organs and normal intelligence, but the testes are abnormally small, the individual is sterile, and he often has breast enlargement and other female body characteristics. Klinefelter syndrome is also found in individuals with more than three sex chromosomes, such as XXYY, XXXY, or XXXXY. These abnormal numbers of sex chromosomes result from multiple nondisjunctions; such men are more likely to have developmental disabilities than XY or XXY individuals.

Human males with an extra Y chromosome (XYY) do not have any well-defined syndrome, although they tend to be taller than average. Females with an extra X chromosome (XXX) cannot be distinguished from XX females except by karyotype.

Females who lack an X chromosome are designated XO; the O indicates the absence of a second sex chromosome. These women have Turner syndrome. They have a characteristic appearance, including short stature and often a web of skin extending between the neck and the shoulders. Women with Turner syndrome are sterile because their sex organs do not fully mature at adolescence. If left untreated, girls with Turner syndrome have poor development of breasts and other secondary sexual characteristics. Artificial administration of estrogen can alleviate these symptoms. Women with Turner syndrome have normal intelligence. The XO condition is the sole known case where having only 45 chromosomes is not fatal in humans.

The sex chromosome abnormalities described here illustrate the crucial role of the Y chromosome in determining sex. In general, a single Y chromosome is enough to produce "maleness," even in combination with several X chromosomes. The absence of a Y chromosome yields "femaleness."

 What is the total number of autosomes you would expect to find in the karyotype of a female with Turner syndrome?

● 44 (plus one sex chromosome)

8.23 New species can arise from errors in cell division

Errors in meiosis or mitosis do not always lead to problems. In fact, biologists hypothesize that such errors have been instrumental in the evolution of many species. Numerous plant species, in particular, seem to have originated from accidents during cell division that resulted in extra sets of chromosomes. The new species is polyploid, meaning that it has more than two sets of homologous chromosomes in each somatic cell. At least half of all species of flowering plants are polyploid, including such useful ones as wheat, potatoes, apples, and cotton.

Let's consider one scenario by which a diploid ($2n$) plant species might generate a tetraploid ($4n$) plant. Imagine that, like many plants, our diploid plant produces both sperm and egg cells and can self-fertilize. If meiosis fails to occur in the plant's reproductive organs and gametes are instead produced by mitosis, the gametes will be diploid. The union of a diploid ($2n$) sperm with a diploid ($2n$) egg during self-fertilization will produce a tetraploid ($4n$) zygote, which may develop into a mature tetraploid plant that can itself reproduce by self-fertilization. The tetraploid plants will constitute a new species, one that has evolved in just one generation.

Although polyploid animal species are less common than polyploid plants, they are known to occur among the fishes and amphibians (**Figure 8.23**). Moreover, researchers in Chile have identified the first candidate for polyploidy among the mammals—a rat whose cells seem to be tetraploid. Tetraploid organisms are sometimes strikingly different from their recent diploid ancestors; they may be larger, for example. Scientists don't yet understand exactly how polyploidy brings about such differences.

 What is a polyploid organism?

● One with more than two sets of homologous chromosomes in its body cells.

▶ **Figure 8.23** The grey tree frog (*Hyla versicolor*), a tetraploid organism

8.24 Alterations of chromosome structure can cause birth defects and cancer

Even if all chromosomes are present in normal numbers, abnormalities in chromosome structure may cause disorders. Breakage of a chromosome can lead to a variety of rearrangements affecting the genes of that chromosome (**Figure 8.24A**). If a fragment of a chromosome is lost, the remaining chromosome will then have a **deletion**. If a fragment from one chromosome joins to a sister chromatid or homologous chromosome, it will produce a **duplication**. If a fragment reattaches to the original chromosome but in the reverse orientation, an **inversion** results.

Inversions are less likely than deletions or duplications to produce harmful effects, because in inversions all genes are still present in their normal number. Many deletions in human chromosomes, however, cause serious physical and mental problems. One example is a specific deletion in chromosome 5 that causes *cri du chat* ("cry of the cat") syndrome. A child born with this syndrome has intellectual disabilities, a small head with unusual facial features, and a cry that sounds like the mewing of a distressed cat. Such individuals usually die in infancy or early childhood.

Another type of chromosomal change is chromosomal **translocation**, the attachment of a chromosomal fragment to a nonhomologous chromosome. As shown in Figure 8.24A, a translocation may be reciprocal; that is, two nonhomologous chromosomes may exchange segments. Like inversions, translocations may or may not be harmful.

Whereas chromosomal changes present in sperm or egg can cause congenital disorders, such changes in a somatic cell may contribute to the development of cancer. For example, a chromosomal translocation in somatic cells in the bone marrow is associated with chronic myelogenous leukemia (CML). CML is one of the most common types of leukemia. (Leukemias are cancers affecting cells that give rise to white blood cells, or leukocytes.) In the cancerous cells of most CML patients, a part of chromosome 22 has switched places with a small

fragment from a tip of chromosome 9 (**Figure 8.24B**). This reciprocal translocation creates a hybrid gene that codes for an abnormal protein. This protein stimulates cell division, leading to leukemia. The chromosome ending up with the activated cancer-causing gene is called the "Philadelphia chromosome," after the city where it was discovered.

Because the chromosomal changes in cancer are usually confined to somatic cells, cancer is not usually inherited. We'll return to cancer in Chapter 11. In Chapter 9, we continue our study of genetic principles, looking first at the historical development of the science of genetics and then at the rules governing the way traits are passed from parents to offspring.

 How is reciprocal translocation different from normal crossing over?

● Reciprocal translocation swaps chromosome segments between nonhomologous chromosomes. Crossing over normally exchanges corresponding segments between homologous chromosomes.

Chromosome 9

Chromosome 22

Reciprocal translocation

Activated cancer-causing gene

"Philadelphia chromosome"

▲ **Figure 8.24B** The translocation associated with chronic myelogenous leukemia

Deletion	Inversion
A segment of a chromosome is removed	A segment of a chromosome is removed and then reinserted "backward" to its original orientation

Duplication	Reciprocal translocation
A segment of a chromosome is copied and inserted into the homologous chromosome	Segments of two nonhomologous chromosomes swap locations with each other

Homologous chromosomes

Nonhomologous chromosomes

▲ **Figure 8.24A** Alterations of chromosome structure

Reviewing the Concepts

Cell Division and Reproduction (8.1–8.2)

8.1 Cell division plays many important roles in the lives of organisms. Cell division is at the heart of the reproduction of cells and organisms because cells come only from pre-existing cells. Some organisms reproduce through asexual reproduction, and their offspring are all genetic copies of the parent and of each other. Others reproduce through sexual reproduction, creating a variety of offspring, each with a unique combination of traits.

8.2 Prokaryotes reproduce by binary fission. Prokaryotic cells reproduce asexually by cell division. As the cell replicates its single chromosome, the copies move apart; the growing membrane then divides the cell.

The Eukaryotic Cell Cycle and Mitosis (8.3–8.11)

8.3 The large, complex chromosomes of eukaryotes duplicate with each cell division. A eukaryotic cell has many more genes than a prokaryotic cell, and they are grouped into multiple chromosomes in the nucleus. Each chromosome contains one very long DNA molecule associated with proteins. Individual chromosomes are visible only when the cell is in the process of dividing; otherwise, they are in the form of thin, loosely packed chromatin fibres. Before a cell starts dividing, the chromosomes duplicate, producing sister chromatids (containing identical DNA) that are joined together. Cell division involves the separation of sister chromatids and results in two daughter cells, each containing a complete and identical set of chromosomes.

8.4 The cell cycle multiplies cells.

8.5 Cell division is a continuum of dynamic changes. Mitosis distributes duplicated chromosomes into two daughter nuclei. After the chromosomes are coiled up, a mitotic spindle made of microtubules moves them to the middle of the cell. The sister chromatids then separate and move to opposite poles of the cell, where two new nuclei form. Cytokinesis, in which the cell divides in two, overlaps the end of mitosis.

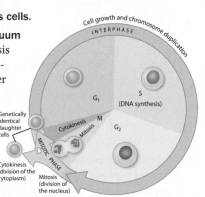

8.6 Cytokinesis differs for plant and animal cells. In animals, cytokinesis occurs by a constriction of the cell (cleavage). In plants, a membranous cell plate splits the cell in two.

8.7 Anchorage, cell density, and chemical growth factors affect cell division. Most animal cells divide only when stimulated by growth factors, and some not at all. Growth factors are proteins secreted by cells that stimulate other cells to divide. In laboratory cultures, most normal cells divide only when attached to a surface. They continue dividing until they touch one another.

8.8 Growth factors signal the cell cycle control system. A set of proteins within the cell controls the cell cycle. Signals affecting critical checkpoints in the cell cycle determine whether a cell will go through the complete cycle and divide. The binding of growth factors to specific receptors on the plasma membrane is usually necessary for cell division.

8.9 Growing out of control, cancer cells produce malignant tumours. Cancer cells divide excessively to form masses called tumours. Malignant tumours can invade other tissues. Radiation and chemotherapy are effective as cancer treatments because they interfere with cell division.

8.10 Are sharks immune to cancer? Sharks do get cancer. The effectiveness of shark cartilage as a treatment for cancer in humans is not supported by scientific literature.

8.11 Review: Mitosis provides for growth, cell replacement, and asexual reproduction. When the cell cycle operates normally, mitotic cell division functions in growth, replacement of damaged and lost cells, and asexual reproduction.

Meiosis and Crossing Over (8.12–8.18)

8.12 Chromosomes are matched in homologous pairs. The somatic (body) cells of each species contain a specific number of chromosomes; for example, human cells have 46, consisting of 23 pairs (two sets) of homologous chromosomes. The chromosomes of a homologous pair of autosomes carry genes for the same characteristics at the same place, or locus. X and Y chromosomes are only partly homologous.

8.13 Gametes have a single set of chromosomes. Cells with two sets of homologous chromosomes are diploid. Gametes—eggs and sperm—are haploid cells with a single set of chromosomes. Sexual life cycles involve the alternation of haploid and diploid stages.

8.14 Meiosis reduces the chromosome number from diploid to haploid. Meiosis, like mitosis, is preceded by chromosome duplication, but in meiosis, the cell divides twice to form four daughter cells. The first division, meiosis I, starts with synapsis, the pairing of homologous chromosomes. In crossing over, homologous chromosomes exchange corresponding segments. Meiosis I separates the members of each homologous pair and produces two daughter cells, each with one set of chromosomes. Meiosis II is essentially the same as mitosis: In each of the cells, the sister chromatids of each chromosome separate. The result is a total of four haploid cells.

8.15 Mitosis and meiosis have important similarities and differences. Both mitosis and meiosis begin with diploid parent cells that have chromosomes duplicated during the previous interphase. But mitosis produces two genetically identical diploid somatic daughter cells, while meiosis produces four genetically unique haploid gametes.

8.16 Independent orientation of chromosomes in meiosis and random fertilization lead to varied offspring. Each chromosome of a homologous pair differs at many points from the other member of the pair. Random arrangements of chromosome pairs at metaphase I of meiosis leads to many different combinations of chromosomes in eggs and sperm. Random fertilization of eggs by sperm greatly increases this variation.

8.17 Homologous chromosomes may carry different versions of genes. The differences between homologous chromosomes are based on the fact that they can bear different versions of genes at corresponding loci.

8.18 Crossing over further increases genetic variability. Genetic recombination, which results from crossing over during prophase I of meiosis, increases variation still further.

Alterations of Chromosome Number and Structure (8.19–8.24)

8.19 A karyotype is a photographic inventory of an individual's chromosomes. To prepare a karyotype, white blood cells are isolated, stimulated to grow, arrested at metaphase, and photographed under a microscope. The chromosomes are arranged into ordered pairs so that any chromosomal abnormalities can be detected.

8.20 An extra copy of chromosome 21 causes Down syndrome. Trisomy 21, the most common chromosome number abnormality in Canada, results in a condition called Down syndrome.

8.21 Accidents during meiosis can alter chromosome number. An abnormal chromosome count is the result of nondisjunction, which can result from the failure of a pair of homologous chromosomes to separate during meiosis I or from the failure of sister chromatids to separate during meiosis II.

8.22 Abnormal numbers of sex chromosomes do not usually affect survival. Nondisjunction of the sex chromosomes during meiosis can result in individuals with a missing or extra X or Y chromosome. In some cases (such as XXY), this leads to syndromes; in other cases (such as XXX), the body is normal.

8.23 New species can arise from errors in cell division. Nondisjunction can produce polyploid organisms, ones with extra sets of chromosomes. Such errors in mitosis can be important in the evolution of new species.

8.24 Alterations of chromosome structure can cause birth defects and cancer. Chromosome breakage can lead to rearrangements—deletions, duplications, inversions, and translocations—that can produce genetic disorders or, if the changes occur in somatic cells, cancer.

Connecting the Concepts

1. Complete the following table to compare mitosis and meiosis.

	Mitosis	Meiosis
Number of chromosomal duplications		
Number of cell divisions		
Number of daughter cells produced		
Number of chromosomes in the daughter cells		
How the chromosomes line up during metaphase		
Genetic relationship of the daughter cells to the parent cell		
Functions performed in the human body		

Testing Your Knowledge

Multiple Choice

2. If an intestinal cell in a grasshopper contains 24 chromosomes, then a grasshopper egg cell contains _____ chromosomes.
   a. 3   b. 6
   c. 12   d. 24
   e. 48

3. Which of the following phases of mitosis is essentially the opposite of prophase in terms of nuclear changes?
   a. telophase   b. metaphase
   c. S phase   d. interphase
   e. anaphase

4. A biochemist measured the amount of DNA in cells growing in the laboratory and found that the quantity of DNA in a cell doubled
   a. between prophase and anaphase of mitosis.
   b. between the G_1 and G_2 phases of the cell cycle.
   c. during the M phase of the cell cycle.
   d. between prophase I and prophase II of meiosis.
   e. between anaphase and telophase of mitosis.

5. Which of the following is *not* a function of mitosis in humans?
   a. repair of wounds
   b. growth
   c. production of gametes from diploid cells
   d. replacement of lost or damaged cells
   e. multiplication of somatic cells

6. A micrograph of a dividing cell from a mouse showed 19 chromosomes, each consisting of two sister chromatids. During which of the following stages of cell division could such a picture have been taken? *(Explain your answer.)*
   a. prophase of mitosis
   b. telophase II of meiosis
   c. prophase I of meiosis
   d. anaphase of mitosis
   e. prophase II of meiosis

7. Cytochalasin B is a chemical that disrupts microfilament formation. This chemical would interfere with
   a. DNA replication.
   b. formation of the mitotic spindle.
   c. cleavage.
   d. formation of the cell plate.
   e. crossing over.

8. It is difficult to observe individual chromosomes during interphase because
   a. the DNA has not been replicated yet.
   b. they are in the form of long, thin strands.
   c. they leave the nucleus and are dispersed to other parts of the cell.
   d. homologous chromosomes do not pair up until division starts.
   e. the spindle must move them to the metaphase plate before they become visible.

9. A fruit fly somatic cell contains 8 chromosomes. This means that _____ different combinations of chromosomes are possible in its gametes.
   a. 4   b. 8
   c. 16   d. 32
   e. 64

10. If a fragment of a chromosome breaks off and then reattaches to the original chromosome but in the reverse direction, the resulting chromosomal abnormality is called
    a. a deletion.
    b. an inversion.
    c. a translocation.
    d. a nondisjunction.
    e. a reciprocal translocation.

11. Why are individuals with an extra chromosome 21, which causes Down syndrome, more numerous than individuals with an extra chromosome 3 or chromosome 16?
    a. There are probably more genes on chromosome 21 than on the others.
    b. Chromosome 21 is a sex chromosome and chromosomes 3 and 16 are not.
    c. Down syndrome is not more common, just more serious.
    d. Extra copies of the other chromosomes are probably fatal.
    e. Chromosome 21 is more likely to produce a nondisjunction error than other chromosomes.

Describing, Comparing, and Explaining

12. An organism called a plasmodial slime mould is one large cytoplasmic mass with many nuclei. Explain how such a "megacell" could form.

13. Briefly describe how three different processes that occur during a sexual life cycle increase the genetic diversity of offspring.

14. Discuss the factors that control the division of eukaryotic cells grown in the laboratory. Cancer cells are easier to grow in the lab than other cells. Why do you suppose this is?

15. In the light micrograph below of dividing cells near the tip of an onion root, identify a cell in interphase, prophase, metaphase, anaphase, and telophase. Describe the major events occurring at each stage.

LM 500×

16. Compare cytokinesis in plant and animal cells. In what ways are the two processes similar? In what ways are they different?

17. Sketch a cell with three pairs of chromosomes undergoing meiosis, and show how nondisjunction can result in the production of gametes with extra or missing chromosomes.

Applying the Concepts

18. Suppose you read in the newspaper that a genetic engineering laboratory has developed a procedure for fusing two gametes from the same person (two eggs or two sperm) to form a zygote. The article mentions that an early step in the procedure prevents crossing over from occurring during the formation of the gametes in the donor's body. The researchers are in the process of determining the genetic makeup of one of their new zygotes. Which of the following predictions do you think they would make? Justify your choice, and explain why you rejected each of the other choices.

    a. The zygote would have 46 chromosomes, all of which came from the gamete donor (its one parent), so the zygote would be genetically identical to the gamete donor.
    b. The zygote *could* be genetically identical to the gamete donor, but it is much more likely that it would have an unpredictable mixture of chromosomes from the gamete donor's parents.
    c. The zygote would not be genetically identical to the gamete donor, but it would be genetically identical to one of the donor's parents.
    d. The zygote would not be genetically identical to the gamete donor, but it would be genetically identical to one of the donor's grandparents.

19. Bacteria are able to divide on a much faster schedule than eukaryotic cells. Some bacteria can divide every 20 minutes, while the minimum time required by eukaryotic cells in a rapidly developing embryo is about once per hour, and most cells divide much less often than that. State several testable hypotheses explaining why bacteria can divide at a faster rate than eukaryotic cells.

20. Red blood cells, which carry oxygen to body tissues, live for only about 120 days. Replacement cells are produced by cell division in bone marrow. How many cell divisions must occur each second in your bone marrow just to replace red blood cells? Here is some information to use in calculating your answer: There are about 5 million red blood cells per cubic millimetre (mm^3) of blood. An average adult has about 5 L (5000 cm^3) of blood. (*Hint:* What is the total number of red blood cells in the body? What fraction of them must be replaced each day if all are replaced in 120 days?)

21. A mule is the offspring of a horse and a donkey. A donkey sperm contains 31 chromosomes and a horse egg cell 32 chromosomes, so the zygote contains a total of 63 chromosomes. The zygote develops normally. The combined set of chromosomes is not a problem in mitosis, and the mule combines some of the best characteristics of horses and donkeys. However, a mule is sterile; meiosis cannot occur normally in its testes (or ovaries). Explain why mitosis is normal in cells containing both horse and donkey chromosomes but the mixed set of chromosomes interferes with meiosis.

Answers to all questions can be found in Appendix E.

Study on the Go

This QR code leads to Study on the Go—mobile study resources, including practice quizzes, videos, and glossary flashcards.

You can access Study on the Go content via your smartphone, allowing you to study whenever and wherever you want. Note: Your login information for MasteringBiology is required.

Go to one of the sites below to download a free app. Once installed, the phone will scan the code and link to a website with *Campbell Biology: Concepts and Connections'* Study on the Go resources.

ScanLife
http://getscanlife.com

NeoReader
http://get.neoreader.com

QuickMark
http://www.quickmark.com.tw/

Patterns of Inheritance

BIG IDEAS

Mendel's Laws

(9.1–9.9)

A few simple and long-established rules explain many aspects of heredity.

Variations on Mendel's Laws

(9.10–9.15)

Some inheritance patterns are more complex than the ones described by Mendel.

The Chromosomal Basis of Inheritance

(9.16–9.19)

Hereditary rules can be understood by following the behaviour of chromosomes.

Sex Chromosomes and Sex-Linked Genes

(9.20–9.23)

Genes found on sex chromosomes display unique patterns of inheritance.

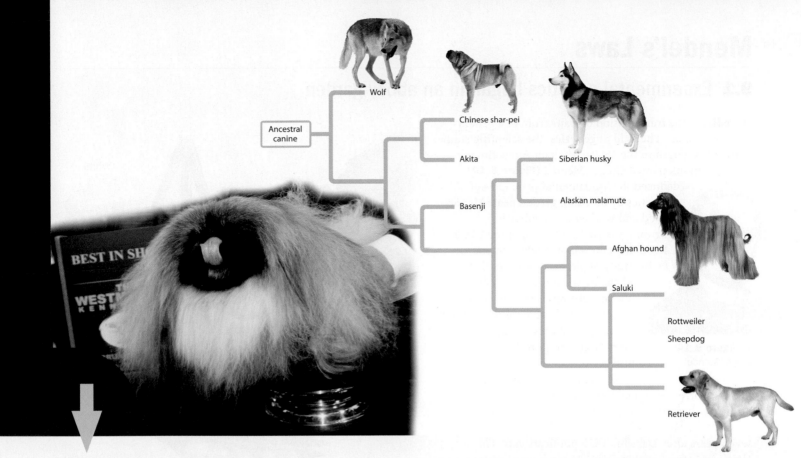

Barking Up the Genetic Tree

The proud pooch shown above is Malachy, winner of the Best in Show trophy at the 136th Westminster Kennel Club Dog Show. Formally known as Champion Palacegarden Malachy, Malachy is considered one of the finest examples of the Pekingese breed. Pekingese breeders expect Malachy's offspring to inherit many of his desirable traits, since they typify the lionlike appearance that distinguishes the breed. Malachy's well-documented pedigree includes award-winning grandparents, great-grandparents, and great-great-grandparents, which all have very similar genetic makeups and appearances.

Malachy is living proof that dogs are more than "man's best friend"; they are also one of humans' longest-running genetic experiments. About 15 000 years ago, in East Asia, humans began to cohabit with ancestral canines—the predecessors of both modern wolves and dogs. As people settled into permanent, geographically isolated settlements, different populations of canines were separated from one another and eventually became inbred. At the same time, different groups of people chose dogs with different traits according to their needs. For example, herders selected dogs that were good at controlling flocks of animals, and hunters chose dogs that were good at retrieving wounded prey. Continued over millennia, this genetic tinkering resulted in an incredibly diverse array of dog body types and behaviours, from tiny, feisty Chihuahuas to huge, docile St. Bernards. But no matter the appearance a dog sports, we can ultimately explain their inborn traits through genetics, the science of heredity. In each breed, a distinct genetic makeup results in a distinct set of physical and behavioural characteristics.

Our understanding of canine genetics took a big leap forward in 2003 when researchers sequenced the complete genome of a dog. Using the genome sequence and a wealth of other data, canine geneticists produced the family tree of dog breeds shown above. Published in 2006, the tree is based on genetic analysis of 414 dogs from 85 recognized breeds. The analysis shows that the canine family tree includes a series of well-defined branch points. Each fork represents purposeful artificial selection that produced a genetically distinct sub-population with specific desired traits. The genetic tree shows that the most ancient breeds, those with genetic makeups most closely resembling the wolf, are Asian species such as the shar-pei and akita. Subsequent genetic splits created distinct breeds in Africa (basenji), the Arctic (Alaskan malamute and Siberian husky), and the Middle East (Afghan hound and saluki). The remaining breeds, primarily of European ancestry, can be grouped by genetic makeup into those bred for guarding (for example, the rottweiler), herding (such as various sheepdogs), and hunting (including the golden retriever and beagle).

Although humans have been applying genetics for thousands of years—by breeding food crops as well as domesticated animals—the biological basis of selective breeding has only recently been understood. In this chapter, we examine the rules that govern how inherited traits are passed from parents to offspring. We look at several kinds of inheritance patterns and how they allow us to predict the ratios of offspring with particular traits. Most importantly, we uncover a basic biological concept: how the behaviour of chromosomes during gamete formation and fertilization (discussed in Chapter 8) accounts for the patterns of inheritance we observe.

Mendel's Laws

9.1 Experimental genetics began in an abbey garden

Heredity is the transmission of traits from one generation to the next. The field of **genetics**, the scientific study of heredity, began in the 1860s, when an Augustinian monk named Gregor Mendel (**Figure 9.1A**) deduced the fundamental principles of genetics by breeding garden peas. Mendel lived and worked in an abbey in Brunn, Austria (now Brno, in the Czech Republic) and was strongly influenced by his study of physics, mathematics, and chemistry at the University of Vienna. His research was both experimentally and mathematically rigorous, and these qualities were largely responsible for his success.

▲ **Figure 9.1A**
Gregor Mendel

In a paper published in 1866, Mendel correctly argued that parents pass on to their offspring discrete "heritable factors." (It is interesting to note that Mendel's landmark publication came just seven years after Darwin's 1859 publication of *The Origin of Species*, making the 1860s a banner decade in the development of modern biology.) In his paper, Mendel stressed that heritable factors, today called genes, retain their individuality generation after generation. That is, genes are like playing cards: A deck may be shuffled, but the cards always retain their original identities, and no card is ever blended with another. Similarly, genes may be rearranged but each gene permanently retains its identity.

Mendel probably chose to study garden peas because they had short generation times, produced large numbers of offspring from each mating, and came in many readily distinguishable varieties. For example, one variety has purple flowers, and another variety has white flowers. A heritable feature that varies among individuals, such as flower colour, is called a **character**. Each variant for a character, such as purple or white flowers, is called a **trait**.

Perhaps the most important advantage of pea plants as an experimental model was that Mendel could strictly control matings. As **Figure 9.1B** shows, the petals of the pea flower almost completely

◀ **Figure 9.1B** The anatomy of a garden pea flower (with one petal removed to improve visibility)

— Petal

— Carpel
Stamen

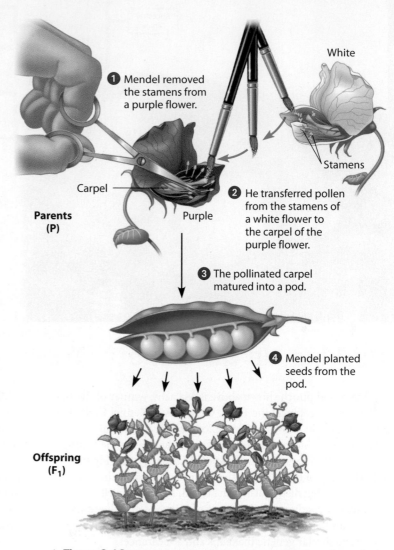

① Mendel removed the stamens from a purple flower.

White

Stamens

Parents (P)

Carpel

Purple

② He transferred pollen from the stamens of a white flower to the carpel of the purple flower.

③ The pollinated carpel matured into a pod.

④ Mendel planted seeds from the pod.

Offspring (F_1)

▲ **Figure 9.1C** Mendel's technique for cross-fertilization of pea plants

enclose the reproductive organs: the stamens and carpel. Consequently, pea plants usually are able to **self-fertilize** in nature. That is, sperm-carrying pollen grains released from the stamens land on the egg-containing carpel of the same flower. Mendel could ensure self-fertilization by covering a flower with a small bag so that no pollen from another plant could reach the carpel. When he wanted **cross-fertilization** (fertilization of one plant by pollen from a different plant), he used the method shown in **Figure 9.1C.** ① He prevented self-fertilization by cutting off the immature stamens of a plant before they produced pollen. ② To cross-fertilize the stamenless flower, he dusted its carpel with pollen from another plant. After pollination,

Character	Traits	
	Dominant	**Recessive**
Flower colour	Purple	White
Flower position	Axial	Terminal
Seed colour	Yellow	Green
Seed shape	Round	Wrinkled
Pod shape	Inflated	Constricted
Pod colour	Green	Yellow
Stem length	Tall	Dwarf

▲ **Figure 9.1D** The seven pea characters studied by Mendel

3 the carpel developed into a pod, containing seeds (peas) that **4** he planted. The seeds grew into offspring plants. Through these methods, Mendel could always be sure of the parentage of new plants.

Mendel's success was due not only to his experimental approach and choice of organism, but also to his selection of characteristics to study. He chose to observe seven characters, each of which occurred as two distinct traits (**Figure 9.1D**). Mendel worked with his plants until he was sure he had **true-breeding** varieties—that is, varieties for which self-fertilization produced offspring all identical to the parent. For instance, he identified a purple-flowered variety that, when self-fertilized, produced offspring plants that all had purple flowers.

Now Mendel was ready to ask what would happen when he crossed his different true-breeding varieties with each other. For example, what offspring would result if plants with purple flowers and plants with white flowers were cross-fertilized? The offspring of two different varieties are called **hybrids**, and the cross-fertilization itself is referred to as a hybridization, or simply a genetic **cross**. The true-breeding parental plants are called the **P generation** (*P* for parental), and their hybrid offspring are called the F_1 **generation** (*F* for filial, from the Latin word for "son"). When F_1 plants self-fertilize or fertilize each other, their offspring are the F_2 **generation**. We turn to Mendel's results next.

? Why was the development of true-breeding varieties critical to the success of Mendel's experiments?

 True-breeding varieties allowed Mendel to predict the outcome of specific crosses and thus to run controlled experiments.

9.2 Mendel's law of segregation describes the inheritance of a single character

Mendel performed many experiments in which he tracked the inheritance of characters that occur in two forms, such as flower colour. The results led him to formulate several hypotheses about inheritance. Let's look at some of his experiments and follow the reasoning that led to his hypotheses.

Figure 9.2A starts with a cross between a true-breeding pea plant with purple flowers and a true-breeding pea plant with white flowers. This is called a **monohybrid cross** because the parent plants differ in only one character—flower colour. At the time that Mendel was working, an existing (but incorrect) theory of inheritance called the blending hypothesis would have predicted that the colour of the F_1 plants would be a mixture of their parents—that is, light purple. Instead, Mendel

observed that F_1 plants all had purple flowers. This blending hypothesis would also have predicted that the original phenotypes would not re-emerge.

Was the white-flowered plant's genetic contribution to the hybrids lost? By mating the F_1 plants with each other, Mendel found the answer to be no. Out of 929 F_2 plants, 705 (about $\frac{3}{4}$) had purple flowers and 224 (about $\frac{1}{4}$) had white flowers, a ratio of about three plants with purple flowers to every one with white flowers (abbreviated as 3:1). Mendel reasoned that the heritable factor for white flowers did not disappear in the F_1 plants, but was masked when the purple-flower factor was present. He also deduced that the F_1 plants must have carried two factors for the flower-colour character, one for purple and one for white.

P generation
(true-breeding parents)

Purple flowers   White flowers

F₁ generation

All plants have
purple flowers

Fertilization
among F₁ plants
(F₁ × F₁)

F₂ generation

$\frac{3}{4}$ of plants
have purple flowers

$\frac{1}{4}$ of plants
have white flowers

▲ **Figure 9.2A** Crosses tracking one character (flower colour)

P generation

Genetic makeup (alleles)

Purple flowers   White flowers

PP pp

Gametes   All P All p

F₁ generation
(hybrids)

All Pp

Gametes $\frac{1}{2}$ P Alleles
segregate $\frac{1}{2}$ p

Fertilization

F₂ generation

Sperm from F₁ plant

P p

Phenotypic ratio
3 purple : 1 white

Eggs
from F₁
plant

P PP Pp

Genotypic ratio
1 PP : 2 Pp : 1 pp

p Pp pp

▲ **Figure 9.2B** An explanation of the crosses in Figure 9.2A

Mendel observed these same patterns of inheritance for six other pea plant characters (see Figure 9.1D). From his results, he developed four hypotheses, described here using modern terminology, such as "gene" instead of "heritable factor."

1. *There are alternative versions of genes that account for variations in inherited characters.* For example, the gene for flower colour in pea plants exists in two versions: one for purple and the other for white. The alternative versions of a gene are called **alleles**.

2. *For each character, an organism inherits two alleles, one from each parent.* These alleles may be the same or different. An organism that has two identical alleles for a gene is said to be **homozygous** for that gene (and is a "homozygote" for that trait). An organism that has two different alleles for a gene is said to be **heterozygous** for that gene (and is a "heterozygote").

3. *If the two alleles of an inherited pair differ, then one determines the organism's appearance and is called the **dominant** allele; the other has no noticeable effect on the organism's appearance and is called the **recessive** allele.* We use uppercase letters to represent dominant alleles and lowercase letters to represent recessive alleles.

4. *A sperm or egg carries only one allele for each inherited character because allele pairs separate (segregate) from each other during the production of gametes.* This statement is called the **law of segregation**. When sperm and egg unite at fertilization, each contributes its allele, restoring the paired condition in the offspring.

Figure 9.2B explains the results in Figure 9.2A. In this example, the letter *P* represents the dominant allele (for purple flowers), and *p* stands for the recessive allele (for white flowers). Both parental plants (at the top of the figure) were true-breeding, and Mendel's first two hypotheses propose that one parental variety had two alleles for purple flowers (*PP*) and the other had two alleles for white flowers (*pp*).

Consistent with hypothesis 4, the gametes of Mendel's parental plants each carried one allele; thus, the parental gametes in Figure 9.2B are either *P* or *p*. As a result of fertilization, the F₁ hybrids each inherited one allele for purple flowers and one for white. Hypothesis 3 explains why all the F₁ hybrids (*Pp*) had purple flowers: The dominant *P* allele has its full effect in the heterozygote, while the recessive *p* allele has no effect.

Mendel's hypotheses also explain the 3:1 ratio in the F₂ generation. Because the F₁ hybrids are *Pp*, they make gametes *P* and *p* in equal numbers. The bottom diagram in Figure 9.2B, called a **Punnett square**, shows the four possible combinations of alleles that could occur when these gametes combine.

The Punnett square shows the proportions of F₂ plants predicted by Mendel's hypotheses. If a sperm carrying allele *P* fertilizes an egg carrying allele *P*, the offspring (*PP*) will produce purple flowers. Mendel's hypotheses predict that this combination will occur in $\frac{1}{4}$ of the offspring. As shown in the Punnett square, the hypotheses also predict that $\frac{1}{2}$ (or two of four) of the offspring will inherit one *P* allele and one *p* allele. These offspring (*Pp*) will all have purple flowers because *P* is dominant. The remaining $\frac{1}{4}$ of F₂ plants will inherit two *p* alleles and will have white flowers.

Because an organism's appearance does not always reveal its genetic composition, geneticists distinguish between an organism's physical traits, called its **phenotype** (such as purple or white flowers), and its genetic makeup, its **genotype** (in this example, PP, Pp, or pp). So now we see that Figure 9.2A shows just phenotypes while Figure 9.2B shows both phenotypes and genotypes in our sample crosses. For the F_2 plants, the ratio of plants with purple flowers to those with white flowers (3:1) is called the phenotypic ratio. The genotypic ratio, as shown by the Punnett square, is 1 PP:2 Pp:1 pp.

Mendel found that each of the seven characteristics he studied exhibited the same inheritance pattern: One parental trait disappeared in the F_1 generation, only to reappear in $\frac{1}{4}$ of the F_2 offspring. The mechanism underlying this inheritance pattern is stated by Mendel's law of segregation: Pairs of alleles segregate (separate) during gamete formation. The fusion of gametes at fertilization creates allele pairs once again. Research since Mendel's time has established that because of the separation of homologous chromosomes during meiosis I (see Modules 8.13–8.15), the law of segregation applies to all sexually reproducing organisms, including humans and Kermode bears. The recessive white colour of the spirit bears is inherited in a similar fashion to the white-flowered peas. We'll return to Mendel and his experiments with pea plants in Module 9.4, but first let's see how some of the concepts we discussed in Chapter 8 fit with what we have said about genetics so far.

 How can two plants with different genotypes for a particular inherited character be identical in phenotype?

● One could be homozygous for the dominant allele and the other heterozygous.

9.3 Homologous chromosomes bear the alleles for each character

Figure 9.3 shows the locations of three genes on a pair of homologous chromosomes (homologues)—chromosomes that carry alleles of the same gene. Recall from Module 8.12 that every diploid cell, whether from pea plant or human, has chromosomes in homologous pairs. One member of each pair comes from the organism's female parent, while the other member of the pair comes from the male parent.

Each labelled band on the chromosomes in the figure represents a gene **locus** (plural, *loci*), a specific location of a gene along the chromosome. The matching colours of the three corresponding loci on the two homologues highlight the fact that homologous chromosomes have genes for the same characters located at the same positions along their lengths. However, as the uppercase and lowercase letters next to the loci indicate, two homologous chromosomes may bear either the same alleles or different ones. This is the connection between Mendel's laws and homologous chromosomes: **Alleles** (alternative versions) of a gene reside at the same locus on homologous chromosomes.

The diagram here also serves as a review of some of the genetic terms we have encountered to this point. We will return to the chromosomal basis of inheritance in more detail beginning with Module 9.16.

▲ **Figure 9.3** Three gene loci on homologous chromosomes

? **An individual is heterozygous, *Bb*, for a gene. According to the law of segregation, each gamete formed by this individual will have *either* the *B* allele *or* the *b* allele. Recalling what you learned about meiosis in Chapter 8, explain the physical basis for this segregation of alleles.**

● The *B* and *b* alleles are located at the same gene locus on homologous chromosomes, which separate during meiosis I and are packaged in separate gametes.

9.4 The law of independent assortment is revealed by tracking two characters at once

Recall from Module 9.2 that Mendel established his law of segregation by following one character from the P generation through the F_1 and F_2 generations. From such monohybrid crosses, Mendel knew that the allele for round seed shape (designated *R*) was dominant to the allele for wrinkled seed shape (*r*) and that the allele for yellow seed colour (*Y*) was dominant to the allele for green seed colour (*y*). Mendel wondered the following: What would happen if he crossed plants that differ in both seed shape and seed colour?

To find out, Mendel set up a mating of parental varieties differing in two characters. Mendel crossed homozygous plants having round yellow seeds (genotype *RRYY*) with plants having wrinkled green seeds (*rryy*). Mendel knew that an *RRYY* plant would produce only gametes with *RY* alleles; an *rryy*

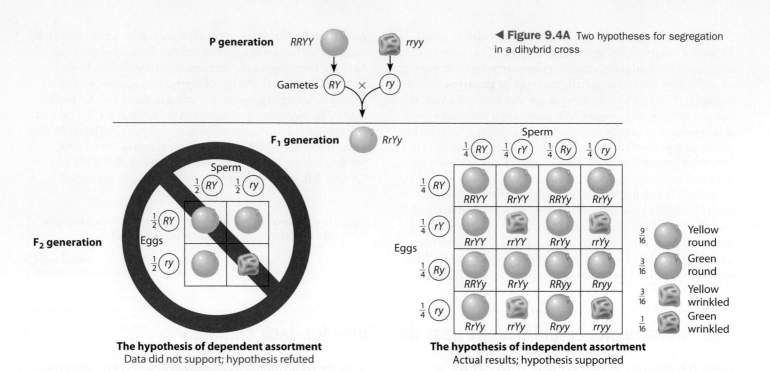

The hypothesis of dependent assortment
Data did not support; hypothesis refuted

The hypothesis of independent assortment
Actual results; hypothesis supported

plant would produce only gametes with *ry* alleles. Therefore, Mendel knew there was only one possible outcome for the F_1 generation: the union of *RY* and *ry* gametes would yield hybrids heterozygous for both characters (*RrYy*)—that is, **dihybrids**. All of these *RrYy* offspring would have round yellow seeds, the double dominant phenotype.

The F_2 generation is a bit trickier. Would the genes for seed colour and seed shape be transmitted from parent to offspring as a package, or would they be inherited separately? To find out, Mendel crossed the *RrYy* F_1 plants with each other. This is called a **dihybrid cross**. He hypothesized two possible outcomes from this experiment: Either the dihybrid cross would exhibit *dependent* assortment, with the genes for seed colour and seed shape inherited together as a set, or it would exhibit *independent* assortment, with the genes inherited independently from each other.

As shown on the left side of **Figure 9.4A**, the hypothesis of dependent assortment leads to the prediction that each F_2 plant would inherit one of two possible sperm (*RY* or *ry*) and one of two possible eggs (*RY* or *ry*), for a total of four combinations. The Punnett square shows that there could be only two F_2 phenotypes—round yellow or wrinkled green—in a 3:1 ratio. However, when Mendel actually performed this cross, he did not obtain these results, thus refuting the hypothesis of dependent assortment.

The alternative hypothesis—that the genes would exhibit independent assortment—is shown on the right side of Figure 9.4A. This leads to the prediction that the F_1 plants would produce four different gametes: *RY*, *rY*, *Ry*, and *ry*. Each F_2 plant would inherit one of four possible sperm and one of four possible eggs, for a total of 16 possible combinations. The Punnett square shows that fertilization among these gametes would lead to four different seed phenotypes—round yellow, round green, wrinkled yellow, or wrinkled green—in a 9:3:3:1 ratio. In fact, Mendel observed such a ratio in the F_2 plants,

indicating that each pair of alleles segregates independently of the other.

The Punnett square on the right-hand side of Figure 9.4A also reveals that a dihybrid cross is equivalent to two monohybrid crosses—one for seed colour and one for seed shape—occurring simultaneously. From the 9:3:3:1 ratio, we can see that there are 12 plants with round seeds to 4 with wrinkled seeds and 12 yellow-seeded plants to 4 green-seeded ones. These 12:4 ratios each reduce to 3:1, which is the F_2 ratio for a monohybrid cross; a monohybrid cross is occurring for each of the two characters. Mendel tried his seven pea characters in various dihybrid combinations and always obtained data close to the predicted 9:3:3:1 ratio. These results supported the hypothesis that each pair of alleles segregates (assorts) independently of other pairs of alleles during gamete formation. In other words, the inheritance of one character has no effect on the inheritance of another. This is called Mendel's **law of independent assortment**. The law of independent assortment can be seen at the chromosome level during metaphase I (shown in Figure 8.14) as the homologous chromosomes line up independently from one another.

Figure 9.4B shows how this law applies to the inheritance of two characters in Labrador retrievers: black versus chocolate coat colour and normal vision versus progressive retinal atrophy (PRA), an eye disorder that leads to blindness. As you would expect, these characters are controlled by separate genes. Black Labs have at least one copy of an allele called *B*, which gives their hairs densely packed granules of a dark pigment. The *B* allele is dominant to *b*, which leads to a less tightly packed distribution of pigment granules. As a result, the coats of dogs with genotype *bb* are chocolate in colour. (If you're wondering about yellow Labs, their colour is controlled by a different gene altogether.) The allele that causes PRA, called *n*, is recessive to allele *N*, which is necessary for normal vision.

Phenotypes	Black coat, normal vision	Black coat, blind (PRA)	Chocolate coat, normal vision	Chocolate coat, blind (PRA)
Genotypes	B_N_	B_nn	bbN_	bbnn

Mating of double heterozygotes (black coat, normal vision)

BbNn × BbNn

Phenotypic ratio of the offspring	**9** Black coat, normal vision	**3** Black coat, blind (PRA)	**3** Chocolate coat, normal vision	**1** Chocolate coat, blind (PRA)

▲ **Figure 9.4B** Independent assortment of two genes in the Labrador retriever

Thus, only dogs of genotype *nn* become blind from PRA. (In the figure, blanks in the genotypes are used where a particular phenotype may result from multiple genotypes. For example, a black Lab may have either genotype *BB* or *Bb*, which we abbreviate as *B_*.)

The lower part of Figure 9.4B shows what happens when we mate two heterozygous Labs, both of genotype *BbNn*. The F_2 phenotypic ratio will be nine black dogs with normal eyes to three black with PRA to three chocolate with normal eyes

to one chocolate with PRA. These results are analogous to the results in Figure 9.4A and demonstrate that the *B* and *N* genes are inherited independently.

? Predict the phenotypes of offspring obtained by mating a black Lab homozygous for both coat colour and normal eyes with a chocolate Lab that is blind from PRA.

● All offspring would be black with normal eyes (BBNN × bbnn → BbNn).

9.5 Geneticists can use the testcross to determine unknown genotypes

Suppose you have a Labrador retriever with a chocolate coat. Referring to Figure 9.4B, you can tell that its genotype must be *bb*, the only combination of alleles that produces the chocolate-coat phenotype. But what if you had a black Lab? It could have one of two possible genotypes—*BB* or *Bb*—and there is no way to tell which is correct simply by looking at the dog. To determine your dog's genotype, you could perform a **testcross**, a mating between an individual of unknown genotype (your black Lab) and a homozygous recessive (*bb*) individual—in this case, a chocolate Lab.

Figure 9.5 shows the offspring that could result from such a mating. If, as shown on the bottom left, the black parent's genotype is *BB*, we would expect all the offspring to be black because a cross between genotypes *BB* and *bb* can produce only *Bb* offspring. On the contrary, if the black parent is *Bb*, as shown on the bottom right, we would expect both black (*Bb*) and chocolate (*bb*) offspring. Thus, the appearance of the offspring reveals the original black dog's genotype.

Mendel used testcrosses to verify that he had true-breeding varieties of plants. The testcross continues to be an important tool of geneticists for determining genotypes.

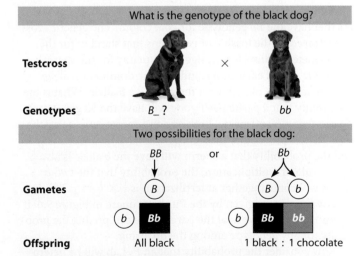

▲ **Figure 9.5** Using a testcross to determine genotype

? You use a testcross to determine the genotype of a Lab with normal eyes. Half the offspring of the testcross are normal and half develop PRA. What is the genotype of the normal parent?

● Heterozygous (*Nn*)

9.6 Mendel's laws reflect the rules of probability

Mendel's strong background in mathematics served him well in his studies of inheritance. He understood, for instance, that the segregation of allele pairs during gamete formation and the re-forming of pairs at fertilization obey the rules of probability—the same rules that apply to the tossing of coins, the rolling of dice, and the drawing of cards. Mendel also appreciated the statistical nature of inheritance. He knew that he needed to obtain large samples—to count many offspring from his crosses—before he could begin to interpret inheritance patterns.

Let's see how the rules of probability apply to inheritance. The probability scale ranges from 0 to 1. An event that is certain to occur has a probability of 1, whereas an event that is certain *not* to occur has a probability of 0. For example, a tossed coin has a $\frac{1}{2}$ chance of landing heads and a $\frac{1}{2}$ chance of landing tails. These two possibilities add up to 1; the probabilities of all possible outcomes for an event to occur must always add up to 1. In another example, in a standard deck of 52 playing cards, the chance of drawing a jack of diamonds is $\frac{1}{52}$ and the chance of drawing any card other than the jack of diamonds is $\frac{51}{52}$, which together add up to 1.

An important lesson we can learn from coin tossing is that for each and every toss of the coin, the probability of heads is $\frac{1}{2}$. Even if heads has landed five times in a row, the probability of the next toss coming up heads is still $\frac{1}{2}$. In other words, the outcome of any particular toss is unaffected by what has happened on previous attempts. Each toss is an independent event.

If two coins are tossed simultaneously, the outcome for each coin is an independent event, unaffected by the other coin. What is the chance that both coins will land heads up? The probability of such a compound event is the product of the probabilities of each independent event; for the two tosses of coins, $\frac{1}{2} \times \frac{1}{2} = \frac{1}{4}$. This statistical principle is called the **rule of multiplication**, and it holds true for genetics as well as coin tosses.

Figure 9.6 represents a cross between F$_1$ Labrador retrievers that have the *Bb* genotype for coat colour. The genetic cross is portrayed by the tossing of two coins that stand in for the two gametes (a dime for the egg and a penny for the sperm); the heads side of each coin stands for the dominant *B* allele and the tails side of each coin the recessive *b* allele. What is the probability that a particular F$_2$ dog will have the *bb* genotype? To produce a *bb* offspring, both egg and sperm must carry the *b* allele. The probability that an egg will have the *b* allele is $\frac{1}{2}$, and the probability that a sperm will have the *b* allele is also $\frac{1}{2}$. By the rule of multiplication, the probability that the two *b* alleles will come together at fertilization is $\frac{1}{2} \times \frac{1}{2} = \frac{1}{4}$. This is exactly the answer given by the Punnett square in Figure 9.6. If we know the genotypes of the parents, we can predict the probability for any genotype among the offspring.

Now consider the probability that an F$_2$ Lab will be heterozygous for the coat-colour gene. As Figure 9.6 shows, there are two ways in which F$_1$ gametes can combine to produce a heterozygous offspring. The dominant (*B*) allele can come from the egg and the recessive (*b*) allele from the sperm, or vice versa. The probability that an event can occur in two or more alternative ways is the sum of the separate probabilities of the

▲ **Figure 9.6** Segregation and fertilization as chance events

different ways; this is known as the **rule of addition**. Using this rule, we can calculate the probability of an F$_2$ heterozygote as $\frac{1}{4} + \frac{1}{4} = \frac{1}{2}$.

By applying the rules of probability to segregation and independent assortment, we can solve some rather complex genetics problems. For instance, we can predict the results of trihybrid crosses, in which three different characters are involved. Consider a cross between two organisms that both have the genotype *AaBbCc*. What is the probability that an offspring from this cross will be a recessive homozygote for all three genes (*aabbcc*)? Since each allele pair assorts independently, we can treat this trihybrid cross as three separate monohybrid crosses:

Aa × *Aa*: Probability of *aa* offspring $= \frac{1}{4}$

Bb × *Bb*: Probability of *bb* offspring $= \frac{1}{4}$

Cc × *Cc*: Probability of *cc* offspring $= \frac{1}{4}$

Because the segregation of each allele pair is an independent event, we use the rule of multiplication to calculate the probability that the offspring will be *aabbcc*:

$$\frac{1}{4}aa \times \frac{1}{4}bb \times \frac{1}{4}cc = \frac{1}{64}$$

We could reach the same conclusion by constructing a 64-section Punnett square, but that would take a lot of time and space!

 A plant of genotype *AABbCC* is crossed with an *AaBbCc* plant. What is the probability of an offspring having the genotype *AABBCC*?

$\bullet \ \frac{1}{16}$ (that is, $\frac{1}{2} \times \frac{1}{4} \times \frac{1}{2}$)

9.7 Genetic traits in humans can be tracked through family pedigrees

While much of the classic work that led to our understanding of genetics was performed on model organisms (such as peas and fruit flies), Mendel's laws apply to the inheritance of many human traits as well. **Figure 9.7A** illustrates alternative forms of three human characters that are each thought to be determined by simple dominant-recessive inheritance at one gene locus. (The genetic basis of many other human characters, such as eye and hair colour, involves several genes and is not well understood.)

If we call the dominant allele of a gene under consideration *A*, the dominant phenotype results from either the homozygous genotype *AA* or the heterozygous genotype *Aa*. Recessive phenotypes always result from the homozygous genotype *aa*.

In genetics, the word *dominant* does not imply that a phenotype is either normal or more common than a recessive phenotype; **wild-type traits**—those prevailing in nature—are not necessarily specified by dominant alleles. Rather, dominance means that a heterozygote (*Aa*), carrying only a single copy of a dominant allele, displays the dominant phenotype. By contrast, the phenotype of the corresponding recessive allele is seen only in a homozygote (*aa*). Recessive traits may in fact be more common in the population than dominant ones. For example, the absence of freckles is more common than their presence.

How can we determine the inheritance pattern of a particular human trait? Since we obviously cannot control human matings and run a testcross, geneticists must analyze the results of matings that have already occurred. First, a geneticist collects as much information as possible about a family's history for the trait of interest. The next step is to assemble this information into a family tree—the family **pedigree**. (You may associate pedigrees with purebred animals—such as racehorses or championship dogs—but they can represent human matings just as well.) To analyze the pedigree, the geneticist applies logic and Mendel's laws.

Let's apply this approach to the example in **Figure 9.7B**, a pedigree that traces the incidence of free versus attached earlobes in a hypothetical family. The letter *F* stands for the allele for free earlobes, and *f* symbolizes the allele for attached earlobes. In the pedigree, □ represents a male, ○ represents a female, and coloured symbols (■ and ●) indicate that the person is affected by the trait under investigation (in this case, attached earlobes). The earliest generation studied is at the top of the pedigree, and the most recent generation is at the bottom.

Even if we didn't already know that *f* was recessive to *F*, we could apply Mendel's laws to deduce it from the pedigree. That is the only way that one of the third-generation sisters

Dominant Traits	Recessive Traits
Freckles	No freckles
Widow's peak	Straight hairline
Free earlobe	Attached earlobe

▲ **Figure 9.7A** Examples of single-gene inherited traits in humans

(at the bottom right) could have attached earlobes when both her parents did not; in the pedigree, this is represented by an affected individual (●) with two parents who are unaffected (□ and ○). We can therefore label all the individuals with attached earlobes in the pedigree—that is, all those with coloured circles or squares—as homozygous recessive (*ff*).

Mendel's laws enable us to deduce the genotypes for most of the people in the pedigree. For example, both of the second-generation parents must have carried the *f* allele (which they passed on to the affected daughter) along with the *F* allele that gave them free earlobes. The same must be true of the first set of grandparents (the top left couple in the pedigree) because they both had free earlobes but their two sons had attached earlobes.

Notice that we cannot deduce the genotype of every member of the pedigree. For example, the sister with free earlobes in the bottom right of the pedigree must have at least one *F* allele, but she could be either *FF* or *Ff*. We cannot distinguish between these two possibilities by using the available data.

? Look at Figure 9.7B and imagine that the sister with free earlobes married a man with free earlobes and they had a daughter. What phenotype of this daughter would allow us to deduce all three genotypes in that family?

● If the daughter has attached earlobes, then she must be *ff* and her two parents must both be *Ff*.

First generation (grandparents) □ *Ff* ○ *Ff* ■ *ff* ○ *Ff*

Second generation (parents, aunts, and uncles) ○ *FF or Ff* ■ *ff* ■ *ff* □ *Ff* ○ *Ff* ● *ff*

Third generation (two sisters) ● *ff* ○ *FF or Ff*

Female Male
● □ Attached
○ □ Free

▲ **Figure 9.7B** A pedigree showing the inheritance of attached versus free earlobes in a hypothetical family

9.8 Many inherited disorders in humans are controlled by a single gene

The genetic disorders listed in Table 9.8 are known to be inherited as dominant or recessive traits controlled by a single gene locus. These human disorders therefore show simple inheritance patterns like the traits Mendel studied in pea plants. The genes discussed in this module are all located on autosomes, chromosomes other than the sex chromosomes X and Y (see Module 8.12).

Recessive Disorders   Most human genetic disorders are recessive. They range in severity from relatively mild, such as albinism (lack of pigmentation), to invariably fatal, such as Tay-Sachs disease. Most people who have recessive disorders are born to normal parents who are both heterozygotes—that is, who are **carriers** of the recessive allele for the disorder but are phenotypically normal.

Using Mendel's laws, we can predict the fraction of affected offspring likely to result from a mating between two carriers. Consider a form of inherited deafness caused by a recessive allele **(Figure 9.8A)**. Suppose two heterozygous carriers (*Dd*) had a child. What is the probability that this child would be deaf? As the Punnett square in Figure 9.8A shows, each child of two carriers has a $\frac{1}{4}$ chance of inheriting two recessive alleles.

▲ **Figure 9.8A** Offspring produced by parents who are both carriers for a recessive disorder, a type of deafness

To put it another way, we can say that about one-fourth of the children from such a mating are likely to be deaf. We can also say that a hearing ("normal") child from such a marriage has a $\frac{2}{3}$ chance of being a *Dd* carrier; that is, two out of three of the

TABLE 9.8 | SOME AUTOSOMAL DISORDERS IN HUMANS

Disorder	Major Symptoms	Incidence		Comments
Recessive Disorders				
Albinism	Lack of pigment in the skin, hair, and eyes	$\frac{1}{22\,000}$		Prone to skin cancer
Cystic fibrosis	Excess mucus in the lungs, digestive tract, and liver; increased susceptibility to infections; death in early childhood unless treated	$\frac{1}{3600}$	Canadian children	See Module 9.8
Galactosemia	Accumulation of galactose in tissues; mental retardation; eye and liver damage	$\frac{1}{100\,000}$		Treated by eliminating galactose from diet
Phenylketonuria (PKU)	Accumulation of phenylalanine in blood; lack of normal skin pigment; intellectual deficiencies	$\frac{1}{12\,000}$	Canadians	See Modules 9.9, 14.4
Sickle-cell disease	Sickled red blood cells; damage to many tissues	$\frac{1}{400}$	African-Canadians	See Module 9.12
Tay-Sachs disease	Lipid accumulation in brain cells; mental deficiency; blindness; death in childhood	$\frac{1}{3600}$	Jews from central Europe and French Canadians	See Module 4.10
Dominant Disorders				
Achondroplasia	Dwarfism	$\frac{1}{25\,000}$		See Module 9.8
Alzheimer's disease (one type)	Mental deterioration; usually strikes late in life	Not known		Familial (inherited) Alzheimer's is a rare form of the disease
Huntington's disease	Mental deterioration and uncontrollable movements; strikes in middle age	$\frac{1}{25\,000}$		See Module 9.8
Hypercholesterolemia	Excess cholesterol in the blood; heart disease	$\frac{1}{500}$	are heterozygous	See Module 9.10

offspring with the hearing phenotype will be carriers. We can apply this same method of pedigree analysis and prediction to any genetic trait controlled by a single gene locus.

The most common life-threatening genetic disease in Canada is **cystic fibrosis (CF)**. Affecting about 4000 Canadians and 70 000 people worldwide, the recessive CF allele is carried by about 1 in 25 Canadians. A person with two copies of this allele has cystic fibrosis, which is characterized by an excessive secretion of very thick mucus from the lungs, pancreas, and other organs. This mucus can interfere with breathing, digestion, and liver function and makes the person vulnerable to recurrent bacterial infections. Although there is no cure for this disease, strict adherence to a daily health regimen—including gentle pounding on the chest and back to clear the airway, inhaled antibiotics, and a special diet—can have a profound impact on the health of the affected person. CF was once invariably fatal in childhood, but tremendous advances in treatment allow over half of Canadians with CF to live well into their forties and older.

Most genetic disorders are not evenly distributed across all ethnic groups. CF, for example, is most common in Caucasians. Such uneven distribution is the result of prolonged geographic isolation of certain populations. For example, the isolated lives of inhabitants of Saguenay–Lac-Saint-Jean, Quebec, a geographically remote inlet of the St. Lawrence Seaway, led to frequent **inbreeding** (matings between close relatives). Within this population, the frequency of the CF gene is much higher than among Canadians. One in 15 people are carriers for the CF allele. The incidence of CF in this location is approximately 2.5 times higher than in the general Canadian population, with 1 in 900 having the disease.

With the increased mobility in most societies today, it is relatively unlikely that two carriers of a rare, harmful allele will meet and mate. However, the probability increases greatly if close blood relatives have children. People with recent common ancestors are more likely to carry the same recessive alleles than are unrelated people. Inbreeding is therefore likely to produce offspring homozygous for recessive traits. Geneticists have observed increased incidence of harmful recessive traits among many types of inbred animals. For example, purebred Labrador retrievers are known to have high incidences of certain genetic defects, such as weak hip, knee, and elbow joints, in addition to eye problems. The detrimental effects of inbreeding are also seen in some endangered species (see Module 14.3).

Dominant Disorders

Although many harmful alleles are recessive, a number of human disorders are caused by dominant alleles. Some are harmless conditions, such as extra fingers and toes (called polydactyly) or webbed fingers and toes.

A more serious dominant disorder is **achondroplasia**, a form of dwarfism in which the head and torso of the body

▲ **Figure 9.8B** Dr. Michael C. Ain, a specialist in the repair of bone defects caused by achondroplasia and related disorders

develop normally, but the arms and legs are short **(Figure 9.8B)**. About 1 out of every 25 000 people have achondroplasia. The homozygous dominant genotype (AA) causes death of the embryo, and therefore only heterozygotes (Aa), individuals with a single copy of the defective allele, have this disorder. (This also means that a person with achondroplasia has a 50% chance of passing on the condition to any children.) Therefore, all those who do not have achondroplasia, more than 99.99% of the population, are homozygous for the recessive allele (aa). This example makes it clear that a dominant allele is not necessarily more common in a population than a corresponding recessive allele.

Dominant alleles that cause lethal diseases are much less common than lethal recessives. One reason for this difference is that the dominant lethal allele cannot be carried by heterozygotes without affecting them. Many lethal dominant alleles result from mutations in a sperm or egg that subsequently kill the embryo. And if the afflicted individual is born but does not survive long enough to reproduce, he or she will not pass on the lethal allele to future generations. This is in contrast to lethal recessive mutations, which are perpetuated from generation to generation by healthy heterozygous carriers.

A lethal dominant allele can escape elimination, however, if it does not cause death until a relatively advanced age. One such example is the allele that causes **Huntington's disease**, a degenerative disorder of the nervous system that usually does not appear until middle age. Once the deterioration of the nervous system begins, it is irreversible and inevitably fatal. Because the allele for Huntington's disease is dominant, any child born to a parent with the allele has a 50% chance of inheriting the allele and the disorder. This example makes it clear that a dominant allele is not necessarily "better" than a corresponding recessive allele.

Until relatively recently, the onset of symptoms was the only way to know if a person had inherited the Huntington's allele. This is no longer the case. By analyzing DNA samples from a large family with a high incidence of the disorder, geneticists tracked the Huntington's allele to a locus near the tip of chromosome 4, and the gene has been sequenced. This information led to development of a test that can detect the presence of the Huntington's allele in an individual's genome. This is one of several genetic tests currently available. We'll explore the topic of personal genetic screening in the next module.

 Peter is a 30-year-old man whose father died of Huntington's disease. Neither Peter's mother nor a much older sister show any signs of Huntington's. What is the probability that Peter has inherited Huntington's disease?

● Since his father had the disease, there is a $\frac{1}{2}$ chance that Peter received the gene. (The genotype of his sister is irrelevant.)

9.9 New technologies can provide insight into one's genetic legacy

Some prospective parents are aware that they have an increased risk of having a baby with a genetic disease. For example, many pregnant women older than age 35 know that they have a heightened risk of bearing children with Down syndrome (see Module 8.20), and some couples are aware that certain genetic diseases run in their families. These potential parents may want to learn more about their own and their baby's genetic makeup. Modern technologies offer ways to obtain such information before conception, during pregnancy, and after birth.

Genetic Testing   Because most children with recessive disorders are born to healthy parents, the genetic risk for many diseases is determined by whether the prospective parents are carriers of the recessive allele. For an increasing number of genetic disorders, including Tay-Sachs disease, sickle-cell disease, and one form of cystic fibrosis, tests are

available that can distinguish between individuals who have no disease-causing alleles and those who are heterozygous carriers. Other parents may know that a dominant but late-appearing disease, such as Huntington's disease, runs in their family. Such people may benefit from genetic tests for dominant alleles. Information from genetic testing (also called genetic screening) can inform decisions about whether to have a child.

Fetal Testing   Several technologies are available for detecting genetic conditions in a fetus. Genetic testing before birth requires the collection of fetal cells. In **amniocentesis**, performed between weeks 14 and 20 of pregnancy, a physician carefully inserts a needle through the abdomen and into the mother's uterus while watching an ultrasound imager to help to avoid the fetus (**Figure 9.9A**, left). The physician extracts about 10 millilitres of the amniotic fluid that bathes

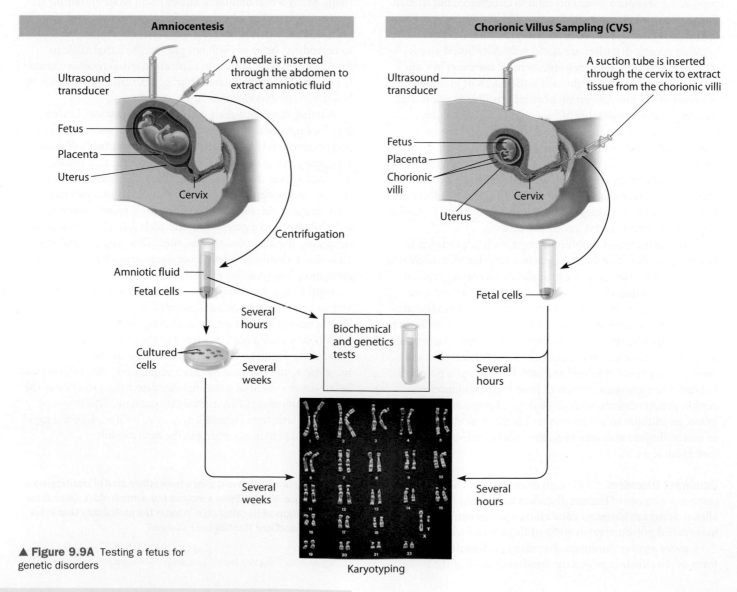

▲ **Figure 9.9A** Testing a fetus for genetic disorders

the developing fetus. Tests for genetic disorders can be performed on fetal cells (mostly from shed skin) that have been isolated from the fluid. Before testing, these cells are usually cultured in the laboratory for several weeks. By then, enough dividing cells can be harvested to allow karyotyping (see Module 8.19) and the detection of chromosomal abnormalities such as Down syndrome. Biochemical tests can also be performed on the cultured cells, revealing conditions such as Tay-Sachs disease.

In another procedure, **chorionic villus sampling (CVS)**, a physician extracts a tiny sample of chorionic villus tissue from the placenta, the organ that carries nourishment and wastes between the fetus and the mother. The tissue can be obtained using a narrow, flexible tube inserted through the mother's vagina and cervix into the uterus (Figure 9.9A, right). Results of karyotyping and some biochemical tests can be available within 24 hours. The speed of CVS is an advantage over amniocentesis. Another advantage is that CVS can be performed as early as the eighth week of pregnancy.

Unfortunately, both amniocentesis and CVS pose some risk of complications, such as maternal bleeding, miscarriage, or premature birth. Complication rates for amniocentesis and CVS are about 1% and 2%, respectively. Because of the risks, these procedures are usually reserved for situations in which the possibility of a genetic disease is significantly higher than average. Newer genetic screening procedures involve isolating tiny amounts of fetal cells or DNA released into the mother's bloodstream. Although few reliable tests are yet available using this method, this promising and complication-free technology may soon replace more invasive procedures.

Blood tests on the mother at 15 to 20 weeks of pregnancy can help to identify fetuses at risk for certain birth defects—and thus candidates for further testing that may require more invasive procedures (such as amniocentesis). The most widely used blood test measures the mother's blood level of alpha-fetoprotein (AFP), a protein produced by the fetus. High levels of AFP may indicate a neural tube defect in the fetus. (The neural tube is an embryonic structure that develops into the brain and spinal cord.) Low levels of AFP may indicate Down syndrome. For a more complete risk profile, a woman's doctor may order a "triple screen test," which measures AFP as well as two other hormones produced by the placenta. Abnormal levels of these substances in the maternal blood may also point to a risk of Down syndrome.

Fetal Imaging
Other techniques enable a physician to examine a fetus directly for anatomical deformities. The most common procedure is **ultrasound imaging**, which uses sound waves to produce a picture of the fetus. **Figure 9.9B** shows an ultrasound scanner, which emits high-frequency sounds, beyond the range of hearing. When the sound waves bounce off the fetus, the echoes produce an image on the monitor. The inset image in Figure 9.9B shows a fetus at about 20 weeks. Ultrasound imaging is noninvasive—no foreign objects are inserted into the mother's body—and has no known risk. In another imaging method, fetoscopy, a needle-thin tube containing a fibre optic viewing scope is

▲ **Figure 9.9B** Ultrasound scanning of a fetus

inserted into the uterus. Fetoscopy can provide highly detailed images of the fetus but, unlike ultrasound, carries risk of complications.

Newborn Screening Some genetic disorders, including CF and sickle-cell disease (see Module 9.12), can be detected at birth by simple tests that are now routinely performed in health centres throughout Canada from blood samples collected after birth. Another common screening program is for phenylketonuria (PKU), a recessively inherited disorder that occurs in about 1 out of every 12 000 births in Canada. Children with this disease cannot properly break down the naturally occurring amino acid phenylalanine, and an accumulation of phenylalanine may lead to intellectual disabilities. However, if the deficiency is detected in the newborn, a special diet low in phenylalanine can usually prevent these disabilities. Unfortunately, few other genetic disorders are currently treatable.

Ethical Considerations As new technologies such as fetal imaging and testing become more widespread, geneticists are working to make sure that they do not cause more problems than they solve. Consider the tests for identifying carriers of recessive diseases. Such information may enable people with family histories of genetic disorders to make informed decisions about having children. But these new methods for genetic screening pose problems, too. If confidentiality is breached, will carriers be stigmatized? For example, will misinformed employers equate "carrier" with disease? The Canadian Coalition for Genetic Fairness is dedicated to protecting all Canadians from genetic discrimination. Geneticists stress that patients seeking genetic testing should receive counselling both before and after the test to clarify their family history, to have their test explained to them, and to help them cope with the results. But with a wealth of genetic information becoming available, a full discussion of the meaning of the results might be time-consuming and costly, raising the question of who should pay for it.

Couples at risk for conceiving children with genetic disorders may now learn a great deal about their unborn children. In particular, CVS gives parents a chance to become informed very early in pregnancy. What is to be done with such information? If fetal tests reveal a serious disorder, the parents must choose between terminating the pregnancy and preparing themselves for a baby with severe problems. Identifying a genetic disease early can give families time to prepare—emotionally, medically, and financially.

Advances in biotechnology offer possibilities for reducing human suffering, For example, the Canadian Gene Cure Foundation funds world-renowned Canadian scientists who are researching cures for a variety of genetic diseases. However, we cannot conduct genetic research without also considering key ethical issues. The dilemmas posed by human genetics reinforce one of this book's central themes: the immense social implications of biology.

 What is the primary benefit of genetic screening by CVS? What is the primary risk?

● CVS allows genetic screening to be performed very early in pregnancy and provides quick results, but it carries a risk of miscarriage.

Variations on Mendel's Laws

9.10 Dominance is not always complete

Mendel's laws explain inheritance in terms of discrete factors—genes—that are passed along from generation to generation according to simple rules of probability. Mendel's laws are valid for all sexually reproducing organisms, including garden peas, Labradors, and human beings. But just as the basic rules of musical harmony cannot account for all the rich sounds of a symphony, Mendel's laws stop short of explaining some patterns of genetic inheritance. In fact, for most sexually reproducing organisms, cases where Mendel's laws can strictly account for the patterns of inheritance are relatively rare. More often, the inheritance patterns are more complex, as we will see in this and the next four modules.

The F_1 offspring of Mendel's pea crosses always looked like one of the two parental varieties. In this situation—called **complete dominance**—the dominant allele has the same phenotypic effect whether present in one or two copies. But for some characters, the appearance of F_1 hybrids falls between the phenotypes of the two parental varieties, an effect called **incomplete dominance**. For instance, as **Figure 9.10A** illustrates, when red snapdragons are crossed with white snapdragons, all the F_1 hybrids have pink flowers. This third phenotype results from flowers of the heterozygote having less red pigment than the red homozygotes.

Incomplete dominance does *not* support the blending hypothesis described in Module 9.2, which would predict that the red and white traits could never be retrieved from the pink hybrids. As the Punnett square at the bottom of Figure 9.10A shows, the F_2 offspring appear in a phenotypic ratio of one red to two pink to one white, because the red and white alleles segregate during gamete formation in the pink F_1 hybrids. In incomplete dominance, the phenotypes of heterozygotes differ from the two homozygous varieties, and the genotypic ratio and the phenotypic ratio are both 1:2:1 in the F_2 generation.

We also see examples of incomplete dominance in humans. One case involves a recessive allele (h) that can cause hypercholesterolemia, dangerously high levels of cholesterol in the blood (see Module 3.16). Normal individuals are HH. Heterozygotes (Hh; about 1 in 500 people) have blood cholesterol levels about twice normal. They are unusually prone to atherosclerosis, the blockage of arteries by cholesterol buildup in artery walls, and they may have heart attacks from blocked heart arteries by their mid-thirties. This form of the disease can often be controlled through changes in diet and by taking statins, a class of medications that can significantly lower blood cholesterol. Hypercholesterolemia is even more serious in homozygous individuals (hh; about one in a million people). Homozygotes have about five times the normal amount of blood cholesterol and may have heart attacks as

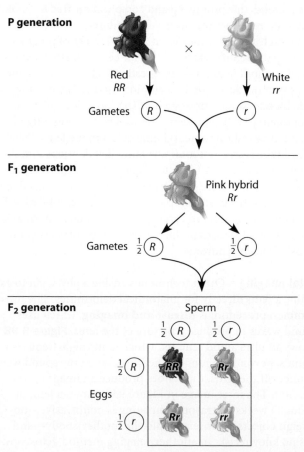

▲ **Figure 9.10A** Incomplete dominance in snapdragon flower colour

Genotypes

HH	*Hh*	*hh*
Homozygous for ability to make LDL receptors	Heterozygous	Homozygous for inability to make LDL receptors

Phenotypes

LDL
LDL receptor
Cell

Normal | Mild disease | Severe disease

▲ **Figure 9.10B** Incomplete dominance in human hypercholesterolemia

early as age 2. Homozygous hypercholesterolemia is harder to treat; options include high doses of statin drugs, organ surgeries or transplants, or physically filtering lipids from the blood.

Figure 9.10B illustrates the molecular basis for hypercholesterolemia. The dominant allele (*H*), which normal individuals carry in duplicate (*HH*), specifies a cell-surface receptor protein called an LDL receptor. Low-density lipoprotein (LDL, sometimes called "bad cholesterol") is transported in the blood. In certain cells, the LDL receptors mop up excess LDL particles from the blood and promote their breakdown. This process helps to prevent the accumulation of cholesterol in arteries. Without the receptors, lethal levels of LDL build up in the blood. Heterozygotes (*Hh*) have only half the normal number of LDL receptors, and homozygous recessives (*hh*) have none.

 Why is a testcross unnecessary to determine whether a snapdragon with red flowers is homozygous or heterozygous?

● Because the homozygotes and heterozygotes differ in phenotype: red flowers for the dominant homozygote and pink flowers for the heterozygote

9.11 Many genes have more than two alleles in the population

So far, we have discussed inheritance patterns involving only two alleles per gene (*H* versus *h*, for example). But most genes can be found in populations in more than two versions, known as multiple alleles. Although a normal individual carries, at most, two different alleles for a particular gene, in cases of multiple alleles, more than two possible alleles exist in the population.

For instance, the **ABO blood group** phenotype in humans involves three alleles of a single gene. Various combinations of three alleles for the ABO blood type produce four phenotypes: A person's blood type may be A, B, AB, or O **(Figure 9.11)**. These letters refer to two carbohydrates, designated A and B, that may be found on the surface of red blood cells. A person's red blood cells may be coated with carbohydrate A (in which case they are said to have type A blood), carbohydrate B (type B), both carbohydrates (type AB), or neither carbohydrate (type O). (In case you are wondering, the *positive* and *negative* notations on blood types—referred to as the Rh blood group system—are due to inheritance of a separate, unrelated gene.) Matching compatible blood types is critical for safe blood transfusions (see Module 28.4).

The four blood groups result from various combinations of the three different alleles: *I^A* (for an enzyme referred to as *I*, which adds carbohydrate A to red blood cells), *I^B* (for B), and *i* (for neither A nor B). Each person inherits one of these alleles from each parent. Because there are three alleles, there are six possible genotypes, as listed in the figure. Both the *I^A* and *I^B* alleles are dominant to the *i* allele. Thus, *I^A I^A* and *I^A i* people have type A blood, and *I^B I^B* and *I^B i* people have type B. Recessive homozygotes, *ii*, have type O blood, with neither carbohydrate. The *I^A* and *I^B* alleles are **codominant**: Both alleles are expressed in heterozygous individuals (*I^A I^B*), who have type

Blood Group (Phenotype)	Genotypes	Carbohydrates Present on Red Blood Cells
A	*I^A I^A* or *I^A i*	Carbohydrate A
B	*I^B I^B* or *I^B i*	Carbohydrate B
AB	*I^A I^B*	Carbohydrate A and Carbohydrate B
O	*ii*	Neither

▲ **Figure 9.11** Multiple alleles for the ABO blood groups

AB blood. In codominance, neither allele masks the presence of the other. Note that codominance (the expression of both alleles) is different from incomplete dominance (the expression of one intermediate trait).

 Maria has type O blood, and her sister has type AB blood. The girls know that both of their maternal grandparents are type A. What are the genotypes of the girls' parents?

● Their mother is *I^A i*; their father is *I^B i*.

9.12 A single gene may affect many phenotypic characters

All of our genetic examples to this point have been cases in which each gene specifies only one hereditary character. In most cases, however, one gene influences multiple characters, a property called **pleiotropy**.

An example of pleiotropy in humans is **sickle-cell disease** (sometimes called sickle-cell anemia). The direct effect of the sickle-cell allele is to make red blood cells produce abnormal hemoglobin proteins. These molecules tend to link together and crystallize, especially when the oxygen content of the blood is lower than usual because of high altitude, overexertion, or respiratory ailments. As the hemoglobin crystallizes, the normally disc-shaped red blood cells deform to a sickle shape with jagged edges **(Figure 9.12A)**. Sickled cells are destroyed rapidly by the body, and their destruction may seriously lower the individual's red cell count, causing anemia and general weakening of the body. Also, because of their angular shape, sickled cells do not flow smoothly in the blood and tend to accumulate and clog tiny blood vessels. Blood flow to body parts is reduced, resulting in periodic fever, severe pain, and damage to various organs, including the heart, brain, and kidneys. Sickled cells also accumulate in the spleen, damaging it. The overall result is a disorder characterized by the cascade of symptoms shown in **Figure 9.12B**. Blood transfusions and certain drugs may relieve some of the symptoms, but there is no cure, and sickle-cell disease kills about 100 000 people in the world each year.

In most cases, only people who are homozygous for the sickle-cell allele suffer from the disease. Heterozygotes, who have one sickle-cell allele and one nonsickle allele, are usually healthy, although in rare cases they may experience some effects when oxygen in the blood is severely reduced, such as at very high altitudes. These effects may occur because the nonsickle and sickle-cell alleles are codominant at the molecular level: Both alleles are expressed in heterozygous individuals, and their red blood cells contain both normal and abnormal hemoglobin.

? How does sickle-cell disease exemplify the concept of pleiotropy?

● Homozygosity for the sickle-cell allele causes abnormal hemoglobin, and the impact of the abnormal hemoglobin on the shape of red blood cells leads to a cascade of symptoms in multiple organs of the body.

An individual homozygous for the sickle-cell allele

↓

Produces sickle-cell (abnormal) hemoglobin

↓

The abnormal hemoglobin crystallizes, causing red blood cells to become sickle-shaped

Sickled cell

SEM 1045×

The multiple effects of sickled cells

Damage to organs	Other effects
Kidney failure	Pain and fever
Heart failure	Joint problems
Spleen damage	Physical weakness
Brain damage (impaired mental function, paralysis)	Anemia
	Pneumonia and other infections

▲ **Figure 9.12B** Sickle-cell disease, an example of pleitropy

SEM 1045×

▲ **Figure 9.12A** In this micrograph, you can see several jagged sickled cells in the midst of normal red blood cells

9.13 A single character may be influenced by many genes

Mendel studied genetic characters that could be classified on an either-or basis, such as purple or white flower colour. However, many characteristics, such as human skin colour and height, vary in a population along a continuum. Many such features result from **polygenic inheritance**, the additive effects of two or more genes on a single phenotypic character.

(This is the converse of pleiotropy, in which a single gene affects several characters.)

Let's consider a hypothetical example. Assume that the continuous variation in human skin colour is controlled by three genes that are inherited separately, like Mendel's pea genes. (Actually, genetic evidence indicates that *at least* three genes control this character.) The "dark-skin" allele for each gene (*A*, *B*, or *C*) contributes one "unit" of darkness to the phenotype and is incompletely dominant to the other allele (*a*, *b*, or *c*). A person who is *AABBCC* would have very dark skin, whereas an *aabbcc* individual would have very light skin. An *AaBbCc* person (resulting, for example, from a mating between an *AABBCC* person and an *aabbcc* person) would have skin of an intermediate shade. Because the alleles have an additive effect, the genotype *AaBbCc* would produce the same skin colour as any other genotype with just three dark-skin alleles, such as *AABbcc,* since both of these individuals have three "units" of darkness.

The Punnett square in **Figure 9.13** shows all possible genotypes of offspring from a mating of two triple heterozygotes (trihybrids), the F₁ generation here. The row of squares below the Punnett square shows the seven skin pigmentation phenotypes that would theoretically result from this mating. The seven bars in the graph at the bottom of the figure depict the relative numbers of each of the phenotypes in the F₂ generation. This hypothetical example shows how inheritance of three genes could lead to a wide variety of pigmentation phenotypes. In real human populations, skin colour has even more variations than shown in the figure, in part for reasons we discuss in the next two modules.

Up to this point in the chapter, we have presented four types of inheritance patterns that are extensions of Mendel's laws of inheritance: incomplete dominance, codominance, pleiotropy, and polygenic inheritance. It is important to realize that these patterns are extensions of Mendel's model, rather than exceptions to it. From Mendel's garden pea experiments came data supporting a particulate theory of inheritance, with the particles (genes) being transmitted according to the same rules of chance that govern the tossing of coins. The particulate theory holds true for all inheritance patterns, even the patterns that are more complex than the ones originally considered by Mendel. In the next module, we consider another important source of deviation from Mendel's standard model: the effect of the environment.

? Based on the model for skin colour in Figure 9.13, an *AaBbcc* individual would be indistinguishable in phenotype from which of the following individuals: *AAbbcc, aaBBcc, AabbCc, Aabbcc,* or *aaBbCc*?

● All except *Aabbcc*

▲ **Figure 9.13** A model for polygenic inheritance of skin colour

9.14 Human pigmentation has repeatedly changed as our ancestors migrated

In the previous module, we discussed how human skin pigmentation was under the control of at least three separate genes. The degree of pigmentation in your skin can be attributed to the number of dark-skin alleles. These alleles actually code for proteins that synthesize **melanin**, a dark pigment. In specialized skin cells called **melanocytes**, having more dark-skin alleles increases melanin production and leads to darker skin tones. For example, people of African descent tend to produce more melanin than those with Scandinavian ancestors. **Figure 9.14** is a map that shows the distribution of pigmentation in indigenous human populations. Have you ever thought about why there is so much variation in human skin colour and why the variations adhere to a geographic pattern? Interestingly, the evolution of human skin pigmentation follows our early ancestors' migration out of Africa; as they experienced different selective pressures, the evolution of pigmentation was driven in different directions (see Module 21.17). More melanin was favourable in certain areas under some circumstances but unfavourable in others. Let's explore how human pigmentation evolved along our ancestors' epic journey.

Our Earliest Ancestors Humans and chimpanzees evolved from a common ancestor (see Module 15.15). Many biologists agree that this common ancestor and its earliest descendants all had light skin covered with dark hair. Living in a forest

habitat, skin pigmentation was neither an advantage nor a disadvantage for these individuals. Today's light-skinned and dark-haired chimpanzees have lived and evolved in a similar environment to their ancestors. Therefore, it is reasonable to predict that the common ancestor and early humans also shared these characteristics.

As humans and chimpanzees diverged, the body hair of humans became considerably less dense in parallel with a major event in human evolution: brain enlargement (see Module 21.14). Why would our ancestors lose their body hair as their brains became larger? Brain activity generates copious amounts of heat, which increases with brain size. Humans needed a way to maintain a constant body temperature by either eliminating or dissipating the excess heat from their bodies. New adaptations, including less hair and more sweat glands, helped the larger brained humans rid themselves of the excess heat.

A new problem arose when early light-skinned humans left the cover of the forests. Without their hairy coats, they became exposed to increased levels of damaging ultraviolet (UV) radiation from the sun.

Effects of UV Radiation Darker skin evolved some time after ancient humans became hairless. It is a widely held belief that exposure to UV radiation was the selective pressure

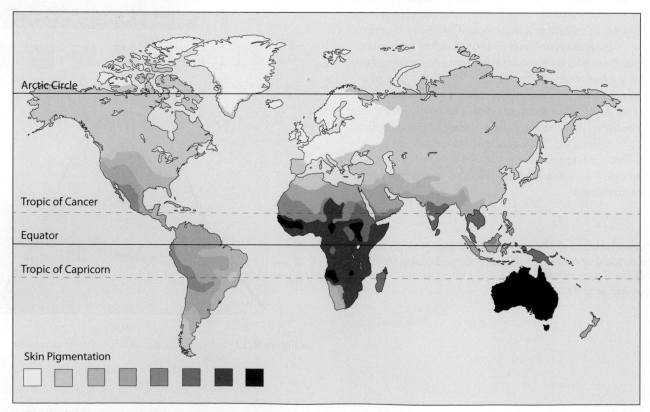

Arctic Circle

Tropic of Cancer

Equator

Tropic of Capricorn

Skin Pigmentation

▲ **Figure 9.14** Map of indigenous human skin pigmentation

leading to this change; originally, scientists thought that skin cancer caused this selection. It is a well-known fact that exposure to high levels of UV radiation damages DNA, causing skin cancer (see Module 10.17). Melanin in the skin reduces the penetration of UV radiation and therefore its damaging effects. But was darker skin an adaptation that reduced the incidence of this disease?

Today, nonmelanoma skin cancer accounts for 94% of all cancer cases and has a very low mortality rate. In 2012, Canada had 81 300 new cases but only 320 deaths. Melanomas have a higher mortality rate than nonmelanoma skin cancers, but the incidence of melanomas is considerably lower. Early hairless humans likely had similar rates of these skin cancers; it is unlikely that nonmelanoma skin cancer exerted significant selective pressure on ancient humans. Because of the low death rate, individuals with these cancers could still reproduce and pass on their genes to the next generation. Therefore, some other factor must have driven the evolution of darker skin pigmentation.

In human skin, UV radiation does more than damage DNA; it can also destroy other compounds, including folic acid or folate (vitamin B_9). Folate is an essential nutrient involved in, among other things, the synthesis of nucleic acids. The need for folate is higher in actively dividing cells, such as those of a developing fetus, which have high rates of DNA synthesis. Deficiencies during pregnancy can affect the fetus and may lead to anemia, birth defects, or miscarriage.

As it penetrates the skin, UV radiation destroys folate, which can lead to folate deficiencies. However, melanin can reduce the destruction of folate in the skin. Therefore, under the intense African sun, darker skin was advantageous and evolved to protect humans and their fetuses from folate deficiencies.

Pigmentation Changes   If darker skin protects humans against folate deficiencies, why did light skin re-emerge as humans migrated toward Europe? Excess UV radiation has damaging effects. But low-dose UV radiation is actually beneficial and facilitates the synthesis of vitamin D_3. Vitamin D_3 is important for the absorption and use of calcium and

phosphorous and is particularly important for bone growth and maintenance. Deficiencies can lead to bone deformities in children as well as bone softening in adults. Fish is a valuable source of dietary vitamin D_3, whereas diets consisting of meat and eggs seldom contain enough vitamin D_3.

To compensate for insufficient dietary sources, vitamin D_3 can be synthesized in the skin in a photochemical reaction. The energy required for this chemical process comes from UV radiation. As such, lighter skinned individuals can synthesize more vitamin D_3 than those with more melanin. For example, a light-skinned Canadian can produce 10 000 international units (IU) of vitamin D_3 in just 20 minutes of sunbathing in summer. In contrast, it would take a dark-skinned Canadian 90 to 120 minutes to produce the same quantity. In autumn, however, sunlight intensity is too low for any Canadian to produce adequate amounts of vitamin D_3. Thus, for most of the year Canadians must rely on dietary sources for this vitamin.

As humans migrated toward higher latitudes, the intensity of sunlight and exposure to UV radiation decreased. Sunlight intensity was greatest in the tropics, where most people could synthesize the amounts of vitamin D_3 they required year-round. At latitudes just above the tropics, darker-skinned individuals could not synthesize vitamin D_3 because their melanin absorbed the vast majority of the UV radiation. As humans migrated into Scandinavia, only those with little melanin could synthesize enough vitamin D_3. Because diets proved to be inadequate sources of vitamin D_3, a new selective pressure became apparent—one that favoured lighter skin. Thus, as some ancient humans made the journey into Asia, Europe, and North America, skin tones became lighter as they moved farther from the tropics.

 What is the likely reason that more pigmentation has re-emerged in the indigenous peoples of South America? South America was the last continent to which humans migrated via North America.

● Darker skin pigmentation evolved in these peoples because it protected individuals from folate deficiencies.

9.15 The environment affects many characters

In Module 9.13, we saw how a set of three hypothetical human skin-colour genes could produce seven different phenotypes for skin colour. If we examine a real human population for skin colour, we might see more shades than just seven. The true range might be similar to the entire spectrum of colour under the bell-shaped curve in Figure 9.13. In fact, no matter how carefully we characterize the genes for skin colour, a purely genetic description will always be incomplete. This is because some intermediate shades of skin colour result from the effects of environmental factors, such as exposure to the sun **(Figure 9.15)**.

Many characters result from a combination of heredity and environment. For example, the leaves of a tree all have the same genotype, but they may vary greatly in phenotype such as size, shape, and colour, depending on exposure to wind and sun and the tree's nutritional state. For humans, nutrition influences height; exercise alters build; suntanning darkens the skin; and experience improves performance on intelligence tests. As geneticists learn more and more about our genes, it is becoming clear that many human phenotypes—such as risk of heart disease and cancer and susceptibility to alcoholism and schizophrenia—are influenced by both genes and environment.

▲ **Figure 9.15** The effect of genes and sun exposure on the skin of one of this book's authors and his family

Whether human characters are more influenced by genes or the environment—nature or nurture—is a very old and hotly contested debate. For some characters, such as the ABO blood group, a given genotype absolutely mandates a very specific phenotype, and the environment plays no role whatsoever. In contrast, a person's counts of red and white blood cells (the numbers of blood cells per millilitre of blood) are influenced greatly by environmental factors such as the altitude, the customary level of physical activity, and the presence of infectious agents.

It is important to realize that the individual features of any organism arise from a combination of genetic and environmental factors. Simply spending time with identical twins will convince anyone that environment, and not just genes, affects a person's traits. However, there is an important difference between these two sources of variation: Only genetic influences are inherited. Any effects of the environment are generally not passed on to the next generation.

 If most characters result from a combination of environment and heredity, why was Mendel able to ignore environmental influences on his pea plants?

● The characters he chose for study were all entirely genetically determined.

The Chromosomal Basis of Inheritance

9.16 Chromosome behaviour accounts for Mendel's laws

Mendel published his results in 1866, but not until long after he died did biologists understand the significance of his work. Cell biologists worked out the processes of mitosis and meiosis in the late 1800s (see Chapter 8 to review these processes). Then, around 1900, researchers began to notice parallels between the behaviour of chromosomes and the behaviour of Mendel's heritable factors. Eventually, one of biology's most important concepts emerged. By combining these observations, the **chromosome theory of inheritance** states that genes occupy specific loci (positions) on chromosomes, and it is the chromosomes that undergo segregation and independent assortment during meiosis. Thus, it is the behaviour of chromosomes during meiosis and fertilization that accounts for inheritance patterns.

We can see the chromosomal basis of Mendel's laws by following the fates of two genes during meiosis and fertilization in pea plants. In **Figure 9.16**, we show the genes for seed shape (alleles R and r) and seed colour (Y and y) as black bars on different chromosomes. Notice that the Punnett square is repeated from Figure 9.4A; we will now follow the chromosomes to see how they account for the results of the dihybrid cross shown in the Punnett square. We start with the F_1 generation, in which all plants

have the $RrYy$ genotype. To simplify the diagram, we show only two of the seven pairs of pea chromosomes and three of the stages of meiosis: metaphase I, anaphase I, and metaphase II.

To see the chromosomal basis of the law of segregation (which states that pairs of alleles separate from each other during gamete formation via meiosis; see Module 9.2), let's follow just the homologous pair of long chromosomes, the ones carrying R and r, taking either the left or the right branch from the F_1 cell. Whichever arrangement the chromosomes assume at metaphase I, the two alleles segregate as the homologous chromosomes separate in anaphase I. And at the end of meiosis II, a single long chromosome ends up in each of the gametes. Fertilization then recombines the two alleles at random, resulting in F_2 offspring that are RR, Rr, and rr. The ratio of round to wrinkled phenotypes is thus 3:1 (12 round to 4 wrinkled), the ratio Mendel observed, as shown in the Punnett square in the figure.

To see the chromosomal basis of the law of independent assortment (which states that each pair of alleles sorts independently of other pairs of alleles during gamete formation; see Module 9.4), follow both the long and short (non-homologous) chromosomes through the figure below. Two

▲ **Figure 9.16** The chromosomal basis of Mendel's laws

alternative, equally likely arrangements of tetrads can occur at metaphase I. The nonhomologous chromosomes (and their genes) assort independently, leading to four gamete genotypes. Random fertilization leads to the 9:3:3:1 phenotypic ratio in the F₂ generation.

? **Which of Mendel's laws have their physical basis in the following phases of meiosis: (a) the orientation of homologous chromosome pairs in metaphase I; (b) the separation of homologues in anaphase I?**

(a) The law of independent assortment; (b) the law of segregation ●

9.17 Genes on the same chromosome tend to be inherited together

In 1908, British biologists William Bateson and Reginald Punnett (originator of the Punnett square) observed an inheritance pattern that seemed inconsistent with Mendelian laws. Bateson and Punnett were working with two characters in sweet peas: flower colour and pollen shape. They crossed doubly heterozygous plants (*PpLl*) that exhibited the dominant traits: purple flowers (expression of the *P* allele) and long pollen grains (expression of the *L* allele). The corresponding recessive traits are red flowers (in *pp* plants) and round pollen (in *ll* plants).

The top part of **Figure 9.17** illustrates Bateson and Punnett's experiment. When they looked at just one of the two characters (that is, either cross $Pp \times Pp$ or cross $Ll \times Ll$), they found that the dominant and recessive alleles segregated, producing a phenotypic ratio of approximately 3:1 for the offspring, in agreement with Mendel's law of segregation. However, when the biologists combined their data for the two characters, they did not see the predicted 9:3:3:1 ratio. Instead, as shown in the table, they found a disproportionately large number of plants with just two of the predicted phenotypes: purple long (almost 75% of the total) and red round (about 14%). The other two phenotypes (purple round and red long) were found in far fewer numbers than expected. What accounts for these results?

The number of genes in a cell is far greater than the number of chromosomes; in fact, each chromosome has hundreds or thousands of genes. Genes located close together on the same chromosome tend to be inherited together and are called **linked genes**. Linked genes generally do not follow Mendel's law of independent assortment.

As shown in the explanation section of the figure, sweet-pea genes for flower colour and pollen shape are located on the same chromosome. Thus, meiosis in the heterozygous ($PpLl$) sweet-pea plant yields mostly two genotypes of gametes (PL and pl) rather than equal numbers of the four types of gametes that would result if the flower-colour and pollen-shape genes were not linked. The large numbers of plants with purple long and red round traits in the Bateson-Punnett experiment resulted from fertilization among the PL and pl gametes. But what about the smaller numbers of plants with purple round and red long traits? As you will see in the next module, the phenomenon of crossing over accounts for these offspring.

 Why do linked genes tend to be inherited together?

ǝɯosoɯoɹɥɔ ǝɯɐs ǝɥʇ uo ɹǝɥʇǝƃoʇ ǝsolɔ pǝʇɐɔol ǝɹɐ ʎǝɥʇ ǝsnɐɔǝꓭ

The Experiment

Purple flower

$PpLl \times PpLl$ Long pollen

Phenotypes	Observed offspring	Prediction (9:3:3:1)
Purple long	284	215
Purple round	21	71
Red long	21	71
Red round	55	24

The Explanation: Linked Genes

3 purple long : 1 red round
Not accounted for: purple round and red long

▲ **Figure 9.17** The experiment revealing linked genes in the sweet pea

9.18 Crossing over produces new combinations of alleles

In Module 8.18, we saw that during meiosis, crossing over between homologous chromosomes produces new combinations of alleles in gametes. Using the experiment shown in Figure 9.17 as an example, **Figure 9.18A** reviews this process, showing that two linked genes can give rise to four different gamete genotypes. Gametes with genotypes PL and pl carry parental-type chromosomes that have not been altered by crossing over. In contrast, gametes with genotypes Pl and pL are recombinant gametes. The exchange of chromosome segments during crossing over has produced new combinations of alleles. We can now understand the results of the Bateson–Punnett experiment presented in

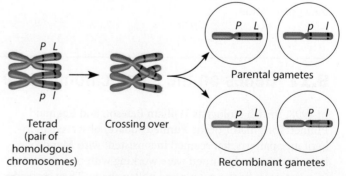

▲ **Figure 9.18A** Review: the production of recombinant gametes

the previous module: The small fraction of offspring with recombinant phenotypes (purple round and red long) must have resulted from fertilization involving recombinant gametes.

▲ **Figure 9.18B** *Drosophila melanogaster*

The discovery of how crossing over creates gamete diversity confirmed the relationship between chromosome behaviour and heredity. Some of the most important early studies of crossing over were performed in the laboratory of American embryologist Thomas Hunt Morgan in the early 1900s. Morgan and his colleagues used the fruit fly *Drosophila melanogaster* in many of their experiments **(Figure 9.18B)**. Often seen flying around ripe fruit, *Drosophila* is a good research animal for genetic studies because it can be easily and inexpensively bred, producing each new generation in a couple of weeks.

Figure 9.18C shows one of Morgan's experiments, a cross between a wild-type fruit fly (recall from Module 9.7 that "wild-type" refers to the traits most common in nature, in this case, grey body and long wings) and a fly with a black body and undeveloped, or vestigial, wings. Morgan knew the genotypes of these flies from previous studies. Here we use the following gene symbols:

G = grey body (dominant)

g = black body (recessive)

L = long wings (dominant)

l = vestigial wings (recessive)

In mating a heterozygous grey fly with long wings (genotype *GgLl*) with a black fly with vestigial wings (genotype *ggll*), Morgan performed a testcross (see Module 9.5). If the genes were not linked, then independent assortment would produce offspring in a phenotypic ratio of 1:1:1:1 ($\frac{1}{4}$ grey body, long wings; $\frac{1}{4}$ black body, vestigial wings; $\frac{1}{4}$ grey body, vestigial wings; and $\frac{1}{4}$ black body, long wings). But because these genes are linked, Morgan obtained the results shown in the top part of Figure 9.18C: Most of the offspring had parental phenotypes, but 17% of the offspring flies were recombinants. The percentage of recombinants is called the **recombination frequency**.

When Morgan first obtained these results, he did not know about crossing over. To explain the ratio of offspring, he hypothesized that the genes were linked and that some mechanism occasionally broke the linkage. Tests of the hypothesis proved him correct, establishing that crossing over was the mechanism that "breaks linkages" between genes.

The lower part of Figure 9.18C explains Morgan's results in terms of crossing over. A crossover between chromatids of homologous chromosomes in parent *GgLl* broke linkages between the *G* and *L* alleles and between the *g* and *l* alleles, forming the recombinant chromosomes *Gl* and *gL*. Later

The Experiment

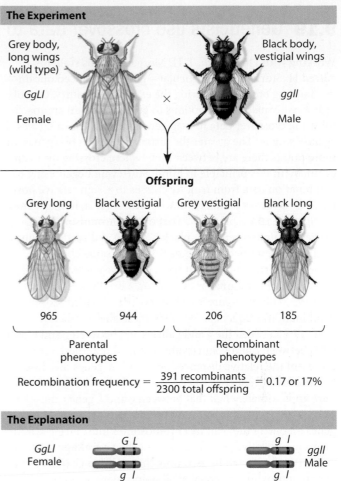

Recombination frequency $= \dfrac{391 \text{ recombinants}}{2300 \text{ total offspring}} = 0.17$ or 17%

The Explanation

▲ **Figure 9.18C** A fruit fly experiment demonstrating the role of crossing over in inheritance

steps in meiosis distributed the recombinant chromosomes to gametes, and random fertilization produced the four kinds of offspring Morgan observed.

? Return to the data in Figure 9.17. What is the recombination frequency between the flower-colour and pollen-length genes?

● 11% ($\frac{38}{42}$)

9.19 Geneticists use crossover data to map genes

Working with *Drosophila*, T. H. Morgan and his students—Alfred H. Sturtevant in particular—greatly advanced our understanding of genetics during the early 20th century. One of Sturtevant's major contributions to genetics was an approach for using crossover data to map gene loci. His reasoning was elegantly simple: The greater the distance between two genes, the more points there are between them where crossing over can occur. With this principle in mind, Sturtevant began using recombination data from fruit fly crosses to assign relative positions of the genes on the chromosomes—that is, to map genes.

Figure 9.19A represents a part of the chromosome that carries the linked genes for black body (*g*) and vestigial wings (*l*) that we described in Module 9.18. This same chromosome also carries a gene that has a recessive allele (we'll call it *c*) determining cinnabar eye colour, a brighter red than the wild-type colour. Figure 9.19A shows the actual crossover (recombination) frequencies between these alleles, taken two at a time: 17% between the *g* and *l* alleles, 9% between *g* and *c*, and 9.5% between *c* and *l*. Sturtevant reasoned that these values represent the relative distances between the genes. Because the crossover frequencies between *g* and *c* and between *l* and *c* are approximately half that between *g* and *l*, gene *c* must lie roughly midway between *g* and *l*. Thus, the sequence of these genes on one of the fruit fly chromosomes must be *g-c-l*. Such a diagram of relative gene locations is called a **linkage map**.

Sturtevant started by assuming that the chance of crossing over is approximately equal at all points along a chromosome. We now know that this assumption is only approximately true; some locations along the chromosome are more prone to crossing over than others. Still, his method of mapping genes

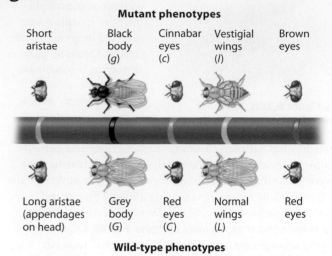

Mutant phenotypes

| Short aristae | Black body (*g*) | Cinnabar eyes (*c*) | Vestigial wings (*l*) | Brown eyes |

| Long aristae (appendages on head) | Grey body (*G*) | Red eyes (*C*) | Normal wings (*L*) | Red eyes |

Wild-type phenotypes

▲ **Figure 9.19B** A partial linkage map of a fruit fly chromosome

worked well, and it proved extremely valuable in establishing the relative positions of many other fruit fly genes. Eventually, enough data were accumulated to reveal that *Drosophila* has four groups of genes, corresponding to its four pairs of homologous chromosomes. **Figure 9.19B** is a genetic map showing just five of the gene loci on part of one chromosome: the loci labelled *g*, *c*, and *l* and two others. Notice that eye colour is a character affected by more than one gene. Here we see the cinnabar-eye and brown-eye genes; still other eye-colour genes are found elsewhere (see Module 9.22). For each of these genes, however, the wild-type allele specifies red eyes.

The linkage-mapping method has proved extremely valuable in establishing the relative positions of many genes in many organisms. The real beauty of the technique is that a wealth of information about genes can be learned simply by breeding and observing the organisms; no fancy equipment is required.

Section of chromosome carrying linked genes

g   *c*   *l*

←——— 17% ———→

←— 9% —→ ←— 9.5% —→

Recombination frequencies

▲ **Figure 9.19A** Mapping genes from crossover data

 ? You design *Drosophila* crosses to provide recombination data for a gene not included in Figure 9.19A. The gene has recombination frequencies of 3% with the vestigial-wing (*l*) locus and 7% with the cinnabar-eye (*c*) locus. Where is it located on the chromosome?

● The gene is located between the vestigial and cinnabar loci, a bit closer to the vestigial-wing locus (since it has a lower recombination frequency).

Sex Chromosomes and Sex-Linked Genes

9.20 Chromosomes determine sex in many species

Many animals, including fruit flies and all mammals, have a pair of **sex chromosomes**, designated X and Y, that determine an individual's sex. **Figure 9.20A** reviews what you learned in Chapter 8 about sex determination in humans. Individuals with one X chromosome and one Y chromosome are males;

XX individuals are females. Human males and females both have 44 autosomes (nonsex chromosomes). As a result of chromosome segregation during meiosis, each gamete contains one sex chromosome and a haploid set of autosomes (22 in humans). All eggs contain a single X chromosome. Of the

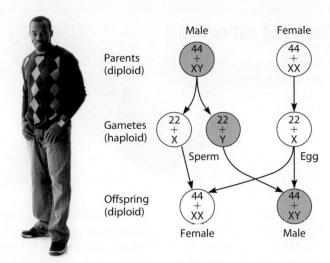

▲ **Figure 9.20A** The X-Y system

sperm cells, half contain an X chromosome and half contain a Y chromosome. An offspring's sex depends on whether the sperm cell that fertilizes the egg bears an X chromosome or a Y chromosome. In the fruit fly's X-Y system, sex is determined by the ratio between the number of X chromosomes and the number of autosome sets, although the Y chromosome is essential for sperm formation.

The genetic basis of sex determination in humans is not yet completely understood, but one gene on the Y chromosome plays a crucial role. This gene, discovered by a British research team in 1990, is called *SRY* (for sex-determining region of Y) and triggers testis development. In the absence of *SRY*, an individual develops ovaries rather than testes. *SRY* codes for proteins that regulate other genes on the Y chromosome. These genes in turn produce proteins necessary for normal testis development.

The X-Y system is only one of several sex-determining systems. For example, grasshoppers, roaches, and some other insects have an X-O system, in which *O* stands for the absence of a sex chromosome (**Figure 9.20B**). Females have two X chromosomes (XX); males have only one sex chromosome (XO). Males produce two classes of sperm (X-bearing and lacking any sex chromosome), and sperm cells determine the sex of the offspring at fertilization.

In contrast to the X-Y and X-O systems, eggs determine sex in certain fishes, butterflies, and birds (**Figure 9.20C**). The sex chromosomes in these animals are designated Z and W. Males have the genotype ZZ; females are ZW. In this system, sex is determined by whether the egg carries a Z or a W.

▲ **Figure 9.20C** The Z-W system

Some organisms lack sex chromosomes altogether. In most ants and bees, sex is determined by chromosome number rather than by sex chromosomes (**Figure 9.20D**). Females develop from fertilized eggs and thus are diploid. Males develop from unfertilized eggs—they are fatherless—and are haploid.

Most animals have two separate sexes; that is, individuals are either male or female. Many plant species have sperm-bearing and egg-bearing flowers borne on different individuals. Some plant species, such as date palms, have the X-Y system of sex determination; others, such as the wild strawberry, have the Z-W system. However, most plant species and some animal species have individuals that produce both sperm and eggs. In such species, all individuals have the same complement of chromosomes.

In Module 9.15, we discussed the role that environment plays in determining many characters. Among some animals, environment can even determine sex. For some species of reptiles, the temperature at which eggs are incubated during a specific period of embryonic development determines whether that embryo will develop into a male or female. For example, if green sea turtle hatchlings incubate above 30°C, nearly all the resulting turtles will be females. In contrast, eggs developing at cooler temperatures (22.5–27°C) will become males. (Some worry that global climate change might have the unexpected consequence of affecting the makeup of turtle populations.) Such temperature-dependent sex determination is an extreme example of the environment affecting the phenotype of an individual.

? **During fertilization in humans, what determines the sex of the offspring?**

● Whether the egg is fertilized by a sperm bearing an X chromosome (producing a female offspring) or a sperm with a Y chromosome (producing a male)

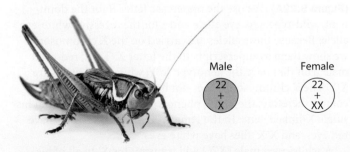

▲ **Figure 9.20B** The X-O system

▲ **Figure 9.20D** Sex determination by chromosome number

9.21 Are human males on the verge of extinction?

▶ **Figure 9.21** The human sex chromosomes

In the previous module we talked about the human sex chromosomes, which determine gender. **Figure 9.21** is a colourized SEM of the human X and Y chromosomes. Although the Y chromosome is significantly smaller than its counterpart, biologists believe the two chromosomes evolved from a pair of homologous autosomes. The considerable reduction in size has led to the rumour that the Y chromosome is shrinking, and that, as it shrinks into nonexistence, the male gender will follow. But is the human Y chromosome actually shrinking away, dooming the entire gender?

Three hundred million years ago, in a mammal ancestor, the X and Y chromosomes were homologous and each contained more than 1000 genes. Today, the human Y chromosome contains only about 50 active genes. This is an average loss of approximately five genes every million years. Extrapolating this rate of decay, in 10 million years the human Y chromosome will have no genes left. Humans are not alone when it comes to shrinking sex chromosomes. In fact, this phenomenon has evolved multiple times in the animal kingdom. For example, the W chromosome in the ZW female chicken is also significantly smaller than its Z chromosome counterpart (see Figure 9.20C). The Y chromosome has completely disappeared in one mammal, the Transcaucasian mole vole (*Ellobius lutescens*). Gender determination in these mammals, however, is by a different mechanism similar to the X-O system of some insects (see Figure 9.20B).

Male-specific genes such as *SRY* (see Module 9.20) became isolated on the Y chromosome after a series of events prevented recombination with its X "homologue." Five separate inversions (see Module 8.24) can be identified in the human Y chromosome. Each inversion event, having flipped a region of the Y chromosome, was also accompanied by a deletion of a segment of the Y chromosome. The combined effect of these events was the rearrangement of the genes on the Y chromosome, and a loss of about 100 million base pairs of DNA. Additionally, with every inversion and deletion, recombination between the X and Y chromosomes became more and more unlikely because the genes no longer line up on both chromosomes. If a recombination event did occur, an XX individual, who should be female, could develop male sex organs. Thus inversions offered an evolutionary advantage by isolating the male-specific genes to the Y chromosome.

Will the Y chromosome shrink into oblivion? Research has shown that this is highly unlikely. By comparing the Y chromosome of humans, chimpanzees, and rhesus monkeys, biologists have determined that the rate of genetic decay is slowing. Humans have one fewer male-specific gene than rhesus monkeys. This change occurred approximately 25 million years ago—before the two lineages diverged. Chimpanzees and humans have the same male-specific genes, meaning no further deletions have occurred since these species diverged nearly 7 million years ago. Additionally, accelerated Y chromosome decay in humans causes infertility, making up 5% to 15% of all male infertility cases. Therefore, the shortened Y chromosome cannot be passed on to a son and fails to persist. Perhaps the disappearance of the Y chromosome would not mean extinction of human males if an X-O system were to evolve, as in the mole vole. The rumour that the shrinking Y chromosome will cause human males to become extinct is, at the very least, improbable.

 With testis development dependent on the *SRY* gene currently on the Y chromosome, how could testes develop if the Y chromosome were to vanish?

● If a translocation moved the *SRY* to another chromosome, testes may still develop.

9.22 Sex-linked genes exhibit a unique pattern of inheritance

Besides bearing genes that determine sex, the sex chromosomes also contain genes for characters unrelated to femaleness or maleness. A gene located on either sex chromosome is called a **sex-linked gene**. Because the human X chromosome contains many more genes than the Y, the term has historically referred specifically to genes on the X chromosome. (Be careful not to confuse the term *sex-linked gene*, which refers to a gene on a sex chromosome, with the term *linked genes*, which refers to genes on the same chromosome that tend to be inherited together.)

The figures in this module illustrate inheritance patterns for white eye colour in the fruit fly, an X-linked recessive trait.

Wild-type fruit flies have red eyes; white eyes are very rare **(Figure 9.22A)**. We use the uppercase letter *R* for the dominant, wild-type, red-eye allele and *r* for the recessive white-eye allele. Because these alleles are carried on the X chromosome, we show them as superscripts to the letter X. Thus, red-eyed male fruit flies have the genotype $X^R Y$; white-eyed males are $X^r Y$. The Y chromosome does not have a gene locus for eye colour; therefore, the male's phenotype results entirely from his single X-linked gene. In the female, $X^R X^R$ and $X^R X^r$ flies have red eyes, and $X^r X^r$ flies have white eyes.

A white-eyed male ($X^r Y$) will transmit his X^r to all of his female offspring but to none of his male offspring. This is

▲ **Figure 9.22A** Fruit fly eye colour determined by sex-linked gene

because his female offspring, in order to be female, must inherit his X chromosome, but his male offspring must inherit his Y chromosome.

As shown in **Figure 9.22B**, when the female parent is a dominant homozygote ($X^R X^R$) and the male parent is $X^r Y$, all the offspring have red eyes, but the female offspring are all carriers of the allele for white eyes ($X^R X^r$). When those offspring are bred to each other, the classic 3:1 phenotypic ratio of red eyes to white eyes appears among the offspring **(Figure 9.22C)**.

However, there is a twist: The white-eyed trait shows up only in males. All the females have red eyes, whereas half the males have red eyes and half have white eyes. All females inherit at least one dominant allele (from their male parent); half of them are homozygous dominant, whereas the other half are heterozygous carriers, like their female parent. Among the males, half of them inherit the recessive allele their mother was carrying, producing the white-eye phenotype.

Because the white-eye allele is recessive, a female will have white eyes only if she receives that allele on both X chromosomes. For example, if a heterozygous female mates with a white-eyed male, there is a 50% chance that each offspring will have white eyes (resulting from genotype $X^r X^r$ or $X^r Y$), regardless of sex **(Figure 9.22D)**. Female offspring with red eyes are heterozygotes, whereas red-eyed male offspring completely lack the recessive allele.

 ? **A white-eyed female *Drosophila* is mated with a red-eyed (wild-type) male. What result do you predict for the numerous offspring?**

● All female offspring will be red-eyed but heterozygous ($X^R X^r$); all male offspring will be white-eyed ($X^r Y$).

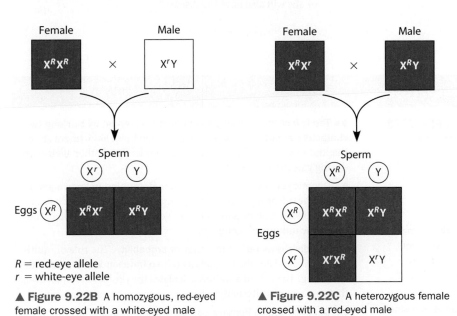

R = red-eye allele
r = white-eye allele

▲ **Figure 9.22B** A homozygous, red-eyed female crossed with a white-eyed male

▲ **Figure 9.22C** A heterozygous female crossed with a red-eyed male

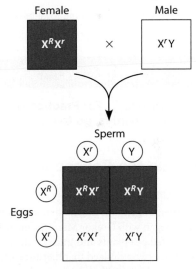

▲ **Figure 9.22D** A heterozygous female crossed with a white-eyed male

---

9.23 Human sex-linked disorders affect mostly males

As in fruit flies, a number of human conditions result from sex-linked (X-linked) recessive alleles. Like a male fruit fly, if a man inherits only one X-linked recessive allele—from his mother—the allele will be expressed. In contrast, a woman has to inherit two such alleles—one from each parent—in order to exhibit the trait. Thus, recessive X-linked traits are expressed much more frequently in men than in women.

Hemophilia is an X-linked recessive trait with a long, well-documented history. Hemophiliacs bleed excessively when injured because they lack one or more of the proteins required for blood clotting. A high incidence of hemophilia plagued the royal families of Europe. Queen Victoria (1819–1901) of England was a carrier of the hemophilia allele. She passed it on to one of her sons and two of her daughters. Through marriage, her daughters then introduced the disease into the royal families of Prussia, Russia, and Spain. Thus, the age-old practice of strengthening international alliances by marriage effectively spread hemophilia through the royal families of several nations.

▲ **Figure 9.23** Hemophilia in the royal family of Russia

The pedigree in **Figure 9.23** traces the disease through one branch of the royal family. As you can see in the pedigree, Alexandra, like her mother and grandmother, was a carrier, and Alexis had the disease.

Another recessive disorder in humans that is sex-linked is **red-green colourblindness**, a malfunction of light-sensitive cells in the eyes. Colourblindness is actually a class of disorders that involves several X-linked genes. A person with normal colour vision can see more than 150 colours. In contrast, someone with red-green colourblindness can see fewer than 25. Mostly males are affected, but heterozygous females have some defects.

Duchenne muscular dystrophy, a condition characterized by a progressive weakening of the muscles and loss of coordination, is another human X-linked recessive disorder. The first symptoms appear in early childhood, when the child begins to have difficulty standing up. He is inevitably wheelchair-bound by age 12. Eventually, muscle tissue becomes severely wasted, and normal breathing becomes difficult. Affected individuals rarely live past their early twenties.

 Neither Tom nor Sue has hemophilia, but their first son does. If the couple has a second child, what is the probability that he or she will also have the disease?

● $\frac{1}{4}$ ($\frac{1}{2}$ chance of a male child × $\frac{1}{2}$ chance that he will inherit the mutant X)

R E V I E W

MasteringBiology® **For Practice Quizzes, BioFlix, MP3 Tutors, and Activities, go to masteringbiology.com.**

Reviewing the Concepts

Mendel's Laws (9.1–9.9)

9.1 Experimental genetics began in an abbey garden. The science of genetics began with Gregor Mendel's quantitative experiments. Mendel crossed pea plants and traced traits from generation to generation. He hypothesized that there are alternative versions of genes (alleles), the units that determine heritable traits.

9.2 Mendel's law of segregation describes the inheritance of a single character. Mendel's law of segregation predicts that each set of alleles will separate as gametes are formed:

Homologous chromosomes — Alleles, residing at the same locus — Fertilization — Meiosis — Gamete from the other parent — Diploid zygote (containing paired alleles) — Paired alleles, different forms of a gene — Haploid gametes (allele pairs separated)

9.3 Homologous chromosomes bear the alleles for each character. When the two alleles of a gene in a diploid individual are different, the dominant allele determines the inherited trait, whereas the recessive allele has no effect.

9.4 The law of independent assortment is revealed by tracking two characters at once. Mendel's law of independent assortment states that the alleles of a pair segregate independently of other allele pairs during gamete formation.

9.5 Geneticists can use the testcross to determine unknown genotypes. The offspring of a testcross, a mating between an individual of unknown genotype and a homozygous recessive individual, can reveal the unknown's genotype.

9.6 Mendel's laws reflect the rules of probability. The rule of multiplication calculates the probability of two independent events both occurring. The rule of addition calculates the probability of an event that can occur in alternative ways.

9.7 Genetic traits in humans can be tracked through family pedigrees. The inheritance of many human traits follows Mendel's laws. Family pedigrees can help to determine individual genotypes.

9.8 Many inherited disorders in humans are controlled by a single gene. Diseases such as cystic fibrosis and sickle-cell disease are inherited by a single gene in simple Mendelian fashion.

9.9 New technologies can provide insight into one's genetic legacy. Carrier screening, fetal testing, fetal imaging, and newborn screening can provide information for reproductive decisions but may create ethical dilemmas.

Variations on Mendel's Laws (9.10–9.15)

9.10 Dominance is not always complete. Mendel's laws are valid for all sexually reproducing species, but genotype often does not dictate phenotype in the simple way his laws describe.

Red
RR

×

White
rr

Incomplete
dominance →

Pink
Rr

9.11 Many genes have more than two alleles in the population. For example, the ABO blood group phenotype in humans is controlled by three alleles that produce a total of four phenotypes.

9.12 A single gene may affect many phenotypic characters:

Single gene — Pleiotropy → Multiple characters

9.13 A single character may be influenced by many genes:

Multiple genes — Polygenic inheritance → Single characters (such as skin colour)

9.14 Human pigmentation has repeatedly changed as our ancestors migrated. Darker skin first evolved to protect against folate deficiencies. Light skin re-emerged and allowed for increased vitamin D_3 synthesis as humans migrated northward.

9.15 The environment affects many characters. Many traits are affected, in varying degrees, by both genetic and environmental factors.

The Chromosomal Basis of Inheritance (9.16–9.19)

9.16 Chromosome behaviour accounts for Mendel's laws. Genes are located on chromosomes, whose behaviour during meiosis and fertilization accounts for inheritance patterns.

9.17 Genes on the same chromosome tend to be inherited together. Such genes are said to be linked; they display non-Mendelian inheritance patterns.

9.18 Crossing over produces new combinations of alleles. Crossing over can separate linked alleles, producing gametes with recombinant chromosomes.

9.19 Geneticists use crossover data to map genes. Recombination frequencies can be used to map the relative positions of genes on chromosomes.

Sex Chromosomes and Sex-Linked Genes (9.20–9.23)

9.20 Chromosomes determine sex in many species. In mammals, a male has XY sex chromosomes, and a female has XX. The Y chromosome has genes for the development of testes, whereas an absence of the Y allows ovaries to develop. Other systems of sex determination exist in other animals and plants.

9.21 Are human males on the verge of extinction? Although the Y chromosome has become considerably smaller, it is unlikely to disappear and cause the extinction of males.

9.22 Sex-linked genes exhibit a unique pattern of inheritance. All genes on the sex chromosomes are said to be sex-linked. However, the X chromosome carries many genes unrelated to sex.

9.23 Human sex-linked disorders affect mostly males. Most sex-linked (X-linked) human disorders are due to recessive alleles and are seen mostly in males. A male receiving a single X-linked recessive allele from his mother will have the disorder; a female must receive the allele from both parents to be affected.

Connecting the Concepts

1. Complete this concept map to help you review some key concepts of genetics.

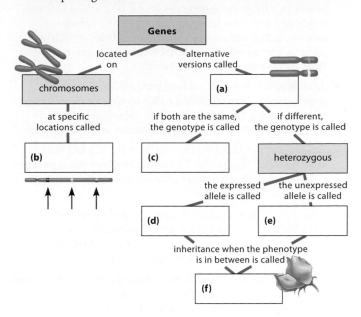

Testing Your Knowledge

Multiple Choice

2. Edward was found to be heterozygous (*Ss*) for sickle-cell trait. The alleles represented by the letters *S* and *s* are
   a. on the X and Y chromosomes.
   b. linked.
   c. on homologous chromosomes.
   d. both present in each of Edward's sperm cells.
   e. on the same chromosome but far apart.

3. Whether an allele is dominant or recessive depends on
   a. how common the allele is, relative to other alleles.
   b. whether it is inherited from the mother or the father.
   c. which chromosome it is on.
   d. whether it or another allele determines the phenotype when both are present.
   e. whether or not it is linked to other genes.

4. Two fruit flies with eyes of the usual red colour are crossed, and their offspring are as follows: 77 red-eyed males, 71 ruby-eyed males, 152 red-eyed females. Which of the following explain the allele for ruby eyes? *(Explain your answer.)*
   a. autosomal (carried on an autosome) and dominant
   b. autosomal and recessive
   c. sex-linked and dominant
   d. sex-linked and recessive
   e. impossible to determine without more information

5. A man who has type B blood and a woman who has type A blood could have children of which of the following phenotypes?
   a. A or B only
   b. AB only
   c. AB or O
   d. A, B, or O
   e. A, B, AB, or O

Additional Genetics Problems

6. Why do more men than women have colourblindness?

7. In fruit flies, the genes for wing shape and body stripes are linked. In a fly whose genotype is *WwSs*, *W* is linked to *S*, and *w* is linked to *s*. Show how this fly can produce gametes containing four different combinations of alleles. Which are parental-type gametes? Which are recombinant gametes? How are the recombinants produced?

8. Adult height in humans is at least partially hereditary; tall parents tend to have tall children. But humans come in a range of sizes, not just tall and short. Which extension of Mendel's model accounts for the hereditary variation in human height?

9. Tim and Jan both have freckles (see Module 9.7), but their son Mike does not. Show with a Punnett square how this is possible. If Tim and Jan have two more children, what is the probability that both will have freckles?

10. Both Tim and Jan (question 9) have a widow's peak (see Module 9.7), but Mike has a straight hairline. What are their genotypes? What is the probability that Tim and Jan's next child will have freckles and a straight hairline?

11. In rabbits, black hair depends on a dominant allele, *B*, and brown hair on a recessive allele, *b*. Short hair is due to a dominant allele, *S*, and long hair to a recessive allele, *s*. If a true-breeding black, short-haired male is mated with a brown, long-haired female, describe their offspring (assume the genes are not linked). What will be the genotypes of the offspring? If two of these F₁ rabbits are mated, what phenotypes would you expect among their offspring? In what proportions?

12. A fruit fly with a grey body and red eyes (genotype *BbPp*) is mated with a fly that has a black body and purple eyes (genotype *bbpp*). What ratio of offspring would you expect if the body-colour and eye-colour genes are on different chromosomes (unlinked)? When this mating is actually carried out, most of the offspring look like the parents, but 3% have a grey body and purple eyes, and 3% have a black body and red eyes. Are these genes linked or unlinked? What is the recombination frequency?

13. A series of matings shows that the recombination frequency between the black-body gene (question 12) and the gene for dumpy (shortened) wings is 36%. The recombination frequency between purple eyes and dumpy wings is 41%. What is the sequence of these three genes on the chromosome?

14. A couple are both phenotypically normal, but their son suffers from hemophilia, a sex-linked recessive disorder. What fraction of their children are likely to suffer from hemophilia? What fraction are likely to be carriers?

15. Heather was surprised to discover she suffered from red-green colourblindness. She told her biology professor, who said, "Your father is colourblind too, right?" How did her professor know this? Why did her professor not say the same thing to the colourblind males in the class?

Applying the Concepts

16. In 1981, a stray black cat with unusual rounded, curled-back ears was adopted by a family in Lakewood, California. Hundreds of descendants of this cat have since been born, and cat fanciers hope to develop the "curl" cat into a show breed. The curl allele is apparently dominant and autosomal (carried on an autosome). Suppose you owned the first curl cat and wanted to breed it to develop a true-breeding variety. Describe tests that would determine whether the curl gene is dominant or recessive and whether it is autosomal or sex-linked. Explain why you think your tests would be conclusive. Describe a test to determine that a cat is true-breeding.

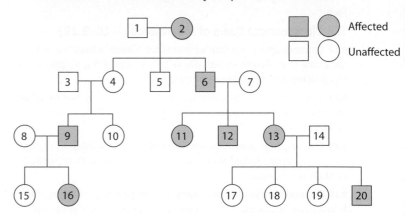

17. For the following pedigree of a hypothetical trait, explain why or why not the trait could be autosomal dominant, autosomal recessive, or X-linked recessive. Explain your answer for each.

Answers to all questions can be found in Appendix E.

Molecular Genetics

BIG IDEAS

The Structure of the Genetic Material

(10.1–10.3)

A series of experiments established DNA as the molecule of heredity.

DNA Replication

(10.4–10.5)

Each DNA strand can serve as a template for another.

The Flow of Genetic Information from DNA to RNA to Protein

(10.6–10.19)

Genotype controls phenotype through the production of proteins.

Translation: A Target for Toxins and Treatments

Proteins perform most of the work done in a cell. Structural proteins are an integral part of every organelle and nearly all metabolic processes within a cell are carried out by protein enzymes. Cells are continually making proteins to fulfill these requirements. Thus, the synthesis of proteins (called translation) is an essential process for every living cell. Preventing translation within a cell interferes with important functions and will lead to cell death. Some organisms produce substances that inhibit translation in their predators as a means of defence. The castor bean plant (*Ricinus communis*), native to Africa and grown in many Canadian gardens, does exactly that. (The castor bean plant is not related to the species of bean plants with which you are likely more familiar.)

A protein called ricin, produced within the castor seeds (beans), is an extremely potent inhibitor of protein synthesis. In fact, it is one of the strongest natural toxins produced. A single chewed seed can kill a child. If the ricin were purified, it would take an amount equivalent to only a few grains of salt to kill an adult. The symptoms of low-dose, nonfatal poisonings depend on the route of exposure, which can be through ingestion, inhalation, or in rare instances, injection. Also, topical exposure through handling beans can irritate the skin. Ricin kills cells by enzymatically cleaving covalent bonds within the large and small ribosomal subunits, rendering the protein-building factories nonfunctional. Some antibiotics kill bacteria through a similar mechanism. Without protein synthesis, cell function is lost and ultimately, the cell will die. An animal is killed when many cells die throughout the body, causing multiple organ failure and cardiovascular collapse.

Ricin was investigated as a potential chemical weapon during World War I. In World War II, a ricin bomb was developed but never used. Recently, with castor beans being readily available and ricin purification relatively simple, concerns about this toxin have re-emerged as a potential tool of murder or terrorism. In James Bond fashion, a ricin-infused BB pellet shot from a rigged umbrella by Bulgarian secret police killed dissident journalist Georgi Markov in 1978. In Canada, ricin is regulated under the *Chemical Weapons Convention Implementation Act* as a Schedule 1 toxin.

Why does the castor bean plant make such a potent poison? Unable to evade herbivores, many plants produce toxic substances that help to deter their consumption. In the castor bean plant, ricin is produced within the seeds, although minute amounts can also be found throughout the plant body. Animals that ingest a sublethal quantity of seeds experience gastrointestinal distress. If they associate the discomfort with eating castor beans, they will avoid the plant in the future.

Modern medicine is experimenting on ways to exploit the toxicity of ricin. The ricin toxin can be covalently joined to antibodies (proteins discussed in Chapter 34) that specifically bind to cancer cells. This treatment strategy uses the specificity of the antibodies to deliver the toxin to and kill only undesirable cells—tumour cells. This treatment, however, is not without its problems. Sometimes the ricin protein binds to normal cells before reaching the tumour target. Scientists are working on ways to reduce this unwanted side effect of the treatment. If scientists can successfully kill tumour cells by blocking their protein synthesis, ricin could become an important weapon in our arsenal against cancer.

This chapter is about molecular biology—the study of DNA and how it serves as the basis of heredity. We'll explore the structure of DNA, how it replicates, and how it controls the phenotypic expression of a cell's genotype by directing RNA and protein synthesis.

The Structure of the Genetic Material

10.1 Experiments showed that DNA is the genetic material

Today, even schoolchildren have heard of DNA, and scientists routinely manipulate DNA in the laboratory and use it to change the heritable characteristics of cells. Early in the 20th century, however, the precise identity of the molecular basis for inheritance was unknown. Biologists knew that genes were located on chromosomes and that the two chemical components of chromosomes were DNA and protein. Therefore, DNA and protein were the likely candidates to be the genetic material. Until the 1940s, the case for proteins seemed stronger because proteins appeared to be more structurally complex: Proteins were known to be made from 20 different amino acid building blocks, whereas DNA was known to be made from a mere four kinds of nucleotides. It seemed to make sense that the more

complex molecule would serve as the hereditary material. Biologists finally established the role of DNA in heredity through experiments with bacteria and the viruses that infect them. This breakthrough ushered in the field of **molecular biology**, which includes the study of heredity at the molecular level.

Early molecular biology experiments showed that chemical components of dead pathogenic (disease-causing) bacteria could transform living harmless bacteria into pathogenic forms. Furthermore, the descendants of the newly transformed bacteria all retained the ability to cause disease. But what was the "transforming factor" that could bring about this change?

The answer to this question came from studying viruses that infect bacteria. **Figure 10.1** shows a **bacteriophage**

Batch 1: Radioactive **protein** shown in yellow

① Hershey and Chase mixed radioactively labelled phages with bacteria. The phages infected the bacterial cells.

② They agitated the cultures in a blender to separate the phages outside of the bacteria from the cells and their contents.

③ They centrifuged the mixture so that the bacteria formed a pellet at the bottom of the test tube.

④ Finally, they measured the radioactivity in the pellet and in the liquid.

Batch 2: Radioactive **DNA** shown in green

▲ **Figure 10.1** The Hershey-Chase experiment

("bacteria-eater") or **phage** for short, which infects the bacterium *Escherichia coli* (*E. coli*). Phages consist solely of DNA and protein (see Figure 10.1), and are able to reprogram their host cells to produce new phages. American biologists Alfred Hershey and Martha Chase devised an experiment to test which phage component, DNA or protein, was responsible for this ability. Their experiment used only a few relatively simple tools: chemicals containing radioactive isotopes (see Module 2.4); a radioactivity detector; a kitchen blender; and a centrifuge, a device that spins test tubes to separate particles of different weights. (These are still basic tools of molecular biology.)

Hershey and Chase used different radioactive isotopes to label the DNA and protein in the phage. First, they grew the phage with *E. coli* in a solution containing radioactive sulphur (yellow in Figure 10.1). Protein contains sulphur but DNA does not, so as new phages were made, the radioactive sulphur atoms were incorporated only into the proteins of the bacteriophage. The researchers grew a separate batch of phages in a solution containing radioactive phosphorus (green). Because nearly all the phage's phosphorus is in DNA, this labelled only the phage DNA.

Armed with the two batches of labelled phage, Hershey and Chase were ready to perform the experiment outlined in Figure 10.1. ❶ They allowed the two batches of phage to infect separate samples of nonradioactive bacteria. ❷ Shortly after the onset of infection, they agitated the cultures in a blender to shake loose any parts of the phages that remained outside the bacterial cells. ❸ Then, they spun the mixtures in a centrifuge. The cells were deposited as a pellet at the bottom of the centrifuge tubes, but phages and parts of phages, being lighter, remained suspended in the liquid. ❹ The researchers then measured the radioactivity in the pellet and in the liquid.

Hershey and Chase found that when the bacteria had been infected with phages containing labelled protein, the radioactivity ended up mainly in the liquid within the centrifuge tube, which contained phages but not bacteria. This result suggested that the phage protein did not enter the cells. But when the bacteria had been infected with phages whose DNA was tagged, then most of the radioactivity was in the pellet of bacterial cells at the bottom of the centrifuge tube. Furthermore, when these bacteria were returned to liquid growth medium and the phage replication cycle continued (see Module 16.3), they soon lysed, or broke open, releasing new phages with radioactive phosphorus in their DNA but no radioactive sulphur in their proteins.

Once DNA was shown to be the molecule of heredity, understanding its structure became the most important quest in biology. In the next two modules, we'll review the structure of DNA and discuss how it was discovered.

 ? What convinced Hershey and Chase that DNA, rather than protein, is the genetic material of a phage?

● Radioactively labelled phage DNA, but not labelled protein, entered the host cell during infection and directed the synthesis of new viruses.

10.2 DNA and RNA are polymers of nucleotides

By the time Hershey and Chase performed their experiments, much was already known about DNA. Scientists had identified all its atoms and knew how they were covalently bonded to one another. What was not understood was the specific arrangement of atoms that gave DNA its unique properties—the capacity to store genetic information, copy it, and pass it from generation to generation. However, only one year after Hershey and Chase published their results, scientists figured out the three-dimensional structure of DNA and the basic strategy of how it works.

Recall from Module 3.12 that DNA and RNA are nucleic acids, consisting of long chains (polymers) of chemical units (monomers) called **nucleotides. Figure 10.2A** shows four representations of various parts of the same molecule. At left is a view of a DNA double helix. One of the strands is opened up (centre) to show two different views of an individual DNA **polynucleotide**, a nucleotide polymer (chain). The view on the far right zooms into a single nucleotide from the chain. Each type of DNA nucleotide has a different nitrogen-containing base: adenine (A), cytosine (C), thymine (T), or guanine (G). Because nucleotides can occur in a polynucleotide in any sequence and polynucleotides vary in length from long to very long, the number of possible polynucleotides is enormous. The chain shown in this figure has the sequence ACTGG, only one of many possible arrangements of the four types of nucleotides that make up DNA.

Looking more closely at our polynucleotide, we see in the centre of Figure 10.2A that each nucleotide consists of three components: a nitrogenous base (in DNA: A, C, T, or G), a sugar (blue), and a phosphate group (yellow). The nucleotides are joined to one another by covalent bonds between the sugar of one nucleotide and the phosphate of the next. This results in a **sugar-phosphate backbone**, a repeating pattern of sugar-phosphate-sugar-phosphate. The nitrogenous bases are arranged like ribs that project from the backbone.

Examining a single nucleotide in even more detail (on the right in Figure 10.2A), you can see the chemical structure of its three components. The phosphate group has a phosphorus atom (P) at its centre and is the source of the word *acid* in *nucleic acid*. The sugar has five carbon atoms, shown in red here for emphasis—four in its ring and one extending above the ring. The ring also includes an oxygen atom. The sugar is called deoxyribose because, compared with the sugar ribose, it is missing an oxygen atom. (Notice that the C2 atom is bonded to an H atom instead of an —OH group, as it is in ribose; see Figure 10.2C. Hence, DNA is "deoxy"—which means "without an oxygen"—compared to RNA.)

The full name for **DNA** is **deoxyribonucleic acid**, with the *nucleic* portion of the word referring to DNA's location in the nuclei of eukaryotic cells. Each nitrogenous base (thymine, in our example at the right in Figure 10.2A) has a single or

Sugar-phosphate backbone

Phosphate group

Nitrogenous base

Covalent bond joining nucleotides

Sugar

A DNA double helix

DNA nucleotide

Nitrogenous base (can be A, G, C, or T)

Thymine (T)

Phosphate group

Sugar (deoxyribose)

DNA nucleotide

Two representations of a DNA polynucleotide

▲ **Figure 10.2A** The structure of a DNA polynucleotide

double ring consisting of nitrogen and carbon atoms with various functional groups attached. Recall from Module 3.2 that a functional group is a chemical group that affects a molecule's function by participating in specific chemical reactions. In the case of DNA, the main role of the functional groups is to determine which other kind of bases each base can hydrogen-bond with. For example, the NH_2 group hanging off cytosine is capable of forming a hydrogen bond to the C=O group hanging off guanine, but not with the NH_2 group protruding from adenine. The chemical groups of the bases are therefore

responsible for DNA's most important property, which you will learn more about in the next module. In contrast to the acidic phosphate group, nitrogenous bases are basic, hence their name.

The four nucleotides found in DNA differ only in the structure of their nitrogenous bases **(Figure 10.2B)**. At this point, the structural details are not as important as the fact that the bases are of two types. **Thymine (T)** and **cytosine (C)** are single-ring structures called pyrimidines. **Adenine (A)** and **guanine (G)** are larger, double-ring structures called purines.

Thymine (T)

Cytosine (C)

Pyrimidines

Adenine (A)

Guanine (G)

Purines

▲ **Figure 10.2B** The nitrogenous bases of DNA

Nitrogenous base
(can be A, G, C, or U)

Phosphate
group

Uracil (U)

Sugar
(ribose)

▲ **Figure 10.2C** An RNA nucleotide

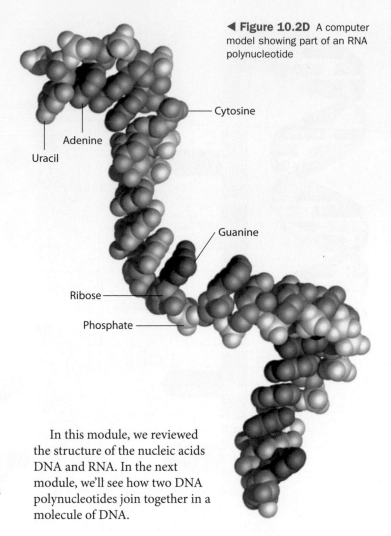

◀ **Figure 10.2D** A computer model showing part of an RNA polynucleotide

Cytosine

Adenine

Uracil

Guanine

Ribose

Phosphate

The one-letter abbreviations can be used either for the bases alone or for the nucleotides containing them.

What about RNA **(Figure 10.2C)**? As its name—*ribonucleic acid*—implies, its sugar is ribose rather than deoxyribose. Notice the ribose in the RNA nucleotide in Figure 10.2C; unlike deoxyribose, the sugar ring has an —OH group attached to the C atom at its lower-right corner. Another difference between RNA and DNA is that instead of thymine, RNA has a nitrogenous base called **uracil (U)**. (You can see the structure of uracil in Figure 10.2C; it is very similar to thymine.) Except for the presence of ribose and uracil, an RNA polynucleotide chain is identical to a DNA polynucleotide chain. **Figure 10.2D** is a computer graphic of a three-dimensional piece of RNA polynucleotide about 20 nucleotides long. In this view, each sphere represents an atom and the colour scheme is the same as in the other figures in this module. The yellow phosphate groups and blue ribose sugars make it easy to spot the sugar-phosphate backbone.

In this module, we reviewed the structure of the nucleic acids DNA and RNA. In the next module, we'll see how two DNA polynucleotides join together in a molecule of DNA.

 ? Compare and contrast DNA and RNA polynucleotides.

● Both are polymers of nucleotides consisting of a sugar, a nitrogenous base, and a phosphate. In RNA, the sugar is ribose; in DNA, it is deoxyribose. Both RNA and DNA have the bases A, G, and C, but DNA has a T and RNA has a U.

10.3 DNA is a double-stranded helix

After the Hershey-Chase experiment convinced most biologists that DNA was the material that stored genetic information, a race was on to determine how the structure of this molecule could account for its role in heredity. By that time, the arrangement of covalent bonds in a nucleic acid polymer was well established, and researchers focused on discovering the three-dimensional shape of DNA. First to the finish line were two scientists who were relatively unknown at the time: American James D. Watson and Englishman Francis Crick.

The brief but celebrated partnership that solved the puzzle of DNA structure began soon after Watson, a 23-year-old newly minted Ph.D., journeyed to University of Cambridge in England, where the more senior Crick was studying three-dimensional protein structure with a technique called X-ray crystallography. A careful study of X-ray crystallographic images of DNA enabled Watson to deduce the basic shape of

DNA to be a helix with a uniform diameter of 2 nanometres (nm), with its nitrogenous bases stacked about one-third of a nanometre apart. (For comparison, the plasma membrane of a cell is about 8 nm thick.) The diameter of the helix suggested that it was made up of two polynucleotide strands, a **double helix**.

Watson and Crick began trying to construct a wire model of a double helix that would conform to what was then known about the chemistry of DNA **(Figure 10.3A)**. They had concluded that the sugar-phosphate backbones must be on the outside of the double helix, forcing the nitrogenous bases to swivel to the interior of the molecule. But how were the bases arranged in the interior of the double helix?

At first, Watson and Crick imagined that the bases paired like with like—for example, A with A and C with C. But that kind of pairing did not fit the X-ray data, which suggested

▲ **Figure 10.3A** Watson and Crick in 1953 with their model of the DNA double helix

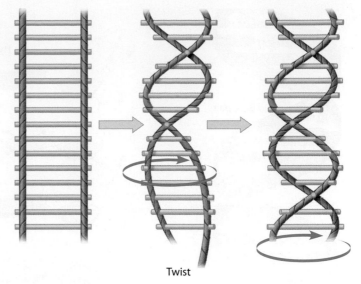

Twist

▲ **Figure 10.3B** A rope ladder model for the double helix

that the DNA molecule has a uniform diameter. An A-A pair, with two double-ring bases, would be almost twice as wide as a C-C pair. It soon became apparent that a double-ringed base (purine) must always be paired with a single-ringed base (pyrimidine) on the opposite strand. Moreover, Watson and Crick realized that the individual structures of the bases dictated the pairings even more specifically. As discussed in the previous module, each base has functional groups protruding from its six-sided ring that can best form hydrogen bonds with one appropriate partner (to review the hydrogen bond, see Module 2.8). Adenine can best form hydrogen bonds with thymine, and guanine with cytosine. In the biologist's shorthand, A pairs with T, and G pairs with C. A is also said to be "complementary" to T, and G to C. Notice that a C-G base pair has functional groups that form three hydrogen bonds, while an A-T base pair has functional groups that form two hydrogen bonds. This difference means that C-G base pairs are somewhat stronger than A-T base pairs.

Watson and Crick's pairing scheme not only fit what was known about the physical attributes and chemical bonding of DNA, but also explained some data obtained several years earlier by American biochemist Erwin Chargaff. Chargaff had discovered that the amount of adenine in the DNA of any one species was equal to the amount of thymine and that the amount of guanine was equal to that of cytosine. Chargaff's rules, as they are called, are explained by the fact that A on one of DNA's polynucleotide chains always pairs with T on the other polynucleotide chain, and G on one chain pairs only with C on the other chain.

You can picture the model of the DNA double helix proposed by Watson and Crick as a rope ladder with wooden rungs, with the ladder twisting into a spiral **(Figure 10.3B)**. The side ropes are the equivalent of the sugar-phosphate backbones, and the rungs represent pairs of nitrogenous bases joined by hydrogen bonds.

Figure 10.3C shows three representations of the double helix. The shapes of the base symbols in the ribbonlike diagram

on the left indicate the bases' complementarity; notice that the shape of any kind of base matches only one other kind of base. In the centre of the diagram is an atomic-level version showing four base pairs, with the helix untwisted. You can see that the two sugar-phosphate backbones of the double helix are oriented in opposite directions. (Notice that the sugars on the two strands are upside down with respect to each other.) On the right is a computer graphic showing most of the atoms of part of a double helix. The atoms that compose the deoxyribose sugars are shown as blue, phosphate groups as yellow, and nitrogenous bases as shades of green and orange.

Although the base-pairing rules dictate the side-by-side combinations of nitrogenous bases that form the rungs of the double helix, they place no restrictions on the sequence of nucleotides along the length of a DNA strand. In fact, the sequence of bases can vary in countless ways, and each gene has a unique order of nucleotides, or base sequence.

In April 1953, Watson and Crick rocked the scientific world with a succinct paper explaining their molecular model for DNA in the journal *Nature*. In 1962, Watson, Crick, and Wilkins received the Nobel Prize for their work. Few milestones in the history of biology have had as broad an impact as the discovery of the double helix, with its A-T and C-G base pairing.

The Watson-Crick model gave new meaning to the words *genes* and *chromosomes*—and to the chromosome theory of inheritance (see Module 9.16). With a complete picture of DNA, we can see that the genetic information in a chromosome must be encoded in the nucleotide sequence of the molecule. One powerful aspect of the Watson-Crick model is that the structure of DNA suggests a molecular explanation for genetic inheritance, as we will see in the next module.

? Along one strand of a double helix is the nucleotide sequence GGCATAGGT. What is the complementary sequence for the other DNA strand?

 CCGTATCCA

▲ **Figure 10.3C** Three representations of DNA

Ribbon model   Partial chemical structure   Computer model

DNA Replication

10.4 DNA replication depends on specific base pairing

One of biology's overarching themes—the relationship between structure and function—is evident in the double helix. The idea that there is specific pairing of bases in DNA was the flash of inspiration that led Watson and Crick to the correct structure of the double helix. At the same time, they saw the functional significance of the base-pairing rules. They ended their classic 1953 paper with this statement: "It has not escaped our notice that the specific pairing we have postulated immediately suggests a possible copying mechanism for the genetic material."

The logic behind the Watson-Crick proposal for how DNA is copied—by specific pairing of complementary bases—is

quite simple. You can see this by covering one of the strands in the parental DNA molecule in **Figure 10.4A**. You can determine the sequence of bases in the covered strand by applying the base-pairing rules to the unmasked strand: A pairs with T (and T with A), and G pairs with C (and C with G).

Watson and Crick predicted that a cell applies the same rules when copying its genes. As shown in Figure 10.4A, the two strands of parental DNA (blue) separate. Each then becomes a template for the assembly of a complementary strand from a supply of free nucleotides (grey) that is always available within the nucleus. The nucleotides line up one at a time along the template strand in accordance with the base-pairing rules.

A parental molecule of DNA   The parental strands separate and serve as templates   Two identical daughter molecules of DNA are formed

Free nucleotides

▲ **Figure 10.4A** A template model for DNA replication

Parental DNA
molecule

Daughter
strand   Parental
          strand

Daughter DNA
molecules

▲ **Figure 10.4B** The untwisting and replication of DNA

Enzymes link the nucleotides to form the new DNA strands. The completed new molecules, identical to the parental molecule, are known as daughter DNA (although no gender should be inferred).

After a double helix replicates, each of the two daughter molecules contains one old strand, which was part of the parental molecule, and one newly created strand. This model for DNA replication is known as the **semiconservative model** because half of the parental molecule is maintained (conserved) in each daughter molecule.

Although the general mechanism of DNA replication is conceptually simple, the actual process is complex, requiring the coordination of more than a dozen enzymes and other proteins. Some of the complexity arises from the need for the helical DNA molecule to untwist as it replicates and for the two new strands to be made roughly simultaneously (**Figure 10.4B**). Another challenge is the speed of the process. *E. coli*, with about 4.6 million DNA base pairs, can copy its entire genome in less than an hour. Humans, with more than 6 billion base pairs in 46 diploid chromosomes, require only a few hours. And yet, the process is amazingly accurate; typically, only about one DNA nucleotide per several billion is incorrectly paired. In the next module, we take a closer look at the mechanisms of DNA replication that allow it to proceed with such speed and accuracy.

 How does complementary base pairing make possible the replication of DNA?

● When the two strands of the double helix separate, free nucleotides can base-pair along each strand, leading to the synthesis of new complementary strands.

10.5 DNA replication proceeds in two directions at many sites simultaneously

Replication of a DNA molecule begins at special sites called origins of replication, short stretches of DNA having a specific sequence of nucleotides where proteins attach to the DNA and separate the strands. As shown in **Figure 10.5A**, replication then proceeds in both directions, creating replication "bubbles." The parental DNA strands (blue) open up as daughter strands (grey) elongate on both sides of each bubble. The DNA molecule of a eukaryotic chromosome has many origins where replication can start simultaneously. Thus, hundreds or thousands of bubbles can be present at once, shortening the total time needed for replication. Eventually, all the bubbles fuse, yielding two completed daughter DNA molecules (see the bottom of Figure 10.5A).

Figure 10.5B shows the molecular building blocks of a tiny segment of DNA, reminding us that the DNA's sugar-phosphate backbones run in opposite directions. Notice that each strand has a 3' ("three-prime") end and a 5' ("five-prime") end. The primed numbers refer to the carbon atoms of the nucleotide sugars (see Figure 10.2A). At one end of each DNA strand, the sugar's 3' carbon atom is attached to an —OH group; at the other end, the sugar's 5' carbon is attached to a phosphate group.

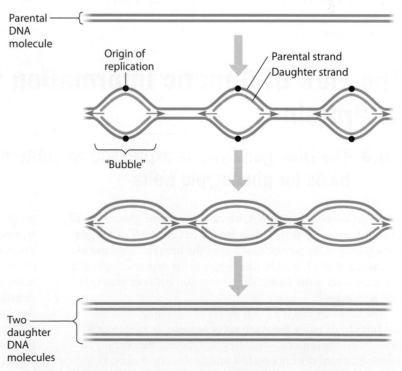

Parental DNA molecule

Origin of replication

Parental strand
Daughter strand

"Bubble"

Two daughter DNA molecules

▲ **Figure 10.5A** Multiple bubbles in replicating DNA

5'end　　　3'end

▲ **Figure 10.5B** The opposite orientations of DNA strands

3'end　　　5'end

The opposite orientation of the strands is important in DNA replication. The enzymes that link DNA nucleotides to a growing daughter strand, called **DNA polymerases**, add nucleotides only to the 3' end of the strand, never to the 5' end. Thus, a daughter DNA strand can grow only in the 5' → 3' direction. You see the consequences of this enzyme specificity in **Figure 10.5C**, where the forked structure represents one side of a replication bubble. One of the daughter strands (shown in grey) can be synthesized in one continuous piece by a DNA polymerase working toward the forking point of the parental DNA. However, to make the other daughter strand, polymerase molecules must work outward from the forking point. The only way this can be accomplished is if the new strand is synthesized in short pieces as the fork opens up. These pieces are called Okazaki fragments, after the Japanese husband-and-wife team of molecular biologists who discovered them. Another enzyme, called **DNA ligase**, then links, or ligates, the pieces together into a single DNA strand.

In addition to their roles in adding nucleotides to a DNA chain, DNA polymerases carry out a proofreading step that quickly removes nucleotides that have base-paired incorrectly during replication. DNA polymerases and DNA ligase, along with the help of many other proteins, help repair DNA damaged by harmful radiation, such as ultraviolet light and X-rays, or toxic chemicals in the environment, such as those found in tobacco smoke.

▲ **Figure 10.5C** How daughter DNA strands are synthesized

DNA replication ensures that all the somatic cells in a multicellular organism carry the same genetic information. It is also the means by which genetic instructions are copied for the next generation of the organism. In the next module, we begin to pursue the connection between DNA instructions and an organism's phenotypic traits.

? What is the function of DNA polymerase in DNA replication?

● As free nucleotides base-pair to a parental DNA strand, the enzyme covalently bonds them to the 3' end of a growing daughter strand.

The Flow of Genetic Information from DNA to RNA to Protein

10.6 The DNA genotype is expressed as proteins, which provide the molecular basis for phenotypic traits

With our knowledge of DNA, we can now define genotype and phenotype more precisely than we did in Chapter 9. An organism's genotype, its genetic makeup, is the heritable information contained in its DNA. The phenotype is the organism's physical traits. So what is the molecular connection between genotype and phenotype?

The answer is that the DNA inherited by an organism specifies traits by dictating the synthesis of proteins. In other words, proteins are the links between the genotype and the phenotype. However, a gene does not build a protein directly. Rather, a gene dispatches instructions in the form of RNA, which in turn

programs protein synthesis. This fundamental concept in biology, termed the sequence hypothesis, is summarized in **Figure 10.6A**. The molecular "chain of command" is from DNA in the nucleus of the cell to RNA to protein synthesis in the cytoplasm. The two main stages are **transcription**, the synthesis of RNA under the direction of DNA, and **translation**, the synthesis of protein under the direction of RNA.

The relationship between genes and proteins was first proposed in 1909, when English physician Archibald Garrod suggested that genes dictate phenotypes through enzymes, the proteins that catalyze chemical reactions. Garrod hypothesized

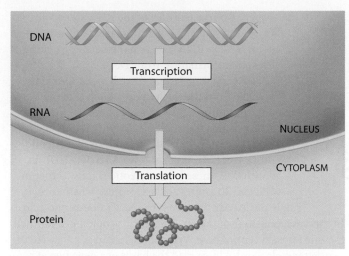

▲ Figure 10.6A The flow of genetic information in a eukaryotic cell

pathways, as in the synthesis of an amino acid or the breakdown of a sugar. As we described in Unit I (see Module 5.14, for example), each step in a metabolic pathway is catalyzed by a specific enzyme. Therefore, individuals lacking one of the enzymes for a pathway are unable to complete it.

The major breakthrough in demonstrating the relationship between genes and enzymes came in the 1940s from the work on the bread mould *Neurospora crassa* (**Figure 10.6B**). Biologists studied strains of the mould that were unable to grow on a simple growth medium. Each of these so-called nutritional mutants turned out to lack an enzyme in a metabolic pathway that produced some molecule the mould needed, such as an amino acid. It was also shown that each mutant was defective in a single gene. This result suggested the one gene–one enzyme hypothesis: the idea that the function of a gene is to dictate the production of a specific enzyme.

The one gene–one enzyme hypothesis has been amply confirmed, but with important modifications. First, it was extended beyond enzymes to include *all* types of proteins. For example, keratin (the structural protein of hair) and the hormone insulin are two examples of proteins that are not enzymes. So biologists began to think in terms of one gene–one protein. However, many proteins are made from two or more polypeptide chains, with each polypeptide specified by its own gene. For example, hemoglobin, the oxygen-transporting protein in your blood, is built from two kinds of polypeptides, encoded by two different genes. Thus, this hypothesis is now stated as follows: The function of a gene is to dictate the production of a polypeptide. Even this description is not entirely accurate, in that the RNA transcribed from some genes is not translated (you'll learn about two such kinds of RNA in Modules 10.11 and 10.12). The flow of information from genotype to phenotype continues to be an active research area.

that an inherited disease reflects a person's inability to make a particular enzyme, and he referred to such diseases as "inborn errors of metabolism." He gave as one example the hereditary condition called alkaptonuria, in which the urine is dark because it contains a chemical called alkapton. Garrod reasoned that individuals without the disorder have an enzyme that breaks down alkapton, whereas alkaptonuric individuals cannot make the enzyme. Garrod's hypothesis was ahead of its time, but research conducted decades later proved him right. In the intervening years, biochemists accumulated evidence that cells make and break down biologically important molecules via metabolic

▲ Figure 10.6B The bread mould *Neurospora crassa* growing in a culture dish

 ? **What are the functions of transcription and translation?**

● Transcription is the transfer of information from DNA to RNA. Translation is the use of the information in RNA to make a polypeptide.

10.7 Genetic information written in codons is translated into amino acid sequences

Genes provide the instructions for making specific proteins. But a gene does not build a protein directly. As you have learned, the bridge between DNA and protein synthesis is the nucleic acid RNA: DNA is transcribed into RNA, which is then translated into protein. Put another way, information within the cell flows as DNA → RNA → protein. This is sometimes stated as "DNA makes RNA makes protein."

Transcription and *translation* are linguistic terms, and it is useful to think of nucleic acids and proteins as having languages. To understand how genetic information passes from genotype to phenotype, we need to see how the chemical language of DNA is translated into the different chemical language of proteins.

What, exactly, is the language of nucleic acids? Both DNA and RNA are polymers (long chains) made of nucleotide monomers (the individual units that make up the polymer). In DNA, there are four types of nucleotides, which differ in their nitrogenous bases (A, T, C, and G). The same is true for RNA, although it has the base U instead of T.

Figure 10.7 focuses on a small region of one gene (gene 3, shown in light blue) carried by a DNA molecule. DNA's language is written as a linear sequence of nucleotide bases on a polynucleotide, a sequence such as the one you see on the enlarged DNA segment in the figure. Specific sequences of bases, each with a beginning and an end, make up the genes on a

DNA strand. A typical gene consists of hundreds or thousands of nucleotides in a specific sequence.

The pink strand underneath the enlarged DNA segment represents the results of transcription: an RNA molecule often called a **transcript**. The process is called transcription because the nucleic acid language of DNA has been rewritten (transcribed) as a sequence of bases on RNA. Notice that the language is still that of nucleic acids, although the nucleotide bases on the RNA molecule are complementary to those on the DNA strand. As we will see in Module 10.9, this is because the RNA was synthesized using the DNA as a template. It is also important to note that only one of the two DNA strands (the **template strand**) is transcribed, as shown in Figure 10.7. The other nontemplate strand is ignored.

The purple chain represents the results of translation, the conversion of the nucleic acid language to the polypeptide language (recall that proteins consist of one or more polypeptides). Like nucleic acids, polypeptides are polymers, but the monomers that compose them are the 20 amino acids common to all organisms. Again, the language is written in a linear sequence, and

the sequence of nucleotides of the RNA molecule dictates the sequence of amino acids of the polypeptide. The RNA acts as a messenger carrying genetic information from DNA.

During translation, there is a change in language from the nucleotide sequence of the RNA to the amino acid sequence of the polypeptide. How is this translation achieved? Recall that there are only four different kinds of nucleotides in DNA (A, G, C, T) and RNA (A, G, C, U). In translation, these four nucleotides must somehow specify all 20 amino acids. Consider whether each single nucleotide base were to specify one amino acid. In this case, only four of the 20 amino acids could be accounted for, one for each type of base. What if the language consisted of two-letter code words? If we read the bases of a gene two at a time—AG, for example, could specify one amino acid, whereas AT could designate a different amino acid—then only 16 arrangements would be possible (4^2), which is still not enough to specify all 20 amino acids. However, if the code word in DNA consists of a triplet, with each arrangement of three consecutive bases specifying an amino acid—AGT specifies one amino acid, for example, while AGA specifies a different one—then there can be 64 (that is, 4^3) possible code words, more than enough to specify the 20 amino acids. Indeed, there are enough triplets to allow more than one coding for each amino acid. For example, the base triplets AAT and AAC could both code for the same amino acid. Thus, triplets of bases are the smallest "words" of uniform length that can specify all the amino acids (see the brackets below the strand of RNA in Figure 10.7).

Experiments have verified that the flow of information from gene to protein is based on a **triplet code**: The genetic instructions for the amino acid sequence of a polypeptide chain are written in DNA and RNA as a series of nonoverlapping three-base "words" called **codons**. Notice in the figure that three-base codons in the DNA are transcribed into complementary three-base codons in the RNA, and then the RNA codons are translated into amino acids that form a polypeptide. We turn to the codons themselves in the next module.

? **What is the minimum number of nucleotides necessary to code for 100 amino acids?**

▲ **Figure 10.7** Transcription and translation of codons

300 ●

10.8 The genetic code dictates how codons are translated into amino acids

During the 1960s, scientists cracked the **genetic code**, the set of rules that relate codons in RNA to amino acids in proteins. The rules were established by a series of elegant experiments that disclosed the amino acid translations of each of the nucleotide-triplet code words. The first codon was deciphered in 1961 by American biochemist Marshall Nirenberg. He synthesized an artificial RNA molecule by linking together identical RNA nucleotides having uracil as their only

base. No matter where this message started or stopped, it could contain only one type of triplet codon: UUU. Nirenberg added this "poly-U" to a test-tube mixture containing ribosomes and the other ingredients required for polypeptide synthesis. This mixture translated the poly-U into a polypeptide containing a single kind of amino acid, phenylalanine (Phe). Thus, Nirenberg learned that the RNA codon UUU specifies the amino acid phenylalanine. By variations on this

Second base

		U	C	A	G	
First base	U	UUU ⎤ Phe UUC ⎦ UUA ⎤ Leu UUG ⎦	UCU ⎤ UCC ⎥ Ser UCA ⎥ UCG ⎦	UAU ⎤ Tyr UAC ⎦ UAA Stop UAG Stop	UGU ⎤ Cys UGC ⎦ UGA Stop UGG Trp	U C A G
	C	CUU ⎤ CUC ⎥ Leu CUA ⎥ CUG ⎦	CCU ⎤ CCC ⎥ Pro CCA ⎥ CCG ⎦	CAU ⎤ His CAC ⎦ CAA ⎤ Gln CAG ⎦	CGU ⎤ CGC ⎥ Arg CGA ⎥ CGG ⎦	U C A G
	A	AUU ⎤ AUC ⎥ Ile AUA ⎦ AUG Met or start	ACU ⎤ ACC ⎥ Thr ACA ⎥ ACG ⎦	AAU ⎤ Asn AAC ⎦ AAA ⎤ Lys AAG ⎦	AGU ⎤ Ser AGC ⎦ AGA ⎤ Arg AGG ⎦	U C A G
	G	GUU ⎤ GUC ⎥ Val GUA ⎥ GUG ⎦	GCU ⎤ GCC ⎥ Ala GCA ⎥ GCG ⎦	GAU ⎤ Asp GAC ⎦ GAA ⎤ Glu GAG ⎦	GGU ⎤ GGC ⎥ Gly GGA ⎥ GGG ⎦	U C A G

Third base (right side label)

▲ **Figure 10.8A** Dictionary of the genetic code (RNA codons)

▲ **Figure 10.8B** Deciphering the genetic information in DNA

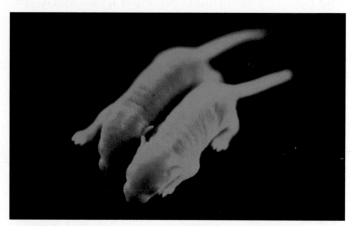

▲ **Figure 10.8C** These mice were engineered to express a green fluorescence protein obtained from a jellyfish

method, the amino acids specified by all the codons were soon determined.

As shown in **Figure 10.8A**, 61 of the 64 triplets code for amino acids. The triplet AUG (green box in the figure) has a dual function: It codes for the amino acid methionine (Met) and also can provide a signal for the start of a polypeptide chain. Three codons (red) do not designate amino acids. They are the stop codons that mark the end of translation.

Notice in Figure 10.8A that there is redundancy in the code but no ambiguity. For example, although codons UUU and UUC both specify phenylalanine (redundancy), neither of them ever represents any other amino acid (no ambiguity). The codons in the figure are the triplets found in RNA. They have a straightforward, complementary relationship to the codons in DNA, with UUU in the RNA matching AAA in the template DNA, for example. The nucleotides making up the codons occur in a linear order along the DNA and RNA, with no gaps or "punctuation" separating the codons.

As an exercise in translating the genetic code, consider the 12-nucleotide segment of DNA in **Figure 10.8B**. Let's read this as a series of triplets. Using the base-pairing rules (with U in RNA instead of T), we see that the RNA codon corresponding to the first transcribed DNA triplet, TAC, is AUG. (Notice that the RNA is nearly identical to the nontemplate DNA strand, only U is present instead of T.) As you can see in Figure 10.8A, AUG specifies, "Place Met as the first amino acid in the polypeptide." The second DNA triplet, TTC, dictates

RNA codon AAG, which designates lysine (Lys) as the second amino acid. We continue until we reach a stop codon (UAG in this example).

The genetic code is nearly universal, shared by organisms from the simplest bacteria to the most complex plants and animals. As you will learn in Chapter 12, such universality is key to modern DNA technologies because it allows scientists to mix and match genes from various species **(Figure 10.8C)**. A language shared by all living things must have evolved early enough in the history of life to be present in the common ancestors of all modern organisms. A shared genetic vocabulary is a reminder of the kinship that connects all life on Earth.

? Translate the RNA sequence CCAUUUACG into the corresponding amino acid sequence.

● Pro-Phe-Thr

10.9 Transcription produces genetic messages in the form of RNA

In eukaryotic cells, transcription, the transfer of genetic information from DNA to RNA, occurs in the nucleus. (The nucleus, after all, contains the DNA; see Figure 10.6A for a review.) An RNA molecule is transcribed from a DNA template by a process that resembles the synthesis of a DNA strand during DNA replication (see Module 10.4).

Figure 10.9A is a close-up view of the process of transcription. As with replication, the two DNA strands must first separate at the place where the process will start. Recall from Module 10.7 that only one of the DNA strands serves as a template for the newly forming RNA molecule; the other strand is unused. The nucleotides that make up the new RNA molecule take their place one at a time along the DNA template strand by forming hydrogen bonds with the nucleotide bases there. Notice that the RNA nucleotides follow the same base-pairing rules that govern DNA replication, except that U, rather than T, pairs with A. The RNA nucleotides are linked by the transcription enzyme **RNA polymerase**, symbolized in the figure by the large grey shape.

Figure 10.9B is an overview of the transcription of an entire prokaryotic gene. (We focus on prokaryotes here; eukaryotic transcription occurs via a similar but more complex process, which we come back to in Chapter 11.) Specific sequences of nucleotides along the DNA mark where transcription of a gene begins and ends. The "start transcribing" signal is a nucleotide sequence called a **promoter**. A promoter is a specific binding site for a protein called sigma factor (the green oval) and RNA polymerase and determines which of the two strands of the DNA double helix is used as the template in transcription. The nontemplate strand of DNA is ignored by RNA polymerase.

❶ The first phase of transcription, called initiation, is the attachment of RNA polymerase to the promoter and the start of RNA synthesis. This process starts with sigma factor binding to specific DNA sequences upstream of the gene. Subsequently, RNA polymerase binds to the sigma factor–DNA complex and transcription can begin. ❷ During the second phase of transcription, elongation, the RNA grows longer. As RNA synthesis

▲ **Figure 10.9B** The transcription of a gene

continues, the RNA strand peels away from its DNA template, allowing the two separated DNA strands to come back together in the region already transcribed. ❸ Finally, in the third phase, termination, the RNA polymerase reaches a sequence of bases in the DNA template called a **terminator**. This sequence signals the end of the gene; at that point, the polymerase molecule detaches from the RNA molecule and the gene.

In addition to producing RNA that encodes amino acid sequences, transcription makes two other kinds of RNA that are involved in building polypeptides. We discuss these three kinds of RNA—messenger RNA, transfer RNA, and ribosomal RNA—in the next three modules.

? What is a promoter? What molecule binds to it?

▲ **Figure 10.9A** A close-up view of transcription

● A promoter is a specific nucleotide sequence at the start of a gene where sigma factor and RNA polymerase attach and begin transcription.

10.10 Eukaryotic RNA is processed before leaving the nucleus as mRNA

The kind of RNA that encodes amino acid sequences is called **messenger RNA (mRNA)** because it conveys genetic messages from DNA to the translation machinery of the cell. Messenger RNA is transcribed from DNA, and the information in the mRNA is then translated into polypeptides. In prokaryotic cells, which lack nuclei, transcription and translation occur in the same place: the cytoplasm. In eukaryotic cells, however, mRNA molecules must exit the nucleus via the nuclear pores and enter the cytoplasm, where the machinery for polypeptide synthesis is located.

Before leaving the nucleus as mRNA, eukaryotic transcripts are modified, or processed, in several ways **(Figure 10.10)**. One kind of RNA processing is the addition of extra nucleotides to the ends of the RNA transcript. These additions include a small cap (a single G nucleotide) at one end and a long tail (a chain of 50 to 250 A nucleotides) at the other end. The cap and tail (yellow in the figure) facilitate the export of the mRNA from the nucleus, protect the mRNA from attack by cellular enzymes, and help ribosomes bind to the mRNA. The cap and tail themselves are not translated into protein.

Another type of RNA processing is made necessary in eukaryotes by noncoding stretches of nucleotides that interrupt the nucleotides that actually code for amino acids. It is as if unintelligible sequences of letters were randomly interspersed in an otherwise intelligible document. Most genes of plants and animals, it turns out, include such internal noncoding regions, which are called **introns** ("intervening sequences"). The coding regions—the parts of a gene that are expressed—are called **exons**. As Figure 10.10 shows, both exons (darker colour) and introns (lighter colour) are transcribed from DNA into RNA. However, before the RNA leaves the nucleus, the introns are removed, and the exons are joined to produce an mRNA molecule with a continuous coding sequence. (The short noncoding regions just inside the cap and tail are considered parts of the first and last exons.) This cutting-and-pasting process is called **RNA splicing**. In most cases, RNA splicing is catalyzed by a complex of proteins and small RNA molecules, but sometimes the RNA transcript itself catalyzes the process. In other words, RNA can sometimes act as an enzyme that removes its own introns! As we will see in the next chapter (in Module 11.5), RNA splicing also provides a means to produce multiple polypeptides from a single gene.

As we have discussed, translation is a conversion between different languages—from the nucleic acid language to the protein language—and it involves more elaborate machinery than transcription. The first important ingredient required for translation is the processed mRNA. Once it is present, the machinery used to translate mRNA requires enzymes and sources of chemical energy, such as ATP. In addition, translation requires two heavy-duty components: ribosomes and a kind of RNA called transfer RNA, the subject of the next module.

▲ **Figure 10.10** The production of eukaryotic mRNA

 ? Explain why most eukaryotic genes are longer than the mRNA that leaves the nucleus.

These genes have introns, noncoding sequences of nucleotides that are spliced out of the initial RNA transcript to produce mRNA.

10.11 Transfer RNA molecules serve as interpreters during translation

Translation of any language requires an interpreter, someone or something that can recognize the words of one language and convert them to another. Translation of a genetic message carried in mRNA into the amino acid language of proteins also requires an interpreter. To convert the words of nucleic acids (codons) to the amino acid words of proteins, a cell employs a molecular interpreter, a special type of RNA called **transfer RNA (tRNA)**.

A cell that is producing proteins has in its cytoplasm a supply of amino acids, either obtained from food or made from other chemicals. But amino acids themselves cannot recognize the codons in the mRNA. The amino acid tryptophan, for example, is no more attracted by codons for tryptophan than by any other codons. It is up to the cell's molecular interpreters, tRNA molecules, to match amino acids to the appropriate codons to form the new polypeptide. To perform this task, tRNA

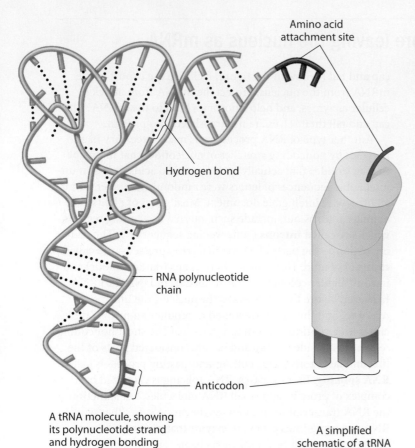

Amino acid
attachment site

Hydrogen bond

RNA polynucleotide
chain

Anticodon

A tRNA molecule, showing
its polynucleotide strand
and hydrogen bonding

A simplified
schematic of a tRNA

▲ **Figure 10.11A** The structure of tRNA

molecules must carry out two functions: (1) picking up the appropriate amino acids and (2) recognizing the appropriate codons in the mRNA. The unique structure of tRNA molecules enables them to perform both tasks.

Figure 10.11A shows two representations of a tRNA molecule. The structure on the left shows the backbone and bases, with hydrogen bonds between bases shown as dotted black lines. The structure on the right is a simplified schematic that emphasizes the most important parts of the structure. Notice from the structure on the left that a tRNA molecule is made of a single strand of RNA—one polynucleotide chain—consisting of about 80 nucleotides. By twisting and folding upon itself, tRNA forms several double-stranded regions in which short stretches of RNA base-pair with other stretches via hydrogen bonds. A single-stranded loop at one end of the folded molecule contains a special triplet of bases called an **anticodon**. The anticodon triplet is complementary to a codon triplet on mRNA. During translation, the anticodon on tRNA recognizes a particular codon on mRNA by using base-pairing rules. At the other end of the tRNA molecule is a site where one specific kind of amino acid can attach.

In the modules that follow, we represent tRNA with the simplified shape shown on the right in Figure 10.11A. This shape emphasizes the two parts of the molecule—the anticodon and the amino acid attachment site—that give tRNA its ability to match a particular nucleic acid word (a codon in mRNA) with its corresponding protein word (an amino acid). Although all tRNA molecules are similar, there is a slightly different variety of tRNA for each amino acid.

Each amino acid is joined to the correct tRNA by a specific enzyme. There is a family of 20 versions of these enzymes, one enzyme for each amino acid. Each enzyme specifically binds one type of amino acid to all tRNA molecules that code for that amino acid, using a molecule of ATP as energy to drive the reaction. The resulting amino acid–tRNA complex can then furnish its amino acid to a growing polypeptide chain, a process that we describe in Module 10.12.

The computer graphic in **Figure 10.11B** shows a tRNA molecule (green) and an ATP molecule (purple) bound to the enzyme molecule (blue). (To help you see the two distinct molecules, the tRNA molecule is shown with a stick representation, while the enzyme is shown as space-filling spheres.) In this figure, you can see the proportional sizes of these three molecules. The amino acid that would attach to the tRNA is not shown; it would be less than half the size of the ATP.

Once an amino acid is attached to its appropriate tRNA, it can be incorporated into a growing polypeptide chain. This is accomplished within ribosomes, the cellular structures directly responsible for the synthesis of protein. We examine ribosomes in the next module.

 What is an anticodon, and what is its function?

● It is the base triplet of a tRNA molecule that couples the tRNA to a complementary codon in the mRNA. This is a key step in translating mRNA to polypeptide.

Enzyme

tRNA

ATP

▲ **Figure 10.11B** A molecule of tRNA (green) binding to an enzyme molecule (blue)

10.12 Ribosomes build polypeptides

We have now looked at many of the components a cell needs to carry out translation: instructions in the form of mRNA molecules, tRNA to interpret the instructions, a supply of amino acids and enzymes (for attaching amino acids to tRNA), and ATP for energy. The final components are the **ribosomes**, structures in the cytoplasm that position mRNA and tRNA close together and catalyze the synthesis of polypeptides.

A ribosome consists of two subunits, each made up of proteins and a kind of RNA called **ribosomal RNA (rRNA)**. In **Figure 10.12A**, you can see the actual shapes and relative sizes of the ribosomal subunits. You can also see where mRNA, tRNA, and the growing polypeptide are located during translation.

The ribosomes of prokaryotes and eukaryotes are very similar in function, but those of eukaryotes are slightly larger and different in composition. The differences are medically significant. Certain antibiotic drugs can inactivate prokaryotic ribosomes while leaving eukaryotic ribosomes unaffected. These drugs, such as tetracycline and streptomycin, are used to combat bacterial infections.

The simplified drawings in **Figures 10.12B** and **10.12C** indicate how tRNA anticodons and mRNA codons fit together on ribosomes. As Figure 10.12B shows, each ribosome has a binding site for mRNA and the two main binding sites (P and A) for tRNA. Figure 10.12C shows tRNA molecules occupying these two sites. The subunits of the ribosome act like a vise, holding the tRNA and mRNA molecules close together, allowing the amino acids carried by the tRNA molecules to be

▲ Figure 10.12A
The true shape of a functioning ribosome

▲ Figure 10.12B
A ribosome with empty binding sites

▲ Figure 10.12C
A ribosome with occupied binding sites

connected to a polypeptide chain. In the next two modules, we examine the steps of translation in detail.

?   How does a ribosome facilitate protein synthesis?

● A ribosome holds mRNA and tRNAs together and connects amino acids from the tRNAs to the growing polypeptide chain.

10.13 An initiation codon marks the start of an mRNA message

Translation can be divided into the same three phases as transcription: initiation, elongation, and termination. The process of polypeptide initiation brings together the mRNA, a tRNA bearing the first amino acid, and the two subunits of a ribosome.

As shown in **Figure 10.13A**, an mRNA molecule is longer than the genetic message it carries. The light pink nucleotides at either end of the molecule are not part of the message, but help the mRNA bind to the ribosome. The initiation process establishes exactly where translation

▲ **Figure 10.13A** A molecule of eukaryotic mRNA

will begin, ensuring that the mRNA codons are translated into the correct sequence of amino acids.

Initiation occurs in two steps (**Figure 10.13B**). ❶ An mRNA molecule binds to a small ribosomal subunit. A special initiator tRNA binds to the specific codon, called the **start codon**, where translation is to begin on the mRNA molecule. The initiator tRNA carries the amino acid methionine (Met); its anticodon, UAC, binds to the start codon, AUG. ❷ Next, a large ribosomal subunit binds to the small

▲ **Figure 10.13B** The initiation of translation

one, creating a functional ribosome. The initiator tRNA fits into one of the two tRNA binding sites on the ribosome. This site, called the **P site**, will hold the growing polypeptide. The other tRNA binding site, called the **A site**, is vacant and ready for the next amino-acid-bearing tRNA.

? **What would happen if a genetic mutation changed a start codon to some other codon?**

● The mRNA transcribed from the mutated gene would be nonfunctional because ribosomes could not initiate translation correctly.

10.14 Elongation adds amino acids to the polypeptide chain until a stop codon terminates translation

Once initiation is complete, amino acids are added one by one to the first amino acid. Each addition occurs in a three-step elongation process **(Figure 10.14)**:

❶ **Codon recognition.** The anticodon of an incoming tRNA molecule, carrying its amino acid, pairs with the mRNA codon in the A site of the ribosome.

❷ **Peptide bond formation.** The polypeptide separates from the tRNA in the P site and attaches by a new peptide bond to the amino acid carried by the tRNA in the A site. The ribosome catalyzes formation of the peptide bond, adding one more amino acid to the growing polypeptide chain.

❸ **Translocation.** The P site tRNA now leaves the ribosome, and the ribosome translocates (moves) the remaining tRNA in the A site, with the growing polypeptide, to the P site. The codon and anticodon remain hydrogen-bonded, and the mRNA and tRNA move as a unit. This movement brings into the A site the next mRNA codon to be translated, and the process can start again with step 1.

Elongation continues until a **stop codon** reaches the ribosome's A site. Stop codons—UAA, UAG, and UGA—do not code for amino acids but instead act as signals to stop translation. This is the termination stage of translation. The completed polypeptide is freed from the last tRNA, and the ribosome splits back into its separate subunits. After translation, the mRNA, tRNA molecules, and ribosomal subunits can all be reused.

? **What happens as a tRNA passes through the A and P binding sites on the ribosome?**

● In the A site, its amino acid receives the growing polypeptide from the tRNA that precedes it. In the P site, it gives up the polypeptide to the tRNA that follows it.

▲ **Figure 10.14** Polypeptide elongation; the small green arrows indicate movement

❶ Codon recognition

❷ Peptide bond formation

New peptide bond

❸ Translocation

10.15 Review: The flow of genetic information in the cell is DNA → RNA → protein

Figure 10.15 summarizes the main stages in the flow of genetic information from DNA to RNA to protein. ❶ In transcription (DNA → RNA), the mRNA is synthesized or transcribed from a DNA template. In eukaryotic cells, transcription occurs in the nucleus, and the messenger RNA must travel from the nucleus to the cytoplasm. In prokaryotes, transcription occurs in the cytoplasm.

❷–❺ Translation (RNA → protein) can be divided into four steps, all of which occur in the cytoplasm in eukaryotic cells. When the polypeptide is complete at the end of the process, the two ribosomal subunits come apart, and the tRNA and mRNA are released (not shown in this figure). Translation is rapid; a single ribosome can make an average-sized polypeptide in less than a minute. Typically, an mRNA molecule is translated simultaneously by a number of ribosomes. Once the start codon emerges from the first ribosome, a second ribosome can attach to it; thus, several ribosomes may trail along on the same mRNA molecule.

As it is made, a polypeptide coils and folds, assuming a three-dimensional shape, its tertiary structure. Several polypeptides may come together, forming a protein with quaternary structure (see Module 3.10).

What is the overall significance of transcription and translation? These are the main processes whereby genes control the structures and activities of cells—or, more broadly, the way the genotype produces the phenotype. The chain of command originates with the information in a gene, a specific linear sequence of nucleotides in DNA. The gene serves as a template, dictating transcription of a complementary sequence of nucleotides in mRNA. In turn, mRNA dictates the linear sequence in which amino acids assemble to form a specific polypeptide. Finally, the proteins that form from the polypeptides determine the appearance and the capabilities of the cell and organism.

? Which of the following molecules or structures does not participate directly in translation: ribosomes, tRNA, mRNA, or DNA?

● DNA

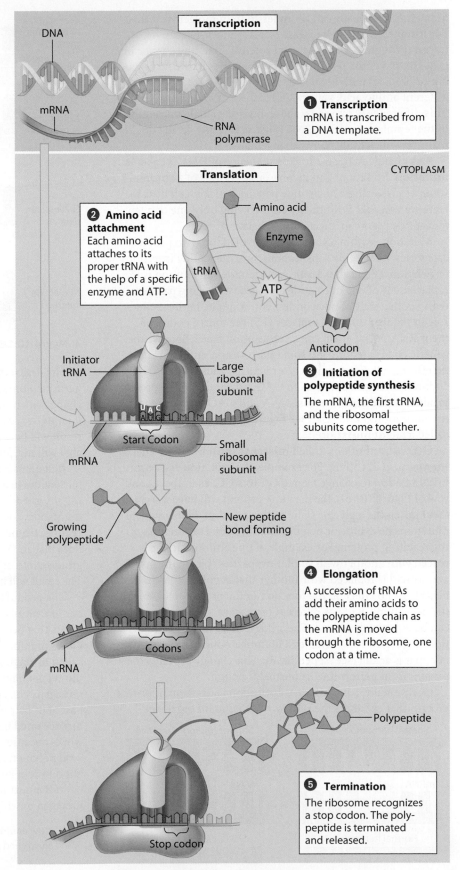

Transcription

DNA

mRNA

RNA polymerase

❶ **Transcription**
mRNA is transcribed from a DNA template.

CYTOPLASM

Translation

❷ **Amino acid attachment**
Each amino acid attaches to its proper tRNA with the help of a specific enzyme and ATP.

Amino acid

Enzyme

tRNA

ATP

Anticodon

Initiator tRNA

Large ribosomal subunit

U A C
AUG

Start Codon

Small ribosomal subunit

mRNA

❸ **Initiation of polypeptide synthesis**
The mRNA, the first tRNA, and the ribosomal subunits come together.

Growing polypeptide

New peptide bond forming

Codons

mRNA

❹ **Elongation**
A succession of tRNAs add their amino acids to the polypeptide chain as the mRNA is moved through the ribosome, one codon at a time.

Polypeptide

❺ **Termination**
The ribosome recognizes a stop codon. The polypeptide is terminated and released.

Stop codon

▲ Figure 10.15 A summary of transcription and translation

10.16 Mutations can change the meaning of genes

Many inherited traits can be understood in molecular terms. For instance, sickle-cell disease (see Module 9.12) can be traced through a difference in a protein to one tiny change in a gene. In one of the two kinds of polypeptides in the hemoglobin protein, an individual with sickle-cell disease has a single different amino acid: valine (Val) instead of glutamate (Glu). This difference is caused by the change of a single nucleotide in the template strand of DNA **(Figure 10.16A)**. In the double helix, one nucleotide *pair* is changed.

Any change in the nucleotide sequence of DNA is called a **mutation**. Mutations can involve large regions of a chromosome or just a single nucleotide pair, as in sickle-cell disease. Here we consider how mutations involving only one or a few nucleotide pairs can affect gene translation.

Mutations within a gene can be divided into two general categories: nucleotide substitutions, and nucleotide insertions or deletions **(Figure 10.16B)**. A nucleotide substitution is the replacement of one nucleotide and its base-pairing partner with another pair of nucleotides. For example, in the second row in Figure 10.16B, A replaces G in the fourth codon of the mRNA. What effect can a substitution have? Because the genetic code is redundant, some substitution mutations have no effect at all. For example, if a mutation causes an mRNA codon to change from GAA to GAG, no change in the protein product would result because GAA and GAG both code for the same amino acid (Glu; see Figure 10.8A). Such a change is called a **silent mutation**.

Other substitutions, called **missense mutations**, do change the amino acid coding. For example, if a mutation causes an mRNA codon to change from GGC to AGC, as in the second row of Figure 10.16B, the resulting protein will have a serine (Ser) instead of a glycine (Gly) at this position. Some missense mutations have little or no effect on the shape or function of the resulting protein. For example, if one amino acid is replaced with another with similar properties (i.e., if one polar amino acid is replaced with another that is polar), there may be little or no effect on the function of the protein. However, if the new amino acid has different properties, protein function can be completely altered. The sickle-cell hemoglobin mutation (Figure 10.16A) involves a nonpolar amino acid replacing one that is acidic (see Appendix B). This change prevents the protein from performing its normal function.

Occasionally, a nucleotide substitution leads to an improved protein that enhances the success of the mutant organism

▲ **Figure 10.16B** Types of mutations and their effects

and its descendants. Much more often, though, mutations are harmful. Some substitutions, called **nonsense mutations**, change an amino acid codon into a stop codon. For example, if an AGA (Arg) codon is mutated to a UGA (stop) codon, the result will be a prematurely terminated protein, which probably will not function properly.

Mutations involving the insertion or deletion of one or more nucleotides in a gene often have disastrous effects. Because mRNA is read as a series of nucleotide triplets (codons) during translation, adding or subtracting nucleotides may alter the **reading frame** (triplet grouping) of the message. All the nucleotides that are "downstream" of the insertion or deletion will be regrouped into different codons (Figure 10.16B, bottom two rows). The result will most likely be a nonfunctional polypeptide.

The production of mutations, called **mutagenesis**, can occur in a number of ways. Spontaneous mutations are due to errors that occur during DNA replication or recombination. Other mutations are caused by physical or chemical agents, called **mutagens**. High-energy radiation, such as X-rays or ultraviolet light, is a physical mutagen. One class of chemical mutagens consists of chemicals that are similar to normal DNA bases but pair incorrectly or are otherwise disruptive when incorporated into DNA. For example, the anti-AIDS drug AZT works because its structure is similar enough to thymine that viral polymerases incorporate it into newly synthesized DNA, but different enough that the drug blocks further replication.

In the next module, we will take a closer look at a specific mutagen to which we are all exposed: UV radiation.

? How could a single nucleotide substitution result in a shortened protein product?

▲ **Figure 10.16A** The molecular basis of sickle-cell disease

Normal hemoglobin DNA — C T T — mRNA — G A A — Normal hemoglobin — Glu

Mutant hemoglobin DNA — C A T — mRNA — G U A — Sickle-cell hemoglobin — Val

● A substitution that changed an amino acid codon into a stop codon would produce a prematurely terminated polypeptide.

10.17 Suntanning damages DNA leading to mutations

For some people, having the perfect tan is very important. Whether basking in a lawn chair or a tanning bed, people can quest for tanned skin year-round. One in four Canadian teenagers (aged 13 to 19) surveyed in 2008 had used tanning beds. However, as a leading cause of skin cancer (the most common type of cancer), tanning is not healthy. The World Health Organization has classified the tanning bed as a known carcinogen—an agent that causes cancer. Using tanning beds before the age of 35 increases the risk of developing the most serious form of skin cancer, melanoma, by 75%. As we discussed in Module 9.14, the skin produces melanin to absorb ultraviolet (UV) radiation. However, the protection is not perfect, and UV radiation can still damage the skin's DNA even if the skin is already tanned.

How exactly does UV radiation cause skin cancer? Before we can answer this question, we must take a look at UV radiation. There are actually different types of UV radiation. In order of decreasing wavelengths, the spectrum of UV radiation is divided into UVA, UVB, and UVC. With the shortest wavelengths, UVC has the most energy; however, this energy is completely absorbed by Earth's atmosphere and does not reach the surface. UVA and UVB can penetrate the atmosphere and do reach the planet's surface. The damaging effects of UVB have been known for decades. However, it was only recently that scientists discovered that UVA can also cause skin cancer by damaging DNA. Dr. Régen Drouin at the University of Sherbrooke in Quebec is investigating the relative impacts of UVA and UVB radiation on the development of skin cancer.

In much the same way that chlorophyll absorbs the energy in a photon of light, DNA absorbs the energy in photons of UV radiation. When a region of DNA with two adjacent pyrimidine bases—for example, two thymine bases—absorbs a photon of UVA or UVB, covalent bonds are formed between them.

The resulting **thymine dimer** physically distorts the DNA double helix, as shown in **Figure 10.17A**. The thymines of the dimer are also no longer able to form hydrogen bonds with the complementary DNA strand.

But all is not lost for the cell. These DNA distortions are readily detected by DNA repair systems within the nucleus. In a process called nucleotide excision repair (NER), cells can repair thymine dimers caused by UV radiation (**Figure 10.17B**).

▲ **Figure 10.17B** Nucleotide excision repair of thymine dimers

▲ **Figure 10.17A** Thymine dimer formation

In a complex process involving 30 different enzymes and proteins, ❶ NER detects distortions in the DNA double helix caused by the thymine dimer. ❷ After recognition, enzymes cut the affected DNA strand on either side of the damage. ❸ A small segment 25 to 30 nucleotides long is removed from the strand. ❹ DNA polymerases replace the missing nucleotides. ❺ NER finishes when DNA ligase joins the pieces into a continuous strand.

If there are few thymine dimers, NER can usually repair them before any deleterious effects occur. If, however, numerous thymine dimers have occurred because of prolonged exposure to UV radiation, NER may not be able to repair them all. Unrepaired thymine dimers can lead to mutations in dividing cells. DNA polymerase cannot recognize the thymines within the dimer because they cannot form hydrogen bonds. As a result, during DNA replication, random nucleotides are added, which potentially leads to one or two nucleotide substitutions. Moreover, because DNA polymerase might not recognize that the dimer consists of two nucleotides, it might insert a single random nucleotide. In this situation, in addition to a potential nucleotide substitution, a nucleotide deletion occurs. Skin cells can become cancerous if these mutations occur in specific genes (see Module 11.15).

Because UV radiation is a known carcinogen, many people are concerned about the use of tanning beds. The Canadian Paediatric Society, along with other health organizations and some Canadian politicians, are trying to implement national legislation that prohibits minors from using tanning beds. Several jurisdictions in Canada have already regulated the usage of tanning beds by teens and more are in the process of doing so. For most Canadians, the decision to use tanning beds is personal. Being well-informed about the risks will enable you to make the right choice.

 How do DNA repair enzymes detect thymine dimers?

● Thymine dimers create a distortion in the DNA double helix that can be detected by repair enzymes.

RUMOUR HAS IT | ## 10.18 Are all mutations detrimental to organisms?

There is a common misconception that all mutations are detrimental. Popular culture often portrays mutation as a horrible event, which must be avoided at all costs. Are mutations always detrimental? What determines the effects of a given mutation on the organism?

Although mutations are often harmful, they can also be extremely useful, both in nature and in the laboratory. It is because of mutations that there is such a rich diversity of genes in the living world, a diversity that makes evolution by natural selection possible. In Unit III, you will learn more about evolution and natural selection. Neither could have occurred without mutation. Individuals with detrimental mutations may be selected against, causing them to produce fewer offspring. Those with beneficial mutations may be selected for and produce more young. On the one hand, a mutation that renders an essential enzyme nonfunctional would likely be selected against. Cells that cannot replicate their DNA will be unable to divide. On the other hand, a mutation that allows an organism to utilize a new nutrient may provide a distinct advantage.

The effect of many mutations is highly situational and may be beneficial in one circumstance but harmful in another. Likewise, evolutionary pressures are highly environment-specific: What is advantageous in one environment may be detrimental in another. Let's consider the single mutation that causes sickle-cell disease, which affects red blood cells (see Module 9.12). Sickle-cell disease is the most common inherited disorder among people of African descent, affecting 1 in 400 African-Canadians. About 1 in 12 African-Canadians is a carrier (an unaffected heterozygote). Among Canadians of other ancestry, the sickle-cell allele is extremely rare.

Because the allele causes such harm in homozygotes, 1 in 12 is an unusually high frequency of carriers. We might expect that the frequency of the sickle-cell allele in the population would be much lower because many homozygotes die before passing their genes to the next generation. The high frequency appears to be a vestige of the roots of African-Canadians. Sickle-cell disease is most common in tropical Africa, where the deadly disease malaria is also prevalent. The parasite that causes malaria spends part of its life cycle inside red blood cells. When it enters those of a person with the sickle-cell allele, it triggers sickling. The body destroys most of the sickled cells, and the parasite does not grow well in those that remain. Consequently, sickle-cell carriers are resistant to malaria. In many parts of Africa, carriers live longer and have more offspring than noncarriers who are exposed to malaria. In this way, malaria has kept the frequency of the sickle-cell allele relatively high in much of the African continent. To put it in evolutionary terms, as long as malaria is a danger, individuals with the sickle-cell allele have a selective advantage.

In the laboratory, mutations are essential tools for geneticists. Whether naturally occurring (as in Gregor Mendel's peas; see Module 9.1) or created in the laboratory (Thomas Morgan used X-rays to make the most of his fruit fly mutants; see Module 9.18), mutations create the different alleles needed for genetic research. Biologists can learn a great deal about the structure and function of organisms by studying the effects of mutations on structural proteins and enzymes.

Some mutations may have dire consequences. For example, changing the allele for an essential enzyme may halt essential processes. However, other mutations prove to be beneficial. Any change that offers a selective advantage in a given environment would be beneficial. Clearly the misconception that all mutations are harmful is biased.

 What determines if a mutation will be detrimental or beneficial?

● The evolutionary pressures of the environment

10.19 Mutations are at the centre of the evolution of antibiotic resistance in bacteria

Antibiotics are drugs that kill infectious microorganisms. Many antibiotics are naturally occurring chemicals derived from soil-dwelling fungi or bacteria. For these microbes, antibiotic production is an adaptation that helps them compete with bacteria for space and nutrients. Penicillin, originally isolated from a fungus, has been widely prescribed since the 1940s. A revolution in human health followed its introduction, rendering many previously fatal diseases easily curable. During the 1950s, some doctors even predicted the end of human infectious diseases.

Why hasn't that optimistic prediction come true? It did not take into account the force of evolution. Improper treatment with antibiotics, including penicillin, has selected for resistant bacteria. Structurally, penicillin belongs to a class of drugs called the **β-lactam antibiotics**. It and its relative, methicillin, contain a four-membered β-lactam ring in their structure **(Figure 10.19A)**. Most β-lactam antibiotics operate by inhibiting the synthesis of peptidoglycan—the structural component of bacterial cell walls. In the presence of the antibiotic, bacterial cells are unable to divide by binary fission because they cannot synthesize new cell wall material for the daughter cells (see Module 8.2).

Bacteria have evolved resistance to these antibiotics with β-lactamase, an enzyme that inhibits the function of β-lactam antibiotics by enzymatically cleaving the β-lactam ring. Modern use of β-lactam antibiotics has driven the continued evolution of these mechanisms within bacteria. In the presence of penicillin, the β-lactamase gene is particularly advantageous. During the treatment of an infection with penicillin, bacteria without β-lactamase are prevented from synthesizing cell wall material and are quickly killed during binary fission. However, bacteria with β-lactamase can protect themselves from the actions of the antibiotic. After the treatment, only resistant bacteria remain, and they may regrow and establish a new infection—one that cannot be treated with penicillin. Through the use and misuse of penicillin, more and more bacteria have β-lactamase and are now resistant. Doctors may overprescribe antibiotics—for example, to patients with viral infections, which do not respond to antibiotic treatment—and patients may misuse prescribed antibiotics by prematurely ceasing to take the medication because they feel better. By not taking the medication for the prescribed amount of time, the patient enables mutant bacteria that would otherwise have been killed

▲ **Figure 10.19B** An MRSA skin infection

more slowly by the drug to survive. Subsequent mutations in such bacteria may lead to full-blown antibiotic resistance. For example, from 1983 to 2003, Canadian hospitals saw the prevalence of penicillin-resistant *Streptococcus pneumoniae* infections (one cause of pneumonia) increase from 2% to more than 20%.

Difficulty in treating infections is a serious public health concern. Penicillin is virtually useless today in its original form and has been chemically altered to form new drugs, including methicillin. At one time, the altered structure of methicillin could not be cleaved by β-lactamase, making it an effective treatment for penicillin-resistant bacteria. Unfortunately, the β-lactamase gene has since mutated; now the changed enzyme can bind to and cleave the β-lactam ring of methicillin. Just as before, the frequency of this new mutation has spread, and methicillin is now much less useful. A formidable superbug known as MRSA (methicillin-resistant *Staphylococcus aureus)* can cause "flesh-eating disease" **(Figure 10.19B)** and potentially fatal systemic (whole-body) infections. Incidents of MRSA infections in both hospital and community settings have increased dramatically in the past decade. The medical community and pharmaceutical companies are engaged in an ongoing race against the powerful force of bacterial evolution.

? Explain why the following statement is incorrect: "**Antibiotics have created resistant bacteria.**"

● The use of antibiotics has increased the frequency of resistance genes that were already naturally present in bacterial populations.

Penicillin

Inactive penicillin

ß-Lactam ring

▲ **Figure 10.19A** The function of β-lactamase

MasteringBiology® **For Practice Quizzes, BioFlix, MP3 Tutors, and Activities, go to masteringbiology.com.**

Reviewing the Concepts

The Structure of the Genetic Material (10.1–10.3)

10.1 Experiments showed that DNA is the genetic material. One key experiment demonstrated that certain phages (bacterial viruses) reprogram host cells to produce more phages by injecting their DNA.

10.2 DNA and RNA are polymers of nucleotides.

	DNA	RNA
Nitrogenous bases	C G A **T**	C G A **U**
Sugar	Deoxy-ribose	Ribose

10.3 DNA is a double-stranded helix. Watson and Crick worked out the three-dimensional structure of DNA: two polynucleotide strands wrapped around each other in a double helix. Hydrogen bonds between bases hold the strands together. Each base pairs with a complementary partner: A with T and G with C.

DNA Replication (10.4–10.5)

10.4 DNA replication depends on specific base pairing. DNA replication starts with the separation of DNA strands. Enzymes then use each strand as a template to assemble new nucleotides into a complementary strand.

10.5 DNA replication proceeds in two directions at many sites simultaneously. Using the enzyme DNA polymerase, the cell synthesizes one daughter strand as a continuous piece. The other strand is synthesized as a series of short pieces, which are then connected by the enzyme DNA ligase.

The Flow of Genetic Information from DNA to RNA to Protein (10.6–10.19)

10.6 The DNA genotype is expressed as proteins, which provide the molecular basis for phenotypic traits. The DNA of a gene—a linear sequence of many nucleotides—is transcribed into RNA, which is translated into a polypeptide.

10.7 Genetic information written in codons is translated into amino acid sequences. Codons are base triplets, which specify the amino acid sequence.

10.8 The genetic code dictates how codons are translated into amino acids. Nearly all organisms use an identical genetic code to convert the codons of a gene to the amino acid sequence of a polypeptide.

10.9 Transcription produces genetic messages in the form of RNA. In the nucleus, the DNA helix unzips, and RNA nucleotides line up and hydrogen-bond along one strand of the DNA, following the base-pairing rules.

10.10 Eukaryotic RNA is processed before leaving the nucleus as mRNA. Noncoding segments of RNA called introns are spliced out, and a cap and tail are added to the ends of the mRNA.

10.11 Transfer RNA molecules serve as interpreters during translation. Translation takes place in the cytoplasm. A ribosome attaches to the mRNA and translates its message into a specific polypeptide, aided by transfer RNAs (tRNAs). Each tRNA is a folded molecule bearing a base triplet called an anticodon on one end; a specific amino acid is added to the other end.

10.12 Ribosomes build polypeptides. Made of rRNA and proteins, ribosomes have binding sites for tRNAs and mRNA.

10.13 An initiation codon marks the start of an mRNA message. An initiator tRNA carrying the amino acid methionine is the first to bind to the mRNA transcript.

10.14 Elongation adds amino acids to the polypeptide chain until a stop codon terminates translation. As the mRNA moves one codon at a time relative to the ribosome, a tRNA with a complementary anticodon pairs with each codon, adding its amino acid to the growing polypeptide chain.

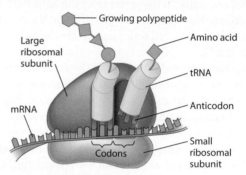

10.15 Review: The flow of genetic information in the cell is DNA → RNA → protein. The sequence of codons in DNA, via the sequence of codons in mRNA, spells out the primary structure of a polypeptide.

10.16 Mutations can change the meaning of genes. Mutations are changes in the DNA nucleotide sequence, caused by errors in DNA replication or recombination, or by mutagens. Substituting, inserting, or deleting nucleotides alters a gene, with varying effects on the organism.

10.17 Suntanning damages DNA leading to mutations. Ultraviolet radiation creates thymine dimers on DNA strands, which may be repaired incorrectly, leading to mutations.

10.18 Are all mutations detrimental to organisms? Although some mutations are detrimental, others may be beneficial. Environmental pressures are a major determinant for whether a mutation will be an advantage or a disadvantage.

10.19 Mutations are at the centre of the evolution of antibiotic resistance in bacteria. Penicillin-resistant bacteria use an enzyme, β-lactamase, to destroy the antibiotic. Mutations in the β-lactamase gene have given bacteria resistance to new forms of these antibiotics, posing a serious health concern.

Connecting the Concepts

1. Check your understanding of the flow of genetic information through a cell by filling in the blanks.

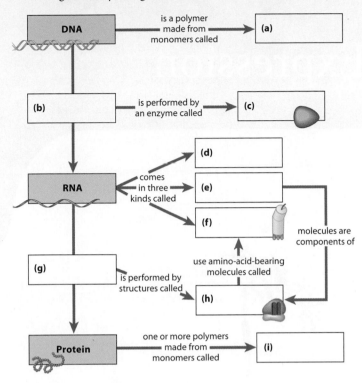

Testing Your Knowledge

Multiple Choice

2. Transcription can produce all but which of the following molecules?
   a. mRNA
   b. tRNA
   c. rRNA
   d. Protein
   e. All of the above are produced by transcription.

3. Tetracycline is a broad-spectrum antibiotic that binds to the small ribosomal subunit, blocking the binding of tRNA. The direct effect would be
   a. prevention of translation.
   b. prevention of the formation of nucleic acids.
   c. interruption of phospholipid synthesis.
   d. prevention of transcription.
   e. interruption of DNA replication.

4. A geneticist found that a particular mutation had no effect on the polypeptide encoded by a gene. This mutation probably involved
   a. deletion of one nucleotide.
   b. alteration of the start codon.
   c. insertion of one nucleotide.
   d. deletion of the entire gene.
   e. substitution of one nucleotide.

5. Which of the following correctly ranks the structures in order of size, from largest to smallest?
   a. gene, chromosome, nucleotide, codon
   b. chromosome, gene, codon, nucleotide
   c. nucleotide, chromosome, gene, codon
   d. chromosome, nucleotide, gene, codon
   e. gene, chromosome, codon, nucleotide

6. The nucleotide sequence of a DNA codon is GTA. A messenger RNA molecule with a complementary codon is transcribed from the DNA. In the process of protein synthesis, a transfer RNA pairs with the mRNA codon. What is the nucleotide sequence of the tRNA anticodon?
   a. CAT
   b. CUT
   c. GUA
   d. CAU
   e. GT

Describing, Comparing, and Explaining

7. Describe the process of DNA replication: the ingredients needed, the steps in the process, and the final product.

8. Describe the process by which the information in a eukaryotic gene is transcribed and translated into a protein. Correctly use these words in your description: tRNA, amino acid, start codon, transcription, RNA splicing, exons, introns, mRNA, gene, codon, RNA polymerase, ribosome, translation, anticodon, peptide bond, stop codon.

Applying the Concepts

9. A cell containing a single chromosome is placed in a medium containing radioactive phosphate so that any new DNA strands formed by DNA replication will be radioactive. The cell replicates its DNA and divides. Then the daughter cells (still in the radioactive medium) replicate their DNA and divide, and a total of four cells are present. Sketch the DNA molecules in all four cells, showing a normal (nonradioactive) DNA strand as a solid line and a radioactive DNA strand as a dashed line.

10. The base sequence of the gene coding for a short polypeptide is CTACGCTAGGCGATTGACT. What would be the base sequence of the mRNA transcribed from this gene? Using the genetic code in Figure 10.8A, give the amino acid sequence of the polypeptide translated from this mRNA. (*Hint:* What is the start codon?)

11. Researchers on the Human Genome Project have determined the nucleotide sequences of human genes and in many cases identified the proteins encoded by the genes. Knowledge of the nucleotide sequences of genes might be used to develop life-saving medicines or treatments for genetic defects. In the United States, both government agencies and biotechnology companies have applied for patents on their discoveries of genes. In Canada, the courts have ruled that a naturally occurring gene cannot be patented. Do you think individuals and companies should be able to patent genes and gene products? Before answering, consider the following: What are the purposes of a patent? How might the discoverer of a gene benefit from a patent? How might the public benefit? What might be some positive and negative results of patenting genes?

Answers to all questions can be found in Appendix E.

Gene Expression

Control of Gene Expression

(11.1–11.11)

Cells can turn genes on and off through a variety of mechanisms.

Cloning of Plants and Animals

(11.12–11.14)

Cloning demonstrates that many body cells retain their full genetic potential.

The Genetic Basis of Cancer

(11.15–11.18)

Changes in genes that control gene expression can lead to out-of-control cell growth.

Cloning to the Rescue?

Both the animals shown above share two unusual features. First, they are both members of endangered species. Second, they are both clones. Here we are using the term *clone* to refer to an individual created by asexual reproduction (that is, reproduction that does not involve fusion of sperm and egg), which is thus genetically identical to a single parent. First demonstrated in the 1950s with frogs, animal cloning became much more commonplace after 1997, when Scottish researcher Ian Wilmut and his colleagues announced the first successful cloning of a mammal: The celebrated sheep Dolly was cloned using a mammary cell from an adult ewe. In the years since Dolly's landmark birth, researchers have cloned a variety of other mammals, including mules, horses, cats, cows, goats, pigs, monkeys, mice, and, most recently, dogs.

Some researchers have concentrated their efforts on cloning members of endangered species. Among the rare animals that have been cloned are a gaur (an Asian ox), a mouflon (a small European sheep), and an African wildcat (*Felis silvestris*). In 2006, South Korean researchers announced the successful cloning of two grey wolves (*Canis lupus*), a species that nearly became extinct in North America in the early 20th century.

One remarkable case was the 2003 cloning of a banteng (a Javanese bovine whose numbers have dwindled to just a few in the wild). Biologists used frozen skin cells from a zoo-raised banteng that had died 23 years previously. They inserted nuclei from the donor into denucleated eggs from ordinary cows. The resulting embryos were implanted into surrogate Angus cows, leading to the birth of a healthy baby banteng (shown here). This case proves the possibility of producing new animals even when a female of the donor species is unavailable. Scientists may someday be able to use similar cross-species methods to clone an animal from a recently extinct species.

The use of cloning to slow or reverse extinction and repopulate endangered species holds tremendous promise. However, conservationists object that cloning may trivialize the tragedy of extinction and detract from efforts to preserve natural habitats. They correctly point out that cloning, like other forms of asexual reproduction, does not increase genetic diversity and is therefore not as beneficial to endangered species as natural reproduction.

Researchers are also concerned that cloned animals are less healthy than those originating from a fertilized egg. In 2003, at age 6, Dolly was euthanized after suffering complications from a lung disease normally seen only in much older sheep. Dolly's premature death, as well as her arthritic condition, led to speculation that her cells were somehow "older" than those of normal sheep. Many other cloned animals exhibit defects. Cloned mice, for instance, are prone to obesity, pneumonia, liver failure, and premature death. Scientists believe that even cloned animals that appear normal are likely to have subtle defects. Recent work traces these problems to physical changes within the chromosomes of the cloned organism that derail the normal regulation of genes. Aging and the environment can play important roles in gene regulation (through mutation, epigenetics, and telomere shortening) and these modifications can be transgenerational.

The ability to clone an animal by using a transplanted nucleus demonstrates an important point: the nuclei of adult body cells contain a complete genome capable of directing the production of all the cell types in an organism. The development of a multicellular organism with many different kinds of cells depends on the turning on and off of genes—the control of gene expression. The health problems associated with cloned animals underscore the fact that proper gene regulation is important to the well-being of all organisms.

Whether an organism is unicellular or multicellular, its cells may alter their patterns of gene expression in response to the organism's needs. We begin this chapter with examples of how and where this may occur. Next we look at the methods and applications of plant and animal cloning. Finally, we discuss cancer, a disease that can be caused by changes in gene expression.

Control of Gene Expression

11.1 Proteins interacting with DNA turn prokaryotic genes on or off in response to environmental changes

Picture an *Escherichia coli* (*E. coli*) bacterium living in your intestine (**Figure 11.1A**). Its environment changes continuously, depending on your dietary whims. For example, if you eat a sweet roll for breakfast, the bacterium will be bathed in sugars and broken-down fats. Later, if you have a salad for lunch, the *E. coli*'s environment will change drastically. How can a bacterium cope with such a constantly shifting flow of resources?

The answer is that **gene regulation**—the turning on and off of genes—can help organisms respond to environmental changes. What does it mean to turn a gene on or off? As we discussed in Chapter 10, genes determine the nucleotide sequences of specific mRNA molecules, and mRNA in turn determines the sequences of amino acids in protein molecules (DNA → RNA → protein). Thus, a gene that is turned on is being transcribed into RNA, and that message is being translated into specific protein molecules. The overall process by which genetic information flows from genes to proteins—that is, from genotype to phenotype—is called **gene expression**. The control of gene expression makes it possible for cells to produce specific kinds of proteins when and where they are needed.

It's no coincidence that we used *E. coli* as our example. Our earliest understanding of gene control came from studies of this bacterium by French biologists François Jacob and Jacques Monod. *E. coli* has a remarkable ability to change its metabolic activities in response to changes in its environment. For example, *E. coli* produces enzymes needed to metabolize a specific nutrient only when that nutrient is available. Bacterial cells that can conserve resources and energy have an advantage over cells that are unable to do so. Thus, natural selection has favoured bacteria that express only the genes whose products are needed by the cell. Let's look at how the regulation of gene transcription helps *E. coli* efficiently use available resources.

Colourized SEM 5000×

▲ **Figure 11.1A** *E. coli* bacteria

The *lac* Operon   Imagine the bacterium in your intestine soon after you drink a glass of milk. One of the main nutrients in milk is the disaccharide sugar lactose. When lactose is plentiful in the intestine, *E. coli* makes the enzymes necessary to absorb the sugar and use it as an energy source. Conversely, when lactose is not plentiful, *E. coli* does not waste its energy producing these enzymes.

Recall that enzymes are proteins; their production is an outcome of gene expression. *E. coli* can make lactose-utilization enzymes because it has genes that code for these enzymes. **Figure 11.1B** presents a model (first proposed in 1961 by Jacob and Monod) to explain how an *E. coli* cell can turn genes coding for lactose-utilization enzymes off or on, depending on whether lactose is available.

E. coli uses three enzymes to take up and start metabolizing lactose, and the genes coding for these three enzymes are regulated as a single unit. The DNA at the top of Figure 11.1B represents a small segment of the bacterium's chromosome. Notice that the three genes that code for the lactose-utilization enzymes (light blue) are next to each other in the DNA.

Adjacent to the group of lactose enzyme genes are two control sequences, short sections of DNA that help to control the enzyme genes. One control sequence is a **promoter**, a site where the transcription enzyme, RNA polymerase, attaches and initiates transcription—in this case, transcription of all three lactose enzyme genes (as depicted in the bottom panel of Figure 11.1B). Between the promoter and the enzyme genes, a DNA control sequence called an **operator** acts as a switch. The operator determines whether RNA polymerase can attach to the promoter and start transcribing the genes.

Such a cluster of genes with related functions, along with the control sequences, is called an **operon**; with rare exceptions, operons exist only in prokaryotes. The key advantage to the grouping of related genes into operons is that a single "on-off switch" can control the whole cluster. The operon discussed here is called the *lac* operon, short for lactose operon. When an *E. coli* bacterium encounters lactose, all the enzymes needed for its metabolism are made at once because the operon's genes are all controlled by a single switch, the operator. But what determines whether the operator switch is on or off?

The top panel of Figure 11.1B shows the *lac* operon in "off" mode, its status when there is no lactose in the cell's environment. Transcription is turned off by a protein called a **repressor** (⬛), a protein that functions by binding to the operator (⬛⬛⬛) and physically blocking the attachment of RNA polymerase (⬛) to the promoter (⬛). On the left side of the figure, you can see where the repressor comes from. A gene called a **regulatory gene** (dark blue), located outside the operon, codes for the repressor. The regulatory gene is expressed continually, so the cell always has a small supply of repressor molecules.

Operon turned off (lactose is absent):

Operon turned on (lactose inactivates the repressor):

▲ **Figure 11.1B** The *lac* operon

How can an operon be turned on if its repressor is always present? As the bottom panel of Figure 11.1B indicates, lactose (⬤) interferes with the attachment of the *lac* repressor to the operator by binding to the repressor and changing its shape. With its new shape (⬤), the repressor cannot bind to the operator, and the operator switch remains on. RNA polymerase can now bind to the promoter (since it is no longer being blocked) and from there transcribes the genes of the operon. The resulting mRNA carries coding sequences for all three enzymes needed for lactose metabolism. The cell can translate the message in this single mRNA into three separate polypeptides because the mRNA has multiple codons signalling the start and stop of translation.

The *lac* operon is so efficient that the addition of lactose to a bacterium's environment results in a thousandfold increase in lactose utilization enzymes in just 15 minutes. The newly produced mRNA and protein molecules will remain intact for only a short time before cellular enzymes break them down. When the synthesis of mRNA and protein stops because lactose is no longer present, the molecules quickly disappear.

Other Kinds of Operons The *lac* operon is only one type of operon in bacteria. Other types also have a promoter, an operator, and several adjacent genes, but they differ in the way the operator switch is controlled. **Figure 11.1C** shows two types of repressor-controlled operons. The *lac* operon's repressor is active when alone and inactive when bound to lactose. A second type of operon, represented here by the *trp* operon, is

controlled by a repressor that is *inactive* alone. To be active, this type of repressor must combine with a specific small molecule. In our example, the small molecule is tryptophan (Trp), an amino acid essential for protein synthesis. *E. coli* can make tryptophan from scratch, using enzymes encoded in the *trp* operon. But it will stop making tryptophan and simply absorb it in prefabricated form from the surroundings whenever possible. When *E. coli* is swimming in tryptophan in the intestines (as occurs when you eat foods such as milk and poultry), the tryptophan binds to the repressor of the *trp* operon. This activates the *trp* repressor, enabling it to switch off the operon. Thus, this type of operon allows bacteria to stop making certain essential molecules when the molecules are already present in the environment, saving materials and energy for the cells.

Another type of operon control involves **activators**, proteins that turn operons *on* by binding to DNA. These proteins act by making it easier for RNA polymerase to bind to the promoter, rather than by blocking RNA polymerase, as repressors do. Activators help to control a wide variety of operons.

Armed with a variety of operons regulated by repressors and activators, *E. coli* and other prokaryotes can thrive in frequently changing environments. Next we examine how more complex eukaryotes regulate their genes.

? A certain mutation in *E. coli* impairs the ability of the *lac* repressor to bind to the *lac* operator. How would this affect the cell?

The cell would wastefully produce the enzymes for lactose metabolism continuously, even when lactose is not present.

lac operon	*trp* operon
Promoter Operator Gene DNA Active repressor	 Active repressor · Tryptophan
Inactive repressor · Lactose	Inactive repressor

▲ **Figure 11.1C** Two types of repressor-controlled operons

11.2 Chromosome structure and chemical modifications can affect gene expression

The cells of all organisms, whether prokaryotes or eukaryotes, must be able to turn genes on and off in response to signals from their external and internal environments. All multicellular eukaryotes also require an additional level of gene control: During the repeated cell divisions that lead from a zygote to an adult in a multicellular organism, individual cells must undergo **differentiation**—that is, they must become specialized in structure and function, with each type of cell fulfilling a distinct role. Your body, for example, contains hundreds of different types of cells. What makes a kidney cell different from, say, a bone cell?

To perform its specialized role, each cell type must maintain a specific program of gene expression in which some genes are expressed and others are not. Almost all the cells in an organism contain an identical genome, yet the subset of genes expressed in each cell type is unique, reflecting its specific function. Each adult human cell expresses only a small fraction of its total genes at any given time. And even one particular cell type can change its pattern of gene expression over time in response to developmental signals or other changes in the environment.

The differences between cell types, therefore, are due not to different genes being present, but to selective gene expression. In this module, we begin our exploration of gene regulation in eukaryotes by looking at the nuclear chromosomes, where almost all of a cell's genes are located.

DNA Packing   The DNA in just a single human chromosome would, if stretched out, average 4 cm in length, thousands of times greater than the diameter of the nucleus. All of this DNA can fit within the nucleus because of an elaborate, multilevel system of packing—coiling and folding—of the DNA in each chromosome. A crucial aspect of DNA packing is the association of the DNA with small proteins called **histones**. In fact, histone proteins account for about half the mass of eukaryotic chromosomes. (Prokaryotes have analogous proteins but lack the degree of DNA packing seen in eukaryotes.)

Figure 11.2A shows a model for the main levels of DNA packing. At the left, notice that the unpacked double-helical molecule of DNA has a diameter of 2 nm. At the first level of packing, histones attach to the DNA double helix. In the electron micrograph near the top left of the figure, notice how the DNA-histone complex has the appearance of beads on a string. Each "bead," called a **nucleosome**, consists of DNA wound around a protein core of eight histone molecules. Short stretches of DNA, called linkers, are the "strings" that join consecutive "beads" of nucleosomes.

At the next level of packing, the beaded string is wrapped into a tight helical fibre. This fibre coils further into a thick supercoil with a diameter of about 300 nm. Looping and folding can further compact the DNA, as you can see in the metaphase chromosome at the right of the figure. Viewed as a whole, Figure 11.2A gives a sense of how successive levels of coiling and folding enable a huge amount of DNA to fit into a cell nucleus.

DNA packing can block gene expression by preventing RNA polymerase and other transcription proteins from contacting the DNA. Cells seem to use higher levels of packing for long-term inactivation of genes. Highly compacted chromatin, which is found not only in mitotic

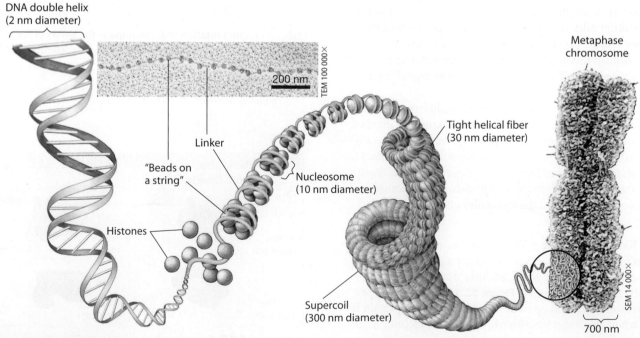

DNA double helix
(2 nm diameter)

200 nm

TEM 100 000×

Linker

"Beads on a string"

Histones

Nucleosome
(10 nm diameter)

Supercoil
(300 nm diameter)

Tight helical fiber
(30 nm diameter)

Metaphase chromosome

SEM 14 000×

700 nm

▲ **Figure 11.2A** DNA packing in a eukaryotic chromosome

chromosomes—such as the duplicated chromosomes found in Figure 11.2A—but also in varying regions of interphase chromosomes, is generally not expressed at all.

Chemical Modifications and Epigenetic Inheritance
In addition to being able to change their level of packing, the cells of many eukaryotic organisms have the capability to establish and maintain chemical modifications to their chromosomes in ways that help to regulate gene expression. For example, the addition of chemical groups to some of the amino acids in histone proteins, or their removal, can cause the proteins to bind DNA more tightly or loosely, altering the ability of transcription machinery to reach those genes.

DNA itself can also be the target of chemical modification. In one such type of modification, certain enzymes add a methyl group ($-CH_3$) to DNA bases, usually cytosine, without changing the actual sequence of the bases. Individual genes are usually more heavily methylated in cells in which they are not expressed, and removal of the extra methyl groups can turn on some of these genes. Thus, DNA methylation appears to play a role in turning genes off. At least in some species, DNA methylation seems to be essential for the long-term inactivation of genes. Such modifications are a normal and necessary mechanism for the regulation of gene expression, and improper methylation can lead to problems for the organism. For example, insufficient DNA methylation can lead to abnormal embryonic development in many species.

Once methylated, genes usually stay that way through successive cell divisions in a given individual. At DNA sites where one strand is already methylated, enzymes methylate the corresponding daughter strand after each round of DNA replication. Methylation patterns are therefore passed on, and cells forming specialized tissues keep a chemical record of what occurred during embryonic development. In this way, modifications to the DNA and histones can be passed along to future generations of cells—that is, they can be inherited. Inheritance of traits transmitted by mechanisms not directly involving the nucleotide sequence is called **epigenetic inheritance**. Whereas mutations in the DNA are permanent changes, modifications to the chromatin, which do not affect the sequence of DNA itself, can be reversed by processes that are not yet fully understood. The importance of epigenetics in gene expression will

be discussed in the next module when we look at how identical twins really are.

X Inactivation
Female mammals, including humans, inherit two X chromosomes, whereas males inherit only one. So why don't females make twice as much of the proteins encoded by genes on the X chromosome compared to the amounts in males? It turns out that in female mammals, one X chromosome in each somatic (body) cell is chemically modified and highly compacted, rendering it almost entirely inactive. Inactivation of an X chromosome involves modification of the DNA (by, for example, methylation) and the histone proteins that help to compact it. A specific gene on the X chromosomes ensures that one and only one of them will be inactivated. This **X chromosome inactivation** is initiated early in embryonic development, when one of the two X chromosomes in each cell is inactivated at random. As a result, the cells of females and males have the same effective dose (one copy) of these genes. The inactive X in each cell of a female condenses into a compact object called a **Barr body**.

Which X chromosome is inactivated is a matter of chance in each embryonic cell, but once an X chromosome is inactivated, all descendant cells have the same copy turned off—an example of epigenetic inheritance. Consequently, females consist of a mosaic of two types of cells: those with the active X derived from the father and those with the active X derived from the mother. If a female is heterozygous for a gene on the X chromosome (a sex-linked gene; see Module 9.22), about half her cells will express one allele, while the others will express the alternative allele.

A striking example of this mosaic phenomenon is the tortoiseshell cat, which has orange and black patches of fur (**Figure 11.2B**). The relevant fur-colour gene is on the X chromosome, and the tortoiseshell phenotype requires the presence of two different alleles, one for orange fur and one for black fur. Normally, only females can have both alleles because only they have two X chromosomes. If a female is heterozygous for the tortoiseshell gene, she will have the tortoiseshell phenotype. Orange patches are formed by populations of cells in which the X chromosome with the orange allele is active; black patches have cells in which the X chromosome with the black allele is active.

In this module, we have seen how the physical structure of chromosomes can affect which genes are expressed in a cell. In the next module, we will discuss whether the chromosomal structure of identical twins is completely alike.

? If a nerve cell and a skin cell in your body have the same genes, how can the cells be so different?

● Each cell type must be expressing certain genes that are present in, but not expressed in, the other cell type.

Early Embryo

X chromosomes

Allele for orange fur   Allele for black fur

Cell division and random X chromosome inactivation

Adult

Two cell populations

Active X
Inactive X

Orange fur

Inactive X
Active X

Black fur

▲ **Figure 11.2B** A tortoiseshell pattern on a female cat, a result of X chromosome inactivation

11.3 Are identical twins really identical?

In humans, giving birth to twins is a relatively uncommon event. However, the use of fertility drugs increases the probability of multiple births. Twins can be the result of two possible occurrences at or shortly after the time of conception. **Fraternal twins** (also known as **dizygotic twins**) occur when two eggs are released during ovulation as opposed to the typical one. A separate sperm fertilizes each egg and the fraternal twins are no more related than any other siblings. On the contrary, **identical twins** (also called **monozygotic twins**, see Figure 11.3) are the result of a single early stage embryo splitting into two separate embryos (see Module 30.4). These twins originate from the same fertilization event. It is a commonly held belief that identical twins share the same genetic information and are therefore, completely identical.

This seems logical enough. After all, when a cell divides by mitosis, both daughter cells are genetically identical. The daughter cells of the zygote's first division have the same genetic information. If separated, forming identical twins, each should have the same DNA. However, anyone who knows identical twins can attest to the fact that they are not the same in all respects. Identical twins often have different personalities, different likes, and even different looks. But how can two individuals with the same DNA be so different?

Until recently, the differences between identical twins have been attributed to environment. Exposure to different conditions through diet or extracurricular activities was used to explain any subtle differences. Although this is true, recent studies suggest that differences may also involve a genetic element as well. Identical twins raised in the same environment may chemically modify their identical genomes differently—a phenomenon known as **epigenetics**. Researchers are amassing more and more evidence of the importance of epigenetic information in the regulation of gene expression. It is often the case that one identical twin acquires a genetically influenced disease, such as schizophrenia, but the other does not, despite their identical genomes. Researchers suspect that epigenetics may be behind such differences.

As we discussed in the previous module, DNA methylation can increase or decrease the expression of a gene without changing the DNA sequence. Alterations in normal patterns of DNA methylation are seen in some cancers, where they are associated with inappropriate gene expression. Although the genomes are identical, DNA methylation will be different in each twin. If the DNA of one twin becomes methylated in a pattern seen in cancer, there is no reason to suspect the same pattern will occur in the second twin.

▲ **Figure 11.3** Identical twins may not be so identical

In addition to epigenetics, other changes to the genome can occur independently in each twin. Significant large-scale structural modifications occur to the human genome. Such changes include the copying of large segments (100 kilobases or greater) of DNA, often several times. Variations in the number of copies are called copy-number variations, and can be different in each identical twin. These copy-number variations can further lead to differences in gene expression.

Identical twins begin life with identical genomes. However, as they age, their genomes undergo unique epigenetic changes. Differing patterns of DNA methylation and gene copying produce differences in the regulation of gene expression. The older the twins, the greater the epigenetic differences in their DNA. It would appear that twins invariably grow apart over time, at least genetically speaking, and the rumour that identical twins have identical genomes is untrue.

 What two changes can contribute to differences between identical twins?

● DNA methylation and copy-number variations

11.4 Complex assemblies of proteins control eukaryotic transcription

The packing and unpacking of chromosomal DNA provide a coarse adjustment for eukaryotic gene expression by making a region of DNA either more or less available for transcription. The fine-tuning begins with the initiation of RNA synthesis—transcription. In both prokaryotes and eukaryotes, the initiation of transcription (whether transcription starts or not) is the most important stage for regulating gene expression.

Like prokaryotes (see Module 11.1), eukaryotes employ regulatory proteins—activators and repressors—that bind to specific segments of DNA and either promote or block the binding of RNA polymerase, turning the transcription of genes on or off. However, most eukaryotic genes have individual promoters and other control sequences and are not clustered together as in operons.

The current model for the initiation of eukaryotic transcription features an intricate array of regulatory proteins that interact with DNA and with one another to turn genes on or off. In eukaryotes, activator proteins seem to be more important than repressors. That is, in multicellular eukaryotes, the "default" state for most genes seems to be "off." A typical animal or plant cell needs to turn on (transcribe) only a small percentage of its genes, those required for the cell's specialized structure and function. Housekeeping genes, those continually active in virtually all cells for routine activities such as glycolysis, may be in an "on" state by default.

To function, eukaryotic RNA polymerase requires the assistance of proteins called **transcription factors**. In the model depicted in **Figure 11.4**, the first step in initiating gene transcription is the binding of activator proteins (⚫) to DNA control sequences

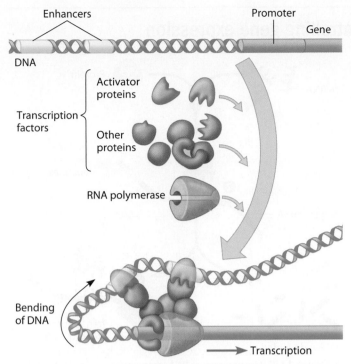

Figure 11.4 begins with labels: Enhancers, Promoter, Gene, DNA, Transcription factors (Activator proteins, Other proteins), RNA polymerase, Bending of DNA, Transcription

▲ **Figure 11.4** A model for the turning on of a eukaryotic gene

called **enhancers** (). In contrast to the operators of prokaryotic operons, enhancers are usually far away on the chromosome from the gene they help to regulate. The binding of activators to enhancers leads to bending of the DNA. Once the DNA is bent, the

bound activators interact with other transcription factor proteins (⬤), which then bind as a complex at the gene's promoter (▬). This large assembly of proteins facilitates the correct attachment of RNA polymerase to the promoter and the initiation of transcription. Only when the complete complex of proteins has assembled can the polymerase begin to move along the gene, producing an RNA strand. As shown in the figure, several enhancers and activators may be involved. Not shown are *repressor* proteins that can bind to DNA sequences called **silencers** and *inhibit* the start of transcription.

If eukaryotic genomes only rarely have operons, how does a eukaryotic cell deal with genes of related function that all need to be turned on or off at the same time? Making the situation even more complex, genes coding for the enzymes of a metabolic pathway are often scattered across different chromosomes. The key to coordinated gene expression in eukaryotes is often the association of a specific combination of control sequences with every gene of a particular metabolic pathway. Copies of the activators that recognize these control sequences bind to them all at once (since they are all identical), promoting simultaneous transcription of the genes, no matter where they are in the genome. In the next module, we consider another method of gene regulation that is unique to eukaryotes.

? **What must occur before RNA polymerase can bind to a promoter and transcribe a specific eukaryotic gene?**

● Enhancers must bind to transcription factors to facilitate the attachment of RNA polymerase to the promoter.

11.5 Eukaryotic RNA may be spliced in more than one way

Although regulation of transcription is the most important step in gene regulation in most cells, transcription alone does not equal gene expression. Several other points along the path from DNA to protein can be regulated. Within a eukaryotic cell, for example, RNA transcripts are processed into mRNA before moving to the cytoplasm for translation by the ribosomes. RNA processing includes the addition of a cap and a tail, as well as the removal of any introns—noncoding DNA segments that interrupt the genetic message—and the splicing together of the remaining exons (see Module 10.10).

Some scientists think that the splicing process may help to control the flow of mRNA from nucleus to cytoplasm because until splicing is completed, the RNA is attached to the molecules of the splicing machinery and cannot pass through the nuclear pores. Moreover, in some cases, the cell can carry out splicing in more than one way, generating different mRNA molecules from the same RNA transcript. Notice in **Figure 11.5**, for example, that one mRNA molecule ends up with the green exon and the other with the brown exon. With this sort of **alternative RNA splicing**, an organism can produce more than one type of polypeptide from a single gene.

One interesting example of two-way splicing is found in the fruit fly, where the differences between males and females are largely due to different patterns of RNA splicing. And as you will learn in Chapter 12, results from the Human Genome Project

suggest that alternative splicing is very common in humans. Included among the many instances already known is one gene whose transcript can be spliced to encode *seven* alternative versions of a protein, each of which is made in a different type of cell.

? **How does alternative RNA splicing enable a single gene to encode more than one kind of polypeptide?**

● Each kind of polypeptide is encoded by an mRNA molecule containing a different combination of exons.

Figure 11.5 labels: Exons, DNA (1, 2, 3, 4, 5), Introns, RNA transcript (Cap, 1, 2, 3, 4, 5, Tail), RNA splicing, or, mRNA (1 2 3 5 / 1 2 4 5)

▲ **Figure 11.5** The production of two different mRNAs from the same gene

11.6 Small RNAs play multiple roles in controlling gene expression

Recall that only 1.5% of the human genome—and a similarly small percentage of the genomes of many other multicellular eukaryotes—codes for proteins. Another very small fraction of DNA consists of genes for ribosomal RNA and transfer RNA. Until recently, most of the remaining DNA was thought to be untranscribed and therefore considered to be lacking any genetic information. This DNA was previously referred to as junk DNA. However, a flood of recent data has contradicted this view. It turns out that a significant amount of the genome is transcribed into functioning but non-protein-coding RNAs, including a variety of small RNAs. While many questions about the functions of these RNAs remain unanswered, researchers are uncovering more evidence of their biological roles every day.

In 1993, researchers discovered small RNA molecules, called **microRNAs (miRNAs)**, that can bind to complementary sequences on mRNA molecules **(Figure 11.6)**. Each miRNA, typically about 20 nucleotides long, ❶ forms a complex with protein. The miRNA-protein complex can ❷ bind to any mRNA molecule with the complementary sequence. Then the complex either ❸ degrades the target mRNA or ❹ blocks its translation. It has been estimated that miRNAs may regulate the expression of at least one-third of all human genes, a striking figure given that miRNAs were unknown a mere 20 years ago.

Researchers can take advantage of miRNA to artificially control gene expression. For example, injecting miRNA into a cell can turn off expression of a gene with a sequence that matches the miRNA, a procedure called **RNA interference (RNAi)**. The RNAi pathway may have evolved as a natural defence against infection by certain viruses with RNA genomes (see Chapter 16). In 2006, two American researchers were awarded a Nobel Prize for their discovery and categorization of RNA interference.

Biologists are excited about these recent discoveries, which hint at a large, diverse population of RNA molecules in the cell

▲ **Figure 11.6** Mechanisms of RNA interference

that play crucial roles in regulating gene expression—and have gone largely unnoticed until now. Our new understanding may lead to important clinical applications. For example, in 2009, researchers discovered a particular microRNA that is essential to the proper functioning of the pancreas. Without it, insulin-producing beta cells die off, which can lead to diabetes. Clearly, we must revise the long-standing view that because they code for proteins, messenger RNAs are the most important RNAs in terms of cellular function.

? **If a gene has the sequence AATTCGCG, what would be the sequence of an miRNA that turns off the gene?**

● The gene will be transcribed as the mRNA sequence UUAAGCGC; an miRNA of sequence AAUUCGCG would bind to and disable this mRNA.

11.7 Later stages of gene expression are also subject to regulation

Even after a eukaryotic mRNA is fully processed and transported to the cytoplasm, there are several additional opportunities for regulation. Such control points include mRNA breakdown, initiation of translation, protein activation, and protein breakdown.

Breakdown of mRNA Molecules of mRNA do not remain intact forever. Enzymes in the cytoplasm eventually break them down, and the timing of this event is an important factor regulating the amounts of various proteins that are produced

in the cell. Long-lived mRNAs can be translated into many more protein molecules than short-lived ones. Prokaryotic mRNAs have very short lifetimes; they are typically degraded by enzymes within a few minutes after their synthesis. This is one reason bacteria can change their protein production so quickly in response to environmental changes. In contrast, the mRNA of eukaryotes can have lifetimes of hours or even weeks.

A striking example of long-lived mRNA is found in vertebrate red blood cells, which manufacture large quantities of the protein hemoglobin. In most species of vertebrates, the mRNAs for hemoglobin are unusually stable. They probably last as long as the red blood cells that contain them—about a month or a bit longer in reptiles, amphibians, and fishes—and are translated again and again. Mammals are an exception. When their red blood cells mature, they lose their ribosomes (along with their other organelles) and thus cease to make new hemoglobin. However, mammalian hemoglobin itself lasts about as long as the red blood cells last, around four months.

Initiation of Translation
The process of translating an mRNA into a polypeptide also offers opportunities for regulation. Among the molecules involved in translation are a great many proteins that control the start of polypeptide synthesis. Red blood cells, for instance, have an inhibitory protein that prevents translation of hemoglobin mRNA unless the cell has a supply of heme, the iron-containing chemical group essential for hemoglobin function. (It is the iron atom of the heme group to which oxygen molecules actually attach.) By controlling the start of protein synthesis, cells can avoid wasting energy if the needed components are currently unavailable.

Protein Activation
After translation is complete, some polypeptides require alterations before they become functional. Post-translational control mechanisms in eukaryotes often involve the cleavage (cutting) of a polypeptide to yield a smaller final product that is the active protein, able to carry out a specific function in the organism. In **Figure 11.7**, we see the example of the hormone insulin, which is a protein. Insulin is synthesized in the cells of the pancreas as one long polypeptide that has no hormonal activity. After translation is completed, the polypeptide folds up, and covalent bonds form between the sulphur (S) atoms of sulphur-containing amino acids (see Figure 3.9B, which shows bonds in another protein). Two H atoms are lost as each bond forms, linking together parts of the polypeptide in a specific way. Finally, a large centre portion is cut away, leaving two shorter chains held together by the sulphur linkages. This combination of two shorter polypeptides is the form of insulin that functions as a hormone. By controlling the timing of such protein modifications, the rate of insulin synthesis can be fine-tuned.

Protein Breakdown
The final control mechanism operating after translation is the selective breakdown of proteins. Though mammalian hemoglobin may last as long as the red blood cell housing it, the lifetimes of many other proteins are closely regulated. Some of the proteins that trigger metabolic changes in cells are broken down within a few minutes or hours. This regulation allows a cell to adjust the kinds and amounts of its proteins in response to changes in its environment. It also enables the cell to maintain its proteins in prime working order. Indeed, when proteins are damaged, they are usually broken down right away and replaced by new ones that function properly.

So far in this chapter, you have learned about several ways that eukaryotes can control gene expression. The next module summarizes all of these processes.

 Review Figure 11.7. If the enzyme responsible for cleaving inactive insulin is deactivated, what effect will this have on the form and function of insulin?

● The final molecule will have a shape different from that of active insulin and therefore will not be able to function as a hormone.

Folding of the polypeptide and the formation of S—S linkages

Cleavage

Initial polypeptide (inactive)

Folded polypeptide (inactive)

Active form of insulin

▲ **Figure 11.7** Protein activation: the role of polypeptide cleavage in producing the active insulin protein

11.8 Review: Multiple mechanisms regulate gene expression in eukaryotes

Figure 11.8 provides a review of eukaryotic gene expression and highlights the multiple control points where the process can be turned on or off, sped up, or slowed down. Picture the series of pipes that carry water from your local water supply, perhaps a reservoir, to a faucet in your home. At various points, valves control the flow of water. We use this model in the figure

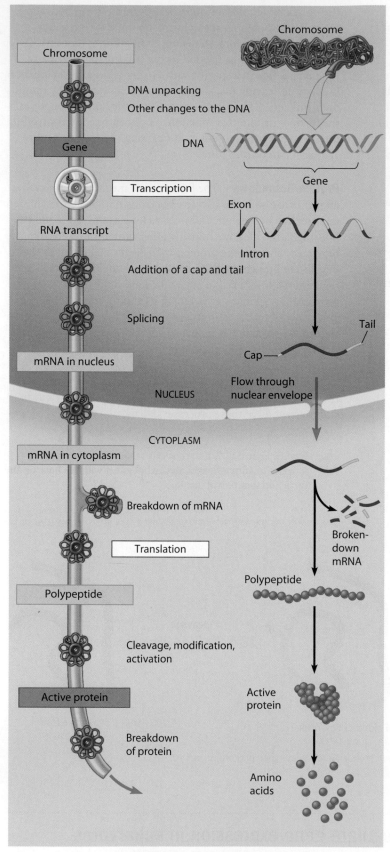

Chromosome

DNA unpacking

Other changes to the DNA

Gene

Transcription

RNA transcript

Addition of a cap and tail

Splicing

mRNA in nucleus

NUCLEUS

CYTOPLASM

mRNA in cytoplasm

Breakdown of mRNA

Translation

Polypeptide

Cleavage, modification, activation

Active protein

Breakdown of protein

Chromosome

DNA

Gene

Exon

Intron

Tail

Cap

Flow through nuclear envelope

Broken-down mRNA

Polypeptide

Active protein

Amino acids

▲ **Figure 11.8** The gene expression "pipeline" in a eukaryotic cell

to illustrate the flow of genetic information from a chromosome—a reservoir of genetic information—to an active protein that has been synthesized in the cell's cytoplasm. The multiple mechanisms that control gene expression are analogous to the control valves in water pipes. In the figure, each gene expression "valve" is indicated by a control knob. Note that these knobs represent *possible* control points; for most proteins, only a few control points may be important. The most important control point, in both eukaryotes and prokaryotes, is usually the start of transcription. In the diagram, the large yellow knob represents the mechanisms that regulate the start of transcription.

Although the initiation of transcription is the most important control point, there are several other opportunities for regulation. RNA processing in the nucleus adds nucleotides to the ends of the RNA (cap and tail) and splices out introns. As we discussed in Module 11.5, a growing body of evidence suggests the importance of control at this stage. Once mRNA reaches the cytoplasm, additional stages that can be regulated include mRNA translation and eventual breakdown, possible alteration of the polypeptide to activate it, and the eventual breakdown of the protein.

Despite its numerous steps, Figure 11.8 actually oversimplifies the control of gene expression. What it does not show is the web of control that connects different genes, often through their products. We have seen examples in both prokaryotes and eukaryotes of the actions of gene products (usually proteins) on other genes or on other gene products within the same cell. The genes of operons in *E. coli*, for instance, are controlled by repressor or activator proteins encoded by regulatory genes on the same DNA molecule. In eukaryotes, many genes are controlled by proteins encoded by regulatory genes on other chromosomes. The numerous interactions of these various proteins, taken in total, result in flexible yet precise control of gene expression.

In eukaryotes, cellular differentiation results from the selective turning on and off of genes. In the next module, we examine the stage in the life cycle of a multicellular eukaryote when cellular differentiation by selective gene expression is most vital: the development of a multicellular embryo from a unicellular zygote.

? **Of the nine regulatory "valves" in Figure 11.8, which five can also operate in a prokaryotic cell?**

● (1) Control of transcription; (2) control of mRNA breakdown; (3) control of translation; (4) control of protein activation; and (5) control of protein breakdown

11.9 Cell signalling and cascades of gene expression direct animal development

Some of the first glimpses into the relationship between gene expression and embryonic development came from studies of mutants of the fruit fly *Drosophila melanogaster* (see Module 9.18). **Figure 11.9A** shows the heads of two fruit flies. The one on the right, a mutant, developed in a strikingly abnormal way: It has two legs where its antennae should be! Research on this and other developmental mutants has led to the identification of many of the genes that program development in the normal fly. This genetic approach has revolutionized developmental biology.

Among the earliest events in fruit fly development are ones that determine which end of the egg cell will become the head and which end will become the tail. As you can see in **Figure 11.9B**, ❶ these events occur in the ovaries of the mother fly and involve communication between an unfertilized egg cell and cells adjacent to it in its follicle (egg chamber). The back-and-forth signalling between the cells triggers expression of certain genes in the two cell types. ❷ One important result is the localization of a specific type of mRNA (pink) at the end of the egg where the fly's head will develop, thus defining the animal's head-to-tail axis. (Similar events lead to the positioning of the top-to-bottom and side-to-side axes.) Molecular interactions and further gene expression bring about growth of the egg.

After the egg is fertilized and laid, repeated rounds of mitosis transform the zygote into an embryo. The early embryo makes proteins that diffuse through its cell layers. Cell signalling—now among the cells of the embryo—helps to drive the process. ❸ The result is the subdivision of the embryo's body into segments.

Now the finer details of the fly can take shape. Protein products of some of the axis-specifying genes and segment-forming genes activate yet another set of genes. These genes, called homeotic genes, determine what body parts will develop from each segment. A **homeotic gene** is a master control gene that regulates batteries of other genes that actually determine the anatomy of parts of the body. For example, one set of homeotic genes in fruit flies instructs cells in the segments of the head and thorax (midbody) to form antennae and legs, respectively. Elsewhere, these homeotic genes remain turned off, while others are turned on. (See Module 30.8 for a discussion of evidence that homeotic genes evolved early in the history of animals.) ❹ The eventual outcome is an adult fly. Notice that the adult's body segments correspond to those of the embryo in step 3. It was mutation of a homeotic gene that was responsible for the abnormal fly in Figure 11.9A.

Cascades of gene expression, with the protein products of one set of genes activating other sets of genes, are a common theme in development.

? **What determines which end of a developing fruit fly will become the head?**

● A specific kind of mRNA localizes at the end of the unfertilized egg that will become the head.

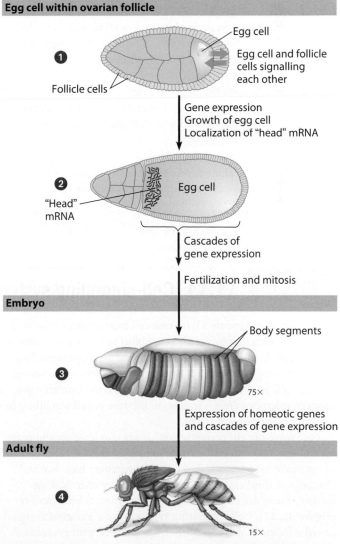

Egg cell within ovarian follicle

❶ Egg cell · Follicle cells · Egg cell and follicle cells signalling each other

Gene expression
Growth of egg cell
Localization of "head" mRNA

❷ "Head" mRNA · Egg cell

Cascades of gene expression

Fertilization and mitosis

Embryo

❸ Body segments · 75×

Expression of homeotic genes and cascades of gene expression

Adult fly

❹ 15×

▲ **Figure 11.9B** Key steps in the early development of the head-to-tail axis in a fruit fly

Eye

Antenna

Extra pair of legs

SEM 50×   SEM 50×

▲ **Figure 11.9A** A normal fruit fly (left) compared with a mutant fruit fly (right) with legs coming out of its head

11.10 Signal transduction pathways convert messages received at the cell surface to responses within the cell

Cell-to-cell signalling, with proteins or other kinds of molecules carrying messages from signalling cells to receiving (target) cells, is a key mechanism in the coordination of cellular activities. In most cases, a signalling molecule acts by binding to a receptor protein in the plasma membrane of the target cell and initiating a signal transduction pathway in the cell. A **signal transduction pathway** is a series of molecular changes that converts a signal on a target cell's surface to a specific response inside the cell.

Figure 11.10 shows the main elements of a signal transduction pathway in which the target cell's response is the expression of a gene. ❶ The signalling cell secretes a signalling molecule. ❷ This molecule binds to a receptor protein embedded in the target cell's plasma membrane. ❸ The binding activates the first in a series of relay proteins within the target cell. Each relay molecule activates another. ❹ The last relay molecule in the series activates a transcription factor that ❺ triggers transcription of a specific gene. ❻ Translation of the mRNA produces a protein.

Signal transduction pathways are crucial to many cellular functions. Throughout your study of biology, you'll see their importance again and again. We encountered them when we studied the cell cycle control system in Module 8.8; we'll revisit them when we discuss cancer later in this chapter (see, for example, Module 11.17); and we'll see how they relate to hormone function in plants (Chapter 24) and animals (Chapter 29).

? How can a signalling molecule from one cell alter gene expression in a target cell without even entering the target cell?

● By binding to a receptor protein in the membrane of the target cell and triggering a signal transduction pathway that activates transcription factors

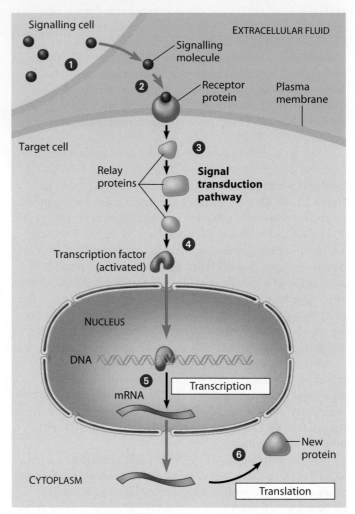

▲ Figure 11.10 A signal transduction pathway that turns on a gene

---

11.11 Cell-signalling systems appeared early in the evolution of life

As explained in Module 11.10, one cell can communicate with another by secreting molecules that bind to surface proteins on a target cell. How ancient and widespread are such signalling systems among Earth's organisms? To answer these questions, we can look at communication between microorganisms, for modern microbes are a window on the role of cell signalling in the evolution of life on Earth.

One topic of cell "conversation" is sex—at least for the yeast *Saccharomyces cerevisiae*, which people have used for millennia to make bread, wine, and beer. Researchers have learned that cells of this yeast identify their mates by chemical signalling. There are two sexes, or mating types, called **a** and **α** **(Figure 11.11)**. Cells of mating type **a** secrete a chemical signal called **a** factor, which can bind to specific receptor proteins on nearby **α** cells. At the same time, **α** cells secrete **α** factor, which binds to receptors on **a** cells. Without actually entering

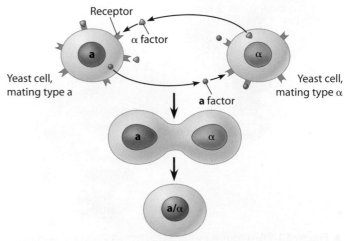

▲ Figure 11.11 Communication between mating yeast cells

the target cells, the two mating factors cause the cells to grow toward each other and bring about other cellular changes. The result is the fusion, or mating, of two cells of opposite type. The new **a/α** cell contains all the genes of both original cells, a combination of genetic resources that provides advantages to the cell's descendants, which arise by subsequent cell divisions.

The signal transduction pathways involved in this yeast mating system have been extensively studied, as have many other pathways in yeasts and other organisms. Amazingly, the molecular details of signal transduction in yeast and mammals are strikingly similar, even though the last common ancestor of these two groups of organisms lived more than a billion years ago. These similarities—and others more recently uncovered between signalling systems in bacteria and plants—suggest that early versions of the cell-signalling mechanisms used today evolved well before the first multicellular creatures appeared on Earth. Scientists think that signalling mechanisms evolved first in ancient prokaryotes and single-celled eukaryotes and then became adapted for new uses in their multicellular descendants.

 In what sense is the joining of yeast mating types "sex"?

● The process results in the creation of a diploid cell that is a genetic blend of two parental haploid cells.

Cloning of Plants and Animals

11.12 Plant cloning shows that differentiated cells may retain all of their genetic potential

One of the most important "take home lessons" from this chapter is that differentiated cells express only a small percentage of their genes. So then how do we know that all the genes are still present? And if all the genes are still there, do differentiated cells retain the potential to express them?

One way to approach these questions is to see if a differentiated cell can **dedifferentiate**, or reverse its differentiation, and then be stimulated to generate a whole new organism. In plants, this ability is common. In fact, if you have ever grown a plant from a small cutting, you've seen evidence that a differentiated plant cell can undergo cell division and give rise to all the tissues of an adult plant. On a larger scale, the technique described in **Figure 11.12** can be used to produce hundreds or thousands of genetically identical plants from the cells of a single plant. For example, when cells from a carrot are transferred to a culture medium, a single cell can begin dividing and eventually grow into an adult plant, a genetic replica of the parent plant. Such an organism, produced through asexual reproduction from a single parent, is called a **clone**. The fact that a mature plant cell can dedifferentiate and then give rise to all the different kinds of specialized cells of a new plant shows that differentiation does not necessarily involve irreversible changes in the plant's DNA.

Plant cloning is now used extensively in agriculture. For some plants, such as orchids, cloning is the only commercially practical means of reproducing plants. In other cases, cloning has been used to reproduce a plant with desirable traits, such as high fruit yield or the ability to resist a plant pathogen.

But is this sort of cloning possible in animals? A good indication that differentiation need not impair an animal cell's genetic potential is the natural process of **regeneration**, the regrowth of lost body parts. As discussed in the chapter-opening essay of Chapter 25, when a newt loses a leg, certain cells in the leg stump dedifferentiate, divide, and then redifferentiate, giving rise to a new leg. Many animals, especially among the invertebrates, can regenerate lost parts, and in a few relatively simple animals, isolated differentiated cells can dedifferentiate and then develop into an entire organism (see Module 30.1). Further evidence for the complete genetic potential of animal cells comes from cloning experiments, our next topic.

▼ **Figure 11.12** Growth of a carrot plant from a differentiated root cell

Root of carrot plant

Single cell

Root cells cultured in growth medium

Cell division in culture

Plantlet

Adult plant

 How does the cloning of plants from differentiated cells support the view that differentiation is based on the control of gene expression rather than on irreversible changes in the genome?

● Cloning shows that all the genes of a fully differentiated plant are still present, but some may be turned off.

11.13 Nuclear transplantation can be used to clone animals

Animal cloning can be achieved through a procedure called **nuclear transplantation (Figure 11.13)**. First performed in the 1950s using cells from frog embryos, nuclear transplantation involves replacing the nucleus of an egg cell or a zygote with the nucleus of an adult somatic cell. The recipient cell may then begin to divide. By about five days later, repeated cell divisions have formed a blastocyst, a hollow ball of about 100 cells. At this point, the blastocyst may be used for different purposes, as indicated by the two branches in Figure 11.13.

If the animal to be cloned is a mammal, further development requires implanting the blastocyst into the uterus of a surrogate mother (Figure 11.13, upper branch). The resulting animal will be genetically identical to the donor of the nucleus—a "clone" of the donor. This type of cloning, which results in the birth of a new living individual, is called **reproductive cloning**. The world-famous sheep Dolly (mentioned in the chapter-opening essay) was produced using reproductive cloning. The researchers used an electric shock to fuse 277 specially treated adult sheep udder cells with eggs

from which they had removed the nuclei. After several days of growth, 29 of the resulting embryos were implanted in the uteruses of surrogate mothers. One of the embryos developed into Dolly. As expected, Dolly resembled her genetic parent, the nucleus donor, not the egg donor or the surrogate mother.

In a different cloning procedure (Figure 11.13, lower branch), **embryonic stem cells (ES cells)** are harvested from the blastocyst. In nature, embryonic stem cells give rise to all the different kinds of specialized cells of the body. In the laboratory, embryonic stem cells are easily grown in culture, where, given the right conditions, they can perpetuate themselves indefinitely. When the major aim is to produce embryonic stem cells for therapeutic treatments, the process is called **therapeutic cloning**. In the next module, we discuss an application of therapeutic cloning.

 What are the intended products of reproductive cloning and therapeutic cloning?

● Reproductive cloning is used to produce new individuals. Therapeutic cloning is used to harvest embryonic stem cells.

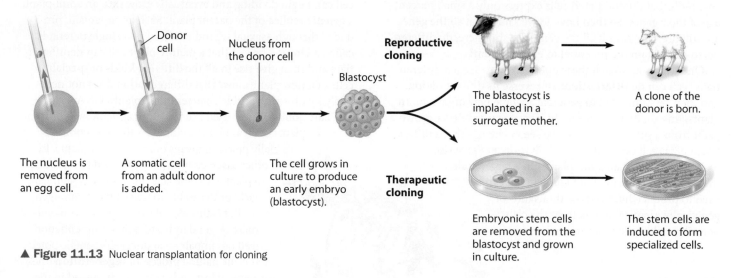

▲ **Figure 11.13** Nuclear transplantation for cloning

- The nucleus is removed from an egg cell.
- A somatic cell from an adult donor is added.
- Donor cell
- Nucleus from the donor cell
- The cell grows in culture to produce an early embryo (blastocyst).
- Blastocyst
- **Reproductive cloning** — The blastocyst is implanted in a surrogate mother. A clone of the donor is born.
- **Therapeutic cloning** — Embryonic stem cells are removed from the blastocyst and grown in culture. The stem cells are induced to form specialized cells.

11.14 Therapeutic cloning can produce stem cells with great medical potential

Therapeutic cloning produces embryonic stem cells, cells that in the early animal embryo differentiate to give rise to all the cell types in the body. When grown in laboratory culture, embryonic stem cells can divide indefinitely (like cancer cells; see Module 8.9). Furthermore, the right conditions can induce changes in gene expression that cause differentiation into a variety of cell types (**Figure 11.14**).

The adult body also has stem cells, which serve to replace nonreproducing specialized cells as needed. In contrast to embryonic stem cells, **adult stem cells** are able to give rise to many but not all cell types in the organism. For example, bone marrow contains several types of stem cells, including one that can generate all the different kinds of blood cells. Although

adult animals have only tiny numbers of stem cells, scientists are learning to identify and isolate these cells from various tissues and, in some cases, to grow them in culture.

Recently, researchers have discovered stem cells in human skin, hair, eyes, and oral tissues. However, the developmental potential of adult stem cells is limited to certain cell types, so embryonic stem cells are considered more promising than adult stem cells for medical applications, at least for now. In 2007, three research groups reported transforming mouse skin cells into embryonic stem cells simply by causing the skin cells to express four "stem cell" master regulatory genes. The researchers used retroviruses as vectors to introduce extra copies of these genes into the skin cells.

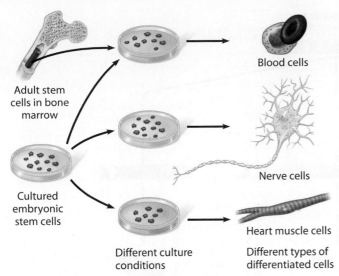

Blood cells

Nerve cells

Heart muscle cells

Adult stem cells in bone marrow

Cultured embryonic stem cells

Different culture conditions

Different types of differentiated cells

▲ **Figure 11.14** Differentiation of stem cells in culture

The ultimate aim of therapeutic cloning is to supply cells for the repair of damaged or diseased organs: for example, insulin-producing pancreatic cells for people with diabetes or

certain kinds of brain cells for people with Parkinson's disease or Alzheimer's disease. Adult stem cells from donor bone marrow have long been used as a source of immune system cells in patients whose own immune systems have been destroyed by genetic disorders or radiation treatments for cancer. More recently, clinical trials using bone marrow stem cells have shown slight success in promoting regeneration of heart tissue in patients whose hearts have been damaged by heart attacks. In the future, a donor nucleus from a patient with a particular disease could allow production of embryonic stem cells for treatment that match the patient and are thus not rejected by his or her immune system.

While many people believe that reproductive cloning of humans is unethical, opinions vary more widely about the morality of therapeutic cloning using embryonic stem cells. The research and the debate continue.

 In nature, how do embryonic stem cells differ from adult stem cells?

● Embryonic cells give rise to all the different kinds of cells in the body. Adult stem cells generate only a few related types of cells.

The Genetic Basis of Cancer

11.15 Cancer results from mutations in genes that control cell division

In Module 8.9, you learned that cancerous cells have escaped from the control mechanisms that normally limit their growth. Scientists have learned that such escape is often due to changes in gene expression.

The abnormal behaviour of cancer cells was observed years before anything was known about the cell cycle, its control, or the role genes play in making cells cancerous. One of the earliest clues to the cancer puzzle was the discovery, in 1911, of a virus that causes cancer in chickens. Recall that viruses are simply molecules of DNA or RNA surrounded by protein and in some cases a membranous envelope. Viruses that cause cancer can become permanent residents in host cells by inserting their nucleic acid into the DNA of host chromosomes (see Module 16.5).

The genes that a cancer-causing virus inserts into a host cell can make the cell cancerous. Such a gene, which can cause cancer when present in a single copy in the cell, is called an **oncogene** (from the Greek *onkos*, tumour). Over the last century, researchers have identified a number of viruses that harbour cancer-causing genes. One example is the human papillomavirus (HPV), which is associated with several types of cancer, most frequently cervical cancer.

Proto-oncogenes In 1976, scientists made a startling discovery. They found that the cancer-causing chicken virus discovered in 1911 contains an oncogene that is an altered version of a normal gene found in chicken cells. Subsequent research has shown that the chromosomes of many animals, including humans, contain genes that can be converted to oncogenes. A normal gene that has the potential to become an oncogene is

called a **proto-oncogene**. (These terms can be confusing, so they bear repeating: a *proto-oncogene* is a normal, healthy gene that, if changed, can become a cancer-causing *oncogene*.) Thus, a cell can acquire an oncogene either from a virus or from the mutation of one of its own genes.

Searching for the normal role of these genes, researchers found that many proto-oncogenes code for growth factors—proteins that stimulate cell division—or for other proteins that somehow affect growth factor function or some other aspect of the cell cycle. When all these proteins are functioning normally, in the right amounts at the right times, they help to properly control cell division and cellular differentiation.

How might a proto-oncogene—a gene that has an essential function in normal cells—become an oncogene, a cancer-causing gene? In general, an oncogene arises from a genetic change that leads to an increase either in the amount of the proto-oncogene's protein product or in the activity of each protein molecule. **Figure 11.15A** illustrates three kinds of changes in DNA that can produce oncogenes. Let's assume that the starting proto-oncogene codes for a protein that stimulates cell division. On the left in the figure, a mutation (green) in the proto-oncogene itself creates an oncogene that codes for a hyperactive protein, which is produced in the usual amount but whose stimulating effect is stronger than normal. In the centre, an error in DNA replication or recombination generates multiple copies of the gene, which are all transcribed and translated; the result is an excess of the normal stimulatory protein. On the right, the proto-oncogene has been moved from its normal location in the cell's DNA to another location. At its new site,

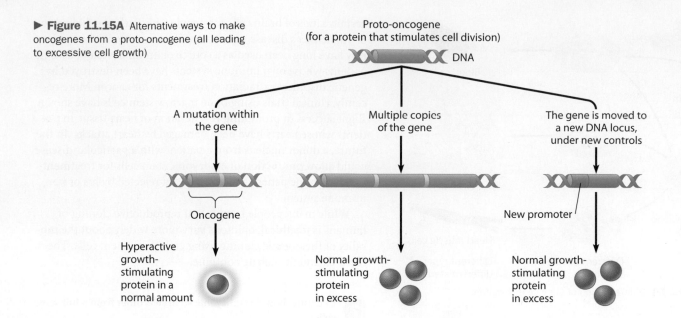

► **Figure 11.15A** Alternative ways to make oncogenes from a proto-oncogene (all leading to excessive cell growth)

Proto-oncogene
(for a protein that stimulates cell division)

DNA

A mutation within the gene

Multiple copies of the gene

The gene is moved to a new DNA locus, under new controls

Oncogene

New promoter

Hyperactive growth-stimulating protein in a normal amount

Normal growth-stimulating protein in excess

Normal growth-stimulating protein in excess

Tumour-suppressor gene

Mutated tumour-suppressor gene

Normal growth-inhibiting protein

Defective, nonfunctioning protein

Cell division under control

Cell division not under control

▲ **Figure 11.15B** The effect of a mutation in a tumour-suppressor gene

the gene is under the control of a different promoter, one that causes it to be transcribed more often than normal; the normal protein is again made in excess. So in all three cases, normal

gene expression is changed, and the cell is stimulated to divide excessively.

Tumour-Suppressor Genes   In addition to genes whose products normally *promote* cell division, cells contain genes whose normal products *inhibit* cell division. Such genes are called **tumour-suppressor genes** because the proteins they encode help to prevent uncontrolled cell growth. Any mutation that decreases the normal activity of a tumour-suppressor protein may contribute to the onset of cancer, in effect stimulating growth through the absence of suppression (**Figure 11.15B**). Scientists have also discovered a class of tumour-suppressor genes that function in the repair of damaged DNA. When these genes are mutated, other cancer-causing mutations are more likely to accumulate.

?   How do proto-oncogenes relate to oncogenes?

● A proto-oncogene is a normal gene that, if mutated, can become a cancer-causing oncogene.

11.16 Multiple genetic changes underlie the development of cancer

More than 23 000 Canadians will be stricken by cancer of the colon (the main part of the large intestine) this year. One of the best-understood types of human cancer, colon cancer illustrates an important principle about how cancer develops: More than one somatic mutation is needed to produce a full-fledged cancer cell. As in many cancers, the development of malignant (spreading) colon cancer is gradual. (See Module 8.9 to review cancer terms.)

Figure 11.16A illustrates this idea by using colon cancer as an example. ❶ Colon cancer begins when an oncogene arises or is activated through mutation, causing unusually frequent division of apparently normal cells in the colon lining. ❷ Later, one or more additional DNA mutations, such as the inactivation of a

tumour-suppressor gene, cause the growth of a small benign tumour (a polyp) in the colon wall. ❸ Still more mutations eventually lead to formation of a malignant tumour, a tumour that has the potential to metastasize (spread). The requirement for several mutations—the actual number is usually four or more—explains why cancers can take a long time to develop.

Thus, the development of a malignant tumour is paralleled by a gradual accumulation of mutations that convert proto-oncogenes to oncogenes and knock out tumour-suppressor genes. Multiple changes must occur at the DNA level for a cell to become fully cancerous. Such changes usually include the appearance of at least one active oncogene and the mutation or loss

DNA changes:	An oncogene is activated	A tumour-suppressor gene is inactivated	A second tumour-suppressor gene is inactivated
Cellular changes:	Increased cell division ❶	Growth of a polyp ❷	Growth of a malignant tumour ❸

Colon wall

▲ **Figure 11.16A** Stepwise development of a typical colon cancer

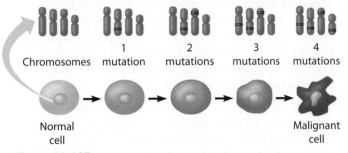

Chromosomes — 1 mutation — 2 mutations — 3 mutations — 4 mutations

Normal cell → → → → Malignant cell

▲ **Figure 11.16B** Accumulation of mutations in the development of a cancer cell

of several tumour-suppressor genes. In **Figure 11.16B**, colours distinguish the normal cell (tan) from cells with one or more mutations leading to increased cell division and cancer (red). Once a cancer-promoting mutation occurs (the red band on the chromosome), it is passed to all the descendants of the cell carrying it.

The fact that more than one somatic mutation is generally needed to produce a full-fledged cancer cell may help to explain why the incidence of cancer increases with age. If cancer results from an accumulation of mutations that occur throughout life, then the longer we live, the more likely we are to develop cancer. Cancer researchers hope to learn about mutations that cause cancer through the Cancer Genome Project, a 10-year effort to map all human cancer-causing genes.

? Epithelial cells, those that line body cavities, are frequently replaced and so divide more often than most other types of body cells. Will epithelial cells become cancerous more or less frequently than other types of body cells?

● More frequent cell divisions will result in more frequent mutation and thus a greater chance of cancer.

11.17 Faulty proteins can interfere with normal signal transduction pathways

To understand how oncogenes and defective tumour-suppressor genes can contribute to uncontrolled cell growth, we need to look more closely at the normal functions of proto-oncogenes and tumour-suppressor genes. Genes in both categories often code for proteins involved in signal transduction pathways leading to gene expression (see Module 11.10).

The figures within this module (excluding, for the moment, the white boxes) illustrate two types of signal transduction pathways leading to the synthesis of proteins that influence the cell cycle. In **Figure 11.17A**, the pathway leads to the stimulation of cell division. The initial signal is a growth factor (⬤), and the target cell's ultimate response is the production of a protein that stimulates the cell to divide. By contrast, **Figure 11.17B** shows an inhibitory pathway, in which a growth-*inhibiting* factor (▼) causes the target cell to make a protein that inhibits cell division. In both cases, the newly made proteins function by interacting with components of the cell cycle control system (see Module 8.8), although the figures here do not show these interactions.

Now, let's see what can happen when the target cell undergoes a cancer-causing mutation. The white box in Figure 11.17A shows the protein product of an oncogene resulting from mutation of a proto-oncogene called *ras*. The normal product of *ras* is a relay protein. Ordinarily, a stimulatory pathway like this will not operate unless the growth factor is available. However, an oncogene protein that is a hyperactive version of a protein in the pathway may

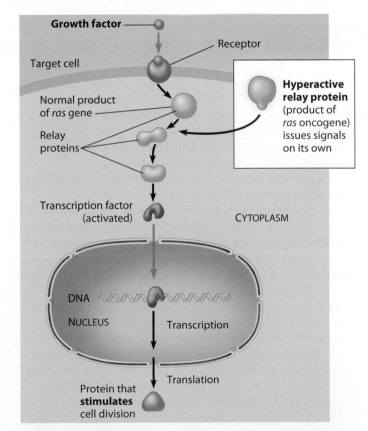

▲ **Figure 11.17A** A stimulatory signal transduction pathway and the effect of an oncogene protein

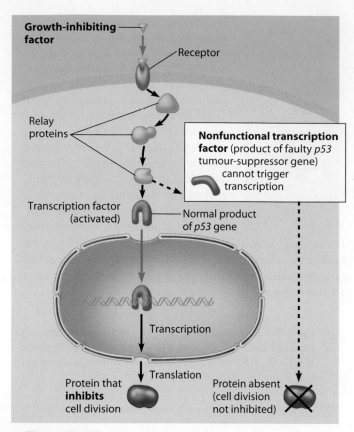

Growth-inhibiting factor

Receptor

Relay proteins

Nonfunctional transcription factor (product of faulty *p53* tumour-suppressor gene) cannot trigger transcription

Transcription factor (activated)

Normal product of *p53* gene

Transcription

Translation

Protein that **inhibits** cell division

Protein absent (cell division not inhibited)

▲ **Figure 11.17B** An inhibitory signal transduction pathway and the effect of a faulty tumour-suppressor protein

trigger the pathway even in the absence of a growth factor. In this example, the oncogene protein is a hyperactive version of the *ras* relay protein that issues signals on its own. In fact, abnormal versions or amounts of any of the pathway's components—from the growth factor itself to the transcription factor—could have the same final effect: overstimulation of cell division.

The white box in Figure 11.17B indicates how a mutant tumour-suppressor protein can affect cell division. In this case, the mutation affects a gene called *p53*, which codes for an essential transcription factor. This mutation leads to the production of a faulty transcription factor, one that the signal transduction pathway cannot activate. As a result, the gene for the inhibitory protein at the bottom of the figure remains turned off, and excessive cell division may occur.

Mutations of the *ras* and *p53* genes have been implicated in many kinds of cancer. In fact, mutations in *ras* occur in about 30% of human cancers, and mutations in *p53* occur in more than 50%. As we see next, carcinogens are responsible for many mutations that lead to cancer.

> **?** Contrast the action of an oncogene with that of a cancer-causing mutation in a tumour-suppressor gene.

● An oncogene encodes an abnormal protein that stimulates cell division via a signal transduction pathway; a mutant tumour-suppressor gene encodes a defective protein unable to function in a pathway that normally inhibits cell division.

11.18 Lifestyle choices can reduce the risk of cancer

In 2011, cancer surpassed heart disease for the first time to become the leading cause of death in all Canadian provinces and territories. Death rates due to certain forms of cancer—including stomach, cervical, and uterine cancers—have decreased in recent years, but the overall cancer death rate is on the rise, currently increasing at about 1% per decade. Table 11.18 lists the most common cancers in Canada and the associated risk factors for each.

The fact that multiple genetic changes are required to produce a cancer cell helps to explain the observation that cancers can run in families. An individual inheriting an oncogene or a mutant allele of a tumour-suppressor gene is one step closer to accumulating the necessary mutations for cancer to develop than an individual without any such mutations.

But the majority of cancers are not associated with a mutation that is passed from parent to offspring; they arise from new mutations caused by environmental factors. Cancer-causing agents, factors that alter DNA and make cells cancerous, are called **carcinogens**. Most mutagens, substances that cause mutations, are carcinogens. Two of the most potent mutagens are X-rays and ultraviolet radiation in sunlight. X-rays are a significant cause of leukemia and brain cancer. Exposure to UV radiation from the sun is known to cause skin cancer, including a deadly type called melanoma. Some

viruses, such as human papillomavirus, are known carcinogens that can lead to cervical cancer (see Module 16.9). To help to minimize infection risk, Health Canada has approved two vaccines and supported a widespread immunization effort for young teens.

The one substance known to cause more cases and types of cancer than any other single agent is tobacco. More people die of lung cancer (nearly 20 100 Canadians in 2012) than any other form of cancer. Most tobacco-related cancers come from smoking, but the passive inhalation of secondhand smoke is also a risk. As Table 11.18 indicates, tobacco use, sometimes in combination with alcohol consumption, causes a number of other types of cancer in addition to lung cancer. In nearly all cases, cigarettes are the main culprit, but smokeless tobacco products, such as snuff and chewing tobacco, are linked to cancer of the mouth and throat.

How do carcinogens cause cancer? In many cases, the genetic changes that cause cancer result from decades of exposure to the mutagenic effects of carcinogens. Carcinogens can also produce their effect by promoting cell division. Generally, the higher the rate of cell division, the greater the chance for mutations resulting from errors in DNA replication or recombination. Some carcinogens seem to have both effects. For instance, the hormones linked to breast and uterine cancers promote cell division

TABLE 11.18 | CANCER IN CANADA

Cancer	Risk Factor	Estimated Number of New Cases in 2012
Lung and larynx	Tobacco smoke	26 650
Prostate	African heritage; possibly dietary fat	26 500
Colon, rectum	High dietary fat; tobacco smoke; alcohol	23 300
Breast	Estrogen	22 900
Lymphomas	Viruses (for some types)	8740
Urinary bladder	Tobacco smoke	7800
Melanoma of the skin	Ultraviolet light	5800
Kidney	Tobacco smoke	5600
Leukemias	X-rays; benzene; virus (for one type)	5600
Thyroid	Iodine deficiency; female; radiation exposure	5600
Uterus	Estrogen	5300
Stomach and esophagus	Table salt; tobacco smoke	5150
Pancreas	Tobacco smoke; obesity	4600
Oral cavity	Tobacco in various forms; alcohol	4000
Brain and nerve	Trauma; X-rays	2800
Ovary	Obesity; many ovulation cycles	2600
Multiple myeloma	African heritage; male; obesity	2400
Liver	Alcohol; hepatitis viruses	2000
Cervix	Sexually transmitted viruses; tobacco smoke	1350
Testis	Undescended testis	940
All others		16 700

and may also cause genetic changes that lead to cancer. In other cases, several different agents, such as viruses and one or more carcinogens, may together produce cancer.

Avoiding carcinogens is not the whole story, for there is growing evidence that some food choices significantly reduce cancer risk. For instance, eating 20–30 grams (g) of plant fibre daily—roughly equal to the amount of fibre in four slices of whole-grain bread, 1 cup of bran flakes, one apple, and $\frac{1}{2}$ cup of carrots combined—and at the same time reducing animal fat intake may help to prevent colon cancer. There is also evidence that other substances in fruits and vegetables, including vitamins C and E and certain compounds related to vitamin A, may offer protection against a variety of cancers. Cabbage and its relatives, such as broccoli and cauliflower (see Figure 13.2), are thought to be especially rich in substances that help to prevent cancer, although the identities of these substances are not yet established. Determining how diet influences cancer has become a major research goal.

The battle against cancer is being waged on many fronts, and there is reason for optimism in the progress being made. It is especially encouraging that we can help to reduce our risk of acquiring and to increase our chance of surviving some of the most common forms of cancer by the choices we make in our daily life. Not smoking, exercising adequately, avoiding overexposure to the sun, and eating a high-fibre, low-fat diet can all help to prevent cancer. Furthermore, seven types of cancer can be easily detected: cancers of the skin and oral cavity (via physical exam), breast (via self-exams and mammograms for higher-risk women), prostate (via rectal exam), cervix (via Pap smear), testes (via self-exam), and colon (via colonoscopy). Regular visits to the doctor can help to identify tumours early, thereby significantly increasing the possibility of successful treatment.

 Which of the most common cancers affect primarily males? Which affect primarily females?

Males: prostate, testis; females: breast, uterus, cervix

REVIEW

MasteringBiology® **For Practice Quizzes, BioFlix, MP3 Tutors, and Activities, go to masteringbiology.com.**

Reviewing the Concepts

Control of Gene Expression (11.1–11.11)

11.1 Proteins interacting with DNA turn prokaryotic genes on or off in response to environmental changes. In prokaryotes, genes for related enzymes are often controlled together in units called operons.

Regulatory proteins bind to control sequences in the DNA and turn operons on or off in response to environmental changes.

11.2 Chromosome structure and chemical modifications can affect gene expression. In multicellular eukaryotes, different types of cells make different proteins because different combinations of genes are active in each type. A chromosome contains DNA wound around clusters of histone proteins, forming a string of beadlike nucleosomes. DNA packing tends to block gene expression by preventing access of transcription proteins to the DNA. One example of DNA packing is X chromosome inactivation in the cells of female mammals.

11.3 Are identical twins really identical? Chemical modification of DNA bases or histone proteins can result in epigenetic inheritance. Such differences may account for differences between identical twins.

11.4 Complex assemblies of proteins control eukaryotic transcription. A variety of regulatory proteins interact with DNA and with each other to turn the transcription of eukaryotic genes on or off.

11.5 Eukaryotic RNA may be spliced in more than one way. After transcription, alternative RNA splicing may generate two or more types of mRNA from the same transcript.

11.6 Small RNAs play multiple roles in controlling gene expression. MicroRNAs, bound to proteins, can prevent gene expression by forming complexes with mRNA molecules.

11.7 Later stages of gene expression are also subject to regulation. The lifetime of an mRNA molecule helps to determine how much protein is made, as do factors involved in translation. A protein may need to be activated in some way, and eventually the cell will break it down.

11.8 Review: Multiple mechanisms regulate gene expression in eukaryotes. Figure 11.8 reviews the multiple stages of eukaryotic gene expression, each stage offering opportunities for regulation.

11.9 Cell signalling and cascades of gene expression direct animal development. A series of RNAs and proteins produced in the embryo control the development of an animal from a fertilized egg.

11.10 Signal transduction pathways convert messages received at the cell surface to responses within the cell. Signals received at the plasma membrane are carried to the nucleus along complex signal transduction pathways. The nucleus initiates a response based on the combination of signals it receives.

11.11 Cell-signalling systems appeared early in the evolution of life. Similarities among organisms suggest that signal transduction pathways evolved early in the history of life on Earth.

Cloning of Plants and Animals (11.12–11.14)

11.12 Plant cloning shows that differentiated cells may retain all of their genetic potential. A clone is an individual created by asexual reproduction and thus genetically identical to a single parent.

11.13 Nuclear transplantation can be used to clone animals. Inserting DNA from a host cell into a nucleus-free egg can result in an early embryo that is a clone of the DNA donor. Implanting a blastocyst into a surrogate mother allows for the birth of a cloned mammal.

11.14 Therapeutic cloning can produce stem cells with great medical potential. The goal of therapeutic cloning is to produce embryonic stem cells. Such cells may eventually be used for a variety of therapeutic purposes. Like embryonic stem cells, adult stem cells can both perpetuate themselves in culture and give rise to differentiated cells. Unlike embryonic stem cells, adult stem cells normally give rise to only a limited range of cell types.

The Genetic Basis of Cancer (11.15–11.18)

11.15 Cancer results from mutations in genes that control cell division. Cancer cells, which divide uncontrollably, result from mutations in genes whose protein products affect the cell cycle. A mutation can change a proto-oncogene, a normal gene that helps to control cell division, into an oncogene, which causes cells to divide excessively. Mutations that inactivate tumour-suppressor genes have similar effects.

11.16 Multiple genetic changes underlie the development of cancer. Cancers result from a series of genetic changes.

11.17 Faulty proteins can interfere with normal signal transduction pathways. Many proto-oncogenes and tumour-suppressor genes code for proteins active in signal transduction pathways regulating cell division.

11.18 Lifestyle choices can reduce the risk of cancer. Reducing exposure to carcinogens, which induce cancer-causing mutations, and making other lifestyle choices can help to reduce cancer risk.

Connecting the Concepts

1. Complete the following concept map to test your knowledge of gene regulation.

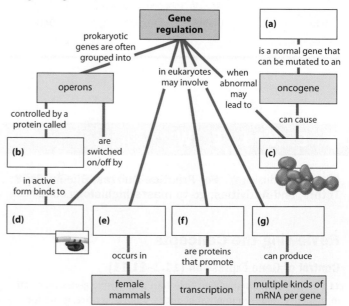

Testing Your Knowledge

Multiple Choice

2. Why is control of gene expression more complex in multicellular eukaryotes than in prokaryotes? *(Explain your answer.)*
   a. Eukaryotic cells are much smaller.
   b. In a multicellular eukaryote, different cells are specialized for different functions.
   c. Prokaryotes are restricted to stable environments.
   d. Eukaryotes have fewer genes, so each gene must do several jobs.
   e. Eukaryotic genes code for proteins.

3. Your bone cells, muscle cells, and skin cells look different because
   a. each cell contains different kinds of genes.
   b. they are present in different organs.
   c. different genes are active in each kind of cell.
   d. they contain different numbers of genes.
   e. each cell has different mutations.

4. Which of the following methods of gene regulation do eukaryotes and prokaryotes have in common?
   a. elaborate packing of DNA in chromosomes
   b. activator and repressor proteins, which attach to DNA
   c. the addition of a cap and tail to mRNA after transcription
   d. *lac* and *trp* operons
   e. the removal of noncoding portions of RNA

5. A homeotic gene does which of the following?
   a. It serves as the ultimate control for prokaryotic operons.
   b. It regulates the expression of groups of other genes during development.
   c. It represses the histone proteins in eukaryotic chromosomes.
   d. It helps to splice mRNA after transcription.
   e. It inactivates one of the X chromosomes in a female mammal.

6. All of your cells contain proto-oncogenes, which can change into cancer-causing genes. Why do cells possess such potential time bombs?
   a. Viruses infect cells with proto-oncogenes.
   b. Proto-oncogenes are genetic "junk" with no known function.
   c. Proto-oncogenes are unavoidable environmental carcinogens.
   d. Cells produce proto-oncogenes as a by-product of mitosis.
   e. Proto-oncogenes normally control cell division.

7. Which of the following is a valid difference between embryonic stem cells and the stem cells found in adult tissues?
   a. In laboratory culture, only adult stem cells are immortal.
   b. In nature, only embryonic stem cells give rise to all the different types of cells in the organism.
   c. Only adult stem cells can differentiate in culture.
   d. Embryonic stem cells are generally more difficult to grow in culture than adult stem cells.
   e. Only embryonic stem cells are found in every tissue of the adult body.

Describing, Comparing, and Explaining

8. A mutation in a single gene may cause a major change in the body of a fruit fly, such as an extra pair of legs or wings. Yet it probably takes the combined action of hundreds or thousands of genes to produce a wing or leg. How can a change in just one gene cause such a big change in the body?

Applying the Concepts

9. You obtain an egg cell from the ovary of a white mouse and remove the nucleus from it. You then obtain a nucleus from a liver cell from an adult black mouse. You use the methods of nuclear transplantation to insert the nucleus into the empty egg. After some prompting, the new zygote divides into an early embryo, which you then implant into the uterus of a brown mouse. A few weeks later, a litter of mice is born. What colour will they be? Why?

10. Mutations can alter the function of the *lac* operon (see Module 11.1). Predict how the following mutations would affect the function of the operon in the presence and absence of lactose:
   a. Mutation of regulatory gene; repressor cannot bind to lactose.
   b. Mutation of operator; repressor will not bind to operator.
   c. Mutation of regulatory gene; repressor will not bind to operator.
   d. Mutation of promoter; RNA polymerase will not attach to promoter.

11. A chemical called dioxin is produced as a by-product of some chemical manufacturing processes. This substance was present in Agent Orange, a defoliant sprayed on vegetation during the Vietnam War. There has been a continuing controversy over its effects on soldiers exposed to it during the war. Animal tests have suggested that dioxin can be lethal and can cause birth defects, cancer, organ damage, and immune system suppression. But its effects on humans are unclear, and even animal tests are inconclusive. Researchers have discovered that dioxin enters a cell and binds to a protein that in turn attaches to the cell's DNA. How might this mechanism help to explain the variety of dioxin's effects?

Answers to all questions can be found in Appendix E.

DNA Technology and Genomics

BIG IDEAS

Gene Cloning

(12.1–12.5)

A variety of laboratory techniques can be used to copy and combine DNA molecules.

Genetically Modified Organisms

(12.6–12.10)

Transgenic cells, plants, and animals are used in agriculture and medicine.

Crime scene DNA   Suspect's DNA

Longer STR fragments

Shorter STR fragments

DNA Profiling

(12.11–12.16)

Genetic markers can be used to definitively match a DNA sample to an individual.

Genomics

(12.17–12.21)

The study of complete DNA sets helps us learn about evolutionary history.

LEICESTERSHIRE CONSTABULARY

MURDER

1983   1986

LYNDA ROSE-MARIE MANN
Aged 15 of Narborough

On Tuesday 22nd November, 1983, Lynda's body was found in a copse alongside the Black Pad footpath which runs between King Edward Avenue and Forest Road at Narborough. The last positive sighting prior to the discovery of her body was at 7.30 pm the previous evening in Cuttback Avenue, Narborough.

DAWN AMANDA ASHWORTH
Aged 15 of Enderby

On Saturday 2nd August, 1986, Dawn's body was found in a field close to Ten Pound Lane, Enderby. The last positive sighting of Dawn was at 4.35 pm on Thursday 31st July, 1986, in Carlton Avenue, Narborough.

£20,000   REWARD

A reward of up to £20,000 has been offered for information leading to the arrest and conviction of the person or persons responsible for the murders of **Lynda Mann and Dawn Ashworth**

If you think you can assist the police in any way, please ring the Incident Room on

LEICESTER 482400 or 482401

If you would prefer to pass your information anonymously, please ring the special answering machine on

LEICESTER 482482 at any time

Printed and Published by the Chief Constable, Leicestershire Constabulary

DNA and Crime Scene Investigations

On November 22, 1983, the sleepy English village of Narborough awoke to news of a horrific crime: A 15-year-old girl had been raped and murdered on a country lane. Despite an extensive investigation and the presence of semen on the victim's body and clothes, the trail of evidence ran cold and the crime went unsolved.

Three years later, the horror resurfaced when another 15-year-old girl was raped and murdered less than a mile away from the first crime scene. When tests indicated that semen from the new crime scene could match the 1983 sample, police began to search for a double murderer. After another extensive investigation, a local man was arrested and charged with both crimes. Under considerable pressure from police, the suspect confessed to the second murder, but he denied committing the first.

In an attempt to pin both murders on the suspect, investigators turned to Alec Jeffreys, a biology professor at nearby Leicester University, who had recently developed the first DNA identification system. Because the DNA sequence of every person is unique (except for identical twins), DNA analysis can be used to determine with near certainty whether two DNA samples are from the same individual. Jeffreys compared DNA from the 1983 and 1986 semen samples. The DNA analysis confirmed that the same person had committed both crimes. However, when Jeffreys analyzed the suspect's DNA, it did not match either crime scene sample, proving the suspect's innocence. He was released, becoming the first person ever to be exonerated by DNA evidence.

The police were back at square one. In an attempt to collect more evidence, they asked every young male from the surrounding area to donate blood for DNA testing. Although nearly 5000 men were sampled, none matched the evidence from the crime scenes. The case finally broke when a pub-goer described how a local named Colin Pitchfork had bullied him into submitting blood on Pitchfork's behalf. The police arrested Pitchfork and took a sample of his blood. Indeed, his DNA matched the samples from the two crime scenes. Colin Pitchfork pleaded guilty to both crimes, closing the first murder case ever to be solved by DNA evidence.

The Narborough murders were the first of a great many criminal investigations that have relied on DNA evidence. DNA technology—methods for studying and manipulating genetic material—has rapidly revolutionized the field of forensics, the scientific analysis of evidence for legal investigations. Since its introduction, DNA analysis has become a standard law enforcement tool and has provided crucial evidence (of both innocence and guilt) in many famous cases.

As we will see in this chapter, DNA technology has practical applications beyond its use in forensic science. Applications of DNA technology include the use of gene cloning in the production of medical and industrial products, the development of genetically modified organisms for agriculture, and even the investigation of genealogical questions. Equally important, DNA technology is invaluable in many areas of biological research, such as cancer and evolution. As we discuss these various applications, we'll consider the specific techniques involved, how they are applied, and some of the social, legal, and ethical issues that are raised by the new technologies.

Gene Cloning

12.1 Genes can be cloned in recombinant plasmids

Although it may seem like a modern field, **biotechnology**, the manipulation of organisms or their components to make useful products, actually dates back to the dawn of civilization. Consider such ancient practices as the use of microbes to make beer, wine, and cheese, and the selective breeding of livestock, dogs, and other animals. But when people use the term *biotechnology* today, they are usually referring to **DNA technology**, modern laboratory techniques for studying and manipulating genetic material. Using these techniques, scientists can, for instance, modify specific genes and move them between organisms as different as bacteria, plants, and animals.

The field of DNA technology grew out of discoveries made about 60 years ago by American geneticists Joshua Lederberg and Edward Tatum. They performed a series of experiments with *Escherichia coli* (*E. coli*) that demonstrated that two individual bacteria can combine genes—a phenomenon that was previously thought to be limited to sexually reproducing eukaryotic organisms. With this work, they pioneered bacterial genetics, a field that within 20 years made *E. coli* the most thoroughly studied and understood organism at the molecular level.

In the 1970s, the field of biotechnology exploded with the invention of methods for making recombinant DNA in a test tube. **Recombinant DNA** is formed when scientists combine nucleotide sequences (pieces of DNA) from two different sources—often different species—to form a single DNA molecule. Today, recombinant DNA technology is widely used in the field of **genetic engineering**, the direct manipulation of genes for practical purposes. Scientists have genetically engineered bacteria to mass-produce a variety of useful chemicals, from cancer drugs to pesticides. Scientists have also transferred genes from bacteria into plants and from one animal species into another (**Figure 12.1A**).

To manipulate genes in the laboratory, biologists often use bacterial **plasmids**, which are small, circular DNA molecules that replicate (duplicate) separately from the much larger bacterial chromosome (see Module 17.8). Because plasmids can carry virtually any gene and are passed from one generation of bacteria to the next, they are key tools for **gene cloning**, the production of multiple identical copies of a gene-carrying piece of DNA. Gene-cloning methods are central to the production of useful products via genetic engineering.

Consider a typical genetic engineering challenge: A molecular biologist at a pharmaceutical company has identified a gene that codes for a valuable product, a hypothetical substance called protein V. The biologist wants to manufacture large amounts of protein V. **Figure 12.1B** illustrates how the techniques of gene cloning can be used to accomplish this goal.

To begin, the biologist isolates two kinds of DNA: ❶ a bacterial plasmid that will serve as the **vector**, or gene carrier, and

▲ **Figure 12.1A** Glowing fish produced by transferring a gene originally obtained from a jellyfish (cnidarian)

❷ the DNA containing the gene of interest—in this case, gene *V* (shown in red in the figure)—along with other, unwanted genes. Often, the plasmid comes from the bacterium *E. coli*. The DNA containing gene *V* could come from a variety of sources, such as a different bacterium, a plant, a nonhuman animal, or even human tissue cells growing in laboratory culture.

The researcher treats both the plasmid and the gene *V* source DNA with an enzyme that cuts DNA. ❸ An enzyme is chosen that cleaves the plasmid in only one place. ❹ The other DNA, which is usually much longer in sequence, may be cut into many fragments, one of which carries gene *V*. The figure shows the processing of just one DNA fragment and one plasmid, but actually, millions of plasmids and DNA fragments, most of which do not contain gene *V*, are treated simultaneously. The cuts leave single-stranded ends, as we'll explain in Module 12.2.

❺ The cut DNA from both sources—the plasmid and target gene—are mixed. The single-stranded ends of the plasmid base-pair with the complementary ends of the target DNA fragment (see Module 10.4 if you need a refresher on the DNA base-pairing rules). ❻ The enzyme **DNA ligase** joins the two DNA molecules by covalent bonds. This enzyme, which the cell normally uses in DNA replication (see Module 10.5), is a "DNA pasting" enzyme that catalyzes the formation of covalent bonds between adjacent nucleotides, joining the strands. The result is a recombinant DNA plasmid containing gene *V*, as well as many other recombinant DNA plasmids carrying other genes not shown here.

❼ The recombinant plasmid containing the targeted gene is mixed with a culture of bacteria. Under the right conditions, a bacterium takes up the plasmid DNA by transformation (see Module 17.7). ❽ This recombinant bacterium then reproduces to form a **clone** of cells, a group of identical cells descended from a single ancestral cell, each carrying a copy of gene *V*. This step is the actual gene cloning. In our example, the biologist will eventually grow a cell clone large enough to produce protein V in marketable quantities.

❾ Gene cloning can be used to produce a variety of desirable products. Copies of the gene itself can be the immediate product, to be used in further genetic engineering projects. For example, a pest-resistance gene present in one plant species might be cloned and transferred into plants of another species. Other times, the protein product of the cloned gene is harvested and used. For example, an enzyme that creates a faded look in blue jeans can be harvested in large quantities from bacteria carrying the cloned gene. (That's right: No stones are used to make stonewashed jeans!) Sometimes, the products of cloned genes can be used for illegal purposes. The performance-enhancing substances erythropoietin and human

E. coli bacterium

Plasmid

Bacterial chromosome

① A plasmid is isolated.

A cell with DNA containing the gene of interest

② The cell's DNA is isolated.

DNA

Gene of interest

③ The plasmid is cut with an enzyme.

④ The cell's DNA is cut with the same enzyme.

Gene of interest

⑤ The targeted fragment and plasmid DNA are combined.

⑥ DNA ligase is added, which joins the two DNA molecules.

Recombinant DNA plasmid

Gene of interest

⑦ The recombinant plasmid is taken up by a bacterium through transformation.

Recombinant bacterium

⑧ The bacterium reproduces.

Clone of cells

Genes may be inserted into other organisms.

Examples of gene use

A gene for pest resistance is inserted into plants.

A gene is used to alter bacteria for cleaning up toxic waste.

Examples of protein use

A protein is used to make "stone-washed" blue jeans.

⑨ Harvested proteins may be used directly.

A protein is used to dissolve blood clots in heart attack therapy.

▲ **Figure 12.1B** An overview of gene cloning

growth hormone are produced by bacteria containing the human genes for these hormones.

In the next four modules, we discuss the methods outlined in Figure 12.1B. You may find it useful to turn back to this summary figure as each technique is discussed.

> **?** Why does the rapid reproduction of bacteria make them a good choice for cloning a foreign gene?

● A foreign gene located within plasmid DNA inside a bacterium is replicated each time the cell divides, resulting in rapid accumulation of many copies of the gene.

12.2 Enzymes are used to "cut and paste" DNA

In the gene-cloning procedure outlined in Figure 12.1B, a recombinant DNA molecule is created by combining two ingredients: a bacterial plasmid and the gene of interest. To understand how these DNA molecules are spliced together, you need to learn how enzymes cut and paste DNA. The cutting tools are bacterial enzymes called **restriction enzymes**. In nature, these enzymes protect bacterial cells against intruding DNA from other organisms or viruses. They work by chopping up the foreign DNA, a process that restricts the ability of the invader to do harm to the bacterium. (The bacterial cell's own DNA is protected from restriction enzymes through chemical modification by other enzymes.)

Biologists have identified hundreds of different restriction enzymes. Each restriction enzyme is specific, recognizing a particular short DNA sequence, usually four to eight nucleotides long. For example, a restriction enzyme called *Eco*RI (found naturally in *E. coli*) recognizes only the DNA sequence GAATTC, whereas the enzyme called *Bam*HI recognizes only GGATCC. The DNA sequence recognized by a particular restriction enzyme is called a **restriction site**. Once a restriction site is recognized, the restriction enzyme cuts both strands of the DNA at specific points within the sequence. All copies of a particular DNA molecule always yield the same set of DNA fragments when exposed to the same restriction enzyme. In other words, a restriction enzyme cuts a DNA molecule in a precise, reproducible way.

Figure 12.2 ❶ shows a piece of DNA containing one recognition sequence for the restriction enzyme *Eco*RI. In this case, the restriction enzyme cuts each DNA strand between the bases A and G within the sequence, producing pieces of DNA called **restriction fragments**. ❷ Notice that the DNA is cut unevenly; the staggered cuts yield two double-stranded DNA fragments with single-stranded ends, called "sticky ends." Sticky ends are the key to joining DNA restriction fragments originating from different sources because these short extensions can form hydrogen-bonded base pairs with complementary single-stranded stretches of DNA.

❸ A piece of DNA (grey, with the red area showing the gene of interest) from another source is now added. Notice that the grey DNA has single-stranded ends identical in base sequence to the sticky ends on the blue DNA. The grey "foreign" DNA has ends with this particular base sequence because it was cut from a larger molecule by the same restriction enzyme used to cut the blue DNA. ❹ The complementary ends on the blue and grey fragments allow them to stick together by base pairing. (The hydrogen bonds are not shown in the figure.) This union between the blue and grey DNA fragments is temporary; it can be made permanent by the "pasting" enzyme DNA ligase. ❺ The final outcome is a stable molecule of recombinant DNA.

The ability to cut DNA with restriction enzymes and then paste it back together with DNA ligase is the key to the gene-cloning procedure outlined in Figure 12.1B and most other modern genetic engineering methods. This particular cloning procedure, which uses a mixture of fragments from the

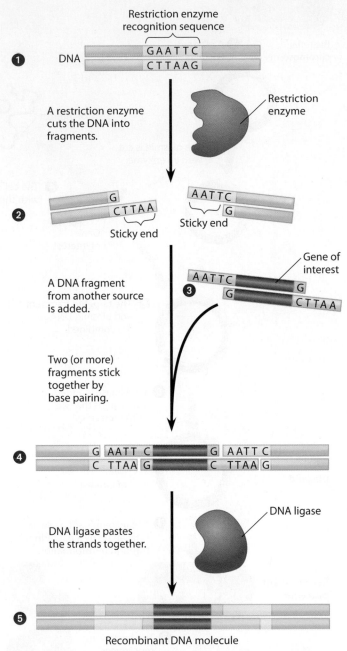

▲ Figure 12.2 Creating recombinant DNA by using a restriction enzyme and DNA ligase

entire genome of an organism, is called a "shotgun" approach. Thousands of different recombinant plasmids are produced, and a clone of each is made. The complete set of plasmid clones, each carrying copies of a particular segment from the initial genome, is a type of library. The next three modules discuss such libraries in more detail.

? What are "sticky ends"?

● Single-stranded regions whose unpaired bases can hydrogen-bond to the complementary sticky ends of other fragments created by the same restriction enzyme.

12.3 Cloned genes can be stored in genomic libraries

Each bacterial clone from the procedure in Figure 12.1B consists of identical cells with plasmids carrying one particular fragment of target DNA. The entire collection of all the cloned DNA fragments from a genome is called a **genomic library**. On the left side of **Figure 12.3**, the red, yellow, and green DNA

A genome is cut up with a restriction enzyme

or

Recombinant plasmid

Recombinant phage DNA

Bacterial clone

Phage clone

Plasmid library

Phage library

▲ **Figure 12.3** Genomic libraries

segments represent three of the thousands of different library "books" that are "shelved" in plasmids inside bacterial cells. A typical cloned DNA fragment is big enough to carry one or a few genes, and together, the fragments include the entire genome of the organism from which the DNA was derived.

Bacteriophages (also called phages)—viruses that infect bacteria—can also serve as vectors when cloning genes (Figure 12.3, right). When a phage is used, the DNA fragments are inserted into phage DNA molecules. The recombinant phage DNA can then be introduced into a bacterial cell through the normal infection process (see Figure 17.7B). Inside the cell, phage DNA is replicated, producing new phage particles, each carrying the foreign DNA. Another type of vector commonly used in library construction is a bacterial artificial chromosome (BAC). BACs are essentially large plasmids containing only the genes necessary to ensure replication. The primary advantage of BACs is that they can carry more foreign DNA than other vectors. In the next module, we look at another source of DNA for cloning: eukaryotic mRNA.

? In what sense does a genomic library have multiple copies of each "book"?

● Each "book"—a piece of DNA from the genome that was the source of the library—is present in every recombinant bacterium or phage in a clone.

12.4 Reverse transcriptase can help to make genes for cloning

Rather than starting with an entire eukaryotic genome, a researcher can focus on the genes expressed in a particular kind of cell by using its mRNA as the starting material for cloning. As shown in **Figure 12.4**, ❶ the chosen cells transcribe their genes and ❷ process the transcripts, removing introns and splicing exons together, producing mRNA. ❸ The researcher isolates the mRNA and makes single-stranded DNA transcripts from it using the enzyme **reverse transcriptase**, a retrovirus enzyme (gold in the figure; see Module 16.5). ❹ Another enzyme is added to break down the mRNA, and ❺ DNA polymerase (the enzyme that replicates DNA; see Module 10.5) is used to synthesize a second DNA strand.

The double-stranded DNA that results from such a procedure, called **complementary DNA (cDNA)**, represents only the subset of genes that had been transcribed into mRNA in the starting cells. Among other purposes, such a cDNA library is useful for studying the genes responsible for the specialized functions of a particular cell type, such as brain or liver cells. Because cDNAs lack introns, they are shorter than the full versions of the genes and therefore easier to work with.

In the next module, you will learn how to find one particular piece of DNA from among the thousands that are stored in a genomic or cDNA library.

? Why is a cDNA gene made using reverse transcriptase often shorter than the natural form of the gene?

● Because cDNAs are made from spliced mRNAs, which lack introns

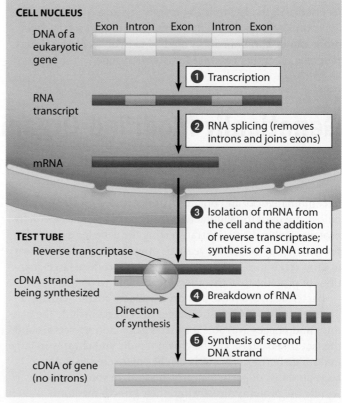

CELL NUCLEUS

DNA of a eukaryotic gene

Exon Intron Exon Intron Exon

❶ Transcription

RNA transcript

❷ RNA splicing (removes introns and joins exons)

mRNA

❸ Isolation of mRNA from the cell and the addition of reverse transcriptase; synthesis of a DNA strand

TEST TUBE

Reverse transcriptase

cDNA strand being synthesized

Direction of synthesis

❹ Breakdown of RNA

❺ Synthesis of second DNA strand

cDNA of gene (no introns)

▲ **Figure 12.4** Making an intron-lacking gene from eukaryotic mRNA

12.5 Nucleic acid probes identify clones carrying specific genes

Often, the most difficult task in gene cloning is finding the right "books" in a genomic library—that is, identifying clones containing a desired gene from among all those created. For example, a researcher might want to pull out just the clone of bacteria carrying the red gene in Figure 12.3. If bacterial clones containing a specific gene actually translate the gene into protein, they can be identified by testing for the protein product. However, not every desired gene produces detectable proteins. In such cases, researchers can also test directly for the gene itself.

Methods for detecting a gene directly depend on base pairing between the gene and a complementary sequence on another nucleic acid molecule, either DNA or RNA. When at least part of the nucleotide sequence of a gene is known, this information can be used to a researcher's advantage. Taking a simplified example, if we know that a hypothetical gene contains the sequence TAGGCT, a biochemist can synthesize a short single strand of DNA with the complementary sequence (ATCCGA) and label it with a fluorescent tag. Historically, a radioisotope label was used, but this practice is far less common today. This labelled, complementary molecule is called a **nucleic acid probe** because it is used to find a specific gene or other nucleotide sequence within a mass of DNA. (In practice, probe molecules are usually considerably longer than six nucleotides to reduce the chances that the sequence occurs in multiple genes.)

Figure 12.5 shows how a probe works. The DNA sample to be tested is treated with heat or chemicals to separate the DNA strands. When the labelled DNA probe is added to these strands, it tags the correct molecules—that is, it finds the correct books in the genomic library—by hydrogen-bonding to the complementary sequence in the gene of interest. Such a probe can be simultaneously applied to many bacterial clones to screen all of them at once for a desired gene.

▲ **Figure 12.5** How a DNA probe tags a gene by base pairing

In one technique, a piece of filter paper is pressed against bacterial colonies (clones) growing on a petri dish. The filter paper picks up cells from each colony. A chemical treatment is used to break open the cells and separate the DNA strands. The DNA strands are then soaked in probe solution. Any bacterial colonies carrying the gene of interest will be tagged on the filter paper, marking them for easy identification. Once the researcher identifies a colony carrying the desired gene, the cells can be grown further, and the gene of interest, or its protein product, can be collected in large amounts.

? How does a probe consisting of labelled DNA or RNA enable a researcher to find the bacterial clones carrying a particular gene?

● The probe molecules bind to and label DNA only from the cells containing the gene of interest, which has a complementary DNA sequence.

Genetically Modified Organisms

12.6 Recombinant cells and organisms can mass-produce gene products

Recombinant cells and organisms constructed by DNA technology are used to manufacture many useful products, chiefly proteins (**Table 12.6**). By transferring the gene for a desired protein into a bacterium, yeast, or other kind of cell that is easy to grow in culture, a genetic engineer can produce large quantities of proteins that are otherwise difficult to obtain.

Bacteria are often the best organisms for manufacturing a protein product. Major advantages of bacteria include the plasmids and phages available for use as gene-cloning vectors and the fact that bacteria can be grown rapidly and cheaply in large tanks. Furthermore, bacteria can be engineered to produce large amounts of particular proteins and, in some cases, to secrete the proteins directly into their growth medium,

simplifying the task of collecting and purifying the products. As Table 12.6 shows, a number of proteins of importance in human medicine and agriculture are being produced in the bacterium E. coli.

Despite the advantages of using bacteria, it is sometimes desirable or necessary to use eukaryotic cells to produce a protein product. Often, the first-choice eukaryotic organism for protein production is the yeast used in making bread and beer, *Saccharomyces cerevisiae*. As bakers and brewers have recognized for centuries, yeast cells are easy to grow. And like E. coli, yeast cells can take up foreign DNA and integrate it into their genomes. Yeast cells also have plasmids that can be used as gene vectors, and yeast is often better

TABLE 12.6	SOME PROTEIN PRODUCTS OF RECOMBINANT DNA TECHNOLOGY		
Product	**Made In**	**Use**	
Human insulin	*E. coli*	Treatment for diabetes	
Human growth hormone (HGH)	*E. coli*	Treatment for growth defects	
Epidermal growth factor (EGF)	*E. coli*	Treatment for burns, ulcers	
Interleukin-2 (IL-2)	*E. coli*	Possible treatment for cancer	
Bovine growth hormone (BGH)	*E. coli*	Improving weight gain in cattle	
Cellulase	*E. coli*	Breaking down cellulose for animal feeds	
Taxol	*E. coli*	Treatment for ovarian cancer	
Interferons (alpha and gamma)	*S. cerevisiae, E. coli*	Possible treatment for cancer and viral infections	
Hepatitis B vaccine	*S. cerevisiae*	Prevention of viral hepatitis	
Erythropoietin (EPO)	Mammalian cells	Treatment for anemia	
Factor VIII	Mammalian cells	Treatment for hemophilia	
Tissue plasminogen activator (TPA)	Mammalian cells	Treatment for heart attacks and some strokes	

▲ **Figure 12.6A** A goat carrying a gene for a human blood protein that is secreted in the milk

than bacteria at synthesizing and secreting eukaryotic proteins. *S. cerevisiae* is currently used to produce a number of proteins. In certain cases, the same product—for example, interferons used in cancer research—can be made in either yeast or bacteria. In other cases, such as the hepatitis B vaccine, yeast alone is used.

The cells of choice for making some gene products come from mammals. Many proteins that mammalian cells normally secrete are glycoproteins, proteins with chains of sugars attached. Because only mammalian cells can attach the sugars correctly, mammalian cells must be used for making these products. For example, recombinant mammalian cells growing in laboratory cultures are currently used to produce human erythropoietin (EPO), a hormone that stimulates the production of red blood cells. EPO is used as a treatment for anemia, but the drug is also abused by some athletes who seek the advantage of artificially high levels of oxygen-carrying red blood cells (called "blood doping").

Recently, pharmaceutical researchers have been exploring the mass production of gene products by whole animals or plants rather than cultured cells. Genetic engineers have used recombinant DNA technology to insert genes for desired human proteins into other mammals, where the protein encoded by the recombinant gene may be secreted in the animal's milk. For example, a gene for antithrombin—a human protein that helps to prevent inappropriate blood clotting—has been inserted into the genome of a goat **(Figure 12.6A)**; isolated from the milk, the protein can be administered to patients with a rare hereditary disorder in which this protein is lacking. The pig in **Figure 12.6B** has been genetically modified to produce

human hemoglobin; this vital blood protein can be supplied to patients via blood transfusion.

However, genetically engineered animals are difficult and costly to produce. Typically, a biotechnology company starts by injecting the desired DNA into a large number of embryos, which are then implanted into surrogate mothers. With luck, one or a few recombinant animals may result; success rates for such procedures are very low. Once a recombinant organism is successfully produced, it may be cloned. The result can be a genetically identical herd—a grazing pharmaceutical "factory" of "pharm" animals that produce otherwise rare biological substances for medical use.

We continue an exploration of the medical applications of DNA technology in the next module.

? Why can't glycoproteins be mass-produced by engineered bacteria or yeast cells?

● Because bacteria and yeast cells cannot correctly attach the sugar groups to the protein of glycoproteins

▲ **Figure 12.6B** A pig that has been genetically modified to produce a useful human protein

12.7 DNA technology has changed the pharmaceutical industry and medicine

DNA technology, and gene cloning in particular, is widely used to produce medicines and to diagnose diseases.

Therapeutic Hormones   Consider the first two products in Table 12.6—human insulin and human growth hormone (HGH). About 200 000 people with diabetes in Canada depend on insulin treatment. Before 1982, the main sources of this hormone were slaughtered pigs and cattle. Insulin extracted from these animals is chemically similar, but not identical, to human insulin, and it causes harmful side effects in some people. Genetic engineering has largely solved this problem by developing bacteria that synthesize and secrete the human form of insulin. In 1983, Humulin **(Figure 12.7A)**—human insulin produced by bacteria—became the first recombinant DNA drug (often referred to as a biologic drug) approved by Health Canada.

▲ **Figure 12.7A**
Human insulin produced by bacteria

Treatment with HGH is a boon to children born with a form of dwarfism caused by inadequate amounts of HGH. Because growth hormones from other animals are not effective in humans, children with HGH deficiency historically have had to rely on scarce supplies from human cadavers or else face dwarfism. In 1985, however, molecular biologists made an artificial gene for HGH by joining a human DNA fragment to a chemically synthesized piece of DNA; using this gene, they were able to produce HGH in *E. coli*. HGH from recombinant bacteria is now widely used.

Another important pharmaceutical product produced by genetic engineering is tissue plasminogen activator (TPA). If administered soon after a heart attack, this protein helps to dissolve blood clots and reduces the risk of subsequent heart attacks.

Diagnosis of Disease   DNA technology is being used increasingly to diagnose disease. Among the hundreds of genes for human diseases that have been identified are those for sickle-cell disease, hemophilia, cystic fibrosis, and Huntington's disease. Affected individuals with such diseases often can be identified before the onset of symptoms, even before birth. It is also possible to identify symptomless carriers of potentially harmful recessive alleles (see Module 9.8). Additionally, DNA technology can pinpoint infections. For example, DNA analysis can help to track down and identify elusive viruses such as HIV, the virus that causes AIDS.

Vaccines   DNA technology is also helping medical researchers develop vaccines. A **vaccine** is a harmless variant (mutant) or derivative of a pathogen—usually a bacterium or virus—that is used to stimulate the immune system to mount a lasting defence against that pathogen (see Module 34.4). For many viral diseases, prevention by vaccination is the only medical way to prevent illness.

Genetic engineering can be used in several ways to make vaccines. One approach is to use genetically engineered cells or organisms to produce large amounts of a protein molecule that is found on the pathogen's outside surface. This method has been used to make the vaccine against the hepatitis B virus. Hepatitis is a disabling and sometimes fatal liver disease, and the hepatitis B virus may also cause liver cancer. **Figure 12.7B** shows a tank for growing yeast cells that have been engineered to carry the gene for the virus's surface protein. Made by the yeast, this protein will be the main ingredient of the vaccine.

Another way to use DNA technology in vaccine development is to make a harmless artificial mutant of the pathogen by altering one or more of its genes. When a harmless mutant is used as a so-called live vaccine, it multiplies in the body and may trigger a strong immune response. Artificial-mutant vaccines may cause fewer side effects than vaccines that have traditionally been made from natural mutants.

Yet another method for making vaccines employs a virus related to the one that causes smallpox. Smallpox was once a dreaded human disease, but it was eradicated worldwide in the 1970s by widespread vaccination with a harmless variant of the smallpox virus. Using this harmless virus, genetic engineers could replace some of the genes encoding proteins that induce immunity to smallpox with genes that induce immunity to other diseases. In fact, the virus could be engineered to carry genes needed to vaccinate against several diseases simultaneously. In the future, one inoculation may prevent a dozen diseases.

Genetic engineering rapidly transformed the field of medicine and continues to do so today. But genetically modified organisms affect our lives in other ways, as we'll see next.

 Human growth hormone and insulin produced by DNA technology are used in the treatment of _____ and _____, respectively.

dwarfism; diabetes ●

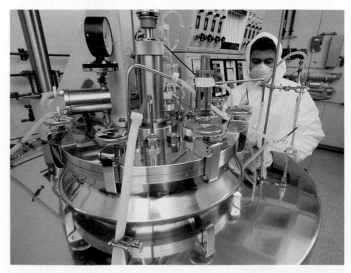

▲ **Figure 12.7B**   Equipment used in the production of a vaccine against hepatitis B

12.8 Genetically modified organisms are transforming agriculture

Since ancient times, people have selectively bred agricultural crops to make them more useful. Today, DNA technology is quickly replacing traditional breeding programs as scientists work to improve the productivity of agriculturally important plants and animals. Genetic engineers have produced many varieties of **genetically modified (GM) organisms**, organisms that have acquired one or more genes by artificial means. If the newly acquired gene is from another organism, typically of another species, the recombinant organism is called a **transgenic organism**.

The most common vector used to introduce new genes into plant cells is a plasmid from the soil bacterium *Agrobacterium tumefaciens* called the **Ti plasmid (Figure 12.8A)**. **❶** With the help of a restriction enzyme and DNA ligase, the gene for a desired trait (indicated in red in the figure) is inserted into a modified version of the plasmid. **❷** Then the recombinant plasmid is put into a plant cell, where the DNA carrying the new gene integrates into the plant chromosome. **❸** Finally, the recombinant cell is cultured and grown into a plant.

With an estimated 1 billion people facing malnutrition, GM crops may be able to help a great many hungry people by improving food production, pest resistance, and the nutritional value of crops. For example, in India, the insertion of a salinity-resistance gene has enabled new varieties of rice to grow in water three times as salty as seawater. Similar research is under way in Australia to help to improve wheat yields in salty soil. In Hawaii, the ring spot virus seemed poised to devastate the papaya industry until a GM variety resistant to the virus was introduced in 1992. Golden Rice, a transgenic variety created in 2000 with a few daffodil genes, produces yellow grains containing beta-carotene, which our body uses to make vitamin A. A new strain (Golden Rice 2) uses corn genes to boost beta-carotene levels even higher **(Figure 12.8B)**. This rice could help to prevent vitamin A deficiency—and the resulting blindness—among the half of the world's people who depend on rice as their staple food.

In addition to agricultural applications, genetic engineers are now creating plants that make human proteins for medical use. A recently developed transgenic rice strain harbours genes for milk proteins that can be used in rehydration formulas to treat infant diarrhea, a serious problem in developing countries. Other pharmaceutical trials currently under way involve using modified corn to treat cystic fibrosis, safflower to treat diabetes, and duckweed to treat hepatitis. Although these trials seem promising, no plant-made drugs intended for use by humans have yet to be approved or sold.

▲ **Figure 12.8B** A mix of conventional rice (white), the original Golden Rice (light gold), and Golden Rice 2 (dark gold)

Agricultural researchers are also producing transgenic animals, as mentioned in Module 12.6. To do this, scientists remove egg cells from a female and fertilize them. They then inject a previously cloned gene directly into the nuclei of the fertilized eggs. Some of the cells integrate the foreign DNA into their genomes. The engineered embryos are then surgically implanted in a surrogate mother. If an embryo develops successfully, the result is an animal containing a gene from a third "parent," which may even be of another species.

The goals in creating a transgenic animal are often the same as the goals of traditional breeding—for instance, to make a sheep with better quality wool or a cow that will mature in less time. In 2006, researchers succeeded in transferring a fat metabolism gene from a roundworm into a pig. Meat from the resulting swine had levels of healthy omega-3 fatty acids—which are believed to reduce the risk of heart disease—four to five times higher than meat from normal pigs. Scientists at the University of Guelph have created a transgenic pig, which is better for the environment. The "Enviropig™" is a Yorkshire pig

▲ **Figure 12.8A** Using the Ti plasmid to genetically engineer plants

Agrobacterium tumefaciens

Ti plasmid

Restriction site

DNA containing the gene for a desired trait

❶ The gene is inserted into the plasmid by using a restriction enzyme and DNA ligase.

Recombinant Ti plasmid

❷ The recombinant plasmid is introduced into a plant cell in culture.

Plant cell

DNA carrying the new gene within the plant chromosome

❸ The plant cell is cultured and grows into a plant.

A plant with the new trait

▲ **Figure 12.8C** Enviropig™

that produces the enzyme phytase from *E. coli*, which digests phytic acid, a phosphorus-containing compound. The phytase enzyme makes a previously indigestible molecule a valuable source of phosphorus for the pig. As a result, the Enviropig™ does not require phosphorus supplements in its diet and excretes less in its feces **(Figure 12.8C)**. Lower phosphorus levels in the feces reduces the impact of this nutrient on the eutrophication of water systems (see Module 40.10).

To date, the vast majority of the GM organisms that contribute to our food supply are not animals but crop plants. As we'll discuss next, some people question whether such genetically modified organisms are beneficial to our society.

 What is the function of the Ti plasmid in the creation of transgenic plants?

● It is used as the vector for introducing foreign genes into a plant cell.

12.9 Genetically modified organisms raise concerns about human and environmental health

As soon as scientists realized the power of DNA technology, they began to worry about potential dangers. Early concerns focused on the possibility that recombinant DNA technology might create new pathogens. What might happen, for instance, if cancer cell genes were transferred into infectious bacteria or viruses? To guard against such rogue microbes, scientists developed a set of guidelines that were adopted as formal government regulations in Canada and some other countries. One safety measure is a set of strict laboratory procedures designed to protect researchers from infection by engineered microbes and to prevent the microbes from accidentally leaving the laboratory **(Figure 12.9A)**. In addition, strains of microorganisms to be used in recombinant DNA experiments are genetically crippled to ensure that they cannot survive outside the laboratory. Finally, certain obviously dangerous experiments have been banned.

▲ **Figure 12.9A** Scientists in the National Microbiology Laboratory, a maximum security facility in Winnipeg

Today, most public concern about possible hazards centres not on recombinant microbes but on genetically modified organisms (GMOs) used for food. Some fear that crops carrying genes from other species might be hazardous to human health or the environment. Others fear that the protein products of transplanted genes might lead to allergic reactions.

About a decade ago, negotiators from 130 countries, including Canada, agreed on a Biosafety Protocol that requires all exporters to identify GM organisms present in bulk food shipments and allows importing countries to decide whether they pose environmental or health risks. Although the majority of several staple crops grown in North America—including corn and soybeans—are genetically modified, products made from GMOs are not required to be labelled in any way. Chances are, you eat a food containing GMOs nearly every day, but the lack of labelling means there is little chance that you would be able to say for certain. However, labelling of foods containing more than trace amounts of GMOs is required in Europe, Japan, Australia, and some other countries. Critics of GM crops point out that labelling would allow consumers to decide for themselves whether or not they wish to be exposed to GM foods. In Canada, labelling is mandatory for anything that may pose a health or safety risk; however, if there is no risk, the labelling of GM products is voluntary. Some biotechnology advocates, however, respond that similar demands were not made when "transgenic" crop plants produced by traditional breeding techniques were put on the market. For example, triticale was created decades ago by combining the genomes of wheat and rye—two plants that do not interbreed in nature. Triticale is now grown worldwide.

Advocates of a cautious approach toward GM crops also fear that transgenic plants might pass their new genes to close relatives in nearby wild areas (**Figure 12.9B**). We know that lawn and crop grasses, for example, commonly exchange genes with wild relatives via pollen transfer. If crop plants carrying genes for resistance to herbicides, diseases, or insect pests pollinated wild ones, the offspring might become "superweeds" that would be very difficult to control. Concern has also been raised that the widespread use of GM seeds may reduce natural genetic diversity, leaving crops susceptible to catastrophic die-offs in the event of a sudden change to the environment or introduction of a new pest.

Today, governments and regulatory agencies throughout the world are grappling with how to facilitate the use of biotechnology in agriculture, industry, and medicine while ensuring that new products and procedures are safe. In Canada, such applications of biotechnology are evaluated for potential risks by multiple government agencies. Meanwhile, these same agencies and the public must consider the ethical implications of biotechnology.

In the case of GM plants and certain other applications of DNA technology, zero risk is probably unattainable. Scientists

and the public need to weigh the possible benefits versus risks on a case-by-case basis. The best scenario would be for us to proceed with caution, basing our decisions on sound scientific information rather than on either irrational fear or blind optimism.

▲ **Figure 12.9B** Genetically engineered crop plants growing near their wild relatives

? What is one of the concerns about engineering crop plants by adding genes for herbicide resistance?

● The possibility that the genes could escape via cross-pollination to weeds that are closely related to the crop species

---

12.10 Gene therapy may someday help to treat a variety of diseases

In this chapter, we have discussed transgenic viruses, bacteria, yeast, plants, and animals. What about transgenic humans? Why would anyone want to insert genes into a living person?

One reason to tamper with the human genome is the potential for treating a variety of diseases by **gene therapy**—alteration of an afflicted individual's genes for therapeutic purposes. In people with disorders traceable to a single defective gene, it might be possible to replace or supplement the defective gene by inserting a normal allele into cells of the tissue affected by the disorder. Once there, the normal allele may be expressed, potentially curing the disease after just a single treatment.

For gene therapy to be permanent, the normal allele would have to be transferred to cells that multiply throughout a person's life. Bone marrow cells, which include the stem cells that give rise to all the cells of the blood and immune system, are prime candidates (see Module 11.14). **Figure 12.10** outlines one possible procedure for gene therapy. ❶ The normal gene is cloned, converted to an RNA version, and then inserted into the RNA genome of a harmless retrovirus vector. ❷ Bone marrow cells are taken from the patient and infected with the virus. ❸ The virus inserts a DNA version of its genome, including the normal human gene, into the cells' DNA (see Module 16.5). ❹ The engineered cells are then injected back into the patient. If the procedure succeeds, the cells will multiply throughout the patient's life and produce a steady supply of the missing protein, curing the patient.

The first successful human gene therapy trial, begun in 2000, used this method to treat 10 young children with severe combined immunodeficiency disease (SCID), a disorder in which the patient lacks a functional immune system. Nine

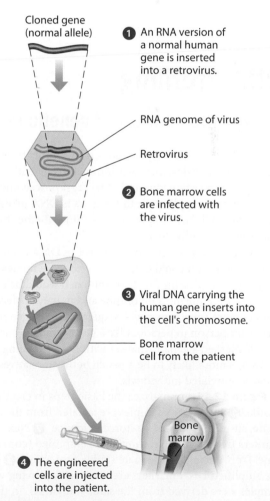

❶ An RNA version of a normal human gene is inserted into a retrovirus.

RNA genome of virus

Retrovirus

❷ Bone marrow cells are infected with the virus.

❸ Viral DNA carrying the human gene inserts into the cell's chromosome.

Bone marrow cell from the patient

Cloned gene (normal allele)

Bone marrow

❹ The engineered cells are injected into the patient.

▲ **Figure 12.10** One type of gene therapy procedure

of these patients showed significant improvement, providing the first definitive success of gene therapy. However, three of the patients subsequently developed leukemia, a cancer of the blood cells, and one died. Researchers discovered that in two of the cases, the inserted DNA appeared to disrupt a gene involved in proliferation and development of blood cells. This insertion somehow caused the leukemia. Active research into treating SCID continues with new, tougher safety guidelines.

A 2009 gene therapy trial involved a disease called Leber's congenital amaurosis (LCA). People with one form of LCA have a defective version of a gene needed to produce rhodopsin, a pigment that enables the eye to detect light. In such people, photoreceptor cells gradually die, causing progressive blindness. An international research team found that a single injection—containing a virus carrying the normal gene—into one eye of affected children improved vision in that eye, sometimes enough to allow normal functioning.

The use of gene therapy raises several technical questions. For example, how can researchers build in gene control mechanisms to ensure that cells with the transferred gene make appropriate amounts of the gene product at the right time and in the right parts of the body? And how can they be sure that the gene's insertion does not harm the cell's normal function?

In addition to technical challenges, gene therapy raises difficult ethical questions. Some critics suggest that tampering with human genes in any way will inevitably lead to the practice of eugenics, the deliberate effort to control the genetic makeup of human populations. Other observers see no fundamental difference between the transplantation of genes into somatic cells and the transplantation of organs.

The implications of genetically manipulating gamete-forming cells or zygotes (already accomplished in lab animals) are more problematic. This possibility raises the most difficult ethical questions of all: Should we try to eliminate genetic defects in our children and their descendants? Should we interfere with evolution in this way? From a biological perspective, the elimination of unwanted alleles from the gene pool could backfire. Genetic variety is a necessary ingredient for the survival of a species as environmental conditions change with time. Genes that are damaging under some conditions may be advantageous under others (one example is the sickle-cell allele; see Module 9.12). Are we willing to risk making genetic changes that could be detrimental to our species in the future? We may have to face this question soon.

> **?** What characteristic of bone marrow makes those cells good targets for gene therapy?

They multiply throughout a person's life.

DNA Profiling

12.11 The analysis of genetic markers can produce a DNA profile

Modern DNA technology methods have rapidly transformed the field of **forensics**, the scientific analysis of evidence for crime scene investigations and other legal proceedings. The most important application to forensics is **DNA profiling**, the analysis of DNA samples to determine whether they came from the same individual.

How do you prove that two samples of DNA come from the same person? You could compare the entire genomes found in the two samples; but, such an approach would be extremely impractical, requiring a lot of time and money. Instead, scientists compare genetic markers, sequences in the genome that vary from person to person. Like a gene, which is one type of genetic marker, a genetic marker within a noncoding stretch of DNA is more likely to be a match between relatives than between unrelated individuals.

Figure 12.11 summarizes the basic steps in creating a DNA profile. ❶ First, DNA samples are isolated from the crime scene, suspects, victims, or stored evidence. ❷ Next, selected markers from each DNA sample are amplified (copied many times), producing an adequate supply for testing. ❸ Finally, the amplified DNA markers are compared, proving which samples were derived from the same individual. In the next three modules, we'll explore the methods behind these steps in detail.

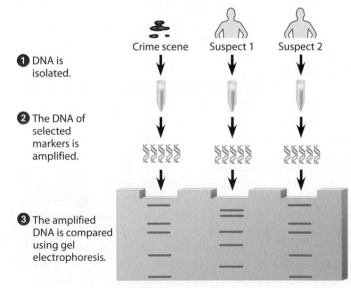

❶ DNA is isolated.

❷ The DNA of selected markers is amplified.

❸ The amplified DNA is compared using gel electrophoresis.

▲ **Figure 12.11** An overview of DNA profiling

> **?** According to the data presented in Figure 12.11, which suspect left DNA at the crime scene?

Suspect 2; notice that the number and location of the DNA markers match between suspect 2's DNA and the crime scene DNA.

12.12 The PCR method is used to amplify DNA sequences

Cloning DNA in host cells is often the best method for preparing large quantities of DNA from a particular gene (see Module 12.1). However, when the source of DNA is scant or impure, the polymerase chain reaction is a much better method. The **polymerase chain reaction** (**PCR**) is a technique by which a specific segment of a DNA molecule can be targeted and quickly amplified in the laboratory. Starting with a minute sample of blood or other tissue, automated PCR can generate billions of copies of a DNA segment in just a few hours, producing enough DNA to allow a DNA profile to be constructed.

In principle, PCR is fairly simple (**Figure 12.12**). A repeated, three-step cycle brings about a chain reaction that doubles the population of identical DNA molecules during each round. The key to amplifying one particular segment of DNA and no others is the use of **primers**, short (usually 15 to 20 nucleotides long), chemically synthesized single-stranded DNA molecules with sequences that are complementary to sequences at each end of the target sequence. One primer is complementary to one strand at one end of the target sequence; the second primer is complementary to the other strand at the other end of the sequence. The primers thus bind to sequences that flank the target sequence, marking the start and end points for the segment of DNA being amplified.

1 In the first step of each PCR cycle, the reaction mixture is heated to separate the strands of the DNA double helices. **2** Next, the strands are cooled. As they cool, primer molecules hydrogen-bond to their target sequences on the DNA. **3** In the third step, a heat-stable DNA polymerase builds new DNA strands by extending the primers in the 5′ → 3′ direction.

These three steps are repeated over and over, doubling the amount of DNA after each three-step cycle. A key prerequisite for automating PCR was the discovery of an unusual DNA polymerase, first isolated from a bacterium living in hot springs, that could withstand the heat at the start of each cycle. Without such a heat-stable polymerase, PCR would be much more difficult because standard DNA polymerases would denature (unfold) during the heating step of each cycle.

Just as impressive as the speed of PCR is its sensitivity. Only minute amounts of DNA need to be present in the starting material, and this DNA can even be in a partially degraded state. The key to the high sensitivity is the primers. Because the primers bind only the sequences associated with the target, the DNA polymerase duplicates only the desired segments of DNA. Other DNA will not be bound by primers and thus not copied by the DNA polymerase.

Devised in 1985, PCR has had a major impact on biological research and biotechnology. PCR has been used to amplify DNA from a wide variety of sources: fragments of ancient DNA from a mummified human, a 40 000-year-old frozen woolly mammoth, and a 30-million-year-old plant fossil; DNA from fingerprints or from tiny amounts of blood, tissue, or semen found at crime scenes; DNA from single embryonic cells for rapid prenatal diagnosis of genetic disorders; and DNA of viral genes from cells infected with viruses that are difficult to detect, such as HIV.

? **Why is amplification of DNA from a crime scene often necessary?**

● The DNA from a crime scene is often scant and impure.

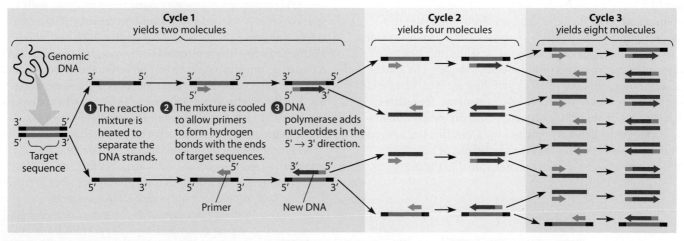

Figure 12.12 DNA amplification by PCR

Cycle 1 yields two molecules
Cycle 2 yields four molecules
Cycle 3 yields eight molecules

Genomic DNA

1 The reaction mixture is heated to separate the DNA strands.
2 The mixture is cooled to allow primers to form hydrogen bonds with the ends of target sequences.
3 DNA polymerase adds nucleotides in the 5′ → 3′ direction.

Target sequence

Primer   New DNA

12.13 Gel electrophoresis sorts DNA molecules by size

Many approaches for studying DNA molecules in the lab make use of **gel electrophoresis**. A gel is a thin slab of jellylike material often made from agarose, a carbohydrate polymer extracted from seaweed. Because agarose contains a dense tangle of cable-like threads (similar to the structure of fibreglass, and resembling a jungle dense with vines), it can act as a molecular sieve that

separates macromolecules—usually proteins or nucleic acids—on the basis of size, electrical charge, or other physical properties.

Figure 12.13 outlines how gel electrophoresis can be used to separate mixtures of DNA fragments obtained from three different sources. A DNA sample from each source is placed in a separate well (or hole) at one end of a flat, rectangular gel. A

▲ **Figure 12.13** Gel electrophoresis of DNA

A mixture of DNA fragments of different sizes

Power source

Gel

Longer (slower) molecules

Shorter (faster) molecules

Completed gel

negatively charged electrode from a power supply is attached near the end of the gel containing the DNA, and a positive electrode is attached near the other end. Because all nucleic acid molecules carry negative charges on their phosphate groups (PO_4^-; see Module 10.2), the DNA molecules all travel through the gel toward the positive pole. However, longer DNA fragments are held back by the thicket of polymer fibres within the gel, so they move more slowly than the shorter fragments. Over time, shorter molecules move farther through the gel than longer fragments. Gel electrophoresis thus separates DNA fragments by length, with shorter molecules migrating toward the bottom faster than longer molecules.

When the current is turned off, a series of bands is left in each "lane" of the gel. Each band is a collection of DNA fragments of the same length. The bands can be made visible by staining, by exposing the bands on photographic film (if the DNA is radioactively labelled), or by measuring fluorescence (if the DNA is labelled with a fluorescent dye).

? **What causes DNA molecules to move toward the positive pole during electrophoresis? Why do large molecules move more slowly than smaller ones?**

● The negatively charged phosphate groups of the DNA are attracted to the positive pole; the gel restricts the movement of longer fragments more.

12.14 STR analysis is commonly used for DNA profiling

If you take another look at the overview of DNA profiling in Figure 12.11, you will see that we have learned about DNA amplification by PCR (step 2) and gel electrophoresis (step 3). Now, let's put them together to see how a DNA profile is made.

To create a DNA profile, a forensic scientist must compare genetic markers from two or more DNA samples. The genetic markers most often used in DNA profiling are inherited variations in the lengths of repetitive DNA segments. **Repetitive DNA** consists of nucleotide sequences that are present in multiple copies in the genome; much of the DNA that lies between genes in humans is of this type. Some regions of repetitive DNA vary considerably from one individual to the next.

For DNA profiling, the relevant type of repetitive DNA consists of short sequences repeated many times in a row; such a series of repeats is called a **short tandem repeat (STR)**. For example, one person might have the sequence AGAT repeated 12 times in a row at one place in the genome, the sequence GATA repeated 45 times in a row at a second place, and so on. Another person is likely to have the same sequences at the same places but with different numbers of repeats. These stretches of repetitive DNA, like any genetic marker, are more likely to be an exact match between relatives than between unrelated individuals.

STR analysis is a method of DNA profiling that compares the lengths of STR sequences at specific sites in the genome. Most commonly, STR analysis compares the number of repeats of specific four-nucleotide DNA sequences at 13 sites scattered throughout the genome. Each of these repeat sites, which typically contain from 3 to 50 four-nucleotide repeats in a row, vary widely from person to person. In fact, some of the short tandem repeats used in the standard procedure can be found in up to 80 different variations in the human population.

Consider the two samples of DNA shown in **Figure 12.14A**, where the top DNA was obtained at a crime scene and the bottom DNA from a suspect's blood. The two segments have the same number of repeats at

STR site 1

AGAT

Crime scene DNA

STR site 2

GATA

The number of short tandem repeats match

The number of short tandem repeats do not match

Suspect's DNA

AGAT

GATA

▲ **Figure 12.14A** Two representative STR sites from crime scene DNA samples

Crime scene DNA   Suspect's DNA

Longer STR fragments

Shorter STR fragments

▲ **Figure 12.14B** DNA profiles generated from the STRs in Figure 12.14A

the first site: 7 repeats of the four-nucleotide DNA sequence AGAT (shown in orange). Notice, however, that they differ in the number of repeats at the second site: 8 repeats of GATA (shown in purple) in the crime scene DNA, compared with 13 repeats in the suspect's DNA. To create a DNA profile, a scientist uses PCR to specifically amplify the regions of DNA that include these STR sites. This can be done by using primers matching nucleotide sequences known to flank the STR sites. The resulting DNA molecules are then compared by gel electrophoresis.

Figure 12.14B shows a gel that could have resulted from the STR fragments in Figure 12.14A. The differences in the locations of the bands reflect the different lengths of the DNA fragments. (A gel from an actual DNA profile would typically contain more than just two bands in each lane.) This gel would provide evidence that the crime scene DNA did not come from the suspect. Notice that electrophoresis allows us to see similarities as well as differences between mixtures of DNA molecules. Thus, data from DNA profiling can provide evidence of either innocence or guilt.

Although other methods have been used in the past, STR analysis of 13 predetermined STR sites is the current standard for DNA profiling in forensic and legal systems. Once determined, the number of repeats at each of these sites can be entered into the Canadian National DNA Data Bank that is administered by the Royal Canadian Mounted Police. Within the human population, so much variation exists within the 13 standard sites that a DNA profile made from them can definitely identify a single person from within the entire human population. In the next module, we'll examine several real-world examples of how this technology has been used.

 What are STRs? What is STR analysis?

STRs are regions of the genome that contain varying numbers of in-a-row repeats of a short nucleotide sequence. STR analysis is a technique for determining whether two DNA samples have identical STRs. ●

12.15 DNA profiling has provided evidence in many forensic investigations

When a violent crime is committed, body fluids or small pieces of tissue may be left at the crime scene or on the clothes of the victim or assailant. If rape has occurred, semen may be recovered from the victim. DNA profiling can match such samples to the person they came from with a high degree of certainty because the DNA sequence of every person is unique, except for identical twins. And with PCR amplification of DNA, a tissue sample as small as 20 cells can be sufficient for testing.

Since its introduction in 1986, DNA profiling has become a standard tool of forensics and has provided crucial evidence in many cases. Of course, DNA evidence can prove innocence as well as guilt. For example, in 1969 Winnipegger David Milgaard was convicted of raping and killing a nursing student in Saskatoon and sentenced to life in prison. After the courts denied several of Milgaard's appeals, a DNA laboratory in the United Kingdom determined that the semen sample left by the killer did not match Milgaard. Milgaard spent 21 years in prison for a crime he did not commit.

The use of DNA profiling extends beyond crimes. For instance, a comparison of the DNA of a child and the purported father can conclusively settle a question of paternity. One of the strangest cases of DNA profiling is that of Cheddar Man, a 9000-year-old skeleton found in a cave near Cheddar, England (Figure 12.15). DNA was extracted from his tooth and analyzed. The DNA profile showed that Cheddar Man was a direct ancestor—through approximately 300 generations—of a present-day schoolteacher who lived fewer than 10 km from the cave!

Just how reliable is DNA profiling? When the standard Canadian National DNA Data Bank set of 13 STR sites (see

Module 12.14) is used, the probability of finding the same DNA profile in randomly selected, unrelated individuals is less than 1 in 10 billion. Put another way, a standard DNA profile can provide a statistical match of a particular DNA sample to just one living human. For this reason, DNA analyses are now accepted as compelling evidence by legal experts and scientists alike. In fact, DNA analysis on stored forensic samples has provided the evidence needed to solve many "cold cases" in recent years.

DNA analysis has also been used to probe the origin of nonhuman materials. The Wildlife Forensic DNA Laboratory at Trent University in Peterborough, Ontario, can identify the species of origin of suspect materials. By conclusively proving

▲ **Figure 12.15** Dr. Chris Stringer, principal researcher of human origin at London's Natural History Museum, holds the skull of Cheddar Man

the origin of contraband animal products, DNA profiling could help to protect endangered species. In another example, a 2005 study determined that DNA extracted from a 27 000-year-old Siberian mammoth was 98.6% identical to DNA from modern African elephants.

Although DNA profiling has provided definitive evidence in many investigations, the method is far from foolproof. Problems can arise from insufficient data, human error, or flawed evidence. While the science behind DNA profiling is irrefutable, the human element remains a possible confounding factor.

 In what way is DNA profiling valuable for determining innocence as well as guilt?

12.16 RFLPs can be used to detect differences in DNA sequences

Recall that a genetic marker is a DNA sequence that varies in a population. Like different alleles of a gene, the DNA sequence at a specific place on a chromosome may exhibit small nucleotide differences, or polymorphisms (from the Greek for "many forms"). Geneticists have catalogued many single-base-pair variations in the genome. Such a variation found in at least 1% of the population is called a **single nucleotide polymorphism** (**SNP**, pronounced "snip"). SNPs occur on average about 1 in 100 to 300 base pairs in the human genome either in the coding sequence of a gene or in a noncoding sequence.

SNPs may alter a restriction site—the sequence recognized by a restriction enzyme. Such alterations change the lengths of the restriction fragments formed by that enzyme when it cuts the DNA. A sequence variation of this type is called a **restriction fragment length polymorphism** (**RFLP**, pronounced "rif-lip"). Thus, RFLPs can serve as genetic markers for particular loci in the genome. RFLPs have many uses. For example, disease-causing alleles can be diagnosed with reasonable accuracy if a closely linked RFLP marker has been found. Alleles for a number of genetic diseases were first detected by means of RFLPs in this indirect way.

Restriction fragment analysis involves two of the methods you have learned about: DNA fragments produced by restriction enzymes (see Module 12.2) are sorted by gel electrophoresis (see Module 12.13). The number of restriction fragments and their sizes reflect the specific sequence of nucleotides in the starting DNA.

At the top of **Figure 12.16**, you can see corresponding segments of DNA from two DNA samples prepared from human tissue. Notice that the DNA sequences differ by a single base pair (highlighted in gold). In this case, the restriction enzyme cuts DNA between two cytosine (C) bases in the sequence CCGG and in its complement, GGCC. Because DNA from the first sample has two recognition sequences for the restriction enzyme, it is cleaved in two places, yielding three restriction fragments (labelled *w*, *x*, and *y*). DNA from the second sample, however, has only one recognition sequence and yields only two restriction fragments (*z* and *y*). Notice that the lengths of restriction fragments, as well as the number of fragments, differ, depending on the exact sequence of bases in the DNA.

To detect the differences between the collections of restriction fragments, we need to separate the restriction fragments in the two mixtures and compare their lengths. This process, called RFLP analysis, is accomplished through gel electrophoresis, which separates the restriction fragments based on size and molecular weight. As shown in the bottom of the figure, the three kinds of restriction fragments from sample 1 separate into three bands in the gel, while those from sample 2 separate into only two bands. Notice that the shortest fragment from sample 1 (*y*) produces a band at the same location as the identical short fragment from the sample 2. So you can see that electrophoresis allows us to see similarities as well as differences between mixtures of restriction fragments—and similarities as well as differences between the base sequences in DNA

▲ **Figure 12.16** RFLP analysis

from two individuals. The restriction fragment analysis in Figure 12.16 clearly shows that the two DNA samples differ in sequence. While RFLP analysis is rarely used today for identification, this method was vital in some of the earliest discoveries of disease-causing genes. For example, the gene for Huntington's disease was found after researchers used RFLPs to track a genetic marker that was closely associated with the disorder.

? You use a restriction enzyme to cut a DNA molecule that has three copies of the enzyme's recognition sequence clustered near one end. When you separate the restriction fragments by gel electrophoresis, how do you expect the bands to look?

● Three bands near the positive pole at the bottom of the gel (small fragments) and one band near the negative pole at the top of the gel (large fragment)

Genomics

12.17 Genomics is the scientific study of whole genomes

By the 1980s, biologists were using RFLPs to help to map important genes in humans and some other organisms. But it didn't take long for biologists to think on a larger scale. In 1995, a team of scientists announced that they had determined the nucleotide sequence of the entire genome of *Haemophilus influenzae* (*H. influenza*), a bacterium that can cause several human diseases, including pneumonia and meningitis. **Genomics**, the science of studying a complete set of genes (a genome) and their interactions, was born.

Since 1995, researchers have used the tools and techniques of DNA technology to develop more and more detailed maps of the genomes of a number of species. The first targets of genomics research were bacteria, which have relatively little DNA. The genome of *H. influenzae*, for example, contains only 1.8 million nucleotides and 1709 genes. But soon, the attention of genomics researchers turned toward more complex organisms with much larger genomes. As of 2009, the genomes of more than 1000 species have been published, and thousands more are in progress. **Table 12.17** lists some of the completed genomes; for diploids, the size refers to the haploid genome. The vast majority of genomes under study are from prokaryotes, including *E. coli* and several hundred other bacteria (some of medical importance), and a few dozen archaea. More than 100 eukaryotic species have been sequenced, including vertebrates, invertebrates, fungi, and plants.

Baker's yeast (*Saccharomyces cerevisiae*) was the first eukaryote to have its full sequence determined, and the roundworm *Caenorhabditis elegans* was the first multicellular organism. Other sequenced animals include the fruit fly (*Drosophila melanogaster*) and the lab mouse (*Mus musculus*), both model organisms for genetics. Plants, such as thale cress, a member of the mustard family (*Arabidopsis thaliana*, an important research organism) and rice (*Oryza sativa*, one of the world's most economically important crops), have also been completed. Other recently completed eukaryotic genomes include sorghum (another important commercial crop) and the honeybee, dog, chicken, and sea urchin.

In 2005, researchers completed the genome sequence for our closest living relative on the evolutionary tree of life, the chimpanzee (*Pan troglodytes*). Comparisons with human DNA revealed that we share 96% of our genome with our closest animal relative. As you will see in Module 12.21, genomic scientists are currently finding and studying the important differences, shedding scientific light on the age-old question of what makes us human.

Why map so many genomes? Not only are all genomes of interest in their own right, but comparative analysis provides invaluable insights into the evolutionary relationships among organisms. Also, having maps of a variety of genomes helps scientists interpret the human genome. For example, when scientists find a nucleotide sequence in the human genome similar to

TABLE 12.17 | SOME IMPORTANT COMPLETED GENOMES

Organism	Year Completed	Size of Haploid Genome (in Base Pairs)	Approximate Number of Genes
Haemophilus influenzae (bacterium)	1995	1.8 million	1700
Saccharomyces cerevisiae (yeast)	1996	12 million	6300
Escherichia coli (bacterium)	1997	4.6 million	4400
Caenorhabditis elegans (nematode)	1998	100 million	20 100
Drosophila melanogaster (fruit fly)	2000	165 million	13 700
Arabidopsis thaliana (thale cress)	2000	120 million	27 000
Mus musculus (mouse)	2001	2.6 billion	22 000
Oryza sativa (rice)	2002	430 million	42 000
Homo sapiens (humans)	2003	3.0 billion	21 000
Rattus norvegius (lab rat)	2004	2.8 billion	25 000
Pan troglodytes (chimpanzee)	2005	3.1 billion	22 000
Macaca mulatta (macaque)	2007	2.9 billion	22 000
Xenopus tropicalis (frog)	2010	1.7 billion	20 000

a yeast gene whose function is known, they have a valuable clue to the function of the human sequence. Indeed, several yeast protein-coding genes are so similar to certain human disease-causing genes that researchers have figured out the functions of the disease genes by studying their normal yeast counterparts. Many genes of disparate organisms are turning out to be astonishingly similar, to the point that one researcher has joked that he now views fruit flies as "little people with wings."

 Why is it useful to sequence nonhuman genomes?

Besides their value in understanding evolution, comparative analysis of nonhuman genes helps scientists interpret human data.

12.18 Is 98% of human DNA actually unused junk?

Chances are that you have heard the term *junk DNA*. The term arises from the fact that in humans, as in most complex eukaryotes, only a small amount of our total DNA contains genes that code for proteins, tRNAs, or rRNAs. Most multicellular eukaryotes, including humans, have a huge amount of DNA that does not code for anything. It is a commonly held belief that if a large portion of our DNA doesn't code for useful products, than it is useless junk. But is this true? Does the vast majority of the DNA in our cells not have a function?

The **Human Genome Project (HGP)** had the goals of determining the nucleotide sequence of all DNA in the human genome and identifying the location and sequence of every gene. The HGP began in 1990 at 20 government-funded research centres in six countries. Several years into the project, private companies joined the effort, which helped to cover the $3 billion cost. At the completion of the final draft of the sequence, more than 99% of the genome had been determined to 99.999% accuracy. (A few hundred gaps of unknown sequences within the human genome that require special investigation still remain.) The DNA sequences determined by the HGP have been deposited in a publicly available database called GenBank.

The chromosomes in the human genome—22 autosomes plus the X and Y sex chromosomes—contain approximately 3.0 billion base pairs of DNA. (See Table 12.17 to compare this number with the genome sizes for a variety of organisms.) To get a sense of how much DNA is in every human cell, imagine that its nucleotide sequence is printed in letters (A, T, C, and G) the size of the font in this book. At this size, the sequence would fill a stack of books 18 stories high! The biggest surprise from the HGP is the small number of human genes. The current estimate is about 21 000 genes, making up about 1.5% of our total DNA **(Figure 12.18)**. The actual number is much lower than earlier estimates of more than 100 000 genes.

The remaining 98.5% of our DNA, the "junk DNA," doesn't seem to be "junk" after all. Like hunting for treasures at a garage sale, the more geneticists rummage through the junk, the more useful DNA sequences they find. *Junk DNA* is now considered antiquated terminology; a better term is **noncoding DNA**.

Recent studies are starting to show that the noncoding DNA in eukaryotes actually performs several important functions.

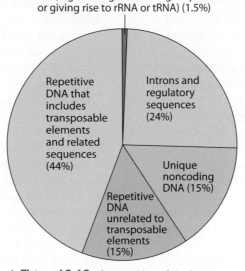

Exons (regions of genes coding for protein or giving rise to rRNA or tRNA) (1.5%)

Repetitive DNA that includes transposable elements and related sequences (44%)

Introns and regulatory sequences (24%)

Repetitive DNA unrelated to transposable elements (15%)

Unique noncoding DNA (15%)

▲ **Figure 12.18** Composition of the human genome

About one-quarter of the noncoding DNA consists of introns and gene control sequences such as promoters and enhancers (see Modules 11.1 and 11.4). An estimated 8% of the human genome has viral origins, the remnants of proviruses (see Module 16.5). A large portion of the DNA between genes consists of repetitive DNA, nucleotide sequences present in many copies in the genome. The repeated units of some of this DNA, such as the STRs used in DNA profiling, are short (see Module 12.14). Stretches of DNA with thousands of short repetitions are also prominent at the centromeres and ends of chromosomes—called **telomeres**—suggesting that this DNA plays a role in chromosome structure. Telomeres also protect the tips of the chromosomes during DNA replication.

In another type of repetitive DNA, each repeated unit is hundreds of nucleotides long, and the copies are scattered around the genome. Most of these sequences seem to be associated with **transposable elements** ("jumping genes"), DNA segments that can move or be copied from one location to another in a chromosome and even between chromosomes. There may be as many as one million transposable elements in the human genome. Researchers believe that transposable elements, through their copy-and-paste mechanism, may be responsible for the regulation of gene expression. Depending on where transposable elements jump, expression of neighbouring genes can be increased or decreased.

Looking at Figure 12.18, one can clearly see that a large portion of noncoding DNA may in fact serve a function. Roughly two-thirds of the genome, including introns and regulatory sequences plus the repetitive DNA including transposable elements, may play important roles in the regulation of the 1.5% of coding DNA. Despite the fact that these elements do not code for proteins, they still play very important roles within the cell. A number of geneticists still believe that some of our DNA serves no function and is in fact junk. But perhaps we just haven't found out what this DNA's function is yet. Genetics used to be a study of genes, now it involves so much more.

? The haploid human genome consists of about _____ base pairs and _____ genes spread over _____ different chromosomes. *(Provide three numbers.)*

3 billion; 21 000; 24 (22 autosomes plus 2 sex chromosomes)

12.19 The whole-genome shotgun method of sequencing a genome can provide a wealth of data quickly

Sequencing an entire genome is a complex task that requires careful work. The Human Genome Project proceeded through three stages that provided progressively more detailed views of the human genome. First, geneticists combined pedigree analyses of large families to map more than 5000 genetic markers (mostly RFLPs) spaced throughout all the chromosomes. The resulting low-resolution *linkage map* (see Module 9.19) provided a framework for mapping other markers and for arranging later, more detailed maps of particular regions. Next, researchers determined the number of base pairs between the markers in the linkage map. These data helped them construct a *physical map* of the human genome. Finally came the most arduous part of the project: determining the nucleotide sequences of the set of DNA fragments that had been mapped. Advances in automated DNA sequencing were crucial to this endeavour.

This three-stage approach is logical and thorough. However, in 1992, molecular biologist J. Craig Venter proposed an alternative strategy called the **whole-genome shotgun method** and set up the company Celera Genomics to implement it. His idea was essentially to skip the genetic and physical mapping stages and start directly with the sequencing step. In the whole-genome shotgun method, an entire genome is chopped by restriction enzymes into fragments that are cloned and sequenced in just one stage (**Figure 12.19**). High-performance computers running specialized mapping software can assemble the millions of overlapping short sequences into a single continuous sequence for every chromosome—an entire genome.

Today, the whole-genome shotgun approach is the method of choice for genomic researchers because it is fast and relatively inexpensive. What originally took 13 years and $3 billion, can now be done in a single day and cost only $1000. However, the data obtained still takes as long to sort through. Whole-genome research also raises some ethical concerns regarding how the

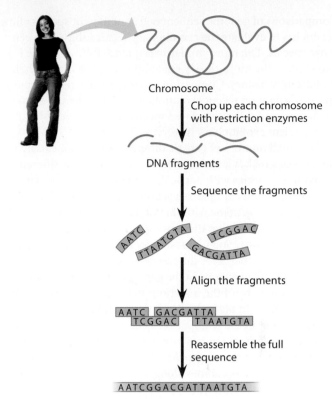

▲ **Figure 12.19**   The whole-genome shotgun method

information may be used (see Module 9.9). Recent research has revealed some limitations of this method, such as difficulties with repetitive sequences, suggesting that a hybrid approach that combines whole-genome shotgunning with physical or genetic maps may prove to be the most useful method in the long run.

 What are the primary advantages of the whole-genome shotgun method?

It is faster and cheaper than the three-stage method of genome sequencing.

12.20 Proteomics is the scientific study of the full set of proteins encoded by a genome

The successes in the field of genomics have encouraged scientists to attempt a similar systematic study of the full protein sets (proteomes) encoded by genomes, an approach called **proteomics**. The number of different proteins in humans far exceeds the number of genes—about 100 000 proteins versus about 21 000 genes. And since proteins, not genes, actually carry out most of the activities of the cell, scientists must study when and where proteins are produced in an organism and how they interact in order to understand the functioning of cells and organisms. Given the huge number of proteins and the myriad ways that their production can be controlled, assembling and analyzing proteomes pose many experimental challenges. Ongoing advances are beginning to provide the tools to meet those challenges.

Genomics and proteomics are enabling biologists to approach the study of life from an increasingly holistic perspective. Biologists are now in a position to compile complete catalogues of genes and proteins—that is, a full listing of all the "parts" that contribute to the operation of cells, tissues, and organisms. With such catalogues in hand, researchers are shifting their attention from the individual parts to how they function together in biological systems.

If every protein is encoded by a gene, how can humans have many more proteins than genes? *Hint*: See Module 11.5.

The RNA transcribed from one gene may be spliced several different ways to produce different mRNAs that are translated into different proteins.

12.21 Genomes hold clues to human evolution

▲ **Figure 12.21** Reconstruction of a Neanderthal female, based on a 36 000-year-old skull

Comparisons of genome sequences from different species allow geneticists to evaluate the evolutionary relationships between those species. The more similar in sequence the same gene is in two species, the more closely related those species are in their evolutionary history. Comparing genes of closely related species sheds light on recent evolutionary events, whereas comparing those of distantly related species helps us understand more ancient evolutionary history.

The small number of genetic differences between closely related species makes it easier to correlate phenotypic differences between the species with particular genetic differences. The completion of the chimpanzee genome in 2005 has allowed us to compare our genome with that of our primate cousins. Such an analysis revealed that these two genomes differ by 1.2% in single-base substitutions. Researchers were surprised when they found a further 2.7% difference because of insertions or deletions of larger regions in the genome of one or the other species, with many of the insertions being duplications or other repetitive DNA. In fact, one-third of the human duplications are not present in the chimpanzee genome, and some of these duplications contain regions associated with human diseases. All of these observations provide clues to the forces that might have swept the two genomes along different paths, but we don't have a complete picture yet.

What about specific genes and types of genes that differ between humans and chimpanzees? Using evolutionary analyses, biologists have identified a number of genes that have evolved faster in humans. Among them are genes involved in defence against malaria and tuberculosis and a gene regulating brain size. One gene that changed rapidly in the human lineage is *FOXP2*, a gene implicated in speech and vocalization. Differences between the *FOXP2* gene in humans and chimpanzees may play a role in the ability of humans, but not chimpanzees, to communicate by speech.

Neanderthals (*Homo neanderthalensis*) were humans' closest relatives (**Figure 12.21**). First appearing at least 300 000 years ago, Neanderthals lived in Europe and Asia until suddenly going extinct a mere 30 000 years ago. Modern humans (*Homo sapiens*) first appeared in Africa around 200 000 years ago and spread into Europe and Asia around 50 000 years ago

(see Module 21.15)—meaning that modern humans and Neanderthals most likely comingled for some time.

In 2010, the completed Neanderthal genome allowed detailed genomic comparisons between two species in the genus *Homo*. Using 38 000-year-old thigh bone fossils of two *H. neanderthalensis* females discovered in a Croatian cave, genomic analysis confirmed Neanderthals as a separate species and as our closest relatives (much closer than chimpanzees). Further comparisons, suggested that Neanderthals and some *H. sapiens* probably did interbreed. Analysis of the sequence of the *FOXP2* gene showed that Neanderthals had the same allele as modern humans, hinting that Neanderthals may have had the same ability to speak as we do. Other genetic analyses of less complete Neanderthal genomes revealed one male to have an unusual allele for a pigment gene that would have given him pale skin and red hair. And, interestingly, analysis of the lactase gene suggests that Neanderthals, like the majority of modern humans, were lactose intolerant as adults.

Comparisons with Neanderthals and chimpanzees are part of a larger effort to learn more about the human genome. Other research efforts are extending genomic studies to many more species. These studies will advance our understanding of all aspects of biology, including health, ecology, and evolution. In fact, comparisons of the completed genome sequences of bacteria, archaea, and eukaryotes supported the theory that these are the three fundamental domains of life—a topic we discuss further in the next unit.

 How can cross-species comparisons of the nucleotide sequences of a gene provide insight into evolution?

● Similarities in gene sequences correlate with evolutionary relatedness; greater genetic similarities reflect a more recent shared ancestry.

R E V I E W

MasteringBiology® **For Practice Quizzes, BioFlix, MP3 Tutors, and Activities, go to masteringbiology.com.**

Reviewing the Concepts

Gene Cloning (12.1–12.5)

12.1 Genes can be cloned in recombinant plasmids. Gene cloning is one application of biotechnology, the manipulation of organisms or their components to make useful products. Researchers can create plasmids containing recombinant DNA and insert those plasmids

into bacteria. If the recombinant bacteria multiply into a clone, the foreign genes are also duplicated and copies of the gene or its protein product can be harvested.

12.2 Enzymes are used to "cut and paste" DNA. Restriction enzymes cut DNA at specific sequences, forming restriction fragments. DNA ligase "pastes" DNA fragments together.

12.3 Cloned genes can be stored in genomic libraries. Genomic libraries, sets of DNA fragments containing all of an organism's genes, can be constructed and stored using cloned bacterial plasmids, phages, or bacterial artificial chromosomes (BACs).

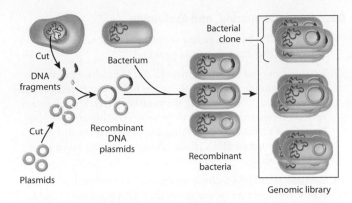

Genomic library

12.4 Reverse transcriptase can help to make genes for cloning.
cDNA libraries contain only the genes that are transcribed by a particular type of cell.

12.5 Nucleic acid probes identify clones carrying specific genes. A short, single-stranded molecule of labelled DNA or RNA can tag a desired gene in a library.

Genetically Modified Organisms (12.6–12.10)

12.6 Recombinant cells and organisms can mass-produce gene products. Bacteria, yeast, cell cultures, and whole animals can be used to make products for medical and other uses.

12.7 DNA technology has changed the pharmaceutical industry and medicine. Researchers use gene cloning to produce hormones, diagnose diseases, and produce vaccines.

12.8 Genetically modified organisms are transforming agriculture. A number of important crop plants are genetically modified.

12.9 Genetically modified organisms raise concerns about human and environmental health. Genetic engineering involves risks, such as ecological damage from GM crops.

12.10 Gene therapy may someday help to treat a variety of diseases. The insertion of healthy genes into unhealthy cells may replace their original function and possibly cure genetic diseases.

DNA Profiling (12.11–12.16)

12.11 The analysis of genetic markers can produce a DNA profile. DNA technology—methods for studying and manipulating genetic material—has revolutionized the field of forensics. DNA profiling—the analysis of DNA fragments—can determine whether two samples of DNA come from the same individual.

12.12 The PCR method is used to amplify DNA sequences. The polymerase chain reaction (PCR) can be used to amplify a DNA sample. The use of specific primers that flank the desired sequence ensures that only a particular subset of the DNA sample will be copied.

12.13 Gel electrophoresis sorts DNA molecules by size.

A mixture of DNA fragments
Longer fragments move slower
A "band" is a collection of DNA fragments of one particular length
Shorter fragments move faster
Power source
DNA is attracted to + pole because of PO_4^- groups

12.14 STR analysis is commonly used for DNA profiling. Short tandem repeats (STRs) are stretches of DNA that contain short nucleotide sequences repeated many times in a row. DNA profiling by STR analysis involves amplifying a set of 13 STRs.

12.15 DNA profiling has provided evidence in many forensic investigations. The applications of DNA profiling include helping to solve crimes and establishing paternity.

12.16 RFLPs can be used to detect differences in DNA sequences. Restriction fragment length polymorphisms (RFLPs) reflect differences in the sequences of DNA samples.

Genomics (12.17–12.21)

12.17 Genomics is the scientific study of whole genomes. Genomics researchers have sequenced many prokaryotic and eukaryotic genomes. Besides being of interest in their own right, nonhuman genomes can be compared with the human genome.

12.18 Is 98% of human DNA actually unused junk? Data from the Human Genome Project (HGP) revealed that the human genome contains about 21 000 genes and a huge amount of noncoding DNA, much of which consists of repetitive nucleotide sequences and transposable elements that can move about within the genome and is important in the regulation of gene expression.

12.19 The whole-genome shotgun method of sequencing a genome can provide a wealth of data quickly. The HGP uses genetic and physical mapping of chromosomes followed by DNA sequencing. Modern genomic analysis often uses the faster whole-genome shotgun method.

12.20 Proteomics is the scientific study of the full set of proteins encoded by a genome. Proteomics is the study of all functional proteins encoded within a genome.

12.21 Genomes hold clues to human evolution. By comparing the genomes of humans, Neanderthals, and chimpanzees, scientists hope to gain insight into our own evolution.

Connecting the Concepts

1. Imagine you have found a small quantity of DNA. Fill in the following diagram, which outlines a series of DNA technology experiments you could perform to study this DNA.

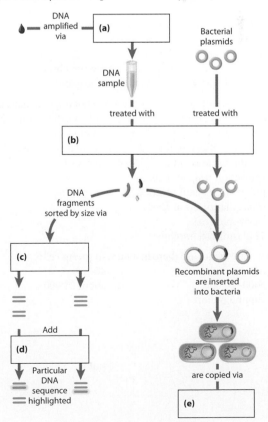

DNA amplified via (a)
DNA sample
Bacterial plasmids
treated with
treated with
(b)
DNA fragments sorted by size via
Recombinant plasmids are inserted into bacteria
(c)
Add
(d)
Particular DNA sequence highlighted
are copied via
(e)

Testing Your Knowledge

Multiple Choice

2. Which of the following would be considered a transgenic organism?
   a. a bacterium that contains a plasmid
   b. a human given a corrected human blood-clotting gene
   c. a fern grown in cell culture from a single fern root cell
   d. a rat with rabbit hemoglobin genes
   e. a human treated with insulin produced by bacteria

3. When a typical restriction enzyme cuts a DNA molecule, the cuts are uneven, giving the DNA fragments single-stranded ends. These ends are useful in recombinant DNA work because
   a. they enable a cell to recognize fragments produced by the enzyme.
   b. they serve as starting points for DNA replication.
   c. the fragments will bond to other fragments with complementary ends.
   d. they enable researchers to use the fragments as molecular probes.
   e. only single-stranded DNA segments can code for proteins.

4. The DNA profiles used as evidence in a murder trial look something like supermarket bar codes. The pattern of bars in a DNA profile shows
   a. the order of bases in a particular gene.
   b. the presence of various-sized fragments of DNA.
   c. the presence of dominant or recessive alleles for particular traits.
   d. the order of genes along particular chromosomes.
   e. the exact location of a specific gene in a genomic library.

5. A biologist isolated a gene from a human cell, attached it to a plasmid, and inserted the plasmid into a bacterium. The bacterium made a new protein, but it was nothing like the protein normally produced in a human cell. Why? *(Explain your answer.)*
   a. The bacterium had undergone transformation.
   b. The gene did not have sticky ends.
   c. The gene contained introns.
   d. The gene did not come from a genomic library.
   e. The biologist should have cloned the gene first.

6. A paleontologist has recovered a tiny bit of organic material from the 400-year-old preserved skin of an extinct dodo. She would like to compare DNA from the sample with DNA from living birds. Which of the following would be most useful for increasing the amount of DNA available for testing?
   a. restriction fragment analysis
   b. polymerase chain reaction
   c. molecular probe analysis
   d. electrophoresis
   e. Ti plasmid technology

7. How many genes are there in a human sperm cell?
   a. 23   b. 46
   c. 5000–10 000   d. about 21 000
   e. about 3 billion

Describing, Comparing, and Explaining

8. Why does DNA profiling rely on comparing specific genetic markers rather than the entire genome?

9. Explain how you might engineer *E. coli* to produce human growth hormone (HGH) by using the following: *E. coli* containing a plasmid, DNA carrying the gene for HGH, DNA ligase, a restriction enzyme, equipment for manipulating and growing bacteria, a method for extracting and purifying the hormone, and an appropriate DNA probe. (Assume that the HGH gene lacks introns.)

10. Recombinant DNA techniques are used to custom-build bacteria for two main purposes: to obtain multiple copies of certain genes and to obtain useful proteins produced by certain genes. Give an example of each of these applications in medicine and agriculture.

Applying the Concepts

11. A biochemist hopes to find a gene in human liver cells that codes for an important blood-clotting protein. She knows that the nucleotide sequence of a small part of the blood-clotting gene is CTGGACTGACA. Briefly outline a possible method she might use to isolate the desired gene.

12. What is left for genetic researchers to do now that the Human Genome Project has determined nearly complete nucleotide sequences for all the human chromosomes? Explain.

13. Today, it is fairly easy to make transgenic plants and animals. What are some important safety and ethical issues raised by this use of recombinant DNA technology? What are some of the possible dangers of introducing genetically engineered organisms into the environment? What are some reasons for and against leaving decisions in these areas to scientists? To business owners and executives? What are some reasons for and against more public involvement? How might these decisions affect you? How do you think these decisions should be made?

14. In the not-too-distant future, gene therapy may be an option for the treatment and cure of some inherited disorders. What do you think are the most serious ethical issues that must be dealt with before human gene therapy is used on a large scale? Why do you think these issues are important?

15. The possibility of extensive genetic testing raises questions about how personal genetic information should be used. For example, should employers or potential employers have access to such information? Why or why not? Should the information be available to insurance companies? Why or why not? Is there any reason for the government to keep genetic files? Is there any obligation to warn relatives who might share a defective gene? Might some people avoid being tested for fear of being labelled genetic outcasts? Or might they be compelled to be tested against their wishes? Can you think of other reasons to proceed with caution?

Answers to all questions can be found in Appendix E.

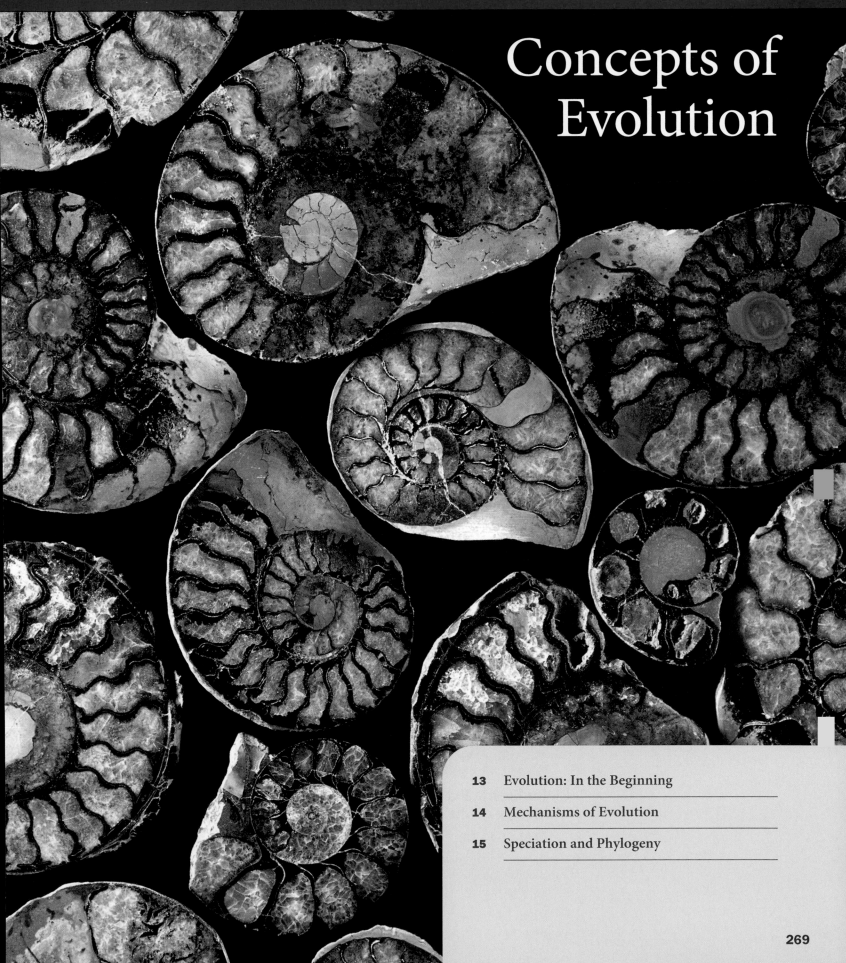

Concepts of Evolution

CHAPTER

13

Evolution:
In the Beginning

BIG IDEAS

Darwin's Theory of Evolution

(13.1–13.7)

Darwin's theory of evolution explains the adaptations of organisms and the unity and diversity of life.

Early Earth and the Origin of Life

(13.8–13.10)

Scientific experiments can test the four-stage hypothesis of how life originated on early Earth.

Major Events in the History of Life

(13.11–13.13)

The fossil record and radiometric dating establish a geologic record of key events in life's history.

Clown, Fool, or Simply Well Adapted?

Is the blue-footed booby really as awkward or foolish as its name implies? With their bright blue feet and trusting demeanour, boobies were certainly noticed by early travellers to the Galápagos Islands, a chain of relatively young volcanic islands located about 900 km off the Pacific coast of South America. Spanish sailors may have called them "bob" (the Spanish word for clown). British seamen may have called them "booby" (slang for "stupid"), as the birds were so approachable that they were easily killed. Either way, their comical feet are hard to miss.

Charles Darwin, whose observations in the Galápagos contributed greatly to his theory of evolution, no doubt encountered this friendly bird. And like the other species he observed, boobies have physical features that suit them to their environment. For example, their large, webbed feet make great flippers, propelling the birds through the water at high speeds. In the clear Galápagos waters, boobies gracefully "fly" beneath the surface. Their feet are thus a huge advantage when hunting fish. On land, however, those same feet are awkward, making for clumsy walking and for an even clumsier flight takeoff: Their wings often touch the ground before they become airborne.

Boobies have other traits that serve them well in their seafaring life. The booby's body and bill are streamlined, like a torpedo, minimizing friction when the bird dives from heights of up to 24 m into the shallow water below. To pull themselves out of this high-speed dive once they hit the water, boobies use their large tail. Specialized glands help boobies manage salt intake. A gland in the bird's eye socket accumulates excess salt from body fluids. This salty liquid then trickles into the nasal cavity. The bird expels this liquid by shaking its head from side to side, a characteristic clownlike movement.

The booby's big webbed feet, streamlined shape, large tail, and specialized salt-excreting glands are all good examples of evolutionary adaptations, inherited traits that enhance an organism's ability to survive and reproduce in a particular environment. As useful as adaptations may be, however, they often represent a trade-off between different needs. The booby's webbed feet are a case in point: extremely functional in water, but clumsy on dry land. But because boobies spend a great deal of time in the water, and especially because they find most of their food there, this adaptation represents a net advantage.

In this chapter, we examine how such adaptations evolve. Thus we begin our study of evolution, the core theme of biology. We explore Darwin's theory of evolution—that Earth's many species are descendants of ancestral organisms that were different from those living today. We end this chapter with a look at how life began on Earth. In Chapter 14 we examine the mechanisms of evolution and in Chapter 15 we discuss how two species diverge from a common ancestor. It is such changes in species over time that have transformed life on Earth from its earliest forms to the vast diversity that we see today. Let's begin this grand journey with Darwin's sea voyage.

Darwin's Theory of Evolution

13.1 A sea voyage helped Darwin frame his theory of evolution

If you visit the Galápagos Islands, a chain of volcanic islands located about 900 km off the coast of Ecuador, you will see many of the same sights that fascinated Darwin more than a century ago: blue-footed boobies waddling around; lumbering giant tortoises (whose Spanish name is *galápagos*) **(Figure 13.1A)**; and marine iguanas basking on dark lava rocks or feeding on algae in the ocean **(Figure 13.1B)**. You will also observe some of the finches Darwin collected—closely related small birds that represent more than a dozen species (distinct types of organisms). A major difference between these birds is the shape of their beaks, which are adapted for crushing seeds, feeding on cactus flowers, or snagging insects. Some finches even find their meals on tortoises, which raise themselves up and stretch out their necks to allow the birds to hop aboard and gobble up parasites.

One of Darwin's lasting contributions is the scientific explanation for the striking ways in which organisms are suited for life in their environment. Let's trace the path Darwin took to his theory of **evolution**, the idea that Earth's many species are descendants of ancestral species that were different from those living today.

Darwin's Cultural and Scientific Context   Some early Greek philosophers suggested that life might change gradually over time. But the Greek philosopher Aristotle, whose views had an enormous impact on Western culture, generally viewed species as perfect and permanent. Judeo-Christian culture reinforced this idea with a literal interpretation of the biblical book of Genesis, which holds that species were individually designed by a divine creator. The idea that all living species are unchanging in form and inhabit an Earth that is only about 6000 years old dominated the intellectual and cultural climate of the Western world for centuries.

In the mid-1700s, the study of **fossils**—the imprints or remains of organisms that lived in the past—revealed a succession of fossil forms in layers of sedimentary rock that differed from current life forms. In the early 1800s, French naturalist Jean Baptiste Lamarck suggested that the best explanation for the relationship of fossils to current organisms is that life evolves. Today, we remember Lamarck mainly for his erroneous view of *how* species evolve. He proposed that by using or not using its body parts, an individual may change its traits and then pass on those changes to its offspring. He suggested, for instance, that the ancestors of the giraffe had lengthened their necks by stretching higher and higher into the trees to reach leaves. Our understanding of genetics refutes Lamarck's idea of the inheritance of acquired characteristics. But the fact remains that by strongly advocating evolution and by proposing that species evolve as a result of interactions with their environment, Lamarck helped to set the stage for Darwin.

Darwin's Sea Voyage   Charles Darwin was born in 1809. Even as a boy, Darwin had a consuming interest in nature. When not reading books about nature, he was fishing, hunting, and collecting insects. His father, an eminent physician, could see no future for his son as a naturalist and sent him to medical school. But Darwin found medicine boring and surgery before the days of anaesthesia horrifying. He quit medical school and enrolled at Cambridge University, intending to become a clergyman. At that time, many scholars of science belonged to the clergy.

Soon after graduation, Darwin's botany professor and mentor recommended him to the captain of the HMS *Beagle*, who was preparing a voyage to chart poorly known stretches of the South American coast. In December 1831, at the age of 22, Darwin began the round-the-world voyage that profoundly influenced his thinking and eventually the thinking of the world **(Figure 13.1C)**.

▲ **Figure 13.1A** A giant tortoise, one of the unique inhabitants of the Galápagos Islands

▲ **Figure 13.1B** A marine iguana feeding on algae in the waters around the Galápagos Islands

Darwin in 1840

HMS *Beagle* in port

▲ **Figure 13.1C** The voyage of the *Beagle* (1831–1836), with insets showing a young Charles Darwin and the ship on which he sailed

While the ship's crew surveyed the coast, Darwin spent most of his time on shore, collecting thousands of plants and animals as well as fossils. He noted the characteristics of plants and animals that made them well suited to such diverse environments as the jungles of Brazil, the grasslands of Argentina, and the desolate and frigid lands at the southern tip of South America. Darwin asked himself why fossils found on the South American continent were more similar to present-day South American species than to fossils found on other continents. During his visit to the Galápagos Islands, Darwin observed many unusual organisms, most of which were not known from anywhere else in the world. Many of these were similar to, but different from, the plants and animals of the nearest mainland. Even the individual islands had species different from those on other islands.

While on the voyage, Darwin was strongly influenced by Charles Lyell's newly published *Principles of Geology*. Having read Lyell's book and witnessed an earthquake that raised part of the coastline of Chile almost a metre, Darwin realized that natural forces gradually changed Earth's surface and that these forces are still operating in modern times. Thus, the growth of mountains as a result of earthquakes could account for the presence of the marine snail fossils that he had collected on mountaintops in the Andes.

By the time Darwin returned to Great Britain five years after the *Beagle* first set sail, his experiences and reading had led him to seriously doubt that Earth and all its living organisms had been specially created only a few thousand years earlier. Darwin had come to realize that Earth was very old and constantly changing. Once in Great Britain, Darwin began to analyze his collections and discuss them with colleagues. He continued to read, correspond with other scientists, and maintain extensive journals of his observations, studies, and thoughts.

Darwin's Writings By the early 1840s, Darwin had composed a long essay describing the major features of his theory of evolution. He realized that his ideas would cause an uproar, however, and he delayed publishing his essay. Even as he procrastinated, Darwin continued to compile evidence in support of his hypothesis. In 1858, Alfred Wallace, a British naturalist doing fieldwork in Indonesia, conceived a hypothesis almost identical to Darwin's. Wallace asked Darwin to evaluate the manuscript he had written to see if it merited publication. Darwin wrote to Lyell, "So all my originality, whatever it may amount to, will be smashed." Lyell and another colleague, however, presented Wallace's paper and excerpts of Darwin's earlier essay together to the scientific community.

In 1859, Darwin published his book titled *On the Origin of Species by Means of Natural Selection*. Commonly referred to as *The Origin of Species*, Darwin's book presented the world with a logical and well-supported explanation for evolution. Darwin provided evidence that present-day species arose from a succession of ancestors. He called this evolutionary history of life "descent with modification." As the descendants of a remote ancestor spread into various habitats over millions and millions of years, they accumulated diverse modifications, or **adaptations**, that fit them to specific ways of life in their environment. Darwin's proposed mechanism for this descent with modification is natural selection, the topic of our next module.

 What was Darwin's phrase for evolution? What does it mean?

● Descent with modification, which means an ancestral species could diversify into many descendant species by the accumulation of adaptations to various environments.

13.2 Darwin proposed natural selection as the mechanism of evolution

Darwin devoted much of *The Origin of Species* to exploring the adaptation of organisms to their environment. First, he discussed familiar examples of domesticated plants and animals. Humans have modified other species by selecting and breeding individuals with desired traits over many generations—a process called **artificial selection**. You can see evidence of artificial selection in the vegetables illustrated in **Figure 13.2**, all varieties of a single species of wild mustard. Crop plants and animals bred as livestock or as pets often bear little resemblance to their wild ancestors. Artificial selection has led to greater yields of crops, meat, and milk, as well as to dogs as different from the ancestral wolf as Chihuahuas, dachshunds, and Afghan hounds.

Darwin explained how a similar selection process could occur in nature, a process he called **natural selection**. He described two observations from which he drew two inferences:

OBSERVATION 1: Members of a population often vary in their inherited traits.

OBSERVATION 2: All species are capable of producing more offspring than the environment can support.

INFERENCE 1: Individuals whose inherited traits give them a higher probability of surviving and reproducing in a given environment tend to leave more offspring than other individuals.

INFERENCE 2: This unequal production of offspring will lead to the accumulation of favourable traits in a population over generations.

Darwin recognized the connection between natural selection and the capacity of organisms to "overreproduce." He had read an essay written in 1798 by economist Thomas Malthus, who contended that much of human suffering—disease, famine, and war—was the consequence of human populations increasing faster than food supplies and other resources. Darwin deduced that the production of more individuals than the limited resources can support leads to a struggle for existence, with only some offspring surviving in each generation. Of the many eggs laid, young born, and seeds spread, only a tiny fraction complete development and leave offspring. The rest are eaten, starved, diseased, unmated, or unable to reproduce for other reasons. The essence of natural selection is this unequal reproduction. Individuals whose traits better enable them to obtain food or escape predators or tolerate physical conditions will survive and reproduce more successfully, passing these adaptive traits to their offspring.

Darwin reasoned that if artificial selection can bring about so much change in a relatively short period of time, then natural selection could modify species considerably over hundreds or thousands of generations. Over vast spans of time, many traits that adapt a population to its environment will accumulate. If the environment changes, however, or if individuals move to a new environment, natural selection will select for adaptations to these new conditions, sometimes producing changes that result in the origin of a completely new species in the process.

It is important to emphasize three key points about evolution by natural selection. First, although natural selection occurs through interactions between individual organisms and the environment, individuals do not evolve. Rather, it is the population—the group of organisms—that evolves over time as adaptive traits become more common in the group and other traits change or disappear.

Second, natural selection can amplify or diminish only heritable traits. Certainly, an organism may become modified through its own interactions with the environment during its lifetime, and those acquired characteristics may help the organism survive. But unless coded for in the genes of an organism's gametes, such acquired characteristics cannot be passed on to offspring. Thus, a championship female bodybuilder will not give birth to a muscle-bound baby.

Third, evolution is not goal directed; it does not lead to perfectly adapted organisms. Natural selection is the result of environmental factors that vary from place to place and over time. A trait that is favourable in one situation may be useless—or even detrimental—in different circumstances. And as you will see, adaptations are often compromises: A blue-footed booby's webbed feet may be efficient in water, but they make for awkward walking on land.

Now let's look at some examples of natural selection.

? **Compare artificial selection and natural selection.**

● In artificial selection, humans choose the desirable traits and breed only organisms with those traits. In natural selection, the environment does the choosing: Individuals with traits best suited to the environment survive and reproduce most successfully, passing on those adaptive traits to offspring.

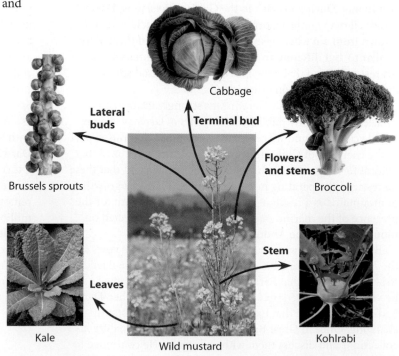

▲ Figure 13.2 Artificial selection: different vegetables produced as humans have selected for variations in different parts of the wild mustard plant

13.3 Scientists can observe natural selection in action

The exquisite camouflage adaptations shown in **Figure 13.3A** by insects that evolved in different environments illustrate the results of natural selection. But do we have examples of natural selection in action?

Indeed, biologists have documented evolutionary change in thousands of scientific studies. A classic example comes from British evolutionary biologists Peter and Rosemary Grant's work with finches in the Galápagos Islands over more than 30 years (see Module 15.9). As part of their research, they measured changes in beak size in a population of a ground finch species. These birds eat mostly small seeds. In dry years, when all seeds are in short supply, birds must eat more large seeds. Birds with larger, stronger beaks have a feeding advantage and greater reproductive success, and the Grants measured an increase in the average beak depth for the population. During wet years, smaller beaks are more efficient for eating the now abundant small seeds, and they found a decrease in average beak depth.

An unsettling example of natural selection in action is the evolution of pesticide resistance in hundreds of insect species. Whenever a new type of pesticide is used to control agricultural pests, the story is similar **(Figure 13.3B)**: A relatively small amount of poison dusted onto a crop may kill 99% of the insects, but subsequent sprayings are less and less effective. The few survivors of the first pesticide wave are insects that are genetically resistant, carrying an allele (alternative form of a gene, coloured red in the figure) that somehow enables them to resist the chemical attack. So the poison kills most members of the population, leaving the resistant individuals to reproduce and pass on the alleles for pesticide resistance to their offspring. The proportion of pesticide-resistant individuals thus increases

▲ **Figure 13.3B** Evolution of pesticide resistance in an insect population

in each generation. Like the finches, the insect population has adapted to environmental change through natural selection.

These examples of evolutionary adaptation highlight two important points about natural selection. First, natural selection is more an editing process than a creative mechanism. A pesticide does not create alleles that allow insects to resist it. Rather, the presence of the pesticide leads to natural selection for insects already in the population that have those alleles. Second, natural selection is contingent on time and place: It favours those heritable traits in a varying population that fit the current, local environment. For instance, mutations that endow houseflies with resistance to the pesticide DDT also reduce their growth rate. Before DDT was introduced, such mutations were a handicap to the flies that had them. But once DDT was part of the environment, the mutant alleles were advantageous, and natural selection increased their frequency in fly populations.

Now that we have seen some direct observations of natural selection, let's turn to the many other types of scientific evidence that support evolution.

? In what sense is natural selection more an editing process than a creative process?

● Natural selection cannot create beneficial traits on demand but instead "edits" variation in a population by selecting for individuals with those traits that are best suited to the current environment.

A flower mantid in Malaysia

A leaf mantid in Costa Rica

▲ **Figure 13.3A** Camouflage as an example of evolutionary adaptation

13.4 The study of fossils provides strong evidence for evolution

Darwin developed his theory of descent with modification by using evidence from artificial selection and from comparisons of the geographic distribution of species and the body structures of different species. (These comparisons are described in the next module.) He also relied on the fossil record. Fossils document differences between past and present organisms and the fact that many species have become extinct.

The photographs on this page illustrate a number of fossils, each of which formed in a somewhat different way. The organic substances of a dead organism usually decay rapidly, but the hard parts of an animal that are rich in minerals, such as the bones and teeth of dinosaurs and the shells of clams and snails, may remain as fossils. The fossilized skull in **Figure 13.4A** is from one of our early relatives, *Homo erectus*, who lived some 1.5 million years ago (mya) in Africa.

Many of the fossils that **paleontologists** (scientists who study fossils) find in their digs are not the actual remnants of organisms at all but are replicas of past organisms. Such fossils result when a dead organism captured in sediment decays and leaves an empty mould that is later filled by minerals dissolved in water. The casts that form when the minerals harden are replicas of the organism, as seen in the 375-million-year-old casts of ammonites shown in **Figure 13.4B**. Ammonites were shelled marine organisms.

Trace fossils are footprints, burrows, and other remnants of an ancient organism's behaviour. The boy in **Figure 13.4C** is standing in a 150-million-year-old dinosaur track in Colorado.

Some fossils actually retain organic material. The leaf in **Figure 13.4D** is about 40 million years old. It is a thin film pressed in rock, still greenish with remnants of its chlorophyll and well enough preserved that biologists can analyze its molecular and cellular structure. In rare instances, an entire organism, including its soft parts, is fossilized. That can happen only when the individual is buried in a medium that prevents bacteria and fungi from decomposing the corpse. The insect in **Figure 13.4E** got stuck in the resin of a tree about 35 mya. The resin hardened

B Ammonite casts

C Dinosaur tracks

A Skull of *Homo erectus*

D Fossilized organic matter of a leaf   E Insect in amber   F "Ice Man"

▲ **Figure 13.4A–F** A gallery of fossils

▲ **Figure 13.4G** Strata of sedimentary rock at the Grand Canyon

into amber (fossilized resin), preserving the insect. Other media can also preserve organisms. Explorers have discovered mammoths, bison, and even prehistoric humans frozen in ice or preserved in acid bogs. Such rare discoveries make the news, as did the 1991 discovery of the "Ice Man" in **Figure 13.4F**, who died 5000 years ago. However, biologists rely mainly on the fossils formed in sedimentary rock to reconstruct the history of life.

The **fossil record**—the sequence in which fossils appear within layers of sedimentary rocks—provides some of the strongest evidence of evolution. Sedimentary rocks form from layers of sand and mud that settle to the bottom of seas, lakes, and swamps. Over millions of years, deposits pile up and compress the older sediments below into rock. When organisms die, they settle along with the sediments and may be preserved as fossils. The rate of sedimentation and the types of particles that settle vary over time. As a result, the rock forms in **strata**, or layers. Younger strata form on top of older ones; thus, the relative ages of fossils can be determined by the layer in which they are found. **Figure 13.4G** shows strata of sedimentary rock at the Grand Canyon. The Colorado River has cut through more than 2000 m of rock, exposing sedimentary layers that can be read like huge pages from the book of life. Scan the canyon wall from rim to floor and you look back through hundreds of millions of years. Each layer entombs fossils that represent some of the organisms from that period of Earth's history. Of course, the fossil record is incomplete: Not all organisms live in areas that favour fossilization, many rocks are distorted by geologic processes, and not all fossils that have been preserved will be found.

The fossil record reveals the historical sequence in which organisms evolved, and radiometric dating (see Module 13.12) helps to determine the ages of rocks and fossils. The oldest known fossils, dating from about 3.5 billion years ago (bya), are prokaryotes. Molecular and cellular evidence also indicates that prokaryotes were the ancestors of all life. More than a billion years passed before fossils of single-celled eukaryotes formed, and approximately a billion more before multicellular eukaryotes appeared. Fossils in younger strata reveal the sequential evolution of various groups of eukaryotic organisms.

Darwin lamented the lack of fossils showing how existing groups of organisms gave rise to new groups. In the 150 years since publication of *The Origin of Species*, however, many fossil discoveries illustrate the transition of existing groups to new groups. For example, a series of fossils traces the gradual modification of jaws and teeth in the evolution of mammals from a reptilian ancestor.

Another series of fossils traces the evolution of whales from four-legged land mammals. Whales living today have forelegs in the form of flippers but lack hind legs. In the past few decades, remarkable fossils of extinct mammals have been discovered in Pakistan, Egypt, and North America that document the transition from life on land to life in the sea **(Figure 13.4H)**. Additional fossils show that *Pakicetus* and *Rodhocetus* (shown in the figure) had a type of ankle bone that is otherwise unique to the group of mammals that includes pigs, hippos, cows, camels, and deer. The ankle bone similarity strongly suggests that whales (and dolphins and porpoises) are most closely related to this group of land mammals.

Next we look at other sources of evidence for evolution.

? **What types of animals do you think would be most represented in the fossil record? Explain your answer.**

● Animals with hard parts, such as shells or bones that readily fossilize, and those that lived in areas where sedimentary rock formed

Pakicetus (terrestrial)

Rodhocetus (predominantly aquatic)

Pelvis and hind limb
Dorudon (fully aquatic)

Pelvis and hind limb

Balaena (recent whale ancestor)

▲ **Figure 13.4H** A transition to life in the sea: fossils of four species that link whales with their land-dwelling ancestors

13.5 Many types of scientific evidence support the evolutionary view of life

Darwin's wide range of evidence convinced many of the scientists of his day that organisms do indeed evolve. Let's continue to explore Darwin's evidence as well as some new types of data that provide overwhelming support for evolution.

Biogeography   It was the geographic distribution of species, known as **biogeography**, that first suggested to Darwin that organisms evolve from ancestral species. Darwin noted that Galápagos animals resembled species of the South American mainland more than they resembled animals on islands that were similar but much more distant. The logical explanation was that the Galápagos species evolved from animals that migrated from South America. These immigrants eventually gave rise to new species as they became adapted to their new environments. Among the many examples from biogeography that make sense only in the historical context of evolution are the marsupials in Australia. This unique collection of pouched mammals, such as kangaroos and koalas, evolved in isolation after geologic activities separated that island continent from the landmasses on which placental mammals diversified.

Comparative Anatomy   Also providing support for evolution and cited extensively by Darwin is comparative anatomy. Anatomical similarities between species give signs of common descent. Similarity in characteristics that results from common ancestry is known as **homology**. As **Figure 13.5A** shows, the same skeletal elements make up the forelimbs of humans, cats, whales, and bats. The functions of these forelimbs differ. A whale's flipper does not do the same job as a bat's wing, so if these structures had been uniquely engineered, we would expect that their basic designs would be very different. The logical explanation is that the arms, forelegs, flippers, and wings of these different mammals are variations on an anatomical structure of an ancestral organism that over millions of years has become adapted to different functions. Biologists call such anatomical similarities in different organisms **homologous structures**—features that often have different functions but are structurally similar because of common ancestry.

Comparative anatomy illustrates that evolution is a remodelling process in which ancestral structures that originally functioned in one capacity become modified as they take on new functions—the kind of process that Darwin called descent with modification.

Comparing early stages of development in different animal species reveals additional homologies not visible in adult organisms. For example, at some point in their development, all vertebrate embryos have a tail posterior to the anus, as well as structures called pharyngeal (throat) pouches. These homologous pouches ultimately develop into structures with very different functions, such as gills in fishes and parts of the ears and throat in humans. Note the pharyngeal pouches and tails of the bird embryo (left) and the human embryo (right) in **Figure 13.5B**.

Some of the most interesting homologies are "leftover" structures that are of marginal or perhaps no importance to the organism. These **vestigial structures** are remnants of features that served important functions in the organism's ancestors. For example, the small pelvis and hind-leg bones of ancient whales (see Figure 13.4H) are vestiges of their walking ancestors. Another example are the eye remnants that are buried under scales in blind species of cave fishes—a vestige of their sighted ancestors.

Molecular Biology   Anatomical homology is not helpful in linking very distantly related organisms such as plants and animals and microorganisms. But in recent decades, advances in **molecular biology** have enabled biologists to read a molecular history of evolution in the DNA sequences of organisms. As we saw in Chapter 10, the hereditary background of an organism is documented in its DNA and in the proteins encoded there. Siblings have greater similarity in their DNA and proteins than do unrelated individuals of the same species. And if two species have homologous genes with sequences that match closely, biologists conclude that these sequences must have been inherited from a relatively recent common ancestor. Conversely, the greater the number of sequence differences between species, the more distant is their last common ancestor. Making these comparisons even easier are the full genome sequences that are becoming available for an ever increasing number of species (see Module 12.19). Molecular comparisons between diverse organisms have allowed biologists to develop hypotheses about the evolutionary divergence of major branches on the tree of life.

Humerus

Radius

Ulna

Carpals

Metacarpals

Phalanges

Human   Cat   Whale   Bat

▲ **Figure 13.5A** Homologous structures: vertebrate forelimbs

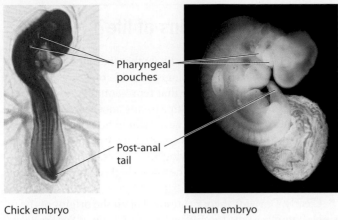

Chick embryo   Human embryo

Pharyngeal pouches

Post-anal tail

▲ **Figure 13.5B** Homologous structures in vertebrate embryos

Darwin's boldest hypothesis was that all life forms are related. Molecular biology provides strong evidence for this claim: All forms of life use the same genetic language of DNA and RNA, and the genetic code—how RNA triplets are translated into amino acids—is essentially universal. Thus, it is likely that all species descended from common ancestors that used this code. But molecular homologies go beyond a shared code. For example, organisms as dissimilar as humans and bacteria share homologous genes that have been inherited from a very distant common ancestor.

? **What is homology? How does the concept of homology relate to molecular biology?**

● Homology is similarity in different species because of evolution from a common ancestor. Similarities in DNA sequences or proteins reflect the evolutionary relationship that is the basis of homology.

13.6 Homologies indicate patterns of descent that can be shown on an evolutionary tree

Darwin was the first to view the history of life as a tree, with multiple branchings from a common ancestral trunk to the descendant species at the tips of the twigs. Biologists represent these patterns of descent with an **evolutionary tree**, although today they often turn the trees sideways, as in **Figure 13.6**.

Homologous structures, both anatomical and molecular, can be used to determine the branching sequence of such a tree. Some homologous characteristics, such as the genetic code, are shared by all species because they date to the deep ancestral past. In contrast, characteristics that evolved more recently are shared only within smaller groups of organisms. For example, all tetrapods (from the Greek *tetra*, four, and *pod*, foot) possess the same basic limb bone structure illustrated in Figure 13.5A, but their ancestors do not.

Figure 13.6 is an evolutionary tree of tetrapods (amphibians, mammals, and reptiles, including birds) and their closest living relatives, the lungfishes. In this diagram, each branch point represents the common ancestor of all species that descended from it. For example, lungfishes and all tetrapods descended from ancestor ❶. Three homologies are shown by the purple hatch marks on the tree—tetrapod limbs, the amnion (a protective embryonic membrane), and feathers. Tetrapod limbs were present in ancestor ❷ and hence are found in all of its descendants (the tetrapods). The amnion was present only in ancestor ❸ and thus is shared only by mammals and reptiles. Feathers were present only in ancestor ❻ and hence are found only in birds.

Each branch point represents the common ancestor of the lineages beginning there and to the right of it.

Lungfishes

Amphibians

Mammals

Tetrapod limbs

❶

❷

Amnion

❸

❹

A hatch mark represents a homologous characteristic shared by all the groups to the right of the mark.

Lizards and snakes

Crocodiles

❺

Ostriches

❻

Feathers

Hawks and other birds

Tetrapods

Amniotes

Birds

▲ **Figure 13.6** An evolutionary tree for tetrapods and their closest living relatives, the lungfishes

Evolutionary trees are hypotheses reflecting our current understanding of patterns of evolutionary descent. Some trees are more speculative because less data may be available. Others, such as the one in Figure 13.6, are supported by strong combinations of fossil, anatomical, and DNA sequence data.

? **Refer to the evolutionary tree in Figure 13.6. Are crocodiles more closely related to lizards or birds?**

● Look for the most recent common ancestor of these groups. Crocodiles are more closely related to birds because they share a more recent common ancestor with birds (ancestor ❺) than with lizards (ancestor ❹).

13.7 Does the theory of evolution explain the origins of life?

Darwin's theory of evolution is widely accepted throughout the scientific community. Reams of evidence have been collected in the past 150 years to support this hypothesis, and more is being collected daily. Unfortunately, many laypeople have misconceptions about the details of Darwin's theory. For example, the theory of evolution is commonly extended to explain the origins of life. But can the theory of evolution explain how life began? Does it even attempt to explain how the first cell evolved?

As you have read in the previous six modules, the theory of evolution can explain how populations have adapted to different environments. The mechanism of natural selection drives evolution by selecting for favourable characters and against those that are unfavourable. For example, insects possessing a gene that offers resistance to an insecticide are favoured in environments exposed to the insecticide (see Module 13.3). However, natural selection can work only on existing characteristics of living organisms. It can explain how a species has adapted to environmental pressures. It cannot explain how the first living cell evolved.

The theory can be used to infer how different species are related. By using evidence such as the fossil record, structural homologies, and molecular similarities, evolutionary biologists can put together a logical sequence of events on how a group of organisms evolved from a common ancestor. The evolutionary tree in Figure 13.6 shows how different groups of vertebrates are related. Also, Darwin's theory explains how all organisms have evolved from a single common ancestor. If all life forms use the same genetic code, it is likely that they all descended from a common ancestor. Biologists could construct an evolutionary or phylogenetic tree that represents all groups of organisms and their relationships to one another (discussed further in Chapter 14). (Such a tree would be extremely large and complex.) Biologists have constructed various detailed (although not exhaustive) phylogenetic trees. None of these trees, however, could explain how the single common ancestor to all life arose.

Clearly, Darwin's theory cannot explain the origins of the single common ancestor. In fact, in *The Origin of Species*, Darwin was very vague about life's origins. If one relies entirely on the book's title and does not read the book, one can easily jump to the wrong conclusions about its contents. The idea that the theory of evolution explains the origins of life, although believed by many, is untrue. Evolution goes far in explaining the amazing diversity of life on Earth; however, it does not try to explain how life originated. Scientists have proposed several other theories as to how this could have occurred, which we'll explore in the next few modules.

 True or false, evolution explains how life began and how it has adapted. Explain.

● False. Evolution explains how species have evolved from an ancestral species. It does not explain how the first common ancestor arose.

Early Earth and the Origin of Life

13.8 Conditions on early Earth made the origin of life possible

Earth is one of eight planets orbiting the sun, which is one of billions of stars in the Milky Way. (Pluto, which used to be the "ninth" planet, was recategorized as a dwarf planet in 2006.) The Milky Way, in turn, is one of billions of galaxies in the universe. The star closest to our sun is 40 trillion kilometres away.

The universe has not always been so spread out. Physicists have evidence that before the universe existed in its present form, all matter was concentrated in one mass. The mass seems to have blown apart with a "big bang" sometime between 12 and 14 bya and has been expanding ever since.

Scientific evidence indicates that Earth formed about 4.6 bya from a vast swirling cloud of dust that surrounded the young sun. As gases, dust, and rocks collided and stuck together, larger bodies formed, and the gravity of the larger bodies in turn attracted more matter, eventually forming Earth and other planets.

Conditions on Early Earth Immense heat would have been generated by the impact of meteorites and compaction by gravity, and young planet Earth probably began as a molten mass. The mass then sorted into layers of varying densities, with the least dense material on the surface, solidifying into a thin crust.

As the bombardment of early Earth slowed about 3.9 bya, conditions on the planet were extremely different from those of today. The first atmosphere was probably thick with water vapour, along with various compounds released by volcanic eruptions, including nitrogen and its oxides, carbon dioxide, methane, ammonia, hydrogen, and hydrogen sulphide. As Earth slowly cooled, the water vapour condensed into oceans. Not only was the atmosphere of young Earth very different from the atmosphere we know today, but lightning, volcanic activity, and ultraviolet radiation were much more intense.

When Did Life Begin? The earliest evidence of life on Earth comes from fossils that are about 3.5 billion years old. One of these fossils from Pavilion Lake in British Columbia is pictured in the inset in **Figure 13.8**; the larger illustration is an artist's rendition of what Earth may have looked like at that time. Life is already present in this painting, as shown by the "stepping stones" that dominate the shoreline. These rocks, called **stromatolites**, were built up by ancient photosynthetic prokaryotes. The prokaryotes that built them bound thin films of sediment together, and then migrated to the surface and started the next layer. Layer upon layer, the stomatolites grow into large formations. Similar layered mats are still being formed today by photosynthetic prokaryotes in a few shallow, salty bays, including what is now Pavilion Lake.

Photosynthesis is not a simple process, so it is likely that significant time had elapsed before life as complex as the organisms that formed the ancient stromatolites had evolved. The evidence that these prokaryotes lived 3.5 bya is strong support for the hypothesis that life in a simpler form arose much earlier, perhaps as early as 3.9 bya.

How Did Life Arise?   From the time of the ancient Greeks until well into the 1800s, it was commonly believed that life arises from nonliving matter. Many people believed, for instance, that flies come from rotting meat and fish from ocean mud. Experiments by the French scientist Louis Pasteur in 1862, however, confirmed that all life arises only by the reproduction of pre-existing life.

Pasteur ended the argument over spontaneous generation of present-day organisms, but he did not address the question of how life arose in the first place. To attempt to answer that question, for which there is no fossil evidence available, scientists develop hypotheses and test their predictions.

Scientists hypothesize that chemical and physical processes on early Earth could have produced very simple cells through a sequence of four main stages:

1. The abiotic (nonliving) synthesis of small organic molecules, such as amino acids and nitrogenous bases

2. The joining of these small molecules into polymers, such as proteins and nucleic acids

▲ **Figure 13.8** A depiction of Earth about 3 bya (inset: photo of a fossilized stromatolite at Pavilion Lake, British Columbia)

3. The packaging of these molecules into "protocells," membrane-enclosed droplets that maintained an internal chemistry different from that of their surroundings

4. The origin of self-replicating molecules that eventually made inheritance possible

In the next two modules, we examine some of the experimental evidence for each of these four stages.

? **Why do 3.5-billion-year-old stromatolites suggest that life originated *before* 3.5 bya?**

● If photosynthetic prokaryotes existed by 3.5 bya, a simpler, nonphotosynthetic cell probably originated well before that time.

13.9 Experiments show that the abiotic synthesis of organic molecules is possible

In 1953, American Stanley Miller performed experiments that attracted global attention. Miller was the first to show that amino acids and other organic molecules could be formed under conditions thought to simulate those of early Earth.

Miller's experiments were a test of a hypothesis about the origin of life developed in the 1920s that conditions on early Earth could have generated organic molecules. Present-day conditions on Earth do not allow the spontaneous synthesis of organic compounds simply because the atmosphere is now rich in oxygen. As a strong oxidizing agent, O_2 tends to disrupt chemical bonds. However, before the early photosynthetic prokaryotes added O_2 to the air, Earth may have had a reducing (electron-adding) atmosphere. The energy for this abiotic synthesis of organic compounds could have come from lightning and intense UV radiation.

Figure 13.9A is a diagram of the apparatus used in Miller's experiment. A flask of warmed water represented the primeval sea. ❶ The water was heated so that some vaporized and moved into a second, higher flask. ❷ The "atmosphere" in this higher flask consisted of water vapour, hydrogen gas (H_2), methane (CH_4), and ammonia (NH_3)—the gases that scientists at the time thought prevailed in the ancient world. Electrodes discharged sparks into the flask to mimic lightning. ❸ A condenser with circulating cold water cooled the atmosphere, raining water and any dissolved compounds back down into the miniature sea. ❹ As material cycled through the apparatus, Miller periodically collected samples for chemical analysis.

Miller identified a variety of organic molecules that are common in organisms, including hydrocarbons (long chains of carbon and hydrogen) and some of the amino acids that make up proteins. Many laboratories have since repeated Miller's classic experiment using various atmospheric mixtures and produced organic compounds.

Sparks simulating lightning

Water vapour

CH₄

"Atmosphere"

NH₃   H₂

❷

Electrode

❸

Condenser

Cold water

❶

H₂O

"Sea"

❹

Sample for
chemical analysis

▲ **Figure 13.9A** The synthesis of organic compounds in Miller's
1953 experiment

There is some evidence that the early atmosphere was
made up primarily of nitrogen and carbon dioxide and was
not as reducing as once assumed. Nevertheless, recent experiments using such atmospheres have also produced organic
molecules. And it is possible that small "pockets" of the early
atmosphere—perhaps near volcanic openings—were reducing.
In 2008, a former graduate student of Miller's discovered some
samples from an experiment that Miller had designed to mimic
volcanic conditions. Reanalyzing these samples using modern

equipment, he identified additional organic compounds
that had been synthesized.
Indeed, as **Figure 13.9B**
shows, many more amino
acids had been produced
under Miller's simulated
volcanic conditions than
were produced in his original 1953 experiment.

▲ **Figure 13.9B** Numbers of
amino acids synthesized in Miller's
original 1953 experiment and found
in a 2008 reanalysis of samples
from his simulated volcanic
eruption

Alternatively, submerged
volcanoes or deep-sea
hydrothermal vents—gaps
in Earth's crust where hot water and minerals gush into deep
oceans—may have provided the initial chemical resources for
life. Such environments are among the most extreme in which
life exists today, and some researchers are exploring the hypothesis that life may have begun in similar regions on early Earth.

Another source of organic molecules may have been meteorites. Fragments of a 4.5-billion-year-old meteorite that fell to
Earth in Australia in 1969 contain more than 80 types of amino
acids, some in large amounts. Recent studies have shown that
this meteorite also contains other key organic molecules, including lipids, simple sugars, and nitrogenous bases such as
uracil. Chemical analyses show that these organic compounds
are not contaminants from Earth. Research will continue on
the possible origins of organic molecules on early Earth.

? Which of the four stages in the hypothetical scenario of the
origin of simple cells was Stanley Miller testing with his
experiments?

● Stage 1: Conditions on early Earth favoured synthesis of organic molecules
important to life, such as amino acids, from simpler ingredients.

13.10 Stages in the origin of the first cells probably included the formation of polymers, protocells, and self-replicating RNA

The abiotic synthesis of small organic molecules would have
been a first step in the origin of life. But what is the evidence
that the next three stages could have occurred on early Earth?

Abiotic Synthesis of Polymers   In a cell, enzymes catalyze
the joining of monomers to build polymers. Could this happen
without enzymes? Scientists have produced polymers in the
laboratory by dripping dilute solutions of amino acids or RNA
monomers onto hot sand, clay, or rock. The heat vaporizes the
water and concentrates the monomers, some of which then
spontaneously bond together in chains. On early Earth, waves
may have splashed organic monomers onto fresh lava or other
hot rocks and then rinsed polypeptides and other polymers
back into the sea.

Formation of Protocells   A key step in the origin of life
would have been the isolation of a collection of organic molecules within a membrane-enclosed compartment. Laboratory

experiments demonstrate that
small membrane-enclosed
sacs or vesicles form when lipids are mixed with water (see
Module 5.2). When researchers add to the mixture a type
of clay thought to have been
common on early Earth, such
vesicles form at a faster rate.
Organic molecules become
concentrated on the surface of
this clay and thus more easily interact. As shown by the
smaller droplets forming in
Figure 13.10A, these abioti-
cally created vesicles are able to grow and divide (reproduce).
Researchers have shown that these vesicles can absorb clay
particles to which RNA and other molecules are attached. In a

LM 700×

▲ **Figure 13.10A** Microscopic
vesicle, with membranes made
of lipids, "giving birth" to smaller
vesicles

① Collection of monomers

② Formation of short RNA polymers: simple "genes"

③ Assembly of a complementary RNA chain, the first step in the replication of the original "gene"

▲ **Figure 13.10B** A hypothesis for the origin of the first genes

similar fashion, protocells on early Earth may have been able to form, reproduce, and create and maintain an internal environment different from their surroundings.

Self-Replicating RNA Today's cells store their genetic information as DNA, transcribe the information into RNA, and then translate RNA messages into proteins. As we saw in Chapter 10, this DNA → RNA → protein assembly system is extremely intricate. Most likely, it emerged gradually through a series of refinements of much simpler processes.

What were the first genes like? One hypothesis is that they were short strands of self-replicating RNA. Laboratory experiments have shown that short RNA molecules can assemble spontaneously from nucleotide monomers. Furthermore, when RNA is added to a solution containing a supply of RNA monomers, new RNA molecules complementary to parts of the starting RNA sometimes assemble. So we can imagine a scenario on early Earth like the one in **Figure 13.10B**: ① RNA monomers adhere to clay particles and become concentrated. ② Some monomers spontaneously join, forming the first small "genes." ③ Then an RNA chain complementary to one of these genes assembles. If the new chain, in turn, serves

as a template for another round of RNA assembly, the result is a replica of the original gene.

This replication process could have been aided by the RNA molecules themselves, acting as catalysts for their own replication. The discovery that some RNAs, which scientists call **ribozymes**, can carry out enzymelike functions supports this hypothesis. Thus, the "chicken and egg" paradox of which came first, genes or enzymes, may be solved if the chicken and egg came together in the same RNA molecules. Scientists use the term *RNA world* for the hypothetical period in the evolution of life when RNA served as both rudimentary genes and catalytic molecules.

Once some protocells contained self-replicating RNA molecules, natural selection would have begun to shape their properties. Those that contained genetic information that helped them grow and reproduce more efficiently than others would have increased in number, passing on their abilities to subsequent generations. Mutations, errors in copying RNA "genes," would result in additional variation on which natural selection could work. At some point during millions of years of selection, DNA, a more stable molecule, replaced RNA as the repository of genetic information, and protocells passed a fuzzy border to become true cells. The stage was then set for the evolution of diverse life forms, changes that we see documented in the fossil record.

? Why would the formation of protocells represent a key step in the evolution of life?

● Segregating mixtures of molecules within compartments could concentrate organic molecules and facilitate chemical reactions. Natural selection could act on protocells once self-replicating "genes" evolved.

Major Events in the History of Life

13.11 The origins of single-celled and multicellular organisms and the colonization of land were key events in life's history

We now begin our study of the broad pattern of changes in life on Earth. **Figure 13.11A** shows a timeline from the origin of Earth 4.6 bya to the present. The coloured bands represent some key origin points in the history of life. Earth's history can be divided into three eons of geologic time. The Archaean and the Proterozoic eons together lasted about 4 billion years. The Phanerozoic eon includes the last half billion years.

Origin of Prokaryotes As we discussed, the earliest evidence of life comes from fossil stromatolites formed by ancient photosynthetic prokaryotes (see Figure 13.8). Prokaryotes (the

gold band in Figure 13.11A) were Earth's sole inhabitants from at least 3.5 bya to about 2 bya. During this time, prokaryotes transformed the biosphere. As a result of prokaryotic photosynthesis, oxygen saturated the seas and began to appear in the atmosphere 2.7 bya (the teal band). By 2.2 bya, atmospheric O_2 began to increase rapidly, causing an "oxygen revolution." Many prokaryotes were unable to live in this aerobic environment and became extinct, while some species survived in anaerobic habitats, where we find their descendants living today. The evolution of cellular respiration, which uses O_2 in harvesting energy from organic molecules, allowed other prokaryotes to flourish.

▲ **Figure 13.11A** Some key events in the history of life on Earth

Origin of Single-Celled Eukaryotes The oldest widely accepted fossils of eukaryotes are about 2.1 billion years old (the salmon-coloured band). As you learned in Module 4.15, the more complex eukaryotic cell originated when small prokaryotic cells capable of aerobic respiration or photosynthesis took up life inside larger cells. After the first eukaryotes appeared, a great range of unicellular forms evolved, giving rise to the diversity of single-celled eukaryotes that continue to flourish today.

Origin of Multicellular Eukaryotes Another wave of diversification followed: the origin of multicellular forms whose descendants include a variety of algae, plants, fungi, and animals. Molecular comparisons suggest that the common ancestor of multicellular eukaryotes arose about 1.5 bya (the light blue band). The oldest known fossils of multicellular eukaryotes are of relatively small algae that lived 1.2 bya.

Larger and more diverse multicellular animals do not appear in the fossil record until about 575 mya. A great increase in the diversity of animal forms occurred 535–525 mya, in a period known as the Cambrian explosion. Most of our knowledge about the diversity of the earliest animals is based largely on the Burgess Shale fossil field in Yoho National Park, British Columbia. The Burgess Shale is rare in that many soft-bodied animals were preserved as well as those with hardened parts. **Figure 13.11B** depicts the array of the animals whose fossilized remains have been identified. Animals are shown on the timeline (Figure 13.11A) by the bright blue band.

Colonization of Land There is fossil evidence that photosynthetic prokaryotes coated damp terrestrial surfaces well over a billion years ago. However, larger forms of life did not begin to colonize land until about 500 mya (the purple band).

Plants colonized land in the company of fungi. Even today, the roots of most plants are associated with fungi that aid in absorption of water and minerals; the fungi receive nutrients

in return (see Module 18.10). Such mutually beneficial associations are evident in some of the oldest plant fossils.

In the next two modules, we see how scientists have determined when these key episodes in Earth's history have occurred in geologic time.

? **For how long did life on Earth consist solely of single-celled organisms?**

● More than 2 billion years: Molecular estimates date the common ancestor of multicellular eukaryotes at 1.5 bya; the oldest known multicellular fossils are about 1.2 billion years old. The earliest known fossils of singled-celled organisms are 3.5 billion years old.

▲ **Figure 13.11B** Life of the Burgess Shale: array of animals whose fossilized remains have been identified

13.12 The actual ages of rocks and fossils mark geologic time

Geologists use several techniques to determine the ages of rocks and the fossils they contain. The method most often used, called **radiometric dating**, is based on the decay of radioisotopes (unstable forms of an element; see Module 2.4). Fossils contain isotopes of elements that accumulated when the organisms were alive. For example, a living organism contains both the common isotope carbon-12 and the radioisotope carbon-14 in the same ratio as is present in the atmosphere. Once an organism dies, it stops accumulating carbon, and the stable carbon-12 in its tissues does not change. Its carbon-14, however, starts to decay to another element. The rate of decay is expressed as a half-life, the time required for 50% of the isotope in a sample to decay. With a half-life of 5730 years, half the carbon-14 in a specimen decays in about 5730 years, half the remaining carbon-14 decays in the next 5730 years, and so on **(Figure 13.12)**. Knowing both the half-life of a radioisotope and the ratio of radioactive to stable isotope in a fossil enables us to determine the age of the fossil.

Carbon-14 is useful for dating relatively young fossils—up to about 75 000 years old. Radioisotopes with longer half-lives are used to date older fossils.

There are indirect ways to estimate the age of much older fossils. For example, potassium-40, with a half-life of 1.3 billion

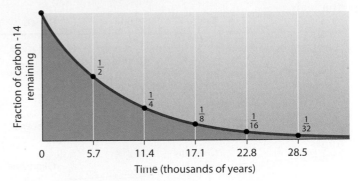

▲ **Figure 13.12** Radiometric dating using carbon-14

years, can be used to date volcanic rocks hundreds of millions of years old. A fossil's age can be inferred from the ages of the rock layers above and below the stratum in which it is found.

By dating rocks and fossils, scientists have established a geologic record of Earth's history.

? Estimate the age of a fossil found in a sedimentary rock layer between two layers of volcanic rock that are determined to be 530 and 520 million years old.

● We can infer that the organism lived approximately 525 mya.

13.13 The fossil record documents the history of life

The fossil record, the sequence in which fossils appear in rock strata, is an archive of evolutionary history (see Module 13.4). Based on this sequence and the ages of rocks and fossils, geologists have established a **geologic record**, as shown in **Table 13.13**, on the next page. As you saw in Figure 13.11A, Earth's history is divided into three eons, the Archaean, Proterozoic, and Phanerozoic. The timeline in Table 13.13 shows the lengths and ages (in mya) of these eons. Note that the Phanerozoic eon, which is only the last 542 million years, is expanded in the table to show the key events in the evolution of multicellular eukaryotic life. This eon is divided into three eras: the Paleozoic, Mesozoic, and Cenozoic, and the eras are subdivided into periods. The boundaries between eras are marked by mass extinctions, when many forms of life disappeared from the fossil record and were replaced by species that diversified from the survivors. Lesser extinctions often mark the boundaries between periods.

Rocks from the Archaean and Proterozoic eons have undergone extensive change over time, and much of their fossil content is no longer visible. Nonetheless, paleontologists have pieced together ancient events in life's history. As mentioned earlier, the oldest known fossils, dating from 3.5 bya, are of prokaryotes; the oldest fossils of eukaryotic cells are from 2.1 bya. Strata from the Ediacaran period (635–542 mya) bear diverse fossils of multicellular algae and soft-bodied animals.

Dating from about 542 mya, rocks of the Paleozoic ("ancient animal") era contain fossils of lineages that gave rise to present-day organisms, as well as many lineages that have become extinct. During the early Paleozoic, virtually all life was aquatic, but by about 400 mya, plants and animals were well established on land.

The Mesozoic ("middle animal") era is also known as the age of reptiles because of its abundance of reptilian fossils, including those of the dinosaurs. The Mesozoic era also saw the first mammals and flowering plants (angiosperms). By the end of the Mesozoic, dinosaurs had become extinct except for one lineage—the birds.

An explosive period of evolution of mammals, birds, insects, and angiosperms began at the dawn of the Cenozoic ("recent animal") era, about 65 mya. Because much more is known about the Cenozoic era than about earlier eras, our table subdivides the Cenozoic periods into finer intervals called epochs.

? What were the dominant animals during the Carboniferous period? When were gymnosperms the dominant plants? (*Hint:* Look at Table 13.13.)

● Amphibians. Gymnosperms were dominant during the Triassic and Jurassic periods (251–145.5 mya).

TABLE 13.13 | THE GEOLOGIC RECORD

Relative Duration of Eons	Era	Period	Epoch	Age (mya)	Important Events in the History of Life
Phanerozoic	Cenozoic	Quaternary	Holocene		Historical time
				0.01	
			Pleistocene		Ice ages; origin of genus *Homo*
				2.6	
		Tertiary	Pliocene		Appearance of bipedal human ancestors
				5.3	
			Miocene		Continued radiation of mammals and angiosperms; earliest direct human ancestors
				23	
			Oligocene		Origins of many primate groups
				33.9	
			Eocene		Angiosperm dominance increases; continued radiation of most present-day mammalian orders
				55.8	
			Paleocene		Major radiation of mammals, birds, and pollinating insects
				65.5	
Proterozoic	Mesozoic	Cretaceous			Flowering plants (angiosperms) appear and diversify; many groups of organisms, including most dinosaurs, become extinct at end of period
				145.5	
		Jurassic			Gymnosperms continue as dominant plants; dinosaurs abundant and diverse
				199.6	
		Triassic			Cone-bearing plants (gymnosperms) dominate landscape; dinosaurs evolve and radiate; origin of mammals
				251	
	Paleozoic	Permian			Radiation of reptiles; origin of most present-day groups of insects; extinction of many marine and terrestrial organisms at end of period
				299	
		Carboniferous			Extensive forests of vascular plants form; first seed plants appear; origin of reptiles; amphibians dominant
				359	
		Devonian			Diversification of bony fishes; first tetrapods and insects appear
				416	
		Silurian			Diversification of early vascular plants
				444	
		Ordovician			Marine algae abundant; colonization of land by diverse fungi, plants, and animals
				488	
		Cambrian			Sudden increase in diversity of many animal phyla (Cambrian explosion)
				542	
		Ediacaran			Diverse algae and soft-bodied invertebrate animals appear
				635	
Archaean				2100	Oldest fossils of eukaryotic cells appear
				2500	
				2700	Concentration of atmospheric oxygen begins to increase
				3500	Oldest fossils of cells (prokaryotes) appear
				3800	Oldest known rocks on Earth's surface
				Approx. 4600	Origin of Earth

MasteringBiology® **For Practice Quizzes, BioFlix, MP3 Tutors, and Activities, go to masteringbiology.com.**

Reviewing the Concepts

Darwin's Theory of Evolution (13.1–13.7)

13.1 A sea voyage helped Darwin frame his theory of evolution. Darwin's theory differed greatly from the long-held notion of a young Earth inhabited by unchanging species. Darwin called his theory descent with modification, which explains that all of life is connected by common ancestry and that descendants have accumulated adaptations to changing environments over vast spans of time.

13.2 Darwin proposed natural selection as the mechanism of evolution.

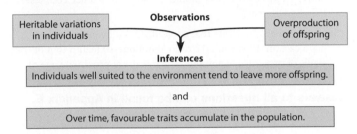

13.3 Scientists can observe natural selection in action. The evolution of resistance to insecticides is an unsettling example of natural selection in action.

13.4 The study of fossils provides strong evidence for evolution. The fossil record reveals the historical sequence in which organisms have evolved.

13.5 Many types of scientific evidence support the evolutionary view of life. Biogeography, comparative anatomy, and molecular biology all document evolution. Homologous structures and DNA sequences reveal evolutionary relationships.

13.6 Homologies indicate patterns of descent that can be shown on an evolutionary tree. Homologous structures have a common origin and are indicative of evolutionary relationships.

13.7 Does the theory of evolution explain the origins of life? Darwin's theory explains how new species adapt and evolve from ancestral species. It does not explain how the first species arose.

Early Earth and the Origin of Life (13.8–13.10)

13.8 Conditions on early Earth made the origin of life possible. Earth formed some 4.6 bya. Fossil stromatolites formed by prokaryotes date back 3.5 billion years.

13.9 Experiments show that the abiotic synthesis of organic molecules is possible. Experiments by Miller have demonstrated that the atmospheric conditions of early Earth could have generated organic molecules.

13.10 Stages in the origin of the first cells probably included the formation of polymers, protocells, and self-replicating RNA. Macromolecules may have polymerized on hot rocks. The first genes may have been catalytic RNA molecules. Protocells containing self-replicating molecules could have been acted on by natural selection.

Major Events in the History of Life (13.11–13.13)

13.11 The origins of single-celled and multicellular organisms and the colonization of land were key events in life's history. The following timeline is based on the fossil record.

13.12 The actual ages of rocks and fossils mark geologic time. Radiometric dating can date rocks and fossils.

13.13 The fossil record documents the history of life. In the geologic record, eras and periods are separated by major transitions in life forms, often caused by extinctions.

Connecting the Concepts

1. Summarize the key points of Darwin's theory of descent with modification, including his proposed mechanism of evolution.

2. Using the figure below, describe the stages that may have led to the origin of life.

Testing Your Knowledge

Multiple Choice

3. Which of the following did not influence Darwin as he synthesized the theory of evolution by natural selection?
   a. examples of artificial selection that produce large and relatively rapid changes in domesticated species
   b. Lyell's *Principles of Geology*, on gradual geologic changes
   c. comparisons of fossils with living organisms
   d. the biogeographic distribution of organisms, such as the unique species on the Galápagos Islands
   e. Mendel's paper describing the laws of inheritance

4. At the end of which period did most dinosaurs become extinct? (*Explain which dinosaur lineage did not.*)
   a. Jurassic period
   b. Cretaceous period
   c. Permian period
   d. Devonion period
   e. Quaternary period

5. Which of the following pairs of structures is least likely to represent homology?
   a. the hemoglobin of a human and that of a baboon
   b. the mitochondria of a plant and those of an animal
   c. the wings of a bird and those of an insect
   d. the tail of a cat and that of an alligator
   e. the foreleg of a pig and the flipper of a whale

6. Which of the following evidence best supports Darwin's claim that all life is descended from a common ancestor? *(Explain your answer.)*
   a. the fossil record
   b. DNA sequence data
   c. evolutionary trees
   d. comparative anatomy
   e. comparative embryology

7. Within a few weeks of treatment with the drug 3TC, a patient's HIV population consists entirely of 3TC-resistant viruses. How can this result best be explained?
   a. HIV can change its surface proteins and resist vaccines.
   b. The patient must have become reinfected with a resistant virus.
   c. A few drug-resistant viruses were present at the start of treatment, and natural selection increased their frequency.
   d. The drug caused the HIV genes to change.
   e. HIV began making drug-resistant versions of its enzymes in response to the drug.

8. You set your time machine for 3 bya and push the start button. When the dust clears, you look out the window. Which of the following describes what you would probably see?
   a. plants and animals very different from those alive today
   b. a cloud of gas and dust in space
   c. green scum in the water
   d. land and water sterile and devoid of life
   e. an endless expanse of red-hot molten rock

9. Ancient photosynthetic prokaryotes were very important in the history of life because they
   a. were probably the first living things to exist on Earth.
   b. produced the oxygen in the atmosphere.
   c. are the oldest known archaea.
   d. were the first multicellular organisms.
   e. showed that life could evolve around deep-sea vents.

10. Which of the following could provide the best data for determining the phylogeny of very closely related species?
    a. the fossil record
    b. a comparison of embryological development
    c. their morphological differences and similarities
    d. a comparison of nucleotide sequences in homologous genes and mitochondrial DNA
    e. a comparison of their ribosomal RNA sequences

11. Major divisions in the geologic record are marked by
    a. radioactive dating.
    b. distinct changes in the types of fossilized life.
    c. continental drift.
    d. regular time intervals measured in millions of years.
    e. the appearance, in order, of prokaryotes, eukaryotes, protists, animals, plants, and fungi.

Describing, Comparing, and Explaining

12. Write a paragraph briefly describing the kinds of scientific evidence for evolution.

13. Which are more likely to be closely related: two species with similar appearance but divergent gene sequences or two species with different appearances but nearly identical genes? Explain.

Applying the Concepts

14. Advocates of "scientific creationism" and "intelligent design" lobby school districts for such things as a ban on teaching evolution, equal time in science classes to teach alternative versions of the origin and history of life, or disclaimers in textbooks stating that evolution is "just a theory." They argue that it is only fair to let students evaluate both evolution and the idea that all species were created by God as the Bible relates or that, because organisms are so complex and well adapted, they must have been created by an intelligent designer. Do you think that alternative views of evolution should be taught in science courses? Why or why not?

15. Measurements indicate that a fossilized skull you unearthed has a carbon-14/carbon-12 ratio about one-sixteenth that of the skulls of present-day animals. What is the approximate age of the fossil? (The half-life of carbon-14 is 5730 years.)

Answers to all questions can be found in Appendix E.

Study on the Go

This QR code leads to Study on the Go—mobile study resources, including practice quizzes, videos, and glossary flashcards for this textbook.

You can access Study on the Go content via your smartphone. Note: Your login information for MasteringBiology is required.

14

Mechanisms of Evolution

BIG IDEAS

The Evolution of Populations

(14.1–14.4)

Genetic variation makes evolution possible within a population.

Mechanisms of Microevolution

(14.5–14.10)

Natural selection, genetic drift, and gene flow can alter gene pools; natural selection leads to adaptive evolution.

Mechanisms of Macroevolution

(14.11–14.16)

Continental drift, mass extinctions, adaptive radiations, and changes in developmental genes have all contributed to macroevolution.

On the Wings of Eagles, Bats, and Pterosaurs

Have you ever wished you could fly? Unfortunately (or perhaps fortunately), we remain earthbound because our ancestors were busy using their arms for other functions that would not easily permit them to become adapted as wings.

But in some species, limbs did become adapted for flight. Forelimbs have been remodelled into wings three separate times in tetrapods (vertebrates with four limbs). Pterosaurs (illustrated here) were the first tetrapods in the air. These flying reptiles evolved about 225 mya, persisted for about 140 million years, and then went extinct along with most of the dinosaurs. Birds evolved from feathered dinosaurs about 150 mya and are still flying. The fossil record of the evolution of bats, the third group of flying vertebrates, is not very complete. The hypothesis is that bats diverged from nocturnal, insectivorous, tree-dwelling mammals some 60 mya. They, too, are still flying today.

Different times, different ancestors, same ability—powered flight. Are the wings of pterosaurs, birds, and bats the same or different? The requirements of powered flight include wings as broad airfoils that can move up and down, forward and backward, and fold against the body when not in use. It appears that in vertebrates, natural selection favoured three different designs to meet these requirements.

Pterosaurs ruled the skies in the Jurassic and Cretaceous periods. Some were as small as songbirds; one was the size of a small airplane, with a wingspan of 12 m. As you can see in the artist's reconstruction of a pterosaur here, the wing was supported along much of its length by one greatly elongated finger. The skin membrane making up the wing was reinforced with thickened fibres.

By contrast, bird wings are composed of feathers, which are outgrowths of the skin along the whole length of the forelimb. The feathers provide much of the wingspan. The supporting structure is an elongated forearm and modified wrist and hand bones. Finger bones are reduced and fused.

Bat wings can be described as "hand wings," made of a membrane supported by the arm and four elongated fingers. The membrane extends to the hind limbs and is attached at the heel. These small mammals are agile flyers, capable of swooping after insects and navigating around obstacles (including humans) by using echolocation.

As different as the architectures of the wings of pterosaurs, birds, and bats are, all three designs represent the remodelling of the same ancestral tetrapod limb. These examples of Darwin's "descent with modification" illustrate again that evolution is an editing process, which can gradually adapt existing structures to new functions. In this case, natural selection led to three different "solutions" to the challenge of powered flight. Indeed, these three kinds of flyers lead to a multitude of evolutionary questions: What were their ancestors like? Were they bipedal, fast-running animals that leaped into the air to capture prey with their arms? Were they tree dwellers whose extended forelimbs helped them glide from limb to limb? How has body form changed as the ability to fly became an adaptation on which natural selection could act? And how did the amazing diversity of pterosaurs, birds, and bats evolve? These questions and more are addressed by biologists who study fossils, genes, development, and phylogeny (the evolutionary history of groups).

In this chapter we examine the mechanisms of evolution. We will look at microevolution, how allelic frequencies change within populations from generation to generation. Following that we'll examine the mechanisms of macroevolution, the major changes (such as the evolution of flight in three different vertebrate lineages) recorded in the history of life over vast tracts of time.

The Evolution of Populations

14.1 Do individuals evolve?

One common belief about evolution is that individual organisms evolve during their lifetimes. This misconception likely arises from an oversimplified description of evolution as "change over time." Some people apply this simplified statement to the individual and argue that a given organism can change itself to adapt to its environment. Is this simplification accurate or does it contribute to the misunderstanding of the mechanisms of evolution?

As is often the case, oversimplifications lead to misunderstandings and misconceptions. This example is no different. It is true that natural selection acts on individuals. Each individual's combination of traits affects its survival and reproductive success. But the evolutionary impact of natural selection is apparent only in the changes in a population of organisms over generations.

A **population** is a group of individuals of the same species that live in the same area and interbreed. We can measure evolution as a change in the prevalence of certain heritable traits in a population over a span of generations. The increasing proportion of resistant insects in areas sprayed with pesticide is one example (see Module 13.3). Natural selection favoured insects with alleles for pesticide resistance; these insects left more offspring, and the population changed, or evolved.

Let's examine some key features of populations. Different populations of the same species may be isolated from one another, with little interbreeding and thus little exchange of genes between them. Such isolation is common for populations confined to widely separated islands or in different lakes. However, populations are not usually so isolated, and they rarely have distinct boundaries. **Figure 14.1** is a nighttime satellite photograph showing the lights of population centres in North America. We know that these populations are not completely isolated; people move around, and there are suburban and rural communities between cities. Nevertheless, people are most likely to choose mates locally. Thus, for humans and other species, members of one population are generally more closely related to one another than to members of other populations.

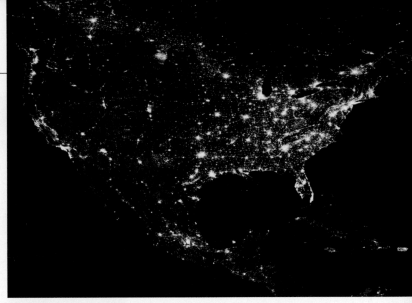

▲ **Figure 14.1** Human population centres in North America

In studying evolution at the population level, biologists focus on what is called the **gene pool**, the total collection of genes in a population at any one time. The gene pool consists of all the alleles in all the individuals making up a population. For many genes, there are two or more alleles in the gene pool. For example, in an insect population, there may be two alleles relating to pesticide breakdown, one that codes for an enzyme that breaks down a certain pesticide and one for a version of the enzyme that does not. In populations living in fields sprayed with pesticide, the allele for the enzyme conferring resistance will increase in frequency and the other allele will decrease in frequency. When the relative frequencies of alleles in a population change like this over a number of generations, evolution is occurring on its smallest scale. Such a change in a gene pool is often called microevolution. We will take a closer look at microevolution later in this chapter. But first, let's look at the genetic variation that makes microevolution possible.

 Why can't an individual evolve?

● Evolution involves changes in the genetic makeup of a population. An individual's genetic makeup rarely changes during its lifetime.

14.2 Mutation and sexual reproduction produce the genetic variation that makes evolution possible

In *The Origin of Species* Darwin provided evidence that life on Earth has evolved over time, and he proposed that natural selection, in favouring some heritable traits over others, was the primary mechanism for that change. But he could not explain the cause of variation among individuals, nor could he account for how those variations passed from parents to offspring.

Just a few years after the publication of *The Origin of Species*, Gregor Mendel wrote a groundbreaking paper on inheritance in pea plants (see Chapter 9). By breeding peas in his abbey garden, Mendel discovered the very hereditary processes required for natural selection. Although the significance of Mendel's work was not recognized during his or Darwin's

lifetime, it set the stage for understanding the genetic differences on which evolution is based.

Genetic Variation You have no trouble recognizing your friends in a crowd. Each person has a unique genome, reflected in individual variations in appearance and other traits. Indeed, individual variation occurs in all species, as illustrated in **Figure 14.2** by the lady beetles and the garter snakes. All four of these snakes were captured in one field. In addition to obvious physical differences, most populations have a great deal of variation that can be observed only at the molecular level.

▲ **Figure 14.2** Variation within a species of Asian lady beetles (above) and within a species of garter snakes (right)

Of course, not all variation in a population is heritable. The phenotype results from a combination of the genotype, which is inherited, and many environmental influences. For instance, if you undertake a strength-training program to build up your muscle mass, you will not pass your environmentally produced physique to your offspring. Only the genetic component of variation is relevant to natural selection.

Many of the characters that vary in a population result from the combined effect of several genes. As we saw in Module 9.13, polygenic inheritance produces characters that vary more or less continuously—in human height, for instance, from very short individuals to very tall ones. By contrast, other features, such as Mendel's purple and white pea flowers or human blood types, are determined by a single gene locus, with different alleles producing distinct phenotypes. But where do these alleles come from?

Mutation   New alleles originate by mutation, a change in the nucleotide sequence of DNA. Thus, mutation is the ultimate source of the genetic variation that serves as raw material for evolution. In multicellular organisms, however, only mutations in cells that produce gametes can be passed to offspring and affect a population's genetic variability.

A mutation that affects a protein's function will probably be harmful. An organism is a refined product of thousands of generations of past selection, and a random change in its DNA is not likely to improve its genome any more than randomly changing some words on a page is likely to improve a story.

On rare occasions, however, a mutant allele may actually improve the adaptation of an individual to its environment and enhance its reproductive success. This kind of effect is more likely when the environment is changing in such a way that mutations that were once disadvantageous are favourable under the new conditions. The evolution of DDT-resistant houseflies (see Module 13.3) illustrates this point.

Chromosomal mutations that delete, disrupt, or rearrange many gene loci at once are almost certain to be harmful (see Module 8.24). But duplication of a gene or small pieces of DNA through errors in meiosis can provide an important source of genetic variation. If a repeated segment of DNA can persist over the generations, mutations in duplicated genes may accumulate, eventually leading to new genes with novel functions. For example, the remote ancestors of mammals carried a single gene for detecting odours, which has been duplicated repeatedly. As a result, mice have about 1300 different olfactory receptor genes. It is likely that such dramatic increases helped early mammals by enabling them to distinguish among many different smells. And duplications of genes that control development are linked to the origin of vertebrate animals from an invertebrate ancestor (see Module 14.14).

In prokaryotes, mutations can quickly generate genetic variation. Because bacteria multiply so rapidly, a beneficial mutation can increase in frequency in a matter of hours or days. And because bacteria are haploid, with a single allele for each gene, a new allele can have an effect immediately.

Mutation rates in animals and plants average about 1 in every 100 000 genes per generation. For these organisms, low mutation rates, long time spans between generations, and diploid genomes prevent most mutations from significantly affecting genetic variation from one generation to the next.

Sexual Reproduction   In organisms that reproduce sexually, most of the genetic variation in a population results from the unique combination of alleles that each individual inherits. (Of course, the origin of those allele variations is past mutations.)

As we saw in Modules 8.16 and 8.18, fresh assortments of existing alleles arise every generation from three random components of sexual reproduction: crossing over, independent orientation of homologous chromosomes at metaphase I of meiosis, and random fertilization. During prophase I, pairs of homologous chromosomes, one set inherited from each parent, trade some of their genes by crossing over. Then each pair of chromosomes separates into gametes independently of other chromosome pairs. Thus, gametes from any individual vary extensively in their genetic makeup. Finally, each zygote made by a mating pair has a unique assortment of alleles resulting from the random union of sperm and egg.

Genetic variation is necessary for a population to evolve, but variation alone does not guarantee that microevolution will occur. In the next module, we'll explore how to test whether evolution is occurring in a population.

? **What is the ultimate source of genetic variation? What is the source of most genetic variation in a population that reproduces sexually?**

● Mutation; unique combinations of alleles resulting from sexual reproduction

14.3 The Hardy-Weinberg equation can test whether a population is evolving

To understand how microevolution works, let's first examine a simple population in which evolution is not occurring and thus the gene pool is not changing. Consider an imaginary population of blue-footed boobies with individuals that differ in foot webbing (**Figure 14.3A**). Let's assume that foot webbing is controlled by a single gene and that the allele for nonwebbed feet (W) is completely dominant to the allele for webbed feet (w). The term *dominant* (see Module 9.2) may seem to suggest that over many generations the W allele will somehow come to "dominate," becoming more and more common at the expense of the recessive allele. In fact, this is not what happens. The shuffling of alleles that accompanies sexual reproduction does not alter the genetic makeup of the population. In other words, no matter how many times alleles are segregated into different gametes and united in different combinations by fertilization, the frequency of each allele in the gene pool will remain constant unless other factors are operating. This equilibrium is known as the **Hardy-Weinberg principle**, named for the two scientists who derived it independently in 1908.

To test the Hardy-Weinberg principle, let's look at two generations of our imaginary booby population. **Figure 14.3B** shows the frequencies of alleles in the gene pool of the original population. We have a total of 500 birds; of these, 320 have the genotype WW (nonwebbed feet), 160 have the heterozygous genotype Ww (also nonwebbed feet, because the nonwebbed allele W is dominant), and 20 have the genotype ww (webbed feet). The proportions or frequencies of the three genotypes are shown in the middle of Figure 14.3B: 0.64 for WW ($\frac{320}{500}$), 0.32 for Ww ($\frac{160}{500}$), and 0.04 for ww ($\frac{20}{500}$).

From these genotype frequencies, we can calculate the frequency of each allele in the population. Because these are diploid organisms, this population of 500 has a total of 1000

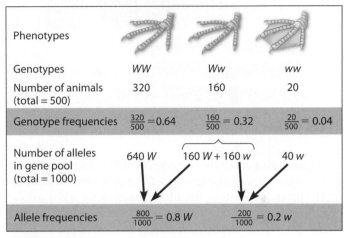

Phenotypes			
Genotypes	WW	Ww	ww
Number of animals (total = 500)	320	160	20
Genotype frequencies	$\frac{320}{500}=0.64$	$\frac{160}{500}=0.32$	$\frac{20}{500}=0.04$
Number of alleles in gene pool (total = 1000)	640 W	160 W + 160 w	40 w
Allele frequencies	$\frac{800}{1000}=0.8\ W$		$\frac{200}{1000}=0.2\ w$

▲ **Figure 14.3B** Gene pool of the original population of imaginary blue-footed boobies

alleles for foot type. To determine the number of W alleles, we add the number in the WW boobies, $2 \times 320 = 640$, to the number in the Ww boobies, 160. The total number of W alleles is thus 800. The frequency of the W allele, which we will call p, is $\frac{800}{1000}$, or 0.8. We can calculate the frequency of the w allele in a similar way; this frequency, called q, is 0.2. The letters p and q are often used to represent allele frequencies. (You will notice that $p + q = 1$. The combined frequencies of all alleles for a gene in a population must equal 1. If there are only two alleles and you know the frequency of one allele, you can calculate the frequency of the other.)

What happens when the boobies of this parent population form gametes? At the end of meiosis, each gamete has one allele for foot type, either W or w. The frequency of the two alleles in the gametes will be the same as their frequencies in the gene pool of the parental population, 0.8 for W and 0.2 for w.

Figure 14.3C shows a Punnett square that uses these gamete allele frequencies and the rule of multiplication (see Module 9.6) to calculate the frequencies of the three genotypes in the next generation. The probability of producing a WW individual (by combining two W alleles from the pool of gametes) is $p \times p = p^2$, or $0.8 \times 0.8 = 0.64$. Thus, the frequency of WW boobies in the next generation would be 0.64. Likewise, the frequency of ww individuals would be $q^2 = 0.04$. For heterozygous individuals, Ww, the genotype can form in two ways, depending on whether the sperm or egg supplies the dominant allele. In other words, the frequency of Ww would be $2pq = 2 \times 0.8 \times 0.2 = 0.32$. Do these frequencies look familiar? Notice that the three genotypes have the same frequencies in the next generation as they did in the parent generation.

▶ **Figure 14.3A**
Imaginary blue-footed boobies, with and without foot webbing

Webbing   No webbing

Gametes reflect allele frequencies of parental gene pool	Sperm	
	W $p = 0.8$	w $q = 0.2$
Eggs W $p = 0.8$	WW $p^2 = 0.64$	Ww $pq = 0.16$
w $q = 0.2$	wW $qp = 0.16$	ww $q^2 = 0.04$

Next generation:

Genotype frequencies	0.64 WW	0.32 Ww	0.04 ww
Allele frequencies		0.8 W	0.2 w

▲ **Figure 14.3C** Gene pool of next generation of imaginary boobies

Finally, what about the frequencies of the alleles in this new generation? Because the genotype frequencies are the same as in the parent population, the allele frequencies p and q are also the same. In fact, we could follow the frequencies of alleles and genotypes through many generations, and the results would continue to be the same. Thus, the gene pool of this population is in a state of equilibrium—Hardy-Weinberg equilibrium.

Now let's write a general formula for calculating the frequencies of genotypes in a population from the frequencies of alleles in the gene pool. In our imaginary blue-footed booby population, the frequency of the W allele (p) is 0.8, and the frequency of the w allele (q) is 0.2. Again note that $p + q = 1$. Also notice in Figures 14.3B and 14.3C that the frequencies of the three possible genotypes in the populations also add up to 1 (that is, $0.64 + 0.32 + 0.04 = 1$). We can represent these relationships symbolically with the Hardy-Weinberg equation:

$$p^2 \quad + \quad 2pq \quad + \quad q^2 \quad = \quad 1$$

Frequency of homozygous dominants	Frequency of heterozygotes	Frequency of homozygous recessives

If a population is in Hardy-Weinberg equilibrium, allele and genotype frequencies will remain constant generation after generation. The Hardy-Weinberg principle tells us that something other than the reshuffling processes of sexual reproduction is required to change allele frequencies in a population. One way to find out what factors *can* change a gene pool is to identify the conditions that must be met if genetic equilibrium is to be maintained. For a population to be in Hardy-Weinberg equilibrium, it must satisfy five main conditions:

1. Very large population
2. No gene flow between populations
3. No mutations
4. Random mating
5. No natural selection

Let's expand on these conditions: (1) The smaller the population, the more likely that allele frequencies will fluctuate by chance from one generation to the next. (2) When individuals move into or out of populations, they add or remove alleles, altering the gene pool. (3) By changing alleles or deleting or duplicating genes, mutations modify the gene pool. (4) If individuals mate preferentially, such as with close relatives (inbreeding), random mixing of gametes does not occur, and genotype frequencies change. (5) The unequal survival and reproductive success of individuals (natural selection) can alter allele frequencies.

Rarely are all five conditions met in real populations, and thus, allele and genotype frequencies often do change. The Hardy-Weinberg equation can be used to test whether evolution is occurring in a population. The equation also has medical applications, as we see next.

? Which is *least* likely to alter allele and genotype frequencies in a few generations of a large, sexually reproducing population: gene flow, mutation, or natural selection? Explain.

● Mutation. Because mutations are rare, their effect on allele and genotype frequencies from one generation to the next is likely to be small.

14.4 The Hardy-Weinberg equation is useful in public health science

Public health scientists use the Hardy-Weinberg equation to estimate how many people carry alleles for certain inherited diseases. Consider a recessive inherited disease, which has an incidence of 1 in 10 000 births. The frequency of individuals born with the disease corresponds to the q^2 term in the Hardy-Weinberg equation. Given 1 occurrence per 10 000 births, $q^2 = \frac{1}{10\,000}$ or 0.0001. Therefore, the frequency of the recessive allele in the population, q, equals the square root of 0.0001, or 0.01. And the frequency of the dominant allele, p, equals $1 - q$, or 0.99. The frequency of carriers, heterozygous people who do not have the disease but may pass on the allele to offspring, is

$2pq$, which equals $2 \times 0.99 \times 0.01$, or 0.0198. Thus, the equation tells us that about 2% (actually 1.98%) of the population are carriers of the recessive allele.

The example above was a hypothetical disease with a frequency that makes the calculations easy to follow. However, the same calculations can be performed for actual genetic disorders. Consider the case of phenylketonuria (PKU), which is an inherited inability to break down the amino acid phenylalanine. PKU occurs in about 1 out of 12 000 babies born in Canada, and if untreated results in severe mental deficiencies. Newborns are now routinely tested for PKU, and symptoms

▶ **Figure 14.4**
A warning to individuals with PKU

INGREDIENTS: CARBONATED WATER, CARAMEL COLOUR, PHOSPHORIC ACID, **ASPARTAME (CONTAINS PHENYLALANINE)** POTASSIUM BENZOATE, NATURAL FLAVOUR, POTASSIUM CITRATE, ACESULFAME-POTASSIUM, CAFFEINE

can be lessened if individuals living with the disease follow a diet that strictly regulates the intake of phenylalanine. Packaged foods with ingredients such as aspartame, a common artificial sweetener that contains phenylalanine, must be labelled clearly (**Figure 14.4**).

PKU is due to a recessive allele, so the frequency of individuals born with PKU corresponds to the q^2 term. Given 1 PKU occurrence per 12 000 births, $q^2 = \frac{1}{12\,000}$ or 0.0000833. Therefore, $q = 0.00913$ and $p = 0.99087$. The frequency of carriers, heterozygous people who do not have PKU but may pass on the PKU allele to offspring, is $2pq$, which equals approximately 0.0181. Thus, the equation tells us that about 1.8% of the Canadian population are carriers of the PKU allele.

 Which term in the Hardy-Weinberg equation—p^2, $2pq$, or q^2— corresponds to the frequency of individuals who have no alleles for the disease PKU?

● The frequency of individuals with no PKU alleles is p^2.

Mechanisms of Microevolution

14.5 Natural selection, genetic drift, and gene flow can cause microevolution

Deviations from the five conditions named in Module 14.3 for Hardy-Weinberg equilibrium can alter allele frequencies in a population (**microevolution**). Although new genes and new alleles originate by mutation, these random and rare events probably change allele frequencies little within a population of sexually reproducing organisms. Nonrandom mating can affect the frequencies of homozygous and heterozygous genotypes, but by itself usually does not affect allele frequencies. The three main causes of evolutionary change are natural selection, genetic drift, and gene flow.

Natural Selection   The condition for Hardy-Weinberg equilibrium that there be no natural selection—that all individuals in a population be equal in ability to reproduce—is probably never met in nature. Populations consist of varied individuals, and some variants leave more offspring than others. In our imaginary blue-footed booby population, birds with webbed feet (genotype *ww*) might survive better and produce more offspring because they are more efficient at swimming and catching food than birds without webbed feet. Genetic equilibrium would be disturbed as the frequency of the *w* allele increased in the gene pool from one generation to the next.

Genetic Drift   Flip a coin a thousand times, and a result of 700 heads and 300 tails would make you suspicious about that coin. But flip a coin 10 times, and an outcome of 7 heads and 3 tails would seem within reason. The smaller the sample, the more likely that chance alone will cause a deviation from an idealized result—in this case, an equal number of heads and tails. Let's apply that logic to a population's gene pool. The frequencies of alleles will be more stable from one generation to the next when a population is large. In a process called **genetic drift**, chance events can cause

allele frequencies to fluctuate unpredictably from one generation to the next. The smaller the population, the more impact genetic drift is likely to have. In fact, an allele can be lost from a small population by such chance fluctuations. Two situations in which genetic drift can have a significant impact on a population are those that produce the bottleneck effect and the founder effect.

Earthquakes, floods, or fires may kill large numbers of individuals, leaving a small surviving population that is unlikely to have the same genetic makeup as the original population. Such a drastic reduction in population size is called a **bottleneck effect**. Analogous to shaking just a few marbles through a bottleneck (**Figure 14.5A**), certain alleles (purple marbles) may be present at higher frequency in the surviving population than in the original population, others

Original population → Bottlenecking event → Surviving population

▲ **Figure 14.5A** The bottleneck effect

▲ **Figure 14.5B** Greater prairie chicken (*Tympanuchus cupido*)

(green marbles) may be present at lower frequency, and some (orange marbles) may not be present at all. After a bottlenecking event, genetic drift may continue for many generations until the population is again large enough for fluctuations due to chance to have less of an impact. Even if a population that has passed through a bottleneck ultimately recovers its size, it may have low levels of genetic variation—a legacy of the genetic drift that occurred when the population was small.

One reason it is important to understand the bottleneck effect is that human actions may create severe bottlenecks for other species, such as the endangered African cheetah (see Figure 14.6). The greater prairie chicken **(Figure 14.5B)** is another example. Millions of these birds once lived on the eastern prairies of North America. But as the prairies were converted to farmland and other uses during the 19th and 20th centuries, the number of greater prairie chickens plummeted. By 1993, only two populations remained, with a total of fewer than 50 birds. Less than 50% of the eggs of these birds hatched. Researchers compared the DNA of the 1993 population with DNA extracted from museum specimens dating back to the 1930s. They surveyed six gene loci and found that the modern birds had lost 30% of the alleles that were present in the museum specimens. Thus, genetic drift as a result of the

bottleneck reduced the genetic variation of the population and may have increased the frequency of harmful alleles, leading to the low egg-hatching rate.

Genetic drift is also likely when a few individuals colonize an island or other new habitat, producing what is called the **founder effect**. The smaller the group, the less likely the genetic makeup of the colonists will represent the gene pool of the larger population they left.

The founder effect explains the relatively high frequency of certain inherited disorders among some human populations established by small numbers of colonists. In 1814, 15 people founded a colony on Tristan da Cunha, a group of small islands in the middle of the Atlantic Ocean. Apparently, one of the colonists carried a recessive allele for retinitis pigmentosa, a progressive form of blindness. Of the 240 descendants who still lived on the islands in the 1960s, four had retinitis pigmentosa, and at least nine others were known to be heterozygous carriers of the allele. The frequency of this allele is 10 times higher on Tristan da Cunha than in the British population from which the founders came.

Gene Flow   Allele frequencies in a population can also change as a result of **gene flow**, where a population may gain or lose alleles when fertile individuals move into or out of a population or when gametes (such as plant pollen) are transferred between populations. Gene flow tends to reduce differences between populations. For example, humans today move more freely about the world than in the past, and gene flow has become an important agent of evolutionary change in previously isolated human populations.

Let's return to the greater prairie chickens and see how gene flow improved their fate. To counteract the lack of genetic diversity, researchers added a total of 271 birds from neighbouring populations. This strategy worked. New alleles entered the population, and the egg-hatching rate improved to more than 90%.

 How might gene flow between populations living in different habitats actually interfere with each population's adaptation to its local environment?

● The introduction of alleles that may not be beneficial in a particular habitat prevents the population living there from becoming fully adapted to its local conditions.

14.6 Natural selection is the only mechanism that consistently leads to adaptive evolution

Genetic drift, gene flow, and even mutation can cause microevolution. But only by chance could these events result in improving a population's fit to its environment. Evolution by natural selection, on the contrary, is a blend of chance and "sorting": chance in the random collection of genetic variation packaged in gametes and combined in offspring, and sorting in that some alleles are favoured over others in a given environment. Because of this sorting effect, only natural selection consistently leads to adaptive evolution—evolution that results in a better fit between organisms and their environment.

The adaptations of organisms include many striking examples. Remember the adaptations of blue-footed boobies to their marine environment and the amazing camouflage of mantids shown in Figure 13.3A. Or consider the remarkable speed of the cheetah **(Figure 14.6)**. The cheetah can accelerate from 0 to 60 km/h in three strides and to a full speed of 110 km/h in seconds. Its entire body—skeleton, muscles, joints, heart, and lungs—is built for speed.

Such adaptations for speed are the result of natural selection. By consistently favouring some alleles over others, natural selection improves the match between organisms and their environment. However, the environment may change over time. As a result, what constitutes a "good match" between an organism and its environment is a moving target, making adaptive evolution a continuous, dynamic process.

Let's take a closer look at natural selection. The commonly used phrases "struggle for existence" and "survival of the fittest" are misleading if we take them to mean direct competition between individuals. There *are* animal species in which individuals lock horns or otherwise do combat to determine mating privilege. But reproductive success is generally more subtle and passive. In a varying population of moths, certain individuals may produce more offspring than others because their wing colours hide them from predators better. Plants in a wildflower population may differ in reproductive success because some attract more pollinators, owing to slight variations in flower colour, shape, or fragrance. In a given environment, such traits can lead to greater **relative fitness**: the contribution an individual makes to the gene pool of the next generation relative to the contributions of other individuals. The fittest individuals in the context of evolution are those that produce the largest number of viable, fertile offspring and thus pass on the

▲ **Figure 14.6** The flexible spine of a cheetah stretching out in the middle of its 7 m stride

most genes to the next generation. In contrast, individuals that produce no offspring have a fitness of zero.

? Explain how the phrase *survival of the fittest* differs from the biological definition of relative fitness.

● Survival alone does not guarantee reproductive success. An organism's relative fitness is determined by its number of fertile offspring and thus its relative contribution to the gene pool of the next generation.

14.7 Natural selection can alter variation in a population in three ways

Evolutionary fitness is related to genes, but it is an organism's phenotype—its physical traits, metabolism, and behaviour—that is directly exposed to the environment. Let's see how natural selection can affect the distribution of phenotypes by using an imaginary

mouse population that has a heritable variation in fur coloration. The bell-shaped curve in the top graph of **Figure 14.7** depicts the frequencies of individuals in an initial population in which fur colour varies along a continuum from very light (only a few

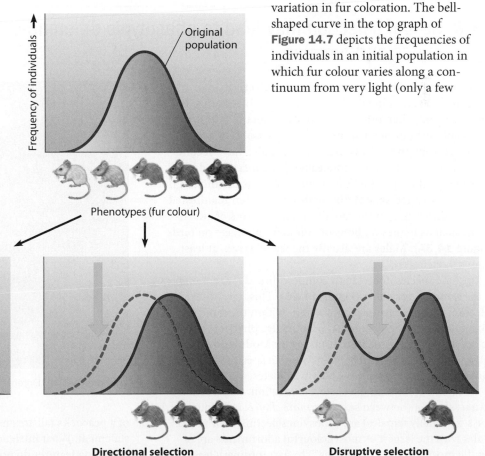

▲ **Figure 14.7** Three possible effects of natural selection on a phenotypic character

individuals) through various intermediate shades (many individuals) to very dark (a few individuals). The bottom graphs show three ways in which natural selection can alter the phenotypic variation in the mouse population. The blue downward arrows symbolize the pressure of natural selection working against certain phenotypes.

Stabilizing selection favours intermediate phenotypes. In the mouse population depicted in the graph on the bottom left, stabilizing selection has eliminated the extremely light and dark individuals, and the population has a greater number of intermediate phenotypes, which may be best suited to an environment with medium grey rocks. Stabilizing selection typically reduces variation and maintains the status quo for a particular character. For example, this type of selection keeps the majority of human birth weights in the range of 3–4 kg. For babies a lot smaller or larger than this, infant mortality may be greater.

Directional selection shifts the overall makeup of the population by acting against individuals at *one* of the phenotypic extremes. For the mouse population in the bottom centre graph, the trend is toward darker fur colour, as might occur if a fire darkened the landscape and now darker fur would more readily camouflage the animal. Directional selection is most common during periods of environmental change or when members of a species migrate to some new habitat with different environmental conditions. The changes

we described in populations of insects exposed to pesticides are an example of directional selection (see Module 13.3). Another example is the increase in beak depth in a population of Galápagos finches following a drought, when the birds that were better able to eat larger seeds were more likely to survive (see Module 13.3).

Disruptive selection typically occurs when environmental conditions vary in a way that favours individuals at *both* ends of a phenotypic range over individuals with intermediate phenotypes. For the mice in the graph on the bottom right, individuals with light and dark fur have increased numbers. Perhaps the mice colonized a patchy habitat where a background of light soil was studded with areas of dark rocks. Disruptive selection can lead to two or more contrasting phenotypes in the same population. For example, in a population of African black-bellied seedcracker finches, large-billed birds, which specialize in cracking hard seeds, and small-billed birds, which feed mainly on soft seeds, survive better than birds with intermediate-sized bills, which are fairly inefficient at cracking both types of seeds.

Next we consider a special case of selection, one that leads to phenotypic differences between males and females.

 What type of selection probably resulted in the colour variations evident in the garter snakes in Figure 14.2?

● Disruptive selection

14.8 Sexual selection may lead to phenotypic differences between males and females

Darwin was the first to examine **sexual selection**, a form of natural selection in which individuals with certain traits are more likely than other individuals to obtain mates. The males and females of an animal species obviously have different reproductive organs. But they may also have secondary sexual characteristics, noticeable differences not directly associated with reproduction or survival. This distinction in appearance, called **sexual dimorphism**, is often manifested in a size difference, but it can also include forms of adornment, such as manes on lions or colourful plumage on birds **(Figure 14.8A)**. Males are usually the showier sex, at least among vertebrates.

In some species, individuals compete directly with members of the same sex for mates **(Figure 14.8B)**. This type of sexual selection is called *intrasexual selection* (within the same sex, most often the males). Contests may involve physical combat but are more often ritualized displays (see Module 36.19). Intrasexual selection is frequently found in species where the winning individual acquires a harem of mates.

In a more common type of sexual selection, called *intersexual selection* (between sexes) or *mate choice*, individuals of one sex (usually females) are choosy in selecting their mates. Males with the largest or most colourful adornments are often the most attractive to females. The extraordinary feathers

▲ **Figure 14.8A** Extreme sexual dimorphism (peacock and peahen)

of a peacock's tail are an example of this sort of "choose me" statement. What intrigued Darwin is that some of these mate-attracting features do not seem to be otherwise adaptive and

▲ **Figure 14.8B** A contest for access to mates between two male elks

▲ **Figure 14.8C** A male grey tree frog calling for mates

may in fact pose some risks. For example, showy plumage may make male birds more visible to predators. But if such secondary sexual characteristics help a male gain a mate, then they will be reinforced over the generations for the most Darwinian of reasons—because they enhance reproductive success. Every time a female chooses a mate based on a certain appearance or behaviour, she perpetuates the alleles that influenced her to make that choice and allows a male with that particular phenotype to perpetuate his alleles.

What is the advantage to females of being choosy? One hypothesis is that females prefer male traits that are correlated with "good genes." In several bird species, research has shown that traits preferred by females, such as bright beaks or long tails, are related to overall male health. The "good genes" hypothesis was also tested in grey tree frogs. Female frogs prefer to mate with males that give long mating calls **(Figure 14.8C)**. Researchers collected eggs from wild grey tree frogs. Half of each female's eggs were fertilized with sperm from long-calling males, the others with sperm from short-calling males. The offspring of long-calling male frogs grew bigger, faster, and survived better than their half-siblings fathered by short-calling males. The duration of a male's mating call was shown to be indicative of the male's overall genetic quality, supporting the hypothesis that female mate choice can be based on a trait that indicates whether the male has "good genes."

 Males with the most elaborate ornamentation may garner the most mates. How might choosing such a mate be advantageous to a female?

● An elaborate display may signal good health and therefore good genes, which in turn could be passed along to the female's offspring.

14.9 Diploidy and balancing selection preserve genetic variation

Natural selection acting on some variants within a population adapts that population to its environment. But what prevents natural selection from eliminating all variation as it selects against unfavourable genotypes? Why aren't less adaptive alleles eliminated as the "best" alleles are passed to the next generation? It turns out that the tendency for natural selection to reduce variation in a population is countered by mechanisms that maintain variation.

Most eukaryotes are diploid: having two sets of chromosomes helps to prevent populations from becoming genetically uniform. The effects of recessive alleles may not often be displayed in a diploid population. A recessive allele is subject to natural selection only when it influences the phenotype, as only occurs in homozygous recessive individuals. In a heterozygote, a recessive allele is, in effect, protected from natural selection. The "hiding" of recessive alleles in the presence of dominant ones can maintain a huge pool of alleles that may not be favoured under present conditions but that could be advantageous if the environment changes.

Genetic variation may also be preserved by natural selection, the same force that generally reduces it. **Balancing selection** occurs when natural selection maintains stable frequencies of two or more phenotypic forms in a population.

Heterozygote advantage is a type of balancing selection in which heterozygous individuals have greater reproductive success than either type of homozygote, with the result that two or more alleles for a gene are maintained in the population. An example of heterozygote advantage is the protection from malaria conferred by the sickle-cell allele (see Module 9.12). The frequency of the sickle-cell allele in Africa is generally highest in areas where malaria is a major cause of death. The environment in those areas favours heterozygotes, who are protected from the most severe effects of malaria. Less favoured are individuals homozygous for the normal hemoglobin allele, who are susceptible to malaria, and individuals homozygous for the sickle-cell allele, who develop sickle-cell disease.

Frequency-dependent selection is a type of balancing selection that maintains two different phenotypic forms in a population. In this case, selection acts against either phenotypic form if it becomes too common in the population. An example of frequency-dependent selection is a scale-eating fish in Lake Tanganyika, Africa, which attacks other fish from behind, darting in to remove a few scales from the side of its prey. As you can see in **Figure 14.9**, some of these fish are "left-mouthed" and others are "right-mouthed." Because their mouth twists to the left, left-mouthed fish always attack their prey's right side—try twisting your lower jaw and lips to the left and imagine which side of a fish you could take a bite from. Similarly, right-mouthed fish attack from the left. Prey fish guard more effectively against attack from whichever phenotype is most common. Thus, scale-eating fish with the less common phenotype have a feeding advantage that enhances survival and reproductive success. As you can see on the graph, the frequency of left-mouthed fish oscillates over time, as frequency-dependent selection keeps each phenotype close to 50%.

Some of the DNA variation in populations probably has little or no impact on reproductive success, such as some nucleotide differences found in noncoding sequences of DNA (see Module 10.10) or changes in protein-coding genes that have little effect on protein function. But even if only a fraction of the variation in a gene pool affects reproductive success, that is still an enormous resource of raw material for natural selection and the adaptive evolution it brings about.

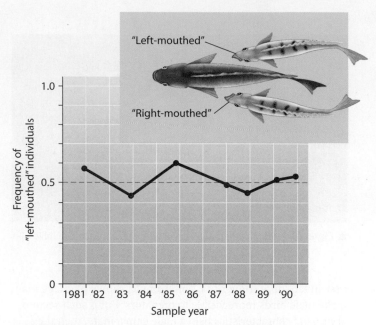

▲ **Figure 14.9** Frequency-dependent selection for left-mouthed and right-mouthed scale-eating fish (*Perissodus microlepis*)

 Why would natural selection tend to reduce genetic variation more in populations of haploid organisms than in populations of diploid organisms?

● All alleles in a haploid organism are phenotypically expressed and are hence screened by natural selection.

14.10 Natural selection cannot fashion perfect organisms

Though natural selection leads to adaptation, there are several reasons why nature abounds with organisms that seem to be less than ideally "engineered" for their lifestyles.

1. *Selection can act only on existing variations.* Natural selection favours only the fittest variants from the phenotypes that are available, which may not be the ideal traits. New, advantageous alleles do not arise on demand.

2. *Evolution is limited by historical constraints.* Each species has a legacy of descent with modification from ancestral forms. Evolution does not scrap ancestral anatomy and build each new complex structure from scratch; it co-opts existing structures and adapts them to new situations. If the ability to fly were to evolve in a terrestrial animal, it might be best to grow an extra pair of limbs that would serve as wings. However, evolution operates on the traits an organism already has. Thus, as birds and bats evolved from four-legged ancestors, their existing forelimbs took on new functions for flight and they were left with only two limbs for walking.

3. *Adaptations are often compromises.* Each organism must do many different things. A blue-footed booby uses its webbed feet to swim after prey in the ocean, but these same feet make for clumsy travel on land.

4. *Chance, natural selection, and the environment interact.* Chance events probably affect the genetic structure of populations to a greater extent than was once recognized. When a storm blows insects over an ocean to an island, the wind does not necessarily transport the individuals that are best suited to the new environment. In small populations, genetic drift can result in the loss of beneficial alleles. In addition, the environment may change unpredictably from year to year, again limiting the extent to which adaptive evolution results in a close match between organisms and the environment.

With all these constraints, we cannot expect evolution to craft perfect organisms. Natural selection operates on a "better than" basis. We can see evidence for evolution in the imperfections of the organisms it produces.

 Humans owe much of their physical versatility and athleticism to their flexible limbs and joints. But we are prone to sprains, torn ligaments, and dislocations. Why?

● Adaptations are compromises: Structural reinforcement has been compromised as agility was selected for.

Mechanisms of Macroevolution

14.11 Continental drift has played a major role in macroevolution

The fossil record documents **macroevolution**, the major events in the history of life on Earth. In this section, we explore some of the factors that helped to shape these evolutionary changes, such as plate tectonics, mass extinctions, and adaptive radiations.

Plate Tectonics   If photographs of Earth were taken from space every 10 000 years and then spliced together, it would make a remarkable movie. The seemingly "rock solid" continents we live on move over time. Since the origin of multicellular eukaryotes roughly 1.5 bya, there have been three occasions in which the landmasses of Earth came together to form a supercontinent, and then later broke apart. Each time the landmasses split, they yielded a different configuration of continents. Geologists estimate that the continents will come together again and form a new supercontinent roughly 250 million years from now.

The continents and seafloors form a thin outer layer of planet Earth, called the crust, which covers a mass of hot, viscous material called the mantle. The outer core is liquid and the inner core is solid (**Figure 14.11A**). According to the theory of **plate tectonics**, Earth's crust is divided into giant, irregularly shaped plates (outlined in black in **Figure 14.11B**) that essentially float on the underlying mantle. In a process called continental drift, movements in the mantle cause the plates to move (black arrows in the figure). In some cases, the plates are moving away from each other. North America and Europe, for example, are drifting apart at a rate of about 2 cm per year. In other cases, two plates are sliding past each other, forming regions where earthquakes are common. In still other cases, two plates are colliding. Massive upheavals may occur, forming mountains along the plate boundaries.

The red dots in Figure 14.11B indicate zones of violent geologic activity, most of which are associated with plate boundaries.

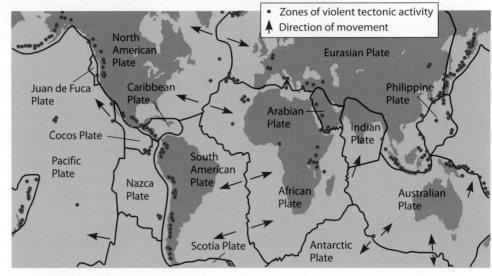

▲ **Figure 14.11B** Earth's tectonic plates

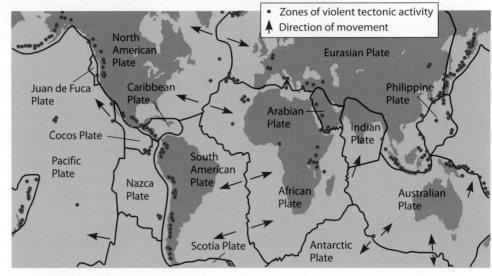

▲ **Figure 14.11A** Cross-sectional view of Earth (with the thickness of the crust exaggerated)

Consequences of Continental Drift   Throughout Earth's history, continental drift has reshaped the physical features of the planet and altered the habitats in which organisms live. **Figure 14.11C** shows continental movements that greatly influenced life during the Mesozoic and Cenozoic eras. ❶ About 250 mya, near the end of the Paleozoic era, plate movements brought all the previously separated landmasses together into a supercontinent we call **Pangaea**, meaning "all land." When the landmasses fused, ocean basins became deeper, lowering the sea level and draining the shallow coastal seas. Then, as now, most marine species inhabited shallow waters, and much of that habitat was destroyed. The interior of the vast continent was cold and dry. Overall, the formation of Pangaea had a tremendous impact on the physical environment and climate. As the fossil record documents, biological diversity was reshaped. Many species were driven to extinction, and new opportunities arose for organisms that survived the crisis.

During the Mesozoic era, Pangaea started to break apart, causing a geographic isolation of colossal proportions. As the continents drifted apart, each became a separate evolutionary arena—a huge island on which organisms evolved in isolation from their previous neighbours. ❷ At first, Pangaea split into northern and southern landmasses, which we call Laurasia and Gondwana, respectively. ❸ By the end of the Mesozoic era, some 65 mya, the modern continents were beginning to take shape. Note that at that time Madagascar became isolated and India was still a large island. Then, around 45 mya, the India plate collided with the Eurasian plate, and the slow, steady buckling at the plate boundary formed the Himalayas, the tallest and youngest of Earth's mountain ranges. ❹ The continents continue to drift today, and the Himalayas are still growing (about 1 cm per year).

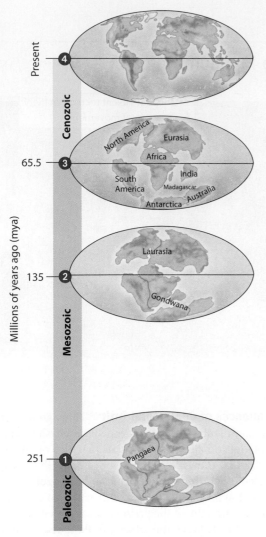

▲ Figure 14.11C Continental drift during the Phanerozoic eon

The pattern of continental mergings and separations solves many biogeographic puzzles, including Australia's great diversity of marsupials (pouched mammals). Fossil evidence suggests that marsupials originated in what is now Asia and reached Australia via South America and Antarctica while the continents were still joined. The subsequent breakup of continents set Australia "afloat" like a great ark of marsupials. The few early eutherians (placental mammals) that lived there became extinct, while on other continents, most marsupials became extinct. Isolated on Australia, marsupials evolved and diversified, filling ecological roles analogous to those filled by eutherians on other continents.

The history of continental drift also explains the distribution of a group of ancient vertebrates called lungfishes **(Figure 14.11D)**. Today, there are six species of lungfishes in the world, four in Africa and one each in Australia and South America (yellow areas in Figure 14.11D). What is the evolutionary history of these animals? Although their present-day distribution may indicate that lungfishes evolved after separation of the supercontinent Gondwana (see Figure 14.11C), their fossil distribution tells a different story. As the orange triangles in Figure 14.11D indicate, fossil lungfishes have been found on all continents except Antarctica. This widespread fossil record indicates that lungfishes evolved when Pangaea was intact.

? Paleontologists have discovered fossils of the same species of Permian freshwater reptiles in West Africa and Brazil, regions that are separated by 3000 km of ocean. How could you explain such finds?

● West Africa and Brazil were connected during the early Mesozoic era, and these reptiles must have ranged across both areas.

▶ Figure 14.11D
Lungfish distribution, a result of continental drift

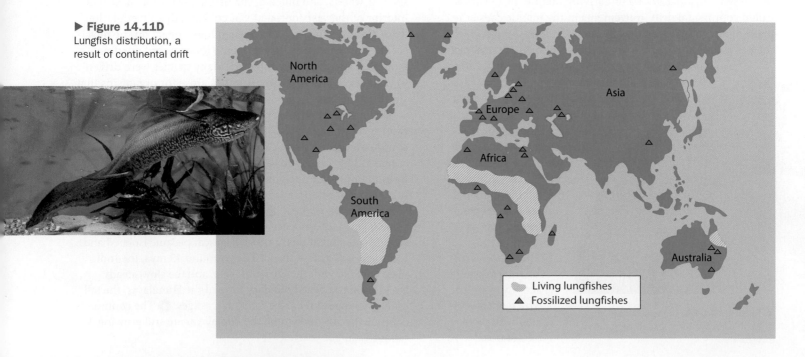

14.12 During mass extinctions, large numbers of species are lost

Extinction is inevitable in a changing world. Indeed, the fossil record shows that the vast majority of species that have ever lived are now extinct. A species may become extinct because its habitat has been destroyed, because of unfavourable climatic changes, or because of changes in its biological community, such as the evolution of new predators or competitors. Extinctions occur all the time, but extinction rates have not been steady.

Mass Extinctions   The fossil record chronicles a number of occasions when global environmental changes were so rapid and disruptive that a majority of species were swept away in a relatively short amount of time. Five mass extinctions have occurred over the past 500 million years. In each of these events, 50% or more of Earth's species became extinct.

Of all the mass extinctions, the ones marking the ends of the Permian and Cretaceous periods have received the most attention. The Permian extinction, which occurred about 251 mya and defines the boundary between the Paleozoic and Mesozoic eras, claimed about 96% of marine animal species and took a tremendous toll on terrestrial life as well. This mass extinction occurred in less than 500 000 years, and possibly in just a few thousand years—an instant in the context of geologic time.

At the end of the Cretaceous period, about 65 mya, the world again lost an enormous number of species—more than half of all marine species and many lineages of terrestrial plants and animals. At that point, dinosaurs had dominated the land and pterosaurs had ruled the air for some 150 million years. After the Cretaceous mass extinction, the pterosaurs and almost all the dinosaurs were gone, leaving behind only the descendants of one lineage, the birds.

Causes of Mass Extinctions   The Permian mass extinction occurred at a time of enormous volcanic eruptions in what is now Siberia. Vast stretches of land were covered with lava hundreds to thousands of metres thick. Besides spewing lava and ash into the atmosphere, the eruptions may have produced enough carbon dioxide to warm the global climate by an estimated 6°C. Reduced temperature differences between the equator and the poles would have slowed the mixing of ocean water, leading to a widespread drop in oxygen concentration in the water. This oxygen deficit would have killed many marine organisms and promoted the growth of anaerobic bacteria that emit a poisonous by-product, hydrogen sulphide. As this gas bubbled out of the water, it would have killed land plants and animals and initiated chemical reactions that would destroy the protective ozone layer. Thus, a cascade of factors may have contributed to the Permian extinction.

One clue to a possible cause of the Cretaceous mass extinction is a thin layer of clay enriched in iridium that separates sediments from the Mesozoic and Cenozoic eras. Iridium is an element very rare on Earth but common in meteorites and other extraterrestrial objects that occasionally fall to Earth. The rocks of the Cretaceous boundary layer have many times more iridium than normal Earth levels. Most paleontologists conclude that the iridium layer is the result of fallout from a huge cloud of dust that billowed into the atmosphere when an asteroid or large comet hit Earth. The cloud would have blocked light and severely disturbed the global climate for months.

Is there evidence of such an asteroid? A large crater, the 65-million-year-old Chicxulub impact crater, has been found in the Caribbean Sea near the Yucatán Peninsula of Mexico **(Figure 14.12)**. About 180 km wide, the crater is the right size to have been caused by an object with a diameter of 10 km. The horseshoe shape of the crater and the pattern of debris in sedimentary rocks indicate that an asteroid or comet struck at a low angle from the southeast. The artist's interpretation in Figure 14.12 represents the impact and its immediate effect—a cloud of hot vapour and debris that could have killed most of the plants and animals in North America within hours. The collision is estimated to have released more than a billion times the energy of the nuclear bombs dropped in Japan during World War II.

In March 2010, an international team of scientists reviewed two decades' worth of research on the Cretaceous extinction

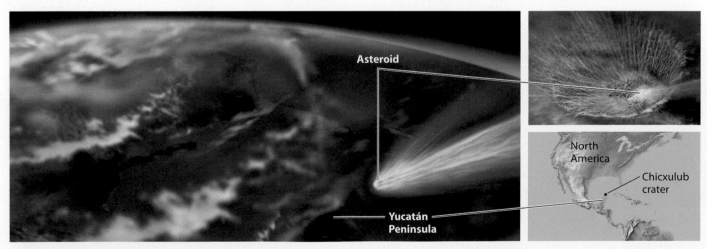

▲ **Figure 14.12** The impact hypothesis for the Cretaceous mass extinction

and endorsed the asteroid hypothesis as the triggering event. Nevertheless, research will continue on other contributing causes and the multiple and interrelated effects of this major ecological disaster.

Consequences of Mass Extinctions   Whatever their causes, mass extinctions affect biological diversity profoundly. By removing large numbers of species, a mass extinction can decimate a thriving and complex ecological community. Mass extinctions are random events that act on species indiscriminately. They can permanently remove species with highly advantageous features and change the course of evolution forever. Consider what would have happened if our early primate ancestors living 65 mya had died out in the Cretaceous mass extinction—or if a few large, predatory dinosaurs had *not* become extinct!

How long does it take for life to recover after a mass extinction? The fossil record shows that it typically takes 5–10 million years for the diversity of life to return to previous levels. In some cases, it has taken much longer: It took about 100 million years for the number of marine families to recover after the Permian mass extinction.

Is a Sixth Mass Extinction Under Way?   As we'll explore in Chapter 41, human actions that result in habitat destruction and climate change are modifying the global environment to such an extent that many species are currently threatened with extinction. In the past 400 years, more than a thousand species are known to have become extinct. Scientists estimate that this rate is 100 to 1000 times the normal rate seen in the fossil record. Does this represent the beginning of a sixth mass extinction?

This question is difficult to answer, partly because it is hard to document both the total number of species on Earth and the number of extinctions that are occurring. It is clear that losses have not reached the level of the other "big five" extinctions. Monitoring, however, does show that many species are declining at an alarming rate, suggesting that a sixth (human-caused) mass extinction could occur within the next few centuries or millennia. And as seen with prior mass extinctions, it may take millions of years for life on Earth to recover.

But the fossil record also shows a creative side to the destruction. Mass extinctions can pave the way for adaptive radiations in which new groups rise to prominence, as we see next.

> **?**   The Permian and Cretaceous mass extinctions mark the ends of the _____ and _____ eras, respectively. (*Hint:* Refer back to Table 13.13.)
>
> ● Paleozoic; Mesozoic

14.13 Adaptive radiations have increased the diversity of life

As will be described in Module 15.8, adaptive radiations are periods of evolutionary change in which many new species evolve from a common ancestor, often following the colonization of new, unexploited areas. Adaptive radiations have also followed each mass extinction, when survivors became adapted to the many vacant ecological roles, or niches, in their communities.

For example, fossil evidence indicates that mammals underwent a dramatic adaptive radiation after the extinction of terrestrial dinosaurs 65 mya (**Figure 14.13**). Although mammals originated 180 mya, fossils older than 65 million years indicate that they were mostly small and not very diverse. Early mammals may have been eaten or outcompeted by the larger and more diverse dinosaurs. With the disappearance of the dinosaurs (except for the bird lineage), mammals expanded greatly in both diversity and size, filling the ecological roles once occupied by dinosaurs.

The history of life has also been altered by radiations that followed the evolution of new adaptations, such as the wings of pterosaurs, birds, and bats (see chapter-opening essay). Major new adaptations facilitated the colonization of land by plants, insects, and tetrapods. The radiation of land plants, for example, was associated with features such as stems that supported the plant against gravity and a waxy coat that protected leaves from water loss. Finally, note that organisms that arise in an adaptive radiation can serve as a new source of food for still other organisms. In this way, the diversification of land plants stimulated a series of adaptive radiations in insects that ate or pollinated plants—helping to make insects the most diverse group of animals on Earth today.

Now that we've looked at geologic and environmental influences, let's consider how genes can affect macroevolution.

> **?**   In addition to the new resources of plants, what other factors likely promoted the adaptive radiation of insects on land?
>
> ● Many unfilled niches on land and the evolution of wings and a supportive, protective, and waterproof exoskeleton

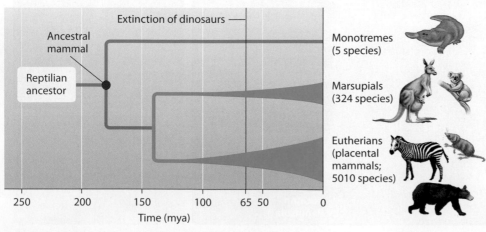

▲ **Figure 14.13**   Adaptive radiation of mammals (width of line reflects numbers of species)

Extinction of dinosaurs

Ancestral mammal

Reptilian ancestor

Monotremes (5 species)

Marsupials (324 species)

Eutherians (placental mammals; 5010 species)

Time (mya)
250   200   150   100   65 50   0

14.14 Genes that control development play a major role in evolution

The fossil record can tell us *what* the great events in the history of life have been and *when* they occurred. Continental drift, mass extinctions, and adaptive radiation provide a big-picture view of *how* those changes came about. But now we are increasingly able to understand the basic biological mechanisms that underlie the changes seen in the fossil record.

Scientists working at the interface of evolutionary biology and developmental biology—the research field abbreviated "**evo-devo**"—are studying how slight genetic changes can become magnified into major morphological differences between species. Genes that program development control the rate, timing, and spatial pattern of change in an organism's form as it develops from a zygote into an adult. A great many of these genes appear to have been conserved throughout evolutionary history: The same or very similar genes are involved in the development of form across multiple lineages.

Changes in Rate and Timing Many striking evolutionary transformations are the result of a change in the rate or timing of developmental events. **Figure 14.14A** shows a photograph of an axolotl, a salamander that illustrates a phenomenon called **paedomorphosis** (from the Greek *paedos*, of a child, and *morphosis*, formation), the retention in the adult of body structures that were juvenile features in an ancestral species. Most salamander species have aquatic larvae (with gills) that undergo metamorphosis in becoming terrestrial adults (with lungs). The axolotl is a salamander that grows to a sexually mature adult while retaining gills and other larval features.

Slight changes in the relative growth of different body parts can change an adult form substantially. As the skulls and photo in **Figure 14.14B** show, humans and chimpanzees are much more alike as fetuses than they are as adults. As development proceeds, accelerated growth in the jaw produces the elongated skull, sloping forehead, and massive jaws of an adult chimpanzee. In the human lineage, genetic changes that slowed the growth of the jaw relative to other parts of the skull produced an adult whose head proportions still resembled that of a child (and that of a baby chimpanzee). Our large skull and complex brain are among our most distinctive features. Compared to the slow growth of a chimpanzee brain after birth, our brain continues to grow at the rapid rate of a fetal brain for the first year of life.

Gills

▲ **Figure 14.14A** An axolotl, a paedomorphic salamander

Chimpanzee infant Chimpanzee adult

Chimpanzee fetus Chimpanzee adult

Human fetus Human adult

▲ **Figure 14.14B** Chimpanzee and human skull shapes compared

Changes in Spatial Pattern Homeotic genes, the master control genes described in Module 11.9, determine such basic features as where a pair of wings or legs will develop on a fruit fly. Changes in homeotic genes or in how or where such genes are expressed can have a profound impact on body form. Consider, for example, the evolution of snakes from a four-limbed lizardlike ancestor. Researchers have found that one pattern of expression of two homeotic genes in tetrapods results in the formation of forelimbs and of vertebrae with ribs, whereas a different pattern of expression of these two genes results in the development of vertebrae with ribs but no limbs, as in snakes.

New Genes and Changes in Genes New developmental genes that arose as a result of gene duplications may have facilitated the origin of new body forms. For example, a fruit fly (an invertebrate) has a single cluster of several homeotic genes that direct the development of major body parts. A mouse (a vertebrate) has four clusters of very similar genes that occur in the same linear order on chromosomes and direct the development of the same body regions as the fly genes (see Figure 30.8B). Two duplications of these gene clusters appear to have occurred in the evolution of vertebrates from invertebrate animals. Mutations in these duplicated genes may then have led to the origin of novel vertebrate characteristics, such as a backbone, jaws, and limbs.

Changes in Gene Regulation Researchers are finding that changes in the form of organisms often are caused by mutations that affect the regulation of developmental genes. As we just discussed, such a change in gene expression was shown to correlate with the lack of forelimbs in snakes.

Additional evidence for this type of change in gene regulation is seen in studies of the three-spine stickleback fish. In British Columbia, these fish live in the ocean and also in lakes that formed when the coastline receded during the past 12 000 years. Ocean populations have bony plates that make up a kind of body armour and a large set of pelvic spines that help to deter predatory fish. The body armour and pelvic spines are reduced or absent in three-spine sticklebacks that live in lakes. The loss of the pelvic spine appears to have been driven by natural selection, because freshwater predators such as dragonfly larvae capture juvenile sticklebacks by grasping onto the spines. **Figure 14.14C** shows specimens of an ocean and a lake stickleback, which have been stained to highlight their bony plates and spines.

Researchers have identified a key gene that influences the development of these spines. Was the reduction of spines in lake populations due to changes in the gene itself or to changes in how the gene is expressed? It turns out that the gene is identical in the two populations, and it is expressed in the mouth region and other tissues of embryos from both populations. Studies have shown, however, that while the gene is also expressed in the developing pelvic region of ocean sticklebacks, it is not turned on in the pelvic

▲ **Figure 14.14C** Stickleback fish from ocean (top) and lake (bottom), stained to show bony plates and spines (arrow indicates the absence of the pelvic spine in the lake fish)

region in lake sticklebacks. This example shows how morphological change can be caused by altering the expression of a developmental gene in some parts of the body but not others.

? Research shows that many differences in body form are caused by changes in gene regulation and not changes in the nucleotide sequence of the developmental gene itself. Why might this be the case?

● A change in sequence may affect a gene's function wherever that gene is expressed—with potentially harmful effects. Changes in the regulation of gene expression can be limited to specific areas in a developing embryo.

14.15 Evolutionary novelties may arise in several ways

Let's see how the Darwinian theory of gradual change can account for the evolution of intricate structures such as eyes or of new body structures such as wings. Most complex structures have evolved in increments from simpler versions having the same basic function—a process of refinement. But sometimes we can trace the origin of evolutionary novelties to the gradual adaptation of existing structures to new functions.

As an example of the process of gradual refinement, consider the amazing camera-like eyes of vertebrates and squids. Although the eyes of vertebrates evolved independently of those of squids, both evolved from a simple ancestral patch of photoreceptor cells through a series of incremental modifications that benefited their owners at each stage. Indeed, there appears to have been a single evolutionary origin of light-sensitive cells, and all animals with eyes—vertebrates and invertebrates alike—share the same master genes that regulate eye development.

Figure 14.15 illustrates the range of complexity in the structure of eyes among molluscs living today. Simple patches of pigmented cells enable limpets to distinguish light from dark, and they cling more tightly to their rock when a shadow falls on them—a behavioural adaptation that reduces the

risk of being eaten. Other molluscs have eyecups that have no lenses or other means of focusing images but can indicate light direction. In those molluscs that do have complex eyes, the organs probably evolved in small steps of adaptation. You can see examples of such small steps in Figure 14.15.

Although eyes have retained their basic function of vision throughout their evolutionary history, evolutionary novelty can also arise when structures that originally played one role gradually acquire a different one. Structures that evolve in one context but become co-opted for another function are sometimes called *exaptations*. This term suggests that a structure can become adapted to alternative functions; it does not mean that a structure evolves in anticipation of future use. Natural selection cannot predict the future; it can only improve an existing structure in the context of its current use. Novel features can arise gradually via a series of intermediate stages, each of which has some function in the organism's current context.

Consider the evolution of birds from a feathered dinosaur ancestor. Feathers could not have evolved as an adaptation for upcoming flights. Their first utility may have been for insulation. It is possible that longer, winglike forelimbs and feathers,

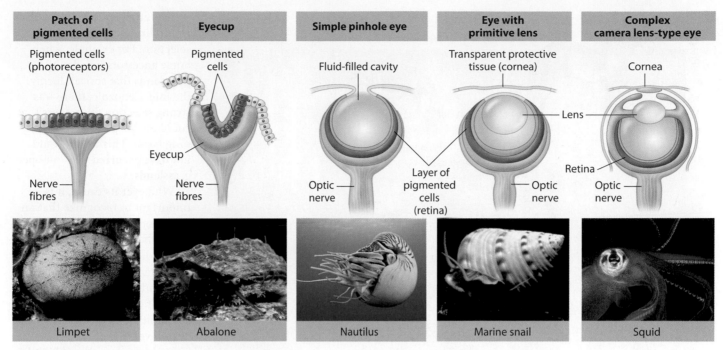

Patch of pigmented cells	Eyecup	Simple pinhole eye	Eye with primitive lens	Complex camera lens-type eye

Pigmented cells (photoreceptors)

Pigmented cells

Fluid-filled cavity

Transparent protective tissue (cornea)

Cornea

Lens

Eyecup

Retina

Nerve fibres

Nerve fibres

Optic nerve

Layer of pigmented cells (retina)

Optic nerve

Optic nerve

Limpet | Abalone | Nautilus | Marine snail | Squid

▲ **Figure 14.15** A range of eye complexity among molluscs

which increased the surface area of these forelimbs, were co-opted for flight after functioning in some other capacity, such as mating displays, thermoregulation, or camouflage (all functions that feathers still serve today). The first flights may have been only short glides to the ground or from branch to branch in tree-dwelling species. Once flight itself became an advantage, natural selection would have gradually remodelled feathers and wings to fit their additional function.

The flippers of penguins are another example of the modification of existing structures for different functions. Penguins cannot fly, but their modified wings are powerful oars that make them strong, fast underwater swimmers.

 Explain why the concept of exaptation does not imply that a structure evolves in anticipation of some future environmental change.

● *Although a structure is co-opted for new or additional functions in a new environment, the structure existed because it worked as an adaptation in the old environment.*

14.16 Evolutionary trends do not mean that evolution is goal directed

The fossil record seems to reveal trends in the evolution of many species. An example is the modern horse (genus *Equus*), a descendant of an ancestor about the size of a large dog that lived some 55 mya. Named *Hyracotherium*, this ancestor had four toes on its front feet, three toes on its hind feet, and teeth adapted to browsing on shrubs and trees. In contrast, the present-day horse is larger, has only one toe on each foot, and has teeth modified for grazing on grasses.

Figure 14.16 shows the fossil record of horses, with the vertical bars representing the period of time each group persisted in the record. If we select only certain species (those highlighted in yellow), it is possible to arrange a sequence of animals that were intermediate in form between *Hyracotherium* and living horses. If these were the only fossils known, they could create the illusion of a single trend in an unbranched lineage, progressing toward larger size, reduced number of toes, and teeth modified for grazing. However, if we consider *all* fossil horses known today, this apparent trend vanishes. Clearly, there was no "trend" toward grazing. Only a few lineages were grazers (green area of figure); the other lineages (tan area), all of which are now extinct, remained multi-toed browsers. The genus *Equus* is the only surviving twig of an evolutionary tree that is so branched that it is more like a bush.

Branching evolution *can* lead to a real evolutionary trend, however. One model of long-term trends compares species to individuals: Speciation is their birth, extinction their death, and new species that diverge from them are their offspring. According to this model of species selection, unequal survival of species and unequal generation of new species play a role in macroevolution similar to the role of unequal reproduction in microevolution (see Module 14.1). In other words, the species that generate the greatest number of new species determine the direction of major evolutionary trends.

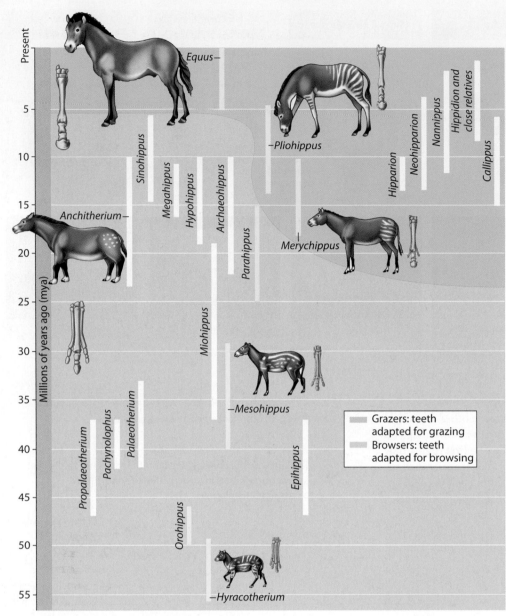

Evolutionary trends can also result directly from natural selection. For example, when horse ancestors invaded the grasslands that spread during the mid-Cenozoic, there was strong selection for grazers that could escape predators by running faster. This trend would not have occurred without open grasslands.

Whatever its cause, it is important to recognize that an evolutionary trend does not imply that evolution is goal directed. Evolution is the result of interactions between organisms and the current environment. If conditions change, an apparent trend may cease or even reverse itself.

In the final section of Unit III, we explore how biologists arrange life's astounding diversity into an evolutionary tree of life.

? A trend in the evolution of mammals was toward a larger brain size. Use the species selection model to explain how such a trend could occur.

● Those species with larger brains persisted longer before extinction and gave rise to more "offspring" species than did species with smaller brains.

▲ **Figure 14.16** The branched evolution of horses

REVIEW

MasteringBiology® **For Practice Quizzes, BioFlix, MP3 Tutors, and Activities, go to masteringbiology.com.**

Reviewing the Concepts

The Evolution of Populations (14.1–14.4)

14.1 Do individuals evolve? Although natural selection works on individuals, only populations can evolve.

14.2 Mutation and sexual reproduction produce the genetic variation that makes evolution possible. Mutations are important in the adaptation of prokaryotes to the environment. In diploid organisms, the shuffling of alleles in sexual reproduction provides most variation.

14.3 The Hardy-Weinberg equation can test whether a population is evolving. The Hardy-Weinberg principle states that allele and genotype frequencies will remain constant if a population is large, mating is random, and there is no mutation, gene flow, or natural selection.

Allele frequencies	$p + q = 1$
Genotype frequencies	$p^2 + 2pq + q^2 = 1$

Dominant homozygotes — Heterozygotes — Recessive homozygotes

14.4 The Hardy-Weinberg equation is useful in public health science. Applying the Hardy-Weinberg equation to genetic disorders within the population allows public health agencies to formulate specific programs.

Mechanisms of Microevolution (14.5–14.10)

14.5 Natural selection, genetic drift, and gene flow can cause microevolution. The bottleneck effect and founder effect lead to genetic drift.

14.6 Natural selection is the only mechanism that consistently leads to adaptive evolution. Relative fitness is the relative contribution an individual makes to the gene pool of the next generation. As a result of natural selection, favourable traits increase in a population.

14.7 Natural selection can alter variation in a population in three ways.

Original population   Evolved population   Pressure of natural selection

Stabilizing selection   **Directional selection**   **Disruptive selection**

14.8 Sexual selection may lead to phenotypic differences between males and females. Secondary sex characteristics can give individuals an advantage in mating.

14.9 Diploidy and balancing selection preserve genetic variation. Diploidy preserves variation by "hiding" recessive alleles. Balancing selection may result from heterozygote advantage or frequency-dependent selection.

14.10 Natural selection cannot fashion perfect organisms. Natural selection can act only on available variation; anatomical structures result from modified ancestral forms; adaptations are often compromises; and chance, natural selection, and the environment interact.

Mechanisms of Macroevolution (14.11–14.16)

14.11 Continental drift has played a major role in macroevolution. The formation and split-up of Pangaea affected the distribution and diversification of organisms.

14.12 During mass extinctions, large numbers of species are lost. The Permian extinction is linked to the effects of extreme volcanic activity, and the Cretaceous extinction, which included most dinosaurs, may have been caused by the impact of an asteroid.

14.13 Adaptive radiations have increased the diversity of life. The origin of many new species often follows mass extinctions, colonization of new habitats, and the evolution of new adaptations.

14.14 Genes that control development play a major role in evolution. "Evo-devo" combines evolutionary and developmental biology. New forms can evolve by changes in the number, sequences, or regulation of developmental genes.

14.15 Evolutionary novelties may arise in several ways. Complex structures may evolve in stages from simpler versions with the same basic function or from the gradual adaptation of existing structures to new functions.

14.16 Evolutionary trends do not mean that evolution is goal directed. An evolutionary trend may be a result of species selection or natural selection in changing environments.

Connecting the Concepts

1. Distinguish between microevolution and macroevolution.

2. Complete this concept map describing potential causes of evolutionary change within populations.

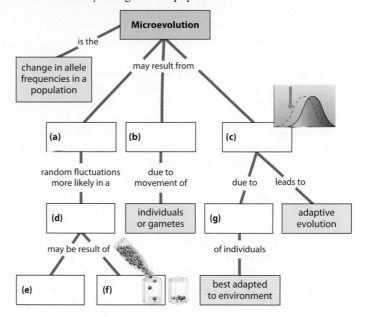

Testing Your Knowledge

Multiple Choice

3. The largest unit within which gene flow can readily occur is a
   a. population.   b. species.
   c. genus.   d. phylum.
   e. hybrid offspring.

4. If an allele is recessive and lethal in homozygotes before they reproduce,
   a. the allele is present in the population at a frequency of 0.001.
   b. the allele will be removed from the population by natural selection in approximately 1000 years.
   c. the allele will likely remain in the population at a low frequency because it cannot be selected against in heterozygotes.
   d. the fitness of the homozygous recessive genotype is 0.
   e. both c and d are correct.

5. In a population with two alleles, *B* and *b*, the allele frequency of *b* is 0.4. *B* is dominant to *b*. What is the frequency of individuals with the dominant phenotype if the population is in Hardy-Weinberg equilibrium?
   a. 0.16
   b. 0.36
   c. 0.48
   d. 0.84
   e. You cannot tell from this information.

6. Mutations are rarely the cause of evolution in populations of plants and animals because they
   a. are often harmful and do not get passed on.
   b. do not directly produce most of the genetic variation present in a diploid population.
   c. occur very rarely.
   d. are passed on only when in cells that lead to gametes.
   e. all of the above

7. In an area of erratic rainfall, a biologist found that grass plants with alleles for curled leaves reproduced better in dry years, and plants with alleles for flat leaves reproduced better in wet years. This situation would tend to _____. (Explain your answer.)
   a. cause genetic drift in the grass population.
   b. preserve genetic variation in the grass population.
   c. lead to stabilizing selection in the grass population.
   d. lead to uniformity in the grass population.
   e. cause gene flow in the grass population.

8. The animals and plants of India are very different from the species in nearby Southeast Asia. Why might this be true?
   a. India was once covered by oceans and Asia was not.
   b. The climates of the two regions are different.
   c. India is in the process of separating from the rest of Asia.
   d. Life in India was wiped out by ancient volcanic eruptions.
   e. India was a separate continent until about 45 mya.

9. Adaptive radiations may be promoted by all the following except one. Which one?
   a. mass extinctions that result in vacant ecological niches
   b. colonization of an isolated region with few competitors
   c. a gradual change in climate
   d. a novel adaptation
   e. another adaptive radiation providing new food sources

10. Evidence indicates that early fish gulped air into primitive lungs, helping them survive in stagnant waters. In some fish, these lungs evolved into swim bladders. A swim bladder is a gas-filled sac that helps fish maintain buoyancy. The evolution of the swim bladder from lungs of an ancestral fish is an example of
    a. an evolutionary trend.
    b. paedomorphosis.
    c. changes in homeotic gene expression.
    d. the gradual refinement of a structure with the same function.
    e. exaptation.

Describing, Comparing, and Explaining

11. Sickle-cell disease is caused by a recessive allele. Roughly 1 out of every 400 African-Canadians (0.25%) is afflicted with sickle-cell disease. Use the Hardy-Weinberg equation to calculate the percentage of African-Canadians who are carriers of the sickle-cell allele. (*Hint:* $q^2 = 0.0025$.)

12. It seems logical that natural selection would work toward genetic uniformity; the genotypes that are most fit produce the most offspring, increasing the frequency of adaptive alleles and eliminating less adaptive alleles. Yet there remains a great deal of genetic variation within populations. Describe some of the factors that contribute to this variation.

13. How can the Darwinian concept of descent with modification explain the evolution of such complex structures as an eye?

14. Explain why changes in the regulation of developmental genes may have played such a large role in the evolution of new forms.

Applying the Concepts

15. A population of snails is preyed on by birds that break the snails open on rocks, eat the soft bodies, and leave the shells. The snails occur in both striped and unstriped forms. In one area, researchers counted both live snails and broken shells. Their data are summarized below:

	Striped	Unstriped	Total	Percentage Striped
Living	264	296	560	47.1
Broken	486	377	863	56.3

Which snail form seems better adapted to this environment? Why? Predict how the frequencies of striped and unstriped snails might change in the future.

16. Cultivated American cotton plants have a total of 52 chromosomes ($2n = 52$). In each cell, there are 13 pairs of large chromosomes and 13 pairs of smaller chromosomes. Old World cotton plants have 26 chromosomes ($2n = 26$), all large. Wild American cotton plants have 26 chromosomes, all small. Propose a testable hypothesis to explain how cultivated American cotton probably originated.

17. The red wolf, *Canis rufus*, which was once widespread in the southeastern and south central United States, was declared extinct in the wild by 1980. Saved by a captive breeding program, the red wolf has been reintroduced in areas of eastern North Carolina. The current wild population estimate is about 100 individuals. It is presently being threatened with extinction because of hybridization with coyotes, *Canis latrans*, which have become more numerous in the area. Red wolves and coyotes differ in terms of morphology, DNA, and behaviour, although these differences may disappear if interbreeding continues. Although designated as an endangered species under the *Endangered Species Act*, some people think that the endangered status of red wolves should be withdrawn and resources should not be spent to protect what is not a "pure" species. Do you agree? Why or why not?

Answers to all questions can be found in Appendix E.

Speciation and Phylogeny

BIG IDEAS

Defining Species

(15.1–15.3)

A species can be defined as a group of populations whose members can produce fertile offspring.

Mechanisms of Speciation

(15.4–15.11)

Speciation can take place with or without geographic isolation, as long as reproductive barriers evolve that keep species separate.

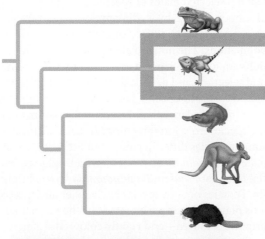

Phylogeny and the Tree of Life

(15.12–15.18)

The evolutionary history of a species is reconstructed using fossils, homologies, and molecular systematics.

The Rise and Fall of Cichlids

Cichlids are so colourful and so diverse. There are algae, insect, and fish eaters, leaf biters, muck feeders, snail crushers, even scale scrapers who steal scales off the flanks of other fish. They are all colours of the rainbow, making them favourites of aquarium enthusiasts. Cichlids are found in many tropical lakes and rivers of Central America, Asia, and Africa. Until recently, there were up to 600 species of these small fish in Lake Victoria, the largest of the Great Lakes of East Africa. Where did they all come from? And why are they disappearing?

Scientists call the Lake Victoria cichlids—this physically, ecologically, and behaviourally diverse assemblage of closely related genera and species—a superflock. Their species number more than all the fish species in all the lakes and rivers of Europe combined. And if you add the more than 1000 species in Lakes Victoria, Tanganyika, and Malawi, you have the biggest diversification of species of any animal group in one geographic region.

The species are young. Studies show that the cichlids of Lake Victoria diversified about 100 000 years ago. (Compare this to bony fish, which have been evolving for about 400 million years.) How did so many cichlid species evolve so fast? There are several hypotheses. The jaw structure and teeth of cichlids vary widely, and these highly adaptable characteristics may

have allowed ancestral species to specialize in different food sources, such as algae, snails, or other fishes. Or perhaps the bright colour patterns of cichlids led to species diversity as females selected mates of specific coloration. The separation of subpopulations by feeding preferences or by female mate choice could have reduced or eliminated breeding between the populations. The now isolated gene pools of these subpopulations could have changed as a result of different mutations, natural selection, and genetic drift. Eventually, the isolated groups became separate species, having lost the ability to interbreed.

Is there evidence that the different colours of cichlids keep the species from interbreeding? In Lake Victoria many pairs of similar species differ in colour but little else. As shown here, males of *Pundamilia nyererei* have a bright red back and dorsal fin. Males of *Pundamilia pundamilia* have a bright blue dorsal fin. Females of both species are smaller and less colourful. Various mate choice experiments have shown that females prefer brightly coloured—and rightly coloured—males.

Studies have shown *P. nyererei* females, who prefer to mate with red males, are more sensitive to red light and *P. pundamilia* females are more sensitive to blue light. For the deeper dwelling *P. nyererei*, the increased sensitivity to red light makes red males more conspicuous and males of other colours less noticeable. Thus, sexual selection for different coloration, as well as specialization in different food sources, most likely contributed to the rise of this multitude of cichlid species.

But what is causing their fall? In the past 30 years, as many as 200 species of cichlids have disappeared from Lake Victoria. Some of these species were driven to extinction by an introduced predator, the Nile perch. But many species not eaten by Nile perch have also disappeared. For decades, the waters of Lake Victoria have become increasingly murky because of pollution, deforestation, and a huge growth in algal populations (which is linked to the loss of algae-eating cichlids). Researchers have found that female cichlids from turbid water are less choosy with regard to male coloration, and males from these areas are less brightly coloured. Thus, the mate choice barriers to breeding that separate closely related species are crumbling.

Interbreeding between two species are producing viable hybrid offspring, and the once isolated gene pools of the parent species are mixing—two species are fusing into one.

This example illustrates that after speciation, species can merge again in response to altered environmental pressures. And hybridization could be considered a type of despeciation. Thus, the great speciation event in Lake Victoria may be coming to an end as the loss of cichlid species continues.

Speciation—the emergence of a new species—is the bridge between microevolution (the changes over time in allele frequencies in a population) and macroevolution (the broader pattern of evolutionary change over longer periods of time). In this chapter, we consider the origin of species—the source of these diverse cichlids and of all the biological diversity on Earth.

Defining Species

15.1 The origin of species is the source of biological diversity

Darwin was eager to explore landforms newly emerged from the sea when he came to the Galápagos Islands. He noted that these volcanic islands, despite their geologic youth, were teeming with plants and animals found nowhere else in the world. He realized that these species, like the islands, were relatively new. He wrote this in his diary: "Both in space and time, we seem to be brought somewhat near to that great fact—that mystery of mysteries—the first appearance of new beings on this Earth."

Even though Darwin titled his seminal work *On the Origin of Species by Means of Natural Selection*, most of his theory of evolution focused on the role of natural selection in the gradual adaptation of a population to its environment. We call this process microevolution—changes in the gene pool of a population from one generation to the next (see Chapter 14). But if microevolution were *all* that happened, then Earth would be inhabited only by a highly adapted version of the first form of life.

The "mystery of mysteries" that fascinated Darwin is **speciation**, the process by which one species splits into two or more species. For example, he saw evidence of speciation in the flightless cormorants of the Galápagos, which he could compare with the flying species he saw elsewhere in his travels. Indeed, more than 40 living species of cormorants have now been identified, with others known from the fossil record. **Figure 15.1** shows one common species found along the Florida coastline and the flightless cormorant found only in the Galápagos.

Each time speciation occurs, the diversity of life increases. Over the course of 3.5 billion years, an ancestral species first gave rise to two or more different species, which then branched to new lineages, which branched again, until we arrive at the millions of species that live, or once lived, on Earth. This origin of species explains both the diversity and the unity of life. When one species splits into two, the new species share many characteristics because they are

▲ **Figure 15.1** Great cormorant (*Phalacrocorax carbo*; top) and the flightless cormorant (*Phalacrocorax harrisi*; bottom)

descended from a common ancestor. Thus, we see not only the uniqueness of the flightless cormorant of the Galápagos but also the similarities between this scrawny-winged bird and its broad-winged relatives.

? **How does microevolution differ from speciation?**

Microevolution involves evolutionary changes within a population; speciation occurs when a population changes enough that it diverges from its parent species and becomes a new species.

15.2 There are several ways to define a species

▲ **Figure 15.2A** Similarity between two species: the eastern meadowlark (left) and western meadowlark (right)

The word *species* is from the Latin for "kind" or "appearance," and indeed, even young children learn to distinguish between kinds of plants and animals—between dogs and cats, or roses and dandelions—from differences in their appearance. Although the basic idea of species as distinct life forms seems intuitive, devising a more formal definition is not so easy.

In many cases, the differences between two species are obvious. A quick comparison of the great cormorant and the flightless cormorant shown in Figure 15.1 would lead you to conclude that these are two different species. In other cases, the physical differences between two species are not so obvious. The two birds in **Figure 15.2A** look much the same: The one on the left is an eastern meadowlark (*Sturnella magna*), and the bird on the right is a western meadowlark (*Sturnella neglecta*). They are distinct species, however, because their songs and other behaviours are different enough that each type of meadowlark breeds only with individuals of its own species.

How similar are members of the same species? Whereas the individuals of many species exhibit fairly limited variation in physical appearance, certain other species—our own, for example—seem extremely varied. The physical diversity within our species (partly illustrated in **Figure 15.2B**) might lead you to guess that there are several human species. Despite these outward appearances, however, humans all belong to the same species, *Homo sapiens*.

The Biological Species Concept   How then, do biologists define a species? And what keeps one species distinct from others? The primary definition of species used in this book is called the **biological species concept**. It defines a **species** as a group of populations whose members have the potential to interbreed in nature and produce fertile offspring (offspring that themselves can reproduce). A businesswoman in Manhattan may be unlikely to meet a dairy farmer in Mongolia, but if the two should happen to meet and mate, they could have viable babies that develop into fertile adults. Thus, members of a biological species are united by being reproductively compatible, at least potentially.

Members of different species do not usually mate with each other. In effect, **reproductive isolation** prevents genetic exchange (gene flow) and maintains the gap between species. But there are some pairs of clearly distinct species that do occasionally interbreed. The resulting offspring are called **hybrids**. An example is the grizzly bear (*Ursus arctos*) and the polar bear (*Ursus maritimus*): Canadian wildlife officials have called the bears' hybrid offspring "grolar bears" or "nanulak," an amalgam of the Inuit names for the polar bear (*nanuk*) and grizzly bear (*aklak*) (**Figure 15.2C**). The two species have been known to interbreed in zoos, and DNA testing confirmed that a wild bear shot in 2006 in the Arctic was the offspring of a polar bear and a grizzly bear. In 2010, yet another nanulak was shot, and scientists determined its mother was a nanulak and its father was

▲ **Figure 15.2B** Diversity within one species

a grizzly. Scientists predict an increase in such hybrids as melting polar sea ice brings the two species into contact more often. Clearly, identifying species solely on the basis of reproductive isolation can be more complex than it may seem.

There are other instances in which applying the biological species concept is problematic. For example, there is no way to determine whether organisms that are now known only through fossils were once able to interbreed. Also, this criterion is useless for organisms such as prokaryotes that reproduce asexually. Because of such limitations, alternative species concepts are useful in certain situations.

Other Definitions of Species   For most organisms—sexual, asexual, and fossils alike—classification is based mainly on physical traits such as shape, size, and other features of morphology (form). This **morphological species concept** has been used to identify most of the 1.8 million species that have been named to date. The advantages of this concept are that it can be applied to asexual organisms and fossils and does not require information on possible interbreeding. The disadvantage, however, is that this approach relies on subjective criteria, and researchers may disagree on which features distinguish a species.

Another species definition, the **ecological species concept**, identifies species in terms of their ecological niches, focusing on unique adaptations to particular roles in a biological

Grizzly bear

Polar bear

Hybrid "nanulak" bear

▲ **Figure 15.2C** Hybridization between two species of bears

community (see Module 34.9). For example, two species of fish may be similar in appearance but distinguishable based on what they eat or the depth of water in which they are usually found.

Finally, the **phylogenetic species concept** defines a species as the smallest group of individuals that share a common ancestor and thus form one branch on the tree of life. Biologists trace the phylogenetic history of such a species by comparing its characteristics, such as morphology or DNA sequences, with those of other organisms. These sorts of analyses can distinguish groups that are generally similar yet different enough to be considered separate species. Of course, agreeing on the amount of difference required to establish separate species remains a challenge.

Each species definition is useful, depending on the situation and the questions being asked. The biological species concept, however, helps to focus on how these discrete groups of organisms arise and are maintained by reproductive isolation. Because reproductive isolation is an essential factor in the evolution of many species, we look at it more closely next.

 Which species concepts could you apply to both asexual and sexual species? Explain.

The morphological, ecological, and phylogenetic species concepts could all be used because they do not rely on the criterion of reproductive isolation.

15.3 Reproductive barriers keep species separate

Clearly, a fly will not mate with a frog or a fern. But what prevents species that are closely related from interbreeding? Reproductive isolation depends on one or more types of reproductive barriers—biological features of the organism that prevent individuals of different species from interbreeding. As shown in **Figure 15.3A**, the various types of reproductive barriers that isolate the gene pools of species can be categorized as either prezygotic or postzygotic, depending on whether they function before or after zygotes (fertilized eggs) form.

Prezygotic Barriers   **Prezygotic barriers** prevent mating or fertilization between species. There are five main types of prezygotic barriers. In the first, called habitat isolation, two species that live in the same area but not in the same kinds of habitats encounter each other rarely, if at all. Two species of garter snake in the genus *Thamnophis* are found in western North America, but one lives mainly in water and the other on land (**Figure 15.3B**). Habitat isolation also affects parasites that are confined to certain host species and thus do not have the opportunity to interbreed.

In a second type of prezygotic barrier, temporal isolation, species breed at different times—different times of the day,

different seasons, or even different years. The frogs shown in **Figure 15.3C** are an example. The breeding season of the wood frog (*Rana sylvatica*) is in early spring when water temperatures are near 7°C, while the northern leopard frog (*Rana pipiens*) breeds later when water temperatures reach 13°C. Thus, even though their geographic ranges overlap in eastern Canada, each type of frog breeds only with individuals of its own species. Many plants also exhibit seasonal differences in reproduction. Some flowering plants are temporally isolated because their flowers open at different times of the day, so pollen cannot be transferred between them.

In behavioural isolation, a third type of prezygotic barrier, there is little or no "mate recognition" between females and males of different species. Special signals that attract mates and elaborate mating behaviours that are unique to a species are probably the most important reproductive barriers between closely related animals. For example, male fireflies of various species signal to females of their kind by blinking their lights in particular rhythms. Females respond only to signals of their own species, flashing back and attracting the males.

Figure 15.3D shows part of a courtship ritual. Many species will not mate until the male and female have performed an

Individuals of different species

Prezygotic Barriers

Habitat isolation: Species live in different habitats within the same area and rarely meet.

Temporal isolation: Breeding occurs at different times of the day or different seasons.

Behavioural isolation: Different courtship rituals or other behaviours prevent mate recognition between species.

Mechanical isolation: Differences in physical structures prevent successful mating.

Gametic isolation: Male and female gametes of different species fail to unite.

Fertilization (zygote forms)

Postzygotic Barriers

Reduced hybrid viability: The development or survival of hybrids is impaired.

Reduced hybrid fertility: Hybrids fail to produce functional gametes.

Hybrid breakdown: Offspring of hybrids are feeble or infertile.

Viable, fertile offspring

▲ **Figure 15.3A** Reproductive barriers between species

▲ **Figure 15.3C** **Temporal isolation:** The wood frog (left) and northern leopard frog (right) breed at different times of the year.

the shells of two species of snails in different directions prevents their genital openings from aligning, resulting in a mechanical barrier to mating.

Mechanical barriers can also contribute to reproductive isolation of plants. Many species have flower structures that are adapted to specific insect or animal pollinators that transfer pollen only between plants of the same species.

Gametic isolation is a fifth type of prezygotic barrier. Sperm of one species may not be able to fertilize the eggs of another species. Gametic isolation is very important when fertilization is external. Male and female sea urchins **(Figure 15.3F)** of many different species release eggs and sperm into the sea, but fertilization occurs only if species-specific molecules on the surfaces of egg and sperm attach to each other. A similar mechanism of molecular recognition enables a flower to discriminate between pollen of its own species and pollen of a different species.

Postzygotic Barriers   In contrast to prezygotic barriers, **postzygotic barriers** operate after hybrid zygotes have formed. In some cases, there is reduced hybrid viability—most hybrid

elaborate ritual that is unlike that of any other species. These blue-footed boobies are involved in a courtship dance in which the male points his beak, tail, and wing tips to the sky. Part of the "script" also calls for the male to high-step, a dance that advertises his bright blue feet.

Mechanical isolation, a fourth type of prezygotic barrier, occurs when female and male sex organs are not compatible; for instance, the male copulatory organs of many insect species have a unique and complex structure that fits the female parts of only one species. **Figure 15.3E** shows how the spiralling of

▲ **Figure 15.3B** **Habitat isolation:** Two species of garter snake do not mate because one lives mainly in water and the other lives on land.

▲ **Figure 15.3D** **Behavioural isolation:** The courtship ritual in blue-footed boobies is a behavioural barrier to mating between species.

▲ **Figure 15.3E Mechanical isolation:** The genital openings (indicated by arrows) of these snails are not aligned, and mating cannot be completed.

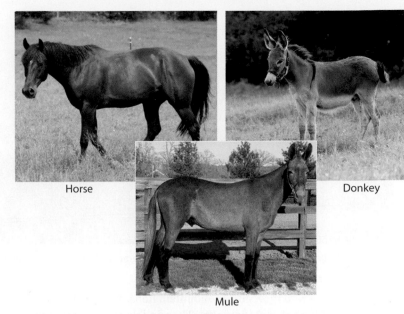

Horse   Donkey

Mule

▲ **Figure 15.3G Reduced hybrid fertility:** A horse and a donkey may produce a hybrid mule.

offspring do not survive. For example, certain salamanders that live in the same habitats may occasionally hybridize, but most hybrids do not complete development.

Another type of postzygotic barrier is reduced hybrid fertility, in which hybrid offspring reach maturity and are vigorous but sterile. A mule, for example, is the robust but sterile offspring of a female horse and a male donkey **(Figure 15.3G)**.

Because infertile hybrids cannot produce offspring with either parent species, genes do not flow between the parent species.

In a third type of postzygotic barrier, called hybrid breakdown, the first-generation hybrid offspring are viable and fertile, but when these hybrids mate with one another or with either parent species, the offspring are feeble or sterile. For example, different species of cotton plants can produce fertile hybrids, but the offspring of the hybrids do not survive.

Next we examine situations that make reproductive isolation and speciation possible.

▲ **Figure 15.3F Gametic isolation:** Gametes of these red and purple urchins are unable to fuse because surface proteins do not match.

? Two closely related fish live in the same lake, but one feeds along the shoreline and the other is a bottom feeder in deep water. This is an example of _____ isolation, which is a _____ reproductive barrier.

● habitat; prezygotic

Mechanisms of Speciation

15.4 In allopatric speciation, geographic isolation leads to speciation

A key event in the origin of a new species is the separation of a population from other populations of the same species. With its gene pool isolated, the splinter population can follow its own evolutionary course. Changes in allele frequencies caused by natural selection, genetic drift, and mutation will not be diluted by alleles entering from other populations (gene flow). The initial block to gene flow may come from a geographic barrier that isolates a population. This mode of speciation is called **allopatric speciation** (from the Greek *allos*, other, and *patra*, fatherland). Populations separated by a geographic barrier are known as allopatric populations.

Geographic Barriers   Several geologic processes can isolate populations. A mountain range may emerge and gradually split a population of organisms that can inhabit only lowlands. A large lake may subside until there are several smaller lakes, isolating certain fish populations. Or, as you saw in Chapter 14, continents themselves can split and move apart. Allopatric speciation can also occur when individuals colonize a remote area and become geographically isolated from the parent population.

How large must a geographic barrier be to keep allopatric populations apart? The answer depends on the ability of the

South rim

A. harrisii

North rim

A. leucurus

▲ **Figure 15.4A** Allopatric speciation of geographically isolated antelope squirrels

organisms to move. Birds, mountain lions, and coyotes can easily cross mountain ranges. The windblown pollen of trees is not hindered by such barriers, and the seeds of many plants may be carried back and forth by animals. In contrast, small rodents may find a canyon or a wide river a formidable barrier. The Grand Canyon and Colorado River **(Figure 15.4A)** separate two species of antelope squirrels. Harris's antelope squirrel (*Ammospermophilus harrisii*) inhabits the south rim. Just a few kilometres away on the north rim, but separated by the deep and wide canyon, lives the closely related white-tailed antelope squirrel (*Ammospermophilus leucurus*).

Evidence of Allopatric Speciation Many studies provide evidence that speciation has occurred in allopatric populations. An interesting example is the 30 species of snapping shrimp in the genus *Alpheus* that live off the Isthmus of Panama, the land bridge that connects South and North America **(Figure 15.4B)**. Snapping shrimp are named for the snapping together of their single oversized claw, which creates a high-pressure blast that stuns their prey. Morphological and genetic data group these shrimp into 15 pairs, with the members of each pair being each other's closest relative. In each case, one member of the pair lives on the Atlantic side of the isthmus, while the other lives on the Pacific side, strongly suggesting that geographic separation of the ancestral species of these snapping shrimp led to allopatric speciation.

? Geologic evidence indicates that the Isthmus of Panama gradually closed about 3 mya. Genetic analyses indicate that the various species of snapping shrimp originated from 9 to 3 mya, with the species pairs that live in deepest water diverging first. How would you interpret these data?

● The deeper species would have been separated into two isolated populations first, which enabled them to diverge into new species first.

A. formosus

A. nuttingi

ATLANTIC OCEAN

Isthmus of Panama

PACIFIC OCEAN

A. panamensis

A. millsae

▲ **Figure 15.4B** Allopatric speciation in snapping shrimp: two of the 15 pairs of shrimp that are separated by the Isthmus of Panama

15.5 Reproductive barriers can evolve as populations diverge

Geographic isolation creates opportunities for speciation, but it does not necessarily lead to new species. Speciation occurs only when the gene pool undergoes changes that establish reproductive barriers such as those described in Module 15.3. What might cause such barriers to arise? The environment of an isolated population may include different food sources, different types of pollinators, and different predators. As a result of natural selection acting on pre-existing variations (or as a result of genetic drift or mutation), a population's traits may change in ways that also establish reproductive barriers.

Researchers have successfully documented the evolution of reproductive isolation with laboratory experiments. While at Yale University, Diane Dodd tested the hypothesis that reproductive barriers can evolve as a by-product of changes in populations as they adapt to different environments. Dodd raised fruit flies on different food sources. Some populations were fed starch; others were fed maltose. After about 40 generations, populations raised on starch digested starch more efficiently, and those raised on maltose digested maltose more efficiently.

		Female				Female	
		Starch	Maltose			Population #1	Population #2
Male	Starch	22	9	Male	Pop#1	18	15
	Maltose	8	20		Pop#2	12	15

Number of matings in experimental groups

Number of matings in starch control groups

▲ **Figure 15.5A** Evolution of reproductive barriers in laboratory populations of fruit flies adapted to different food sources

Pollinator choice in typical monkey flowers

Typical *M. lewisii* (pink)

Typical *M. cardinalis* (red)

Pollinator choice after colour allele transfer

M. lewisii with red-colour allele

M. cardinalis with pink-colour allele

▲ **Figure 15.5B** Transferring an allele between monkey flowers changes flower colour and influences pollinator choice.

Dodd then combined flies from various populations in mating experiments. **Figure 15.5A** shows some of her results. When flies from "starch populations" were mixed with flies from "maltose populations," the flies mated more frequently with like partners (left grid), even when the like partners came from different populations. In one of the control tests (right grid), flies taken from different populations adapted to starch were about as likely to mate with each other as with flies from their own populations. The mating preference shown in the experimental group is an example of a prezygotic barrier. The reproductive barrier was not absolute—some mating between maltose flies and starch flies did occur—but reproductive isolation was under way as these allopatric populations became adapted to different environments.

A reproductive barrier in plants is often pollinator choice. Perhaps populations of an ancestral species became separated in environments that had either more hummingbirds than bees or vice versa. Flower colour and shape would evolve through natural selection in ways that attracted the most common pollinator, and these changes would help to separate the species should they later share the same region. Two species of closely related monkey flower are found in the same area of the Sierra Nevada, but they rarely interbreed. Bumblebees prefer the pink-flowered *Mimulus lewisii*, and hummingbirds prefer the red-flowered *Mimulus cardinalis*. When scientists experimentally exchanged the alleles for flower colour between these two

species, the colour of their flowers changed (**Figure 15.5B**). In a field experiment, the now light orange *M. lewisii* received many more visits from hummingbirds than did the normal pink-flowered *M. lewisii*, and the now pinker *M. cardinalis* flowers received many more visits from bumblebees than the normal red-flowered plants. Thus, a change in flower colour influenced pollinator preference, which normally provides a reproductive barrier between these two species.

Sometimes reproductive barriers can arise even when populations are not geographically separated, as we see next.

? **Females of the Galápagos finch *Geospiza difficilis* respond to the songs of males from their island but ignore songs of males from other islands. How would you interpret these findings?**

● Behavioural barriers to reproduction have begun to develop in these allopatric (geographically separated) finch populations.

15.6 Sympatric speciation takes place without geographic isolation

In **sympatric speciation** (from the Greek *syn*, together, and *patra*, fatherland), a new species arises within the same geographic area as its parent species. How can reproductive isolation develop when members of sympatric populations remain in contact with each other? Sympatric speciation may occur

when mating and the resulting gene flow between populations are reduced by factors such as polyploidy, habitat differentiation, and sexual selection.

Many plant species have originated from accidents during cell division that resulted in extra sets of chromosomes. New species formed in this way are **polyploid**, meaning that their cells have more than two complete sets of chromosomes. **Figure 15.6A** shows one way in which a tetraploid plant (4*n*, with four sets of chromosomes) can arise from a parent species that is diploid. ❶ A failure of cell division after chromosome duplication could double a cell's chromosomes. ❷ If this 4*n* cell gives rise to a tetraploid branch, flowers produced on this branch would produce diploid gametes. ❸ If self-fertilization occurs, as it commonly does in plants, the resulting tetraploid zygotes would develop into plants that can produce fertile tetraploid offspring by self-pollination or by mating with other tetraploids.

A tetraploid cannot, however, produce fertile offspring by mating with a parent plant. The fusion of a diploid (2*n*) gamete from the tetraploid plant and a haploid (*n*) gamete from the diploid parent would produce triploid (3*n*) offspring. Triploid individuals are sterile; they cannot produce normal gametes because the odd number of chromosomes cannot form homologous pairs and separate normally during meiosis (see Module 8.14). Thus, the formation of a tetraploid (4*n*) plant is an instantaneous speciation event: A new species, reproductively isolated from its parent species, is produced in just one generation.

Most polyploid species, however, arise from hybridization of two different species. **Figure 15.6B** illustrates one way in which this can happen. ❶ When haploid gametes from two different species combine, the resulting hybrid is normally sterile because its chromosomes cannot pair during meiosis. ❷ However, the hybrid may reproduce asexually, as many plants can do. ❸ Subsequent errors in cell division may produce chromosome duplications that result in a diploid set of chromosomes (2*n* = 10). Now chromosomes *can* pair in meiosis, and haploid gametes will be produced; thus, a fertile polyploid species has formed. The new species has a chromosome number equal to the sum of the diploid chromosome numbers of its parent species. Again, this new species is reproductively isolated, this time from both parent species.

Does polyploid speciation occur in animals? It appears to happen occasionally. For example, the grey tree frog (see Figure 14.8C) is thought to have originated in this way.

Sympatric speciation in animals is more likely to happen through habitat differentiation or sexual selection. Both these factors may have been involved in the origin of as many as 600 species of small fish called cichlids in Lake Victoria in East Africa, the topic of this chapter's opening essay. Adaptations for exploiting different food sources may have evolved in different subgroups of the original cichlid population. If those sources were in different habitats, mating between the populations would become rare, isolating their gene pools as each population becomes adapted to a different resource. As you will learn in Module 15.10, speciation in these brightly coloured fish may also have

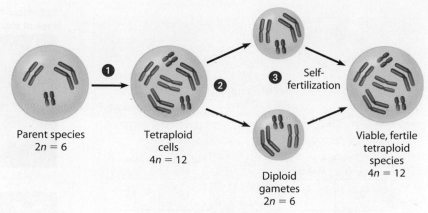

▲ **Figure 15.6A** Sympatric speciation by polyploidy within a single species

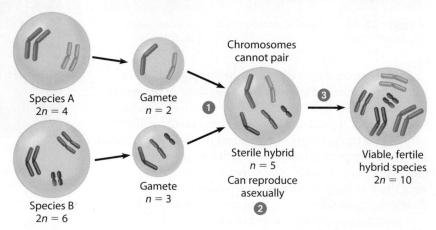

▲ **Figure 15.6B** Sympatric speciation producing a hybrid polyploid from two different species

been driven by the type of sexual selection in which females choose mates based on coloration.

In the waters of British Columbia, a sympatric speciation event is occurring between populations of killer whales (*Orcinus orca*) with distinct behaviours. *Transient* killer whales are migratory and feed on marine mammals, while *residential* killer whales do not migrate and feed mainly on fishes. Although the ranges of these two populations overlap, their actual habitats differ partly because of their feeding habits. Research by Lance Barrett-Lennard at the University of British Columbia has shown that the whales do not interbreed.

Such mate choice can contribute to reproductively isolating populations, keeping the gene pools of newly forming species separate. Of course, both habitat differentiation and sexual selection can also contribute to the formation of reproductive barriers between allopatric populations.

? Revisit the reproductive barriers in Figure 15.3A and choose the barrier that isolates a viable, fertile polyploid plant from its parental species.

● Reduced hybrid fertility

15.7 Most plant species trace their origin to polyploid speciation

Plant biologists estimate that 80% of living plant species are descendants of ancestors that formed by polyploid speciation. Hybridization between two species accounts for most of these species, perhaps because of the adaptive advantage of the diverse genes a hybrid inherits from different parental species.

Many of the plants we grow for food are polyploids, including oats, potatoes, bananas, peanuts, barley, plums, apples, sugarcane, coffee, and wheat. Cotton, also a polyploid, provides one of the world's most popular clothing fibres.

Wheat, the most widely cultivated plant in the world, occurs as 20 different species of *Triticum*. We know that humans were cultivating wheat at least 10 000 years ago because wheat grains of *Triticum monococcum* ($2n = 15$) have been found in the remains of Middle Eastern farming villages from that time. This species has small seed heads and is not highly productive, but some varieties are still grown in the Middle East.

Our most important wheat species is bread wheat (*Triticum aestivum*), a polyploid with 42 chromosomes. **Figure 15.7** illustrates how this species may have evolved; the uppercase letters represent not genes but *sets of chromosomes* that have been traced through the lineage.

❶ The process may have begun with hybridization between two wheats, one the cultivated species *T. monococcum* (AA), the other one of several wild species that probably grew as weeds at the edges of fields (BB). Chromosome sets A and B of the two species would not have been able to pair at meiosis, making the AB hybrid sterile. ❷ However, an error in cell division and self-fertilization would have produced a new species (AABB) with 28 chromosomes. Today, we know this species as emmer wheat (*T. turgidum*), varieties of which are grown widely in Eurasia and western North America. It is used mainly for making macaroni and other noodle products because its proteins hold their shape better than bread-wheat proteins.

The final steps in the evolution of bread wheat are thought to have occurred in early farming villages on the shores of European lakes more than 8000 years ago. ❸ The cultivated emmer wheat, with its 28 chromosomes, hybridized spontaneously with the closely related wild species *T. tauschii* (DD), which has 14 chromosomes. The hybrid (ABD, with 21 chromosomes) was sterile, ❹ but a cell division error in this hybrid and self-fertilization doubled the chromosome number to 42. The result was bread wheat, with two each of the three ancestral sets of chromosomes (AABBDD).

Today, plant geneticists generate new polyploids in the laboratory by using chemicals that induce meiotic and mitotic cell division errors. Researchers can produce new hybrids with special qualities, such as a hybrid combining the high yield of wheat with the hardiness of rye.

? Why are errors in mitosis or meiosis a necessary part of speciation by hybridization between two species?

so that there is a diploid number of each set and normal gametes can form.
gametes. Errors in mitosis or meiosis must somehow duplicate chromosomes
homologous pairs cannot join and separate during meiosis to produce
● *If a hybrid has a single copy of the chromosomes from two species,*

▲ **Figure 15.7** The evolution of bread wheat, *Triticum aestivum*

15.8 Isolated islands are often showcases of speciation

Although sympatric speciation is known to occur in plants and occasionally in animals, most of the diverse life forms on Earth are thought to have originated by allopatric speciation. Isolated island chains offer some of the best evidence of this type of speciation. These groups of islands are often inhabited by unique collections of species. Islands that have physically diverse habitats and that are far enough apart to permit populations to evolve in isolation but close enough to allow occasional dispersions to occur are often the sites of multiple speciation events. The evolution of many diverse species from a common ancestor is known as **adaptive radiation**.

The Galápagos Archipelago, located about 900 km west of Ecuador, is one of the world's great showcases of adaptive radiation. Each island was born naked from underwater volcanoes and was gradually clothed by plants, animals, and microorganisms derived from strays that rode the ocean currents and winds from other islands and the South American mainland.

The Galápagos Islands today have numerous plants, snails, reptiles, and birds that are found nowhere else on Earth. For example, they have 14 species of closely related finches, which are often called Darwin's finches because Darwin collected them during his around-the-world voyage on the *Beagle* (see Module 13.1). These birds share many finchlike traits, but they differ in their feeding habits and their beaks, which are specialized for what they eat. Their various foods include insects, large or small seeds, cactus fruits, and even eggs of other species. The woodpecker finch uses cactus spines or twigs as tools to pry insects from trees. The "vampire" finch is noted for pecking wounds on the backs of seabirds and drinking their blood. **Figure 15.8** illustrates some of these birds, with their distinctive beaks adapted for their specific diets.

How might Darwin's finch species have evolved from a small population of ancestral birds that colonized one of the islands? Completely isolated on the island, the founder population may have changed significantly as natural selection adapted it to the new environment, and thus it became a new species. Later, a few individuals of this species may have migrated to a neighbour island, where, under different conditions, this new founder population was changed enough through natural selection to become another new species. Some of these birds then may have recolonized the first island and coexisted there with the original ancestral species if reproductive barriers kept the species distinct. Multiple colonizations and speciations on the many separate islands of the Galápagos probably followed.

Today, each of the Galápagos Islands has several species of finches, with as many as 10 on some islands. The effects of the adaptive radiation of Darwin's finches are evident not just in their many types of beaks but also in their different habitats—some live in trees and others spend most of their time on the ground. Reproductive isolation because of species-specific songs helps to keep the species separate.

The closely related finches of the Galápagos provide evidence not only of past speciation events, but also of recent modifications. In the next module we see how scientists studying these birds are documenting current evolutionary changes.

? Explain why isolated island chains provide opportunities for adaptive radiations.

● The chance colonization of an island often presents a species with new resources and an absence of predators. Through natural selection acting on existing variation, the island population becomes adapted to this new habitat and may evolve into a new species. Subsequent colonizations of nearby islands would provide additional opportunities for adaptation and genetic drift, which could lead to further speciations.

Cactus-seed-eater (cactus finch)

Tool-using insect-eater (woodpecker finch)

Seed-eater (medium ground finch)

▲ **Figure 15.8** Examples of differences in beak shape and size in Galápagos finches, each adapted for a specific diet

15.9 A long-term field study documents evolution in Darwin's finches

Peter and Rosemary Grant have been conducting field research on Darwin's finches in the Galápagos for more than three decades. In 2009, the Grants received the prestigious Kyoto Prize for their long-term studies of natural selection and evolution in response to environmental changes.

How did the Grants come to work with these finches? They were looking for a pristine, undisturbed place to study variation within populations. In 1973, Peter banded about 60 medium ground finches (*Geospiza fortis*) on Daphne Major, an isolated, uninhabited island in the Galápagos. Returning eight months later with Rosemary and their young daughters, he found all but two of the banded birds. With such an opportunity to work with a small, isolated population, the Grants decided to study these birds for three years. One evolutionary question led to another, and for more than 34 years the Grants have done research on Daphne Major. Each year, the Grants and their student assistants have captured, tagged, measured, and studied every finch on this desolate, 40-hectare island.

What were some of the questions that kept the Grants returning for so many years? In addition to their study of beak size and shape and natural selection (see Module 13.3), the Grants focused on other evolutionary questions: How might competition for food from another species affect beak size? What keeps two finch species distinct despite their ability to interbreed? How might a new finch species originate?

During their long years of study, the Grants found opportunities to answer some of their questions. As the graph in **Figure 15.9** shows, they documented an increase in mean (average) beak size in the medium ground finch population following a severe drought in 1977, when the only seeds available were much tougher to crack than the small seeds that are abundant in wetter years. During the drought, 84% of the population disappeared. The survivors had much larger beaks, and this beak size was inherited by their offspring.

Then, in 1982, a new competitor species, the large ground finch (*G. magnirostris*), arrived on the island. It fed on large, hard seeds, taking more than were harvested by the resident medium ground finches. When another drought occurred in 2003–2004, the populations of both ground finches declined sharply as all seed supplies dwindled. As you can see in Figure 15.9, mean beak size decreased abruptly in the following year. Because of the depletion of large seeds by the competitive large ground finch, the medium ground finches that survived the drought had small beaks that most likely helped them feed more efficiently on very small seeds. Thus, over the 30 years of study, the average beak size of the medium ground finch has shifted in two different directions in response to two different selection pressures—drought and competition.

The Grants also study reproductive barriers between species. They found that occasional interbreeding between the

▲ **Figure 15.9** Changes in mean beak size in the medium ground finch (*Geospiza fortis*)

medium ground finch and the cactus finch happens when a male learns to sing the song of a different species. For example, a cactus finch nestling whose father dies or does not sing much may learn a neighbour's song, even if the neighbour is a medium ground finch. Thus, a medium ground finch female might breed with a cactus finch because he sings her song.

To find out whether these interspecies couples would create a new hybrid species, the Grants followed their offspring. They found that the hybrids have intermediate bill sizes and thus can survive only during wet years when there are plenty of small seeds. During dry years, the hybrids can't crack the larger, harder seeds that the medium ground finches can eat and can't compete with cactus finches for cactus seeds. Thus, the severe selection during drought years helps to keep the medium ground finch and the cactus finch on separate evolutionary paths.

Hybrids, however, can introduce more genetic variation on which natural selection can act. The Grants have documented increases in the variation within the medium ground finch and cactus finch populations when hybrids have bred with members of the parent species.

Peter Grant conjectures about hybrid finches:

Perhaps hybrids occasionally disperse . . . to another island that has neither parent species. The hybrids could start a new population with a range of genetic variation different from the parent species. . . . I see no reason why hybridization hasn't been important right from the beginning, from the first divergence of the ancestral finch stock that reached the islands.

The research goes on. The Grants have teamed up with molecular scientists to identify the genes involved in beak development. The Galápagos continue to provide a laboratory in which varying natural conditions allow scientists to make and test predictions about evolution, natural selection, and speciation.

 What were the advantages of Daphne Major as a research site?

● The resident finch populations were small and isolated, and individual birds and their offspring could be followed over many years.

15.10 Hybrid zones provide opportunities to study reproductive isolation

What happens when separated populations of closely related species come back into contact with one another? Will reproductive barriers be strong enough to keep the species separate? Or will the two species interbreed and become one? Biologists attempt to answer such questions by studying **hybrid zones**, regions in which members of different species meet and mate, producing at least some hybrid offspring.

Figure 15.10A illustrates the formation of a hybrid zone, starting with the ancestral species. ❶ Three populations are connected by gene flow. ❷ A barrier to gene flow separates one population. ❸ This population diverges from the other two. ❹ Gene flow is re-established in the hybrid zone. There are three main possible outcomes for a hybrid zone over time: reinforcement, fusion, or stability. Let's consider each in turn.

 Reinforcement When hybrid offspring are less fit than members of both parent species, we might expect natural selection to strengthen, or *reinforce*, reproductive barriers, thus reducing the formation of unfit hybrids. And we would predict that barriers between species should be stronger where the species overlap (that is, where the species are sympatric).

As an example, consider the closely related pied flycatcher and collared flycatcher illustrated in **Figure 15.10B**. When populations of these two species do not overlap (that is, when they are allopatric), males closely resemble each other, with similar black and white coloration (see left side of Figure 15.10B). However, when populations of the two species are sympatric, male collared flycatchers are still black but with enlarged patches of white, whereas male pied flycatchers are a dull brown (see right side of Figure 15.10B). The photographs at the bottom of the figure show two pied flycatchers, the one on the left from a population that has no overlap with collared flycatchers and the one on the right from a population in an area where both species coexist. When scientists performed mate choice experiments, they found that female flycatchers frequently made mistakes when presented with males from allopatric populations, which look similar. But females never selected mates from the other species when presented with males from sympatric populations, which look different. Thus, reproductive barriers are reinforced when populations of these two species overlap.

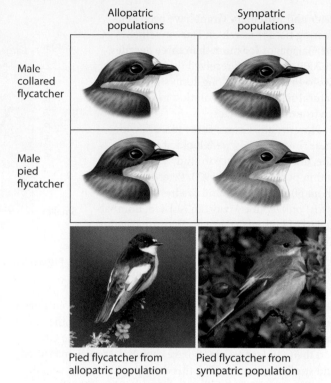

Pied flycatcher from allopatric population | Pied flycatcher from sympatric population

▲ **Figure 15.10B** Reinforcement of reproductive barriers

Fusion What happens when the reproductive barriers between species are not strong and the species come into contact in a hybrid zone? So much gene flow may occur that the speciation process reverses, causing the two hybridizing species to fuse into one.

Such a situation may be occurring among the cichlid species in Lake Victoria that we discussed in the opening essay of this chapter. Many species are reproductively isolated by female mate choice based on male coloration. As shown in **Figure 15.10C**, males of *P. nyererei* have a bright red back

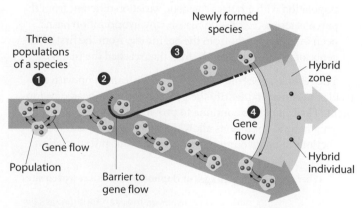

Three populations of a species ❶ ❷ ❸ — Newly formed species — ❹ Gene flow — Hybrid zone — Hybrid individual — Gene flow — Population — Barrier to gene flow

▲ **Figure 15.10A** Formation of a hybrid zone

Pundamilia nyererei | *Pundamilia pundamilia*

Hybrid: *Pundamilia "turbid water"*

▲ **Figure 15.10C** Fusion: males of *Pundamilia nyererei* and *Pundamilia pundamilia* contrasted with a hybrid from an area with turbid water and dorsal fin, whereas males of the closely related species, *P. pundamilia*, have a bright blue dorsal fin. Various mate choice experiments have shown that females prefer brightly coloured—and rightly coloured—males.

Many viable hybrid offspring are produced by interbreeding and the once isolated gene pools of the parent species combine—that is, two species fusing into a single hybrid species (see bottom of Figure 15.10C).

 Stability One might predict that either reinforcement of reproductive barriers or fusion of gene pools would occur in a hybrid zone. However, many hybrid zones are fairly stable,

and hybrids continue to be produced. Although these hybrids allow for some gene flow between populations, each species maintains its own integrity. The island inhabited by medium ground finches and cactus finches, with their occasional hybrid offspring (see Module 15.9), is an example of a stable hybrid zone.

? Why might hybrid zones be called "natural laboratories" in which to study speciation?

● By studying the fate of hybrids over time, scientists can directly observe factors that cause (or fail to cause) reproductive isolation.

15.11 Speciation can occur rapidly or slowly

Biologists continue to make field observations and devise experiments to study evolution in progress. However, much of the evidence for evolution comes from the fossil record. What does this record say about the process of speciation?

Many fossil species appear suddenly in a layer of rock and persist essentially unchanged through several layers (strata) until disappearing just as suddenly. Paleontologists Niles Eldredge and the late Stephen Jay Gould coined the term **punctuated equilibria** to describe these long periods of little change, or equilibrium, punctuated by abrupt episodes of speciation. The top of **Figure 15.11** illustrates the evolution of two lineages of butterflies in a punctuated pattern. Notice that the butterfly species change little, if at all, once they appear.

Other fossil species appear to have diverged gradually over long periods of time. As shown at the bottom of Figure 15.11, differences gradually accumulate, and new species (represented by the two butterflies at the far right) evolve gradually from the ancestral population.

Even when fossil evidence points to a punctuated pattern, species may not have originated as rapidly as it appears. Suppose that a species survived for 5 million years but that most of the changes in its features occurred during the first 50 000 years of its existence. Time periods this short often cannot be distinguished in fossil strata. And should a new species originate from a small, isolated population—as no doubt many species have—the chances of fossils being found are low.

But what about the total length of time between speciation events—between when a new species forms and when its populations diverge enough to produce another new species? In one survey of 84 groups of plants and animals, this time ranged from 4000 to 40 million years. Overall, the time between speciation events averaged 6.5 million years. What are the implications of such long time frames? They tell us that it has taken vast spans of time for life on Earth to evolve and that it takes a long time for life to recover from mass extinctions, as have occurred in the past and may be occurring now (see Module 14.12).

As you've seen, speciation may begin with small differences. However, as species diverge and speciate again and again, these changes may eventually lead to new groups that differ greatly from their ancestors. The cumulative effects of multiple speciations, as well as extinctions, have shaped the dramatic changes documented in the fossil record. Such macroevolutionary changes are the subject of our next chapter.

? How does the punctuated equilibrium model account for the relative rarity of transitional fossils linking newer species to older ones?

● If speciation takes place in a relatively short time or in a small isolated population, the transition of one species to another may be difficult to find in the fossil record.

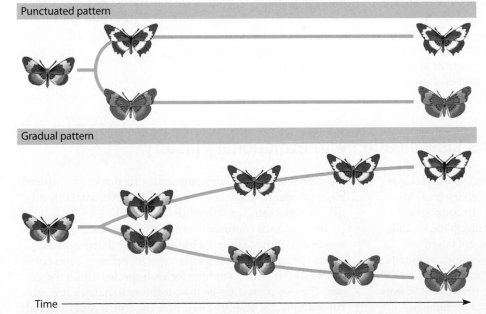

Punctuated pattern

Gradual pattern

Time

▲ **Figure 15.11** Two models for the tempo of speciation

Phylogeny and the Tree of Life

15.12 Phylogenies based on homologies reflect evolutionary history

So far in this chapter, we have looked at the major evolutionary changes that have occurred during the history of life on Earth. Now we shift our focus to how biologists use the pattern of evolution to distinguish and categorize the millions of species that live, and have lived, on Earth.

The evolutionary history of a species or group of species is called **phylogeny** (from the Greek *phylon*, tribe, and *genesis*, origin). The fossil record provides a substantial chronicle of evolutionary change that can help to trace the phylogeny of many groups. It is, however, an incomplete record, as many of Earth's species probably never left any fossils; many fossils that formed were probably destroyed by later geologic processes; and only a fraction of existing fossils have been discovered. Even with its limitations, however, the fossil record is a remarkably detailed account of biological change over the vast scale of geologic time.

In addition to evidence from the fossil record, phylogeny can also be inferred from morphological and molecular homologies among living organisms. As we discussed in Module 13.5, homologies are similarities because of shared ancestry. Homologous structures may look different and function differently in different species, but they exhibit fundamental similarities because they evolved from the same structure in a common ancestor. For instance, the whale limb is adapted for steering in water; the bat wing is adapted for flight. Nonetheless, the bones that support these two structures, which were present in their common mammalian ancestor, are basically the same (see Figure 13.5A).

Generally, organisms that share similar morphologies are likely to be closely related. The search for homologies is not without pitfalls, however, for not all likenesses are inherited from a common ancestor. In a process called **convergent evolution**, species from different evolutionary branches may come to resemble one another if they live in similar environments and natural selection has favoured similar adaptations. In such cases, body structures and even whole organisms may resemble each other.

Similarity because of convergent evolution is called **analogy**. For example, the two mole-like animals shown in **Figure 15.12** are very similar in external appearance. They both have enlarged front paws, small eyes, and a pad of protective thickened skin on the nose. However, the Australian "mole" (top) is a marsupial, meaning that its young complete their embryonic development in a pouch outside the mother's body. The North American mole (bottom) is a eutherian, which means that its young complete development in the mother's uterus. Genetic and fossil evidence indicate that the last common ancestor of these two animals lived 140 mya. And in fact, that ancestor and most of its descendants were not mole-like. Analogous traits evolved independently in these two mole lineages as they each became adapted to burrowing lifestyles.

▲ **Figure 15.12** Australian "mole" (top) and North American mole (bottom)

In addition to molecular comparisons and fossil evidence, another clue to distinguishing homology from analogy is to consider the complexity of the structure being compared. For instance, the skulls of a human and a chimpanzee (see Figure 14.14B) consist of many bones fused together, and the composition of these skulls matches almost perfectly, bone for bone. It is highly improbable that such complex structures have separate origins. More likely, the genes involved in the development of both skulls were inherited from a common ancestor, and these complex structures are homologous.

 Human forearms and a bat's wings are _____. A bat's wings and a bee's wings are _____.

homologous; analogous ●

15.13 Systematics connects classification with evolutionary history

Systematics is a discipline of biology that focuses on classifying organisms and determining their evolutionary relationships. In the 18th century, Carolus Linnaeus introduced a system of naming and classifying species, a discipline we call **taxonomy**. Although Linnaeus's system was not based on evolutionary relationship, many of its features, such as the two-part Latin names for species, remain useful in systematics.

Common names, such as *bird*, *bat*, and *pterosaur*, may work well in everyday communication, but they can be ambiguous because there are many species of each of these kinds of organisms. And some common names are downright misleading. Consider these three "fishes": *jellyfish* (a cnidarian), *crayfish* (a crustacean), and *silverfish* (an insect).

To avoid such confusion, biologists assign each species a two-part scientific name, or **binomial**. The first part is the **genus** (plural, *genera*) to which a species belongs. The second part of the binomial is unique for each species within the genus. The two parts must be used together to name a species. For example, the scientific name for the North American red squirrel is *Tamiasciurus hudsonicus* and for the black-capped

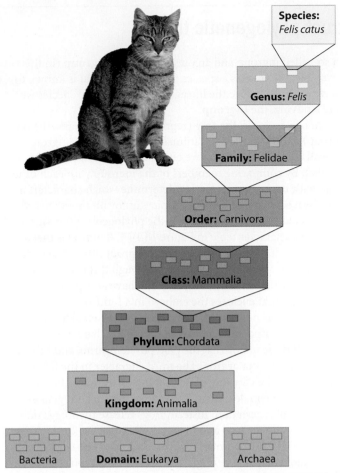

Species: *Felis catus*

Genus: *Felis*

Family: Felidae

Order: Carnivora

Class: Mammalia

Phylum: Chordata

Kingdom: Animalia

Bacteria | **Domain:** Eukarya | Archaea

▲ **Figure 15.13A** Hierarchical classification of the domestic cat

chickadee is *Poecile atricapillus*. Notice that the first letter of the genus name is capitalized and that the binomial is italicized (or underlined if handwritten) and Latinized.

In addition to naming species, Linnaeus also grouped them into a hierarchy of categories. Beyond the grouping of species within genera (as indicated by the binomial), the Linnaean system extends to progressively broader categories of classification. It places similar genera in the same **family**, puts families into **orders**, orders into **classes**, classes into **phyla** (singular, *phylum*), phyla into **kingdoms**, and, more recently, kingdoms into **domains**.

Figure 15.13A uses the domestic cat (*Felis catus*) to illustrate this progressively broader classification system. The genus *Felis* includes the domestic cat and several closely related species of small wild cats (represented by small yellow boxes in the figure). The genus *Felis* is placed in the cat family, Felidae, along with other genera of cats, such as the genus *Panthera*, which includes the cougar, tiger, leopard, and African lion. Family Felidae belongs to the order Carnivora, which also includes the family Canidae (for example, the wolf and coyote) and several other families. Order Carnivora is grouped with many other orders in the class Mammalia, the mammals. Class Mammalia is one of the classes belonging to the phylum Chordata in the kingdom Animalia, which is one of several kingdoms in the domain Eukarya. Each taxonomic unit at any level—family Felidae or class Mammalia, for instance—is called a **taxon** (plural, *taxa*).

Grouping organisms into more inclusive categories seems to come naturally to humans—it is a way to structure our world. Classifying species into higher (broader) taxa, however, is ultimately arbitrary. Higher classification levels are generally defined by morphological characteristics chosen by taxonomists rather than by quantitative measurements that could apply to the same taxon level across all lineages. Because of such difficulties with determining higher taxa, some biologists propose that classification be based entirely on evolutionary relationships, using a PhyloCode, as it is called, which names only groups that include a common ancestor and all its descendants. This approach emphasizes the importance of clades (see Module 15.14) in understanding phylogeny rather than traditional taxa. While PhyloCode would change the way taxa are defined, the names of most groups would remain the same, just without "ranks," such as family, order, or class, attached to them.

Ever since Darwin, systematics has had a goal beyond simple organization: to have classification reflect evolutionary relationships. Biologists traditionally use **phylogenetic trees** to depict hypotheses about the evolutionary history of species. These branching diagrams reflect the hierarchical classification of groups nested within more inclusive groups. **Figure 15.13B** illustrates the connection between classification and phylogeny. This tree shows the classification of some of the taxa in the order Carnivora and the probable evolutionary relationships among these groups. Note that such a phylogenetic tree does not indicate when a particular species evolved but only the pattern of descent from the last common ancestors of the species shown.

Next we explore how phylogenetic trees are constructed.

? How much of the classification in Figure 15.13A do we share with the domestic cat?

● We are classified the same from the domain to the class level. Both cats and humans are mammals. We do not belong to the same order.

Order	Family	Genus	Species

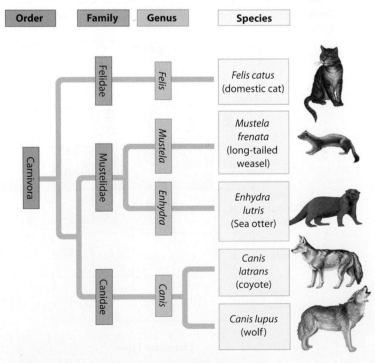

Felidae — Felis — *Felis catus* (domestic cat)

Carnivora — Mustelidae — Mustela — *Mustela frenata* (long-tailed weasel)

Enhydra — *Enhydra lutris* (Sea otter)

Canidae — Canis — *Canis latrans* (coyote)

Canis lupus (wolf)

▲ **Figure 15.13B** Relating classification to phylogeny

15.14 Shared characters are used to construct phylogenetic trees

In reconstructing a group's evolutionary history, biologists first sort homologous features, which reflect evolutionary relationship, from analogous features, which do not. They then infer phylogeny by using these homologous characters.

Cladistics   The most widely used method in systematics is called **cladistics**. Common ancestry is the primary criterion used to group organisms into **clades** (from the Greek *clados*, branch). A clade is a group of species that includes an ancestral species and all its descendants. Such an inclusive group of ancestor and descendants, be it a genus, family, or some broader taxon, is said to be **monophyletic** (meaning "single tribe"). Clades reflect the branching pattern of evolution and can be used to construct phylogenetic trees.

Cladistics is based on the Darwinian concept that organisms both share characteristics with their ancestors and differ from them. For example, all mammals have backbones, but the presence of a backbone does not distinguish mammals from other vertebrates. The backbone predates the branching of the mammalian clade from other vertebrates. Thus, we say that for mammals, the backbone is a **shared ancestral character** that originated in an ancestor of all vertebrates. In contrast, hair, a character shared by all mammals but not found in their ancestors, is considered a **shared derived character**, an evolutionary novelty unique to mammals. Shared derived characters distinguish clades and thus the branch points in the tree of life.

Inferring Phylogenies by Using Shared Characters   The simplified example in **Figure 15.14A** illustrates that the sequence in which shared derived characters appear can be used to construct a phylogenetic tree. The figure compares five animals according to the presence or absence of a set of characters. An important part of cladistics is a comparison between

a so-called ingroup and an outgroup. The **outgroup** (in this example, the frog) is a species from a lineage that is known to have diverged before the lineage that includes the species we are studying, the **ingroup**.

In our example, the frog (representing amphibians, the outgroup) and the other four animals (collectively the ingroup) are all related in that they are tetrapods (vertebrates with limbs). By comparing members of the ingroup with each other and with the outgroup, we can determine which characters are the derived characters—evolutionary innovations—that define the sequence of branch points in the phylogeny of the ingroup.

In the character table in Figure 15.14A, 0 indicates that a particular character is not present in a group; 1 indicates that the character is present. Let's work through this example step by step. All the animals in the ingroup have an amnion, a membrane that encloses the embryo in a fluid-filled sac. The outgroup does not have this character. Now consider the next character—hair and mammary glands. This character is present in all three mammals (the platypus, kangaroo, and beaver) but not the iguana or frog. The third character in the table is gestation, the carrying of developing offspring within the uterus of the female parent. Both the outgroup and iguanas do not exhibit gestation. Instead, frogs release their eggs into the water, and iguanas and most other reptiles lay eggs with a shell. One of the mammals, the platypus, also lays eggs with a shell; and from this we might infer that the platypus represents an early branch point in the mammalian clade. In fact, this hypothesis is strongly supported by structural, fossil, and molecular evidence. The final character is long gestation, in which an offspring completes its embryonic development within the uterus. This is the case for a beaver, but a kangaroo has a very short gestation period and completes its embryonic development while nursing in its mother's pouch.

TAXA

CHARACTERS	Frog	Iguana	Platypus	Kangaroo	Beaver
Amnion	0	1	1	1	1
Hair, mammary glands	0	0	1	1	1
Gestation	0	0	0	1	1
Long gestation	0	0	0	0	1

Character Table

Phylogenetic Tree

▲ **Figure 15.14A** Constructing a phylogenetic tree by using cladistics

We can now translate the data in our table of characters into a phylogenetic tree. As we saw in Module 13.6, such a tree is constructed from a series of two-way branch points. Each branch point (also called a node) represents the divergence of two groups from a common ancestor and the emergence of a lineage possessing a new set of derived characters. By tracing the distribution of shared derived characters, you can see how we inferred the sequence of branching and the evolutionary relationships of this group of animals. Although this example illustrates how physical characters can be used to construct a phylogenetic tree, today many of these trees are drawn on the basis of molecular evidence, such as the whole-genome sequencing we discussed in Module 12.19.

Parsimony   Useful in many areas of science, **parsimony** is the adoption of the simplest explanation for observed phenomena. Systematists use the principle of parsimony to construct phylogenetic trees that require the smallest number of evolutionary changes. For instance, parsimony leads to the hypothesis that a beaver is more closely related to a kangaroo than to a platypus, because in both the beaver and the kangaroo, embryos begin development within the female uterus. It is possible that gestation evolved twice, once in the kangaroo lineage and independently in the beaver lineage, but this explanation is more complicated and therefore less likely. Typical cladistic analyses involve much more complex data sets than we presented in Figure 15.14A (often including comparisons of DNA sequences) and are usually handled by computer programs designed to construct parsimonious trees.

Phylogenetic Trees as Hypotheses   Systematists use many kinds of evidence, such as structural and developmental features, molecular data, and behavioural traits, to reconstruct evolutionary histories. However, even the best tree represents only the most likely hypothesis based on available evidence. As new data accumulate, hypotheses are revised and new trees drawn.

An example of a redrawn tree is shown in **Figure 15.14B**. In traditional vertebrate taxonomy, crocodiles, snakes, lizards, and other reptiles were classified in the class Reptilia, while birds were placed in the separate class Aves. However, such a reptilian clade is not monophyletic—in other words, it does

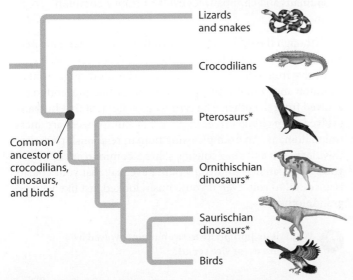

▲ **Figure 15.14B** A phylogenetic tree of reptiles (*indicates extinct lineages)

Labels in figure: Lizards and snakes; Crocodilians; Pterosaurs*; Common ancestor of crocodilians, dinosaurs, and birds; Ornithischian dinosaurs*; Saurischian dinosaurs*; Birds

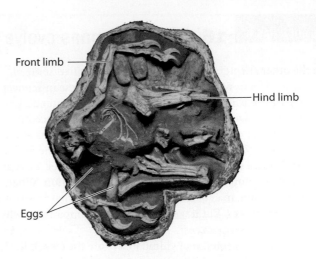

▲ **Figure 15.14C**   Fossil remains of *Oviraptor* and eggs. The orientation of the bones, which surround the eggs, suggests that the dinosaur died while incubating or protecting its eggs.

Labels in figure: Front limb; Hind limb; Eggs

not include an ancestral species and all of its descendants, one group of which includes the birds. Many lines of evidence support the tree shown in Figure 15.16B, showing that birds belong to the clade of reptiles.

Thinking of phylogenetic trees as hypotheses allows us to use them to make and test predictions. For example, if our phylogeny is correct, then features shared by two groups of closely related organisms should be present in their common ancestor. Using this reasoning, consider the novel predictions that can be made about dinosaurs. As seen in the tree in Figure 15.14B, the closest *living* relatives of birds are crocodiles. Birds and crocodiles share numerous features: They have four-chambered hearts, they "sing" to defend territories and attract mates (although a crocodile "song" is more like a bellow), and they build nests. Both birds and crocodiles care for and warm their eggs by brooding. Birds brood by sitting on their eggs, whereas crocodiles cover their eggs with their neck. Reasoning that any feature shared by birds and crocodiles is likely to have been present in their common ancestor (denoted by the red circle in Figure 15.14B) and all of its descendants, biologists hypothesize that dinosaurs had four-chambered hearts, sang, built nests, and exhibited brooding.

Internal organs such as hearts rarely fossilize, and it is, of course, difficult to determine whether dinosaurs sang. However, fossilized dinosaur nests have been found. **Figure 15.14C** shows a fossil of an *Oviraptor* dinosaur thought to have died in a sandstorm while incubating or protecting its eggs. The hypothesis that dinosaurs built nests and exhibited brooding has been further supported by additional fossil discoveries that show other species of dinosaurs caring for their eggs.

The more we know about an organism and its relatives, the more accurately we can portray its phylogeny. In the next module, we consider how molecular biology is providing valuable data for tracing evolutionary history.

? **To distinguish a particular clade of mammals within the larger clade that corresponds to class Mammalia, why is hair not a useful characteristic?**

● Hair is a shared ancestral character common to all mammals and thus is not helpful in distinguishing different mammalian subgroups.

15.15 Did humans evolve from chimpanzees?

In the other chapters of this unit, we have clarified some of the misconceptions surrounding evolution. These misconceptions are primarily based on an incomplete understanding of evolution and how it works. We resolved the misconception that the theory of evolution tries to explain the origins of life in Module 13.7. And in Module 14.1, we dispelled the notion that individual organisms can evolve. In this chapter, we examine another common misconception about evolution. When speaking of human evolution, many people say that we evolved from chimpanzees. But if we evolved from chimpanzees, why are there still chimpanzees?

It is widely accepted that chimpanzees are the closest living relative to our own species. A large amount of evidence supports this relationship, which is why humans and chimpanzees are in close proximity on a phylogenetic tree of primates (see Figure 21.10). The molecular similarity alone is compelling. More than 98% of the DNA of chimpanzees and humans is identical. In genomes that are 3 billion base pairs long, only 35 million nucleotide substitutions, 5 million insertions or deletions, and some chromosomal rearrangement separate the two genomes.

That said, humans did not evolve from chimpanzees—nor did chimpanzees evolve from humans. The appropriate way to state the evolutionary relationship is that humans and chimpanzees evolved from a common ancestor, which was neither chimp nor human. It is important to note that since the ancestral chimpanzee and human diverged from their common ancestor about 6–7 mya, they have both been evolving independently.

Fossilized ape remains are extremely rare and those of a common ancestor of humans and chimpanzees have yet to be found. The partial skull of *Sahelanthropus tchadensis* (**Figure 15.15A**) is a remnant of the oldest known hominin, at 6–7 million years old. It is possible that the common ancestor resembled *S. tchadensis* (**Figure 15.15B**). The appearance of our common ancestor shown in the figure may indicate why

▲ **Figure 15.15B** A common ancestor may have resembled the oldest hominin *Sahelanthropus tchadensis*

people misunderstand the relationship between chimpanzees and humans: Ancestral humans likely looked more like apes than modern humans.

Consider the following two statements:

Humans evolved from chimpanzees.
Humans and chimpanzees evolved from a common ancestor.

Although the difference between these two statements may seem small, it is actually very significant. Although species do evolve from one another, when two species diverge from a common ancestor, it is inappropriate to say that one endpoint evolved from the other. The erroneous statement that humans evolved from chimpanzees implies that chimpanzees are ancestral to humans. An example using human relationships makes this clear: You and your cousins share a common ancestor—your grandparents—but you would never say that your cousin is ancestral to you, even if your cousin looked just like your grandmother.

▲ **Figure 15.15A** The skull of the oldest hominin *Sahelanthropus tchadensis*

 Why is it inappropriate to say humans evolved from chimpanzees (or vice versa)?

Both humans and chimpanzees have been evolving along separate evolutionary paths since they diverged from their common ancestor 6–7 mya.

15.16 An organism's evolutionary history is documented in its genome

The more recently two species have branched from a common ancestor, the more similar their DNA sequences should be. The longer two species have been on separate evolutionary paths, the more their DNA is expected to have diverged.

Molecular Systematics   Using DNA or other molecules to infer relatedness, a method called **molecular systematics** is a valuable approach for tracing phylogeny. Scientists have sequenced more than 110 billion bases of DNA from thousands of species. This enormous database has fuelled a boom in the study of phylogeny and clarified many evolutionary relationships.

For example, consider the red panda, an endangered, Southeast Asian tree-dwelling mammal that feeds mostly on bamboo. It was initially classified as a close relative of the giant panda, and then as a member of the raccoon family. Recent molecular studies, however, suggest that the red panda represents a separate group, which diverged from the lineage that led to the raccoon and the weasel families. Molecular evidence has also begun to sort out the relationships among the species of bears. **Figure 15.16** presents a phylogenetic hypothesis for the families that include bears, raccoons, weasels, and the red panda. Notice that this phylogenetic tree includes a timeline, which is based on fossil evidence and molecular data that can estimate when many of these divergences occurred. Most of the phylogenetic trees we have seen so far indicate only the relative order in which lineages diverged; they do not show the timing of those events.

Bears, raccoons, and the red panda are closely related mammals that diverged fairly recently. But biologists can also use DNA analyses to assess relationships between groups of organisms that are so phylogenetically distant that structural similarities are absent. It is also possible to reconstruct phylogenies among groups of present-day prokaryotes and other microorganisms for which we have no fossil record at all. Molecular biology has helped to extend systematics to the extremes of evolutionary relationships far above and below the species level, ranging from major branches of the tree of life to its finest twigs.

The ability of molecular trees to encompass both short and long periods of time is based on the observation that different genes evolve at different rates. The DNA specifying ribosomal RNA (rRNA) changes relatively slowly, so comparisons of DNA sequences in these genes are useful for investigating relationships between taxa that diverged hundreds of millions of years ago. Studies of the genes for rRNA have shown, for example, that fungi are more closely related to animals than to green plants—something that certainly could not have been deduced from morphological comparisons alone.

In contrast, the DNA in mitochondria (mtDNA) evolves relatively rapidly and can be used to investigate more recent evolutionary events. For example, researchers have used mtDNA sequences to study the relationships between Native American groups. Their studies support earlier evidence that the Pima of Arizona, the Maya of Mexico, and the Yanomami of Venezuela are closely related, probably descending from the first wave of immigrants to cross the Bering Land Bridge from Asia to the Americas about 15 000 years ago.

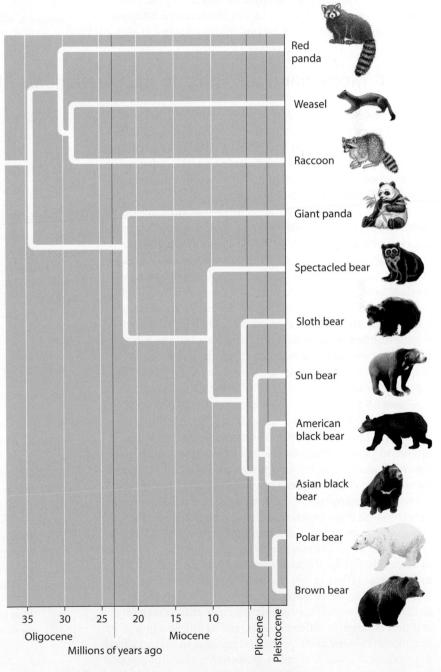

▲ **Figure 15.16**   A phylogenetic tree based on molecular data

Genome Evolution   Now that we can compare entire genomes, including our own, some interesting facts have emerged. As you read earlier, the genomes of humans and chimpanzees are strikingly similar. An even more remarkable fact is that homologous genes (similar genes that species share because of descent from a common ancestor) are widespread and can extend over huge evolutionary distances. While the genes of humans and mice are certainly not identical, 99% of them are detectably homologous. And 50% of human genes are homologous with those of yeast. This remarkable commonality demonstrates that all living organisms share many biochemical and developmental pathways and provides overwhelming support for Darwin's theory of "descent with modification."

Gene duplication has played a particularly important role in evolution because it increases the number of genes in the genome, providing additional opportunities for further evolutionary changes (see Module 14.14). Molecular techniques now allow scientists to trace the evolutionary history of such duplications—in which lineage they occurred and how the multiple copies of genes have diverged from each other over time.

Another interesting fact evident from genome comparisons is that the number of genes has not increased at the same rate as the complexity of organisms. Humans have only about four times as many genes as yeasts. Yeasts are simple, single-celled eukaryotes; humans have a complex brain and a body that contains more than 200 different types of tissues. Evidence is emerging that many human genes are more versatile than those of yeast, but explaining the mechanisms of such versatility remains an exciting scientific challenge.

 What types of molecules should be compared to help to determine whether fungi are more closely related to plants or to animals?

● Because these organisms diverged so long ago, scientists should compare molecules that change or evolve very slowly, such as the DNA that specifies rRNA.

15.17 Molecular clocks help to track evolutionary time

Some regions of genomes appear to accumulate changes at constant rates. Comparisons of certain homologous DNA sequences for taxa known to have diverged during a certain time period have shown that the number of nucleotide substitutions is proportional to the time that has elapsed since the lineages branched. For example, homologous genes of bats and dolphins are much more alike than are homologous genes of sharks and tuna. This is consistent with the fossil evidence that sharks and tuna have been on separate evolutionary paths much longer (more than 420 million years) than have bats and dolphins (perhaps 60 million years). In this case, molecular divergence has kept better track of time than have changes in morphology.

For a gene shown to have a reliable average rate of change, a **molecular clock** can be calibrated in actual time by graphing the number of nucleotide differences against the dates of evolutionary branch points known from the fossil record. The graph line can then be used to estimate the dates of other evolutionary episodes not documented in the fossil record.

Figure 15.17 shows how a molecular clock has been used to date the origin of HIV (human immunodeficiency virus) infection in humans. HIV, the virus that causes AIDS (acquired immunodeficiency syndrome), is descended from viruses that infect chimpanzees and other primates. When did HIV jump to humans? The virus has spread to humans more than once, but the most widespread strain in humans is HIV-1 M. To pinpoint the earliest infection by this strain, researchers compared samples of the virus from various times during the epidemic, including a sample from 1959. The samples showed that the virus has evolved in a clocklike fashion. Extrapolating backward from these data indicates that HIV-1 M first spread to humans during the 1930s.

Some biologists are skeptical about the accuracy of molecular clocks because the rate of molecular change may vary at different times, in different genes, and in different groups of organisms. In some cases, problems may be avoided by calibrating molecular clocks with many genes rather than just one or a few genes. One group of researchers used sequence data from

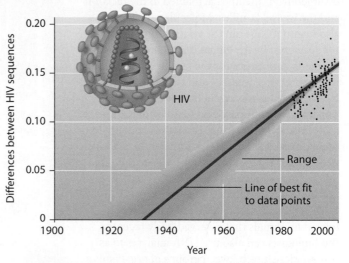

▲ **Figure 15.17** Dating the origin of HIV-1 M with a molecular clock. The data points in the upper-right corner represent different HIV samples taken at known times.

658 genes to construct a molecular clock that covered almost 600 million years of vertebrate evolution. Their estimates of divergence times agreed closely with fossil-based estimates. An abundant fossil record extends back only about 550 million years, and molecular clocks have been used to date evolutionary divergences that occurred a billion or more years ago. But the estimates assume that the clocks have been constant for all that time. Thus, such estimates are highly uncertain.

Evolutionary theory holds that all of life has a common ancestor. Molecular systematics is helping to link all living organisms into a comprehensive tree of life, as we see next.

 What is a molecular clock? What assumption underlies the use of such a clock?

● A molecular clock estimates the actual time of evolutionary events based on the number of DNA changes. It is based on the assumption that some regions of genomes evolve at constant rates.

15.18 Constructing the tree of life is a work in progress

Phylogenetic trees are hypotheses about evolutionary history. Like all hypotheses, they are revised, or in some cases rejected, in accordance with new evidence. As you have learned, molecular systematics and cladistics are remodelling many trees.

Over the years, multiple schemes have been proposed for classifying all of life. Historically, a two-kingdom system divided all organisms into plants and animals. But it was beset with problems. Where do bacteria fit? Or photosynthetic unicellular organisms that move? And what about the fungi?

By the late 1960s, many biologists recognized five kingdoms: Monera (prokaryotes), Protista (a diverse kingdom consisting mostly of unicellular eukaryotes), Plantae, Fungi, and Animalia. However, molecular studies highlighted fundamental flaws in the five-kingdom system. Biologists have since adopted a **three-domain system**, which recognizes three basic groups: two domains of prokaryotes, Bacteria and Archaea, and one domain of eukaryotes, called Eukarya. Kingdoms Fungi, Plantae, and Animalia are still recognized, but kingdoms Monera and Protista are obsolete because they are not monophyletic.

Molecular and cellular evidence indicates that the two lineages of prokaryotes (bacteria and archaea) diverged very early in the evolutionary history of life. Molecular evidence also suggests that archaea are more closely related to eukaryotes than to bacteria. **Figure 15.18A** is an evolutionary tree based largely on rRNA genes. As you just learned, rRNA genes have evolved so slowly that homologies between distantly related organisms can still be detected. This tree shows that ❶ the first major split in the history of life was the divergence of the bacteria from the other two domains, followed by the divergence of domains Archaea and Eukarya.

Every day, scientists are sequencing the whole genomes of many organisms from all three domains. Comparisons of these genomes have shown that, especially during the early history of life, there have been substantial interchanges of genes between organisms in the different domains. These took place through **horizontal gene transfer**, a process in which genes are transferred from one genome to another through mechanisms such as plasmid exchange and viral infection (see Modules 17.7 and 17.8) and even through the fusion of different organisms. Figure 15.18A shows two major episodes of horizontal gene transfer: ❷ gene transfer between a mitochondrial ancestor and the ancestor of eukaryotes and ❸ gene transfer between a chloroplast ancestor and the ancestor of green plants. Module 4.15 describes the endosymbiont theory for the origin of mitochondria and chloroplasts.

Some scientists have argued that horizontal gene transfers were so common that the early history of life should be represented as a tangled network of connected branches. Others have suggested that the early history of life is best represented by a ring, not a tree (**Figure 15.18B**). Based on an analysis of hundreds of genes, some researchers have hypothesized that the eukaryote lineage (gold in the figure) arose when an early archaean (teal) fused with an early bacterium (purple). In this model, eukaryotes are as closely related to bacteria as they are to archaea—an evolutionary relationship that can best be shown in a ring of life. As new data and new methods for analyzing that data emerge at an increasingly fast rate, constructing a comprehensive tree of life will continue to challenge and intrigue scientists.

In the next unit, we examine the enormous diversity of organisms that have populated Earth since life first arose more than 3.5 bya.

? **Why might the evolutionary history of the earliest organisms be best represented by a ring of life?**

● There appear to have been multiple horizontal gene transfers among these earliest organisms before the three domains of life eventually emerged from the ring to give rise to Earth's tremendous diversity of life.

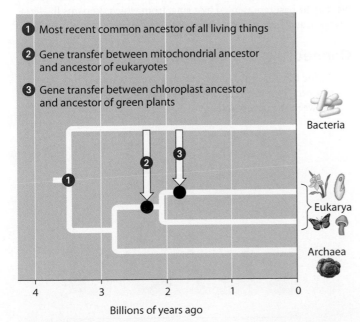

▲ **Figure 15.18A** Two major episodes of horizontal gene transfer in the history of life (dates are uncertain)

▲ **Figure 15.18B** Is the tree of life really a ring of life? In this model, eukaryotes arose when an early archaean fused with an early bacterium.

MasteringBiology® **For Practice Quizzes, BioFlix, MP3 Tutors, and Activities, go to masteringbiology.com.**

Reviewing the Concepts

Defining Species (15.1–15.3)

15.1 The origin of species is the source of biological diversity. Speciation, the process by which one species splits into two or more species, accounts for both the unity and diversity of life.

15.2 There are several ways to define a species. The biological species concept holds that a species is a group of populations whose members can interbreed and produce fertile offspring with each other but not with members of other species. This concept emphasizes reproductive isolation. Most organisms are classified based on observable traits—the morphological species concept.

15.3 Reproductive barriers keep species separate. Such barriers isolate a species' gene pool and prevent interbreeding.

Gametes		Zygote		Viable, fertile offspring

Prezygotic barriers	**Postzygotic barriers**
• Habitat isolation	• Reduced hybrid viability
• Temporal isolation	• Reduced hybrid fertility
• Behavioural isolation	
• Mechanical isolation	• Hybrid breakdown
• Gametic isolation	

Mechanisms of Speciation (15.4–15.11)

15.4 In allopatric speciation, geographic isolation leads to speciation. Geographically separated from other populations, a small population may become genetically unique as its gene pool is changed by natural selection, mutation, or genetic drift.

15.5 Reproductive barriers can evolve as populations diverge. Researchers have documented the beginning of reproductive isolation in fruit fly populations adapting to different food sources and have identified a gene for flower colour involved in the pollinator choice that helps to separate monkey flower species.

15.6 Sympatric speciation takes place without geographic isolation. Many plant species have evolved by polyploidy, duplication of the chromosome number due to errors in cell division. Habitat differentiation and sexual selection, usually involving mate choice, can lead to sympatric (and allopatric) speciation.

15.7 Most plant species trace their origin to polyploid speciation. Many plants, including food plants such as bread wheat, are the result of hybridization and polyploidy.

15.8 Isolated islands are often showcases of speciation. Repeated isolation, speciation, and recolonization events on isolated island chains have led to adaptive radiations of species, many of which are found nowhere else in the world.

15.9 A long-term field study documents evolution in Darwin's finches. Peter and Rosemary Grant have documented changes in beak size resulting from natural selection because of drought and competition, as well as interbreeding between some Galápagos finch species.

15.10 Hybrid zones provide opportunities to study reproductive isolation. Hybrid zones are regions in which populations of different species overlap and produce at least some hybrid offspring. Over time, reinforcement may strengthen barriers to reproduction, or fusion may reverse the speciation process as gene flow between species increases. In stable hybrid zones, a limited number of hybrid offspring continue to be produced.

15.11 Speciation can occur rapidly or slowly. The punctuated equilibria model draws on the fossil record, where species change most as they arise from an ancestral species and then change relatively little for the rest of their existence. Other species appear to have evolved more gradually. The time interval between speciation events varies from a few thousand years to tens of millions of years.

Phylogeny and the Tree of Life (15.12–15.18)

15.12 Phylogenies based on homologies reflect evolutionary history. Homologous structures and molecular sequences provide evidence of common ancestry.

15.13 Systematics connects classification with evolutionary history. Taxonomists assign each species a binomial—a genus and species name. Genera are grouped into progressively broader categories. A phylogenetic tree is a hypothesis of evolutionary relationships.

15.14 Shared characters are used to construct phylogenetic trees. Cladistics uses shared derived characters to define clades. A parsimonious tree requires the fewest evolutionary changes.

15.15 Did humans evolve from chimpanzees? Humans did not evolve from chimpanzees. Both humans and chimpanzees evolved from a common ancestor.

15.16 An organism's evolutionary history is documented in its genome. Molecular systematics uses molecular comparisons to build phylogenetic trees. Homologous genes are found across distantly related species.

15.17 Molecular clocks help to track evolutionary time. Regions of DNA that change at a constant rate can provide estimated dates of past events.

15.18 Constructing the tree of life is a work in progress. Evidence of multiple horizontal gene transfers suggests that the early history of life may be best represented by a ring, from which domains Bacteria, Archaea, and Eukarya emerge.

Connecting the Concepts

1. Name the two types of speciation represented by this diagram. For each type, describe how reproductive barriers may develop between the new species.

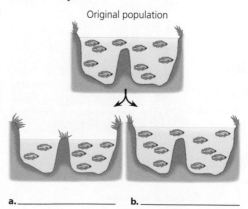

Original population

a._____   b._____

2. Fill in this concept map about systematics.

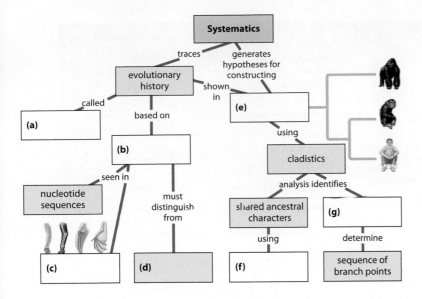

Testing Your Knowledge

Multiple Choice

3. Bird guides once listed the myrtle warbler and Audubon's warbler as distinct species that lived side by side in parts of their ranges. However, recent books show them as eastern and western forms of a single species, the yellow-rumped warbler. Most likely, it has been found that these two kinds of warblers
   a. live in similar habitats and eat similar foods.
   b. interbreed often in nature, and the offspring are viable and fertile.
   c. are almost identical in appearance.
   d. have many genes in common.
   e. sing similar songs.

4. Which concept of species would be most useful to a field biologist identifying new plant species in a tropical forest?
   a. biological
   b. ecological
   c. morphological
   d. phylogenetic
   e. a and b combined

5. A new plant species C, which formed from hybridization of species A ($2n = 16$) with species B ($2n = 12$), would probably produce gametes with a chromosome number of
   a. 12.
   b. 14.
   c. 16.
   d. 28.
   e. 56.

6. If you were using cladistics to build a phylogenetic tree of cats, which would be the best choice for an outgroup?
   a. kangaroo
   b. leopard
   c. domestic cat
   d. iguana
   e. lion

7. Which of the following is an example of a postzygotic reproductive barrier?
   a. One *Ceanothus* shrub lives on acid soil, another on alkaline soil.
   b. Mallard and pintail ducks mate at different times of year.
   c. Two species of leopard frogs have different mating calls.
   d. Hybrid offspring of two species of jimsonweeds always die before reproducing.
   e. Pollen of one species of tobacco cannot fertilize a different species of tobacco.

8. Biologists have found more than 500 species of fruit flies on the various Hawaiian Islands, all apparently descended from a single ancestor species. This example illustrates
   a. polyploidy.
   b. temporal isolation.
   c. adaptive radiation.
   d. sympatric speciation.
   e. postzygotic barriers.

9. A horse ($2n = 64$) and a donkey ($2n = 62$) can mate and produce a mule. How many chromosomes would there be in a mule's body cells?
   a. 31
   b. 62
   c. 63
   d. 126
   e. 252

10. What prevents horses and donkeys from hybridizing to form a new species?
    a. limited hybrid fertility
    b. limited hybrid viability
    c. hybrid breakdown
    d. gametic isolation
    e. prezygotic barrier

11. When hybrids produced in a hybrid zone can breed with each other and with both parent species, and they survive and reproduce as well as members of the parent species, one would predict that
    a. the hybrid zone would be stable.
    b. sympatric speciation would occur.
    c. reinforcement of reproductive barriers would keep the parent species separate.
    d. reproductive barriers would lessen and the two parent species would fuse.
    e. a new hybrid species would form through allopatric speciation.

12. Which of the following factors would not contribute to allopatric speciation?
    a. A population becomes geographically isolated from the parent population.
    b. The separated population is small, and genetic drift occurs.
    c. The isolated population is exposed to different selection pressures than the parent population.
    d. Different mutations begin to distinguish the gene pools of the separated populations.
    e. Gene flow between the two populations continues to occur.

Describing, Comparing, and Explaining

13. Explain how each of the following makes it difficult to clearly define a species: variation within a species, geographically isolated populations, asexual species, and fossil organisms.

14. Explain why allopatric speciation would be less likely on an island close to a mainland than on a more isolated island.

15. What types of molecular comparisons are used to determine the very early branching of the tree of life? *Explain.*

16. Can factors that cause sympatric speciation also cause allopatric speciation? *Explain.*

17. In the waters of British Columbia, female Dall's porpoises (*Phocoenoides dalli*) and male harbour porpoises (*Phocoena phocoena*) will occasionally interbreed. The hybrid offspring are vigorous and survive well. What are two possible reproductive barriers that may keep species that hybridize separate? In 2011, a pregnant female Dall's-harbour hybrid was found dead, washed up on shore. What is the reproductive barrier that is keeping these porpoise species separate?

Applying the Concepts

18. Explain how the murky waters of Lake Victoria may be contributing to the decline in cichlid species. How might these polluted waters affect the formation of new species? How might the loss of cichlid species be slowed?

19. A paleontologist compares fossils from three dinosaurs and Archaeopteryx, the earliest known bird. The following table shows the distribution of characters for each species, where 1 means that the character is present and 0 means it is not. The outgroup (not shown in the table) had none of the characters. Arrange these species on the phylogenetic tree below and indicate the derived character that defines each branch point.

Trait	Velociraptor	Coelophysis	Archaeopteryx	Allosaurus
Hollow bones	1	1	1	1
Three-fingered hand	1	0	1	1
Half-moon-shaped wrist bone	1	0	1	0
Reversed first toe	0	0	1	0

Outgroup

20. Experts estimate that human activities cause the extinction of hundreds of species every year. The natural rate of extinction is thought to average only a few species per year. As we continue to alter the environment, especially by destroying tropical rainforests and altering Earth's climate, the resulting wave of extinctions may rival previous mass extinctions. Considering that life has endured five mass extinctions before, should we be concerned that we may cause a sixth? How would such an extinction differ from previous extinctions? What might be the consequences for the surviving species, including ourselves?

Answers to all questions can be found in Appendix E.

The Evolution of Biodiversity

CHAPTER

16

Viruses and Other Acellular "Life"

BIG IDEAS

Viral Structure and Replication

(16.1–16.6)

Viruses consist of nucleic acids covered by a protein coat and require enzymes from a host cell in order to replicate.

Viral Infections

(16.7–16.12)

All cellular organisms are susceptible to viral infections. However, the mechanisms vary depending on the virus and host types.

Other Infectious Acellular Particles

(16.13–16.14)

The simplest known infectious agents are viroids (naked RNA) and prions (proteins).

Oh Deer! North America's Prion Disease

"Outbreak of Mad Cow Disease Feared!" is a headline that you have probably seen or heard at least once. The technical name for this disease in cattle is bovine spongiform encephalopathy (BSE) because of the spongy appearance of damaged brain tissue in affected areas. BSE leads to abnormal behaviours and ultimately death in cattle. Of even greater concern is the ability of this disease to also affect humans.

What makes this disease different from other infections is that it is not caused by a living cell (such as a parasite or bacterium) or even a virus, but by a simple infectious protein. Prion proteins have a primary structure (that is, an amino acid sequence) similar to healthy proteins found in the body. However, prion proteins are folded differently. Their different shape lowers their solubility in cytoplasm causing the formation of protein crystals.

What causes an outbreak of BSE? The answer is still being debated. Many believe that it is related to the practice of feeding cattle infected animal by-products, including nervous tissue and bone marrow. Once infected, prions cause normal proteins to refold into the prion shape, making the damaging crystals even larger. Cellular damage in the brain leads to a spongy appearance and neurological symptoms, which progresses to a loss of sensory and motor function, and eventually death.

Prion diseases came into the spotlight in the mid-1990s when several people living in or having visited Great Britain were diagnosed with variant Creutzfeldt-Jakob disease (vCJD), a degenerative neurological condition caused by the same prion as BSE. As of 2012, only two cases of vCJD have been confirmed in Canada. Many of those infected had come into direct contact with the BSE prion. How did this happen? Improper handling of infected animal tissues may have contaminated meat. The subsequent ingestion of contaminated meat by humans probably accounts for the majority of these vCJD cases.

Although cases of BSE have been identified in Canada, there is another lesser-known prion disease in our deer, moose, and elk populations that is of rising concern. Chronic wasting disease (CWD) is a prion disease similar to BSE, characterized by dramatic weight loss. CWD was first identified from an emaciated mule deer in Colorado. Since then, this disease has spread to Southern Alberta, Saskatchewan, and many U.S. states. In endemic areas the incidence of infection in the wild population is 10% to 12% and rising annually. In some captive deer populations the incidence can be as high as 80%. This poses a particular risk to wild deer populations in these regions, and their numbers may drastically decline in the coming decades.

The symptoms of CWD are similar to those of BSE. Initially the animal will exhibit psychological disturbances. At about three to four years after infection, the animal will display unusual behaviours. Physical or motor disturbances follow, including a lack of coordination, excessive urination, weight loss, and finally death.

Unlike the BSE prion, which is transmitted directly by the ingestion of contaminated tissues, the CWD prion can be transmitted indirectly when an animal ingests material contaminated by excretions (such as saliva, feces, and urine). Thus, normal grazing behaviours in endemic areas can place animals at risk for infection. This indirect method of transmission leads to its high incidence and makes it very difficult to contain.

Like other prion diseases, CWD has no treatment. The current method of control is the quarantine of herds and euthanization of infected animals. While these containment methods work well in captive herds, it is difficult to control the disease in the wild populations. The Alberta and Saskatchewan governments, working with the Canadian Food Inspection Agency (CFIA) and the Canadian Cooperative Wildlife Health Centre, have established a surveillance program where local hunters submit heads of animals for testing. This testing allows scientists to track the location and spread of CWD in the wild populations.

Currently, there is no evidence that the CWD prion protein can infect humans. However, the World Health Organization and CFIA urge hunters not to consume game that is infected with the CWD prion protein. Because the incubation times of prion diseases in humans may be as long as 50 years, there simply is not enough data to rule out the possibility that CWD can infect people.

Prion diseases are a major focus of research and have prompted the establishment of many institutes across North America and Europe, including the Centre for Prions and Protein Folding Diseases at the University of Alberta. Research into CWD and BSE is essential and may give us a greater understanding of other prion diseases, including such devastating diseases as Alzheimer's disease and Parkinson's disease. A deeper understanding of protein-folding diseases may lead to effective treatments and possibly even cures. We will discuss prions and their diseases in more detail in this chapter, after we examine the biology of viruses.

Viral Structure and Replication

16.1 A virus consists of nucleic acid and proteins

With this chapter, we begin our exploration of biodiversity. We focus primarily on diversity, but we also retrace evolutionary journeys that changed the face of our planet, such as the colonization of land by plants and vertebrates. Let's begin with the viruses and acellular "life."

Viruses are small, acellular particles, which fulfill many of the properties of life listed in Module 1.1. For this reason, viruses were once considered to be the simplest living organisms. Today, many biologists would suggest that viruses are not alive.

Instead, viruses are often described as molecular organisms living a borrowed life. Alone, a virus lacks the metabolic processes found in cells and the enzymatic machinery to replicate itself. However, once inside a host cell, the virus borrows everything it needs to reproduce.

In a sense, a virus is nothing more than "genes in a box": an infectious particle consisting of a bit of nucleic acid wrapped in a protein coat and, in some cases, a membrane envelope **(Figure 16.1)**. Consequently, viruses are extremely small and

(A) Plant virus–tobacco mosaic virus — 18 × 250 nm — 20 nm

(B) Unenveloped animal virus–adenovirus — 70–90 nm (diameter) — 50 nm

(C) Bacteria virus–bacteriophage T4 — 80 × 225 nm — 50 nm

(D) Enveloped animal virus–influenza — 80–200 nm (diameter) — 50 nm

▲ **Figure 16.1** Structure of viruses

typically require an electron microscope to be seen. Although all viruses are small, there is a great deal of variation in size. Megavirus is the largest known virus with a diameter of 440 nm, and the smallest virus (circovirus) has a diameter of only 17 nm and is smaller than a ribosome.

The protein coat, or **capsid**, is built from numerous protein subunits called **capsomeres**. The variety of capsomeres for any given virus is typically small. The capsid of the tobacco mosaic virus (discussed further in Module 16.8) in Figure 16.1 is made of thousands of identical capsomeres. In contrast, the capsids of bacteriophages (viruses that infect bacteria) have different capsomeres in the head, tail, and tail fibres. The shape of the capsid is determined by the way in which the capsomeres bind to each other. Capsomeres are arranged in a spiral in *helical viruses* such as the tobacco mosaic virus (Figure 16.1A). Other viruses have capsomeres that are arranged into a 20-sided polyhedron (Figure 16.1B). Viruses with this shape, such as adenoviruses (see Module 16.4), are referred to as *icosahedral viruses*. Most bacteriophages have complex capsids, consisting of an icosahedral head, which encloses the genetic material, and a helical tail with multiple tail fibres (Figure 16.1C). The capsid of the bacteriophage T4, for example, resembles a lunar landing module.

Many viruses that infect animals, including influenza in the figure, have a membranous **envelope** surrounding their capsid (Figure 16.1D). Viral envelopes are derived from the host cell membranes as the virus is released (see Module 16.6). Envelopes are composed of host cell phospholipids, host proteins, and viral glycoproteins (protein molecules with attached sugars) that facilitate the infection of a new cell (see Module 16.4). Viruses without an envelope are referred to as naked.

The capsid protects the genetic material while the virus is outside of a host cell. There is a great deal of variability in the makeup of viral genomes. Most (but not all) viruses have their genes on a single molecule of nucleic acid, which can be linear or circular. In Chapter 10, we saw that the DNA double helix (double-stranded DNA) is the genetic material in all cells. Viral genomes, however, defy this convention. DNA viruses can have double-stranded DNA (dsDNA), but some have single-stranded DNA (ssDNA). Many viruses don't have DNA at all. The RNA viruses have a genome made of either double-stranded RNA (dsRNA) or single-stranded RNA (ssRNA). In some viruses, the entire genome is on a single molecule of nucleic acid. Most bacteriophages have only a single molecule of DNA. Yet other viruses can have multiple molecules. For example, influenza (the virus that causes the "flu") has a genome on eight RNA molecules. Examples of RNA viruses include those that cause the common cold, measles, mumps, polio, and AIDS. Examples of diseases caused by DNA viruses include hepatitis B, chicken pox, and herpes infections.

 What is the arrangement of capsomeres in the influenza viruses?

Helical ●

16.2 Viruses require host cells for replication

As we discussed in Module 10.1, bacteria and viruses served as models in experiments that uncovered the molecular details of heredity. We'll now take a closer look at viruses, focusing on the relationship between viral structure and replication.

Viruses are parasites that can replicate (reproduce) only inside host cells. In fact, the host cell provides most of the components necessary for replicating, transcribing, and translating the viral nucleic acid. All types of cellular organisms, including bacteria, archaea, and all eukaryotes, can be infected by viruses. Viruses are classified on the basis of their hosts. For example, bacteriophages ("bacteria-eaters"), or **phages** for short, can infect only bacteria. Similarly, archaeal, fungal, plant, and animal viruses are restricted to their respective kingdoms. Within these broad groups, a single virus can infect only a limited number of host species, called its host range.

Host recognition is accomplished by molecular interactions between viral surface proteins and specific host cell surface molecules. This "lock-and-key" interaction is similar to the enzyme-substrate interactions we discussed in Module 5.13. Therefore, a virus can infect any cell with the appropriate surface molecule.

Some viruses have a wide host range. For example, the West Nile virus (WNV), which has made headlines in Canadian news, can infect mosquitoes, birds, horses, and humans, among others. Birds, including robins and crows, are the normal host for WNV. Female mosquitoes typically acquire the infection by feeding on the blood of infected birds such as crows.

The cycle continues when an infected mosquito bites a healthy bird. Infected mosquitoes can also pass on the infection to their offspring. Although an infected mosquito may pass WNV to a human or horse in its saliva during a bite, a mosquito cannot acquire WNV from biting an infected mammal. Because the transmission cycle stops, humans and horses are accidental, dead-end hosts. In birds and mammals, WNV can lead to fatal inflammation of the brain (encephalitis) or its protective covering (meningitis). In mild cases, people usually experience flu-like symptoms. Risk of developing serious health effects is higher among individuals with weaker immune systems: for example, older adults and people with chronic diseases. Information about WNV is regularly updated on the website of the Public Health Agency of Canada.

Other viruses have a narrow host range and can infect only a single species. Measles, for example, is caused by the measles virus, which can infect only humans. The measles virus is transmitted by direct contact or through the inhalation of aerosols (tiny droplets of water suspended in the air, often produced by coughs or sneezes). Symptoms include a blotchy red rash on the face, which progresses down the chest, drowsiness and irritability. Before the MMR (measles, mumps, and rubella) vaccine was introduced in 1963, there were an estimated 400 000 cases of measles every year in Canada. Today, vaccination efforts have nearly eliminated the measles virus and most cases are among individuals who are philosophically opposed to vaccination.

Viral infection can be further limited to specific tissues or organs within a single host. Rhinoviruses (from the Greek word *rhinos*, meaning "nose") are the most common cause of the common cold (see Module 16.11). Only the cells lining the upper respiratory tract (that is, the nasal cavity and back of the throat) are infected by rhinoviruses. The AIDS virus, HIV, can infect only certain types of white blood cells with a specific cell surface marker. T-lymphocytes are among the target cells and their destruction leads to the decreased immune function caused by HIV.

 Why are humans considered an accidental host for the West Nile virus?

● Infected humans cannot infect another host (mosquito or human) with the virus.

16.3 The viral replicative cycle

Regardless of viral structure, genome type, or host specificity, all viral replicative cycles involve the same essential processes **(Figure 16.3)**. Infection begins when ❶ a virus binds to and enters a host cell. Different viruses use different mechanisms of viral entry depending on their structure and host range (see Module 16.4). Regardless of the mode of entry, the virus must first commandeer the host cell if it is to replicate. Immediately after entry, certain viral genes called **early genes** are expressed. (Genes that are expressed later in the replicative cycle are called **late genes**.) Products of these early genes are typically regulatory proteins that seize control of the host cell nucleus. When in control of the nucleus, the virus has full control over the enzymes, ribosomes, and tRNAs required for replication, transcription, and translation of viral molecules. After the virus is in control, the host cell no longer makes its own proteins and focuses on the production of vast quantities of viral molecules, including ❷ genetic material and ❸ capsid proteins (late gene products). In addition to the machinery, the host also provides all the nucleic acids, amino acids, ATP, and any other components needed. The mechanism of nucleic acid replication depends on the type of genetic material and is the topic of Module 16.5.

Within the cytoplasm, newly synthesized viral nucleic acids and capsomeres spontaneously ❹ self-assemble into new viruses. The plans for constructing a complete virus are inherent in the three-dimensional shape of its parts. Scientists can reassemble complete tobacco mosaic viruses simply by recombining isolated RNA and capsomeres. The replicative cycle ends with ❺ the release of new viruses from the host cell. Although the figure shows only the assembly and release of three new viruses, the actual number is significantly more. In fact, hundreds or thousands of new viruses can be released from a single infected host cell. The simplest mechanism involves the rupture or lysis of the infected cell. Many animal viruses do not lyse the cell; instead, they bud off of the membrane and take a small fraction as a new envelope.

After viral release, each new virus can infect another cell within the same host, or, if conditions are right, be transmitted to a new host. Cellular destruction during the replicative cycle and the body's immune response produce most of the symptoms associated with viral infection.

After entry, some viruses may become dormant inside a host cell. For example, after a bout of replication and spread, herpesviruses can become quiescent and symptoms subside. While inside the nuclei of certain nerve cells, herpesvirus DNA may remain permanently dormant, without destroying these

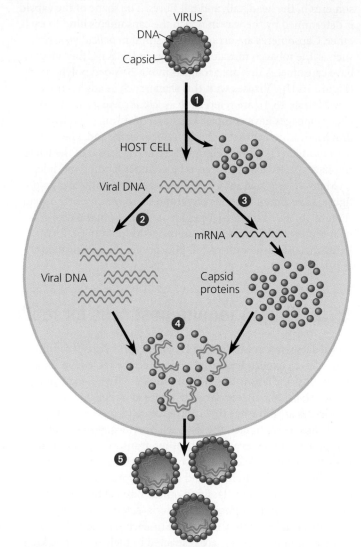

▲ **Figure 16.3** A simplified viral life cycle

cells. From time to time, physical stress, such as a cold or sunburn, or emotional stress may stimulate the herpesvirus DNA to begin production of the virus, which then infects cells at the body's surface and brings about cold sores or genital sores.

In the next few modules, we'll take a closer look at the variations in the replicative cycles of viruses that infect bacteria, plants, and animals.

 What is the primary role of the virus's early gene products?

● They take control of the host cell nucleus.

16.4 Viral entry is a crucial first step

Because a virus is biologically inert outside of a host cell, entry is a crucial step in its replicative cycle. As mentioned in the previous module, there are many mechanisms by which entry occurs. The type of host cell and the structure of the virus affect how this goal is accomplished. Cell walls are a physical barrier to infection, and viruses have evolved methods to circumvent them. In any case, receptors on the virus must interact with specific molecules on the target cell. Cells lacking the right molecules are immune to infection.

Bacteriophages The tail fibres of a bacteriophage bind to specific molecules on the surface of the bacterial cell wall or outer membrane. Once bound, the cell wall is a significant obstacle in preventing internalization of the capsid. But bacteriophages, including the T-even phages, have an entry mechanism that easily circumvents such an obstacle. The capsid functions like a microscopic hypodermic needle, injecting the nucleic acid into the bacterium **(Figure 16.4A)**. After the tail fibres have bound to a bacterium, the capsid's hollow tail sheath contracts and pushes through the cell wall. The nucleic acid travels through the tail sheath and enters the cytoplasm and the complex capsid remains outside of the cell.

Plant Viruses Plant viruses have a similar obstacle to entry into the cells of their hosts. However, instead of an active injection mechanism seen in the bacteriophages, plant viruses gain entry through passive methods. Breaches within the wall of a plant cell offer viruses an opportunity to enter. Many plant viruses exploit insects to transmit them from plant to plant. Chewing or piercing mouthparts of some insects damage plant cells and give some viruses a point of entry. For example, the cucumber mosaic virus is transmitted between squash plants when sap-sucking aphids pierce cells to feed. The cucumber mosaic virus promotes its transmission by stimulating an infected plant to produce odours that attract aphids. With more aphids feeding on the infected plant, the virus is more likely to be carried to new hosts.

Regardless of the mechanism of entry, plant viruses must spread within the host to ensure its transmission. For instance, if more plant tissue is infected, it will be more likely that an insect will bite into an infected region and pick up virus particles. Adjacent plant cells are joined by plasmodesmata, the cytoplasmic connections that penetrate the walls between adjacent plant cells (see Figure 4.21). These openings allow for the easy exchange of molecules between cells. Unfortunately for the plant, viruses also travel through these openings, allowing them to infect large portions of the plant's body. Some viruses can migrate to the developing seeds and infect the plant embryo growing inside. By infecting the embryos, viruses are transmitted vertically, from one generation to the next.

Animal Viruses Recall from Module 16.1, that animal viruses can be enveloped or naked. Each type has a different mechanism of entry. Naked animal viruses, including the adenoviruses, tend to employ passive mechanisms of entry, stimulating endocytosis by the host cell (see Module 5.8). Glycoproteins on the adenovirus capsid first bind to specific molecules on the animal cell membrane. Then the virus sinks into a coated pit and is internalized into a coated vesicle **(Figure 16.4B)**. Once inside, the virus must escape the confines of the vesicle before it can replicate. The internal environment of the vesicle gradually becomes more acidic. The lower pH disrupts the protein capsid and releases viral proteins that mediate the lysis of the vesicle membrane. By exploiting the natural endocytic process, adenovirus gains access to the host machinery it requires. Although the mechanisms of escape for adenovirus is well understood, how other naked viruses accomplish this remains elusive.

Enveloped viruses have little trouble infecting animal cells. The viral envelope, after all, is a piece of plasma membrane

▲ **Figure 16.4A** Bacteriophages inject nucleic acid into host cells

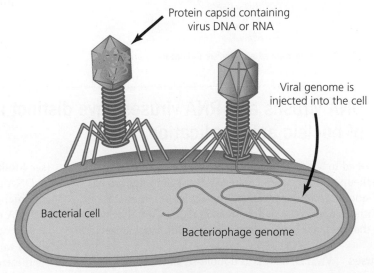

Protein capsid containing virus DNA or RNA

Viral genome is injected into the cell

Bacterial cell

Bacteriophage genome

Herpesviruses, paramyxoviruses, HIV

▲ **Figure 16.4C** Viral envelopes fuse with plasma membranes

▲ **Figure 16.4B** Endocytosis of adenovirus indicated by arrows

taken from a previous host cell. When viral proteins bind to surface molecules on the target cell, the two membranes are brought close together. As shown in **Figure 16.4C**, the juxtaposed membranes fuse with one another and the virus capsid enters the cytoplasm. HIV, the causative agent of AIDS, enters cells of an infected possessive patient's immune system in this manner. Enveloped viruses may also be internalized by the host cell through phagocytosis or, as in the case of the influenza viruses, receptor-mediated endocytosis. The influenza envelope fuses with the vesicle membrane to release the virus in the same way the HIV envelope fuses with the plasma membrane.

Very little is known about how fungal viruses gain entry into their host cells. But the mechanisms they employ would likely be similar to those used by plant viruses or bacteriophages. In the next module, we'll take a closer look at the steps that occur after a virus has entered the cell.

 How do plant viruses move from cell to cell? Why can't animal viruses do the same?

● Plant cells are joined by plasmodesmata, through which plant viruses can move. Animal cells do not have plasmodesmata, making this method of movement impossible.

16.5 DNA viruses and RNA viruses have distinct mechanisms of nucleic acid replication

As mentioned in Module 16.1, viruses have a wide diversity in the makeup of their genetic material. Viral genomes can be made of single- or double-stranded molecules of either DNA or RNA. With such diversity in genetic material, it should be no surprise that there is equal variety in replication mechanisms.

DNA Viruses Viral DNA that is double-stranded can replicate using the same enzymatic machinery as cellular DNA

(see Modules 10.4 and 10.5). Semiconservative replication by DNA polymerases generates multiple copies of the viral genome, which are ready to be assembled into new viruses.

DNA replication in ssDNA viruses requires an additional step compared to the replication of double-stranded DNA, which we discussed in Chapter 10. When DNA polymerase synthesizes a new daughter strand, it is complementary and not identical to the parent molecule. To make copies of the original parent ssDNA, the complementary daughter strand is used as a template. DNA polymerase uses this template strand to generate multiple copies of ssDNA that are identical to the original parent molecule.

RNA Viruses   All cells have polymerases, which they can use to make DNA or RNA from a DNA template. In animals, there are no cellular polymerases that can use RNA as a template. Therefore, animal RNA viruses must produce uniquely viral enzymes to replicate their genome, an RNA template. Plant RNA viruses do not face this problem as they can exploit the RNA-dependent RNA polymerases of their hosts.

Rotavirus, the most common cause of diarrheal disease in children, is a dsRNA virus. Symptoms include severe diarrhea (caused by the death of infected cells), nausea, vomiting, and fever. Infection with rotavirus is often colloquially called the stomach flu. The cells lining the intestinal track internalize this naked virus through endocytosis. As a result, rotavirus damages intestinal lining.

A virally encoded enzyme, **RNA replicase** (an RNA-dependent RNA polymerase), is packaged within the rotavirus particle and becomes functional immediately after entry. RNA replicase uses RNA as a template to produce a complementary strand of RNA. For clarity, the two complementary strands of RNA are identified as the plus-strand and minus-strand. Just as mRNA molecules are synthesized from only one strand of a DNA double helix, only the viral minus–RNA-strand encodes for proteins.

Once rotavirus has entered a host cell, ❶ the plus- and minus-strands of the dsRNA are separated as shown in **Figure 16.5A**. Both are used as templates by RNA replicase. ❷ RNA replicase makes several copies of the minus-strand by using the plus-strand as a template. The newly synthesized minus-strands are ❸ translated by host ribosomes to produce viral proteins. These minus-strands will not be used in the assembly of new viruses. ❹ Using the minus-strand as a template, RNA replicase makes multiple copies of the plus-strand. In a second step, ❺ the same enzyme uses these plus-strands to synthesize multiple dsRNA molecules to be ❻ packaged into new viruses.

The devastating disease AIDS is caused by HIV, an ssRNA virus with some special properties. In outward appearance, HIV resembles the flu or mumps virus **(Figure 16.5B)**. Its membranous envelope and glycoprotein spikes enable HIV to enter and leave a host cell much the way the mumps virus does (see Figure 16.4C). Notice, however, that HIV contains two identical copies of its ssRNA instead of one. HIV also has a different mode of replication. HIV carries molecules of a viral enzyme called **reverse transcriptase**, which catalyzes reverse transcription, the synthesis of DNA on an RNA template. This unusual process, which is opposite the usual DNA to RNA flow of genetic information, characterizes **retroviruses** (*retro* means "backward").

Figure 16.5C illustrates what happens after HIV RNA is uncoated in the cytoplasm of a host cell. ❶ Reverse transcriptase uses the RNA as a template to make a DNA strand and then ❷ adds a second, complementary DNA strand. ❸ The resulting viral dsDNA enters the cell's nucleus and inserts itself into

▲ **Figure 16.5A** dsRNA virus replication

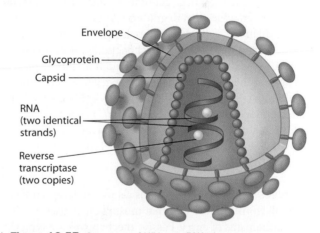

▲ **Figure 16.5B** Structure of HIV, a ssRNA virus

▲ **Figure 16.5C** The behaviour of HIV nucleic acid in a host cell

the chromosomal DNA, becoming a provirus. The host's RNA polymerase ❹ transcribes the proviral DNA into RNA, which can then be ❺ translated by ribosomes into viral proteins. ❻ New viruses assembled from these components leave the cell and can infect other cells.

HIV infects and kills white blood cells that play important roles in the body's immune system. The loss of such cells causes the body to become immunocompromised and

susceptible to other infections that it would normally be able to fight off. Such secondary infections cause the syndrome (a collection of symptoms) that can kill an AIDS patient.

 In which organelles can DNA viruses replicate? Explain your answer.

● DNA viruses must replicate in the nucleus, mitochondria, or chloroplasts because DNA polymerases can be found only in these organelles.

16.6 Viral transmission requires the release from the host cell

Within an infected host cell, the viral genome is replicated and structural proteins are produced. Assembly occurs spontaneously as capsid proteins aggregate and surround the genetic material. Release from the host cell is the final step in the viral replicative cycle. As you might expect, viral mechanisms to exit a cell are as diverse as those used to enter cells. Once released, the viruses can infect other cells or be transmitted to other organisms.

Bacteriophages The bacterial cell wall is an obstacle for bacteriophage release, just as it was for entry. However, bacteriophages have adapted tools to breach such a formidable barrier. Encoded in the bacteriophage genome is a gene for a **lysozyme**. Lysozymes are enzymes that degrade bacterial peptidoglycan, destroying their cell wall. Many animals produce an analogous enzyme to defend themselves against bacterial infection (see Module 34.1). As the cell wall is weakened, it no longer protects the cell against the osmotic uptake of water. The cell ultimately swells and bursts, releasing 100 to 200 phages **(Figure 16.6A)**.

Bacteriophages that infect *Mycobacterium* species, bacteria without a cell wall, do not need lysozyme and typically escape using a mechanism similar to enveloped animal viruses (see the facing page).

Plant Viruses The plant cell wall is also a barrier to viral release. Recall from Module 16.4 that most plant viruses employ passive mechanisms of entry. Passive mechanisms are typically used for viral release as well. Mechanical transmission from one host to another is required. Animals brushing against an infected plant may pick up some viral particle on their skin. By chance, these viruses may be rubbed onto a healthy plant and enter through a damaged cell.

Insect vectors (vehicles of disease transmission) are an effective means of plant virus transmission. You read in Module 16.4 that insects can introduce viruses while feeding on a plant. But before an insect can transmit a virus, it must first collect virus particles by feeding on an infected plant. Insects can harbour plant viruses externally for hours or for weeks internally. (Plant viruses that are harboured internally are typically nonreplicative.) The cauliflower mosaic virus is an external passenger of an aphid vector. Capsid proteins recognize and bind to specific molecules on the cuticle of the aphid's mouthparts. When the aphid feeds, some virus particles are released into the fluids of a healthy plant.

Luteovirus, which is transmitted internally by aphids, infects a wide range of host plants. This mode of transmission is much more complex than externally harboured viruses. To be

▲ **Figure 16.6A** Bacteriophage release from a bacterium

successful, the virus must persist within the tissues of the vector without triggering an immune response. Inside of the vector, virus particles penetrate the intestinal wall and travel to the salivary glands. When the aphid takes another meal, viruses are released in the saliva. Regardless of where the viruses are carried by the insect vector, the end result is the same, the passive infection of a new plant host.

Animal Viruses The mechanism of release differs between naked and enveloped animal viruses. On the one hand, naked animal viruses exit their host cell by exploiting the host immune system. As you will learn in Chapter 34, the host immune system has several mechanisms to kill virus-infected cells. Activated immune cells create pores in the plasma membrane of infected target cells. This allows water to enter the target cell, causing it to burst. This tactic works if the target cell is destroyed before viral assembly is complete. Assembly cannot occur outside of the cytoplasm. However, if assembly is complete, lysis of the target cell releases thousands of new viruses.

Enveloped viruses, on the other hand, do not require lysis of the host cell to escape. Instead, these viruses escape by budding off of the host cell. An infected host cell can release new viruses continually, or at least until it is destroyed by the host immune system. **Figure 16.6B** shows an HIV virus budding off of an infected host cell. Prior to release, viral molecules are inserted into the plasma membrane at the site of budding. The molecules within the envelope (discussed in Module 16.4) include those used for host recognition.

? **How is viral release similar between bacteriophages and naked animal viruses?**

● Both types of viruses typically require the lysis of the host cell.

1 The envelope glycoproteins enable the virus to bind to specific receptors on certain white blood cells.

Glycoprotein | Viral envelope

Capsid

RNA (two identical strands)

Reverse transcriptase

HIV

HIV

Membrane of white blood cell

Cytoplasm

0.25 μm

HIV entering a cell

New HIV leaving a cell

2 The virus fuses with the cell's plasma membrane. The capsid proteins are removed, releasing the viral proteins and RNA.

3 Reverse transcriptase catalyzes the synthesis of a DNA strand complementary to the viral RNA.

4 Reverse transcriptase catalyzes the synthesis of a second DNA strand complementary to the first.

5 The double-stranded DNA is incorporated as a provirus into the cell's DNA.

6 Proviral genes are transcribed into RNA molecules, which serve as genomes for the next viral generation and as mRNAs for translation into viral protein.

7 The viral proteins include capsid proteins and reverse transcriptase (made in the cytosol) and envelope glycoproteins (made in the ER).

8 Vesicles transport the glycoproteins to the cell's plasma membrane.

9 Capsids are assembled around viral genomes and reverse transcriptase molecules.

10 New viruses bud off from the host cell.

HOST CELL

Reverse transcriptase

Viral RNA

RNA-DNA hybrid

DNA

NUCLEUS

Provirus

Chromosomal DNA

RNA genome for the next viral generation

mRNA

▲ **Figure 16.6B** HIV virus leaving a cell

Viral Infections

16.7 Some bacteriophages have two types of replicative cycles

Figure 16.7A outlines our current understanding—as originally outlined by Hershey and Chase (see Module 10.1)—of the replication cycle of the T-even phage, T2. After the virus ❶ attaches to the host bacterial cell, it ❷ injects its DNA into the host. Notice that virtually all the viral protein (yellow) is left outside. Once injected, the viral DNA causes the bacterial cells to ❸ produce new phage proteins and DNA molecules—indeed, complete new phages—which soon ❹ cause the cell to lyse, releasing the newly produced phages. This sort of cycle is called a **lytic cycle** because it results in the lysis (breaking open) of the host cell and the release of the viruses that were produced within the cell. Some phages can also replicate by an alternative route called the lysogenic cycle. During a lysogenic cycle, viral DNA replication occurs without destroying the host cell.

In **Figure 16.7B**, you see the two kinds of cycles for a phage called lambda that infects the bacteria *Escherichia coli*. Both cycles begin when the phage DNA ❶ enters the bacterium and ❷ forms a circle. The DNA then embarks on one of the two pathways. In the lytic cycle described above (left in the figure), ❸ lambda's DNA immediately turns the cell into a virus-producing factory, and ❹ the cell soon lyses and releases its viral products.

❶ A phage attaches itself to a bacterial cell.

❷ The phage injects its DNA into the bacterium.

❸ The phage DNA directs the host cell to make more phage DNA and proteins; new phages assemble.

❹ The cell lyses and releases the new phages.

▲ **Figure 16.7A** A T-even phage replicative cycle

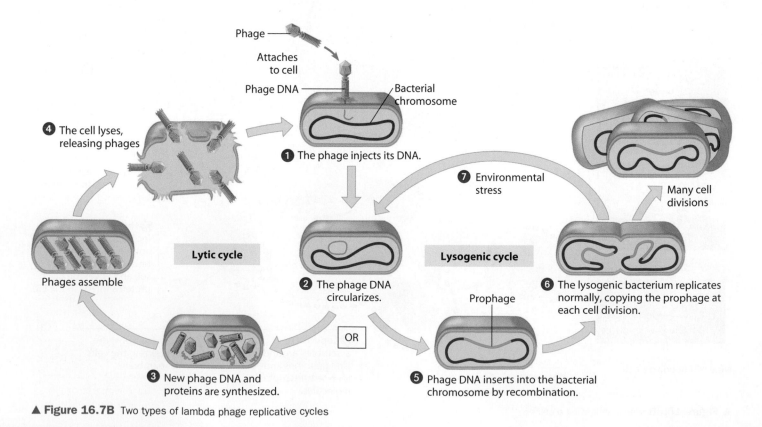

Phage

Attaches to cell

Phage DNA

Bacterial chromosome

❶ The phage injects its DNA.

❼ Environmental stress

Many cell divisions

Lytic cycle

Lysogenic cycle

❹ The cell lyses, releasing phages

Phages assemble

❷ The phage DNA circularizes.

OR

Prophage

❻ The lysogenic bacterium replicates normally, copying the prophage at each cell division.

❸ New phage DNA and proteins are synthesized.

❺ Phage DNA inserts into the bacterial chromosome by recombination.

▲ **Figure 16.7B** Two types of lambda phage replicative cycles

In the **lysogenic cycle**, however, viral DNA is inserted by genetic recombination into the bacterial chromosome. Once inserted, the phage DNA is referred to as a **prophage** (analogous to a provirus), and most of its genes are inactive. ❻ Every time the *E. coli* cell prepares to divide, it replicates the phage DNA along with its own chromosome and passes on the copies to daughter cells. A single infected cell can thereby quickly give rise to a large population of bacterial cells that all carry prophage. The lysogenic cycle enables viruses to spread without killing the host cells on which they depend. The prophages may remain in the bacterial cells indefinitely. ❼ Occasionally, however, an environmental signal—typically, one that indicates an unfavourable turn in the environment, such as an increase in radiation, drought, or certain toxic chemicals—triggers a switchover from the lysogenic cycle to the lytic cycle. This so-called genetic switch causes the viral DNA to be excised from the bacterial chromosome, eventually leading to death of the

host cell as the lytic cycle resumes. If a prophage fails to excise under these conditions, it will be unable to replicate and die along with the bacterium.

Sometimes, the few prophage genes active in a lysogenic bacterium can cause medical problems. For example, the bacteria that cause diphtheria, botulism, and scarlet fever would be harmless to humans if it were not for the prophage genes they carry. Bacteria produce the toxins responsible for making people ill only when they express these prophage genes. In the next modules, we will explore viruses that infect plants and animals.

? **Describe one way a virus can perpetuate its genes without destroying its host cell. What is this type of replication cycle called?**

● Some viruses can insert their DNA into a chromosome of the host cell, which replicates the proviral genes when it replicates its own DNA prior to cell division. This is called the lysogenic cycle.

16.8 Plant viruses can have a serious impact on agriculture

Viruses that infect plants can stunt plant growth and diminish crop yields. Most known plant viruses are RNA viruses. To infect a plant, a virus must first get past the plant's outer protective layer of cells (the epidermis). Once a virus enters a plant cell and begins replicating, it can spread throughout the entire plant through plasmodesmata.

Most plant viruses are named and classified based on the plants they infect and the symptoms of the diseases that they cause. For instance, the tobacco mosaic virus (the first virus that was identified) causes focal lesions that give a spotty or mottled appearance to the leaves of tobacco plants. And the tomato bushy stunt virus causes tomato plants to grow short and branch excessively.

Viral infections can be problematic for many crops. Several Canadian crops are at risk of viral infection. For example, grapevine leafroll-associated virus (GLRaV) is the most common viral disease of grapevines worldwide. GLRaV has been found in nearly 12% of grapevines in both Ontario and British Columbia and has significant impacts on vine health and grape quality. Infection causes a thickening and curling of the leaves, as well as a loss of chlorophyll, giving the leaves a red (red grape varieties) or yellow (white grape varieties) colour **(Figure 16.8A)**. The corresponding reduction in photosynthesis impairs plant growth and fruit development. Crop yield may be reduced as much as 70%. The fruit that are produced are lower in sugar content (by 25% to 50%), have a higher acidity, and have a poor colour. Ultimately, wine quality is also negatively affected by poor fruit quality.

Transmission of GLRaV can occur over long distances through the propagation of infected plants, by planting infected cuttings or seeds, when replacing vines or establishing a new vineyard. Mealybugs and scale bugs have been shown to transmit infection in a laboratory setting. The common mealybug (*Pseudococcus maritimus*) is a known vector for GLRaV in California. The common mealybug is found in the

▲ **Figure 16.8A** Symptoms of grapevine leafroll-associated virus infection

grape-producing Okanagan Valley, but whether or not it can infect new plants on Canadian vineyards is unknown.

Another plant virus has been problematic for Canadian potato farmers. Potato virus Y (PVY) is a mosaic virus, which can seriously affect potato crops. Symptoms include the mottled leaves typical of the mosaic viruses. This appearance is accompanied by the dropping of leaves and rings of dead tissue can develop on tubers with more powerful strains **(Figure 16.8B)**. The more virulent strains can cause entire crop yields to be lost.

Winged aphids are the primary transmission vectors for PVY. As aphids move from plant to plant, they can quickly spread the infection across an entire field. Because transmission is so rapid, the use of insecticides offers little protection against PVY. Mineral oil sprays can reduce but not prevent the spread by aphids. Seed potatoes can also harbour the virus and grow into infected plants. The best control strategy is to use seed potatoes that are certified PVY-free. An outbreak of PVY in New Brunswick in 1989 was traced to seed potatoes grown in Prince Edward Island. Testing by Agriculture Canada,

▲ **Figure 16.8B** Effects of potato virus Y

which was responsible at the time, did not identify the virus until 1990, after the seed had been planted. The Canadian government established a quarantine zone in both provinces that prevented selling potato crops on domestic and foreign markets. Farmers suffered significant losses. Later, Agriculture Canada agreed to pay out more than $15 million in compensation to the Maritime farmers affected by the government's mistake. The outbreak of PVY led to the formation of the

CFIA in 1997, which took over the responsibility of testing from Agriculture Canada.

 Why is the transmission rate for plant viruses potentially high in an agricultural setting?

● Viruses can quickly spread by physical contact or by feeding insects moving within the dense population of plants.

16.9 Some animal viruses cause serious disease

Most infections by animal viruses are asymptomatic and do not cause significant disease in healthy hosts. For example, cytomegalovirus (CMV) infection typically produces no symptoms and goes unnoticed in most people. Other viruses are even beneficial to their host. The development of most mammals involves the formation of a placenta, an interface between the mother and developing embryo (see Module 30.15). For many mammals, proper placenta development requires a protein called syncytin. Interestingly, syncytin is not made from a human gene but rather one belonging to a provirus. This viral protein causes cells of the placenta to fuse, forming a syncytium (pale yellow in Figures 30.15D and 30.15E). Failure to produce this viral protein prevents proper placental formation and abortion of the embryo.

Viruses that do cause serious disease symptoms in their host can do so through a number of mechanisms. Typically, there is a period of time after initial infection before symptoms manifest. The inoculation dose is variable, but usually

small. With only a few infected cells, the host usually does not exhibit any symptoms. The few viruses that initiate an infection require time to replicate and infect more host cells. For viruses that require the host immune system to release them from the cells, this can take as long as two weeks. As more host cells become infected and damaged, symptoms become noticeable. However, some viruses may lie dormant for years before initiating disease. Recently, a number of baby boomers have developed liver disease caused by the hepatitis C virus, which they acquired much earlier in life. Sources of infection include experimenting with needle drugs or in some cases, contaminated blood transfusions. (The Canadian blood supply was not tested for hepatitis C until the 1980s.) In many of these people, the virus is now causing liver failure after remaining dormant for decades.

Symptoms can arise from the death of infected cells. The amount of damage a virus causes our body depends partly on how quickly our immune system responds to fight the infection and partly on the ability of the infected tissue to repair itself. We usually recover completely from rotavirus because our intestinal tract tissue can efficiently replace damaged cells by mitosis. In contrast, the poliovirus attacks nerve cells, which are not usually replaceable. The damage to such cells, unfortunately, is permanent. In such cases, we try to prevent the disease with vaccines (see Module 34.4).

Toxic molecules produced by certain viruses can also cause symptoms. Rotavirus, for example, produces a toxin that triggers the vomiting centre of the brain. Another rotavirus toxin stimulates secretion in the intestinal tract. Excess secretion increases the water content of the feces, exacerbating the diarrheal symptoms.

Other viruses cause disease by transforming healthy cells into cancerous tumour cells. Most cancer-causing viruses cause acute, short-lasting symptoms, but the virus persists after symptoms have cleared. For example, human papillomavirus (HPV) is the most common sexually transmitted infection (STI, formerly referred to as a sexually transmitted disease or STD) in Canada and can be detected during routine Pap smears **(Figure 16.9)**. An estimated 75% of sexually active adults will have at least one HPV infection in their lives. More than 100 types of HPV have been identified, of which a few are known to cause genital warts or cervical cancer. Two HPV early genes interfere with proteins that regulate the cell cycle and stimulate mitosis and tumour development. Genes that cause cancer are called **oncogenes**. HPV's oncogenes allow nondividing cells in the G_0 phase to re-enter the cell cycle and resume division in an uncontrolled manner (see Module 8.8).

Currently, two vaccines against HPV, which can prevent infection and therefore cervical cancer, are approved for use in Canada. In 2006, the National Advisory Committee on Immunization recommended vaccination for all girls

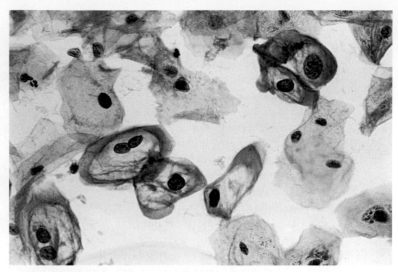

▲ **Figure 16.9** HPV causes a halo around the nucleus

between 9 and 26 years. In 2012, vaccination recommendations were extended to boys of the same age. This decision was made because both genders contribute to the spread of HPV through sexual contact.

Many viral infections are difficult to treat, as these molecular organisms do not respond to antibiotics. Many infections must simply run their course. The prevention of infection through vaccination remains our best defence against viruses. Scientists are working diligently to develop new vaccines against some of the new emerging viruses, the topic of the next module.

 What is one way that viral oncogenes cause cancer?

● Oncogene products can affect the regulation of the cell cycle and cause uncontrolled division in affected cells.

16.10 Emerging viruses threaten human health

Viruses that appear suddenly or are new to medical scientists are called **emerging viruses**. There are many familiar examples. HIV, the AIDS virus, is a classic example: This virus appeared in New York and California in the early 1980s, seemingly out of nowhere. The deadly Ebola virus, recognized initially in 1976 in central Africa, is one of several emerging viruses that cause hemorrhagic fever, an often fatal illness characterized by fever, vomiting, massive bleeding, and circulatory system collapse. A number of other dangerous new viruses cause encephalitis, an inflammation of the brain. One example is the West Nile virus, which appeared for the first time in North America in 1999 and has since spread to all Canadian provinces. Severe acute respiratory syndrome (SARS) first appeared in China in 2002. Within eight months, the virus had spread globally, infecting about 8000 people (more than 400 in Canada), of whom some 10% died. Researchers quickly identified the infectious agent as a previously unknown, single-stranded RNA coronavirus, so named for its crownlike "corona" of spikes. In 2003, scientists at the Michael Smith Genome Sciences Centre at the University of British Columbia were the first in the world to sequence the genome of the SARS virus.

From where and how do such viruses burst on the human scene, giving rise to rare or previously unknown diseases? Three processes contribute to the emergence of viral diseases: mutation, contact between species, and spread from isolated populations.

The mutation of existing viruses is a major source of new viral diseases. RNA viruses tend to have unusually high rates of mutation because errors in replicating their RNA genomes are not subject to the kind of proofreading and repair mechanisms that help to reduce errors in DNA replication. Some mutations enable existing viruses to evolve into new strains (genetic varieties) that can cause disease in individuals who have developed immunity to ancestral strains. That is why we need yearly flu vaccines: Mutations create new influenza virus strains to which previously vaccinated people have no immunity (see Module 34.5).

New viral diseases often arise from the spread of existing viruses from one host species to another. Scientists estimate that about three-quarters of new human diseases have originated in other animals. For example, in 1997, at least 18 people in Hong Kong were infected with a strain of flu virus called H5N1, which was previously seen only in birds. A mass culling of all of Hong Kong's 1.5 million domestic birds appeared to stop that outbreak. Beginning in 2002, however, new cases of human infection by this bird strain began to crop up around Southeast Asia. As of 2009, the disease caused by this virus, now called avian flu, has killed more than 250 people, and more than 100 million birds have either died from the disease or been killed to prevent the spread of infection.

In January of 2014, the first documented case of avian flu in North America claimed the life of a young Alberta woman after she returned from a trip to Beijing. To date, all instances of H5N1 infection in humans have been linked to contact with infected birds and human-to-human transmission has not yet been observed. While in China, however, this woman reportedly had no contact with poultry. Scientists remain puzzled as to how she acquired the infection.

In 2009, scientists in Mexico became aware of a rapidly spreading new strain of flu called H1N1 **(Figure 16.10)**. This particular virus evolved through genetic reshuffling of multiple flu viruses, including some that infect humans, birds, and pigs (hence the name *swine flu*, even though humans cannot contract the virus directly from pigs). A vaccine against the 2009 H1N1 was rushed into production and became available in the fall of that year. This reshuffling can result in new strains of viruses, which are able to infect new host species.

The spread of a viral disease from a small, isolated human population can also lead to widespread epidemics. For instance, AIDS went unnamed and virtually unnoticed for decades before it began to spread around the world. In this case, technological and social factors—including affordable international travel, blood transfusions, sexual promiscuity, and the abuse of intravenous drugs—allowed a previously rare human disease to become a global scourge. If we ever do manage to control HIV and other emerging viruses, that

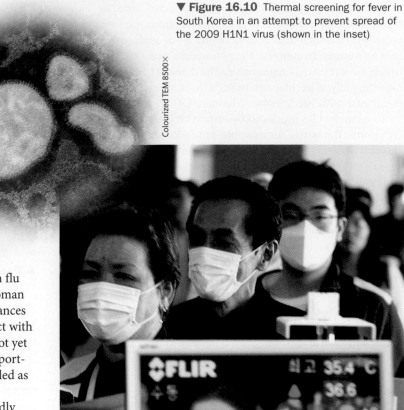

▼ **Figure 16.10** Thermal screening for fever in South Korea in an attempt to prevent spread of the 2009 H1N1 virus (shown in the inset)

Colourized TEM 8500×

success will likely follow from our understanding of molecular biology.

? Why are emerging viruses considered a greater threat than those we know about?

● Emerging viruses can spread quickly, giving scientists a very short amount of time to develop and test vaccines.

16.11 Can you catch a cold from going outside in the cold?

Spring in Canada is usually welcomed with the shedding of toques and winter coats and venturing outside. If you have ever gone outside in the spring with wet hair or no jacket, you have probably had at least one person say to you, "you'll catch your death of cold!"

What does it mean to "catch a cold"? The common cold has multiple causes, the most common cause being the rhinoviruses. Rhinoviruses are a group of naked ssRNA viruses that infect the cells lining the upper respiratory tract shown

in **Figure 16.11**. Infection occurs when aerosolized (meaning "within small droplets of water") viruses are inhaled and make contact with the lining of the upper respiratory tract. Symptoms such as cough, runny nose, and fever arise from the defensive secretion of mucus and cell damage caused by viral release.

The rumour that you can catch a cold simply by going outside in cold temperatures has been a common belief for more than a century. It can be traced back to the father of

▲ **Figure 16.11** Rhinovirus infects the upper respiratory tract

microbiology, Louis Pasteur. In 1878, Pasteur observed that chickens were immune to anthrax. He predicted that immunity was due to the high body temperature (approximately 41°C) of the chickens. To test this hypothesis, he exposed two groups of chickens to *Bacillus anthracis*, the bacterium that causes anthrax. One group of chickens was chilled in a basin of cool water to lower their body temperature while the other group served as the unmanipulated control. Chickens that were chilled were no longer immune and developed anthrax. The results of this experiment have been misinterpreted and twisted by many to start this rumour. Other experiments using chilled animals showed that they were more susceptible to a wide variety of illnesses than animals in a warm control group. These results added momentum to the rumour.

Experiments were performed in the 1950s on chilled human volunteers at the Common Cold Research Unit in Salisbury, England. After being experimentally administered infected mucus from an ill person, subjects bathed and wandered the chilly damp halls in wet socks and bathing suits. These subjects, as cold and miserable as they were, were no more likely to develop a cold than those in the warm control group. Rhinovirus and its role as the most common cause of the common cold were discovered in 1968. With this new information, human experiments were repeated. This time, subjects were inoculated with purified rhinovirus. The results were the same: Chilled patients had the same odds of developing a cold as warm subjects.

Why do other animals get sick when chilled but people don't? When animals become chilled, their immune system becomes suppressed. In this state, they are less able to fight off invading pathogens and become sick more easily. However,

chilling has the opposite effect on humans. Dr. Pang Shek at the University of Toronto has shown that exposure to cold actually stimulates the immune system of human subjects. And this boost may actually help to prevent illness.

Despite the multiple studies unequivocally disproving the rumour that going out in cold weather will give you a cold, this misconception still exists. A 2003 survey found that 40% of parents still believed that underdressing in cold weather was an important risk factor for catching a cold. More than half believed there is a causative role for going outside with wet hair. After all, the frequency of colds does increase in the winter months. There are two possible reasons for this trend; neither of which involves the chilly weather. In the cold, short days of winter, people are more likely to huddle indoors, in their homes, or at shopping malls and schools. As we congregate, we increase our exposure to others who may be infected, increasing our risk of catching the virus. Recent studies have shown that vitamin D deficiency may also increase our risk of infection. Staying indoors, we are exposed to less sunlight and UV radiation, which is required for vitamin D synthesis in the skin.

The next time someone warns you about catching a cold if you have damp hair or no jacket, you can tell them that your risk is no greater than theirs. However, you can reduce your risk with routine exercise and by taking supplements containing vitamin D.

 ? Why do the rhinoviruses infect only the cells lining the upper respiratory tract?

● The specific molecules that they recognize and bind to are expressed only on these cells.

16.12 How did viruses originate?

Determining the origins of viruses is an extraordinarily difficult task and we may never have a definitive answer. Viruses are not preserved in the fossil record, so scientists can study only present-day viruses. However, some information about viruses has been preserved within the genetic record of eukaryotes in the form of proviruses. Tracing evolutionary history is also made difficult by the fact that viruses can inherit genes horizontally from other viruses as well as their hosts. Although viruses share reproductive strategies and have common characteristics, they are not a monophyletic group (refer to Chapter 15). And the different lineages undoubtedly have different evolutionary origins.

There are three major hypotheses about the origins of viruses, and each may be true for some viruses. The *reduction* or *regressive hypothesis* suggests that viruses originated as parasitic cellular organisms. Through natural selection, genes that were unnecessary to complete their life cycle were lost. Some pathogenic bacteria such as *Chlamydia* and *Rickettsia* can reproduce only inside of a host cell. These bacteria must acquire certain amino acids, nucleosides, as well as ATP from their host cells in order to reproduce. Given their intracellular environment and supply of macromolecules and chemical energy, synthetic pathways become redundant and may be lost. If an ancestral cell lost other redundant components, including its membrane and cell wall, or enzymes such as nucleic acid polymerases and ribosomes, it may have eventually been reduced to a virus.

Other viruses may have evolved from pieces of nucleic acid that escaped from a cell. The plasmids found in many bacteria encode genes and can replicate autonomously from the host cell (see Module 17.8). Plasmids can be transferred from one cell to another during bacterial conjugation. Within the genome of bacteria and eukaryotes, genetic elements called **transposable elements** can jump from location to location (see Module 12.18). These transposable elements can be moved or copied to a different location on the same chromosome or another chromosome altogether. The *escape* or *cellular origin*

hypothesis speculates that similar mobile genetic elements became encapsulated by self-encoded proteins, escaped from the original cell, and became the ancestors of some viruses.

Both the reduction and escape hypothesis assume that cells evolved first. A logical approach, as viruses are obligate intracellular pathogens. However, the *co-evolution* or *virus-first hypothesis* suggests the opposite. According to this hypothesis, viruses evolved from the primordial gene pool, alongside evolving cells. Ancestral viruses would have been dependent on ancestral cells, having a similar relationship to that which modern viruses have with cells today. Most biologists agree that the first genetic material was RNA and that RNA could replicate without cells. It is possible that single-stranded RNA viruses are the descendants of the initial genetic material.

Each of these hypotheses may explain the origins of only a fraction of viruses. And they all have some inexplicable drawbacks, yet they are currently the best explanations available. As mentioned earlier, we may never have a clear understanding of how viruses evolved. Regardless of their evolutionary history, the existence of viruses has greatly affected the evolution of life on this planet. Horizontal DNA transfer can provide organisms with a source of novel genes and gene products (see Module 15.18). Viruses may also have been involved in the evolution of eukaryotic cells. Some biologists believe that the nucleus evolved after a virus infected an ancestral prokaryote. This mechanism is analogous to the evolution of mitochondria and chloroplasts as described by endosymbiosis (see Module 4.15).

 In terms of viral origin, in what way is the co-evolution hypothesis different from the reduction or escape hypotheses?

● The reduction and escape hypotheses both imply that cells existed before viruses and the co-evolution hypothesis suggests that viruses and cells evolved at the same time.

Other Infectious Acellular Particles

16.13 Viroids are infectious RNA molecules

Viruses may be small and simple, but they dwarf another class of pathogens: **viroids**. Viroids are small, circular, single-stranded RNA molecules that infect plants. No known viroids infect animals. Unlike the nucleic acid of a virus, viroids are not encased in a capsid coat and do not encode proteins. By convention, the RNA strand of a viroid is considered the sense (+) strand (+RNA), despite the fact that no proteins are encoded.

Similar to a virus, a viroid replicates inside host cells by using cellular enzymes. Some viroids enter the chloroplasts and use the organelle's enzymes to replicate. One mechanism of viroid replication is shown in **Figure 16.13A**. ❶ A template

(–) RNA strand is created using host RNA polymerase. ❷ The template strand is copied repeatedly, producing a long, linear molecule of repeating +RNA. ❸ Ribozymes, catalytic RNA molecules, separate the individual copies of +RNA, which ❹ recircularize to produce new viroids.

Viroids are transmitted passively and mechanically, similar to the transmission of plant viruses. Contact between plants can spread the infection directly. In agriculture, pruning tools and farm equipment can easily spread viroids from one plant to another. Insects can also act as a vector for transmission. Once a plant becomes infected, viroids can move through plasmodesmata and infect neighbouring cells. Before long, the

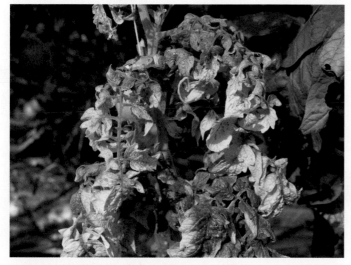

Infectious viroid RNA
(+RNA)

4 Recircularization

+RNA

1 RNA polymerase makes a template strand
(−RNA)

−RNA

3 Cleavage by ribozyme

+RNA

+RNA

−RNA

2 Synthesis of positive strand
(+RNA)

▲ **Figure 16.13A** Viroid replication

▲ **Figure 16.13B** Tomatoes infected with TCDVd

entire plant body can contain viroid RNA. Some viroids can even move into developing seeds and be transmitted vertically to the next generation.

Typical symptoms of a viroid infection may include reduced and malformed growth of plant structures, reduced fruit yield, and spotty discolorations of the leaves and stems. Exactly how a viroid causes disease symptoms in a plant remains poorly understood. Without the production of proteins, the RNA of the viroid itself must have some effects on the host cell. It is probable that symptoms arise from the silencing of specific genes through a mechanism similar to RNA interference (see Module 11.6). Occasionally, host enzymes that cleave double-stranded RNA, a defence against some viruses, generate short viroid RNA sequences. These sequences may function like miRNA, binding to a complementary host cell mRNA molecule and inhibiting its translation. Unfortunately, which proteins in the host are affected remains a mystery.

The potato spindle tuber viroid (PSTVd) became common in eastern Canada after its first appearance in 1930. Infection causes leaves to become chlorotic (yellowed) and shrivelled, slowing growth. The tubers of PSTVd-infected plants are spindle-shaped, small and narrow, giving the viroid its name. During the 1950s, PSTVd became widespread in New Brunswick after infected seed potatoes were planted in large numbers. Improved seed regulations were put in place in the 1970s. All seed stocks were tested for the viroid and any positive stocks were destroyed. Viroid-free "elite" seed stocks have been propagated from disease-free plants or tubers and meticulously maintained. Zero tolerance for PSTVd in seed stocks ensured crops would be healthy. Unlike potato virus Y (see Module 16.8), PSTVd has been successfully eradicated from Canada. Similar success stories can be told about the eradication of tomato chlorotic dwarf viroid **(Figure 16.13B)** from Canadian greenhouses.

? How are viroids different from viruses?

● Viroids are small RNA molecules that are not coated with a capsid.

16.14 Prions are infectious protein molecules

An important lesson to learn from viroids (RNA) is that a single molecule can be an infectious agent. Even more surprising are infectious proteins called **prions**, which cause a number of degenerative brain diseases in various animal species. While viroids are known to infect only plants, prions infect only animals. In addition to chronic wasting disease in deer and elk (see the chapter-opening essay), prion diseases include scrapie in sheep and goats, mad cow disease (formally called bovine spongiform encephalopathy, or BSE), and Creutzfeldt-Jakob disease (CJD) in humans. The same prion protein can cause scrapie, BSE, and CJD, but not chronic wasting disease.

A prion is thought to be a misfolded form of a protein normally present in brain cells. When the prion enters a cell containing the normal form of protein, the prion somehow converts the normal protein molecules to the misfolded prion versions **(Figure 16.14)**. The abnormal proteins clump together and crystalize, which may cause damage to brain tissue (although how this occurs is the subject of much debate and ongoing research). To date, there is no cure for prion diseases, and the only hope for developing effective treatments lies in understanding and preventing the process of infection.

▲ **Figure 16.14** A normal protein (left) and a misfolded prion protein (right)

Two forms of CJD can afflict humans. Variant CJD, or vCJD, which we discussed in the chapter-opening essay, is caused from the ingestion of meat from BSE-infected cattle. The cattle were believed to have contracted the prion from being fed scrapie-infected sheep by-products that were improperly processed. Classical CJD is a similar disease but is not associated with the ingestion of prion proteins. Instead, classical CJD develops spontaneously. CJD is exceedingly rare, with approximately 30 cases per year in Canada.

Classical CJD is typically diagnosed between the ages of 45 and 70 and progresses rapidly. Initial symptoms include a loss of coordination, mood swings, and depression. As damage accumulates within the brain, aphasia (impaired language ability), dementia (mental deterioration), and death occur as quickly as six months after diagnosis. In comparison, vCJD usually affects individuals earlier in life, at around age 30. Recently diagnosed patients have a life expectancy of approximately one year. Early stages of vCJD are similar to the classical form but are often accompanied by aggression and other behavioural changes.

After the discovery of three cases of BSE in 2003, many countries closed their borders to Canadian beef. Many borders were reopened after two to four years, but others still remain closed. The financial losses for the beef industry during this period were estimated at more than $4 billion. Today, the beef industry is closely monitored for signs of BSE. A handful of cases have been reported since 2003, but the CFIA ensured that no parts of the infected animals entered the food supply.

Kuru, another human prion disease, was discovered among the Fore tribe of Papua New Guinea in 1953. The name *kuru* is derived from the Fore word meaning "shake," as tremors occur in nearly all sufferers. Kuru is transmitted in a similar fashion to vCJD—through the ingestion of contaminated animals. However, the diseased animals that are eaten are humans. Cannibalism was a common practice in the Fore tribe, as they believed that it returned the life force of the dead back to the village. The disease started when a tribe member who had spontaneously developed a form of CJD was consumed after death. Gender stratification within the tribe dictated that men eat first. After eating the muscles, which are less likely to be contaminated, women were left to eat tissues with higher levels of the prion proteins, including the brain. As a result, the prevalence of kuru was several times higher in women than in men. The Fore tribe abandoned cannibalistic practices in the 1960s and kuru has since disappeared.

In the next chapter, we will continue our survey of living organisms, starting with the first cellular organisms, the prokaryotes.

 What makes prions different from all other known infectious agents?

Prions are infectious proteins and have no nucleic acid. ●

R E V I E W

MasteringBiology® **For Practice Quizzes, BioFlix, MP3 Tutors, and Activities, go to masteringbiology.com.**

Reviewing the Concepts

Viral Structure and Replication (16.1–16.6)

16.1 A virus consists of nucleic acid and proteins. Viruses are molecular organisms consisting of nucleic acid (DNA or RNA) and a protein coat. Many animal viruses also have a membranous envelope.

16.2 Viruses require host cells for replication. Viruses are obligate intracellular pathogens and require host enzymes to replicate their genetic material and proteins. Viruses have specific host ranges and are classified based on which organisms they can infect.

16.3 The viral replicative cycle. The replicative cycle starts with lock-and-key recognition of host cell surface molecules. Following binding, the virus (or its genetic material) enters the cell. Nucleic acid replication, protein replication, and assembly occur within the host. The replicative cycle ends when new viruses are released.

16.4 Viral entry is a crucial first step. Bacteriophage capsids cannot penetrate the rigid cell wall and so they inject the DNA into the host cell. Plant viruses enter by passive mechanisms through damaged cells. Naked animal viruses are internalized by endocytosis. Enveloped viruses fuse with the plasma or vesicle membrane.

16.5 DNA viruses and RNA viruses have distinct mechanisms of nucleic acid replication. DNA viruses can use the host's DNA polymerase to replicate, but RNA viruses require unique viral enzymes. Reverse transcriptase makes a complementary DNA strand from the ssRNA genome in retroviruses. The enzyme RNA replicase in dsRNA viruses can make RNA by using an RNA template.

16.6 Viral transmission requires the release from the host cell. Viral release can occur when the host cell lyses or when an insect feeds on a damaged plant cell. Enveloped animal viruses bud off of the plasma membrane, taking a small piece as its new envelope.

Viral Infections (16.7–16.12)

16.7 Some bacteriophages have two types of replicative cycles. The lytic cycle causes cell lysis and release of many new viruses. In the lysogenic cycle, however, the viral DNA is inserted into the host chromosome. The inserted provirus is copied with every division of the host cell.

16.8 Plant viruses can have a serious impact on agriculture. Plant viruses are classified based on their host and the disease they cause.

The grapevine leafroll-associated virus is problematic in vineyards, and potato virus Y can cause extensive losses for farmers.

16.9 Some animal viruses cause serious disease. Most animal viruses go unnoticed but some cause serious disease. Symptoms can be caused by cell death, by toxins, or by oncogenes that transform infected cells into cancerous tumour cells.

16.10 Emerging viruses threaten human health. New viruses or mutated viruses can appear very quickly and pose a great threat to the human population. For example, SARS travelled the globe in a matter of months, and swine flu could have become a global epidemic.

16.11 Can you catch a cold from going outside in the cold? The rumour about catching a cold by going outside without a jacket or with wet hair is untrue. The majority of common colds are caused by rhinoviruses.

16.12 How did viruses originate? Three main hypotheses attempt to explain the origin of viruses. The reduction hypothesis states that viruses have a cellular ancestor. The escape hypothesis suggests that viruses evolved from mobile genetic elements that escaped from a cell. The co-evolution hypothesis says that viruses evolved from the primordial gene pool along with cells.

Other Infectious Acellular Particles (16.13–16.14)

16.13 Viroids are infectious RNA molecules. Viroids are small, circular, ssRNA molecules that infect plants.

16.14 Prions are infectious protein molecules. Prions are infectious proteins that cause neurological diseases in animals.

Connecting the Concepts

1. Complete the following generalized viral replicative cycle.

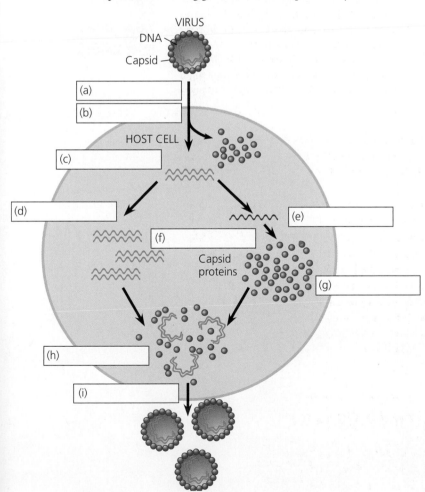

2. Complete the following concept map to review the concepts of RNA viral genome replication.

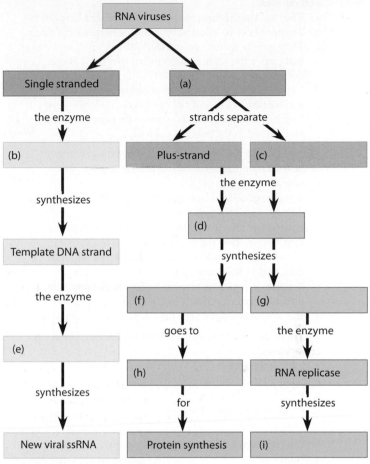

Testing Your Knowledge

Multiple Choice

3. Scientists have discovered how to put together a bacteriophage with the protein coat of phage T2 and the DNA of phage lambda. If this composite phage were allowed to infect a bacterium, which of the following would the phages produced in the host cell have? *(Explain your answer.)*
   a. the protein of T2 and the DNA of lambda
   b. the protein of lambda and the DNA of T2
   c. a mixture of the DNA and proteins of both phages
   d. the protein and DNA of T2
   e. the protein and DNA of lambda

4. What determines the host range of a virus?
   a. the proteins or glycoproteins on its surface and that of the host
   b. whether its nucleic acid is RNA or DNA
   c. the proteins in the host's cytoplasm
   d. whether or not the host has a cell wall
   e. the enzymes produced by the virus before it infects the cell

5. If you designed an antiviral treatment to be given before virus contact, which step of the replicative cycle could you inhibit that would protect the largest number of host cells?
   a. the assembly of new viruses
   b. the recognition of surface molecules by capsid proteins
   c. the replication of viral nucleic acid
   d. viral release from the cell
   e. synthesis of viral proteins

6. Why are people who have had a herpesvirus-mediated cold sore or genital sore subject to recurrences throughout the remainder of their lives?
   a. They are later re-infected by a closely related herpesvirus.
   b. They are later re-infected by the same herpesvirus strain.
   c. They were originally co-infected with an unrelated virus that causes the same symptoms but that has a longer dormant period.
   d. Copies of the herpesvirus genome are permanently maintained in the host cell cytoplasm.
   e. Copies of the herpesvirus genome are permanently maintained in the host cell nucleus.

7. With respect to the flow of genetic information, which of the following statements about reverse transcriptase is correct?
   a. It causes genetic information to flow in the opposite direction as DNA polymerase.
   b. It causes genetic information to flow in the opposite direction as RNA polymerase.
   c. It causes genetic information to flow in the opposite direction as RNA replicase.
   d. It causes genetic information to flow in the opposite direction as a ribosome.
   e. It is not involved with the flow of genetic information.

8. Which of the following viruses typically enter a cell through endocytosis?
   a. bacteriophages
   b. plant viruses
   c. naked animal viruses
   d. enveloped animal viruses
   e. fungal viruses

9. Which virus is the most common cause of the common cold?
   a. rotavirus   b. herpesvirus
   c. luteovirus   d. rhinovirus
   e. adenovirus

10. What is the proposed mechanism by which a viroid causes disease symptoms?
    a. Viroid RNA binds to host mRNA, causing it to be destroyed before translation.
    b. Viroid RNA binds to host mRNA, causing it to be destroyed after it is translated.
    c. Viroid RNA binds to ribosomes and prevents their function.
    d. Viroid RNA interferes with the host cell's RNA polymerase.
    e. Viroid RNA interferes with the host cell's DNA polymerase.

Describing, Comparing, and Explaining

11. Describe the two replicative cycles of the lambda bacteriophage. What triggers the switch between these cycles?

12. Compare and contrast the three major hypotheses regarding the origins of viruses.

13. Explain how insects can be vectors for plant viruses.

Applying the Concepts

14. How do air travel and today's global community make the threat of emerging viruses even more serious to human health?

15. Explain why antibiotics that inhibit metabolism cannot prevent viral spread between cells or hosts.

Answers to all questions can be found in Appendix E.

 Study on the Go

This QR code leads to Study on the Go— mobile study resources, including practice quizzes, videos, and glossary flashcards for this textbook.

   You can access Study on the Go content via your smartphone. Note: Your login information for MasteringBiology is required.

17

Bacteria and Other Prokaryotes

BIG IDEAS

Prokaryote Diversity

(17.1–17.6)

Prokaryotes, the smallest
organisms known,
are extraordinarily diverse.

Bacterial Genetics

(17.7–17.8)

Bacteria are able to exchange genetic
information, which may involve discrete
genetic elements called plasmids.

Bacteria

(17.9–17.15)

Bacteria are ubiquitous and have
a huge impact on humans.

How We Enter the World Can Affect Our Well-Being

We are constantly exposed to countless numbers of bacteria in our daily lives. Bacteria are everywhere, on every surface we touch, in the air we breathe and the food we eat, and even on and within our bodies. Although bacteria are commonly looked at in a negative light, only a small fraction of those we encounter are harmful. Most are typically harmless and a few "good" bacteria are even helpful. Within your intestinal tract lives an entire community consisting of hundreds of bacterial species called a microbiome. The microbiome contains 10 times as many bacteria as there are cells in your body—approximately 100 trillion.

Because of their beneficial effects, some good bacteria are used as probiotics—organisms that promote health. *Lactobacillus* is a common probiotic bacterium found in fermented foods such as yogourt, which can help to prevent intestinal disease. After completing a course of antibiotics to fight an infection, many patients develop diarrhea. In addition to fighting the infection, antibiotics can also disturb the microbiome. *Clostridium*, which is normally present in low numbers, becomes abundant and leads to intestinal inflammation and diarrhea. To minimize microbiome disturbances, physicians often suggest taking probiotics during and after any antibiotic treatments.

When present in the intestinal microbiome, *Lactobacillus* and other good bacteria can do more than help to prevent short-term discomfort: They can promote lifelong health. Disturbances of the microbiome have been associated with several diseases, including inflammatory bowel disease, asthma, allergies, and diabetes. However, to be effective in this way, good bacteria must establish within the microbiome during infancy when the immune system develops. The microbiome plays a major role in the proper stimulation of the developing immune system during this time. By practising on the good bacteria within the microbiome, our immune system learns how to respond properly when exposed to something more serious. Moreover, this early exposure also helps to prevent inappropriate immune responses, which may lead to those diseases mentioned above. But how do we get these bacteria into our intestinal tracts?

In 2013, Dr. Meghan Azad at the University of Alberta provided part of the answer to this question. Azad and her colleagues found that the mode of delivery greatly influences the newborn's microbiome. The microbiomes of infants born by natural vaginal birth have more good bacteria than those delivered by Caesarean section. During natural birth, an infant acquires numerous bacteria, including *Lactobacillus*, from the natural flora living within the mother's vagina. Delivery by Caesarean section, however, does not expose the child to these beneficial organisms and as a result, their microbiomes have fewer good bacteria.

Breastfeeding also contributes to the development of a healthy microbiome. It is well known that breast milk offers many benefits to the infant compared to formula. The developing immune system is supplemented with maternal antibodies contained within breast milk. Furthermore, breast milk not only nourishes the infant, but also contains specific nutrients for the beneficial bacteria within the growing microbiome.

Interestingly, it may be possible that the microbiome starts to develop even before birth. Biologists originally thought that mammalian fetuses developed within a bacteria-free environment and that babies were born with no microbiome. However, experiments have detected *Lactobacillus* given to the mother within the meconium (first feces) of her baby. How the bacteria found its way into the developing fetus remains a mystery.

In Canada, approximately 27% of infants are delivered by Caesarean section and less than 15% are exclusively breastfed for the recommended six months. Although most Caesarean sections are performed for valid medical reasons, many are elected. The consequences of these choices may have a significant impact later in these children's lives. Their risks of developing inflammatory bowel disease, asthma, allergies, or diabetes may increase by up to 80% compared to a child delivered vaginally.

This chapter begins with an overview of the extraordinary diversity seen among the prokaryotic organisms. Then, with our focus on bacteria, we will discuss how these minute organisms can exchange DNA and the many ways in which they affect our lives.

Prokaryote Diversity

17.1 Prokaryotes are diverse and widespread

In this chapter, you will learn about prokaryotes, organisms that have a cellular organization fundamentally different from that of eukaryotes (see Modules 4.3 and 4.4). Whereas eukaryotic cells have a membrane-enclosed nucleus and numerous other membrane-enclosed organelles, prokaryotic cells lack these structural features. Prokaryotes are also typically much smaller than eukaryotes. You can get an idea of the size of most prokaryotes from **Figure 17.1**, a colourized scanning electron micrograph of the point of a pin (purple) covered with numerous bacteria (orange). Most prokaryotic cells have diameters in the range of 1–5 μm, much smaller than most eukaryotic cells (typically 10–100 μm).

Despite their small size, prokaryotes have an immense impact on our world. They are found wherever there is life, including in and on the bodies of multicellular organisms. The collective biological mass (biomass) of prokaryotes is at least 10 times that of all eukaryotes! Prokaryotes also thrive in habitats too cold, too hot, too salty, too acidic, or too alkaline for any eukaryote. And scientists are just beginning to investigate the extensive prokaryotic diversity in the oceans.

Although prokaryotes are a constant presence in our environment, we hear most about the relatively few species that cause illnesses. We focus on bacterial **pathogens**, disease-causing agents, in Module 17.13. But benign or beneficial prokaryotes are far more common than harmful prokaryotes. For example, each of us harbours several hundred species of prokaryotes in and on our body. Many of the bacteria that live on our skin perform helpful housekeeping functions such as decomposing dead skin cells. Some of our intestinal residents supply essential vitamins and enable us to obtain nutrition

▶ **Figure 17.1** Bacteria on the point of a pin

Colourized SEM 525×

from food molecules that we can't otherwise digest. Bacteria also guard the body against pathogenic intruders.

Prokaryotes are also essential to the health of the environment. They help to decompose dead organisms and other organic waste material, returning vital chemical elements to the environment. They are indispensable components of the chemical cycle that makes nitrogen available to plants and other organisms. If prokaryotes were to disappear, the chemical cycles that sustain life would halt, and all forms of eukaryotic life would also be doomed. In contrast, prokaryotic life would undoubtedly persist in the absence of eukaryotes, as it once did for billions of years.

As you learned in Module 15.18, there are two very different kinds of prokaryotes, which are classified in the domains **Archaea** and **Bacteria**. In the next few modules, we will take a look at the diversity of each domain.

 If prokaryotes have 10 times the biomass of eukaryotes, why can we not see these organisms?

● Because of their very small size. We cannot see individual eukaryotic cells, which range from 10–100 μm, and prokaryotes are much smaller, ranging from 1–5 μm.

17.2 Prokaryotes have unparalleled nutritional diversity

One way to organize the vast diversity of prokaryotes is by their mode of nutrition—how they obtain energy for cellular work and carbon to build organic molecules. Prokaryotes exhibit much more nutritional diversity than eukaryotes. This allows them to inhabit almost every nook and cranny on Earth.

Source of Energy   As shown in **Figure 17.2**, two sources of energy are used by prokaryotes. Like plants, prokaryotic *phototrophs* capture energy from sunlight. Prokaryotic cells do not have chloroplasts, but some prokaryotes have thylakoid membranes where photosynthesis takes place.

Prokaryotes called *chemotrophs* harness the energy stored in chemicals, either organic molecules or inorganic chemicals such as hydrogen sulphide (H_2S), elemental sulphur (S), iron (Fe)-containing compounds, or ammonia (NH_3).

Source of Carbon   Organisms that make their own organic compounds from inorganic sources are autotrophic (see Module 7.1). **Autotrophs**, including plants and some prokaryotes and protists, obtain their carbon atoms from carbon dioxide (CO_2). Most prokaryotes, as well as animals, fungi, and some protists, are **heterotrophs**, meaning they obtain their carbon atoms from the organic compounds of other organisms.

ENERGY SOURCE	
Sunlight	**Chemicals**

CARBON SOURCE

CO_2

Photoautotrophs

LM 65×

Oscilliatoria

Chemoautotrophs

Unidentified "rock-eating" bacteria

Organic compounds

Photoheterotrophs

Colourized TEM 6000×

Rhodopseudomonas

Chemoheterotrophs

Colourized TEM 4000×

A *Bdellovibrio* attacking a larger cell

▲ **Figure 17.2** Sources of energy and carbon in prokaryotic modes of nutrition

Mode of Nutrition The terms used to describe how an organism obtains energy and carbon are combined to describe its mode of nutrition (see Figure 17.2).

Photoautotrophs harness sunlight for energy and use CO_2 for carbon. Cyanobacteria, such as the example shown in Figure 17.2, are photoautotrophs. As in plants, photosynthesis in cyanobacteria uses chlorophyll *a* and produces O_2 as a by-product.

Photoheterotrophs obtain energy from sunlight but get their carbon atoms from organic sources. This unusual mode of nutrition is found in only a few types of bacteria called purple nonsulphur bacteria. Many of them, including the example shown in Figure 17.2, are found in aquatic sediments.

Chemoautotrophs harvest energy from inorganic chemicals and use carbon from CO_2 to make organic molecules. Because they don't depend on sunlight, chemoautotrophs can

thrive in conditions that seem totally inhospitable to life. Near hydrothermal vents, where scalding water and hot gases surge into the sea 2000 m below the surface, chemoautotrophic bacteria use sulphur compounds as a source of energy. The organic molecules they produce using CO_2 from the seawater support diverse animal communities. The chemoautotrophs shown in Figure 17.2 live between layers of rocks buried 100 m below Earth's surface. Chemoautotrophs are also found in more predictable habitats, such as the soil.

Chemoheterotrophs, which acquire both energy and carbon from organic molecules, are by far the largest and most diverse group of prokaryotes. Almost any organic molecule is food for some species of chemoheterotrophic prokaryote.

 Which term would describe your mode of nutrition?

● Chemoheterotrophy

17.3 Archaea and bacteria are the two main branches of prokaryotic evolution

As you learned in Module 15.18, researchers recently discovered that many prokaryotes once classified as bacteria are actually more closely related to eukaryotes and belong in a domain of their own. As a result, prokaryotes are now classified in two domains: Bacteria and Archaea (from the Greek *archaios*, ancient). Many bacterial and archaeal genomes have now been sequenced. When compared with each other and with the genomes of eukaryotes, these genome sequences strongly support the three-domain view of life. Some genes of archaea are similar to bacterial genes, others to eukaryotic genes, and still others seem to be unique to archaea.

Table 17.3 summarizes some of the main differences between the three domains. Differences between the ribosomal RNA (rRNA) sequences provided the first clues of a deep division among prokaryotes. Other differences in the cellular machinery for gene expression include differences in RNA polymerases (the enzymes that catalyze the synthesis of RNA) and in the presence of introns within genes. The cell walls and membranes of bacteria and archaea are also distinctive. Bacterial cell walls contain peptidoglycan (see Module 17.2), while archaea do not. Archaea cell walls contain a unique molecule that is similar

Characteristic	Bacteria	Archaea	Eukarya
rRNA sequences	Some unique to bacteria	Some unique to archaea; some match eukaryotic sequences	Some unique to eukaryotes; some match archaeal sequences
RNA polymerase	One kind; relatively small and simple	Several kinds; complex	Several kinds; complex
Introns	Rare	In some genes	Present
Peptidoglycan in cell wall	Present	Absent	Absent
Histones associated with DNA	Absent	Present in some species	Present

to peptidoglycan. Furthermore, the lipids forming the backbone of plasma membranes differ between the two domains. Intriguingly, for most of the features listed in the table, archaea have at least as much in common with eukaryotes as they do with bacteria.

Now that you are familiar with the general characteristics of prokaryotes and the features underlying their spectacular success, let's take a look at prokaryotic diversity. We begin with domain Archaea.

 As different as bacteria and archaea are, both groups are characterized by _____ cells, which lack nuclei and other membrane-enclosed organelles.

● prokaryotic

17.4 Archaea thrive in extreme environments—and in other habitats

Archaea are abundant in many habitats, including places where few other organisms can survive. The archaeal inhabitants of extreme environments have unusual proteins and other molecular adaptations that enable them to metabolize and reproduce effectively. Scientists are only beginning to learn about these adaptations.

A group of archaea called the **extreme halophiles** ("salt lovers") thrive in very salty places, such as the Great Salt Lake in Utah, the Dead Sea, and seawater-evaporating ponds used to produce salt. Many species flourish when the salinity of the water is 15% to 30% and can tolerate even higher salt concentrations. Because seawater, with a salt concentration of about 3%, is hypertonic enough to shrivel most cells, these archaea have very little competition from other organisms. Extremely salty environments may turn red, purple, or yellow as a result of the dense growth and colourful pigments of halophilic archaea.

Another group of archaea, the **extreme thermophiles** ("heat lovers"), thrive in very hot water; some even live near deep-ocean vents, where temperatures are above 100°C, the boiling point of water at sea level! One such habitat is the Nevada geyser shown in **Figure 17.4A**. Other thermophiles thrive in acid. Many hot, acidic pools in Yellowstone National Park harbour such archaea, which give the pools a vivid greenish colour. One of these organisms, *Sulfolobus*, can obtain energy by oxidizing sulphur or a compound of sulphur and iron; the mechanisms involved may be similar to those used billions of years ago by the first cells.

A third group of archaea, the **methanogens**, live in anaerobic (oxygen-lacking) environments and give off methane as a waste product. Many thrive in anaerobic mud at the bottom of lakes and swamps. You may have seen methane, also called marsh gas, bubbling up from a swamp. A large amount of methane is generated in solid waste landfills, where methanogens flourish in the anaerobic conditions. Many municipalities collect this methane and use it as a source of energy (Figure 17.4B). Great numbers of

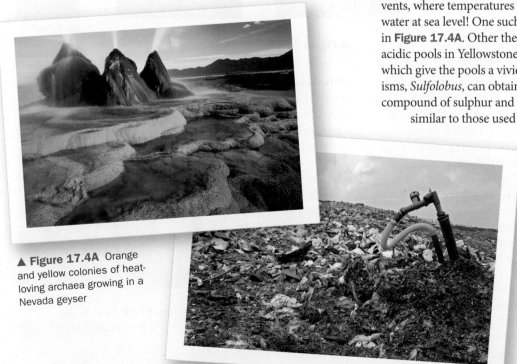

▲ Figure 17.4A Orange and yellow colonies of heat-loving archaea growing in a Nevada geyser

▲ Figure 17.4B Pipes for collecting gas from a landfill

methanogens also inhabit the digestive tracts of cattle, deer, and other animals that depend heavily on cellulose for their nutrition. Because methane is a greenhouse gas (see Module 7.13), landfills contribute to climate change. We will examine the rumour about methanogens in livestock contributing to climate change in Module 41.5.

Accustomed to thinking of archaea as inhabitants of extreme environments, scientists have been surprised to discover their abundance in more moderate conditions, especially in the oceans. Archaea live at all depths, making up a substantial fraction of the prokaryotes in waters more than 150 m beneath the surface and half of the prokaryotes that live below 1000 m. Archaea are thus one of the most abundant cell types in Earth's largest habitat.

Because bacteria have been the subject of most prokaryotic research for over a century, much more is known about them than about archaea. For this reason, bacteria will be the focus for the remainder of this chapter and whenever we discuss prokaryotes throughout this text. Now that the evolutionary and ecological importance of archaea has come into focus, we can expect research on this domain to turn up many more surprises about the history of life and the roles of microbes in ecosystems.

 Some archaea are referred to as "extremophiles." Why?

● Because they can thrive in extreme environments too hot, too salty, or too acidic for other organisms.

17.5 External features contribute to the success of bacteria

Some of the diversity of bacteria is evident in their external features, including shape, cell walls, and projections such as flagella. These features are useful for identifying bacteria as well as helping the organisms survive in their environments.

Cell Shape   Determining cell shape by microscopic examination is an important step in identifying bacteria. The micrographs in **Figure 17.5A** show three of the most common bacterial cell shapes. Spherical bacterial cells are called **cocci** (singular, *coccus*). Cocci that occur in chains, like those in Figure 17.5A, are called streptococci (from the Greek *streptos*, twisted). The bacterium that causes strep throat in humans is a streptococcus. Other cocci occur in clusters; they are called staphylococci (from the Greek *staphyle*, cluster of grapes).

Rod-shaped bacteria are called **bacilli** (singular, *bacillus*). Most bacilli occur singly, like the *Escherichia coli* cells in the middle photo in Figure 17.5A. (*E. coli* resides in our digestive tract.) However, the cells of some species occur in pairs or chains. Bacilli may also be threadlike, or filamentous.

A third bacterial cell shape is spiral, like a corkscrew. Spiral bacteria that are relatively short and rigid are called *spirilla*; those with longer, more flexible cells, like the one shown on the right in Figure 17.5A, which causes Lyme disease, are called *spirochetes*. The bacterium that causes syphilis is also a spirochete. Spirochetes include some giants by prokaryotic standards: cells 0.5 mm long (though they are very thin).

Some bacteria, such as *Mycobacterium* species, lack a rigid cell wall and therefore have no consistent shape. These bacteria are described as pleomorphic (meaning "more forms").

Cell Wall   Nearly all bacteria have a cell wall, a feature that enables them to live in a wide range of environments. The cell wall provides physical protection and prevents the cell from bursting in a hypotonic environment (see Module 5.5). The cell walls of bacteria fall into two general types, which scientists can identify with a technique called the **Gram stain (Figure 17.5B)**. Gram-positive bacteria have simpler walls

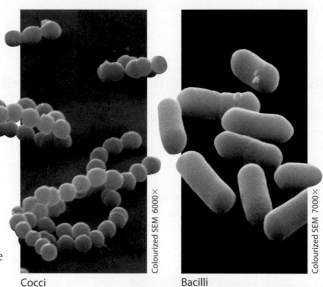

Colourized SEM 6000×

Colourized SEM 7000×

Colourized SEM 5000×

Cocci   Bacilli   Spirochete

▲ **Figure 17.5A** Bacteria shapes

with a relatively thick layer of a unique material called **peptidoglycan**, a polymer of sugars cross-linked by short polypeptides. The walls of gram-negative bacteria stain differently. They have less peptidoglycan and are more complex, with an outer membrane that contains phospholipids bonded to carbohydrates. The cell walls of archaea do not contain peptidoglycan but can also be gram-positive or gram-negative.

LM 1000×

▲ **Figure 17.5B** Gram-positive (purple) and gram-negative (pink) bacteria

In medicine, Gram stains are often used to detect the presence of bacteria and indicate the type of antibiotic to prescribe.

Tonsil cell

Capsule

Bacterium

Colourized TEM 50 000×

▲ **Figure 17.5C** Capsule

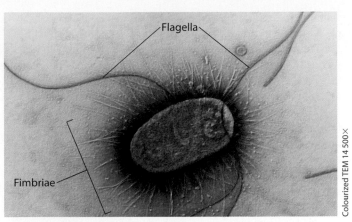

Flagella

Fimbriae

Colourized TEM 14 500×

▲ **Figure 17.5D** Flagella and fimbriae

Among disease-causing bacteria, gram-negative species are generally more threatening than gram-positive species because lipid molecules of the outer membrane of gram-negative bacteria are often toxic. The membrane also protects the gram-negative bacteria against the body's defences and hinders the entry of antibiotic drugs into the bacterium.

The cell wall of many bacteria is covered by a capsule, a sticky layer of polysaccharide or protein. The capsule enables bacteria to adhere to a surface or to other individuals in a colony. Capsules can also shield pathogenic bacteria from attacks by their host's immune system. The capsule surrounding the *Streptococcus* bacterium shown in **Figure 17.5C** enables it to attach to cells that line the human respiratory tract—in this image, a tonsil cell.

Projections   Some bacteria have external structures that extend beyond the cell wall. Many bacteria and archaea are equipped with flagella, adaptations that enable them to move about in response to chemical or physical signals in their environment. For example, bacteria can move toward nutrients or

other members of their species or away from a toxic substance. Flagella may be scattered over the entire cell surface or concentrated at one or both ends of the cell. Unlike the flagellum of eukaryotic cells (described in Module 4.17), the prokaryotic flagellum is a naked protein structure that lacks microtubules. The flagellated bacterium in **Figure 17.5D** is *E. coli*, as seen in a TEM.

Figure 17.5D also illustrates the hairlike projections called **fimbriae** that enable some bacteria to stick to a surface or to one another. Fimbriae allow many pathogenic bacteria to latch onto the host cells they colonize. For example, *Neisseria gonorrheae*, which causes the sexually transmitted infection gonorrhea, uses fimbriae to attach to cells in the reproductive tract. During sexual intercourse, *N. gonorrheae* bacteria may also attach to sperm cells and travel to a woman's oviducts; an infection in these narrow tubes can impair fertility.

 How could a microscope help you distinguish the cocci that cause "staph" infections from those that cause "strep" throat?

● It would show clusters of cells for *Staphylococcus* and chains of cells for *Streptococcus*.

17.6 Bacteria include a diverse assemblage of prokaryotes

Domain Bacteria is currently divided into five groups based on comparisons of genetic sequences. In this module, we sample some of the diversity in each group.

Proteobacteria are all gram-negative and share a particular rRNA sequence. With regard to other characteristics, however, this large group encompasses enormous diversity. For example, all four modes of nutrition are represented.

Chemoheterotrophic proteobacteria include pathogens such as *Salmonella*, one cause of food poisoning; *Vibrio cholerae*, which causes cholera; and species of *Bordetella* that cause pertussis (whooping cough).

LM 200×

▲ **Figure 17.6A**
Thiomargarita namibiensis

E. coli, which is a common resident of the intestines of humans and other mammals and a favourite research organism, is also a member of this group. Proteobacteria even include bacteria that attack other bacteria. *Bdellovibrio* (see Figure 17.2) charge their prey at up to 100 μm/sec (comparable to a human running 600 km/hr) and bore into the prey by spinning at 100 revolutions per second.

Thiomargarita namibiensis (**Figure 17.6A**), an example of a photoautotrophic species of proteobacteria, uses H_2S to generate organic molecules from CO_2. The small greenish globules you see in the photo are sulphur wastes. *T. namibiensis* is a giant among prokaryotes. Single cells are typically 100–300 μm in diameter, roughly 100 times the length of an *E. coli* cell and large enough to be seen with the unaided eye. Other proteobacteria, including *Rhodopseudomonas* (see Figure 17.2), are photoheterotrophs; they cannot convert CO_2 to sugars.

Chemoautotrophic soil bacteria such as *Nitrosomonas* obtain energy by oxidizing inorganic nitrogen compounds. These and related species of proteobacteria are essential to the chemical cycle that makes nitrogen available to plants.

Proteobacteria also include *Rhizobium* species that live symbiotically in root nodules of legumes such as soybeans and peas (see Module 39.5). *Rhizobium* endosymbionts fix nitrogen; that is, they convert atmospheric nitrogen gas to a form usable by their legume host.

A second major group of bacteria, **gram-positive bacteria**, rivals the proteobacteria in diversity. One subgroup, the actinomycetes (from the Greek *mykes*, fungus, for which these bacteria were once mistaken), forms colonies of branched chains of cells. Actinomycetes are very common in the soil, where they decompose organic matter. Soil-dwelling species in the genus *Streptomyces*, shown in **Figure 17.6B**, are cultured by pharmaceutical companies as a source of many antibiotics, including streptomycin. Gram-positive bacteria also include many solitary species, such as *Bacillus anthracis* (see Figure 17.9). The pathogens *Staphylococcus* and *Streptococcus* are also gram-positive bacteria. Mycoplasmas are gram-positive bacteria that lack cell walls and are the tiniest of all known cells, with diameters as small as 0.1 μm (about five times the diameter of a ribosome).

The **cyanobacteria** are the only group of bacteria with plantlike, oxygen-generating photosynthesis. Ancient cyanobacteria generated the oxygen that changed Earth's atmosphere hundreds of millions of years ago. Today, cyanobacteria provide an enormous amount of food for freshwater and marine ecosystems. Some species, such as the cyanobacterium *Anabaena* in **Figure 17.6C**, have specialized cells that fix nitrogen. Many species of cyanobacteria have symbiotic relationships

▲ **Figure 17.6C** *Anabaena*, a filamentous cyanobacterium

▲ **Figure 17.6D** *Chlamydia* cells (indicated by arrows) inside an animal cell

▲ **Figure 17.6E** *Treponema pallidum*, the spirochete that causes syphilis

with organisms such as fungi, mosses, and a variety of marine invertebrates.

The **chlamydiae** (singular, *chlamydia*), which live inside eukaryotic host cells, form a fourth bacterial group **(Figure 17.6D)**. *Chlamydia trachomatis* is a common cause of blindness in developing countries and also causes nongonococcal urethritis, the most common sexually transmitted infection in Canada.

Spirochetes, the fifth group, are helical bacteria that spiral through their environment by means of rotating, internal filaments. Some spirochetes are notorious pathogens: *Treponema pallidum*, shown in **Figure 17.6E**, causes syphilis, and *Borrelia burgdorferi* (see Figure 17.5A) causes Lyme disease.

▲ **Figure 17.6B** *Streptomyces*, the source of many antibiotics

? How are *Thiomargarita namibiensis* similar to cyanobacteria?

● They are both photoautotrophic.

Bacterial Genetics

17.7 Bacteria can transfer DNA in three ways

Bacteria are valuable as microbial models in genetics research. As prokaryotic cells, bacteria allow researchers to investigate molecular genetics in the simplest living organisms.

Most of a bacterium's DNA is found in a single chromosome, a closed loop of DNA with associated proteins. In the diagrams here, we show the chromosome much smaller than it actually is relative to the cell. A bacterial chromosome is hundreds of times longer than its cell; it fits inside the cell because it is tightly folded.

Bacterial cells reproduce by replication of the bacterial chromosome followed by binary fission (see Module 8.2). Because binary fission is an asexual process involving only a single parent, the bacteria in a colony are genetically identical to the parental cell. But this does not mean that bacteria lack ways to produce new combinations of genes. In fact, in the bacterial world, there are three mechanisms by which genes can move from one cell to another: transformation, transduction, and conjugation. Let's discuss each of these in turn.

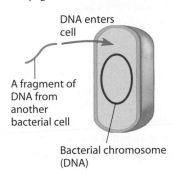

DNA enters cell

A fragment of DNA from another bacterial cell

Bacterial chromosome (DNA)

▲ **Figure 17.7A**
Transformation

Phage

A fragment of DNA from another bacterial cell (previous phage host)

▲ **Figure 17.7B**
Transduction

Figure 17.7A illustrates **transformation**, the uptake of foreign DNA from the surrounding environment. In Module 10.1, the "transforming factor" that converted one strain of bacterium to another was DNA. A harmless strain of bacteria took up pieces of DNA left from the dead cells of a disease-causing strain. The DNA from the pathogenic bacteria carried a gene that made the cells resistant to an animal's defences, and when the previously harmless bacteria acquired this gene, it could cause pneumonia in infected animals.

Bacteriophages, the viruses that infect bacteria, provide the second means of bringing together genes of different bacteria. The transfer of bacterial genes by a phage is called **transduction**. During a lytic infection (see Module 16.7), when new viruses are being assembled in an infected bacterial cell, a fragment of DNA belonging to the host cell may be mistakenly packaged within the phage's coat instead of the phage's DNA. When the phage infects a new bacterial cell, the DNA stowaway from the previous host cell is injected into the new host (**Figure 17.7B**).

Figure 17.7C is an illustration of what happens at the DNA level when two bacterial cells "mate." This physical union of two bacterial cells—of the same or different species—and the DNA transfer between them is called **conjugation**. The donor cell has hollow appendages called sex pili, one of which is attached to the recipient cell in the figure. The outside layers

Mating bridge

Sex pili

▶ **Figure 17.7C**
Conjugation

Donor cell   Recipient cell

of the cells have fused, and a cytoplasmic bridge has formed between them. Through this mating bridge, donor cell DNA (light blue in the figure) passes to the recipient cell. The donor cell replicates its DNA as it transfers it, so the cell doesn't end up lacking any genes. The DNA replication is a special type that allows one copy to peel off and transfer into the recipient cell.

Once new DNA gets into a bacterial cell, by whatever mechanism, part of it may then integrate into the recipient's chromosome. As **Figure 17.7D** indicates, integration occurs by crossing over between the donor and recipient DNA molecules, a process similar to crossing over between eukaryotic chromosomes (see Module 8.18). Here we see that two crossovers result in a piece of the donated DNA replacing part of the recipient cell's original DNA. The leftover pieces of DNA are broken down and degraded, leaving the recipient bacterium with a recombinant chromosome.

Vertical gene transfer describes the familiar generation-to-generation, Mendelian inheritance of genes within a species. In contrast, the modes of gene transfer discussed above are all examples of **horizontal gene transfer**. That is, the transfer of genetic information between two organisms that does not require a reproductive event. Because the two bacteria can be of different species, horizontal gene transfer can lead to rapid adaptation and evolution in the recipients of new genes.

? The three modes of gene transfer between bacteria are _____, which is transfer via a virus; _____, which is the uptake of DNA from the surrounding environment; and _____, which is bacterial "mating."

transduction; transformation; conjugation ●

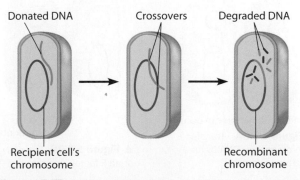

Donated DNA   Crossovers   Degraded DNA

Recipient cell's chromosome   Recombinant chromosome

▲ **Figure 17.7D** The integration of donated DNA into the recipient cell's chromosome

17.8 Bacterial plasmids can serve as carriers for gene transfer

The ability of a donor *E. coli* cell to carry out conjugation is usually due to a specific piece of DNA called the **F factor** (*F* for *fertility*). The F factor carries genes for making sex pili and other requirements for conjugation; it also contains an origin of replication, where DNA replication starts.

Let's see how the F factor behaves during conjugation. In **Figure 17.8A**, the F factor (light blue) is integrated into the donor bacterium's chromosome. When this cell conjugates with a recipient cell, the donor chromosome starts replicating at the F factor's origin of replication, indicated by the blue dot on the DNA. The growing copy of the DNA peels off the chromosome and heads into the recipient cell. Thus, part of the F factor serves as the leading end of the transferred DNA, but right behind it are genes from the donor's original

Plasmids

Colourized TEM 1730×

▲ **Figure 17.8C** Plasmids and part of a bacterial chromosome released from a ruptured *E. coli* cell

4210×

chromosome. The rest of the F factor stays in the donor cell. Once inside the recipient cell, the transferred donor genes can recombine with the corresponding part of the recipient chromosome by crossing over. If crossing over occurs, the recipient cell may be genetically changed, but it usually remains a recipient because the two cells break apart before the F factor is transferred.

Alternatively, as **Figure 17.8B** shows, an F factor can exist as a **plasmid**, a small, circular DNA molecule separate from the bacterial chromosome. Every plasmid has an origin of replication, required for its replication within the cell. Some plasmids, including the F factor plasmid, can bring about conjugation and move to another cell. When the donor cell in Figure 17.8B mates with a recipient cell, the F factor replicates and at the same time transfers one whole copy of itself, in linear rather than circular form, to the recipient cell. The transferred plasmid becomes circular in the recipient cell, and the cell becomes a donor.

E. coli and other bacteria have many different kinds of plasmids. You can see several from one cell in **Figure 17.8C**, along with part of the bacterial chromosome, which extends in loops from the ruptured cell. Some plasmids carry genes that can affect the survival of the cell, which we'll discuss in the next module.

? Why do you think plasmids are useful tools for genetic engineering?

F factor (integrated)

— Donor

— Origin of F replication

— Bacterial chromosome

F factor starts replication and transfer of chromosome

Recipient cell

Only part of the chromosome transfers

Recombination can occur

▲ **Figure 17.8A** Transfer of chromosomal DNA by an integrated F factor

F factor (plasmid)

— Donor

— Bacterial chromosome

F factor starts replication and transfer

The plasmid completes its transfer and circularizes

The cell is now a donor

▲ **Figure 17.8B** Transfer of an F factor plasmid

Scientists can take advantage of the ability of plasmids to carry foreign genes, to replicate, and to be inherited by progeny cells.

Bacteria

17.9 Populations of bacteria can adapt rapidly to changes in the environment

Certainly a large part of the success of bacteria is their potential to reproduce quickly in a favourable environment. Dividing by binary fission (see Module 8.2), a single prokaryotic cell becomes 2 cells, which then become 4, 8, 16, and so on. While many bacteria produce a new generation within 1–3 hours, some species can produce a new generation in only 20 minutes under optimal conditions. If reproduction continued unchecked at this rate, a single bacterium could give rise to a colony outweighing Earth in only three days!

Salmonella bacteria, which cause food poisoning, are commonly found on raw poultry and eggs, but the bacterial population is often too small to cause symptoms. Refrigeration slows (but does not stop) bacterial reproduction. However, when raw poultry is left in the warm environment of the kitchen, bacteria multiply rapidly and can quickly reach a risky population size. Similarly, bacteria that remain on the counter, cutting board, or kitchen implements may continue to reproduce. So be sure to cook poultry thoroughly (an internal temperature of 75°C is considered safe), and clean anything that has come into contact with the raw poultry with soap and hot water.

Each time DNA is replicated prior to binary fission, spontaneous mutations occur. As a result, rapid reproduction generates a great deal of genetic variation in a bacterium population. If the environment changes, an individual that possesses a beneficial gene can quickly take advantage of the new conditions. For example, exposure to antibiotics may select for antibiotic resistance in a bacterial population.

The amount of DNA in a bacterial cell is on average only about one-thousandth as much as that in a eukaryotic cell. The genome of a typical bacterium is one long, circular chromosome. (In an intact cell, it is packed into a distinct region; see Figure 4.3.) As you read in the previous module, many bacteria also have extra DNA molecules called plasmids (see Module 17.8). Some plasmids carry genes that enhance survival under certain conditions. Plasmids of one class, called **R plasmids**, pose serious problems for human medicine. Transferable R plasmids carry genes for enzymes that destroy antibiotics such as penicillin and tetracycline. Bacteria containing R plasmids are resistant (hence the designation *R*) to antibiotics that would otherwise kill them. The widespread use of antibiotics in medicine and agriculture has tended to kill off bacteria that lack R plasmids, whereas those with R plasmids have multiplied. As a result, an increasing number of bacteria that cause human diseases, such as food poisoning and gonorrhea, are becoming resistant to antibiotics (see Module 10.19). The ability of many bacteria to conjugate and transfer plasmids within and even between species provides another rapid means of adaptation to changes in the environment.

If environmental conditions become too harsh to sustain active metabolism—for example, when food or moisture is depleted—some bacteria form specialized resistant cells.

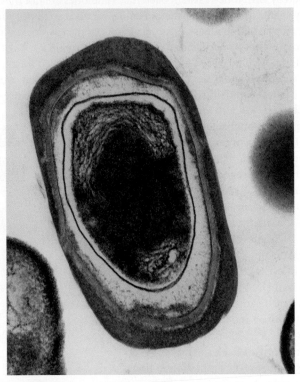

▲ **Figure 17.9** An endospore within an anthrax bacterium cell

Figure 17.9 shows an example of such an organism, *Bacillus anthracis*, the bacterium that causes a disease called anthrax in cattle, sheep, and humans. There are actually two cells here, one inside the other. The outer cell, which will later disintegrate, produced the specialized inner cell, called an **endospore**. The endospore, which has a thick, protective coat, dehydrates and becomes dormant. It can survive all sorts of trauma, including extreme heat or cold. When the endospore receives cues that the environmental conditions have improved, it absorbs water and resumes growth.

Endospores can remain dormant for centuries or longer. Endospores extracted from the intestine of a bee that was trapped in amber have germinated after 20 million years. Not even boiling water kills most of these resistant cells, making it difficult to get rid of spores in a contaminated area. The food-canning industry kills endospores of dangerous bacteria such as *Clostridium botulinum*, the source of the potentially fatal disease botulism, by heating the food to a temperature of 110–150°C with high-pressure steam.

We will consider the rumour about antimicrobial cleaners causing the evolution of superbacteria in the next module.

? **Why does rapid reproduction produce high genetic variation in populations of bacteria?**

● Each time DNA replicates, spontaneous mutations occur.

17.10 Are antibacterial hand soaps creating strains of superbugs?

In the opening essay of this chapter, we discussed the challenges posed by antibiotic-resistant bacteria. Antibiotics are not the only agents used to kill bacteria. Handwashing is an important step in preventing illness. Your local grocery store is stocked with numerous antibacterial hand soaps that claim to kill 99.9% of bacteria. Alcohol-based hand sanitizers are positioned throughout campuses and other public places. Rumour has it that overuse of these sanitizing products, as with the irresponsible use of antibiotics, will also lead to the evolution of resistant bacteria.

The origin of resistance starts with genetic mutation (see Module 10.16). Mutations arise most commonly by errors in DNA replication, which typically occur once every 100 million bases, written as 10^{-8}. Normally, all but 1% of these errors are repaired immediately. Thus, about 1 mutation out of every 10 billion bases of synthesized DNA remains and is passed on to the next generation. In a typical bacterium, 1 mutation will go unrepaired every 1000 cell divisions. In other words, 1 bacterium out of every 1000 will pass on a mutation to the next generation. Occasionally, one of these mutations bestows resistance to the bacterium and its offspring. The action of mutagens can accelerate this process by increasing the rate of mutations. Alternatively, as you learned in Module 17.7, bacteria can obtain genes horizontally through transformation, transduction, or conjugation.

Why do bacteria acquire resistance against some antimicrobial agents but not others? The answer lies in how the antimicrobial agent works. Bacteria can adapt against antibiotics that affect specific bacterial components, as discussed in the chapter-opening essay. But can bacteria evolve resistance against the antibacterial soaps and hand sanitizers as rumoured?

Plain hand soap and alcohol-based hand sanitizers work in a more general fashion than antimicrobial agents. Soap contains sodium lauryl (dodecyl) sulphate (SLS), a fatty acid salt, which mixes with lipids and makes them soluble. Thus, SLS solubilizes oils and dirt from your hands, which are easily rinsed away in water. SLS also solubilizes the lipids in plasma membranes, causing them to disintegrate. In gram-negative bacteria and enveloped viruses, the outer membrane is removed and the organisms are destroyed.

Alcohol-based hand sanitizers appeared almost everywhere during the swine flu scare in 2010. At concentrations of 60% to 70%, these sanitizers are more effective at killing skin bacteria than plain soap and water. Alcohol kills bacteria by disintegrating plasma membranes and denaturing proteins.

▲ **Figure 17.10** A triclosan-free hand cleanser

Resistance against both detergents and alcohol-based sanitizers would require a fundamental change in the structure of proteins and the plasma membrane. A change of this magnitude is highly unlikely to occur. So the fear of soap or alcohol-based hand sanitizers generating resistant bacteria is unwarranted. And the rumour that these cleaners can promote resistance in bacteria is incorrect.

There is an element of truth in this rumour, however, with some antibacterial hand soap. Many products labelled "antibacterial" contain triclosan, an antimicrobial agent. Triclosan interacts specifically with an enzyme involved in maintenance of the bacterial cell wall and prevents its function. However, mutations may arise that alter the enzyme's structure, preventing triclosan from binding and thus granting resistance. Such mutations have already occurred in some strains of *Escherichia coli* and *Streptococcus pneumonia*, making them triclosan-resistant. Another concern about triclosan is that it may create resistance to antibiotics even without exposure. Antimicrobial agents targeting the same enzyme or pathway may also be rendered ineffective by the mutations that protect the bacterium from triclosan.

One study demonstrated that *E. coli* O157:H7, the cause of hamburger disease, gained some level of resistance to 7 of 15 antimicrobial agents tested. However, many scientists remain skeptical. To err on the side of caution, the Canadian Medical Association is encouraging federal legislation that restricts the sale of products containing triclosan. Aware of the issues with triclosan, some companies go so far as to advertise their products as being triclosan-free (**Figure 17.10**).

The rumour that bacteria evolve resistance to antibacterial soap is plausible if the soap contains triclosan. However, the risk of bacterial resistance against plain soap and alcohol-based hand sanitizers is improbable. Plain hand soap is as effective at reducing bacteria load on the skin as antibacterial soap, but without the risks. Other studies demonstrate that alcohol-based hand sanitizers are superior to both. The best way to keep your hands clean is to wash often in plain soapy water and when unavailable, use alcohol-based hand sanitizers. When buying hand soap and other cleaners, read the labels carefully and choose wisely.

? Why are bacteria unlikely to evolve resistance against alcohol-based hand sanitizers?

● Alcohol denatures proteins and disrupts plasma membranes. Becoming resistant would require alterations in the physical properties of these cellular components.

17.11 Biofilms are complex associations of bacteria

In many natural environments, bacteria attach to surfaces in highly organized colonies called **biofilms**. A biofilm may consist of one or several species of bacteria, and it may include protists and fungi as well. Biofilms can form on almost any support, including rocks, soil, organic material (including living tissue), metal, and plastic. You have a biofilm on your teeth: Dental plaque is a biofilm that can cause tooth decay. Biofilms can even form without a solid foundation—for example, on the surface of stagnant water.

Biofilm formation (**Figure 17.11A**) begins when prokaryotes secrete signalling molecules that attract nearby cells into a cluster. ❶ Once the cluster becomes sufficiently large, the cells produce a gooey polysaccharide matrix ❷ that glues them to the support and to each other, making the biofilm extremely difficult to dislodge. For example, if you don't scrub your shower, a biofilm could grow around the drain—running water alone is not strong enough to wash it away. As the biofilm gets larger and more complex, it becomes a "city" of microbes. ❸ Communicating by chemical signals, members of the community coordinate the division of labour, including defence against invaders and other activities. Channels in the biofilm allow nutrients to reach cells in the interior and allow wastes to leave, and a variety of environments develop within it.

Biofilms are common among bacteria that cause disease in humans. For instance, ear infections and urinary tract infections are often the result of biofilm-forming bacteria. Cystic fibrosis patients are vulnerable to pneumonia caused by bacteria that form biofilms in their lungs. Biofilms of harmful bacteria can also form on implanted medical devices such as catheters, replacement joints, or pacemakers. The complexity of biofilms makes these infections especially difficult to defeat. Antibiotics may not be able to penetrate beyond the outer layer of cells, leaving much of the community intact. For example, some biofilm bacteria produce an enzyme that breaks down penicillin faster than it can diffuse inward.

▲ **Figure 17.11B** A biofilm fouling the insides of a pipe

Biofilms that form in the environment can be difficult to eradicate, too. A variety of industries spend billions of dollars every year trying to get rid of biofilms that clog and corrode pipes, gum up filters and drains, and coat the hulls of ships (**Figure 17.11B**). Biofilms in water distribution pipes may survive chlorination, the most common method of ensuring that drinking water does not contain any harmful microorganisms. For example, biofilms of *Vibrio cholerae*—the bacterium that causes cholera—found in water pipes were capable of withstanding levels of chlorine 10 to 20 times higher than the concentrations routinely used to chlorinate drinking water.

? Why are biofilms difficult to eradicate?

Polysaccharide matrix

▲ **Figure 17.11A** Biofilm growth

● The biofilm sticks to the surface it resides on, and the cells that make up the biofilm stick to each other; the outer layer of cells may prevent antimicrobial substances from penetrating into the interior of the biofilm.

17.12 Bacteria can help to clean up the environment

The characteristics that have made bacteria so widespread and successful—their nutritional diversity, adaptability, and capacity for forming biofilms—also make them useful for cleaning up contaminants in the environment. **Bioremediation** is the use of organisms to remove pollutants from soil, air, or water.

Prokaryotic decomposers are the mainstays of sewage treatment facilities. Raw sewage is first passed through a series of screens and shredders, and solid matter settles out from the liquid waste. This solid matter, called sludge, is then gradually added to a culture of anaerobic prokaryotes, including both bacteria and archaea. The microbes decompose the organic matter in the sludge into material that can be placed in a landfill or used as fertilizer.

Liquid wastes are treated separately from the sludge. In **Figure 17.12A**, you can see a trickling filter system, one type of mechanism for treating liquid wastes. The long horizontal pipes rotate slowly, spraying liquid wastes onto a thick bed of rocks, the filter. Biofilms of aerobic bacteria and fungi growing on the rocks remove much of the organic material dissolved in the waste. Outflow from the rock bed is sterilized and then released, usually into a river or ocean.

Bioremediation has also become a useful tool for cleaning up toxic chemicals released into the soil and water. Naturally occurring bacteria capable of degrading pollutants such as oil, solvents, and pesticides are often present in contaminated soil and water, but their activity is limited by environmental

Rotating
spray arm

Rock bed coated
with aerobic
bacteria and fungi

Liquid wastes

Outflow

▲ **Figure 17.12A** The trickling filter system at a sewage treatment plant

Chemical dispersants were used in the massive Gulf of Mexico oil spill in 2010. Like detergents that help to clean greasy dishes, these chemicals break oil into smaller droplets that offer more surface area for microbial attack.

? **What is bioremediation?**

● The use of organisms to clean up pollution

▲ **Figure 17.12B** Treatment of an oil spill in Alaska

factors such as nutrient availability. In **Figure 17.12B**, workers are spraying an oil-polluted beach in Alaska with fertilizers to stimulate soil bacteria to speed up the breakdown of oil.

17.13 Some bacteria cause disease

All organisms, people included, are almost constantly exposed to pathogenic bacteria. Most often, our body's defences prevent pathogens from affecting us (see Chapter 34). Occasionally, however, a pathogen establishes itself in the body and causes illness. Even some of the bacteria that are normal residents of the human body can make us ill when our defences have been weakened by poor nutrition or by a viral infection. In May 2000, an infamous and tragic outbreak of the dangerous O157:H7 strain of the bacterium *E. coli* occurred in Walkerton, Ontario. Improper treatment and testing of the town's water supply allowed contaminated water to enter the public drinking water. In a matter of days, nearly half of the town's population of about 5000 became ill with diarrhea and other intestinal symptoms, such as cramps and nausea. Seven people died from their infections. This tragedy remains Canada's worst bacterial outbreak on record.

Most bacteria that cause illness do so by producing a poison—either an exotoxin or an endotoxin. **Exotoxins** are proteins that bacterial cells secrete into their environment. They include some of the most powerful poisons known. For example, *Staphylococcus aureus*, shown in **Figure 17.13**, produces several exotoxins. Although *S. aureus* is commonly found on the skin and in the nasal passages, if it enters the body through a wound, it can cause serious disease. One of its exotoxins destroys the white blood cells that attack invading bacteria, resulting in the pus-filled skin bumps characteristic of methicillin-resistant *S. aureus* infections (MRSA; see

21 942×

▲ **Figure 17.13** *Staphylococcus aureus*, an exotoxin producer

Module 10.19). Food may also be contaminated with *S. aureus* exotoxins, which are so potent that less than a millionth of a gram causes vomiting and diarrhea.

Endotoxins are lipid components of the outer membrane of gram-negative bacteria that are released when the cell dies or is digested by a defensive cell. All endotoxins induce the same general symptoms: fever, aches, and sometimes a dangerous drop in blood pressure (septic shock). Septic shock triggered by an endotoxin of *Neisseria meningitides*, which causes bacterial meningitis, can kill a healthy person in a matter of days or even hours. Because the bacteria are easily transmitted among people living in close contact, many universities and colleges require students to be vaccinated against this disease. Other examples of endotoxin-producing bacteria include the species of *Salmonella* that cause food poisoning and typhoid fever.

17.14 Koch's postulates are used to prove that a bacterium causes a disease

To test the hypothesis that a certain bacterium is the cause of a disease, a researcher must satisfy four conditions. This method of hypothesis testing, formulated by microbiologist Robert Koch in the late 19th century, is known as Koch's postulates. For a human disease, the researcher must be able to (1) find the candidate bacterium in every case of the disease; (2) isolate the bacterium from a person who has the disease and grow it in pure culture; (3) show that the cultured bacterium causes the disease when transferred to a healthy subject (usually an animal); and (4) isolate the bacterium from the experimentally infected subject. So when Australian microbiologist Barry Marshall hypothesized that chronic gastritis (an inflammation of the stomach lining that can lead to ulcers) was caused by a bacterium called *Helicobacter pylori*, he knew he would need to fulfill these criteria.

Over the course of several years, Marshall satisfied the first two requirements, but his efforts to infect animals failed to produce results. Taking another approach to the problem, he designed an experiment to test whether antibiotics would cure ulcers. However, the scientific community was highly skeptical of Marshall's hypothesis. Doctors and scientists had long believed that chronic gastritis was caused by lifestyle factors such as stress, diet, and smoking and saw no reason to pursue alternative explanations. As a result, Marshall had difficulty obtaining funding, and his research stalled.

Marshall didn't give up, continuing to accumulate evidence supporting his hypothesis. But he was frustrated watching so many patients suffer life-threatening complications from peptic (stomach) ulcers when his research might yield a simple cure. At last, Marshall decided to take a radical course of action—he would experiment on himself. He concocted a nasty brew of *H. pylori* and swallowed it. Several days later, he became ill from gastritis (step 3 of Koch's postulates). His stomach lining proved to be teeming with *H. pylori* (step 4). Marshall then cleared up his infection with antibiotics. He subsequently received funding to continue his research, and other scientists followed up with further studies. Several years after

▲ **Figure 17.14** Marshall (left) and colleague Robin Warren celebrating the success of Marshall's unorthodox experiment

Marshall's big gulp, an international conference of disease specialists finally accepted his conclusions about *H. pylori*.

In 1993, before Marshall established the pathogenicity of *H. pylori*, it was estimated that half of Canadians had this bacterium in their stomachs. Today, most confirmed cases are cured with antibiotics shortly after diagnosis. Now, the number of estimated cases has dropped to only 25% to 30%. However, 75% of First Nations peoples test positive for *H. pylori*. Barry Marshall and collaborator Robin Warren were awarded the 2005 Nobel Prize in Medicine for their discovery of *H. pylori* and its role in peptic ulcers (**Figure 17.14**).

BIOLOGY AND SOCIETY ## 17.15 Bacteria can be used as biological weapons

War has beleaguered humankind since the dawn of civilization. And warfare has evolved with the advent of new lethal technologies. Biological warfare, the use of deadly biological agents, has received a great deal of attention lately. In October 2001, endospores of *Bacillus anthracis*, the bacterium that causes anthrax, were mailed to members of the news media and the United States Senate. These attacks, which resulted in five deaths, raised public awareness of the potential for biological agents such as viruses and bacteria to be used as weapons.

B. anthracis forms hardy endospores (see Figure 17.9) that are commonly found in the soil of agricultural regions, where large grazing animals can become infected. People who work in agriculture, leather tanning, or wool processing occasionally catch the easily treated cutaneous (skin) form of anthrax from infected animals. Inhalation anthrax, which affects the lungs, is the deadly form of the disease. "Weaponizing" anthrax involves manufacturing a preparation of endospores that disperses easily in the air, where they will be inhaled by the target population. Endospores that enter the lungs germinate, and the bacteria multiply, producing an exotoxin that eventually accumulates to lethal levels in the blood. *B. anthracis* can be controlled by certain antibiotics, but the antibiotics kill only the bacteria—they can't eliminate the toxin already in the body. As a result, inhalation anthrax has a very high death rate.

Biological warfare is often misconceived as a new battle-front. However, biological weapons have been used for millennia. The Assyrians (2500 before present [BP]) poisoned water wells of enemies with a toxic fungus that induced deliria in those who drank from the well. Soldiers of Hannibal of Carthage (2200 BP) threw clay pots filled with venomous snakes onto enemy ships where they would bite enemy sailors upon their release. Several armies, including the Mongol and Turkish, catapulted plague-ridden corpses over garrisoned city walls, exposing city inhabitants to *Yersinia pestis*, the bacterium that causes plague. This strategy was used until 1710 when the Russians attacked the city of Reval (now Tallinn). Today, *Y. pestis* bacteria are carried by rodents in many parts of the world and are transmitted by fleas. People contract the disease known as plague when infected fleas bite them. When diagnosed in time, plague can be treated by antibiotics.

In the bubonic form of plague, egg-size swellings called buboes grow in the groin, armpits, and neck, and black blotches appear where the bacteria proliferate in clots under the skin (**Figure 17.15**). If bacteria spill into the bloodstream, death from the bacterial toxins is certain. Inhalation of *Y. pestis* causes the pneumonic form of plague. Bacteria infect cells in the lungs, becoming airborne as the disintegrating lung tissue is coughed out in droplets. As a result, pneumonic plague is

▶ **Figure 17.15**
Swellings (buboes) characteristic of the bubonic form of plague

easily transmitted from person to person and can become epidemic, the worst scenario for an attack by bioweapons.

Unlike other biological agents, the weapon form of *C. botulinum* is the exotoxin it produces, botulinum, rather than the living microbes. Botulinum is the deadliest poison known. Just 3 g of pure toxin, less than a sugar cube, is enough to kill every Canadian. Botulinum blocks transmission of the nerve signals that cause muscle contraction, resulting in paralysis of the muscles required for breathing. As a weapon, it would most likely be broadcast as an aerosol. *B. anthracis*, *Y. pestis*, and the exotoxin of *C. botulinum* are among the biological agents that are considered the highest-priority threats by many governments today.

 Why is *Bacillus anthracis* an effective bioweapon?

It is easy to obtain from the soil and forms potentially deadly endospores that resist destruction and can be easily dispersed.

R E V I E W

MasteringBiology® **For Practice Quizzes, BioFlix, MP3 Tutors, and Activities, go to masteringbiology.com.**

Reviewing the Concepts

Prokaryote Diversity (17.1–17.6)

17.1 Prokaryotes are diverse and widespread. Prokaryotes are the most numerous organisms. Although small, they have an immense impact on the environment and on our own health.

17.2 Prokaryotes have unparalleled nutritional diversity.

Nutritional Mode	Energy Source	Carbon Source
Photoautotroph	Sunlight	CO_2
Chemoautotroph	Inorganic chemicals	CO_2
Photoheterotroph	Sunlight	Organic compounds
Chemoheterotroph	Organic compounds	Organic compounds

17.3 Archaea and bacteria are the two main branches of prokaryotic evolution. Although archaea and bacteria are both prokaryotic, they are different in many ways.

17.4 Archaea thrive in extreme environments—and in other habitats. Domain Archaea includes extreme halophiles ("salt lovers"), extreme

thermophiles ("heat lovers"), and methanogens that thrive in anaerobic conditions. They are also a major life form in the ocean.

17.5 External features contribute to the success of bacteria. Bacteria can be classified by shape and by reaction to a Gram stain. Almost all prokaryotes have a cell wall. Other external features may include a sticky capsule, flagella that provide motility, or fimbriae that attach to surfaces. These external features enable bacteria to be successful in a wide range of environments.

17.6 Bacteria include a diverse assemblage of prokaryotes. Domain Bacteria is currently organized into five major groups: proteobacteria, gram-positive bacteria, cyanobacteria, chlamydiae, and spirochetes.

Bacterial Genetics (17.7–17.8)

17.7 Bacteria can transfer DNA in three ways. DNA can be transferred from one bacterium to another through transformation, transduction, or conjugation.

17.8 Bacterial plasmids can serve as carriers for gene transfer. Plasmids, discrete genetic elements, can hold valuable genes for bacteria, including those required for conjugation.

Bacteria (17.9–17.15)

17.9 Populations of bacteria can adapt rapidly to changes in the environment. Rapid bacteria population growth by binary fission generates a great deal of genetic variation, increasing the likelihood that some members of the population will survive changes in the environment. Some prokaryotes form specialized cells called endospores that remain dormant through harsh conditions.

17.10 Are antibacterial hand soaps creating strains of superbugs? Bacteria can become resistant to triclosan, an ingredient of some antibacterial soaps. Plain hand soap and alcohol-based hand sanitizers irreversibly damage proteins and plasma membranes, which bacteria cannot acquire resistance to.

17.11 Biofilms are complex associations of bacteria. Bacteria attach to surfaces and form biofilm communities that are difficult to eradicate, causing both medical and environmental problems.

17.12 Bacteria help to clean up the environment. Bacteria are often used for bioremediation, the restoration of environments, including in sewage treatment facilities.

17.13 Some bacteria cause disease. Pathogenic bacteria often cause disease by producing exotoxins or endotoxins.

Exotoxin	Endotoxin
Secreted by cell	Component of gram-negative plasma membrane

SEM 26 500×

SEM 4000×

Staphylococcus aureus   *Salmonella enteritidis*

17.14 Koch's postulates are used to prove that a bacterium causes a disease. Barry Marshall used the postulates to show that peptic ulcers are usually caused by a bacterium, *Helicobacter pylori*.

17.15 Bacteria can be used as biological weapons. Bacteria, such as the species that cause anthrax and plague, and bacterial toxins, such as botulinum, can be used as biological weapons.

Connecting the Concepts

1. Explain how each of the following characteristics contributes to the success of prokaryotes: cell wall, capsule, flagella, fimbriae, endospores.

2. Explain why the prokaryotes, Bacteria and Archaea, are not in the same domain. In your answer, compare and contrast the three domains.

Testing Your Knowledge

Multiple Choice

3. You are trying to identify a bacterium that is 1 μm wide and 5 μm long. Which of the following terms describes its shape?
   a. coccus   b. bacillus
   c. spiral   d. pleomorphic
   e. oval

4. A bacterium that can synthesize its own organic molecules and harvests energy from inorganic molecules can be described as
   a. photoautotrophic.
   b. chemoautotrophic.
   c. photoheterotrophic.
   d. chemoheterotrophic.
   e. photochemotrophic.

5. The bacteria that cause tetanus can be killed only by prolonged heating at temperatures considerably above boiling. This suggests that tetanus bacteria
   a. have cell walls containing peptidoglycan.
   b. protect themselves by secreting antibiotics.
   c. secrete endotoxins.
   d. are autotrophic.
   e. produce endospores.

6. Which of the following statements about bacterial virulence (ability to cause disease) is false?
   a. Infections by gram-negative bacteria are more serious than those by gram-positive bacteria.
   b. Bacteria that have capsules are more virulent than those without.
   c. The presence of a cell wall makes a bacterium more virulent.
   d. If a bacterium can attach to host cells with fimbriae, it will be more virulent.
   e. Infections by bacteria that produce endospores are more serious, as they can escape treatments by antibiotics.

7. Which of the following traits do archaea and bacteria share?
   1. composition of the cell wall
   2. presence of plasma membrane
   3. lack of a nuclear envelope
   4. identical rRNA sequences
   a. 1 only
   b. 4 only
   c. 1 and 3
   d. 2 and 3
   e. 1, 2, and 3

8. Penicillin is an antibiotic that inhibits enzymes from catalyzing the synthesis of peptidoglycan, so which prokaryotes should be least vulnerable to the effects of penicillin?
   a. *Mycoplasma*   b. gram-positive bacteria
   c. gram-negative bacteria d. endospore-bearing bacteria
   e. bacteria with a capsule

9. Which of the following bacteria are not pathogenic?
   a. *Chlamydia*   b. *Rhizobium*
   c. *Streptococcus*   d. *Salmonella*
   e. *Bacillus anthracis*

Describing, Comparing, and Explaining

10. Explain why bacteria populations can adapt rapidly to changes in their environment.

11. Describe how a scientist would prove that a bacterium causes a disease.

12. Describe how bacteria form biofilms. What are some of the impacts biofilms have on humans?

Applying the Concepts

13. Imagine you are on a team designing a moon base that will be self-contained and self-sustaining. Once supplied with building materials, equipment, and organisms from Earth, the base will be expected to function indefinitely. One of the team members has suggested that everything sent to the base be sterilized so that no bacteria of any kind are present. Do you think this is a good idea? Predict some of the consequences of eliminating all bacteria from an environment.

14. What actions can people take to minimize the risk of bacteria developing antibiotic resistance? Explain how each action would help to prevent resistance.

Answers to all questions can be found in Appendix E.

Biodiversity of Protists and Fungi

BIG IDEAS

Diversity of Protists

(18.1–18.9)

Most protists are microscopic, unicellular eukaryotes. Yet some protists are large multicellular organisms.

Diversity of Fungi

(18.10–18.16)

Fungi are a diverse group of organisms that acquire nutrients through absorption. Many fungi have complex life cycles.

The Whiskey-Loving Fungus

The air around any whiskey distillery warehouse is heavy with whiffs of spices, caramel, and fresh-cut lumber, blended with a hint of ethanol from the liquid gold aging inside. Another distinct characteristic of the area around these warehouses is a black fungus with an unusual thirst, growing on the surfaces of nearby walls, rocks, and trees. This mould was originally misidentified in 1881; but, in 2007, Dr. James Scott of the University of Toronto recognized the mould actually belonged to a new genus of sac fungus and renamed it *Baudoinia compniacensis*. It has long been thought that the fungus consumes ethanol, and it has been colloquially called the alcoholic fungus or angel's share fungus.

Whiskey is a spirit (hard liquor) made from the distillation of fermented grain products. Although Scotland is famous for its Scotch whisky (the spelling without the *e* is usually reserved for Scotch), most grain-producing nations, including Canada, also produce whiskey. Residents in the vicinity of the Hiram Walker distillery in Lakeshore, Ontario, complained of a black mould growing on their houses and blamed the distillery. Structures as far away as 1.5 km showed signs of the mould. Closer to the warehouses, the mould covered more area and grew thicker. (Similar fungus growth occurs near distillery warehouses throughout North America and Europe.) But how was the fungus getting the ethanol?

Aging is an important step in whiskey production and is required by law. To be called Canadian whiskey, the grain alcohol must age in oak casks for at least three years. Aging longer produces a finer product and it is not uncommon for distillers to age their whiskey for 10 years or more. But oak casks are not airtight and vapours can escape through the porous walls. The aging spirit loses approximately 2% ethanol by volume every year. The evaporative loss is called the angel's share and is what you smell when around a whiskey warehouse. After aging for 10 years, what started as 80% grain alcohol has matured into 62% whiskey. (Most cask strength whiskeys are diluted to 40% before bottling.)

The ethanol vapour that diffuses from warehouses actually provides a supplemental carbon source for nearby fungi. In the absence of ethanol, *B. compniacensis* generated energy from glucose using glycolysis followed by the citric acid cycle and oxidative phosphorylation. However, when exposed to small concentrations of ethanol vapour (10 parts per million [ppm] in vapour), different enzymes are turned on that convert ethanol into acetaldehyde, which enters a modified citric acid cycle. An alternative energy generating cycle and two carbon sources (ethanol and glucose) allows for robust growth of *B. compniacensis* in areas with low ethanol concentrations in the atmosphere, namely around distillery warehouses and bakeries. Another fungus, the wine cellar mould (*Racodium cellare*), common in underground cellars, also uses ethanol as an alternative carbon source.

Interestingly, higher concentrations of ethanol actually inhibit the growth of *B. compniacensis*. Exposure to 100 ppm ethanol in vapour inhibited growth of the mould by one-third. It appears that this fungus is not greedy and truly wants only the angel's share. In the second half of this chapter, we continue our look at fungi in more detail. But first, let's explore the diversity of some other eukaryotic microorganisms, the protists.

Diversity of Protists

18.1 Protists are an extremely diverse assortment of eukaryotes

Protists are a diverse collection of mostly unicellular eukaryotes. Biologists used to classify all protists in a kingdom called Protista, but now it is thought that these organisms constitute multiple kingdoms within domain Eukarya. While our knowledge of the evolutionary relationships among these diverse groups remains incomplete, *protist* is still useful as a convenient term to refer to eukaryotes that are not plants, animals, or fungi.

Protists obtain their nutrition in a variety of ways **(Figure 18.1A)**. Some protists are autotrophs, producing their food by photosynthesis; these are called algae (another useful term that is not taxonomically meaningful). Many algae, including the one shown on the left in Figure 18.1A, are multicellular. Other protists, informally called *protozoans*, are heterotrophs, eating bacteria and other protists. Some heterotrophic protists are funguslike and obtain organic molecules by absorption, and some are parasitic. Parasites derive their nutrition from a living host, which is harmed by the interaction. *Giardia*, shown in the middle of Figure 18.1A, is a human parasite. Still other protists are **mixotrophs**, capable of both photosynthesis and heterotrophy, depending on availability of light and nutrients. An example is *Euglena*, shown on the right in Figure 18.1A.

Protist habitats are also diverse. Most protists are aquatic, and they are found almost anywhere there is moisture, including terrestrial habitats such as damp soil and leaf litter. Others inhabit the bodies of various host organisms. For example, **Figure 18.1B** shows one of the protists that are endosymbionts in the intestinal tract of termites (see Module 39.2).

As eukaryotes, protists are more complicated than any prokaryotes. Their cells have a membrane-enclosed nucleus (containing multiple chromosomes) and other organelles characteristic of eukaryotic cells. The flagella and cilia of protistan

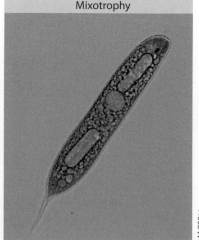

◀ **Figure 18.1B** A protist from a termite gut covered by thousands of flagella, viewed with scanning electron microscope (left) and light microscope (below).

SEM 560×

LM 325×

cells have a 9 + 2 pattern of microtubules, another typical eukaryotic trait (see Module 4.17).

Because most protists are unicellular, they are justifiably considered the simplest eukaryotes. However, the cells of many protists are among the most elaborate in the world. This level of cellular complexity is not really surprising, for each unicellular protist is a complete eukaryotic organism analogous to an entire animal or plant.

With their extreme diversity, protists are difficult to categorize. Recent molecular and cellular studies have shaken the foundations of protistan taxonomy as much as they have that of the prokaryotes. Intuitive groupings such as protozoans and algae are phylogenetically meaningless because the nutritional modes used to categorize them are spread across many different lineages. It is now clear that there are multiple clades

▶ **Figure 18.1A**
Protist modes of nutrition

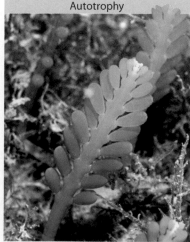
Autotrophy

Caulerpa, a green alga

Heterotrophy

Colourized SEM 2000×

Giardia, a parasite

Mixotrophy

LM 700×

Euglena

of protists, with some lineages more closely related to plants, fungi, or animals than they are to other protists. We have chosen to organize our brief survey of protist diversity by using one current hypothesis of protist phylogeny, which proposes five monophyletic "supergroups": Chromalveolata, Rhizaria, Excavata, Unikonta, and Archaeplastida. While there is general agreement on some of these groupings, others are hotly debated—the classification of protists is very much a work in progress. Before embarking on our tour of protists, however, let's consider how their extraordinary diversity originated.

? **What is a general definition for "protist"?**

● A eukaryote that is not an animal, fungus, or plant

18.2 Secondary endosymbiosis is the key to much of protist diversity

As Module 18.1 indicates, protists are bewilderingly diverse. What is the origin of this enormous diversity? To explain, let's first review the endosymbiont theory for the origin of mitochondria and chloroplasts (see Module 4.15). According to that theory, eukaryotic cells evolved when prokaryotes with special capabilities established residence within other, larger prokaryotes. The evidence for this theory includes the structural and molecular similarities between prokaryotic cells and present-day mitochondria and chloroplasts. Mitochondria and chloroplasts even replicate their own DNA and reproduce by a process similar to that of prokaryotes.

Scientists think that heterotrophic eukaryotes evolved first; these had mitochondria but not chloroplasts. As shown in **Figure 18.2**, autotrophic eukaryotes are thought to have arisen later from a lineage of heterotrophic eukaryotes descended from ❶ an individual that engulfed an autotrophic cyanobacterium through primary endosymbiosis. If the cyanobacterium continued to function within its host cell, its photosynthesis would have provided a steady source of food for the heterotrophic host and thus given it a significant selective advantage. And because the cyanobacterium had its own DNA, it could reproduce to make multiple copies of itself within the host cell. In addition, cyanobacteria could be passed on when the host reproduced. Over time, ❷ the descendants of the original cyanobacterium evolved into chloroplasts. The chloroplast-bearing lineage of eukaryotes later diversified into ❸ the autotrophs green algae and red algae (see Module 18.2).

On subsequent occasions during eukaryotic evolution, ❹ green algae and red algae themselves became endosymbionts following ingestion by heterotrophic eukaryotes. Heterotrophic host cells enclosed the algal cells in food vacuoles ❺ but the algae—or parts of them—survived and became cellular organelles. The presence of the endosymbionts, which also had the ability to replicate themselves, gave their hosts a selective advantage. This process, in which an autotrophic eukaryotic protist became endosymbiotic in a heterotrophic eukaryotic protist, is called **secondary endosymbiosis**. Secondary endosymbiosis appears to be a major key to protist diversity. Figure 18.2 shows how secondary endosymbiosis of green algae could give rise to mixotrophs, such as the *Euglena* in Figure 18.1A. Secondary endosymbiosis of red algae led to nutritional diversity in other groups of protists.

? Distinguish between primary and secondary endosymbiosis.

● In primary endosymbiosis, the endosymbiont is a prokaryote. In secondary endosymbiosis, the endosymbiont is a eukaryote.

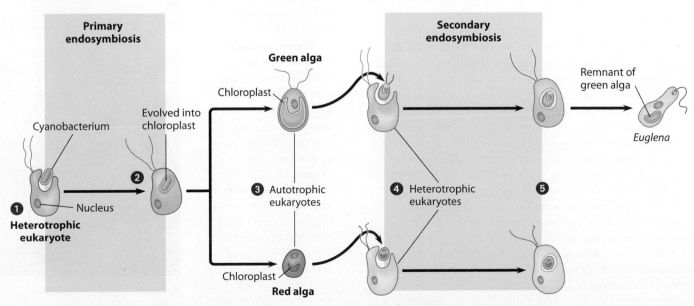

▲ **Figure 18.2** The theory of the origin of protistan diversity through endosymbiosis (mitochondria not shown)

18.3 Chromalveolates represent the range of protist diversity

Our sample of protist diversity begins with the supergroup **Chromalveolata** (the chromalveolates). This large, extremely diverse group includes autotrophic, heterotrophic, and mixotrophic species and multicellular as well as unicellular species. Although some evidence supports Chromalveolata as monophyletic, it remains a controversial grouping.

Autotrophic chromalveolates include **diatoms**, unicellular algae that have a unique glassy cell wall containing silica. The cell wall of a diatom consists of two halves that fit together like the bottom and lid of a shoe box **(Figure 18.3A)**. Both freshwater and marine environments are rich in diatoms, and the organic molecules these microscopic algae produce are a key source of food in all aquatic environments. Some diatoms store food reserves in the form of lipid droplets as well as carbohydrates. In addition to being a rich source of energy, the lipids make the diatoms buoyant, which keeps them floating near the surface in the sunlight. Massive accumulations of fossilized diatoms make up thick sediments known as diatomaceous earth, which is mined for use as a filtering medium and as a grinding and polishing agent.

Dinoflagellates, a group that includes unicellular autotrophs, heterotrophs, and mixotrophs, are also very common components of marine and freshwater plankton (communities of microorganisms that live near the water's surface). Blooms—population explosions—of autotrophic dinoflagellates sometimes cause warm coastal waters to turn pinkish orange, a phenomenon known as "red tide" **(Figure 18.3B)**. Toxins produced by some red-tide dinoflagellates have killed large numbers of fish. Humans who consume molluscs that have accumulated the toxins by feeding on dinoflagellates may be affected as well. One genus of photosynthetic dinoflagellates resides within the cells of reef-building corals, providing at least half the energy used by the corals. Without these algal partners, corals could not build and sustain the massive reefs that provide the food, living space, and shelter that support the splendid diversity of the reef community.

Brown algae are large, complex chromalveolates. Like diatoms and some dinoflagellates, they are autotrophic. Brown algae owe their characteristic brownish colour to some of the pigments in their chloroplasts. All are multicellular, and most are marine. Brown algae include many of the species commonly called seaweeds. We use the word *seaweeds* here to refer to marine algae that have large multicellular bodies but lack

Colourized SEM 200×

▲ **Figure 18.3A**
Diatom, a unicellular alga

▲ **Figure 18.3B** A red tide caused by *Gymnodinium*, a dinoflagellate

the roots, stems, and leaves found in most plants. (Some red and green algae are also referred to as seaweeds.) **Figure 18.3C** shows an underwater bed of brown algae called **kelp** off the coast of California. Anchored to the seafloor by rootlike structures, kelp may grow to heights of 60 m, taller than a 15-story building. Fish, sea lions, sea otters, and grey whales regularly use these kelp "forests" as their feeding grounds. These communities will be discussed further in Module 38.10.

Water moulds are heterotrophic unicellular chromalveolates that typically decompose dead plants and animals in freshwater habitats. Because many species resemble fungi **(Figure 18.3D)**, water moulds were classified as fungi until molecular comparisons revealed their kinship to protists. Parasitic water moulds sometimes grow on the skin or gills of fish. Water moulds also include

▲ **Figure 18.3C** Brown algae: a kelp "forest"

plant parasites called downy mildews. "Late blight" of potatoes, a disease caused by a downy mildew, led to a devastating famine in Ireland in the mid-1800s. A closely related pathogen has swept through tomato crops throughout North America since 2009, depriving fast-food burgers of a standard topping and home gardeners of a favourite summertime treat.

Ciliates, named for their use of cilia to move and to sweep food into their mouth, are a group of unicellular protists that includes heterotrophs and mixotrophs. You may have seen the common freshwater protist *Paramecium* (see Figure 4.11A) in a biology lab. Like many ciliates, the example shown in **Figure 18.3E** swims by beating its cilia in a wavelike motion. Other ciliates "crawl" over a surface by using cilia that are arranged in bundles along the length of the cell.

Another subgroup of Chromalveolata is made up of parasites, including some that cause serious diseases in humans. For example, *Plasmodium*, which causes malaria, kills nearly a million people a year. You can read more about *Plasmodium*

▲ **Figure 18.3D** Water mould (white threads) decomposing a goldfish

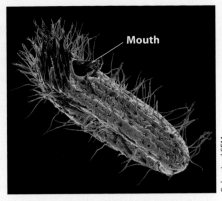

▲ **Figure 18.3E** A freshwater ciliate showing cilia distributed over the cell surface and around the mouth

in Canada in the chapter-opening essay for Chapter 39. Some stages of *Plasmodium*'s complex life cycle take place in certain species of mosquitoes, which transmit the parasite to humans.

? **Which subgroups of chromalveolates include autotrophs?**

● Diatoms, dinoflagellates, and brown algae

RUMOUR HAS IT ## 18.4 Can algae provide a renewable source of energy?

There is no question that our culture runs on fossil fuels. But, have you ever wondered what the "fossils" are in fossil fuels? They are organic remains of organisms that lived hundreds of millions of years ago. Diatoms are thought to be the main source of oil, while coal was formed from primitive plants (see Module 19.7). Rapid consumption is depleting the world's supply of readily accessible fossil fuels. We are on the verge of an energy crisis. In 2006, the world reached its highest level of conventional oil production to date, after which the production started to slow down. When oil production decreases, its price increases. Higher oil prices make even the costly extraction from Alberta's oil sands profitable. Many scientists are looking for alternative, affordable energy sources. You may have heard of corn being used for biodiesel. Rumour has it that algae can also be used as a renewable source of energy. So, will we be filling our tanks at the neighbourhood algae station one day?

Renewable biofuels include both ethanol and biodiesel, and their production is a very active area of research. Ethanol is produced by the fermentation of starches within corn and wheat, whereas biodiesel, or green diesel, can be processed from vegetable oil, canola oil, waste cooking oil, and animal fats. Although biodiesel is available only at a few stations in British Columbia and Ontario, ethanol-blended gasoline is in every pump in the country. You have probably used biofuels and may not have known it. Canadian Renewable Fuels Regulations require that all gasoline sold in Canada contains at least 5% ethanol. The hope of these regulations is to reduce our dependence on fossil fuel energy. Also, reduced fossil fuel

consumption would decrease the release of CO_2 from sequestered sources and mitigate climate change.

The use of corn and wheat for the production of biofuels has been brought into question. Problems arise when forested land is cleared to grow biofuel crops; an act that actually increases global climate change. Using food, such as corn or wheat, to produce fuel, means that more food has to be grown to feed the country. Planting more crops would require the conversion of natural ecosystems into farmland. Moreover, ethanol-blended gasoline may produce as many emissions as traditional gasoline.

A solution to the biofuel dilemma may be algae. Algae produce energy by the process of photosynthesis, which converts light energy to chemical energy, and then stores the chemical energy in sugar. Some algal species store excess chemical energy in lipid droplets that could be extracted and converted to biodiesel—green oil. Alternatively, carbohydrates produced by algae could be used to make ethanol. Unlike biofuel crops such as corn or oil palms, algae don't require large areas of fertile soil, and they grow quickly. Some designs even include using the CO_2 emissions from coal-fired power plants—a major contributor to climate change—as the carbon source for their photosynthesis.

Lipid droplets in diatoms and other algae are a potential source of renewable energy. After all, the energy we extract from fossil fuels was originally stored in organisms through the process of photosynthesis. Why wait millions of years? If unicellular algae could be grown on a large scale, the oil could be harvested and processed into biodiesel. When supplied with light, carbon dioxide, and nutrients, unicellular algae reproduce rapidly. In one scenario, algae could be grown indoors in closed "bioreactor" vessels (chambers containing living organisms, which allow scientists to collect specific biochemical products) under tightly controlled environmental conditions (**Figure 18.4**). Outdoor systems using closed bioreactors or open-air ponds are also being developed. An open-air pond can produce far more oil, and therefore biodiesel, than traditional crops per unit area, up to 100 times more than canola and 800 times more than corn. Bioreactors could increase production even further; however, some energy input would be required.

There are numerous technical hurdles to overcome before the industrial-scale production of biofuel from algae becomes a reality. Investigators must identify the most productive of the hundreds of algal species and test whether they are suitable for mass culturing methods. With further research, scientists may be able to improve desirable characteristics such as growth rate or oil yield through genetic engineering. In addition, manufacturers need to develop cost-effective methods of harvesting the algae and extracting and processing the oil. With this in mind, the rumour about algae being a source of renewable energy is absolutely true. We just need to develop ways to use it. When that happens, there might be an algae-powered vehicle in your future.

▲ **Figure 18.4** Green algae in a bioreactor

? What characteristics of unicellular algae make them attractive candidates for the production of biofuels?

● Rapid reproduction; would not occupy farmland needed to grow food crops

18.5 Rhizarians include a variety of amoebas

The clade **Rhizaria** was recently proposed based on similarities in DNA, although some scientists disagree and think that rhizarians should be placed in Chromalveolata. The two largest groups in Rhizaria, foraminiferans and radiolarians, are among the organisms referred to as amoebas. **Amoebas** move and feed by means of **pseudopodia** (singular, *pseudopodium*), which are temporary extensions of the cell. Molecular systematics now indicates that amoebas are dispersed across many taxonomic groups. Most of the amoebas in Rhizaria are distinguished from other amoebas by their threadlike (rather than lobe-shaped) pseudopodia.

Foraminiferans (forams) (**Figure 18.5A**) are found both in the ocean and in fresh water. They have porous shells, called tests, composed of organic material hardened by calcium carbonate. The pseudopodia, which

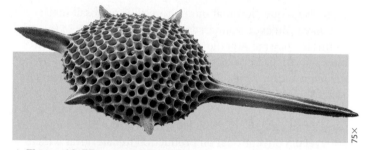

▲ **Figure 18.5B** A radiolarian skeleton

75×

function in feeding and locomotion, extend through small pores in the test (see Figure 18.5A inset). Ninety percent of identified forams are fossils. The fossilized tests, which are a component of sedimentary rock, are excellent markers for correlating the ages of rocks in different parts of the world.

Like forams, **radiolarians** produce a mineralized support structure, in this case an internal skeleton made of silica (**Figure 18.5B**). The cell is also surrounded by a test composed of organic material. Most species of radiolarians are marine. When they die, their hard parts, like those of forams, settle to the bottom of the ocean and become part of the sediments. In some areas, radiolarians are so abundant that sediments, known as radiolarian ooze, are hundreds of metres thick.

▲ **Figure 18.5A** A foraminiferan (inset SEM shows a foram test)

LM 700×

? What minerals compose foram tests and radiolarian skeletons?

● Forams: calcium carbonate; radiolarians: silica

18.6 Some excavates have modified mitochondria

Excavata (the excavates) has recently been proposed as a clade on the basis of molecular and morphological similarities. The name refers to an "excavated" feeding groove possessed by some members of the group. Many excavates have modified mitochondria that lack functional electron transport chains and use anaerobic pathways such as glycolysis to extract energy. Heterotrophic excavates include the termite endosymbiont shown in Figure 18.1B. There are also autotrophic species and mixotrophs, such as *Euglena* (see Figure 18.1A).

Some excavates are parasites. *Giardia intestinalis* (see Figure 18.1A) is the most common waterborne parasite in North America. *Giardia* has two life stages: a dormant cyst that can survive in surface waters and an active trophozoite that colonizes the intestines of its hosts. Cysts are passed in the feces of infected animals and may enter nearby water systems. When ingested by a new host, cysts release two trophozoites that reproduce asexually by mitosis and establish an infection. People most often pick up *Giardia* by drinking water contaminated with dormant cysts. For example, a hiker might become infected after drinking contaminated water from a seemingly pristine stream and end up with a bout of severe diarrhea. (Boiling the water before drinking it will kill *Giardia*.)

Another excavate, *Trichomonas vaginalis* (**Figure 18.6A**), is a common sexually transmitted parasite that causes an

▲ **Figure 18.6B** A parasitic excavate: *Trypanosoma* (with blood cells)

Colourized SEM 1500×

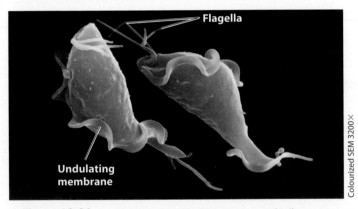

Flagella

Undulating
membrane

Colourized SEM 3200×

▲ **Figure 18.6A** A parasitic excavate: *Trichomonas vaginalis*

estimated 5 million new infections each year. The parasite travels through the reproductive tract by moving its flagella and undulating part of its membrane. In women, the protists feed on white blood cells and bacteria living on the cells lining the vagina. *T. vaginalis* also infects the cells lining the male reproductive tract, but limited availability of food results in very small population sizes. Consequently, males typically have no symptoms of infection, although they can repeatedly infect their female partners. The only treatment available is a drug called metronidazole. Disturbingly, drug resistance seems to be evolving in *T. vaginalis*, especially on college and university campuses.

Members of the excavate genus *Trypanosoma* are parasites that can be transmitted to humans by insects. For instance, the trypanosome shown in **Figure 18.6B** causes sleeping sickness, a potentially fatal disease spread by the African tsetse fly. The squiggly cells in the photo are cells of *Trypanosoma*; the circular cells are human red blood cells.

 How do the nutritional modes of *Euglena* and *Trichomonas* differ?

Euglena is mixotrophic; *Trichomonas* is strictly heterotrophic. ●

18.7 Unikonts include protists that are closely related to fungi and animals

Unikonta is a controversial grouping that joins two well-established clades: **amoebozoans**, which are protists, and a second clade that includes animals and fungi. You'll learn about the amoebozoans in this module, and then return to the second clade in later modules of this chapter.

Amoebozoans, including many species of free-living amoebas, some parasitic amoebas, and the slime moulds, have lobe-shaped pseudopodia. The amoeba in **Figure 18.7A** is poised

Colourized TEM 2000×

▲ **Figure 18.7A** An amoeba beginning to ingest an algal cell

to ingest an alga. Its pseudopodia arch around the prey and will enclose it in a food vacuole (see Module 4.10). Free-living amoebas creep over rocks, sticks, or mud at the bottom of a pond or an ocean. A parasitic species of amoeba causes amoebic dysentery, a potentially fatal diarrheal disease.

The yellow, branching growth on the dead log in **Figure 18.7B** is an amoebozoan called a **plasmodial slime mould**. These protists are common where there is moist, decaying organic matter and are often brightly pigmented. Although it is large and has many extensions, the organism in Figure 18.7B is not multicellular. Rather, it is a **plasmodium**, a single, multinucleate mass of cytoplasm undivided by plasma membranes. (Don't confuse this word with the

▲ Figure 18.7B A plasmodial slime mould: *Physarum*

chromalveolate *Plasmodium*, which causes malaria.) Because most of the nuclei go through mitosis at the same time, plasmodial slime moulds are used to study molecular details of the cell cycle.

The plasmodium extends pseudopodia through soil and rotting logs, engulfing food by phagocytosis as it grows. Within the fine channels of the plasmodium, cytoplasm streams first one way and then the other in pulsing flows that probably help to distribute nutrients and oxygen. When food and water are in short supply, the plasmodium stops growing and differentiates into reproductive structures (shown in the inset in Figure 18.7B) that produce spores.

When conditions become favourable, the spores release haploid cells that fuse to form a zygote, and the life cycle continues.

Cellular slime moulds are also common on rotting logs and decaying organic matter. Most of the time, these organisms exist as solitary amoeboid cells. When food is scarce, the amoeboid cells swarm together, forming a sluglike aggregate that wanders around for a short time. Some of the cells then dry up and form a stalk supporting an asexual reproductive structure in which yet other cells develop into spores. The cellular slime mould *Dictyostelium*, shown in **Figure 18.7C**, is a useful model for researchers studying the genetic mechanisms and chemical changes underlying cellular differentiation.

? Contrast the plasmodium of a plasmodial slime mould with the sluglike stage of a cellular slime mould.

● A plasmodium is not multicellular but is one cytoplasmic mass with many nuclei; the sluglike stage of a cellular slime mould consists of many cells.

▲ Figure 18.7C An aggregate of amoeboid cells (left) and the reproductive structure of a cellular slime mould, *Dictyostelium*

18.8 Archaeplastids include red algae, green algae, and land plants

Almost all the members of the supergroup **Archaeplastida** are autotrophic. As you learned in Module 18.2, autotrophic eukaryotes are thought to have arisen by primary endosymbiosis of a cyanobacterium that evolved into chloroplasts. The descendants of this ancient protist evolved into red algae and green algae, which are key photosynthesizers in aquatic food webs. Archaeplastida also includes land plants, which evolved from a group of green algae.

The warm coastal waters of the tropics are home to the majority of species of **red algae**. Their red colour comes from an accessory pigment that masks the green of chlorophyll. Although a few species are unicellular, most red algae are multicellular. Multicellular red algae are typically soft-bodied, but some have cell walls encrusted with hard, chalky deposits. Encrusted species, such as the one in **Figure 18.8A**, are common on coral reefs, and their hard parts are important in building and maintaining the reef. Other red algae are

▲ Figure 18.8A An encrusted red alga

commercially important. Carrageenan, a gel that is used to stabilize many products, including ice cream, chocolate milk, and pudding, is derived from species of red algae. Sheets of a red alga, known as nori, are used to wrap sushi. Agar, a polysaccharide used as a substrate for growing bacteria, also comes from red algae.

Green algae, which are named for their grass-green chloroplasts, include unicellular and colonial species as well as multicellular seaweeds. The micrograph on the right in **Figure 18.8B** shows *Chlamydomonas*, a unicellular alga common in freshwater lakes and ponds. It is propelled through the water by two flagella. (Such cells are said to be biflagellated.) *Volvox*, shown on the left, is a colonial green alga. Each *Volvox* colony is a hollow ball composed of hundreds or thousands of biflagellated cells. As the flagella move, the colony tumbles slowly through the water. Some of the large colonies shown here contain small daughter colonies that will eventually be released.

Ulva, or sea lettuce, is a multicellular green alga. Like many multicellular algae and all land plants, *Ulva* has a complex life cycle that includes an **alternation of generations (Figure 18.8C)**. In this type of life cycle, a multicellular diploid ($2n$) form alternates with a multicellular haploid (n) form. Notice in the figure that multicellular

Volvox LM 80×   *Chlamydomonas* SEM 2600×

▲ **Figure 18.8B** Green algae, colonial (left) and unicellular (right)

diploid forms are called **sporophytes**, because they produce spores. The sporophyte generation alternates with a haploid generation that features a multicellular haploid form called a **gametophyte**, which produces gametes. In *Ulva*, the gametophyte and sporophyte organisms are identical in appearance; both look like the one in the photograph, although they differ in chromosome number. The haploid gametophyte produces gametes by mitosis, and fusion of the gametes begins the sporophyte generation. In turn, cells in the sporophyte undergo meiosis and produce haploid, flagellated spores. The life cycle is completed when a spore settles to the bottom of the ocean and develops into a gametophyte. In the next chapter, you will learn about the alternation of generation life cycles in land plants.

▲ **Figure 18.8C** The life cycle of *Ulva*, a multicellular green alga

? How does chromosome number differ in the gametophyte and sporophyte in the alternation of generations life cycle?

● The gametophyte is haploid (*n*); the sporophyte is diploid (2*n*).

18.9 Multicellularity evolved several times in eukaryotes

Increased complexity often makes more variations possible. Thus, the origin of the eukaryotic cell led to an evolutionary radiation of new forms of life. As you have seen in this chapter, unicellular protists, which are structurally complex eukaryotic cells, are much more diverse in form than the simpler prokaryotes. The evolution of multicellular bodies broke through another threshold in structural organization.

Multicellular organisms—seaweeds, plants, animals, and most fungi—are fundamentally different from unicellular ones. In a unicellular organism, all of life's activities occur within a single cell. In contrast, a multicellular organism has various specialized cells that perform different functions and are dependent on one another. For example, some cells give the organism its shape, while others make or procure food, transport materials, enable movement, or reproduce. The division of labour among different cells within the multicellular body allows cells to focus on fewer tasks than a single-celled organism, which makes them more efficient. Furthermore, a larger body size provides extra protection from variable environmental conditions. By isolating the body's internal environment from the outside, individuals are better able to cope with a variable environment. Dr. Richard Dawkins, emeritus fellow at the

University of Oxford, is a proponent of the theory that multicellularity and the regulated internal environment are beneficial in protecting the germ line of the organism, improving the chance of passing its genes to the next generation.

As you have seen in this chapter so far, multicellular organisms have evolved from three different ancestral lineages: chromalveolates (containing brown algae), unikonts (containing fungi and animals), and archaeplastids (with red algae, green algae, and land plants). **Figure 18.9A** summarizes some current hypotheses for the early phylogeny of land plants and animals, which are all multicellular, and fungi, which are mostly multicellular.

A group of green algae called charophytes are the closest living relatives of the land plants. Around 500 million years ago, the move onto land began, probably as green algae living along the edges of lakes gave rise to ancestral plants.

According to one hypothesis, two separate unikont lineages led to fungi and animals. Based on molecular clock calculations, scientists estimate that the ancestors of animals and fungi diverged more than 1 billion years ago. A combination of morphological and molecular evidence suggests that a group of unikonts called choanoflagellates are the closest living protist relatives of animals. The bottom half of **Figure 18.9B** shows that the cells of choanoflagellates strongly resemble the "collar cells" with which sponges, the group that is closest to the root of the animal tree, obtain food. Similar cells have been found in other animals, but not in fungi or plants. Some species of choanoflagellates live as colonies, federations of independent cells sticking loosely together. Scientists hypothesize that the common ancestor of living animals may have been a stationary colonial choanoflagellate similar to the one shown in Figure 18.9B.

A different group of unikont protists is thought to have given rise to the fungi. Molecular evidence suggests that a group of single-celled protists called nucleariids—amoebas that feed on algae and bacteria—are the closest living relatives of fungi (top of Figure 18.9B). We will explore the diversity of the kingdom Fungi in the following modules.

? In what way do multicellular organisms differ fundamentally from unicellular ones?

● In unicellular organisms, all the functions of life are carried out within a single cell. Multicellular organisms have specialized cells that perform different functions.

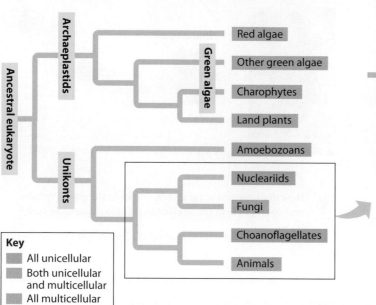

▲ **Figure 18.9A** A hypothesis for the phylogeny of plants, fungi, and animals

A nucleariid, closest living protistan relative of fungi

▲ **Figure 18.9B** The closest living protist relatives of fungi (top) and animals (bottom)

Diversity of Fungi

18.10 Fungi absorb food after digesting it outside their bodies

In the second half of this chapter, we turn our attention to the kingdom **Fungi**. You have probably seen fungi at some time, whether they were mushrooms sprouting in a lawn, bracket fungi attached to a tree like small shelves, or fuzzy patches of mould on leftover food. Despite the differences in their visible body forms, each of these fungi is obtaining food from its substrate in the same way. All fungi are heterotrophs that acquire their nutrients by **absorption**. They secrete powerful enzymes that digest macromolecules into monomers and then absorb the small nutrient molecules into their cells. For example, enzymes secreted by fungi growing on a loaf of bread digest the bread's starch into glucose molecules, which the fungal cells absorb. Some fungi produce enzymes that digest cellulose and lignin, the major structural components of

plants. Consequently, they are essential decomposers in most ecosystems.

The feeding structures of a fungus are a network of thread-like filaments called **hyphae** (singular *hypha*). Hyphae branch repeatedly as they grow, forming a mass known as a **mycelium** (plural, *mycelia*) **(Figure 18.10A)**. The "umbrellas" that you recognize as fungi, such as those in **Figure 18.10B**, are reproductive structures. Like the rest of the fungal body, the reproductive structures are made up of hyphae. In the type of fungus shown, mushrooms arise as small buds on a mycelium that extends throughout the food source, hidden from view. When a bud has developed sufficiently, the rapid absorption of water (for example, after a rainfall) creates enough hydraulic pressure to pop the mushroom to the surface. Above ground,

▲ Figure 18.10A Mycelium on fallen conifer needles

SEM 72×

the mushroom produces tiny reproductive cells called spores at the tips of specialized hyphae, and the spores are then dispersed on air currents.

Fungal hyphae are surrounded by a cell wall. Unlike plants, which have cellulose cell walls, most fungi have cell walls made of **chitin**, a strong, flexible nitrogen-containing polysaccharide, identical to the chitin found in the external skeletons of insects. In most fungi, the hyphae consist of chains of cells separated by cross-walls that have pores large enough to allow ribosomes, mitochondria, and even nuclei to flow from cell to cell. Some fungi lack cross-walls entirely and have many nuclei within a single mass of cytoplasm.

Fungi cannot run or fly in search of food. But their mycelium makes up for the lack of mobility by being able to grow at a phenomenal rate, branching throughout a food source and extending its hyphae into new territory. If you were to break open the log beneath the mushrooms in Figure 18.10B, for example, you would see strands of hyphae throughout the wood. Because its hyphae grow longer without getting thicker, the fungus develops a huge surface area from which it can secrete digestive enzymes and through which it can absorb food.

Not all fungi are decomposers. In the rest of this chapter, you will encounter some fungi that are parasites and others that live symbiotically with other organisms. Of special significance is the mutualistic symbiosis between fungi and plant roots called a mycorrhiza (meaning "fungus root"; plural, *mycorrhizae*), which will be discussed further in Module 39.5. Mycorrhizae absorb phosphorus and other essential minerals from the soil and make them available to the plant. Sugars

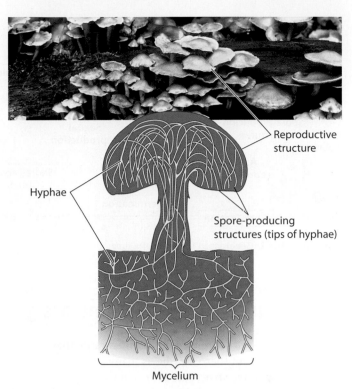

Reproductive structure

Hyphae

Spore-producing structures (tips of hyphae)

Mycelium

▲ Figure 18.10B Fungal reproductive and feeding structures

produced by the plant through photosynthesis nourish the fungus, making the relationship mutually beneficial. About 30% of known species of fungi are parasites, obtaining their nutrients at the expense of living plants or animals (see Module 39.6). Fungal parasites of plants are a serious concern among farmers.

? Contrast how fungi digest and absorb their food with your own digestion.

● A fungus digests its food externally by secreting enzymes onto the food and then absorbing the small nutrients that result from digestion. In contrast, humans and most other animals eat relatively large pieces of food and digest the food within their bodies.

18.11 Fungi produce spores in both asexual and sexual life cycles

Fungal reproduction typically involves the release of vast numbers of haploid spores, which are transported easily over great distances by wind or water. A spore that lands in a moist place where food is available germinates and produces a new haploid fungus. As you can see in **Figure 18.11**, however, spores can be produced either sexually or asexually.

In many fungi, sexual reproduction involves mycelia of different mating types. Hyphae from each mycelium release signalling molecules and grow toward each other. ❶ When the hyphae meet, their cytoplasms fuse. But this fusion of cytoplasm is often not followed immediately by the fusion of "parental" nuclei. Thus, many fungi have what is called a **heterokaryotic stage** (from the Greek, meaning "different nuclei"), in which cells contain two genetically distinct haploid

nuclei. Hours, days, or even centuries may pass before the parental nuclei fuse, ❷ forming the usually short-lived diploid phase. ❸ Zygotes undergo meiosis, producing haploid spores. As you'll learn in the next module, the specialized structures in which these spores are formed are used to classify fungi.

In asexual reproduction, ❹ spore-producing structures arise from haploid mycelia that have undergone neither a heterokaryotic stage nor meiosis. Many fungi that reproduce sexually can also produce spores asexually. In addition, asexual reproduction is the only known means of spore production in some fungi, informally known as **imperfect fungi**. Many species commonly called mould and yeasts are imperfect fungi. The term **mould** refers to any rapidly growing fungus that reproduces asexually by producing spores, often at the tips

Key

- ☐ Haploid (*n*)
- ■ Heterokaryotic (*n* + *n*) (unfused nuclei)
- ☐ Diploid (2*n*)

Heterokaryotic stage

❶ Fusion of cytoplasm

Fusion of nuclei

❷

Zygote (2*n*)

Meiosis

Sexual reproduction

Spore-producing structures

Spores (*n*)

Asexual reproduction

Mycelium

Spore-producing structures

❹

Germination

Germination

❸

Spores (*n*)

▲ **Figure 18.11** Generalized life cycle of a fungus

of specialized hyphae. These familiar furry carpets often appear on aging fruit and bread, and in seldom-cleaned shower stalls. The term **yeast** refers to any single-celled fungus. Yeasts reproduce asexually by cell division, often by budding—pinching off small "buds" from a parent cell. Yeasts inhabit liquid or moist habitats, such as plant sap and animal tissues. We will examine fungal reproduction more closely in Module 18.13, but first let's look at the classification of fungi.

? What is the heterokaryotic stage of a fungus?

● The stage in which each cell has two different nuclei (from two different parents), with the nuclei not yet fused.

18.12 Fungi are classified into five groups

Biologists who study fungi have described more than 100 000 species, but there may be as many as 1.5 million. Sexual reproductive structures are often used to classify species. Molecular analysis has helped scientists understand the phylogeny of fungi. The lineages that gave rise to fungi and animals are thought to have diverged from a flagellated unikont ancestor more than 1 billion years ago (see Module 18.9). The oldest undisputed fossils of fungi, however, are only about 460 million years old, perhaps because the ancestors of terrestrial fungi were microscopic and fossilized poorly.

Figure 18.12A shows a current hypothesis of fungal phylogeny. The multiple lines leading to the chytrids and the zygomycetes indicate that these groups are probably not monophyletic. For now, though, most biologists still talk in terms of the five groups (rather than phyla) of fungi shown here.

The **chytrids**, the only fungi with flagellated spores, are thought to represent the earliest lineage of fungi. They are common in lakes, ponds, and soil. Some species are decomposers; others parasitize protists, plants, or animals. Some researchers have linked the widespread decline of amphibian species to a highly infectious fungal disease caused by a species of chytrid. Populations of frogs in British Columbia and around the world have suffered massive mortality from this emerging disease.

The **zygomycetes**, or **zygote fungi**, are characterized by their protective zygosporangium, where zygotes produce haploid spores by meiosis. This diverse group includes fast-growing moulds, such as black bread mould (**Figure 18.12B**) and moulds that rot produce, such as peaches, strawberries, and sweet potatoes. Some zygote fungi are parasites on animals.

The **glomeromycetes** (from the Latin *glomer*, ball) form a distinct type of mycorrhiza in which hyphae that invade plant roots branch into tiny treelike structures known as arbuscules (**Figure 18.12C**). About 90% of all plants have such symbiotic partnerships with glomeromycetes, which deliver phosphate and other minerals to plants while receiving organic nutrients in exchange.

The **ascomycetes**, or **sac fungi**, are named for saclike structures called asci (from the Greek *asco*, pouch) that produce

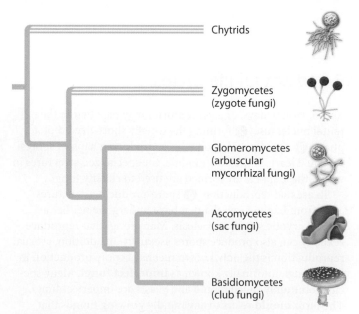

Chytrids

Zygomycetes (zygote fungi)

Glomeromycetes (arbuscular mycorrhizal fungi)

Ascomycetes (sac fungi)

Basidiomycetes (club fungi)

▲ **Figure 18.12A** A proposed phylogenetic tree of fungi

▲ **Figure 18.12B** Zygomycete: *Rhizopus stolonifer*, black bread mould

▲ **Figure 18.12C** Glomeromycete: an arbuscule in a root cell

Mushrooms

A puffball

Shelf fungi

▲ **Figure 18.12E** Basidiomycetes (club fungi)

spores in sexual reproduction. They live in a variety of marine, freshwater, and terrestrial habitats and range in size from unicellular yeasts to elaborate morels and cup fungi **(Figure 18.12D)**. Ascomycetes include some of the most devastating plant pathogens. Other species of ascomycetes live with green algae or cyanobacteria in symbiotic associations called lichens, which we discuss in Module 18.16.

When you think of fungi, you probably picture mushrooms, puffballs, or shelf fungi **(Figure 18.12E)**. These are examples of **basidiomycetes**, or **club fungi**. They are named for their club-shaped, spore-producing structure, called a basidium (meaning "little pedestal" in Latin; plural, *basidia*; see Figure 18.13C). Many species excel at breaking down the lignin found in wood and thus play key roles as decomposers. For example, shelf

fungi often break down the wood of weak or damaged trees and continue to decompose the wood after the tree dies. The basidiomycetes also include two groups of particularly destructive plant parasites, the rusts and smuts.

In the next module, we explore the life cycles of some representative fungi.

? What is one reason that chytrids are thought to have diverged earliest in fungal evolution?

● Chytrids are the only fungi that have flagellated spores, a characteristic of the ancestor of fungi.

Edible morels

Cup fungus

▲ **Figure 18.12D** Ascomycetes

18.13 Fungal groups differ in their life cycles and reproductive structures

The life cycle of black bread mould (see Figure 18.12B) is typical of zygomycetes. As hyphae grow through its food, the fungus reproduces asexually, forming spores in sporangia at

the tips of upright hyphae. When the food is depleted, the fungus reproduces sexually. As shown in **Figure 18.13A**, ❶ hyphae from mycelia of different mating types fuse (fungi

Zygosporangium ($n + n$)

1 Hyphae of different mating types Cells fuse **2** **3**

Fusion of nuclei

Meiosis

Young zygosporangium (heterokaryotic)

Sporangium (on stalk arising from the zygosporangium) **4** Spores (n)

Key
Haploid (n)
Heterokaryotic ($n + n$)
Diploid ($2n$)

▲ **Figure 18.13A** Sexual reproduction of a zygote fungus

do not have gametes that are distinguishably male or female) and **2** produce a cell containing multiple nuclei from two parents. **3** This young zygosporangium develops into a thick-walled structure that can tolerate dry or harsh environments. When conditions are favourable, the parental nuclei fuse to form diploid zygotes, which undergo meiosis, **4** producing haploid spores.

Like the zygomycetes, ascomycetes, such as those shown in Figure 18.12D, reproduce asexually when conditions are suitable. **Figure 18.13B** shows the typical life cycle of a sac fungus.

In many species, sexual reproduction takes place in the fall **1**, with the haploid

Key
Haploid (n)
Heterokaryotic ($n + n$)
Diploid ($2n$)

Dispersal
3
Autumn
Germination
ASEXUAL REPRODUCTION
Hypha
2
Mating type (+)
FUSION OF CYTOPLASM
Conidiophore
Ascus (heterokaryotic)
4
Mycelia
Heterokaryotic hyphae
Mycelium
Spring
Germination
SEXUAL REPRODUCTION
Dispersal
FUSION OF NUCLEI
1
Diploid nucleus (zygote)
Asci
Eight ascospores
Ascocarp
5
Four haploid nuclei
MEIOSIS

▲ **Figure 18.13B** Life cycle of a sac fungus

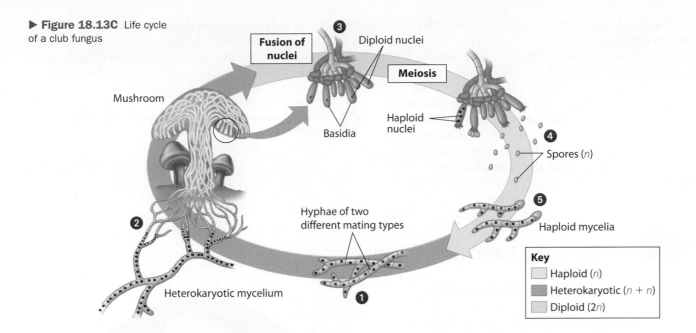

▶ **Figure 18.13C** Life cycle of a club fungus

Fusion of nuclei

Diploid nuclei

Meiosis

Mushroom

Basidia

Haploid nuclei

❸

Spores (n)

❹

❺

Haploid mycelia

Hyphae of two different mating types

❷

Heterokaryotic mycelium

❶

Key
- Haploid (n)
- Heterokaryotic (n + n)
- Diploid (2n)

spores maturing into mycelia in the early spring. The genetic diversity of these sexually produced spores increases the likelihood that at least one genotype will successfully establish itself in the environment encountered in the new season. ❷ The surviving individuals then reproduce asexually ❸ for several generations through the spring and summer before undergoing sexual reproduction. ❹ Diploid zygotes form on specialized structures on the heterokaryotic hyphae called asci (singular, *ascus*), ❺ which may be clustered in a larger fruiting body, the ascocarp.

Now let's follow the life cycle of a club fungus, a basidiomycete, starting at the centre bottom of **Figure 18.13C** ❶ The heterokaryotic stage begins when hyphae of two different mating types fuse, ❷ forming a heterokaryotic mycelium, which grows and produces the mushroom. In the club-shaped cells called basidia, which line the gills of a mushroom, ❸ the haploid nuclei fuse, forming diploid nuclei. Each diploid nucleus

then undergoes meiosis, producing haploid spores. ❹ A single mushroom can release as many as a billion spores. If spores land on moist matter that can serve as food, ❺ they germinate and grow into haploid mycelia.

Much of the success of fungi is due to their reproductive capacity, both in the asexual production of spores and in sexual reproduction, which increases genetic variation and facilitates adaptation to harsh or changing conditions.

? Under what conditions is asexual reproduction advantageous? Under what conditions is sexual reproduction advantageous?

● In asexual reproduction, a successful genotype can be propagated to take advantage of consistent, favourable conditions. Sexual reproduction reshuffles alleles, providing numerous genotypes that will be "tested" by the environment. This is an advantage when environmental conditions are changing.

18.14 Fungi have enormous ecological benefits

As you have read, fungi have been major players in terrestrial communities ever since they moved onto land in the company of plants. As symbiotic partners in mycorrhizae, fungi supply essential nutrients to plants and are enormously important in natural ecosystems and agriculture.

Fungi, along with bacteria, are essential decomposers in ecosystems, breaking down organic matter and restocking the environment with vital nutrients essential for plant growth. So many fungal spores are in the air that as soon as a leaf falls or an insect dies, it is covered with spores and is soon infiltrated by fungal hyphae **(Figure 18.14)**. If fungi and bacteria in a forest suddenly stopped decomposing, leaves, logs, feces, and dead animals would pile up on the forest floor. Plants—and the animals that eat plants—would starve

▲ **Figure 18.14** A fungal mycelium

because elements taken from the soil would not be replenished through decomposition.

Almost any organic (carbon-containing) substance can be consumed by fungi. During World War II, the moist tropical heat of Southeast Asia and islands in the Pacific Ocean provided ideal conditions for fungal decomposition of wood and natural fibres such as canvas and cotton. Packing crates, military uniforms, and tents quickly disintegrated, causing supply problems for the military forces. Synthetic substances are more resistant to fungal attack, but some fungi have the useful ability to break down toxic pollutants, including

the pesticide DDT and certain chemicals that cause cancer. Scientists are also investigating the possibility of using fungi that can digest petroleum products to clean up oil spills and other chemical messes.

? Name two essential roles that fungi play in terrestrial ecosystems.

● In mycorrhizae, fungi help plants acquire nutrients from the soil. When soil fungi decompose dead animals, fallen leaves, and other organic materials, they release nutrients that fertilize plant growth.

18.15 Fungi have many practical uses

Fungi have a number of culinary uses. Most of us have eaten mushrooms, although we may not have realized that we were ingesting reproductive structures of subterranean fungi. The distinctive flavours of certain cheeses, including Roquefort and blue cheese **(Figure 18.15A)**, come from fungi used to ripen them. Truffles, which are produced by certain mycorrhizal fungi associated with tree roots, are highly prized by gourmets. And humans have used yeasts for thousands of years to produce alcoholic beverages and cause bread to rise.

Fungi are medically valuable as well. Like the bacteria called actinomycetes (see Module 17.6), some fungi produce antibiotics that we use to treat bacterial diseases. In fact, the first antibiotic discovered was penicillin, which is made by the common mould called *Penicillium*. In **Figure 18.15B**, the clear area between the mould and the bacterial growth is where the antibiotic produced by *Penicillium* has inhibited the growth of the bacteria (*Staphylococcus aureus*).

Fungi also figure prominently in research in molecular biology and in biotechnology. Researchers often use yeasts to study the molecular genetics of eukaryotes because they are easy to culture and manipulate. Yeasts have also been genetically modified to produce human proteins for research and medical use.

Fungi may play a major role in the future production of biofuels from plants. Ideally, the biofuels would be derived from plants or plant parts that could not be used to feed people or livestock, such as straw, certain grasses, and wood. These plant materials are primarily

Staphylococcus aureus (bacteria) — *Penicillium* (mould) — Zone of inhibited growth

▲ **Figure 18.15B** A culture of *Penicillium* and bacteria

made up of cellulose and lignin, large molecules that are difficult to decompose. Researchers are currently investigating a variety of fungi that produce enzymes capable of digesting the toughest plant parts. Basidiomycetes called white rot fungi (because the enzymatic breakdown of lignin bleaches the brown colour out of wood) are promising candidates for this application **(Figure 18.15C)**.

? What do you think is the function of the antibiotics that fungi produce in their natural environments?

● The antibiotics probably block the growth of microorganisms, especially bacteria that compete with the fungi for nutrients and other resources.

▲ **Figure 18.15A** Blue cheese

▲ **Figure 18.15C** White rot fungus

18.16 Lichens are symbiotic associations of fungi and photosynthetic organisms

The rock in **Figure 18.16A** is covered with a living crust of **lichens**, symbiotic associations of millions of unicellular green algae or cyanobacteria held in a mass of fungal hyphae. The partners are so closely entwined that they appear to be a single organism. How does this merger come about? When the growing hyphal tips of a lichen-forming fungus come into contact with a suitable partner, the hyphae quickly fork into a network of tendrils that encircle and overgrow the algal cells **(Figure 18.16B)**. The fungus invariably benefits from the symbiosis, receiving food from its photosynthetic partner. In fact, fungi with the ability to form lichens rarely thrive on their own in nature. In many lichens that have been studied, the alga or cyanobacterium also benefits, as the fungal mycelium provides a suitable habitat that helps it absorb and retain water and minerals. In other lichens, it is not clear whether the relationship benefits the photosynthetic partner or is only advantageous to the fungus.

Lichens are rugged and able to live where there is little or no soil. As a result, they are important pioneers on new land. Dr. Daniel McCarthy at Brock University has been able to trace the retreat of alpine glaciers in the Canadian Rocky and Selkirk Mountains by examining the growth of these pioneers. By measuring the size of lichens growing on the rocky surfaces, McCarthy has estimated their age and, therefore, how long the surface has been exposed. Lichens grow into tiny rock crevices, where the acids they secrete help to break down the rock to soil, paving the way for future plant growth. Some lichens can tolerate severe cold, and carpets of them cover the Arctic tundra. Caribou feed on lichens known as reindeer moss **(Figure 18.16C)** in their winter feeding grounds in northern Canada.

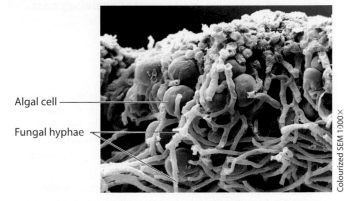

Algal cell
Fungal hyphae

Colourized SEM 1000×

▲ **Figure 18.16B** The close relationship between fungal and algal partners in a lichen

▲ **Figure 18.16C** Reindeer moss, a lichen

Lichens can also withstand severe drought. They are opportunists, growing in spurts when conditions are favourable. When it rains, a lichen quickly absorbs water and photosynthesizes at a rapid rate. In dry air, it dehydrates and photosynthesis may stop, but the lichen remains alive more or less indefinitely. Some lichens are thousands of years old, rivalling the oldest plants and fungi as the oldest organisms on Earth.

As tough as lichens are, many do not withstand air pollution. Because they get most of their minerals from the air, in the form of dust or compounds dissolved in raindrops, lichens are very sensitive to airborne pollutants. The death of lichens is often a sign that air quality in an area is deteriorating. McCarthy, in collaboration with the Ontario Ministry of the Environment, has also developed a technique to use lichens as biomonitors for air quality.

Fungi are the second group of eukaryotes we have surveyed so far. (Protists were the first.) Strong evidence suggests that they evolved from unikont protists, a group that also gave rise to the fourth and most diverse group of eukaryotes, the animals, which we study in Chapters 20 and 21. But first, let's survey the diversity of the plant kingdom.

 What benefit do fungi in lichens receive from their partners?

▲ **Figure 18.16A** Several of the 200 to 300 species of lichen that live in Antarctica

● Access to the sugar molecules that algae or cyanobacteria produce by photosynthesis

Reviewing the Concepts

Diversity of Protists (18.1–18.9)

18.1 **Protists are an extremely diverse assortment of eukaryotes.** Protists are mostly unicellular eukaryotes that are found in a variety of aquatic or moist habitats. They may be autotrophic, heterotrophic, or mixotrophic. Molecular systematists are exploring protistan phylogeny, but at present it is highly tentative.

18.2 **Secondary endosymbiosis is the key to much of protist diversity.** Endosymbiosis of prokaryotic cells resulted in the evolution of eukaryotic cells containing mitochondria. By a similar process, heterotrophic eukaryotic cells engulfed cyanobacteria, which became chloroplasts. Secondary endosymbiosis of eukaryotic cells by red and green algae gave rise to diverse lineages of protists.

18.3 **Chromalveolates represent the range of protist diversity.** Chromalveolates include diatoms, dinoflagellates, brown algae water moulds, ciliates, and a group whose members are all parasites.

18.4 **Can algae provide a renewable source of energy?** Researchers are working on methods of growing diatoms and other algae as a source of biofuels.

18.5 **Rhizarians include a variety of amoebas.** Rhizarian amoebas have threadlike pseudopodia and include forams, which have calcium carbonate shells, and radiolarians, which have internal skeletons made of silica.

18.6 **Some excavates have modified mitochondria.** Some excavates are anaerobic protists that have modified mitochondria; they include parasitic *Giardia*, *Trichomonas vaginalis*, and *Trypanosoma*. Other excavates include *Euglena*, a mixotroph, and termite endosymbionts.

18.7 **Unikonts include protists that are closely related to fungi and animals.** Amoebozoans, the protistan unikonts, include amoebas with lobe-shaped pseudopodia, plasmodial slime moulds, and cellular slime moulds. Fungi and animals are also unikonts.

18.8 **Archaeplastids include red algae, green algae, and land plants.** Red algae, which are mostly multicellular, include species that contribute to the structure of coral reefs and species that are commercially valuable. Green algae may be unicellular, colonial, or multicellular. The life cycles of many algae involve the alternation of haploid gametophyte and diploid sporophyte generations. Archaeplastida also includes land plants, which arose from a group of green algae called charophytes.

18.9 **Multicellularity evolved several times in eukaryotes.** Multicellular organisms have cells specialized for different functions. Multicellularity evolved in ancestral lineages of chromalveolates (brown algae), unikonts (fungi and animals), and archaeplastids (red and green algae and land plants).

Diversity of Fungi (18.10–18.16)

18.10 **Fungi absorb food after digesting it outside their bodies.** Fungi are heterotrophic eukaryotes that digest their food externally and absorb the resulting nutrients. A fungus usually consists of a mass of threadlike hyphae, called a mycelium.

18.11 **Fungi produce spores in both asexual and sexual life cycles.** In some fungi, fusion of haploid hyphae produces a heterokaryotic stage containing nuclei from two parents. After the nuclei fuse, meiosis produces haploid spores.

18.12 **Fungi are classified into five groups.** Fungi evolved from a protist ancestor. Fungal groups include chytrids, zygomycetes, glomeromycetes, ascomycetes, and basidiomycetes.

18.13 **Fungal groups differ in their life cycles and reproductive structures.** Each fungal group has slight modifications to the general life cycle and distinctive reproductive structures.

18.14 **Fungi have enormous ecological benefits.** Fungi are essential decomposers and also participate in mycorrhizae.

18.15 **Fungi have many practical uses.** Some fungi provide food or antibiotics.

18.16 **Lichens are symbiotic associations of fungi and photosynthetic organisms.** The photosynthesizers are algae or cyanobacteria.

Connecting the Concepts

1. Fill in the blanks on the phylogenetic tree to show current hypotheses for the origin of multicellular organisms.

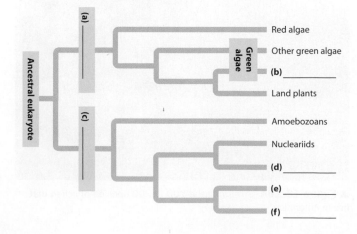

2. Complete the diagram of a general fungal life cycle. Be certain to note missing stages, the ploidy of each, and the processes that produce each stage.

Testing Your Knowledge

Multiple Choice

3. Glycolysis is the only metabolic pathway common to nearly all organisms. To scientists, this suggests that it
   a. evolved many times during the history of life.
   b. was first seen in early eukaryotes.
   c. appeared early in the history of life.
   d. must be very complex.
   e. appeared rather recently in the evolution of life.

4. Which pair of protists has support structures composed of silica?
   a. dinoflagellates and diatoms
   b. diatoms and radiolarians
   c. radiolarians and forams
   d. forams and amoebozoans
   e. amoebozoans and dinoflagellates

5. Which of the following groups is incorrectly paired with an example of that group?
   a. excavates—trypanosome causing sleeping sickness
   b. chromalveolates—parasites such as *Plasmodium*
   c. chromalveolates—brown algae
   d. unikonts—water mould
   e. archaeplastids—red algae

6. The grey-black, filamentous, haploid mycelium, which grows on stale bread, is most likely what kind of fungus?
   a. chytrid
   b. basidiomycete
   c. yeast
   d. zygomycete
   e. ascomycete

7. In the general fungus life cycle, membrane fusion produces what distinct stage?
   a. the mycelium
   b. the heterokaryotic stage
   c. the zygote
   d. the spore
   e. the fruiting body

8. The club fungi are also called
   a. chytridiomycetes.
   b. zygomycetes.
   c. glomeromycetes.
   d. ascomycetes.
   e. basidiomycetes.

9. Under a microscope, a piece of a mushroom would look most like
   a. a tangle of string.
   b. jelly.
   c. grains of sugar or salt.
   d. a piece of glass.
   e. foam.

10. In lichens, the photosynthetic partner benefits from the provision of _____ from the fungal partner.
    a. carbohydrates
    b. water and minerals
    c. fixed nitrogen
    d. antibiotics
    e. carbon dioxide

Describing, Comparing, and Explaining

11. Explain how protist diversity may have arisen through secondary endosymbiosis.

12. *Chlamydomonas* is a unicellular green alga. How does it differ from a photosynthetic bacterium, which is also single-celled? How does it differ from a protozoan, such as an amoeba? How does it differ from larger green algae, such as sea lettuce (*Ulva*)?

13. Explain how the heterokaryotic stage of a generalized fungal life cycle is distinct from the haploid and diploid stages.

Applying the Concepts

14. The buildup of CO_2 in the atmosphere resulting from the burning of fossil fuels is regarded as a major contributor to global warming (see Module 7.13). Diatoms and other microscopic algae in the oceans counter this buildup by using large quantities of atmospheric CO_2 in photosynthesis, which requires small quantities of iron. Experts suspect that a shortage of iron may limit algal growth in the oceans. Some scientists have suggested that one way to reduce CO_2 buildup might be to fertilize the oceans with iron. The iron would stimulate algal growth and thus the removal of more CO_2 from the air. A single supertanker of iron dust, spread over a wide enough area, might reduce the atmospheric CO_2 level significantly. Do you think this approach would be worth a try? Why or why not?

15. Many fungi produce antibiotics, such as penicillin, which are valuable in medicine. But of what value might the antibiotics be to the fungi? Similarly, fungi often produce compounds with unpleasant tastes and odours as they digest their food. What might be the value of these chemicals to the fungi? How might production of antibiotics and odours have evolved?

Answers to all questions can be found in Appendix E.

Biodiversity of Plants

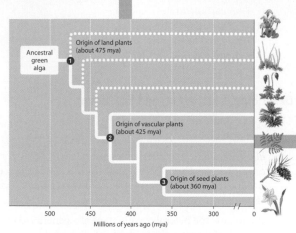

Ancestral green alga

❶ Origin of land plants (about 475 mya)

❷ Origin of vascular plants (about 425 mya)

❸ Origin of seed plants (about 360 mya)

500   450   400   350   300   0

Millions of years ago (mya)

Plant Evolution

(19.1–19.3)

A variety of adaptations enable plants to live on land.

Plant Diversity

(19.4–19.8)

Different plant phyla have modified the general alternation of generations life cycle.

The Flowering Plants

(19.9–19.14)

More than 90% of known plant species are flowering plants.

Phytoremediation: Planting for Cleaner Soil

Plants are absolutely essential for our survival. Not only do they feed us, they also clothe us, heal us, and provide us with shelter. Plants such as cotton and hemp provide us with fibres, which can be spun into textiles. Isolated plant compounds have medicinal purposes. For example, aspirin is a modified form of salicylic acid isolated from willow bark. Trees provide us with many building materials. Scientists are devising other ways in which plants can benefit us. One plant with potential is tall fescue (*Festuca arundinacea*), which is being used to clean up oil contaminants in Sarnia, Ontario.

Plants can efficiently pull minerals and other compounds from the soil into their roots and eventually move them throughout their body. Most often, the compounds absorbed are nutrients that help the plant grow. But some species of plants, such as the sunflower, can absorb lead, zinc, and other heavy metals in concentrations that would kill most other types of plants. Using plants to clean the soil as they grow is called phytoremediation. These plants are ideally suited for detoxifying soil because the heavy metals they remove become concentrated in the plant body, which can be easily discarded. In using plants to clean up toxic wastes, we are benefiting from millions of years of plant evolution. Unable to move about in search of food, plants have evolved amazing abilities to pull water and nutrients out of the soil and air.

Petroleum hydrocarbons are a large family of chemical contaminants, which human activities have made ubiquitous in our environment. Phytoremediation of these toxic contaminants invariably causes stress to the plants. Although remediating plants sequester toxins from the soil, they do so at a cost. As contaminants accumulate in plant tissues, they begin to affect cellular processes by triggering stress responses. Stress in plants can affect growth by reducing the rate of photosynthesis and increasing cellular respiration. Petroleum compounds can also directly affect these processes and further inhibit growth. The consequence of reduced plant growth is a lower capacity for phytoremediation. But Dr. Bruce Greenberg at the University of Waterloo has developed an enhanced phytoremediation strategy by using growth-promoting rhizobacteria in combination with tall fescue, a contaminant-tolerant plant. Dr. Greenberg demonstrated a 90% reduction of soil petroleum hydrocarbons from an Imperial Oil site in Sarnia, Ontario. Remediation by fescue alone was only half as effective. Rhizobacteria improve the effectiveness of phytoremediation by alleviating the plants' stress response. Without contaminant-induced stress, plant growth and therefore phytoremediation are greatly improved.

Phytoremediation is also useful for cleaning up after natural disasters. After Hurricane Katrina slammed into New Orleans on August 29, 2005, most of the city was flooded with noxious runoff containing raw sewage, heavy metals, toxic chemicals, and petroleum. The effect on the local environment was devastating, especially the contamination of the city's topsoil. Volunteers from a grassroots relief organization called Common Ground planted tens of thousands of sunflowers in the hardest hit wards of New Orleans. Once fully grown, the metal-laden crops were harvested and hauled away to a hazardous-waste landfill. Besides easing cleanup efforts, the sunflowers provided an uplifting message to the community, bringing beauty and life back to an area weary with grief and loss.

As you'll learn in this chapter, evolution in the plant kingdom began with structural and reproductive adaptations for life on land. From a modest beginning, plants have diversified into 290 000 present-day species with adaptations that enable them to live in all kinds of environmental conditions.

Plant Evolution

19.1 Plants have adaptations for life on land

As you learned in Module 18.9, plants and green algae called charophytes are thought to have evolved from a common ancestor. Like plants, charophytes are photosynthetic eukaryotes, and many species have complex, multicellular bodies (**Figure 19.1A**). In this module, you will learn about the characteristics that distinguish plants from their algal relatives. As you will see, many of the adaptations that evolved after plants diverged from algae facilitated survival and reproduction on dry land. Some plant groups, including water weeds such as *Anacharis* that are used in aquariums, returned to aquatic habitats during their evolution. However, most present-day plants live in terrestrial environments.

▲ **Figure 19.1A** *Chara*, an elaborate charophyte

The algal ancestors of plants may have carpeted moist fringes of lakes or coastal salt marshes more than 500 mya. These shallow-water habitats were subject to occasional drying, and natural selection would have favoured algae that could survive periodic droughts. Some species accumulated multiple adaptations that enabled them to live permanently above the waterline. The modern-day green alga *Coleochaete* (**Figure 19.1B**), which grows at the edges of lakes as disclike, multicellular colonies, may resemble one of these early plant ancestors.

Adaptations making life on dry land possible had accumulated by about 475 mya, the age of the oldest known plant fossils. The evolutionary novelties of these first land plants opened the new frontier of a terrestrial habitat. On the one hand, early

LM 450×

▲ **Figure 19.1B** *Coleochaete*, a simple charophyte

plant life would have thrived in the new environment. Bright sunlight was virtually limitless on land, the atmosphere had an abundance of carbon dioxide (CO_2), and at first there were relatively few pathogens and plant-eating animals.

On the other hand, life on land poses a number of challenges. Because terrestrial organisms are surrounded by air rather than water, they must be able to maintain moisture inside their cells, support the body in a nonbuoyant medium, and reproduce and disperse offspring without water. As nonmotile organisms, plants must also anchor their bodies in the soil and obtain resources from both soil and air. Thus, the water-to-land transition required fundamental changes in algal structure and life cycle.

Figure 19.1C, on the facing page, compares how plants such as moss, ferns, and pines differ from multicellular algae such as *Chara*. Many algae are anchored by a holdfast, but generally they have no rigid tissues and are supported by the surrounding water. The whole algal body obtains CO_2 and minerals directly from the water. Almost all of the organism receives light and can perform photosynthesis. For reproduction, flagellated sperm swim to fertilize an egg. The offspring are dispersed by water as well.

Maintaining Moisture The above-ground parts of most land plants are covered by a waxy coating, called a cuticle, that prevents water loss. Gas exchange cannot occur directly through the cuticle, but CO_2 and O_2 diffuse across the leaf surfaces through the tiny pores called stomata (see Module 7.2). Two surrounding cells regulate each stoma's opening and closing. Stomata are usually open during sunlight hours, allowing gas exchange, and closed at other times, preventing water loss by evaporation. You'll learn more about the role of stomata in water regulation in Chapter 23.

Obtaining Resources from Two Locations A typical plant must obtain chemicals from both soil and air, two very different media. Water and mineral nutrients are mainly found in the soil; light and CO_2 are available above ground. Most plants have discrete organs—roots, stems, and leaves—that help to meet this resource challenge.

Plant roots provide anchorage and absorb water and mineral nutrients from the soil. Plant roots may also absorb environmental contaminants such as heavy metals and

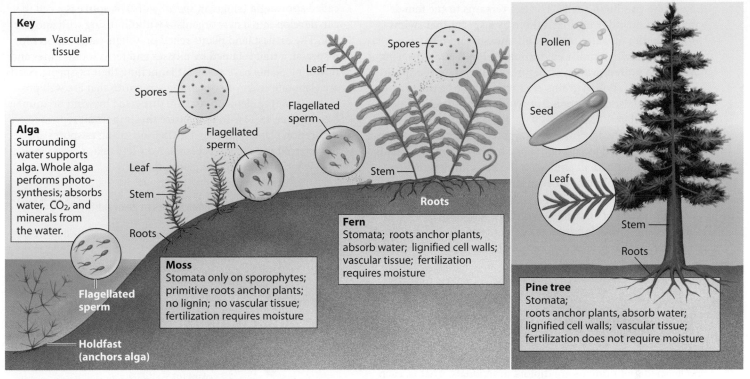

Key
— Vascular tissue

Alga
Surrounding water supports alga. Whole alga performs photosynthesis; absorbs water, CO_2, and minerals from the water.

Flagellated sperm

Holdfast (anchors alga)

Spores

Leaf

Stem

Roots

Flagellated sperm

Moss
Stomata only on sporophytes; primitive roots anchor plants; no lignin; no vascular tissue; fertilization requires moisture

Flagellated sperm

Spores

Leaf

Stem

Roots

Fern
Stomata; roots anchor plants, absorb water; lignified cell walls; vascular tissue; fertilization requires moisture

Pollen

Seed

Leaf

Stem

Roots

Pine tree
Stomata; roots anchor plants, absorb water; lignified cell walls; vascular tissue; fertilization does not require moisture

▲ **Figure 19.1C** Comparing the terrestrial adaptations of moss, fern, and pine with *Chara*, a multicellular green alga

hydrocarbons. Scientists can exploit this ability and use plants to help detoxify contaminated soil by planting in affected areas, a process called **phytoremediation** (see the opening essay of this chapter). Above ground, a plant's stems bear leaves, which obtain CO_2 from the air and light from the sun, enabling them to perform photosynthesis. Growth-producing regions of cell division, called **apical meristems**, are found near the tips of stems and roots. The elongation and branching of a plant's stems and roots maximize exposure to the resources in the soil and air.

A plant must be able to connect its subterranean and aerial parts, conducting water and minerals upward from its roots to its leaves and distributing sugars produced in the leaves throughout its body. Most plants, including ferns, pines, and flowering plants, have **vascular tissue**, a network of thick-walled cells joined into narrow tubes that extend throughout the plant body (traced in red in Figure 19.1C). The photograph of part of an aspen leaf in **Figure 19.1D** shows the leaf's network of veins, which are fine branches of vascular tissue. There are two types of vascular tissue. **Xylem** includes dead cells that form microscopic pipes conveying water and minerals up from the roots. **Phloem**, which consists entirely of living cells, distributes sugars throughout the plant. In contrast to plants with elaborate vascular tissues, mosses lack a complex transport system (although some mosses do have simple vascular tissue). With limited means for distributing water and minerals from soil to the leaves, the height of nonvascular plants is severely restricted.

Supporting the Plant Body Because air provides much less support than water, plants must be able to hold themselves up

against the pull of gravity. The cell walls of some plant tissues, including xylem, are thickened and reinforced by a chemical called **lignin**. The absence of lignified cell walls in mosses and other plants that lack vascular tissue is another limitation on their height.

Reproduction and Dispersal Reproduction on land presents complex challenges. For *Chara* and other algae, the surrounding water ensures that gametes and offspring stay moist. Plants, however, must keep their gametes and developing embryos from drying out in the air. Like the earliest land plants, mosses and ferns still produce gametes in male and female structures called **gametangia** (singular, *gametangium*), which consist of protective jackets of cells surrounding

▲ **Figure 19.1D** The network of veins in a leaf

the gamete-producing cells. The egg remains in the female gametangium and is fertilized there by a sperm that swims through a film of water. As a result, mosses and ferns can reproduce only in a moist environment. Pines and flowering plants have **pollen grains**, structures that contain the sperm-producing cells. Pollen grains are carried close to the egg by wind or animals; moisture is not required for bringing sperm and egg together.

In all plants, the fertilized egg (zygote) develops into an embryo while attached to and nourished by the parent plant. This multicellular, dependent embryo is the basis for designating plants as **embryophytes** (*phyte* means "plant"), distinguishing them from algae.

The life cycles of all plants involve the alternation of a haploid generation, which produces eggs and sperm, and a diploid generation, which produces spores within protective structures called **sporangia** (singular, *sporangium*). A **spore** is a cell that can develop into a new organism without fusing with another cell. The earliest land plants relied on tough-walled spores for dispersal, a trait retained by mosses and ferns today. Pines and flowering plants have seeds for launching their offspring. Seeds are elaborate embryo-containing structures that are well protected from the elements and are dispersed by wind or animals (see Module 19.11). To emphasize this important reproductive difference, plants that disperse their offspring as spores are often referred to as seedless plants. Now let's take a closer look at the evolution of the major plant groups.

? **What adaptations enable plants to grow tall?**

● Vascular tissues to transport materials from below-ground parts to above-ground parts and vice versa; lignified cell walls to provide structural support

19.2 Haploid and diploid generations alternate in plant life cycles

Plant life cycles are very different from ours. In Module 8.13, you learned that humans are diploid individuals. That is, each of us has two sets of chromosomes, one from each parent. The only haploid stages in the human life cycle are sperm and eggs. Plants have an **alternation of generations**: The diploid and haploid stages are distinct, multicellular bodies. The haploid generation of a plant produces gametes and is called the **gametophyte**. The diploid generation produces spores and is called the **sporophyte**. In a plant's life cycle, these two generations alternate in producing each other.

The life cycles of all plants follow the pattern shown in **Figure 19.2**. Be sure that you understand this diagram; then review it after studying each life cycle to see how the pattern applies. ❶ A haploid gametophyte plant produces gametes (sperm and eggs) by mitosis—not by meiosis, as in animals. ❷ Fertilization results in a diploid zygote. ❸ The zygote grows by mitotic cell division and develops into the multicellular diploid sporophyte plant. ❹ The sporophyte produces haploid spores by meiosis. ❺ A spore then develops by mitosis into a multicellular haploid gametophyte.

Although some algae exhibit alternation of generations, the closest algal relatives of plants, the charophytes, do not. Thus, this life cycle appears to have evolved independently in plants; it is a derived character of land plants.

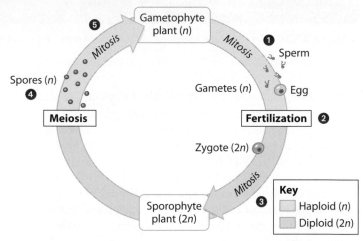
▲ **Figure 19.2** Alternation of generations

The next module highlights the diversity of the plant kingdom. In subsequent modules, we will illustrate specific life cycles of the major plant groups.

? **How does gamete production differ in plants and animals?**

● Animals produce gametes by meiosis; in plants, gametes are produced by mitosis.

19.3 Plant diversity reflects the evolutionary history of the plant kingdom

Figure 19.3A highlights some of the major events in the history of the plant kingdom and presents a widely held view of the relationships between surviving lineages of plants.

❶ After plants originated from an algal ancestor approximately 475 mya, early diversification gave rise to seedless, nonvascular plants, including mosses, liverworts,

and hornworts **(Figure 19.3B)**. These plants, which are informally called **bryophytes**, resemble other plants in having apical meristems and embryos that are retained on the parent plant, but they lack true roots and leaves. Without lignified cell walls, bryophytes with an upright growth habit lack support. A mat of moss actually consists of many plants

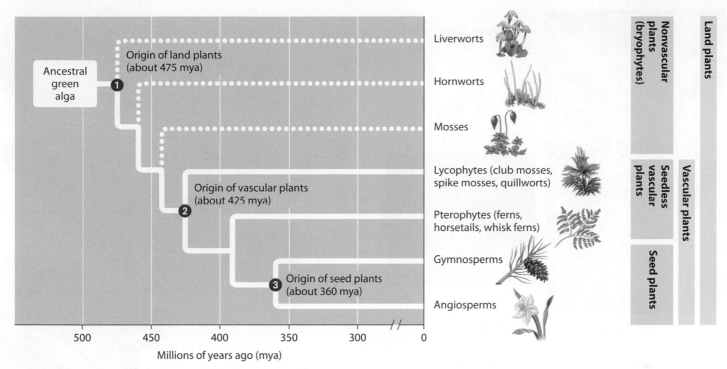

▲ **Figure 19.3A** Some highlights of plant evolution (dotted lines indicate uncertain evolutionary relationships)

growing in a tight pack. Like people crowded together in a small space, their bodies hold one another upright. The mat is spongy and retains water. Other bryophytes grow flat against the ground. Growth in dense mats facilitates fertilization by flagellated sperm swimming through a film of water left by rain or dew.

❷ The origin of **vascular plants** occurred about 425 mya. Their lignin-hardened vascular tissues provide strong support, enabling stems to stand upright and grow tall on land. Two clades of vascular plants are informally called **seedless**

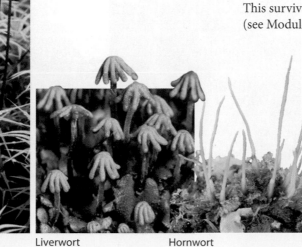

Moss   Liverwort   Hornwort

▲ **Figure 19.3B** Bryophytes

vascular plants (Figure 19.3C): the lycophytes (such as club mosses) and the widespread pterophytes (ferns and their relatives). A fern has well-developed roots and rigid stems. Ferns are common in temperate forests, but they are most diverse in the tropics. In some tropical species, called tree ferns, upright stems can grow several metres tall. Like bryophytes, however, ferns and club mosses require moist conditions for fertilization, and they disperse their offspring as spores that are carried by air currents.

❸ The first vascular plants with seeds evolved about 360 mya. Today, the seed plant lineage accounts for more than 90% of the approximately 290 000 species of living plants. Seeds and pollen are key adaptations that improved the ability of plants to diversify in terrestrial habitats. A **seed** consists of an embryo packaged with a food supply within a protective covering. This survival packet facilitates wide dispersal of plant embryos (see Module 19.11). As you learned in Module 19.1, pollen brings sperm-producing cells into contact with egg-producing parts without water. And unlike flagellated sperm, which can swim a few centimetres at most, pollen can travel great distances.

Gymnosperms (from the Greek *gymnos*, naked, and *sperma*, seed) were among the earliest seed plants. Seeds of gymnosperms are said to be "naked" because they are not produced in specialized chambers. The largest clade of gymnosperms is the conifers, consisting mainly of cone-bearing trees, such as pine, spruce, and fir. (The term *conifer* means "cone-bearing.") Some examples of less common gymnosperms

◀ **Figure 19.3C** Seedless vascular plants

Fern (a pterophyte)

Club moss (a lycophyte). Spores are produced in the upright tan-coloured structures.

A jacaranda tree

Barley, a grass

▲ **Figure 19.3E** Angiosperms

are the ornamental ginkgo tree, desert shrubs in the genus *Ephedra*, and the palmlike cycads **(Figure 19.3D)**. Gymnosperms flourished alongside the dinosaurs in the Mesozoic era.

The most recent major episode in plant evolution was the appearance of flowering plants, or **angiosperms** (from the Greek *angion*, container, and *sperma*, seed), at least 140 mya. Flowers are complex reproductive structures that develop seeds within protective chambers. The great majority of living plants—some 250 000 species—are angiosperms, which include a wide variety of plants, such as grasses, flowering shrubs, and flowering trees **(Figure 19.3E)**.

In summary, four key adaptations for life on land distinguish the main lineages of the plant kingdom. (1) Dependent embryos are present in all plants. (2) Lignified vascular tissues mark a lineage that gave rise to most living plants. (3) Seeds are found in a lineage that includes all living gymnosperms and angiosperms and that dominates the plant kingdom today.

(4) Flowers mark the angiosperm lineage. As you will see in the next several modules, the life cycles of living plants reveal additional details about plant evolution.

? Identify which of the following traits is shared by all plants: flowers, seeds, retained embryo, or vascular tissue.

● An embryo retained on the parent plant

▼ **Figure 19.3D** Gymnosperms

Ginkgo

Cycad

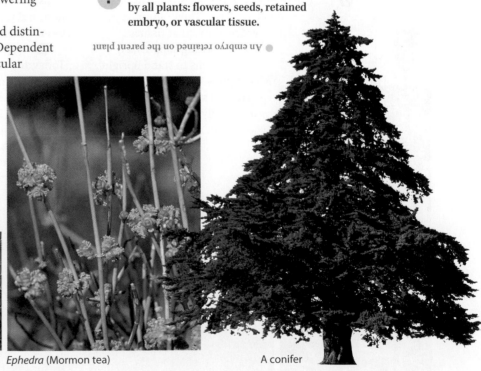

Ephedra (Mormon tea)

A conifer

Plant Diversity

19.4 The life cycle of a moss is dominated by the gametophyte

In a moss, the green, cushiony growth we see consists of gametophytes. Follow the moss life cycle in **Figure 19.4**. ❶ Gametes develop in male and female gametangia, usually on separate plants. The flagellated sperm are released from the male gametangium and swim through a film of water to the egg in the female gametangium. After fertilization, ❷ the zygote remains in the gametangium. ❸ There it divides by mitosis, developing into a sporophyte embryo and then a mature sporophyte, which remains attached to the gametophyte. The sporophyte acquires nutrients from the gametophyte through this attachment. ❹ Meiosis occurs in the sporangia at the tips of the sporophyte stalks. After meiosis, haploid spores are released from the sporangium. ❺ The spores undergo mitosis and develop into gametophyte plants.

? **How do moss sperm travel from male gametangia to female gametangia, where fertilization of eggs occurs?**

● The flagellated sperm swim through a film of water.

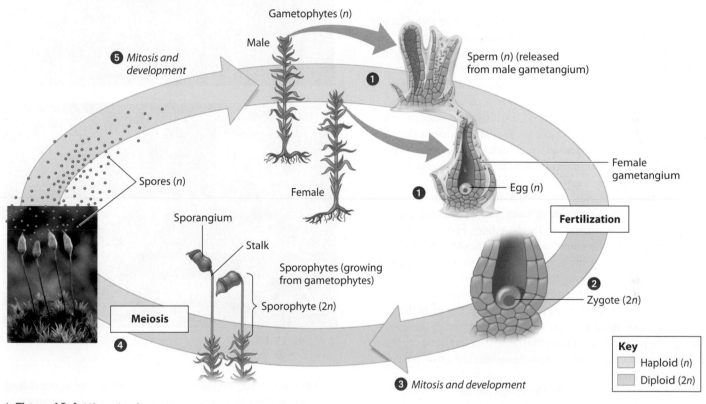

▲ **Figure 19.4** Life cycle of a moss

RUMOUR HAS IT   ## 19.5 Does moss grow only on the north side of trees?

Imagine that you are walking in a forest just south of your hometown and become lost. After the immediate sense of doom subsides, you remember an old adage about moss. Rumour has it that moss dislikes the sun and because the sun is typically to the south (at least in the Northern Hemisphere), moss grows on the north side of trees. According to this, if you walk in the direction the moss is growing, you should find your way home. But will this small plant point you in the right direction? Maybe. Whether moss can guide you will depend largely on where you live.

The green gametophytes of moss lack vascular tissue and require water for fertilization (see Module 19.3). The flagellated sperm swims to the egg in a film of water. These requirements typically restrict mosses to grow only in viable humid habitats. Mosses definitely do not avoid the sun as the rumour suggests. In fact, they depend on the sun to fuel photosynthesis, just like most other plants. Nevertheless, mosses can survive with only indirect sunlight. In other words, they are shade-tolerant. They typically grow in shady areas because of the higher humidity. In some cases, there may be suitable areas that are highly localized within an ecosystem. These areas, called microclimates, have different environmental conditions than the surrounding areas (see Module 38.14).

Microclimates may be large or small. An example of a larger microclimate would be the south-facing slopes of the Canadian

▲ **Figure 19.5A** A valley showing two microclimates

▲ **Figure 19.5B** Moss growing on trees in a drier climate (top) and humid climate (bottom)

Rockies. These faces would be much warmer than those facing other directions because they receive more direct sunlight. **Figure 19.5A** shows a valley in which the south-facing side is dry and barren; its north-facing side, however, is cooler, more humid, and covered in ferns and mosses. Smaller microclimates may include the coast of a lake or a riverbank, where the humidity would be higher and the air cooler than several metres away. A smaller example yet would be under a single leaf. The leaf slows air movement, which can trap moisture underneath the leaf and create environmental conditions different from those in an area only a few centimetres away.

Thus, there is an element of truth to the rumour that moss grows only on the north side of trees, but only under certain environmental conditions. In the Northern Hemisphere, the sun is typically to the south (see Figure 35.5A). The sun hitting the south-facing surface warms it up, increasing the rate of evaporation and drying the air. On the shady northern surface, however, evaporation is slower and the air remains more humid in this microclimate. Based on the growth requirements for most mosses, mosses would prefer the north-facing microclimates. (The opposite is true in the southern hemisphere: In the right climate, moss should grow on the south side of trees.)

In some Canadian forests, the adage appears to be correct **(Figure 19.5B)**. However, it certainly is not a reliable rule and growth is not restricted to only the northern side. Within any shady or damp forest, moss may grow on all surfaces. In many parts of Canada, the reliability of moss directing you northward is extremely poor. Along the coastal region of British Columbia, you would likely find a thick carpet of moss growing on all surfaces of the tree, which is also shown in Figure 19.5B. In contrast, you may be challenged to find any moss while hiking in the Nk'Mip Desert of the Okanagan Valley.

Although it may be true the moss grows on the north side of trees, supporting this rumour, in many climates it can grow on the east, west, and south sides, too. If you go hiking in unfamiliar territory, take a map and compass or a GPS device. They are far more reliable and will help you more than relying on moss.

 Why do many mosses prefer shady habitats?

In areas without direct sunlight, there is less evaporation and the microclimate is generally cooler and more humid, which mosses prefer.

19.6 Ferns, like most plants, have a life cycle dominated by the sporophyte

All we usually see of a fern is the sporophyte. But let's start with the gametophyte in the fern life cycle in **Figure 19.6**. ❶ Fern gametophytes often have a distinctive heartlike shape, but they are quite small (about 0.5 cm across) and inconspicuous. ❷ Like mosses, ferns have flagellated sperm that require moisture to reach an egg. Although eggs and sperm are usually

▲ **Figure 19.6** Life cycle of a fern

⑥ *Mitosis and development*

Gametophyte (*n*)
(underside; actual size 0.5 cm)

② Sperm (*n*)
(released from male gametangium)

Female gametangium (*n*)

Egg (*n*)

Meiosis

Fertilization

Spores (*n*)

⑤

Clusters of sporangia

Zygote (2*n*)

③ *Mitosis and development*

④

Mature sporophyte
(independent of gametophyte)

New sporophyte (2*n*)

Gametophyte (*n*)

Key
Haploid (*n*)
Diploid (2*n*)

produced in separate locations on the same gametophyte, a variety of mechanisms promote cross-fertilization between gametophytes. **③** The zygote remains on the gametophyte as it develops into a new sporophyte. **④** Unlike moss, the gametophyte dies and the sporophyte becomes an independent plant. **⑤** The black dots in the photograph are clusters of sporangia, in which cells undergo meiosis, producing haploid spores. **⑥** The spores are released and develop into gametophytes by mitosis.

Today, about 95% of all plants, including all seed plants, have a dominant sporophyte in their life cycle. But before

we resume this story, let's look back at a time in plant history, before seed plants rose to dominance, when ferns and other seedless vascular plants covered much of the land surface.

? **What is the major difference between the moss and fern life cycles?**

● In mosses, the dominant plant body is the gametophyte. In ferns, the
sporophyte is dominant and is independent of the gametophyte.

19.7 Seedless vascular plants dominated vast "coal forests"

During the Carboniferous period (about 360–299 mya), the two clades of seedless vascular plants, lycophytes (for example, club mosses) and pterophytes (such as ferns and their relatives), grew in vast forests in the low-lying wetlands of what is now Eurasia and North America. At that time, these continents

were close to the equator and had warm, humid climates that supported broad expanses of lush vegetation.

Figure 19.7 shows an artist's reconstruction of one of these forests based on fossil evidence. Tree ferns are visible in the foreground. Most of the large trees are lycophytes, giants that

▲ **Figure 19.7** A reconstruction of an extinct forest dominated by seedless plants

organic deposits called peat. Later, seawater covered the swamps, marine sediments covered the peat, and pressure and heat gradually converted the peat to coal, black sedimentary rock made up of fossilized plant material. Coal deposits from the Carboniferous period are the most extensive ever formed. (The name *Carboniferous* comes from the Latin *carbo*, coal, and *fer*, bearing.) Coal, oil, and natural gas are called **fossil fuels** because they were formed from the remains of ancient organisms. (Oil and natural gas were formed from marine organisms.) Since the Industrial Revolution, coal has been a crucial source of energy for human society. However, burning these fossil fuels releases CO_2 and other greenhouse gases into the atmosphere, which are now causing a warming climate (see Modules 41.3 and 41.4).

grew as tall as a 12-story building, with diameters of more than 2 m. (For a sense of scale, dragonflies such as the one shown in the foreground had wing spans of up to 1 m.) As you'll learn in Chapter 21, vertebrates were adapting to terrestrial habitats in parallel with plants; amphibians and early reptiles lived among these trees.

Photosynthesis in these immense swamp forests fixed large amounts of carbon from CO_2 into organic molecules, dramatically reducing CO_2 levels in the atmosphere. Because atmospheric CO_2 traps heat, this change caused global cooling. Photosynthesis generated great quantities of organic matter. As the plants died, they fell into stagnant swamps and did not decay completely. Their remains formed thick

As temperatures dropped during the late Carboniferous period, glaciers formed. The global climate turned drier, and the vast swamps and forests began to disappear. The climate change provided an opportunity for the early seed plants, which grew along with the seedless plants in the Carboniferous swamps. With their wind-dispersed pollen and protective seeds, seed plants could complete their life cycles on dry land.

 How did the tropical swamp forests contribute to global cooling in the Carboniferous period?

● Photosynthesis by the abundant plant life reduced atmospheric CO_2, a gas that traps heat.

19.8 A pine tree is a sporophyte with gametophytes in its cones

In seed plants, a specialized structure within the sporophyte houses all reproductive stages, including spores, eggs, sperm, zygotes, and embryos. In gymnosperms such as pines and other conifers, this structure is called a **cone**. If you look at the longitudinal section of the cones in **Figure 19.8**, you'll see that the cone resembles a short stem bearing thick leaves. The resemblance is not surprising—cones are shoots that were modified by natural selection to serve a different function. Each modified leaf, or scale, of the cone contains sporangia that produce spores by meiosis. Unlike seedless plants, however, the spores are not released. Rather, spores give rise to haploid gametophytes within the shelter of the cone. The gametophytes later

produce gametes, which unite to form a new sporophyte (see Figure 19.2).

A pine tree bears two types of cones, which produce spores that develop into male and female gametophytes. The smaller ones, called pollen cones (❶ in Figure 19.8), produce the male gametophytes. Pollen cones contain many sporangia, each of which makes numerous haploid spores by meiosis. Male gametophytes, or pollen grains, develop from the spores. Mature pollen cones release millions of microscopic pollen grains in great clouds. You may have seen yellowish conifer pollen covering cars or floating on puddles after a spring rain. Pollen grains, which are carried by the wind, house cells that will develop into sperm

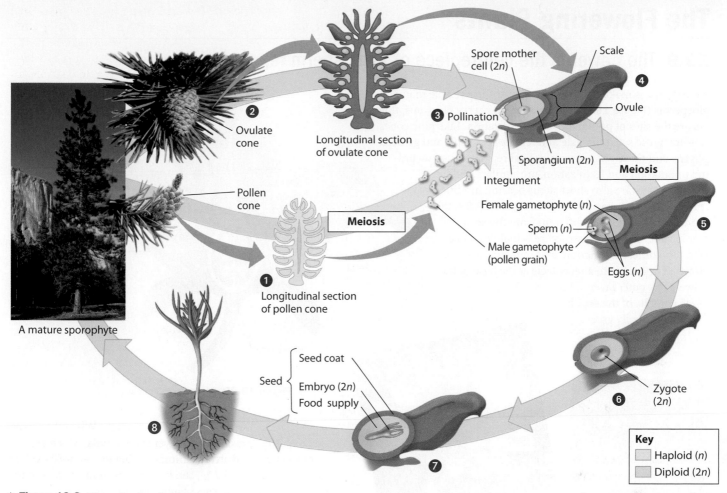

▲ Figure 19.8 Life cycle of a pine tree

Key
Haploid (*n*)
Diploid (2*n*)

if by chance they land on a cone that contains a female gametophyte.

2 An ovulate cone, which produces the female gametophyte, is larger than a pollen cone. Each of its stiff scales bears a pair of **ovules**. (Only one is shown in the diagram.) Each ovule contains a sporangium surrounded by a protective covering called the integument. **3 Pollination** occurs when a pollen grain lands on an ovulate scale and enters an ovule. After pollination, the scales of the cone grow together, sealing it until the seeds are mature. Meiosis then occurs in a spore "mother cell" within the ovule. Over the course of many months, **4** one surviving haploid spore cell develops into the female gametophyte, which makes eggs. **5** Meanwhile, a tiny tube grows out of each pollen grain, digests its way through the ovule, and eventually releases sperm, which are simply nuclei rather than independent cells, near an egg. Fertilization typically occurs more than a year after pollination.

6 Usually, all eggs in an ovule are fertilized, but ordinarily only one zygote develops fully into a sporophyte embryo. **7** The ovule matures into a seed, which contains the embryo's food supply (the remains of the female gametophyte) and has a tough **seed coat** (the ovule's integument). In a

typical pine, seeds are shed about two years after pollination. **8** The seed is dispersed by wind, and when conditions are favourable, it germinates, and its embryo grows into a pine seedling.

In summary, all the reproductive stages of conifers are housed in cones borne on sporophytes. The ovule is a key adaptation—a protective device for all the female stages in the life cycle, as well as the site of pollination, fertilization, and embryonic development. The ovule becomes the seed, an important terrestrial adaptation and a major factor in the success of the conifers and flowering plants.

In the next Big Idea, we consider flowering plants, the most diverse and geographically widespread of all plants. Angiosperms dominate most landscapes today, and it is their flowers that account for their unparalleled success.

? **What key adaptations have contributed to the overwhelming success of seed plants?**

● Pollen transfers sperm to eggs without the need for water. Seeds protect, nourish, and help to disperse plant embryos. The female gametophytes of seed plants are protected on the sporophyte plant.

The Flowering Plants

19.9 The flower is the centrepiece of angiosperm reproduction

No organisms make a showier display of their sex life than angiosperms (**Figure 19.9A**). From roses to cherry blossoms, flowers are the sites of pollination and fertilization. Like pine cones, flowers house separate male and female sporangia and gametophytes, and the mechanisms of sexual reproduction, including pollination and fertilization, are similar. And like cones, flowers are also short stems bearing modified leaves. However, as you can see in **Figure 19.9B**, the modifications are quite different from the scales of a pine cone. Each floral structure is highly specialized for a different function, and the structures are attached in a circle to a receptacle at the base of the flower. The outer layer of the circle consists of the **sepals**, which are usually green.

▲ **Figure 19.9B** The parts of a flower

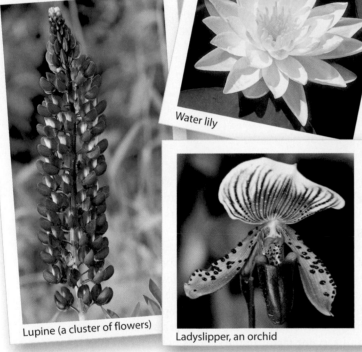

Water lily

Lupine (a cluster of flowers)

Ladyslipper, an orchid

▲ **Figure 19.9A** Some examples of floral diversity

They enclose the flower before it opens. When the sepals are peeled away, the next layer is the **petals**, which are conspicuous and attract animal pollinators. As we'll explore further in Module 19.13, showy petals are a major reason for the overwhelming success of angiosperms.

Plucking off a flower's petals reveals the filaments of the **stamens**. The **anther**, a sac at the top of each filament, contains male sporangia and will eventually release pollen. At the centres of the flower is the **carpel**, the female reproductive structure. It includes the **ovary**, a unique angiosperm adaptation that encloses the ovules. If you cut open the ovary of a flower, you can see its white, egg-shaped ovules. As in pines, each ovule contains a sporangium that will produce a female gametophyte and eventually become a seed. The ovary typically matures into a fruit, which aids in seed dispersal, as we'll discuss shortly. In the next module, you will learn how the alternation of generations life cycle proceeds in angiosperms.

 Where are the male and female sporangia located in flowering plants?

● Anthers contain the male sporangia; ovules contain the female sporangia.

19.10 The angiosperm plant is a sporophyte with gametophytes in its flowers

In angiosperms, as in gymnosperms, the sporophyte generation is dominant and produces the gametophyte generation within its body. **Figure 19.10** illustrates the life cycle of a flowering plant and highlights features that have been especially important in angiosperm evolution. (We will discuss these

features, as well as double fertilization in angiosperms, in more detail in Modules 22.10 to 22.14.) Starting at the meiosis box at the top of Figure 19.10, ❶ meiosis in the anthers of the flower produces haploid spores that undergo mitosis and form the male gametophytes, or pollen grains. ❷ Meiosis in the ovule produces a haploid spore that undergoes mitosis and forms the few cells of the female gametophyte, one of which becomes an egg. ❸ Pollination occurs when a pollen grain, carried by the wind or an animal, lands on the stigma. As in gymnosperms, a tube grows from the pollen grain to the ovule, and a sperm fertilizes the egg, ❹ forming a zygote. Also, as in gymnosperms, ❺ a seed develops from each ovule. Each seed consists of an embryo (a new sporophyte) surrounded by a food supply and a seed coat derived from the integuments. While the seeds develop, ❻ the ovary's wall thickens, forming the fruit that encloses the seeds. When conditions are favourable, ❼ a seed germinates. As the embryo begins to grow, it uses the food supply from the seed until it can begin to photosynthesize. Eventually, it develops into a mature sporophyte plant, completing the life cycle.

The evolution of flowers that attract animals, which carry pollen more reliably than the wind, was a key adaptation of angiosperms. The success of angiosperms was also enhanced by their ability to reproduce rapidly. Fertilization in angiosperms usually occurs about 12 hours after pollination, making it possible for the plant to produce seeds in only a few days or weeks. As we mentioned in Module 19.8, a typical pine takes years to produce seeds. Rapid seed production is especially advantageous in harsh environments such as deserts, where growing seasons are extremely short.

Another feature contributing to the success of angiosperms is the development of fruits, which protect and help to disperse the seeds, as we see in the next module.

? **What is the difference between pollination and fertilization?**

● Pollination is the transfer of pollen by wind or animals from stamens to the tips of carpels. Fertilization is the union of egg and sperm; the sperm are released from the pollen tube after the tube grows and makes contact with an ovule.

▲ **Figure 19.10** Life cycle of an angiosperm

19.11 The structure of a fruit reflects its function in seed dispersal

A **fruit**, the ripened ovary of a flower, is an adaptation that helps to disperse seeds. Some angiosperms depend on wind for seed dispersal. For example, the fruit of a dandelion **(Figure 19.11A)** has a parachute-like extension that carries the tiny seed away from the parent plant on wind currents. Hook-like modifications of the outer layer of the fruit or seed coat allow some angiosperms to hitch a ride on animals. The fruits of the cocklebur plant **(Figure 19.11B)**, for example, may be carried for miles before they open and release their seeds.

Many angiosperms produce fleshy, edible fruits that are attractive to animals as food. While the seeds are developing, these fruits are green and effectively camouflaged against green foliage. When ripe, the fruit turns a bright colour, such as

red or yellow, advertising its presence to birds and mammals. When the catbird in **Figure 19.11C** eats a berry, it digests the fleshy part of the fruit, but most of the tough seeds pass unharmed through its digestive tract. The bird may then deposit the seeds, along with a supply of natural fertilizer, some distance from where it ate the fruit.

The dispersal of seeds in fruits is one of the main reasons that angiosperms are so successful. Humans have also made extensive use of fruits and seeds, as we see next.

? What is a fruit?

 A ripened ovary of a flower, which contains, protects, and aids in the dispersal of seeds

Fruit

Seed dispersal

▲ **Figure 19.11A** Dandelion seeds can be launched into the air by a light breeze

▲ **Figure 19.11B** Cocklebur fruits may be carried by animal fur

▲ **Figure 19.11C** Seeds within edible fruits are often dispersed in animal feces

---

19.12 Angiosperms sustain us—and add spice to our diets

We depend on the fruits and seeds of angiosperms for much of our food. Corn, rice, wheat, and other grains, the main food sources for most of the world's people and their domesticated animals, are dry fruits. Many food crops are fleshy fruits, including apples, cherries, oranges, tomatoes, squash, and cucumbers. (In scientific terms, a fruit is an angiosperm structure containing seeds, so some of what many people consider vegetables are actually fruits.) While most people can easily recognize grains and fleshy fruits as plant products, fewer realize that spices such as nutmeg, cinnamon, cumin, cloves, ginger, and licorice come from angiosperms. **Figure 19.12** shows the source of a condiment found on most Canadian dinner tables: black pepper. The pepper fruits are harvested before ripening, and then dried and ground into powder or sold whole as "peppercorns." In medieval Europe, peppercorns were so valuable that they were used

as currency. Rent and taxes could be paid in peppercorns; as a form of wealth, peppercorns were included in dowries and left in wills. The search for a sea route to obtain pepper and other precious spices from India and Southeast Asia led to the Age of Exploration and had a lasting impact on European history.

? Suppose you found a cluster of pepper berries like the ones in Figure 19.12. How would you know that they are fruits?

 Each berry has seeds inside it.

▲ **Figure 19.12** Berries (fruits) of *Piper nigrum*

19.13 Pollination by animals has influenced angiosperm evolution

Most of us associate flowers with colourful petals and sweet fragrances, but not all flowers have these accessories. **Figure 19.13A**, for example, shows flowers of a red maple, which have many stamens but no petals (carpels are borne on separate flowers). Compare those flowers to the large, vibrantly coloured columbine in **Figure 19.13B**. Such an elaborate flower costs the columbine an enormous amount of energy to produce, but the investment pays off when a pollinator, attracted by the flower's colour or scent, carries the plant's pollen to another flower of the same species. Red maple, on the contrary, devotes substantial energy to making massive amounts of pollen for release into the wind, a far less certain method of pollination. Both species have adaptations to achieve pollination, which is necessary for reproductive success, but they allocate their resources differently.

▲ **Figure 19.13A** Flowers of red maple, whose pollen is carried by the wind

Plant scientists estimate that about 90% of angiosperms employ animals to transfer their pollen. Birds, bats, and many different species of insects (notably bees, butterflies, moths, and beetles) serve as pollinators. These animals visit flowers in search of a meal, which the flowers provide in the form of nectar, a high-energy fluid. For pollinators, the colourful petals and alluring odours are signposts that mark food resources.

The cues that flowers offer are keyed to the sense of sight and smell of certain types of pollinators. For example, birds are attracted by bright red and orange flowers but not to particular scents, while most beetles are drawn to fruity odours but are indifferent to colour. The petals of bee-pollinated flowers may be marked with guides in contrasting colours that lead to the nectar. In some flowers, the nectar guides are pigments that reflect ultraviolet light, a part of the electromagnetic spectrum that is invisible to us and most other animals, but readily apparent to bees. Flowers that are pollinated by night-flying animals such as bats and moths typically have large, light-coloured, highly scented flowers that can easily be found at night. Some flowers even produce an enticing imitation of the smell of rotting flesh, thereby attracting pollinators such as carrion flies and beetles.

▲ **Figure 19.13C** A bee picking up pollen from a scotch broom flower as it feeds on nectar

Many flowers have additional adaptations that improve pollen transfer, and thus reproductive success, once a pollinator arrives. The location of the nectar, for example, may manipulate the visitor's position in a way that maximizes pollen pickup and deposition. In **Figure 19.13C**, the pollen-bearing stamens of a scotch broom flower arch over the bee as it harvests nectar. Some of the pollen the bee picks up here will rub off onto the stigmas of other flowers it visits. In the columbine, as well as in many other flowers, the nectar can be reached only by pollinators with long tongues, a group that includes butterflies, moths, birds, and some bees.

Pollination is effective only if the pollen transfer occurs between members of the same species, but relatively few pollinators visit one species of flower exclusively. Biologists hypothesize that it takes time, through trial and error, for a pollinator to learn to extract nectar from a flower. Insects, for instance, can remember only one extraction technique at a time. Thus, pollinators are most successful at obtaining food if they visit another flower with the same cues immediately after mastering a technique for nectar extraction.

Although floral characteristics are adaptations that attract pollinators, they are a source of enjoyment to people, as well. Humans use flowering plants, including many species of trees, for a variety of purposes. As we consider in the next module, however, the most essential role of plants in our lives is as food.

▲ **Figure 19.13B** Showy columbine flower

❓ **What type of pollinator do you think would be attracted to the columbine in Figure 19.13B?**

● Long-tongued birds, because the flower is red and has a long floral tube

19.14 Plant diversity is vital to the future of the world's food supply

Plants have always been a mainstay of the human diet, but the way we obtain our plant food has changed enormously. Early humans made use of any edible plant species that was available, probably eating different plants as the seasons changed, as do present-day hunter-gatherers. During the development of agriculture, people in different parts of the world domesticated the tastiest, most easily cultivated species, gradually increasing their productivity through generation after generation of artificial selection. In modern agriculture, plant-breeding techniques have further narrowed the pool of food plant diversity by creating a select few genotypes possessing the most desirable characteristics. Most of the world's population is now fed by varieties of rice, wheat, corn, and soybeans that require specific cultivation techniques.

Agriculture has also changed the landscape. Over thousands of years, the expanding human population created farms by clear-cutting or burning forests. More recently, deforestation has accelerated to replace the vast expanses of cropland that have been severely degraded by unsustainable agricultural practices. But converting more land to farms is not the only way to ensure an adequate food supply for the future. Plant diversity offers possibilities for developing new crops and improving existing ones. As part of the Global Crop Diversity Trust, some farmers in Canada plant varieties of crops simply to preserve genetic diversity. For example, 295 varieties of apples are grown on Salt Spring Island, British Columbia. Crop diversity is also protected in seed banks at Plant Gene Resources of Canada. The seed bank in Saskatoon, Saskatchewan, alone protects more than 1000 plant species. A greenhouse in Harrow, Ontario, conserves over 1500 varieties of strawberries and more than 850 types of apples. And, in Fredericton, New Brunswick, over 140 varieties of heirloom potatoes are protected.

Some new crops may come from the hundreds of species of nutritious fruits, nuts, and grains that people gather and use

▲ Figure 19.14B Satellite photo of Amazonian rainforest. The fishbone pattern marks a network of roads carved through the forest when farmers and loggers came to the area.

▲ Figure 19.14A Sugar plums (left) and safou (right), two wild fruits that may be ripe for domestication

locally. In a recent study of potential food sources in Africa, scientists identified dozens of wild plants that might be suitable for domestication and regional production (Figure 19.14A). Promising candidates include intriguingly named fruits such as chocolate berries, gingerbread plums, and monkey oranges. In addition, some regions already have unique domesticated or semi-domesticated crops with the potential for greater production, especially in marginal farmland. For example, some African grains tolerate heat and drought, and many grow better on infertile soil than grains cultivated elsewhere. One species is so tough that it grows on sand dunes where the annual rainfall is less than 70 mm per year!

Modifying crops to enable them to thrive in less than ideal conditions—either through traditional breeding methods or biotechnology—is another approach (see Module 22.1). Genes that enable plants to grow in salty soil, to resist pests, or to tolerate heat and drought would also be useful. But where might such genes be found? All crop plants were originally derived from wild ancestors. Those ancestors and their close relatives are a rich source of genetic diversity that could be used to bolster existing crops.

Both of these approaches to crop diversification are undermined by the ongoing loss of natural plant diversity caused by habitat destruction. Besides clear-cutting to create farmland, forests are being lost to logging, mining, and air pollution. Roads slice vast tracts of lands into fragments that are too small to support a full array of species (Figure 19.14B). As a result, species that could potentially be domesticated are instead being lost. So are many wild relatives of crop species and with them a priceless pool of genetic diversity. The introduction of invasive species has also contributed to a dramatic decrease in the diversity of native plants. These losses are just one example of the impact of declining biodiversity on the future of our species. The Canadian branch of Botanic Gardens Conservation International strives to protect plant species that are endemic

to Canada. We will return to this problem—and possible solutions—in Chapter 41.

 Name two ways that the loss of plant diversity might affect the world's future supply of food.

● Potential crop plants could be lost; potentially useful genes carried by wild ancestors or close relatives of crop plants could be lost.

REVIEW

Reviewing the Concepts

Plant Evolution (19.1–19.3)

19.1 Plants have adaptations for life on land.

Leaves carry out photosynthesis.

Reproductive structures, as in flowers, contain spores and gametes.

Cuticle covering leaves and stems reduces water loss.

Stomata in leaves allow gas exchange between plant and atmosphere.

Lignin hardens cell walls of some plant tissues.

Stem supports plant; may perform photosynthesis.

Vascular tissues in shoots and roots transport water, minerals, and sugars; provide support.

Roots anchor plant; mycorrhizae (root-fungus associations) help absorb water and minerals from the soil.

19.2 Haploid and diploid generations alternate in plant life cycles. The haploid gametophyte produces eggs and sperm by mitosis. The zygote develops into the diploid sporophyte, in which meiosis produces haploid spores. Spores grow into gametophytes.

19.3 Plant diversity reflects the evolutionary history of the plant kingdom. Nonvascular plants (bryophytes) include the mosses, hornworts, and liverworts. Vascular plants have supportive conducting tissues. Ferns are seedless vascular plants with flagellated sperm. Seed plants have sperm-transporting pollen grains and protect embryos in seeds. Gymnosperms, such as pines, produce seeds in cones. The seeds of angiosperms develop within protective ovaries.

Plant Diversity (19.4–19.8)

19.4 The life cycle of a moss is dominated by the gametophyte. A mat of moss is mostly gametophytes, which produce eggs and swimming sperm. The zygote develops on the gametophyte into the smaller sporophyte.

19.5 Does moss grow only on the north side of trees? The rumour that moss grows only on the north side of trees is largely unfounded. Moss tends to grow in more humid microclimates, which may exist on the northern side of trees at higher latitudes.

19.6 Ferns, like most plants, have a life cycle dominated by the sporophyte. The sporophyte is the dominant generation. Sperm, produced by the gametophyte, swim to the egg.

19.7 Seedless vascular plants dominated vast "coal forests." Seedless vascular plants dominated during the Carboniferous period. Their fossilized remains include coal, oil, and natural gas and are known as fossil fuels.

19.8 A pine tree is a sporophyte with gametophytes in its cones. A pine tree is a sporophyte; tiny gametophytes grow in its cones. A sperm from a pollen grain fertilizes an egg in the female gametophyte. The zygote develops into a sporophyte embryo, and the ovule becomes a seed, with stored food and a protective coat.

The Flowering Plants (19.9–19.14)

19.9 The flower is the centrepiece of angiosperm reproduction. A flower usually consists of sepals, petals, stamens (which produce pollen), and carpels (which contain ovules).

19.10 The angiosperm plant is a sporophyte with gametophytes in its flowers. The sporophyte is independent, with tiny, dependent gametophytes protected in flowers. Ovules become seeds, and ovaries become fruits.

19.11 The structure of a fruit reflects its function in seed dispersal. Fruits increase the dispersal of seeds by wind or animals.

19.12 Angiosperms sustain us—and add spice to our diets. Many of our foods are actually angiosperm fruit.

19.13 Pollination by animals has influenced angiosperm evolution. Flowers attract pollinators by colour and scent. Visiting pollinators are rewarded with nectar and pollen.

19.14 Plant diversity is vital to the future of the world's food supply. As plant biodiversity is lost through extinction and habitat destruction, potential crop species and valuable genes are lost.

Connecting the Concepts

1. In this abbreviated diagram, identify the four major plant groups and the key terrestrial adaptation associated with each of the three major branch points.

2. Complete the diagram of a general plant life cycle. Be certain to note missing stages, the ploidy of each, and the processes that produce each stage.

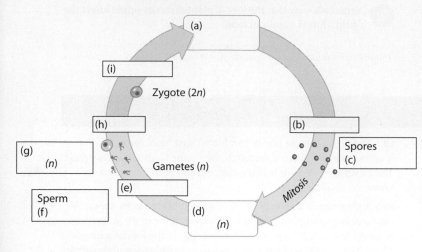

Zygote (2n)

(a)

(i)

(h)

(g)
(n)

Sperm
(f)

(e)

(b)

Spores
(c)

Gametes (n)

Mitosis

(d)
(n)

Testing Your Knowledge

Multiple Choice

3. Angiosperms are different from all other plants because only they have
   a. a vascular system.
   b. flowers.
   c. a life cycle that involves alternation of generations.
   d. seeds.
   e. a dominant sporophyte phase.

4. Which of the following produce eggs and sperm? (*Explain your answer.*)
   a. the sexual reproductive structures of a fungus
   b. fern sporophytes
   c. moss gametophytes
   d. the anthers of a flower
   e. moss sporangia

5. The eggs of seed plants are fertilized within ovules, and the ovules then develop into
   a. seeds.   b. spores.
   c. gametophytes.   d. fruit.
   e. sporophytes.

6. The diploid sporophyte stage is dominant in the life cycles of all of the following *except* a
   a. pine tree.   b. dandelion.
   c. rose bush.   d. fern.
   e. moss.

7. Which group of plants has a sporophyte that is completely dependent on the gametophyte?
   a. mosses   b. ferns
   c. gymnosperms   d. angiosperms
   e. flowering plants

8. Which of the following foods, commonly thought of as a vegetable, is actually a fruit? (*Explain your answer.*)
   a. zucchini   b. lettuce
   c. celery   d. carrot
   e. potato

9. Which of the following terms describes all the others?
   a. angiosperm   b. gymnosperm
   c. vascular plant   d. fern
   e. seed plant

10. Which of the following is a plant with flagellated sperm and a sporophyte-dominated life cycle?
    a. cycad   b. moss
    c. charophyte   d. fern
    e. liverwort

Describing, Comparing, and Explaining

11. Compare the adaptations of a seed plant with those of an alga in terms of their fitness to grow and reproduce successfully on dry land.

12. Compare the structure of gymnosperm and angiosperm seeds. For each group, indicate how pollen reaches the ovule, where the seeds develop, what are the origins of the structures within the seed, and how are the seeds dispersed.

13. How do animals help flowering plants reproduce? How do the animals benefit?

Applying the Concepts

14. Give five main reasons why plants and fungi (covered in Chapter 18) are classified in different kingdoms.

15. In March 2011, an earthquake and tsunami caused the release of radioactive materials from the Fukushima Daiichi nuclear power plant in Japan, scattering radioactive fallout for hundreds of kilometres. In assessing the biological effects of the radiation, researchers found mosses to be especially valuable as organisms for monitoring the damage. As mentioned in Module 10.16, radiation damages organisms by causing mutations. Explain why it is faster to observe the genetic effects of radiation on mosses than on plants from other groups. Imagine that you are conducting tests shortly after a nuclear accident. Using potted moss plants as your experimental organisms, design an experiment to test the hypothesis that the frequency of mutations decreases with the organism's distance from the source of radiation.

Answers to all questions can be found in Appendix E.

Biodiversity of Invertebrate Animals

BIG IDEAS

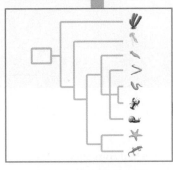

Animal Evolution and Diversity

(20.1–20.4)

Animal body plans can be used to build a phylogenetic tree.

Invertebrate Diversity

(20.5–20.15)

In this chapter, you will learn about animals without backbones.

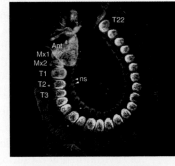

Animal Phylogeny and Diversity Revisited

(20.16–20.17)

Scientists are using molecular data to revise the phylogenetic tree for animals.

Is That an Animal?

Very few places in Canada offer as diverse a range of invertebrate animals (those without backbones) as an intertidal pool on the rocky west coast of Vancouver Island (pictured here) or the coast of the Bay of Fundy in New Brunswick or Nova Scotia. The intertidal region is exposed at low tide and submerged when the tide comes in. Many bizarre creatures make these areas their homes. But would you categorize all the animals that live there as animals?

When the tide goes out, seawater collects in depressions in the rocky shore, forming an intertidal pool. If observers carefully navigate the slippery terrain, these small pools provide extraordinary vantage points to view intertidal communities teaming with life. Pacific intertidal pools are often filled with a diverse array of animals, plants, algae, and microscopic organisms. But identifying many of the animals might not be easy. For example, the pink and orange sponges that encrust the rock may be overlooked or mistaken as algae. Nonetheless, sponges are animals that feed on organic debris floating in the water.

Sea anemones, which look like flowers, are commonplace in intertidal pools. The green sea anemone (*Anthopleura xanthogrammica*) in the photograph forms symbiotic relationships with the algae living in its tissues. The algae provide sugars to the anemone in exchange for protection from grazing by snails. A clonal anemone (*Anthopleura elegantissima*) sometimes appears to be moving in two directions. This movement indicates that it is dividing by fission. Both sides pull in opposite directions, and they eventually separate, forming two animals, which are clones of each other.

Several species of sea stars are easily recognizable inhabitants of the intertidal pools. The purple sea star (*Pisaster ochraceus*)— which can be purple, red, or orange, as evident in the photograph above—can often be seen feeding on molluscs. Using hundreds of tiny suction cup–like tube feet, the sea star can pull open the shell of the mussel or pull a snail off the rocky substrate. Tube feet use very little energy when compared to the muscles of a mollusc. And when a hungry sea star moves over its prey, it usually wins the "tug-of-war," which may last for several days.

Various types of crustaceans, including the red rock crab (*Cancer productus*), are present in many intertidal pools. Although crabs are readily recognized as animals, other crustaceans may not be. Many species of barnacles that live in the intertidal region of the west coast are not easily identified as crustaceans. Goose barnacles have a long stalk attached to the substrate, whereas acorn barnacles, often seen on piers, have no stalk and may attach to other organisms. When submerged, their jointed appendages can be seen scoping through the water to capture food.

The animals listed here are only a few examples of what can be found in a Vancouver Island intertidal pool. Why do intertidal pools have so many different invertebrate animals? One main reason is the highly variable environmental conditions in the intertidal region. As the tide subsides, the sun can warm the temperature of the intertidal pools. Furthermore, as freshwater from streams and rainfall mixes with the seawater, large gradients of salinity develop within the pools. The broad range of environmental conditions throughout the intertidal region can support an equally wide range of invertebrate species. There is also a continual inflow of nutrients being delivered by streams. This nutrient supply helps to sustain the large number of organisms in the intertidal pools.

Although intertidal pools have a wealth of animal diversity, they represent a minute proportion of the diversity of invertebrate life. Millions of invertebrate animals live on Earth, but we have identified only a small fraction of them. In this chapter, we will look at 9 major phyla of the roughly 35 phyla in the animal kingdom (systematists disagree on the precise number). We'll see that identifying, classifying, and arranging this diversity remains a work in progress. But first let's define what an animal is!

Animal Evolution and Diversity

20.1 What is an animal?

Animals are multicellular, heterotrophic eukaryotes that (with a few exceptions) obtain nutrients by ingestion. Now that's a mouthful—and speaking of mouthfuls, **Figure 20.1A** shows a rock python just beginning to ingest a gazelle. **Ingestion** means eating food. This mode of nutrition contrasts animals with fungi, which absorb nutrients after digesting food outside their bodies. Animals digest food within their bodies after ingesting other organisms, dead or alive, whole or by the piece.

Animals also have cells with distinctive structures and specializations. Animal cells lack the cell walls that provide strong support in the bodies of plants and fungi. Animal cells are held together by extracellular structural proteins, the most abundant of which is collagen, and by unique types of intercellular junctions (see Module 4.20). In addition, all but the simplest animals have muscle cells for movement and nerve cells for conducting impulses.

Other unique features are seen in animal reproduction and development. Most animals are diploid and reproduce sexually; eggs and sperm are the only haploid cells, as shown in the life cycle of a sea star in **Figure 20.1B**. ❶ Male and female adult animals make haploid gametes by meiosis. (Recall that in both plants and fungi, meiosis produces spores.) When an egg and sperm fuse during fertilization ❷, a zygote is produced. ❸ The zygote divides by mitosis, ❹ forming an early embryonic stage called a **blastula**, which is usually a hollow ball of cells. ❺ In the sea star and most other animals, one side of the blastula folds inward, forming a stage called a **gastrula**. ❻ The internal sac formed by gastrulation becomes the digestive tract, lined by a cell layer called the **endoderm**. The embryo also has an **ectoderm**, an outer cell layer that gives rise to the outer covering of the animal and, in some phyla, to the central nervous system. Most animals have a third embryonic layer, known as the **mesoderm**, which forms the muscles and most internal organs.

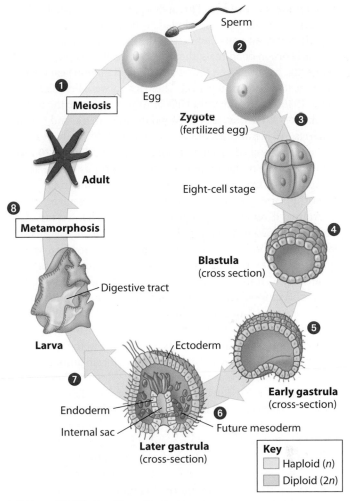

▲ **Figure 20.1B** The life cycle of a sea star

After the gastrula stage, many animals develop directly into adults. Others, such as the sea star, ❼ develop into one or more larval stages first. A **larva** is an immature individual that looks different from the adult animal. ❽ The larva undergoes a major change of body form, called **metamorphosis**, when becoming an adult capable of reproducing sexually. You will read more about animal development in Chapter 30.

This transformation of a zygote into an adult animal is controlled by clusters of homeotic genes (see Modules 11.9 and 14.14). The study of these master control genes has helped scientists investigate the phylogenetic relationships among the highly diverse animal forms we are about to survey.

? List the distinguishing characteristics of animals.

● Bodies composed of multiple eukaryotic cells; ingestion of food (heterotrophic nutrition); absence of cell walls; unique cell junctions; nerve and muscle cells (generally); sexual reproduction and life cycles with unique embryonic stages; unique developmental genes; gametes alone representing the haploid stage of the life cycle

▲ **Figure 20.1A** Ingestion, the animal way of life

20.2 Animal diversification began more than half a billion years ago

As you learned in Module 18.12, the lineage that gave rise to animals is thought to have diverged from a flagellated unikont ancestor more than 1 bya. This ancestor may have resembled modern choanoflagellates, colonial protists that are the closest living relatives of animals. But despite the molecular data indicating this early origin of animals, the oldest generally accepted animal fossils that have yet been found are 575–550 million years old, from the late Ediacaran period. These fossils were first discovered in the 1940s, in the Ediacara Hills of Australia (hence the name). Similar fossils have since been found in Asia, Africa, and North America. All are impressions of soft-bodied animals that varied in shape and ranged in length from 1 cm to 1 m **(Figure 20.2A)**. Although some of the fossils may belong to groups of invertebrates that still exist today, such as sponges and cnidarians, most do not appear to be closely related to any living organism.

Animal diversification appears to have accelerated rapidly from 535 to 525 mya, during the Cambrian period. Because many animal body plans and new phyla appear in the fossils from such an evolutionarily short time span, biologists call this episode the Cambrian explosion. The most celebrated source of Cambrian fossils in the world is a fine-grained deposit of sedimentary rock in British Columbia's Yoho National Park. The Burgess Shale, as it is known, provided a cornucopia of perfectly preserved animal fossils. In contrast to the uniformly soft-bodied Ediacaran animals, many Cambrian animals had hard body parts such as shells and spikes. Many of these fossils are clearly related to existing animal groups. For example, scientists have classified more than one-third of the species found in the Burgess Shale as arthropods, including the one labelled in **Figure 20.2B**. (Present-day arthropods include crabs, shrimp, and insects.) Another striking fossil represented in this reconstruction is an early member of our own phylum, Chordata. Other fossils are more difficult to place, and some are downright weird, such as the spiky creature called *Hallucigenia* and *Anomalocaris* (dominating the left half of the illustration), a formidable predator that grew to an estimated 60 cm in length. The circular structure on the underside of the animal's head is its mouth.

▲ **Figure 20.2B**
A drawing based on fossils from the early Cambrian period; fossil *Hallucigenia* (inset)

What ignited the Cambrian explosion? Scientists have proposed several hypotheses, including increasingly complex predator-prey relationships and an increase in atmospheric oxygen. But whatever the cause of the rapid diversification, it is highly probable that the set of homeotic genes—the genetic framework for complex bodies—was already in place. As you learned in Module 14.14, much of the diversity in body form among the animal phyla is associated with variations in where and when homeotic genes are expressed within developing embryos. The role of these master control genes in the evolution of animal diversity will be discussed further in Module 20.17.

Most animals are **invertebrates**, so called because they lack a vertebral column (backbone): Of the 35 or so animal phyla, only one phylum is made up of vertebrates; the rest are invertebrates. You'll learn about invertebrates in this chapter and vertebrates in Chapter 21. But first let's look at some of the anatomical features biologists use to classify this vast animal diversity.

? **What are two major differences between the fossil animals from the Ediacaran and the Cambrian periods?**

Dickinsonia costata (about 8 cm across)

Spriggina floundersi (about 3 cm long)

▲ **Figure 20.2A** Ediacaran fossils

● Ediacaran animals were all soft-bodied; many Cambrian animals had hard parts such as shells. Few Ediacaran animals can be classified as members of present-day groups; many Cambrian animals are clearly related to present-day groups.

20.3 Animals can be characterized by basic features of their "body plan"

One way that biologists categorize the diversity of animals is by certain general features of body structure, which together describe what is called an animal's "body plan." Distinctions between body plans help biologists infer the phylogenetic relationships between animal groups.

Symmetry is a prominent feature of the body plan. Some animals have **radial symmetry**: As illustrated by the sea anemone on the left in **Figure 20.3A**, the body parts radiate from the centre like the spokes of a bicycle wheel. Any imaginary slice through the central axis divides a radially symmetric animal into mirror images. Thus, the animal has a top and a bottom, but not right and left sides. As shown by the lobster in the figure, an animal with **bilateral symmetry** has mirror-image right and left sides; a distinct head, or **anterior**, end; a tail, or **posterior**, end; a back, or **dorsal**, surface; and a bottom, or **ventral**, surface.

The symmetry of an animal reflects its lifestyle. A radial animal is typically sedentary or passively drifting, meeting its environment equally on all sides. In bilaterally symmetric animals, the brain, sense organs, and mouth are usually located in the head. This arrangement facilitates mobility. As the animal travels headfirst through the environment, its eyes and other sense organs contact the environment first.

Body plans also vary in the organization of tissues. True tissues are collections of specialized cells, usually isolated from other tissues by membrane layers, that perform specific functions. An example is the nervous tissue of your brain and spinal cord. Sponges lack true tissues; but, in other animals, the cell layers formed during gastrulation (see Figure 20.1B) give rise to true tissues and organs. Some animal embryos have only ectoderm and endoderm; most also have mesoderm, making a body with three tissue layers.

Animals arising from embryos with three tissue layers may be characterized by the presence or absence of a **body cavity**. This fluid-filled space *between* the digestive tract and outer body wall cushions the internal organs and enables them to grow and move independently of the body wall. In soft-bodied animals, a noncompressible fluid in the body cavity forms a **hydrostatic skeleton** that provides a rigid structure against which muscles contract, moving the animal.

In the figures to the right, colours indicate the embryonic tissue layers from which the adult arose: ectoderm (blue), mesoderm (red), and endoderm (yellow). The cross-section of a segmented worm in **Figure 20.3B** shows a body cavity called a **true coelom**, which is completely lined by tissue derived from mesoderm. A roundworm **(Figure 20.3C)** has a body cavity called a **pseudocoelom**. A pseudocoelom is not completely lined by tissue derived from mesoderm. Despite the name, pseudocoeloms function just like coeloms. A flatworm **(Figure 20.3D)** reveals a body that is solid except for the cavity of the digestive sac—it lacks a coelom.

Animals that arise from three tissue layers can be separated into two groups based on details of their embryonic development, such as the fate of the opening formed during gastrulation that leads to the developing digestive tract. In **protostomes** (from the Greek *protos*, first, and *stoma*, mouth), this opening becomes the mouth; in **deuterostomes** (from the Greek *deutero*, second), this opening becomes the anus, and the mouth forms from a second opening. Other differences between protostomes and deuterostomes include the pattern of early cell divisions and the way the coelom forms.

Next we see how biologists use these general features of body plan to infer relationships between animal groups.

? **List four features that can describe an animal's body plan.**

● Symmetry, number of embryonic tissue layers, body cavity type, patterns of embryonic development

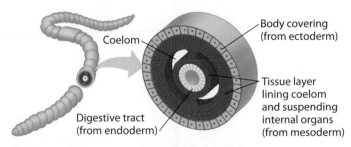

▲ **Figure 20.3B** True coelom (a segmented worm)

Coelom — Body covering (from ectoderm) — Digestive tract (from endoderm) — Tissue layer lining coelom and suspending internal organs (from mesoderm)

▲ **Figure 20.3C** Pseudocoelom (a roundworm)

Body covering (from ectoderm) — Muscle layer (from mesoderm) — Digestive tract (from endoderm) — Pseudocoelom

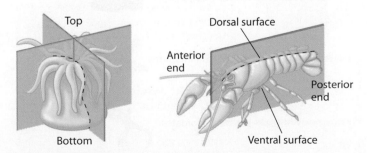

Top — Dorsal surface — Anterior end — Posterior end — Ventral surface — Bottom

▲ **Figure 20.3A** Radial (left) and bilateral (right) symmetry

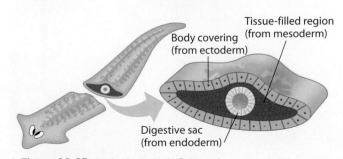

Tissue-filled region (from mesoderm) — Body covering (from ectoderm) — Digestive sac (from endoderm)

▲ **Figure 20.3D** No body cavity (a flatworm)

20.4 The body plans of animals can be used to build phylogenetic trees

Because animals diversified so rapidly on the scale of geologic time, it is difficult to sort out the evolutionary relationships among the various phyla by using only the fossil record. Traditionally, biologists have proposed hypotheses about animal phylogeny based on morphological studies of living animals as well as fossils, often using the characteristics of body plan and embryonic development described in the preceding module.

Figure 20.4 presents a morphology-based phylogenetic tree of the major phyla of the animal kingdom. At the far left is the hypothetical ancestral colonial protist. The tree has a series of branch points that represent shared derived characters. The first branch point splits the sponges from the clade of **eumetazoans** ("true animals"), the animals with true tissues. The next branch point separates the animals with radial symmetry from those with bilateral symmetry. Notice that most animal phyla have bilateral

symmetry and thus belong to the clade called **bilaterians**. This morphology-based tree then divides the bilaterians into two clades based on embryology: protostomes and deuterostomes.

All phylogenetic trees are hypotheses for the key events in the evolutionary history that led to the animal phyla now living on Earth. Increasingly, researchers are adding molecular comparisons to their data sets for identifying clades. In Module 20.16, we will see that such data are leading to new hypotheses for grouping animal phyla. But first let's look at the unique characteristics of each phylum and meet some examples.

? **What shared derived character separates bilaterians from cnidarians?**

Bilateral symmetry ●

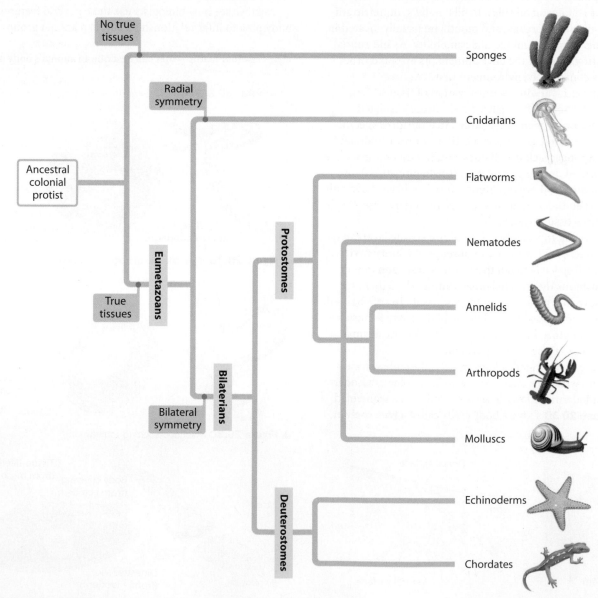

▲ **Figure 20.4** A hypothesis of animal phylogeny based on morphological comparisons

Invertebrate Diversity

20.5 Sponges have a relatively simple, porous body

Sponges (phylum Porifera) are the simplest of all animals. They have no nerves or muscles, though their individual cells can sense and react to changes in the environment. The majority of species are marine, although some are found in fresh water. Some sponges are radially symmetric, but most lack body symmetry. The size and internal structure of sponges vary. For example, the purple tube sponge shown in **Figure 20.5A** can reach heights of 1.5 m. The body of *Scypha*, a small sponge only about 1–3 cm tall resembles a simple sac. Other sponges, such as the azure vase sponge, have folded body walls and irregular shapes. Some freshwater sponges, such as *Spongilla*, grow as thin encrustations on rocks.

A simple sponge resembles a thick-walled sac perforated with holes. (*Porifera* means "pore-bearer" in Latin.) Water enters through the pores into a central cavity, and then flows out through a larger opening **(Figure 20.5B)**. More complex sponges have branching water canals.

The body of a sponge consists of two layers of cells separated by a gelatinous region. Since the cell layers are loose associations of cells, they are not considered true tissues. The inner cell layer consists of flagellated "collar" cells called **choanocytes** (tan in Figure 20.5B), which help to sweep water through the sponge's body. Notice the resemblance of choanocytes to the choanoflagellate in Figure 18.9B. **Amoebocytes** (blue), which wander through the middle body region, produce supportive skeletal fibres (yellow) composed of a flexible protein called spongin and mineralized particles called spicules. Most sponges have both types of skeletal components, but some, including those used as bath sponges, contain only spongin.

Sponges are examples of **suspension feeders** (also known as filter feeders), animals that collect food particles from water passed through some type of food-trapping equipment. Sponges feed by filtering food particles suspended in the water that streams through their porous bodies. To obtain enough food to grow by 100 g, a sponge must filter roughly 1000 litres (L) of seawater. Choanocytes trap food particles in mucus on the membranous collars that surround the base of their flagella and then engulf the food by phagocytosis (see Module 5.8). Amoebocytes pick up food packaged in food vacuoles from choanocytes, digest it, and carry the nutrients to other cells.

Adult sponges are **sessile**, meaning they are anchored in place—they cannot escape from predators. Researchers have found that sponges produce defensive compounds such as toxins and antibiotics that deter pathogens, parasites, and predators. Some of these compounds may prove useful to humans as new drugs.

Biologists hypothesize that sponge lineages arose very early from the multicellular organisms that gave rise to the animal kingdom. The choanocytes of sponges and the cells of living choanoflagellates are similar, supporting the molecular evidence that animals evolved from a flagellated protist ancestor. Sponges are the only animal phylum covered in this book that lack true tissues; thus, they are not members of the clade Eumetazoa ("true animals"). You will learn about the simplest Eumetazoans in the next module.

? **Why is it thought that sponges represent the earliest branch of the animal kingdom?**

● Sponges lack true tissues, and their choanocytes resemble certain flagellated protists.

Spongilla

Scypha

Water flow

Pores

A purple tube sponge

An azure vase sponge

▲ **Figure 20.5A** Sponges

Central cavity

Water flow

Skeletal fiber

Water flow

Choanocyte in contact with an amoebocyte

Pore

Choanocyte

Amoebocyte

Flagellum

Water flow

▲ **Figure 20.5B** The structure of a simple sponge

20.6 Cnidarians are radial animals with tentacles and stinging cells

Among eumetazoans, one of the oldest groups is phylum Cnidaria, which includes the hydras, sea anemones, corals, and jellies (also called jellyfish). **Cnidarians** are characterized by radial symmetry and bodies arising from only two tissue layers. The simple body of most cnidarians has an outer epidermis and an inner cell layer that lines the digestive cavity. A jelly-filled middle region may contain scattered amoeboid cells. Contractile tissues and nerves occur in their simplest forms in cnidarians.

Cnidarians exhibit two kinds of radially symmetric body forms. Hydras, common in freshwater ponds and lakes, and sea anemones have a cylindrical body with tentacles projecting from one end. This body form is a **polyp (Figure 20.6A)**. The other type of cnidarian body is the **medusa**, exemplified by the marine jelly in **Figure 20.6B**. While polyps are mostly sedentary, medusae move freely about in the water. They are shaped like an umbrella with a fringe of tentacles around the lower edge. A few jellies have tentacles 60–70 m long dangling from an umbrella up to 2 m in diameter, but the diameter of most jellies is 2–40 cm.

Some cnidarians pass sequentially through both a polyp stage and a medusa stage in their life cycles. Others exist only as medusae; still others, including hydras and sea anemones, exist only as polyps.

Despite their flowerlike appearance, cnidarians are carnivores that use their tentacles to capture small animals and protists and to push the prey into their mouths. In a polyp, the mouth is on the top of the body, at the hub of the radiating tentacles (see Figure 26.3A). In a medusa, the mouth is in the centre of the undersurface. The mouth leads into a multifunctional compartment called a **gastrovascular cavity** (from the Greek *gaster*, belly, and Latin *vas*, vessel), where food is digested. The mouth is the only opening in the body, so it is also the exit for undigested food and other wastes. Fluid in the gastrovascular cavity circulates nutrients and oxygen to internal cells and removes metabolic wastes (hence the "vascular" in gastrovascular; see Module 28.1). The fluid also acts as a hydrostatic skeleton, supporting the body and helping to give a cnidarian its shape, much like water can give shape to a balloon. When the animal closes its mouth, the volume of the cavity is fixed. Then contraction of selected cells changes the shape of the animal and can produce movement.

Phylum Cnidaria (from the Greek *cnide*, nettle) is named for its unique stinging cells, called **cnidocytes**, that function in defence and in capturing prey. Each cnidocyte contains a fine thread coiled within a capsule **(Figure 20.6C)**. When it is discharged, the thread can sting or entangle prey. Some large marine cnidarians use their stinging threads to catch fish. A group of cnidarians called cubozoans have highly toxic cnidocytes. The sea wasp, a cubozoan found off the coast of northern Australia, is the deadliest organism on Earth: One animal may produce enough poison to kill as many as 60 people.

Coral animals are polyp-form cnidarians that secrete a hard external skeleton. Each generation builds on top of the skeletons of previous generations, constructing the characteristic shapes of "rocks" we call coral. Reef-building corals depend on sugars produced by symbiotic algae to supply them with enough energy to maintain the reef structure in the face of erosion and reef-boring animals.

? What are three functions of a cnidarian's gastrovascular cavity?

● Digestion, circulation (transport of oxygen, nutrients, and wastes), and physical support and movement

A hydra
(about 2–25
mm tall)

A sea anemone
(about 6 cm in diameter)

▲ **Figure 20.6A** Polyp body form

A marine jelly
(about 6 cm in diameter)

▲ **Figure 20.6B**
Medusa body form

Tentacle

"Trigger"

Discharge
of thread

Prey

Coiled thread

Capsule

Cnidocyte

▲ **Figure 20.6C** Cnidocyte action

20.7 Flatworms are the simplest bilateral animals

The vast majority of animal species belong to the clade Bilateria, which consists of animals with bilateral symmetry and three embryonic tissue layers. In Modules 20.7 through 20.12, you'll learn about phyla belonging to the protostome group of bilaterians. **Flatworms**, phylum Platyhelminthes (from the Greek *platys*, flat, and *helmis*, worm), are the simplest of the bilaterians. These thin, often ribbonlike animals range in length from about 1 mm to 20 m and live in marine, freshwater, and damp terrestrial habitats. In addition to free-living forms, there are many parasitic species. Like cnidarians, most flatworms have a gastrovascular cavity with only one opening. Fine branches of the gastrovascular cavity distribute food throughout the animal.

There are three major groups of flatworms. Worms called planarians represent the **free-living flatworms** (**Figure 20.7A**). A planarian has a head with a pair of light-sensitive eyecups and a flap at each side that detects chemicals. Dense clusters of nerve cells form a simple brain, and a pair of nerve cords connects with small nerves that branch throughout the body.

When a planarian feeds, it sucks in food through a mouth at the tip of a muscular tube that projects from a surprising location—the mid-ventral surface of the body (as shown in the figure). Planarians live on the undersurfaces of rocks in freshwater ponds and streams. Using cilia on their ventral surface, they crawl about in search of food. They also have muscles that enable them to twist and turn.

A second group of flatworms, the **flukes**, live as parasites in other animals. Many flukes have suckers that attach to their host and a tough protective covering. Reproductive organs occupy nearly the entire interior of these worms.

Many flukes have complex life cycles that facilitate dispersal of offspring to new hosts. Larvae develop in an intermediate host. The larvae then infect the final host in which they live as adults. For example, the North American liver fluke (*Metorchis conjunctus*) has two intermediate hosts: snails and freshwater fish, including white suckers (*Catostomus commersoni*). The final hosts are fish-eating mammals, in which the worms lodge themselves in the bile ducts and cause liver damage. This fluke is of particular concern in northern Canadian communities, where white suckers are often fed to sled dogs and occasionally eaten by humans.

Tapeworms are another parasitic group of flatworms. Adult tapeworms inhabit the digestive tracts of vertebrates, including humans. In contrast with planarians and flukes, most tapeworms have a very long, ribbonlike body with repeated units. As **Figure 20.7B** shows, the anterior end, called the scolex, is armed with hooks and suckers that grasp the host. Notice that there is no mouth. Bathed in the partially digested food in the intestines of their hosts, they simply absorb nutrients across their body surface and have no digestive tract. Because of this adaptation to their parasitic lifestyle, tapeworms are an exception to our definition of animals in Module 20.1; other animals ingest nutrients. Behind the scolex is a long ribbon of repeated units filled with both male and female reproductive structures. The units at the posterior end, which are full of ripe eggs, break off and pass out of the host's body in feces. The complex life cycle of the beef tapeworm is discussed in Module 39.9.

The term *worm* is commonly applied to any slender, elongated invertebrate. Thus, flatworms are just one of three major animal phyla known as worms. You'll learn about roundworms in the next module and segmented worms in Module 20.10.

> ❓ Flatworms and cnidarians differ in symmetry, with flatworms being _____ and cnidarians being _____; but, the animals of both phyla have a _____.
>
> ● bilateral; radial; gastrovascular cavity

Units with reproductive structures

Hooks

Sucker

Scolex (anterior end)

Colourized SEM 65×

▲ **Figure 20.7B** A tapeworm, a parasitic flatworm

Gastrovascular cavity

Nerve cords

Mouth

Eyecups

Nervous tissue clusters

Bilateral symmetry

▲ **Figure 20.7A** A free-living flatworm, the planarian (most are about 5–10 mm long)

20.8 Nematodes have a pseudocoelom and a complete digestive tract

Nematodes, also called roundworms, make up the phylum Nematoda. As bilaterians, these animals have bilateral symmetry and an embryo with three tissue layers. In contrast with flatworms, roundworms have a fluid-filled body cavity (a pseudocoelom, not completely lined with mesoderm) and a digestive tract with two openings.

Nematodes are cylindrical with a blunt head and tapered tail. They range in size from less than 1 mm to more than 1 m. Several layers of tough, nonliving material called a **cuticle** cover the body and prevent the nematode from drying out. In parasitic species, the cuticle protects the nematode from the host's digestive system. When the worm grows, it periodically sheds its cuticle (moults) and secretes a new, larger one. What looks like a corduroy coat on the nematode in **Figure 20.8A** is its cuticle.

Colourized SEM 400×

Mouth

▲ **Figure 20.8A**
A free-living nematode

You can also see the mouth at the tip of the blunt anterior end of the nematode in Figure 20.8A. Nematodes have a **complete digestive tract** extending as a tube from the mouth to the anus near the tip of the tail. Food travels only one way through the system and is processed as it moves along. In animals with a complete digestive tract, the anterior regions of the tract churn and mix food with enzymes, while the posterior regions absorb nutrients and then dispose of wastes. This division of labour makes the process more efficient and allows each part of the digestive tract to be specialized for its particular function.

Fluid in the pseudocoelom of a nematode distributes nutrients absorbed from the digestive tract throughout the body. The pseudocoelom also functions as a hydrostatic skeleton, and contraction of longitudinal muscles produces a whiplike motion that is characteristic of nematodes.

Although about 25 000 species of nematodes have been named, estimates of the total number of species range as high as 500 000. Free-living nematodes live virtually everywhere there is rotting organic matter, and their numbers are huge. Ninety thousand individuals were found in a single rotting apple lying on the ground; half a hectare of topsoil contains billions of nematodes. Nematodes are important decomposers in soil and on the bottom of lakes and oceans. Some are predators, eating other microscopic animals.

Little is known about most free-living nematodes. A notable exception is the soil-dwelling species *Caenorhabditis elegans*, an important research organism. A *C. elegans* adult hermaphrodite has only 959 somatic cells and an adult male only 1031—in contrast with the human body, which consists of some 10 trillion cells. By following every cell division in the developing *C. elegans* embryo, biologists have been able to trace the lineage of every cell in the adult worm. The genome of *C. elegans* has been sequenced, and ongoing research contributes to our understanding of how genes control animal development, the functioning of nervous systems, and even some of the mechanisms of aging.

Other nematodes thrive as parasites in the moist tissues of plants and in the body fluids and tissues of animals. The largest known nematodes are parasites of whales and measure more than 7 m long! Many species are serious agricultural pests that attack the roots of plants or parasitize animals. The dog heartworm, a common parasite, is deadly to dogs and can also infect other pets such as cats and ferrets (see Module 39.8).

Humans are host to at least 50 species of nematodes, including a number of disease-causing organisms. *Trichinella spiralis* causes a disease called trichinosis in a wide variety of mammals, including humans. People usually acquire the worms by eating undercooked pork or wild game containing the juvenile worms (**Figure 20.8B**). Cooking meat until it is no longer pink kills the worms. Hookworms, which grapple onto the intestinal wall and suck blood, infect millions of people worldwide. Although hookworms are small (about 10 mm long), a heavy infestation can cause severe anemia.

You might expect that an animal group as numerous and widespread as nematodes would include a great diversity of body form. In fact, the opposite is true. Most species look very much alike. In sharp contrast, animals in the phylum Mollusca, which we examine next, exhibit enormous diversity in body form.

 ? What is the advantage of a complete digestive tract?

● Different parts of the digestive tract can be specialized for different functions.

▲ **Figure 20.8B** Juvenile *Trichinella spiralis*, a parasitic nematode, in infected muscle

20.9 Diverse molluscs are variations on a common body plan

Snails, slugs, oysters, clams, octopi, and squids are just a few of the great variety of animals known as **molluscs** (phylum Mollusca). Molluscs are soft-bodied animals (from the Latin *molluscus*, soft), but most are protected by a hard shell.

You may wonder how animals as different as octopi and clams could belong in the same phylum, but these and other molluscs have inherited several common features from their ancestors. **Figure 20.9A** illustrates the basic body plan of a mollusc, consisting of three main parts: a muscular **foot** (grey in the drawing), which functions in locomotion; a **visceral mass** (orange) containing most of the internal organs; and a **mantle** (purple), a fold of tissue that drapes over the visceral mass and secretes a shell in molluscs such as clams and snails. In many molluscs, the mantle extends beyond the visceral mass, producing a water-filled chamber called the mantle cavity, which houses the gills (left side in Figure 20.9A).

▲ Figure 20.9A The general body plan of a mollusc

Figure 20.9A shows yet another body feature found in many molluscs—a unique rasping organ called a **radula**, which is used to scrape up food. In a snail, for example, the radula extends from the mouth and slides back and forth like a backhoe, scraping and scooping algae off rocks. You can observe a radula in action by watching a snail graze on the glass wall of an aquarium.

▲ Figure 20.9B
Trochophore larva

Most molluscs have separate sexes, with reproductive organs located in the visceral mass. The life cycle of many marine molluscs includes a ciliated larva called a trochophore **(Figure 20.9B)**. As you will learn in Module 20.16, trochophore larvae are a significant characteristic in determining phylogenetic relationships among the invertebrate phyla.

In contrast with flatworms, which have no body cavity, and nematodes, which have a pseudocoelom, molluscs have a true coelom (white in Figure 20.9A). Also, unlike flatworms and nematodes, molluscs have a **circulatory system**—an organ system that pumps blood and distributes nutrients and oxygen throughout the body.

These basic body features have evolved in markedly different ways in different groups of molluscs. The three most diverse groups are the gastropods (including snails and slugs), bivalves (including clams, scallops, and oysters), and cephalopods (including squids and octopi).

Gastropods   The largest group of molluscs is called the **gastropods** (from the Greek *gaster*, belly, and *pod*, foot), found in fresh water, salt water, and terrestrial environments. In fact, they include the only molluscs that live on land. Most gastropods are protected by a single, spiralled shell into which the animal can retreat when threatened. Many gastropods have a distinct head with eyes at the tips of tentacles, like the land snail in **Figure 20.9C**. Terrestrial snails lack the gills typical of aquatic molluscs; instead, the lining of the mantle cavity functions as a lung, exchanging gases with the air.

Most gastropods are marine, and shell collectors delight in their variety. Slugs, however, are unusual molluscs in that they have lost their shell during their evolution. The long, colourful projections on the sea slug in Figure 20.9C function as gills.

Bivalves   The **bivalves** (from the Latin *bi*, double, and *valva*, leaf of a folding door) include numerous species of clams,

A sea slug (about 5 cm long)

A land snail

▲ Figure 20.9C Gastropods

A scallop
(about 10 cm
in diameter)

Mussels (each about 6 cm long)

▲ **Figure 20.9D** Bivalves

oysters, mussels, and scallops. They have shells divided into two halves that are hinged together. Most bivalves are suspension feeders. The mantle cavity contains gills that are used for feeding as well as gas exchange. The mucus-coated gills trap fine food particles suspended in the water, and cilia sweep the particles to the mouth. Most bivalves are sedentary, living in sand or mud. They may use their muscular foot for digging and anchoring. Mussels are sessile, secreting strong threads that attach them to rocks, docks, and boats **(Figure 20.9D)**. The scallop in Figure 20.9D can skitter along the seafloor by flapping its shell, rather like the mechanical false teeth sold in novelty shops. Notice the many bluish eyes peering out between the two halves of its hinged shell. The eyes are set into the fringed edges of the animal's mantle.

Cephalopods   The **cephalopods** (from the Greek *kephale*, head, and *pod*, foot) differ from gastropods and bivalves in being adapted to the lifestyle of fast, agile predators. The chambered nautilus in **Figure 20.9E** is a descendant of ancient groups with external shells, but in other cephalopods, the shell is small and internal (as in squids) or missing altogether (as in octopi). If you have a pet bird, you may have hung the internal shell of another cephalopod, the cuttlefish, in its cage. Such "cuttlebones" are commonly given to caged birds as a source of calcium. Cephalopods use beaklike jaws and a radula to crush or rip prey apart. The mouth is at the base of the foot, which is drawn out into several long tentacles for catching and holding prey.

The squid in Figure 20.9E ranks with fishes as a fast, streamlined predator. Some squid can reach swimming speeds of more than 40 km/h; the fastest human could reach only 8.24 km/h. It darts about by drawing water into its mantle cavity and then forcing a jet of water out through a muscular siphon. It steers by pointing the siphon in different directions. Octopi live on the seafloor, where they prowl about in search of crabs and other food.

All cephalopods have large brains and sophisticated sense organs that contribute to their success as mobile predators. The eyes of squid and octopi are among the most complex sense organs in the animal kingdom. Each eye contains a lens that focuses light and a retina on which clear images form. Octopi are considered among the most intelligent invertebrates and have shown remarkable learning abilities in laboratory experiments (the topic of Chapter 31's opening essay).

The so-called colossal squid, which lives in the ocean depths near Antarctica, is the largest of all invertebrates. Specimens are rare, but in 2007, a male colossal squid measuring 10 m and weighing 450 kg was hauled in by a fishing boat. Females are generally even larger, and scientists estimate that the colossal squid averages around 13 m in overall length. The giant squid, which rivals the colossal in length, is thought to average about 10 m. Most information about these impressive animals has been gleaned from dead specimens that washed ashore. In 2004, however, Japanese zoologists succeeded in capturing the first video footage of a giant squid in its natural habitat.

?   Identify the mollusc group that includes each of these examples: garden snail, clam, and squid.

Gastropod, bivalve, cephalopod

A squid (internal shell)

◀ **Figure 20.9E**
Cephalopods

A chambered nautilus (about 21 cm in diameter)

20.10 Annelids are segmented worms

A segmented body resembling a series of fused rings is the hallmark of phylum Annelida (from the Latin *anellus*, ring). **Segmentation**, the subdivision of the body along its length into a series of repeated parts (segments), played a central role in the evolution of many complex animals. A segmented body allows for greater flexibility and mobility, and it probably evolved as an adaptation facilitating movement. An earthworm, a typical **annelid**, uses its flexible, segmented body to crawl and burrow rapidly into the soil.

Annelids range in length from less than 1 mm to 3 m, the length of some giant Australian earthworms. They are found in damp soil, the sea, and most freshwater habitats. Some aquatic annelids swim in pursuit of food, but most are bottom-dwelling scavengers that burrow in sand and mud. There are three main groups of annelids: earthworms and their relatives, polychaetes, and leeches.

Earthworms and Their Relatives Figure 20.10A illustrates the segmented anatomy of an earthworm. Internally, the coelom is partitioned by membrane walls (only a few are fully shown here). Many of the internal body structures are repeated within each segment. The nervous system (yellow) includes a simple brain and a ventral nerve cord with a cluster of nerve cells in each segment. Excretory organs called metanephridia (green, see Module 28.16), which dispose of fluid wastes, are also repeated in each segment (only a few are shown in this diagram). The digestive tract, however, is not segmented; it passes through the segment walls from the mouth to the anus.

Many invertebrates, including most molluscs and all arthropods (which you will meet in the next module), have what is called an **open circulatory system**, in which blood is pumped through vessels that open into body cavities, where organs are bathed directly in blood. Annelids and vertebrates, in contrast, have a **closed circulatory system**, in which blood remains enclosed in vessels as it distributes nutrients and oxygen throughout the body. As you can see in the diagram at the lower left, the main vessels of the earthworm circulatory system—a dorsal blood vessel and a ventral blood vessel—are connected by segmental vessels. The pumping organ, or "heart," is simply an enlarged region of the dorsal blood vessel plus five pairs of segmental vessels near the anterior end.

Each segment is surrounded by longitudinal and circular muscles. Earthworms move by coordinating the contraction of these two sets of muscles (see Figure 33.1D). The muscles work against the coelomic fluid in each segment, which acts as a hydrostatic skeleton. Each segment also has four pairs of stiff bristles that provide traction for burrowing.

Earthworms are hermaphrodites; that is, they have both male and female reproductive structures. However, they do not fertilize their own eggs. Mating earthworms align their bodies facing in opposite directions and exchange sperm. Fertilization occurs some time later, when a specialized organ, visible as the thickened region of the worm in Figure 20.10A, secretes a cocoon made of mucus. The cocoon slides along the worm, picking up the worm's own eggs and the sperm it received from its partner. The cocoon then slips off the worm into the soil, where the embryos develop.

▲ **Figure 20.10A** Segmentation and internal anatomy of an earthworm

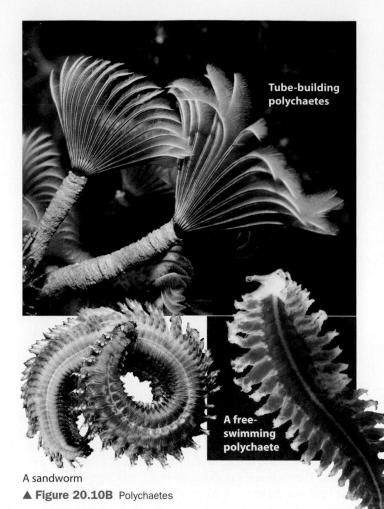

Tube-building polychaetes

A free-swimming polychaete

A sandworm

▲ **Figure 20.10B** Polychaetes

Polychaetes

The **polychaetes** (from the Greek *polys*, many, and *chaeta*, hair), which are mostly marine, form the largest group of annelids.

Many polychaetes live in tubes and extend feathery appendages coated with mucus that trap suspended food particles. Tube-dwellers usually build their tubes by mixing mucus with bits of sand and broken shells. Some species of tube-dwellers are colonial, such as the group shown in **Figure 20.10B**. The circlet of feathery appendages seen at the mouth of each tube extends from the head of the worm inside. The free-swimming polychaete in Figure 20.10B travels in the open ocean by moving the paddlelike appendages on each segment. In polychaetes such as the sandworm that live in the sediments, stiff bristles (called *chaetae*) on the appendages help the worm wriggle about in search of small invertebrates to eat. In many polychaetes, the appendages are richly supplied with blood vessels and are either associated with the gills or function as gills themselves.

Leeches

The third main group of annelids is the **leeches**, which are notorious for their bloodsucking habits. This notoriety is undeserved, however, as most species are free-living carnivores that eat small invertebrates such as snails and insects. The majority of leeches inhabit fresh water, but there are also marine species and a few terrestrial species that inhabit moist vegetation in the tropics. Leeches range in length from 1 to 30 cm.

Some bloodsucking leeches use razorlike jaws to slit the skin of an animal. The host is usually oblivious to this attack because the leech secretes an anaesthetic as well as an anticoagulant into the wound. The leech then sucks as much blood as it can hold, often more than 10 times its own weight. After this gorging, a leech can last for months without another meal.

▲ **Figure 20.10C**
A medicinal leech applied to drain blood from a patient

Until the 1920s, physicians used leeches for bloodletting. For centuries, illness was thought to result from an imbalance in the body's fluids, and the practice of bloodletting was originally conceived to restore the natural balance. Later, physicians viewed bloodletting as a kind of spring cleaning for the body to remove any toxins or "bad blood" that had accumulated. Leeches are still occasionally applied to remove blood from bruised tissues (**Figure 20.10C**) and to help relieve swelling in fingers or toes that have been sewn back on after accidents. Blood tends to accumulate in a reattached finger or toe until small veins have a chance to grow back into it.

The anticoagulant produced by leeches has also proved to be medically useful. It is used to dissolve blood clots that form during surgery or as a result of heart disease. Because it is

Earthworms eat their way through the soil, extracting nutrients as soil passes through their digestive tube. Undigested material, mixed with mucus secreted into the digestive tract, is eliminated as castings (feces) through the anus. Farmers and gardeners value earthworms because the animals aerate the soil and their castings improve the soil's texture. In his final book, Charles Darwin estimated that a single acre (0.4 hectare) of British farmland had about 50 000 earthworms, producing more than 16 tonnes of castings per year.

However, in areas where earthworms have been introduced, they do not always improve the soil conditions. In Canada, most earthworms did not survive glaciation during the last ice age. Only eight species of earthworms are native to the warmer regions of Canada. The other 19 species found in Canadian soil have been recently introduced from European origins. Although these non-native worms may benefit our lawns, gardens, and agricultural lands, they are posing a major problem in forests across Canada. Invasive earthworms alter natural nutrient cycling as they burrow through the soil by mixing the upper layer of decomposing organic material with the inorganic layers beneath it. These changes significantly modify the structure of the forest floor and may disturb the entire forest community. New soil conditions may support the growth of a different plant community, which in turn attracts different animals.

difficult to obtain this chemical from natural sources, it is now being produced through genetic engineering.

The segments of an annelid are all very similar. In the next group we explore, the arthropods, body segments and their appendages have become specialized, serving a variety of functions.

? Tapeworms and bloodsucking leeches are parasites. What are the key differences between them?

● Whereas both are composed of repeated segments, the segments of a tapeworm are filled mostly with reproductive organs and are shed from the posterior end of the animal. Tapeworms are flatworms with no body cavity and, in their parasitic lifestyle, not even a gastrovascular cavity. Leeches have a true coelom and a complete digestive tract.

20.11 Arthropods are segmented animals with jointed appendages and an exoskeleton

More than a million species of **arthropods**—including crayfish, lobsters, crabs, barnacles, spiders, ticks, and insects—have been identified. Biologists estimate that the arthropod population of the world numbers about a billion billion (10^{18}) individuals! In terms of species diversity, geographic distribution, and sheer numbers, phylum Arthropoda must be regarded as the most successful animal phylum.

The diversity and success of arthropods are largely related to their segmentation, their hard exoskeleton, and their jointed appendages, for which the phylum is named (from the Greek *arthron*, joint, and *pod*, foot). As indicated in the drawing of a lobster in **Figure 20.11A**, the appendages are variously adapted for sensory reception, defence, feeding, walking, and swimming. The arthropod body, including the appendages, is covered by an **exoskeleton**, an external skeleton that protects the animal and provides points of attachment for the muscles that move the appendages. This exoskeleton is a cuticle, a nonliving covering that in arthropods is hardened by layers of protein and chitin, a polysaccharide. The exoskeleton is thick around the head, where its main function is to house and protect the brain. It is paper-thin and flexible in other locations, such as the joints of the legs. As it grows, an arthropod must periodically shed its old exoskeleton and secrete a larger one, a complex process called **moulting**.

In contrast with annelids, which have similar segments along their body, the body of most arthropods arises from

▲ **Figure 20.11B** A horseshoe crab (up to about 30 cm wide)

several distinct groups of segments that fuse during development: the head, thorax, and abdomen. In some arthropods, including the lobster, the exoskeleton of the head and thorax is partly fused, forming a body region called the cephalothorax. Each of the segment groups is specialized for a different function. In a lobster, the head bears sensory antennae, eyes, and jointed mouthparts on the ventral side. The thorax bears a pair of defensive appendages (the pincers) and four pairs of legs for walking. The abdomen has swimming appendages.

Like molluscs, arthropods have an open circulatory system in which a tubelike heart pumps blood through short arteries into spaces surrounding the organs. A variety of gas exchange organs have evolved. Most aquatic species have gills. Terrestrial insects have internal air sacs that branch throughout the body (see Module 27.3).

Fossils and molecular evidence suggest that living arthropods represent four major lineages that diverged early in the evolution of arthropods. The figures in this module illustrate representatives of three of these lineages. The fourth, the insects, will be discussed in Module 20.12.

Chelicerates **Figure 20.11B** shows a **horseshoe crab**, a species that has survived with little change for hundreds of millions of years. This "living fossil" is the only surviving member of a group of marine **chelicerates** (from the Greek *chele*, claw, and *keras*, horn) that were abundant in the sea some 300 mya. The oldest horseshoe crab fossils, dating back 445 million years, were found near Churchill, Manitoba, by Canadian paleontologist

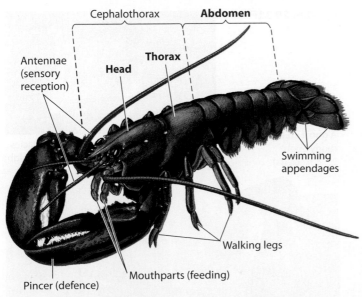

Cephalothorax   **Abdomen**

Antennae (sensory reception)   **Head**   **Thorax**

Swimming appendages

Walking legs

Mouthparts (feeding)

Pincer (defence)

▲ **Figure 20.11A** The structure of a lobster, an arthropod

A scorpion

A black widow spider
(about 1 cm wide)

A dust mite
(about 0.4 mm long)

Colourized SEM

▲ **Figure 20.11C** Arachnids

David Rudkin. One member of this group, the water scorpion, could grow up to 3 m long. Horseshoe crabs are common in the warmer waters of the Atlantic and Gulf coasts of North America.

Living chelicerates also include the scorpions, spiders, ticks, and mites collectively called **arachnids**. Most arachnids live on land. Scorpions (**Figure 20.11C**, left) are nocturnal hunters. Their ancestors were among the first terrestrial carnivores, preying on other arthropods that fed on early land plants. Scorpions have a large pair of pincers for defence and capturing prey. The tip of the tail bears a poisonous stinger. Scorpions eat mainly insects and spiders and attack people only when prodded or stepped on. Only a few species are dangerous to humans, but the sting is painful nonetheless.

Spiders, a diverse group of arachnids, hunt insects or trap them in webs of silk that they spin from specialized glands on their abdomen (see Figure 20.11C, centre). Mites make up another large group of arachnids. On the right in Figure 20.11C is a micrograph of a dust mite, a ubiquitous scavenger in our homes. Thousands of these microscopic animals can thrive in a few square centimetres of carpet or in one of the dustballs that form under a bed. Dust mites do not carry infectious diseases, but many people are allergic to them.

Millipedes and Centipedes   The animals in this lineage have similar segments over most of their body and superficially resemble annelids; however, their jointed legs identify them as arthropods. **Millipedes (Figure 20.11D)** are wormlike terrestrial creatures that eat decaying plant matter. They have two pairs of short legs per body segment. **Centipedes (Figure 20.11E)** are terrestrial carnivores with a pair of poison claws used in defence and to paralyze prey such as cockroaches and flies. Each of their body segments bears a single pair of long legs.

Crustaceans   The **crustaceans** are nearly all aquatic. Lobsters and crayfish are in this group, along with numerous barnacles, crabs, and shrimps **(Figure 20.11F)**. Barnacles

▶ **Figure 20.11F**
Crustaceans

◀ **Figure 20.11D**
A millipede (about 7 cm long)

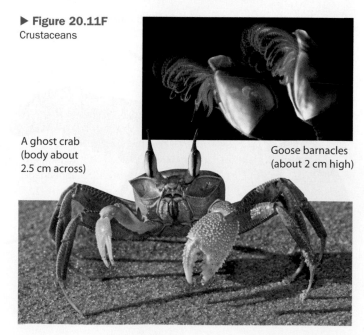

A ghost crab (body about 2.5 cm across)

Goose barnacles (about 2 cm high)

▶ **Figure 20.11E**
A Peruvian giant centipede (can reach 30 cm in length)

are marine crustaceans with a cuticle that is hardened into a shell containing calcium carbonate, which may explain why they were once classified as molluscs. Their jointed appendages project from their shell to strain food from the water. Most barnacles anchor themselves to rocks, boat hulls, pilings, or even whales. The adhesive they produce is as strong as any glue ever invented. Other crustaceans include small copepods and krill, which serve as food sources for many fishes and whales.

We turn next to the fourth lineage of arthropods, the insects, whose numbers dwarf all other groups combined.

20.12 Insects are the most successful group of animals

The evolutionary success of insects is unrivalled by any other group of animals. More than a million species of insects have been identified, making up over 70% of all animal species. Entomologists (scientists who study insects) think that fewer than half the total number of insect species have been identified, and some believe there could be as many as 30 million. Insects are distributed worldwide and have a remarkable ability to survive challenging terrestrial environments. Although they have also flourished in freshwater habitats, insects are rare in the seas, where crustaceans are the dominant arthropods.

What characteristics account for the extraordinary success of insects? One answer lies in the features they share with other arthropods—body segmentation, an exoskeleton, and jointed appendages. Other key features include flight, a waterproof coating on the cuticle, and a complex life cycle. In addition, many insects have short generation times and large numbers of offspring. For example, *Culex pipiens*, the most widely distributed species of mosquito, has a generation time of roughly 10 days, and a single female can lay many hundreds of eggs over the course of her lifetime. Thus, natural selection acts rapidly, and alleles that offer a reproductive advantage can quickly be established in a population.

Life Cycles One factor in the success of insects is a life cycle that includes metamorphosis, during which the animal takes on different body forms as it develops from larva to adult. Only the adult insect is sexually mature and has wings. More than 80% of insect species, including beetles, flies, bees, and moths and butterflies, undergo **complete metamorphosis**. The larval stage (such as caterpillars, which are the larvae of moths and butterflies, and maggots, which are fly larvae) is specialized for eating and growing. A larva typically moults several times as it grows, and then exists as an encased, nonfeeding pupa while its body rebuilds from clusters of embryonic cells that have been held in reserve. The insect then emerges as an adult that is specialized for reproduction and dispersal. Adults and larvae eat different foods, permitting the species to make use of a wider range of resources and avoiding intergenerational competition. **Figure 20.12A** shows the larva, pupa, and adult of the rhinoceros beetle (*Oryctes nasicornis*), named for the horn on the male's head.

▼ **Figure 20.12A** Complete metamorphosis of a European rhinoceros beetle

Larva (grub, up to 12 cm length)

Adult (up to 4 cm length)

Pupa

Other insect species undergo **incomplete metamorphosis**, in which the transition from larva to adult is achieved through multiple moults, but without forming a pupa. In some species, including grasshoppers and cockroaches, the juvenile forms resemble the adults. In others, the body forms and lifestyles are very different. The larvae of dragonflies, for example, are aquatic, but the adults live on land.

Modular Body Plan Like other arthropods, insects have specialized body regions—a head, a thorax, and an abdomen (**Figure 20.12B**). These regions arise from the fusion of embryonic segments during development. Early in development,

Head Thorax Abdomen

Antenna

Specialized jumping legs

Wings (extensions of cuticle)

Eye

Mouthparts

Walking legs

▲ **Figure 20.12B** Modular body plan of insects, as seen in a grasshopper

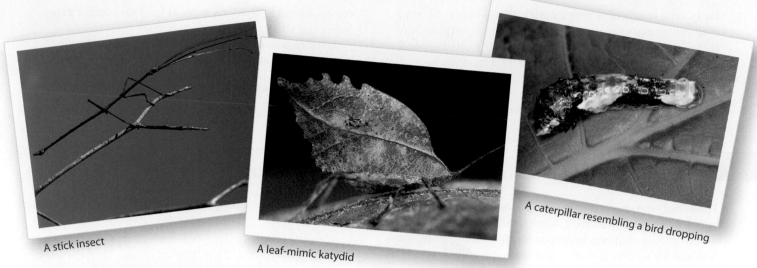

A stick insect

A leaf-mimic katydid

A caterpillar resembling a bird dropping

▲ **Figure 20.12C** Remarkable resemblances

the embryonic segments are identical to each other. However, as discussed in Module 11.9, they soon diverge as different genes are expressed in different segments, giving rise to the three distinct body parts and to a variety of appendages, including antennae, mouthparts, legs, and wings. The insect body plan is essentially modular: Each embryonic segment is a separate building block that develops independently of the other segments. As a result, a mutation that changes homeotic gene expression can change the structure of one segment or its appendages without affecting any of the others. In the evolution of the grasshopper, for example, genetic changes in one thoracic segment produced the specialized jumping legs but did not affect the other two leg-producing segments. Wings, antennae, and mouthparts have all evolved in a similar fashion, by the specialization of independent segments through changes in the timing and location of homeotic gene expression (see Module 14.14). Much of the extraordinary diversification of insects resulted from modifications of the appendages that adapted them for specialized functions.

The head typically bears a pair of sensory antennae, a pair of eyes, and several pairs of mouthparts. The mouthparts are adapted for particular kinds of eating—for example, for chewing plant material (in grasshoppers); for biting and tearing prey (praying mantis); for lapping up fluids (houseflies); or for piercing into and sucking the fluids of plants (aphids) or animals (mosquitoes). When flowering plants appeared, adaptations for nectar feeding became advantageous (see Module 19.13). As a result of this variety in mouthparts, insects have adaptations that exploit almost every conceivable food source.

Most adult insects have three pairs of legs, which may be adapted for walking, jumping, grasping prey, digging into the soil, or even paddling on water. Insects are the only invertebrates that can fly; most adult insects have one or two pairs of wings. (Some insects, such as fleas, are wingless.) Flight, which is an effective means of dispersal and escape from predators, was a major factor in the success of insects. And because the wings are extensions of the cuticle, insects have acquired the ability to fly without sacrificing any legs. By contrast, the wings of birds and bats are modified limbs. With a single pair of walking legs, those animals are generally clumsy when on the ground.

Protective Colour Patterns   In many groups of insects, adaptations of body structures have been coupled with protective coloration. Many different animals, including insects, have camouflage, colour patterns that blend into the background. But insects also have elaborate disguises that include modifications to their antennae, legs, wings, and bodies. For instance, there are insects that resemble twigs, leaves, and bird droppings (**Figure 20.12C**). Some even do a passable imitation of vertebrates. The "snake" in **Figure 20.12D** is actually a hawk moth caterpillar. The colours of its dorsal side are an effective camouflage. When disturbed, however, it flips over to reveal the snake-like eyes of its ventral side, even puffing out its thorax to enhance the deception. "Eyespots" that resemble vertebrate eyes are common in several groups of moths and butterflies. **Figure 20.12E** shows a member of a genus known informally as owl butterflies. A flash of these large "eyes" startles would-be predators. In other species, eyespots deflect the predator's attack away from vital body parts.

How could evolution have produced these complex colour patterns? It turns out that the genetic mechanism by which eyespots evolve is very similar to the mechanism by which specialized appendages evolve. Butterfly wings have a modular construction similar to that of embryonic body segments. Each section can change independently of the others and can

▲ **Figure 20.12D** A hawk moth caterpillar

therefore have a unique pattern. And like the specialization of appendages, eyespots result from different patterns of homeotic gene expression during development.

The study of insects has given evolutionary developmental biologists valuable insight into the genetic mechanisms that have generated the amazing diversity of life. We'll return to this topic in Module 20.17. But first let's explore the rumour that cricket chirps can be used as a thermometer. After that, we'll complete our survey of the invertebrate phyla.

 Contrast incomplete and complete metamorphosis.

● Complete metamorphosis has a pupal stage; incomplete metamorphosis does not.

▲ **Figure 20.12E** An owl butterfly (left) and a long-eared owl (right)

20.13 Can you determine the temperature from cricket chirps?

Have you ever been outside and wondered what the temperature was? Without a thermometer or weather app, you might have thought there was no way of knowing. Or, perhaps you have heard the rumour that you can determine the temperature by counting cricket chirps. Crickets chirp common sounds in many rural and urban areas at dusk and into the night. And if you listen to the right species and count its chirps, you *can* figure out the approximate temperature.

It is a commonly held but inaccurate belief that cricket chirps are produced when the insect rubs its legs together. Instead, it is the wings that produce the chirping sounds. The facing surfaces of each wing have a comb of tiny teeth. When the wings are moved side to side, the teeth of the combs rub against each other, producing the chirp. You can simulate this sound by scraping your thumbnail across the teeth of a comb.

Male crickets chirp as a form of communication. There are actually four different types of chirps. Loud and frequent calling chirps draw females closer. These chirps are loud to drown out the calls of other males competing for the attention of female crickets. In the evening, it is these calling chirps that are most commonly heard. When a female cricket has approached, the hopeful male uses quiet courting chirps to entice her. After mating with the female, copulatory chirps are sung. If a rival male is detected, aggressive chirps show dominance and may intimidate a subordinate male into leaving.

How does temperature affect the frequency of calling chirps? Like most insects, crickets are ectotherms and acquire most of their body heat from the environment (see Module 25.16). In other words, the cricket's body temperature matches that of the surrounding air. As you will read in Unit VI, neurons send signals to muscles to cause them to contract. Both neurons and muscles are temperature sensitive and generally work faster when warmer. Therefore, when the male cricket is warmer, the neurons that trigger chirping do so at a faster frequency. Not only does temperature affect the frequency of male chirps, it also affects the preferred chirping frequency of the females. Natural selection has led to the harmonization of male chirp frequency and female preference. If females did not alter their preferences, they would be receptive for mating at only a narrow range of ambient temperatures.

▲ **Figure 20.13** Snowy tree cricket (*Oecanthus fultoni*)

By adapting their preference to ambient temperature, successful mating can occur over a broader temperature range.

American physicist Amos Dolbear published an article in 1897 that first described the relationship between ambient temperature and cricket chirps. The rumour is true then, but there is a catch. To be accurate, you need to listen to the right species. There are approximately 2000 species of crickets (96 of which live in Canada) and each has a distinct chirp. Most calculations are based on the snowy tree cricket (**Figure 20.13**), which lives in Southern Ontario and British Columbia and is sometimes referred to as the thermometer cricket. Field crickets, common throughout Canada, give a close but less accurate measurement. If you count the number of calling chirps in an eight-second period and add five (a formula known as Dolbear's Law), your answer will be a close approximation of the ambient temperature in degrees Celsius. For example, if you count 15 chirps in 8 seconds, the temperature is close to 20°C (15 + 5). If you are listening to a different species, however, your calculations may not be as accurate.

 Why does the frequency of cricket chirp change with temperature?

● A change in the air temperature changes the cricket's body temperature, which ultimately affects how frequently neurons and muscles move the wings across each other.

20.14 Echinoderms have spiny skin, an endoskeleton, and a water vascular system for movement

Echinoderms, such as sea stars, sand dollars, and sea urchins, are slow-moving or sessile marine animals. Most are radially symmetric as adults. Both the external and the internal parts of a sea star, for instance, radiate from the centre like spokes of a wheel. The bilateral larval stage of echinoderms, however, tells us that echinoderms are not closely related to cnidarians or other animals that never show bilateral symmetry.

The phylum name Echinodermata (from the Greek *echin*, spiny, and *derma*, skin) refers to the prickly bumps or spines of a sea star or sea urchin. These are extensions of the hard calcium-containing plates that form the **endoskeleton**, or internal skeleton, under the thin skin of the animal.

Unique to echinoderms is the **water vascular system**, a network of water-filled canals that branch into extensions called tube feet (**Figure 20.14A**). Tube feet function in locomotion, feeding, and gas exchange. A sea star pulls itself slowly over the seafloor by using its suction cup–like tube feet. Its mouth is centrally located on its undersurface. When the sea star shown

▲ **Figure 20.14C** A sea urchin

in **Figure 20.14B** encounters an oyster or clam, its favourite food, it grips the bivalve with its tube feet and pulls until the mollusc's muscle tires enough to create a narrow opening between the two valves of the shell. The sea star then turns its stomach inside out, pushing it through its mouth and into the opening. The sea star's stomach digests the soft parts of its prey inside the mollusc's shell. When the meal is completed, the sea star withdraws its stomach from the empty shell.

Sea stars and some other echinoderms are capable of regeneration. Arms that are lost are readily regrown.

In contrast with sea stars, sea urchins are spherical and have no arms. They do have five rows of tube feet that project through tiny holes in the animal's globelike case. If you look carefully in **Figure 20.14C**, you can see the long, threadlike tube feet projecting among the spines of the sea urchin. Sea urchins move by pulling with their tube feet. They also have muscles that pivot their spines, which can aid in locomotion. Unlike the carnivorous sea stars, most sea urchins eat algae.

Other echinoderm groups include brittle stars, which move by thrashing their long, flexible arms; sea lilies, which live attached to the substrate by a stalk; and sea cucumbers, odd elongated animals that resemble their vegetable namesake more than they resemble other echinoderms.

Though echinoderms have many unique features, we see evidence of their relation to other animals in their embryonic development. As we discussed in Modules 20.3 and 20.4, differences in patterns of development have led biologists to identify echinoderms and chordates (which include vertebrates) as a clade of bilateral animals called deuterostomes. Thus, echinoderms are more closely related to our phylum, the chordates, than to the protostome animals, such as molluscs, annelids, and arthropods. We examine the chordates next.

▲ **Figure 20.14A** The water vascular system (canals and tube feet) of a sea star (top view)

▲ **Figure 20.14B** A sea star feeding on a clam

? Contrast the skeleton of an echinoderm with that of an arthropod.

An echinoderm has an endoskeleton; an arthropod has an exoskeleton.

20.15 Our own phylum, Chordata, is distinguished by four features

You may be surprised to find the phylum that includes humans in a chapter on invertebrate diversity. However, vertebrates evolved from invertebrate ancestors and continue to share the distinctive features that identify members of the phylum Chordata. The embryos, and often the adults, of chordates possess the following: (1) a **dorsal, hollow nerve cord**; (2) a **notochord**, a flexible, supportive, longitudinal rod located between the digestive tract and the nerve cord; (3) **pharyngeal slits** located in the pharynx, the region just behind the mouth; and (4) a muscular **post-anal tail** (a tail posterior to the anus). You can see these four features in **Figure 20.15A** and **Figure 20.15B**. The two chordates shown, a tunicate and a lancelet, are called invertebrate chordates because they do not have a backbone.

Adult **tunicates** are stationary and look more like small sacs than anything we usually think of as a chordate (Figure 20.15A). Tunicates often adhere to rocks and boats, and they are common on coral reefs. The adult has no trace of a notochord, nerve cord, or tail, but it does have prominent pharyngeal slits that function in feeding. The tunicate larva, however, is a swimming, tadpole-like organism that exhibits all four distinctive chordate features.

Tunicates are suspension feeders. Seawater enters the adult animal through an opening at the top, passes through the pharyngeal slits into a large cavity in the animal, and exits back into the ocean via an excurrent siphon on the side of the body (see the photo in Figure 20.15A). Food particles are trapped in a net made of mucus and then transported to the intestine, where they are digested. Because they shoot a jet of water through their excurrent siphon when threatened, tunicates are often called sea squirts.

Lancelets, another group of marine invertebrate chordates, also feed on suspended particles. Lancelets are small, bladelike

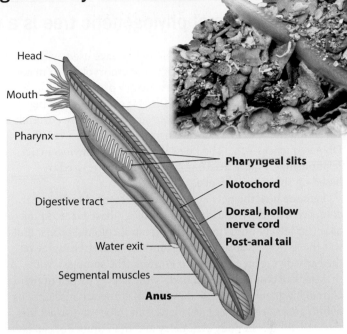

▲ **Figure 20.15B** A lancelet (5–15 cm long)

chordates that live in marine sands (Figure 20.15B). When feeding, a lancelet wriggles backward into the sand with its head sticking out. As in tunicates, a net of mucus secreted across the pharyngeal slits traps food particles. Water flowing through the slits exits via an opening in front of the anus.

Lancelets clearly illustrate the four chordate features. They also have segmental muscles that flex their body from side to side, producing slow swimming movements. These serial muscles are evidence of the lancelet's segmentation. Although not unique to chordates, body segmentation is also a chordate characteristic.

What is the relationship between the invertebrate chordates and the vertebrates? Until recently, biologists believed that the tunicates represented the earliest branch of the chordate lineage. However, molecular evidence indicates that the lancelets are the basal chordates and the tunicates are actually are the closest living nonvertebrate relatives of vertebrates. Recent studies on embryological development, as well as whole genome analysis and miRNA analysis, have led biologists to reorganize their understanding of the relationships among the chordate groups.

The invertebrate chordates have helped us identify the four chordate hallmarks. We'll look at the vertebrate members of this phylum in the next chapter. Next, we review the invertebrates by revisiting the phylogenetic tree presented in Module 20.4.

? **What four features do we share with invertebrate chordates, such as lancelets?**

▲ **Figure 20.15A** A tunicate

● Human embryos and invertebrate chordates all have (1) a dorsal, hollow nerve cord; (2) a notochord; (3) pharyngeal slits; and (4) a post-anal tail.

Animal Phylogeny and Diversity Revisited

20.16 An animal phylogenetic tree is a work in progress

As you learned in Module 20.4, biologists have used evidence from the fossil record, morphology, and embryology to make hypotheses about the evolutionary history of animal groups. The evolutionary tree in Figure 20.4 was constructed using the best evidence at the time. However, scientists are currently collecting new evidence, including molecular data—chiefly DNA sequences—that shed new light on these phylogenetic relationships. **Figure 20.16** presents a slightly revised tree based on this new evidence.

Let's see how the new hypotheses represented by the tree compare with the traditional, morphology-based tree. At the base (far left) of both trees is the ancestral colonial protist that was the hypothetical ancestor of animals. Both trees agree on the early divergence of phylum Porifera (the sponges), with their lack of true tissues and body symmetry. The rest of the animal kingdom represents the clade of eumetazoans, animals with true tissues. The eumetazoans split into two distinct lineages that differ in body symmetry and the number of cell layers formed in gastrulation. The hydras, jellies, sea anemones, and corals of phylum Cnidaria are radially symmetric and have two cell layers. The other lineage consists of bilateral animals, the bilaterians. The two trees agree on all of these early branchings. Both trees also recognize the deuterostomes, which include the echinoderms and chordates, as a clade.

The purple branches in Figure 20.16 show how molecular data have changed the hypotheses represented by Figure 20.4. As you can see, the revised tree distinguishes two clades within the protostomes: lophotrochozoans and ecdysozoans. The lophotrochozoans, while grouped on the basis of molecular similarities, are named for the feeding apparatus (called a lophophore) of some phyla in the group (which we did not discuss) and for the trochophore larva found in molluscs and annelids (see Figure 20.9B). Lophotrochozoans include the flatworms, molluscs, annelids, and many other phyla that we did not survey. The ecdysozoans include the nematodes and arthropods. Both of these phyla have exoskeletons that must be shed for the animal to grow. This moulting process is called ecdysis, the basis for the name ecdysozoan.

Both the tree here and the one in Figure 20.4 represent hypotheses for the key events in the evolutionary history that led to the animal phyla now living on Earth. Like other phylogenetic trees, this latest one serves to stimulate research and discussion, and it is subject to revision as new information is

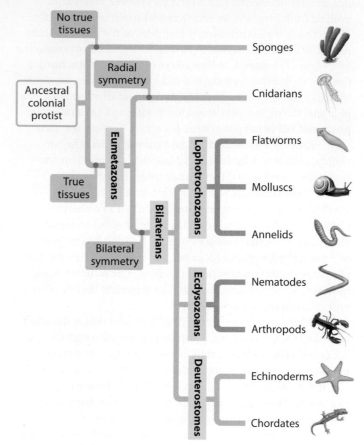

▲ **Figure 20.16** A molecular-based phylogenetic tree

acquired. As biologists continue to revise some branch points, however, the tree's overall message remains the same: The animal kingdom's great diversity arose through the process of evolution, and all animals exhibit features reminiscent of their evolutionary history. In the next module, we look at one of the common threads of evolutionary history, the generation of diversity from shared ancestral genes.

? **Compare the placement of annelids, arthropods, and molluscs in Figures 20.4 and 20.16. How do they differ?**

● In the morphology-based tree, annelids and arthropods are hypothesized to be more closely related to each other than to molluscs, largely based on their segmented bodies. In the molecular-based tree, arthropods are separated from both annelids and molluscs and are placed in the ecdysozoan clade.

20.17 The genes that build animal bodies are ancient

This chapter, a brief tour of invertebrate life, has introduced you to some of the immense variety of animal bodies—flowerlike sea anemones, echinoderms in the shapes of stars and cucumbers, and arthropods with countless configurations

of appendages and colour patterns, to name just a few. How can we explain the evolution of such strikingly different forms from a common protistan ancestor? As exciting new discoveries in the genetics and evolution of development (evo-devo) are integrated with existing lines of evidence from the fossil record, comparative anatomy, and molecular biology, a new understanding of the evolution of animal diversity is beginning to emerge.

Until recently, scientists assumed that the construction of complex organs such as eyes and hearts required more complex instructions than for simple organs. Consequently, they expected the results of the Human Genome Project (see Module 12.18) to reflect the complexity of the human body, estimating that we have about 100 000 genes. As you may recall, geneticists were taken aback to learn how few genes humans have (about 21 000), especially in comparison with other animals (about 14 000 in fruit flies).

It is now clear that important genes responsible for building animal bodies are shared by virtually every member of the animal kingdom—they have existed for at least half a billion years. These ancient genes are the master control genes called homeotic genes, the body-building genes you learned about earlier.

Let's look at one investigation into the involvement of homeotic genes in the evolution of animal diversity, in this case, the origin of the arthropod body plan. How did the enormous variety of distinct body segments bearing specialized appendages evolve? According to one hypothesis, the ancestors of arthropods had a small number of body segment types whose development was controlled by a small number of homeotic genes. New genes that originated on the arthropod branch of the tree, perhaps by duplication of existing homeotic genes, expanded the diversity of segment and appendage types.

To test the hypothesis, a team of scientists compared homeotic genes in arthropods with those of their closest living relatives, known as velvet worms. Velvet worms are one of the small animal phyla (containing 110 species) that we omitted from our coverage of animal diversity. The wormlike bodies of velvet worms bear fleshy antennae and numerous short, identical appendages that are used for walking **(Figure 20.17A)**.

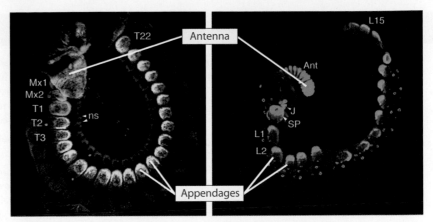

▲ **Figure 20.17B** Expression of homeotic genes in the embryos of a centipede (left) and a velvet worm (right). (The labels identify distinct body segments.)

If velvet worms have only a subset of the homeotic genes found in arthropods, then the hypothesis is supported—arthropods acquired additional genes after the lineages diverged. However, results showed that velvet worms *do* have all the arthropod homeotic genes. The researchers concluded that body segment diversity did *not* result from new homeotic genes that arose in arthropods.

What other explanation might account for arthropod diversity? Recall from Module 14.14 that changes in the regulation of developmental gene expression—when and where the master control genes are transcribed and translated into proteins—can result in morphological changes. **Figure 20.17B** shows differences in gene expression patterns in a centipede embryo (left; also see Figure 20.11E) and a velvet worm embryo (right). The green stain indicates expression of a homeotic gene that is involved in the formation of appendages in a wide range of taxa. Two homeotic genes unique to arthropods and their close relatives are expressed in the body regions stained red or yellow. As you can see, the velvet worm deploys these unique genes only in the posterior tip of its body. In the centipede, and in other groups of arthropods that have been studied, the locations where these genes are expressed correspond with the boundaries between one segment type and the next.

Experiments such as this have demonstrated that the evolution of new structures and new types of animals does not require new genes. Rather, the genetic differences that result in new forms arise in the segments of DNA that control when and where ancient homeotic genes are expressed. To put it simply, building animal bodies is not just about which genes are present—it's about how they are used.

The work of evo-devo researchers is deepening our understanding of how Earth's enormous wealth of biological diversity evolved. With the next chapter, we conclude our exploration of diversity with the evolution of our own group, the vertebrates.

? Researchers found that velvet worms and arthropods share the same set of homeotic genes. What conclusion did they draw from this result?

▲ **Figure 20.17A** *Peripatus*, a velvet worm

● The evolution of diverse arthropod body segment types was not the result of new genes in arthropods.

Reviewing the Concepts

Animal Evolution and Diversity (20.1–20.4)

20.1 What is an animal? Animals are multicellular eukaryotes that have distinctive cell structures and specializations and obtain their nutrients by ingestion. Animal life cycles and embryonic development also distinguish animals from other groups of organisms.

20.2 Animal diversification began more than half a billion years ago. The oldest animal fossils are from the late Ediacaran period and are 575–550 million years old. Animal diversification accelerated rapidly during the Cambrian explosion from 535–525 mya.

20.3 Animals can be characterized by basic features of their "body plan." Body plans may vary in symmetry (radial or bilateral), body cavity (none, pseudocoelom, or true coelom), and embryonic development (protostomes or deuterostomes).

20.4 The body plans of animals can be used to build phylogenetic trees.

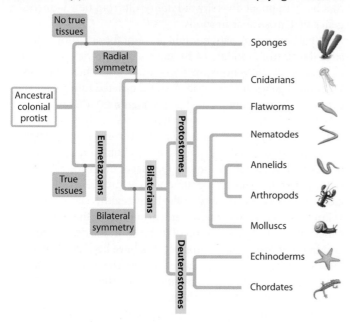

Invertebrate Diversity (20.5–20.15)

20.5 Sponges have a relatively simple, porous body. Members of the phylum Porifera have no true tissues. Their flagellated choanocytes filter food from water passing through pores in the body.

20.6 Cnidarians are radial animals with tentacles and stinging cells. Members of the phylum Cnidaria have true tissues and a gastrovascular cavity. Their two body forms are polyps (such as hydras) and medusae (jellies).

20.7 Flatworms are the simplest bilateral animals. Members of the phylum Platyhelminthes are bilateral animals with no body cavity. A planarian has a gastrovascular cavity and a simple nervous system. Flukes and tapeworms are parasitic flatworms with complex life cycles.

20.8 Nematodes have a pseudocoelom and a complete digestive tract. A protective cuticle covers members of the phylum Nematoda. Many nematodes (roundworms) are free-living decomposers; others are plant or animal parasites.

20.9 Diverse molluscs are variations on a common body plan. Members of the phylum Mollusca include gastropods (such as snails and slugs), bivalves (such as clams), and cephalopods (such as octopi and squids). All have a muscular foot and a mantle, which encloses the visceral mass and may secrete a shell. Many molluscs feed with a rasping radula.

20.10 Annelids are segmented worms. Members of the phylum Annelida include earthworms, polychaetes, and leeches.

20.11 Arthropods are segmented animals with jointed appendages and an exoskeleton. The four lineages of the phylum Arthropoda are chelicerates (arachnids such as spiders), the lineage of millipedes and centipedes, the aquatic crustaceans (lobsters and crabs), and the terrestrial insects.

20.12 Insects are the most successful group of animals. Their development often includes metamorphosis. Insects have a three-part body (head, thorax, and abdomen) and three pairs of legs; most have wings. Specialized appendages and protective colour patterns, which frequently result from evolutionary changes in the timing and location of homeotic gene expression, have played a major role in this group's success.

20.13 Can you determine the temperature from cricket chirps? Ambient temperature changes the frequency of the calling chirps of crickets. Crickets chirp more frequently in warmer temperatures than in cooler temperatures. Dolbear's Law describes this relationship mathematically.

20.14 Echinoderms have spiny skin, an endoskeleton, and a water vascular system for movement. Members of the phylum Echinodermata, such as sea stars, have bilateral symmetry as larvae but are radially symmetric as adults.

20.15 Our own phylum, Chordata, is distinguished by four features. Chordates have a dorsal, hollow nerve cord; a stiff notochord; pharyngeal slits; and a muscular post-anal tail. The simplest chordates are tunicates and lancelets, marine invertebrates that use their pharyngeal slits for suspension feeding.

Animal Phylogeny and Diversity Revisited (20.16–20.17)

20.16 An animal phylogenetic tree is a work in progress. Phylogeny is a constantly evolving science. A revised phylogenetic tree based on molecular data distinguishes two protostome clades: the lophotrochozoans and the ecdysozoans.

20.17 The genes that build animal bodies are ancient. Changes in the regulation of homeotic gene expression have been significant factors in the evolution of animal diversity.

Connecting the Concepts

1. The table below lists the common names of the nine animal phyla surveyed in this chapter. For each phylum, list the key characteristics and some representatives.

Phylum	Characteristics	Representatives
Sponges		
Cnidarians		
Flatworms		
Nematodes		
Molluscs		
Annelids		
Arthropods		
Echinoderms		
Chordates		

Testing Your Knowledge

Multiple Choice

2. Bilateral symmetry in animals is best correlated with
   a. an ability to see equally in all directions.
   b. the presence of a skeleton.
   c. motility and active predation and escape.
   d. development of a true coelom.
   e. adaptation to terrestrial environments.

3. Jon found an organism in a pond and thinks it's a freshwater sponge. His friend Liz thinks it looks more like an aquatic fungus. Which of the following should they do to determine whether it is an animal or a fungus?
   a. See if it can swim.
   b. Figure out whether it is autotrophic or heterotrophic.
   c. See if it is a eukaryote or a prokaryote.
   d. Look for cell walls under a microscope.
   e. Determine whether it is unicellular or multicellular.

4. Which of the following groupings includes the largest number of species? *(Explain your answer.)*
   a. invertebrates   b. chordates
   c. arthropods   d. insects
   e. vertebrates

5. Which of the following animal groups does not have tissues derived from mesoderm?
   a. annelids
   b. amphibians
   c. echinoderms
   d. cnidarians
   e. flatworms

6. Molecular comparisons place nematodes and arthropods in clade Ecdysozoa. What characteristic do they share that is the basis for the name Ecdysozoa?
   a. a complete digestive tract   b. body segmentation
   c. moulting of an exoskeleton   d. bilateral symmetry
   e. a true coelom

Matching

7. Include the vertebrates   a. annelids

8. Medusa and polyp body forms   b. nematodes

9. The simplest bilateral animals   c. sponges

10. The most primitive animal group   d. arthropods

11. Earthworms, polychaetes, and leeches   e. flatworms

12. Largest phylum of all   f. cnidarians

13. Closest relatives of chordates   g. molluscs

14. Body cavity is a pseudocoelom   h. echinoderms

15. Have a muscular foot and a mantle i. chordates

Describing, Comparing, and Explaining

16. Compare the structure of a planarian (a flatworm) and an earthworm with regard to the following: digestive tract, body cavity, and segmentation.

17. Name two phyla of animals that are radially symmetric and two that are bilaterally symmetric. How do the general lifestyles of radial and bilateral animals differ?

18. One of the key characteristics of arthropods is their jointed appendages. Describe four functions of these appendages in four different arthropods.

19. Contrast the phylogenetic tree from Module 20.4 with the one from Module 20.16 (see previous page for both phylogenetic trees). What are the similarities and differences? Why have scientists revised the tree?

Applying the Concepts

20. A marine biologist has dredged up an unknown animal from the seafloor. Describe some of the characteristics that could be used to determine the animal phylum to which the creature should be assigned.

21. Biologists are often asked to identify organisms by people who discover them in their backyards or while walking through a park. Suppose that you are a biologist who answers a phone call from a woman who asks about a worm she found. Which of the nine phyla discussed in this chapter contain worms? What are three questions that you should ask in order to determine which phylum the worm belongs to without actually seeing it for yourself? How will these questions lead you to an answer?

Answers to all questions can be found in Appendix E.

Biodiversity of Vertebrate Animals

Vertebrate Evolution and Diversity

(21.1–21.9)

The major clades of chordates are distinguished by traits such as hinged jaws, two pairs of limbs, fluid-filled eggs with shells, and milk.

Primate Diversity

(21.10–21.11)

Humans have many characteristics in common with other primates, including forward-facing eyes, limber shoulder and hip joints, and opposable thumbs.

Hominin Evolution

(21.12–21.17)

Hominins, species that are on the human branch of the evolutionary tree, include approximately 20 extinct species.

Did Ancient Humans Cause Extinctions Too?

Thinking about prehistoric giants might conjure up images of dinosaurs. However, giant mammals roamed North America much more recently. Extinction of the dinosaurs opened up spaces, which mammals then occupied, bringing about the age of mammals. By the Quaternary period, 2.6 mya, North America was home to many giant mammals. Among them were the woolly rhinoceros, woolly mammoths, sabre-toothed cats, and giant ground sloths. A large body size is beneficial for mammals in colder climates as it minimizes heat loss to the environment.

But things changed 11 000 years ago in the Late Quaternary period. Nearly three-quarters of North American giant mammals became extinct. What happened to cause such a large extinction rate? Most scientists believe two main events, working alone or in combination, contributed to the demise of these animals. First, glaciation between 50 000 and 11 000 years ago covered most of North America with an extensive sheet of ice. The peak of glaciation occurred roughly 18 000 years ago. The second event was the human migration to North America. Evidence suggests that humans came across the Bering Strait between 35 000 and 15 000 years ago. However, the details of human colonization of the new world remain a matter of great debate.

How can scientists discern whether humans or environmental conditions caused the extinction of these hairy giants? Until recently, most believed that overhunting was the primary mechanism of extinction. Dr. Duane Froese at the University of Alberta is part of an international team of scientists that has evidence to the contrary. The team's findings demonstrate that each species responded differently to both climatic change and human encroachment. Neither alone can explain the disappearance of many of these giants.

Climatic changes associated with glaciation altered the distribution of plant life and shrank the habitats of the giant mammals. Habitat loss is a major concern for conservationists today. Smaller habitats cannot support large populations and animals must emigrate or die. This effect is greater for large animals that require more resources.

Overhunting did, as previously thought, have significant impacts on certain species. Ancient humans heavily hunted giant sloths and wild horses, contributing to their extinction. However, the same cannot be said for other species. The ranges of the wooly rhinoceros and Eurasian muskox did not overlap significantly with that of humans. With little to no human contact, it is far more likely that climatic changes and habitat loss were the major factors in their extinction. The reasons behind the extinction of the woolly mammoth still remain elusive. It is likely that both humans and the environment played a part.

Today, bison are the largest land animal in North America and the last of the giant mammals. Bison survived the glaciation and thrived after the glaciers retreated 10 000 years ago. Later, overhunting by North American settlers nearly caused their demise.

The incredible diversity of animal life arose through hundreds of millions of years of evolution, as natural selection shaped adaptations to Earth's diverse and changing environments. In this chapter, we continue our tour of the animal kingdom by exploring our own group, the vertebrates. We end the chapter, and our unit on the diversity of life, with a look at our predecessors—the primates who first walked on two legs; evolved a large, sophisticated brain; and eventually dominated Earth.

Vertebrate Evolution and Diversity

21.1 Derived characters define the major clades of chordates

Using a combination of anatomical, molecular, and fossil evidence, biologists have developed hypotheses for the evolution of chordate groups. **Figure 21.1** illustrates a current view of the major clades of chordates and lists some of the derived characters that define the clades. You can see that the lancelets are thought to be the first group to branch from the chordate lineage. Despite their unique adult morphology, molecular evidence suggests that the tunicates are more closely related to the vertebrates than are the lancelets.

The next transition was the development of a head that consists of a brain at the anterior end of the dorsal nerve cord, eyes, and other sensory organs. These innovations opened up a completely new way of feeding for chordates: active predation.

The origin of a skull and backbone came next. The **vertebrates** are distinguished by a more extensive skull and a backbone, or **vertebral column**, composed of a series of bones called **vertebrae** (singular, *vertebra*). These skeletal elements enclose the main parts of the nervous system. The skull forms a case for the brain, and the vertebrae enclose the nerve cord.

The vertebrate skeleton is an endoskeleton, made of either flexible cartilage or a combination of hard bone and cartilage. Bone and cartilage are mostly nonliving material. But because there are living cells that secrete the nonliving material, the endoskeleton can grow with the animal.

The next major transition was the origin of jaws, which opened up new feeding opportunities. The evolution of lungs or lung derivatives, followed by muscular lobed fins with skeletal support, opened the possibility of life on land. **Tetrapods**, jawed vertebrates with two pairs of limbs, were the first vertebrates on land. The evolution of **amniotes**, tetrapods with a terrestrially adapted egg, completed the transition to land.

In the next several modules, we'll survey the vertebrates, from the jawless hagfish to the fishes to the tetrapods to the amniotes.

? **List the hierarchy of clades to which mammals belong.**

Chordates, vertebrates, jawed vertebrates, tetrapods, amniotes

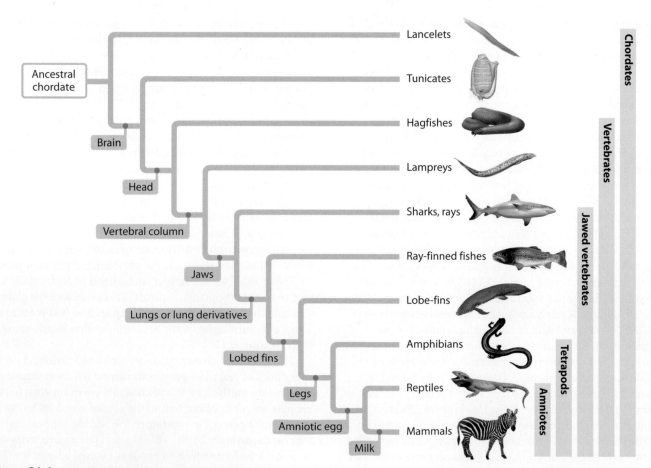

▲ **Figure 21.1** A phylogenetic tree of chordates, showing key derived characters

21.2 Hagfishes and lampreys lack hinged jaws

The most ancestral vertebrates are hagfishes and lampreys. In hagfishes (**Figure 21.2A**, see the opening essay of Chapter 26), the notochord—a strong, flexible rod that runs most of the length of the body—is the body's main support in the adult. The notochord also persists in the adult lamprey, but rudimentary vertebral structures are also present. The classification of hagfish remains controversial. Some biologists consider hagfish to be **craniates** (chordates with heads) and not vertebrates because they lack any vertebral structures, rudimentary or otherwise. However, recent evidence suggests that hagfish and lampreys belong to a group of vertebrates called Cyclostomata (meaning "circular mouth"). Neither hagfishes nor lampreys have jaws.

Present-day hagfishes (roughly 40 species) scavenge dead or dying vertebrates on the cold, dark seafloor. Although nearly blind, they have excellent senses of smell and touch. They feed by entering the animal through an existing opening or by creating a hole using sharp, toothlike structures on the tongue that grasp and tear flesh. For leverage, the hagfish may tie its tail in a knot, and then slide the knot forward to tighten it against the prey's body. The knot trick is also part of its antipredator behaviour. When threatened, a hagfish exudes an enormous amount of slime from special glands on the sides of its body (see Figure 21.2A, inset). The slime may make the hagfish difficult to grasp, or it may repel the predator. After the danger has passed, the hagfish ties itself into a knot and slides the knot forward, peeling off the layer of slime.

Fishers who use nets have long been familiar with hagfishes. With their keen chemical senses, hagfishes are quick to detect bait and entrapped fish. Many fishers have hauled in a net filled with feasting hagfishes, unsalable fish, and bucketfuls of slime. Dr. Douglas Fudge at the University of Guelph investigates hagfish slime production and the potential it may have in the development

▲ **Figure 21.2B** A sea lamprey, with its rasping mouth and larval stage (insets)

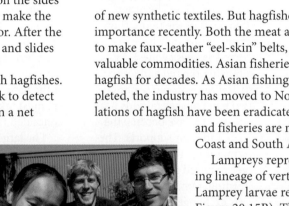

of new synthetic textiles. But hagfishes have gained economic importance recently. Both the meat and the skin, which is used to make faux-leather "eel-skin" belts, purses, and boots, are valuable commodities. Asian fisheries have been harvesting hagfish for decades. As Asian fishing grounds have been depleted, the industry has moved to North America. Some populations of hagfish have been eradicated along the West Coast, and fisheries are now looking to the East Coast and South America for fresh stocks.

Lampreys represent the oldest living lineage of vertebrates (**Figure 21.2B**). Lamprey larvae resemble lancelets (see Figure 20.15B). They are suspension feeders that live in freshwater streams, where they spend much of their time buried in sediment. Most lampreys migrate to the sea or lakes as they mature into adults.

Most species of lamprey are parasites, having mouths surrounded by several rings of sharp teeth to latch onto their hosts. After attaching itself to the side of a fish, the lamprey uses its rasping tongue to penetrate the skin, and feeds on its victim's blood and tissues. After invading the Great Lakes via canals, these voracious vertebrates multiplied rapidly, decimating fish populations as they spread. Since the 1960s, streams that flow into the lakes have been treated with a chemical that reduces lamprey numbers, and fish populations have been recovering.

Slime glands

? **What structure, common to all chordates, do the Cyclostomata use to support the length of their body?**

▲ **Figure 21.2A** Hagfish and slime demonstrated by Douglas Fudge and his students (inset)

● The notochord

21.3 Jawed vertebrates with gills and paired fins include sharks, ray-finned fishes, and lobe-finned fishes

Jawed vertebrates appeared in the fossil record in the mid-Ordovician period, about 470 mya, and steadily became more diverse. Their success probably relates to their paired fins and tail, which allowed them to swim after prey, as well as to their jaws, which enabled them to catch and eat a wide variety of prey instead of feeding as mud-suckers or suspension feeders. Sharks, fishes, amphibians, reptiles (including birds), and mammals—the vast majority of living vertebrates—have jaws supported by two skeletal parts held together by a hinge.

Where did these hinged jaws come from? According to one hypothesis, they evolved by modification of skeletal supports of the anterior pharyngeal (gill) slits. The first part of **Figure 21.3A** shows the skeletal rods supporting the gill slits in a hypothetical ancestor. The main function of these gill slits was trapping suspended food particles. The other two parts of the figure show changes that may have occurred as jaws evolved. By following the red and green structures, you can see how two pairs of skeletal rods near the mouth have become the jaws and their supports. The remaining gill slits, no longer required for suspension feeding, remained as sites of gas exchange.

Three lineages of jawed vertebrates with gills and paired fins are commonly called fishes. The sharks and rays of the class Chondrichthyes, which means "cartilage fish," have changed little in over 300 million years. As shown in Figure 21.1, lungs or lung derivatives (that is, swim bladders) are the key derived character of the clade that includes the ray-finned fishes and the lobe-fins. Muscular fins supported by stout bones further characterize the lobe-fins.

Chondrichthyans Sharks and rays, the **chondrichthyans**, have a flexible skeleton made of cartilage. The largest sharks are suspension feeders that eat small, floating plankton.

▲ **Figure 21.3A** A hypothesis for the origin of vertebrate jaws

Gill slits / Skeletal rods / Skull / Mouth / Hinged jaw

▶ **Figure 21.3C** A manta ray, a chondrichthyan

Most sharks, however, are adept predators—fast swimmers with a streamlined body, powerful jaws, and knifelike teeth (**Figure 21.3B**). A shark has sharp vision and a keen sense of smell. Its head has electrosensors, organs that can detect the minute electric fields produced by muscle contractions in nearby animals. Sharks and most other aquatic vertebrates have a **lateral line system**, a row of sensory organs running along each side that are sensitive to changes in water pressure and can detect minor vibrations caused by animals swimming nearby.

While the bodies of sharks are streamlined for swimming in the open ocean, rays are adapted for life on the bottom. Their bodies are dorsoventrally flattened, with the eyes on the top of the head. Once settled, they flip sand over their bodies with their broad pectoral fins and lie half-buried for much of the day. The tails of stingrays bear sharp spines with venom glands at the base. Where stingrays are common, swimmers and divers must take care not to step on or swim too closely over a concealed ray. The sting is painful and in rare cases fatal.

The largest rays swim through the open ocean filtering plankton (**Figure 21.3C**). Some of these fishes are truly gigantic, measuring up to 6 m across the fins. The fin extensions in front of the mouth, which led to the common name *devilfish*, help to funnel in water for suspension feeding.

Ray-Finned Fishes In **ray-finned fishes**, which include the familiar tuna, trout, and goldfish, the skeleton is made of bone—connective tissue reinforced with a hard matrix of calcium phosphate. Their fins are supported by thin, flexible skeletal rays. Most have flattened scales covering their skin and secrete a coating of mucus that reduces drag during swimming. **Figure 21.3D** highlights key features of a ray-finned fish, such as the rainbow trout shown in the photograph. On each side of the head, a protective flap called an **operculum** covers a chamber housing the gills. Movement of the operculum

▶ **Figure 21.3B** A sandbar shark, a chondrichthyan

Gill openings

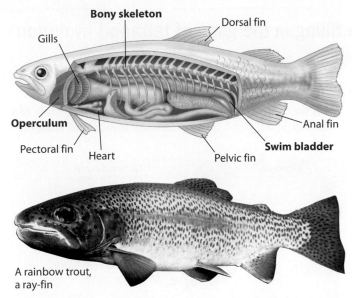

Bony skeleton

Gills

Dorsal fin

Operculum

Anal fin

Pectoral fin   Heart   Pelvic fin   Swim bladder

A rainbow trout,
a ray-fin

▲ **Figure 21.3D** The anatomical features of a ray-finned fish

and mouth allows the fish to breathe without swimming. (By contrast, sharks must generally swim to pass water over their gills.) Ray-finned fishes also have a lung derivative that helps to keep them buoyant—the **swim bladder**, a gas-filled sac. Darwin had proposed that lungs evolved from swim bladders, but odd as it sounds, the opposite appears to be true. In some lineages of bony fishes, swim bladders evolved from balloonlike lungs, which the ancestral fishes may have used in shallow water to supplement gas exchange by their gills.

Ray-finned fishes, which emerged during the Devonian period along with the lobe-fins, include the greatest number of species of any vertebrate group, more than 27 000, and more species are discovered all the time. They have adapted to virtually every aquatic habitat on Earth. From the basic structural adaptations that gave them great maneuverability, speed, and feeding efficiency, various groups have evolved specialized body forms, fins, and feeding adaptations. **Figure 21.3E** shows a sample of the variety. The flounder's flattened body is nearly invisible on the seabed. Pigment cells in its skin match the background for excellent camouflage. Notice that both eyes are on the same side of its head. The larvae of flounders and other flatfishes have eyes on both sides of the head. During development, one eye migrates to join the other on the side that will become the top. The balloon fish doesn't always look like a spiky beach ball. It raises its spines and inflates its body to deter predators. The small fins of the seahorse help it manoeuvre in dense vegetation, and the long tail is used for grasping onto a support. Seahorses have an unusual method of reproduction. The female deposits eggs in the male's abdominal brood pouch. His sperm fertilize the eggs, which develop inside the pouch.

Lobe-Finned Fishes   The key derived character of the **lobe-fins** is a series of rod-shaped bones in their muscular

pectoral and pelvic fins. During the Devonian period, they lived in coastal wetlands and may have used their lobed fins to "walk" underwater. Today, three lineages of lobe-fins survive: The coelacanth is a deep-sea dweller once thought to be extinct. The lungfishes are represented by a few Southern Hemisphere genera that generally inhabit stagnant waters and gulp air into lungs connected to the pharynx **(Figure 21.3F)**. The third lineage, the tetrapods, adapted to life on land during the mid-Devonian period and gave rise to terrestrial vertebrates, as we will see next.

? **From what structure might the swim bladder of ray-finned fishes have evolved?**

● Simple lungs of an ancestral species

A seahorse

A balloon fish

A flounder

▲ **Figure 21.3E** A variety of ray-finned fishes

▲ **Figure 21.3F** A lobe-finned lungfish (about 1 m long)

21.4 New fossil discoveries are filling in the gaps of tetrapod evolution

During the late Devonian period, a line of lobe-finned fishes gave rise to tetrapods (meaning "four feet" in Greek), which today are defined as jawed vertebrates that have limbs and feet that can support their weight on land. Adaptation to life on land was a key event in vertebrate history; all subsequent groups of vertebrates—amphibians, mammals, and reptiles (including birds)—are descendants of these early land-dwellers.

In Chapter 19, we examined how the dramatic differences between aquatic and terrestrial environments shaped plant bodies and life cycles. Like plants, vertebrates faced obstacles on land in regard to gas exchange, water conservation, structural support, and reproduction. But vertebrates had other challenges as well. Sensory organs that worked in water had to be adapted or replaced by structures that received stimuli transmitted through air. And, crucially, a new means of locomotion was required.

Lobe-finned fishes were long considered the most likely immediate ancestors of tetrapods. Their fleshy paired fins contain bones that appear to be homologous to tetrapod limb bones, and some of the modern lobe-fins have lungs that extract oxygen from the air. Alfred Romer, a renowned American paleontologist, hypothesized that these features enabled lobe-finned fishes to survive by moving from one pool of water to another as aquatic habitats shrank during periods of drought. With Romer's gift for vivid imagery, it was easy to imagine the fish dragging themselves short distances across the Devonian landscape, those with the best locomotor skills surviving such journeys to reproduce. In this way, according to the hypothesis, vertebrates gradually became fully adapted to a terrestrial existence. But fossil evidence of the transition was scarce.

For decades, the most informative fossils available were *Eusthenopteron*, a 385-million-year-old specimen that was clearly a fish, and *Ichthyostega*, which lived 365 mya and had advanced tetrapod features **(Figure 21.4A)**. The ray-finned tail and flipperlike hind limbs of *Ichthyostega* indicated that it spent considerable time in the water, but its well-developed front limbs with small, fingerlike bones and powerful shoulders showed that it was capable of locomotion on land. Unlike the shoulder bones of lobe-finned fishes, which are connected directly to the skull, *Ichthyostega* had a neck, a feature advantageous for terrestrial life. *Eusthenopteron* and *Ichthyostega* represented two widely separated points in the transition from fins to limbs. But what happened in between?

Recent fossil finds have begun to fill in the gap. Scientists have discovered lobe-fin fossils that are more similar to tetrapods than to *Eusthenopteron*, including a 380-million-year-old fish called *Panderichthys* (see Figure 21.4A). With its long snout, flattened body shape, and eyes on top of its head, *Panderichthys* looked a bit like a crocodile. It had lungs as well as gills and an opening that allowed water to enter through the top of the skull, a possible indication of a shallow-water habitat. Its paired fins had fishlike rays, but the dorsal and anal fins had been lost, and the tail fin was much smaller than in *Eusthenopteron*. Certain features of its skull were more like those of a tetrapod. Although it had no neck, the bones connecting forelimb to skull were intermediate in shape between that of a fish and a tetrapod.

Panderichthys could have been capable of leveraging its fins against the bottom as it propelled itself through shallow water. It was a fish, but a tetrapod-like fish.

On the contrary, *Acanthostega* **(Figure 21.4B)** was more of a fishlike tetrapod, and it turned scientists' ideas about tetrapod

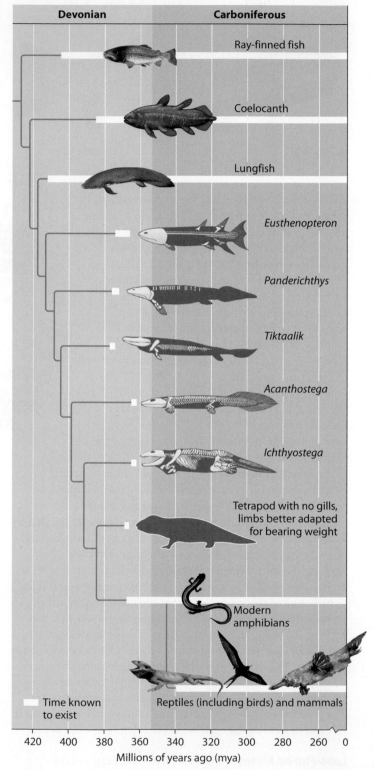

▲ **Figure 21.4A** Some of the transitional forms in tetrapod evolution

evolution upside down. Like *Ichthyostega*, *Acanthostega* had a neck, structural modifications that strengthened its backbone and skull, and four limbs with toes. But its limbs could not have supported the animal on land, nor could its ribs have prevented its lungs from collapsing out of water. The startling conclusion was that the first tetrapods were not fish with lungs that had gradually evolved legs as they dragged themselves from pool to pool in search of water. Instead, they were fish with necks and four limbs that raised their heads above water and could breathe oxygen from the air. **Figure 21.4C** shows an artist's rendering, with fanciful colours.

In 2006, a team of scientists added another important link to the chain of evidence. Using information from the dates and habitats of previous specimens, they predicted that transitional forms might be found in rock formed from the sediments of shallow river environments during a particular time in the late Devonian period. They found a suitable area to search in Ellesmere Island, Nunavut, which was located near the equator during that time. There they discovered several remarkable fossils of an animal they named *Tiktaalik* ("large freshwater fish" in the language of the Inuit from that region). The specimens were exquisitely preserved; even the fishlike scales are clearly visible. *Tiktaalik* straddled the border between *Panderichthys* and *Acanthostega* (see Figure 21.4A). Its paddlelike forelimbs were part fin, part foot. The fin rays had not been replaced by toes. The joints would have served to prop the animal up but would not have enabled it to walk. It had well-developed gills like a fish but a tetrapod-like neck. It was a perfectly intermediate form.

Currently, *Tiktaalik* and *Panderichthys* are the oldest known tetrapod organisms. However, there is evidence that animals walked on land at least 10 million years earlier. Fossilized footprints that can only have been made by a tetrapod have been discovered in the Zachelmie trackways in the Holy Cross Mountains of Poland. Clearly, our understanding of tetrapod evolution

Bones supporting gills

Tetrapod limb skeleton

▲ **Figure 21.4B** *Acanthostega*, a Devonian transitional form

remains incomplete and the search for the first tetrapod continues.

With these images of early tetrapods gleaned from the fossil record in mind, let's look at the environmental conditions that drove their evolution. Plants had colonized the land 100 million years earlier, followed by arthropods. By the time *Tiktaalik* appeared, shallow water would have been a complex environment, with fallen trees and other debris from land plants, along with rooted aquatic plants, providing food and shelter for a variety of organisms. Even a metre-long predator such as *Tiktaalik* would have found plenty to eat. But warm, stagnant water is low in oxygen. The ability to supplement its oxygen intake by air breathing—by lifting the head out of the water—would have been an advantage (see Module 27.5).

Once tetrapods had adaptations that enabled them to leave the water for extended periods of time, they diversified rapidly. Food and oxygen were plentiful in the Carboniferous swamp forests (see Module 19.7). From one of the many lines of tetrapods that settled ashore, modern amphibians evolved.

? How did *Acanthostega* change scientists' concept of tetrapod evolution?

● It showed that the first tetrapods were more fishlike than previously thought. They did not spend time on land.

▼ **Figure 21.4C** The first tetrapod, a four-limbed fish that lived in shallow water and could breathe air

21.5 Amphibians are tetrapods—vertebrates with two pairs of limbs

▲ **Figure 21.5A** A red spotted newt

Amphibians include salamanders, frogs, and caecilians. Some present-day salamanders are entirely aquatic, but those that live on land walk with a side-to-side bending of the body that probably resembles the swagger of early terrestrial tetrapods (**Figure 21.5A**). Frogs are more specialized for moving on land, using their powerful hind legs to hop along the terrain. Caecilians (**Figure 21.5B**) are nearly blind and are legless, adaptations that suit their burrowing lifestyle. However, they evolved from a legged ancestor.

▲ **Figure 21.5B** A caecilian

Most amphibians are found in damp habitats, where their moist skin supplements their lungs for gas exchange. Amphibian skin usually has poison glands that play a role in defence. Poison dart frogs have particularly deadly poisons, and their vivid coloration warns away potential predators (**Figure 21.5C**)

In Greek, the word *amphibios* means "living a double life," a reference to the metamorphosis of many frogs. A frog spends much of its time on land, but it lays its eggs in water. During the breeding season, many species fill the air with their mating calls. As you can see in **Figure 21.5D**, frog eggs are encapsulated in a jellylike material. Consequently, they must be surrounded by moisture to prevent them from drying out. The larval stage, called a tadpole, is a legless, aquatic algae-eater

▲ **Figure 21.5C** An adult poison dart frog

▶ **Figure 21.5E** A tadpole undergoing metamorphosis

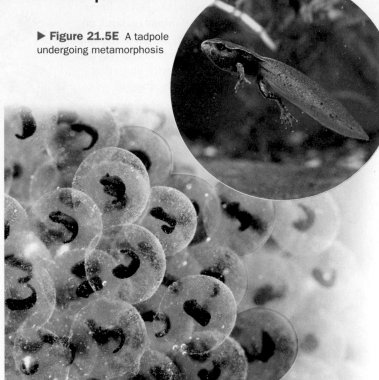

▲ **Figure 21.5D** Frog eggs; a tadpole is developing in the centre of each ball of jelly

with gills, a lateral line system resembling that of fishes, and a long, finned tail (**Figure 21.5E**). In changing into a frog, the tadpole undergoes a radical metamorphosis. When a young frog crawls onto shore and continues life as a terrestrial insect-eater, it has four legs and air-breathing lungs instead of gills (see Figure 21.5C). Not all amphibians live such a double life, however. Some species are strictly terrestrial, and others are exclusively aquatic. *Toad* is a term generally used to refer to frogs that have rough skin and live entirely in terrestrial habitats.

For the past 25 years, zoologists have been documenting a rapid and alarming decline in amphibian populations throughout the world. In 2009, roughly 30% of all known species were at risk for extinction. Multiple causes are contributing to the decline, including habitat loss, climate change, and the spread of a pathogenic fungus (see Module 18.12).

Amphibians were the first vertebrates to colonize the land. The early amphibians probably feasted on insects and other invertebrates in the lush forests of the Carboniferous period (see Figure 19.7). As a result, amphibians became so widespread and diverse that the Carboniferous period is sometimes called the age of amphibians. However, the distribution of amphibians was limited by their vulnerability to dehydration. Adaptations that evolved in the next clade of vertebrates we discuss, the amniotes, enabled them to complete their life cycles entirely on land.

? In what ways are amphibians not completely adapted for terrestrial life?

● Their eggs are not well protected against dehydration; many species have an aquatic larval form; their skin is not waterproof and must remain moist to permit gas exchange.

21.6 Reptiles are amniotes—tetrapods with a terrestrially adapted egg

Reptiles (including birds) and mammals are **amniotes**. The major derived character of this clade is the amniotic egg (Figure 21.6A). The **amniotic egg** contains specialized extra-embryonic membranes, so called because they are not part of the embryo's body. The *amnion*, for which the amniotic egg is named, is a fluid-filled sac surrounding the embryo (Figure 21.6B). The *yolk sac* contains a rich store of nutrients for the developing embryo, like the yellow yolk of a chicken egg. Additional nutrients are available from the albumen ("egg white"). The *chorion* and the membrane of the *allantois* enable the embryo to obtain oxygen from the air for aerobic respiration and dispose of the carbon dioxide produced. The allantois is also a disposal sac for other metabolic waste products. With a waterproof shell to enclose the embryo and its life-support system, reptiles were the first vertebrates to be able to complete their life cycles on land. As we saw in Module 19.3, the seed played a similar role in the evolution of plants.

The clade of amniotes called **reptiles** includes lizards, snakes, turtles, crocodilians, and birds, along with a number of extinct groups such as most of the dinosaurs (see Figure 15.14B). Lizards are the most numerous and diverse reptiles other than birds. Snakes, which are closely related to lizards, may have become limbless as their ancestors adapted to a burrowing lifestyle. Turtles have changed little since they evolved, although their ancestral lineage is still uncertain. Crocodiles and alligators (crocodilians) are the largest living reptiles—the saltwater crocodiles measure up to 6.3 m in length and weigh more than a tonne. Crocodilians spend most of the time in water, breathing air through upturned nostrils.

In addition to an amniotic egg protected in a waterproof shell, reptiles have several other adaptations for terrestrial living not found in amphibians. Reptilian skin, covered with scales waterproofed with the tough protein keratin, keeps the body from drying out. Reptiles cannot breathe through their dry skin and obtain most of their oxygen with their lungs, using their rib cage to help ventilate their lungs.

Lizards, snakes, crocodilians, and turtles are sometimes said to be "cold-blooded" because they do not use their metabolism

▲ **Figure 21.6B** An amniotic egg

to produce body heat. Nonetheless, these animals may regulate their temperature through their behaviour. The bearded dragon of the Australian outback (Figure 21.6C) commonly warms up in the morning by sitting on warm rocks and basking in the sun. If the lizard gets too hot, it seeks shade. Animals that absorb external heat rather than generating much of their own are said to be **ectothermic** (from the Greek *ektos*, outside, and *therme*, heat), a term that is more appropriate than the term *cold-blooded*. Because the energy demands of ectothermic animals are low, reptiles are well suited to deserts, where food is scarce.

Like the amphibians from which they evolved, reptiles were once much more prominent than they are today. Following the decline of amphibians, reptilian lineages expanded rapidly, creating a dynasty that lasted 200 million years. Most dinosaurs died out during the period of mass extinctions about 65 mya (see Module 14.12). Descendants of one dinosaur lineage, however, survive today as the reptilian group we know as birds.

? What is an amniotic egg?

● A shelled egg in which an embryo develops in a fluid-filled amniotic sac and is nourished by a yolk

▲ **Figure 21.6A** A bull snake laying eggs

▲ **Figure 21.6C** A bearded dragon basking in the sun

21.7 Do chameleons change colour for camouflage?

Chameleons are intriguing lizards whose abilities are fairly well known. Their eyes can move independently of each other and focus on two objects simultaneously. They walk with a humorous back-and-forth gait. It is, however, their ability to change colour for which they are best known. Rumour has it that they do so for camouflage to blend in with their surroundings. But is this explanation true?

How do chameleons change colour? Chameleons have specialized pigmented cells within their skin called chromatophores, which give the skin its colour. Some of these cells contain melanin, a dark pigment. Other cells contain pigments of different colours. The colours present depend on the species of chameleon. Chromatophores can change shape under the control of the animal's nervous and endocrine systems. When relaxed, the coloured pigment is condensed and not visible through the skin. If all chromatophores are relaxed, the natural colour of the lizard can be seen. When the cells are excited, they expand and their coloured pigments become visible. The cells can change shape, and therefore so does the colour of the chameleon, in just seconds.

If a green chameleon sends a signal to its blue chromatophores, the animal quickly turns blue. To visualize this, imagine a crowd of people, all wearing green jackets, opening up blue umbrellas all at once. The crowd would appear blue. The crowd would appear green again when the people close their umbrellas. Striped patterns can be produced when specific chromatophores are excited and others are not.

The natural colour of most chameleons is typically a shade of green or light brown. With these hues, they already blend in with their arboreal surroundings fairly well. They do not need to change colour to do so. If chameleons do not change colour for camouflage, why do they? Most biologists agree that colour change is actually an effective form of communication between members of the species. Also, colours can reflect the animal's mood or temperature.

The panther chameleon (*Furcifer pardalis*), native to Madagascar, is normally greenish blue in colour with a white stripe along its side (**Figure 21.7**, upper left image). Male chameleons are very territorial and when a rival male draws near, excitation of red chromatophores signals an aggressive or threatened state. The upper right image is a male panther chameleon displaying aggressive colours. The lower image is a male displaying coloration associated with courting. To impress a female, males display a colourful mosaic of reds, blues, and greens. Females also change colour and may do so to signal their receptiveness to mating.

▲ **Figure 21.7** Some colorations of the male panther chameleon

Colour change can also be an effective way to regulate body temperature. As mentioned in the previous module, lizards are ectothermic and acquire their body heat from the environment. By adopting a darker colour, a chameleon can absorb more heat while basking in the sun. You can feel this when you wear a dark shirt on a sunny day.

The rumour that chameleons change colour to blend in with their surroundings is untrue. Colour changes are actually used for communication and thermoregulation. In the next module, we'll return to our discussion on vertebrate diversity by looking at a lineage of the reptiles, the birds.

 If a chameleon had red and blue chromatophores, how could it change its skin from red to purple?

● Skin would appear red when only red chromatophores are excited. By simultaneously exciting red and blue cells, the skin would appear purple.

21.8 Birds are feathered reptiles with adaptations for flight

Almost all **birds** can fly, and nearly every part of a bird's body reflects adaptations that enhance flight. The forelimbs have been remodelled as feather-covered wings that act as airfoils, providing lift and manoeuvrability in the air (see Figure 33.1E). Large flight muscles anchored to a central ridge along the breastbone provide power. Some species, such as the frigate bird in **Figure 21.8A**, have wings adapted to soaring on air currents, and they flap their wings only occasionally. Others, such as hummingbirds, excel at manoeuvring but must flap almost continuously to stay aloft. The few flightless birds include the ostrich, which is the largest bird in the world, and the penguins of the Southern Hemisphere.

Many features help to reduce weight for flight: Present-day birds lack teeth; their tail is supported by only a few small vertebrae; their feathers have hollow shafts; and their bones have a honeycombed structure, making them strong but light. For example, the frigate bird has a wingspan of more than 2 m, but its whole skeleton weighs only about 113 g.

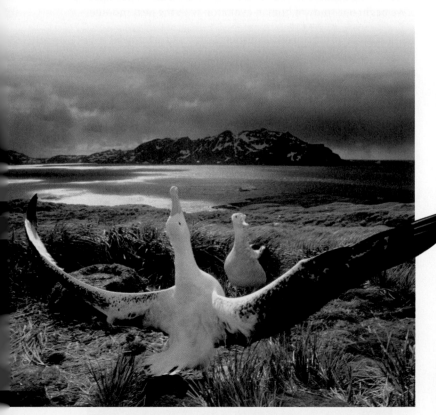

▲ **Figure 21.8A** A soaring frigate bird

Flying requires a great amount of energy, and present-day birds have a high rate of metabolism. Unlike other living reptiles, they are **endothermic**, using heat generated by metabolism to maintain a warm, steady body temperature. Insulating feathers help to maintain their warm body temperature. In support of their high metabolic rate, birds have a highly efficient circulatory system, and their lungs are even more efficient at extracting oxygen from the air than are the lungs of mammals. These adaptations have allowed birds to inhabit a wider range of habitats than their reptilian ancestors.

▲ **Figure 21.8B** A male wandering albatross performing a courtship display for a potential mate

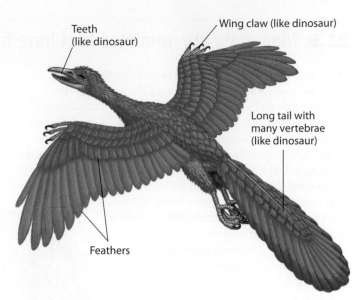

▲ **Figure 21.8C** *Archaeopteryx*, an extinct bird

Flying also requires acute senses and fine muscle control. Birds have excellent eyesight, perhaps the best of all vertebrates, and the visual and motor areas of the brain are well developed.

Birds typically display very complex behaviours, particularly during breeding season. Courtship often involves elaborate rituals. The male frigate bird in Figure 21.8A, for example, inflates its red throat pouch like an enormous balloon to attract females. The wandering albatross in **Figure 21.8B** employs a different kind of courtship display. In many species of birds, males and females take turns incubating the eggs and then feeding the young. Some birds migrate great distances each year to different feeding or breeding grounds.

Strong evidence indicates that birds evolved from a lineage of small, two-legged dinosaurs called theropods. **Figure 21.8C** is an artist's reconstruction based on a 150-million-year-old fossil of the oldest known, most primitive bird, called *Archaeopteryx* (from the Greek *archaios*, ancient, and *pteryx*, wing). Like living birds, it had feathered wings, but otherwise it was more like a small two-legged dinosaur of its era—with teeth, wing claws, and a tail with many vertebrae.

Over the past decade, Chinese paleontologists have excavated fossils of many feathered theropods, including specimens that predate *Archaeopteryx* by 5–10 million years. Such findings imply that feathers, which are homologous to reptilian scales, evolved long before powered flight. Early feathers may have functioned in insulation or courtship displays. As more of these fossils are discovered, scientists are gaining new insight into the evolution of flight.

? **List some adaptations of birds that enhance flight.**

● Reduced weight, endothermy with high metabolism, efficient respiratory and circulatory systems, feathered wings shaped like airfoils, good eyesight

21.9 Mammals are amniotes that have hair and produce milk

There are two major lineages of amniotes: one that led to the reptile clade and one that produced the mammals. Two features—hair and mammary glands that produce milk—are the distinguishing traits of **mammals**. Like birds, mammals are endothermic. Hair provides insulation that helps to maintain a warm body temperature. Efficient respiratory and circulatory systems (including a four-chambered heart) support the high rate of metabolism characteristic of endotherms. Differentiation of teeth adapted for eating many kinds of foods is also characteristic of mammals; different kinds of teeth specialize in cutting, piercing, crushing, or grinding. The three major lineages of mammals—monotremes (egg-laying mammals), marsupials (mammals with a pouch), and eutherians (placental mammals)—differ in their reproductive patterns.

The only existing egg-laying mammals, known as **monotremes**, are echidnas (spiny anteaters) and the platypus. The female platypus usually lays two eggs and incubates them in a nest. After hatching, the young lick up milk secreted onto the mother's fur **(Figure 21.9A)**.

All other mammals are born rather than hatched. During development, the embryos remain inside the mother and receive their nourishment directly from her blood. Mammalian embryos produce extraembryonic membranes that are homologous to those found in the amniotic egg, including the amnion, which retains its function as a protective fluid-filled sac. The chorion, yolk sac, and allantois have different functions in mammals than in reptiles (see Module 30.15). Membranes from the embryo join with the lining of the uterus to form a **placenta**, a structure in which nutrients from the mother's blood diffuse into the embryo's blood.

Marsupials have a brief gestation and give birth to tiny, embryonic offspring that complete development while attached to the mother's nipples. The nursing young are usually housed in an external pouch **(Figure 21.9B)**. Nearly all marsupials live in Australia, New Zealand, and Central and South America. The opossum is the only North American marsupial. **Eutherians** are mammals that bear fully developed live young. They are commonly called **placental mammals** because their placentas are more complex than those of marsupials, and the young complete their embryonic development in the mother's uterus attached to the placenta. The large silvery membrane still clinging to the newborn zebra in **Figure 21.9C** is the amniotic sac. Elephants, rodents, rabbits, dogs, cows, whales, bats, and humans are all examples of eutherians.

▲ **Figure 21.9A** Monotremes: a platypus with newly hatched young

The first true mammals arose about 200 mya and were probably small, nocturnal insect-eaters. Of the three main groups of living mammals, monotremes are the oldest lineage. Marsupials diverged from eutherians about 180 mya. During the Mesozoic era, mammals remained about the size of today's shrews, which are very small insectivores weighing as little as 2 g. After the extinction of large dinosaurs at the end of the Cretaceous period, however, mammals underwent an adaptive radiation, giving rise to large terrestrial herbivores and predators, as well as bats and aquatic mammals such as porpoises and whales. Humans belong to the mammalian order Primates, along with monkeys and apes. We begin our study of human evolution with the next module.

? What are the two distinguishing features of mammals?

Hair and mammary glands, which produce milk

▲ **Figure 21.9B** Marsupials: a grey kangaroo with her young in her pouch

▲ **Figure 21.9C** Eutherians: a zebra with newborn

Primate Diversity

21.10 The human story begins with our primate heritage

The mammalian order Primates includes the lemurs, tarsiers, monkeys, and apes. The earliest primates were probably small arboreal (tree-dwelling) mammals that arose before 65 mya, when dinosaurs still dominated the planet. Most living primates are still arboreal, and the primate body has a number of features that were shaped, through natural selection, by the demands of living in trees. Although humans never lived in trees, the human body retains many of the traits that evolved in our arboreal ancestors. The squirrel-sized slender loris in **Figure 21.10A** illustrates a number of distinguishing primate features. It has limber shoulder and hip joints, enabling it to climb and to swing from one branch to another. The five digits of its grasping feet and hands are highly mobile; the separation of its big toe from the other toes and its flexible thumb give the loris the ability to hang onto branches and manipulate food. Its hands and feet have great sensitivity to touch, which also aids in manipulation. Lorises have a short snout and eyes set close together on the front of the face. The position of the eyes makes their two fields of vision overlap, enhancing depth perception, an important trait for manoeuvring in trees. We humans share all these basic primate traits with the slender loris except for the widely spaced big toe.

▼ **Figure 21.10A**
A slender loris

As shown in the phylogenetic tree in **Figure 21.10B**, the slender loris belongs to one of three main groups of living primates. The lorises and pottos of tropical Africa and southern Asia are placed in one group along with the lemurs. Ranging from the pygmy mouse lemur, which weighs 25 g, to the sifaka **(Figure 21.10C)**, which may weigh as much as 8 kg, lemurs are a diverse group. Of the 50 species of lemurs originally present on the island of Madagascar, 18 have become extinct since humans first colonized the island about 2000 years ago. Because of continuing deforestation and hunting, all lemurs are currently endangered species.

The tarsiers form a second group of primates. Limited to Southeast Asia, these small, nocturnal tree-dwellers have flat faces with large eyes **(Figure 21.10D)**. Fossil evidence indicates that tarsiers are more closely related to anthropoids, the third group of primates, than to the lemur-loris-potto group.

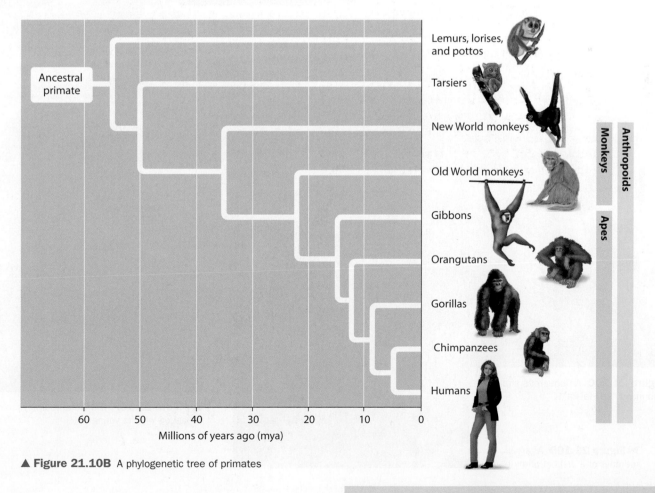

▲ **Figure 21.10B** A phylogenetic tree of primates

The **anthropoids** (from the Greek *anthropos*, man, and *eidos*, form) include monkeys and apes. As shown in Figure 21.10B, the fossil record indicates that anthropoids began diverging from other primates about 50 mya. Anthropoids have a fully **opposable thumb**; that is, they can touch the tip of all four fingers with their thumb. In monkeys and most apes, the opposable thumb functions in a grasping power grip; but, in humans, a distinctive bone structure at the base of the thumb allows it to be used for more precise manipulation.

Notice that monkeys do not constitute a monophyletic group. The first monkeys probably evolved in the Old World (Africa and Asia) and may have reached South America by rafting on logs from Africa. The monkeys of the Old World and New World (the Americas) have been evolving separately for over 30 million years. Both New and Old World monkeys are active during the day and usually live in bands held together by social behaviour.

New World monkeys, found in Central and South America, are all arboreal. Their nostrils are wide open and far apart, and many, such as the black spider monkey, an inhabitant of rainforests in eastern South America (**Figure 21.10E**, right), have a long prehensile tail—specialized for grasping tree limbs. The squirrel-sized golden lion tamarin (Figure 21.10E, left) is a New World monkey that inhabits lowland rainforests of eastern Brazil. In the 1970s, habitat destruction reduced this species to the brink of extinction. Thanks to an intense international conservation effort, numbers have rebounded to about 1200 in the wild.

Old World monkeys lack a prehensile tail, and their nostrils open downward. They include macaques (**Figure 21.10F**), mandrills, baboons, and rhesus monkeys. Many species are arboreal, but some, such as the baboons of the African savanna, are ground dwelling.

Monkeys differ from most apes in having forelimbs that are about equal in length to their hind limbs. Old

A golden lion tamarin (note nostrils that open to the side)

▲ **Figure 21.10E** New World monkeys

A black spider monkey (note prehensile tail)

▲ **Figure 21.10C** A Coquerel's sifaka (pronounced "she-fa'-ka")

▶ **Figure 21.10D** A tarsier, member of a distinct primate group

▲ **Figure 21.10F** Old World monkeys: a macaque with its young

World monkeys and apes, which you will learn about in the next module, diverged about 20–25 mya. The human lineage probably diverged from an ancestor shared with chimpanzees around 6–7 mya (see Module 15.15).

? To which mammalian order do we belong? What are the three main groups of this order?

Primates: (1) lorises, pottos, and lemurs; (2) tarsiers; and (3) anthropoids

21.11 Humans and four other groups of apes are classified as anthropoids

In addition to monkeys, the anthropoid group includes apes: gibbons, orangutans, gorillas, chimpanzees (and bonobos), and humans (**Figure 21.11**). Apes lack a tail and have relatively long arms and short legs. Compared to other primates, they have larger brains relative to body size, and consequently their behaviour is more flexible. Gorillas, chimpanzees, and humans have a high degree of social organization. Except for the human lineage, the apes have a smaller geographic range than the monkeys; they evolved and diversified only in Africa and Southeast Asia and are confined to tropical regions, mainly rainforests.

The nine species of gibbons, all found in Southeast Asia, are entirely arboreal. Gibbons are the smallest, lightest, and most acrobatic of the apes. They are also the only nonhuman apes that are monogamous, with mated pairs remaining together for life.

The orangutan is a shy, solitary ape that lives in the rainforests of Sumatra and Borneo. The largest living arboreal mammal, it moves rather slowly through the trees, supporting its stocky body with all four limbs. Orangutans may occasionally venture onto the forest floor.

The gorilla is the largest ape: Some males are almost 2 m tall and weigh about 200 kg. Found only in African rainforests, gorillas usually live in groups

of up to about 20 individuals. They spend nearly all their time on the ground. Gorillas can stand upright on their hind legs; but, when they walk on all fours, their knuckles contact the ground.

Like the gorilla, the chimpanzee and a closely related species called the bonobo are knuckle walkers. These apes spend as much as a quarter of their time on the ground. Both species inhabit tropical Africa. Chimpanzees have been studied extensively, and many aspects of their behaviour resemble human behaviour. For example, chimpanzees make and use simple tools. The individual in Figure 21.11 is using a blade of grass to "fish" for termites. Chimpanzees also raid other social

▼ **Figure 21.11** Nonhuman anthropoids

A gibbon

An orangutan

A chimpanzee

A gorilla and offspring

groups of their own species, exhibiting behaviour formerly thought to be uniquely human.

Molecular evidence indicates that chimpanzees and gorillas are more closely related to humans than they are to other apes. Humans and chimpanzees are especially closely related; their genomes are 99% identical. Nevertheless, human and chimpanzee genomes have been evolving separately since the two lineages diverged from their last common ancestor.

 What are the five groups of apes within the anthropoid category?

Gibbons, orangutans, gorillas, chimpanzees, and humans ●

Hominin Evolution

21.12 The hominin branch of the primate tree includes species that coexisted

Paleoanthropology, the study of human origins and evolution, focuses on the tiny slice of biological history that has occurred since the divergence of human and chimpanzee lineages from their common ancestor. Paleoanthropologists have unearthed fossils of approximately 20 species of extinct **hominins**, species that are more closely related to humans than to chimpanzees and are therefore on the human branch of the evolutionary tree. (The older term *hominid* is still used by some anthropologists.) These fossils have shown that many of the characters that distinguish humans from other apes first emerged long before *Homo sapiens* appeared.

Thousands of hominin fossils have been discovered, and each new find sheds light on the story of human evolution. However, paleoanthropologists are still vigorously debating hominin classification and phylogenetic relationships. Therefore, **Figure 21.12** presents some of the known hominins in a timeline rather than in a tree diagram like the one in Figure 21.10B. The vertical bars indicate the approximate time period when each species existed, as currently known from the fossil record.

One inference about human phylogeny can immediately be made from Figure 21.12: Hominins did not evolve in a straight line leading directly to *H. sapiens*. At times several hominin species coexisted, and some must have been dead ends that did not give rise to new lineages.

The oldest hominin yet discovered, *Sahelanthropus tchadensis*, lived from about 7 to 6 mya, around the time when the human and chimpanzee lineages diverged. However, most of

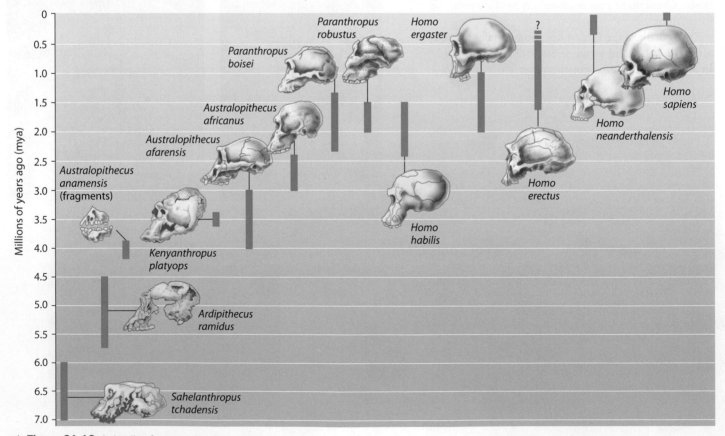

▲ **Figure 21.12** A timeline for some hominin species

the hominin fossils that have been found are less than 4 million years old. Thus, the 4.4-million-year-old fossils of *Ardipithecus ramidus*, painstakingly uncovered and reconstructed by international teams of scientists over the past 15 years, represent an unprecedented perspective on early hominin evolution. *Ardipithecus* was a woodland creature that moved in the trees by walking along branches on the flat parts of its hands and feet. It was equally capable of moving on the ground, and its skeletal features suggest that it walked upright.

Hominin diversity increased dramatically in the period between 4 and 2 mya. The first fossil member of our own genus, *Homo*, dates from that time. By 1 mya, only species of *Homo* existed. Eventually, all *Homo* species except one—our own—ended in extinction.

 Based on the fossil evidence represented in Figure 21.12, how many hominin species coexisted 1.7 million years ago?

Five: P. boisei, P. robustus, H. habilis, H. ergaster, H. erectus

21.13 Australopiths were bipedal and had small brains

Present-day humans and chimpanzees clearly differ in two major features: Humans are bipedal (walk upright) and have much larger brains. When did these features emerge? In the early 20th century, paleoanthropologists hypothesized that increased brain size was the initial change that separated hominins from apes. Bipedalism and other adaptations came later as hominin intelligence led to changes in food-gathering methods, parental care, and social interactions.

The evidence needed to test this hypothesis would come from hominin fossils. Hominin skulls would reveal brain size. Evidence of upright stance might be found by examining the limb and pelvic structures. Another clue to bipedalism is the location of the opening in the base of the skull through which the spinal cord exits. In chimpanzees and other species that are primarily quadrupeds, the spinal cord exits toward the rear of the skull, at an angle that allows the eyes to face forward (**Figure 21.13A**, left). In bipeds, including humans, the spinal cord emerges from the floor of the braincase, so the head can be held directly over the body (Figure 21.13A, right).

In 1924, a scientist working in South Africa discovered a skull that he interpreted as having both apelike and human characteristics. He claimed that the skull represented a new genus and species of bipedal human relatives, which he named *Australopithecus africanus* ("southern ape of Africa"). However, the skull had been blasted out of its geologic context before the scientist received it, making it difficult to establish the fossil's age.

It was another 50 years before convincing evidence to test the hypothesis was unearthed. A team of paleoanthropologists working in the Afar region of Ethiopia discovered a knee joint from a bipedal hominin—and it was more than 3 million years old. The following year, the same researchers found a significant portion of a 3.24-million-year-old female skeleton, which they nicknamed Lucy. Lucy and similar fossils (hundreds have since been discovered) were classified as *Australopithecus afarensis*. The fossils show that *A. afarensis* had a small brain, walked on two legs, and existed as a species for at least 1 million years.

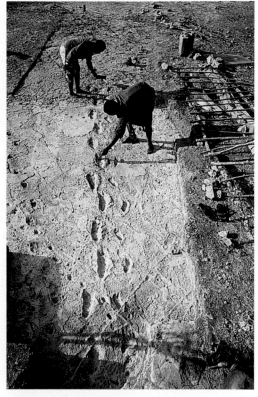

▲ **Figure 21.13B** Evidence of bipedalism in early hominins: footprints in ancient ash

Not long after Lucy was found, another team of paleoanthropologists discovered unique evidence of bipedalism in ancient hominins. While working in what is now Tanzania in East Africa, they found a 3.6-million-year-old layer of hardened volcanic ash criss-crossed with tracks of hyenas, giraffes, and several extinct species of mammals—including upright-walking hominins (**Figure 21.13B**). After the ash had settled, rain had dampened it. The feet of two hominins, one large and one small, walking close together, made impressions in the ash as if it were wet sand on a beach. The ash, composed of a cementlike

▲ **Figure 21.13A** The angle of the spinal cord's exit from a chimpanzee skull (left) and a human skull (right)

material, solidified soon after and was buried by more ash from a later volcanic eruption. The hominins strolling across that ancient landscape may have been *A. afarensis*, which lived in the region at the time, but we will never know for certain.

A. africanus, represented by many other specimens besides the original skull, did prove to be bipedal, and an earlier species, *A. anamensis* (see Figure 21.12), may have been, too. In other features, though, australopiths were decidedly more like apes than humans. Lucy's brain size relative to her body size was about the same as that of a chimpanzee. Our arms are shorter than our legs, but Lucy's proportions were the opposite, and her fingers and toes were long and curved compared to ours—all suggesting that her

species spent some of their time in trees. Another lineage known as "robust" australopiths—*Paranthropus boisei* and *Paranthropus robustus* in Figure 21.12—were also small-brained bipeds.

Paleoanthropologists are now certain that bipedalism is a very old trait. There is evidence that even *Sahelanthropus*, the oldest hominin yet discovered, was capable of walking upright. It was only much later that the other major human trait—an enlarged brain—appeared in the human lineage.

 How can paleoanthropologists conclude that a species was bipedal based on only a fossil skull?

● By the location of the opening where the spinal cord exits the skull

21.14 Larger brains mark the evolution of *Homo*

By measuring the capacity of fossil skulls, paleoanthropologists can estimate the size of the brain, which, relative to body size, roughly indicates the animal's intelligence. The brain volume of *H. sapiens*, at an average 1300 cm³, is approximately triple that of australopiths **(Figure 21.14A)**. As evolutionary biologist Stephan J. Gould put it, "Mankind stood up first and got smart later."

The evolution of larger brains among the hominins came at a cost—weaker jaws. The powerful jaw muscles of nonhuman primates, such as gorillas and chimpanzees, attach to a ridge or crest of bone on the skull. Similar ridges are apparent on the fossilized skulls of early hominins—those with small brains. However, during the course of evolution, the skull ridges and powerful jaw muscles disappeared at about the same time that

brain size started to increase. Some biologists suggest that powerful jaws and a powerful brain were incompatible, and that brain size could increase only after the jaw muscles became smaller.

At 400–450 cm³, the brains of australopiths were too small to qualify them as members of the genus *Homo*, but how big is big enough? What distinguishes humanlike from apelike brain capacity? When a team of paleoanthropologists found crude stone tools along with hominin fossils, they decided that the toolmaker must be one of us and dubbed their find *Homo habilis* ("handy man"). Its brain volume of 510–690 cm³ was a significant jump from australopiths, but some scientists did not consider this large enough to be included in the genus *Homo*. Many *H. habilis* fossils ranging in age from about 1.6 to 2.4 million years have since been found, some appearing more humanlike than others.

Homo ergaster, dating from 1.9 to 1.6 mya, marks a new stage in hominin evolution. With a further increase in brain size, ranging from 750 to 850 cm³, *H. ergaster* was associated with more sophisticated stone tools. Its limb proportions and rib cage were similar to those of modern humans, and its short, straight fingers indicate that it did not climb trees. Its long, slender legs and hip joints were well adapted for long-distance walking.

Fossils of *H. ergaster* were originally thought to come from early members of another species, *Homo erectus*. In *H. erectus* ("upright man"), average brain volume had increased to 940 cm³; the range of sizes overlaps that of *H. ergaster*. Members of *H. erectus* were the first hominins to extend their range beyond Africa. The oldest known fossils of hominins outside Africa, discovered in 2000 in the former Soviet Republic of Georgia, are *H. erectus* dating back 1.8 million years. Others have been found in China and Indonesia. Most fossil evidence indicates that *H. erectus* became

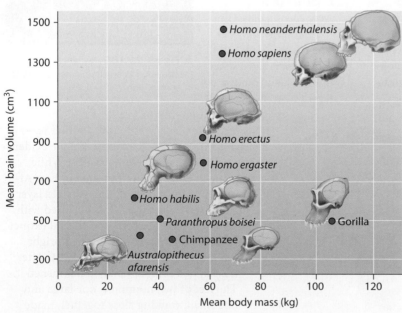

▲ **Figure 21.14A** Brain volume versus body mass in anthropoids

extinct at some point about 200 000 years ago, but recent discoveries raise the possibility that a population survived until 50 000 years ago.

Homo neanderthalensis, commonly called Neanderthals, are perhaps the best known hominins. They had a brain even larger than ours and hunted big game with tools made from stone and wood. Neanderthals were living in Europe as long as 350 000 years ago and later spread to the Near East **(Figure 21.14B)**, but by 28 000 years ago, the species was extinct.

Since the discovery of fossilized remains of *H. neanderthalensis* in the Neander Valley in Germany 150 years ago, people have wondered how Neanderthals are related to us. Were they the ancestors of Europeans? Close cousins? Or part of a different branch of evolution altogether? By comparing mitochondrial DNA sequences from Neanderthals and living humans, researchers showed that Neanderthals are not the ancestors of Europeans. Rather, the last common ancestor of humans and Neanderthals lived around 500 000 years ago. However, a comparison of the nuclear genome sequence of *H. sapiens* with that from Neanderthal fossils, completed in 2010, suggests that Neanderthals and some *H. sapiens* that had left Africa probably did interbreed. Further analysis of Neanderthal DNA may reveal details about the physical appearance, physiology, and brain structure of these intriguing hominins.

▲ **Figure 21.14B** Sites where Neanderthal fossils have been found

In the next module, we look at the origin and worldwide spread of our own species, *H. sapiens.*

? Place the following hominins in order of increasing brain volume: *Australopithecus afarensis, H. erectus, H. ergaster, H. habilis, H. sapiens.*

Australopithecus afarensis, H. habilis, H. ergaster, H. erectus, H. sapiens

21.15 From origins in Africa, *Homo sapiens* spread around the world

Evidence from fossils and DNA studies is coming together to support a compelling hypothesis about how our own species, *H. sapiens*, emerged and spread around the world.

The ancestors of humans originated in Africa. Older species (perhaps *H. ergaster* or *H. erectus*) gave rise to newer species and ultimately to *H. sapiens*. The oldest known fossils of our own species have been discovered in Ethiopia and include fossils that are 160 000 and 195 000 years old. These early humans lacked the heavy browridges of *H. erectus* and Neanderthals (*H. neanderthalensis*), and they were more slender.

Molecular evidence about the origin of humans supports the conclusions drawn from fossils. In addition to showing that living humans are more closely related to one another than to Neanderthals, DNA studies indicate that Europeans and Asians share a more recent common ancestor and that many African lineages represent earlier branches on the human tree. These findings strongly suggest that all living humans have ancestors that originated as *H. sapiens* in Africa.

This conclusion is further supported by analyses of mitochondrial DNA, which is maternally inherited, and Y chromosomes, which are transmitted from fathers to sons—as well as recently sequenced autosomal DNA. Such studies suggest that all living humans inherited their mitochondrial DNA from a common ancestral woman who lived approximately 160 000–200 000 years ago. Mutations on the Y chromosomes can serve as markers for tracing the ancestry and relationships among males alive today. By comparing the Y chromosomes of males from various geographic regions, researchers were able to infer divergence from a common African ancestor.

These lines of evidence suggest that our species emerged from Africa in one or more waves, spreading first into Asia 50 000–60 000 years ago, and then to Europe, Southeast Asia, and Australia **(Figure 21.15)**. The date of the first arrival of humans in the New World is hotly debated.

The rapid expansion of *H. sapiens* may have been spurred by the evolution of human cognition as our species evolved in Africa. Although Neanderthals and other hominins were able to produce sophisticated tools, they showed little creativity and not much capability for symbolic thought, as far as we can tell. In contrast, researchers are beginning to find evidence of increasingly sophisticated thought as *H. sapiens* evolved. In 2002, researchers reported the discovery in South Africa of 77 000-year-old art, and by 36 000 years ago, *H. sapiens* were producing spectacular cave paintings.

▲ **Figure 21.15** The spread of modern *Homo sapiens* (dates given as years before present [BP])

As *H. sapiens* spread around the globe, populations adapted to the new environments they encountered. Consequently, some differences among people are attributable to their deep ancestry. We'll look at one such adaptation in Module 21.16.

 What types of evidence indicate that *Homo sapiens* originated in Africa?

● Fossils and analyses of mitochondrial DNA and chromosomal DNA

21.16 Who were the "hobbits"?

New findings continually update our understanding of human evolution. Perhaps the most surprising was the 2004 discovery of the nearly complete skeleton of a tiny hominin on Flores, one of the Indonesian islands. In size and brain capacity, the adult female was comparable to Lucy—about 1 m tall, with a chimp-sized brain—and quickly acquired the nickname "hobbit." Despite its diminutive size, its skull **(Figure 21.16)** displays some humanlike traits, and it apparently made and used stone tools. Most astonishingly, it lived as recently as 18 000 years ago.

The researchers who discovered the "hobbit" proposed that it was a previously unknown human species that evolved from a population of *Homo erectus* into a dwarf form on the island. They named it *Homo floresiensis*. Some scientists agreed with them, but others vehemently disputed their conclusions. One counterargument suggested that the hobbit was simply an *H. sapien* adult with a genetic disorder.

Since the initial discovery, researchers have unearthed the bones of an estimated 14 *H. floresiensis* individuals, but no additional skulls have been located. Numerous scientists have pored over the fossils, and the more this species is studied, the more mysterious it becomes. For example, on the one hand, the feet are very long in proportion to the legs, the toes are long and curved, and the foot lacks an arch—all apelike characteristics. On the other hand, the big toe aligns with the others, unlike the ape toe, which diverges at an angle. But if *H. floresiensis*

▲ **Figure 21.16** The skull of an adult "hobbit" (*Homo floresiensis*)

is determined to be a very primitive *Homo*, more like *H. habilis* than *H. erectus*, then new questions are raised. It must have left Africa even earlier than *H. erectus* and managed to extend its range thousands of kilometres without the long, striding legs and sophisticated tools of that species. If that was the case, then undiscovered hominin fossils much older than *H. erectus* must exist somewhere between Africa and Indonesia.

As researchers target new sites to explore and excavation continues in the cave where the hobbits were found, the mystery continues. The final answers await the discovery of more fossils.

 What characteristics prompted the discoverers of the "hobbit" to classify it in the genus *Homo*?

● Humanlike skull characteristics and the apparent use of stone tools

21.17 Our knowledge of animal diversity is far from complete

When an Englishman sent home the skin of a platypus more than 200 years ago, it was one of thousands of previously unknown species of organisms pouring into Europe from naturalists exploring Africa, Asia, and North and South America, as well as Australia. You might think that after centuries of scientific exploration, only tiny organisms such as microbes and insects remain to be found. But the days of exploring new ecosystems and discovering new species are not over. In fact, better access to remote areas, coupled with new mapping technologies, has renewed the pace of discovery. According to a report issued in 2009, 18 516 species were described for the first time in 2007. As you might expect from Module 20.12, over half of them were insects, but the list also includes more than 1200 vertebrates.

The Mekong region of Southeast Asia, an area of diverse landscapes surrounding the Mekong River as it flows from southern China to the China Sea, is one of many treasure troves of previously unknown species that are currently being explored. In 2011, 126 new species were described in this region. In fact, more than 1000 species have been found there over the past 15 years, including the leopard gecko shown in **Figure 21.17A**, which is one of more than 400 new species of vertebrates that scientists have turned up there. To the southeast, remote mountains on the island of New Guinea are also yielding hundreds of discoveries, including a frog with a droopy nose **(Figure 21.17B)** and the tiny wallaby shown

in **Figure 21.17C**. The first new species of monkey found in more than a century was discovered in the eastern Himalayas. Discoveries of new primate species are extremely rare, but four others have also been made recently: two new lemur species in Madagascar and two new monkeys, an Old World species in Tanzania and a New World species in Bolivia.

Previously undescribed species are being reported almost daily from every continent and a wide variety of habitats. And researchers are just beginning to explore the spectacular diversity of the oceans. The Census of Marine Life, a decade-long collaboration among scientists from 80 nations, has reported the discovery of more than 6000 new species. Thousands more are expected to be found as new technology enables scientists to investigate deep-sea habitats. Recent expeditions have also gleaned hundreds of new species from the seas surrounding Antarctica, and the collapse of Antarctic ice shelves has allowed researchers their first glimpse of life on a seafloor that had previously been hidden from view. Even places that are regularly visited by people offer surprises. For example, more than 100 new marine species were identified recently on a coral reef near Australia.

When a new species is described, taxonomists learn as much as possible about its physical and genetic characteristics and assign it to the appropriate groups in the Linnaean system. As a result, most new species automatically acquire a series of names from domain through genus. But every species also has

► **Figure 21.17A** Leopard gecko, a newly discovered lizard from northern Vietnam

► **Figure 21.17B** Pinocchio frog, recently discovered in New Guinea

▲ **Figure 21.17C** Dwarf wallaby, a rabbit-sized member of the kangaroo family a unique identifier, and the honour of choosing it belongs to the discoverer. Species are often named for their habitat or a notable feature.

In a new twist, naming rights for recently discovered species have been auctioned off to raise money for conservation organizations, which undertake many of the projects that survey biological diversity. The right to name a new species of monkey cost the winning bidder $650 000, and donors spent more than $2 million for the honour of naming 10 new species of fish. Naming rights are available for smaller budgets, too—the top bid to name a new species of shrimp was $2900. The proceeds from these auctions go toward funding

new expeditions and preserving the habitats of the newly discovered species. In many cases, such discoveries are made as roads and settlements reach farther into new territory. Consequently, many species are endangered soon after they are discovered. We'll consider the various threats to biological diversity in Chapter 41.

 What factors are responsible for the recent increase in the number of new species found?

Technology; encroachment of human activities into wilderness areas

REVIEW

MasteringBiology® **For Practice Quizzes, BioFlix, MP3 Tutors, and Activities, go to masteringbiology.com.**

Reviewing the Concepts

Vertebrate Evolution and Diversity (21.1–21.9)

21.1 Derived characters define the major clades of chordates. Tunicates and lancelets have no skull or vertebral column.

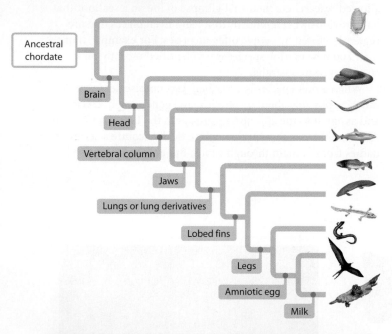

Ancestral chordate

- Brain
- Head
- Vertebral column
- Jaws
- Lungs or lung derivatives
- Lobed fins
- Legs
- Amniotic egg
- Milk

21.2 Hagfishes and lampreys lack hinged jaws. Hagfish have a skull but no spine. A notochord and rudimentary vertebrae support lampreys.

21.3 Jawed vertebrates with gills and paired fins include sharks, ray-finned fishes, and lobe-finned fishes. Sharks and rays have a skeleton made of cartilage. Ray-fins and lobe-fins have lungs or lung derivatives.

21.4 New fossil discoveries are filling in the gaps of tetrapod evolution. Scientists believe the first tetrapods were fishlike animals that could lift their heads to breathe air.

21.5 Amphibians are tetrapods—vertebrates with two pairs of limbs. The first terrestrial vertebrates had strong ties to the water.

21.6 Reptiles are amniotes—tetrapods with a terrestrially adapted egg. The extraembryonic amnion allowed eggs to be laid on land, cutting the reproductive tie to water.

21.7 Do chameleons change colour for camouflage? The natural colour of chameleons already blends in with their surroundings. Chameleons change colour to communicate, not to camouflage themselves.

21.8 Birds are feathered reptiles with adaptations for flight. The birds, having evolved from a dinosaur lineage, belong to the reptilian clade.

21.9 Mammals are amniotes that have hair and produce milk. The earliest mammals laid eggs like their reptilian ancestors and gestation evolved after mammals diverged.

Primate Diversity (21.10–21.11)

21.10 The human story begins with our primate heritage. Primates had evolved as small arboreal mammals by 65 mya. Primate characters include limber joints, grasping hands and feet with flexible digits, a short snout, and forward-pointing eyes that enhance depth perception. The three groups of living primates are the lorises, pottos, and lemurs; the tarsiers; and the anthropoids (monkeys and apes).

21.11 Humans and four other groups of apes are classified as anthropoids. Apes, which have larger brains than other primates and lack tails, include gibbons, orangutans, gorillas, chimpanzees, and humans. Humans share 99% of our genome with chimpanzees, our closest living relatives.

Hominin Evolution (21.12–21.17)

21.12 The hominin branch of the primate tree includes species that coexisted. Paleoanthropologists have found about 20 species of extinct hominins, species that are more closely related to humans than to chimpanzees. Some of these species lived at the same time.

21.13 Australopiths were bipedal and had small brains. The angle at which the spinal cord exits the skull allowed scientists to predict the bipedal nature of these early hominins.

21.14 Larger brains mark the evolution of *Homo*. The genus *Homo* includes hominins with larger brains and evidence of tool use. *H. ergaster* had a larger brain than *H. habilis*. *H. erectus*, with a larger brain than *H. ergaster*, was the first hominin to spread out of Africa. *H. neanderthalensis* lived in Europe as recently as 30 000 years ago.

21.15 From origins in Africa, *Homo sapiens* spread around the world. Evidence from fossils and DNA studies has enabled scientists to trace early human history.

21.16 Who were the "hobbits"? Fossils of small hominins named *Homo floresiensis* that were found in Indonesia are controversial. Scientists are trying to determine their relationship to other hominins.

21.17 Our knowledge of animal diversity is far from complete. Thousands of new species are discovered each year.

Connecting the Concepts

1. In the primate phylogenetic tree below, fill in groups (a)–(e). Which of the groups are anthropoids? Which of the groups are apes?

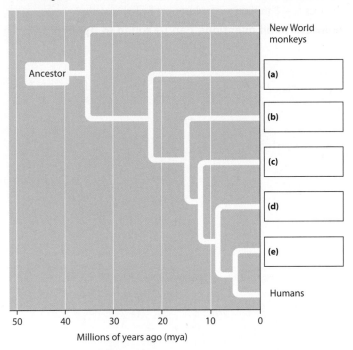

2. In the chordate phylogenetic tree below, fill in the key derived character that defines each clade.

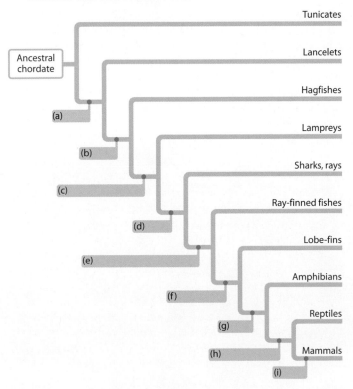

Testing Your Knowledge

Multiple Choice

3. A lamprey, a shark, a lizard, and a rabbit share all the following characteristics except
   a. pharyngeal slits in the embryo or adult.
   b. vertebrae.
   c. hinged jaws.
   d. a dorsal, hollow nerve cord.
   e. a post-anal tail.

4. Why were the *Tiktaalik* fossils an exciting discovery for scientists studying tetrapod evolution?
   a. They are the earliest froglike animal discovered to date.
   b. They show that tetrapods successfully colonized land much earlier than previously thought.
   c. They have a roughly equal combination of fishlike and tetrapod-like characteristics.
   d. They demonstrate conclusively that limbs evolved as lobe-fins dragged themselves from pond to pond during droughts.
   e. They reveal new information about the breeding behaviour of early tetrapods.

5. Fossils suggest that the first major trait distinguishing hominins from other primates was
   a. a larger brain.
   b. erect posture.
   c. forward-facing eyes with depth perception.
   d. grasping hands.
   e. toolmaking.

6. Which of the following correctly lists possible ancestors of humans from the oldest to the most recent?
   a. *Homo erectus, Australopithecus, Homo habilis*
   b. *Australopithecus, Homo habilis, Homo erectus*
   c. *Australopithecus, Homo erectus, Homo habilis*
   d. *Homo ergaster, Homo erectus, Homo neanderthalensis*
   e. *Homo habilis, Homo erectus, Australopithecus*

7. Which of these is not a member of the anthropoids?
   a. chimpanzee
   b. ape
   c. tarsier
   d. human
   e. New World monkey

8. Studies of DNA support which of the following?
   a. Members of the group called australopiths were the first to migrate from Africa.
   b. Neanderthals are more closely related to humans in Europe than to humans in Africa.
   c. *Homo sapiens* originated in Africa.
   d. *Sahelanthropus* was the earliest hominin.
   e. Chimpanzees are more similar to gorillas and orangutans than to humans.

9. The earliest members of the genus *Homo*
   a. had a larger brain compared to other hominins.
   b. probably hunted dinosaurs.
   c. lived in Europe.
   d. lived about 4 mya.
   e. were the first hominins to be bipedal.

Describing, Comparing, and Explaining

10. Compare the adaptations of amphibians and reptiles for terrestrial life.

11. Birds and mammals are both endothermic, and both have four-chambered hearts. Most reptiles are ectothermic and have three-chambered hearts. Why don't biologists group birds with mammals? Why do most biologists now consider birds to be reptiles?

12. What adaptations inherited from our primate ancestors enable humans to make and use tools?

Applying the Concepts

13. A good scientific hypothesis is based on existing evidence and leads to testable predictions. What hypothesis did the paleontologists who discovered *Tiktaalik* test? What evidence did they use to predict where they would find fossils of transitional forms?

14. Explain some of the reasons why humans have been able to expand in number and distribution to a greater extent than most other animals.

15. Anthropologists are interested in locating areas in Africa where fossils 4–8 million years old might be found. Why?

Answers to all questions can be found in Appendix E.

Plants: Structure and Function

CHAPTER 22

Plant Structure, Growth, and Reproduction

BIG IDEAS

Plant Structure and Function

(22.1–22.6)

Plant bodies contain specialized cells grouped into tissues, organs, and organ systems.

Plant Growth

(22.7–22.9)

All plants increase their length via primary growth, and woody plants thicken via secondary growth.

Reproduction of Flowering Plants

(22.10–22.15)

Sexual reproduction in angiosperms involves pollination, development of fruit and seeds, seed dispersal, germination, and growth.

Look Up, Way Up

Cathedral Grove on Vancouver Island is home to the tallest trees in Canada. The Grove is protected by MacMillan Provincial Park and represents a small remnant of an ancient Douglas fir ecosystem. Ancient western redcedars (*Thuja plicata*) and Douglas firs (*Pseudotsuga menziesii*) grow to towering heights. Some trees in the forest reach a staggering 75 m and can be 6 m in diameter. Even at this height, these trees are not the tallest around. A coast redwood (*Sequoia sempervirens*) named Hyperion is the tallest tree. It lives in an undisclosed location and measures at over 115 m. Nonetheless, the trees in the Cathedral Grove are an impressive testimonial of plant growth, and this area was recently nominated to be one of the Seven Wonders of Canada.

Revered by First Nations peoples, the western redcedars have been sacred for thousands of years. Redcedars were vital to the peoples living on the island. The Kakawaka'wakw people referred to the redcedar as the "tree of life." Legend has it that a generous man gave the people anything they wanted. When he died, a giant redcedar grew to provide for the Aboriginal peoples. Its stringy bark was used for weaving mats, baskets, and clothes. The wood is naturally waterproof and resistant to insects and rotting, which makes for excellent building materials. Massive logs were used to build sea-going dugout canoes. Lumber was used to build houses. Religious artifacts, including spiritual masks, were carved from the venerated wood.

The Cathedral Grove is an old-growth forest, which has been growing for centuries without significant disturbance and contains trees varying in age. The oldest trees in the forest are well over 800 years old, but most are younger than 350 because a forest fire ravaged the area about 350 years ago. A few of the largest trees were protected by their thick bark and survived to repopulate the forest. Still, a 350-year-old redcedar or Douglas fir reaches an impressive height of 45–55 m with a diameter of nearly 4 m.

Most of the giant redcedars and Douglas firs outside of protected areas have been logged for their wood. A large tree can contain several hundred cubic metres of wood. Logging of redcedars has long been protested on Vancouver Island and elsewhere. Unfortunately, other human activities also threaten trees in MacMillan Provincial Park. A short walk through the park will bring you to a small sign next to a massive stump. The sign explains how vandals set a 700-year-old tree ablaze in 1972. The tree was cut down to prevent the fire from spreading. The depression in which the tree now lies, called "Giant's Grave," was formed by the force of its impact. The stump serves as a reminder of how we, as individuals, can have significant impacts on the environment.

During a windstorm on New Year's Day in 1997, hundreds of trees within the park were uprooted by the hurricane-force winds. Many of the fallen trees still lie across paths today. These trees serve as nurse logs, providing nutrients for plants in the undergrowth. Openings in the canopy above allow light to reach the forest floor, perhaps for the first time in hundreds of years. With the influx of nutrients and increased light availability, perhaps the young redcedars or firs today may grow to tower above in a few hundred years.

This chapter begins our exploration of plant form and function. In it, we will look at the structure, growth, and reproduction of plants. Although we focus on angiosperms—the flowering plants—the massive western redcedars grow in a similar fashion but to a much larger scale. By studying angiosperm structure in relation to growth and reproduction, we can gain insight into the relationships between structure and function in all plants.

Plant Structure and Function

22.1 People have manipulated plants since prehistoric times

To tell the story of human society, you have to talk about plants. From the dawn of civilization to the frontiers of genetic engineering, human progress has always depended on expanding our use of plants for food, fuel, clothing, and countless other trappings of modern life.

To illustrate, let's consider humankind's relationship with a single crop: wheat. Today, wheat accounts for about 20% of all calories consumed worldwide. In Canada, it is one of the most valuable cash crops, with Canadian farmers exporting an average of 17 million tonnes each year. And we do more than just eat wheat. For example, researchers developed a new material made from wheat that can be used to make biodegradable packaging materials, and a protein that protects the wheat plant from cold can be added to ice cream to help prevent freezer burn.

The roots of today's prosperous relationship between people and wheat can be traced back to the earliest human settlements. Throughout much of prehistory, humans were nomadic hunter-gatherers, moving and foraging with the changing seasons. People gathered and ate seeds from wild grasses and cereals, but didn't plant them. About 10 000 years ago, a major shift occurred as people in several parts of the world began to domesticate wild plants (see Module 15.7). This domestication allowed for the production of surplus food and the formation of year-round farming villages. Farming, in turn, led to the establishment of cities and the emergence of modern civilizations.

When and where did this crucial shift take place? The origin of wheat cultivation has been traced to a region of the Middle East dubbed the Fertile Crescent, near the upper reaches of the Tigris and Euphrates Rivers (**Figure 22.1**). Archaeological excavations of sites older than 10 000 years have found remnants of wild wheat. But in younger sites, cultivated wheat also appears, displacing wild varieties in the archaeological record over the course of more than a millennium.

▲ **Figure 22.1** The Fertile Crescent region (shaded green), the original site of the cultivation of wheat

Once begun, cultivation rapidly replaced gathering in the Middle East. These habits quickly spread. By 7000 years ago, bread wheat was cultivated in Egypt, India, China, and northern Europe. Farming became the dominant way of life across Europe by 6000 years ago. For most of the subsequent millennia, little changed in the production of wheat. Individual farmers tinkered to produce slightly superior varieties, but these were small, incremental improvements.

A major leap forward occurred in the latter half of the 20th century. Faced with the rapidly expanding human population and a dwindling availability of farmland, an international effort was undertaken to improve wheat and other staple crops. The methods were straightforward: controlled cross-pollinations between varieties with desirable traits, selection of the few plants possessing the best combinations of characteristics, cross-pollination of these plants, and so on. Through such repeated selective breeding experiments, today's wheat varieties were created. The improved traits of modern wheat include a short stature with double the grain per 0.4 hectare (h) of full-sized varieties; the ability to grow in a wide variety of climates and soil conditions (such as dry or acidic soils); short generation times; and resistance to more than 30 pests and pathogens. As a result of the so-called green revolution, wheat yield (tonnes of grain per 0.4 h planted) more than doubled from 1940 to 1980, while the cost of wheat production was cut in half.

In Western Canada, a special variety of wheat called winter wheat has been the focus of research by scientists such as Dr. Brian Fowler at the University of Saskatchewan. Winter wheat is planted in autumn and the seeds germinate before the ground freezes. The cold-hardy plants then lay dormant under the cover of snow until spring, when growing commences. By July, a high-yield crop is ready for harvest. Winter wheat is also more environmentally sound than traditional summer crops. Fields do not have to be tilled prior to planting winter wheat. The stubble of the previous crop helps to retain the snow cover, preventing winterkill (caused by exposure) and increasing water availability in the spring. Not tilling also reduces soil erosion, a major concern in agricultural centres in Canada and throughout the world. Folwer and the governments of the Canadian Prairie provinces encourage farmers to plant winter wheat as a sustainable, environmentally friendly crop option.

Wheat and other crops continue to be the target of considerable research today, primarily through the methods of genetic engineering and genomics (see Module 12.8). One goal is to enhance the nutritional value of food crops. In the case of wheat, some wild varieties are much more nutritious than domesticated varieties, with 10% to 15% higher concentrations of protein, iron, and zinc. In 2006, researchers identified and cloned a gene responsible for this difference. (Domestic wheat contains the gene, but at least one copy of it is inactive.) The hope is to transfer the active version of this gene into domesticated varieties, increasing their nutritional content.

Another group of researchers developed genetically modified (GM) wheat with triple the usual amount of the polysaccharide amylose, a component of dietary fibre. They achieved this by turning off a gene that normally breaks down amylose in wheat. High-fibre strains may be a health boon because eating more fibre has been linked to reduced colorectal cancer, heart disease, diabetes, and obesity. Other genetic engineers are attempting to identify genes that confer resistance to a new strain of wheat rust, a virulent fungal pathogen that threatens the world's wheat crops.

As we continue to refine modern DNA technology methods, we will continue to deepen our understanding of wheat and other crops. Keeping in mind this staple crop as one example, we will explore the structure of angiosperms in the next five modules.

? When and where did humans first cultivate wheat?

● About 10 000 years ago in the Middle East

22.2 The two major groups of angiosperms are the monocots and the eudicots

Angiosperms have dominated the land for more than 100 million years, and there are about 250 000 known species of flowering plants living today. Most of our foods come from a few hundred domesticated species of flowering plants. Among these foods are roots, such as beets and carrots; the fruits of trees and vines, such as apples, nuts, berries, and squashes; the fruits and seeds of legumes, such as peas and beans; and grains, the fruits of grasses such as wheat, rice, and corn (maize).

On the basis of several structural features, plant biologists (also called botanists) traditionally placed most angiosperms into two groups, called monocots and dicots. The names *monocot* and *dicot* refer to the first leaves on the plant embryo. These embryonic leaves are called seed leaves, or **cotyledons**. A **monocot** embryo has one seed leaf; a **dicot** embryo has two seed leaves. The great majority of dicots, called the **eudicots** ("true" dicots), are evolutionarily related, having diverged from a common ancestor about 125 mya; a few smaller groups of dicots have evolved independently. In this chapter, we will focus on monocots and eudicots **(Figure 22.2)**.

Monocots are a large group of related plants that include the orchids, bamboos, palms, and lilies, as well as the grains and other grasses. You can see the single cotyledon inside the seed on the top left in Figure 22.2. The leaves, stems, flowers, and roots of monocots are also distinctive. Most monocots have leaves with parallel veins. Monocot stems have vascular tissues (internal tissues that transport water and nutrients) organized into bundles that are arranged in a scattered pattern. The flowers of most monocots have their petals and other parts in multiples of three. Monocot roots form a shallow fibrous system—a mat of threads—that spreads out below the soil surface. With most of their roots in the top few centimetres of soil, monocots, especially grasses, make excellent ground cover that reduces erosion. Fibrous root systems are well adapted to shallow soils where rainfall is light.

Most flowering shrubs and trees are eudicots, such as the majority of our ornamental plants and many of our food crops, including nearly all of our fruits and vegetables. You can see the two cotyledons of a typical eudicot in the seed on the lower left in Figure 22.2. Eudicot leaves have a multibranched

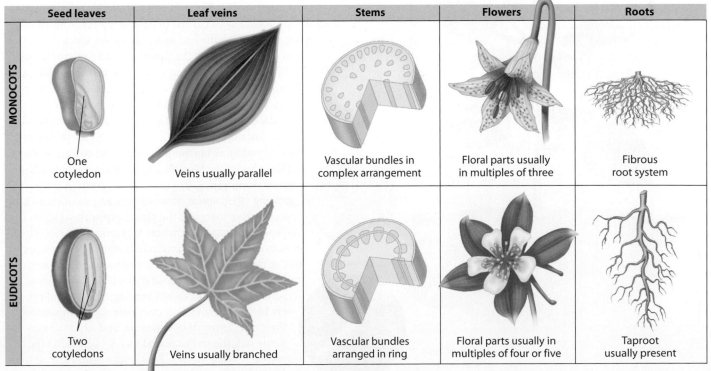

	Seed leaves	Leaf veins	Stems	Flowers	Roots
MONOCOTS	One cotyledon	Veins usually parallel	Vascular bundles in complex arrangement	Floral parts usually in multiples of three	Fibrous root system
EUDICOTS	Two cotyledons	Veins usually branched	Vascular bundles arranged in ring	Floral parts usually in multiples of four or five	Taproot usually present

▲ **Figure 22.2** A comparison of monocots and eudicots

network of veins, and eudicot stems have vascular bundles arranged in a ring. Eudicot flowers usually have petals and other parts in multiples of four or five. The large, vertical root of a eudicot, which is known as a taproot, goes deep into the soil, as you know if you've ever tried to pull up a dandelion. Taproots are well adapted to soils with deep groundwater.

As we saw in the preceding unit on animals, a close look at a structure often reveals its function. Conversely, function provides insight into the "logic" of a structure. In the modules that follow, we'll take a detailed look at the correlation between plant structure and function.

 The terms *monocot* and *eudicot* refer to the number of _____ on the developing embryo in a seed.

cotyledons (seed leaves)

22.3 A typical plant body contains three basic organs: roots, stems, and leaves

Plants, like most animals, have organs composed of different tissues, which in turn are composed of one or more cell types. An **organ** consists of several types of tissues that together carry out particular functions. In this and the next module, we'll focus on plant organs. We will then work our way down the structural hierarchy and examine plant tissues (in Module 22.5) and cells (in Module 22.6).

The basic structure of plants reflects their evolutionary history as land-dwelling organisms. Most plants must draw resources from two very different environments: They must absorb water and minerals from the soil, while simultaneously obtaining CO_2 and light from above ground. The subterranean roots and aerial shoots (stems and leaves) of a typical land plant, such as the generalized flowering plant shown in **Figure 22.3**, perform these vital functions.

A plant's **root system** anchors it in the soil, absorbs and transports minerals and water, and stores food. Near the root tips, a vast number of tiny tubular projections called **root hairs** enormously increase the root surface area for absorption of minerals and water. As shown on the far right of the figure, each root hair is an extension of an epidermal cell (a cell in the outer layer of the root). It is difficult to move an established plant without injuring it because transplantation often damages the plant's delicate root hairs.

The **shoot system** of a plant is made up of stems, leaves, and adaptations for reproduction, which in angiosperms are the flowers. (We'll return to flowers in Module 22.10.) The **stems** are the parts of the plant that are generally above the ground and that support and separate the leaves (thereby promoting photosynthesis) and flowers (responsible for reproduction). In the case of a tree, the stems are the trunk and all the branches, including the smallest twigs. Leaves attach to points on the stem called **nodes**, and the section of a stem between two nodes is an **internode**. The **leaves** are the main photosynthetic organs in most plants, although green stems also perform photosynthesis. Most leaves consist of a flattened blade and a stalk, or petiole, which joins the leaf to a node of the stem.

The two types of buds in the figure are undeveloped shoots. When a plant stem is growing in length, the **terminal bud** (also called the apical bud), at the tip (apex) of the stem has developing leaves and a compact series of nodes and internodes. The **axillary buds**, one in each of the angles formed by a leaf and the stem, are usually dormant. In many plants, the terminal bud produces hormones that inhibit growth of the axillary buds (see Module 24.4), a phenomenon called **apical dominance**. By concentrating resources on growing taller, apical dominance is an evolutionary adaptation that increases the plant's exposure to light. This is especially important where vegetation is dense. However, branching is also important for increasing the exposure of the shoot system to the environment, and under certain conditions, the axillary buds begin growing. Some develop into shoots bearing flowers, and others become nonreproductive branches complete with their own terminal buds, leaves, and axillary buds. Removing the terminal bud usually stimulates the growth of axillary buds. This is why pruning fruit trees and "pinching back" houseplants makes them bushier.

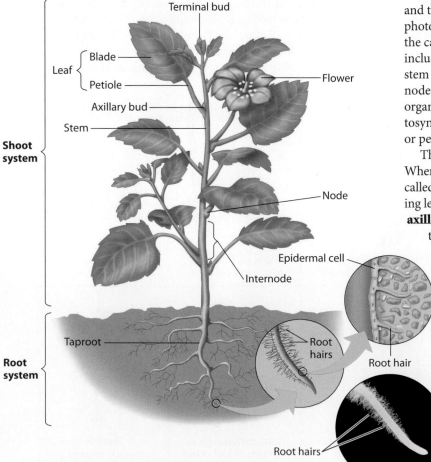

▲ **Figure 22.3** The body plan of a flowering plant (a eudicot)

The drawing in Figure 22.3 gives an overview of plant structure, but it by no means represents the enormous diversity of angiosperms. Next, let's look briefly at some variations on the basic themes of root and stem structure.

? Name the two organ systems and three basic organs found in typical plants.

● Root system and shoot system: roots, stems, leaves

22.4 Many plants have modified roots, stems, and leaves

▲ Figure 22.4A The modified root of a sugar beet plant

Over evolutionary history, the three basic plant organs—roots, stems, and leaves—have become adapted for a variety of functions. Carrots, turnips, sugar beets, and sweet potatoes, for instance, all have unusually large taproots that store food in the form of carbohydrates such as starch (**Figure 22.4A**). The plants consume the stored sugars during flowering and fruit production. For this reason, root crops are harvested before flowering.

Figure 22.4B shows three examples of modified stems. The strawberry plant has a horizontal stem called a stolon (or "runner") that grows along the ground. Stolons enable a plant to reproduce asexually, as plantlets form at nodes along their length. That is why strawberries, if left unchecked, can rapidly fill your garden. You've seen a different stem modification if you have ever dug up an iris plant or cooked with fresh ginger; the large, brownish, rootlike structures are actually **rhizomes**, horizontal stems that grow near the soil surface. Rhizomes store food and, having buds, can also form new plants. About every three years, gardeners can dig up iris rhizomes, split them, and replant to get multiple genetically identical plants. A potato plant has rhizomes that end in

▲ Figure 22.4C Modified leaves: the tendrils of a pea plant (left) and cactus spines (right)

enlarged structures specialized for storage called **tubers** (the potatoes we eat). Potato "eyes" are axillary buds on the tubers that can grow when planted, allowing potatoes to be easily propagated. Plant bulbs are underground shoots containing swollen leaves that store food. As you peel an onion, you are removing layers of leaves attached to a short stem.

Plant leaves, too, are highly varied. Grasses and many other monocots, for instance, have long leaves without petioles. Some eudicots, such as celery, have enormous petioles—the stalks we eat—which contain a lot of water and stored food. The left photograph in **Figure 22.4C** shows

Strawberry plant

Stolon (runner)

▲ Figure 22.4B Three kinds of modified stems: stolons, rhizomes, and tubers

Rhizome

Iris plant

Taproot

Rhizome

Tuber

Potato plant

a modified leaf called a **tendril**, with its tips coiled around a support structure. Tendrils help plants climb. (Some tendrils, as in grapevines, are modified stems.) The spines of the barrel cactus (right photo) are modified leaves that protect the plant from being eaten by animals. The main part of the cactus is the stem, which is adapted for photosynthesis and water storage.

So far, we have examined plants as we see them with the unaided eye. Next, we move further down the structural hierarchy to explore plant tissues.

 In what sense do cactus spines deviate from the typical function of plant leaves?

● Cactus spines are protective but are not the main sites of photosynthesis (as leaves are on most plants).

22.5 Three tissue systems make up the plant body

Like the organs of most animals, the organs of plants contain tissues with characteristic functions. A **tissue** is a group of cells that together perform a specialized function. For example, **xylem** tissue contains water-conducting cells that convey water and dissolved minerals upward from the roots, while **phloem** tissue contains cells that transport sugars and other organic nutrients from leaves or storage tissues to other parts of the plant.

Each plant organ—root, stem, or leaf—has three types of tissues: dermal, vascular, and ground tissues. Each of these three categories forms a **tissue system**, a functional unit connecting all of the plant's organs. Each tissue system is continuous throughout the entire plant body, but the systems are arranged differently in leaves, stems, and roots **(Figure 22.5)**. In this module, we examine the tissue systems of young roots and shoots. Later we will see that the tissue systems are somewhat different in older roots and stems.

The **dermal tissue system** (brown in the figure) is the plant's outer protective covering. Like our own skin, it forms the first line of defence against physical damage and infectious organisms. In many plants, the dermal tissue system consists of a single layer of tightly packed cells called the **epidermis**. The epidermis of leaves and most stems has a waxy coating called the **cuticle**, which helps to prevent water loss. The second tissue system is the **vascular tissue system** (purple). It is made up of xylem and phloem tissues and provides support and long-distance transport between the root and shoot systems. Tissues that are neither dermal nor vascular make up the **ground tissue system** (yellow). It accounts for most of the bulk of a young plant, filling the spaces between the epidermis and vascular tissue system. Ground tissue internal to the vascular tissue is called **pith**, and ground tissue external to the vascular tissue is called **cortex**. The ground tissue system has diverse functions, including photosynthesis, storage, and support.

The close-up views on the right side of Figure 22.5 show how these three tissue systems are organized in typical plant roots, stems, and leaves. The close-up view at the bottom left shows in cross-section the three tissue systems in a young eudicot root. Water and minerals that are absorbed from the soil must enter through the epidermis. In the centre of the root, the vascular tissue system forms a **vascular cylinder**, with the cross-sections of xylem cells radiating from the centre like spokes of a wheel and phloem cells filling in the wedges between the spokes. The ground tissue system of the root, the region between the vascular cylinder and epidermis, consists entirely of cortex. The cortex cells store food as starch and take up minerals that have entered the root through the epidermis.

The innermost layer of the cortex is the **endodermis**, a cylinder one cell thick. The endodermis is a selective barrier, determining which substances pass between the rest of the cortex and the vascular tissue (as you'll see in Module 23.2).

The bottom right close-up view of Figure 22.5 shows a cross-section of a young monocot root. It has several similarities to the eudicot root: an outer layer of epidermis (dermal tissue) surrounding a large cortex (ground tissue), with a vascular cylinder (vascular tissue) at the centre. But in a monocot root, the vascular tissue consists of a central core of cells surrounded by a ring of xylem and a ring of phloem.

As the centre close-ups of Figure 22.5 indicates, the young stem of a eudicot looks quite different from that of a monocot. Both stems have their vascular tissue system arranged in numerous **vascular bundles**. However, in monocot stems the bundles are scattered, whereas in eudicots they are arranged in a ring. This ring separates the ground tissue into cortex and pith regions. The cortex fills the space between the vascular ring and the epidermis. The pith fills the centre of the stem and is often important in food storage. In a monocot stem, the ground tissue is not separated into these regions because the vascular bundles don't form a ring.

The top close-up of Figure 22.5 illustrates the arrangement of the three tissue systems in a typical eudicot leaf. The epidermis is interrupted by tiny pores called **stomata** (singular, *stoma*), which allow exchange of CO_2 and O_2 between the surrounding air and the photosynthetic cells inside the leaf. Also, most of the water vapour lost by a plant passes through stomata. Each stoma is flanked by two **guard cells**, which regulate the opening and closing of the stoma.

The ground tissue system of a leaf, called the **mesophyll**, is sandwiched between the upper and lower epidermis. Mesophyll consists mainly of cells specialized for photosynthesis. The green structures in the diagram are their chloroplasts. In this eudicot leaf, notice that cells in the lower area of mesophyll are loosely arranged, with a labyrinth of air spaces through which CO_2 and O_2 circulate. The air spaces are particularly large in the vicinity of stomata, where gas exchange with the outside air occurs. In many monocot leaves and in some eudicot leaves, the mesophyll is not arranged in distinct upper and lower areas.

In both monocots and eudicots, the leaf's vascular tissue system is made up of a network of veins. As you can see in Figure 22.5, each **vein** is a vascular bundle composed of xylem and phloem tissues surrounded by a protective sheath of cells. The veins' xylem and phloem, continuous with the vascular bundles of the stem, are in close contact with the leaf's

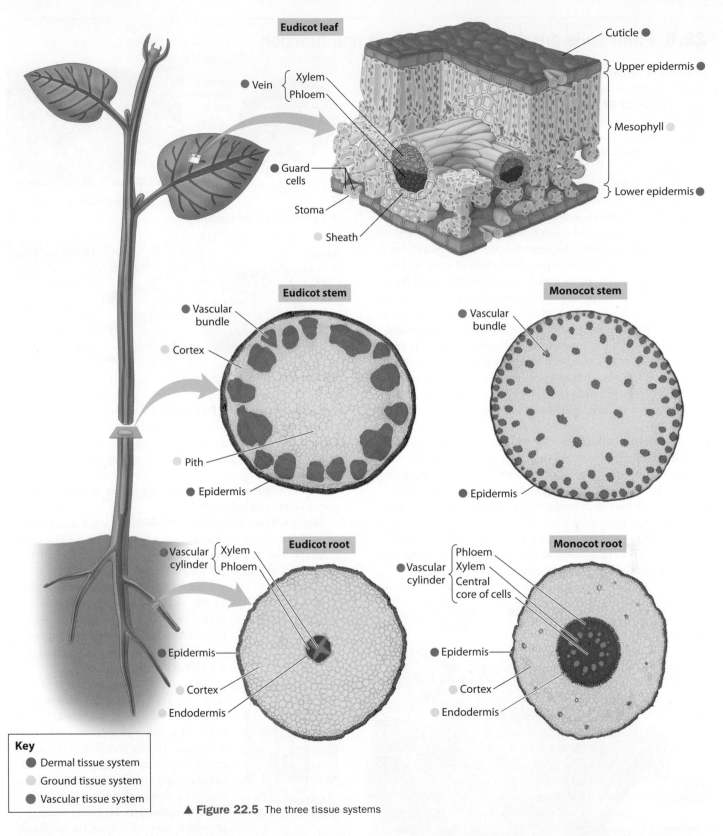

Eudicot leaf

Cuticle ●

Upper epidermis ●

Mesophyll ○

Lower epidermis ●

Vein ● { Xylem / Phloem }

Guard cells ●

Stoma

Sheath ○

Eudicot stem

Vascular bundle ●

Cortex ○

Pith ○

Epidermis ●

Monocot stem

Vascular bundle ●

Epidermis ●

Eudicot root

Vascular cylinder ● { Xylem / Phloem }

Epidermis ●

Cortex ○

Endodermis ○

Monocot root

Vascular cylinder ● { Phloem / Xylem / Central core of cells }

Epidermis ●

Cortex ○

Endodermis ○

Key
● Dermal tissue system
○ Ground tissue system
● Vascular tissue system

▲ **Figure 22.5** The three tissue systems

photosynthetic tissues. This ensures that those tissues are supplied with water and mineral nutrients from the soil and that sugars made in the leaves are transported throughout the plant. The vascular structure also functions as a skeleton that reinforces the shape of the leaf.

In the last three modules, we have examined plant structure at the level of organs and tissues. In the next module, we will complete our descent into the structural hierarchy of plants by taking a look at plant cells.

? **For each of the following structures in your body, name the most analogous plant tissue system: circulatory system, skin, and adipose tissue (body fat).**

● Vascular tissue system, dermal tissue system, ground tissue system

22.6 Plant cells are diverse in structure and function

In addition to features shared with other eukaryotic cells (see Module 4.4), most plant cells have three unique structures **(Figure 22.6A)**: chloroplasts, the sites of photosynthesis; a central vacuole containing fluid that helps to maintain cell turgor (firmness); and a protective cell wall made from the structural carbohydrate cellulose surrounding the plasma membrane.

The enlargement on the right in Figure 22.6A highlights the adjoining cell walls of two cells. Many plant cells, especially those that provide structural support, have a two-part cell wall; a primary cell wall is laid down first, and then a more rigid secondary cell wall forms between the plasma membrane and the primary wall. The primary walls of adjacent cells in plant tissues are held together by a sticky layer called the middle lamella. Pits, where the cell wall is relatively thin, allow migration of water between adjacent cells. Plasmodesmata are open channels in adjacent cell walls through which cytoplasm and various molecules can flow from cell to cell (see Module 4.21).

The structure of a plant cell and the nature of its wall often correlate with the cell's main functions. As you consider the five major types of plant cells shown in Figures 22.6B–22.6F, notice the structural adaptations that make their specific functions possible.

Parenchyma cells (Figure 22.6B) are the most abundant type of cell in most plants. They usually have only primary cell walls, which are thin and flexible. Parenchyma cells perform most metabolic functions of a plant, such as photosynthesis, aerobic respiration, and food storage. Most parenchyma cells can divide and differentiate into other types of plant cells under certain conditions, such as during the repair of an injury. In the laboratory, it is even possible to regenerate an entire plant from a single parenchyma cell (as you'll see in Module 22.15).

▲ **Figure 22.6B** Parenchyma cell

▲ **Figure 22.6C** Collenchyma cell

Collenchyma cells (Figure 22.6C) resemble parenchyma cells in that they lack secondary walls, but they have unevenly thickened primary walls. These cells provide flexible support in actively growing parts of the plant; young stems and petioles often have collenchyma cells just below their surface (the "string" of a celery stalk, for example). These living cells elongate as stems and leaves grow.

Sclerenchyma cells (Figure 22.6D) have thick secondary cell walls usually strengthened with lignin, the main chemical component of wood (see Module 19.1). Mature sclerenchyma cells cannot elongate and thus are found only in regions of the plant that have stopped growing in length. When mature, most sclerenchyma cells are dead, their cell walls forming a rigid "skeleton" that supports the plant much as steel beams do in the interior of a building.

Figure 22.6D shows two types of sclerenchyma cells. One, called a **fibre**, is long and slender and is usually arranged in bundles. Some plant tissues with abundant fibre cells are commercially important; hemp fibres, for example, are used to make rope and clothing. **Sclereids**, which are shorter than fibre cells, have thick, irregular, and very hard secondary walls. Sclereids impart the hardness to nutshells and seed coats and the gritty texture to the soft tissue of a pear.

The xylem tissue of angiosperms includes two types of water-conducting cells: tracheids and vessel elements. Both have rigid, lignin-containing secondary cell walls. As **Figure 22.6E** shows,

▲ **Figure 22.6A** The structure of a plant cell

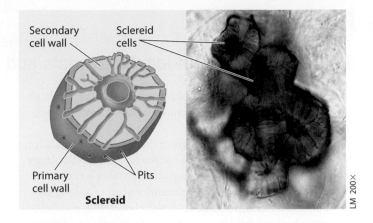

▲ **Figure 22.6D** Sclerenchyma cells: fibre (left) and sclereid (right)

the **tracheids** are long, thin cells with tapered ends. **Vessel elements** are wider, shorter, and less tapered. Chains of tracheids or vessel elements with overlapping ends form a system of tubes that conveys water from the roots to the stems and leaves as part of xylem tissue. The tubes are hollow because both tracheids and vessel elements are dead when mature, with only their cell walls remaining. Water passes through pits in the walls of tracheids and vessel elements and through openings in the end walls of vessel elements. With their thick, rigid walls, these cells also function in support.

Food-conducting cells, known as **sieve-tube elements** (or sieve-tube members), are also arranged end to end, forming tubes as part of phloem tissue **(Figure 22.6F)**. Unlike water-conducting cells, however, sieve-tube elements remain alive at maturity, though they lose most organelles, including the nucleus and ribosomes. This reduction in cell contents enables nutrients to pass more easily through the cell. The end walls between sieve-tube elements, called **sieve plates**, have pores that allow fluid to flow from cell to cell along the sieve tube. Alongside each sieve-tube element is at least one **companion cell**, which is connected to the sieve-tube element by numerous plasmodesmata. One companion cell may serve multiple sieve-tube elements by producing and transporting proteins to all of them.

Now that we have reached the lowest level in the structural hierarchy of plants—cells—let's review by moving back up. Cells of plants are grouped into tissues with characteristic functions. For example, xylem tissue contains water-conducting cells that convey water and dissolved minerals upward from the roots as well as sclerenchyma cells, which provide support, and parenchyma cells, which store various materials. Xylem and phloem tissues are organized into the vascular tissue system, which provides structural support and long-term transport throughout the plant body. The vascular, dermal, and ground tissue systems connect all the plant organs: roots, stems, and leaves. This review completes our survey of basic plant anatomy. Next, we examine how plants grow.

? Identify which of the following cell types can give rise to all others in the list: collenchyma, sclereid, parenchyma, vessel element, or companion cell.

Parenchyma ●

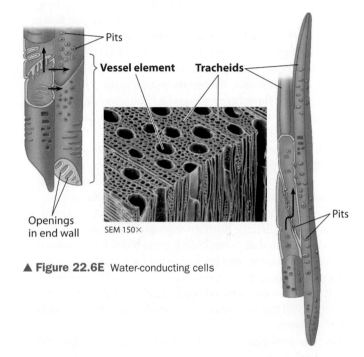

▲ **Figure 22.6E** Water-conducting cells

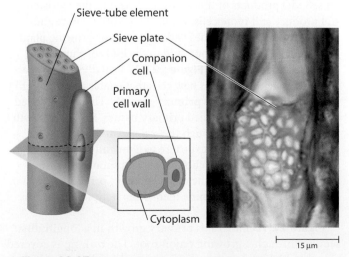

▲ **Figure 22.6F** Food-conducting cell (sieve-tube element)

Plant Growth

22.7 Primary growth lengthens roots and shoots

So far, we have looked at the structure of plant tissues and cells in mature organs. We will now consider how such organization arises through plant growth.

The growth of a plant differs from that of an animal in a fundamental way. Most animals are characterized by **determinate growth**; that is, they cease growing after reaching a certain size. Most species of plants, however, continue to grow as long as they live, a condition called **indeterminate growth**. Indeterminate growth allows a plant to continuously increase its exposure to sunlight, air, and soil.

Indeterminate growth does not mean that plants are immortal; they do, of course, die. Flowering plants are categorized as annuals, biennials, or perennials, based on the length of their life cycle, the time from germination through flowering and seed production to death. **Annuals** complete their life cycle in a single year or less. Our most important food crops (including grains and legumes) are annuals, as are a great number of wildflowers. **Biennials** complete their life cycle in two years, with flowering and seed production usually occurring during the second year. Beets, parsley, turnips, and carrots are biennials, but we usually harvest them in their first year and so miss seeing their flowers. **Perennials** are plants that live and reproduce for many years. They include trees, shrubs, and some grasses.

Some plants are among the oldest organisms alive. Some of the coast redwoods are estimated to be 2000 to 3000 years old, and another conifer, the bristlecone pine, can live thousands of years longer than that. Some buffalo grass of the North American prairies is believed to have been growing for 10 000 years from seeds that sprouted at the end of the last ice age. When a plant dies, it is not usually from old age, but from an infection or some environmental trauma, such as fire, severe drought, or consumption by animals.

Growth in all plants is made possible by tissues called meristems. A **meristem** consists of undifferentiated (unspecialized) cells that divide when conditions permit, generating additional cells. Some products of this division remain in the meristem and produce still more cells, while others differentiate and are incorporated into tissues and organs of the growing plant. Meristems at the tips of roots and in the buds of shoots are called **apical meristems (Figure 22.7A)**. Cell division in the apical meristems produces new cells that enable a plant to grow in length, a process called **primary growth**. Tissues produced by primary growth are called primary tissues. Primary growth enables roots to push through the soil and allows shoots to grow upward, increasing exposure to light and CO_2. Although apical meristems lengthen both roots and shoots, there are important differences in the mechanisms of primary growth in each system. We will examine them separately, starting at the bottom with roots.

Figure 22.7B illustrates primary growth in a longitudinal section through a growing onion root. The root tip is covered by a thimblelike **root cap** that protects the delicate, actively

dividing cells of the apical meristem. Growth in length occurs just behind the root tip, where three zones of cells at successive stages of primary growth are located. Moving away from the root tip, they are called the zone of cell division, the zone of elongation, and the zone of differentiation. The three zones of cells overlap, with no sharp boundaries between them.

The zone of cell division includes the root apical meristem and cells that derive from it. New root cells are produced in this region, including the cells of the root cap. In the zone of elongation, root cells elongate, sometimes to more than 10 times their original length. It is cell elongation that pushes the root tip farther into the soil. The cells lengthen, rather than expand equally in all directions, because of the circular arrangement of cellulose fibres in parallel bands in their cell walls. The enlargement diagrams at the left of the root indicate how this works. The cells elongate by taking up water, and as they do, the cellulose fibres (shown in red) separate, somewhat like an expanding accordion. The cells cannot expand greatly in width because the cellulose fibres do not stretch much.

The three tissue systems of a mature plant (dermal, ground, and vascular) complete their development in the zone of differentiation. Cells of the vascular cylinder differentiate into

▲ **Figure 22.7A** Locations of apical meristems, which are responsible for primary growth

Vascular cylinder · Cortex

Root hair · · Epidermis

Zone of differentiation

Cellulose fibres

Zone of elongation

Zone of cell division (including apical meristem)

Root cap

LM 200×

Key

● Dermal tissue system ● Ground tissue system ● Vascular tissue system

▲ **Figure 22.7B** Primary growth of a root

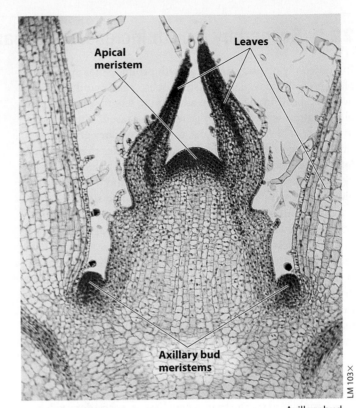

Apical meristem

Leaves

Axillary bud meristems

LM 103×

Apical meristem

Axillary bud meristems

① ②

Growth →

▲ **Figure 22.7C** Primary growth of a shoot

primary xylem and **primary phloem**. Differentiation of cells—the specialization of their structure and function—results from differential gene expression (see Module 11.2). Cells in the vascular cylinder, for instance, develop into primary xylem or phloem cells because certain genes are turned on and are expressed as specific proteins, whereas other genes in these cells are turned off. Genetic control of differentiation is one of the most active areas of plant research.

The micrograph in **Figure 22.7C** shows a section through the end of a growing shoot that was cut lengthwise from its tip to just below its uppermost pair of axillary buds. A growing shoot tip can be divided into the same three zones as seen in the root. However, the labelling is more complex and not all can be seen in the figure. You can see the apical meristem, which is a dome-shaped mass of dividing cells at the tip of the terminal bud. Elongation occurs just below this meristem, and the elongating cells push the apical meristem upward, instead of downward as in the root. As the apical meristem

advances upward, some of its cells remain behind, and these become new axillary bud meristems at the base of the leaves. Initially, the apical bud meristems are dormant. In time, they may be activated and become the apical meristem of a growing branch.

The drawings in Figure 22.7C show two stages in the growth of a shoot. Stage ① is just like the micrograph. At the later stage shown in sketch ②, the apical meristem has been pushed upward by elongating cells underneath.

Primary growth accounts for a plant's lengthwise growth. The stems and roots of many plants increase in thickness, too, and in the next module, we see how this usually happens.

? A plant grows taller because of cell division within the _____ at the tips of the shoots. Such lengthening is called _____.

● apical meristem; primary growth

22.8 Secondary growth increases the diameter of woody plants

In nonwoody plants, primary growth produces nearly all the plant body. Woody plants (such as trees, shrubs, and vines), however, grow in diameter in addition to length, thickening in older regions where primary growth has ceased. This increase in thickness of stems and roots, called **secondary growth**, is caused by the activity of dividing cells in tissues that are called **lateral meristems**. These dividing cells are arranged into two cylinders, known as the vascular cambium and the cork cambium, that extend along the length of roots and stems.

The **vascular cambium** is a cylinder of meristem cells one cell thick between the primary xylem and primary phloem. In **Figure 22.8A**, left, this region of the stem is just beginning secondary growth. Except for the vascular cambium, the stem at this stage of growth is virtually the same as a young stem undergoing primary growth (compare this figure with the eudicot stem in Figure 22.5). Secondary growth adds layers of vascular tissue on either side of the vascular cambium, as indicated by the black arrows.

The drawings at the centre and the right show the results of secondary growth. Tissues produced by secondary growth are called secondary tissues. In the centre drawing, the vascular cambium has given rise to two new tissues: **secondary xylem** at its interior and **secondary phloem** at its exterior. Each year, the vascular cambium gives rise to layers of secondary xylem and secondary phloem that are larger in circumference than the previous layer (see the drawing at the right). In this way, the vascular cambium thickens roots and stems.

Secondary xylem makes up the **wood** of a tree, shrub, or vine. Over the years, a woody stem gets thicker and thicker as its vascular cambium produces layer upon layer of secondary xylem. The cells of the secondary xylem have thick walls rich in lignin, giving wood its characteristic hardness and strength.

Annual growth rings, such as those in the cross-section in **Figure 22.8B**, result from the layering of secondary xylem. The layers are visible as rings because of uneven activity of the vascular cambium during the year. In woody plants that live in Canada, the vascular cambium becomes dormant each year during winter, and secondary growth is interrupted. When secondary growth resumes in the spring, a cylinder of early wood forms. Early wood cells are made up of the first new xylem cells to develop and are usually larger in diameter and thinner-walled than those produced later in summer. The boundary between the large cells of early wood and the smaller cells of the late wood produced during the previous growing season is usually a distinct ring visible in cross-sections of tree trunks and roots. Therefore, a tree's age can be estimated by counting its annual rings. Dendrochronology (*dendros* is Greek for "tree") is the science of analyzing tree ring growth patterns. The rings may have varying thicknesses, reflecting climate conditions and therefore the amount of seasonal growth in a given year. In fact, growth ring patterns in older trees are one source of evidence for recent global climate change.

Now let's return to Figure 22.8A and see what happens to the parts of the stem that are *external* to the vascular cambium. Unlike xylem, the external tissues do not accumulate over the years. Instead, they are sloughed off at about the same rate they are produced.

Notice at the left of the figure that the epidermis and cortex, both the result of primary growth, make up the young stem's external covering. When secondary growth begins (centre drawing), the epidermis is sloughed off and replaced with a new outer layer called **cork** (brown). Mature cork cells are dead and have thick, waxy walls that protect the underlying tissues of the stem from water loss, physical damage, and pathogens.

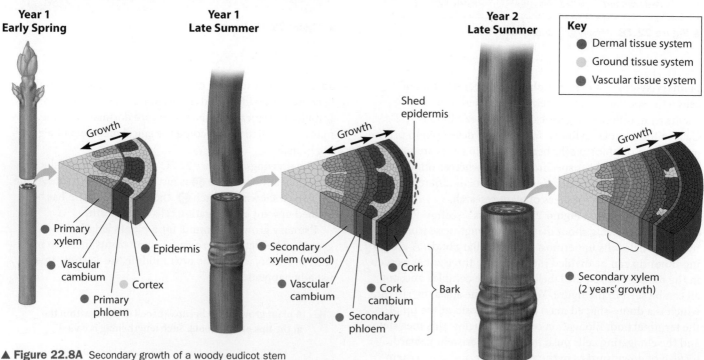

▲ **Figure 22.8A** Secondary growth of a woody eudicot stem

Cork is produced by meristem tissue called the **cork cambium** (light brown), which first forms from parenchyma cells in the cortex. As the stem thickens and the secondary xylem expands, the original cork and cork cambium are pushed outward and fall off, as is evident in the cracked, peeling bark of many tree trunks. A new cork cambium forms to the inside. When no cortex is left, it forms from parenchyma cells in the phloem.

Everything external to the vascular cambium is called **bark**. As indicated in the diagram at the right in Figure 22.8B, its main components are the secondary phloem, the cork cambium, and the cork. The youngest secondary phloem (next to the vascular cambium) functions in sugar transport. The older secondary phloem dies, as does the cork cambium you see here. Pushed outward, these tissues and cork produced by the cork cambium help to protect the stem until they, too, are sloughed off as part of the bark. Keeping pace with secondary growth, cork cambium keeps regenerating from the younger secondary phloem and keeps producing a steady supply of cork.

The log on the left in Figure 22.8B shows the results of several decades of secondary growth. The bulk of a trunk like this is dead tissue. The living tissues in it are the vascular cambium, the youngest secondary phloem, the cork cambium, and cells in the wood rays, which you can see radiating from the centre of the log in the drawing on the right. The **wood rays** consist of parenchyma cells that transport water and nutrients, horizontally; store organic nutrients; and aid in wound repair. The **heartwood**, in the centre of the trunk, consists of older layers of secondary xylem. These cells no longer transport water; they are clogged with resins and other compounds that make heartwood resistant to rotting. Because heartwood doesn't conduct water, a large tree can survive even if the centre of its trunk is hollow **(Figure 22.8C)**. The lighter-coloured **sapwood** is younger secondary xylem that does conduct xylem fluid (sap).

Thousands of useful products are made from wood—from construction lumber to fine furniture, musical instruments, paper, insulation, and a long list of chemicals, including turpentine, alcohols, artificial vanilla flavouring, and preservatives. Among the qualities that make wood so useful are a unique combination of strength, hardness, lightness, high insulating properties, durability, and workability. In many cases, there is simply no good substitute for wood. A wooden oboe, for instance, produces far richer sounds than a plastic one. Fence posts made of locust tree wood actually last much longer in the ground than metal ones. Ball bearings are sometimes made of a very hard wood called lignum vitae. Unlike metal bearings, they require no lubrication because a natural oil completely penetrates the wood.

▲ **Figure 22.8C** A giant sequoia that survived for 88 years with a tunnel cut through its heartwood

In a sense, wood is analogous to the hard endoskeletons of many land animals. It is an evolutionary adaptation that enables a shrub or tree to remain upright and keep growing year after year on land—sometimes to attain enormous heights, as we saw in the chapter-opening essay. In the next Big Idea, we discuss some additional adaptations that enable plants to live on land—those that facilitate reproduction. But first we examine a tree-based rumour.

? Why can some large trees survive after a tunnel has been cut through their centre?

● The centre of an older tree consists of old layers of secondary xylem that no longer transport materials through the plant. It can thus be removed without harming the tree.

Rings

Wood rays

Heartwood

Sapwood

Vascular cambium

Bark { Secondary phloem
Cork cambium
Cork

▲ **Figure 22.8B** Anatomy of a log

22.9 Is there a palm tree that can walk?

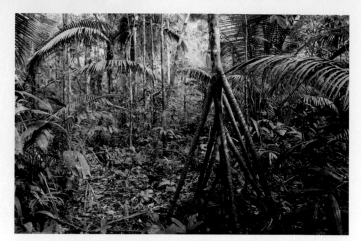

▲ **Figure 22.9A** The walking palm (*Socratea exorrhiza*)

If you have ever walked through a Costa Rican jungle, you may have felt as though something was following you. Chances are you were probably right. But did you think that your stalker was a palm tree? Rumour has it that a particular palm tree in the jungles of Central and South America can actually walk. Can a tree exhibit such an extraordinarily untree-like behaviour and actually move?

The suspect tree, shown in **Figure 22.9A**, is the walking palm (*Socratea exorrhiza*). It is easily recognizable by its unusual root structure. Unlike most palm trees, the base of the walking palm's trunk is not at ground level. Instead, its trunk is supported more than 1 m above ground by numerous stiltlike roots. The walking palm grows to an average height of 15 m and has a diameter of 12 cm.

Soil in tropical rainforests can be nutritionally poor and there may only be a few centimetres of topsoil. Rapid decomposition of dead organic matter and leaching by rainfall prevent the accumulation of essential nutrients. Many palm trees that grow there have a variety of special adaptations that provide them with the nutrients they require. For example, a shallow root system maximizes nutrient uptake by many palms.

But the walking palm has a unique adaptation. It can actually move to increase its nutrient absorption.

As new stilt roots rapidly grow (70 cm per month) from the base of the trunk, the diameter of the root cone enlarges. (Roots on the perimeter of the cone are the youngest.) The amount of nutrients a new root can take up depends on the quality of soil into which it plants itself. If soil in one area is relatively nutrient-rich, more roots will grow, extending the cone in that direction. At the same time, roots on the opposite side of the root cone, in nutrient-poor soil, eventually die and rot away. As this process continues, the root cone and tree trunk actually move toward higher quality soil.

The stilt roots also appear to benefit younger trees growing in the undergrowth. The falling of a large dead tree is a fairly frequent occurrence in a tropical rainforest. A young palm reaching for light may end up pinned by the fallen trunk of a dead neighbour. Figure 22.9B shows how a young tree resumes its vertical ascent after being pinned. Very shortly after ❶ being pinned, ❷ new roots start growing from the trunk. As the new roots grow, they lift the tip upright. More roots grow to support the young tree and ❸ the parts that were pinned eventually die and rot away. The final result has the young tree growing vertically a short distance away from its original position. Small seedlings are able to right themselves in a few months and larger juvenile trees in only a few years.

Although the rumour about the walking palm tree is true, you do not need to be afraid of the palm chasing anyone down. The top speed of this remarkable palm is a mere 1 m per year. In the next modules, we'll focus our attention on flowering plants and their reproduction.

? It is hypothesized that the walking palm can also move toward areas with brighter sunlight. What advantage would this offer the plant?

● By moving to an area with increased light, the palm can increase its rate of photosynthesis and growth, providing it can acquire enough nutrients.

Original position

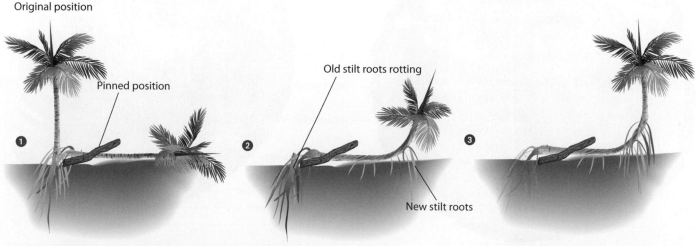

Pinned position

❶   ❷

Old stilt roots rotting

❸

New stilt roots

▲ **Figure 22.9B** A young walking palm righting itself

Reproduction of Flowering Plants

22.10 The flower is the organ of sexual reproduction in angiosperms

It has been said that an oak tree is merely an acorn's way of making more acorns. Indeed, evolutionary fitness for any organism is measured only by its ability to produce healthy, fertile offspring. Thus, from an evolutionary viewpoint, all the structures and functions of a plant can be interpreted as mechanisms contributing to reproduction. In the remaining modules, we explore the reproductive biology of angiosperms, beginning here with a brief overview. (This would be a good time to review Modules 19.9 and 19.10, where this information was first presented.) Flowers, the reproductive shoots of angiosperms, can vary greatly in shape **(Figure 22.10A)**. Despite such variation, nearly all flowers contain four types of modified leaves called floral organs: sepals, petals, stamens, and carpels **(Figure 22.10B)**. The **sepals**, which enclose and protect the flower bud, are usually green and more leaflike than the other floral organs (picture the green at the base of a rosebud). The **petals** are often colourful and advertise the flower to pollinators. The stamens and carpels are the reproductive organs, containing the sperm and eggs, respectively.

A **stamen** consists of a stalk (filament) tipped by an anther. Within the **anther** are sacs in which pollen is produced via meiosis. Pollen grains house the cells that develop into sperm.

A **carpel** has a long slender neck (style) with a sticky stigma at its tip. The **stigma** is the landing platform for pollen. The base of the carpel is the **ovary**, which contains one or more **ovules**, each containing a developing egg and supporting cells. The term **pistil** is sometimes used to refer to a single carpel or a group of fused carpels.

Figure 22.10C shows the life cycle of a generalized angiosperm. ❶ Fertilization occurs in an ovule within a flower. ❷ As the ovary usually develops into a fruit, ❸ the ovule develops into the seed containing the embryo. The fruit protects the seed and aids in dispersing it. Completing the life cycle, ❹ the seed then **germinates** (begins to grow) in a

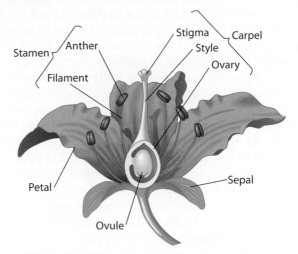

▲ **Figure 22.10B** The structure of a flower

suitable habitat; ❺ the embryo develops into a seedling; and the seedling grows into a mature plant.

In the next four modules, we examine key stages in the angiosperm sexual life cycle in more detail. We will see a number of variations in the basic themes presented here.

? Pollen develops within the _____ of _____. Ovules develop within the _____ of _____.

● anthers; stamens; ovaries; carpels

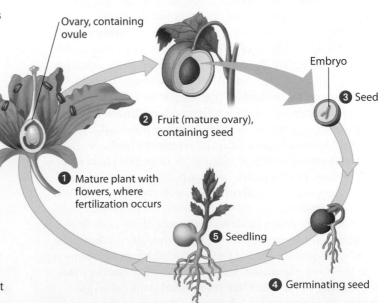

▲ **Figure 22.10A** Some variations in flower shape

▲ **Figure 22.10C** Life cycle of a generalized angiosperm

22.11 The development of pollen and ovules culminates in fertilization

The life cycles of plants are characterized by an alternation of generations, in which haploid (*n*) and diploid (*2n*) generations take turns producing each other (see Modules 19.2 and 19.10). The roots, stems, leaves, and most of the reproductive structures of angiosperms are diploid. The diploid plant body is called the **sporophyte**. A sporophyte of an angiosperm produces special structures, the anthers and ovules, in which cells undergo meiosis to produce haploid cells called spores. Each spore then divides via mitosis and becomes a multicellular **gametophyte**, the plant's haploid generation. The gametophyte produces gametes by mitosis. At fertilization, gametes from the male and female gametophytes unite, producing a diploid zygote. The life cycle is completed when the zygote divides by mitosis and develops into a new sporophyte. In angiosperms, the sporophyte is the dominant generation: It is larger, more obvious, and longer-living than the gametophyte. In this module, we take a look at the microscopic gametophytes of a flowering plant.

Pollen grains are the male gametophytes. The cells that develop into pollen grains are found within a flower's anthers (top left in **Figure 22.11**). Each cell first undergoes meiosis, forming four haploid spores. Each spore divides once by mitosis, forming a two-cell, haploid pollen grain. The **tube cell** will form the tube or conduit from a flower's stigma to an ovule inside the ovary that the sperm will travel through. The other cell, the **generative cell**, will ultimately divide once more to produce two sperm cells. The generative cell is internalized into the tube cell, and a thick wall forms around them. The resulting pollen grain is ready for release from the anther.

Moving to the top right of the figure, we can follow the development of the flower parts that form the female gametophyte and eventually the egg. In most species, the ovary of a flower contains several ovules, but only one is shown here. An ovule contains a central cell (gold) surrounded by a protective covering of smaller cells (yellow). The central cell enlarges and undergoes meiosis, producing four haploid spores. Three of the spores usually degenerate, but the surviving one enlarges and divides by mitosis, producing a multicellular structure known as the **embryo sac**. Housed in several layers of protective cells (yellow) produced by the sporophyte plant, the embryo sac is the female gametophyte. The sac contains a large central cell with two haploid nuclei. One of its other cells is the haploid egg, ready to be fertilized.

The first step leading to fertilization is **pollination** (at the centre of the figure), the delivery of pollen from anther to stigma. Most angiosperms depend on insects, birds, or other animals to transfer pollen. Most major crops rely on insects, mainly bees. But the pollen of some plants—such as grasses and many trees—is windborne (as anyone bothered by pollen allergies knows). Other plants, including the tomato, can self-pollinate when pollen lands on the stigma of the same flower.

After pollination, the pollen grain germinates on the stigma. Its tube cell gives rise to the pollen tube, which grows downward into the ovary. Meanwhile, the generative cell divides by mitosis, forming two sperm. Only at this point is the pollen grain mature. When the pollen tube reaches the base of the ovule, it enters the ovary and discharges its two sperm near the embryo

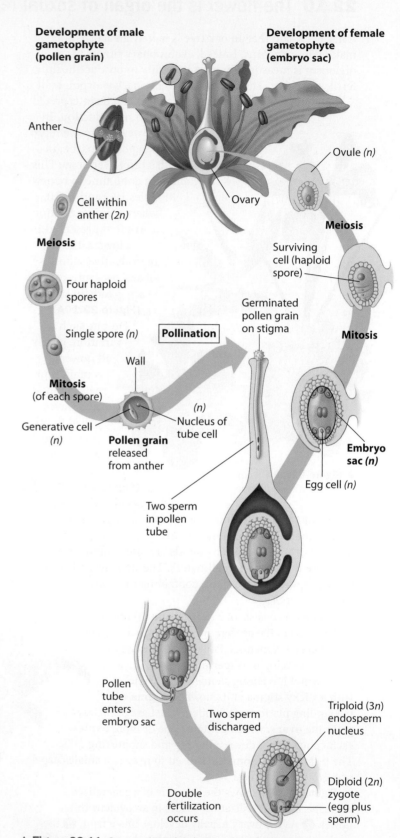

▲ **Figure 22.11** Gametophyte development and fertilization in an angiosperm

sac. One sperm fertilizes the egg, forming the diploid zygote. The other contributes its haploid nucleus to the large diploid central cell of the embryo sac. This cell, now with a triploid (3*n*) nucleus, will give rise to a food-storing tissue called **endosperm**.

The union of two sperm cells with different nuclei of the embryo sac is called **double fertilization**, and the resulting production of endosperm is unique to angiosperms. Endosperm will develop only in ovules containing a fertilized egg, thereby preventing angiosperms from squandering nutrients.

> **?** Fertilization unites the sperm cell, which develops within the male gametophyte (or _____), with the egg cell, which develops within the female gametophyte (or _____).
>
> ● pollen grain; embryo sac

22.12 The ovule develops into a seed

After fertilization, the ovule, containing the triploid central cell and the diploid zygote, begins developing into a seed. As the embryo develops from the zygote, the seed stockpiles proteins, oils, and starch to varying degrees, depending on the species. This is what makes seeds such a major source of nutrition for many animals.

As shown in **Figure 22.12A**, embryonic development begins when the zygote divides by mitosis into two cells. Repeated division of one of the cells then produces a ball of cells that becomes the embryo. The other cell divides to form a thread of cells that pushes the embryo into the endosperm. The bulges you see on the embryo are the developing cotyledons. You can tell that the plant in this drawing is a eudicot, since it has two cotyledons.

The result of embryonic development in the ovule is a mature seed (Figure 22.12A, bottom right). Near the end of its

Common bean (eudicot)

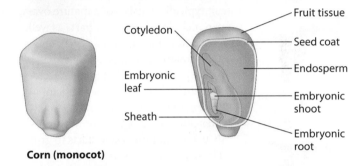

Corn (monocot)

▲ **Figure 22.12B** Seed structure

▲ **Figure 22.12A** Development of a eudicot plant embryo

maturation, the seed loses most of its water and forms a hard, resistant **seed coat** (brown). The embryo, surrounded by its endosperm food supply (gold), becomes dormant; it will not develop further until the seed germinates. Seed dormancy, a condition in which growth and development are suspended temporarily, is a key evolutionary adaptation. Dormancy allows time for a plant to disperse its seeds and increases the chance that a new generation of plants will begin growing only when environmental conditions, such as temperature and moisture, favour survival.

The dormant embryo contains a miniature root and shoot, each equipped with an apical meristem. After the seed germinates, the apical meristems will sustain primary growth as long as the plant lives. Also present in the embryo are the three tissues that will form the epidermis, cortex, and primary vascular tissues.

Figure 22.12B contrasts the internal structures of eudicot and monocot seeds. In the eudicot (a bean), the embryo is an elongated structure (light beige) with two thick cotyledons (tan). The embryonic root develops just below the point at which the cotyledons are attached to the rest of the embryo. The embryonic shoot, tipped by a pair of miniature embryonic leaves, develops just above the point of attachment. The bean seed contains no endosperm because its cotyledons absorb the endosperm nutrients as the seed forms. The nutrients start passing from the cotyledons to the embryo when it germinates.

A kernel of corn, an example of a monocot, is actually a fruit containing one seed. Everything you see in the drawing is the seed, except the kernel's outermost covering. The covering is dried fruit tissue, the former wall of the ovary, and is tightly bonded to the seed coat. Unlike the bean, the corn seed contains a large endosperm and a single, thin cotyledon. The cotyledon absorbs the endosperm's nutrients during germination.

Also unlike the bean, the embryonic root and shoot in corn each have a protective sheath.

? **What is the role of the endosperm in a seed?**

● The endosperm provides nutrients to the developing embryo.

22.13 The ovary typically develops into a fruit

In the previous two modules, we followed the angiosperm life cycle from the flower on the sporophyte plant through the transformation of an ovule into a seed. While the seeds are developing from ovules, hormonal changes triggered by fertilization cause other flower structures (typically the ovary) to thicken and mature into a fruit. A **fruit** is a specialized vessel that houses and protects seeds and helps to disperse them from the parent plant. Although a fruit typically consists of a mature ovary, it can include other flower parts as well. A pea pod is a fruit, as is a peach, orange, tomato, cherry, or corn kernel.

The photographs in **Figure 22.13A** illustrate the changes in a pea plant leading to pod formation. ❶ Soon after pollination, ❷ the flower drops its petals, and the ovary starts to grow. The ovary expands tremendously, and its wall thickens, ❸ forming the pod, or fruit, which holds the peas, or seeds.

Figure 22.13B matches the parts of a pea flower with what they become in the pod. The wall of the ovary becomes the pod. The ovules, within the ovary, develop into the seeds. The small, threadlike structure at the end of the pod is what remains of the upper part of the flower's carpel. The sepals of the flower often stay attached to the base of the green pod. Peas are usually harvested at this stage of

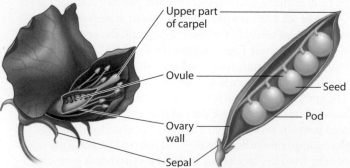

▲ **Figure 22.13A** Development of a fruit, a pea pod

Maple fruits

▲ **Figure 22.13C** A collection of fleshy (top) and dry (bottom) fruits

Upper part of carpel

Ovule

Seed

Ovary wall

Pod

Sepal

▲ **Figure 22.13B** The correspondence between flower and fruit in the pea plant

fruit development. If the pods are allowed to develop further, they become dry and brownish and will split open, releasing the seeds.

As shown in the examples in **Figure 22.13C**, mature fruits can be either fleshy or dry. Oranges, plums, and grapes are examples of fleshy fruits, in which the wall of the ovary becomes soft during ripening. When walking through the produce aisle at your local grocer, you may categorize some products as vegetables that are actually fruit. The fleshy cucumber or squashes, for example, contain seeds and are therefore fruit. Dry fruits include beans, nuts, and grains. The dry, wind-dispersed fruits of grasses, harvested while on the plant, are major staple foods for humans. The cereal grains of wheat, rice, corn, and other grasses, though easily mistaken for seeds, are each actually a fruit with a dry outer covering (the former wall of the ovary) that adheres to the seed coat of the seed within.

As discussed in Module 19.11, various adaptations of fruits help to disperse seeds (see Figures 19.11A–19.11C). The seeds of some flowering plants, such as dandelions and maples, are contained within fruits that function like kites or propellers, adaptations that enhance dispersal by wind.

Some fruits, such as coconuts, are adapted to dispersal by water. And many angiosperms rely on animals to carry seeds. Some of these plants have fruits modified as burrs that cling to animal fur (or the clothes of humans). Other angiosperms produce edible fruits, which are usually nutritious, sweet tasting, and vividly coloured, advertising their ripeness. When an animal eats the fruit, it digests the fruit's fleshy part, but the tough seeds usually pass unharmed through the animal's digestive tract. Animals may deposit the seeds, along with a supply of fertilizer, kilometres from where the fruit was eaten.

? Seed is to _____ as _____ is to ovary.

● ovule; fruit

22.14 Seed germination continues the life cycle

The germination of a seed is often used to symbolize the beginning of life; but, as we have seen, the seed already contains a miniature plant, complete with embryonic root and shoot. Thus, at germination, the plant does not begin life but rather resumes the growth and development that were temporarily suspended during seed dormancy.

Germination usually begins when the seed takes up water. The hydrated seed expands, rupturing its coat. The inflow of water also triggers metabolic changes in the embryo that make it start growing again. Enzymes begin digesting stored nutrients in the endosperm or cotyledons, and these nutrients are transported to the growing regions of the embryo.

The figures below trace germination in a eudicot (a garden bean) and a monocot (corn). In **Figure 22.14A**, notice that the embryonic root of a bean emerges first and grows downward from the germinating seed. Next, the embryonic shoot emerges. The bend just below the cotyledons protects the delicate shoot tip by holding it downward, rather than pushing it up through the abrasive soil. As the shoot breaks through the soil surface, its tip is lifted gently out of the soil as exposure to light stimulates the bend to straighten. The first foliage leaves then expand from the shoot tip and begin making food by photosynthesis. The cotyledons emerge from the soil and become leaflike photosynthetic structures. In many other plants, such as peas, the cotyledons remain behind in the soil and decompose.

Corn and other monocots use a different mechanism for breaking ground at germination (**Figure 22.14B**). A protective sheath surrounding the shoot pushes upward and breaks through the soil. The shoot tip then grows up through the tunnel provided by the sheath. The corn cotyledon remains in the soil and decomposes.

In the wild, only a small fraction of fragile seedlings endure long enough to reproduce. Production of enormous numbers of seeds compensates for the odds against individual survival. Asexual reproduction, generally simpler and less hazardous for offspring than sexual reproduction, is an alternative means of plant propagation, as we see next.

? Which meristems provide additional cells for early growth of a seedling after germination?

● The apical meristems of the shoot and root

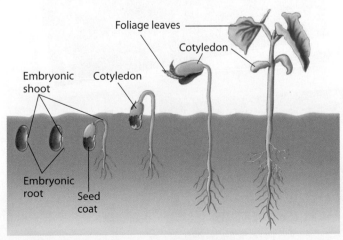

▲ **Figure 22.14A** Bean germination (a eudicot)

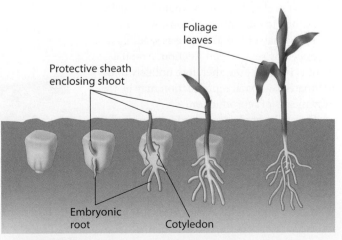

▲ **Figure 22.14B** Corn germination (a monocot)

22.15 Asexual reproduction produces plant clones

Asexual reproduction in angiosperms and other plants is an extension of their capacity to grow throughout life. A plant's meristematic tissues can sustain growth indefinitely. In addition, parenchyma cells can divide and differentiate into the various types of cells.

In nature, asexual reproduction in plants often involves **fragmentation**, the separation of a parent plant into parts that develop into whole plants. A garlic bulb **(Figure 22.15A)** is actually an underground stem that functions in storage. A single large bulb fragments into several parts, called cloves. Each clove can give rise to a separate plant, as indicated by the green shoots emerging from some of them. The white, paper-thin sheaths are leaves that are attached to the stem. Each of the small trees you see in Figure 22.15B is a sprout from the roots of a western redcedar tree (discussed in the chapter-opening essay). Each small tree develops its own root system separate from the parent tree.

▲ **Figure 22.15A** Cloves of a garlic bulb

The ring of plants in **Figure 22.15C** is a clone of creosote bushes growing in the Mojave Desert in Southern California. In this case, the word **clone** refers to a group of genetically identical organisms. All these bushes came from generations of asexual reproduction by roots. Making the oldest trees seem youthful, this clone apparently began with a single plant that germinated from a seed about 12 000 years ago. The original plant probably occupied the centre of the ring.

Some aspen groves, such as those shown in **Figure 22.15D**, consist of thousands of trees descended by asexual reproduction from the root system of a single parent. (Genetic differences between groves that arose from different parents result in different timing for the development of fall colour.)

Many plants can reproduce both sexually and asexually. What advantages can asexual reproduction offer? For one thing, a particularly fit parent plant can clone many copies of itself, all of which would be equally well suited to current conditions. Also, the offspring may not be as fragile as seedlings produced by sexual reproduction. And if a plant is isolated (and therefore unlikely to be pollinated), asexual reproduction may be the only means of reproduction.

The ability of plants to reproduce asexually provides many opportunities for growers to produce large numbers of plants with minimal effort and expense. For example, most of our fruit trees and houseplants are asexually

▲ **Figure 22.15B** Sprouts from the roots of western redcedar trees

propagated from cuttings. Several other plants are propagated from root sprouts (for example, raspberries) or pieces of underground stems (such as potatoes) or by grafting a bud from one plant onto a closely related plant (for example, most varieties of wine grapes).

Plants can also be asexually propagated in the laboratory. The test tube in **Figure 22.15E** contains a geranium plantlet that was grown from a few meristem cells cut from a mature plant

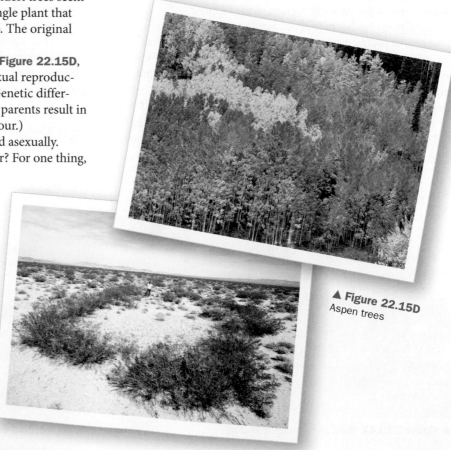

▲ **Figure 22.15D** Aspen trees

▶ **Figure 22.15C** A ring of creosote bushes

and cultured in a growth medium containing nutrients and hormones. Using this method, researchers can clone a single plant into thousands of copies. Orchids and certain pine trees used for mass plantings are commonly propagated this way.

As discussed in Module 12.8, plant cell culture methods also enable researchers to grow plants from genetically engineered plant cells. Foreign genes are incorporated into a single parenchyma cell, and the cell is then cultured so that it multiplies and develops into a new plant. The resulting genetically modified (GM) plant may then be able to grow and reproduce normally. The commercial adoption of GM crops by farmers has been one of the most rapid cases of technology transfer in the history of agriculture; but, as discussed in Module 12.9, it is not without controversy.

Aside from the issues raised by GM plants, modern agriculture faces some potentially serious problems. Nearly all of today's crop plants have very little genetic variability. In fact,

we grow most crops in monocultures, cultivating a single plant variety on large areas of land. Given these conditions, plant scientists fear that a small number of diseases could devastate large crop areas. In response, plant breeders are working to maintain "gene banks," storage sites for seeds of many different plant varieties that can be used to breed new hybrids.

? **Which mode of reproduction (sexual or asexual) would generally be more advantageous in a location where the composition of the soil is constantly changing? Why?**

● Sexual, because it generates genetic variation among the offspring, which enhances the potential for adaptation to a changing environment

▲ **Figure 22.15E**
Test-tube cloning

R E V I E W

MasteringBiology® **For Practice Quizzes, BioFlix, MP3 Tutors, and Activities, go to masteringbiology.com.**

Reviewing the Concepts

Plant Structure and Function (22.1–22.6)

22.1 People have manipulated plants since prehistoric times. Humans share a long and prosperous history with angiosperms (flowering plants).

22.2 The two major groups of angiosperms are the monocots and the eudicots. These two groups differ in the number of seed leaves and the structure of roots, stems, leaves, and flowers.

22.3 A typical plant body contains three basic organs: roots, stems, and leaves. The structure of a flowering plant allows it to draw resources from both soil and air.

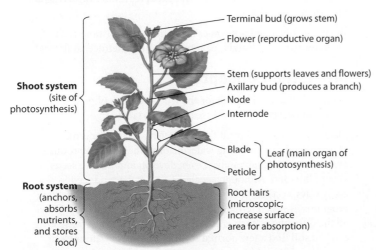

Terminal bud (grows stem)

Flower (reproductive organ)

Shoot system (site of photosynthesis)

Stem (supports leaves and flowers)
Axillary bud (produces a branch)
Node
Internode

Blade ⎱ Leaf (main organ of
Petiole ⎰ photosynthesis)

Root system (anchors, absorbs nutrients, and stores food)

Root hairs (microscopic; increase surface area for absorption)

22.4 Many plants have modified roots, stems, and leaves. In addition to their primary functions, plant organs may store food, promote asexual reproduction, and provide protection.

22.5 Three tissue systems make up the plant body. Roots, stems, and leaves are each made up of dermal, vascular, and ground tissues. Dermal tissue covers and protects the plant. In leaves, dermal tissue has stomata, pores with guard cells that regulate exchange of gases and water vapour with the environment. The vascular tissue system contains xylem and phloem, which function in support and

transport. Xylem conveys water and dissolved minerals, and phloem transports sugars. The ground tissue system functions in storage, photosynthesis, and support.

22.6 Plant cells are diverse in structure and function. The major types of plant cells are parenchyma, collenchyma, sclerenchyma (including fibre and sclereid cells), water-conducting cells (tracheids and vessel elements), and food-conducting cells (sieve-tube elements).

Plant Growth (22.7–22.9)

22.7 Primary growth lengthens roots and shoots. Meristems, areas of unspecialized, dividing cells, are where plant growth originates. Apical meristems at the tips of roots and in terminal and axillary buds of shoots initiate primary growth by producing new cells. A root or shoot lengthens as the cells elongate and differentiate.

22.8 Secondary growth increases the diameter of woody plants. An increase in a plant's diameter, called secondary growth, arises from cell division in a cylinder of meristem cells called the vascular cambium. The vascular cambium thickens a stem by adding layers of secondary xylem, or wood, next to its inner surface. Outside the vascular cambium, the bark includes secondary phloem, cork cambium, and protective cork cells produced by the cork cambium.

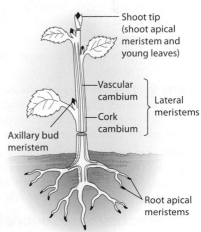

Shoot tip (shoot apical meristem and young leaves)

Vascular cambium
Cork cambium
Axillary bud meristem

Lateral meristems

Root apical meristems

22.9 Is there a palm tree that can walk? The walking palm tree sends out new stilt roots in search of more fertile soils. As older roots die and rot away, the root cone and trunk are able to move from their original location.

Reproduction of Flowering Plants (22.10–22.15)

22.10 The flower is the organ of sexual reproduction in angiosperms. The angiosperm flower consists of sepals, petals, stamens, and carpels. Pollen grains develop in anthers, at tips of stamens. The tip of the carpel, the stigma, receives pollen grains. The ovary, at the carpel's base, houses the egg-producing ovule.

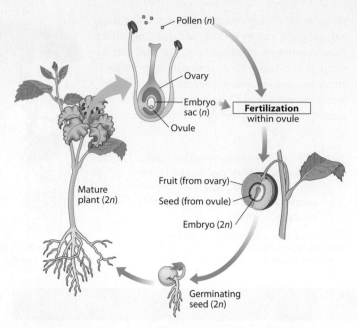

Pollen (n)

Ovary

Embryo sac (n)

Ovule

Fertilization
within ovule

Mature plant (2n)

Fruit (from ovary)

Seed (from ovule)

Embryo (2n)

Germinating seed (2n)

22.11 The development of pollen and ovules culminates in fertilization. Haploid spores are formed within ovules and anthers. The spores in anthers give rise to male gametophytes—pollen grains—which produce sperm.

A spore in an ovule produces the embryo sac, the female gametophyte. Each embryo sac has an egg cell. Pollination is the arrival of pollen grains onto a stigma. A pollen tube grows into the ovule, and sperm pass through it and fertilize both the egg and a second cell. This process is called double fertilization.

Endosperm nucleus (3n)
(2 polar nuclei plus sperm)

Zygote (2n)
(egg plus sperm nucleus)

22.12 The ovule develops into a seed. After fertilization, the ovule becomes a seed, and the fertilized egg within it divides and becomes an embryo. The other fertilized cell develops into the endosperm, which stores food for the embryo.

22.13 The ovary typically develops into a fruit. Fruits help to protect and disperse seeds.

22.14 Seed germination continues the life cycle. A seed starts to germinate when it takes up water and expands. The embryo resumes growth and absorbs nutrients from the endosperm. An embryonic root emerges, and a shoot pushes upward and expands its leaves.

22.15 Asexual reproduction produces plant clones. Asexual reproduction can occur by fragmentation or outgrowths of root systems. Propagating plants asexually from cuttings or bits of tissue can increase agricultural productivity but reduces genetic diversity.

Connecting the Concepts

1. Create a diagram that shows the relationships between the following: root system, root hairs, shoot system, leaves, petioles, blades, stems, nodes, internodes, and flowers.

Testing Your Knowledge

Multiple Choice

2. Which of the following is closest to the centre of a woody stem? (*Explain your answer.*)
   a. vascular cambium
   b. primary phloem
   c. secondary phloem
   d. primary xylem
   e. secondary xylem

3. A pea pod is formed from _____. A pea inside the pod is formed from _____.
   a. an ovule; a carpel
   b. an ovary; an ovule
   c. an ovary; a pollen grain
   d. an anther; an ovule
   e. an endosperm; an ovary

4. While walking in the woods, you encounter an unfamiliar nonwoody flowering plant. If you want to know whether it is a monocot or eudicot, it would *not* help to look at the
   a. number of seed leaves, or cotyledons, present in its seeds.
   b. shape of its root system.
   c. number of petals in its flowers.
   d. arrangement of vascular bundles in its stem.
   e. size of the plant.

5. In angiosperms, each pollen grain produces two sperm. What do these sperm do?
   a. Each one fertilizes a separate egg cell.
   b. One fertilizes an egg, and the other fertilizes the fruit.
   c. One fertilizes an egg, and the other is kept in reserve.
   d. Both fertilize a single egg cell.
   e. One fertilizes an egg, and the other fertilizes a cell that develops into stored food.

Matching

6. Attracts pollinator   a. pollen grain

7. Develops into seed   b. ovule

8. Protects flower before it opens   c. anther

9. Produces sperm   d. ovary

10. Produces pollen   e. sepal

11. Houses ovules   f. petal

Describing, Comparing, and Explaining

12. How does a fruit (containing seeds) develop from a flower?

13. Name two kinds of asexual reproduction. Explain two advantages of asexual reproduction over sexual reproduction. What is the primary drawback?

14. What part of a plant are you eating when you consume each of the following: celery stalk, peanut, strawberry, lettuce, and beet?

Applying the Concepts

15. Plant scientists are looking for the wild ancestors of potatoes, corn, and wheat. Why is this search important?

16. Many fruits you can buy at the produce market are referred to as being seedless, including watermelons. These plants produce ovules, however, they rarely, if ever, develop into mature seeds after pollination. Although seedless fruit can be produced in many ways, seedless watermelon plants are the result of breeding programs in which tetraploid and diploid parents are bred. Why do the offspring of such crosses fail to produce viable seeds? Why can you still find a few normal seeds in a seedless watermelon?

Answers to all questions can be found in Appendix E.

 Study on the Go

This QR code leads to Study on the Go—mobile study resources, including practice quizzes, videos, and glossary flashcards for this textbook.

You can access Study on the Go content via your smartphone. Note: Your login information for MasteringBiology is required.

CHAPTER

23

Nutrition in Plants

BIG IDEAS

The Uptake and Transport of Plant Nutrients

(23.1–23.5)

Plants absorb and transport substances—such as water, minerals, CO_2, and sugar—required for growth.

Plant Nutrients and the Soil

(23.6–23.12)

Plants require many essential minerals for proper health.

An Unexpected Carnivore

To an insect, the leaves of a Venus flytrap offer an inviting platform for resting in the warm sun. Woe to the insect that takes the plant up on its invitation! Shortly after the insect touches down, the leaves will snap shut and seal themselves around the victim. Digestive juices will then begin to eat away at the insect's body, until all that remains is the prey's tough exoskeleton. Finally, the leaves will reabsorb the fluids and relax their grasp, allowing the prey's ghostly remains to blow away.

Although the Venus flytrap is likely the most familiar example, more than 600 species of plants are carnivores—that is, they feed on animals. Most are small and consume only insects. However, some carnivorous plants are large enough to capture frogs and even small mammals. Another example is the provincial flower of Newfoundland and Labrador: the purple pitcher plant (*Sarracenia purpurea*). This plant grows east of the Great Divide (located in the Rocky Mountains) in all provinces excluding British Columbia.

If you are intrigued by these meat-eaters, you have something in common with Charles Darwin, who published a book about them. Through his investigations, Darwin answered a question you, too, may have: Why would plants have adaptations to entrap and digest animals? The surprising answer is that carnivorous plants absorb and use nutrients from this food, just as we do. Animals are a good source of protein, a nitrogen-rich macromolecule. Thus, carnivory enables plants to thrive in poor soil, especially where nitrogen is scarce. For example, the carnivorous pitcher plant lives in bogs, which contain mostly humus and mosses and lack the essential minerals and nitrogen required for healthy plant life. Insects fulfill these dietary needs.

Unlike the Venus flytrap, pitcher plants trap their prey without moving parts. The tubular leaves grow from the underground rhizome. When mature, the leaves form the characteristic pitchers, which collect rainwater. Using a variety of lures (nectar, scent, and colour), pitcher plants entice insects to investigate a potential meal. The inner walls of the pitcher are covered in small, downward-pointing hairlike extensions of the epidermal cells. When an unsuspecting insect ventures too far into the trap, the directionality of the hairs makes its escape difficult. Exhausted, the insect falls into the water below and drowns.

Pitcher plants do not produce digestive enzymes like the Venus flytrap. Instead, they rely on a veritable microscopic community that resides within the pitcher's water. Many microorganisms, including bacteria, protists, and small insect larvae (a juvenile stage of the insect life cycle), live within the aquatic habitat supplied by the pitcher plant. These microorganisms form a complex food web whose source of nutrients comes from the trapped insects. The larvae of midges and flies quickly devour the drowned insect. Resident bacteria and protists consume the debris and wastes from the insects. The microorganisms digest the insect carcass, ultimately breaking it down into its mineral components, which are absorbed by the *Sarracenia* leaves. In return for the habitat supporting the microcommunity within its rain-filled leaves, the purple pitcher plant has a continual source of essential nutrients, such as nitrogen, potassium, and phosphorous.

Carnivorous plants have an array of special adaptations, which allow them to acquire nutrients from animals. Most other plants, however, absorb their essential nutrients from the soil by using their roots. In this chapter, we explore how other non-carnivorous plants obtain essential nutrients and how they transport them throughout their roots, stems, and leaves.

The Uptake and Transport of Plant Nutrients

23.1 Plants acquire nutrients from air, water, and soil

Watch a plant grow from a tiny seed, and you can't help wondering where all the mass comes from. If you had to take a guess, what would you think is the source of the raw materials that make up a plant's body? Soil? Water? Air?

Aristotle thought that soil provided all the substance for plant growth. The 17th-century physician Jan Baptista van Helmont performed an experiment to test this hypothesis. He planted a willow seedling in a pot containing 91 kg of soil. After five years, the willow had grown into a tree weighing 76.8 kg, but only 0.06 kg of soil had disappeared from the pot. Van Helmont concluded that the willow had grown mainly from added water. A century later, an English physiologist named Stephen Hales postulated that plants are nourished mostly by air.

As it turns out, there is truth in all these early hypotheses about plant nutrition; air, water, and soil all contribute to plant growth **(Figure 23.1A)**. About 96% of the plant's dry weight is organic (carbon-containing) material. The carbon within this material comes from carbon dioxide (CO_2) absorbed across the plant's leaves. Meanwhile, a plant gets water (H_2O), minerals, and some oxygen (O_2) from the soil.

What happens to the materials a plant takes up from the air and soil? The sugars that a plant makes by photosynthesis are composed of the elements carbon, oxygen, and hydrogen. In Chapter 7, we saw that the carbon and oxygen used in photosynthesis come from atmospheric CO_2 and that the hydrogen comes from water molecules. Plant cells use the sugars made by photosynthesis in constructing all the other organic materials

they need, but primarily for carbohydrates. The trunk of the giant sequoia tree in **Figure 23.1B**, for instance, consists mainly of sugar derivatives, such as the cellulose of cell walls.

Plants use cellular respiration to break down some of the sugars they make, obtaining energy from them in a process that consumes O_2. A plant's leaves take up some O_2 from the air, but Figure 23.1A does not show this because plants are actually net producers of O_2, giving off more of this gas than they use. When water is split during photosynthesis, O_2 gas is produced and released through the leaves. The O_2 being taken up from the soil by the plant's roots in Figure 23.1A is actually atmospheric O_2 that has diffused into the soil; it is used in cellular respiration in the roots themselves.

A plant's ability to move water from its roots to its leaves and its ability to deliver sugars to specific areas of its body are amazing evolutionary adaptations. Figure 23.1B highlights an extreme example; the topmost leaves of a giant sequoia can be more than 100 m above the roots. In the next four modules, we follow the movement of water, dissolved mineral nutrients, and sugar throughout the plant body.

? **What inorganic substance is obtained in the greatest quantities from the soil?**

● Water

▼ **Figure 23.1B** A giant sequoia, a product of photosynthesis

▲ **Figure 23.1A** The uptake of nutrients by a plant

23.2 The plasma membranes of root cells control solute uptake

With its surface area enormously expanded by thousands of root hairs **(Figure 23.2A)**, a plant root has a remarkable ability to extract water and minerals from soil. Recall from Module 22.3 that root hairs are extensions of epidermal cells that cover the root. They provide a huge surface area in contact with nutrient-containing soil; in fact, the root hairs of a single sunflower plant, if laid end to end, could stretch for several kilometres.

All substances that enter a plant root are in solution (that is, dissolved in water). For water and solutes to be transported from the soil throughout the plant, they must move through the epidermis and cortex of the root and then into the water-conducting xylem tissue in the central cylinder of the root. Any route the water and solutes take from the soil to the xylem requires that they pass through some of the plasma membranes of the root cells. Because plasma membranes are selectively permeable, only certain solutes reach the xylem. This plasma membrane selectivity provides a checkpoint that transports needed minerals from the soil and keeps out many unneeded or toxic substances.

▲ **Figure 23.2A** Root hairs of a radish seedling

You can see two possible routes to the xylem in the bottom part of **Figure 23.2B**. The long blue arrow indicates an *intracellular* route. Water and selected solutes cross the cell wall and plasma membrane of an epidermal cell (usually at a root hair). The cells within the root are all interconnected by plasmodesmata; there is a continuum of living cytoplasm among the root cells. Therefore, once inside the epidermal cell, the solution can move inward from cell to cell without crossing any other plasma membranes, diffusing through the interconnected cytoplasm all the way into the root's endodermis. An endodermal cell then discharges the solution directly into the xylem (light purple), or into the phloem, from which it enters the xylem.

The long pink arrow in Figure 23.2B indicates an alternative *extracellular* route. In this route, the solution moves inward within the hydrophilic walls and extracellular spaces of the root cells, but does not enter the cytoplasm of the epidermis or cortex cells. The solution does not cross any plasma membranes, and there is no selection of solutes until the solution reaches the endodermis. Here, a continuous waxy barrier called the **Casparian strip** stops water and solutes from entering the xylem through the cell walls, instead forcing them to cross a plasma membrane into an endodermal cell (short blue arrow). Ion selection occurs at this membrane instead of in the epidermis, and once the selected solutes and water are in the endodermal cell, they can be discharged into the xylem.

Actually, water and solutes rarely follow just the two kinds of routes in Figure 23.2B. They may take any combination of these routes, and they may pass through numerous plasma membranes and cell walls en route to the xylem. Because of the Casparian strip, however, there are no nonselective routes; the water and solutes must cross a selectively permeable plasma membrane at some point. In other words, no solutes enter the vascular tissue uncontrolled; all must pass through at least one checkpoint. Next, we see how water and minerals move upward within the xylem from roots to shoots.

? **What is the function of the Casparian strip?**

● It regulates the passage of minerals (inorganic ions) into the xylem by blocking access via cell walls and requiring all minerals to cross a selectively permeable plasma membrane.

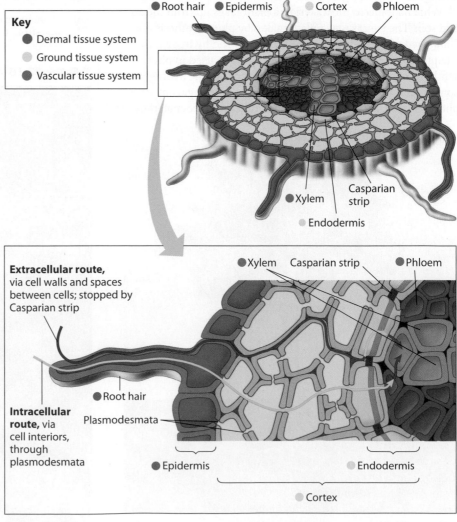

Key
● Dermal tissue system
● Ground tissue system
● Vascular tissue system

● Root hair ● Epidermis ● Cortex ● Phloem

● Xylem
Casparian strip
● Endodermis

Extracellular route, via cell walls and spaces between cells; stopped by Casparian strip

Intracellular route, via cell interiors, through plasmodesmata

● Xylem   Casparian strip   ● Phloem

● Root hair
Plasmodesmata

● Epidermis   ● Endodermis

● Cortex

▲ **Figure 23.2B** Routes of water and solutes from soil to root xylem

23.3 Transpiration pulls water up xylem vessels

As a plant grows upward toward sunlight, it needs to extract an increasing supply of water and dissolved mineral ions from the soil. Imagine having to haul 20 L of water weighing 20 kg up five flights of stairs. Now imagine doing that every 20 minutes, all day long. To thrive, a typical tree must constantly transport that quantity of water from its roots to the rest of the plant.

We saw in Figure 22.6E that xylem tissue of angiosperms includes two types of conducting cells: tracheids and vessel elements. **Xylem sap**, a solution of water and inorganic nutrients, flows through the long, thin conduits formed by these dead cells from the roots to the tips of the leaves.

What force moves xylem sap up against the downward pull of gravity? Is it pushed or pulled upward? Plant biologists have found that the roots of some plants do exert a slight upward push on xylem sap. The root cells actively pump inorganic ions into the xylem, and the root's endodermis holds the ions there. As ions accumulate in the xylem, water tends to enter by osmosis, pushing xylem sap upward ahead of it. This force, called **root pressure**, can push xylem sap up a few metres.

For the most part, however, xylem sap is not pushed from below by root pressure but pulled upward. The pulling force is **transpiration**, which is the loss of water from the leaves and other aerial parts of a plant by evaporation.

Figure 23.3 illustrates transpiration and its effect on water movement (blue arrows) in a tree. ❶ Water molecules (red dots) exit the leaf through stomata (singular, *stoma*), microscopic pores on the surface of a leaf (see also Figure 22.5 and Figure 23.4). When the stomata are open, water diffuses out of the leaves because the surrounding air is usually drier than the inside of the leaf. You can see this yourself on chilly mornings when the cold air causes the evaporating water to condense as dew.

Transpiration can pull xylem sap up the tree because of two special properties of water: cohesion and adhesion. Both of these properties arise from the charge polarity of water molecules (see Modules 2.8 and 2.11). **Cohesion** is the sticking together of molecules of the same kind. ❷ In the case of water, hydrogen bonds stick the H_2O molecules to one another. ❸ The cohering water molecules within the xylem tubes form continuous strings, extending all the way from the leaves down to the roots. In contrast, **adhesion** is the sticking together of molecules of different kinds. ❹ Water molecules tend to adhere to hydrophilic cellulose molecules in the walls of xylem cells via hydrogen bonds.

What effect does transpiration have on a string of water molecules that tend to adhere to the walls of the xylem tubes? Because the air outside the leaf is drier than the moist air spaces within the leaf, the water molecule at the end of the string diffuses outward, exiting the leaf. Cohesion resists the pulling force of diffusion, but it is not strong enough to overcome it. The outer water molecule breaks off, and the opposing forces of cohesion and transpiration put tension on the remainder of the string of water molecules. As long as transpiration continues, the string is kept tense and is pulled upward as one molecule exits the leaf and the one right behind it is tugged up into its place. Adhesion of the water molecules to the walls of the xylem cells assists the upward movement of the xylem sap by counteracting the downward pull of gravity.

Plant biologists call this explanation for the ascent of xylem sap the **transpiration-cohesion-adhesion mechanism**. We can summarize it as follows: Transpiration exerts a pull on a tense, unbroken chain of water molecules that is held together by cohesion and helped upward by adhesion. Transpiration is an efficient means of moving large volumes of water upward from roots to shoots. In fact, via transpiration, xylem sap can move up a tree at speeds approaching 80 km/h. And yet, all

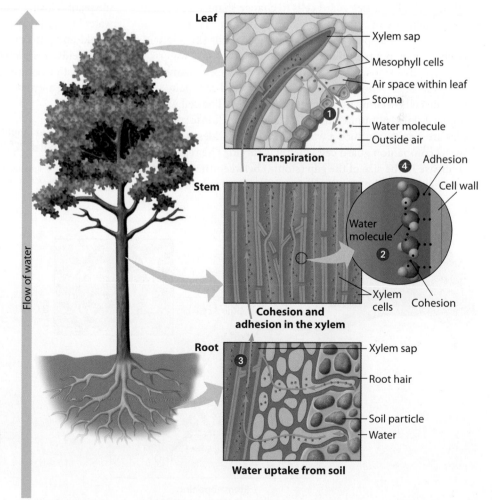

Flow of water

Leaf
- Xylem sap
- Mesophyll cells
- Air space within leaf
- Stoma
- Water molecule
- Outside air

Transpiration

Stem

- Adhesion
- Cell wall
- Water molecule
- Xylem cells
- Cohesion

Cohesion and adhesion in the xylem

Root
- Xylem sap
- Root hair
- Soil particle
- Water

Water uptake from soil

▲ **Figure 23.3** The flow of water up a tree

transport of xylem sap requires no energy expenditure by the plant. Physical properties—cohesion, adhesion, and evaporation—move water and dissolved minerals from a plant's roots to its shoots.

? Describe the roles of cohesion and adhesion in the ascent of xylem sap.

● Cohesion causes water molecules to stick together in a continuous string; adhesion helps xylem sap stick to the inside walls of the xylem cells.

23.4 Guard cells control transpiration

Adaptations that increase photosynthesis—such as large leaf surface areas—have the serious drawback of increasing water loss by transpiration. A plant must make a trade-off between its tremendous need for water and its need to make food by photosynthesis. As long as water moves up from the soil fast enough to replace the water that is lost, transpiration presents no problem. But if the soil dries out and transpiration exceeds the delivery of water to the leaves, the leaves will wilt. Unless the soil and leaves are rehydrated, the plant will eventually die.

The leaf stomata, which can open and close, are evolutionary adaptations that help plants adjust their transpiration rates to changing environmental conditions. As shown in **Figure 23.4**, a pair of guard cells flank each stoma. The guard cells control the opening of a stoma by changing shape, like an inflatable set of doors that widen or narrow the gap between the two cells.

What actually causes guard cells to change shape and thereby open or close stomata? Figure 23.4 illustrates the principle. A stoma opens (left) when its guard cells (in colour) actively take up potassium ions (K^+, orange dots), and water then enters by osmosis (blue arrows). (For a review of osmosis, see Module 5.4.) When the vacuoles in the guard cells gain water, the cells become more turgid and bowed. The cell wall of a guard cell is not uniformly thick, and the cellulose molecules are oriented in such a way that the cell buckles away from its companion guard cell when it is turgid. The result is an increase in the size of the gap (stoma) between the two cells. Conversely, when the guard cells lose K^+, they also lose water

by osmosis and become flaccid and less bowed, closing the space between them (right).

In general, guard cells keep the stomata open during the day and closed at night. During the day, CO_2 can enter the leaf from the atmosphere and thus keep photosynthesis going when sunlight is available. At night, when there is no light for photosynthesis and therefore no need to take up CO_2, the stomata are closed, saving water.

At least three cues contribute to stomatal opening at dawn. One is light, which stimulates guard cells to accumulate K^+ and become turgid. A low level of CO_2 in the leaf can have the same effect. A third cue is an internal timing mechanism—a biological clock—found in the guard cells; even if you keep a plant in a dark closet, stomata will continue their daily rhythm of opening and closing. (We'll return to biological clocks in plants in Module 24.11.)

Even during the day, the guard cells may close the stomata if the plant is losing water too fast. This response reduces further water loss and may prevent wilting, but it also slows down CO_2 uptake and photosynthesis—one reason that droughts reduce crop yields. In summary, guard cells arbitrate the photosynthesis-transpiration compromise on a moment-to-moment basis by integrating a variety of stimuli.

? Some leaf moulds secrete a chemical that causes guard cells to accumulate K^+. How does this help the mould infect the plant?

● Accumulation of K^+ by guard cells causes the stomata to stay open. The mould can then grow into the leaf interior via the stomata.

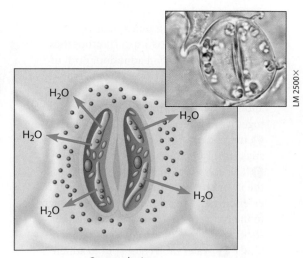

Stoma opening   Stoma closing

▲ **Figure 23.4** How guard cells control stomata

23.5 Phloem transports sugars

A plant has two separate transport systems: xylem (the topic of Module 23.3) and phloem. Xylem transports xylem sap (water and dissolved minerals), while the main function of phloem is to transport the products of photosynthesis dissolved in **phloem sap**. In angiosperms, phloem contains food-conducting cells called sieve-tube elements arranged end to end to form long tubes (see Figure 22.6F). The art and micrograph in **Figure 23.5A** show two sieve-tube elements and the sieve plate between them. Perforations in sieve plates connect the cytoplasm of these living cells into one continuous solution. Phloem sap can thus move freely from one cell to the next. In addition to sugars, phloem sap may also contain inorganic ions, amino acids, and hormones in transit from one part of the plant to another, but its main solute is usually the disaccharide sugar sucrose.

In contrast to xylem sap, which flows only upward from the roots, phloem sap moves throughout the plant in various directions. However, sieve tubes always carry sugars from a sugar source to a sugar sink. A **sugar source** is a plant organ that is a net producer of sugar, by photosynthesis or breakdown of starch. Leaves are the primary sugar sources in most mature plants. A **sugar sink** is an organ that is a net consumer or storer of sugar. Growing roots, buds, stems, and fruits are sugar sinks. A storage organ, such as a tuber or a bulb, may be a source or a sink, depending on the season. When stockpiling carbohydrates in the summer, it is a sugar sink. After breaking dormancy in the spring, it is a source, as its starch is broken down to sugar, which is carried to the growing shoot tips of the plant. Thus, each food-conducting tube in phloem tissue has a source end and a sink end, but these may change with the season or the developmental stage of the plant.

What causes phloem sap to flow from a sugar source to a sugar sink? Flow rates may be as high as 1 m/hr, which is much

▲ **Figure 23.5B** Pressure flow in plant phloem from a sugar source to a sugar sink (and the return of water to the source via xylem)

▲ **Figure 23.5A** Food-conducting cells of phloem

too fast to be accounted for by diffusion. (By diffusion alone, phloem sap would travel less than 1 metre per year.) Biologists have tested a number of hypotheses for phloem sap movement. A hypothesis called the **pressure flow mechanism** is now widely accepted for angiosperms. **Figure 23.5B** illustrates how this mechanism works, using a beet plant growing in the summer as an example. The pink dots in the phloem tube represent sugar molecules; notice their concentration gradient from top to bottom. The blue colour represents a parallel gradient of water pressure in the phloem sap.

At the sugar source (the beet leaves, in this example), ❶ sugar is loaded from a photosynthetic cell into a phloem tube by active transport. Sugar loading at the source end raises the solute (sugar) concentration inside the phloem tube. ❷ The high solute concentration draws water into the tube by osmosis, usually from the xylem. The inward flow of water raises the water pressure at the source end of the phloem tube.

At the sugar sink (the beet root, in this case), both sugar and water leave the phloem tube. ❸ As sugar departs the phloem, lowering the solute (sugar) concentration at the sink end, ❹ water follows by osmosis back into the xylem. The exit

Aphids feeding on a branch

Aphid with phloem droplet

▲ **Figure 23.5C** Aphids feeding, a process used to study the flow of phloem sap

Stylet of aphid

Aphid's stylet inserted into a phloem cell

Severed stylet dripping phloem sap

of water lowers the water pressure in the tube. The building of water pressure at the source end of the phloem tube and the reduction of that pressure at the sink end cause phloem sap to flow from source to sink—down a gradient of water pressure. Sieve plates allow free movement of solutes as well as water. Thus, sugar is carried along from source to sink at the same rate as the water. As indicated on the right side of Figure 23.5B, xylem tubes recycle the water back from sink to source.

The pressure flow mechanism explains why phloem sap always flows from a sugar source to a sugar sink, regardless of their locations in the plant. However, the mechanism is somewhat difficult to test because most experimental procedures disrupt the structure and function of the phloem tubes. Some of the most interesting studies have taken advantage of natural phloem probes: insects called aphids.

Figure 23.5C shows an aphid feeding by inserting its needlelike mouthpart, called a stylet, into the phloem of a tree branch. The aphid excretes droplets of phloem sap containing excess fluid and unabsorbed solutes. The micrograph in the centre shows an aphid's stylet inserted into the plant's sugar-conducting phloem. The pressure within the phloem force-feeds the aphid, swelling it to several times its original size. Plant biologists have used this process to study the flow of phloem sap. While the aphid is feeding, it can be anaesthetized and severed from its stylet. The stylet then serves the researcher as a miniature tap that drips phloem sap for hours (similar to the way a tap in a pressurized keg of beer allows the liquid to flow out for hours). The photograph at the lower right shows a droplet of phloem sap on the cut end of a stylet. Studies using this technique support the pressure flow model: The closer the stylet is to a sugar source, the

faster the sap flows and the greater its sugar concentration. This is what we would expect if pressure is generated at the source end of the phloem tube by the active pumping of sugar into the tube.

We now have a broad picture of how a plant absorbs substances from the soil and transports materials from one part of its body to another: Water and inorganic ions enter from the soil and are distributed by xylem. The xylem sap is pulled upward by transpiration. Carbon dioxide enters leaves through stomata and is incorporated into sugars. A second transport system, phloem, distributes the sugars. Pressure flow drives the phloem sap from leaves and storage sites to other parts of the plant, where the sugars are used or stored.

In Chapter 7, we discussed how plants convert raw materials to organic molecules by photosynthesis. We have yet to say much about the kinds of inorganic nutrients a plant needs and what it does with them. This is the subject of plant nutrition, which we discuss in the next section.

? **Contrast the forces that move phloem sap with the forces that move xylem sap.**

● Pressure is generated at the source end of a sieve tube by the loading of sugar and the resulting osmotic flow of water into the phloem. This pressure pushes phloem sap from the source end and to the sink end of the tube. In contrast, transpiration generates a pulling force that drives the ascent of xylem sap.

Plant Nutrients and the Soil

23.6 Plant health depends on the acquisition of essential inorganic nutrients

In contrast to animals, which require a diet of complex organic (carbon-containing) foods, plants survive and grow solely on CO_2 and inorganic substances (that is, plants are autotrophs; see Module 7.1). The ability of plants to assimilate CO_2 from the air, extract water and inorganic ions from the soil, and synthesize organic compounds is essential not only to the survival of plants but also to the survival of humans and other animals.

A chemical element is considered an **essential nutrient** if a plant must obtain it from its environment to complete its life cycle—that is, to grow from a seed and produce another generation of seeds. A method called hydroponic culture can be used to determine which chemical elements are essential nutrients. As shown in **Figure 23.6**, plants are grown without soil by bathing the roots in mineral solutions. Air is bubbled into the water to give the roots oxygen for cellular respiration. By omitting a particular element from the medium, a researcher can test whether that element is essential to the plant.

If the element left out of the solution is an essential nutrient, then the incomplete medium will make the plant abnormal in appearance compared with control plants grown on a complete nutrient medium. The most common symptoms of a nutrient deficiency are stunted growth and discoloured leaves. Hydroponic techniques have identified 17 essential nutrients that plants require in variable amounts. Most research has involved crop plants and houseplants; little is known about the nutritional needs of uncultivated plants.

Nine of the **essential elements** are called **macronutrients** because plants require relatively large amounts of them. Six of the nine macronutrients—carbon, oxygen, hydrogen, nitrogen, sulphur, and phosphorus—are the major ingredients of organic compounds forming the structure of a plant. These six elements make up almost 98% of a plant's dry weight. The other three macronutrients—calcium, potassium, and magnesium—make up another 1.5%.

How does a plant use calcium, potassium, and magnesium? Calcium has several functions. For example, it is important in the formation of cell walls, and it combines with certain proteins to form the glue that holds plant cells together in tissues. Calcium also helps to maintain the structure of cell membranes and helps to regulate their selective permeability. Potassium is crucial as a cofactor required for the activity of several enzymes. (Recall from Module 5.13 that a cofactor is an atom or molecule that cooperates with an enzyme in catalyzing a reaction.) Potassium is also the main solute for osmotic regulation in plants; we saw how potassium ion movements regulate the opening and closing of stomata in Module 23.4. Magnesium is a component of chlorophyll and thus is essential for photosynthesis.

Elements that plants need in very small amounts are called **micronutrients**. The eight known micronutrients are chlorine, iron, manganese, boron, zinc, copper, nickel, and molybdenum. (If you compare these nutrients with those listed in Table 2.1, you'll notice that most of them are also essential for animals.) Micronutrients function in plants mainly as cofactors. Iron, for example, is a component of cytochromes, proteins in the electron transport chains of chloroplasts and mitochondria. Micronutrients can generally be recycled repeatedly, so plants need only minute quantities of these elements from the soil. The requirement for molybdenum, for example, is so modest that there is only one atom of this rare element for every 60 million atoms of hydrogen in dried plant material. Yet a deficiency of molybdenum or any other micronutrient can weaken or kill a plant.

Complete solution containing all minerals (control)   Solution lacking potassium (experimental)

▲ **Figure 23.6** A hydroponic culture experiment

? You conduct an experiment like the one in Figure 23.6 to test whether a certain plant species requires a particular chemical element as a micronutrient. Why is it important that the glassware be completely clean?

● Because micronutrients are required in only minuscule amounts, even the smallest amount of dirt in the experimental flask may contain enough of the element you are testing to allow normal growth and invalidate your results.

23.7 Fertilizers can help to prevent nutrient deficiencies

The quality of soil—especially the availability of nutrients—determines the health of a growing plant and, for plants we consume, the quality of our own nutrition ("You are what you eat"). **Figure 23.7A** shows a healthy corn leaf (top) as well as three leaves from plants suffering various nutrient deficiencies. Such mineral shortages can stunt plant growth, and if grain is produced at all, it will likely have low nutritional value. In this way, nutritional deficiencies in plants can be passed on to livestock or human consumers.

Fortunately, the symptoms of nutrient deficiency are often distinctive enough for a grower to diagnose its cause. Many growers make visual diagnoses and then check their conclusions by having soil and plant samples chemically analyzed at a provincial or local laboratory.

Nitrogen shortage is the most common nutritional problem for plants. Soils are usually not deficient in nitrogen, but they are often deficient in the nitrogen compounds that plants can use: dissolved nitrate ions (NO_3^-) and ammonium ions (NH_4^+). Stunted growth and yellow-green leaves, starting at the tips of older leaves, are signs of nitrogen deficiency (see Figure 23.7A, second leaf from top). Other common nutrient shortfalls in plants include phosphorus (third leaf from top) and potassium (bottom leaf) deficiencies.

Once a diagnosis of a nutrient deficiency is made, treating the problem is usually simple. **Fertilizers** are compounds given to plants to promote growth. Fertilizers come in two basic types: inorganic and organic. Inorganic fertilizers (also called mineral fertilizers) can contain naturally occurring inorganic compounds (such as mined limestone or phosphate rock) or synthetic inorganic compounds (such as ammonium nitrate). Inorganic fertilizers come in a wide variety of formulations, but most emphasize their "N-P-K ratio," the amounts of the three nutrients most often deficient in depleted soils: nitrogen (N), phosphorus (P), and potassium (K). For example, 5–6–7 fertilizer contains 5 percent nitrogen (often as ammonium or nitrate), 6 percent phosphorus (as phosphoric acid),

and 7 percent potassium (as the mineral potash). Many crops benefit from an all-purpose 5–5–5 formula, but some plants thrive only under special fertilizer formulations and regimes. For example, in Canada, high-nitrogen fertilizers are applied in spring to promote shoot and leaf growth and

Healthy

N-deficient

P-deficient

K-deficient

▲ **Figure 23.7A** The most common mineral deficiencies, as seen in corn leaves

photosynthesis. However, plants require more phosphorous between May and July to promote root growth. (Phosphorous will also promote blooming in houseplants and gardens.) To harden plants for the Canadian winter, people should not apply fertilizer after July.

Organic fertilizers are composed of chemically complex organic matter such as **compost**, which is a soil-like mixture of decomposed organic matter. (Organic fertilizers may or may not be *certified organic*, a label which means that the product meets a strict set of guidelines.) Many gardeners maintain a free-standing compost pile or an enclosed compost bin to which they add leaves, grass clippings, yard waste, and kitchen scraps (but not most animal products, such as meat, fat, bone, or animal droppings). Over time, the vegetable matter breaks down because of the action of naturally occurring microbes, fungi, and animals **(Figure 23.7B)**. Occasional turning and watering will speed the composting process, producing home-grown fertilizer in several months. The compost can then be applied to outdoor gardens or indoor pots.

? **What is the most common nutrient deficiency in plants? What are the signs?**

Nitrogen deficiency; stunted growth and yellowing leaves

▼ **Figure 23.7B** Steam produced by the metabolic activity of organisms within a compost pile

23.8 Fertile soil supports plant growth

Along with climate, the major factor determining whether a plant can grow well in a particular location is the quality of the soil (see Module 23.7). Fertile soil can support abundant plant growth by providing conditions that enable plant roots to absorb water and dissolved nutrients.

Distinct layers of soil are visible in a road cut or a deep hole, such as the cross-section shown in **Figure 23.8A**. You can see three distinct soil layers, called horizons, in the cut. The A horizon, or **topsoil**, is subject to extensive weathering (freezing, drying, and erosion, for example). Topsoil is a mixture of rock particles of various sizes, living organisms, and **humus**, the remains of partially decayed organic material produced by the decomposition of dead organisms, feces, fallen leaves, and other organic matter by bacteria and fungi. The rock particles provide a large surface area that retains water and minerals while also forming air spaces containing oxygen that can diffuse into plant roots. Fertile topsoil is home to an astonishing number and variety of living organisms. About 5 billion bacteria, algae and other protists, fungi, and small animals such as earthworms, roundworms, and burrowing insects live in every teaspoon. Along with plant roots, these organisms loosen and aerate the soil and contribute organic matter to the soil as they live and die. Nearly all plants depend on bacteria and fungi in the soil to break down organic matter into inorganic molecules that roots can absorb. Besides providing nutrients, humus also tends to retain water while keeping the topsoil porous enough for good aeration of the plant roots. Topsoil is rich in organic materials and is therefore most important for plant growth. Plant roots branch out in the A horizon and usually extend into the next layer, the B horizon.

The soil's B horizon contains fewer organisms and much less organic matter than the topsoil and is less subject to weathering. Fine clay particles and nutrients dissolved in soil water drain down from the topsoil and often accumulate in the B horizon. The C horizon is composed mainly of partially broken-down rock that serves as the "parent" material for the upper layers of soil.

Figure 23.8B illustrates the intimate association between a plant's root hairs, soil water, and the tiny particles of topsoil. The root hairs are in direct contact with the water that surrounds the particles. This water is actually a solution containing dissolved inorganic ions. Oxygen diffuses into the water from small air spaces in the soil. Roots absorb this soil solution.

Cation exchange is a mechanism by which the root hairs take up certain positively charged ions (cations). Inorganic cations—such as calcium (Ca^{2+}), magnesium (Mg^{2+}), and potassium (K^+)—adhere by electrical attraction to the negatively charged surfaces of clay particles. This adhesion helps to prevent these positively charged nutrients from draining away during heavy rain or irrigation. In cation exchange **(Figure 23.8C)**, root hairs release hydrogen ions (H^+) into the soil solution. The hydrogen ions displace cations on the clay particle surfaces, and root hairs can then absorb them. The acidification of the soil by human activities can have severe impacts on a root's ability to absorb essential nutrients. Soils with low pH do not retain cations well, and the cations can leach out of the soil before being absorbed by plants. The end result is poor plant growth or even death.

In contrast to cations, negative ions (anions)—such as nitrate (NO_3^-)—are usually not bound tightly by soil particles. Unbound ions are readily available to plants, but they

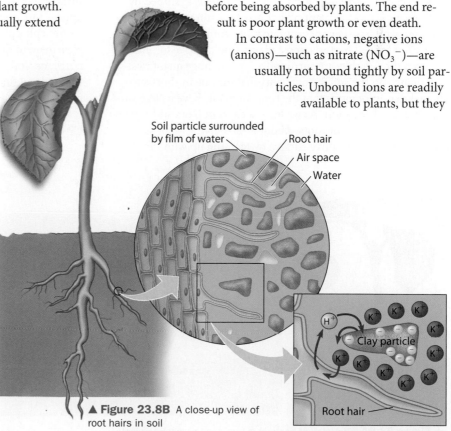

▲ Figure 23.8A Three soil horizons visible beneath grass

▲ Figure 23.8B A close-up view of root hairs in soil

Soil particle surrounded by film of water
Root hair
Air space
Water

H^+
K^+
Clay particle
Root hair

▲ Figure 23.8C Cation exchange

tend to drain out of the soil quickly because of irrigation or rainfall. If they do, the soil may become deficient in nitrogen. In the next module, we will discuss how plants obtain nitrogen despite this loss of nitrate.

It may take centuries for a soil to become fertile through the breakdown of rock and the accumulation of organic material.

The loss of soil fertility is one of our most pressing environmental problems.

? How do roots actively increase the availability of mineral nutrients that are cations?

23.9 Most plants depend on bacteria to supply nitrogen and on fungi to supply phosphorous

As discussed in the two previous modules, nitrogen deficiency is the most common nutritional problem in plants. This is puzzling when you consider that the atmosphere is nearly 80% nitrogen. But even though plants are bathed in gaseous nitrogen (N_2), they cannot absorb it directly from the air. To be used by plants, N_2 must be converted to ammonium (NH_4^+) or nitrate (NO_3^-).

Within soil, ammonium and nitrate are produced from atmospheric N_2 or from organic matter by bacteria. As shown in **Figure 23.9A**, certain soil bacteria, called nitrogen-fixing bacteria, convert atmospheric N_2 to ammonia (NH_3), a metabolic process called **nitrogen fixation**. In soil, ammonia picks up an H^+ to form an ammonium ion (NH_4^+). A second group of bacteria, called ammonifying bacteria, adds to the soil's supply of ammonium by decomposing organic matter.

Plant roots can absorb nitrogen as ammonium. However, plants acquire their nitrogen mainly in the form of nitrate (NO_3^-), which is produced in the soil by a third group of soil bacteria called nitrifying bacteria. After nitrate is absorbed by roots, enzymes within plant cells convert the nitrate back to ammonium, which is then incorporated into amino acids. Thus, were it not for soil bacteria, most plants would starve for nitrogen even though they are surrounded by it in huge quantities.

Reliance on the soil for nutrients that may be in short supply makes it imperative that the roots of plants have a large surface area for absorption. As we have seen, root hairs add a great deal of surface to plant roots. About 80% of living plant species gain even more absorptive surface by teaming up with fungi.

The micrograph in **Figure 23.9B** shows a root of a eucalyptus tree. The root is covered with a twisted mat of fungal filaments. Together, the roots and the fungus form a mutually beneficial relationship called a **mycorrhiza** ("fungus root"; see Module 39.5). The fungus benefits from a steady supply of sugar supplied by the host plant. In return, the fungus increases the surface area for water uptake and selectively absorbs phosphate and other minerals from the soil and supplies them to the plant. Fungi are very efficient at gathering nutrients from soil. Even in phosphorous-deficient soils, the mycorrhizal fungus is able to supply enough phosphorous to meet the plant's needs.

▲ Figure 23.9B Part of a eucalyptus mycorrhiza (white bar = fungal mycelium thickness)

113×

? What is the danger in applying a compound that kills bacteria to the soil around plants?

▲ Figure 23.9A The roles of bacteria in supplying nitrogen to plants

23.10 Is organically farmed food better for your health and for the environment?

If you find tomatoes labelled "organic" at a local farmers' market and at a giant grocery store chain, can you be sure they were both grown in the same way? What does the "organic" label mean? Food sold under Canada's organic logo must be grown and processed according to strict guidelines established and regulated by the Canadian Food Inspection Agency. It is a common belief that eating organic food is better for your health and for the environment. But does this impression have scientific merit?

The primary goal of organic farming is to achieve sustainable agriculture: a system embracing conservation-minded, environmentally safe, and profitable farming methods, without the use of pesticides or herbicides. Organic farming involves agricultural practices that promote biological diversity by maintaining soil quality through natural methods (rotating crops, planting cover crops, amending the soil with organic matter, and using few or no synthetic fertilizers), by providing habitat for predators of pests rather than relying mainly on synthetic pesticides, and by avoiding genetically modified organisms.

The ultimate aim of many organic farmers is to restore as much to the soil as is drawn from it, creating fields that are bountiful and self-sustaining. Many have chosen organic farming to both protect the environment and answer the growing demand for more naturally produced foods. The benefits of organic farming are clear: fewer synthetic chemicals in the environment and less risk of exposing farm workers and wildlife to potential toxins, while leaving the environment of the soil intact (see Module 24.9). Because organic fruits and vegetables are usually picked when ripe and sold locally, they may be fresher and taste better than conventional produce.

However, an organic label is no guarantee of extra health benefits. To date, there has not been a single scientific report that suggests an increased health benefit of organically grown food. Many people believe they ingest fewer chemical contaminants by choosing organic produce. Any difference, however, is insignificant relative to our daily exposure to pollutants and contaminants from other sources. For example, automobile exhaust is a major contributor of air pollution, to which we are frequently exposed **(Figure 23.10)**. Typically, our exposure is highest during daily rush-hour commutes or while waiting in a drive-through for a morning coffee and doughnut. Relative to air pollution, reducing exposure to chemical toxins in food has an insignificant impact.

Interest in organic farming is increasing in the Canadian Prairies. Before much of the area was converted into farmland, the Canadian Prairies were home to extremely diverse ecosystems with hundreds of species. Today, the prairies are a mosaic of fields, each composed of a single crop, with very few natural grasslands remaining. Single crop farms support fewer species and have low biodiversity as a result. However, organic farmers continue to improve their practices. Some are trying new growing methods that promote greater biological diversity among the plants and wildlife in their fields.

▲ **Figure 23.10** Air pollution in Calgary

Some studies have shown increased biodiversity in organic farms relative to similar conventional farms. However, other studies have shown no conclusive difference in biodiversity between regions of different farming techniques. With conflicting reports, it is difficult to make a definitive claim either way. Only about 3500 Canadian farms, accounting for 1% of Canadian farmland, are certified organic. Any benefits to biodiversity of this area are diluted by the surrounding traditional farmland. However, the organic farming industry is growing at a rate of 10% to 15% per year, making it one of the fastest-growing segments of agriculture. As more farms replace traditional practices to become farms producing certified organic foods, the benefit of organic farming to the environment may become more evident.

The idea that eating organic food is a healthier choice may be misconceived. Until scientific research can show significant benefits, this rumour will remain just that. Many who choose to eat organic foods claim that they feel healthier for doing so. Although this might be true on an individual basis, it is merely anecdotal evidence and not proof.

If you are environmentally conscious and want to make "greener" choices, buying foods from local farmers is a wise choice. Many of the foods we consume are grown far away and have to be shipped to our locations, often covering thousands of kilometres. In North America, foods are commonly transported by trucks or trains, which contribute to air pollution. Your choice to eat local foods will reduce air pollution and may be beneficial to the environment in the long term.

 If you buy "organic" apples, does that tell you anything about how they were grown or how healthy they are?

● An "organic" label indicates that the grower has been certified to follow standards meant to promote long-term agricultural sustainability. The organic designation does not mean that the produce is healthier than conventionally grown produce.

23.11 Vertical farming may help to supply the rapidly growing human population

Because the world's population reached 7 billion in October 2011 and is still growing, there is an ever-pressing need to increase agricultural yield. By the year 2050, an estimated 9 billion people will require 30% more food than we currently produce. Meeting these needs will require an additional 3.4 million hectares of farmland (about 85% of Canada's area). There is simply not enough cultivable land on Earth.

Expansion of agricultural land would also place high demands on worldwide water resources. Globally, about 75% of all freshwater use is dedicated to crop irrigation. Although irrigation can turn a desert into a garden, there is not enough water to irrigate the area required for 2050 food production. Without enough land or water, we cannot expand horizontally. We must, therefore, expand vertically. But how can we grow crops on top of each other? The answer may be as literal as the question suggests. It starts with technology already available today—greenhouses and urban agriculture.

Manipulating lighting, temperature, and water conditions, greenhouses give growers complete control over their internal environments. Furthermore, natural insect predators can be used instead of chemical pesticides and fungicides. Recreating optimal growing conditions for any crop can make any space productive. For example, greenhouses in Antarctica and on skyscraper rooftops turn these otherwise barren spaces into invaluable sources of fresh produce.

The Science Barge, docked in Yonkers, New York, is an example of urban agriculture that grows fresh produce year-round. Using solar and wind power, no pesticides, and irrigated with rainwater, this vessel represents an important step in the development of sustainable urban agriculture. Expanding on this idea, imagine a greenhouse that has multiple stories, growing a different crop on every floor (**Figure 23.11**). This is the concept of vertical farming.

To improve crop yields, most farmers use inorganic, commercially produced fertilizers containing essential minerals. As discussed in Module 23.7, fertilizers are usually enriched in nitrogen, phosphorus, and potassium, the macronutrients most commonly deficient in farm and garden soils. However, because these minerals are soluble in water, they may not be retained in the soil for long. The excess minerals are often leached from the soil by rainwater or irrigation. This mineral runoff may pollute groundwater, streams, and lakes. Vertical farms, using closed-loop hydroponic techniques (introduced in Module 23.6), can recycle water and unabsorbed nutrients, thereby eliminating this waste.

Transporting crops from the field to the consumers can be a significant cost for many growers. Moving grain by truck to elevators and then by train to distribution centres requires expensive equipment and fuel. Vertical farms can be built in urban centres, adjacent to consumers, reducing such costs. Imagine a building with barley growing on one floor, hops on another, and a microbrewery located on a third. The entire

▲ **Figure 23.11** The vertical farming concept

beer-making process, from barley to beverage, could operate under a single roof, and the only item requiring transport is the final product.

Vertical farms could be designed to optimize natural light, minimizing the need for artificial illumination. Hydroponic systems maximize the effectiveness of fertilizer. Buildings making use of these advantages can become highly productive. With the footprint of only one city block, a 30-story vertical farm can, in theory, produce enough food to sustain 50 000 people. And with enough towers, a building with a total footprint the size of a small town could feed the entire population of Canada.

While the technology exists, only Vancouver has built a vertical farm to date. Several cities across the globe have expressed interest, including Toronto and Montreal. As the population grows and food shortages become more frequent, vertical farming may become a necessity. However, when you factor in savings on water, fertilizers, pesticides, and transportation, it may be profitable to be proactive rather than reactive.

 What are three cost-saving benefits of vertical farming?

● Vertical farms save money by recycling water, preventing nutrient loss, and reducing costs associated with transportation.

23.12 Some plants have evolved other methods to acquire nutrients

Throughout this chapter we have described how plants obtain essential nutrients from the soil in which they grow. Although this describes how most plant species obtain nutrients, some highly adapted plants acquire their nutrients differently. Some plants are able to absorb nutrients from sources other than soil.

For example, an epiphyte is a plant that grows on another plant, usually anchored to branches or trunks of living trees. Examples of epiphytes include staghorn ferns and orchids, like the one shown in **Figure 23.12A**. With roots that are above ground, epiphytes absorb water and minerals from rain.

Some plants have adaptations that allow them to penetrate the vascular tissues of other plants. These parasitic plants absorb sugars and minerals from their living hosts. (This relationship is explored further in Chapter 39.) **Figure 23.12B** shows part of an oak tree parasitized by mistletoe. All the leaves you see here are mistletoe; the oak has lost its leaves for winter. Mistletoe is photosynthetic, but it supplements its diet by siphoning sap from the vascular tissue of the host tree.

A few plants are carnivores, as discussed in the chapter-opening essay. They grow in acid bogs and other habitats where soils are extremely poor in nitrogen and other minerals. In these acidic soils, organic matter decays so slowly that little inorganic

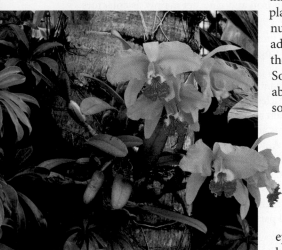

▲ **Figure 23.12A** Orchids are epiphytes that grow on the trunks of trees

▲ **Figure 23.12B** Mistletoe growing on an oak tree

▲ **Figure 23.12C** A sundew plant trapping a winged ant

nitrogen is available for plant roots to take up. Carnivorous plants obtain most of their nitrogen and some minerals by killing and digesting insects and other small animals. Few species illustrate the correlation of structure and function better than carnivorous plants. The sundew plant has modified leaves, each bearing many club-shaped filaments **(Figure 23.12C)**. A sticky, sugary secretion at the tips of the filaments attracts insects and traps them. The presence of an insect triggers the leaf to bend and envelop its prey. The filaments then secrete digestive enzymes, and the plant absorbs nutrients released as the insect is digested.

The Venus flytrap has hinged leaves that close around small insects. As insects walk on the insides of these leaves, they touch sensory hairs that trigger rapid closure of the trap. The leaf then secretes digestive enzymes and absorbs nutrients from the prey. Using insects as a source of nitrogen is a nutritional adaptation that enables carnivorous plants to thrive in soils where most other plants cannot.

? Carnivorous plants are most common in locales where the soil is deficient in _____ and _____.

nitrogen; minerals

R E V I E W

MasteringBiology® **For Practice Quizzes, BioFlix, MP3 Tutors, and Activities, go to masteringbiology.com.**

Reviewing the Concepts

The Uptake and Transport of Plant Nutrients (23.1–23.5)

23.1 Plants acquire nutrients from air, water, and soil. As a plant grows, its roots absorb water, minerals (inorganic ions), and some O_2 from the soil. Its leaves take in carbon dioxide from the air.

23.2 The plasma membranes of root cells control solute uptake. Root hairs greatly increase a root's absorptive surface. Water and solutes can move through the root's epidermis and cortex by going either through cells or between them. However, all water and solutes must pass through the selectively permeable plasma membranes of cells of the endodermis to enter the xylem (water-conducting tissue) for transport upward.

23.3 Transpiration pulls water up xylem vessels. Transpiration can move xylem sap, consisting of water and dissolved inorganic nutrients, to the top of the tallest tree.

Transpiration (regulated by guard cells surrounding stomata)

H_2O

Cohesion and adhesion in xylem (cohesion of H_2O molecules to each other and adhesion of H_2O molecules to cell walls)

Water uptake (via root hairs)

H_2O

Flow of water

23.4 Guard cells control transpiration. By changing shape, guard cells generally keep stomata open during the day (allowing transpiration) but closed at night (preventing excess water loss).

23.5 Phloem transports sugars. By a pressure flow mechanism, phloem transports food molecules made by photosynthesis. At a sugar source, sugar is loaded into a phloem tube. The sugar raises the solute concentration in the tube, and water follows, raising the pressure in the tube. As sugar is removed at a sugar sink, water follows. The increase in pressure at the sugar source and the decrease at the sugar sink cause phloem sap to flow from source to sink.

Sugar

Water

Source cell (in leaf)

Sieve plate

Sink cell (in storage root)

Sugar

Water

Plant Nutrients and the Soil (23.6–23.12)

23.6 Plant health depends on the acquisition of essential inorganic nutrients. A plant must obtain usable sources of the chemical elements—inorganic nutrients—it requires from its surroundings. Macronutrients, such as carbon and nitrogen, are needed in large amounts, mostly to build organic molecules. Micronutrients, including iron and zinc, act mainly as cofactors of enzymes.

23.7 Fertilizers can help to prevent nutrient deficiencies. Nutrient deficiencies can often be recognized and then fixed by using appropriate fertilizers.

23.8 Fertile soil supports plant growth. Fertile soil contains a mixture of small rock and clay particles that hold water and ions and also allow O_2 to diffuse into plant roots. Humus (decaying organic material) provides nutrients and supports the growth of organisms that enhance soil fertility. Anions (negatively charged ions), such as nitrate (NO_3^-), are readily available to plants because they are not bound to soil particles. However, anions tend to drain out of soil rapidly. Cations (positively charged ions), such as K^+, adhere to soil particles. In cation exchange, root hairs release H^+, which displaces cations from soil particles; the root hairs then absorb the free cations.

23.9 Most plants depend on bacteria to supply nitrogen and on fungi to supply phosphorous. Relationships with other organisms help plants obtain nutrients. Bacteria in the soil convert atmospheric N_2 to forms that can be used by plants. Mycorrhizal fungi absorb most of the phosphorous in the soil and pass it on to the plant root.

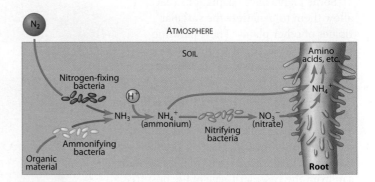

N_2

ATMOSPHERE

SOIL

Amino acids, etc.

Nitrogen-fixing bacteria

H^+

NH_4^+

NH_3 NH_4^+ (ammonium)

Nitrifying bacteria

NO_3^- (nitrate)

Ammonifying bacteria

Organic material

Root

23.10 Is organically grown food better for your health and for the environment? To earn the certified organic designation, food must be grown and processed following a strict set of guidelines. Though these guidelines make organically grown food better for the environment, human health benefits have not been documented.

23.11 Vertical farming may help to supply the rapidly growing human population. To meet the demands of an ever-growing human population, farming vertically in skyscrapers may be an essential strategy in the future.

23.12 Some plants have evolved other methods to acquire nutrients. Epiphytes are plants that grow on other plants. Parasitic plants siphon sap from host plants. Carnivorous plants can obtain nitrogen by digesting insects.

Connecting the Concepts

1. Fill in the blanks in this concept map to help you tie together key concepts concerning transport in plants.

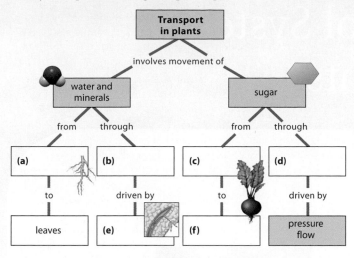

Testing Your Knowledge

Multiple Choice

2. Plants require the smallest amount of which of the following nutrients?
   a. oxygen
   b. phosphorus
   c. carbon
   d. iron
   e. hydrogen

3. Which of the following activities of soil bacteria does *not* contribute to creating usable nitrogen supplies for plant use?
   a. the fixation of atmospheric nitrogen
   b. the conversion of ammonium ions to nitrate ions
   c. the decomposition of dead animals
   d. the assembly of amino acids into proteins
   e. the generation of ammonium from proteins in dead leaves

4. By trapping insects, carnivorous plants obtain _____, which they need _____. *(Pick the best answer.)*
   a. water; because they live in dry soil
   b. nitrogen; to make sugar
   c. phosphorus; to make protein
   d. sugars; because they can't make enough by photosynthesis
   e. nitrogen; to make protein

5. The opening of the stomata during daylight involves
   a. the movement of potassium ions into the guard cells.
   b. an increase in turgor pressure of the guard cells.
   c. an efflux of protons from the guard cells.
   d. a shape change of the guard cells.
   e. All of the above will complete this statement correctly.

6. A corn plant that is grown in phosphate-deficient soil will first exhibit which of the following symptoms?
   a. yellowing of the midrib of the leaf
   b. yellowing of the edges (fringe) of the leaf
   c. reddish-purple coloration of the leaf edges
   d. necrosis (tissue death) at the edges of the leaf
   e. reddish-purple coloration of the midrib of the leaf

Describing, Comparing, and Explaining

7. Describe the movement of xylem sap and phloem sap.

8. Explain how guard cells limit water loss from a plant on a hot, dry day. How can this be harmful to the plant?

Applying the Concepts

9. Acid rain contains an excess of hydrogen ions (H^+). One effect of acid rain is to deplete the soil of plant nutrients such as calcium (Ca^{2+}), potassium (K^+), and magnesium (Mg^{2+}). Offer a hypothesis to explain why acid rain washes these nutrients from the soil. How might you test your hypothesis?

10. In some situations, the application of nitrogen fertilizer to crops has to be increased each year because the fertilizer decreases the rate of nitrogen fixation in the soil. Propose a hypothesis to explain this phenomenon. Describe a test for your hypothesis. What results would you expect from your test?

11. Transpiration is fastest when humidity is low and temperature is high, but in some plants it seems to increase in response to light as well. During one 12-hour period when cloud cover and light intensity varied frequently, a scientist studying a certain crop plant recorded the data in the table below. (The transpiration rates are grams of water per square metre of leaf area per hour.)

Time (hr)	Temperature (°C)	Humidity (%)	Light (% of full sun)	Transpiration Rate (g/m² · hr)
8 AM	14	88	22	57
9	14	82	27	72
10	21	86	58	83
11	26	78	35	125
12 PM	27	78	88	161
1	33	65	75	199
2	31	61	50	186
3	30	70	24	107
4	29	69	50	137
5	22	75	45	87
6	18	80	24	78
7	13	91	8	45

Do these data support the hypothesis that the plants transpire more when the light is more intense? If so, is the effect independent of temperature and humidity? Explain your answer. (*Hint:* Look for overall trends in each column, and then compare pairs of data within each column and between columns.)

Answers to all questions can be found in Appendix E.

Control Systems in Plants

BIG IDEAS

Plant Hormones

(24.1–24.9)

Chemical signals help to regulate many important processes within a plant's body.

Responses to Stimuli

(24.10–24.14)

Plants respond to environmental stimuli in a variety of ways.

The Plant Social Network

Communication between animals is well known and fairly well understood, but what about among the plants? Recent research about plant behaviour and communication has produced some very exciting and intriguing results. We are slowly starting to understand the basics of how plants communicate with others. Plants can communicate with members of their own species, with plants of different species, and even with animals. How can plants communicate without uttering a word? Plants "talk" through the release of volatile chemicals.

Volatile chemicals, produced within the leaves, escape through the stomata into the atmosphere. This chemical "voice" can be perceived by nearby individuals and elicit a response. This occurrence is similar to an animal releasing a pheromone into the environment, which triggers a response in another of its species. Usually pheromones are used in mating to entice or stimulate a potential partner. The difference is that a plant can release a variety of chemical cues that are perceived by different species as well as its own.

Plants that are wounded by grazing herbivores often send out a chemical signal to neighbouring companions. For example, the acacia tree in Africa releases a chemical SOS when being grazed upon by herbivores. (The smell of freshly cut grass is a similar distress call caused by injury.) When the smell is detected by neighbouring acacias, they start augmenting their defences in case the hungry herbivore moves over to them. To defend themselves, the acacia produces alkaloids and cyanide, which make their leaves taste bitter and toxic.

Plants also use these chemical signals to distinguish family members within a population. Dr. Susan Dudley at McMaster University discovered that the sea rocket common to the Great Lakes area (shown in the photograph) can distinguish its kin from strangers. A sea rocket growing beside a stranger grows an extensive root mass to give it a competitive edge. However, a neighbouring family member does not elicit this aggressive strategy. In this case, chemical signals identify kinship and conservative root growth minimizes competition with familial neighbours. Whether the signals are deliberately sent remains unknown. Regardless, other plants respond to them.

Plants can also communicate with members of different species. Whether this type of communication is intentional or more like eavesdropping remains unknown. Nevertheless, detecting a signal warning of herbivory would be beneficial to any plant in the vicinity, regardless of species. Plants that can "listen in" on warnings from others gain benefit by ramping up their own defences against herbivores. Wild tobacco plants have been shown to increase nicotine production after a neighbouring sagebrush has been injured by a herbivore. Nicotine is extremely toxic to most insect herbivores. Many plants can attract the predators of their herbivores. For example, after being fed upon by caterpillars, plants can release chemicals that attract wasps to come and kill the caterpillar. You will learn more about how plants communicate with animals in the last module of this chapter.

Also in this chapter, we explore other chemical signals within a plant called plant hormones. Similar to the hormones of animals, plant hormones control how the organism functions, including plant growth, movement, flowering, fruit development, and even defence.

Plant Hormones

24.1 Experiments on how plants turn toward light led to the discovery of a plant hormone

The shoots of a house plant sitting on a windowsill grow toward light **(Figure 24.1A)**. If you rotate the plant, it soon reorients its growth until the leaves again face the window. Any growth response that results in plant organs curving toward or away from stimuli is called a **tropism** (from the Greek *tropos*, turn). The growth of a shoot in response to light is called **phototropism**. Phototropism has an obvious evolutionary advantage: directing growing seedlings and the shoots of mature plants toward the sunlight that drives photosynthesis.

Microscopic observations of plants growing toward light reveal the cellular mechanism that underlies phototropism. **Figure 24.1B** shows a grass seedling curving toward light that comes from one side. As the enlargement shows, cells on the darker side of the seedling are larger—actually, they have elongated faster—than those on the brighter side. The different cellular growth rates made the shoot bend toward the light. If a seedling is illuminated uniformly from all sides or if it is kept in the dark, the cells all elongate at a similar rate and so the seedling grows straight upward.

A **hormone** is a chemical signal produced in one part of the body and transported to other parts via the circulatory system, where it acts on target cells to elicit a response. In Chapter 29, you will learn about animal hormones. Like animals, plants also produce chemical signals that elicit effects on distant cells. Studies of plant responses to light led to the first evidence of a plant hormone. Some key discoveries about plant hormones emerged from a series of classic experiments conducted by two scientists with a very famous name.

Showing That Light Is Detected by the Shoot Tip
In the late 1800s, Charles Darwin and his son Francis conducted some of the earliest experiments on phototropism. They observed that grass seedlings could bend toward light only if the tips of their shoots were present. The first five grass plants in **Figure 24.1C** summarize the Darwins' findings. ❶ When they removed the tip of a grass shoot, the shoot did not curve toward the light as did the control. ❷ The shoot also remained straight when the Darwins placed an opaque cap on its tip. ❸ However, the shoot curved normally when they placed a transparent cap on its tip or ❹ an opaque shield around its base. The Darwins concluded that the tip of the shoot was responsible for sensing light. They also recognized that the growth response, the bending of the shoot, occurs in cells that are below the tip.

▲ **Figure 24.1A**
A houseplant growing toward light

Illuminated side of shoot — Shaded side of shoot

Light

Light

Control | Tip removed ❶ | Tip covered by opaque cap ❷ | Tip covered by transparent cap ❸ | Base covered by opaque shield ❹

Darwin and Darwin (1880)

▲ **Figure 24.1B** Phototropism in a grass seedling

▲ **Figure 24.1C** Early experiments on phototropism: detection of light by shoot tips and evidence for a chemical signal

Therefore, they speculated that some signal must be transmitted from the tip downward to the growth region of the shoot.

A few decades later, Danish plant biologist Peter Boysen-Jensen further tested the chemical signal idea of the Darwins. ❺ In one group of seedlings, Boysen-Jensen inserted a block of gelatin between the tip and the lower part of the shoot (Figure 24.1C). The gelatin prevented cellular contact but allowed chemicals to diffuse through. The seedlings with gelatin blocks behaved normally, bending toward light. ❻ In a second set of seedlings, Boysen-Jensen inserted a thin piece of the mineral mica under the shoot tip. Mica is an impermeable barrier, and the seedlings with mica had no phototropic response. These experiments supported the hypothesis that the signal for phototropism is a mobile chemical.

Isolating the Chemical Signal

In 1926, Frits Went, a Dutch graduate student, modified Boysen-Jensen's techniques and extracted the chemical messenger for phototropism in grasses. As shown in **Figure 24.1D**, Went first removed the tips of grass seedlings and placed them on blocks of agar, a gelatin-like material. He reasoned that the chemical messenger (pink in the figure) from the shoot tips should diffuse into the agar and that the blocks should then be able to substitute for the shoot tips. Went tested the effects of the agar blocks on tipless seedlings, which he kept in the dark to eliminate the effect of light. ❶ First, he centred the treated agar blocks on the cut tips of a batch of seedlings. These plants grew straight upward. They also grew faster than the decapitated control seedlings, which hardly grew at all. Went concluded that the agar had absorbed the chemical messenger produced in the shoot tip and that the chemical had passed into the shoot and stimulated it to grow. ❷ He then placed agar blocks off centre on another batch of tipless seedlings. These plants bent away from the side with the chemical-laden agar block, as though growing toward light. ❸ Control seedlings with blank agar blocks (whether offset or not) grew no more than the control. Went concluded that the agar block contained a chemical produced in

the shoot tip, that this chemical stimulated growth as it passed down the shoot, and that a shoot curved toward light because of a higher concentration of the growth-promoting chemical on the darker side. Went called this chemical messenger, or hormone, auxin. In the 1930s, biochemists determined the chemical structure of Went's auxin.

The classical hypothesis for what causes grass shoots to grow toward light, based on these early experiments, is that an uneven distribution of auxin moving down from the shoot tip causes cells on the darker side to elongate faster than cells on the brighter side. Studies with plants other than grass shoots, however, do not always support this hypothesis. For example, there is no evidence that light from one side causes an uneven distribution of auxin in the stems of sunflowers or other eudicots. There is, however, a greater concentration of substances that may act as growth inhibitors on the lighted side of a stem.

The discovery of auxin stimulated discoveries of a wide variety of plant hormones. The next six modules will introduce some of the major plant hormones and the roles they play in the lives of plants.

? How do the experiments illustrated in Figures 24.1C and 24.1D provide evidence that phototropism depends on a chemical signal?

● Light is detected by the shoot tip, but the bending response occurs farther down the shoot. The fact that the signal can pass through a barrier that prevents cell contact but allows chemicals to pass suggests that the signal is a chemical.

The shoot tip is placed on an agar block. A chemical (later called auxin) diffuses from the shoot tip into the agar.

Agar

❶ The block with the chemical stimulates growth.

Control

❷ Offset blocks with the chemical stimulate curved growth.

❸ Other controls: Blocks with no chemical have no effect.

No light

❺ Tip separated by gelatin block

❻ Tip separated by mica

Boysen-Jensen (1913)

Went (1926)

▲ **Figure 24.1D** Went's experiments: isolation of the chemical signal

24.2 Five major types of hormones regulate plant growth and development

Plant hormones are produced in very low concentrations. But similar to animal hormones, a tiny amount of hormone can have a profound effect on growth and development. The binding of a hormone to a specific cell-surface receptor triggers a signal transduction pathway (see Module 11.10) that amplifies the hormonal signal and leads to one or more responses within the cell. In general, plant hormones control whole-body activities such as growth and development by affecting the division, elongation, and differentiation of cells.

Plant biologists have identified five major types of plant hormones, previewed in **Table 24.2**. There are other hormones important to plants that we will not discuss in this chapter, and some of the "hormones" listed in the table actually represent a group of related hormones; such cases will be mentioned in the

text. Notice that all five types of hormones stimulate or inhibit cell division and elongation, thereby influencing growth.

As Table 24.2 indicates, each hormone has multiple effects, depending on its site of action, its concentration, and the developmental stage of the plant. In most situations, no single hormone acts alone. Instead, it is usually the balance of several hormones—their relative concentrations—that controls the growth and development of a plant. These interactions will become apparent as we survey the five major types of plant hormones and their functions.

 ? Hormones elicit cellular responses by binding to cell-surface receptors and triggering _____.

signal transduction pathways ●

TABLE 24.2 | MAJOR TYPES OF PLANT HORMONES

Hormone (Module)	Major Functions	Where Produced or Found in the Plant
Auxins (24.3)	Stimulate stem elongation; affect root growth, differentiation, branching, development of fruit, apical dominance, phototropism, and gravitropism (response to gravity)	Meristems of apical buds, young leaves. embryos within seeds
Cytokinins (24.4)	Affect root growth and differentiation; stimulate cell division and growth; stimulate germination; delay aging	Made in the roots and transported to other organs
Gibberellins (24.5)	Promote seed germination, bud development, stem elongation, and leaf growth; stimulate flowering and fruit development: affect root growth and differentiation	Meristems of apical buds and roots, young leaves, embryos
Abscisic acid (ABA) (24.6)	Inhibits growth: closes stomata during water stress; helps to maintain dormancy	Leaves, stems, roots, green fruits
Ethylene (24.7)	Promotes fruit ripening; opposes some auxin effects; promotes or inhibits growth and development of roots, leaves, and flowers, depending on species	Ripening fruits, nodes of stems, aging leaves and flowers

24.3 Auxin stimulates the elongation of cells in young shoots

The term **auxin** is used for any chemical substance that promotes seedling elongation, although auxins have multiple functions in flowering plants. The major natural auxin in plants is indoleacetic acid (IAA), although several other compounds, including some synthetic ones, have auxin activity. When we use the term *auxin* in this text, however, we are referring specifically to IAA.

Figure 24.3A shows the effect of auxin on a mustard plant called *Arabidopsis thaliana*. The plant on the right is a wild-type *Arabidopsis*. The plant on the left contains a mutation in the auxin gene. The result of this mutation is a lack of auxin protein, which in turn results in stunted growth.

The apical meristem at the tip of a shoot (see Module 22.7) is a major site of auxin synthesis. As auxin moves downward, diffusing from cell to cell, it stimulates growth of the stem by making cells elongate. As the blue curve in **Figure 24.3B** shows, auxin promotes cell elongation in stems only within

▶ **Figure 24.3A** The effect of auxin (IAA): comparing a wild-type *Arabidopsis* plant (right) with one that underproduces auxin (left)

▲ **Figure 24.3B** The effect of auxin concentration on cell elongation

a certain concentration range. Above a certain concentration (0.9 g of auxin per litre of solution, in this case), it usually inhibits cell elongation in stems, probably by inducing the production of ethylene, a hormone that generally counters the effects of auxin (see Module 24.7).

The red curve on the graph shows the effect of auxin on root growth. On the one hand, an auxin concentration too low to stimulate shoot cells will cause root cells to elongate. On the other hand, an auxin concentration high enough to make stem cells elongate is in the concentration range that inhibits root cell elongation. Higher concentrations benefit the plant by promoting stem growth while inhibiting root growth nearer to the sites of auxin production. These effects of auxin on cell elongation reinforce two points: (1) the same chemical messenger may have different effects at different concentrations in one target cell, and (2) a given concentration of the hormone may have different effects on different target cells. In fact, some herbicides (including the infamous Vietnam War defoliant Agent Orange used between 1961 and 1971) contain synthetic auxins at high concentrations that kill plants through hormonal overdose.

How does auxin make plant cells elongate? One hypothesis is that auxin initiates elongation by weakening cell walls. As shown in **Figure 24.3C**, ❶ auxin may stimulate certain proteins in a plant cell's plasma membrane to pump hydrogen ions into the cell wall, lowering the pH within the wall. The low pH ❷ activates enzymes that separate cross-linking molecules from cellulose microfibrils in the wall (see Figure 3.7). ❸ The cross-linking molecules are now more exposed to enzymes that loosen the cell wall. ❹ The cell then swells with water and elongates because its weakened wall no longer resists the cell's tendency to take up water via osmosis. After this initial elongation caused by the uptake of water, the cell sustains the growth by synthesizing more cell wall material and cytoplasm. These processes are also stimulated by auxin.

Auxin produces a number of other effects in addition to stimulating cell elongation and causing stems and roots to lengthen. For example, it induces cell division in the vascular cambium, thus promoting growth in stem diameter (see Module 22.8). Also, auxin produced by developing seeds promotes the growth of fruit. Sometimes commercial fruit growers add synthetic auxins. For instance, greenhouse tomatoes typically have fewer seeds than tomatoes grown outdoors, resulting in poorly developed fruits. Therefore, growers spray synthetic auxins on tomato vines to induce normal fruit development, making it possible to grow commercial tomatoes in greenhouses.

? Suppose you had a tiny pH electrode that could measure the pH of a plant cell's wall. How could you use it to test the hypothesis in Figure 24.3C for how auxin stimulates cell elongation?

● The hypothesis predicts that addition of auxin to the cell should lower the pH of the cell wall (make it more acidic). You could test this prediction with your pH electrode by measuring the cell wall pH in the presence of auxin (experimental group) or the absence of auxin (control group).

▲ **Figure 24.3C** A hypothesis to explain how auxin stimulates cell elongation

24.4 Cytokinins stimulate cell division

Cytokinins are a group of closely related hormones that promote cytokinesis, or cell division. A number of cytokinins have been extracted from plants; the most common is zeatin, so named because it was first discovered in corn (*Zea mays*). Also, several synthetic cytokinins have been manufactured. Natural cytokinins are produced in actively growing tissues, particularly in roots, embryos, and fruits. Cytokinins made in the roots reach target tissues in stems by moving upward in xylem sap.

Plant biologists have found that cytokinins enhance the division, growth, and development of plant cells grown in culture. Cytokinins also retard the aging of flowers and leaves. Thus, florists use cytokinin sprays to keep cut flowers fresh.

Cytokinins and auxin interact in the control of *apical dominance*, the ability of the terminal bud of a shoot to suppress the growth of the axillary buds (see Module 22.3). **Figure 24.4A** shows the results of a simple experiment that demonstrates this effect. Both basil plants pictured are the same age. The one on the left has an intact terminal bud on the main shoot; the one on the right had the terminal bud of the main shoot removed several weeks earlier. In the plant on the left, apical dominance inhibited growth of the axillary buds (the buds that produce side branches). As a result, the shoot grew in height but did not branch out to the sides very much. In the plant on the right, the lack of a terminal bud on the main shoot resulted in the activation of the axillary buds, making the plant grow more branches and become bushy.

The leading hypothesis to explain the hormonal regulation of apical dominance—known as the direct inhibition hypothesis—proposes that auxin and cytokinin act antagonistically (with the action of one opposing the action of the other) in regulating axillary bud growth. According to this view, auxin transported down the shoot from the terminal bud directly inhibits axillary buds from growing, causing a shoot to lengthen at the expense of lateral branching

▲ **Figure 24.4A** Apical dominance in a bean plant resulting from the action of auxin and cytokinins

(Figure 24.4B). Meanwhile, cytokinins entering the shoot system from the roots counter the action of auxin by signalling axillary buds to begin growing when auxin concentrations are low (see Figure 24.4B). Thus, the ratio of auxin to cytokinin is viewed as the critical factor in controlling axillary bud inhibition. Many observations and experiments are consistent with the direct inhibition hypothesis. It now appears, however, that the effects of auxin are partially indirect. Recent research suggests that the flow of auxin down the

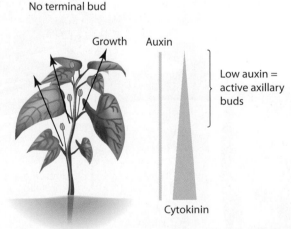

▲ **Figure 24.4B** The direct inhibition hypothesis

shoot triggers the synthesis of a newly discovered plant hormone that represses bud growth. Thus, the direct inhibition hypothesis does not account for all experimental findings, and it is likely that plant biologists have not uncovered all the pieces of this puzzle. The role of plant hormones in apical dominance remains an area of active research.

24.5 Gibberellins affect stem elongation and have numerous other effects

Farmers in Asia have long noticed that some rice seedlings in their paddies grew so tall and spindly that they toppled over before they could produce grain. In the 1920s, Japanese scientists discovered that a fungus of the genus *Gibberella* caused this "foolish seedling disease." By the 1930s, Japanese scientists had determined that the fungus produced hyperelongation of rice stems by secreting a chemical, which was given the name **gibberellin**. In the 1950s, researchers discovered that gibberellin exists naturally in plants, where it is a growth regulator. Foolish seedling disease occurs when rice plants infected with the *Gibberella* fungus get an overdose of gibberellin.

Dwarf plant (untreated)   Dwarf plant treated with gibberellins

▲ **Figure 24.5A** Reversing dwarfism in pea plants with gibberellins

More than 100 different gibberellins have been identified in plants. Roots and young leaves are major sites of gibberellin production. One of the main effects of gibberellins is to stimulate cell elongation and cell division in stems and leaves. This action generally enhances that of auxin and can be demonstrated when certain dwarf plant varieties (such as the dwarf pea plant variety studied by Mendel; see Module 9.1) grow to normal height after treatment with gibberellins **(Figure 24.5A)**.

Gibberellin-induced stem elongation can also cause bolting, the rapid growth of a floral stalk **(Figure 24.5B)**. Bolting can frustrate gardeners because it often renders the plant unpalatable. In many plants, both auxin and gibberellins must be present for fruit to develop. The most important commercial application of gibberellins

▲ **Figure 24.5B** A parsley plant bolting, a result of too much gibberellin

▲ **Figure 24.5C** Gibberellin-treated grapes (left) and untreated grapes (right)

is in the production of the Thompson variety of seedless grapes. Gibberellins make the grapes grow farther apart in a cluster (which increases air flow and decreases rotting) and produces larger grapes, a trait desired by most shoppers **(Figure 24.5C)**.

Gibberellins are also important in seed germination in many plants. Many seeds that require special environmental conditions to germinate, such as exposure to light or cold temperatures, will germinate when sprayed with gibberellins. In nature, gibberellins in seeds are probably the link between environmental cues and the metabolic processes that renew growth of the embryo. For example, when water becomes available to a grass seed, it causes the embryo in the seed to release gibberellins, which promote germination by mobilizing nutrients stored within the seed. In some plants, gibberellins seem to be interacting antagonistically with another hormone, abscisic acid, which we discuss next.

24.6 Abscisic acid inhibits many plant processes

In the 1960s, one research group studying bud dormancy and another team investigating leaf abscission (the dropping of autumn leaves) isolated the same compound, **abscisic acid (ABA)**. Ironically, ABA is no longer thought to play a primary role in either bud dormancy or leaf abscission (for which it was named), but it is a plant hormone of great importance in other functions. In contrast to the growth-stimulating hormones we have studied so far—auxin, cytokinins, and gibberellins—ABA *slows* growth. ABA often counteracts the actions of growth hormones; it is the ratio of ABA to one or more growth hormones that often determines the final outcome.

Seed dormancy (a period of inactivity of the seed) is an evolutionary adaptation that ensures that a seed will germinate only when there are favourable conditions of light, temperature, and moisture. What prevents a seed dispersed in autumn from germinating immediately, only to be killed by winter? For that matter, what prevents seeds from germinating in the dark, moist interior of fruit? ABA is the answer. Levels of ABA may increase a hundredfold during seed maturation. The high levels of ABA in maturing seeds inhibit germination. Many types of dormant seeds therefore germinate only when ABA is removed or inactivated in some way. For example, some seeds require prolonged exposure to cold to trigger ABA inactivation. In these plants, the breakdown of ABA in the winter is required for seed germination in the spring. The seeds of some desert plants remain dormant in parched and/or frozen soil until a downpour washes ABA out of the seeds, allowing them to germinate. For example, the arctic heather in **Figure 24.6** grew from seeds that were dormant in frozen soils for months.

As we saw in the previous module, gibberellins promote seed germination. For many plants, it is actually the ratio of

▲ Figure 24.6 Arctic heather blooming in Nunavut after the spring thaw

ABA to gibberellins that determines whether the seed will remain dormant or germinate.

In addition to its role in dormancy, ABA is the primary internal signal that enables plants to withstand drought. When a plant begins to wilt, ABA accumulates in its leaves and causes stomata to close rapidly (see Module 23.4). This closing of stomata reduces transpiration and prevents further water loss. In some cases, water shortage can stress the root system before the shoot system. ABA transported from roots to leaves may function as an "early warning system."

 Which two hormones regulate seed dormancy and germination? What are their opposing effects?

● Abscisic acid maintains seed dormancy. Gibberellins promote seed germination.

24.7 Ethylene triggers fruit ripening and other aging processes

During the 1800s, leakage from gas streetlights caused the leaves on nearby trees to drop prematurely. In 1901, scientists demonstrated that this effect was due to the gas **ethylene**, a by-product of coal combustion. We now know that plants produce their own ethylene, which functions as a hormone that triggers a variety of aging responses, including fruit ripening and pro-grammed cell death. Ethylene is also produced in response to stresses such as drought, flooding, injury, and infection.

Fruit Ripening A burst of ethylene production in a fruit triggers its ripening. In an example of positive feedback, ethylene triggers ripening, which then triggers more ethylene production, resulting in a surge of released gas. And because ethylene is a gas, the signal to ripen can spread from fruit to fruit: One bad apple really can spoil the bunch! The ripening process includes the enzymatic breakdown of cell walls, which softens the fruit, and the conversion of starches and acids to sugars,

which makes the fruit sweet. The production of new scents and colours attracts animals, which eat the fruits and disperse the seeds.

You can make some fruits ripen faster if you store them in a bag so that the ethylene gas accumulates. **Figure 24.7A** shows two bananas that began unripe and were stored for the same time period in bags under different conditions: alone (above) and with an ethylene-releasing peach (below). As you can see, the ethylene released by the ripening peach resulted in a riper (darker) banana. On a commercial scale,

▲ Figure 24.7A The effect of ethylene on the ripening of bananas

many kinds of fruit—tomatoes, for instance—are often picked green and then ripened in huge storage bins into which ethylene gas is piped.

In other cases, growers take measures to slow down the ripening action of natural ethylene. Stored apples are often flushed with CO_2, which inhibits ethylene synthesis. Also, air is circulated around the apples to prevent ethylene from accumulating. In this way, apples picked in autumn can be stored for sale the following summer.

The Falling of Leaves Like fruit ripening, the changes that occur in deciduous trees each autumn—colour changes, drying, and the loss of leaves—are also aging processes. Leaves lose their green colour because chlorophyll is broken down during autumn. Fall colours result from a combination of new red pigments made in autumn and the exposure of yellow and orange pigments that were already present in the leaf but masked by dark green chlorophyll. Autumn leaf drop is an adaptation that helps to keep the tree from drying out in winter. Without its leaves, a tree loses less water by evaporation when its roots cannot take up water from the frozen ground. Before leaves fall, many essential elements are salvaged from them and stored in the stem, where they can be recycled into new leaves the following spring.

When an autumn leaf falls, the base of the leaf stalk separates from the stem. The separation region is called the abscission layer. As indicated in **Figure 24.7B**, the abscission layer consists of a narrow band of cells with thin walls that are further weakened when enzymes digest the cell walls. The leaf drops off when its weight, often helped by wind, splits the abscission layer apart. Notice the protective layer of cells next to the abscission layer. Even before the leaf falls, these cells form a leaf scar on the stem. Dead cells covering the scar help to protect the plant from infectious organisms.

Leaf drop is triggered by environmental stimuli, including the shortening days of autumn and, to a lesser extent, cooler temperatures. These stimuli apparently cause a change in the balance of ethylene and auxin. The auxin prevents abscission and helps to maintain the leaf's metabolism; but, as a leaf ages, it produces less auxin. Meanwhile, cells begin producing ethylene, which stimulates formation of the abscission layer. The ethylene primes the abscission layer to split by promoting the synthesis of enzymes that digest cell walls in the layer.

Leaf stalk (petiole)

Stem

Protective layer

Abscission layer

Stem | Leaf stalk

LM 20×

▲ **Figure 24.7B** The abscission layer at the base of a leaf

We have now completed our survey of the five major types of plant hormones. Before moving on to the topic of plant behaviour, let's explore the rumour that only deciduous trees lose their leaves.

 Plant biologists sometimes refer to ethylene as the "aging hormone." What is the basis for this term?

● Many of ethylene's functions, including fruit ripening and leaf abscission, are associated with aging-like changes in cells.

RUMOUR HAS IT **24.8 Is it only deciduous trees and shrubs that lose their leaves?**

There are a number of misconceptions surrounding different types of trees and shrubs. As you read in Chapter 19, both trees and shrubs are seed plants, which can be found among two groups of plants: the gymnosperms (conifers) and the angiosperms (flowering plants). The cone-bearing gymnosperm trees are referred to as the conifers. Angiosperm trees are commonly called broadleaf trees. Another pair of terms that is commonly used to describe trees is evergreen or deciduous. Evergreen trees are those that have leaves

year-round, whereas deciduous trees lose all of their leaves seasonally.

Common misconceptions surround the terminology. Many people think that all conifers are evergreen trees and all broadleaf trees are deciduous. This overgeneralization, however, is not correct for all species. Most conifers are indeed evergreens. The pines, firs, and spruce trees that may grow in your neighbourhood are forever green, keeping their leaves (needles) year-round. However, there are species of gymnosperms that

▲ **Figure 24.8A** The larch loses its needles in autumn

▲ **Figure 24.8B** The Pacific madrone covered in snow

are deciduous. The larch (*Larix laricina*), for example, is a gymnosperm tree that grows throughout Canada (**Figure 24.8A**). The larch loses its needles every autumn after they turn a brilliant gold—it is deciduous.

It is true that the vast majority of broadleaf trees in Canada are deciduous. It is difficult for delicate leaves to survive our harsh winters. Therefore, each autumn, broadleaf trees across Canada lose their leaves in a spectacular display of yellows, reds, and oranges. One notable exception is the Pacific madrone (*Arbutus menziesii*). Native to the milder climate of Vancouver Island and neighbouring mainland, the evergreen Pacific madrone holds its thick, leathery leaves for multiple growing seasons. **Figure 24.8B** shows a snow-laden branch with fruit, commonly called snowberries. Rhododendrons, *Euonymus*, and boxwood are all examples of evergreen shrubs. If you travel south to warmer climates, you are certain to find other examples of broadleaf evergreen trees such as the magnolia tree. The leaves of all broadleaf evergreens share a similar durable structure.

But is it only deciduous trees that lose leaves? Dropping leaves in fall is an adaptation to protect trees during the winter months. The leaves of a deciduous tree or shrub have a lifespan limited to a few months during the summer. Similarly, the leaves of evergreens also have a finite lifespan, at the end of which they drop from the bases of the older branches. Spruce needles may last up to six years, and healthy spruce trees continually shed old leaves, but mostly in the spring. Pine needles can last between two and five years and are shed more frequently in the fall. Leaf drop in evergreens is readily apparent by the masses of brown, dried needles that collect at their bases. Because only the older, worn-out leaves drop from the tree and younger leaves remain, evergreen trees appear forever green. As you read in the previous module, ethylene and auxin are involved in the abscission of leaves. This is true in both deciduous and evergreen trees.

To clear up any misunderstandings, not all conifers are evergreen and not all broadleaf trees and shrubs are deciduous. The misconception that only deciduous trees lose their leaves is untrue. All trees lose leaves. Deciduous trees just lose them all at once. In the next module, we will look at the agricultural uses of some plant hormones.

 Why do the leaves of broadleaf evergreen trees tend to be thick and leathery?

● Thick, leathery leaves are an adaptation that makes them more durable and longer lasting.

24.9 Plant hormones have many agricultural uses

Although a lot remains to be learned about plant hormones, much of what we do know has a direct application to agriculture. As already mentioned, the control of fruit ripening and the production of seedless fruits are two of several major uses of these chemicals. Plant hormones also enable farmers to control when plants will drop their fruit. For instance, synthetic auxins are often used to prevent orange and grapefruit trees from dropping their fruit before they can be picked.

Figure 24.9 shows a fruit grower spraying a grove with auxins. The quantity of auxin must be carefully monitored because too much of the hormone may stimulate the plant to release more ethylene, making the fruit ripen and drop off sooner. Indeed, large doses of auxins are sometimes used to *promote* premature fruit drop. With apple and olive trees, for example, auxin may be sprayed on some fruit to cause them to drop prematurely; then the remaining fruit will grow larger. Ethylene is used similarly on peaches and plums, and it is sometimes sprayed on berries, grapes, and cherries to loosen the fruit so it can be picked by machines.

In combination with auxin, gibberellins are used to produce seedless fruits, as mentioned in Module 24.5. Sprayed on other kinds of plants, at an earlier stage, gibberellins can have the opposite effect: the *promotion* of seed production. A large dose of gibberellins will induce many biennial plants, such as carrots, beets, and cabbage, to flower and produce seeds during their first year of growth, rather than in their second year as is normally the case.

Research on plant hormones has also been used to develop herbicides. One of the most widely used weed killers is the synthetic auxin 2,4-D, which disrupts the normal balance of hormones that regulate plant growth. Monocots can rapidly inactivate this herbicide, but eudicots cannot; so 2,4-D can be used to selectively remove dandelions and other broadleaf eudicot weeds from a lawn or grainfield. By applying herbicides to cropland, a farmer can reduce the amount of tillage required to control weeds, thus reducing soil erosion, fuel consumption, and labour costs.

Modern agriculture relies heavily on the use of synthetic chemicals. Without chemically synthesized herbicides to control weeds and synthetic plant hormones to help grow and preserve fruits, less food would be produced and food prices could increase. At the same time, there is growing concern that the heavy use of certain artificial chemicals in food production may pose environmental and health hazards. One of these chemicals is dioxin, a by-product of 2,4-D synthesis. Though 2,4-D itself does not appear to be toxic to mammals, dioxin is a serious hazard when it leaks into the environment, causing birth defects, liver disease, and leukemia in laboratory animals. This is one of many reasons behind the growth of organic farming discussed in Module 23.10.

▲ **Figure 24.9** Using auxins to prevent early fruit drop

? What is the main commercial incentive to treat products with plant hormones? What behaviour of consumers helps to drive this use of hormone sprays in agriculture?

● The need to compete in the market by increasing production and lowering cost; shopping for the lowest price for produce

Responses to Stimuli

24.10 Tropisms orient plant growth toward or away from environmental stimuli

Having surveyed the hormones that carry signals within a plant, we now shift our focus to the responses of plants to physical stimuli from the environment. With the exception of the walking palm (see Module 22.9), plants cannot migrate to water or a sunny spot, and a seed cannot manoeuvre itself into an upright position if it lands upside down in the soil. Because of their immobility, plants must respond to environmental stimuli through developmental and physiological mechanisms. Tropisms are directed growth responses that cause parts of a plant to grow toward a stimulus (a positive tropism) or away from a stimulus (a negative tropism). In Module 24.1, we discussed positive phototropism, the growth of a plant shoot toward light. Two other types of tropisms are gravitropism, a response to gravity, and thigmotropism, a response to touch.

Response to Light As we saw in Module 24.1, the mechanism for phototropism is a greater rate of cell elongation on the darker side of a stem. In grass seedlings, the signal linking the light stimulus to the cell elongation response is auxin. Researchers have shown that illuminating a grass shoot from one side causes auxin to migrate across the shoot tip from the bright side to the dark side. The shoot tip contains a protein pigment that detects the light and somehow passes the "message" to molecules that affect auxin transport. (We discuss protein light receptors in Module 24.13.)

Response to Gravity **Gravitropism**, the directional growth of a plant in response to gravity, is responsible for the fact that no matter how a seed lands on the ground, shoots grow upward (negative gravitropism) and roots grow downward (positive gravitropism). The corn seedlings in **Figure 24.10A** were both germinated in the dark. The one on the left was left untouched; notice that its shoot grew straight up and its root straight down. The seedling on the right was germinated in the same way, but two days later it was turned on its side so that the shoot and root were horizontal. By the time the photo was taken, the shoot had turned back upward, exhibiting a negative response to gravity, and the root had turned down, exhibiting positive gravitropism.

One hypothesis for how plants tell up from down is that gravity pulls special organelles containing dense starch grains to the low points of cells. The uneven distribution of organelles may in turn signal the cells to redistribute auxin. This effect has been documented in roots. A higher auxin concentration

▲ **Figure 24.10B** The "sensitive plant" (*Mimosa pudica*)

on the lower side of a root inhibits cell elongation (see the red line in Figure 24.3B). As cells on the upper side continue to elongate, the root curves downward. This tropism continues until the root is growing straight down.

Response to Touch **Thigmotropism**, directional growth in response to touch, is illustrated when the tendril of a pea plant (which is actually a modified leaf) contacts a string or wire and coils around it for support (see Figure 22.4C, left). Tendrils grow straight until they touch an object. Contact then stimulates the cells to grow at different rates on opposite sides of the tendril (slower in the contact area), making the tendril coil around the support. Most climbing plants have tendrils that respond by coiling and grasping when they touch rigid objects. Thigmotropism enables these plants to use such objects for support while growing toward sunlight.

Some plants show remarkable abilities to respond to touch. When stimulated by contact, the "sensitive plant" (*Mimosa pudica*) rapidly folds its leaflets together (**Figure 24.10B**). This response, which takes only a second or two, results from a rapid loss of turgor by cells within the joints of the leaf. It takes about 10 minutes for the cells to regain their turgor and restore the open form of the leaf.

Tropisms all have one function in common: They help plant growth stay in tune with the environment. In the next module, we see that plants also have a way of keeping time with their environment.

▶ **Figure 24.10A** Gravitropism in a corn seedling

? Why are tropisms called "growth responses"?

  Because the movement of a plant organ toward or away from an environmental stimulus generally takes place by growing. An organ bends when cells on one side grow faster than cells on the other side, and it elongates in one direction when cells grow evenly.

24.11 Plants have internal clocks

Your pulse rate, blood pressure, body temperature, rate of cell division, blood cell counts, alertness, urine composition, metabolic rate, sex drive, and responsiveness to medications all fluctuate rhythmically with the time of day. Plants also display rhythmic behaviour; examples include the opening and closing of stomata (see Module 23.4) and the "sleep movements" of many species that fold their leaves or flowers in the

evening and unfold them in the morning. Some of these cyclic variations continue even under artificially constant conditions, implying that plants have a built-in ability to sense time.

Innate Biological Rhythms An innate biological cycle of about 24 hours is called a **circadian rhythm** (from the Latin *circa*, about, and *dies*, day). A circadian rhythm persists even when an organism is sheltered from environmental cues. A bean plant, for example, exhibits sleep movements at about the same intervals even if kept in constant light or darkness. Thus, circadian rhythms occur with or without external stimuli such as sunrise and sunset. Research on a variety of organisms indicates that circadian rhythms are controlled by internal timekeepers known as **biological clocks**.

Although a biological clock continues to mark time in the absence of environmental cues, it requires daily signals from the environment to remain tuned to a period of *exactly* 24 hours. This is because innate circadian rhythms generally differ somewhat from a 24-hour period. Consider bean plants, for instance. As shown in **Figure 24.11**, the leaves of a bean plant are normally horizontal at noon and folded downward at midnight. When the plant is held in darkness, however, its sleep movements change to a cycle of about 26 hours.

The light/dark cycle of day and night provides the cues that usually keep biological clocks precisely synchronized with the outside world. But a biological clock cannot immediately adjust to a sudden major change in the light/dark cycle. We observe this problem ourselves when we cross several time zones in an airplane: When we reach our destination, we have "jet lag"; our internal clock is not synchronized with the clock on the wall. Moving a plant across several time zones produces a similar lag. The plant will, for example, display leaf movements that are synchronized to the clock in its original location. In the case of either the plant or the human traveller, resetting the clock usually takes several days.

The Nature of Biological Clocks   Just what is a biological clock? Researchers are actively investigating this question. In humans and other mammals, the clock is located within a cluster of nerve cells in the hypothalamus of the brain (see Module 31.13). But for most other organisms, including plants, we know little about where the clocks are located or what kinds

▲ **Figure 24.11** Sleep movements of a bean plant

of cells are involved. A leading hypothesis is that biological timekeeping in plants may depend on the synthesis of a protein that regulates its own production through feedback control. After the protein accumulates to a sufficient concentration, it turns off its own gene. When the concentration of the protein falls, transcription restarts. The result would be a cycling of the protein's concentration over a roughly 24-hour period—a clock! Some research indicates that such a molecular mechanism may be common to all eukaryotes. However, much research remains to be done in this area.

Unlike most metabolic processes, biological clocks and the circadian rhythms they control are affected little by temperature. Somehow, a biological clock compensates for temperature shifts. This adjustment is essential, for a clock that speeds up or slows down with the rise and fall of outside temperature would be an unreliable timepiece.

In attempting to answer questions about biological clocks, it is essential to distinguish between the clock and the processes it controls. You could think of the sleep movements of leaves as the "hands" of a biological clock, but they are not the essence of the clockwork itself. You can restrain the leaves of a bean plant for several hours so that they cannot move. But on release, they will rush to the position appropriate for the time of day. Thus, we can interfere with an organism's rhythmic activity, but its biological clock goes right on ticking. In the next module, we'll learn more about the interface between a plant's internal biological clock and the external environment.

?   It has been hypothesized that biological clocks in plants are controlled by the synthesis of a protein that, once it accumulates to a sufficient concentration, shuts off its own gene. What kind of feedback does such a mechanism represent?

● Negative feedback, where the result of a process (in this case, a protein) shuts off that process (the transcription and translation of the gene)

24.12 Plants mark the seasons by measuring photoperiod

A biological clock not only times a plant's everyday activities, but may also influence seasonal events that are important in a plant's life cycle. Flowering, seed germination, and the onset and ending of dormancy are all stages in plant development that usually occur at specific times of the year. The

environmental stimulus plants most often use to detect the time of year is called **photoperiod**, the relative lengths of day and night.

Plants whose flowering is triggered by photoperiod fall into two groups. One group, the **short-day plants**, generally flower in late summer, fall, or winter, when light periods shorten. Chrysanthemums and poinsettias are examples of short-day plants. In contrast, **long-day plants**, such as spinach, lettuce, iris, and many cereal grains, usually flower in late spring or early summer, when light periods lengthen. Spinach, for instance, flowers only when daylight lasts at least 14 hours. Some plants, such as dandelions, tomatoes, and rice, are day-neutral; they flower when they reach a certain stage of maturity, regardless of day length.

In the 1940s, researchers discovered that flowering and other responses to photoperiod are actually controlled by the length of continuous *darkness*, not the length of continuous daylight. That is, "short-day" plants will flower only if it stays dark long enough, and "long-day" plants will flower only if the dark period is short enough. Therefore, it would seem more appropriate to call the two types "long-night" plants and "short-night" plants. However, the day-length terms are embedded firmly in the literature of plant biology and so will be used here.

Figure 24.12 illustrates the evidence for the night-length effect and shows the difference between the flowering response of a short-day plant and a long-day plant. The top part of the figure represents short-day plants. Notice that a short-day plant will not flower ❶ until it is exposed to a *continuous* dark period ❷ exceeding a critical length (about 14 hours, in this case). The continuity of darkness is important. The short-day plant will not blossom if the nighttime part of the photoperiod is interrupted ❸ by even a brief flash of light. There is no effect if the daytime portion of the photoperiod is broken by a brief exposure to darkness.

Florists apply this information about short-day plants to bring us flowers out of season. Chrysanthemums, for instance, are short-day plants that normally bloom in the autumn, but their blooming can be stalled until Mother's Day in May by punctuating each long night with a flash of light, thus turning one long night into two short nights. Easter lilies are also forced by growers to bloom at one particular time of year, which may vary by as much as five weeks from year to year, due to the relationship of Easter to the lunar calendar.

The bottom part of the figure demonstrates the effect of night length on a long-day plant. In this case, flowering occurs when the night length is *shorter* ❹ than a critical length (less than 10 hours, in this example). A dark interval that is too long ❺ will prevent flowering. Additionally, flowering

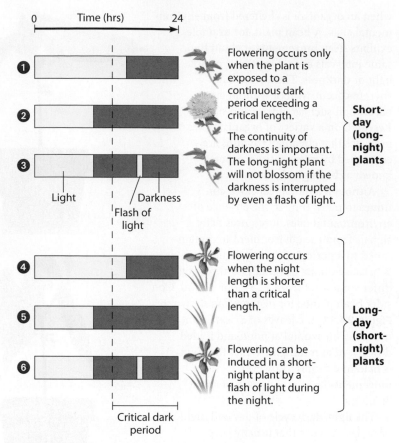

▲ **Figure 24.12** Photoperiodic control of flowering

can be induced in a long-day plant by a flash of light ❻ during the night.

Many plant species have critical night lengths, but how that critical night length affects flowering varies with the type of plant. In short-day plants, the critical night length is the *minimum* number of hours of darkness required for flowering; less darkness prevents flowering. In long-day plants, this critical night length is the *maximum* number of hours of darkness required for flowering; less darkness promotes flowering.

? **A particular short-day plant won't flower in the spring. Suppose a short dark interruption splits the long-light period of spring into two short-light periods. What result do you predict?**

● The plants still won't flower because it is actually night length, not day length, that counts in the photoperiodic control of flowering.

24.13 Phytochromes are light detectors that may help to set the biological clock

The discovery that photoperiod (specifically night length) determines the seasonal responses of plants leads to another question: How does a plant actually measure photoperiod? Much remains to be learned, but photoreceptive pigments called phytochromes are part of the answer. **Phytochromes** are proteins with a light-absorbing component. (Do not confuse phytochrome pigments

with those within the photosystems discussed in Chapter 7.) Because the light absorbed is at the red end of the spectrum, while light in the blue/green range is reflected, the molecules appear blue or bluish green (see Module 7.6).

Phytochromes were discovered during studies on how different wavelengths of light affect seed germination. Red

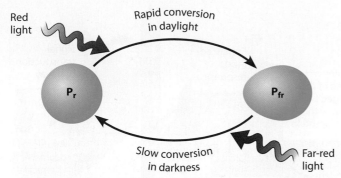

▲ **Figure 24.13A** Interconversion of the two forms of phytochrome

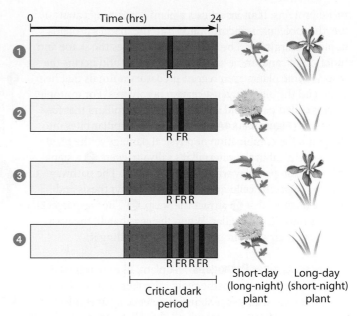

▲ **Figure 24.13B** The reversible effects of red and far-red light

light, with a wavelength of 660 nm, was found to be most effective at increasing germination. Light of a longer wavelength, called far-red light (730 nm, near the edge of human visibility), both inhibited germination and reversed the effect of red light.

How do phytochromes respond differently to different wavelengths of light? The key to this ability is that a phytochrome molecule changes back and forth between two forms that differ slightly in structure. One form, known as P_r, absorbs red light, and the other, known as P_{fr}, absorbs far-red light. As diagrammed in **Figure 24.13A**, when the P_r form absorbs red light (660 nm), it is quickly converted to P_{fr}, and when P_{fr} absorbs far-red light (730 nm), it is slowly converted back to P_r.

Each night, new phytochrome molecules are synthesized only in the P_r form. Thus, molecules of P_r slowly accumulate in the continuous darkness that follows sunset. After sunrise, the red wavelengths of sunlight cause much of the phytochrome to be rapidly converted from the P_r form to P_{fr}. Sunlight contains both red light and far-red light, but the conversion to P_{fr} is faster than the conversion to P_r. Therefore, the ratio of P_{fr} to P_r increases in the sunlight. It is this sudden increase in P_{fr} each day at dawn that resets a plant's biological clock. Interactions between phytochrome and the biological clock enable plants to measure the passage of night and day. In doing so, the clock monitors photoperiod and, when detecting seasonal changes in day and night length, cues responses such as seed germination, flowering, and the beginning and ending of bud dormancy.

The consequences of this phytochrome switch are shown in **Figure 24.13B**. Bar ❶ shows the results we saw in the previous module for both short-day and long-day plants that receive a

flash of light during their critical dark period. The letter *R* on the light flash stands for red light. The other three bars show how flashes of far-red (FR) light affect flowering. Bar ❷ reveals that the effect of a flash of red light that interrupts a period of darkness can be reversed by a subsequent flash of far-red light: Both types of plants behave as though there is no interruption in the night length. Bars ❸ and ❹ indicate that no matter how many flashes of red or far-red light a plant receives, only the wavelength of the *last* flash of light affects the plant's measurement of night length.

Plants also have a group of blue-light photoreceptors that control such light-sensitive plant responses as phototropism and the opening of stomata at daybreak. Light is an especially important environmental factor in the lives of plants, and diverse receptors and signalling pathways have evolved that mediate a plant's responses to light.

? How do phytochrome molecules help the plant recognize dawn each day?

 Phytochrome molecules are mainly in the P_r form during the night. Dawn is signalled by the sudden conversion of P_r to P_{fr} because of the absorption of the red wavelengths of sunlight.

24.14 Defences against herbivores and infectious microbes have evolved in plants

Plants are at the base of most food webs and are subject to attack by a wide range of **herbivores** (animals that eat mainly plants). Also, some pathogens can damage or kill plants. However, a wide variety of defences, many regulated by hormones, have evolved in plants.

Defences Against Herbivores   Plants counter herbivores with physical defences, such as thorns, and chemical defences, such as distasteful or toxic compounds. For example, some plants produce an amino acid called canavanine. Canavanine resembles arginine, one of the 20 amino acids normally used to make proteins. If an insect eats a plant containing canavan-ine, the molecule is incorporated into the insect's proteins in place of arginine. The substitution changes the shape and function of canavanine-containing proteins and harms the insect. Some plants even recruit predatory animals that help to defend the plants against certain herbivores. For example, insects called parasitoid wasps can kill caterpillars that feed on plants (Figure 24.14A). ❶ When a caterpillar bites into the plant, the combination of physical damage to the plant and a chemical in the caterpillar's saliva triggers ❷ a signal transduction pathway within the plant cells. The pathway leads to a specific cellular response: ❸ the synthesis and release of gases that ❹ attract the wasp. ❺ The wasp injects its eggs into the caterpillar. When the eggs hatch, the wasp larvae eat their way out of the caterpillar, killing it.

Defences Against Pathogens

A plant, like an animal, is subject to infection by pathogenic microbes: viruses, bacteria, and fungi. A plant's first line of defence against infection is the physical barrier of the plant's "skin," the epidermis. The same is true for animals, as you will read in Chapter 34. However, microbes can cross this barrier through wounds or through natural openings such as stomata. Once infected, the plant uses chemicals as a second line of defence. Plant cells damaged by the infection release microbe-killing molecules and chemicals that signal nearby cells to mount a similar chemical defence. In addition, infection stimulates chemical changes in the plant cell walls, which toughen the walls and thus slow the spread of the microbes within the plant.

This chemical defence system is enhanced by the plant's inherited ability to recognize certain pathogens. A kind of "compromise" has coevolved between plants and most of their pathogens: The pathogen gains enough access to its host to perpetuate itself without severely harming the plant. Otherwise, hosts and pathogens would soon perish together. The plant is said to be resistant to that pathogen, and the pathogen is said to be avirulent for the plant.

Recognition between R and Avr proteins, leading to a strong local response

Systemic acquired resistance

▲ **Figure 24.14B** Defence responses against an avirulent pathogen

This resistance to destruction by a specific pathogen is based on the ability of the plant and the microbe to make a complementary pair of molecules. A plant has many R genes (for *resistance*), and each pathogen has a set of Avr genes (for *avirulence*). Researchers hypothesize that an R gene encodes an R protein, a receptor protein in the plant's cells, and that the complementary Avr gene encodes an Avr protein, a signal molecule of the pathogen that binds specifically to the R protein in the plant cell. Recognition of pathogen-derived molecules by R proteins triggers a signal transduction pathway that leads to both local and plant-wide defence responses.

Figure 24.14B shows this interaction and subsequent events in the plant. ❶ The binding of the pathogen's signal molecule (magenta) to the plant's receptor (purple) triggers ❷ a signal transduction pathway, which leads to ❸ a defence response that is much stronger than would occur without the matchup of the R and Avr proteins. The cells at the site of infection mount a vigorous chemical defence, tightly seal off the area, and then kill themselves.

The defence response at the site of infection helps to protect the rest of the plant in yet another way. Among the signal molecules produced there are ❹ hormones that sound an alarm throughout the plant. ❺ At destinations distant from the original site, these hormones trigger signal transduction pathways leading to ❻ the production of additional defensive chemicals. This defence response, called **systemic acquired resistance**, provides protection against a diversity of pathogens for days.

Researchers suspect that one of the alarm hormones is salicylic acid, a compound whose pain-relieving effects led early cultures to use the salicylic-acid-rich bark of willows (*Salix*) as a medicine. Aspirin is a chemical derivative of this compound. With the discovery of systemic acquired resistance, biologists have learned one function of salicylic acid in plants.

? What is released at a site of infection that triggers the development of general resistance to pathogens?

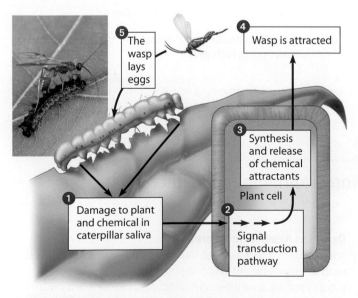

▲ **Figure 24.14A** Recruitment of a wasp in response to a herbivore

● Hormones

W

MasteringBiology® **For Practice Quizzes, BioFlix, MP3 Tutors, and Activities, go to masteringbiology.com.**

Reviewing the Concepts

Plant Hormones (24.1–24.9)

24.1 Experiments on how plants turn toward light led to the discovery of a plant hormone. Hormones coordinate the activities of plant cells and tissues. Experiments carried out by Darwin and others showed that the tip of a grass seedling detects light and transmits a signal down to the growing region of the shoot.

24.2 Five major types of hormones regulate plant growth and development. By triggering signal transduction pathways, small amounts of hormones regulate plant growth and development.

24.3 Auxin stimulates the elongation of cells in young shoots. Plants produce the auxin indoleacetic acid in the apical meristems at the tips of shoots. At different concentrations, auxin stimulates or inhibits the elongation of shoots and roots. It may act by weakening cell walls, allowing them to stretch when cells take up water. Auxin also stimulates the development of vascular tissues and cell division in the vascular cambium, promoting growth in stem diameter.

24.4 Cytokinins stimulate cell division. Cytokinins, produced by roots, embryos, and fruits, promote cell division. Cytokinins from roots may balance the effects of auxin from apical meristems, causing lower buds to develop into branches.

24.5 Gibberellins affect stem elongation and have numerous other effects. Gibberellins stimulate the elongation of stems and leaves and the development of fruits. Gibberellins released from embryos function in some of the early events of seed germination.

24.6 Abscisic acid inhibits many plant processes. Abscisic acid (ABA) inhibits germination. The ratio of ABA to gibberellins often determines whether a seed remains dormant or germinates. Seeds of many plants remain dormant until their ABA is inactivated or washed away. ABA also acts as a "stress hormone," causing stomata to close when a plant is dehydrated.

24.7 Ethylene triggers fruit ripening and other aging processes. As fruit cells age, they give off ethylene gas, which hastens ripening. A changing ratio of auxin to ethylene, triggered mainly by shorter days, probably causes autumn colour changes and the loss of leaves from deciduous trees.

24.8 Is it only deciduous trees and shrubs that lose their leaves? Evergreen trees can be either conifers or broadleaf trees. Their thick, leathery leaves last for multiple growing seasons but have a limited lifespan. Evergreen trees continually lose old leaves, but not all at once.

24.9 Plant hormones have many agricultural uses. Auxin can delay or promote fruit drop. Auxin and gibberellins are used to produce seedless fruits. A synthetic auxin called 2,4-D kills weeds. There are questions about the safety of using such chemicals.

Responses to Stimuli (24.10–24.14)

24.10 Tropisms orient plant growth toward or away from environmental stimuli. Plants sense and respond to environmental changes. Tropisms are growth responses that change the shape of a plant or make it grow toward or away from a stimulus.

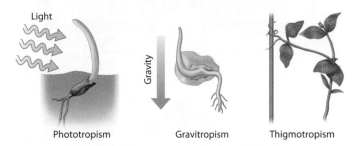

Phototropism   Gravitropism   Thigmotropism

Phototropism, bending in response to light, may result from auxin moving from the light side to the dark side of a stem. A response to gravity, or gravitropism, may be caused by settling of organelles on the low sides of shoots and roots, which may trigger a change in hormone distribution. Thigmotropism, a response to touch, is responsible for coiling of tendrils and vines around objects.

24.11 Plants have internal clocks. An internal biological clock controls sleep movements and other daily cycles in plants. These cycles, called circadian rhythms, persist with periods of about 24 hours even in the absence of environmental cues, but such cues are needed to keep them synchronized with day and night.

24.12 Plants mark the seasons by measuring photoperiod. The timing of flowering is one of the seasonal responses to photoperiod, the relative lengths of night and day.

Short-day (long-night) plants   Long-day (short-night) plants

24.13 Phytochromes are light detectors that may help to set the biological clock. Light-absorbing proteins called phytochromes may help plants set their biological clocks and monitor the photoperiod.

24.14 Defences against herbivores and infectious microbes have evolved in plants. Plants use chemicals to defend themselves against both herbivores and pathogens. So-called avirulent plant pathogens interact with host plants in a specific way that stimulates both local and systemic defences in the plant. Local defences include microbe-killing chemicals and the sealing off of the infected area. Hormones trigger generalized defence responses in other organs (systemic acquired resistance).

Connecting the Concepts

1. Test your knowledge of the five major classes of plant hormones (auxins, cytokinins, gibberellins, abscisic acid, and ethylene) by matching one hormone to each lettered box. (*Note:* Some hormones will match up with more than one box.)

Testing Your Knowledge

Multiple Choice

2. During winter or periods of drought, which one of the following plant hormones inhibits growth and seed germination?
   a. ethylene
   b. abscisic acid
   c. gibberellin
   d. auxin
   e. cytokinin

3. A certain short-day plant flowers only when days are less than 12 hours long. Which of the following would cause it to flower?
   a. a 9-hour night and 15-hour day with 1 minute of darkness after 7 hours
   b. an 8-hour day and 16-hour night with a flash of white light after 8 hours
   c. a 13-hour night and 11-hour day with 1 minute of darkness after 6 hours
   d. a 12-hour day and 12-hour night with a flash of red light after 6 hours
   e. 24 hours of continuous light

4. Auxin causes a shoot to bend toward light by
   a. causing cells to shrink on the dark side of the shoot.
   b. stimulating growth on the dark side of the shoot.
   c. causing cells to shrink on the lighted side of the shoot.
   d. stimulating growth on the lighted side of the shoot.
   e. inhibiting growth on the dark side of the shoot.

5. In autumn, the amount of _____ increases and the amount of _____ decreases in fruits and leaf stalks, causing a plant to drop fruit and leaves.
   a. ethylene; auxin
   b. gibberellin; abscisic acid
   c. ethylene; abscisic acid
   d. auxin; ethylene
   e. gibberellin; auxin

6. Plant hormones act by affecting the activities of
   a. genes.
   b. membranes.
   c. enzymes.
   d. genes, membranes, and enzymes.
   e. genes and enzymes.

7. Buds and sprouts often form on tree stumps. Which hormone would stimulate their formation?
   a. auxin
   b. cytokinin
   c. abscisic acid
   d. ethylene
   e. gibberellin

8. A plant's defence response at the site of initial infection by a pathogen will be especially strong if the
   a. pathogen is virulent.
   b. plant makes a receptor protein that recognizes a signal molecule from the microbe.
   c. pathogen is a fungus.
   d. plant has an *Avr* gene that is the right match for one of the microbe's *R* genes.
   e. right combination of hormones travel from the infection site to other parts of the plant.

Matching

9. Bending of a shoot toward light   a. phytochrome

10. Growth response to touch   b. photoperiod

11. Cycle with a period of about 24 hours   c. sleep movement

12. Pigment that helps to control flowering   d. circadian rhythm

13. Relative lengths of night and day   e. thigmotropism

14. Growth response to gravity   f. phototropism

15. Folding of plant leaves at night   g. gravitropism

Describing, Comparing, and Explaining

16. If apples are to be stored for long periods, it is best to keep them in a place with good air circulation. Explain why.

17. Why does a houseplant become bushier if you pinch off its terminal buds?

Applying the Concepts

18. A plant nursery manager tells the new night security guard to stay out of a room where chrysanthemums (which are short-day plants) are about to flower. Around midnight, the guard accidentally opens the door to the chrysanthemum room and turns on the lights for a moment. How might this affect the chrysanthemums? How could the guard correct the mistake?

19. A plant biologist observed a peculiar pattern when a tropical shrub was attacked by caterpillars. After a caterpillar ate a leaf, it would skip over nearby leaves and attack a leaf some distance away. Simply removing a leaf did not trigger the same change nearby. The biologist suspected that a damaged leaf sent out a chemical that signalled other leaves. How could this hypothesis be tested?

20. Imagine the following scenario: A plant biologist has developed a synthetic chemical that mimics the effects of a plant hormone. The chemical can be sprayed on apples before harvest to prevent flaking of the natural wax that is formed on the skin. This makes the apples shinier and gives them a deeper red colour. What kinds of questions do you think should be answered before farmers start using this chemical on apples? How might the scientist go about finding answers to these questions?

Answers to all questions can be found in Appendix E.

Structure and Function of Animals

CHAPTER 25

Unifying Concepts of Animal Structure and Function

BIG IDEAS

Structure and Function in Animal Tissues

(25.1–25.7)

The structural hierarchy in an animal begins with cells and tissues, whose forms correlate with their functions.

Organs and Organ Systems

(25.8–25.12)

Tissues are arranged into organs, which may be functionally coordinated in organ systems.

External Exchange and Internal Regulation

(25.13–25.19)

Complex animals have internal surfaces that facilitate exchange with the environment. Feedback control maintains homeostasis in many animals.

Day 1   Day 7   Day 11   Day 13   Day 17   Day 21   Day 31

Is Human Limb Regeneration Out of Reach?

Not many people make it past their teens without obtaining some sort of cut or abrasion. You probably have at least one scar as a permanent reminder of an injury, even if you cannot recall it. Skin is one of only a few organs in our bodies that are capable of regeneration. However, this process is not perfect. The new skin is visibly different from the original. Hair follicles and glands that are irreparably damaged during the insult do not regenerate. Therefore, the new skin will be functionally different as well.

Regeneration is not uncommon; it occurs throughout the animal kingdom. The vast majority of examples are invertebrates. Free-living flatworms such as *Dugesia* are well known for their ability to completely regenerate after an injury. Cutting these worms in half, a seemingly devastating injury, results in both halves regenerating into separate and fully functional animals in only two weeks. In fact, some flatworms use this mechanism to reproduce asexually. Segments as small as 10 000 cells (less than 1/250th of a worm) can regrow into a fully functional animal.

Scattered within *Dugesia*'s tissues are small clusters of undifferentiated *totipotent stem cells*. These cells are similar to those found in embryos, having the potential to become any other cell type. Recall that within the genome of every cell is all the information required to generate an entire organism. Cells specialize within a tissue by turning on specific subsets of these genes. Every tissue has a unique subset of active genes giving rise to their uniqueness. After an injury, these clusters form a *blastema*, which ultimately replaces any missing tissues and organs. Images of *Dugesia* with two heads show the result of an injury that split the head when each half regenerated its missing structures.

Few vertebrates can regenerate. However, a few amphibians, such as the red spotted newt (*Notophthalmus viridescens*), have incredible regenerative abilities. Shortly after amputation, cells at the injury site *dedifferentiate*. That is, they revert to an earlier stage of development and re-enter the cell cycle. These totipotent cells form the *blastema* that will ultimately replace the limb. Research by Dr. Morton Globus at the University of Waterloo was instrumental in the understanding of this process and the complex signals involved. The new limb will be completely functional within 40 days. Regeneration in the newt seems to be perfect, with no visible scarring or loss of function. The new limbs are complete with all tissue and organs in their appropriate location.

In humans and other terrestrial vertebrates (reptiles, birds, and mammals), blastemas do not form at limb amputation sites. Instead, rapid healing with scar formation rather than regeneration follows injury. Promoting blastema formation in humans, and therefore exploring the potential of regeneration, is a very active area of research.

This chapter opens the unit with an overview of animal structure and function. We'll explore the hierarchy of cells, tissues, organs, and organ systems. And we'll see how an animal's structure enhances exchange with the external environment as well as the regulation of the internal environment.

Structure and Function in Animal Tissues

25.1 Structure fits function at all levels of organization in the animal body

When discussing structure and function, biologists distinguish anatomy from physiology. **Anatomy** is the study of the form of an organism's structures; **physiology** is the study of the functions of those structures. A biologist interested in anatomy, for instance, might focus on the arrangement of muscles and bones in a red spotted newt's legs. A physiologist might study how a newt's muscles function. Despite their different approaches, both scientists are working toward a better understanding of the connection between structure and function, such as how the structural adaptations of the tissues in the newt allow for regeneration of an amputated limb.

Structure in the living world is organized in hierarchical levels. We followed the progression from molecules to cells in Unit I. In Unit V, we traced the hierarchy in plants from cells to the organisms as a whole. Now, let's follow the same hierarchy in animals. (In Unit VII, we pick up the trail again, moving from organisms to ecosystems.) As we discussed in Module 1.2, emergent properties—novel properties that were not present at the preceding level of the hierarchy of life—arise as a result of the structural and functional organization of each level's component parts.

Figure 25.1 illustrates structural hierarchy in a Kermode spirit bear. **Part A** shows a single muscle cell in the bear's heart. This cell's main function is to contract, and the stripes in the cell indicate the precise alignment of strands of proteins that perform that function. Each muscle cell is also branched, providing for multiple connections to other cells that ensure coordinated contractions of all the muscle cells in the heart.

Together, these heart cells make up a tissue **(Part B)**, the second structural level. A **tissue** is an integrated group of similar cells that perform a common function. The cells of a tissue are specialized, and their structure enables them to perform a specific task—in this instance, coordinated contraction.

Part C, the heart itself, illustrates the organ level of the hierarchy. An **organ** is made up of two or more types of tissues that together perform a specific task. In addition to muscle tissue, the heart includes nervous, epithelial, and connective tissue.

Part D shows the circulatory system, the organ system of which the heart is a component. An **organ system** consists of multiple organs that together perform a vital body function. Other parts of the circulatory system include the blood and the blood vessels: arteries, veins, and capillaries.

In **Part E**, the bear itself forms the final level of this hierarchy. An **organism** contains a number of organ systems, each specialized for certain tasks and all functioning together as an integrated, coordinated unit. For example, the bear's circulatory system cannot function without oxygen supplied by the respiratory system and nutrients supplied by the digestive system. And it takes the coordination of several other organ systems to enable this animal to walk or hunt for food.

As we see throughout our study of the anatomy and physiology of animals, form fits function at each level of the structural hierarchy. In the next several modules, we focus on the tissue

A Cellular level
Muscle cell

B Tissue level
Muscle tissue

C Organ level
Heart

D Organ system level
Circulatory system

E Organism level
Many organ systems functioning together

▲ **Figure 25.1** A structural hierarchy in a Kermode spirit bear

level of this biological hierarchy. In the later modules of this chapter, we will examine how animals maintain a stable internal environment through homeostasis. But first, let's explore how evolution shapes an animal's body form.

 ? Explain how the ability to pump blood is an emergent property of a heart, which is at the organ level of the biological hierarchy.

● The specific structural organization and integration of the individual muscle, connective, epithelial, and nervous tissues of a heart enable the function of pumping blood.

25.2 An animal's form reflects natural selection

An animal's size and shape are fundamental aspects of form that affect the way an animal interacts with its environment. Although biologists often refer to "body plan" or "design" in discussing animal form, they are not implying a process of conscious invention. The body plan of an animal is the result of millions of years of evolution. Natural selection fits form to function by selecting the variations that best meet the challenges of an animal's environment.

How might physical laws affect the evolution of an animal's form? Consider some of the properties of water that limit the possible shapes for fast swimmers. Water is about a thousand times denser than air. Thus, any bump on the body surface that causes drag slows a swimmer much more than it would a runner or a flyer. What shape, then, is best suited for rapid movement through the dense medium of water?

Tuna and other fast fishes can swim at speeds up to 80 km/hr. Sharks, penguins, dolphins, and seals are also fast swimmers. As illustrated by the examples in **Figure 25.2**, such animals share a streamlined, tapered body form. The similar shape found in speedy fishes, sharks, and aquatic birds and mammals is an example of convergent evolution (see Module 15.12).

Natural selection often shapes similar adaptations when diverse organisms face the same environmental challenge, such as the resistance of water to fast swimming.

Physical laws also influence body form of terrestrial animals with regard to maximum size. As body dimensions increase, thicker skeletons are required to support the body. In addition, as bodies increase in size, the muscles required for movement become an ever-larger proportion of the total body mass. At some point, mobility becomes limited. By considering the fraction of body mass in leg muscles and the force such muscles can generate, scientists can estimate maximum running speed for a wide range of body plans. Such calculations suggest that *Tyrannosaurus rex*, a dinosaur that was more than 6 m tall, could probably only lumber from place to place, a far cry from the thunderous sprint depicted in the movie *Jurassic Park*. Although alternative interpretations of *T. rex*'s musculature may cast doubt and controversy on how fast the *T. rex* could actually run.

? Explain how a seal, a penguin, and a shark illustrate convergent evolution.

● All three have a streamlined, tapered shape, the result of natural selection adapting each to fast swimming in its dense, aquatic environment.

▲ **Figure 25.2** Convergent evolution of body shape in fast swimmers

Seal

Shark

Penguin

25.3 Tissues are groups of cells with a common structure and function

In almost all animals, the cells of the body are organized into tissues. The term *tissue* is from a Latin word meaning "weave," and some tissues resemble woven cloth in that they consist of cells surrounded by a meshwork of nonliving fibres and other extracellular substances. Other tissues are held together by a sticky glue that coats the cells or by special junctions between adjacent plasma membranes (see Module 4.20). The structure of tissues relates to their specific functions.

The specialization of complex body parts such as organs and organ systems is largely based on varied combinations of

a limited set of cells and tissue types. For example, your lungs and blood vessels have very distinct functions, but they are lined by tissues that are of the same basic type.

Your body is built from four main types of tissues: epithelial, connective, muscle, and nervous. We examine the structure and function of these tissue types in the next four modules.

? How is a tissue different from a cell and an organ?

 Tissues are collections of similar cells that perform a common function. Several different tissue types usually produce the structure of an organ.

25.4 Epithelial tissue covers the body and lines its organs and cavities

Epithelial tissues, or epithelia (singular, *epithelium*), are sheets of closely packed cells that cover your body surface and line your internal organs and cavities. The tightly knit cells form a protective barrier and, in some cases, a surface for exchange with the fluid or air on the other side. One side of an epithelium is attached to a basal lamina, a dense mat of extracellular matrix consisting of fibrous proteins and sticky polysaccharides that separates the epithelium from the underlying tissues. The other side, called the apical surface, faces the outside of an organ or the inside of a tube or a passageway. These two distinct surfaces of epithelia allow for directional exchange with the external environment.

Epithelial tissues are named according to the number of cell layers they have and according to the shape of the cells on their apical surface. A simple epithelium has a single layer of cells, whereas a stratified epithelium has multiple layers. A pseudostratified epithelium has a single layer but appears stratified because the cells vary in length. The shape of the cells may be squamous (flat like ceramic tiles), cuboidal (like dice), or columnar (like pillars). **Figure 25.4** shows examples of different types of epithelia. In each case, the pink colour identifies the cells of the epithelium itself.

The structure of each type of epithelium fits its function. Simple squamous epithelium **(Part A)** is thin and leaky and thus suitable for exchanging materials by diffusion. You would find it lining your capillaries and the air sacs of your lungs.

Both cuboidal and columnar epithelia have cells with a relatively large amount of cytoplasm, facilitating their role of secretion or absorption of materials. **Part B** shows a simple cuboidal epithelium forming a tube in the kidney. Such epithelia are also found in glands, such as the thyroid and salivary glands. A simple columnar epithelium **(Part C)** lines your intestines, where it secretes digestive juices and absorbs nutrients.

The many layers of the stratified squamous epithelium in **Part D** make it well suited for lining surfaces subject to abrasion, such as your outer skin and the linings of your mouth and esophagus. Stratified squamous epithelium regenerates rapidly by division of the cells near the basal lamina. New cells move toward the apical surface as older cells slough off.

The pseudostratified ciliated columnar epithelium in **Part E** forms a mucous membrane that lines the upper portions of your respiratory tract and helps to keep your lungs clean. Dust, pollen, and other particles are trapped in the mucus it secretes and then are swept up and out of your respiratory tract by the beating of the cilia on its cells.

? **How does the specific shape of the lung epithelium facilitate gas exchange?**

● The single thin layer allows for easy diffusion of gases, and the massive surface area allows for more gas exchange.

A **Simple squamous epithelium** (lining the air sacs of the lung)

Basal lamina (extracellular matrix) / Apical surface of epithelium / Underlying tissue / Cell nuclei

B **Simple cuboidal epithelium** (forming a tube in the kidney)

C **Simple columnar epithelium** (lining the intestines)

E **Pseudostratified ciliated columnar epithelium** (lining the upper respiratory tract)

D **Stratified squamous epithelium** (lining the esophagus)

▲ **Figure 25.4** Types of epithelial tissue

25.5 Connective tissue binds and supports other tissues

In contrast to epithelium, **connective tissue** consists of a sparse population of cells scattered throughout an extracellular material called a matrix. The cells produce and secrete the matrix, which usually consists of a web of fibres embedded in a liquid, jelly, or solid. Connective tissues may be grouped into six major types. **Figure 25.5** shows micrographs of each type and illustrates where each would be found in your arm, for example.

The most widespread connective tissue in your body is called **loose connective tissue (Part A)** because its matrix is a loose weave of fibres. Many of the fibres consist of the strong, ropelike protein collagen. Other fibres are more elastic, making the tissue resilient as well as strong. Loose connective tissue serves mainly to bind epithelia to underlying tissues and to hold organs in place. In the figure, we show the loose connective tissue that lies directly under the skin.

Fibrous connective tissue (Part B) has densely packed parallel bundles of collagen fibres, an arrangement that maximizes its strength. This tissue forms tendons, which attach your muscles to bone, and ligaments, which connect your bones at joints.

Adipose tissue (Part C) stores fat in large, closely packed adipose cells held in a matrix of fibres. This tissue pads and insulates your body and stores energy. Each adipose cell contains a large fat droplet that swells when fat is stored and shrinks when fat is used as fuel.

The matrix of **cartilage (Part D)**, a connective tissue that forms a strong but flexible skeletal material, consists of collagen fibres embedded in a rubbery material. Cartilage commonly surrounds the ends of bones, providing a shock-absorbing surface. It also supports your ears and nose and forms the cushioning discs between your vertebrae.

Bone (Part E) has a matrix of collagen fibres embedded in a hard mineral substance made of calcium, magnesium, and phosphate. The combination of fibres and minerals makes bone strong without being brittle. The microscopic structure of compact regions of bones contains repeating circular layers of matrix, each with a central canal containing blood vessels and nerves. Like other tissues, bone contains living cells and can therefore grow as you grow and mend when broken.

Blood (Part F) transports substances throughout your body and thus functions differently from other connective tissues. Its extensive extracellular matrix is a liquid called plasma, which consists of water, salts, and dissolved proteins. Suspended in the plasma are red blood cells, which carry oxygen; white blood cells, which function in defence against disease; and platelets, which aid in blood clotting.

? Why does blood qualify as a type of connective tissue?

● Because it consists of a relatively sparse population of cells surrounded by a noncellular matrix, which in this case is a fluid called plasma

A Loose connective tissue (under the skin)
- Cell nucleus
- Collagen fibre
- Elastic fibres

B Fibrous connective tissue (forming a tendon)
- Cell nucleus
- Collagen fibres

C Adipose tissue
- Fat droplets with adipose cells

D Cartilage (at the end of a bone)
- Cartilage-forming cells
- Matrix

E Bone
- Central canal
- Matrix
- Bone-forming cells

F Blood
- White blood cells
- Red blood cell
- Plasma (a fluid matrix)

▲ **Figure 25.5** Types of connective tissue

25.6 Muscle tissue functions in movement

Muscle tissue is the most abundant tissue in most animals. It consists of long cells called muscle fibres, each containing many molecules of the contractile proteins, actin and myosin (see Module 33.8). **Figure 25.6** shows micrographs of the three types of vertebrate muscle tissue.

Skeletal muscle (Part A) can be found in all vertebrate animals and in some active invertebrates. In the vertebrates, it attaches to bones with tendons and is responsible for voluntary movements, such as walking or bouncing a ball. The arrangement of the contractile units along the length of the muscle fibres gives the cells a striped, or striated, appearance, as you can see in the micrograph below. In active invertebrates—for example, insects—powerful skeletal muscle can be used for flight.

Cardiac muscle (Part B) can be found only in the hearts of vertebrates. It is striated like skeletal muscle but is under involuntary control, meaning that one cannot consciously control its contraction. Cardiac muscle fibres are branched, interconnecting at specialized junctions that rapidly relay the signal to contract from cell to cell during a heartbeat.

Smooth muscle (Part C) is found in all animals. It gets its name because it lacks striations. Smooth muscle cells are spindle-shaped and contract more slowly than skeletal muscles, but can sustain contractions for a longer period of time. Within vertebrates, smooth muscle is found in the walls of the digestive tract, arteries, and other internal organs. It is responsible for involuntary body activities, such as the movement of food through your intestines. In invertebrate animals, however, smooth muscle is under voluntary control. Many of these animals use smooth muscle for locomotion, in place of skeletal muscle.

? What muscle types are used for locomotion in a gecko that is quickly climbing a wall and in an earthworm that is slowly crawling through the dirt?

● The gecko is using skeletal muscle and the earthworm is using smooth muscle to move.

A Skeletal muscle — Unit of muscle contraction, Muscle fibre (cell), Nuclei

B Cardiac muscle — Muscle fibre, Nucleus, Junction between two cells

C Smooth muscle — Muscle fibre, Nucleus

▲ **Figure 25.6** The three types of muscle tissue

25.7 Nervous tissue forms a communication network

Nervous tissue senses stimuli and rapidly transmits information. Nervous tissue is found in your brain and spinal cord, as well as in the nerves that transmit signals throughout your body.

The structural and functional unit of nervous tissue is the nerve cell, or **neuron**, which is uniquely specialized to conduct electrical nerve impulses. As you can see in the micrograph in **Figure 25.7**, a neuron consists of a cell body (containing the cell's nucleus and other organelles) and a number of slender extensions. Dendrites and the cell body receive nerve impulses from other neurons. Axons, which are often bundled together into nerves, transmit signals toward other neurons or to an effector, such as a muscle cell.

Nervous tissue actually contains many supporting cells in addition to neurons. Some of these cells surround and insulate axons, promoting faster transmission of signals. Others help to nourish neurons and regulate the fluid around them.

Dendrites, Cell body, Axon

Fluorescent LM 430×

▲ **Figure 25.7** A neuron

? How does the long length of some axons (such as those that extend from your lower spine to your toes) relate to the function of a neuron?

● It allows for the transmission of a nerve signal over a long distance directly to specific muscle cells.

Organs and Organ Systems

25.8 Organs are made up of tissues

In all but the simplest animals, tissues are arranged into organs that perform specific functions. The heart, for example, while mostly muscle, also has epithelial, connective, and nervous tissues. Epithelial tissue lining the heart chambers prevents leakage and provides a smooth surface over which blood can flow. Connective tissue makes the heart elastic and strengthens its walls. Neurons regulate the contractions of cardiac muscle.

In some organs, tissues are organized in layers, as you can see in the diagram of the small intestine in **Figure 25.8**. The lumen, or interior space, of the small intestine is lined by a columnar epithelium that digests and absorbs nutrients. Notice the fingerlike projections that increase the surface area of this lining. Underneath the epithelium (and extending into the projections) is connective tissue, which contains blood vessels. The two layers of smooth muscle, oriented in different directions, propel food through the intestine. The smooth muscle, in turn, is surrounded by another layer of connective tissue and epithelial tissue.

An organ represents a higher level of structure than the tissues composing it, and it performs functions that none of its component tissues can carry out alone. These functions emerge from the coordinated interactions of tissues.

? Explain why a disease that damages connective tissue can impair most of the body's organs.

● Connective tissue is a component of most organs and therefore, all may be affected by this disease.

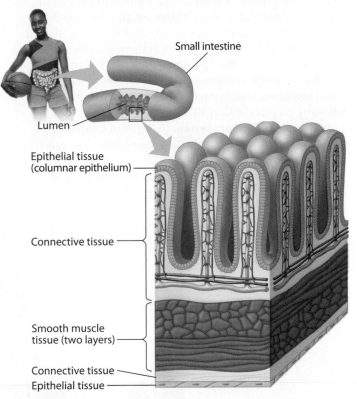

▲ **Figure 25.8** Tissue layers of the wall of the small intestine

Labels: Small intestine · Lumen · Epithelial tissue (columnar epithelium) · Connective tissue · Smooth muscle tissue (two layers) · Connective tissue · Epithelial tissue

---

25.9 Bioengineers are learning to produce tissues and organs for transplants

Injuries, diseases, and birth defects often leave individuals with disfiguring or life-threatening conditions. Scientists are increasingly turning to bioengineering in their search for ways to repair or replace damaged tissues and organs.

As we discussed in the opening essay of this chapter, regenerating tissue on our own is currently not possible. However, scientists are working on other exciting options. One of the most successful tissue-engineering advances has come in the form of artificial skin, a type of human-engineered tissue designed for everyone from burn victims to diabetic patients with skin ulcers. The tissue is grown from human fibroblasts, tissue-generating cells often harvested from newborn foreskin tissue. These cells are applied along a tiny protein scaffolding, where they multiply and produce a three-dimensional skin substitute containing active living cells.

In 2006, researchers reported the first successful transplantation and long-term functioning of laboratory-grown bladders **(Figure 25.9)**. Such bladders have now been implanted in seven children and adults. These organs were grown from the patients' own cells, thus avoiding the risk of rejection. Organs grown from a patient's cells may someday reduce the shortage of organs available for transplants.

▲ **Figure 25.9** A laboratory-grown bladder

In another remarkable advance in tissue engineering, some imaginative researchers filled recycled inkjet print cartridges with a cell solution instead of ink and, using desktop printers, actually "printed" cells in layers on a biodegradable gel. The gel can be removed, leaving a three-dimensional cellular structure. Sheets of artificial tissues or even pieces of organs may someday be produced by such printing techniques. Researchers may also use such cellular systems for testing drugs or for basic research into cell growth and interactions.

? Why is it beneficial to grow replacement tissues or organs from a patient's own cells?

● The patient's body does not reject the tissue as foreign.

25.10 Organ systems work together to perform life's functions

Just as it takes several different tissues to build an organ, it takes the integration of several organs into organ systems to perform the body's functions. **Figure 25.10** illustrates the organ systems found in humans and other mammals. As you read through the brief descriptions of these systems and study their components in the figure, remember that all the organ systems are interdependent and work together to create a functional organism. These systems will be discussed within the following chapters of Unit VI.

A The **integumentary system** (covered in Chapter 25) protects your body against physical injury, infection, excessive heat or cold, and drying out.

B The **digestive system** (Chapter 26) ingests and digests your food, absorbs nutrients, and eliminates undigested material.

C The **respiratory system** (Chapter 27) exchanges gases with the environment, supplying your blood with O_2 and disposing of CO_2.

D The **circulatory system** (Chapter 28) delivers O_2 and nutrients to your body cells and transports CO_2 to the lungs and metabolic wastes to the kidneys.

E The **urinary system** (Chapter 28) removes waste products from your blood and excretes urine. It also regulates the chemical makeup, pH, and water balance of your blood.

F The **endocrine system** (Chapter 29) secretes hormones that regulate the activities of your body, thus maintaining an internal steady state called homeostasis.

G The **reproductive system** (Chapter 30) produces gametes and sex hormones. The female system supports a developing embryo and produces milk.

A Integumentary system

Hair

Skin

Nails

B Digestive system

Mouth
Esophagus
Liver
Stomach
Small intestine
Large intestine
Anus

E Urinary system

Kidney
Ureter
Urinary bladder
Urethra

C Respiratory system

Nasal cavity
Larynx
Pharynx
Trachea
Bronchus
Lung

D Circulatory system

Heart
Blood vessels

F Endocrine system

Hypothalamus
Pituitary gland
Thyroid gland
Parathyroid gland
Thymus
Adrenal gland
Pancreas
Testis (male)
Ovary (female)

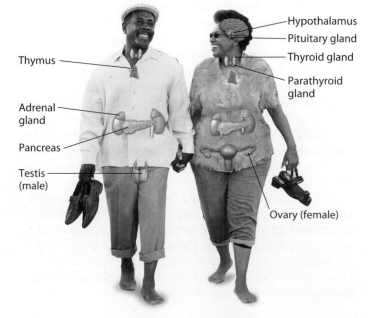

▲ **Figure 25.10** Human organ systems and their component parts

H The **nervous system** (Chapters 31 and 32) coordinates your body's activities by detecting stimuli, integrating information, and directing the body's responses.

I The **skeletal system** (Chapter 33) supports your body, protects organs such as your brain and lungs, and provides the framework for muscles to produce movement.

J The **muscular system** (Chapter 33) moves your body, maintains posture, and produces heat.

K The **lymphatic system** (Chapter 34) returns excess body fluid to the circulatory system and functions as part of the immune system. The **immune system** (Chapter 34) defends your body against infections and cancer.

The ability to perform life's functions emerges from the organization and coordination of all the body's organ systems. Indeed, the whole is greater than the sum of its parts.

? Which two organ systems are most directly involved in regulating all other systems?

● The nervous system and the endocrine system

G Reproductive system

Female

Oviduct
Ovary
Uterus
Vagina

Male

Seminal vesicles
Prostate gland
Vas deferens
Penis
Urethra
Testis

H Nervous system

Brain
Sense organ (ear)
Spinal cord
Nerves

I Skeletal system

Bone
Cartilage

J Muscular system

Skeletal muscles

K Lymphatic and Immune systems

Lymph nodes
Appendix
Bone marrow
Thymus
Spleen
Lymphatic vessels

25.11 The integumentary system protects the body

Most of the organ systems introduced in Module 25.10 are examined in more detail in the chapters of this unit. Here we take a brief look at the integumentary system, which consists of the skin and epidermal derivatives such as horns, hooves, nails, scales (reptiles), feathers (birds), or hair (mammals).

Structure of Skin   As shown in **Figure 25.11**, your skin consists of two layers: the epidermis and the dermis. The epidermis is a stratified squamous epithelium (many layers of flat cells; see Module 25.4). Rapid cell division near the base of the epidermis serves to replenish the skin cells that are constantly abraded from your body surface. As these new cells are pushed upward in the epidermis by the addition of new cells below them, they fill with the fibrous protein keratin, release a waterproofing glycolipid, and eventually die. These dead, tightly joined cells remain at the surface of your skin for up to two weeks. This continuous process means that you get a brand new epidermis every few weeks.

The dermis is the inner layer of the skin. It consists of a fairly dense connective tissue with many resilient elastic fibres and strong collagen fibres. The dermis contains hair follicles, oil and sweat glands, muscles, nerves, sensory receptors (shown in Figure 32.1A), blood vessels, and many immune cells called macrophages. The ink particles injected by a tattoo needle are held in place by macrophages and the dense extracellular matrix. Beneath the skin lies the hypodermis, a layer of adipose tissue. (The hypodermis is the site of many of the injections you receive with a hypodermic needle.)

Functions of Skin   The structure of the skin corresponds to its functions. The keratin-filled, tightly joined cells at the surface of the epidermis provide a waterproof covering that protects your body from dehydration and prevents penetration by microbes. And as close encounters with the environment, including wearing clothing, abrade the epidermis, replacement cells move up.

The sensory receptors in the skin provide important environmental information to your brain: Is this surface too hot, or cold, or sharp? Your touch receptors help you to manipulate food and tools and to feel your way around in the dark. The profusion of small blood vessels and the 2.5 million sweat glands in the dermis also facilitate the important function of temperature regulation, as Figure 25.15 illustrates.

One of the metabolic functions of the skin is the synthesis of vitamin D, which is required for absorbing calcium. Ultraviolet (UV) light (also referred to as UV radiation) catalyzes the conversion of a derivative of cholesterol to vitamin D in the cells in the lower layers of your epidermis. Adequate sunlight is needed for this synthesis. But sunlight also has damaging effects on the skin. In response to UV radiation, skin cells make more melanin, which moves to the outer layers of the skin and is visible as a tan. A tan is not indicative of good health; it signals that skin cells have been damaged. DNA changes caused by the UV rays can lead to premature aging of the skin, cataracts in the eyes, and skin cancers.

Hair and Nails   In mammals, hair is an important component of the integumentary system. Hair is a flexible shaft of flattened, keratin-filled dead cells, which were produced by a hair follicle. Associated with hair follicles are oil glands, whose secretions lubricate the hair, condition the surrounding skin, and inhibit the growth of bacteria. Look at the hair follicle in Figure 25.11 and you will see that it is wrapped in nerve endings. Hair plays important sensory functions, as its slightest movement is relayed to the nervous system. (You can get a sense of this sensitivity by lightly touching the hair on your arm.)

Hair insulates the bodies of most mammals—although in humans this insulation is limited to the head. Land mammals react to cold by raising their fur, which traps a layer of air and increases the insulating power of the fur. Look again at the hair follicle in the figure. The muscle attached to it is responsible for raising the hair when you get cold. The resulting "goose bumps" are a vestige of hair raising inherited from our furry ancestors.

Fingernails and toenails are the final component of your integumentary system. These protective coverings are also composed of keratin. Fingernails facilitate fine manipulation (and are useful for chewing when nervous). In other mammals, the digits may end in claws or hooves.

The integumentary system encloses and protects an animal from its environment. But animals cannot be isolated systems; they must exchange gases, take in food, and eliminate wastes. In Chapters 26 and 27, we explore some of the structural adaptations that provide for these functions.

In the next module, we will discuss a rumour about the properties of polar bear hair.

▲ **Figure 25.11** A section of mammalian skin, the major organ of the integumentary system

Labels: Hair, Epidermis, Dermis, Hypodermis (under the skin), Adipose tissue, Blood vessels, Sweat pore, Muscle, Nerve, Sweat gland, Oil gland, Hair follicle

? Describe three structures associated with a hair follicle that contribute to the functions of hair.

● The nerve endings sense when the hair is moved; the muscle raises the hair (producing goose bumps in humans but warming other mammals); and the oil gland produces lubricating and antibacterial secretions.

25.12 Do polar bears have fibre optic hair?

Polar bears (*Ursus maritimus*, **Figure 25.12A**) are well adapted to survive in the Canadian Arctic. Large, hairy feet work like snowshoes on land and like paddles in the water. A thick layer of insulating fat under the bears' skin prevents heat loss and provides an energy store. The most obvious adaptation to the environment is their coat of hair, common to all mammals as discussed in the previous module. Polar bear fur consists of a thick underfur and long, coarse guard hairs.

The actual functions of polar bear hair have been misunderstood for decades. At one time, it was thought that the overlaying guard hairs were transmitting UV light to the skin. This ability was attributed to presumed fibre optic characteristics of the hairs. This hypothesis was supported by three groups of scientists and was based on circumstantial evidence.

Underneath its thick coat, the polar bear's skin is black. Although the coat appears white to the eye, the hairs are actually colourless and hollow **(Figure 25.12B)**. The reason we see these hairs as white is because we see the reflection of the entire visible spectrum by the hairs. (Within the visible spectrum of light, the combination of all wavelengths is seen as white.) Under UV light, the pelt appears black, which suggests the hair is absorbing this radiation.

With these observations, some scientists inferred that the guard hairs were capturing UV light and carrying it to the skin. The dark skin would then convert this energy into heat, warming the animal. Each hair was likened to a fibre optic cable conducting energy to the animal's skin. Previously, claims were made that 95% of the UV radiation could be converted to heat, satisfying 25% of the bears' needs. Thus began the solar polar bear hypothesis.

After the initial report, this untested hypothesis was promulgated in popular science magazines for decades. Though interesting, these magazines do not rely on the same peer review process that scientific literature uses. Peer review requires scientists in the field to read manuscripts and comment on their validity, meaning the manuscripts will be approved for publication only if they are accurate and complete. This process weeds out weak scholarship. For example, the well-respected journal *Nature* accepts only 8% of all submitted manuscripts. The intent of peer review is to guarantee that the science being published has a minimum standard of quality.

Nearly 20 years after the untested hypothesis of the solar polar bear was made, it was clearly disproved in scientific literature. Polar bear hair was demonstrated to be a poor conductor of UV light—less than 1% of the light travels farther than 0.5 cm. Thus, the minute amount of UV light that reaches a bear's skin could not contribute significantly to warming the bear. The black appearance of the pelt under UV light is actually due to the light's absorption by keratin, a major component of mammalian hair.

The hollow guard hairs are, indeed, an adaptation for the cold climate. However, they are not unique to polar bears. Other mammals adapted to colder climates—caribou and grizzly bears, for example—also have hollow hair shafts. The hollow hair has a higher insulative value than solid-core hair and is easier for the bear to shake dry after it emerges from the icy seawater. The white appearance also provides good camouflage for a polar bear against a snowy background.

From this polar bear example, you can clearly see that a series of observations can have more than one interpretation. Had the reports of the solar polar bear been peer reviewed, this rumour might not have lasted so long in popular media.

? Why is it unlikely that the dark skin of the polar bear absorbs enough radiation to significantly warm the animal?

● The keratin in the hair absorbs the majority of UV radiation and reflects the majority of visible light that hits it. Therefore, very little radiation actually reaches the bear's pigmented skin.

▲ **Figure 25.12A** The polar bear, a Canadian icon

Colourized SEM 304×

▲ **Figure 25.12B** Polar bear hair in cross-section

External Exchange and Internal Regulation

25.13 Structural adaptations enhance exchange with the environment

Every living organism is an open system, meaning that it exchanges matter and energy with its surroundings. You, for example, take in O_2 and water and food, and in exchange, you breathe out CO_2, urinate, defecate, sweat, and radiate heat. The exchange of materials with the environment must extend to the level of each individual cell. Exchange of gases, nutrients, and wastes occurs as substances dissolved in an aqueous solution move across the plasma membrane of every cell.

A freshwater hydra has a body wall only two cell layers thick (see Figure 26.3A). The outside layer is in contact with its water environment; the inner layer is bathed by fluid in its saclike gastrovascular cavity. This internal fluid circulates in and out of the hydra's mouth. Thus, every body cell exchanges materials directly with an aqueous environment.

Another common body plan that maximizes exchange with the environment is a flat, thin shape. For instance, a parasitic tapeworm (see Figure 20.7B) may be several metres long, but because it is very thin, most of its cells are bathed in the intestinal fluid of its host—the source of its nutrients.

The saclike body of a hydra or the paper-thin one of the tapeworm works well for animals with a simple body structure. However, most animals are composed of compact masses of cells and have an outer surface that is relatively small compared with the animal's overall volume. (For a reminder of the relationship of surface area to volume, see Module 4.2.) As an extreme example, the ratio of a whale's outer surface area to its volume is hundreds of thousands of times smaller than that of a small animal like a hydra. Still, every cell in the whale's body must be bathed in fluid, have access to oxygen and nutrients, and be able to dispose of its wastes. How is all this accomplished?

In whales and other complex animals, the evolutionary adaptation that provides for sufficient exchange with the environment is in the form of extensively branched or folded surfaces. In almost all cases, these surfaces lie within the body, protected by the integumentary system from dehydration or damage and allowing for a streamlined body shape. In humans, the digestive, respiratory, and circulatory systems rely on exchange surfaces within the body that each have a surface area more than 25 times that of the skin. Indeed, if you lined up all the tiny capillaries across which exchange between the blood and body cells occurs within your body, they would circle the globe!

Figure 25.13A is a schematic model illustrating four of the organ systems of a compact, complex animal. Each system has a large, specialized internal exchange surface. We have placed the circulatory system in the middle because of its central role in transporting substances between the other three systems. The green arrows show exchange of materials between the organism and its environment. The blue arrows indicate exchange between the circulatory system and the other systems.

Actually, direct exchange does not occur between the blood and the cells of tissues and organs. Body cells are bathed in a solution called **interstitial fluid** or lymph (see the circular enlargement in Figure 25.13A). Exchange takes place through

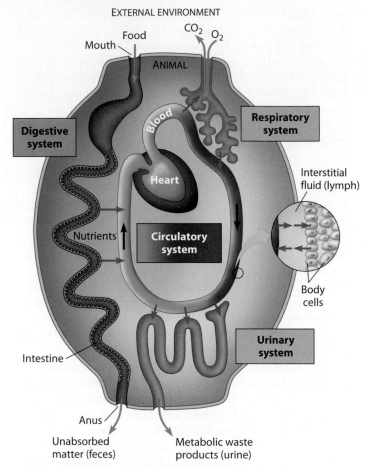

▲ **Figure 25.13A** A schematic representation showing indirect exchange between the environment and the cells of a complex animal

this fluid. In other words, to get from the blood to body cells, or vice versa, materials pass through the interstitial fluid.

The digestive system, especially the intestine, has an expanded surface area resulting from folds and projections of its inner lining (see Figure 25.8). Nutrients are absorbed from the lumen of the intestine into the cells lining this large surface area. They then pass through the interstitial fluid and into capillaries, tiny branched blood vessels that form an exchange network with the digestive surfaces. This system is so effective that enough nutrients move into the circulatory system to support the rest of the cells in the body.

The extensive, epithelium-lined tubes of the urinary system are equally effective at increasing the surface area for exchange. Enmeshed in capillaries, excretory tubes extract metabolic wastes that the blood brings from throughout the body. The wastes move out of the blood, into the excretory tubes, and pass out of the body in urine.

The respiratory system also has an enormous internal surface area across which gases are exchanged. Your lungs are not shaped like big balloons, as they are sometimes depicted, but rather like millions of tiny balloons at the tips of finely branched air tubes.

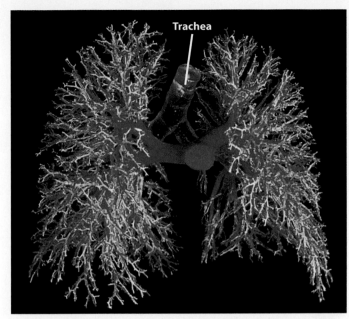

Trachea

▲ **Figure 25.13B** A resin model of the finely branched air tubes (white) and blood vessels (red) of the human lungs

Figure 25.13B shows a resin model of the human lungs. Blood vessels that convey blood from the heart to the lungs divide into tiny blood vessels that radiate throughout the lungs, shown in the model as the red branches. The white branches represent tiny air tubes that end in multilobed sacs lined with thin epithelium and surrounded by capillaries. Oxygen readily moves from the air in the lungs across this epithelium and into the blood in the capillaries. The blood returns to the heart and is then pumped throughout the body to supply all cells with oxygen.

Both Figures 25.13A and 25.13B highlight two basic concepts in animal biology: First, any animal with a complex body—one with most of its cells not in direct contact with its external environment—must have internal structures that provide sufficient surface area to service those cells. Second, the organ systems of the body are interdependent; it takes their coordinated actions to produce a functional organism.

 How do the structures of the lungs, small intestine, and kidneys relate to the function of exchange with the environment?

● These organs all have a huge number of sacs, projections, or tubes that greatly increase the surface area across which exchange of materials can occur.

25.14 Animals regulate their internal environment

More than a century ago, French physiologist Claude Bernard recognized that *two* environments are important to an animal: the external environment surrounding the animal and the internal environment, where its cells actually live. The internal environment of a vertebrate is the interstitial fluid that fills the spaces around the cells. Many animals maintain relatively constant conditions in their internal environment. Your own body maintains the salt and water balance of your internal fluids, maintains a stable pH around 7.4, and also keeps your body temperature at about 37°C. A bird, such as the ptarmigan shown in **Figure 25.14**, also maintains salt and water balance and a body temperature of about 40°C, even in winter. The bird uses energy from its food to generate body heat, and it has a thick, insulating coat of down feathers. A gecko does not generate its own body heat, but it can maintain a fairly constant body temperature by basking in the sun or resting in the shade. It does, however, regulate the salt and water balance of its body fluids.

Today, Bernard's concept of the internal environment is included in the principle of **homeostasis**, which means "a steady state." As Figure 25.14 illustrates, conditions may fluctuate widely in the external environment, but homeostatic mechanisms regulate internal conditions, resulting in much smaller changes in the animal's internal environment. Both birds and mammals have control systems that keep body temperature within a narrow range, despite large changes in the temperature of the external environment.

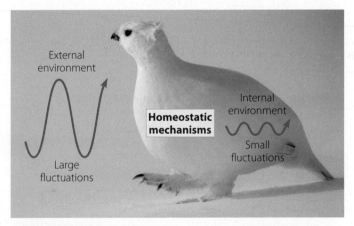

External environment

Large fluctuations

Homeostatic mechanisms

Internal environment

Small fluctuations

▲ **Figure 25.14** A model of homeostasis in a white-tailed ptarmigan in its snowy habitat

The internal environment of an animal always fluctuates slightly. Homeostasis is a dynamic state, an interplay between outside forces that tend to change the internal environment and internal control mechanisms that oppose such changes. An animal's homeostatic control systems maintain internal conditions within a range where life's metabolic processes can occur. In the next module, we explore a general mechanism for how many of these control systems function.

 Look back at Figure 25.13A. What are some ways in which the circulatory system contributes to homeostasis?

● By its exchanges with the digestive, respiratory, and urinary systems, the blood helps to maintain the proper balance of materials in the interstitial fluid surrounding body cells.

25.15 Homeostasis depends on negative feedback

Most of the control mechanisms of homeostasis are based on **negative feedback**, in which a change in a variable triggers mechanisms that reverse that change. To identify the components of a negative-feedback system, consider the simple example of the regulation of room temperature. You set the thermostat at a comfortable temperature—call this its set point. When a sensor in the thermostat detects that the temperature has dropped below this set point, the thermostat turns on the furnace. The response (heat) reverses the drop in temperature. Then, when the temperature rises to the set point, the thermostat turns the furnace off. Physiologists would call the thermostat a control centre, which senses a stimulus (room temperature below the set point) and activates a response.

Many of the control centres that maintain homeostasis in animals are located in the brain. For example, your "thermostat" operates by negative feedback to switch on and off mechanisms that maintain your body temperature around 37°C. As shown in the upper part of **Figure 25.15**, when the thermostat senses a rise in temperature above the set point, it activates cooling mechanisms, such as the dilation of blood vessels in your skin and sweating. Once body temperature returns to normal, the thermostat shuts off these cooling mechanisms. When your body temperature falls below the set point (lower part of the figure), the thermostat activates warming mechanisms, such as constriction of blood vessels in the skin to reduce heat loss and shivering to generate heat. Again, a return to normal temperature shuts off these mechanisms.

In the next four modules, we'll investigate homeostasis further, including how animals maintain a stable temperature as well as water and salt balance. As you examine the body's organ systems in detail in the chapters of this unit, you will encounter many examples of homeostatic control and negative feedback, as well as constant reminders of the relationship between structure and function.

▲ **Figure 25.15** Feedback control of body temperature

? How would adding an air conditioner contribute to the homeostatic control of room temperature?

● The air conditioner would cool the room when temperature exceeded the set point. Such opposing, or antagonistic, pairs of control circuits are common homeostatic mechanisms in the body.

25.16 An animal's regulation of body temperature helps to maintain homeostasis

Internal metabolism and the external environment provide heat for **thermoregulation**—the process by which animals maintain an internal temperature within a tolerable range. Most mammals and birds, a few other reptiles, some fishes, and many insect species are **endotherms**, meaning they are warmed mostly by heat generated by their own metabolism. In contrast, most amphibians, lizards, many fishes, and most invertebrates are **ectotherms**, meaning they gain most of their heat by absorbing it from external sources.

Keep in mind, though, that endothermic and ectothermic modes of thermoregulation are not mutually exclusive. For example, a bird is mainly endothermic, but it may warm itself in the sun on a cold morning much as an ectothermic lizard does. In the following two modules, we examine some of the ways that animals regulate their body temperatures.

? A lizard warming itself on a hot rock is an example of an _____. Why?

● Ectotherm. Lizards absorb most of their body heat from their surroundings.

25.17 Heat is gained or lost in four ways

An animal can exchange heat with the environment by four physical processes. *Conduction* is the direct transfer of thermal motion (heat) between molecules of objects in direct contact with each other, as when an animal is physically touching an object in its environment. Heat is always transferred from an object of higher temperature to one of lower temperature. In **Figure 25.17**, heat conducted from the warm rock (red arrows) elevates the lizard's body temperature.

Convection is the transfer of heat by the movement of air or liquid past a surface. In the figure, a breeze removes heat from the lizard's tail (orange arrows) by convection.

Radiation is the emission of electromagnetic waves. Radiation can transfer heat between objects that are not in direct contact, as when an animal absorbs heat radiating from the sun (yellow arrows). The lizard also radiates some of its own heat into the external environment.

Evaporation is the loss of heat from the surface of a liquid that is losing some of its molecules as a gas. A lizard loses heat as moisture evaporates from its nostrils (blue arrow).

▲ **Figure 25.17** Mechanisms of heat exchange

? If you are sweating on a hot day and turn a fan on yourself, which two mechanisms contribute to your cooling?

● Evaporation (of sweat) and convection (fan moving air)

25.18 Thermoregulation involves adaptations that balance heat gain and loss

Different animals are adapted to different environmental temperatures. Within their optimal temperature range, endotherms and many ectotherms maintain a fairly constant internal temperature despite external temperature fluctuations. Five general categories of adaptations help animals thermoregulate.

Metabolic Heat Production In cold weather, hormonal changes tend to boost the metabolic rate of birds and mammals, increasing their heat production. Simply moving around more or shivering produces heat as a metabolic by-product of the contraction of skeletal muscles. Honeybees survive cold winters by clustering together and shivering in their hive. The metabolic activity of all the bees together generates enough heat to keep the cluster alive.

Insulation A major thermoregulatory adaptation in mammals and birds is insulation—hair (often called fur), feathers, and fat layers—which reduces the flow of heat between an animal and its environment. Most land mammals and birds react to cold by raising their fur or feathers, which traps a thicker layer of air next to the warm skin, improving the insulation. (In humans, our muscles raise our hair in the cold, causing goose bumps, a

vestige from our furry ancestors.) (See Module 25.11). Aquatic mammals (such as seals) and aquatic birds (such as penguins) are insulated by a thick layer of fat called blubber.

Circulatory Adaptations Heat loss can be altered by changing the amount of blood flowing to the skin. In a bird or mammal (and some ectotherms), nerve signals cause surface blood vessels to constrict or dilate, depending on the external temperature (see Module 25.15). When the vessels are constricted, less blood flows from the warm body core to the body surface, reducing the rate of heat loss through radiation. Conversely, dilation (opening) of surface blood vessels increases the rate of heat loss. Large, thin ears capable of radiating a lot of heat have evolved in elephants, helping to cool their large bodies in their native tropical climates (**Figure 25.18A**). Flapping their ears increases heat dissipation by convection. Dilation is what causes your face to become flushed after exercising rigorously or sitting in a hot tub.

Figure 25.18B illustrates a circulatory adaptation found in many birds and mammals. In **countercurrent heat exchange**, warm and cold blood flow in opposite (countercurrent)

▼ **Figure 25.18A** Heat dissipation via ear flapping (convection) and via water spray (evaporative cooling)

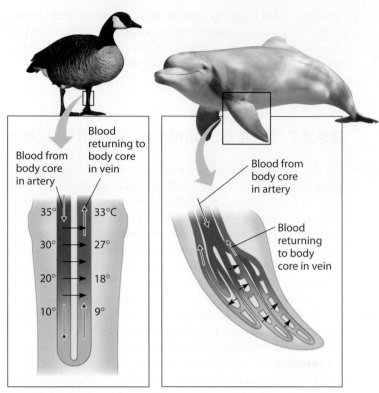

▲ **Figure 25.18B** Countercurrent heat exchange

directions in two adjacent blood vessels. Warm blood (red) from the body core cools as it flows down the goose's leg or the dolphin's flipper. But the arteries carrying the warm blood are in close contact with veins conveying cool blood (blue) back toward the body core. As shown in the figure by the black arrows, heat passes from the warmer blood to the cooler blood along the whole length of these side-by-side vessels (because heat always flows from where it is warmer to where it is cooler). By the time blood leaves the leg or flipper and returns to the body core, it is almost as warm as the body core. Thus, even when the animal is standing on ice or swimming in frigid water, heat loss through the extremities is minimal.

Some endothermic bony fishes and sharks also have countercurrent exchange mechanisms. All fishes lose heat as blood passes through the gills. In large, powerful swimmers such as the great white shark, cold blood returning from the gills is transported in large vessels lying just under the skin. Small branches of these vessels deliver oxygenated blood to the deep muscles. Each branch runs side by side with a vessel carrying warm blood outward from the inner body. The resulting countercurrent heat exchange retains heat around the main swimming muscles and enables the vigorous, sustained activity of these endothermic animals.

Evaporative Cooling   Many animals live in places where thermoregulation requires cooling as well as warming. Some animals have adaptations that greatly increase evaporative

cooling, such as panting, sweating, or spreading saliva on body surfaces. As shown in Figure 25.18A, elephants spray water over their bodies to aid evaporation. Humans sweat and other animals (such as dogs) lose heat as moisture evaporates during panting.

Behavioural Responses   Both endotherms and ectotherms control body temperature through behavioural responses. Some birds and butterflies migrate seasonally to more suitable climates. Other animals, such as desert lizards, warm themselves in the sun when it is cold and find cool, damp areas or burrows when it is hot. Many animals bathe, which brings immediate cooling by convection and continues to cool for some time by evaporation. In another example, humans dress for warmth. We will examine other animal behaviours in Chapter 36.

 ?   **Compare countercurrent heat exchange with the countercurrent exchange of oxygen in fish gills (see Module 27.4).**

● In both cases, countercurrent exchange enhances transfer all along the length of a blood vessel—transfer of heat from one vessel to another in the case of a heat exchanger and transfer of oxygen between water and vessels in the case of gills.

25.19 Animals balance their level of water and solutes through osmoregulation

Osmoregulation is the homeostatic control of the uptake and loss of water and solutes, dissolved substances such as salt (NaCl) and other ions. Animal cells cannot survive substantial water gain or loss: They swell and burst if there is a significant

net uptake of water; they shrivel and die if there is a substantial net loss of water. Osmosis is one process whereby animals regulate their uptake and loss of fluids. Recall from Module 5.4 that osmosis is a movement of water across a selectively permeable

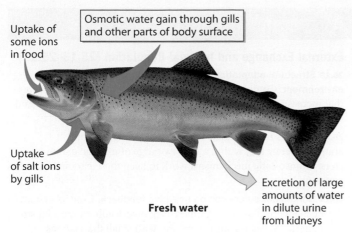

Uptake of some ions in food

Osmotic water gain through gills and other parts of body surface

Uptake of salt ions by gills

Fresh water

Excretion of large amounts of water in dilute urine from kidneys

▲ **Figure 25.19A** Osmoregulation in a rainbow trout, a freshwater fish

Gain of water and salt ions from food and by intake of seawater

Osmotic water loss through gills and other parts of body surface

Excretion of salt from gills

Salt water

Excretion of excess ions and small amounts of water in concentrated urine from kidneys

▲ **Figure 25.19B** Osmoregulation in a bluefin tuna, a saltwater fish

membrane from a solution with lower solute concentration to a solution with higher solute concentration. So, because water movement also affects solute concentrations, osmoregulation controls both solute and water levels.

Some sea-dwelling animals—such as squids, sea stars, and most other marine invertebrates—have body fluids with a solute concentration equal to that of seawater. Called **osmoconformers**, such animals do not undergo a net gain or loss of water. They therefore face no substantial challenges in water balance. However, because they differ considerably from seawater in the concentrations of certain specific solutes, they must actively transport these solutes to maintain homeostasis. For example, the resting state of squid neurons requires a higher concentration of sodium ions (Na^+) outside the cell than inside.

Many animals—land animals (such as elephants), freshwater animals (such as trout), and marine vertebrates (such as sharks)—have body fluids whose solute concentration differs from that of their environment. Therefore, they must actively regulate water movement. Such animals are called **osmoregulators**.

The freshwater fish in **Figure 25.19A** has a much higher solute concentration in its internal fluids than does fresh water. Therefore, a freshwater fish constantly gains water by osmosis through its body surface, especially through its gills. It also loses salt by diffusion to its more dilute environment. To compensate, freshwater fish actively take in salt through their gills. Although such fish do not drink water, food helps to supply some additional ions. To dispose of excess water and to conserve solutes, the fish's kidneys produce large amounts of **urine**, the waste material produced by its urinary system.

The saltwater fish in **Figure 25.19B** has different osmoregulatory challenges. Because its internal fluids are lower in total solutes than seawater, a saltwater fish loses water by osmosis across its body surfaces. It also gains salt by diffusion and from the food it eats. The fish balances the water loss by drinking large amounts of seawater, and it balances solutes by pumping out excess salt through its gills. It also saves water by producing only small amounts of concentrated urine, in which it disposes of some excess ions.

In parallel with osmoregulation, animals must also maintain a stable pH of their body fluids and cells (see Module 2.15). Small changes in pH can have large implications on enzyme and cell function. Environmental acidification, whether it is in water or soil, greatly influences an organism's ability to effectively control its body pH. Acidic external conditions can interfere with the removal of excess hydrogen ions from body fluids, effectively lowering their pH. Subsequently, ion transporters involved in osmoregulation may also be affected negatively, exacerbating the physiological stress on an individual.

Land animals face an additional homeostatic challenge. Because of the threat of dehydration, adaptations that prevent or reduce this danger provide important evolutionary advantages. Insects have tough exoskeletons impregnated with waterproof wax, which helps to conserve water. Most terrestrial vertebrates, including humans, have an outer skin formed of multiple layers of dead, water-resistant cells, which also minimizes surface water loss. As we will see in Module 28.18, the kidney also plays a major role in conserving water. Essential to survival on land are adaptations that protect fertilized eggs and developing embryos from drying out. Many insects (such as pesky summertime mosquitoes) lay their eggs in moist areas, and the eggs of many species (such as birds, turtles, and other reptiles) are surrounded by a tough, watertight shell. Likewise, the embryos of reptiles and mammals develop in a water-filled amniotic sac surrounded by protective membranes. In addition to reproductive adaptations, land animals maintain water balance by drinking and eating moist foods and by producing water metabolically through cellular respiration. Despite such adaptations, however, most terrestrial animals lose water in many ways: in urine and feces, across their skin, and from the surfaces of gas exchange organs.

? **Why are no freshwater animals osmoconformers?**

● Osmoconformers have solute concentrations equal to that of their environment. The body fluid of a freshwater osmoconformer would be very low in ions and would be too dilute to support life's processes.

Reviewing the Concepts

Structure and Function in Animal Tissues (25.1–25.7)

25.1 Structure fits function at all levels of organization in the animal body. Complex organisms are composed of systems of organs, which in turn, are made up of tissues and cells. The structure (anatomy) and function (physiology) of each are directly related.

25.2 An animal's form reflects natural selection. Physical laws affect the evolution of an animal's size and shape. Convergent evolution occurs when different animals evolve similar character traits in comparable environments.

25.3 Tissues are groups of cells with a common structure and function. Several cells may work together in a coordinated fashion to perform the specific function of the tissue.

	25.4 Epithelial tissue covers the body and lines its organs and cavities.	25.5 Connective tissue binds and supports other tissues.	25.6 Muscle tissue functions in movement.	25.7 Nervous tissue forms a communication network.
Function				
Structure	Sheets of closely packed cells	Sparse cells in extra-cellular matrix	Long cells (fibers) with contractile proteins	Neurons with branching extensions; supporting cells
Example	Columnar epithelium	Loose connective tissue	Skeletal muscle	Neuron

Organs and Organ Systems (25.8–25.12)

25.8 Organs are made up of tissues. Emergent properties of organs arise when different tissues interact to perform functions they cannot complete alone.

25.9 Bioengineers are learning to produce tissues and organs for transplants. Culturing organs in a laboratory from a patient's own cells means there will be no rejection.

25.10 Organ systems work together to perform life's functions. The integumentary system covers the body. Skeletal and muscular systems support and move it. The digestive and respiratory systems obtain food and oxygen, respectively, and the circulatory system transports these materials. The urinary system disposes of wastes, and the immune and lymphatic systems protect the body from infection. The nervous and endocrine systems control and coordinate body functions. The reproductive system produces offspring.

25.11 The integumentary system protects the body. The skin maintains a barrier between the external and internal environments. Epidermal derivatives (scales, feathers, and hair) may be involved in other functions such as protection, flight, and insulation.

25.12 Do polar bears have fibre optic hair? Polar bear hair was once thought to act like fibre optic cables, conducting UV radiation to the skin. Though the hairs are transparent and hollow, they do not conduct light of any wavelength.

External Exchange and Internal Regulation (25.13–25.19)

25.13 Structural adaptations enhance exchange with the environment. Complex animals have specialized internal structures that increase surface area. Exchange of materials between blood and body cells takes place through the interstitial fluid.

25.14 Animals regulate their internal environment. Many animals operate best within a narrow range of internal parameters. Homeostatic mechanisms work to keep these parameters constant.

25.15 Homeostasis depends on negative feedback. Control systems detect change and direct responses. Negative-feedback mechanisms keep internal variables fairly constant, with small fluctuations around set points.

25.16 An animal's regulation of body temperature helps to maintain homeostasis. Thermoregulation maintains body temperature within a tolerable range. Endotherms derive body heat mainly from their metabolism; ectotherms absorb heat from their surroundings.

25.17 Heat is gained or lost in four ways. Heat exchange with the environment occurs by conduction, convection, radiation, and evaporation.

25.18 Thermoregulation involves adaptations that balance heat gain and loss. Adaptations for thermoregulation include increased metabolic heat production, insulation, circulatory adaptations, evaporative cooling, and behavioural responses.

25.19 Animals balance their level of water and solutes through osmoregulation. Osmoconformers have the same internal solute concentration as seawater. Osmoregulators control their solute concentrations.

Connecting the Concepts

1. This chapter introduced several key concepts: Structure correlates with function; an animal's body has a hierarchy of organization with emergent properties at each level; and complex bodies have structural adaptations that increase surface area for exchange. Label the tissue layers shown in this section of the small intestine, and describe how this diagram illustrates these three concepts.

a. _____

b. _____

c. _____

d. _____
e. _____

Testing Your Knowledge

Multiple Choice

2. The cells in the human body are in contact with an internal environment consisting of
   a. blood.
   b. connective tissue.
   c. interstitial fluid.
   d. matrix.
   e. mucous membranes.

3. Which of the following body systems facilitates (but doesn't regulate) the functions of the other systems?
   a. respiratory system
   b. endocrine system
   c. digestive system
   d. urinary system
   e. circulatory system

4. Negative-feedback mechanisms are
   a. most often involved in maintaining homeostasis.
   b. activated only when a variable rises above a set point.
   c. analogous to a furnace that produces heat.
   d. found only in birds and mammals.
   e. all of the above.

5. Which of the following best illustrates homeostasis? *(Explain your answer.)*
   a. Most adult humans are between 1.5 and 1.8 m tall.
   b. The lungs and intestines have large surface areas.
   c. All the cells of the body are about the same size.
   d. When the salt concentration of the blood goes up, the kidneys expel more salt.
   e. When oxygen in the blood decreases, you feel dizzy.

6. Which of the following tissues can be found only in vertebrate animals?
   a. skeletal muscle
   b. loose connective tissue
   c. cardiac muscle
   d. adipose tissue
   e. epidermis

7. The main difference between endotherms and ectotherms is
   a. how they conserve water.
   b. whether they are warm or cold.
   c. the source of most of their body heat.
   d. whether they live in a warm or cold environment.
   e. whether they maintain a fairly stable body temperature.

8. Which of the following is not an adaptation for reducing the rate of heat loss to the environment?
   a. contraction of flight muscles before a moth takes off
   b. reduction of blood flow to surface blood vessels
   c. feathers or fur
   d. countercurrent heat exchange
   e. a thick layer of fat

9. A freshwater fish would be expected to
   a. pump salt out through its gills.
   b. produce copious quantities of dilute urine.
   c. diffuse urea out through the gills.
   d. have scales and a covering of mucus that reduce water loss to the environment.
   e. do all of the above.

Matching *(Terms in the right-hand column may be used more than once.)*

10. Closely packed cells covering a surface
11. Adipose tissue, blood, and cartilage
12. Scattered cells embedded in matrix
13. Senses stimuli and transmits signals
14. Cells are called fibres
15. Cells may be squamous, cuboidal, or columnar
16. Skeletal, cardiac, or smooth

a. connective tissue
b. muscle tissue
c. nervous tissue
d. epithelial tissue

Describing, Comparing, and Explaining

17. Briefly explain how the structure of each of these tissues is well suited to its function: stratified squamous epithelium in the skin, neurons in the brain, simple squamous epithelium lining the lung, and bone in the skull.

18. Describe ways in which the bodies of complex animals are structured for exchanging materials with the environment. Do all animals share such features?

19. Describe how the fur coat of the polar bear is well adapted for life in the Canadian Arctic.

Applying the Concepts

20. Suppose at the end of a hard run on a hot day you find that there are no drinks left in the cooler. If, out of desperation, you dunk your head into the cooler, how might the ice-cold water affect the rate at which your body temperature returns to normal?

21. Hypohidrosis is a condition where an individual has a reduced ability to sweat. How can people with hypohidrosis maintain their body temperature on a hot summer day?

Answers to all questions can be found in Appendix E.

 Study on the Go

This QR code leads to Study on the Go—mobile study resources, including practice quizzes, videos, and glossary flashcards for this textbook.

You can access Study on the Go content via your smartphone. Note: Your login information for MasteringBiology is required.

CHAPTER
26

Nutrition in Animals

BIG IDEAS

Obtaining and Processing Food

(26.1–26.4)

Animals ingest food, digest it in specialized compartments, absorb nutrients, and eliminate wastes.

The Human Digestive System

(26.5–26.12)

Food is processed sequentially in the mouth, stomach, and small intestine, where nutrients are absorbed.

Nutrition

(26.13–26.18)

A healthy diet fuels activities, provides organic building blocks, and provides nutrients a body cannot manufacture.

Having Dinner with an Ancient Fish

During a break from your studies, you may enjoy going for dinner with your friends. As you chew and swallow each morsel, you probably spend little time thinking about how your digestive system processes it. The need to acquire nutrients from other organisms is a defining feature of all animals. But, how this task is accomplished varies greatly throughout the animal kingdom.

Though diets and techniques may vary, most chordates (animals in the phylum Chordata, including humans) acquire nutrients in much the same way as we do. They ingest food through their mouths. As it passes through the digestive tract, the nutrients are digested into smaller molecules for absorption across the intestinal wall. Finally, indigestible wastes are eliminated. You will learn more about this process as you read through this chapter.

One example of an animal with unusual nutrient acquisition techniques is the hagfish. Hagfish are jawless, spineless chordates that have been described as the most hideous animals in the sea. These ancient relatives of the vertebrates have a cranium, but they diverged from the common ancestor before the evolution of vertebrae (the spinal column or backbone).

Living on the ocean floor, hagfish are scavengers, feeding primarily on dead animals. Although finding a whale carcass on the ocean floor is a rare occurrence, whenever humans have found one, they have always also found hagfish feeding on it. Like an earthworm digging through the soil, hagfish burrow into the decaying flesh of the carcass with their rasplike teeth, eating as they go.

Interestingly, hagfish are not limited to absorbing nutrients in their guts. Recent studies by Dr. Carol Bucking at the University of Ottawa have shown that hagfish are able to absorb nutrients directly across their skin. This ability is not unusual in itself. Several marine invertebrates and some parasites, including tapeworms, gather nutrients across their skin from their surroundings. What is unusual, however, is that hagfish are the only known chordates with this ability. In fact, they absorb as many nutrients across their slime-coated skin as through their intestines. Moreover, hagfish epidermal absorption is selective. Only useful nutrients, such as amino acids and glucose liberated during the decay process, are absorbed. A similar mechanism prevents the absorption of unusable material from the intestinal tract, ultimately excreting it in the feces.

What is the benefit of such an ability for the hagfish? While the creature burrows through a carcass, its ability to absorb nutrients doubles in efficiency, since they come from both inside and outside of the hagfish's body. Furthermore, nutrients that are absorbed across the skin enter the bloodstream and can be readily used. The ingested meal, however, can be digested slowly, providing nutrients for a prolonged period of time between meals. Finding a dead whale is an irregular event for a hagfish. Rationing nutrients, by storing meals in the gut, can help the animal survive prolonged periods of time that may occur between meals.

In this chapter, we consider nutrition and diet in the context of the human digestive system. This discussion will help you determine whether you are eating the right foods in the proper proportions needed to provide your body with the nutrients it needs for good health. But first, let's look at the variety of ways in which animals obtain and process food.

Obtaining and Processing Food

26.1 Animals obtain and ingest their food in a variety of ways

All animals eat other organisms—dead or alive, whole or in pieces. In general, animals fall into one of three dietary categories. **Herbivores**, such as cattle, gorillas, sea urchins, and snails, eat mainly autotrophs—plants and algae. **Carnivores**, such as lions, hawks, spiders, and whales, mostly eat other animals. Animals that consume *both* plants and animals are called **omnivores** (from the Latin *omni*, all, and *vorus*, devouring). Omnivores include humans, as well as crows, cockroaches, and raccoons.

Several types of feeding mechanisms have evolved among animals. Many aquatic animals are **suspension feeders**, which filter small organisms or food particles from water. For example, humpback whales use comblike plates called baleen to strain krill and small fish from the enormous volumes of water they take into their mouths. Clams and oysters are also suspension feeders. A film of mucus on their gills traps tiny morsels suspended in the water, and cilia on the gills sweep the food to the mouth. Figure 26.1A shows the feathery tentacles of a suspension-feeding tube worm.

Substrate feeders live in or on their food source and eat their way through it. **Figure 26.1B** shows a leaf miner caterpillar, the larva of a moth. The dark spots on the leaf are a trail of feces that the caterpillar leaves in its wake. Other substrate feeders include maggots (fly larvae), which burrow into animal carcasses, similar to the hagfish you read about in the opening essay, and earthworms, which eat their way through soil, digesting partially decayed organic material and helping to aerate and fertilize the soil as they go.

Fluid feeders suck nutrient-rich fluids from a living host. Aphids, for example, tap into the sugary sap in plants. Bloodsuckers, such as mosquitoes and ticks, pierce animals with needle-like mouthparts. The female mosquito in **Figure 26.1C** has just filled her abdomen with a meal of human blood. (Only female mosquitoes suck blood; males are also fluid feeders, but they feed on plant nectar.) In contrast to such parasitic fluid feeders, some fluid feeders actually benefit their hosts. For example, hummingbirds and bees move pollen between flowers as they fluid-feed on nectar.

Rather than filtering food from water, eating their way through a substrate, or sucking fluids from other animals or plants, most animals are **bulk feeders**, meaning they ingest large pieces of food. **Figure 26.1D** shows a grey heron preparing to swallow its prey whole. A bulk feeder may use such utensils as tentacles, pincers, claws, poisonous fangs, or jaws and teeth to kill its prey or to tear off pieces of meat or vegetation. Whatever the type of food or feeding mechanism, the processing of food involves four stages, as we see next.

▲ **Figure 26.1C** A fluid feeder: a mosquito sucking blood

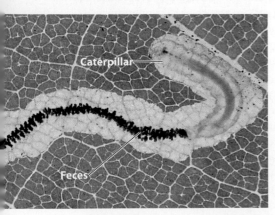

▲ **Figure 26.1A** A suspension feeder: a tube worm filtering food through its tentacles

Caterpillar

Feces

▲ **Figure 26.1B** A substrate feeder: a caterpillar eating its way through the soft tissues inside an oak leaf

> **?** Kermode spirit bears eat berries, nuts, green plants, and salmon. Name their diet category and type of feeding mechanism.
>
> Omnivore and bulk feeder ●

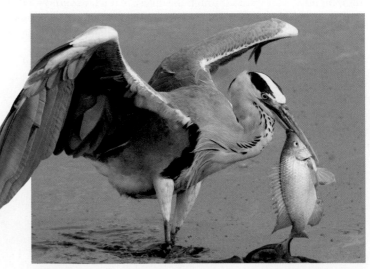

▲ **Figure 26.1D** A bulk feeder: a grey heron preparing to swallow a fish headfirst

26.2 Overview: Food processing occurs in four stages

So far we have discussed what animals eat and how they feed. As shown in **Figure 26.2A**, ❶ **ingestion**, the act of eating, is only the first of four main stages of food processing. The second stage, ❷ **digestion**, is the breaking down of food into molecules small enough for the body to absorb. Digestion typically occurs in two phases. First, food may be mechanically broken into smaller pieces. In animals with teeth, the process of chewing or tearing breaks large chunks of food into smaller ones. The second phase of digestion is the chemical breakdown process called hydrolysis. Catalyzed by specific enzymes, hydrolysis breaks the chemical bonds in food molecules by adding water to them (see Module 3.3).

Most of the organic matter in food consists of proteins, fats, and carbohydrates—all macromolecules. Animals cannot use these materials directly for two reasons. First, these molecules are too large to pass through plasma membranes into the cells. Second, an animal needs small components to make the molecules of its own body. Most food molecules—for instance, the proteins in the cat's food shown in the figure below—are different from those that make up an animal's body.

All organisms use the same building blocks to make their macromolecules. For instance, cats, caterpillars, and humans all make their proteins from the same 20 amino acids. Digestion breaks the polymers in food into monomers. As shown in **Figure 26.2B**, proteins are split into amino acids, polysaccharides and disaccharides are broken down into monosaccharides, and nucleic acids are split into nucleotides (and their components). Fats are not polymers, but they are split into their components, glycerol and fatty acids. The animal can then use these small molecules to make the specific macromolecules it needs (see Module 6.17).

In the third stage of food processing, ❸ **absorption**, the cells lining the digestive tract take up, or absorb, the products of digestion—small molecules such as amino acids and simple sugars (monosaccharides). From the digestive tract, absorbed nutrients travel in the blood to body cells, where they are used to build a cell's macromolecules or broken down further

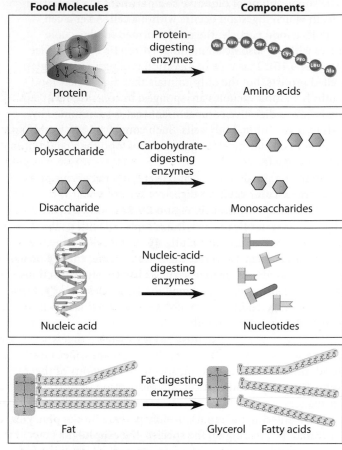

▲ **Figure 26.2B** Chemical digestion: the breakdown of organic macromolecules to their components

to provide energy. In an animal that eats much more than its body immediately uses, many of the nutrient molecules are stored throughout the body until required (see Module 26.14). Our muscles and liver make and store glycogen, a carbohydrate, whereas fats are stored in adipose cells. In the fourth and last stage of food processing, ❹ **elimination**, undigested material passes out of the digestive tract.

How can an animal digest food without digesting its own cells and tissues? After all, digestive enzymes hydrolyze the same biological molecules that animals are made of—and it is obviously important to avoid digesting ourselves! The evolutionary adaptation found in most animal species is the chemical digestion of food within specialized compartments. We discuss digestive compartments in the next module.

? **What are the two typical phases of digestion?**

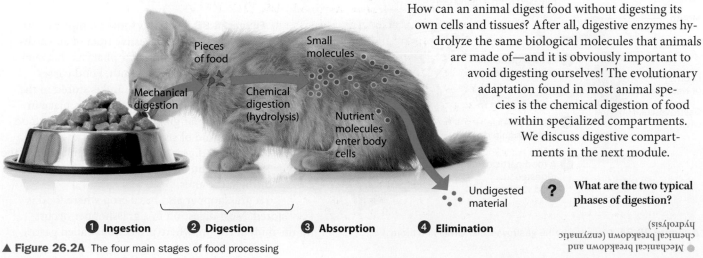

▲ **Figure 26.2A** The four main stages of food processing

❶ Ingestion   ❷ Digestion   ❸ Absorption   ❹ Elimination

26.3 Digestion occurs in specialized compartments

The simplest type of digestive compartment is a food vacuole, in which digestion occurs within a cell. After a cell engulfs a food particle, the newly formed food vacuole fuses with a lysosome containing hydrolytic enzymes (see Module 4.10). This type of digestion is common in single-celled protists, but the only animals that digest their food entirely in food vacuoles are sponges. In contrast, most animals have a digestive compartment that is surrounded by, rather than within, body cells. Such compartments enable an animal to devour much larger pieces of food than could fit in a food vacuole.

Simpler animals such as cnidarians and flatworms have a **gastrovascular cavity**, a digestive compartment with a single opening, the **mouth**. **Figure 26.3A** shows a hydra digesting a water flea, which it has captured with its tentacles and stuffed into its mouth. ❶ Gland cells lining the gastrovascular cavity secrete digestive enzymes that ❷ break down the food into smaller particles in hydrolytic reactions. ❸ Other cells engulf these small food particles, and ❹ digestion is completed in food vacuoles. Undigested material is expelled through the mouth.

Most animals have an **alimentary canal**, a digestive tract with two openings, a mouth and an anus. Because food moves in one direction, specialized regions of the tube can carry out digestion and absorption of nutrients in sequence.

Food entering the mouth usually passes into the **pharynx**, or throat. Depending on the species, the **esophagus** may channel food to a crop, gizzard, or stomach. A **crop** is a pouchlike organ in which food is softened and stored. **Stomachs** and **gizzards** may also store food temporarily, but they are more muscular and they churn and grind the food. Chemical digestion and nutrient absorption occur mainly in the **intestine**. Undigested materials are expelled through the **anus**.

Earthworm

Mouth
Pharynx
Esophagus
Crop
Gizzard
Intestine
Anus

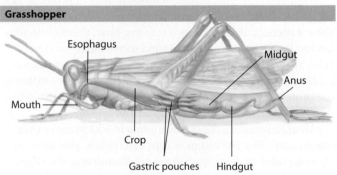

Grasshopper

Esophagus
Midgut
Anus
Mouth
Crop
Gastric pouches
Hindgut

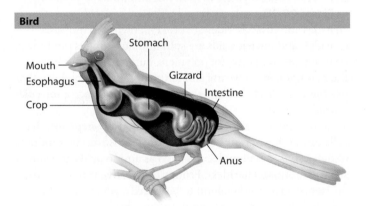

Bird

Stomach
Mouth
Gizzard
Esophagus
Intestine
Crop
Anus

▲ **Figure 26.3B** Three examples of alimentary canals

Tentacles
Mouth
❶ Digestive enzymes being released from a gland cell
❷ Food digested to small particles
Food (a water flea)
Gastrovascular cavity
❸ A food particle being engulfed
❹ A food particle digested in a food vacuole

▲ **Figure 26.3A** Digestion in the gastrovascular cavity of a hydra

Figure 26.3B illustrates three examples of alimentary canals. The digestive tract of an earthworm includes a muscular pharynx that sucks food in through the mouth. Food passes through the esophagus and is stored in the crop. Mechanical digestion takes place in the muscular gizzard, which pulverizes food with the aid of small bits of sand and gravel. Chemical digestion and absorption occur in the intestine, and undigested material is expelled through the anus.

A grasshopper also has a crop where food is stored. Most digestion in a grasshopper occurs in the midgut region, where projections called gastric pouches function in digestion and absorption. The hindgut mainly reabsorbs water and compacts wastes. Many birds have three separate chambers: a crop, a stomach, and a gravel-filled gizzard, in which food is pulverized. Chemical digestion and absorption occur in the intestine.

? **What is an advantage of an alimentary canal, compared to a gastrovascular cavity?**

● An alimentary canal has specialized regions, which can carry out digestion and absorption sequentially.

26.4 Evolutionary adaptations of vertebrate digestive systems relate to diet

Natural selection has favoured adaptations that fit the structure of a vertebrate's digestive system to the function of digesting the kind of food the animal eats. Large, expandable stomachs are common adaptations in carnivores, which may go a long time between meals and must eat as much as they can when they do catch prey. A 60 kg cougar (*Felis concolor*) can eat 9 kg of meat in one meal! After such a feast, the cougar may not hunt again for a few days.

The length of an animal's digestive tract also correlates with diet. In general, herbivores and omnivores have longer alimentary canals, relative to their body size, than carnivores. Vegetation is more difficult to digest than meat because it contains plant cell walls. A longer canal provides more time for digestion and more surface area for the absorption of nutrients.

Most herbivorous animals have special chambers that house great numbers of bacteria and protists. Nearly all animals lack the enzymes needed to digest the cellulose in plants. The microbes break down cellulose to simple sugars, which the animals then absorb or obtain by digesting the microbes.

Many herbivorous mammals—horses, elephants, and koalas, for example—house cellulose-digesting microbes in a large cecum. **Figure 26.4** compares the digestive tract of a carnivore, the coyote (*Canis latrans*), with that of a herbivore, the koala (*Phascolarctos cinereus*). These two mammals are about the same size, but the koala's intestine is much longer and includes the longest cecum (one third of the entire intestinal tract) of any animal of its size. With the aid of bacteria in its cecum, the koala gets almost all its food and water from the leaves of eucalyptus trees.

In rabbits and some rodents, cellulose-digesting bacteria live in the large intestine as well as in the cecum. Many of the nutrients produced by these microbes are initially lost in the feces because they do not go through the small intestine, the main site of nutrient absorption (see Module 26.9). Rabbits and rodents recover these nutrients by eating some of their feces, thus passing the food through the alimentary canal a second time. The feces from the second round of digestion, the familiar rabbit "pellets," are more compact and are not reingested.

The most elaborate adaptations for a herbivorous diet have evolved in the mammals called **ruminants**, which include cattle, sheep, and deer. The stomach of a ruminant has four chambers containing symbiotic microbes. A cow periodically regurgitates food from the first two chambers

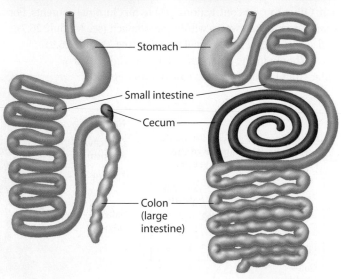

Stomach

Small intestine

Cecum

Colon (large intestine)

Carnivore   **Herbivore**

▲ **Figure 26.4** The alimentary canal in a carnivore (coyote) and a herbivore (koala)

and "chews its cud," exposing more plant fibres to its microbes for digestion. The cud is then swallowed and moves to the last stomach chambers, where digestion is completed. A cow actually obtains many of its nutrients by digesting the microbes along with the nutrients they produce. The microbes reproduce so rapidly that their numbers remain stable despite this constant loss.

Next, let's look at the details of the human digestive system as an example.

? **Name two advantages of a long alimentary canal in herbivores.**

● It provides increased time for the processing of difficult-to-digest plant material and increased surface area for absorption of nutrients.

The Human Digestive System

26.5 The human digestive system consists of an alimentary canal and accessory organs

As an introduction to our own digestive system, **Figure 26.5** illustrates the human alimentary canal and its accessory glands. The schematic diagram on the left gives you an overview of the sequence of the digestive organs and the locations of the accessory organs. Accessory organs—the salivary glands, gallbladder, liver, and pancreas—are labelled in blue on the figure. They secrete digestive juices that enter the alimentary canal through ducts.

Food is ingested and chewed in the mouth, or **oral cavity**, and then pushed by the tongue into the pharynx. Once food is swallowed, muscles propel it through the alimentary canal by **peristalsis**, alternating waves of contraction and relaxation of the smooth muscles lining the canal (see Module 26.6). It is peristalsis that enables you to process and digest food even while lying down. After chewing a bite of food, it takes only 5–10 seconds for it to pass from the pharynx down the esophagus and into your stomach. Other muscle contractions help to mix luminal contents. For example, churning waves within the stomach (see Module 26.7) and segmentation in the small intestine (see Module 26.9).

As shown in the enlargement, below right, muscular ringlike valves, called **sphincters**, regulate the passage of food into and out of the stomach. The sphincter controlling the passage out of the stomach works like a drawstring to close the stomach off, keeping food there for about 2–6 hours, long enough for stomach acids and enzymes to begin digestion. The final steps of digestion and nutrient absorption occur in the small intestine over a period of 5–6 hours. Undigested material moves slowly through the large intestine (taking 12–24 hours), and feces are stored in the rectum and then expelled through the anus.

In the next several modules, we follow a snack—an apple and some crackers and cheese—through your alimentary canal to see in more detail what happens to the food in each of the processing stations along the way.

? By what process does food move from the pharynx to the stomach of an astronaut in the weightless environment of a space station?

● Peristalsis

▲ **Figure 26.5** The human digestive system

26.6 Digestion begins in the oral cavity

Both mechanical digestion and chemical digestion begin in your oral cavity. Chewing cuts, smashes, and grinds food, making it easier to swallow and exposing more food surface to digestive enzymes. As **Figure 26.6A** shows, you have several kinds of teeth. Starting at the front on one side of the upper or lower jaw, there are two bladelike incisors. You use these for biting into your apple. Behind the incisors is a single pointed canine tooth. (Canine teeth are much bigger in carnivores, which use them to kill and rip apart prey.) Next come two premolars and three molars, which grind and crush your food. You use these to pulverize your apple, cheese, and crackers. The third molar, a "wisdom" tooth, does not appear in all people, and in some people it pushes against the other teeth and must be removed.

As you anticipate your snack, your multiple **salivary glands** may start delivering saliva through ducts to the oral cavity even before you take a bite. This is a response to the sight or smell or even thought of food. The presence of food in the oral cavity continues to stimulate salivation. In a typical day, your salivary glands secrete more than a litre of saliva. You can see the duct opening in Figure 26.6A. All three pairs of major salivary glands are visible in Figure 26.5.

Saliva contains several substances important in food processing. A slippery glycoprotein (carbohydrate-protein complex) protects the soft lining of your mouth and lubricates food for easier swallowing. Buffers neutralize food acids, helping to prevent tooth decay. Antibacterial agents kill many of the bacteria that enter your mouth with food. Saliva also contains the digestive enzyme amylase, which begins hydrolyzing the starch in your cracker into the disaccharide maltose (see Table 26.9).

Also prominent in the oral cavity is the tongue, a muscular organ covered with taste buds. Besides enabling you to taste your meal, the tongue manipulates food and helps to shape it into a ball called a **bolus**. When swallowing, the tongue pushes the bolus to the back of your oral cavity and into the pharynx.

Openings into both the esophagus and the trachea (windpipe) are in the pharynx, the region you call your throat. Most of the time, as shown on the left in **Figure 26.6B**, the esophageal opening is closed off by a sphincter (blue arrows). Air enters the larynx and flows past the vocal cords in your voice box, through the trachea, to your lungs (black arrows).

This situation changes when you start to swallow. The tongue pushes the bolus of food into the pharynx, triggering the swallowing reflex (centre of Figure 26.6B).

▲ **Figure 26.6A** The human oral cavity

Labels: Incisors, Canine, Premolars, Molars, "Wisdom" tooth, Tongue, Salivary glands, Opening of a salivary gland duct

The larynx, the upper part of the respiratory tract, moves upward. This movement tips a flap of cartilage called the epiglottis over the opening to the larynx, preventing food from entering the trachea. You can see this motion in the bobbing of your larynx (also called your Adam's apple) during swallowing. The esophageal sphincter relaxes, and the bolus enters the esophagus (green arrows in the throat). As shown on the right side of Figure 26.6B, the esophageal sphincter then contracts above the bolus, and the epiglottis tips up again, reopening the breathing tube.

The length of the esophagus varies by species. For example, fishes have no lungs to bypass and have a very short esophagus. It will come as no surprise that giraffes have a very long esophagus. Next, we will examine what happens to the food once it reaches the stomach.

? Chewing functions in the _____ phase of digestion. What does the amylase in saliva do?

● mechanical; begins the chemical digestion of starch

Labels: Tongue, Bolus of food, Pharynx, Epiglottis up, Esophageal sphincter, Larynx down, Trachea (windpipe), Esophagus, Epiglottis down, Larynx up, Epiglottis up, Larynx down

Starting to swallow (sphincter contracted) | **Swallowing reflex (sphincter relaxed)** | **Swallowing completed (sphincter contracted)**

▲ **Figure 26.6B** The human swallowing reflex

26.7 The stomach stores food and breaks it down with acid and enzymes

Having a stomach is the main reason you do not need to eat constantly. With its accordion-like folds and highly elastic wall, your stomach can stretch to accommodate more than 2 L of food and drink, usually enough to satisfy your needs for hours.

Mechanical digestion continues in the stomach. Powerful churning motions of the muscle layers thoroughly mix the stomach contents. The churning process mixes the solid food you ingest with the gastric juices, forming a liquid material called **chyme**. You may feel hunger pangs when your stomach has been empty for hours and strongly contracts.

Some chemical digestion occurs in the stomach. The stomach secretes **gastric juice**, which is made up of a protein-digesting enzyme, mucus, and strong acid. The pH of gastric juice is about 2, acidic enough to dissolve iron nails (see Module 2.15). One function of the acid is to break apart the cells in food and denature (unravel) proteins. The acid also kills many bacteria and other microbes that are swallowed with food.

The interior surface of the stomach wall is highly folded, and as the diagram in **Figure 26.7** shows, it is dotted with pits leading into tubular gastric glands. The gastric glands have three types of cells that secrete different components of gastric juice. Mucous cells (shown here in dark pink) secrete mucus, which lubricates and protects the cells lining the stomach. Parietal cells (yellow) secrete both hydrogen and chloride ions (essentially hydrochloric acid [HCl]) into the stomach lumen. Chief cells (light pink) secrete pepsinogen, an inactive form of the enzyme pepsin.

The diagram on the far right of the figure indicates how active pepsin is formed. ❶ Pepsinogen, H^+, and Cl^- are secreted into the lumen of the stomach. ❷ Next, the HCl converts some pepsinogen to pepsin. ❸ Pepsin itself then helps to activate more pepsinogen, starting a chain reaction. This series of events is an example of positive feedback, in which the end product of a process promotes the formation of more end product.

Now what does all this active pepsin do? Pepsin begins the chemical digestion of proteins—those in your cheese snack, for instance. It splits the polypeptide chains of proteins into smaller polypeptides, which will be broken down further in the small intestine. In recent years, scientists have discovered gastric forms of amylase and lipase that are functional in the low pH environment of the stomach. These enzymes play a minor role in the overall digestion of carbohydrates and lipids. These steps are included in the summary of digestion in Table 26.9.

What prevents gastric juice from digesting away the stomach lining? Secreting pepsin in the inactive form of pepsinogen helps to protect the cells of the gastric glands, and mucus helps to protect the stomach lining from both pepsin and acid. Regardless, the epithelium of the stomach is constantly eroded. But do not worry, enough new cells are generated by mitosis to replace your stomach lining completely about every three days.

Another protection for the stomach is that gastric glands do not secrete acidic gastric juice constantly. Their activity is regulated by a combination of nerve signals and hormones. When you see, smell, or taste food, a signal from your brain stimulates your gastric glands. And as food arrives in your stomach, it stretches the stomach walls and triggers the release of the hormone

▲ **Figure 26.7** The stomach and its production of gastric juice

gastrin. Gastrin circulates in the bloodstream, returning to the stomach (green dashed line in the top section of Figure 26.7), where it stimulates additional secretion of gastric juice. As much as 3 L of gastric juice may be secreted in a day.

What prevents too much gastric juice from being secreted? A negative-feedback mechanism like the one we described in Module 25.15 inhibits the secretion of gastric juice when the stomach contents become too acidic. The acid inhibits the release of gastrin, and with less gastrin in the blood, the gastric glands secrete less gastric juice.

The sphincter between the stomach and the small intestine regulates the passage of chyme, which leaves the stomach and enters the small intestine a squirt at a time, which we will discuss in Module 26.9.

? If you add pepsinogen to a test tube containing protein dissolved in distilled water, not much protein will be digested. What inorganic chemical could you add to the tube to accelerate protein digestion? What effect will it have?

● HCl or some other acid will convert inactive pepsinogen to active pepsin, which will begin digestion of the protein and also activate more pepsinogen.

26.8 Digestive ailments include acid reflux and gastric ulcers

A stomachful of digestive juice laced with enzymes and strong acid breaks apart the cells in your food, kills bacteria, and begins the digestion of proteins. At the same time, these chemicals can be dangerous to unprotected cells. The opening between the esophagus and the stomach is usually closed until a bolus arrives. Occasionally, however, acid reflux occurs. This backflow of chyme into the lower end of the esophagus causes the feeling we call heartburn—actually "esophagus-burn."

Some people suffer acid reflux frequently and severely enough to harm the lining of the esophagus, a condition called GERD (gastroesophageal reflux disease). GERD can often be treated with lifestyle changes. Doctors usually recommend that patients stop smoking, avoid alcohol, lose weight, eat small meals, refrain from lying down for 2–3 hours after eating, and sleep with the head of the bed raised. Medications to treat GERD include antacids, which reduce stomach acidity, and drugs called H2 blockers, such as Pepcid AC or Zantac, which impede acid production. Proton pump inhibitors, such as Prilosec, have a different mechanism of action and are very effective at stopping acid production. When lifestyle changes and medications fail to alleviate the symptoms, surgery to strengthen the lower esophageal sphincter may be an option.

Can all that acid also cause problems in the stomach? Increased blood flow, caused by acid secretion, protects the stomach epithelium from the damaging effects of any acid that crosses the epithelium. A gel-like coat of mucus also helps the stomach wall from the corrosive effect of the digestive juice. When these fail, open sores called gastric ulcers can develop in the stomach wall. The symptoms are usually a gnawing pain in the upper abdomen, which may occur a few hours after eating.

Gastric ulcers were formerly thought to be caused by too much acid and linked to factors such as aspirin, smoking, alcohol, coffee, and, in particular, psychological stress. However, in 1982, researchers Barry Marshall and Robin Warren reported that an acid-tolerant bacterium called *Helicobacter pylori* causes ulcers **(Figure 26.8)**. Their hypothesis was poorly received. Marshall then experimented on himself by drinking a mixture laced with *H. pylori* bacteria—and soon developed gastritis, a mild inflammation of the stomach (see Module 17.14). Although Marshall and Warren were awarded the 2005 Nobel Prize for their discovery, we do not recommend this kind of experiment!

The low pH of the stomach kills most microbes, but not *H. pylori*. This bacterium burrows beneath the mucus and can

Colourized SEM 10 700×

Bacteria

Mucous layer of stomach

▲ **Figure 26.8** An ulcer-causing bacterium, *Helicobacter pylori*

neutralize the acid before it can kill it. Growth of *H. pylori* seems to result in a localized loss of protective mucus and damage to the cells lining the stomach. Numerous white blood cells move into the stomach wall to fight the infection, and their presence is associated with gastritis. Gastric ulcers develop when pepsin and hydrochloric acid destroy cells faster than the cells can regenerate. Eventually, the stomach wall may erode to the point that it actually has a hole in it. This hole can lead to a life-threatening infection within the abdomen or internal bleeding. *H. pylori* is found in up to 90% of ulcer and gastritis sufferers. Some studies also link *H. pylori* to certain kinds of stomach cancer.

Gastric ulcers usually respond to a combination of antibiotics and bismuth (the active ingredient in Pepto-Bismol), which eliminates the bacteria and promotes healing.

When partially digested food leaves the stomach, it is accompanied by gastric juices, and so the first section of the small intestine—the duodenum—is also susceptible to ulcers, as is the esophagus in cases of severe GERD. Secretions of the pancreas work to neutralize this chyme and protect the small intestine.

 In contrast to most microbes, the species that causes ulcers thrives in an environment with a very low _____.

Hd ●

26.9 The small intestine is the major organ of chemical digestion and nutrient absorption

So what is the status of your snack as it passes out of the stomach and into the small intestine? At this point in its journey through the digestive tract, the food has been mechanically reduced to smaller pieces and mixed with digestive juices; it now resembles a thick soup. Chemically, the digestion of starch in the cracker began in the mouth, and the breakdown of protein in the cheese began in the stomach. The rest of the digestion of the macromolecules in your snack occurs in the **small intestine**. The nutrients that result from this digestion are absorbed into the blood from the small intestine. With a length of more than 6 m, the small intestine is the longest organ of the alimentary canal. Its name does not come from its length but from its diameter, which is only about 2.5 cm; the large intestine is much shorter but has twice the diameter.

Sources of Digestive Enzymes and Bile   The first 25 cm or so of the small intestine is called the **duodenum**. This is where chyme squirted from the stomach mixes with digestive juices from the pancreas, liver, and gallbladder, as well as from gland cells in the intestinal wall itself **(Figure 26.9A)**. The **pancreas** produces pancreatic juice, a mixture of digestive enzymes and an alkaline solution rich in bicarbonate. The bicarbonate acts as a buffer to neutralize the acidity of chyme as it enters the small intestine. (As you will learn in Chapter 29, the pancreas also produces hormones that regulate blood glucose levels.) Segmentation contractions of the small intestinal wall serve to mix the chyme with the pancreatic secretions.

In addition to its many other functions, the **liver** produces bile. **Bile** contains bile salts that break up fats into small droplets that are more susceptible to attack by digestive enzymes. The **gallbladder** stores and concentrates bile until it is needed in the small intestine. In response to chyme, hormones produced by the duodenum stimulate the release of bile from the liver and gallbladder, as well as digestive juices from the pancreas.

As already mentioned, the intestinal wall itself also produces digestive enzymes. Some of these enzymes are secreted into the lumen of the small intestine; others are bound to the surface of epithelial cells.

Digestion in the Small Intestine   Table 26.9 summarizes the processes of enzymatic digestion that occur in the small intestine. All four types of macromolecules—carbohydrates, proteins, nucleic acids, and fats—are digested in the small intestine. As we discuss the digestion of each, the table will help you keep track of the enzymes involved.

Remember that the digestion of carbohydrates, such as those in your cracker, began in the oral cavity and continued in the stomach. Their digestion is completed in the small intestine. An enzyme called pancreatic amylase hydrolyzes polysaccharides into the disaccharide maltose. The enzyme maltase then splits maltose into the monosaccharide glucose. Maltase is one of a family of enzymes, each specific for the hydrolysis

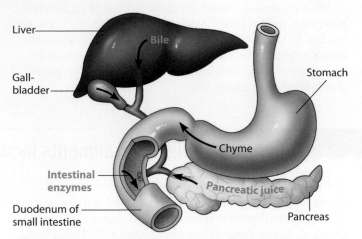

▲ **Figure 26.9A** The duodenum and associated digestive organs

of a different disaccharide. For example, sucrase hydrolyzes the sucrose (table sugar) in your apple, and lactase digests lactose. Lactose is common in milk and cheese. Children generally produce much more lactase than do adults; as a result, many adults have difficulty digesting milk products. If you are lactose intolerant, you will likely experience digestive discomfort shortly after eating the cheese in your snack.

The small intestine also completes the digestion of proteins that was begun in the stomach. The pancreas and the duodenum produce enzymes that completely dismantle polypeptides into amino acids. The enzymes trypsin and chymotrypsin break polypeptides into smaller polypeptides. Several types of enzymes called peptidases then split off one amino acid at a time from these smaller polypeptides. Working together, this enzyme team digests proteins much faster than any single enzyme could.

Yet another team of enzymes, the nucleases, hydrolyzes nucleic acids. Nucleases from the pancreas split DNA and RNA (which are present in the cells of food sources) into their component nucleotides. The nucleotides are then broken down into nitrogenous bases, sugars, and phosphates by other enzymes.

Digestion of fats is a special problem because fats are insoluble in water and tend to clump together in large globules. How is this problem solved? First, bile salts in bile separate and coat smaller fat droplets, a process called emulsification. When there are many small droplets, a larger surface area of fat is exposed to lipase, a pancreatic enzyme that breaks fat molecules down into fatty acids and glycerol.

By the time the mixture of chyme and digestive juices has moved through your duodenum, chemical digestion of your snack is just about complete. The main function of the rest of the small intestine is to absorb nutrients and water.

Absorption in the Small Intestine   Structurally, the small intestine is well suited for its task of absorbing nutrients. As **Figure 26.9B** shows, the inner wall of the small intestine has large circular folds with numerous small, fingerlike projections

TABLE 26.9 | ENZYMATIC DIGESTION

	Mouth	Stomach	Small Intestine		
Protein					
		Acid hydrolysis and pepsin	Trypsin and chymotrypsin	Various peptidases	
Large polypeptides	→————————————————————————————→		Smaller polypeptides	→————→	Amino acids
Carbohydrates					
	Salivary amylase	Gastric amylase	Pancreatic amylase	Maltase, sucrase, and lactase	
Polysaccharides	→————————————————————————————→		Maltose (and other di-saccharides)	→————→	Monosaccharides
Nucleic acids					
			Nucleases	Other enzymes	
DNA and RNA	→————————————————————————————→		Nucleotides	→————→	Nitrogenous bases, sugars, and phosphates
Fats					
		Gastric lipase	Bile salts	Pancreatic lipase	
Fat globules	→————————————————————————————→		Emulsified fat droplets	→————→	Glycerol and fatty acids

called **villi** (singular, *villus*). Each of the epithelial cells on the surface of a villus has many tiny projections, called **microvilli**. This combination of folds and projections greatly increases the surface area across which nutrients are absorbed. Indeed, the lining of your small intestine has a huge surface area—roughly 300 m², about the size of a tennis court.

Some nutrients are absorbed by facilitated diffusion; others are pumped against concentration gradients into the epithelial

Intestinal wall

Vein carrying blood to the liver

Muscle layers

Lumen

Large circular folds

Villi

Nutrient absorption

Lumen of intestine

Epithelial cells

Blood capillaries

Lymph vessel

Villi

Nutrient absorption

Microvilli

Amino acids and sugars

Fatty acids and glycerol

Fats

Blood

Lymph

Epithelial cells of a villus

▲ **Figure 26.9B** Structure and function of the small intestine cells. Once inside the epithelial cell, glucose and amino acids are transported into the capillary network within each villus. Lipids, however, must be processed further before they can enter circulation. Notice that a small lymph vessel (shown in yellow in the figure) penetrates the core of each villus. After fatty acids and glycerol are absorbed by an epithelial cell, these building blocks are recombined into fats, which are then coated with proteins and transported into a lymph vessel. These vessels are part of the lymphatic system—a network of vessels filled with a clear fluid called lymph that eventually empties into large veins near the heart.

Notice that each villus also has a network of capillaries. Many absorbed nutrients, such as amino acids and sugars, pass directly out of the intestinal epithelium and then across the thin walls of the capillaries into the blood and are carried directly to the liver.

As nutrients are absorbed from the intestinal lumen, the solute concentration of the tissue rises. As a result, the tissues become hypertonic relative to the lumen and water is absorbed by osmosis (see Module 5.4). The small intestine absorbs 90% of the water by this mechanism. The remaining water is reabsorbed in the large intestine, as we see in Module 26.11.

? Amylase is to _____ as _____ is to DNA.

polysaccharides; nuclease

26.10 One of the liver's many functions is processing nutrient-laden blood from the intestines

The liver has a strategic location in your body—between the intestines and the heart. As shown in **Figure 26.10**, capillaries from the small and large intestines converge into veins that lead into the **hepatic portal vein**. This large vessel transports blood to the liver, thus giving the liver first access to nutrients absorbed in the intestines. The liver removes excess glucose from the blood and converts it to glycogen (a polysaccharide), which is stored in liver cells. In balancing the storage of glycogen with the release of glucose to the blood, your liver plays a key role in regulating metabolism.

The liver also converts many of the nutrients it receives to new substances. Liver cells synthesize many important proteins. Among these are plasma proteins important in blood clotting and in maintaining the osmotic balance of the blood, as well as lipoproteins that transport fats and cholesterol to body cells. If your diet includes too much junk food and too many calories, the liver converts the excess to fat, which is stored in your body.

The liver has a chance to modify and detoxify substances absorbed by the digestive tract before the blood carries these materials to the rest of the body. It converts toxins such as alcohol or other drugs to inactive products that are excreted in the urine. These breakdown products are what are looked for in urine tests for various drugs. As liver cells detoxify alcohol or process some over-the-counter and prescription drugs, however, they can be damaged. The combination of alcohol and certain drugs, such as acetaminophen, is particularly harmful.

As you already learned, the liver produces bile, which aids in the digestion of fats. And as you will learn in Module 28.15, it processes nitrogen-containing wastes from the breakdown of proteins for disposal in urine.

Heart

Liver

Hepatic portal vein

Intestines

▲ **Figure 26.10** The hepatic portal vein carrying blood from the intestines to the liver

? What two functions of the liver relate to the hepatic portal vein?

As blood is delivered directly from the intestines, the liver can process and regulate the absorbed nutrients and remove toxic substances.

26.11 The large intestine compacts the feces

The **large intestine**, or **colon**, is about 1.5 m long and averages 5 cm in diameter. As the enlargement in **Figure 26.11** shows, at the junction where the small intestine leads into the large intestine there is a small pouch called the **cecum**. Compared with many other mammals, humans have a small cecum. The **appendix**, a small, fingerlike extension of the cecum, contains a mass of white blood cells that make a minor contribution to immunity. Despite this role, the appendix itself is prone to infection (appendicitis). If this occurs, emergency surgery is usually required to remove the appendix and prevent the spread of infection.

By the time your snack leaves the small intestine, the useful nutrients have been absorbed and the bulk of the fluids reclaimed. The material that reaches your large intestine is largely waste to be eliminated. The primary function of the large intestine is to process unusable wastes into feces. By absorbing still more of the water as material moves along by peristalsis, the colon makes the feces more solid. The feces consist mainly of indigestible plant fibres—cellulose from your apple, for instance—and bacteria that normally live in the colon.

Feces are stored in the final portion of the colon, the **rectum**, until they can be eliminated. Strong contractions of the colon create the urge to defecate. Two rectal sphincters, one voluntary and the other involuntary, regulate the opening of the anus.

 What intestinal disturbance arises when not enough water is absorbed throughout the intestinal tract?

Unclaimed water remains in the feces, resulting in diarrhea ●

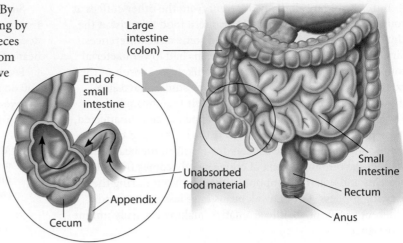

▲ **Figure 26.11** The relationship of the small and large intestines

---

RUMOUR HAS IT | ## 26.12 Is there really a coffee made from monkey dung?

If you enjoy a cup of coffee in the morning or to stay awake in class, you may have heard a rumour about a particular coffee that is collected from monkey feces. These stories, however, are not exactly true. The beans for Kopi Luwak are actually from the feces of a catlike animal, the luwak or Asian palm civet (*Paradoxurus hermaphroditus*; see **Figure 26.12A**), not a monkey. The luwak feeds on the fruit of several plants, including coffee cherries. These animals have a penchant for the ripest and reddest coffee cherries, as do farmers on traditional coffee plantations.

Once ingested, the cherries spend approximately 36 hours moving through the luwak's digestive tract. During this time, the fleshy, red pod is readily digested. The beans inside, however, are protected by a tough, indigestible seed coat. As a result,

the beans are excreted intact in the feces (**Figure 26.12B**). *Kopi* is the Indonesian word for "coffee," thus Kopi Luwak literally means "civet coffee," for obvious reasons.

How did brewing luwak feces ever become a feasible idea? In the 18th century in the Dutch East Indies, native farmers were prohibited from picking coffee fruit, called cherries, for their own use. After observing the luwaks' feeding and their passing of undigested coffee beans, the locals had a source to fulfill their caffeine fix. Soon, the Dutch plantation owners were drawn to the unique attributes of this coffee, which was brewed after the undigested beans were washed and roasted. Kopi Luwak is renowned for its smooth, nutty flavour and, most of all, its price. Less than 230 kg of Kopi Luwak can be produced annually. And, selling at between $600 and $6000 per kilogram, it is the most expensive coffee in the world. You can order a cup at a Calgary coffee shop for $20. Unfortunately, Kopi Luwak's high price and increasing popularity has prompted the establishment of luwak "farms" where animals are often held under less than suitable conditions.

▲ **Figure 26.12A** The luwak feeding on coffee cherries

▲ **Figure 26.12B** Luwak feces with undigested coffee beans

But is Kopi Luwak really different from the other coffees at your local café? Dr. Massimo Marcone, a food scientist at the University of Guelph, has discovered some clear differences. First, despite its fecal origin, these beans had lower bacterial counts than traditional coffee beans—likely as a result of the extensive washing procedure. Marcone's studies have also shown that the beans are altered on their trip through the luwak. Although the beans outward appearance is unaffected, some proteolytic enzymes penetrate the beans' seed coat. Some coffee proteins are broken down within the bean. The distinct flavour and aroma of coffee largely comes from the proteins and volatile compounds that leach out during the brewing process. Kopi Luwak beans have less protein and a different gamut of volatile aromatics, making it a truly unique experience.

Surprisingly, Kopi Luwak is not the only coffee collected from animal feces. Feces from the muntjac, a small Indonesian deer, and the Jacu bird of Brazil also contain undigested coffee beans. Small markets also exist for these beans.

Feces-generated coffee is certainly not the norm though. You do not need to be concerned about where your morning eye-opener has been. Chances are that the beans in your $2 cup were nowhere near the bowels of a civet.

 Although coffee beans pass through a luwak's digestive tract mostly unaffected, the seeds do undergo a slight change. What might this change be and what advantage might it offer to the coffee plant?

● Digestion removes or weakens the seed coat, making the germination process easier for the seedling inside.

Nutrition

26.13 Overview: An animal's diet must satisfy three needs

All animals—whether herbivores such as koalas, carnivores such as coyotes, or omnivores such as humans—have the same basic nutritional needs. All animals must obtain (1) fuel to power all body activities; (2) organic molecules to build the animal's own molecules; and (3) essential nutrients, substances the animal cannot make for itself.

We have seen that digestion dismantles the macromolecules in food. Cells can then use the resulting small molecules for energy or assemble them into their own complex

molecules—the proteins, carbohydrates, lipids, and nucleic acids needed to build and maintain cell structure and function.

Eating too little food, too much food, or the wrong mixture of foods can endanger an animal's health. Starting with the need for fuel and paying particular attention to humans, we discuss basic nutritional needs in the rest of this chapter.

 What are the three needs that an adequate diet fills?

● Fuel, organic building materials, and essential nutrients

26.14 Chemical energy powers the body

It takes energy to read this book. It also takes energy to digest your snack, walk to class, and perform all the other activities of your body. Cellular respiration produces the body's energy currency, ATP, by oxidizing organic molecules obtained from food (see Chapter 6). Usually, cells use carbohydrates and fats as fuel sources. Fats are especially rich in energy: The oxidation of a gram of fat liberates more than twice the energy liberated from a gram of carbohydrate or protein. The energy content of food is measured in **kilocalories** (1 **kcal** = 1000 calories). The calories listed on food labels or referred to in regard to nutrition are actually kilocalories and are often written as Calories (capital C).

The rate of energy consumption by an animal is called its **metabolic rate**. It is the sum of all the energy used by biochemical reactions over a given time interval. Cellular metabolism must continuously drive several processes for an animal to remain alive. These include cell maintenance, breathing, the beating of the heart, and, in birds and mammals, the maintenance of body temperature. The number of kilocalories a resting animal requires to fuel these essential processes for a given time is called the **basal metabolic rate (BMR)**.

The BMR for humans averages 1300–1500 kcal per day for adult females and about 1600–1800 kcal per day for adult males. This is about equivalent to the rate of energy use by a 75 watt light bulb. But this is only a basal (base) rate—the amount of energy you "burn" lying motionless. Any activity, even working at your desk, consumes kilocalories in addition to the BMR. The more active you are, the greater your actual metabolic rate and the greater the number of kilocalories your body uses per day.

Table 26.14 gives you an idea of the amount of activity it takes for a 68 kg person to use up the kilocalories contained in several common foods. What happens when you take in more Calories than you use? Rather than discarding the extra energy, your cells store it in various forms. Your liver and muscles store energy in the form of glycogen, a polymer of glucose molecules. Most of us store enough glycogen to supply about a day's worth of basal metabolism. Your body also stores excess energy as fat. This happens even if your diet contains little fat because the liver converts excess carbohydrates and proteins to fat. The average human's energy needs can be fuelled by the oxidation of only 0.3 kg of

	Jogging	Swimming	Walking
Speed of exercise	**12 km/h (8 min/mi)**	**3 km/h (30 min/mi)**	**4 km/h (24 min/mi)**
Kcal "burned" per hour	**850**	**408**	**252**
Quarter-pounder with cheese (113.4 g), 417 kcal	29.5 min	61 min	99.3 min
Pepperoni pizza (1 large slice), 280 kcal	19.8 min	42 min	66.7 min
Non-diet soft drink (355 mL can), 152 kcal	10.7 min	22 min	36.2 min
Whole wheat bread (1 slice), 65 kcal	4.6 min	10 min	15.5 min
These data are for a person weighing 68 kg.			

fat per day. Most healthy people have enough stored fat to sustain them through several weeks of starvation. We discuss fat storage and its consequences in Module 26.17. But first let's consider the essential nutrients that must be supplied in the diet.

? **What is the difference between metabolic rate and basal metabolic rate?**

 Metabolic rate is the total energy used for all activities in a unit of time; BMR is the minimum number of kilocalories that a resting animal needs to maintain life's basic processes for a unit of time.

26.15 An animal's diet must supply essential nutrients

Besides providing fuel and organic raw materials, an animal's diet must also supply **essential nutrients**. These are materials that must be obtained in preassembled form because the animal's cells cannot make them from *any* raw material. Some nutrients are essential for all animals, whereas others are needed only by certain species. For example, vitamin C is an essential nutrient for humans and other primates, guinea pigs, and some birds and snakes, but most animals can make vitamin C as needed. There are four classes of essential nutrients: essential fatty acids, essential amino acids, vitamins, and minerals.

Essential Fatty Acids   Our cells make fats and other lipids by combining fatty acids with other molecules, such as glycerol (see Module 3.14). We can make most of the fatty acids we need. Those we cannot make, called **essential fatty acids**, must be obtained from our diet. Important essential fatty acids include linoleic acid (also called omega-6) and linolenic acid (omega-3). Both omega-3 and omega-6 fatty acids are needed to make some of the phospholipids of cell membranes. They also have numerous health benefits, including fighting cancers and heart disease. Because seeds, grains, and vegetables generally provide ample amounts of essential fatty acids, deficiencies are rare.

Essential Amino Acids   Proteins are built from 20 different kinds of amino acids. Adult humans can make 12 of these amino acids from other compounds. The remaining eight, known as the **essential amino acids**, must be obtained from the diet. Infants also require a ninth, histidine. A deficiency of a single essential amino acid impairs protein synthesis and can lead to protein deficiency.

The simplest way to get all the essential amino acids is to eat meat and animal by-products such as eggs, milk, and cheese. The proteins in these products are said to be "complete," meaning they provide all the essential amino acids in the

proportions needed by the human body. In contrast, most plant proteins are "incomplete," or deficient in one or more essential amino acids. If you are vegetarian (by choice, or, as for much of the world's population, by economic necessity), the key to good nutrition is to eat a varied diet of plant proteins that together supply sufficient quantities of all the essential amino acids.

Simply by eating a combination of beans and corn, for example, vegetarians can get all the essential amino acids **(Figure 26.15)**. The combination of a legume (such as beans,

Essential amino acids

Methionine
Valine
(Histidine)
Threonine
Phenylalanine
Leucine
Isoleucine
Tryptophan
Lysine

Corn

Beans and other legumes

▲ Figure 26.15 Essential amino acids from a vegetarian diet

peanuts, or soybeans) and a grain often provides the right balance. Most societies have, by trial and error, developed balanced diets that prevent protein deficiency. The Latin American staple of rice and beans is an example.

Dietary Deficiencies   A diet that is chronically deficient in calories or lacks one or more essential nutrients results in **malnutrition**. Failing to obtain adequate nutrition can have serious health consequences.

Living in an industrialized country where food is plentiful and most people can afford it, you may find it hard to relate to starvation. However, hunger is still a concern for many Canadians. The number of people relying on food banks appears to be on the rise. In March 2010, more than 850 000 people received assistance. Globally, almost 1 billion people do not have enough to eat, and an estimated 4.5 million die of hunger each year, most of them children. Undernutrition, which occurs when diets do not supply sufficient chemical energy, may occur when food supplies are disrupted by drought, wars, or other crises and when severe poverty prevents people from obtaining sufficient food.

The most common type of human malnutrition is protein deficiency resulting from a diet that must depend on a single plant staple—just corn, rice, or potatoes, for instance. Protein deficiency often begins when a child's diet shifts from breast milk alone to food that is mostly starch or other carbohydrates. Such children, if they survive infancy, often have impaired physical and mental development.

Depending on food availability and choices, it is even possible for an overnourished (obese) individual to be malnourished. For example, malnutrition can result from a steady diet of junk food, which offers little nutritional value.

Another cause of undernutrition is anorexia nervosa, an eating disorder in which individuals, most often females, starve themselves compulsively, in response to an intense fear of gaining weight. Bulimia is a pattern of binge eating followed by purging through induced vomiting, abuse of laxatives, or excessive exercise. Both disorders are serious health problems and can even lead to death.

In the next module, we continue our look at essential nutrients—this time vitamins and minerals.

 ? **Look carefully at Figure 26.15. A diet consisting strictly of corn would probably result in a deficiency of which essential amino acids?**

● Tryptophan and lysine

26.16 A healthy human diet includes 13 vitamins and many essential minerals

A **vitamin** is an organic nutrient required in your diet but only in very small amounts. For example, 1 tablespoon of vitamin B_{12} could provide the daily requirement for nearly a million people. Depending on the vitamin, the required daily amount ranges from about 0.01 to 100 mg. To help you imagine how small these amounts are, consider that a small peanut weighs about 1 g, so 100 mg would be one-tenth of a small peanut. And some vitamin requirements are one-ten-thousandth of that!

Table 26.16A lists 13 essential vitamins and their major dietary sources. As you can see from the functions in the body and symptoms of deficiency listed in the table, vitamins are absolutely necessary to your health—helping to keep your skin healthy, your nervous system in good working order, and your vision clear, among dozens of other actions.

Vitamins are classified as water-soluble or fat-soluble. Water-soluble vitamins include the B vitamins and vitamin C. Many B vitamins function in the body as coenzymes, enabling the catalytic functions of enzymes that are used over and over in metabolic reactions. Vitamin C is required in the production of connective tissue.

Most animals have the ability to synthesize vitamin C. Humans, however, are among the few species that lacks this ability on account of a single genetic defect. Therefore, we must obtain adequate vitamin C in our diets. Not enough vitamin C leads to the condition known as scurvy, the deterioration of the skin and teeth. If left untreated, scurvy frequently leads to death. In the 16th century, French explorer Jacques Cartier led explorations of the St. Lawrence Region. During these explorations, a poor diet caused many of his men to fall ill with scurvy. With the help of Canadian Aboriginals and their tea-like concoction of white cedar needles and bark, presumably containing vitamin C, Cartier's men were saved.

Fat-soluble vitamins include vitamins A, D, E, and K. Vitamin A is a component of the visual pigments in your eyes. Among populations subsisting on simple rice diets, people are often afflicted with vitamin A deficiency, which can cause blindness or death. Vitamin D aids in calcium absorption and bone formation. Your dietary requirement for vitamin D is variable because you synthesize this vitamin from other molecules when your skin is exposed to sunlight. Currently, the Canadian Cancer Society recommends a daily dose of 1000 IU during the months of autumn and winter when exposure to sunlight is limited. Vitamin E functions as an antioxidant that helps to prevent damage to your cells. Vitamin K is necessary for proper blood clotting.

Minerals are simple inorganic nutrients, also required in small amounts—from less than 1 mg to about 2500 mg per day. Table 26.16B lists your daily mineral requirements. As you can see from the table, you need the first seven minerals in amounts greater than 200 mg per day (about two-tenths of that small peanut). You need the rest in much smaller quantities. The table includes the dietary sources for each mineral, and lists the functions and the symptoms of deficiency for most of these minerals.

Along with bony fish and tetrapods, humans require relatively large amounts of calcium and phosphorus to construct

TABLE 26.16A | VITAMIN REQUIREMENTS OF HUMANS

Vitamin	Major Dietary Sources	Functions in the Body	Symptoms of Deficiency
Water-Soluble Vitamins			
Vitamin B_1 (thiamine)	Pork, legumes, peanuts, whole grains	Coenzyme use in removing CO_2 from organic compounds	Beriberi (tingling, poor coordination, reduced heart function)
Vitamin B_2 (riboflavin)	Dairy products, meats, enriched grains, vegetables	Component of coenzyme FAD	Skin lesions, such as cracks at corners of mouth
Vitamin B_3 (niacin)	Nuts, meats, grains	Component of coenzymes NAD^+ and $NADP^+$	Skin and gastrointestinal lesions, delusions, confusion
Vitamin B_5 (pantothenic acid)	Meats, dairy products, whole grains, fruits, vegetables	Component of coenzyme A	Fatigue, numbness, tingling of hands and feet
Vitamin B_6 (pyridoxine)	Meats, vegetables, whole grains	Coenzyme used in amino acid metabolism	Irritability, convulsions, muscular twitching, anemia
Vitamin B_7 (biotin)	Legumes, other vegetables, meats	Coenzyme in synthesis of fats, glycogen, and amino acids	Scaly skin inflammation, neuromuscular disorders
Vitamin B_9 (folic acid)	Green vegetables, oranges, nuts, legumes, whole grains	Coenzyme in nucleic acid and amino acid metabolism	Anemia, birth defects
Vitamin B_{12} (cobalamin)	Meats, eggs, dairy products	Production of nucleic acids and red blood cells	Anemia, numbness, loss of balance
Vitamin C (ascorbic acid)	Citrus fruits, broccoli, tomatoes	Used in collagen synthesis; antioxidant	Scurvy (degeneration of skin, teeth), delayed wound healing
Fat-Soluble Vitamins			
Vitamin A (retinol)	Dark green and orange vegetables and fruits, dairy products	Component of visual pigments; maintenance of epithelial tissues	Blindness, skin disorders, impaired immunity
Vitamin D	Dairy products, egg yolk	Aids in absorption and use of calcium and phosphorus	Rickets (bone deformities) in children; bone softening in adults
Vitamin E (tocopherol)	Vegetable oils, nuts, seeds	Antioxidant; helps prevent damage to cell membranes	Nervous system degeneration
Vitamin K	Green vegetables, tea; also made by colon bacteria	Important in blood clotting	Defective blood clotting

and maintain our skeleton. Too little calcium, especially before the age of 30, can result in the degenerative bone disease osteoporosis (see Module 33.5). In all animals, calcium is also necessary for the normal functioning of nerves and muscles, and phosphorus is an ingredient of ATP and nucleic acids.

Iron is a component of hemoglobin, the oxygen-carrying protein found in your red blood cells. Vertebrates need iodine to make thyroid hormones, which regulate metabolic rate. Worldwide, iodine deficiency is a serious human health problem (see Module 2.2). Insufficient iodine during pregnancy is the leading cause of motor and intellectual deficiencies in the unborn child. These conditions are preventable with iodine supplementation. In North America, table salt is iodized to help prevent iodine deficiencies.

Sodium, potassium, and chlorine are important in nerve function and help to maintain the osmotic balance of your cells. Most of us ingest far more salt (sodium chloride) than we need. The average Canadian consumes about two to three times the required amount of sodium. Packaged (prepared) foods and most junk foods contain large amounts of sodium chloride, even if they do not taste very salty. Ingesting too much sodium has been associated with high blood pressure and other health risks. However, an actual link

between high salt intake and high blood pressure is currently under debate.

A varied diet usually includes enough vitamins and minerals and is considered the best source of these nutrients. Such diets meet the **Recommended Dietary Allowances (RDAs)**, minimum amounts of nutrients that are needed each day, as determined by a national scientific panel. Health Canada makes specific recommendations for certain population groups, such as additional B_{12} for people over age 50, folic acid for pregnant women, and extra vitamin D for people with dark skin (which blocks the synthesis of this vitamin) and for those exposed to insufficient sunlight.

The subject of vitamin dosage has led to heated scientific and popular debate. Some people argue that RDAs are set too low, and some believe, probably mistakenly, that massive doses of vitamins confer health benefits. In general, any excess water-soluble vitamins consumed will be eliminated in urine. But high doses of niacin have been shown to cause liver damage, and large doses of vitamin C can result in gastrointestinal upset. Excessive amounts of fat-soluble vitamins accumulate in body fat. Thus, overdoses may have toxic effects. Excess vitamin A and K are both linked to liver damage. In addition to the dangers of high salt intake, excessive consumption of

TABLE 26.16B | MINERAL REQUIREMENTS OF HUMANS

Mineral*	Dietary Sources	Functions in the Body	Symptoms of Deficiency
Calcium (Ca)	Dairy products, dark green vegetables, legumes	Bone and tooth formation, blood clotting, nerve and muscle function	Impaired growth, loss of bone mass
Phosphorus (P)	Dairy products, meats, grains	Bone and tooth formation, acid-base balance, nucleotide synthesis	Weakness, loss of minerals from bone, calcium loss
Sulphur (s)	Proteins from many sources	Component of certain amino acids	Impaired growth, fatigue, swelling
Potassium (K)	Meats, dairy products, many fruits and vegetables, grains	Acid-base balance, water balance, nerve function	Muscular weakness, paralysis, nausea, heart failure
Chlorine (Cl)	Table salt	Acid-base balance, water balance, nerve function, formation of gastric juice	Muscle cramps, reduced appetite
Sodium (Na)	Table salt	Acid-base balance, water balance, nerve function	Muscle cramps, reduced appetite
Magnesium (Mg)	Whole grains, green leafy vegetables	Enzyme cofactor; ATP bioenergetics	Nervous system disturbances
Iron (Fe)	Meats, eggs, legumes, whole grains, green leafy vegetables	Component of hemoglobin and of electron carriers; enzyme cofactor	Iron-deficiency anemia, weakness, impaired immunity
Fluorine (F)	Drinking water, tea, seafood	Maintenance of tooth structure	Higher frequency of tooth decay
Iodine (I)	Seafood, iodized salt	Component of thyroid hormones	Goiter (enlarged thyroid gland), congenital intellectual deficiencies

(Left bracket label spanning Calcium through Magnesium: *Greater than 200 mg per day required*)

*Additional minerals required in trace amounts are chromium (Cr), cobalt (Co), copper (Cu), manganese (Mn), molybdenum (Mo), selenium (Se), and zinc (Zn). All of these minerals, as well as those in the table, are harmful when consumed in excess.

all the listed minerals may be harmful. For example, in some regions of Africa where the water supply is especially iron-rich, as much as 10% of the population have liver damage as a result of iron overload.

Nevertheless, when we discuss health concerns relating to vitamins and minerals, most of the time we are concerned with deficiencies. Remember that a diet that does not include adequate quantities of fresh fruits and vegetables, either as a result of poor food choices or limited supplies or resources, is unlikely to provide the nutrients needed for good health.

 Which of the vitamins and minerals listed in these tables are involved with the formation or maintenance of bones and teeth?

● Vitamin C, vitamin D, calcium, phosphorus, and fluorine

EVOLUTION CONNECTION

26.17 The human health problem of obesity may reflect our evolutionary past

Overnourishment, consuming more food energy than the body needs for normal metabolism, causes **obesity**, the excessive accumulation of fat. The World Health Organization now recognizes obesity as a major global health problem. The increased availability of fattening foods and large portions, combined with more sedentary lifestyles, puts excess weight on bodies. A standard method of determining healthy weight is body mass index (BMI), a ratio of weight to height **(Figure 26.17A)**. A BMI of 25–29 is considered overweight, and above 30 is obese. In Canada, the percentage of obese (very overweight) people has been increasing in recent years, reaching 17.5% in 2010. A further 33.1% of Canadians are overweight. Weight problems often begin at a young age: About 26% of Canadian children and adolescents are either overweight or obese.

Obesity contributes to a number of health problems, including type 2 diabetes, cancer of the colon and breast, and cardiovascular disease. Obesity is estimated to be a factor in more than 9% of Canadian deaths. The results of a 15-year study, published in 2010, indicates that obesity now equals smoking in its contribution to disease and effect on health-related quality of life.

The obesity epidemic has stimulated an increase in scientific research on the causes and possible treatments for weight-control problems. Inheritance is one factor in obesity, which helps to explain why certain people have to struggle harder than others to control their weight. Dozens of genes have been identified that code for weight-regulating hormones. **Figure 26.17B** compares a normal mouse to one that is obese because of genetic causes. Scientists continue to study the signalling pathways that regulate both long-term and short-term appetite and the body's storage of fat. This research gives us reason to be somewhat optimistic that obese people who have inherited defects in these weight-controlling mechanisms may someday be treated with a new generation of drugs. But so far, the diversity of defects in these complex systems has made it difficult to develop drugs that are effective and free from serious side effects.

Some of our current struggles with obesity may be a consequence of our evolutionary history. Most of us crave foods that are fatty: fries, chips, burgers, cheese, and ice cream. Though fat hoarding can be a health liability today, it may actually have been advantageous in our evolutionary past. Only in the past few centuries have

▲ **Figure 26.17B** A genetically obese mouse (left) and a normal mouse (right)

large numbers of people had access to a reliable supply of high-calorie food. Our ancestors on the African savanna were hunter-gatherers who probably survived mainly on seeds and other plant products, a diet only occasionally supplemented by hunting game or scavenging meat from animals killed by other predators. In such a feast-and-famine existence, natural selection may have favoured those individuals with a physiology that induced them to gorge on rich, fatty foods on those rare occasions when such treats were available. Individuals with genes promoting the storage of fat during feasts may have been more likely than their thinner peers to survive famines.

So perhaps our modern taste for fats and sugars reflects the selective advantage it conveyed in our evolutionary history. Although we know it is unhealthful, many of us find it difficult to overcome the ancient survival behaviour of stockpiling for the next famine.

▼ **Figure 26.17A** Body mass index (BMI): one measure of healthy weight

 How was fat hoarding beneficial for early hunter-gatherers?

● Hunter-gatherers typically fed in feast-famine nature. The ability to store high-calorie fat after rare opportunities to gorge themselves allowed for its use during times when food was scarce.

26.18 Diet can influence risk of cardiovascular disease and cancer

Food influences far more than your size and appearance. Diet also plays an important role in a person's risk of developing serious illnesses, including cardiovascular disease and cancer. Some risk factors associated with cardiovascular disease, such as family history, are unavoidable, but others, such as smoking and lack of exercise, you can influence through your behaviour. Diet is another behavioural factor that affects cardiovascular health. For instance, a diet rich in saturated fats is linked to high blood cholesterol, which in turn is linked to cardiovascular disease.

Cholesterol travels through the body in particles made up of thousands of molecules of cholesterol and other lipids bound to proteins in complexes called lipoproteins (see Module 3.16). Recall that high blood levels of one type of particle called **low-density lipoprotein (LDLs)** generally correlate with a tendency to develop blocked blood vessels, high blood pressure, and consequent heart attacks. In contrast to LDLs, **high-density lipoprotein (HDLs)** may decrease the risk of vessel blockage, perhaps because HDLs convey excess cholesterol to the liver, where it is broken down. Some research indicates that reducing LDLs while maintaining or increasing HDLs lowers the risk of cardiovascular disease. How do you increase your levels of "good" cholesterol? You can exercise more, which tends to increase HDL levels. And you can abstain from smoking, because smoking has been shown to lower HDL levels.

How do you decrease your levels of "bad" cholesterol? You can avoid a diet high in saturated fats, which tend to increase LDL levels. Saturated fats (see Module 3.14) are found in eggs, butter, and most meats. Saturated fats are also found in artificially saturated ("hydrogenated") vegetable oils as in margarine. The hydrogenation process, which solidifies vegetable oils, also produces a type of fat called trans fat. Trans fats tend not only to increase LDL levels but also to lower HDL levels, a two-pronged attack on cardiovascular health. Trans fats may also accumulate in the myelin of neurons, affecting the conduction of action potentials (see the opening essay for Chapter 3). By contrast, eating mainly unsaturated fats, such as those found in fatty fish like salmon, certain nuts, and most liquid vegetable oils, including corn, soybean, and olive oils, tends to lower LDL levels and raise HDL levels. These oils are also important sources of vitamin E, whose antioxidant effect may help to prevent blood vessel blockage, and omega-3 fatty acids, which appear to protect against cardiovascular disease.

As discussed in Module 11.18, diet also seems to influence our risk for certain cancers. Some research suggests a link between diets heavy in fats or carbohydrates and the incidence of breast cancer. The incidence of colon cancer and prostate cancer may be linked to a diet rich in saturated fat or red meat. Other foods may help to fight cancer. For example, some fruits and vegetables (Figure 26.18) are rich in antioxidants, chemicals that help to protect cells from damaging molecules known as free radicals. Antioxidants may help to prevent cancer, although this link is still debated by scientists. Foods that are particularly high in antioxidants include berries, beans, nuts, and dried fruit.

Despite the progress researchers have made in studying nutrition and health, it is often difficult to design controlled experiments that establish the link between the two. Experiments that may damage participants' health are clearly unethical. Some studies rely on self-reported food intake, and the accuracy of participants' memories may influence the outcome. Scientists often do studies that correlate certain health characteristics with groups that have particular diets or lifestyles.

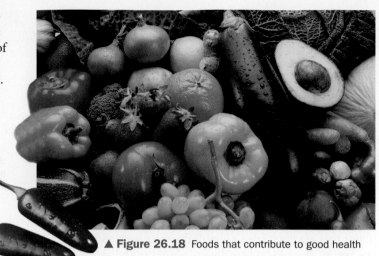

▲ **Figure 26.18** Foods that contribute to good health

For example, many French people eat high-fat diets and drink wine, yet have lower rates of obesity and heart disease than do North Americans. When researchers notice apparent contradictions like these, they attempt to control for other variables and isolate the factors responsible for such observations, such as the fact that the French eat smaller portions; eat more unprocessed, fresh foods; and snack infrequently.

Even with large, controlled intervention trials, results may be contradictory or inconclusive. For instance, an eight-year study of almost 49 000 postmenopausal women found that low-fat diets failed to reduce the risk of breast and colon cancer and did not affect the incidence of cardiovascular disease. LDL and cholesterol levels did decrease slightly in the low-fat group, however.

The relationship between foods and health is complex, and we have much to learn. The Canadian Cancer Society (CCS) suggests that following the dietary guidelines in **Table 26.18**, in combination with physical activity, can help to lower cancer risk. The CCS's main recommendation is to "eat a variety of healthful foods, with an emphasis on plant sources."

 If you are trying to minimize the damaging effects of blood cholesterol on your cardiovascular system, your goal is to _____ your LDLs and _____ your HDLs.

● decrease; increase

TABLE 26.18	DIETARY GUIDELINES FOR REDUCING CANCER RISK
Maintain a healthy weight throughout life.
Eat five or more servings of a variety of fruits and vegetables daily.
Choose whole grains over processed (refined) grains.
Limit consumption of processed and red meats.
If you drink alcoholic beverages, limit yourself to a maximum of one or two drinks a day (a drink = 12 ounces of beer, 5 ounces of wine, or 1.5 ounces of 80% distilled spirits).

Reviewing the Concepts

Obtaining and Processing Food (26.1–26.4)

26.1 Animals obtain and ingest their food in a variety of ways. Animals may be herbivores, carnivores, or omnivores and may obtain food by suspension, substrate, fluid, or bulk feeding.

26.2 Overview: Food processing occurs in four stages. The stages are ingestion, digestion, absorption, and elimination.

26.3 Digestion occurs in specialized compartments. Food may be digested in food vacuoles, gastrovascular cavities, or alimentary canals, which run from mouth to anus with specialized regions.

26.4 Evolutionary adaptations of vertebrate digestive systems relate to diet. Herbivores may have longer alimentary canals than carnivores and compartments that house cellulose-digesting microbes.

The Human Digestive System (26.5–26.12)

26.5 The human digestive system consists of an alimentary canal and accessory organs. The rhythmic muscle contractions of peristalsis squeeze food along the alimentary canal.

26.6 Digestion begins in the oral cavity. The teeth break up food, saliva moistens it, and an enzyme in saliva begins the hydrolysis of starch. The tongue pushes the bolus of food into the pharynx.

26.7 The stomach stores food and breaks it down with acid and enzymes. Pepsin in gastric juice begins to digest protein.

26.8 Digestive ailments include acid reflux and gastric ulcers. Too much or too little stomach acid can lead to disease development. Excess acid in the esophagus can lead to GERD. The bacterium *Helicobacter pylori* can cause stomach ulcers.

26.9 The small intestine is the major organ of chemical digestion and nutrient absorption. Enzymes from the pancreas and cells of the intestinal wall digest food molecules. Bile, made in the liver and stored in the gallbladder, emulsifies fat for attack by enzymes. Folds of the intestinal lining and fingerlike villi (with microscopic microvilli) increase the area across which absorbed nutrients move into capillaries and lymph vessels.

26.10 One of the liver's many functions is processing nutrient-laden blood from the intestines. The liver regulates nutrient levels in the blood, produces bile, detoxifies alcohol and drugs, and synthesizes blood proteins.

26.11 The large intestine compacts the feces. Some bacteria in the colon produce vitamins. Feces are stored in the rectum before elimination.

26.12 Is there really a coffee made from monkey dung? The world's most expensive coffee beans are collected from the feces of the catlike Asian palm civet. Washed, roasted, and brewed, these beans create a unique cup of coffee.

Nutrition (26.13–26.18)

26.13 Overview: An animal's diet must satisfy three needs. The diet must provide chemical energy, raw materials for biosynthesis, and essential nutrients.

26.14 Chemical energy powers the body. Metabolic rate, the rate of energy consumption, includes the basal metabolic rate (BMR) plus the energy used for other activities.

26.15 An animal's diet must supply essential nutrients. Essential fatty acids are easily obtained from the diet. The eight essential amino acids can be obtained from animal protein or the proper combination of plant foods. Malnutrition results from a diet lacking in sufficient calories or essential nutrients.

26.16 A healthy human diet includes 13 vitamins and many essential minerals. Most vitamins function as coenzymes. Minerals are inorganic nutrients that play a variety of roles. A varied diet usually meets the RDAs for these nutrients.

26.17 The human health problem of obesity may reflect our evolutionary past. The dramatic rise in obesity is linked to a lack of exercise and abundance of fattening foods and may partly stem from an evolutionary advantage of fat hoarding.

26.18 Diet can influence risk of cardiovascular disease and cancer. The ratio of HDLs to LDLs is influenced by diet.

Connecting the Concepts

1. Label the parts of the human digestive system below and indicate the functions of these organs and glands.

2. Complete the following map summarizing the nutritional needs of animals that are met by a healthy diet.

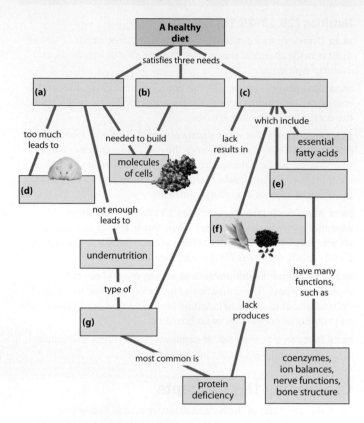

Testing Your Knowledge
Multiple Choice

3. Earthworms, which are substrate feeders,
   a. feed mostly on mineral substrates.
   b. filter small organisms from the soil.
   c. are bulk feeders.
   d. are herbivores that eat autotrophs.
   e. eat their way through the soil, feeding on partially decayed organic matter.

4. The energy content of fats
   a. is released by bile salts.
   b. may be lost unless a herbivore eats some of its feces.
   c. is, per gram, twice that of carbohydrates or proteins.
   d. can reverse the effects of undernutrition.
   e. Both c and d are correct.

5. After performing dissections of a tadpole and an adult of the same frog species you notice differences in the structure of their intestines. The tadpole has a very long intestine relative to its body size, while the adult has a short intestine relative to its body size. Which of the following would you predict?
   a. The animal is carnivorous throughout its life.
   b. The animal is herbivorous throughout its life.
   c. The animal is herbivorous as a tadpole, and carnivorous as an adult.
   d. The animal is carnivorous as a tadpole, and herbivorous as an adult.
   e. You cannot tell the diet of an animal by looking at the structure of its intestines.

6. Which of the following statements properly describes the structure and function of the small intestine?
   a. The small intestine has numerous pits that secrete HCl in order to denature proteins.
   b. The small intestine has fingerlike projections that secrete numerous enzymes to digest macromolecules.
   c. The small intestine has fingerlike projections that increase the surface area for absorption of digested nutrients.
   d. The small intestine has lymphatic vessels that are responsible for transporting monosaccharides to the circulatory system.
   e. The small intestine epithelium absorbs water and forms feces.

7. Which of the following statements is false?
   a. A healthy human has enough stored fat to supply calories for several weeks.
   b. The synthesis of essential amino acids occurs in the liver.
   c. The interconversion of glucose and glycogen takes place in the liver.
   d. After glycogen stores are filled, excessive calories are stored as fat, regardless of their original food source.
   e. Carbohydrates and fats are normally used as fuel before proteins are used.

8. Which of the following is mismatched with its function?
   a. most B vitamins—coenzymes
   b. vitamin E—antioxidant
   c. vitamin K—blood clotting
   d. iron—component of thyroid hormones
   e. phosphorus—bone formation, nucleotide synthesis

9. Why is it necessary for healthy vegetarians to combine different plant foods or eat some eggs or milk products?
   a. to make sure they obtain sufficient calories
   b. to provide sufficient vitamins
   c. to make sure they ingest all essential fatty acids
   d. to make their diet more interesting
   e. to provide all essential amino acids for protein synthesis

Describing, Comparing, and Explaining

10. A peanut butter and jelly sandwich contains carbohydrates, proteins, and fats. Describe what happens to the sandwich when you eat it. Discuss ingestion, digestion, absorption, and elimination.

Applying the Concepts

11. How might our craving for fatty foods, which is helping to fuel the obesity crisis, have evolved through natural selection?

12. What are the benefits of eating fresh fruit and vegetables as part of a diet?

13. The media report numerous claims and counterclaims about the benefits and dangers of certain foods, dietary supplements, and diets. Have you modified your eating habits on the basis of nutritional information disseminated by the media? Why or why not? How should we evaluate whether such nutritional claims are valid?

14. Worldwide, almost 1 billion people go to bed hungry most nights, and millions of people have starved to death in recent decades. In some cases, war, poor crop yields, and disease epidemics strip people of food. Many say instead that it is not inadequate food production but unequal food distribution that causes food shortages. What responsibility do nations have for feeding their citizens? For feeding the people of other countries? What do you think you can do to lessen world hunger?

Answers to all questions can be found in Appendix E.

CHAPTER

27

Gas Exchange

BIG IDEAS

Mechanisms of Gas Exchange

(27.1–27.6)

Gas exchange occurs across thin, moist surfaces in respiratory organs such as gills, tracheal systems, and lungs.

The Human Respiratory System

(27.7–27.10)

Air travels through branching tubes to the lungs, where gases are exchanged with the blood.

Transport of Gases in the Human Body

(27.11–27.13)

The circulatory system transports O_2 to body tissues and returns CO_2 to the lungs.

A Frozen Mammoth "Breathes" Again After 43 000 Years

Woolly mammoths (*Mammuthus primigenius*) are a species of mammoth that roamed the Canadian and Siberian Arctic until 12 000 and 4000 years ago, respectively. Closely related to modern elephants, mammoths diverged from a common ancestor approximately 7 million years ago (mya). At the beginning of the Pleistocene ice ages (~2 mya), mammoth ancestors left their southern homes for the Great White North.

Although relatively common in the fossil record, most mammoth remains are not actually fossilized. Instead, the permafrost graves in which they are found have preserved their organic remains, including their soft tissues. Several adaptations allowed mammoths to survive in their northern habitat. Evident from their remains are long, shaggy hair and smaller ears, which would have effectively reduced heat loss.

Although not preserved well, the blood vessels in the mammoth limbs, similar to those of other arctic mammals, were likely arranged countercurrently—that is, with their arteries in close proximity to their veins. Arterial blood leaving the heart is at core body temperature. As blood travels toward the extremities, heat is transferred directly to the veins and the cold blood returning from the feet is warmed. Consequently, the body's core remains warm while the feet are much cooler, meaning the body as a whole loses less heat to the icy ground.

However, the cold feet of arctic animals pose a problem for oxygen delivery. As you will read in this chapter, hemoglobin binds oxygen and transports it throughout the body. The strength of this binding (affinity) is affected by several factors, including temperature. Oxygen release requires heat and is enhanced by warmer temperatures and inhibited by cold.

Slight adaptations of hemoglobin structure and function are evident in modern arctic mammals, including arctic fox (*Vulpes lagopus*), caribou (*Rangifer tarandus*), and muskoxen (*Ovibos moschatus*). Subtle differences in the hemoglobin genes produce proteins that are less sensitive to cold, increasing oxygen delivery to cooler extremities. These animals are all living examples, but what about the woolly mammoth? How can we possibly examine the hemoglobin of an extinct species?

To answer this question, Dr. Kevin Campbell of the University of Manitoba studied the frozen remains of mammoths that died 25 000 to 43 000 years ago. Within the soft tissues of these specimens was the key: DNA. Campbell's first step involved the amplification of the mammoth hemoglobin genes, which identified three amino acid–changing DNA substitutions. By inserting the ancient hemoglobin genes into *E. coli* bacteria, researchers successfully resurrected functional mammoth hemoglobin. When compared to that of modern elephants, the amino acid changes (highlighted in various colours in the upper right figure) in mammoth hemoglobin slightly altered its properties, causing it to release oxygen more readily at lower temperatures. Therefore, within the cold feet of the woolly mammoth, oxygen needs were met. This study represents the first demonstration of a physiological adaptation within an extinct species. The mammoth's adaptations, which allow it to survive the cold arctic winters, are similar but not identical to living arctic species and represent good examples of convergent evolution.

In this chapter, we explore the various types of gas exchange systems that have evolved in animals. We then take a closer look at the structures and functions of the human respiratory system. We conclude with a preview of the circulatory system, which delivers the oxygen essential for life to all body cells.

Mechanisms of Gas Exchange

27.1 Overview: Gas exchange in humans involves breathing, transport of gases, and exchange with body cells

▲ **Figure 27.1** The three phases of gas exchange in a human

Gas exchange makes it possible for you to put to work the food molecules the digestive system provides. **Figure 27.1** presents an overview of the three phases of gas exchange in humans and other animals with lungs. ❶ Breathing: As you inhale, a large, moist internal surface is exposed to the air entering the lungs. Oxygen (O_2) diffuses across the cells lining the lungs and into surrounding blood vessels. At the same time, carbon dioxide (CO_2) diffuses from the blood into the lungs. As you exhale, CO_2 leaves your body.

❷ Transport of gases by the circulatory system: The O_2 that diffused into the blood attaches to hemoglobin in red blood cells. The red vessels in the figure are transporting O_2-rich blood from the lungs to capillaries in the body's tissues. CO_2 is also transported in blood, from the tissues back to the lungs, carried in the blue vessels shown here. Circulatory systems will be the focus of Chapter 28.

❸ Exchange of gases with body cells: Your cells take up O_2 from the blood and release CO_2 to the blood. As you learned in Chapter 6, O_2 functions in cellular respiration in the mitochondria as the final electron acceptor in the stepwise breakdown of fuel molecules. H_2O and CO_2 are waste products, and ATP is produced that will power cellular work. The gas exchange occurring as we breathe is often called respiration; do not confuse this exchange with cellular respiration.

Cellular respiration requires a continuous supply of O_2 and the disposal of CO_2. Gas exchange involves both the respiratory and circulatory systems in servicing your body's cells.

> **?** **Humans cannot survive for more than a few minutes without O_2. Why?**

● Cells require a steady supply of O_2 for cellular respiration to produce enough ATP to function. Without enough ATP, cells and the organism die.

27.2 Animals exchange O_2 and CO_2 across moist body surfaces

The part of an animal's body where gas exchange with the environment occurs is called the respiratory surface. Respiratory surfaces are made up of living cells, and like all cells, their plasma membranes must be wet to function properly. Thus, respiratory surfaces are always moist.

Gas exchange takes place by diffusion. The surface area of the respiratory surface must be large enough to take up sufficient O_2 for every cell in the body. Usually, a single layer of cells forms the respiratory surface. This thin, moist layer allows O_2 to diffuse rapidly into the circulatory system or directly into body tissues and also allows CO_2 to diffuse out.

The four figures in this module illustrate, in simplified form, four types of respiratory organs, structures in which gas exchange with the external environment occurs. In each of

these figures, the circle represents a cross-section of the animal's body through the respiratory surface. The yellow areas represent the respiratory surfaces; the green areas represent body surfaces with little or no role in gas exchange. The boxed enlargements show gas exchange occurring across the respiratory surface.

Some animals use their entire outer skin as a gas exchange organ. The earthworm in **Figure 27.2A** is an example. The cross-sectional diagram shows its whole body surface as yellow; there are no specialized gas exchange surfaces. O_2 diffuses into a dense network of thin-walled capillaries lying just beneath the skin. Earthworms and other skin-breathers must live in damp places or in water because their whole body surface has to stay moist. Animals that breathe only through their skin

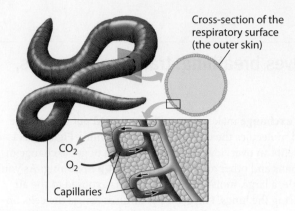

Cross-section of the
respiratory surface
(the outer skin)

CO_2
O_2

Capillaries

▲ **Figure 27.2A** The skin: the outer body surface

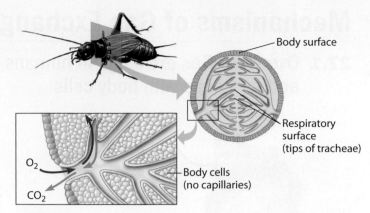

Body surface

Respiratory
surface
(tips of tracheae)

O_2

Body cells
(no capillaries)

CO_2

▲ **Figure 27.2C** A tracheal system: air tubes that extend throughout
the body

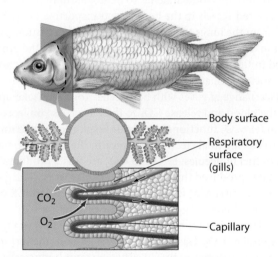

Body surface

Respiratory
surface
(gills)

CO_2

O_2

Capillary

▲ **Figure 27.2B** Gills: extensions of the body surface

Body surface

Respiratory
surface
(within lung)

CO_2 O_2

CO_2 O_2

Capillary

▲ **Figure 27.2D** Lungs: internal thin-walled sacs

are generally small, and many are long and thin or flattened. These shapes provide a high ratio of respiratory surface to body volume, allowing for sufficient gas exchange for all the cells in the body.

In most animals, the skin surface is not extensive enough to exchange gases for all cells within the body. Consequently, certain parts of the body have become adapted as highly branched respiratory surfaces with large surface areas. Such gas exchange organs include gills, tracheal systems, and lungs.

Gills have evolved in most aquatic animals. **Gills** are extensions, or outfoldings, of the body surface specialized for gas exchange. Many marine worms have flaplike gills that extend from each body segment. The gills of clams and crayfish are clustered in one body location. A fish **(Figure 27.2B)** has a set of featherlike gills on each side of its head. As indicated in the enlargement, gases diffuse across the gill surface between the water and the blood. Because the respiratory surfaces of aquatic animals extend into the surrounding water, keeping the surface moist is not a problem.

In most terrestrial animals, the respiratory surface is folded into the body rather than projecting from it. The infolded surface opens to the air only through narrow tubes, an

arrangement that helps to retain the moisture that is essential for the cells of the respiratory surfaces to function.

The **tracheal system** of insects **(Figure 27.2C)** is an extensive system of branching internal tubes called tracheae, with a moist, thin epithelium forming the respiratory surface at their tips. As you will see in Module 27.3, the smallest branches exchange gases directly with body cells. Thus, gas exchange in insects requires no assistance from the circulatory system.

Most terrestrial vertebrates have **lungs (Figure 27.2D)**, which are internal sacs lined with moist epithelium. As the diagram indicates, the inner surfaces of the lungs are extensively subdivided, forming a large respiratory surface. Gases are carried between the lungs and the body cells by the circulatory system.

We examine tracheae, gills, and lungs more closely in the next several modules.

? What are two ways that the structure of the respiratory surface of a gill or lung fit its function?

● These respiratory surfaces are moist and thin so that gases can easily diffuse across them and into or out of the closely associated capillaries. They are highly branched or subdivided, providing a large surface area for exchange.

27.3 The tracheal system of insects provides direct exchange between the air and body cells

There are three big advantages to breathing air: Air contains a much higher concentration of O_2 than does water, air is much lighter and easier to move than water, and the diffusion rate is faster in air than in water. Thus, a terrestrial animal expends much less energy than an aquatic animal ventilating its respiratory surface. The main problem facing an air-breathing animal, however, is the loss of water to the air by evaporation.

The tracheal system of insects, with respiratory surfaces at the tips of tiny branching tubes inside the body, greatly reduces evaporative water loss. **Figure 27.3A** illustrates the tracheal system in a grasshopper. The largest tubes, called tracheae, open to the outside and are reinforced by rings of chitin, as shown in the close-up on the bottom right of the figure. (An insect's tough exoskeleton is also made of chitin.) Enlarged portions of tracheae form air sacs (shown in pink) near organs that require a large supply of O_2, which includes the wings.

▲ **Figure 27.3B** A grasshopper in flight

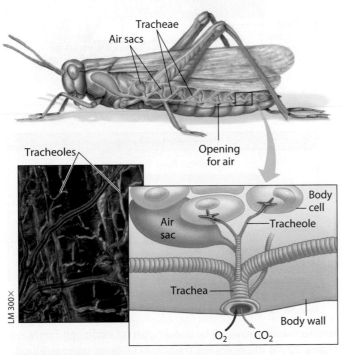

▲ **Figure 27.3A** The tracheal system of an insect

The micrograph on the left in Figure 27.3A shows how these tubes branch repeatedly. The smallest branches, called tracheoles, extend to nearly every cell in the insect's body. Their tiny tips have closed ends and contain fluid (blue in the drawing). Gas is exchanged with body cells by diffusion across the moist epithelium that lines these tips. The structure of a tracheal system matches its function of exchanging gases directly with body cells. Thus, the circulatory system of insects is not involved in transporting gases.

For a small insect, diffusion through the tracheae brings in enough O_2 to support cellular respiration. Larger insects may ventilate their tracheal systems with rhythmic body movements that compress and expand the air tubes like bellows. An insect in flight **(Figure 27.3B)** has a very high metabolic rate and consumes 10 to 200 times more O_2 than it does at rest. In many insects, alternating contraction and relaxation of the flight muscles rapidly pumps air through the tracheal system.

? In what basic way does the process of gas exchange in insects differ from that in both fishes and humans?

● The circulatory system of insects is not involved in transporting gases to and from the body cells.

27.4 Gills are adapted for gas exchange in aquatic environments

Oceans, lakes, and other bodies of water contain O_2 as a dissolved gas. The gills of fishes and many invertebrate animals, including lobsters and clams, tap this source of O_2.

An advantage of exchanging gases in water is that there is no problem keeping the respiratory surface moist. A disadvantage, however, is that the concentration of oxygen dissolved in water is only about 3% of that in an equivalent volume of air. And the warmer and saltier the water, the less

O_2 it holds. Thus, gills—especially those of large, active fishes and squids in warm oceans—must be very efficient to obtain enough O_2 from the surrounding water.

Structure of Fish Gills The drawings in **Figure 27.4A** show the architecture of fish gills, which are among the most efficient gas exchange organs in the aquatic world. There are four supporting gill arches on each side of the body. Two rows of

Water flow

Operculum
(gill cover)

Blood vessels

Gill arch

Gill filaments

Oxygen-poor
blood

Oxygen-rich
blood

Lamella

Water flow
between
lamellae

Blood flow through
capillaries in a lamella

▲ **Figure 27.4A** The structure of fish gills and countercurrent gas exchange

gill filaments project from each gill arch. Each filament bears many flattened plates called lamellae (singular, *lamella*), which are the actual respiratory surfaces. A lamella is full of tiny capillaries that are so narrow that blood cells pass through them in single file. Thus, every red blood cell comes in close proximity to O_2 dissolved in the surrounding water.

What you can't see in the drawings are the movements that ventilate the gills. We use the term **ventilation** to refer to any mechanism that increases the flow of water or air over the respiratory surface (in gills, tracheae, or lungs). Increasing this flow ensures a fresh supply of O_2 and the removal of CO_2. Blue arrows in the drawings represent the one-way flow of water into the mouth, across the gills, and out the side of the fish's body. Swimming fish simply open their mouths and let water flow over their gills. Fish also pump water across the gills by the coordinated opening and closing of the mouth and operculum, the stiff flap that covers and protects the gills. Because water is dense and contains so little oxygen, most fish expend considerable energy in ventilating their gills.

Countercurrent Exchange The flow of blood inside a gill in a direction opposite the movement of water past the gill makes it possible for O_2 to diffuse into the blood by an efficient process called **countercurrent exchange**. The name reflects the fact that substances (or heat, see Module 25.18) are exchanged between two fluids that are moving *counter* to each other. Let's see how this arrangement enhances the exchange of gases in a fish gill.

In the enlargement on the top right of Figure 27.4A, notice that the direction that water flows over the surface of the lamellae (blue arrows) is opposite that of the blood flow within each

Countercurrent exchange

Water flow, showing % O_2

100 70 40 15

Diffusion of O_2 from water to blood

80 60 30 5

Blood flow in simplified capillary, showing % O_2

▲ **Figure 27.4B** Countercurrent exchange of O_2 across a fish gill

Concurrent exchange

Water flow, showing % O_2

100 70 50 50

Diffusion of O_2 from water to blood

5 35 50 60

Blood flow in simplified capillary, showing % O_2

▲ **Figure 27.4C** Less efficient concurrent exchange at a hypothetical fish gill

lamella (black arrows). The countercurrent exchange diagram in **Figure 27.4B** illustrates the transfer of O_2 from water to blood. The percentages shown indicate the changing amount of O_2 dissolved in each fluid. Notice that as blood flows through a lamella and picks up more and more O_2, it comes in contact with water that is closer to beginning its passage over the gills and thus has more O_2 available. As a result, a concentration gradient is maintained that favours the diffusion of O_2 from the water to the blood along the entire length of the capillary.

This countercurrent exchange mechanism is so efficient that fish gills can remove more than 80% of the O_2 dissolved in the water flowing through them. For comparison, a hypothetical situation where water and blood flow in the same direction (concurrent) is shown in **Figure 27.4C**. In this circumstance, the gills could not remove more than 50% of the oxygen as the oxygen gradient between the fluids reaches an equilibrium.

The mechanism of countercurrent exchange is also important in temperature regulation, as you saw in Chapter 25.

No matter how efficient they may be, gills are unsuitable for an animal living on land. An expansive surface of wet membrane extending out from the body and exposed to air would lose too much water to evaporation. Therefore, most terrestrial animals house their respiratory surfaces within the body, opening to the atmosphere through narrow tubes, as we see next.

27.5 The evolution of lungs facilitated the movement of tetrapods onto land

The colonization of land by vertebrates was one of the pivotal milestones in the history of life. The evolution of legs from fins may be the most obvious change in body design, but the refinement of lung breathing was just as important. And although skeletal changes were undoubtedly required in the transition from fins to legs, the evolution of lungs for breathing on land also required skeletal changes. Interestingly, current fossil evidence supports the hypothesis that the earliest changes in the front fins and shoulder girdle of tetrapod ancestors may actually have been breathing adaptations that enabled a fish in shallow water to push itself up to gulp in air.

Paleontologists have uncovered numerous transitional forms in tetrapod evolution (see Module 21.4). It now seems clear that tetrapods first evolved in shallow water from what some researchers jokingly call "fishapods." These ancient forms had both gills and lungs (see Module 21.3). The adaptations for air breathing evident in their fossils include a flat skull with a strong, elongated snout, as well as a muscular neck and shoulders that enabled the animal to lift its head clear of water and into the unsupportive air. Strengthening of the lower jaw may have facilitated the pumping motion presumed to be used by early air-breathing tetrapods and still employed by frogs to inflate their lungs. The recently discovered 375-million-year-old fossil of *Tiktaalik* (**Figure 27.5**) illustrates some of these air-breathing adaptations.

The first tetrapods on land diverged into three major lineages: amphibians, reptiles (including birds), and mammals. Most amphibians have small lungs and rely heavily on the diffusion of gases across body surfaces. Reptiles and mammals rely on lungs for gas exchange. In general, the size and

▲ **Figure 27.5** A cast of a fossil of *Tiktaalik* discovered on Ellesmere Island, Nunavut

complexity of lungs are correlated with an animal's metabolic rate and thus oxygen need. For example, the lungs of birds and mammals, whose high body temperatures are maintained by a high metabolic rate, have a greater area of exchange surface than the lungs of similar-sized amphibians and nonbird reptiles, which have a much lower metabolic rate.

In the next module, we examine a rumour that turtles have an unusual respiratory surface.

? How might adaptations for breathing air be linked to the evolution of tetrapod limbs?

● Fossil evidence indicates that changes in the neck, shoulder girdle, and limb bones may have helped early tetrapod ancestors lift their heads above water to gulp air.

27.6 Can turtles really breathe through their backsides?

So far in this chapter, you have learned about different specialized respiratory surfaces used by various animals. Some animals can absorb O_2 and eliminate CO_2 directly across their skin. Other animals use specialized organs such as gills, lungs, or the tracheal system of insects. Rumour has it that turtles can breathe through a completely different structure: their backsides. Young dragonfly larvae ventilate their gills by bringing water in through openings at their back end, so why not

turtles? As unusual as it sounds, this rumour has been validated by scientific evidence.

Although not true for all turtles, two species of aquatic turtles in Australia have been observed breathing water through their backsides. Shown in **Figure 27.6**, the Fitzroy River turtle (*Rheodytes leukops*), informally known as the bum-breathing turtle, is one species capable of a form of gas exchange called cloacal gill respiration.

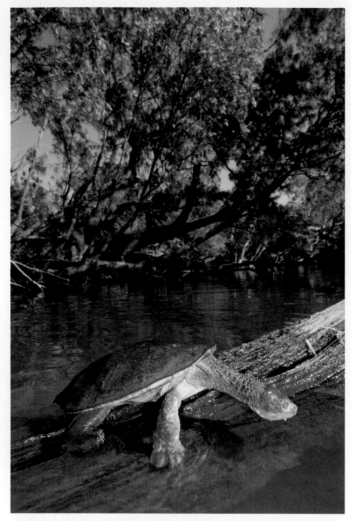

▲ **Figure 27.6** The Fitzroy River "bum-breathing" turtle

submerged, the turtle starts breathing through its bottom—more specifically, its **cloaca**. In turtles, products of the digestive, urinary, and reproductive systems exit the body through this single opening.

Most turtles have a pair of pouches coming off of their large intestine called bursae (singular, *bursa*). The function of these bursae varies among species. The bursae of Fitzroy River turtles function like gills and absorb O_2 from water. As with any respiratory surface, ventilation is imperative to provide a fresh O_2 supply. Using two internal muscle groups, water is pulled through the cloaca into the bursae, similar to negative pressure breathing (see Module 27.9). When observed in the laboratory, the cloacal bursae are ventilated between 15 and 60 times per minute. Cloacal gill respiration can meet up to 70% of the total oxygen demands, allowing for prolonged submersions under water.

How could such an unusual mechanism of gas exchange evolve? Having two mechanisms of respiration was likely advantageous for these animals. Aquatic respiration through the cloaca allowed for prolonged stints underwater, potentially avoiding terrestrial predators. Meanwhile, air breathing facilitated movement onto land to lay eggs and reproduce. If a second respiratory surface is beneficial, why did cloacal bursae assume this role?

As you have read in previous modules, efficient gas exchange requires a surface with a rich blood supply. The intestinal tract is highly vascularized to facilitate the efficient absorption of nutrients. Exposing this surface to water by bringing it in through the cloaca may have provided these animals with a new O_2-absorbing surface. Ultimately, in these two turtle species, regions of the digestive tract became sufficient surfaces for gas exchange.

We explore the mammalian respiratory system next, with humans as an example.

 The bursae of the Fitzroy River turtle are lined with numerous projections. What is the evolutionary advantage of these structures?

● By increasing the surface area of the cloacal bursae, these projections increase the amount of oxygen that can be absorbed.

Like other reptiles, the Fitzroy River turtle uses its lungs for respiration while at the water's surface or on land. Yet, while submerged for extended periods, up to several days, their oxygen demands must be met through another mechanism. When

The Human Respiratory System

27.7 In mammals, branching tubes convey air to lungs located in the chest cavity

As in all mammals, your lungs are located in your chest, or thoracic cavity, and are protected by the supportive rib cage. The thoracic cavity is separated from the abdominal cavity by a sheet of muscle called the **diaphragm**. You will see how the diaphragm helps to ventilate your lungs in Module 27.9.

Figure 27.7A shows the human respiratory system (along with the esophagus and heart, for orientation). Air enters your respiratory system through the nostrils. It is filtered by hairs and warmed, humidified, and sampled for odours as it flows through a maze of spaces in the nasal cavity. You can also draw in air through your mouth, but mouth breathing does not allow the air to be processed by your nasal cavity.

From the nasal cavity or mouth, air passes to the **pharynx**, where the paths for air and food cross. As you will remember from the previous chapter, when you swallow food, the **larynx** (the upper part of the respiratory tract) moves upward and tips the epiglottis over the opening of your **trachea**, or windpipe (see Figure 26.6B). The rest of the time, the air passage in the pharynx is open for breathing.

The larynx is often called the voice box. When you exhale, the outgoing air rushes by a pair of **vocal cords** in the larynx, and you can produce sounds by voluntarily tensing muscles that stretch the cords so they vibrate. You produce high-pitched sounds when your vocal cords are tightly stretched and

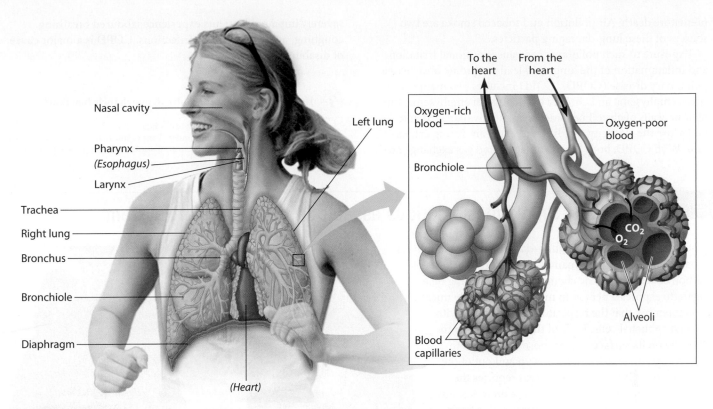

▲ **Figure 27.7A** The anatomy of the human respiratory system (left) and details of the alveoli (right)

vibrating very fast. When the cords are less tense, they vibrate slowly and produce low-pitched sounds.

From the larynx, air passes into your trachea. Rings of cartilage (shown in Figure 27.7A in blue) reinforce the walls of the larynx and trachea, keeping this part of the airway open. The trachea forks into two **bronchi** (singular, *bronchus*), one leading to each lung. Within the lung, each bronchus branches repeatedly into finer and finer tubes called **bronchioles**. Bronchitis is a condition in which these small tubes become inflamed and constricted, making breathing difficult.

As the enlargement on the right of Figure 27.7A shows, the bronchioles dead-end in grapelike clusters of air sacs called **alveoli** (singular, *alveolus*). Each of your lungs contains millions of these tiny sacs. Together they have a surface area of about 100 m², 50 times that of your skin. The inner surface of each alveolus is lined with a thin layer of epithelial cells. The O_2 in inhaled air dissolves in a film of moisture on the epithelial cells. It then diffuses across the epithelium and into the dense web of blood capillaries that surrounds each alveolus. **Figure 27.7B** is a scanning electron micrograph showing the network of capillaries enclosing the alveoli. (The alveoli in this micrograph appear as empty spaces because the blood vessels were injected with a solution that hardened to form casts of the capillaries, and the tissues of the alveoli were then dissolved.) This close association between capillaries and alveoli also enables CO_2 to diffuse the opposite way—from the capillaries, across the epithelium of the alveolus, into the air space, and finally out in the exhaled air.

The major branches of your respiratory system are lined by a moist epithelium covered by cilia and a thin film of mucus. The cilia and mucus are the respiratory system's cleaning system. The beating cilia move mucus with trapped dust, pollen, and other contaminants upward to the pharynx, where it is usually swallowed.

Respiratory Problems   Alveoli are so small that specialized secretions called **surfactants** are required to keep them from sticking shut from the surface tension of their moist surface. Surfactant also facilitates the expansion of the alveoli during inhalation. Respiratory distress syndrome caused by a lack of lung surfactant is a common disease seen in babies born six weeks or more before their due dates. Surfactants typically appear in the lungs after 33 weeks of embryonic development; birth normally occurs at 38 weeks. Artificial surfactants are now administered through a breathing tube to treat such preterm infants.

Alveoli are highly susceptible to airborne contaminants. Defensive white blood cells patrol them and engulf foreign particles. However, if too much particulate matter reaches the alveoli, the delicate lining of these small sacs becomes damaged and the efficiency of gas exchange drops. Studies have shown a significant association between exposure to fine particles and

Colourized SEM 280×

▲ **Figure 27.7B** A colourized electron micrograph showing the network of capillaries that surround the alveoli in the lung premature death. Air pollution and tobacco smoke are two sources of these lung-damaging particles.

Exposure to such pollutants can cause continual irritation and inflammation of the lungs and lead to chronic obstructive pulmonary disease (COPD). COPD includes two main conditions: emphysema and chronic bronchitis. In emphysema, the delicate walls of alveoli become permanently damaged and the lungs lose the elasticity that helps to expel air during exhalation. With COPD, both lung ventilation and gas exchange are severely impaired. Patients experience laboured breathing, coughing, and frequent lung infections. COPD is a major cause of disability and death.

? **How does the structure of alveoli match their function?**

● Alveoli have a thin, moist epithelium across which dissolved O_2 and CO_2 can easily diffuse into or out of the surrounding capillaries. The huge collective surface area of all the alveoli enables the passage of many gas molecules.

27.8 Smoking is a serious assault on the respiratory system

One of the worst sources of lung-damaging air pollutants is tobacco smoke, which is mainly microscopic particles of carbon coated with toxic chemicals. A single drag on a cigarette exposes a person to more than 4000 chemicals.

Remember that the respiratory tract is lined with ciliated epithelial cells. Each of these cells has up to 200 cilia on its surface, the purpose of which is to sweep contaminant-laden mucus up and out of the airways. To be effective, this process requires the coordinated action of millions of cilia on thousands of cells. Tobacco smoke irritates these cells, slowing and eventually paralyzing their cilia. As cilia function slows down, so does their ability to remove mucus. In heavy smokers, cilia function is stopped altogether. This can lead to frequent coughing, the respiratory system's attempt to clear the mucus no longer moved by the cilia. Smoke's toxins also kill the white blood cells that reside in the respiratory tract and engulf foreign particles. Thus, smoking disables the normal cleansing and protective mechanisms of the respiratory system.

Smoking is a leading cause of emphysema (see Module 27.7), which causes breathlessness and constant fatigue as the body is forced to spend more and more energy just breathing.

Some of the toxins in tobacco smoke cause lung cancer. The photographs in **Figure 27.8** show a cutaway view of a pair of healthy human lungs (left) and the lungs of a cancer victim (right), whose lungs are black from the long-term buildup of smoke particles. Smokers account for 90% of all lung cancer cases. Most victims die within one year of diagnosis. Smoking is also linked to an increased risk of numerous other cancers.

Cardiovascular disease is the second highest cause of smoking-related deaths. Smokers have a higher rate of heart attacks and stroke. Smoking raises blood pressure and increases harmful cholesterol levels in the blood.

Every year in Canada, smoking kills over 37 000 people, more than all the deaths caused by accidents, alcohol and drug abuse, HIV, and murders combined. On average, adults who smoke die nine years earlier than nonsmokers. Studies show that nonsmokers exposed to secondary cigarette smoke are also at risk. Young children are particularly susceptible, with increased risk of asthma, bronchitis, and pneumonia. Studies by Dr. Carole Yauk, from Carleton University in Ottawa, have shown that second-hand smoke can cause mutations in the germ cells that produce sperm within the testes. These mutations may be passed on to offspring and increase their risk of childhood cancers.

Shortly after quitting smoking, cilia function returns and normal mucus clearing begins again. About 15 years after quitting, a former smoker's risk of most diseases linked to smoking is similar to that of people who have never smoked. No lifestyle choice has a more positive impact on the long-term health of you and those with whom you live than not smoking.

▲ **Figure 27.8** Healthy lungs (left) and cancerous lungs (right)

? **What causes "smoker's cough"?**

● Smoke damages cilia, inhibiting their ability to sweep mucus and trapped particles from the respiratory tract. The body tries to compensate by coughing.

27.9 Negative pressure breathing ventilates your lungs

Breathing is the alternate inhalation and exhalation of air. This ventilation of your lungs maintains high O_2 and low CO_2 concentrations at the respiratory surface.

Figure 27.9 shows the changes that occur during breathing. Put your hands on your rib cage and inhale: You can feel your ribs move upward and out as muscles between the ribs

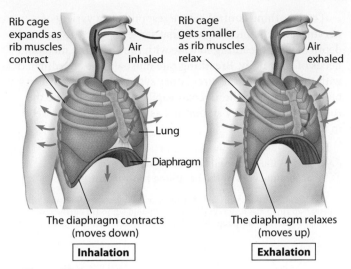

Rib cage expands as rib muscles contract

Air inhaled

Lung

Diaphragm

The diaphragm contracts (moves down)

Inhalation

Rib cage gets smaller as rib muscles relax

Air exhaled

The diaphragm relaxes (moves up)

Exhalation

▲ **Figure 27.9** Negative pressure breathing

contract. At the same time, your diaphragm contracts and moves downward, expanding the chest cavity. The volume of your lungs increases with the expanding chest cavity, which lowers the air pressure in the alveoli to less than atmospheric pressure. Flowing from a region of higher pressure to one of lower pressure, air is pulled through the nostrils and down the breathing tubes to the alveoli. This type of ventilation is called **negative pressure breathing** because inhalation is caused by an active reduction in pressure.

The diagram on the right in Figure 27.9 shows what happens when you exhale. Your rib muscles and diaphragm both relax, decreasing the volume of the rib cage and chest cavity, which increases the air pressure inside the lungs, forcing air

out. Notice that the diaphragm curves farther upward into the chest cavity when relaxed.

Each year, you take between 4 million and 10 million breaths. The volume of air in each breath when you breathe quietly, called the **tidal volume**, is about 500 mL. The volume of air breathed during maximal inhalation and exhalation is called **vital capacity**. It averages about 3.4 L and 4.8 L for university-age females and males, respectively. (Women tend to have smaller rib cages and lungs.) When you breathe deeply during exercise, you are tapping into your vital capacity. The lungs actually hold more air than the vital capacity. Because the alveoli do not completely collapse, a residual volume of "dead" air remains in the lungs even after you blow out as much air as you can. As lungs lose resilience (springiness) with age or as the result of disease, such as emphysema, less air exits on exhalation and residual volume increases at the expense of vital capacity.

Because the lungs do not completely empty, each inhalation mixes fresh air with oxygen-depleted air. Thus, you can extract only about 25% of the O_2 in the air you inhale. The gas exchange system of birds is much more efficient than that of humans. Unlike the in-and-out flow of air in the human alveoli, the air in the lungs of birds moves in one direction through tiny passageways where gas exchange occurs. Because of this one-way flow of air, oxygen-depleted air does not remain in a bird's lungs after exhalation. Thus, birds can extract more oxygen from a volume of inhaled air, enough oxygen to fly over the Himalayas.

? **Explain how negative pressure breathing ventilates your lungs.**

● The lungs expand along with the expanding chest cavity during inhalation. This increase in volume lowers the pressure in the lungs, which draws air into the lungs. During exhalation, the process is reversed.

27.10 Breathing is automatically controlled

Although you can voluntarily hold your breath or breathe faster and deeper, most of the time your breathing is under involuntary control. **Figure 27.10** illustrates how a **breathing control centre** in a part of the brain called the medulla oblongata ensures that your breathing rate is coordinated with your body's need for oxygen. **❶** Nerves from the breathing control centre signal the diaphragm and rib muscles to contract, causing you to inhale. When you are at rest, these nerve signals result in about 10 to 14 inhalations per minute. Between inhalations, the muscles relax, and you exhale.

❷ The control centre regulates breathing rate in response to changes in the CO_2 level of the blood. When you exercise vigorously, for instance, your metabolism speeds up and your cells generate more CO_2 as a waste product. The CO_2 goes into the blood, where it reacts with water to form carbonic acid. The acid slightly lowers the pH of the blood and the fluid bathing the brain, the cerebrospinal fluid. When the medulla senses this pH drop, its breathing control centre increases both the rate and depth of your breathing. As a result, more CO_2 is eliminated in the exhaled air, and the pH of the blood returns to normal.

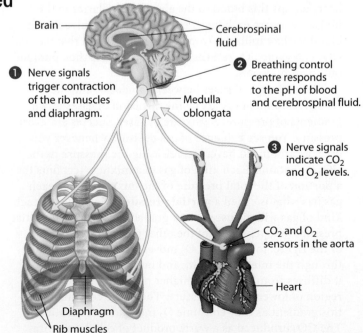

Brain

Cerebrospinal fluid

❶ Nerve signals trigger contraction of the rib muscles and diaphragm.

❷ Breathing control centre responds to the pH of blood and cerebrospinal fluid.

Medulla oblongata

❸ Nerve signals indicate CO_2 and O_2 levels.

CO_2 and O_2 sensors in the aorta

Heart

Diaphragm

Rib muscles

▲ **Figure 27.10** How the breathing control centre regulates breathing

The O_2 concentration in the blood usually has little effect on the breathing control centre. Because the same process that consumes O_2—cellular respiration—also produces CO_2, a rise in CO_2 is generally a good indication of a decrease in blood oxygen. Thus, by responding to lowered pH, the breathing control centre increases blood oxygen level.

❸ Secondary control over breathing is exerted by sensors in the aorta and carotid arteries that monitor concentrations of O_2 as well as CO_2. When the O_2 level in the blood becomes very low, these sensors signal the control centre via nerves to increase the rate and depth of breathing. This response may occur, for example, at high altitudes, where the air is so thin that you cannot get enough O_2 by breathing normally.

The breathing control centre responds to a variety of nervous and chemical signals that serve to keep the rate and depth of your breathing in tune with the changing metabolic needs of your body. Breathing rate must also be coordinated with the activity of the circulatory system, which transports blood to and from the alveolar capillaries. We examine the role of the circulatory system in gas exchange more closely in the next module.

 How is the increased need for O_2 during exercise accommodated by the breathing control centre?

During exercise, cells release more CO_2 to the blood, which forms carbonic acid, lowering the pH of the blood. The breathing centre senses the decrease in pH and sends impulses to increase breathing rate, thus supplying more O_2.

Transport of Gases in the Human Body

27.11 Blood transports respiratory gases

How does oxygen get from your lungs to all the other tissues in your body, and how does carbon dioxide travel from the tissues to your lungs? To answer these questions, we must jump ahead a bit to the subject of Chapter 28 and look at the basic organization of the human circulatory system.

Figure 27.11 shows the main components of your circulatory system and their roles in gas exchange. Let's start with the heart, in the middle of the diagram. The right side of the heart (drawn on the left of the diagram as if you are looking at the animal facing you) handles O_2-poor blood (coloured blue). The left side handles O_2-rich blood (red). As indicated in the lower left of the diagram, O_2-poor blood returns to the heart from capillaries in body tissues. The heart pumps this blood to the alveolar capillaries in the lungs. Gases are exchanged between air in the alveoli and blood in the capillaries (top of diagram). Blood that has lost CO_2 and gained O_2 returns to the heart and is then pumped out to body tissues.

The exchange of gases between capillaries and the cells around them occurs by the diffusion of gases down gradients of pressure. A mixture of gases, such as air, exerts pressure. You see evidence of gas pressure whenever you open a carbonated beverage, releasing the pressure of the CO_2 it contains. Each kind of gas in a mixture accounts for a portion of the total pressure of the mixture. Thus, each gas has what is called a **partial pressure**. Molecules of each kind of gas will diffuse down a gradient of their own partial pressure independently of the other gases. At the bottom of the figure, for instance, O_2 moves from O_2-rich blood, through the interstitial fluid, and into tissue cells because it diffuses from a region of higher partial pressure to a region of lower partial pressure. The tissue cells maintain this gradient as they consume O_2 in cellular respiration. The CO_2 produced as a waste product of cellular respiration diffuses down its own partial pressure gradient out of

▲ **Figure 27.11** Gas transport and exchange in the body

tissue cells and into the capillaries. Diffusion down partial pressure gradients also accounts for gas exchange in the alveoli.

27.12 Hemoglobin carries O₂ and has other functions

Oxygen is not very soluble in water, and most animals transport it bound to proteins called respiratory pigments. These molecules have distinctive colours, hence the name *pigment*. Many molluscs and arthropods use a blue, copper-containing pigment. Almost all vertebrates and many invertebrates use **hemoglobin**, an iron-containing pigment that is red in colour.

Each of your red blood cells is packed with about 250 million molecules of hemoglobin. A single, vertebrate hemoglobin molecule consists of four polypeptide chains of two different types, depicted with two shades of purple in **Figure 27.12A**. Attached to each polypeptide is a chemical group called a heme (coloured blue in the figure), at the centre of which is an iron atom (black). Each iron atom binds one O₂ molecule.

What actually causes hemoglobin to bind O₂ at the lungs and release it at the tissues? When the first hemoglobin subunit binds to O₂, it causes a shape change in other subunits. The new shape increases their affinity for oxygen, and the second O₂ molecule binds easier than the first. This continues until the hemoglobin is saturated with four O₂ molecules. This process is called cooperativity.

Whether a hemoglobin molecule is bound to O₂ also depends on the surrounding partial pressure of O₂ (P_{O_2}). If you were to measure the percentage of hemoglobin molecules carrying O₂ over a range of partial pressures, you could generate an oxygen dissociation curve (**Figure 27.12B**). In the lungs of a person at sea level, where P_{O_2} is approximately 105 mmHg, the hemoglobin loads up with O₂, becoming nearly 100% saturated with oxygen (red line), which will be transported to the tissues.

P_{O_2} in the tissue reflects how much O₂ the cells are using and determines how much O₂ is unloaded. A resting tissue has an average P_{O_2} of 40 mmHg (blue line). At this P_{O_2}, only 25% of hemoglobin molecules release their oxygen for use by the tissue. Although this may seem like a small amount of oxygen delivered, it is enough to supply the tissue. Active tissues such as working muscles consume more oxygen, lowering the P_{O_2} of their surroundings to 20 mmHg

(green line). In this scenario, the hemoglobin saturation drops to 30%, and 70% of its O₂ is unloaded at these demanding tissues.

In the opening essay to this chapter, you read about how hemoglobin adaptations allow animals to meet their oxygen demands in arctic temperatures. Low oxygen (*hypoxic*) environments also provide challenges for effective oxygen transport. P_{O_2} decreases as elevation increases. The summit of Mount Logan, the tallest mountain in Canada at 5959 m above sea level, is considerably hypoxic having a P_{O_2} less than half of that at sea level. At this P_{O_2}, the blood's hemoglobin is 80% saturated (see Figure 27.12B) and can drop off only 5% to resting tissues. If you have hiked through the mountains, you may have noticed that your breathing rate increased so your body could get enough oxygen to your tissues.

As you read in Module 27.11, diffusion of O₂ and CO₂ occurs down partial pressure gradients, driving gas exchange. The partial pressure of oxygen is highest in the atmosphere and lowest at the tissues where it is used by working cells. Under hypoxic conditions, the gradient is much smaller and diffusion is significantly reduced. Specific adaptations of hemoglobin have increased its affinity for oxygen. This hemoglobin collects much more O₂ at the lungs despite a smaller gradient. Most migrating birds, which may fly between 3000 and 9000 m, have hemoglobin with a higher affinity for oxygen.

Hemoglobin is a multipurpose molecule. It also helps to transport CO₂ and assists in buffering the blood. Most of the CO₂ that diffuses from tissue cells into a capillary enters red blood cells, where some (approximately 5%) of it combines with hemoglobin. Another 5% binds to other proteins in the blood plasma. The rest reacts with water, forming carbonic acid (H_2CO_3), which then breaks apart into a hydrogen ion

▲ Figure 27.12A Hemoglobin loading and unloading O₂

▲ Figure 27.12B An oxygen dissociation curve for human hemoglobin (partial pressure is measured in millimetres of mercury [mmHg])

(H^+) and a bicarbonate ion (HCO_3^-). This reversible reaction is shown below:

$$CO_2 + H_2O \rightleftharpoons H_2CO_3 \rightleftharpoons H^+ + HCO_3^-$$

Carbon dioxide   Water   Carbonic acid   Hydrogen ion   Bicarbonate ion

Hemoglobin binds most of the H^+ produced by this reaction, minimizing the change in blood pH. (As discussed in Module 27.10, the slight drop in pH on account of the increased production of CO_2 during exercise is the stimulus to increase breathing rate.) The bicarbonate ions diffuse into the plasma, where they are carried to the lungs.

As blood flows through capillaries in the lungs, the reaction is reversed. CO_2 is released from the hemoglobin or other proteins, which it was bound to. Bicarbonate ions combine with H^+ to form carbonic acid; carbonic acid is converted to CO_2 and water; and CO_2 diffuses from the blood to the alveoli and leaves the body in exhaled air.

We have seen how O_2 and CO_2 are transported between your lungs and body tissue cells via the bloodstream. In the next module, we consider a special case of gas exchange between two circulatory systems.

? O_2 in the blood is transported bound to _____ within _____ _____cells, and CO_2 is mainly transported as _____ ions within the plasma.

hemoglobin; red blood; bicarbonate ●

27.13 The human fetus exchanges gases with the mother's blood

Figure 27.13 is a drawing of a human fetus inside a mother's uterus. The fetus literally swims in a protective watery bath, the amniotic fluid. Its nonfunctional lungs are full of fluid. How does the fetus exchange gases with the outside world? It does this by way of the placenta, a composite organ that includes tissues from both fetus and mother. A large network of capillaries fans out into the placenta from blood vessels in the umbilical cord of the fetus. These capillaries exchange gases with the maternal blood that circulates in the placenta, and the mother's circulatory system transports the gases to and from her lungs. The structure of the placenta brings maternal and fetal blood in close proximity to facilitate gas exchange, but the two do not actually mix. Aiding O_2 uptake by the fetus is fetal hemoglobin, which attracts O_2 more strongly than does adult hemoglobin.

One of the reasons that smoking is considered a health risk during pregnancy is because it reduces, perhaps by as much as 25%, the supply of oxygen reaching the placenta. Lower oxygen levels delay fetal development and growth, resulting in a higher incidence of premature birth, low birth weight, and brain and lung defects. Avoiding cigarette smoke protects the health of both mothers and babies.

Let's move on to what happens when a baby is born. Very soon after delivery, placental gas exchange with the mother ceases, and the baby's lungs must begin to work. Carbon dioxide acts as the signal. As soon as CO_2 stops diffusing from the fetus into the placenta, CO_2 levels rise in the fetal blood. The resulting drop in blood pH stimulates the breathing control centre in the infant's brain, and the newborn gasps and takes its first breath.

A human birth and the radical changes in gas exchange mechanisms that accompany it are extraordinary events, resulting from millions of years of evolutionary adaptation. For a human baby to switch almost instantly from living in water and exchanging gases with maternal blood to breathing air directly requires truly remarkable adaptations in the respiratory system. Also required are adaptations of the circulatory system, which, as we have seen, support the respiratory system in its gas exchange function. We will turn to the circulatory system in Chapter 28.

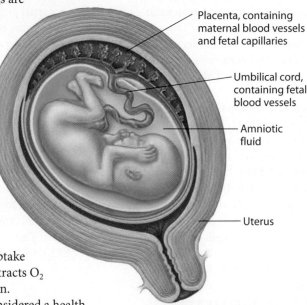

Placenta, containing maternal blood vessels and fetal capillaries

Umbilical cord, containing fetal blood vessels

Amniotic fluid

Uterus

▲ **Figure 27.13** A human fetus and placenta in the uterus

? How does fetal hemoglobin enhance oxygen transfer from mother to fetus across the placenta?

 Because fetal hemoglobin has a greater affinity for O_2 than does adult hemoglobin, it helps to "pull" the O_2 from maternal blood to fetal blood.

MasteringBiology® **For Practice Quizzes, BioFlix, MP3 Tutors, and Activities, go to masteringbiology.com.**

Reviewing the Concepts

Mechanisms of Gas Exchange (27.1–27.6)

27.1 Overview: Gas exchange in humans involves breathing, transport of gases, and exchange with body cells. Gas exchange, the interchange of O_2 and CO_2 between an organism and its environment, provides O_2 for cellular respiration and removes its waste product, CO_2.

27.2 Animals exchange O_2 and CO_2 across moist body surfaces. Respiratory surfaces must be thin and moist for diffusion of O_2 and CO_2 to occur. Some animals use their entire skin as a gas exchange organ. In most animals, a tracheal system, gills, or lungs provide large respiratory surfaces for gas exchange.

27.3 The tracheal system of insects provides direct exchange between the air and body cells. A network of finely branched tubes transports O_2 directly to body cells and moves CO_2 from them.

27.4 Gills are adapted for gas exchange in aquatic environments. Gills absorb O_2 dissolved in water. In a fish, gas exchange is enhanced by ventilation and the countercurrent flow of water and blood.

27.5 The evolution of lungs facilitated the movement of tetrapods onto land. Skeletal adaptations of air-breathing fish may have helped early tetrapods move onto land.

27.6 Can turtles really breathe through their backsides? Although most turtles cannot, at least two aquatic species are able to breathe water through their cloaca.

The Human Respiratory System (27.7–27.10)

27.7 In mammals, branching tubes convey air to lungs located in the chest cavity. Inhaled air passes through the pharynx and larynx into the trachea, bronchi, and bronchioles to the alveoli. Mucus and cilia in the respiratory passages protect the lungs.

27.8 Smoking is a serious assault on the respiratory system. Smoking causes lung cancer, heart disease, and strokes.

27.9 Negative pressure breathing ventilates your lungs. The contraction of rib muscles and the diaphragm expands the chest cavity, reducing air pressure in the alveoli and drawing air into the lungs.

27.10 Breathing is automatically controlled. A breathing control centre in the brain keeps breathing in tune with body needs, sensing and responding to the CO_2 level in the blood. A drop in blood pH triggers an increase in the rate and depth of breathing.

Transport of Gases in the Human Body (27.11–27.13)

27.11 Blood transports respiratory gases. The heart pumps O_2-poor blood to the lungs, where it picks up O_2 and drops off CO_2. O_2-rich blood returns to the heart and is pumped to body cells, where it drops off O_2 and picks up CO_2.

27.12 Hemoglobin carries O_2 and has other functions. Hemoglobin binds O_2 and carries it throughout the body. It can also bind other

molecules. A small amount of CO_2 is transported by hemoglobin, and protons can bind, making hemoglobin an effective buffer.

27.13 The human fetus exchanges gases with the mother's blood. Fetal hemoglobin enhances oxygen transfer from maternal blood in the placenta. At birth, rising CO_2 in fetal blood stimulates the breathing control centre to initiate breathing.

Connecting the Concepts

1. Complete the following concept map to review some of the concepts of gas exchange.

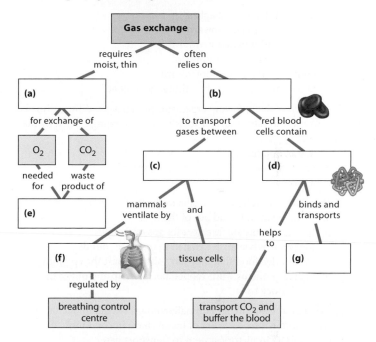

2. Label the parts of the human respiratory system.

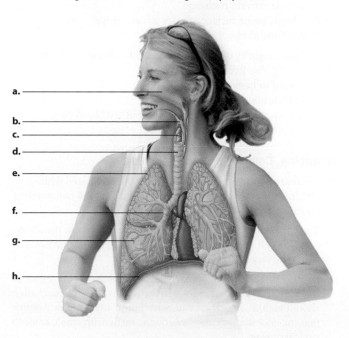

a.
b.
c.
d.
e.
f.
g.
h.

Testing Your Knowledge

Multiple Choice

3. When you hold your breath, which of the following first leads to the urge to breathe?
   - a. falling CO_2
   - b. falling O_2
   - c. rising CO_2
   - d. rising pH of the blood
   - e. both c and d

4. Countercurrent gas exchange in the gills of a fish
   - a. speeds up the flow of water through the gills.
   - b. maintains a gradient that enhances diffusion.
   - c. enables the fish to obtain oxygen without swimming.
   - d. means that blood and water flow at different rates.
   - e. allows O_2 to diffuse against its partial pressure gradient.

5. When you inhale, the diaphragm
   - a. relaxes and moves upward.
   - b. relaxes and moves downward.
   - c. contracts and moves upward.
   - d. contracts and moves downward.
   - e. is not involved in the breathing movements.

6. In which of the following organisms does oxygen diffuse directly across a respiratory surface to cells, without being carried by the blood?
   - a. a grasshopper
   - b. a whale
   - c. an earthworm
   - d. a sparrow
   - e. a mouse

7. What is the function of the cilia in the trachea and bronchi?
   - a. to sweep air into and out of the lungs
   - b. to increase the surface area for gas exchange
   - c. to vibrate when air is exhaled to produce sounds
   - d. to dislodge food that may have slipped past the epiglottis
   - e. to sweep mucus with trapped particles up and out of the respiratory tract

8. What do the alveoli of mammalian lungs, the gill filaments of fish, and the tracheal tubes of insects have in common?
   - a. use of a circulatory system to transport gases
   - b. respiratory surfaces that are infoldings of the body wall
   - c. countercurrent exchange
   - d. a large, moist surface area for gas exchange
   - e. all of the above

9. The vast majority of carbon dioxide in the blood is transported
   - a. as CO_2 dissolved in the plasma.
   - b. bound to hemoglobin.
   - c. as bicarbonate ions.
   - d. as CO_2 dissolved in the cytoplasm of red blood cells.
   - e. as carbonic acid.

Describing, Comparing, and Explaining

10. What are two advantages of breathing air, compared with obtaining dissolved oxygen from water? What is a comparative disadvantage of breathing air?

11. Trace the path of an O_2 molecule in its journey from the air to a muscle cell in your arm, naming all the structures involved along the way.

12. Explain three key evolutionary adaptations that have facilitated cloacal gill respiration in the Fitzroy River turtle. These changes should include structural and behavioural adaptations. Assume that the ancestor was another aquatic turtle with small, smooth cloacal bursae.

Applying the Concepts

13. Carbon monoxide (CO) is a colourless, odourless gas found in furnace and automobile engine exhaust and cigarette smoke. CO binds to hemoglobin 210 times more tightly than does O_2. (You also learned in Module 6.11 that CO binds with an electron transport protein and disrupts cellular respiration.) Explain why CO is such a deadly gas.

14. Partial pressure reflects the relative amount of gas in a mixture and is measured in millimetres of mercury (mmHg). Llamas are native to the Andes Mountains in South America. The partial pressure of O_2 (abbreviated P_{O_2}) in the atmosphere where llamas live is about half of the P_{O_2} at sea level. As a result, the P_{O_2} in the lungs of llamas is about 50 mmHg, whereas the P_{O_2} in human lungs at sea level is about 100 mmHg.

    A dissociation curve for hemoglobin shows the percentage of saturation (the amount of O_2 bound to hemoglobin) at increasing values of P_{O_2}. As you see in the graph below, the dissociation curves for llama and human hemoglobin differ. Compare these two curves and explain how the hemoglobin of llamas is an adaptation to living where the air is "thin."

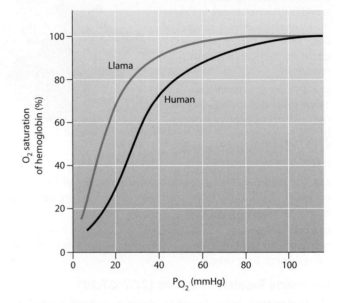

15. Mountain climbers often spend weeks adjusting to the low O_2 concentration at high altitudes before and during their ascent of high peaks. During that time, their bodies begin to produce more red blood cells. Some runners and cyclists prepare for competition by training at high altitudes or by sleeping in a tent in which P_{O_2} is kept artificially low. Explain why this training strategy may improve an athlete's performance.

16. One of the many mutant opponents that the movie monster Godzilla contends with is Mothra, a giant mothlike creature with a wingspan of 7–8 m. Such science fiction creatures can be critiqued on the grounds of biomechanical and physiological principles. Focusing on the principles of gas exchange that you learned about in this chapter, what problems would Mothra face? Why do you think truly giant insects are improbable?

Answers to all questions can be found in Appendix E.

Circulation
and Waste Removal

Circulatory Systems

(28.1–28.2)

Internal transport systems carry materials between exchange surfaces and body cells.

Blood and Blood Vessels

(28.3–28.10)

Red blood cells carry oxygen, white blood cells fight infections, and platelets function in blood clotting. Blood flows through arteries to capillaries, where exchange occurs with body cells, and returns to the heart in veins.

The Human Cardiovascular System and Heart

(28.11–28.14)

The heart pumps blood through the pulmonary circuit and the systemic circuit.

The Circulatory System and Waste Removal

(28.15–28.19)

The circulatory system is closely associated with the kidneys, organs for the removal of nitrogenous waste.

Sperm Whales, Extreme Free-Divers

Free-diving is a component of many aquatic activities that require individuals to hold their breath underwater for extended periods of time. In competitive apnea (breath-holding), free-divers try to attain the deepest dive on a single breath taken at the surface. In January 2013, the human record for free-diving, without any equipment, was 101 m. To reach such a depth and return to the surface, free-divers must hold their breath for upward of four minutes.

There are two fundamental reasons why other air-breathing mammals dive: food and sex. Thus, successful dives lead to meals or mates. While submerged, mammals experience a series of cardiovascular changes collectively called the dive reflex. Although the magnitude of these reactions varies, similar changes occur in all mammals. The dive reflex increases the efficiency of oxygen consumption and lengthens the dive duration. Much of what we know about the dive reflex comes from research on Steller sea lions (*Eumetopias jubatus*) by Dr. Andrew Trites and others at the University of British Columbia. Trites, director of the Marine Mammal Research Consortium, uses trained sea lions and sophisticated equipment to measure various cardiovascular parameters during dives. A typical dive for a sea lion is about 50 m. However, dives of more than 400 m have been recorded. These records, however, pale in comparison to that of the ultimate free-diver: The sperm whale (*Physeter macrocephalus*) has been seen at depths of 3000 m and may stay submerged for 90 minutes!

First, during the whale's dive reflex, blood is redirected to essential organs—including the brain, heart, and lungs—and away from nonessential organs. The whale restricts blood flow to its extremities and many of its skeletal muscles. Yet these muscles do not become oxygen starved. The extremely dark muscles of a sperm whale have a very high concentration of O_2-storing myoglobin to fulfill their needs during the dive.

The heart rate of a diving whale can slow by as much as 95%, as the 100 kg heart is pumping blood to fewer organs. During this state, known as bradycardia, the heart rate of a sperm whale can drop to one or two beats per minute during a dive. (At the surface, a typical sperm whale heart rate is between 10 and 30 beats per minute.) With fewer heartbeats, less oxygen is consumed and more is available for the brain.

Lastly, a special network of blood vessels of the sperm whale creates a countercurrent heat exchanger in the brain. This network of blood vessels maintains the brain at a consistent temperature, ensuring proper function. Additionally, this network minimizes heat loss to the cold ocean water.

When compared to the sperm whale, humans are poorly adapted to aquatic life. However, we still possess a similar, albeit much weaker, cardiovascular response when diving. This can be seen in humans simulating a dive in the laboratory. Presence of the dive reflex in all mammals suggests it was of importance to the common ancestor of early mammals.

We begin this chapter with a survey of some of the solutions to transport that natural selection has favoured in different animals. This is followed by a discussion of the structure and function of the vertebrate circulatory system. The chapter closes by examining how wastes are removed from the blood by the kidneys.

Circulatory Systems

28.1 Circulatory systems facilitate exchange with all body tissues

To sustain life, an animal must acquire nutrients, exchange gases, and dispose of waste products, and these needs ultimately extend to every cell in the body. In most animals, these functions are facilitated by a **circulatory system**. As you saw in Figure 25.13A, a circulatory system is necessary in any animal whose body is too large or too complex for such exchange to occur by diffusion alone. Diffusion is inadequate for transporting materials over distances greater than a few cell widths—far less than the distance oxygen must travel between your lungs and brain or the distance nutrients must go between your small intestine and the muscles in your arms and legs. An internal transport system must bring resources close enough to cells for diffusion to be effective.

Several types of internal transport have evolved in animals. For example, in cnidarians and most flatworms, a central gastrovascular cavity serves both in digestion and in distribution of substances throughout the body. As you saw in Figure 26.3A, the body wall of a hydra is only two or three cells thick, so all the cells can exchange materials directly with the water surrounding the animal or with the fluid in its gastrovascular cavity. Nutrients and other materials have only a short distance to diffuse between cell layers.

A gastrovascular cavity is not adequate for animals with thick, multiple layers of cells. Such animals require a true circulatory system, which consists of a muscular pump (**heart**), a circulatory fluid, and a set of tubes (vessels) to carry the circulatory fluid.

Two basic types of circulatory systems have evolved in animals: closed and open systems. Earthworms, squids, octopuses, and vertebrates (such as ourselves) all have a **closed circulatory system**. It is called "closed" because the circulatory fluid, **blood**, is confined to vessels, keeping it distinct from the interstitial fluid called lymph. There are three kinds of vessels: **Arteries** carry blood away from the heart to body organs and tissues; **veins** return blood to the heart; and **capillaries** convey blood between arteries and veins within each tissue. The vertebrate circulatory system is often called a **cardiovascular system** (from the Greek *kardia*, heart, and Latin *vas*, vessel). How extensive are the vessels in your cardiovascular system? If all your blood vessels were lined up end to end, they would circle Earth's equator twice.

The cardiovascular system of a fish **(Figure 28.1A)** illustrates some key features of a closed circulatory system. The heart of a fish has two main chambers. The **atrium** (plural, *atria*) receives blood from the veins and the **ventricle** pumps blood to the gills via large arteries. As in all figures depicting closed circulatory systems in this book red represents oxygen-rich blood and blue represents oxygen-poor blood. It is important to note that arteries do not always carry O_2-rich blood just as veins do not always carry O_2-poor blood. After passing through the gill capillaries, the blood, now oxygen-rich, flows into large arteries that carry it to all other parts of the body. The large arteries branch into **arterioles**, small vessels that give rise to capillaries. Networks of capillaries called **capillary beds** infiltrate every tissue in the body. The thin walls of the capillaries allow chemical exchange between the blood and the interstitial fluid. The capillaries converge into **venules**, which in turn converge into larger veins that return blood to the heart.

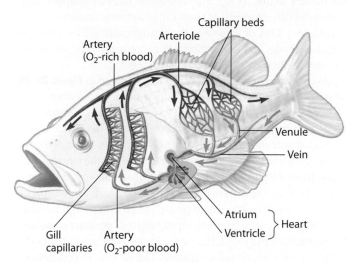

▲ **Figure 28.1A** The closed circulatory system of a fish

Many invertebrates, including most molluscs and all arthropods, have an **open circulatory system**. The system is called "open" because fluid is pumped through open-ended vessels and flows out among the tissues; there is no distinction between the circulatory fluid and interstitial fluid. This single fluid is referred to as **hemolymph** and it has the functions of both blood and lymph. In an insect, such as the grasshopper **(Figure 28.1B)**, pumping of the tubular heart drives body fluid into the head and the rest of the body (black arrows). Body movements help to circulate the fluid as materials are exchanged with body cells. When the heart relaxes, fluid enters through several pores. Each pore has a valve that closes when the heart contracts, preventing backflow of the circulating fluid. In insects, as you learned in Module 27.3, respiratory gases are conveyed to and from body cells by the tracheal system (not shown here), not by the circulatory system.

In the next module, we compare the cardiovascular systems of different vertebrate groups.

? What are the key differences between an open circulatory system and a closed circulatory system?

● The vessels in an open circulatory system do not form an enclosed circuit from the heart, through the body, and back to the heart, and the circulatory fluid is not distinct from interstitial fluid, as is the blood in a closed circulatory system.

▲ **Figure 28.1B** The open circulatory system of a grasshopper

28.2 Vertebrate cardiovascular systems reflect evolution

The colonization of land by vertebrates was a major episode in the history of life. As aquatic vertebrates became adapted for terrestrial life, nearly all of their organ systems underwent major changes. One of these was the change from gill breathing to lung breathing, and this switch was accompanied by important changes in their closed circulatory systems.

As illustrated in Figure 28.1A and diagrammed in **Figure 28.2A**, blood passes through the heart of a fish once in each circuit through the body, an arrangement called **single circulation**. Blood pumped from the ventricle travels first to the gill capillaries. Blood pressure drops considerably as blood flows through the numerous, narrow gill capillaries. An artery carries the oxygen-rich blood from the gills to capillaries in the tissues and organs, from which the blood returns to the atrium of the heart. The animal's swimming movements help to propel the blood through the body.

A single circuit would not supply enough pressure to move blood through the capillaries of the lungs and then to the body capillaries of a terrestrial vertebrate. The evolutionary adaptation that resulted in a more vigorous flow of blood to body organs is called **double circulation**, in which blood is pumped a second time after it loses pressure in the lungs. The **pulmonary circuit** carries blood between the heart and gas exchange tissues in the lungs, and the **systemic circuit** carries blood between the heart and the rest of the body.

You can see an example of these two circuits in **Figure 28.2B**. (Notice that the right side of the animal's heart is on the left in the diagram. It is customary to draw the system as though it is in a body facing you from the page.) Frogs and other amphibians have a three-chambered heart. The right atrium receives blood returning from the systemic capillaries in the body's organs. The ventricle pumps blood to capillary beds in the lungs and skin. Because gas exchange occurs both in the lungs and across

the thin, moist skin, this is called a pulmocutaneous circuit. Oxygen-rich blood returns to the left atrium. Although blood from the two atria mixes in the single ventricle, a ridge diverts most of the oxygen-poor blood to the pulmocutaneous circuit and most of the oxygen-rich blood to the systemic circuit.

In the three-chambered heart of turtles, snakes, and lizards, the ventricle is partially divided, and less mixing of blood occurs. The ventricle is completely divided in crocodilians.

In all birds and mammals (for example, the Kermode bear in **Figure 28.2C**), the heart has four chambers: two atria and two ventricles. The right side of the heart handles only oxygen-poor blood; the left side receives and pumps only oxygen-rich blood. The evolution of a powerful four-chambered heart was an essential adaptation to support the high metabolic rates of birds and mammals, which are endothermic. Endotherms use about 10 times as much energy as equal-sized ectotherms (see Module 25.16). Therefore, their circulatory system needs to deliver much more fuel and oxygen to body tissues. This requirement is met by a large heart that is able to pump a large volume of blood through separate systemic and pulmonary circulations. It is important to note that birds and mammals descended from different reptilian ancestors, and their four-chambered hearts evolved independently—an example of convergent evolution, in which natural selection favours the same adaptation in response to similar environmental challenges.

We discuss blood and blood vessels in more detail in the next several modules.

? What is the difference between the single circulation of a fish and the double circulation of a land vertebrate?

● In a fish, blood travels from gill capillaries to body capillaries before returning to the heart. In a land vertebrate, blood returns to the heart and is pumped a second time between the pulmonary and systemic circuits.

▲ **Figure 28.2A** The single circulation and two-chambered heart of a fish

▲ **Figure 28.2B** The double circulation and three-chambered heart of an amphibian

▲ **Figure 28.2C** The double circulation and four-chambered heart of a bird or mammal

28.3 Blood consists of red and white blood cells suspended in plasma

Your body has about 5 L of blood. Blood consists of several types of cells suspended in a liquid called **plasma**. When a blood sample is taken, the cells can be separated from the plasma by spinning the sample in a centrifuge, after adding a chemical to prevent the blood from clotting. The cellular elements (cells and cell fragments), which make up about 45% of the volume of blood, settle to the bottom of the centrifuge tube, underneath the transparent, straw-coloured plasma (**Figure 28.3A**).

Plasma is about 90% water. Among its many solutes are inorganic salts in the form of dissolved ions. The functions of these ions (also called electrolytes) include keeping the pH of blood at about 7.4 and maintaining the osmotic balance between blood and interstitial fluid.

Plasma proteins also help to maintain osmotic balance. Some proteins act as buffers. **Fibrinogen** is a plasma protein that functions in blood clotting, and immunoglobulins are proteins important in body defence (immunity).

Plasma also contains a wide variety of substances in transit from one part of the body to another, such as nutrients, waste products, O_2, CO_2, and hormones.

There are two classes of cells suspended in blood plasma: **red blood cells** and **white blood cells**. Also suspended in plasma are **platelets**, cell fragments that are involved in the process of blood clotting.

All blood cells are formed within the red marrow inside bones such as the ribs, vertebrae, sternum, and pelvis. Red marrow is a spongy tissue in which unspecialized cells called **stem cells** differentiate into blood cells. **Multipotent stem cells** are so named because they have the ability to form multiple types of cells, in this case all the blood cells and platelets. When a stem cell divides, one daughter cell remains a stem cell while the other can take on a specialized function.

As shown in **Figure 28.3B**, multipotent stem cells in bone marrow give rise to two different types of stem cells: lymphoid stem cells and myeloid stem cells. Lymphoid stem cells produce two different types of lymphocytes, which function in the immune system (discussed in Chapter 34). Myeloid stem cells can differentiate into other white blood cells, platelets, and red blood cells. The stem cells continually produce all the blood cells needed throughout life.

Red blood cells are also called **erythrocytes**. The structure of a red blood cell suits its main function, which is to carry oxygen. Human red blood cells are small biconcave discs, thinner in the centre than at the sides. Their small size and shape create a large surface area across which oxygen can diffuse. Red blood cells of mammals lack a nucleus, allowing more room to pack in hemoglobin. Each tiny red blood cell contains about 250 million molecules of hemoglobin and thus can transport about a billion O_2 molecules. A single drop of your blood

Plasma (55%)	
Constituent	**Major functions**
Water	Solvent for carrying other substances
Ions (blood electrolytes) Sodium Potassium Calcium Magnesium Chloride Bicarbonate	Osmotic balance, pH buffering, and maintaining ion concentration of interstitial fluid
Plasma proteins	Osmotic balance and pH buffering
Fibrinogen	Clotting
Immunoglobulins (antibodies)	Defence
Substances transported by blood Nutrients (e.g., glucose, fatty acids, vitamins) Waste products of metabolism Respiratory gases (O_2 and CO_2) Hormones	

Centrifuged blood sample

Cellular elements (45%)		
Cell type	**Number** per μL (mm³) of blood	**Functions**
Red blood cells (erythrocytes)	5–6 million	Transport of O_2 and some CO_2
White blood cells (leukocytes)	5000–10 000	Defence and immunity
Basophils Eosinophils Lymphocytes Neutrophils Monocytes		
Platelets	250 000– 400 000	Blood clotting

▲ **Figure 28.3A** The composition of blood

Multipotent stem cells (in bone marrow)

Lymphoid stem cells

Myeloid stem cells

Erythrocytes

Basophils

Platelets

Eosinophils

Lymphocytes

Monocytes   Neutrophils

▲ **Figure 28.3B** Differentiation of blood cells from multipotent stem cells

contains about 25 million cells (a drop is about 50 μL), which means you have about 25 trillion red blood cells in your 5 L of blood. Think about how many molecules of O_2 are travelling through your bloodstream!

Adequate numbers of red blood cells are essential for healthy body function. After circulating for three or four months, red blood cells are broken down and their molecules recycled. Much of the iron removed from the hemoglobin is returned to the bone marrow, where new red blood cells are formed at the amazing rate of 2 million per second.

An abnormally low amount of hemoglobin or a low number of red blood cells is a condition called **anemia**. Anemics feel tired because the blood cannot deliver enough oxygen to the body's cells. Anemia can result from a variety of factors, including excessive blood loss, vitamin or mineral deficiencies, and certain forms of cancer. Iron deficiency is the most common cause. Women are more likely to develop iron deficiency than men because of blood loss during menstruation. Pregnant women are generally prescribed iron supplements to support the developing fetus and placenta.

Individuals living at high altitudes, where oxygen levels are low, adapt by producing more red blood cells. In response to low oxygen at the tissues, the kidneys produce a hormone called **erythropoietin**. Erythropoietin stimulates the production of red blood cells and increases oxygen delivery. Many athletes train at high altitudes to benefit from this effect.

There are five major types of white blood cells, or **leukocytes**, as pictured in Figure 28.3A: monocytes, neutrophils, basophils, eosinophils, and lymphocytes. Their collective function is to fight infections. For example, monocytes and neutrophils are **phagocytes**, which engulf and digest bacteria and debris from your own dead cells. White blood cells actually spend much of their time moving through interstitial fluid, where most of the battles against infection are waged. There are also great numbers of white blood cells in the lymphatic system. These cells are examined in more detail in Chapter 34.

Leukemia is cancer of the white blood cells, or leukocytes. Because cancerous cells grow uncontrollably, a person with leukemia has an unusually high number of leukocytes, most of which are defective. These overabundant cells crowd out the bone marrow cells that are developing into red blood cells and platelets, causing severe anemia and impaired clotting.

 For every one white blood cell in normal human blood, there are about _____ to _____ red blood cells.

● 500, 1000

28.4 Donating blood and bone marrow saves lives

Roughly every minute of every day, a Canadian requires blood. These individuals include, among others, accident victims, surgery patients, transplant patients, patients with blood disorders, and those undergoing cancer treatment. Without donors, the prognosis for these individuals becomes dire. Fortunately, organizations such as the Canadian Blood Services devote countless hours to ensure that patients can have the blood they need.

If you choose to donate, your blood will go through an important screening process before it can be used. Before you can donate, a small drop of blood is collected from a pinprick to determine your blood type and hemoglobin level. Blood is also screened for a multitude of diseases, including hepatitis and HIV, ensuring the safest product possible for those in need of a transfusion.

Recall the ABO blood types (based on surface carbohydrates) and Rh blood groups (based on the presence, "+," or absence,

"−," of the Rh protein) discussed in Module 9.11. For example, someone with carbohydrate A and protein Rh has type A positive blood. Therefore, there are eight human blood types: A, B, AB, and O, each of which can be either Rh+ or Rh−. Matching compatible blood types is critical for safe blood transfusions. If a donor's blood cells have a carbohydrate (A or B) that is foreign to the recipient, then the recipient's immune system produces blood proteins called antibodies (see Module 34.10) that bind specifically to the foreign carbohydrates and cause the donor blood cells to clump together, potentially killing the recipient. The clumping reaction is also the basis of a blood-typing test performed in the laboratory (**Figure 28.4A**). Similarly, if Rh− individuals receive Rh+ blood, they may produce antibodies to the Rh protein and clumping will occur. An Rh+ recipient, on the other hand, can receive either Rh− or Rh+ blood without concern. Individuals who have AB positive blood

Recipient's Blood Group (Phenotype)	Carbohydrates Present on Red Blood Cells	Antibodies Present in Blood	Reaction When Donor Blood from Groups Below Is Mixed with Antibodies from Groups at Left			
			O	A	B	AB
A	Carbohydrate A	Anti-B	No reaction	No reaction	Clumping reaction	Clumping reaction
B	Carbohydrate B	Anti-A	No reaction	Clumping reaction	No reaction	Clumping reaction
AB	Carbohydrate A and Carbohydrate B	None	No reaction	No reaction	No reaction	No reaction
O	Neither	Anti-A Anti-B	No reaction	Clumping reaction	Clumping reaction	Clumping reaction

No reaction Clumping reaction ⚠

▲ **Figure 28.4A** Clumping reaction of donor blood groups mixed with recipient antibodies

type can receive blood from anyone without fear of clumping, making them "universal recipients." In contrast, donated type O negative blood never causes clumping, making these individuals "universal donors." Recipients with O negative blood type, however, can receive blood from only type O negative donors.

Donations can take different forms. Whole blood is easily collected at any one of the thousands of clinics held annually. Before use, the white blood cells of the donor's immune system (see Chapter 34) are removed to prevent unwanted complications. Surgery patients are the primary recipients of whole blood.

Permanent donation centres across the country use complicated techniques to extract only some of the specific blood components described in the previous module from donors. For example, blood plasma can be collected by an apheresis machine (**Figure 28.4B**), which returns all blood cells to the donor. Plasma is used to treat burn patients. Alternatively, a similar machine can extract platelets for the treatment of

some leukemia and cancer patients, and patients with blood clotting disorders.

Leukemia is usually fatal unless treated, and not all cases respond to the standard cancer treatments of radiation and chemotherapy. An alternative treatment involves destroying the cancerous bone marrow completely and replacing it with healthy bone marrow. Injection of as few as 30 stem cells can repopulate the blood and immune system. Patients may be treated with their own bone marrow. Marrow from the patient is harvested, processed to remove as many cancerous cells as possible, and reinjected. Alternatively, a suitable donor, often a sibling, may provide the marrow. Bone marrow must also be typed to determine compatibility. Marrow typing, based on the self proteins discussed in Modules 34.9 and 34.12, is more complicated than blood typing and must be done in a laboratory. Unlike blood testing, marrow typing is performed only when you volunteer for marrow donation. Patients that receive marrow from a donor require lifelong treatment with drugs that suppress the tendency of some of the transplanted marrow cells to reject the cells of the recipient.

Unfortunately, fewer than one-third of patients have a relative who is a suitable donor. These patients must rely on unrelated, volunteer donors. Canadian Blood Services's OneMatch Stem Cell and Marrow Network is a part of an international network of registries, consisting of more than 11 million donors. These international registries significantly improve the chance of finding a suitable donor. To join, an informed donor provides a cheek swab sample that is tested for molecular markers. If a match occurs, bone marrow stem cells could be collected through apheresis or by harvesting bone marrow directly. Both carry minimal risks and side effects.

? What type of donated blood product is used to treat a patient with hemophilia, a blood clotting disorder?

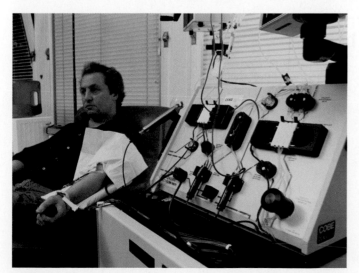

▲ **Figure 28.4B** An apheresis machine collecting blood plasma

Platelets ●

28.5 Blood clots plug leaks when blood vessels are injured

1 Platelets adhere to the exposed connective tissue.

2 A platelet plug forms.

3 A fibrin clot forms.

Endothelium

Connective tissue

Platelet

Platelet plug

Fibrin clot

▲ **Figure 28.5A** The blood-clotting process

You may get cuts and scrapes from time to time, yet you don't bleed to death from such minor injuries because your blood contains self-sealing materials that are activated when blood vessels are injured. These sealants are platelets and the previously mentioned plasma protein fibrinogen.

What happens when you sustain an injury? Your body's immediate response is to constrict the damaged blood vessel, thereby reducing blood loss and allowing time for repairs to begin. **Figure 28.5A** shows the stages of the clotting process. **1** When the endothelium (shown as tan) lining a blood vessel is damaged, connective tissue in the vessel wall is exposed to blood. Platelets (purple) rapidly adhere to the exposed tissue and release chemicals that make nearby platelets sticky. **2** Soon a cluster of sticky platelets forms a plug that quickly provides protection against additional blood loss. Clotting factors in the plasma and those released from the clumped platelets set off a chain of reactions that culminate in the formation of a reinforced patch, called a scab when located on the skin. In this complex process, an activated enzyme converts fibrinogen to a threadlike protein called **fibrin**. **3** Threads of fibrin (white) reinforce the plug, forming a fibrin clot.

Figure 28.5B is a micrograph of a fibrin clot. Within an hour after a fibrin clot forms, the platelets contract, pulling the torn edges closer together and reducing the size of the area in need of repair. Chemicals released by platelets also stimulate cell division in smooth muscle and connective tissue, initiating the healing process.

The clotting mechanism is so important that any defect in it can be life-threatening. In the inherited disease hemophilia, excessive, sometimes fatal bleeding occurs from even minor cuts or bruises. In other people, the formation of blood clots in the *absence* of injury can be a problem. Anticlotting factors in the blood normally prevent spontaneous clotting. If blood clots form within a vessel, they can block the flow of blood. Such a clot, called a thrombus, can be dangerous if it blocks a blood vessel of the heart or brain (see Module 28.14). Aspirin, heparin, and warfarin are anticoagulant drugs that work by different mechanisms to prevent undesirable clotting in patients at risk for heart attack or stroke.

Colourized SEM 4000×

▲ **Figure 28.5B** A fibrin clot

? What is the role of platelets in blood clot formation?

● Platelets adhere to exposed connective tissue and release various chemicals that help a platelet plug form and activate the pathway leading to a fibrin clot. (Also, some of the chemicals promote healing in other ways.)

28.6 Is the blood in our veins blue?

Blue blood is a medieval English idiom describing an individual of noble descent. In contrast to labourers who worked long days in the sun becoming tanned, royalty had pale skin. Superficial veins, highly visible through untanned skin, have a bluish colour. And so it was thought that blood of aristocrats was blue. The rumour that arterial blood is oxygenated and red, and venous blood is deoxygenated and blue, has evolved from this.

Students of animal biology and anatomy usually spend time studying the circulatory system. Diagrams prove to be a useful tool in illustrating the flow of blood throughout the body. Many textbooks, including this one, use colours to clearly distinguish between oxygenated and deoxygenated blood. For contrast, these colours are typically red and blue, respectively (see Figure 27.11 for an example). This convention has unfortunately propagated

the misconception that venous blood is blue. The use of more anatomical colours would be difficult for students to distinguish. Furthermore, it is common practice to use red and blue injectants for arteries and veins respectively in the preparation of animals for student dissections—a practice which further reinforces this misconception.

Although the veins just under the skin do have a blue tint, the colour does not come from the blood inside. Both veins and arteries have thick walls consisting of many layers of tissue. As such, they are completely opaque, preventing any light from passing through. Therefore, when you can see a vein under your skin, you are seeing its exterior, not its contents. As light penetrates your skin, low energy wavelengths are quickly absorbed. Blue wavelengths, however, have enough energy to reflect off

▲ **Figure 28.6** The colour of blood: arterial (oxygenated, left) and venous (deoxygenated, right)

produced by the large concentration of hemoglobin in our red blood cells (see Module 27.12). Hemoglobin is a pigmented molecule, meaning that it reflects light, specifically the red wavelengths. **Figure 28.6** shows the colour of hemoglobin under two conditions. Arterial blood on the left contains highly oxygenated hemoglobin and is bright red in colour. Venous blood on the right is deoxygenated and dark red. Although Hollywood may not always get the hue correct, blood (at least that of humans) is typically portrayed as red.

the veins and be perceived by your retina (see Module 32.10). As a result, we perceive the veins with a bluish tint.

Despite the diagrams in this and other textbooks, the truth is that blood is always red. The colour of blood is

 If superficial veins appear blue, why do capillaries appear red? (*Hint:* You may want to read Module 28.10.)

● Capillaries do not have the thick walls that are found in arteries and veins. Therefore, the blood inside is visible and appears red.

28.7 The structure of blood vessels fits their functions

Now that we have explored the structure and function of blood, let's look at the extensive series of vessels that transports it throughout your body.

Functions of Blood Vessels The blood vessels of the circulatory system must have an intimate connection with all of the body's tissues. The micrograph in **Figure 28.7A** shows a capillary that carries oxygenated, nutrient-rich blood to smooth muscle cells. Notice that red blood cells pass single file through the capillary, coming close enough to the surrounding tissue that O_2 and nutrients can diffuse out of them into the muscle cells.

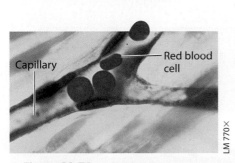

▲ **Figure 28.7A** A capillary in smooth muscle tissue

In **Figure 28.7B**, the downward arrows show the route that molecules take in diffusing from blood in a capillary to tissue cells. As we discussed in Module 25.13, cells are immersed in interstitial fluid. Molecules such as O_2 (●) and nutrients (●) diffuse out of a capillary into the interstitial fluid and then from the fluid into a tissue cell.

In addition to transporting O_2 and nutrients, blood vessels convey metabolic wastes to waste disposal organs: CO_2 to the lungs and a variety of other metabolic wastes to the kidneys. The upward arrows in Figure 28.7B represent the diffusion of waste molecules (●) out of a tissue cell, through the interstitial fluid, and into the capillary.

The circulatory system plays several key roles in maintaining a constant internal environment (homeostasis). By

● O_2
● Nutrient
● CO_2

▲ **Figure 28.7B** Diffusion between blood and tissue cells

exchanging molecules with the interstitial fluid, it helps to control the makeup of the environment in which the tissue cells live. We have already seen the circulatory system's role in thermoregulation (Module 25.18). We will look at other roles including hormone distribution and body defence in later chapters.

Structure of Blood Vessels **Figure 28.7C** illustrates the structures of the different kinds of blood vessels and how the vessels are connected. Look first at the capillaries (centre). Appropriate to its function of exchanging materials, a capillary has a very thin wall of a single layer of epithelial cells (the endothelium), which is wrapped in a thin basal lamina (see Module 25.4). The inner surface of the capillary is smooth, which keeps the blood cells from being abraded as they tumble along.

Arteries, arterioles, veins, and venules have thicker walls than capillaries. Their walls have the same smooth endothelium but are reinforced by two other tissue layers. The middle layer consists mainly of smooth muscle. An outer layer of connective tissue with elastic fibres enables the vessels to stretch and recoil. Both these layers are thicker and sturdier in arteries, providing the strength and elasticity to accommodate the rapid flow and high pressure of blood pumped by the heart. Arteries are also able to regulate blood flow by constricting or relaxing their smooth muscle layer. The thinner-walled veins convey blood back to the heart at low velocity and pressure. Within large veins, flaps of tissue act as one-way valves, which permit blood to flow only toward the heart.

? **How does the structure of a capillary relate to its function?**

▲ **Figure 28.7C** Structural relationships of blood vessels

● The small diameter and thin walls of capillaries facilitate the exchange of substances between blood and interstitial fluid.

28.8 Blood pressure and velocity reflect the structure and arrangement of blood vessels

Now that you've looked at the structure of blood vessels, let's explore the forces that move your blood through these vessels.

Blood Pressure   **Blood pressure** is the force that blood exerts against the walls of your blood vessels. Created by the pumping of the heart, blood pressure drives the flow of blood from the heart through arteries and arterioles to capillary beds.

When the ventricles contract, blood is forced into the arteries faster than it can flow into the arterioles. This stretches the elastic walls of the arteries. You can feel this rhythmic stretching of the arteries when you measure your heart rate by taking your **pulse**. You can see this surge in pressure (expressed in millimetres of mercury, mmHg) as the pressure peaks in the top graph of **Figure 28.8A**. The pressure caused by ventricular contraction is called systolic pressure. The elastic arteries snap back during diastole, which keeps a minimum pressure on the blood and a continuous flow of blood into arterioles and capillaries. The dips in pressure in the top graph represent diastolic pressure.

The diagram at the centre of Figure 28.8A shows the relative sizes and numbers of blood vessels as blood flows from the aorta through arteries to capillaries and back through veins to the venae cavae. Blood pressure is highest in the aorta and arteries and declines abruptly as the blood enters the arterioles. The pressure drop results mainly from the resistance to blood flow caused by friction between the blood and the walls of the millions of narrow arterioles and capillaries.

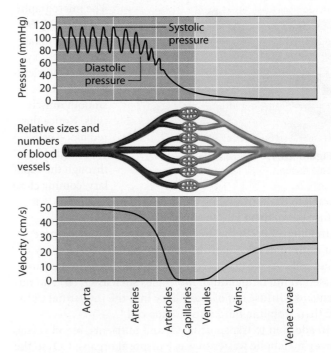

▲ **Figure 28.8A** Blood pressure and velocity in the blood vessels

Blood pressure in the arteries depends on the volume of blood pumped into the aorta and also on the restriction of blood flow into the narrow openings of the arterioles. These openings are controlled by smooth muscles. When the muscles

Typical blood pressure:
120 systolic
70 diastolic

Rubber cuff inflated with air

Pressure in the cuff above 120

120

Artery

Artery closed

❶

❷

Pressure in the cuff at 120

120

Sounds audible in the stethoscope

❸

Pressure in the cuff at 70

70

Sounds stop

❹

▲ **Figure 28.8B** Measuring blood pressure

relax, the arterioles dilate, and blood flows through them more readily, causing a fall in blood pressure. Physical and emotional stress can raise blood pressure by triggering nervous and hormonal signals that constrict these blood vessels. Regulatory mechanisms coordinate cardiac output and changes in the arteriole openings to maintain adequate blood pressure as demands on the circulatory system change.

Blood pressure is generally measured in an artery in the arm at the same height as the heart. As indicated in **Figure 28.8B**, ❶ a typical blood pressure for a healthy young adult is about 120/70. The first (sometimes referred to as the top) number is the systolic pressure; the second (or bottom) number is the diastolic pressure.

Figure 28.8B shows how blood pressure is measured using a sphygmomanometer, or blood pressure cuff. ❷ Once wrapped around the upper arm, where large arteries are accessible, the cuff is inflated until the pressure is strong enough to close the artery and cut off blood flow to the lower arm. ❸ A stethoscope is used to listen for sounds of blood flow below the cuff as the cuff is gradually deflated. The first sound of blood gurgling through the constricted artery indicates that the pressure exerted by the cuff has fallen just below that in the artery. The pressure at this point is the systolic pressure. The sound of blood flowing unevenly through the artery continues until the pressure of the cuff falls below the pressure of the artery during diastole. ❹ Blood now flows continuously through the artery, and the sound of blood flow ceases. The reading at this point is the diastolic pressure.

Optimal blood pressure for adults is below 120 mmHg for systolic pressure and below 80 mmHg for diastolic pressure. Lower values are generally considered better, except in rare cases where low blood pressure may indicate a serious underlying condition (such as an endocrine disorder, malnutrition, or internal bleeding). High blood pressure, known as **hypertension**, may indicate a serious cardiovascular disorder and lead to kidney disease (see Module 28.17).

Blood Velocity The blood's velocity (rate of flow, expressed in centimetres per second, cm/s) is illustrated in the bottom graph of Figure 28.8A. As the figure shows, velocity declines rapidly in the arterioles, drops to almost zero in the capillaries, and then speeds up in the veins. What accounts for these changes? As larger arteries divide into smaller and more numerous arterioles, the total combined cross-sectional area of the many vessels is much greater than the diameter of the one artery that feeds into them. If there were only one arteriole per artery, the blood would actually flow faster through the arteriole, the way water does when you add a narrow nozzle to a garden hose. However, there are many arterioles per artery, so the effect is like taking the nozzle off the hose: As you increase the diameter of a pipe, the flow rate goes down.

The cross-sectional area is greatest in the capillaries, and the velocity of blood is slowest through them. The steady, leisurely flow of blood in the capillaries enhances the exchange of substances with body cells.

By the time blood reaches the veins, its pressure has dropped to near zero. The blood has encountered so much resistance as it passes through the millions of tiny arterioles and capillaries that the force from the pumping heart no longer propels it. How, then, does blood return to the heart, especially when it must travel up the legs against gravity? Whenever the body moves, muscles squeeze blood through the veins. **Figure 28.8C** shows how veins are often sandwiched between skeletal muscles and how one-way valves allow the blood to flow only toward the heart. Breathing also

Direction of blood flow in vein

Valve (open)

Contracting skeletal muscle

Valve (closed)

▲ **Figure 28.8C**
Blood flow in a vein

helps to return blood to the heart. When you inhale, the change in pressure within your chest cavity causes the large veins near your heart to expand and fill.

Next we look at how local blood flow at the capillaries can be controlled.

28.9 Smooth muscle controls the distribution of blood

You learned in the previous module that smooth muscles in arteriole walls can influence blood pressure by changing the resistance to blood flow out of the arteries and into arterioles. The smooth muscles in the arteriole walls also regulate the distribution of blood to the capillaries of the various organs. At any given time, only about 5% to 10% of your body's capillaries have blood flowing through them. However, each tissue has many capillaries, so every part of your body is supplied with blood at all times. Capillaries in a few organs, such as the brain, heart, kidneys, and liver, usually carry a full load of blood. In many other sites, however, blood supply varies as blood is diverted from one place to another, depending on need.

Figure 28.9 illustrates a second mechanism that regulates the flow of blood into capillaries. Notice that in both parts of this figure there is a capillary called a thoroughfare channel, through which blood streams directly from arteriole to venule. This channel is always open. Rings of smooth muscle located at the entrance to capillary beds, called precapillary sphincters, regulate the passage of blood into the branching capillaries. As you can see in the figure, ① blood flows through the entire capillary bed when its precapillary sphincters are relaxed. ② It bypasses the capillary bed when the sphincters are contracted.

During the dive reflex discussed in the chapter-opening essay, for example, it is the precapillary sphincters that redirect blood away from the skin. After a meal, precapillary sphincters in the wall of your digestive tract relax, letting a large quantity of blood pass through the capillary beds. The products of digestion are absorbed into the blood, which delivers them to the rest of the body. During strenuous exercise, many of the capillaries in the digestive tract are closed off, and blood is supplied more generously to your skeletal muscles. This is one reason why heavy exercise right after eating may cause indigestion or abdominal cramps (and why you shouldn't swim too soon after eating—just like mom always said). Blood flow to your skin is regulated to help control body temperature and plays an important role in thermoregulation discussed in Module 25.15. An increase in blood supply to the skin helps to release the excess heat generated by exercise.

Nerve impulses, hormones, and chemicals produced locally influence the contraction of the smooth muscles that regulate the flow of blood to capillary beds. For example, the chemical histamine released by cells at a wound site causes smooth muscle relaxation, increasing blood flow and the supply of infection-fighting white blood cells.

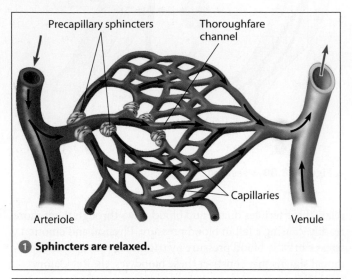

Precapillary sphincters   Thoroughfare channel

Capillaries

Arteriole   Venule

① Sphincters are relaxed.

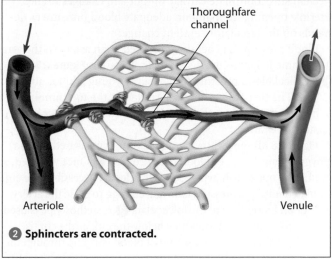

Thoroughfare channel

Arteriole   Venule

② Sphincters are contracted.

▲ Figure 28.9 The control of capillary blood flow by precapillary sphincters

Next we consider how substances are exchanged when blood flows through a capillary.

28.10 Capillaries allow the transfer of substances through their walls

Capillaries are the only blood vessels with walls thin enough for substances to cross between the blood and the interstitial fluid that bathes the body cells. This transfer of materials is the most important function of the circulatory system, so let's examine the process more carefully.

Capillary Structure and Function

Take a look at **Figure 28.10A**. It shows a cross-section of a capillary that serves skeletal muscle cells, illustrated with a micrograph and a labelled drawing. The drawing will help you interpret the micrograph. The capillary wall consists of adjoining epithelial cells that enclose a lumen, or interior space. The lumen is just large enough for red blood cells to tumble through in single file. The nucleus you see in the figure belongs to one of the two cells making up this portion of the capillary wall. (The other cell's nucleus does not appear in this particular cross-section.) Interstitial fluid, shown in blue in the drawing, fills the space between the capillary and the muscle cells.

The exchange of substances between the blood and the interstitial fluid occurs in several ways. Some nonpolar molecules, such as O_2 and CO_2, simply diffuse through the epithelial cells of the capillary wall. Larger molecules may be carried across an epithelial cell in vesicles that form by endocytosis on one side of the cell and then release their contents by exocytosis on the other side (see Module 5.8).

In addition, the capillary wall is leaky; there are small pores in the wall and narrow clefts between the epithelial cells making up the wall (see Figure 28.10A). Water and small solutes, such as sugars and salts, move freely through these pores and clefts. Blood cells and dissolved proteins generally remain inside the capillary because they are too large to fit through these passageways. Much of the exchange between blood and interstitial fluid is the result of the pressure-driven flow of

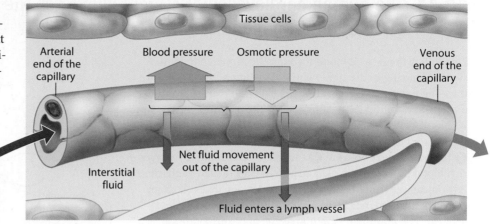

▲ **Figure 28.10B** The movement of fluid out of a capillary and into a lymph vessel

fluid (consisting of water and dissolved solutes) through these openings.

The diagram in **Figure 28.10B** shows part of a capillary with blood flowing from its arterial end (near an arteriole) to its venous end (near a venule). What are the active forces that drive fluid into or out of the capillary? One of these forces is blood pressure, which tends to push fluid outward. The other is osmotic pressure, a force that tends to pull fluid back because the blood has a higher concentration of solutes than the interstitial fluid. Proteins dissolved in the blood account for much of this high solute concentration. On average, blood pressure is greater than the opposing forces, leading to a net loss of fluid from capillaries.

Fluid Return via the Lymphatic System

Each day, you lose approximately 4–8 L of fluid from your capillaries to the surrounding tissues. The lost fluid is picked up by your lymphatic system, which includes a network of tiny vessels intermingled among the capillaries (the tan-coloured vessel in Figure 28.10B). After diffusing into these vessels, the fluid, now called lymph, is returned to your circulatory system through ducts that join with large veins in your neck. You learned in Module 26.9 that lymph vessels also transport fats from the small intestine to the blood. You can see a diagram of the lymphatic system in Figure 34.3.

Now that we have examined the structure and function of blood and blood vessels, we turn our focus to the heart and human cardiovascular system.

? Explain how a severe protein deficiency in the diet that decreases the concentration of blood plasma proteins can cause edema, the accumulation of fluid in body tissues.

▲ **Figure 28.10A** A capillary in cross-section

● Decreased blood protein concentration reduces the osmotic gradient across the capillary walls, thus reducing the pull of fluid back into the capillaries.

The Human Cardiovascular System and Heart

28.11 The human cardiovascular system illustrates the double circulation of mammals

Let's follow the flow of blood through the human circulatory system. Starting in the right ventricle in **Figure 28.11A**, we trace the pulmonary circuit first. ❶ The right ventricle pumps oxygen-poor blood to the lungs via ❷ the **pulmonary arteries**. As blood flows through ❸ capillaries in the lungs, it takes up O_2 and unloads CO_2. Oxygen-rich blood flows back through ❹ the **pulmonary veins** to ❺ the left atrium. Next, the oxygen-rich blood flows from the left atrium into ❻ the left ventricle. As you can see from the figure, arteries do not always contain oxygenated blood, nor is the blood within veins always deoxygenated. The pulmonary circuit has the opposite condition.

Now let's trace the systemic circuit. As Figure 28.11A shows, the left ventricle pumps oxygen-rich blood into ❼ the **aorta**. The aorta is our largest blood vessel, with a diameter of about 2.5 cm, roughly equal to the diameter of a quarter. The first branches from the aorta are the coronary arteries (not shown), which supply blood to the heart muscle itself. Next there are large branches leading to ❽ the head, chest, and arms, and the abdominal regions and legs. For simplicity, Figure 28.11A does not show the individual organs, but within each organ, arteries lead to arterioles that branch into capillaries. The capillaries

▲ **Figure 28.11A** Blood flow through the double circulation of the human cardiovascular system

▲ **Figure 28.11B** Blood flow through the human heart

rejoin as venules, which lead to veins. ❾ Oxygen-poor blood from the upper part of the body is channelled into a large vein called the **superior vena cava**, and from the lower part of the body it flows through the **inferior vena cava**. The two venae cavae empty into ❿ the right atrium. As the blood flows from the right atrium into the right ventricle, we complete our journey, only to start the pulmonary circuit again at the right ventricle.

Remember that the path of any single red blood cell is always heart to lung capillaries to heart to body tissue capillaries and back to heart. In one systemic circuit, a blood cell may travel to the brain; in the next (after a pulmonary circuit), it may travel to the legs. A red blood cell never travels from the brain to the legs without first returning to the heart and being pumped to the lungs to be recharged with oxygen.

Figure 28.11B shows the path of blood through the human heart. About the size of a clenched fist, your heart is enclosed in a sac just under the sternum (breastbone). The heart is formed mostly of cardiac muscle tissue. Its thin-walled atria collect blood returning to the heart. The thicker-walled ventricles pump blood to the lungs and to all other body tissues. Notice that the left ventricle walls are thicker than the right, a reflection of how much farther it pumps blood in the body. Flaplike valves between the atria and ventricles and at the openings to the pulmonary artery and the aorta regulate the direction of blood flow. We'll look at these valves and the functioning of the heart in the next module.

? Why does blood in the pulmonary veins have more O_2 than blood in the venae cavae, which are also veins?

● Pulmonary veins carry blood from the lungs, where it picks up O_2, to the heart. The venae cavae carry blood returning to the heart after delivering O_2 to body tissues.

28.12 The heart contracts and relaxes rhythmically

The four-chambered heart is the hub of the circulatory system. It separately but simultaneously pumps oxygen-poor blood to the lungs and oxygen-rich blood to the body. Its pumping action occurs as a rhythmic sequence of contraction and relaxation, called the **cardiac cycle**. When the heart contracts, it pumps blood; when it relaxes, blood fills its chambers.

The Cardiac Cycle How long does a cardiac cycle take? If you have a heart rate of 72 beats per minute, your cardiac cycle takes about 0.8 seconds. **Figure 28.12** shows that when the heart is relaxed, in the phase called ❶ **diastole**, blood flows into all four of its chambers. Blood enters the right atrium from the venae cavae and the left atrium from the pulmonary veins (see Figure 28.11A). The valves between the atria and the ventricles (atrioventricular [AV] valves) are open. The valves leading from the ventricles to the aorta or pulmonary artery (semilunar valves) are closed. Diastole lasts about 0.4 seconds, during which the ventricles nearly fill with blood.

The contraction phase of the cardiac cycle is called **systole**. ❷ Systole begins with a very brief (0.1 seconds) contraction of the atria that completely fills the ventricles with blood (atrial systole). ❸ Then the ventricles contract for about 0.3 seconds (ventricular systole). The force of their contraction closes the AV valves, opens the semilunar valves located at the exit from each ventricle, and pumps blood into the large arteries. Blood flows into the relaxed atria during the second part of systole, as the green arrows in step 3 indicate.

Because it pumps blood to your whole body, the left ventricle contracts with greater force than the right. Both ventricles,

however, pump the same volume of blood. The volume of blood that each ventricle pumps per minute is called **cardiac output**. This volume is equal to the amount of blood pumped each time a ventricle contracts (about 70 mL) multiplied by the **heart rate** (number of beats per minute). At an average resting heart rate of 72 beats per minute, cardiac output would be calculated as 70 mL/beat × 72 beats/min = about 5 L/min, roughly equivalent to the total volume of blood in your body. Thus, a single blood cell can travel the entire circuit in just 1 minute.

Heart rate and cardiac output vary, depending on age, fitness, and other factors. Both increase, for instance, during heavy exercise, in which cardiac output can increase fivefold, enabling the circulatory system to provide the additional oxygen needed by hardworking muscles. A well-trained athlete's heart may strengthen and enlarge with a resulting increase in the volume of blood a ventricle pumps. Thus, a resting heart rate of an athlete may be as low as 40 beats/min and still produce a normal cardiac output of about 5 L/min. During competition, a trained athlete's cardiac output may increase sevenfold.

Heart Valves Notice again in Figure 28.12 how the heart valves act as one-way doors at the exits of the atria and ventricles during a cardiac cycle. Made of flaps of connective tissue, these valves open when pushed from one side and close when pushed from the other. The powerful contraction of the ventricles forces blood against the AV valves, which closes them and keeps blood from flowing back into the atria. The semilunar valves are pushed open when the ventricles contract. When the ventricles relax, blood in the arteries starts to flow back toward the heart, causing the flaps of the semilunar valves to close and preventing blood from flowing back into the ventricles.

You can follow the closing of the two sets of heart valves either with a stethoscope or by pressing your ear tightly against the chest of a friend (or a friendly dog). The sound pattern is "lub-dup, lub-dup, lub-dup." The "lub" sound comes from the recoil of blood against the closed AV valves. The "dup" is produced by the recoil of blood against the closed semilunar valves.

Someone who is trained can detect the hissing sound of a **heart murmur**, which may indicate a defect in one or more of the heart valves. A murmur occurs when a stream of blood squirts backward through a valve. Some people are born with murmurs, while others have their valves damaged by infection (from rheumatic fever, for instance). Most valve defects do not reduce the efficiency of blood flow enough to warrant surgery. Those that do can be corrected by replacing the damaged valves with synthetic ones or with valves taken from an organ donor (human or other animal, usually a pig).

The next module explores the control of the cardiac cycle.

Diastole

❶ The heart is relaxed.

The semilunar valves are closed.

0.1 s

0.4 s

0.3 s

The AV valves are open.

Systole

❷ The atria contract.

❸ The ventricles contract.

The semilunar valves are open.

The AV valves are closed.

▲ **Figure 28.12** A cardiac cycle in a human with a heart rate of about 72 beats a minute

? During a cardiac cycle of 0.8 seconds, the atria are generally relaxed for _____ seconds.

0.7

28.13 The SA node sets the tempo of the heartbeat

In vertebrates, the cardiac cycle originates in the heart itself. Your cardiac muscle cells have their own beat. Each contracts and relaxes without any signal from the nervous system. But if each of these cells has its own intrinsic rhythm, how are their contractions coordinated so that your heart beats as an integrated unit? The answer lies with a group of cells that make up the pacemaker, or **SA (sinoatrial) node**, which sets the rate at which all the muscle cells of your heart contract.

The SA node, situated in the upper wall of the right atrium, generates electrical impulses much like those produced by nerve cells. These signals spread rapidly through the specialized junctions between cardiac muscle cells (see Module 25.6). **Figure 28.13A** shows the sequence of electrical events in the heart. ❶ Signals (shown in the figure in tan) from the SA node spread quickly through both atria, making them contract in unison. ❷ The impulses pass to a relay point called the **AV (atrioventricular) node**, located between the right atrium and right ventricle. Here the signals are delayed about 0.1 seconds, which ensures that the atria empty completely before the ventricles contract. ❸ Specialized muscle fibres (orange) then relay the signals to the apex of the heart and ❹ up through the walls of the ventricles, triggering the strong contractions that drive the blood out of the heart.

The electrical impulses in the heart generate electrical changes in the skin, which can be detected by electrodes and recorded as an electrocardiogram (ECG or EKG). The tan portion of the graphs under each heart in Figure 28.13A indicates the part of an ECG that matches the electrical event shown in the heart. In step 4, the portion of the ECG to the right of the tan "spike" is the electrical activity that readies the ventricles for the next round of contraction.

An ECG can provide data about heart health, such as the existence of arrhythmias. These are abnormal heart rhythms, including heart rates that are too slow or too fast and fibrillations (flutterings) of the atria or ventricles. In certain kinds of heart disease, the heart's self-pacing system fails to maintain a normal heart rhythm. In such cases, doctors can implant in the chest an artificial pacemaker **(Figure 28.13B)** invented by Dr. Wilfred Bigelow, a Canadian. A pacemaker

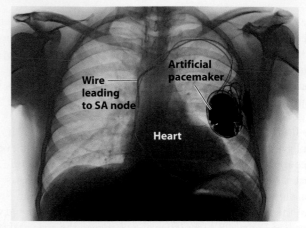

▲ **Figure 28.13B** An artificial pacemaker implanted in the chest

is a device that emits electrical signals to trigger normal heartbeats.

During a heart attack, the SA node is often unable to maintain a normal rhythm. Electrical shocks applied to the chest by a defibrillator may reset the SA node and restore proper cardiac function. The availability of automatic external defibrillators (AEDs) has saved thousands of lives. Unlike hospital defibrillators, AEDs are designed to be used by laypeople and are placed in public places (such as airports, movie theatres, and shopping malls) where they are quickly accessible.

A variety of cues help to regulate the SA node. Two sets of nerves with opposite effects can direct this pacemaker to speed up or slow down, depending on physiological needs and emotional cues. Heart rate is also influenced by hormones, such as adrenaline, the "fight-or-flight" hormone released at times of stress (see Module 29.1). An increased heart rate provides more blood to muscles that may be needed to "fight or flee."

? A slight decrease in blood pH causes the SA node to increase the heart rate. How would this control mechanism benefit a person during strenuous exercise? (*Hint*: See Module 27.10.)

● More CO₂ in the blood, as would occur with increased exercise, causes pH to drop. An accelerated heart rate enhances delivery of O₂-rich blood to body tissues and CO₂-rich blood to the lungs for removal of CO₂. (Breathing rate is also speeded up by this mechanism.)

▶ **Figure 28.13A** The sequence of electrical events in a heartbeat (top) and the corresponding electrocardiogram (bottom). (tan represents electrical signals.)

❶ Signals from the SA node spread through the atria.

❷ Signals are delayed at the AV node.

❸ Specialized muscle fibres pass signals to the heart apex.

❹ Signals spread throughout the ventricles.

SA node (pacemaker)

Right atrium

AV node

Specialized muscle fibres

Apex

ECG

28.14 What is a heart attack?

Like all of your cells, your heart muscle cells require nutrients and oxygen-rich blood to survive. Indeed, their needs are high, as your heart contracts more than 100 000 times a day. Where blood exits the heart via the aorta, several coronary arteries (shown in red in **Figure 28.14A**) immediately branch off to supply the heart muscle. If one or more of these blood vessels become blocked, heart muscle cells will quickly die (grey area in Figure 28.14A). A **heart attack**, also called a myocardial infarction, is the damage or death of cardiac muscle tissue, usually as a result of such blockage. (Rarely, a severe spasm of a coronary artery, possibly related to the use of a drug such as cocaine, may trigger a heart attack.) Approximately one-third of heart attack victims die almost immediately, as their damaged heart can no longer provide the brain and other vital tissues with sufficient oxygen. For those who survive, the ability of the damaged heart to pump blood may be seriously impaired.

Nearly one-third of all deaths in Canada are caused by **cardiovascular disease**—disorders of the heart and blood vessels. A **stroke** is the death of brain tissue on account of a lack of O_2 resulting from the rupture or blockage of arteries in the head. The suddenness of a heart attack or stroke belies the fact that the arteries of most victims became impaired gradually by a chronic cardiovascular disease known as **atherosclerosis** (from the Greek *athero*, paste, and *sclerosis*, hardness). During the course of this disease, fatty deposits called plaques develop in the inner walls of arteries, narrowing the passages through which blood can flow (**Figure 28.14B**). As a plaque grows, it incorporates fibrous connective tissue and cholesterol, and the walls of the artery become thick and stiff. A blood clot is more

▲ **Figure 28.14A** Blockage of a coronary artery, resulting in a heart attack

likely to become trapped in a vessel that has been narrowed in this way. Furthermore, plaques may rupture and cause blood clots to form, or fragments of the ruptured plaque may become lodged in other narrowed arteries.

Treatments are available for cardiovascular disease, and more continue to be developed. Heart attack victims are treated with clot-dissolving drugs, which stop many heart attacks and help to prevent damage. Diagnostic tests ranging from cholesterol and blood pressure measurements to sophisticated imaging techniques such as CT and MRI help to identify those at risk. Drugs are available that can reduce risk factors such as high cholesterol and blood pressure.

Recently, researchers have found that inflammation plays a central role in atherosclerosis and blood clot formation, and this has led to new ways of diagnosing and treating cardiovascular disease. A substance known as C-reactive protein (CRP) is produced by the liver during episodes of acute inflammation, and significant levels of CRP in the blood appear to be a predictor of cardiovascular disease. Aspirin, an anticoagulant that blocks the body's inflammatory response, is typically given during a cardiac episode and is often prescribed in low doses to help prevent the recurrence of heart attacks and stroke.

Angioplasty (insertion of a tiny catheter with a small balloon that is inflated to compress plaques and widen clogged arteries) and stents (small wire mesh tubes that prop arteries open) are common treatments for atherosclerosis. In bypass surgery, a more drastic remedy, blood vessels removed from a patient's legs are sewn into the heart to detour blood around clogged arteries. In extreme cases, a heart transplant may be necessary. With the severe shortage of donor hearts, various artificial pumping devices are being developed.

Fortunately, the death rate from cardiovascular disease has been greatly reduced over the past 50 years. Health education, early diagnosis, and reduction of risk factors, particularly smoking, have contributed to this decline.

To some extent, the tendency to develop cardiovascular disease appears to be inherited. There are three behaviours under your control, however, that significantly affect the risk. Smoking doubles the risk of heart attack and harms the circulatory system in other ways. Exercise can cut the risk of heart disease in half. Also, eating a heart-healthy

▲ **Figure 28.14B** Atherosclerosis: a normal artery (left) and an artery partially closed by plaque (right)

diet, low in cholesterol and trans and saturated fats, can reduce the risk of atherosclerosis (see Module 26.18).

Closely associated with the circulatory system, the major function of the urinary system is to remove waste products from the blood. We discuss this function in the next five modules.

The Circulatory System and Waste Removal

28.15 The circulatory system transports different nitrogenous wastes in animals depending on evolutionary history and habitat

In Chapter 27, you learned the circulatory system's role in transporting oxygen to the tissues and one waste product, carbon dioxide, away from the tissues. But carbon dioxide is not the only waste product of cellular metabolism. Toxic nitrogenous (nitrogen-containing) wastes result from the breakdown of proteins and nucleic acids. The circulatory system also transports nitrogenous wastes from the tissues to the excretory system that ultimately removes them from the body.

The form of an animal's nitrogenous wastes depends on its evolutionary history and its habitat. As **Figure 28.15** indicates, most aquatic animals dispose of their nitrogenous wastes as **ammonia**. Among the most toxic of all metabolic by-products, ammonia (NH_3) is formed when amino groups ($-NH_2$) are removed from amino acids and nucleic acids. Ammonia is too toxic to be stored in the body, but it is highly soluble and diffuses rapidly down concentration gradients. If an animal is surrounded by water, ammonia readily diffuses out of its cells and body. Small, soft-bodied invertebrates, such as jellies (cnidarians), excrete ammonia across their whole body surface. Fishes and larger invertebrates, such as crabs, excrete it mainly across their gills.

Ammonia excretion does not work well for land animals. Because it is so toxic, ammonia must be transported and excreted in large volumes of very dilute solutions. It is therefore more efficient for land animals to convert ammonia to less toxic compounds, either *urea* or *uric acid*, that can be safely transported by the circulatory system and stored in the body and released periodically by the excretory system. The disadvantage of excreting urea or uric acid is that the animal must use energy to produce these compounds from ammonia.

As shown in Figure 28.15, mammals, most adult amphibians, sharks, some bony fishes, and turtles excrete **urea**. Urea is produced in the vertebrate liver by a metabolic cycle that combines ammonia with carbon dioxide. The circulatory system transports urea to the kidneys. Urea is highly soluble in water. It is also some 100 000 times less toxic than ammonia, so it can be held in a concentrated solution in the body and disposed of with relatively little water loss. Some animals can switch between excreting ammonia and urea, depending on environmental conditions. Certain toads, for example, excrete ammonia (thus saving energy) when in water as tadpoles, but they excrete mainly urea (reducing water loss) when they become land-dwelling adults.

Urea can be stored in a concentrated solution, but it must be diluted with water for disposal. By contrast, land animals that excrete **uric acid** (insects, land snails, and many reptiles, including birds) avoid the water loss problem almost completely. As you can see in the figure, uric acid is a considerably more complex molecule than either urea or ammonia. Like urea, uric acid is relatively nontoxic. But unlike either ammonia or urea, uric acid is largely insoluble in water, and thus water is not used to dilute it. In most cases, uric acid is excreted as a semisolid paste. (The white material in bird droppings is mostly uric acid—which explains why this substance can cause so much damage to the paint job on a car.) An animal must

▲ **Figure 28.15** Nitrogen-containing metabolic waste products

expend more energy to excrete uric acid than to excrete urea, but the higher energy cost is balanced by the great savings in body water.

An animal's type of reproduction also influences whether it excretes urea or uric acid. Urea can diffuse out of a shell-less amphibian egg or be carried away from a mammalian embryo in the mother's blood. However, the shelled eggs produced by birds and other reptiles are not permeable to liquids. The evolution of uric acid as a waste product therefore conveyed a selective advantage because it precipitates out of solution and can remain as a harmless solid that is left behind when the animal hatches.

Regardless of the form of nitrogenous waste excreted or the organ of excretion, the circulatory system is one of two essential systems that rid the body of these toxic by-products. The other system, the excretory system, is the topic of the next four modules.

? Aquatic turtles excrete both urea and ammonia; land turtles excrete mainly uric acid. What could account for this difference?

● Although uric acid as a waste product evolved in terrestrial reptiles with their shelled eggs, natural selection favoured the energy savings of ammonia and urea for aquatic turtles.

28.16 Overview: The key processes of the urinary system are filtration, reabsorption, secretion, and excretion

Survival in any environment requires a precise balance between the competing demands of waste disposal and an animal's need for water. The excretory system plays a central role in homeostasis, forming and excreting urine while regulating the amount of water and solutes in body fluids. Animal excretory systems produce and dispose of urine by using four major processes, shown in **Figure 28.16A**. First, during **filtration**, the pressure of the blood forces water and other small molecules through a capillary wall into the start of an excretory organ, forming **filtrate**. This connection illustrates the intimate relationship between the circulatory and excretory systems.

Two processes then refine the filtrate. In **reabsorption**, water and valuable solutes—including glucose, salt, other ions, and amino acids—are reclaimed from the filtrate and returned to the blood. In **secretion**, substances in the blood are transported into the filtrate. When there is an excess of H^+ in the blood, for example, these ions are secreted into the filtrate, thus keeping the blood from becoming acidic. Secretion also eliminates certain drugs and other toxic substances from the blood. In both reabsorption and secretion, water and solutes move between the tubule and capillaries by passing through the interstitial fluid (see Module 28.7).

Fourth, in **excretion**, urine—the waste-containing product of filtration, reabsorption, and secretion—is released from the body.

These four steps of urine production are common to all animal excretory systems. The complexity of these systems, however, varies widely between animal groups. Planarians (flatworms) have rudimentary kidney structures called protonephridia (singular, *protonephridium*), which are a system of blind-ended tubules (**Figure 28.16B**). At the end of each tubule sits a ciliated

▶ **Figure 28.16B**
Protonephridia in a flatworm

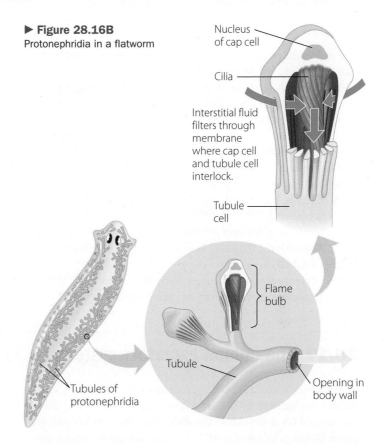

cell, called a flame bulb, which moves interstitial fluid into a network of tubules (filtration, blue arrows). The urine is refined (reabsorption and secretion) as it moves throughout the network.

▲ **Figure 28.16A** Major processes of the excretory system

Components of a metanephridium:

Collecting tubule

Internal opening

Bladder

External opening

▲ **Figure 28.16C** Metanephridia in an earthworm

Coelom

Capillary network

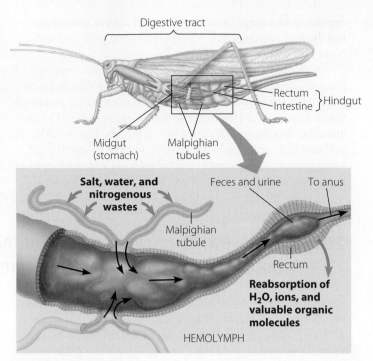

Digestive tract

Midgut (stomach)

Malpighian tubules

Rectum
Intestine }Hindgut

Salt, water, and nitrogenous wastes

Feces and urine

To anus

Malpighian tubule

Rectum

Reabsorption of H_2O, ions, and valuable organic molecules

HEMOLYMPH

▲ **Figure 28.16D** Malpighian tubules in an insect

The processed filtrate is released through openings in the body wall (excretion, yellow arrow).

Within each segment of an earthworm are two slightly more complex kidneys called metanephridia (singular, *metanephridium*). Metanephridia consist of a collecting tubule that is closely associated with a capillary network of the circulatory system (**Figure 28.16C**). Coelomic fluid enters the collecting tubule through a ciliated internal opening. The filtrate is processed as it passes through the tubule and empties into a small bladder where it can be stored before it is released through an external opening.

Insects have a different excretory system that is closely associated with the digestive system. Malpighian tubules (**Figure 28.16D**) are outpocketings of the digestive tract, bathed in hemolymph, the single body fluid of animals with open circulatory systems. Wastes, including uric acid, are

transported from the hemolymph into the Malpighian tubule, which empty into the lumen of the digestive tract where they are eliminated along with the feces. This excretion mechanism minimizes water loss and has proven to be a key adaptation leading to the success of insects on land.

? Urine differs in composition from the fluid that enters a nephron tubule by filtration because of the processes of _____ and _____.

● reabsorption; secretion

28.17 The human excretory system

In humans, the main processing centres of the urinary system are the two kidneys. Each is a compact organ a bit smaller than a fist, located on either side of the abdomen. The kidneys contain about 80 km of tubules (small tubes) that are closely associated with an intricate network of tiny blood capillaries. The human body contains only about 5 L of blood, but because this blood circulates repeatedly, about 1100–2000 L pass through the capillaries in our kidneys every day. From this enormous circulation of blood, every day our kidneys extract about 180 L of filtrate, consisting of water, urea, and a number of valuable solutes, including glucose, amino acids, ions, and vitamins. If we excreted all the filtrate as urine, we would lose vital nutrients and dehydrate rapidly. Instead, our kidneys refine the filtrate, concentrating the urea and recycling most of the water and useful solutes to the blood. In a typical day, we excrete only about 1.5 L of urine.

In the human kidneys, numerous tubules are organized in close association with a dense network of capillaries (**Figure 28.17**). Starting with the whole system in **Part A**, blood

to be filtered enters each kidney via a renal artery, shown in red; blood that has been filtered leaves the kidney in the renal vein, shown in blue. Urine leaves each kidney through a duct called a **ureter**. Both ureters drain into the **urinary bladder**. During urination, urine is expelled from the bladder through a tube called the **urethra**, which empties to the outside near the vagina in females and through the penis in males. Sphincter muscles near the junction of the urethra and the bladder control urination.

As shown in **Part B**, the kidney has two main regions, an outer **renal cortex** and an inner **renal medulla**. Each kidney contains about a million tiny functional units called **nephrons**, one of which is shown in **Part C**. A nephron consists of a single folded tubule and associated blood vessels. Performing the kidney's functions in miniature, the nephron extracts a tiny amount of filtrate from the blood and then refines the filtrate into a much smaller quantity of urine. Each nephron starts and ends in the kidney's cortex; some extend

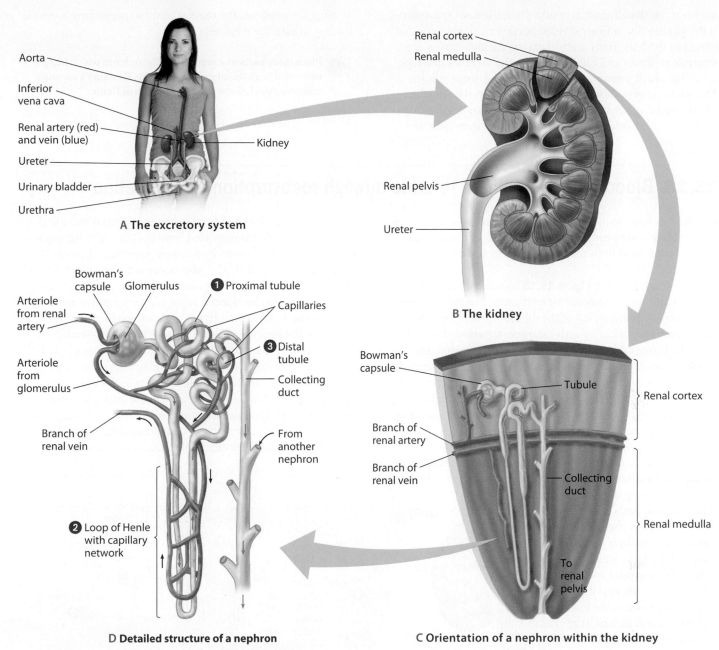

A The excretory system

- Aorta
- Inferior vena cava
- Renal artery (red) and vein (blue)
- Ureter
- Urinary bladder
- Urethra
- Kidney

B The kidney

- Renal cortex
- Renal medulla
- Renal pelvis
- Ureter

D Detailed structure of a nephron

- Bowman's capsule
- Glomerulus
- ❶ Proximal tubule
- Arteriole from renal artery
- Capillaries
- ❸ Distal tubule
- Arteriole from glomerulus
- Collecting duct
- Branch of renal vein
- From another nephron
- ❷ Loop of Henle with capillary network

C Orientation of a nephron within the kidney

- Bowman's capsule
- Tubule
- Renal cortex
- Branch of renal artery
- Branch of renal vein
- Collecting duct
- Renal medulla
- To renal pelvis

▲ **Figure 28.17** Anatomy of the human excretory system

into the medulla, as in Part C. The receiving end of the nephron is a cup-shaped swelling, called **Bowman's capsule**. At the other end of the nephron is the **collecting duct**, which carries urine to the renal pelvis.

Part D shows a nephron in more detail, along with its blood vessels. Bowman's capsule envelops a ball of capillaries called the **glomerulus** (plural, *glomeruli*). The glomerulus and Bowman's capsule make up the blood-filtering unit of the nephron. Here, blood pressure forces water and solutes from the blood in the glomerular capillaries across the wall of Bowman's capsule and into the nephron tubule. This process creates the filtrate, leaving blood cells and large molecules such as plasma proteins behind in the capillaries. Hypertension, or high blood pressure (see Module 28.8) can lead to kidney disease by damaging the delicate capillaries of the glomeruli. If

this occurs, the nephrons do not produce enough filtrate and the overall function of the kidneys decreases.

The rest of the nephron refines filtrate. The tubule has three sections: ❶ the **proximal tubule** (in the cortex); ❷ the **loop of Henle**, a hairpin loop with a capillary network that carries filtrate toward—and in some cases into—the medulla and then back toward the cortex; and ❸ the **distal tubule** (called distal because it is the most distant from Bowman's capsule). The distal tubule drains into a collecting duct, which receives filtrate from many nephrons. From the kidney's many collecting ducts, the processed filtrate, or urine, passes into a chamber called the renal pelvis and then into the ureter, from which it is then expelled.

The intricate association between blood vessels and tubules is the key to nephron function. As shown in Part D, the nephron has two distinct networks of capillaries. One network is the glomerulus, a finely divided portion of an arteriole that branches from the renal artery. Leaving the glomerulus, the arteriole re-forms and carries blood to the second capillary network, which surrounds the proximal and distal tubules. This second network works with the tubule in refining the filtrate. Some of the vessels in this network parallel the loop of Henle, with blood flowing downward and then back up.

Leaving the nephron, the capillaries converge to form a venule leading toward the renal vein.

 Place these parts of a nephron in the order in which filtrate moves through them: proximal tubule, Bowman's capsule, collecting duct, distal tubule, and loop of Henle.

● Bowman's capsule, proximal tubule, loop of Henle, distal tubule, collecting duct

28.18 Blood filtrate is refined to urine through reabsorption and secretion

Let's take a closer look at how a single nephron and collecting duct in the kidney produce urine from a blood filtrate that initially consists of both wanted substances and unwanted substances.

The broad arrows in **Figure 28.18** indicate where reabsorption and secretion occur along the nephron tubule. The purple arrows pointing out of the tubule represent reabsorption, which may occur by active transport, passive diffusion, or osmosis (see Chapter 5). The blue arrows pointing into the tubule represent secretion. For simplicity, this figure omits the capillary network that surrounds the tubule. The direction of flow within the collecting tubule is countercurrent to that in the capillary, increasing the efficiency of transfer in a similar way to how it increases oxygen absorption across a fish's gill (see Module 27.4).

The pink area of the figure represents the interstitial fluid, through which solutes and water move between the tubule and capillaries. The intensity of the colour corresponds to the concentration of solutes in the interstitial fluid: The concentration is lowest in the cortex of the kidney and becomes progressively greater toward the inner medulla. By maintaining this solute gradient, the kidney can extract and save most of the water from the filtrate. All along the tubule, wherever you see an indication that water is passing out of the filtrate into the interstitial fluid, the water is moving by osmosis. Water flows this way because the solute concentration of the interstitial fluid exceeds that of the filtrate.

To get an overview of the process, let's first discuss the activities of the proximal and distal tubules. ❶ The proximal tubule actively transports nutrients such as glucose and amino acids from the filtrate into the interstitial fluid to be reabsorbed into the capillaries.

NaCl (salt) is reabsorbed from both the proximal and distal tubules. As NaCl is transported from the filtrate to the interstitial fluid, water follows by osmosis. Secretion of excess H^+ and reabsorption of HCO_3^- also occur at the proximal and distal tubules, helping to regulate the blood's pH. Potassium concentration in the blood is regulated by secretion of excess K^+ into the distal tubule. Drugs and poisons that were processed in the liver are secreted into the proximal tubule.

The loop of Henle and the collecting duct have one major function: water reabsorption. ❷ The long loop of Henle carries the filtrate deep into the medulla and then back to the cortex. The presence of NaCl and some urea in the interstitial fluid maintains the high concentration gradient in the medulla, which in turn increases water reabsorption by osmosis. Water leaves the tubule because the interstitial fluid in the medulla has a higher

Filtrate composition
H_2O
Salts (NaCl and others)
HCO_3^-
H^+
Urea
Glucose
Amino acids
Some drugs

Reabsorption
Secretion
Filtrate movement

▶ **Figure 28.18** Reabsorption and secretion in a nephron

solute concentration than the filtrate. As soon as the water from the filtrate passes into the interstitial fluid, it moves into nearby blood capillaries and is carried away to be recycled in the body. This prompt removal is essential because the water would otherwise dilute the interstitial fluid surrounding the loop and destroy the concentration gradient necessary for water reabsorption.

Just after the filtrate rounds the hairpin turn in the loop of Henle, water reabsorption stops because the tubule there is impermeable to water. As the filtrate moves back toward the cortex, NaCl leaves the filtrate, first passively and then actively as the cells of the tubule pump NaCl into the interstitial fluid. It is primarily this movement of salt that creates the solute gradient in the interstitial fluid of the medulla.

3 Final refining of the filtrate occurs in the collecting duct. Because it actively reabsorbs NaCl, the collecting duct

is important in determining how much salt is excreted in the urine. In the medulla, the collecting duct becomes permeable to urea and some leaks out, adding to the high concentration gradient in the interstitial fluid. As the filtrate moves through the collecting duct, more water is reabsorbed before the final product, urine, passes into the renal pelvis. In sum, the nephron returns much of the water that filters into it from the blood. This water conservation is one of the major functions of the kidneys.

 What would happen if reabsorption in the proximal and distal tubules were to cease?

● Needed solutes and water would be lost in the urine, depriving the body of substances it requires.

28.19 Kidney dialysis can be life-saving

A person can survive with one functioning kidney; but, if both kidneys fail, the buildup of toxic wastes and the lack of regulation of blood ion concentrations, pH, and pressure will lead to certain and rapid death. More than 60% of all cases of kidney disease are caused by hypertension and diabetes, but the prolonged use of pain relievers (even common, over-the-counter ones), alcohol, and other drugs are also possible causes.

Knowing how the nephron works helps us understand how some of its functions can be performed artificially when the kidneys are damaged. In **dialysis**, blood is filtered by a machine, which mimics the action of a nephron (**Figure 28.19**). Like the nephrons of the kidney, the machine sorts small molecules of the blood, keeping some and discarding others. The patient's blood is pumped from an artery through a

series of selectively permeable tubes. The tubes are immersed in a dialyzing solution that resembles the chemical makeup of the interstitial fluid that bathes the nephrons. As the blood circulates through the tubing, urea and excess ions diffuse out. Needed substances diffuse from the dialyzing solution into the blood. The machine continually discards the used dialyzing solution as wastes build up.

Dialysis treatment is life sustaining for people with kidney failure, but it is costly, takes a lot of time (about 4–6 hours three times a week), and must be continued for life—or until the patient is able to undergo kidney transplantation. In some cases, a kidney from a living compatible donor (usually a close relative) or a deceased organ donor can be transplanted into a person with kidney failure. Unfortunately, the number of people who need kidneys is much greater than the number of kidneys available, and the average wait for a kidney donation in Canada ranges from three years in Alberta to eight years in Ontario.

 How does the composition of dialyzing solution compare with that of the patient's blood plasma?

● Dialyzing solution has a solute concentration similar to that of interstitial fluid. The solution contains no urea, which allows urea from the patient's blood to diffuse into it.

Line from artery to apparatus
Pump
Tubing made of a selectively permeable membrane
Line from apparatus to vein
Dialyzing solution
Fresh dialyzing solution
Used dialyzing solution (with urea and excess ions)

▲ **Figure 28.19** Kidney dialysis

MasteringBiology® **For Practice Quizzes, BioFlix, MP3 Tutors, and Activities, go to masteringbiology.com.**

Reviewing the Concepts

Circulatory Systems (28.1–28.2)

28.1 Circulatory systems facilitate exchange with all body tissues. Gastrovascular cavities function in both digestion and transport. In open circulatory systems, a heart pumps fluid through open-ended vessels to bathe tissue cells directly. In closed circulatory systems, a heart pumps blood, which travels through arteries to capillaries to veins and back to the heart.

28.2 Vertebrate cardiovascular systems reflect evolution. A fish's two-chambered heart pumps blood in a single circuit. Land vertebrates have double circulation with a pulmonary and a systemic circuit. Amphibians and many reptiles have three-chambered hearts; birds and mammals have four-chambered hearts.

Blood and Blood Vessels (28.3–28.10)

28.3 Blood consists of red and white blood cells suspended in plasma. Plasma contains various inorganic ions, proteins, nutrients, wastes, gases, and hormones. Red blood cells (erythrocytes) transport O_2 bound to hemoglobin. White blood cells (leukocytes) fight infections.

28.4 Donating blood and bone marrow saves lives. Donating through Canadian Blood Services is quick, painless, and life-saving. Donations can include whole blood or specific blood components. An international bone marrow registry maximizes the chance of a patient finding a suitable donor.

28.5 Blood clots plug leaks when blood vessels are injured. Platelets adhere to connective tissue of damaged vessels and help to convert fibrinogen to fibrin, forming a clot that plugs the leak.

28.6 Is the blood in our veins blue? Oxygenated blood is bright red and deoxygenated blood is actually dark red, not blue.

28.7 The structure of blood vessels fits their functions. Arteries have thick, muscular walls to withstand high blood pressure. Capillaries are thin walled to facilitate exchange of materials. Veins have valves to prevent the backflow of blood as it returns to the heart.

28.8 Blood pressure and velocity reflect the structure and arrangement of blood vessels. Blood pressure depends on cardiac output and the resistance of vessels. Pressure is highest in the arteries. Blood velocity is slowest in the capillaries. Muscle contractions and one-way valves keep blood moving through veins to the heart.

28.9 Smooth muscle controls the distribution of blood. Constriction of arterioles and precapillary sphincters controls blood flow through capillary beds.

28.10 Capillaries allow the transfer of substances through their walls. Blood pressure forces fluid and small solutes out of the capillary at the arterial end. Excess fluid is returned to the circulatory system through lymph vessels.

The Human Cardiovascular System and Heart (28.11–28.14)

28.11 The human cardiovascular system illustrates the double circulation of mammals. The mammalian heart has two thin-walled atria and two thick-walled ventricles. The right side of the heart receives and pumps oxygen-poor blood; the left side receives oxygen-rich blood from the lungs and pumps it to all other organs.

28.12 The heart contracts and relaxes rhythmically. During diastole of the cardiac cycle, blood flows from the veins into the heart chambers; during systole, contractions of the atria push blood into the ventricles, and then stronger contractions of the ventricles propel blood into the large arteries. Cardiac output is the amount of blood per minute pumped by a ventricle. Heart valves prevent the backflow of blood.

28.13 The SA node sets the tempo of the heartbeat. The SA node, or pacemaker, generates electrical signals that trigger contraction of the atria. The AV node relays these signals to the ventricles. An electrocardiogram records the electrical changes.

28.14 What is a heart attack? A heart attack is damage or death of cardiac muscle, usually resulting from a blocked coronary artery.

The Circulatory System and Waste Removal (28.15–28.19)

28.15 The circulatory system transports different nitrogenous wastes in animals depending on evolutionary history and habitat. The circulatory system transports nitrogenous wastes (ammonia, urea, or uric acid) to the organs that excrete them. Aquatic invertebrates and fish readily excrete ammonia across gills or other surfaces. Terrestrial animals must convert ammonia into less toxic forms such as urea (mammals) or uric acid (birds) to store them before they can be released.

28.16 Overview: The key processes of the urinary system are filtration, reabsorption, secretion, and excretion. In filtration, blood pressure forces water and many small solutes into the nephron. In reabsorption, water and valuable solutes are reclaimed from the filtrate. In secretion, excess H^+ and toxins are added to the filtrate. In excretion, urine is expelled.

28.17 The human excretory system. The urinary system expels wastes and regulates water and ion balance. Nephrons extract a filtrate from the blood and refine it to urine. Urine leaves the kidneys via the ureters, is stored in the urinary bladder, and is expelled through the urethra.

28.18 Blood filtrate is refined to urine through reabsorption and secretion. Nutrients, salt, and water are reabsorbed from the proximal and distal tubules within the nephron. Secretion of H^+ and reabsorption of HCO_3^- help to regulate pH. High NaCl concentration in the medulla promotes reabsorption of water.

28.19 Kidney dialysis can be life-saving. A dialysis machine removes wastes from blood and maintains solute concentration.

Connecting the Concepts

1. Use the following diagram to review the flow of blood through a human cardiovascular system. Label the indicated parts, highlight the vessels that carry oxygen-rich blood, and then trace the flow of blood by numbering the circles from 1 to 10, starting with 1 in the right ventricle. (When two locations are equivalent

in the pathway, such as right and left lung capillaries or capillaries of top and lower portion of the body, assign them both the same number.)

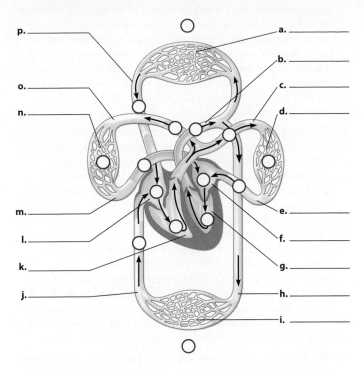

p. _____
o. _____
n. _____
m. _____
l. _____
k. _____
j. _____

a. _____
b. _____
c. _____
d. _____
e. _____
f. _____
g. _____
h. _____
i. _____

2. In this schematic of urine production in a nephron, label the four processes involved and list some of the substances that are moved in each process.

(a) → (b) → (c) →

Bowman's capsule

From renal artery →

To renal vein ←

Glomerulus

Tubule

Loop of Henle

Capillaries

Collecting duct

(d) →

Testing Your Knowledge

Multiple Choice

3. Blood pressure is highest in _____, and blood moves most slowly in _____.
   a. veins; capillaries
   b. arteries; capillaries
   c. veins; arteries
   d. capillaries; arteries
   e. arteries; veins

4. When the doctor listened to Janet's heart, he heard "lub-hiss, lub-hiss" instead of the normal "lub-dup" sounds. The hiss is most likely because of _____. (Explain your answer.)
   a. a clogged coronary artery
   b. a defective atrioventricular (AV) valve
   c. a damaged pacemaker (SA node)
   d. a defective semilunar valve
   e. high blood pressure

5. Which of the following is the main difference between your cardiovascular system and that of a fish?
   a. In a fish, blood is oxygenated by passing through a capillary bed.
   b. Your heart has two chambers; a fish heart has four.
   c. Your circulation has two circuits; fish circulation has one.
   d. Your heart chambers are called atria and ventricles.
   e. Yours is a closed system; the fish's is an open system.

6. Paul's blood pressure is 150/90. The 150 indicates _____, and the 90 indicates _____.
   a. pressure in the left ventricle; pressure in the right ventricle
   b. arterial pressure; heart rate
   c. pressure during ventricular contraction; pressure during heart relaxation
   d. systemic circuit pressure; pulmonary circuit pressure
   e. pressure in the arteries; pressure in the veins

7. Which of the following *initiates* the process of blood clotting?
   a. damage to the lining of a blood vessel
   b. exposure of blood to the air
   c. conversion of fibrinogen to fibrin
   d. attraction of leukocytes to a site of infection
   e. conversion of fibrin to fibrinogen

8. Which of the following is *not* a true statement about open and closed circulatory systems?
   a. Both systems have some sort of a heart that pumps a circulatory fluid through the body.
   b. A frog has an open circulatory system; other vertebrates have closed circulatory systems.
   c. The blood and interstitial fluid are separate in a closed system but are indistinguishable in an open system.
   d. The open circulatory system of an insect does not transport O_2 to body cells; closed circulatory systems do transport O_2.
   e. Some of the circulation of blood in both systems results from body movements.

9. If blood was supplied to all of the body's capillaries at one time,
   a. blood pressure would fall dramatically.
   b. resistance to blood flow would increase.
   c. blood would move too rapidly through the capillaries.
   d. the amount of blood returning to the heart would increase.
   e. the increased gas exchange in the lungs and in the supply of O_2 to muscles would allow for strenuous exercise.

10. Birds and insects excrete uric acid, whereas mammals and most amphibians excrete mainly urea. What is the chief advantage of uric acid over urea as a waste product?
    a. Uric acid is more soluble in water.
    b. Uric acid is a much simpler molecule.
    c. It takes less energy to make uric acid.
    d. Less water is required to excrete uric acid.
    e. More solutes are removed excreting uric acid.

11. In each nephron of the kidney, the glomerulus and Bowman's capsule
    a. filter the blood and capture the filtrate.
    b. reabsorb water into the blood.
    c. break down harmful toxins and poisons.
    d. reabsorb ions and nutrients.
    e. refine and concentrate the urine for excretion.

12. As filtrate passes through the loop of Henle, salt is removed and concentrated in the interstitial fluid of the medulla. This high concentration enables nephrons to
    a. excrete the maximum amount of salt.
    b. neutralize toxins that might be found in the kidney.
    c. control the pH of the interstitial fluid.
    d. excrete a large amount of water.
    e. reabsorb water very efficiently.

Describing, Comparing, and Explaining

13. Trace the path of blood starting in a pulmonary vein, through the heart, and around the body, returning to the pulmonary vein. Name, in order, the heart chambers and types of vessels through which the blood passes.

14. Here is a blood sample that has been spun in a centrifuge. List, as completely as you can, the components you would find in the straw-coloured fluid at the top of this tube and in the dense red portion at the bottom.

Applying the Concepts

15. Some babies are born with a small hole in the wall between the left and right ventricles. How might this affect the oxygen content of the blood pumped out of the heart into the systemic circuit?

16. Juan has a disease in which damaged kidneys allow some of his normal plasma proteins to be removed from the blood. How might this condition affect the osmotic pressure (the driving force of osmosis) of blood in capillaries, compared with that of the surrounding interstitial fluid? One of the symptoms of this kidney malfunction is an accumulation of excess interstitial fluid, which causes Juan's arms and legs to swell. Can you explain why this occurs?

17. Some years ago, a 19-year-old woman received a bone marrow transplant from her 1-year-old sister. The woman was suffering from a deadly form of leukemia and was almost certain to die without a transplant. The parents had decided to have another child in a final attempt to provide their daughter with a matching donor. Although the ethics of the parents' decision were criticized, doctors report that this situation is not uncommon. In your opinion, is it acceptable to have a child to provide an organ or tissue donation? Why or why not?

18. Physiologists speculate about cardiovascular adaptations in dinosaurs—some of which had necks almost 10 m long. Such animals would have required a systolic pressure of nearly 760 mmHg to pump blood to the brain when the head was fully raised. Some analyses suggest that dinosaurs' hearts were not powerful enough to generate such pressures, leading to the speculation that long-necked dinosaurs fed close to the ground rather than raising their heads to feed on high foliage. Scientists also debate whether dinosaurs had a reptile-like or birdlike heart. Most modern reptiles have a three-chambered heart with just one ventricle. Birds, which evolved from a lineage of dinosaurs, have a four-chambered heart. Some scientists believe that the circulatory needs of these long-necked dinosaurs provide evidence that dinosaurs must have had a four-chambered heart. Why might they conclude this?

19. The kidneys remove many drugs from the blood, and these substances show up in the urine. Some employers require a urine drug test at the time of hiring and/or at intervals during the term of employment. Why do some employers feel that drug testing is necessary? Do you think that passing a drug test is a valid criterion for employment? If so, for what types of jobs? Would you take a drug test to get or keep a job? Why or why not?

20. Kidneys were the first organs to be transplanted successfully. A donor can live a normal life with a single kidney, making it possible for individuals to donate a kidney to an ailing relative or even an unrelated individual. In some countries, poor people sell kidneys to transplant recipients through organ brokers. What are some of the ethical issues associated with organ commerce?

Answers to all questions can be found in Appendix E.

CHAPTER

29

Hormones and Endocrine Systems

BIG IDEAS

The Nature of Chemical Regulation

(29.1–29.2)

Hormones affect cells by using two distinct mechanisms.

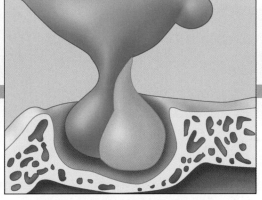

The Vertebrate Endocrine System

(29.3–29.4)

The hypothalamus exerts master control over many other endocrine glands.

Hormones and Homeostasis

(29.5–29.13)

Hormones, often in antagonistic pairs, regulate whole-body processes.

To Win the Race and Fall from Grace

In many sports, professional and amateur alike, strength and endurance are deciding factors for victory. More muscle mass can provide a competitive edge. Unfortunately, for some athletes working out does not meet their perceived need. In many sports, including track and field, weightlifting, football, and baseball, some athletes have resorted to illegal and unethical performance-enhancing drugs. The International Olympic Committee (IOC) bans more than 200 agents from competitive sport. On the list are 85 hormone products, including steroids and peptide hormones such as growth hormone (GH). In 2009, Dr. Anthony Galea (above) pleaded guilty to a felony charge of bringing GH from Canada into the United States to treat athletes. Why are so many hormones on this list? The answer lies in the roles hormones play in regulating bodily functions such as muscle growth and metabolism.

As you will read in this chapter, GH is a natural regulator of human growth and metabolism. Released by the anterior pituitary gland throughout life, GH has a primary role in the promotion of growth during childhood. GH causes a moderate increase in blood sugar to fuel growing tissues. Although GH can affect all body tissues, it has a larger influence on skeletal muscle and bone tissue.

Illegal use of GH by athletes increases their muscle mass. Prolonged abuse can cause disfiguring growth of the hands, feet, and facial bones, which is similar to a condition known as acromegaly. Abuse of GH may also cause an enlarged heart, and in rare cases, the increased blood sugar can reduce the body's responsiveness to insulin, increasing the risk of developing type 2 diabetes.

The actual benefit of GH abuse is under debate. Some studies show marked improvement in performance, whereas others have shown little to no effect. The increase in muscle mass is due primarily to an increase in water retention and does not correlate with an increase in strength. Questionable benefits and severe consequences make GH a poor performance-enhancing drug with big risks and few gains.

A pharmaceutical arms race exists between the IOC and drug developers. As one side generates new tests to detect performance-enhancing drugs, the other is inventing new, undetectable substances. At one point, this arms race was focused on human GH. The initial source of GH was the pituitary glands of human cadavers. Now it can be mass-produced by genetically engineered bacteria and is more readily available.

Blood normally contains GH, making detection of the hormone's abuse problematic. A test was only recently developed based on the discovery that multiple isoforms of human GH are naturally produced. Each isoform is slightly different and its relative amount in the blood remains constant. The GH manufactured using bacteria, however, is of a single isoform. The new test looks for a disproportionate amount of a single isoform, which indicates GH abuse.

In this chapter, we explore how chemical signals maintain an animal's dynamic steady state. We begin with an overview of how hormones work in all vertebrates and then turn to the major components of the human endocrine system. Along the way, we consider many examples of the effects of hormonal imbalance.

The Nature of Chemical Regulation

29.1 Chemical signals coordinate body functions

Animals rely on many kinds of chemical signals to regulate their body activities. A **hormone** is a substance that acts as one such chemical signal. Hormones are carried by the circulatory system (usually in the blood) to other parts of the body, where they may communicate regulatory messages. Hormones are made and secreted mainly by organs called **endocrine glands**. Collectively, all of an animal's hormone-secreting cells constitute its **endocrine system**, one of two body systems for communication and chemical regulation.

Hormones reach all cells of the body, and the endocrine system is especially important in controlling whole-body activities. For example, hormones coordinate the body's responses to stimuli such as dehydration, low blood glucose levels, or stress, as with the rapid increase in heartbeat and awareness that you feel when faced with a sudden threat. Hormones also regulate long-term developmental processes, such as the appearance of characteristics that distinguish an adult animal from a juvenile animal and bring about the physical and behavioural changes that underlie sexual maturity.

Figure 29.1A sketches the activity of a hormone-secreting cell. Membrane-enclosed secretory vesicles in the endocrine cell are full of molecules of the hormone (•:). The endocrine cell secretes the molecules directly into blood vessels. From there, hormones may travel via the circulatory system to all parts of the body, but only certain types of cells, called **target cells**, have receptors for that specific hormone. (A hormone is ignored by nontarget cells that lack the specific receptor.) A single hormone molecule may dramatically alter a target cell's metabolism by turning on or off the production of a number of enzymes. A tiny amount of a hormone can govern the activities of enormous numbers of target cells in a variety of organs. (In the next module, we look at *how* hormones trigger responses in their target cells.)

Chemical signals play a major role in coordinating the internal functioning of animals. Hormones are the body's long-distance chemical regulators and convey information via the bloodstream to target cells that may or may not be close to the cell that initiates the signal. Other chemical signals—local regulators—are secreted into the interstitial fluid and affect only nearby target cells. Still other chemical signals, called pheromones, carry messages between different individuals of a species, as in mate attraction.

The other system of internal communication and regulation is the nervous system, the subject of Chapter 31. Unlike the endocrine system, which sends chemical signals through the bloodstream, the nervous system transmits electrical signals via nerve cells. These rapid messages control split-second responses. The flick of a frog's tongue as it catches a fly and the jerk of your hand away from a flame result from high-speed nerve signals. The endocrine system coordinates slower but longer-lasting responses. In some cases, the endocrine system takes hours or even days to act, partly because of the time it takes for hormones to be made and transported to all of their target organs and partly because the cellular response may take time.

Although it is convenient to distinguish between the endocrine and nervous systems, in reality the lines between these two regulatory systems are blurred. In particular, certain specialized nerve cells called **neurosecretory cells** perform functions of both systems. Like all nerve cells, neurosecretory cells conduct nerve signals, but they also make and secrete hormones into the blood. A neurosecretory cell thus functions similarly to the endocrine cell shown in Figure 29.1A.

A few chemicals serve both as hormones in the endocrine system and as chemical signals in the nervous system. Adrenaline (epinephrine), for example, functions in vertebrates as the "fight-or-flight" hormone (so called because it prepares the body for sudden action) and as a *neurotransmitter*. A neurotransmitter is a chemical that carries information from one nerve cell (*neuron*) to another or from a neuron to another kind of cell that will react. When a nerve signal reaches the end of a neuron, it triggers the secretion of neurotransmitter molecules (•: in **Figure 29.1B**). Unlike most hormones, however, neurotransmitters usually do not travel in the bloodstream but instead move between adjacent neurons (see Module 31.10). In the rest of this chapter, we explore the endocrine system and its hormones.

? How do hormones usually travel between an endocrine gland and their target cells?

▲ **Figure 29.1A** Hormones from an endocrine cell travel through the bloodstream to affect a target cell

 Via the bloodstream

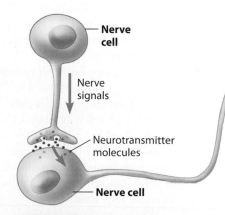

▲ **Figure 29.1B** Neurotransmitter from one neuron to another

29.2 Hormones affect target cells by using two main signalling mechanisms

Two major classes of molecules function as hormones in vertebrates. The first class, the **amino-acid-derived hormones**, includes proteins, peptides (polypeptides of only 3–30 amino acids), and amines (modified versions of single amino acids). They are almost all water-soluble. Hormones of the second main class, the **steroid hormones**, are small lipid-soluble molecules made from cholesterol (see Module 3.15).

Regardless of their chemical structure, signalling by any of these molecules involves three key events: reception, signal transduction, and response. *Reception* of the signal occurs when a hormone binds to a specific receptor protein on or in the target cell. Each signal molecule has a specific shape that can be recognized by its target cell receptors. The binding of a signal molecule to a receptor protein triggers events within the target cell—*signal transduction*—that convert the signal from one form to another. The result is a *response*, a change in the cell's behaviour. Cells that lack receptors for a particular chemical signal do not respond to that signal.

Both amino-acid-derived (water-soluble) and steroid (lipid-soluble) hormones carry out these three key steps; however, they do so by different mechanisms. We now take a closer look at how each type of hormone elicits cellular responses.

Water-soluble hormones cannot pass through the phospholipid bilayer of the plasma membrane, but they can bring about cellular changes indirectly, without entering their target cells. The receptor proteins for most water-soluble hormones are embedded in the plasma membrane of target cells and project outward from the cell surface **(Figure 29.2A).** ❶ A water-soluble hormone molecule in the interstitial fluid (◯) binds to the receptor protein, activating it. ❷ This initiates a signal transduction pathway, a series of changes in cellular proteins (relay molecules) that converts an extracellular chemical signal to a specific intracellular response. ❸ The final relay molecule (◯) activates a protein (◭) that carries out the cell's response, either in the cytoplasm (such as activating an enzyme) or in the nucleus (turning on or off genes). One hormone may trigger a variety of responses in target cells because each cell may contain different receptors for that hormone, diverse signal transduction pathways with distinct relay molecules, or several proteins that can initiate different responses.

While water-soluble hormones bind to receptors in the plasma membrane, lipid-soluble steroid

hormones pass through the phospholipid bilayer and bind to receptors inside the cell. As shown in **Figure 29.2B,** ❶ a steroid hormone (▽) enters a cell by diffusion. If the cell is a target cell, the hormone ❷ binds to an open receptor protein in the cytoplasm or nucleus. Rather than triggering a signal transduction pathway, as happens with a water-soluble hormone, the hormone-receptor complex itself usually carries out the transduction of the hormonal signal: The complex acts as a transcription factor—a gene activator or repressor (see Module 11.1). ❸ The hormone-receptor complex attaches to specific sites on the cell's DNA in the nucleus. (These sites are enhancers; see Module 11.4.) ❹ The binding to DNA stimulates gene regulation, turning genes either on (by promoting transcription of certain genes into RNA) or off.

Because a hormone can bind to a variety of receptors in various kinds of target cells, different kinds of cells can respond differently to the same hormone. The main effect of adrenaline on heart muscle cells, for example, is cellular contraction, which speeds up the heartbeat; its main effect on liver and muscle cells, however, is glycogen breakdown, providing glucose (an energy source) to body cells. Together, these effects speed the delivery of energy to cells throughout the body, allowing for a rapid response to the stress that triggered the release of the hormone.

Occasionally, we encounter substances in the environment that can interfere with the normal function of our own

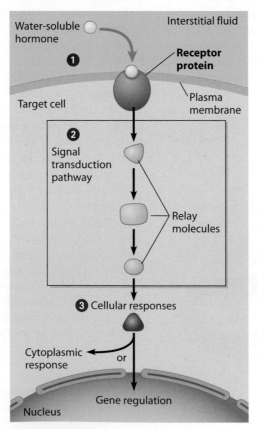

▲ **Figure 29.2A** A hormone that binds a plasma membrane receptor

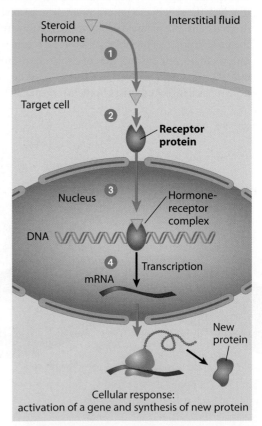

▲ **Figure 29.2B** A hormone that binds an intracellular receptor

chemical signals. These chemicals, called endocrine disruptors, can mimic or interfere with the effects of hormones. For example, bisphenol A (BPA), which is found in some number 7 polycarbonate plastics, has made headlines in recent years. These plastics have been widely used in the manufacturing of reusable water bottles, baby bottles, and the lining of some food cans. Over time, BPA can leech out of the plastic container and contaminate its contents, which are consumed. Statistics Canada has reported that over 90% of Canadians have BPA in their systems. Although human levels are normally low, the level of exposure that is considered safe is currently under debate.

Unfortunately, the effects of BPA exposure are also poorly understood. Peer-reviewed studies have suggested exposure increases risk for developing breast, ovarian, and prostate cancers in adults. Unborn fetuses and infants under 18 months, a critical period in development, seem to exhibit the most severe consequences. Even small disruptions of the delicate hormone balance during this time may have lifelong consequences. Too much estrogen alters the normal development of neurons in the brain, which may lead to behavioural problems. Exposure to BPA in the womb (from maternal consumption) and as a newborn (from baby bottles) may have similar consequences. In light of this evidence, Canada was the first country to declare BPA a toxic substance; it has banned the sale of polycarbonate baby bottles.

We will discuss a rumour about phytoestrogens, another potential endocrine disruptor, in Module 29.12. Before that, let's take a look at the vertebrate endocrine system in more detail.

? **What are two major differences between the action of steroid hormones and the action of nonsteroid hormones?**

● (1) Steroid hormones bind to receptors inside the cell; other hormones bind to plasma membrane receptors. (2) Steroid hormones always affect gene expression; other hormones have this or other effects.

The Vertebrate Endocrine System

29.3 Overview: The vertebrate endocrine system consists of more than a dozen major glands

Some endocrine glands (such as the thyroid) are specialists that primarily secrete hormones into the blood. Other glands (such as the pancreas) serve dual roles, having both endocrine and nonendocrine functions. Still other organs (such as the stomach) are primarily nonendocrine but have some cells that secrete hormones.

Figure 29.3 shows the locations of the major human endocrine glands. **Table 29.3** summarizes the actions of the main hormones they produce and how the glands are regulated. (When reviewing the information in this table, keep in mind that this chapter covers only the major endocrine glands and hormones; there are other hormone-secreting structures—the heart, liver, and stomach, for example—and other hormones that we will not discuss.)

Notice the distribution of the chemical classes of hormone (proteins, peptides, amines, and steroids) in Table 29.3. Only the sex organs and the cortex of the adrenal gland produce steroid hormones, the main type of hormone that actually enters target cells. Most of the endocrine glands produce water-soluble hormones, which generally bind to plasma membrane receptors and act via signal transduction.

Thyroid gland

Parathyroid glands (embedded within thyroid)

Thymus

Adrenal glands (atop kidneys)

Pancreas

Testes (male)

Hypothalamus

Pituitary gland

Ovaries (female)

▲ **Figure 29.3** The major endocrine glands in vertebrates (humans)

TABLE 29.3 | MAJOR HUMAN ENDOCRINE GLANDS AND SOME OF THEIR HORMONES

Gland (module)	Hormone	Chemical Class	Representative Actions	Regulated by
Hypothalamus (29.4)	Hormones released by the posterior pituitary and hormones that regulate the anterior pituitary (see below)			
Pituitary gland (29.4)				
Posterior lobe (releases hormones made by hypothalamus)	Oxytocin	Peptide	Stimulates contraction of uterus during labour and ejection of milk from mammary glands	Nervous system
	Antidiuretic hormones (ADH)	Peptide	Promotes retention of water by kidneys	Water/salt balance
Anterior lobe	Growth hormone (GH)	Protein	Stimulates growth (especially bones) and metabolic functions	Hypothalamic hormones
	Prolactin (PRL)	Protein	Stimulates milk production and secretion in females	Hypothalamic hormones
	Follicle-stimulating hormone (FSH)	Protein	Stimulates production of ova and sperm	Hypothalamic hormones
	Luteinizing hormone (LH)	Protein	Stimulates ovaries and testes	Hypothalamic hormones
	Thyroid-stimulating hormone (TSH)	Protein	Stimulates thyroid gland	Thyroxine in blood; hypothalamic hormones
	Adrenocorticotropic hormone (ACTH)	Peptide	Stimulates adrenal cortex to secrete glucocorticoids	Glucocorticoids; hypothalamic hormones
Pineal gland (29.3)	Melatonin	Amine	Involved in rhythmic activities (daily and seasonal)	Light/dark cycles
Thyroid gland (29.6–29.7)	Thyroxine (T_4) and triiodothyronine (T_3)	Amine	Stimulate and maintain metabolic processes	TSH
	Calcitonin	Peptide	Lowers blood calcium level	Calcium in blood
Parathyroid glands (29.7)	Parathyroid hormone (PTH)	Peptide	Raises blood calcium level	Calcium in blood
Thymus (29.3)	Thymosin	Peptide	Stimulates T cell development	Not known
Adrenal gland (29.10)				
Adrenal medulla	Adrenaline and noradrenaline	Amine	Increase blood glucose; increase metabolic activities; constrict certain blood vessels	Nervous system
Adrenal cortex	Glucocorticoids	Steroid	Increase blood glucose	ACTH
	Mineralocorticoids	Steroid	Promote reabsorption of Na^+ and excretion of K^+ in kidneys	K^+ in blood
Pancreas (29.8–29.9)	Insulin	Protein	Lowers blood glucose	Glucose in blood
	Glucagon	Protein	Raises blood glucose	Glucose in blood
Testes (29.11)	Androgens	Steroid	Support sperm formation; promote development and maintenance of male secondary sex characteristics	FSH and LH
Ovaries (29.11)	Estrogens	Steroid	Stimulate uterine lining growth; promote development and maintenance of female secondary sex characteristics	FSH and LH
	Progesterone	Steroid	Promotes uterine lining growth	FSH and LH

Hormones have a wide range of targets. Some—like the sex hormones, which promote male and female characteristics—affect most of the tissues of the body. Other hormones, such as glucagon from the pancreas, have only a few kinds of target cells (liver and fat cells for glucagon). Some hormones have other endocrine glands as their targets. For example, the pituitary gland produces thyroid-stimulating hormone, which in turn promotes activity of the thyroid gland. This mode of action is referred to as a hormone cascade.

The close association between the endocrine system and the nervous system is apparent in both Figure 29.3 and Table 29.3. For example, the hypothalamus, which is part of the brain, secretes many hormones that regulate other endocrine glands, especially the pituitary. We explore structural and functional connections between the endocrine system and the nervous system further in Module 29.4.

Endocrine glands that we do not discuss at length in this chapter include the pineal and the thymus. The **pineal gland** is a pea-sized mass of tissue near the centre of the brain. The pineal gland synthesizes and secretes melatonin, a hormone that links environmental light conditions with biological rhythms, particularly the sleep–wake circadian rhythms. Melatonin is sometimes called "the dark hormone" because it is secreted at night. In diurnal (day-active) animals, melatonin production peaks in the middle of the night and then gradually falls. Some people ingest melatonin supplements as sleep aids, but scientists have not established the effectiveness of this treatment. Although there is good evidence that nightly increases in natural melatonin play a significant role in promoting sleep, we do not yet know exactly what effects melatonin has on body cells and precisely how sleep–wake cycles are controlled.

The **thymus gland** lies under the breastbone in humans and is quite large during childhood. But it was not until the 1960s that researchers discovered its importance in the immune system. Thymus cells secrete several important hormones, including a peptide that stimulates the development of T cells (see Module 34.7). Beginning at puberty, when the immune system reaches maturity, the thymus shrinks drastically. However, it continues to secrete its T cell–stimulating hormones throughout life.

In the rest of this chapter, we explore several of the endocrine glands listed in Figure 29.3 and Table 29.3. We focus on the hormones produced by each organ and how they help to maintain homeostasis within the human body.

? **Of the glands listed in Table 29.3, which are the only ones to secrete steroid hormones?**

● The testes, ovaries, and adrenal cortex

29.4 The hypothalamus, which is closely tied to the pituitary, connects the nervous and endocrine systems

As we saw earlier, the distinction between the endocrine system and the nervous system often blurs, especially when we consider the hypothalamus and its intricate association with the pituitary gland. The **hypothalamus (Figure 29.4A)** is the main control centre of the endocrine system. As part of the brain, the hypothalamus receives information from nerves about the internal condition of the body and about the external environment. It then responds by sending out appropriate nervous or endocrine signals. Its hormonal signals directly control the pituitary gland, which in turn secretes hormones that influence numerous body functions. The hypothalamus thus exerts master control over the endocrine system by using the pituitary to relay directives to other glands.

As Figure 29.4A shows, the pea-sized **pituitary gland** consists of two distinct parts: a posterior lobe and an anterior lobe, both situated in a pocket of skull bone just under the hypothalamus. The **posterior pituitary** is composed of nervous tissue and is actually an extension of the hypothalamus. It stores and secretes two hormones that are made in the hypothalamus. In contrast, the **anterior pituitary** is composed of endocrine cells that synthesize and secrete numerous hormones directly into the blood. Several of these hormones control the activity of other endocrine glands. The hypothalamus exerts control over the anterior pituitary by secreting two kinds of hormones into short blood vessels that connect the two organs: releasing hormones and inhibiting hormones. A **releasing hormone** stimulates the anterior pituitary to secrete one or more specific hormones, and an **inhibiting hormone** induces the anterior pituitary to stop secreting one or more specific hormones.

Figures 29.4B and 29.4C emphasize the structural and functional connections between the hypothalamus and the pituitary. As **Figure 29.4B** indicates, a set of neurosecretory

Brain
Hypothalamus
Posterior pituitary
Anterior pituitary
Bone

▲ **Figure 29.4A** Location of the hypothalamus and pituitary

▲ **Figure 29.4B** Hormones of the posterior pituitary

▲ **Figure 29.4C** Hormones of the anterior pituitary

cells extends from the hypothalamus into the posterior pituitary. These cells synthesize the peptide hormones **oxytocin** and **antidiuretic hormone (ADH)**. These hormones (▲▲) are channelled along the neurosecretory cells into the posterior pituitary. When released into the blood from the posterior pituitary, oxytocin causes uterine muscles to contract during childbirth and mammary glands to eject milk during nursing. ADH helps cells of the kidney tubules reabsorb water, thus decreasing urine volume when the body needs to retain water. We will examine the role of ADH more in Module 29.5.

Figure 29.4C shows a second set of neurosecretory cells in the hypothalamus. These cells secrete releasing and inhibiting hormones (•∴) that control the anterior pituitary. A system of small blood vessels carries these hormones from the hypothalamus to the anterior pituitary. In response to hypothalamic releasing hormones, the anterior pituitary synthesizes and releases many different peptide and protein hormones (▲▲). These protein hormones, in turn, influence a broad range of body activities. **Thyroid-stimulating hormone (TSH)**, adrenocorticotropic hormone (ACTH), follicle-stimulating hormone (FSH), and luteinizing hormone (LH)

▲ **Figure 29.4D** Gigantism, caused by an excess of growth hormone during childhood

all activate other endocrine glands. Feedback mechanisms control the secretion of these hormones by the anterior pituitary. Another anterior pituitary hormone, **prolactin (PRL)**, produces very different effects in different species (see Module 29.13); in mammals, prolactin stimulates the mammary glands.

Of all the pituitary secretions, none has a broader effect than the protein mentioned in the chapter-opener essay: **growth hormone (GH)**. GH promotes protein synthesis and the use of body fat for energy metabolism in a wide variety of target cells. In young mammals, GH promotes the development and enlargement of all parts of the body. Normally, secretion peaks during the teenage years and subsequently decreases to low levels throughout adulthood. How the timing of GH release is controlled remains poorly understood. However, releasing and inhibiting hormones from the hypothalamus are both involved.

As you read in the opening essay of this chapter, abnormal production of GH can result in several human disorders. Deficiencies in GH production lead to pituitary dwarfism, which means that tissues receive inadequate growth signals. Treatment with exogenous GH can help to prevent this condition. In contrast, excess GH production during childhood increases growth, leading to gigantism **(Figure 29.4D)**.

If GH levels do not decline after childhood, as they should, a disfiguring condition known as acromegaly develops.

In addition to the functions discussed above, GH is contributing to new biotechnologies that are continually being developed to improve agricultural yields. For example, GH stimulates milk production in mammals so treatment with bovine GH has been proposed to increase milk production on dairy farms. Although a desirable outcome, GH-fed cattle experience multiple related health problems. Also, the milk produced by treated cows is of lesser quality and has been shown to contain GH. The risks of consuming GH-containing milk to humans are unknown. In light of this, the Canadian government has not approved GH for use in Canada's dairy or cattle industries.

The **endorphins**, other hormones produced by the anterior pituitary as well as other parts of the brain, are the body's natural painkillers. These chemical signals bind to receptors in the brain and dull the perception of pain. The effect on the nervous system is similar to that of the drug morphine, earning endorphins the nickname "natural opiates" (although it would be more accurate to call opiates "artificial endorphins"). Some researchers speculate that the so-called runner's high results partly from the release of endorphins when stress and pain in the body reach critical levels. Some research also suggests that endorphins may be released during deep meditation, by acupuncture treatments, or even by eating spicy foods.

Figure 29.4E shows how the hypothalamus operates through the anterior pituitary to direct the activity of another endocrine organ, the thyroid gland. The hypothalamus secretes a releasing hormone known as **TRH (TSH-releasing hormone)**. In turn, TRH stimulates the anterior pituitary to produce thyroid-stimulating hormone (TSH). Under the influence of TSH, the thyroid secretes the hormone thyroxine into the blood. Thyroxine is converted to another

hormone that increases the metabolic rate of most body cells, warming the body as a result.

Precise regulation of the TRH-TSH-thyroxine system keeps the hormones at levels that maintain homeostasis. The hypothalamus takes some cues from the environment; for instance, cold temperatures tend to increase its secretion of TRH. In addition, as the red arrows in Figure 29.4E indicate, negative-feedback mechanisms control the secretion of thyroxine. When thyroxine increases in the blood, it acts on the hypothalamus and anterior pituitary, inhibiting TRH and TSH secretion and consequently thyroxine synthesis.

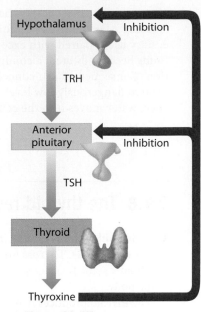

▲ **Figure 29.4E** Control of thyroxine secretion

To summarize what we discussed in this module: The anterior and posterior pituitary, directed by the hypothalamus, stimulates a number of other endocrine glands with specific functions. In the rest of the modules in this chapter, we explore several of these endocrine glands, the hormones they produce, and their effects on the vertebrate body.

 Alcohol inhibits secretion of ADH by the anterior pituitary. How do you think this action of alcohol would affect urination?

● Since ADH stimulates reabsorption of water in the kidneys, alcohol increases the volume of urine produced.

Hormones and Homeostasis

29.5 Hormones regulate the excretory system

In Chapter 28, you learned how the kidneys filter the blood and remove nitrogenous wastes from the body in urine. The production of urine must be regulated to avoid excess water loss and maintain tissue solute concentrations. Control comes from the levels of hormones that act on the kidney's nephrons. If you start to become dehydrated, the solute concentration of your body fluids rises. When this concentration gets too high, the brain increases levels of a hormone called antidiuretic hormone (ADH) in your blood. This hormone signals the nephrons in your kidneys to reabsorb more water from the filtrate. This reabsorption increases the amount of water returning to your blood (where it is needed) and decreases the amount of water excreted (resulting in concentrated urine). Dark-coloured urine may indicate that you have not been drinking enough water.

On the other hand, if you drink a lot of water, the solute concentration of your body fluids becomes too dilute. In response, blood levels of ADH drop, causing the nephrons to reabsorb less water from the filtrate, resulting in dilute, watery urine. This process explains why your urine is very clear after you drink a lot of water. (Increased urination is called diuresis, and it is because ADH acts against this state that it is called antidiuretic hormone.) Diuretics, such as alcohol, are substances that inhibit the release of ADH and therefore result in excessive urinary water loss. Drinking alcohol will make you urinate more frequently, and the resulting dehydration contributes to the symptoms of a hangover. Caffeine is also a diuretic; you may have noticed that drinking coffee, tea, or cola causes you to urinate soon afterward. The drug ecstasy has the opposite effect by increasing ADH release and inhibiting urine production. If ecstasy use is paired with excess water consumption, bodily fluids become diluted, a condition known as water intoxication. Consequently, salt concentrations of body fluids can drop to dangerously low levels. To correct the salt imbalance, water moves into the cells by osmosis, making them swell. Swelling of brain cells can lead to seizures, coma, or even death.

 Some of the drugs classified as diuretics make the epithelium of the collecting duct less permeable to water. How would this affect kidney function?

● The collecting ducts would reabsorb less water, and thus the diuretic would increase water loss in the urine.

29.6 The thyroid regulates development and metabolism

Your **thyroid gland** is located in your neck just under your larynx (voice box). Thyroid hormones perform several important homeostatic functions that affect virtually all the tissues of the body.

The thyroid produces two very similar amine hormones, both of which contain the element iodine. One of these, **thyroxine**, is called T_4 because it contains four iodine atoms; the other, **triiodothyronine**, is called T_3 because it contains three iodine atoms. In target cells, most T_4 is converted to T_3. One of the crucial roles of both hormones is in development and maturation. In a bullfrog, for example, these hormones trigger the profound reorganization of body tissues that occurs as a tadpole—a strictly aquatic organism—transforms into an adult frog, which may spend much of its time on land (**Figure 29.6A**). Thyroid hormones are equally important in mammals, especially in bone and nerve cell development. T_3 and T_4 also help to maintain normal blood pressure, heart rate, muscle tone, digestion, and reproductive function. Throughout the body, these hormones tend to increase the rate of oxygen consumption and cellular metabolism.

Too much or too little of the thyroid hormones in the blood can result in serious metabolic disorders. An excess of T_3 and T_4 in the blood (*hyper*thyroidism) can make a person overheat, sweat profusely, become irritable, develop high blood pressure, and lose weight. The most common form of hyperthyroidism is Graves' disease; protruding eyes caused by fluid accumulation behind the eyeballs are a typical symptom. Conversely, insufficient amounts of T_3 and T_4 (*hypo*thyroidism) can cause weight gain, lethargy, and intolerance to cold.

Hypothyroidism can result from a defective thyroid gland or from dietary disorders. For example, severe iodine deficiency during childhood can cause cretinism, which results in retarded skeletal growth and poor mental development. And in adults, insufficient iodine in the diet can cause **goiter**, an enlargement of the thyroid (see

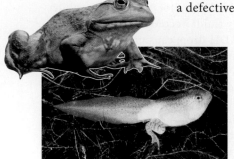

▲ **Figure 29.6A** The maturation of a tadpole (below) into an adult frog (above), as regulated by thyroid hormones

Figure 2.2A). In such cases, the thyroid gland cannot synthesize adequate amounts of its T_3 and T_4 hormones. The lack of T_3 and T_4 interrupts the feedback loops that control thyroid activity (**Figure 29.6B**). The blood never carries enough of the T_3 and T_4 hormones to shut off the secretion of TRH or TSH. The thyroid enlarges because TSH continues to stimulate it.

Fortunately, both hypo- and hyperthyroidism can be successfully treated. For example, many cases of goiter can be treated simply by adding iodine to the diet. Seawater is a rich source of iodine, and goiter rarely occurs in people living near the seacoast, where the soil is iodine-rich and a lot of iodine-rich seafood is consumed. Goiter is less common today than in the past thanks to the incorporation of iodine into table salt, but it still affects thousands of people in developing nations. Treatment for hyperthyroidism (an overactive thyroid) takes advantage of the fact that the thyroid accumulates iodine: Patients drink a solution containing a small dose of radioactive iodine, which kills off some thyroid cells. This "radioactive cocktail" can kill off just enough cells to reduce thyroid output and relieve symptoms.

 By what mechanism does thyroxine switch off its own production?

● By negative feedback: It inhibits the secretion of TRH from the hypothalamus and TSH from the pituitary.

▲ **Figure 29.6B** How iodine deficiency causes goiter

29.7 Hormones from the thyroid and parathyroid glands maintain calcium homeostasis

To work properly, many body functions require an appropriate level of calcium in the blood and interstitial fluid. Without calcium, nerve signals cannot be transmitted from cell to cell, muscles cannot function properly, blood cannot clot, and cells cannot transport molecules across their membranes. The thyroid and parathyroid glands function in the homeostasis of calcium ions (Ca^{2+}), keeping the concentration of the ions within a narrow range.

You have four disc-shaped **parathyroid glands**, all embedded in the surface of the thyroid. Two peptide hormones, **calcitonin** from the thyroid and **parathyroid hormone (PTH)** from the parathyroids, regulate blood calcium levels. Calcitonin and PTH are said to be **antagonistic hormones** because the actions of one oppose the actions of the other: In this example, calcitonin lowers the calcium level in the blood, whereas PTH raises it. As **Figure 29.7** indicates, this pair of antagonistic hormones operate by means of feedback systems

that keep the calcium level near the homeostatic set point of 10 mg of Ca^{2+} per 100 mL of blood.

❶ When the blood Ca^{2+} level drops below the set point, ❷ the parathyroids release PTH into the blood. ❸ PTH stimulates the release of calcium ions from bones and increases Ca^{2+} reabsorption by the kidneys. The kidneys also play an indirect role in calcium homeostasis, which involves vitamin D. We obtain this vitamin in inactive form from food and also from chemical reactions in our skin when it is exposed to sunlight. Transported in the blood, inactive vitamin D undergoes sequential steps of activation in the liver and kidneys. ❹ The active form of vitamin D, secreted by the kidneys, acts as a hormone. It stimulates the intestines to increase uptake of Ca^{2+} from food. ❺ The combined effects of PTH on the bones, kidneys, and intestines result in a higher Ca^{2+} level in the blood.

The top part of the diagram shows how calcitonin from the thyroid gland reverses the effects of PTH. ❻ A rise in blood

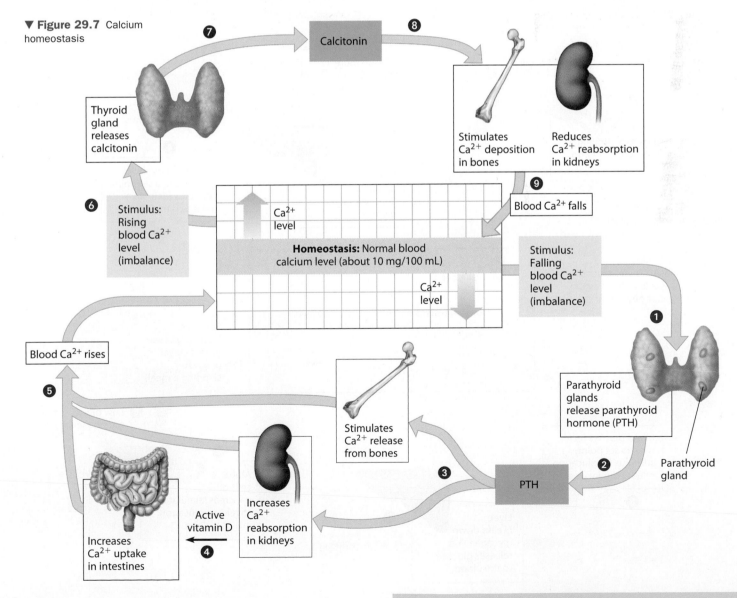

▼ **Figure 29.7** Calcium homeostasis

Thyroid gland releases calcitonin

❼ Calcitonin ❽

Stimulates Ca^{2+} deposition in bones

Reduces Ca^{2+} reabsorption in kidneys

❻ Stimulus: Rising blood Ca^{2+} level (imbalance)

Ca^{2+} level

Homeostasis: Normal blood calcium level (about 10 mg/100 mL)

Ca^{2+} level

❾ Blood Ca^{2+} falls

Stimulus: Falling blood Ca^{2+} level (imbalance)

❶

Blood Ca^{2+} rises

❺

Stimulates Ca^{2+} release from bones

Parathyroid glands release parathyroid hormone (PTH)

Parathyroid gland

Increases Ca^{2+} uptake in intestines

Active vitamin D ❹

Increases Ca^{2+} reabsorption in kidneys

❸

PTH

❷

Ca^{2+} above the set point ❼ induces the thyroid gland to secrete calcitonin. ❽ Calcitonin, in turn, has two main effects: It causes more Ca^{2+} to be deposited in the bones, and it makes the kidneys reabsorb less Ca^{2+} as they form urine. ❾ The result is a lower Ca^{2+} level in the blood.

In summary, a sensitive balancing system maintains calcium homeostasis. The system depends on feedback control by two antagonistic hormones. Failure of the system can have far-reaching effects. For example, a shortage of PTH causes the blood calcium level to drop dramatically, leading to convulsive contractions of the skeletal muscles. This condition, known as tetany, can be fatal. In such cases, a rapid intravenous infusion of calcium can be life-saving.

? Why are calcitonin and PTH referred to as antagonistic hormones?

Antagonistic hormones have opposite effects on the body. In this case, calcitonin lowers blood calcium levels, whereas PTH raises blood calcium levels.

29.8 Pancreatic hormones regulate blood glucose levels

The **pancreas** produces two hormones that play a large role in managing the body's energy supplies. Clusters of endocrine cells, called islets of Langerhans, are scattered throughout the pancreas. Each islet has a population of beta cells, which produce the hormone **insulin**, and a population of alpha cells, which produce another hormone, **glucagon**. Insulin and glucagon—both protein hormones—are secreted directly into the blood. Insulin was discovered in the 1920s by two Canadian scientists, Dr. Frederick Banting, and Dr. Charles Best at the University of Toronto. This discovery improved the quality of life of millions of people worldwide. Banting and Dr. John Macleod (who provided laboratory space and was included after a controversial decision that omitted Best) were awarded the Nobel Prize for Physiology or Medicine in 1923.

As shown in **Figure 29.8**, insulin and glucagon are antagonistic hormones that regulate the concentration of glucose in

▼ **Figure 29.8** Glucose homeostasis

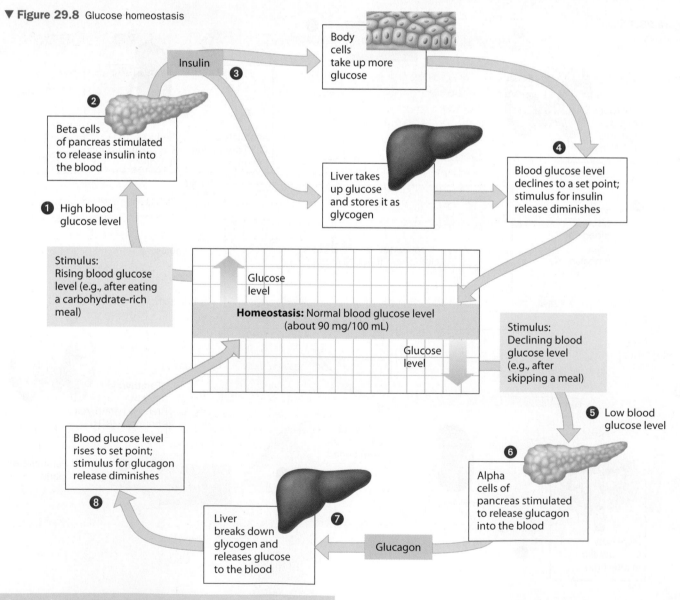

Body cells take up more glucose

Insulin ❸

❷ Beta cells of pancreas stimulated to release insulin into the blood

Liver takes up glucose and stores it as glycogen

❹ Blood glucose level declines to a set point; stimulus for insulin release diminishes

❶ High blood glucose level

Stimulus: Rising blood glucose level (e.g., after eating a carbohydrate-rich meal)

Glucose level

Homeostasis: Normal blood glucose level (about 90 mg/100 mL)

Glucose level

Stimulus: Declining blood glucose level (e.g., after skipping a meal)

❺ Low blood glucose level

❻ Alpha cells of pancreas stimulated to release glucagon into the blood

Blood glucose level rises to set point; stimulus for glucagon release diminishes ❽

Liver breaks down glycogen and releases glucose to the blood ❼

Glucagon

the blood. The two hormones counter each other in a feedback circuit that precisely manages the amount of circulating glucose available to use as cellular fuel versus the amount of glucose stored as the polymer glycogen in body cells. Through such feedback, the concentration of glucose in the blood determines the relative amounts of insulin and glucagon secreted by the islet cells.

In the top half of the diagram, you see what happens when the glucose concentration of the blood rises above the set point of about 90 mg of glucose per 100 mL of blood, as it does shortly after we eat a carbohydrate-rich meal. ❶ The rising blood glucose level ❷ stimulates the beta cells in the pancreas to secrete more insulin into the blood. ❸ The insulin stimulates nearly all body cells to take up glucose from the blood, which decreases the blood glucose level. Liver cells (and skeletal muscle cells) take up much of the glucose and use it to form glycogen, which they store. Insulin also stimulates cells to metabolize the glucose for immediate energy use, for the storage of energy in fats, or for the synthesis of proteins. ❹ When the blood glucose level falls to the set point, the beta cells lose their stimulus to secrete insulin.

Following the bottom half of the diagram, you see what happens when ❺ the blood glucose level starts to dip below the set point, as it may between meals or during strenuous exercise. ❻ The pancreatic alpha cells respond by secreting glucagon. ❼ Glucagon is a fuel mobilizer, signalling liver cells to break glycogen down into glucose, convert amino acids and fat-derived glycerol to glucose, and release the glucose into the blood. ❽ Then, when the blood glucose level returns to the set point, the alpha cells slow their secretion of glucagon.

In the next module, we see what can happen when this delicately balanced system breaks down.

? **How is the insulin-glucagon relationship similar to the calcitonin-PTH relationship?**

● In both cases, the two hormones are antagonists that help to maintain homeostasis by counteracting each other's effects. Their actions keep the blood concentration of a key chemical (glucose for insulin-glucagon; calcium ions for calcitonin-PTH) near the set point.

29.9 Diabetes is a major concern for First Nations peoples in Canada

Diabetes mellitus is a serious hormonal disease in which body cells are unable to absorb glucose from the blood, regardless of how much is present. As digestion and absorption of starch continues, glucose accumulates in the blood. Blood glucose levels become so high that glucose can be measured in the urine. (Normally, the kidneys leave no glucose in the urine.) Diabetes mellitus literally means "overflowing with honey," which describes the excess production of sweet urine. Diagnosis requires a glucose tolerance test, in which diabetics show high blood glucose levels for extended periods after a meal **(Figure 29.9A)**.

There are three types of diabetes mellitus. Type 1 (insulin-dependent) diabetes is an autoimmune disease in which the body's own immune system attacks and destroys the insulin-producing pancreatic beta cells. As a result, the pancreas does not produce enough insulin, and glucose builds up in the blood. Type 1 patients are treated with injections of human insulin several times daily.

In type 2 (non-insulin-dependent) diabetes, insulin is produced, but target cells fail to take up glucose from the blood, causing blood glucose levels to remain elevated. Many type 2 diabetics can manage their disease with exercise and diet; some require medication.

Third, gestational diabetes affects about 4% of pregnant women, whether or not they have shown symptoms of diabetes before. If left untreated, gestational diabetes can lead to dangerously large babies, which can greatly complicate delivery. If diagnosed, diet and insulin injections can prevent most problems.

Diabetes affects over 1.9 million Canadians, with 90% of cases being type 2. It is estimated that a further 900 000 people with diabetes remain undiagnosed, unaware that they have a serious illness. The prevalence of type 2 diabetes in Canadian Aboriginal people is alarmingly high; three to five times that of the general population. The lone exception are the Inuit, whose prevalence is lower than the general population. However, the rate among the Inuit has been increasing in recent decades. Furthermore, First Nations women have a much higher chance (over fourfold) of developing gestational diabetes than the national average. This may exacerbate the problem in First Nations peoples because infants born to mothers with gestational diabetes have an increased risk of obesity and for developing type 2 diabetes.

Why are Canadian First Nations more likely to develop diabetes? The causes of diabetes are not well understood. Multiple risk factors have been identified, including genetic susceptibility and environmental factors. The Aboriginal peoples can

▲ **Figure 29.9A** Results of glucose tolerance tests

be traced back to Asia when their ancestors crossed a land bridge at the Bering Strait between 13 000 and 16 000 years ago. Asians also have a higher incidence of diabetes than Caucasians: about two times greater.

True for all peoples, type 2 diabetes is almost always associated with being overweight and underactive, although whether obesity causes diabetes (and if so, how) remains unknown. Many First Nations peoples have replaced their traditional nomadic lifestyle with a more sedentary existence. With reduced activity level, obesity is on the rise in these communities. Socioeconomic factors affecting many Aboriginal communities, such as poverty and poor access to education and health care, also contribute to the problem. Surveys show that fewer than 40% of Aboriginal diabetics attend diabetes clinics to get the information they need. However, national programs are in place to help provide access to information and care to all First Nations peoples (Figure 29.9B).

If left untreated, diabetes can lead to severe complications. Heart and kidney disease are common, as are blood vessel and nerve damage that necessitate lower limb amputations. Not only are First Nations peoples more likely to develop diabetes, they are more likely to develop severe complications. Diabetics among the First Nations in Manitoba are 12 times more likely to develop kidney disease and 18 times more likely to require amputation than non-Aboriginal diabetics. Early diagnosis may prevent or delay the onset of complications.

Diabetes has been declared an epidemic in Canada's First Nations. With its high incidence, accompanied by early onset and late detection, risk of complications is extraordinarily high

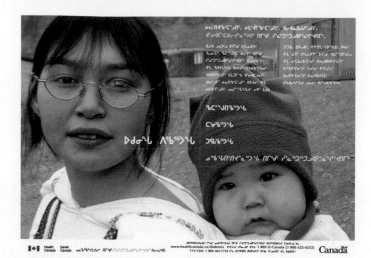

▲ **Figure 29.9B** The Aboriginal Diabetes Initiative raises awareness of this health concern

in these communities. Only with increased access to pertinent information, health clinics, and a change in lifestyle, will this problem be solved. Without these changes, prevalence in First Nations peoples is expected to increase.

 How can increased awareness and understanding help to prevent diabetes in First Nations communities?

● Understanding risk factors and altering lifestyle to avoid them will help to reduce the risk of developing diabetes.

29.10 The adrenal glands mobilize responses to stress

The endocrine system includes two **adrenal glands**, one sitting on top of each kidney. As you can see in **Figure 29.10** (inset, top left), each adrenal gland is actually made up of two glands fused together: a central portion called the **adrenal medulla** and an outer portion called the **adrenal cortex**. Though the cells they contain and the hormones they produce are different, both the adrenal medulla and the adrenal cortex secrete hormones that enable the body to respond to stress.

The adrenal medulla produces the "fight-or-flight" hormones that we discussed earlier; they ensure a rapid, short-term response to stress. You have probably felt your heart beat faster and your skin develop goose bumps when sensing danger. Facing an unexpected threat, like a pop quiz, can cause these short-term stress symptoms. Positive emotions—extreme pleasure, for instance—can produce the same effects. These reactions are triggered by two amine hormones secreted by the adrenal medulla, **adrenaline** (epinephrine) and **noradrenaline** (norepinephrine).

As shown in the figure, stressful stimuli, whether negative or positive, activate certain nerve cells in the hypothalamus. ❶ These cells send nerve signals via the spinal cord to the adrenal medulla, ❷ stimulating it to secrete adrenaline and noradrenaline into the blood. Adrenaline and noradrenaline have somewhat different effects on tissues, but both contribute to the short-term stress response. Both hormones stimulate liver cells to release glucose, thus making more fuel available for cellular work. They also prepare the body for action by raising the blood pressure, breathing rate, and metabolic rate. In addition, adrenaline and noradrenaline change blood flow patterns, making some organs more active and others less so. For example, adrenaline dilates blood vessels in the brain and skeletal muscles, thus increasing alertness and the muscles' ability to react to stress. At the same time, adrenaline and noradrenaline constrict blood vessels elsewhere, thereby reducing activities that are not immediately involved in the stress response, such as digestion. The short-term stress response prepares the body for a quick and decisive reaction—as would be needed to confront a sudden danger—but it occurs and subsides rapidly.

In contrast to adrenaline and noradrenaline secreted by the adrenal medulla, hormones secreted by the adrenal cortex can provide a slower, longer-lasting response to stress that can last for days. The adrenal cortex responds to endocrine signals—chemical signals in the blood—rather than to nerve cell signals. As shown in Figure 29.10, ❸ the hypothalamus secretes a releasing hormone that ❹ stimulates target cells in the anterior pituitary to secrete the hormone **adrenocorticotropic hormone (ACTH)**. ❺ In turn, ACTH stimulates cells of the adrenal cortex to synthesize and secrete a family of steroid hormones called the **corticosteroids**. The two main types in humans are the mineralocorticoids and the glucocorticoids. Both help to maintain homeostasis when the body experiences long-term stress.

Mineralocorticoids act mainly on salt and water balance. One of these hormones (aldosterone) stimulates the kidneys to reabsorb sodium ions and water, with the overall effect of increasing the volume of the blood and raising blood pressure as a response to prolonged stress.

Glucocorticoids function mainly in mobilizing cellular fuel, thus reinforcing the effects of glucagon. Glucocorticoids promote the synthesis of glucose from noncarbohydrates such as proteins and fats. When the body cells consume more glucose than the liver can provide from glycogen stores, glucocorticoids stimulate the breakdown of muscle proteins, making amino acids available for conversion to glucose by the liver. This makes more glucose available in the blood as cellular fuel in response to stress.

Very high levels of glucocorticoids can suppress the body's defence system, including the inflammatory response that occurs at infection sites (see Module 34.2). For this reason, physicians may use glucocorticoids to treat excessive inflammation. The glucocorticoid cortisone, for example, was once regarded as a miracle drug for treating serious inflammatory conditions such as arthritis. Cortisone and other glucocorticoids can relieve swelling and pain from inflammation; but, by suppressing immunity, they can also make a person highly susceptible to infection.

Physicians often prescribe oral glucocorticoids to relieve pain from athletic injuries. However, glucocorticoids are potentially very dangerous; prolonged use can depress the activity of the adrenal glands and cause side effects such as a weakened immune system, easy bruising, weak bones, weight gain, muscle breakdown, and increased risk of diabetes. It is safer, but

▲ **Figure 29.10** How the adrenal glands control our responses to stress

still potentially dangerous, to inject a glucocorticoid at the site of injury. With this treatment, the pain usually subsides, but its underlying cause remains. Masking the pain covers up the pain's message that tissue is damaged.

? Adrenaline and noradrenaline are responsible for the _____ stress response while the mineralocorticoids and glucocorticoids are responsible for the _____ stress response.

● short-term; long-term

29.11 The gonads secrete sex hormones

The sex hormones are steroid hormones that affect growth and development and also regulate reproductive cycles and sexual behaviour. The **gonads**, or sex glands (ovaries in the female and testes in the male), secrete sex hormones in addition to producing gametes (ova and sperm).

The gonads of mammals produce three major categories of sex hormones: estrogens, progestins, and androgens. Females and males have all three types, but in different proportions. Females have a high ratio of estrogens to androgens. In humans, **estrogens** maintain the female reproductive system and promote the development of female features such as smaller body size, higher-pitched voice, breasts, and wider hips. In all mammals, **progestins**, such as progesterone, are primarily involved in preparing and maintaining the uterus to support an embryo.

In general, **androgens** stimulate the development and maintenance of the male reproductive system. Males have a high ratio of androgens to estrogens, with their main androgen being **testosterone**. In humans, androgens produced by male embryos during the seventh week of development stimulate the development of male genitalia. During puberty, high concentrations of androgens trigger the development of male characteristics, such as a lower-pitched voice, facial hair, and large skeletal muscles. The muscle-building action of androgens and other anabolic steroids has enticed some athletes to abuse them at great risk to their health.

Research has established that the process of sex determination by androgens occurs in a highly similar manner in all vertebrates, suggesting that androgens had this role early in evolution. In elephant seals, male androgens promote development of large bodies weighing 2 tonnes, an inflatable enlargement of the nasal cavity, a thick hide that can withstand bloody conflicts, and aggressive behaviour toward other males. The two males in **Figure 29.11** are fighting by slamming their bodies against each other. In so doing, one will establish dominance over the other and the right to mate with many females.

The synthesis of sex hormones by the gonads is regulated by the hypothalamus and anterior pituitary. In response to a releasing factor from the hypothalamus, the anterior pituitary secretes follicle-stimulating hormone (FSH) and luteinizing hormone (LH). These stimulate the ovaries or testes to synthesize and secrete the sex hormones, among other effects. We examine the complex effects of these hormones when we focus on human reproduction in the next chapter. In the next module, we look at the rumour that hormone-like molecules in our food affect gender development.

? Name the human male and female gonads and the primary hormone(s) that each produce(s).

● Ovaries (estrogens and progestins) and testes (androgens)

▼ **Figure 29.11** Male elephant seals in combat

29.12 Does consuming soy products cause feminization in males?

It has long been known that plant products can have a wide range of effects on humans, including salicin (used to develop aspirin) from willows, which reduces pain and fever, and digitalis from foxgloves, which treats heart failure. Some of these products are endocrine disruptors, which mimic natural signals within the body, including hormone signals (see Module 29.2). For example, phytoestrogens have a similar molecular structure to human estrogens and may be able to mimic their function. The rumour we explore in this module states that consumption of phytoestrogens can have feminizing effects in males because they elevate estrogen levels. But are phytoestrogens really an endocrine disruptor?

Soy foods, such as tofu (Figure 29.12), are the primary dietary source of phytoestrogens. The promotion of female sex characteristics by estrogen was discussed in the previous module. Scientific literature includes a few case reports (documents about individual patients) that anecdotally demonstrate the feminizing effects of phytoestrogens in males, including increased estrogen levels, lower testosterone levels, breast development, and erectile dysfunction. However, case studies should never be used as the basis for developing conclusions. A proper conclusion requires extensive research and clinical trials involving hundreds, or even thousands, of individuals. Yet the rumour persists, promulgated on the Internet on websites devoted to inform the public about the "evils" of soy products.

Why do plants make phytoestrogens? The answer to this question is poorly understood because most research to date about phytoestrogens focuses on their effects on dietary health. It is thought that these molecules are an important component of the plant's defence against bacterial infection and possibly herbivory. A few studies suggest that phytoestrogens can reduce fertility in herbivores. During stressful periods of low rainfall, some plants have been shown to increase phytoestrogen production. At the same time, reproduction among herbivores grazing on these plants decreases. With fewer herbivore offspring, the plants benefit by a reduction in grazing pressure. From this observation, some scientists concluded that molecules that mimic estrogen decrease fertility, further supporting the rumour. However, the observed reduction in herbivore fertility might have been a direct result of the harsh environment and not the ingestion of phytoestrogens.

In recent years, several clinical studies have failed to find a correlation between the ingestion of phytoestrogens and feminization in males. A few studies did report a statistically significant increase in circulating estrogen levels in boys consuming soy foods daily for six months. However, the high estrogen level in these boys was still within the normal range and there was no evidence of feminization. Thus, it is highly unlikely that phytoestrogens are endocrine disruptors and it is equally unlikely that consumption of soy foods will cause feminization in males.

In fact, a large body of scientific literature supports numerous health benefits associated with soy foods. Consumption of soy foods has been shown to reduce the risk of certain cancers and cardiovascular disease and to lower cholesterol

▲ Figure 29.12 Soy foods contain phytoestrogens

levels. The cancer rate is lower in Asian populations that consume soy foods on a regular basis. As antioxidants, phytoestrogens help to protect our cells from potentially cancer-causing oxidizing agents. Prenatal exposure to dietary soy reduces the fetus's chance of obesity and heart disease later in life. New research is investigating phytoestrogens as a suitable hormone replacement therapy for menopausal women.

The evidence that phytoestrogen containing soy foods are actually beneficial is accumulating. Evidence of their feminizing effects are not, and yet this rumour still persists. This hearsay is another example of how you should always think critically about the things you read and hear.

 How could the phytoestrogens produced in a plant affect humans?

● The molecular structure is similar enough that phytoestrogens may bind to estrogen receptors in the body and elicit a gene response.

29.13 A single hormone can perform a variety of functions in different animals

Hormones play important roles in all vertebrates, and some of the same hormones can be found in vertebrates that are only distantly related. Interestingly, the same hormone can have different actions in different animals—a strong indication that hormonal regulation was an early evolutionary adaptation.

The peptide hormone prolactin (PRL), produced and secreted by the anterior pituitary under the direction of the hypothalamus, is a good example. Prolactin produces diverse effects in different vertebrate species. In humans, PRL performs several important functions related to childbirth. During late pregnancy, PRL stimulates mammary glands to grow and produce milk. (A brief surge in prolactin levels just before menstruation causes breast swelling and tenderness in some women.) Suckling by a newborn stimulates further release of PRL, which in turn increases the milk supply (Figure 29.13). High prolactin levels during nursing tend to prevent the ovaries from releasing eggs, decreasing the chances of a new pregnancy occurring during the time of breastfeeding. This may be an evolutionary adaptation that helps to ensure that adequate care is given to newborns.

PRL plays a wide variety of other roles unrelated to childbirth. In some nonhuman mammals, PRL stimulates nest building. In birds, PRL regulates fat metabolism and reproduction. In amphibians, it stimulates movement toward water in preparation for breeding and affects metamorphosis. In fish that migrate between saltwater and fresh water (salmon, for example), PRL helps to regulate salt and water balance in the gills and kidneys.

Such diverse effects suggest that prolactin is an ancient hormone whose functions diversified through evolution. Over millions of years, the prolactin molecule stayed the same, but

▶ **Figure 29.13** Suckling promotes prolactin production

its role changed dramatically—a good example of how evolution can both preserve unity (in terms of the structure of the molecule itself) and promote diversity (in terms of the varying roles it plays).

? PRL promotes the production of milk. Newborn suckling promotes PRL production. This connection is an example of _____ feedback.

positive

REVIEW

Reviewing the Concepts

The Nature of Chemical Regulation (29.1–29.2)

29.1 Chemical signals coordinate body functions. Hormones are signalling molecules, usually carried in the blood, that cause specific changes in target cells. All hormone-secreting cells make up the endocrine system, which works with the nervous system in regulating body activities.

29.2 Hormones affect target cells by using two main signalling mechanisms.

The Vertebrate Endocrine System (29.3–29.4)

29.3 Overview: The vertebrate endocrine system consists of more than a dozen major glands. Some glands are specialized for

hormone secretion only; some also do other jobs. Some hormones have a very narrow range of targets and effects; others have numerous effects on many kinds of target cells.

29.4 The hypothalamus, which is closely tied to the pituitary, connects the nervous and endocrine systems. The releasing and inhibiting hormones from the hypothalamus control the secretion of several other hormones.

Hormones and Homeostasis (29.5–29.13)

29.5 Hormones regulate the excretory system. Antidiuretic hormone causes the kidneys to reabsorb more water, reducing urine volume. Diuretics, such as alcohol, inhibit ADH release and increase urine volume.

29.6 The thyroid regulates development and metabolism. Two amine hormones from the thyroid gland, T_4 and T_3, regulate an animal's development and metabolism. Negative feedback maintains homeostatic levels of T_4 and T_3 in the blood. Thyroid imbalance can cause disease.

29.7 Hormones from the thyroid and parathyroid glands maintain calcium homeostasis. Blood calcium level is regulated by a well-balanced antagonism between calcitonin from the thyroid and parathyroid hormone from the parathyroid glands.

29.8 Pancreatic hormones regulate blood glucose levels.

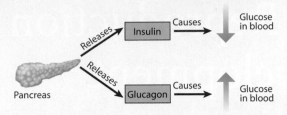

29.9 Diabetes is a major concern for First Nations peoples in Canada. Diabetes mellitus results from a lack of insulin or a failure of cells to respond to it. Canadian First Nations peoples are three to five times more likely to develop type 2 diabetes.

29.10 The adrenal glands mobilize responses to stress. Nerve signals from the hypothalamus stimulate the adrenal medulla to secrete adrenaline and noradrenaline, which quickly trigger the fight-or-flight response. ACTH from the pituitary causes the adrenal cortex to secrete glucocorticoids and mineralocorticoids, which boost blood pressure and energy in response to long-term stress.

29.11 The gonads secrete sex hormones. Estrogens, progestins, and androgens are steroid sex hormones produced by the gonads in response to signals from the hypothalamus and pituitary. Estrogens and progestins (mainly progesterone) stimulate the development of female characteristics and maintain the female reproductive system. Androgens, such as testosterone, trigger the development of male characteristics.

29.12 Does consuming soy products cause feminization in males? The rumour that the phytoestrogens in soy foods cause feminization of males is not supported by scientific evidence. In fact, there may be many benefits to eating these foods.

29.13 A single hormone can perform a variety of functions in different animals. A single hormone, such as prolactin, can assume diverse roles.

Connecting the Concepts

Match each hormone (top) with the gland where it is produced (centre) and its effect on target cells (bottom).

1. thyroxine   4. insulin   7. PTH
2. adrenaline   5. melatonin   8. ADH
3. androgens   6. FSH

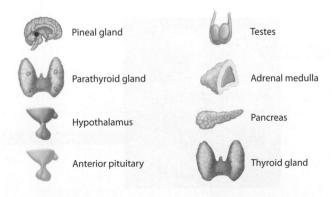

Pineal gland
Parathyroid gland
Hypothalamus
Anterior pituitary
Testes
Adrenal medulla
Pancreas
Thyroid gland

a. lowers blood glucose
b. stimulates ovaries
c. triggers fight-or-flight
d. promotes male characteristics
e. regulates metabolism
f. influences sleep–wake rhythms
g. raises blood calcium level
h. boosts water retention

Testing Your Knowledge

Multiple Choice

9. Which of the following controls the activity of all the others?
   a. thyroid gland
   b. pituitary gland
   c. adrenal cortex
   d. hypothalamus
   e. ovaries

10. The pancreas increases its output of insulin in response to
    a. an increase in body temperature.
    b. changing cycles of light and dark.
    c. a decrease in blood glucose.
    d. a hormone secreted by the anterior pituitary.
    e. an increase in blood glucose.

11. Which of the following hormones have antagonistic (opposing) effects? Choose all that apply.
    a. parathyroid hormone and calcitonin
    b. glucagon and thyroxine
    c. growth hormone and adrenaline
    d. ACTH and cortisone
    e. adrenaline and noradrenaline

12. For which of the following reasons is the body able to maintain a relatively constant level of thyroxine in the blood? *(Explain your answer.)*
    a. Because thyroxine stimulates the pituitary to secrete thyroid-stimulating hormone (TSH)
    b. Because thyroxine inhibits the secretion of TSH-releasing hormone (TRH) from the hypothalamus
    c. Because TRH inhibits the secretion of thyroxine by the thyroid gland
    d. Because thyroxine stimulates the hypothalamus to secrete TRH
    e. Because thyroxine stimulates the pituitary to secrete TRH

13. Which of the following hormones has the broadest range of targets?
    a. ADH   b. oxytocin
    c. TSH   d. adrenaline
    e. ACTH

Describing, Comparing, and Explaining

14. Explain how the hypothalamus controls body functions through its action on the pituitary gland. How does control of the anterior and posterior pituitary differ?

15. Explain how the same hormone might have different effects on two different target cells and no effect on nontarget cells.

Applying the Concepts

16. A strain of transgenic mice remains healthy as long as you feed them regularly and do not let them exercise. After they eat, their blood glucose level rises slightly and then declines to a homeostatic level. However, if these mice fast or exercise at all, their blood glucose drops dangerously. Which hypothesis best explains their problem? *(Explain your answer.)*
    a. The mice have insulin-dependent diabetes.
    b. The mice lack insulin receptors on their cells.
    c. The mice lack glucagon receptors on their cells.
    d. The mice cannot synthesize glycogen from glucose.

17. How could a hormonal imbalance result in a person who is genetically male but physically female?

Answers to all questions can be found in Appendix E.

Animal Reproduction and Development

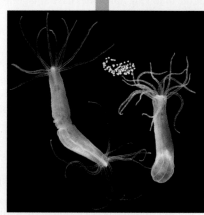

Asexual and Sexual Reproduction

(30.1–30.2)

Some animals can reproduce asexually, but most reproduce by the fusion of egg and sperm.

Principles of Embryonic Development

(30.3–30.8)

A zygote develops into an embryo through a series of carefully regulated processes.

Human Reproduction

(30.9–30.14)

Human males and females have structures that produce, store, and deliver gametes.

Human Development

(30.15–30.18)

A human fetus develops within the uterus for 9 months.

Love Potion Might Save Endangered Frog Species

Captive breeding programs are essential for the conservation of species at risk of extinction. If populations are too small, finding a mate in nature may become more difficult. Also, habitat loss can drastically reduce the survival of offspring born in the wild. By artificially creating stable and favourable breeding conditions, conservationists significantly improve the chances of survival for an endangered species. Captive offspring may be reintroduced to the wild to supplement the native population.

One success story involves the Vancouver Island marmot (*Marmota vancouverensis*), a mascot of the 2010 Winter Olympic Games. Captive breeding programs at the Toronto and Calgary Zoos have produced over 120 litters and more than 440 pups. Reintroduction of these marmots to Vancouver Island has increased the population from 30 to 320 individuals. The success of any reintroduction program, however, hinges on the animals' willingness to reproduce in captivity.

Amphibians are extremely sensitive to environmental contaminants, climate change, and habitat loss. Roughly one-third of British Columbian frog species are at risk; for example, only 300 wild Oregon spotted frogs (*Rana pretiosa*) still live in the province. For many of these species, a captive breeding program may be their only hope of survival.

Unfortunately, many frog species are reluctant to breed in captivity where specific environmental cues required to initiate breeding cycles may not be present. Such cues stimulate the release of gonadotropin-releasing hormone (GnRH) from the hypothalamus, initiating the reproductive cycle. Recreating important environmental cues has been effective for some species. Unfortunately, we do not know what cues every species requires. Instead, hormone treatments are used to artificially stimulate breeding. Injections of human hormones have been used to mimic the effects of luteinizing hormone (LH) and stimulate gamete release with limited success. Though frogs produce LH, human LH is more readily available for this purpose and is effective in some amphibians. However, human hormones may not be fully compatible with all frogs. Furthermore, the stress of captivity affects the frogs' production of reproductive hormones and breeding cycles.

Recently, Dr. Vance Trudeau at the University of Ottawa developed a novel hormone treatment affectionately called Vance's love potion. Unlike traditional hormone injections, this new treatment includes the peptide GnRH and a dopamine antagonist (a molecule that blocks dopamine, a neurotransmitter that inhibits reproduction). The idea behind this treatment is to stimulate the natural release of LH from the pituitary gland. Essentially, the animals are tricked into a breeding cycle, despite the lack of key environmental cues. Both females and males are injected so as to enter the breeding cycle simultaneously. Three to five days after treatment, the animals exhibit courting behaviours and start spawning.

To date, Vance's love potion has worked on every frog species tested. Successful breeding of captive frogs is a major step in ensuring their future. However, if the destruction of their habitats is not stopped, it might not be enough. For more information on species at risk in Canada, visit the online Species at Risk Public Registry.

We begin this chapter with a brief introduction to the diverse ways that animals reproduce, followed by a close look at the processes of fertilization and embryonic development in vertebrates. In the second half of the chapter, we discuss the reproductive system and embryonic development of our own species.

Asexual and Sexual Reproduction

30.1 Asexual reproduction results in the generation of genetically identical offspring

Individual animals have a finite lifespan. A species transcends this limit only by **reproduction**, the creation of new individuals from existing ones. Animals reproduce in a great variety of ways, but there are two principal modes: asexual and sexual.

Asexual reproduction (reproduction without sex) is the creation of genetically identical offspring by a lone parent. Because asexual reproduction proceeds without the fusion of egg and sperm, the resulting offspring are genetic copies of the one parent.

Several types of asexual reproduction are found among animals. Many invertebrates, such as the hydra in **Figure 30.1A**, reproduce asexually by **budding**, a process by which new individuals form outgrowths of existing ones. The sea anemone in the centre of **Figure 30.1B** is undergoing **fission**, the separation of a parent into two or more individuals of about equal size. Asexual reproduction can also result from the process of **fragmentation**, the breaking of the parent body into several pieces, followed by **regeneration**, the regrowth of lost body parts.

In sea stars (starfish) of the genus *Linckia*, for example, a whole new individual can develop from a broken-off arm plus a bit of the central body. Thus, a single animal with five arms, if broken apart, could potentially give rise to five offspring via asexual reproduction in a matter of weeks. In some species of sea sponges, if a single sponge is pushed through a wire mesh, each of the resulting clumps of cells can regrow into a new sponge. (Besides the natural means of asexual reproduction discussed here, many species have been the target of artificial asexual reproduction; see the discussion of cloning in Chapter 11.)

▲ **Figure 30.1A** Asexual reproduction via budding in a hydra

▲ **Figure 30.1B** Asexual reproduction of a sea anemone (*Anthopleura elegantissima*) by fission

In nature, asexual reproduction has several potential advantages. For one, it allows animals that do not move from place to place or that live in isolation to produce offspring without finding mates. Another advantage is that it enables an animal to produce many offspring quickly; no time or energy is lost in production of eggs and sperm or in mating. Asexual reproduction perpetuates a particular genotype faithfully, precisely, and rapidly. Therefore, it can be an effective way for animals that are genetically well suited to an environment to quickly expand their populations and exploit available resources.

A potential disadvantage of asexual reproduction is that it produces genetically uniform populations. Genetically similar individuals may thrive in one particular environment, but if the environment changes and becomes less favourable, all individuals may be affected equally, and the entire population may die out.

 What kinds of environments would likely be advantageous to asexually reproducing organisms? Why?

● Relatively unchanging environments favour asexual reproduction because well-suited individuals can rapidly multiply and use available resources.

30.2 Sexual reproduction results in the generation of genetically unique offspring

Sexual reproduction is the creation of offspring through the process of **fertilization**, the fusion of two haploid (*n*) sex cells, or **gametes**, to form a diploid (2*n*) **zygote** (fertilized egg). (Recall from Chapter 8 that *n* refers to the haploid number of chromosomes and 2*n* refers to the diploid number; for humans, $n = 23$ and $2n = 46$.) The male gamete, the **sperm**, is a relatively small cell that moves by means of a flagellum. The female gamete, the **egg**, is a much larger cell that is not self-propelled. The zygote—and the new individual it develops into—contains a unique combination of genes inherited from the parents via the egg and sperm.

Most animals reproduce mainly or exclusively by sexual reproduction, which increases genetic variability among offspring. Although a few species, such as *Daphnia*, can switch between asexual and sexual reproduction, depending on environmental factors. As we discussed in Modules 8.16 and 8.18, meiosis and random fertilization can generate enormous genetic variation. And such variation is the raw material of evolution by natural selection. The variability produced by the reshuffling of genes in sexual reproduction may provide greater adaptability to changing environments. According to this hypothesis, when an environment changes suddenly or

Eggs

Two offspring arising by fission

▲ **Figure 30.2A** Asexual (left) and sexual (right) reproduction in the starlet sea anemone (*Nematostella vectensis*)

Egg

▲ **Figure 30.2C** Frogs in an embrace that triggers the release of eggs and sperm (the sperm are too small to be seen)

drastically, more offspring will survive and reproduce if they aren't all genetically very similar.

Animals that can reproduce both asexually and sexually benefit from both modes. In **Figure 30.2A**, you can see two sea anemones of the same species; the one on the left is reproducing asexually (via fission) while the one on the right is releasing eggs. Many other marine invertebrates can also reproduce by both modes. Why would such dual reproductive capabilities be advantageous to an organism? From several well-studied cases, it is known that certain animals reproduce asexually when there is ample food and when water temperatures are favourable for rapid growth and development. Asexual reproduction usually continues until cold temperatures signal the approach of winter or until the food supply dwindles or the habitat starts to dry up. At that point, the animals switch to a sexual reproduction mode, resulting in a generation of genetically varied individuals with better potential to adapt to the changing conditions.

Although sexual reproduction has advantages, it presents a problem for nonmobile animals and for those that live solitary lives: how to find a mate. One solution that has evolved is **hermaphroditism**, in which each individual has both female and male reproductive systems. (The term comes from the Greek myth in which Hermaphroditus, the son of the gods Hermes and Aphrodite, fused with a woman to form one

individual of both sexes.) Although some hermaphrodites, such as tapeworms, can fertilize their own eggs, most must mate with another member of the same species. For hermaphrodites, every individual encountered is a potential mate. When hermaphrodites mate (for example, the two earthworms in **Figure 30.2B**), each animal serves as both male and female, donating and receiving sperm. Mating can therefore result in twice as many offspring than if only one individual's eggs were fertilized.

The mechanics of fertilization play an important part in sexual reproduction. Many aquatic invertebrates and most fishes and amphibians exhibit **external fertilization**: The parents discharge their gametes into the water, where fertilization then occurs, often without the male and female even making physical contact. Timing is crucial because the eggs and sperm must be available for fertilization at the same time. For many species—certain clams that live in freshwater rivers and lakes, for instance—environmental cues such as temperature and day length cause a whole population to release gametes all at once. Males or females may also emit a chemical signal (a pheromone) as they release their gametes. The signal triggers gamete release in members of the opposite sex. Most fishes and amphibians with external fertilization have specific courtship rituals that trigger simultaneous gamete release in the same vicinity by the female and male. An example of such a mating ritual is the clasping of a female frog by a male (**Figure 30.2C**).

In contrast to external fertilization, **internal fertilization** occurs when sperm are deposited in or close to the female reproductive tract and gametes unite within the tract. Nearly all terrestrial animals exhibit internal fertilization, which is an adaptation that enables sperm to reach an egg despite a dry external environment. Internal fertilization usually requires **copulation**, or sexual intercourse. It also requires complex reproductive systems, including organs for gamete storage and transport and organs that facilitate copulation. We next consider the development of an embryo (after fertilization).

? **In terms of genetic makeup, what is the most important difference between the outcome of sexual reproduction and that of asexual reproduction?**

● The offspring of sexual reproduction are genetically diverse, whereas the offspring of asexual reproduction are genetically identical.

▲ **Figure 30.2B** Hermaphroditic earthworms mating

Principles of Embryonic Development

30.3 Fertilization results in a zygote and triggers embryonic development

In the next six modules, we examine the results of reproduction: the formation and development of an embryo. Embryonic development begins with fertilization, the union of a sperm and an egg to form a diploid zygote. Fertilization combines haploid sets of chromosomes from two individuals and also activates the egg by triggering metabolic changes that start embryonic development.

The Properties of Sperm Cells   **Figure 30.3A** is a micrograph of an unfertilized human egg that is surrounded by sperm. Among all of these sperm, only one will enter and fertilize the egg. All the other sperm—the ones shown here and millions more that were ejaculated with them—will die. The one sperm that penetrates the egg adds its unique set of genes to those of the egg and contributes to the next generation.

Figure 30.3B illustrates the structure of a mature mammalian sperm cell, a clear case of form fitting function. The sperm's streamlined shape is an adaptation for swimming through fluids in the vagina, uterus, and oviduct of the female. Its head contains a haploid nucleus and is tipped with a vesicle, the **acrosome**, which lies just inside the plasma membrane. The acrosome contains enzymes that help the sperm penetrate the egg. The middle piece of the sperm contains mitochondria. The sperm absorbs high-energy nutrients, especially the sugar fructose, from the semen. Thus fuelled, its mitochondria provide ATP for movement of the tail, which is actually a flagellum. By the time a sperm has reached the egg, it has consumed much of the energy available to it. But

▲ **Figure 30.3B** The structure of a mammalian sperm cell

a successful sperm will have enough energy left to penetrate the egg and deposit its nucleus in the egg's cytoplasm.

The Process of Fertilization   **Figure 30.3C** illustrates the sequence of events in fertilization. This diagram is based on fertilization in sea urchins (phylum Echinodermata—see Module 20.14), on which a great deal of research has been done. Similar processes occur in other animals, including humans. The diagram traces one sperm through the successive activities of fertilization. Notice that to reach the egg nucleus, the sperm nucleus must pass through three barriers: the egg's jelly coat (yellow), a middle region of glycoproteins called the vitelline layer (pink), and the egg cell's plasma membrane (brown).

Let's follow the steps shown in the figure. ❶ The contact of a sperm with the jelly coat of the egg triggers the release of

▶ **Figure 30.3A** A mammalian egg cell surrounded by sperm

Colourized SEM 1000×

a cloud of enzyme molecules by exocytosis (see Module 5.8) from the sperm's acrosome. ❷ The enzyme molecules digest a tunnel through the jelly. When the sperm head reaches the vitelline layer, ❸ species-specific protein molecules on its surface bind with specific receptor proteins on the vitelline layer. The binding between these proteins ensures that sperm of other species cannot fertilize the egg. This specificity is especially important when fertilization is external because the sperm of other species may be present in the water. After the specific binding occurs, the sperm proceeds through the vitelline layer, and ❹ the sperm's plasma membrane fuses with that of the egg. Fusion of the two membranes ❺ makes it possible for the sperm nucleus to enter the egg.

Fusion of the sperm and egg plasma membranes triggers a number of important changes in the egg. Two such changes prevent other sperm from entering the egg. About one second after the membranes fuse, the entire egg plasma membrane becomes impenetrable to other sperm cells. Shortly thereafter, ❻ the vitelline layer hardens and separates from the plasma membrane. The space quickly fills with water, and the vitelline layer becomes impenetrable to sperm. If these events did not occur

and an egg were fertilized by more than one sperm, the resulting zygote nucleus would contain too many chromosomes, and the zygote could not develop normally.

❼ About 20 minutes after the sea urchin sperm nucleus enters the egg, the sperm and egg nuclei fuse. Gearing up for the enormous growth and development that will soon follow, DNA synthesis and cellular respiration begin. The first cell division occurs after about 90 minutes, marking the end of the fertilization stage.

Note that the sperm provided chromosomes to the zygote, but little else. The zygote's cytoplasm and various organelles were all provided by the mother through the egg. In the next module, we begin to trace the development of the zygote into a new animal.

> **?** Why is the vitelline layer particularly important among aquatic animals that use external fertilization?

● Protein receptors on the vitelline layer match with species-specific proteins on the sperm, ensuring that sperm of a different species will not fertilize the egg.

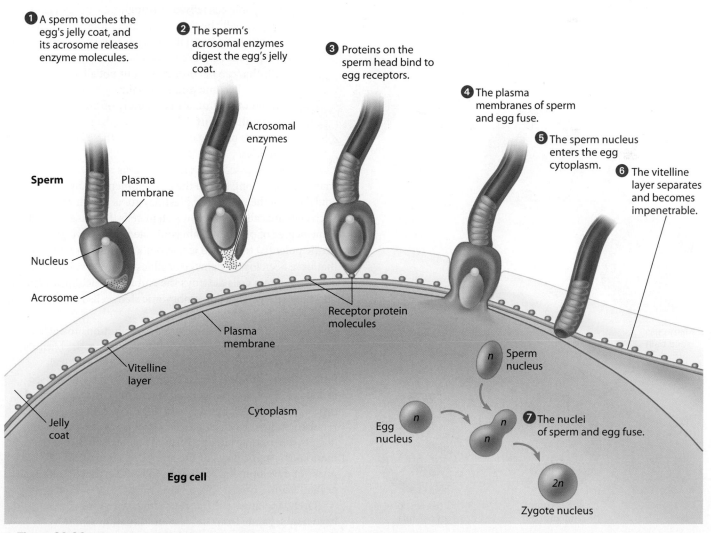

❶ A sperm touches the egg's jelly coat, and its acrosome releases enzyme molecules.

❷ The sperm's acrosomal enzymes digest the egg's jelly coat.

❸ Proteins on the sperm head bind to egg receptors.

❹ The plasma membranes of sperm and egg fuse.

❺ The sperm nucleus enters the egg cytoplasm.

❻ The vitelline layer separates and becomes impenetrable.

Acrosomal enzymes

Sperm Plasma membrane

Nucleus

Acrosome

Receptor protein molecules

Plasma membrane

Vitelline layer

Jelly coat

Cytoplasm

Egg cell

n Sperm nucleus

n Egg nucleus

n n ❼ The nuclei of sperm and egg fuse.

2n Zygote nucleus

▲ **Figure 30.3C** The process of fertilization in a sea urchin

30.4 Cleavage produces a ball of cells from the zygote

Animals consist of many thousands, millions, even trillions of cells that are precisely organized into complex tissues and organs. The transformation from a zygote to this multicellular state is truly phenomenal. Order and precision are required at every step, and both are clearly displayed in the first two major phases of embryonic development: cleavage and gastrulation.

Cleavage is a rapid succession of cell divisions that produces a ball of cells—a multicellular embryo—from the zygote. Nutrients stored in the egg nourish the dividing cells. DNA replication, mitosis, and cytokinesis occur rapidly, but gene transcription virtually shuts down and few new proteins are synthesized. The embryo does not enlarge significantly; instead, cleavage partitions the cytoplasm of the one-celled zygote into many smaller cells, each with its own nucleus.

Figure 30.4 illustrates cleavage in a sea urchin. (A similar process occurs in humans.) As the first three steps show, the number of cells doubles with each cleavage division. In a sea urchin, a doubling occurs about every 20 minutes, and the whole cleavage process takes about three hours to produce a solid ball of cells. Notice that as cleavage proceeds, the total size of the ball remains constant even as the number of cells double. As a result, each cell in the ball is much smaller than the original cell that formed the zygote. As cleavage continues, a fluid-filled cavity called the **blastocoel** forms in the centre of the embryo. At the completion of cleavage, the embryo, now a hollow ball of cells, is called a **blastula**.

It is important to discuss the concept of *potency* when discussing embryonic development. A cell's **potency** is a description of its ability to change, or differentiate, into another cell type. The cells of early embryos have varying potentials to become other cell types. The zygote can, and ultimately will, give rise to every cell in the body. As such, the zygote is **totipotent**.

As the embryonic cells divide throughout early development, they gradually become more and more specialized. This limits the potential cell types that they can become. **Pluripotent** cells are descendants of the totipotent cells that can become most, but not all, cell types. As cells become more specialized, being able to differentiate into a small family of similar cells, they are **multipotent**. We will see in the next module that cells of the gastrula fall into these latter two categories.

As discussed in Chapter 11, cells removed from a human blastocyst long before the development of any organs (the equivalent of the sea urchin blastula) are useful in research. Such cells are called embryonic stem cells. Because they retain some degree of potency, embryonic stem cells have great therapeutic potential to replace just about any kind of mature cells that have been lost to damage or illness. But harvesting the embryonic stem cells destroys the embryo, which raises ethical questions. Research using embryonic stem cells remains one of the hottest areas of biological study.

Cleavage makes two important contributions to early development. It creates a multicellular embryo, the blastula, from a single-celled zygote and partitions the multicellular embryo into developmental regions. As we discussed in Module 11.9, a variety of cell signalling cascades control gene expression during early development. During cleavage, regulatory chemicals become localized in particular groups of cells, where they later activate the genes that direct the formation of specific parts of the animal. Gastrulation, the next phase of development, further refines the embryo's cellular organization.

Rarely, and apparently at random, a cell in the early embryo may separate from the rest and function as if it were the original zygote; the result is the development of identical

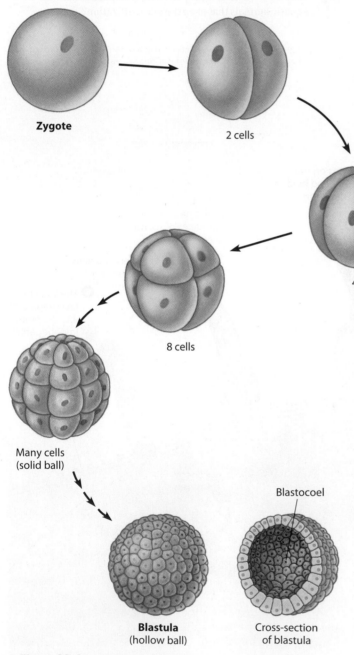

Zygote

2 cells

4 cells

8 cells

Many cells (solid ball)

Blastocoel

Blastula (hollow ball)

Cross-section of blastula

▲ **Figure 30.4** Cleavage in a sea urchin

(monozygotic) twins. (Nonidentical, or dizygotic, twins result from a completely different mechanism: Two eggs are fertilized separately, producing two genetically unique zygotes that develop in the uterus simultaneously.) In exceedingly rare cases, the separation and resetting that produce identical twins can occur twice, producing identical triplets.

? **How does the reduction of cell size during cleavage increase oxygen supply to the cells' mitochondria?** (*Hint:* Review Module 4.2.)

● Smaller cells have a greater plasma membrane surface area relative to cellular volume, and this facilitates diffusion of oxygen from the environment to the cell's cytoplasm.

30.5 Gastrulation produces a three-layered embryo

After cleavage, the rate of cell division slows dramatically. Groups of cells then undergo **gastrulation**, the second major phase of embryonic development. During gastrulation, cells take up specific locations that will allow later formation of all the organs and tissues. As gastrulation proceeds, the embryo is organized into a three-layered stage called a **gastrula**.

The three layers produced by gastrulation are embryonic tissues called **ectoderm**, **endoderm**, and **mesoderm**. The ectoderm forms the outer layer (skin) of the gastrula. The endoderm forms an embryonic digestive tract. And the mesoderm lies between the ectoderm and endoderm. Eventually, these three cell layers develop into all the parts of the adult animal. For instance, our nervous system and the outer layer (epidermis) of our skin come from ectoderm; the innermost lining of our digestive tract arises from endoderm; and most other organs and tissues, such as the kidney, heart, muscles, and the inner layer of our skin (dermis), develop from mesoderm. Table 30.5 lists the major organs and tissues that arise in most vertebrates from the three main embryonic tissue layers.

The mechanics of gastrulation vary somewhat, depending on the species and the amount of nutritional yolk. We have chosen the frog, a vertebrate that has long been a favourite of researchers, to demonstrate how gastrulation produces three cell layers. The top of **Figure 30.5** shows the frog blastula, formed by cleavage (as discussed in the previous module). The frog blastula is a partially hollow ball of unequally sized cells. The cells toward one end, called the animal pole, are smaller than those near the opposite end, the vegetal pole. The three colours on the blastula in the figure indicate regions of cells that will give rise to the primary cell layers in the gastrula at the bottom of the figure:

TABLE 30.5	DERIVATIVES OF THE THREE EMBRYONIC TISSUE LAYERS
Embryonic Layer	**Organs and Tissues in the Adult**
Ectoderm	Epidermis of skin; epithelial lining of mouth and rectum; sense receptors in epidermis; cornea and lens of eye; nervous system
Endoderm	Epithelial lining of digestive tract (except mouth and rectum); epithelial lining of respiratory system; liver; pancreas; thyroid; parathyroids; thymus; lining of urethra, urinary bladder, and reproductive system
Mesoderm	Skeletal system; muscular system; circulatory system; excretory system; reproductive system (except gamete-forming cells); dermis of skin; lining of body cavity

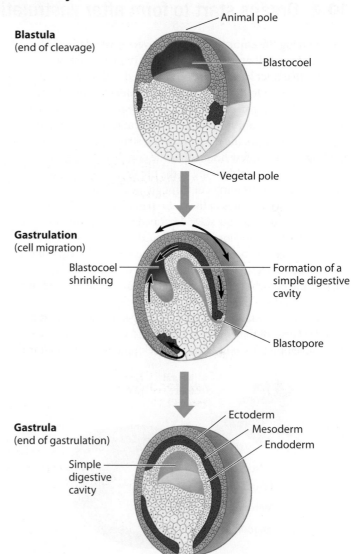

▲ **Figure 30.5** Development of the frog gastrula

ectoderm (blue), endoderm (yellow), and mesoderm (red). (Notice that each layer may be more than one cell thick.)

During gastrulation (shown in the centre of Figure 30.5), cells migrate to new positions that will form the three layers. Gastrulation begins when a small groove, called the blastopore, appears on one side of the blastula. In the blastopore, cells of the future endoderm (yellow) move inward from the surface and fold over to produce a simple digestive cavity. Meanwhile, the cells that will form ectoderm (blue) spread downward over more of the surface of the embryo, and the cells that will form mesoderm (red) begin to spread into a thin layer inside the embryo, forming a middle layer between the other two.

As shown at the bottom of the figure, gastrulation is completed when cell migration has resulted in a three-layered embryo. Ectoderm covers most of the surface. Mesoderm forms a layer between the ectoderm and the endoderm.

Although gastrulation differs in detail from one animal group to another, the process is driven by the same general mechanisms in all species. The timing of these events also varies with the species. In many frogs, for example, cleavage and gastrulation together take about 15–20 hours.

> **?** The first two phases of embryonic development are _____, which forms the blastula, followed by _____, which forms the _____.

30.6 Organs start to form after gastrulation

In organizing the embryo into three layers, gastrulation sets the stage for the shaping of an animal. After gastrulation, the digestive tract has already been formed. All other organ systems have yet to develop. Once the ectoderm, endoderm, and mesoderm form, cells in each layer begin to differentiate into tissues and embryonic organs. The cutaway drawing in **Figure 30.6A** shows the developmental structures that appear in a frog embryo a few hours after the completion of gastrulation. The orientation drawing at the upper left of the figure indicates a corresponding cut through an adult frog.

We see two structures in the embryo in Figure 30.6A that were not present at the gastrula stage described in the last module. An organ called the notochord has developed in the mesoderm, and a structure that will become the hollow nerve cord is beginning to form in the ectoderm (in the region that is coloured green). Recall that the notochord and the dorsal, hollow nerve cord are two of the hallmarks of the chordates (see Module 20.15).

Made of a substance similar to cartilage, the **notochord** extends for most of the embryo's length and provides support for other developing tissues. Later in development, the notochord will function as a core around which mesodermal cells gather and form the spine of vertebrates.

The area shown in green in the cutaway drawing of Figure 30.6A is a thickened region of ectoderm called the neural plate. From it arises a pair of pronounced ectodermal ridges, called neural folds, visible in both the drawing and the micrograph below it. If you now look at the series of diagrams in **Figure 30.6B**, you will see what happens as the neural folds and neural plate develop further. The neural plate rolls up and forms a tube, which sinks beneath the surface of the embryo and is covered by an outer layer of ectoderm. If you look carefully at the figure, you will see that cells of the ectoderm fold inward by changing shape, first elongating and then becoming wedge-shaped. The result is a tube of ectoderm—the **neural tube**—which is destined to become the brain and spinal cord.

Figure 30.6C shows a later frog embryo (about 12 hours older than the one in Figure 30.6A), in which the neural tube

▲ **Figure 30.6A** The beginning of organ development in a frog: the notochord, neural folds, and neural plate

Neural fold   Neural plate

Notochord
Ectoderm
Mesoderm
Endoderm

Neural folds

13.5×

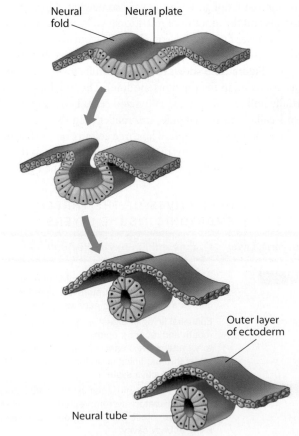

Neural fold   Neural plate

Outer layer of ectoderm

Neural tube

▲ **Figure 30.6B** Formation of the neural tube

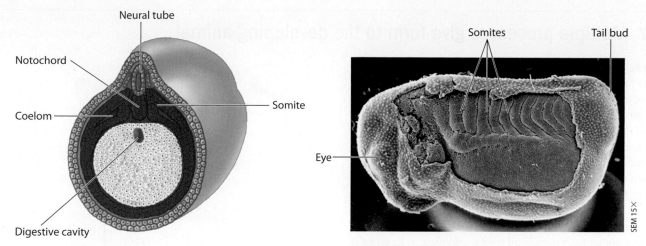

▲ Figure 30.6C An embryo with completed neural tube, somites, and coelom

has formed. Notice in the drawing that the neural tube lies directly above the notochord. The relative positions of the neural tube, notochord, and digestive cavity give us a preview of the basic body plan of a frog. The spinal cord will lie within extensions of the dorsal (upper) surface of the spine (which will replace the notochord), and the digestive tract will be ventral to (beneath) the backbone. We see this same arrangement of organs in all vertebrates.

The importance of these processes is underscored by human birth defects that result from improper signalling between embryonic tissues. For example, spina bifida is a condition that results from the failure of the tube of ectoderm cells to close properly and form the spine during the first month of fetal development. Infants born with spina bifida often have permanent nerve damage that results in paralysis of the lower limbs.

Besides the appearance of the neural tube and digestive cavity, Figure 30.6C shows several other fundamental changes in the frog embryo. In the micrograph, which is a side view, you can see that the embryo is more elongated than the one in Figure 30.6A. You can also see the beginnings of an eye and a tail (called the tail bud). Part of the ectoderm has been removed to reveal a series of internal ridges called somites. The **somites** are blocks of mesoderm that will give rise to segmental structures (constructed of repeating units), such as the vertebrae and associated muscles of the spine. In the cross-sectional drawing, notice that the mesoderm next to the somites is developing a hollow space—the body cavity, or **coelom**. Segmented body parts and a coelom are basic features of all chordates.

In this and the previous two modules, we have observed the sequence of changes that occur as an animal begins to take shape. The same three phases occur in nearly all animals. To summarize, the three key phases in embryonic development are as follows:

- cleavage, which creates a multicellular blastula from a zygote
- gastrulation, which organizes the embryo into a gastrula with three distinct layers
- organ formation, which generates embryonic organs from the three embryonic tissue layers

If we followed a frog's development beyond the stage represented in Figure 30.6C, within a few hours we would be able to monitor muscular responses and a heartbeat and see a set of gills with blood circulating in them. A long tail fin would grow from the tail bud. The timing of the later stages in frog development varies enormously; but, in many species, by five to eight days after development begins, we would see all the body tissues and organs of a tadpole develop from cells of the ectoderm, mesoderm, and endoderm. Eventually, the structures of the tadpole (**Figure 30.6D**) would transform into the tissues and organs of an adult frog.

Watching embryos develop helps us appreciate the enormous changes that occur as one tiny cell, the zygote, gives rise to a highly structured, many-celled animal. Your own body, for instance, is a complex organization of some 60 trillion cells, all of which arose from a zygote smaller than the period at the end of this sentence. Discovering how this incredibly intricate arrangement is achieved is one of biology's greatest challenges. Through research that combines the experimental manipulation of embryos with cell biology and molecular genetics, developmental biologists have begun to work out the mechanisms that underlie development. We examine several of these mechanisms in the next module.

 What is the embryonic basis for the dorsal, hollow nerve cord that is common to all members of our phylum?

● The neural tube, which becomes the brain and spinal cord, develops from a dorsal ectodermal plate that folds to form an interior tube.

▲ Figure 30.6D A tadpole with some early adult features

30.7 Multiple processes give form to the developing animal

The development of an animal embryo depends on several cellular processes. For example, as you learned in the last module, changes in cell shape help to form the neural tube (see Figure 30.6B).

Most developmental processes depend on signals passed between neighbouring cells and cell layers, telling embryonic cells precisely what to do and when to do it. The mechanism by which one group of cells influences the development of an adjacent group of cells is called **induction**. Induction may be mediated by diffusible signals or, if the cells are in direct contact, by cell-surface interactions. Induction plays a major role in the early development of virtually all tissues and organs. Its effect is to switch on or off a set of genes whose expression makes the receiving cells differentiate into a specific tissue. Many inductions involve a sequence of inductive steps from different surrounding tissues that progressively determine the fate of cells. The neural tube, for example, forms only after an inductive signal is received from the underlying notochord. In the developing animal, a sequence of inductive signals leads to increasingly greater specialization of cells as organs begin to take shape.

Cell migration is also essential in development. For example, during gastrulation, cells "crawl" within the embryo by extending and contracting cellular protrusions, similar to the pseudopodia of amoeboid cells. Migrating cells may follow inductive chemical trails secreted by cells near their specific destination. Once a migrating cell reaches its destination, surface proteins enable it to recognize similar cells. The cells join together and secrete glycoproteins that glue them in place. Finally, they differentiate, taking on the characteristics of a particular tissue.

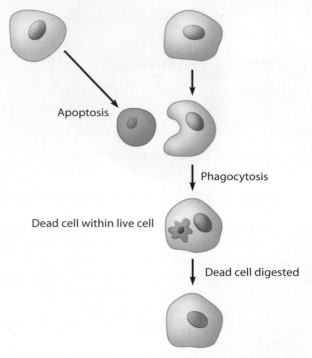

▲ **Figure 30.7B** Apoptosis and phagocytosis at the cellular level

Another important developmental process is apoptosis, the timely and tidy suicide of cells. Apoptosis is a type of programmed cell death. Animal cells make proteins that have the ability, when activated, to kill the cell that produces them. In humans, the timely death of specific cells in developing hands and feet creates the spaces between fingers and toes **(Figure 30.7A)**. In **Figure 30.7B**, the cell on the left shrinks and dies because suicide proteins have been activated. Meanwhile, signals from the dying cell make an adjacent cell phagocytic. This cell engulfs and digests the dead cell, keeping the embryo free of harmful debris.

> **?** Induction often involves signal transduction pathways. What do you suppose their role is? (You may wish to review Module 11.10.)

▲ **Figure 30.7A** Apoptosis in a developing human hand

● They mediate between the chemical signal received by the cell and the resulting changes in gene expression and other responses by the cell.

 EVOLUTION CONNECTION

30.8 Pattern formation during embryonic development is controlled by ancient genes

So far, we have discussed the formation of individual organs. What directs the formation of large body features, such as the limbs? The shaping of an animal's major parts involves **pattern formation**, the emergence of a body form with specialized organs and tissues in the right places. Research indicates that master control genes (see Modules 11.9 and 14.14) respond to chemical signals that tell a cell where it is relative to other cells in the embryo. These positional signals determine which master control genes will be expressed and, consequently, which body parts will form. Research has shown that such control genes arose early in the evolution of animals and so play similar roles across diverse animal groups. The field of biology that studies the evolution of developmental processes is called evo-devo.

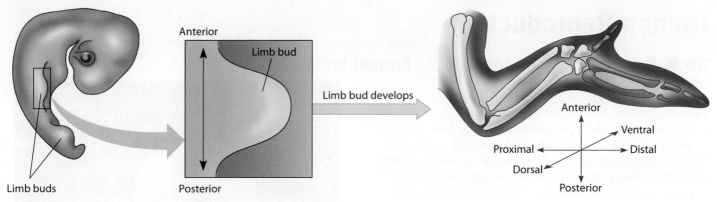

▲ Figure 30.8A The normal development of a wing

Vertebrate limbs, such as bird wings, begin as embryonic structures called limb buds **(Figure 30.8A)**. Each component of a chick wing, such as a specific bone or muscle, develops with a precise location and orientation relative to three axes: the proximal-distal axis (the "shoulder-to-fingertip" axis), the anterior-posterior axis (the "thumb-to-little finger" axis), and the dorsal-ventral axis (the "knuckle-to-palm" axis). The embryonic cells within a limb bud respond to positional information indicating location along these three axes. Only with this information will the cell's genes direct the synthesis of the proteins needed for normal differentiation in that cell's specific location.

Among the most exciting biological discoveries in recent years is that a class of similar genes—**homeotic genes**—help to direct embryonic pattern formation in a wide variety of organisms. Researchers studying homeotic genes in fruit flies found a common structural feature: Every homeotic gene they looked at contained a common sequence of 180 nucleotides. Very similar sequences have since been found in virtually every eukaryotic organism examined so far, including yeasts, plants, and humans—and even some prokaryotes. These nucleotide sequences are called **homeoboxes**, and each is translated into a segment (60 amino acids long) of the protein product of the homeotic gene. The homeobox polypeptide segment binds to specific sequences in DNA, enabling homeotic proteins that contain it to turn groups of genes on or off during development.

Figure 30.8B highlights some striking similarities in the chromosomal locations and the developmental roles of some homeobox-containing homeotic genes in two quite different animals. The figure shows portions of chromosomes that carry homeotic genes in the fruit fly and the mouse. The coloured boxes represent homeotic genes that are very similar in flies and mice. Notice that the order of genes on the fly chromosome is the same as on the four mouse chromosomes and that the gene order on the chromosomes corresponds to analogous body regions in both animals. These similarities suggest that the original version of these homeotic genes arose very early in the history of life and that the genes have remained remarkably unchanged for eons of animal evolution. By their presence in such diverse creatures, homeotic genes illustrate one of the central themes of biology: unity in diversity because of shared evolutionary history.

A major goal of developmental research is to learn how the one-dimensional information encoded in the nucleotide sequence of a zygote's DNA directs the development of the three-dimensional form of an animal. Pattern formation requires cells to receive and interpret environmental cues that vary from one location to another. These cues, acting together along three axes, tell cells where they are in the three-dimensional realm of a developing organ. In Modules 30.15 and 30.16, we will see the results of this process as we watch an individual of our own species take shape.

First we will look at the principles of human reproduction.

? How is pattern formation already apparent in the limb bud?

● The major axes of the animal—anterior-posterior, dorsal-ventral, and proximal-distal—are already set at the gastrula stage.

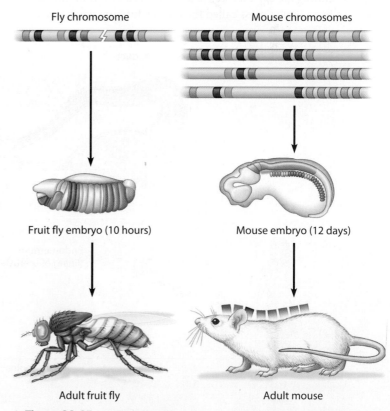

▲ Figure 30.8B Comparison of fruit fly and mouse homeotic genes

Human Reproduction

30.9 Reproductive anatomy of the human female

Although we tend to focus on the anatomical differences between the human male and female reproductive systems, there are also some important similarities. Both sexes have a pair of **gonads**, the organs that produce gametes. Also, both sexes have ducts that store and deliver gametes as well as structures that facilitate copulation. In this and the next module, we examine the anatomical features of the human reproductive system, beginning with female anatomy.

A woman's gonads, her **ovaries**, are each about 2.5 cm long, with a bumpy surface (**Figure 30.9A**). The bumps are **follicles**, each consisting of one or more layers of cells that surround, nourish, and protect a single developing egg cell. In addition to producing egg cells, the ovaries produce hormones (see Table 29.3). Specifically, the follicle cells produce the female sex hormone estrogen. (In this chapter, we use the word *estrogen* to refer collectively to several closely related chemicals that affect the body similarly.)

A female is born with 1–2 million follicles, but only several hundred will release egg cells during her reproductive years. Starting at puberty, one follicle (or, rarely, more than one, as is the case with fraternal multiples) matures and releases an immature egg cell about every 28 days. This monthly cycle continues until a female reaches menopause, which usually occurs around age 50. An immature egg cell is ejected from the follicle in a process called **ovulation**, shown in **Figure 30.9B**.

After ovulation, the follicular tissue that had been surrounding the egg that was just ejected grows within the ovary to form a solid mass called the **corpus luteum**; you can see

▲ **Figure 30.9B** Ovulation

one in the ovary on the left in Figure 30.9A. The corpus luteum secretes additional estrogen as well as progesterone, a hormone that helps to maintain the uterine lining during pregnancy. If the released egg is not fertilized, the corpus luteum degenerates, and a new follicle matures during the next cycle. We discuss ovulation and female hormonal cycles further in later modules.

Notice in Figure 30.9A that each ovary lies next to the opening of an **oviduct**, also called a fallopian tube. The oviduct opening resembles a funnel fringed with fingerlike projections. The projections touch the surface of the ovary, but the

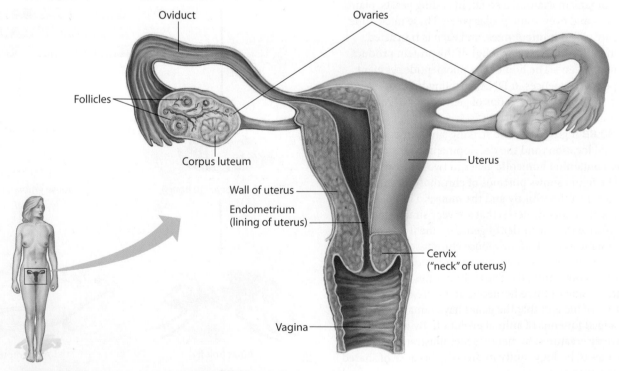

▲ **Figure 30.9A** Front view of female reproductive anatomy (upper portion)

ovary is actually separated from the opening of the oviduct by a tiny space in the abdominal cavity. When ovulation occurs, the egg cell passes across the space and into the oviduct, where cilia sweep it toward the uterus. If sperm are present, fertilization may occur in the upper part of the oviduct. The resulting zygote starts to divide, thus becoming an embryo, as it moves along within the oviduct.

The **uterus**, also known as the womb, is the actual site of pregnancy. The uterus is only about 7.5 cm long in a woman who has never been pregnant, but during pregnancy it expands considerably as the baby develops. The uterus has a thick muscular wall, and its inner lining, the **endometrium**, is richly supplied with blood vessels. An embryo implants in the endometrium, and development is completed there. The term **embryo** is used for the stage in development from the first division of the zygote until most organs have appeared, about the ninth week in humans. From the ninth week until birth, a developing human is called a **fetus**.

The uterus is the normal site of pregnancy. However, in about 1% of pregnancies, the embryo implants somewhere else, resulting in an **ectopic pregnancy**. Most ectopic pregnancies occur in the oviduct and are called tubal pregnancies. An ectopic pregnancy is a serious medical emergency that requires surgical intervention; otherwise, it can rupture surrounding tissues, causing severe bleeding and even death of the mother.

The narrow neck at the bottom of the uterus is the **cervix**, which opens into the vagina. It is recommended that women have a yearly Pap test in which cells are removed from around the cervix and examined under a microscope for signs of cervical cancer. Regular Pap smears greatly increase the chances of detecting cervical cancer early and therefore treating it successfully. The cervix opens to the **vagina**, a thin-walled, but strong, muscular chamber that serves as the birth canal through which the baby is born. The vagina is also the repository for sperm during sexual intercourse. Glands near the vaginal opening secrete mucus during sexual arousal, lubricating the vagina and facilitating intercourse.

You can see more features of female reproductive anatomy in **Figure 30.9C**, a side view. **Vulva** is the collective term for the external female genitalia. Notice that the vagina opens to the outside just behind the opening of the urethra, the tube through which urine is excreted. A pair of slender skin folds, the **labia minora**, border the openings, and a pair of thick, fatty ridges, the **labia majora**, protect the vaginal opening. Until sexual intercourse or vigorous physical activity ruptures it, a thin piece of tissue called the hymen partly covers the vaginal opening.

Several female reproductive structures are important in sexual arousal, and stimulation of them can produce highly pleasurable sensations. The vagina, labia minora, and a small erectile organ called the **clitoris** all engorge with blood and enlarge during sexual activity. The clitoris of the female is homologous to the male penis, consisting of a short shaft supporting a rounded **glans**, or head, covered by a small hood of skin called the **prepuce**. In Figure 30.9C, blue highlights the spongy erectile tissue within the clitoris that fills with blood during arousal. The clitoris, especially the glans, has an enormous number of nerve endings and is very sensitive to touch. Keep in mind the details of female reproductive anatomy as you read the next module, and you will notice many similarities in the human male.

? Where does fertilization occur? In which organ does the fetus develop?

● The oviduct; the uterus

▲ **Figure 30.9C** Side view of female reproductive anatomy (with nonreproductive structures in italic)

30.10 Reproductive anatomy of the human male

Figures 30.10A and **30.10B** present front and side views of the male reproductive system. The male gonads, or **testes** (singular, *testis*), are each housed outside the abdominal cavity in a sac called the **scrotum**. In humans, the testes are often referred to as testicles.

Now let's track the path of sperm from one of the testes out of the male's body. From each testis, where sperm production begins, sperm pass into a coiled tube called the **epididymis**,

which stores the sperm while they continue to develop. Sperm leave the epididymis during **ejaculation**, the expulsion of sperm-containing fluid from the penis. At that time, muscular contractions propel the sperm from the epididymis through another duct called the **vas deferens**. The vas deferens (which is the target of a vasectomy; see Module 30.14) passes upward into the abdomen and loops around the urinary bladder. Next to the bladder, the vas deferens joins a short duct from a gland, the seminal vesicle. The two ducts unite to form a short **ejaculatory duct**, which joins its counterpart conveying sperm from the other testis. Each ejaculatory duct empties into the urethra, which conveys both urine and sperm out through the penis, although not at the same time. Thus, unlike the female, the male has a direct connection between the reproductive and urinary systems.

In addition to the testes and ducts, the reproductive system of human males contains three sets of glands: the seminal vesicles, the prostate gland, and the bulbourethral glands. The two **seminal vesicles** secrete a thick fluid that contains fructose, which provides most of the energy used by the sperm as they propel themselves through the female reproductive tract. The **prostate gland** secretes a thin fluid that further nourishes the sperm. The two **bulbourethral glands** secrete a clear, alkaline mucus.

Together, the sperm and the glandular secretions make up **semen**, the fluid ejaculated from the penis during **orgasm**, a series of rhythmic, involuntary contractions of the reproductive structures. About 2–5 mL of semen are discharged during a typical ejaculation. About 95% of the fluid consists

▲ **Figure 30.10A** Front view of male reproductive anatomy (with nonreproductive structures in italic)

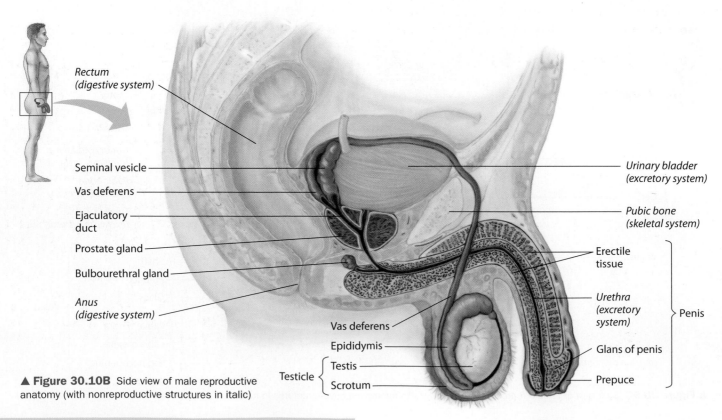

▲ **Figure 30.10B** Side view of male reproductive anatomy (with nonreproductive structures in italic)

of glandular secretions. The other 5% is made up of sperm (typically 200–500 million of them), only one of which may eventually fertilize an egg. The alkalinity of the semen balances the acidity of any traces of urine in the urethra and neutralizes the acidic environment of the vagina, protecting the sperm and increasing their motility.

The human **penis** consists mainly of erectile tissue (shown in blue in Figures 30.10A and 30.10B) that can fill with blood to cause an erection during sexual arousal. Erection is essential for insertion of the penis into the vagina. Like the clitoris, the penis consists of a shaft that supports the glans, or head. The glans is richly supplied with nerve endings and is highly sensitive to stimulation. A fold of skin called the prepuce, or foreskin, covers the glans. Circumcision, the surgical removal of the prepuce, arose from religious traditions. The number of parents opting for circumcision has been declining in Canada in recent years. There is a small (less than 1%) chance of complication from the surgery. However, recent studies have suggested that circumcision does have a medical advantage: The procedure significantly reduces a man's chance of contracting and passing on sexually transmitted diseases, including AIDS.

Figure 30.10C illustrates the process of ejaculation and summarizes the production of semen and its expulsion. Ejaculation occurs in two stages. ❶ At the peak of sexual arousal, muscle contractions in multiple glands force secretions into the urethra and propel sperm from the epididymis. At the same time, a sphincter muscle at the base of the bladder contracts, preventing urine from leaking into the urethra from the bladder. Another sphincter also contracts, closing off the entrance of the urethra into the penis. The section of the urethra between the two sphincters fills with semen and expands. ❷ In the second stage of ejaculation, the expulsion stage, the sphincter at the base of the penis relaxes, admitting semen into the penis. At the same time, a series of strong muscle contractions around the base of the penis and along the urethra expels the semen from the body.

Figure 30.10D shows how hormones control sperm production by the testes. The hypothalamus secretes a releasing hormone that regulates release of follicle-stimulating hormone (FSH) and luteinizing hormone (LH) by the anterior pituitary

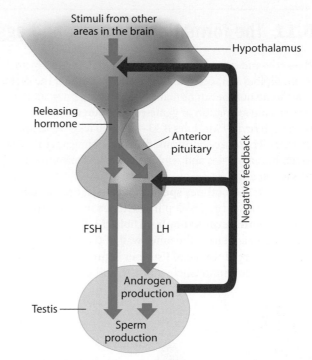

▲ **Figure 30.10D** Hormonal control of the testis

(see Module 29.4). FSH increases sperm production by the testes, while LH promotes the secretion of androgens, mainly testosterone. Androgens stimulate sperm production. In addition, androgens carried in the blood help to maintain homeostasis by a negative-feedback mechanism (red arrows), inhibiting secretion of both the releasing hormone and LH. Under the control of this chemical regulating system, the testes produce hundreds of millions of sperm every day, from puberty well into old age. Next we will see how sperm and eggs are made.

? Arrange the following organs in the correct sequence for the travel of sperm: epididymis, testis, urethra, and vas deferens.

● Testis, epididymis, vas deferens, urethra

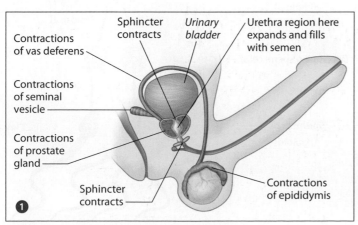

▲ **Figure 30.10C** The two stages of ejaculation

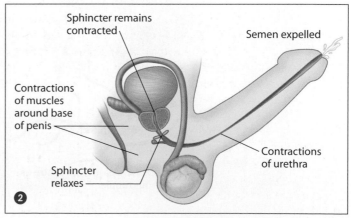

30.11 The formation of sperm and egg cells requires meiosis

Both sperm and egg are haploid (n) cells that develop by meiosis from diploid ($2n$) cells in the gonads. Recall that the diploid chromosome number in humans is 46; that is, $2n = 46$. Before we turn to the formation of gametes, **gametogenesis**, you may want to review Modules 8.13–8.15 as background for our discussion. There are significant differences in gametogenesis between human males and females, so we will examine the processes separately.

Figure 30.11A outlines **spermatogenesis**, the formation of sperm cells. Sperm develop in the testes in coiled tubes called the **seminiferous tubules**. Diploid cells that begin the process are located near the outer wall of the tubules (at the top of the enlarged wedge of tissue in Figure 30.11A). These cells multiply continuously by mitosis, and each day about

3 million of them differentiate into **primary spermatocytes**, the cells that undergo meiosis. Meiosis I of a primary spermatocyte produces two **secondary spermatocytes**, each with the haploid number of chromosomes ($n = 23$). Meiosis II then forms four cells, each with the haploid number of chromosomes. A sperm cell develops by differentiation of each of these haploid cells and is gradually pushed toward the centre of the seminiferous tubule. From there it passes into the epididymis, where it matures, becomes motile, and is stored until ejaculation. In human males, spermatogenesis takes about two months.

In Module 30.12, we will examine the rumour stating that the heat of a laptop affects spermatogenesis. First, we will finish our discussion of gametogenesis in females.

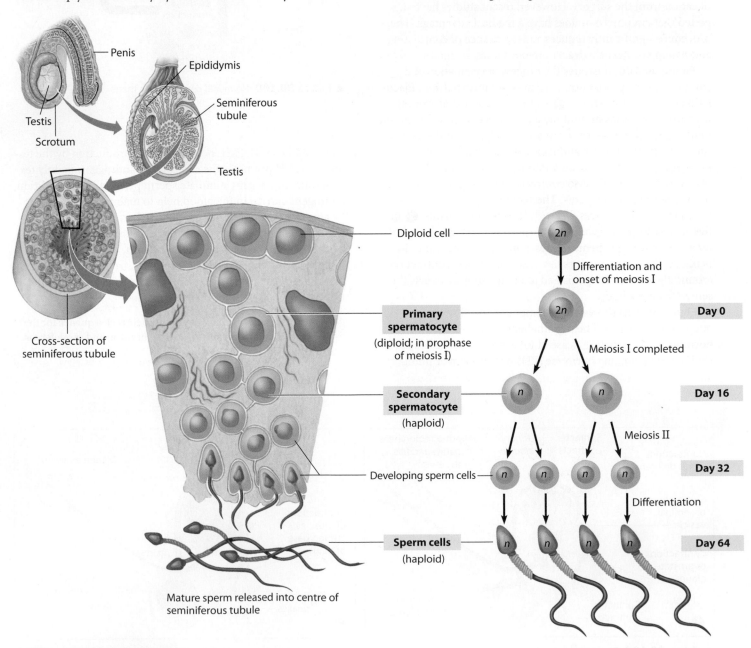

▲ **Figure 30.11A** Spermatogenesis

The right side of **Figure 30.11B** shows **oogenesis**, the development of a mature egg (also called an ovum; plural, *ova*). Most of the process occurs in the ovary. Oogenesis actually begins prior to birth, when a diploid cell in each developing follicle begins meiosis. At birth, each follicle contains a dormant **primary oocyte**, a diploid cell that is resting in prophase of meiosis I. A primary oocyte can be hormonally triggered to develop further. Between puberty and menopause, about every 28 days, FSH (follicle-stimulating hormone) from the pituitary stimulates one of the dormant follicles to develop. The follicle enlarges, and the primary oocyte completes meiosis I and begins meiosis II. Meiosis then halts again at metaphase II. In the female, the division of the cytoplasm in meiosis I is unequal, with a single **secondary oocyte** receiving almost all of it. The smaller of the two daughter cells, called the first polar body, receives almost no cytoplasm.

The secondary oocyte is released by the ovary during ovulation. It enters the oviduct, and if a sperm cell penetrates it, the secondary oocyte completes meiosis II. Meiosis II is also unequal, yielding a second polar body and the mature egg (ovum). The haploid nucleus of the mature egg can then fuse with the haploid nucleus of the sperm cell, producing a zygote.

Although not shown in Figure 30.11B, the first polar body may also undergo meiosis II, forming two cells. These and the second polar body receive virtually no cytoplasm and quickly degenerate, leaving the mature egg with nearly all the cytoplasm and thus the bulk of the nutrients contained in the original diploid cell.

The left side of Figure 30.11B is a cutaway view of an ovary. The series of follicles here represents the changes one follicle undergoes over time. An actual ovary would have thousands of dormant follicles, each containing a primary oocyte. Usually, only one follicle has a dividing oocyte at any one time. Meiosis I occurs as the follicle matures. About the time the secondary oocyte forms, the pituitary hormone LH triggers ovulation, the rupture of the follicle and expulsion of the secondary oocyte. The ruptured follicle then develops into a corpus luteum ("yellow body"). Unless fertilization occurs, the corpus luteum degenerates before another follicle starts to develop.

Oogenesis and spermatogenesis are alike in that they both produce haploid gametes. However, these two processes differ in some important ways. First, only one mature egg results from each diploid cell that undergoes meiosis. The other products of oogenesis, the polar bodies, degenerate. By contrast, in spermatogenesis, all four products of meiosis develop into mature gametes. Second, although the cells from which sperm develop continue to divide by mitosis throughout the male's life, this is probably not the case for the comparable cells in the human female as the oocytes are all present at birth. Third, oogenesis has long "resting" periods, whereas spermatogenesis produces mature sperm in an uninterrupted sequence.

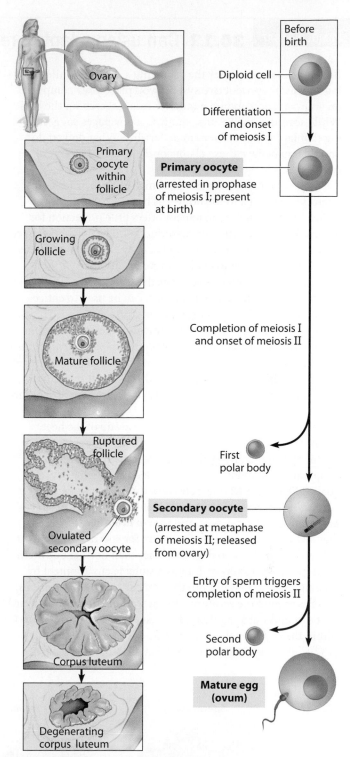

▲ **Figure 30.11B** Oogenesis and the development of an ovarian follicle

? What are two processes in the development of sperm and eggs that are responsible for the genetic variation among gametes? (*Hint:* Review Module 8.16.)

Crossing over and the random alignment of homologous chromosomes during meiosis, specifically meiosis I

30.12 Can using a laptop reduce male fertility?

If you are male, consider the following scenario: While studying the male reproductive system, you place your computer on your lap and conduct a quick Internet search on the topic. While scanning the results, you find a few pages suggesting that laptop use reduces male fertility. What do you do? Should you believe these claims or dismiss them as mere rumour?

The reason males of many mammals have their testes in a scrotum, external to the body, has been debated since the 1920s. This unusual arrangement offers little protection for organs that are essential for reproduction. The gonads of other animals are secure within the body cavity. Several hypotheses have been postulated to explain this circumstance.

The *display* hypothesis suggests the scrotum is a sign of virility that, like the tail of a peacock, can be used to entice potential mates. The *training* hypothesis states the sperm become hardier in the harsh environment of the cool scrotum. The classical explanation for scrotal position is the *temperature* hypothesis, which is based on the optimal temperature of spermatogenesis. Despite multiple hypotheses about the scrotum, one explanation alone cannot clarify its presence or absence in all mammals.

Anyone who has used a computer is aware of the heat it generates. A man holding a laptop on his lap has a much warmer groin than normal, and is hyperthermic. High temperatures have long been suspected of reducing sperm quality. **Figure 30.12** illustrates how quality is measured by examining **sperm count** (numbers of sperm present), **sperm morphology** (their shape), and **sperm mobility** (how well they swim). The optimal temperature for sperm development in humans is 35°C, two degrees cooler than normal body temperature. The scrotum maintains a suitable environment by keeping the testes away from the body. Or, in cold conditions, muscles around the scrotum contract, pulling the testes toward the body and warming them. Because the ovaries are retained within the abdominal cavity, oogenesis functions optimally at 37°C. It is less likely that heat from a laptop will warm a woman's abdomen, and therefore her ovaries, to a point where oogenesis will be negatively affected.

A body temperature of 37°C actually inhibits the release of spermatogenesis-promoting androgens (see Module 30.10). Also, enzymes involved in meiosis within the developing sperm are not as active at body temperature. Heat given off by a computer further inhibits the function of these enzymes and therefore negatively affect spermatogenesis. Even sitting for prolonged periods or wearing briefs has been shown to warm the testes and lower sperm count.

The effects of hyperthermia are not permanent. When temperature returns to normal, spermatogenesis can recover. However, recovery may take as long as five months in humans. In bighorn sheep (*Ovis canadensis*), males experience seasonal sterility during hot summer months. With cooler autumn temperatures, their fertility quickly returns to normal in time for mating season.

Although the first of its kind, a study published in January 2012 showed that a laptop Wi-Fi connection further decreases sperm mobility. Wi-Fi devices produce electromagnetic fields similar to those emitted by cellphones. And the effects of this radiation—reducing sperm mobility and damaging sperm DNA—are well documented. Because radiation decreases exponentially with distance from the source, placing a laptop on a table rather than your lap reduces the radiation the groin absorbs to insignificant levels. It is unknown whether this radiation has effects on ovaries.

This rumour is factual and the evidence supporting it has grown with the discovery that Wi-Fi connections also have an impact. Knowing this, you may be more inclined to keep your laptop off of your lap.

 Setting a laptop on a pillow instead of directly on a lap separates the computer from the user's groin. Does this eliminate the problem?

● Not completely; though the Wi-Fi radiation will be reduced, the pillow traps body heat that still warms the testes.

Sperm count — Low — Normal

Sperm morphology — Abnormal — Normal

Sperm motility — Abnormal — Normal forward progression

▲ **Figure 30.12** Three measures of sperm quality

30.13 Hormones synchronize cyclic changes in the ovary and uterus

Oogenesis is one part of a female mammal's **reproductive cycle**, a recurring sequence of events that produces eggs, makes them available for fertilization, and prepares the body for pregnancy. The reproductive cycle is actually one integrated cycle involving cycles in two different reproductive organs: the ovaries and the uterus. In discussing oogenesis in the last module, we described the **ovarian cycle**, cyclic events that occur about every 28 days in the human ovary. Concurrent changes in the uterus define the **menstrual cycle**. Hormonal messages link the two cycles, synchronizing follicle growth in the ovaries with the establishment of a uterine lining that can support a growing embryo. The hormone story is complex and involves intricate feedback mechanisms. **Table 30.13** lists the major hormones and their roles. **Figure 30.13** shows how the events of the ovarian cycle (Part C) and menstrual cycle (Part E) are synchronized through the actions of multiple hormones (shown in Parts A, B, and D). Notice the time scale at the bottom of Part E; it also applies to Parts B–D.

An Overview of the Ovarian and Menstrual Cycles   Let's begin with the structural events of the ovarian and menstrual cycles. For simplicity, we have divided the ovarian cycle (Part C of the figure) into two phases separated by ovulation: the pre-ovulatory phase, when a follicle is growing and a secondary oocyte is developing, and the post-ovulatory phase, after the follicle has become a corpus luteum.

Events in the menstrual cycle (Part E) are synchronized with the ovarian cycle. By convention, the first day of a woman's "period" is designated day 1 of the menstrual cycle. Uterine bleeding, called **menstruation**, usually lasts for three to five days. Notice that this corresponds to the beginning of the pre-ovulatory phase of the ovarian cycle. During menstruation, the endometrium (the blood-rich inner lining of the uterus) breaks down and leaves the body through the vagina. The menstrual discharge consists of blood, small clusters of endometrial cells, and mucus. After menstruation, the endometrium regrows. It continues to thicken through the time of ovulation, reaching a maximum thickness at about 20–25 days. If an embryo has not implanted in the uterine lining, menstruation begins again, marking the start of the next ovarian and menstrual cycles.

Now let's consider the hormones that regulate the ovarian and menstrual cycles. The ebb and flow of the hormones listed in Table 30.13 synchronize events in the ovarian cycle (the growth of the follicle and ovulation) with events in the menstrual cycle (preparation of the uterine lining for possible implantation of an embryo). A releasing hormone from the hypothalamus in the brain regulates secretion of the two pituitary hormones FSH and LH. Changes in the blood levels of FSH, LH, and two other hormones—estrogen and progesterone—coincide with specific events in the ovarian and menstrual cycles.

Hormonal Events Before Ovulation   Focusing on Part A of Figure 30.13, we see that the releasing hormone from the hypothalamus stimulates the anterior pituitary ❶ to increase its output of FSH and LH. True to its name, ❷ FSH stimulates the growth of an ovarian follicle, in effect starting the ovarian cycle. In turn, the follicle secretes estrogen. Early in the pre-ovulatory phase, the follicle is small (Part C) and secretes relatively little estrogen (Part D). As the follicle grows, ❸ it secretes more and more estrogen, and the rising but still relatively low level of estrogen exerts negative feedback on the pituitary. This keeps the blood levels of FSH and LH low for most of the pre-ovulatory phase (Part B). As the time of ovulation approaches, hormone levels change drastically, with estrogen reaching a critical peak (Part D) just before ovulation. This high level of estrogen exerts positive feedback on the hypothalamus (green arrow in Part A), which then ❹ makes the pituitary secrete surges of FSH and LH. By comparing Parts B and D of the figure, you can see that the peaks in FSH and LH occur just after the estrogen peak. It may help to place a piece of paper over the figure and slide it slowly to the right. As you uncover the figure, you will see the follicle getting bigger and the estrogen level rising to its peak, followed almost immediately by the LH and FSH surges. ❺ Then, just to the right of the peaks, comes the dashed line representing ovulation.

Hormonal Events at Ovulation and After   LH stimulates the completion of meiosis I, transforming the primary oocyte in the follicle into a secondary oocyte. It also signals enzymes to rupture the follicle, allowing ovulation to occur, and triggers

TABLE 30.13	HORMONES OF THE OVARIAN AND MENSTRUAL CYCLES	
Hormone	**Secreted by**	**Major Roles**
Releasing hormone	Hypothalamus	Regulates secretion of LH and FSH by pituitary
Follicle-stimulating hormone (FSH)	Pituitary	Stimulates growth of ovarian follicle
Luteinizing hormone (LH)	Pituitary	Stimulates growth of ovarian follicle and production of secondary oocyte; promotes ovulation; promotes development of corpus luteum and secretion of other hormones
Estrogen	Ovarian follicle	Low levels inhibit pituitary; high levels stimulate hypothalamus; promotes growth of endometrium
Estrogen and progesterone	Corpus luteum	Maintain endometrium; high levels inhibit hypothalamus and pituitary; sharp drops promote menstruation

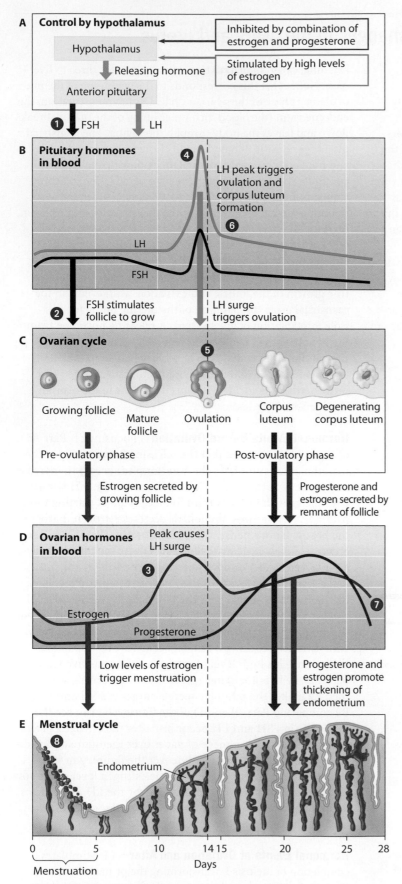

A Control by hypothalamus

Hypothalamus

Releasing hormone

Anterior pituitary

Inhibited by combination of estrogen and progesterone

Stimulated by high levels of estrogen

1 FSH   LH

B Pituitary hormones in blood

4

LH peak triggers ovulation and corpus luteum formation

6

LH

FSH

2 FSH stimulates follicle to grow

LH surge triggers ovulation

C Ovarian cycle

5

Growing follicle

Mature follicle

Ovulation

Corpus luteum

Degenerating corpus luteum

Pre-ovulatory phase

Post-ovulatory phase

Estrogen secreted by growing follicle

Progesterone and estrogen secreted by remnant of follicle

D Ovarian hormones in blood

Peak causes LH surge

3

Estrogen

Progesterone

7

Low levels of estrogen trigger menstruation

Progesterone and estrogen promote thickening of endometrium

E Menstrual cycle

8

Endometrium

0   5   10   14 15   20   25   28

Days

Menstruation

▲ **Figure 30.13** The reproductive cycle of the human female

the development of the corpus luteum from the ruptured follicle (hence its name, luteinizing hormone). LH also promotes the secretion of progesterone and estrogen by the corpus luteum. In Part D of the figure, you can see the progesterone peak and the second (lower and wider) estrogen peak after ovulation.

High levels of estrogen and progesterone in the blood following ovulation have a strong influence on both the ovary and the uterus. The combination of the two hormones exerts negative feedback on the hypothalamus and pituitary, producing **6** falling FSH and LH levels. The drop in FSH and LH prevents follicles from developing and ovulation from occurring during the post-ovulatory phase. Also, the LH drop is followed by the gradual degeneration of the corpus luteum. Near the end of the post-ovulatory phase, unless an embryo has implanted in the uterus, the corpus luteum stops secreting estrogen and progesterone. **7** As blood levels of these hormones decline, the hypothalamus once again can stimulate the pituitary to secrete more FSH and LH, and a new cycle begins.

Control of the Menstrual Cycle Hormonal regulation of the menstrual cycle is simpler than that of the ovarian cycle. The menstrual cycle (Part E) is directly controlled by estrogen and progesterone alone. You can see the effects of these hormones by comparing Parts D and E of the figure. Starting around day 5 of the cycle, the endometrium thickens in response to the rising levels of estrogen and, later, progesterone. When the levels of these hormones drop, the endometrium begins to slough off. **8** Menstrual bleeding begins soon after, on day 1 of a new cycle.

We have now described what happens in the human ovary and uterus in the absence of fertilization. As we will see later, the ovarian and menstrual cycles are put on hold if fertilization and pregnancy occur. Early in pregnancy, the developing embryo, implanted in the endometrium, releases a hormone (human chorionic gonadotropin [hCG]). This hormone acts like LH in that it maintains the corpus luteum, which continues to secrete progesterone and estrogen, keeping the endometrium intact. (hCG also boosts testosterone production in males, so its use is banned by many sports organizations.) We will return to the events of pregnancy in Modules 30.15 and 30.16.

? **Which hormonal change triggers the onset of menstruation?**

● The drop in the levels of estrogen and progesterone. These changes are caused by negative feedback of these hormones on the hypothalamus and pituitary after ovulation.

which protects the embryo. The amnion usually breaks just before childbirth, and the amniotic fluid leaves the mother's body through her vagina ("her water broke").

In humans and most other mammals, the **yolk sac** contains no yolk, but it is given the same name as the homologous structure in birds. In a bird egg, the yolk sac contains a large mass of yolk. Isolated within a shelled egg outside of the mother's body, a developing bird will obtain nourishment from the yolk rather than from a placenta. In mammals, the yolk sac, which remains small, has other important functions: It produces the embryo's first blood cells and its first germ cells, the cells that will give rise to the gamete-forming cells in the gonads.

The **allantois** also remains small in mammals. It forms part of the umbilical cord—the lifeline between the embryo and the placenta. It also forms part of the embryo's urinary bladder. In birds and other reptiles, the allantois expands around the embryo and functions in waste disposal.

The outermost extraembryonic membrane, the **chorion**, completely surrounds the embryo and other extraembryonic membranes. The chorion becomes part of the placenta, where it functions in gas exchange. Cells in the chorion secrete a hormone called **human chorionic gonadotropin (hCG)**, which maintains production of estrogen and progesterone by the corpus luteum of the ovary during the first few months of pregnancy. Without these hormones, menstruation would occur, and the embryo would abort spontaneously. Levels of hCG in maternal blood are so high that some is excreted in the urine, where it can be detected by pregnancy tests.

The Placenta   Looking again at Figure 30.15D, notice the knobby outgrowths on the outside of the chorion. In Figure 30.15E, these outgrowths, now called **chorionic villi**, are larger and contain mesoderm. In Figure 30.15F, the mesoderm cells have formed into embryonic blood vessels in the chorionic villi. By this stage, the placenta is fully developed. Starting with the chorion and extending outward, the placenta is a composite organ consisting of chorionic villi closely associated with the blood vessels of the mother's endometrium. The villi are actually bathed in tiny pools of maternal blood. The mother's blood and the embryo's blood are not in direct contact. Instead, the chorionic villi absorb nutrients and oxygen from the mother's blood and pass these substances to the embryo via the chorionic blood vessels that are shown in red. The chorionic vessels shown in blue carry wastes away from the embryo. The wastes diffuse into the mother's bloodstream and are excreted by her kidneys.

The placenta is a vital organ with both embryonic and maternal parts that mediates exchange of nutrients, gases, and the products of excretion between the embryo and the mother. However, the placenta cannot always protect the embryo from substances circulating in the mother's blood. A number of viruses—the German measles virus and HIV, for example—can cross the placenta. German measles can cause serious birth defects; 25% of HIV-infected mothers transmit the infection to their children during pregnancy or childbirth. Most drugs, both prescription and not, also cross the placenta, and many can harm the developing embryo. Alcohol and the chemicals in tobacco smoke, for instance, raise the risk of miscarriage and birth defects. Alcohol can cause a set of birth defects called fetal alcohol spectrum disorder, which includes mental deficiencies and affects 9 in 1000 Canadian babies.

?   **Why does testing for hCG in a woman's urine or blood work as an early test of pregnancy?**

● Because this hormone is secreted by the chorion of an embryo

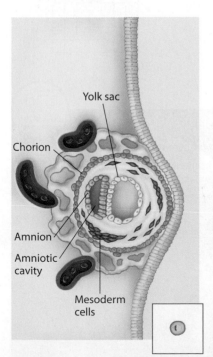

▲ **Figure 30.15D** Embryonic layers and extraembryonic membranes starting to form (nine days)

Yolk sac
Chorion
Amnion
Amniotic cavity
Mesoderm cells

▲ **Figure 30.15E** Three-layered embryo and four extraembryonic membranes (16 days)

Embryo:
Endoderm
Mesoderm
Ectoderm
Chorionic villi
Chorion
Amnion
Allantois
Yolk sac

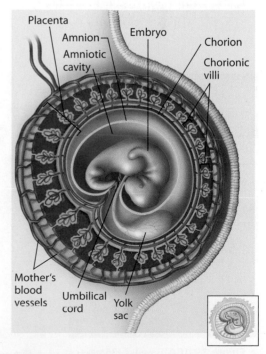

▲ **Figure 30.15F** Placenta formed (31 days)

Placenta
Amnion
Amniotic cavity
Embryo
Chorion
Chorionic villi
Mother's blood vessels
Umbilical cord
Yolk sac

30.16 Human development from conception to birth is divided into three trimesters

In the previous module, we followed human development through the first four weeks. In this module, we use photographs to illustrate the rest of human development in the uterus. For convenience, we divide the period of human development from conception to birth into three **trimesters** of about three months each.

First Trimester   The first trimester is the time of the most radical change for both mother and embryo. **Figure 30.16A** shows a human embryo about five weeks after fertilization. In that brief time, this highly organized multicellular embryo has developed from a single cell. Not shown are the extraembryonic membranes that surround the embryo or most of the umbilical cord that attaches it to the placenta. This embryo is about 7 mm long and has a number of features in common with the somite stage of a frog embryo (see Figure 30.6C). The embryo has a notochord and a coelom, both formed from mesoderm. Its brain and spinal cord have begun to take shape from a tube of ectoderm. The human embryo also has four stumpy limb buds, a short tail, and elements of gill pouches. The gill pouches appear during embryonic development in all chordates; in land vertebrates, they eventually develop into parts of the throat and middle ear. Overall, a month-old human embryo is similar to other vertebrates at the somite stage of development.

Figure 30.16B shows a developing human, now called a fetus, about nine weeks after fertilization. The large pinkish structure on the left is the placenta, attached to the fetus by the umbilical cord. The clear sac around the fetus is the amnion. By this time, the fetus looks decidedly human, rather than generally vertebrate. It is about 5.5 cm long, and all the major structures of the adult are present in rudimentary form. The somites have developed into the segmental muscles and bones of the back and ribs. The limb buds have become tiny arms and legs with fingers and toes. The first trimester is when most of the body's organs form. Because these important structures are taking shape, during this stage an embryo is particularly susceptible to damage by radiation, drugs, or alcohol, all of which can lead to birth defects.

Although still less than 6 cm long, the fetus can move its arms and legs, turn its head, frown, and make sucking motions with its lips. By the end of the first trimester, the fetus

Timeline of Human Fetal Development

January	February	March	April
0 Conception	35 days	63 days	98 days

▲ **Figure 30.16A** 5 weeks (35 days)

▲ **Figure 30.16B** 9 weeks (63 days)

▲ **Figure 30.16C** 14 weeks (98 days)

looks like a miniature human being, although its head is still oversized for the rest of the body. The sex of the fetus is usually evident by this time, and its heartbeat can be detected.

Second Trimester The main developmental changes during the second and third trimesters include an increase in size and general refinement of the human features—nothing as dramatic as the changes of the first trimester. **Figure 30.16C** shows a fetus at 14 weeks, 2 weeks into the second trimester. The fetus is now about 6 cm long. During the second trimester, the placenta takes over the task of maintaining itself by secreting progesterone, rather than receiving it from the corpus luteum. At the same time, the placenta stops secreting hCG, and the corpus luteum, no longer needed to maintain pregnancy, degenerates.

At 20 weeks **(Figure 30.16D)**, well into the second trimester, the fetus is about 19 cm long, weighs about 500 g, and has the face of an infant, complete with eyebrows and eyelashes. Its arms, legs, fingers, and toes have lengthened. It also has fingernails and toenails and is covered with fine hair. Fetuses of this age are usually quite active. The mother's abdomen has become markedly enlarged, and she may often feel her baby move. Because of the limited space in the uterus, the fetus flexes forward into the so-called fetal position. By the end of the second trimester, the fetus's eyes are open and its teeth are forming.

Third Trimester The third trimester (28 weeks to birth) is a time of rapid growth as the fetus gains the strength it will need to survive outside the protective environment of the uterus. Babies born prematurely—as early as 24 weeks—may survive, but they require special medical care after birth. During the third trimester, the fetus's circulatory system and respiratory system undergo changes that will allow the switch to air breathing (see Module 27.13). The fetus gains the ability to maintain its own temperature, and its bones begin to harden and its muscles thicken. It also loses much of its fine body hair, except on its head. The fetus becomes less active as it fills the space in the uterus. As the fetus grows and the uterus expands around it, the mother's abdominal organs become compressed and displaced, leading to frequent urination, digestive blockages, and strain in the back muscles. At birth **(Figure 30.16E)**, babies average about 50 cm in length and weigh 3–4 kg.

? Certain drugs cause their most serious damage to an embryo very early in pregnancy, often before the mother even realizes she is pregnant. Why?

● Because organ systems, such as the circulatory and nervous systems, begin to develop early in the first trimester.

▲ **Figure 30.16D** 20 weeks (140 days)

▲ **Figure 30.16E** At birth (280 days)

30.17 Childbirth is induced by hormones and other chemical signals

The series of events that expel an infant from the uterus is called **labour**. Several hormones play key roles in this process (**Figure 30.17A**). One hormone, estrogen, reaches its highest level in the mother's blood during the last weeks of pregnancy. An important effect of this estrogen is to trigger the formation of numerous oxytocin receptors on cells of the uterus. Cells of the fetus produce the hormone oxytocin, and late in pregnancy, the mother's pituitary gland secretes it in increasing amounts. Oxytocin stimulates the smooth muscles in the wall of the uterus, producing the series of increasingly strong, rhythmic contractions characteristic of labour. It also stimulates the placenta to make prostaglandins, local tissue regulators that stimulate the uterine muscle cells to contract even more.

The induction of labour involves **positive feedback**, a type of control in which a change triggers mechanisms that amplify that change. In this case, oxytocin and prostaglandins cause uterine contractions that in turn stimulate the release of more oxytocin and prostaglandins. The result is a steady increase in contraction intensity, climaxing in forceful muscle contractions that propel a baby from the uterus.

Figure 30.17B shows the three stages of labour. As the process begins, the cervix (neck of the uterus) gradually opens, or dilates. ❶ The first stage, dilation, is the time from the onset of labour until the cervix reaches its full dilation of about 10 cm. Dilation is the longest stage of labour, lasting 6–12 hours or even considerably longer.

❷ The period from full dilation of the cervix to delivery of the infant is called the expulsion stage. Strong uterine contractions, lasting about one minute each, occur every two to three minutes, and the mother feels an increasing urge to push or bear down with her abdominal muscles. Within a period of 20 minutes to an hour or so, the infant is forced down and out of the uterus and vagina. An attending physician or midwife

(or nervous partner!) clamps and cuts the umbilical cord after the baby is expelled. ❸ The final stage is the delivery of the placenta ("afterbirth"), usually within 15 minutes after the birth of the baby.

Hormones continue to be important after the baby and placenta are delivered. Decreasing levels of progesterone and estrogen allow the uterus to start returning to its state before

❶ Dilation of the cervix

❷ Expulsion: delivery of the infant

❸ Delivery of the placenta

▲ **Figure 30.17A** The hormonal induction of labour

▲ **Figure 30.17B** The three stages of labour

pregnancy. In response to suckling by the newborn, as well as falling levels of progesterone after birth, the pituitary secretes prolactin and oxytocin. These two hormones promote milk production and release (called lactation) by the mammary glands. At first, a yellowish fluid called colostrum, rich in

protein and antibodies, is secreted. After two to three days, the production of regular milk begins.

? The onset of labour is marked by dilation of the _____.

● cervix

BIOLOGY AND SOCIETY

30.18 Reproductive technologies increase our reproductive options

About 15% of couples who want children are unable to conceive, even after 12 months of unprotected intercourse. Such a condition, called **infertility**, can have many causes. A man's testes may not produce enough sperm (a "low sperm count"), or those that are produced may be defective. Underproduction of sperm is frequently caused by the man's scrotum being too warm, so a switch of underwear from briefs (which hold the scrotum close to the body) to boxers may help. In other cases, infertility is caused by **impotence**, also called erectile dysfunction, the inability to maintain an erection. Temporary impotence can result from alcohol or drug use or from psychological problems. Permanent impotence can result from nervous system or circulatory problems. Female infertility can result from a lack of eggs, a failure to ovulate, or blocked oviducts (often caused by scarring, a result of some sexually transmitted diseases). Egg health also deteriorates with age and may contribute to infertility in many Canadians that delay having children. The average age for first-time mothers in Canada is now 29.3, compared to 23.4 in 1976. Other women are able to conceive but cannot support a growing embryo in the uterus. The resulting multiple miscarriages can take a heavy emotional toll.

Reproductive technologies can help many cases of infertility. Drug therapies (including Viagra) and penile implants can be used to treat impotence. If a man produces no functioning sperm, the couple may elect to use another man's sperm that has been donated to a sperm bank.

If a woman has normal eggs that are not being released properly, hormone injections can induce ovulation. Such treatments frequently result in multiple pregnancies. If a woman has no eggs of her own, then they, too, can be obtained from a donor for fertilization and implantation into the uterus. While sperm can be collected without any danger to the donor, collection of eggs involves surgery and therefore some pain and risk for the donating woman.

If a woman produces eggs but is unable to support a growing fetus, she and her partner may hire a surrogate mother. In such cases, the couple enters into a legal contract with a woman who agrees to be implanted with the couple's embryo and carry it to birth.

Many infertile couples turn to fertilization procedures called **assisted reproductive technologies**. In these procedures, eggs (secondary oocytes) are surgically removed from a woman's ovaries after hormonal stimulation and are then fertilized and returned to the woman's body. Eggs, sperm, and embryos from such procedures can be frozen for later pregnancy attempts.

With *in vitro* fertilization (**IVF**), the most common assisted reproductive technology procedure, a woman's eggs are mixed with sperm in culture dishes (*in vitro* means "in glass") and incubated for several days to allow fertilized eggs to start

▲ **Figure 30.18** *In vitro* fertilization

developing (**Figure 30.18**). When they have developed into embryos of at least eight cells each, the embryos are carefully inserted into the woman's uterus. Dr. Jocelynn Cook of the University of Ottawa has shown that twins and triplets are three times more likely in IVF pregnancies. Today, single embryo transfers are recommended by most obstetricians.

If mature sperm are defective, of low number, or even absent, fertilization can often be achieved by a technique called intracytoplasmic sperm injection (ICSI). In this form of IVF, the head of a sperm is drawn up into a needle and injected directly into an egg to achieve fertilization.

Abnormalities arising as a consequence of an IVF procedure appear to be quite rare, although some research has shown small but significant risks of lower birth weights and higher rates of birth defects. Despite such risks and the high cost (typically $10 000 per attempt, whether or not it succeeds), IVF techniques are now performed at medical centres throughout the world and result in the birth of thousands of babies each year. Provincial health care plans in some provinces, including Quebec and Ontario, are starting to cover part of the costs of IVF to ease the financial burden.

In this chapter, we have watched a single-celled product of sexual reproduction, the zygote, become transformed into a new organism, complete with all organ systems. One of the first of those organ systems to develop is the nervous system. In the next chapter, we will see how the nervous system functions together with the endocrine system to regulate virtually all body activities.

 Explain how IVF can involve up to three different people in the birth of a child.

● One woman (1) may become pregnant with an embryo created using the sperm of a man (2) and the mature egg of a second woman (3).

Reviewing the Concepts

Asexual and Sexual Reproduction (30.1–30.2)

30.1 Asexual reproduction results in the generation of genetically identical offspring. Asexual reproduction can proceed by budding, fission, or fragmentation and regeneration and enables one individual to produce many offspring rapidly.

30.2 Sexual reproduction results in the generation of genetically unique offspring. Sexual reproduction involves the fusion of gametes from two parents, resulting in genetic variation among offspring. This may enhance survival of a population in a changing environment.

Principles of Embryonic Development (30.3–30.8)

30.3 Fertilization results in a zygote and triggers embryonic development. During fertilization, a sperm releases enzymes that pierce the egg's coat. Sperm surface proteins bind to egg receptor proteins, sperm and egg plasma membranes fuse, and the two nuclei unite. Changes in the egg membrane prevent entry of additional sperm, and the fertilized egg (zygote) develops into an embryo.

30.4 Cleavage produces a ball of cells from the zygote. Cleavage is a rapid series of cell divisions that results in a blastula.

30.5 Gastrulation produces a three-layered embryo. In gastrulation, cells migrate and form a rudimentary digestive cavity and three layers of cells.

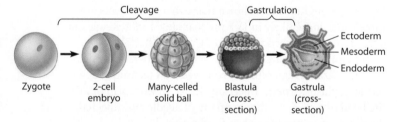

30.6 Organs start to form after gastrulation. After gastrulation, the three embryonic tissue layers give rise to specific organ systems.

30.7 Multiple processes give form to the developing animal. Tissues and organs take shape in a developing embryo as a result of cell shape changes, cell migration, and programmed cell death. Through induction, adjacent cells and cell layers influence one another's differentiation via chemical signals.

30.8 Pattern formation during embryonic development is controlled by ancient genes. Pattern formation, the emergence of the parts of a structure in their correct relative positions, involves the response of genes to spatial variations of chemicals in the embryo. Homeotic genes contain homeoboxes, nucleotide sequences that appeared early in the evolutionary history of animals.

Human Reproduction (30.9–30.14)

30.9 Reproductive anatomy of the human female. The human reproductive system consists of a pair of ovaries (in females) or testes (in males), ducts that carry gametes, and structures for copulation. A woman's ovaries contain follicles that nurture eggs and produce sex hormones. Oviducts convey eggs to the uterus, where a fertilized egg develops. The uterus opens into the vagina, which receives the penis during intercourse and serves as the birth canal.

30.10 Reproductive anatomy of the human male. A man's testes produce sperm, which are expelled through ducts during ejaculation. Several glands contribute to the formation of fluid that nourishes and protects sperm.

30.11 The formation of sperm and egg cells requires meiosis. Spermatogenesis and oogenesis produce sperm and eggs, respectively. Primary spermatocytes are made continuously in the testes; these diploid cells undergo meiosis to form four haploid sperm. In females, each month, one primary oocyte forms a secondary oocyte, which, if penetrated by a sperm, completes meiosis and becomes a mature egg. The haploid nucleus of the mature egg then fuses with the haploid nucleus of the sperm, forming a diploid zygote.

30.12 Can using a laptop reduce male fertility? The scrotum helps to maintain the optimal temperature for spermatogenesis. Laptops generate heat, which can negatively affect sperm quality. Radiation emitted from Wi-Fi devices has a further impact on sperm count and motility.

30.13 Hormones synchronize cyclic changes in the ovary and uterus. Approximately every 28 days, the hypothalamus signals the anterior pituitary to secrete FSH and LH, which trigger the growth of a follicle and ovulation, the release of an egg. The follicle becomes the corpus luteum, which secretes both estrogen and progesterone. These two hormones stimulate the endometrium (the uterine lining) to thicken, preparing the uterus for implantation. They also inhibit the hypothalamus, reducing FSH and LH secretion. If the egg is not fertilized, the drop in LH shuts down the corpus luteum and its hormones. This triggers menstruation, the breakdown of the endometrium. The hypothalamus and pituitary then stimulate another follicle, starting a new cycle. If fertilization occurs, a hormone from the embryo maintains the uterine lining and prevents menstruation.

30.14 Contraception can prevent unwanted pregnancy. Several forms of contraception can prevent pregnancy, with varying degrees of success.

Human Development (30.15–30.18)

30.15 The embryo and placenta take shape during the first month of pregnancy. Human development begins with fertilization in the oviduct. Cleavage produces a blastocyst, whose inner cell mass becomes the embryo. The blastocyst's outer layer, the trophoblast, implants in the uterine wall. Gastrulation occurs, and organs develop from the three embryonic layers. Meanwhile, the four extraembryonic membranes develop: the amnion, the chorion, the yolk sac, and the allantois. The embryo floats in the fluid-filled amniotic cavity, while the chorion and embryonic mesoderm form the embryo's part of the placenta. The placenta's chorionic villi absorb food and oxygen from the mother's blood.

30.16 Human development from conception to birth is divided into three trimesters. The most rapid changes occur during the first trimester. At nine weeks, the embryo is called a fetus. The second and third trimesters are times of growth and preparation for birth.

30.17 Childbirth is induced by hormones and other chemical signals. Estrogen makes the uterus more sensitive to oxytocin, which acts with prostaglandins to initiate labour. The cervix dilates, the baby is expelled by strong muscular contractions, and the placenta follows.

30.18 Reproductive technologies increase our reproductive options. In *in vitro* fertilization, eggs are extracted and fertilized in the lab. The resulting embryo is implanted into a woman.

Connecting the Concepts

1. This graph plots the rise and fall of pituitary and ovarian hormones during the human ovarian cycle. Identify each hormone (A–D) and the reproductive events with which each one is associated (P–S). For A–D, choose from estrogen, LH, FSH, and progesterone. For P–S, choose from ovulation, growth of follicle, menstruation, and development of corpus luteum. How would the right-hand side of this graph be altered if pregnancy occurred? What other hormone is responsible for triggering this change?

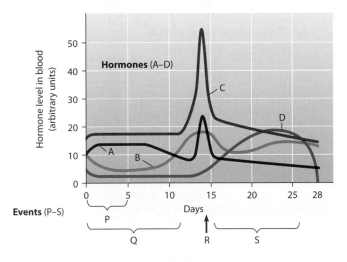

Testing Your Knowledge

Multiple Choice

2. After a sperm penetrates an egg, it is important that the vitelline layer separate from the egg so that it can
   a. secrete important hormones.
   b. enable the fertilized egg to implant in the uterus.
   c. prevent more than one sperm from entering the egg.
   d. attract additional sperm to the egg.
   e. activate the egg for embryonic development.

3. In an experiment, a researcher coloured a bit of tissue on the outside of a frog gastrula with an orange fluorescent dye. The embryo developed normally. When the tadpole was placed under an ultraviolet light, which of the following glowed bright orange? (*Explain your answer.*)
   a. the heart   b. the pancreas
   c. the brain   d. the stomach
   e. the liver

4. How does a zygote differ from a mature egg?
   a. A zygote has more chromosomes.
   b. A zygote is smaller.
   c. A zygote consists of more than one cell.
   d. A zygote is much larger.
   e. A zygote divides by meiosis.

5. A woman had several miscarriages. Her doctor suspected that a hormonal insufficiency was causing the lining of the uterus to break down, as it does during menstruation, terminating her pregnancies. Treatment with which of the following might help her remain pregnant?
   a. oxytocin   b. follicle-stimulating hormone
   c. testosterone   d. luteinizing hormone
   e. prolactin

Matching

6. Turns into the corpus luteum   a. vas deferens

7. Female gonad   b. prostate gland

8. Site of spermatogenesis   c. endometrium

9. Site of fertilization in humans   d. testis

10. Site of human gestation   e. follicle

11. Sperm duct   f. uterus

12. Secretes seminal fluid   g. ovary

13. Lining of uterus   h. oviduct

Describing, Comparing, and Explaining

14. Compare sperm formation with egg formation. In what ways are the processes similar? In what ways are they different?

15. The embryos of reptiles (including birds) and mammals have systems of extraembryonic membranes. What are the functions of these membranes, and how do fish and frog embryos survive without them?

Applying the Concepts

16. You have been given a grant to develop a method of thermal contraception. What are some of the main questions that you would have to answer to prove the usefulness of such a method? Explain why it would be important to answer these questions.

17. As a frog embryo develops, the neural tube forms from ectoderm along what will be the frog's back, directly above the notochord. To study this process, a researcher extracted a bit of notochord tissue and inserted it under the ectoderm where the frog's belly would normally develop. What can the researcher hope to learn from this experiment? Predict the possible outcomes. What experimental control would you suggest?

18. Should parents undergoing *in vitro* fertilization have the right to choose which embryos to implant based on genetic criteria, such as the presence or absence of disease-causing genes? Should they be able to choose based on the sex of the embryo? How could you distinguish acceptable from unacceptable criteria? Do you think such options should be legislated?

Answers to all questions can be found in Appendix E.

Neurons and Nervous Systems

Nervous System Structure and Function

(31.1–31.2)

Neurons receive and process inputs and communicate responses.

An Overview of Animal Nervous Systems

(31.3–31.6)

The vertebrate nervous system can be understood as a structural and functional hierarchy.

Nerve Signals and Their Transmission

(31.7–31.12)

Nerve signals are electrical messages generated by the movement of ions across membranes.

The Human Brain

(31.13–31.19)

Modern research techniques are illuminating how the interplay of brain regions controls our actions and behaviour.

What Has Eight Legs and Is Smarter Than a Dog?

The answer to this question is not two dogs and may seem unlikely: It's an octopus. The end of this chapter includes a discussion on memory, the storage of information within the brain. Although memory is not necessarily indicative of intelligence, the two are linked. Intelligence requires the rapid and accurate retrieval of memories. Better memory increases recall speed and is perceived as higher intelligence.

Humans are unquestionably intelligent, but what about other animals? Many pet owners tout the intellect of their companions. But animal intelligence is very difficult to confirm and quantify and remains a controversial concept. Still, biologists and psychologists work together to identify animal analogues to human intellect. Several vertebrates demonstrate signs of intelligence, and its evolutionary history can be outlined among these animals. Chimpanzees are closely related to humans and also highly intelligent. Other vertebrates that perform well on tests of intelligence include dolphins and ravens. But are any invertebrates intelligent? Dr. Jennifer Mather at the University of Lethbridge has spent much of her career investigating and documenting octopus intelligence.

Octopi in general are remarkably smart animals. Because they are more closely related to clams and snails, their intelligence has clearly evolved along a separate lineage from the vertebrates. However, the two lineages share the many features discussed below.

Relative to their body size, octopi have a large, complex brain. Specific memory centres dedicated to learning, analogous to those in vertebrates, store short-term and long-term memories. And these memories can be used to solve new problems, a common measure of intelligence. Whether they are retrieving and eating lobsters that are caught in traps or navigating their way through a maze, octopi quickly learn and remember these skills. Throughout their learning process, the octopi try many techniques. Unsuccessful methods are quickly abandoned for new ones. Less intelligent animals tend to keep repeating the same futile method until they become frustrated and leave.

Octopi demonstrate many other signs of intelligence, including observational learning, tool use, and play. In studies, octopi observe their neighbours and learn complex skills such as how to open a container to retrieve a meal or solve a puzzle (above right). Octopi are also the only invertebrates known to use tools. The veined octopus (*Amphioctopus marginatus*) will carry two shell halves. Smaller individuals may carry clam shells whereas larger octopi often carry empty halves of coconuts. If threatened by a predator, it will quickly flip the shells around and use them as shelter (above left).

Play involves an active mind and is observed only in highly intelligent animals. An empty pill bottle floating in the aquarium of octopi quickly draws attention. An octopus will blow a jet of water to move the bottle into the aquarium's current. When the current returns the bottle, like bouncing a ball, they push the bottle back again.

With an intellect that rivals your family's dog, octopi are likely the most intelligent invertebrates. In this chapter, we explore the structure, function, and evolution of animal nervous systems. We will start with an overview of nerve cells, which function similarly in nearly all animals. Then we will focus on the vertebrate nervous system and the structure and function of the human brain.

Nervous System Structure and Function

31.1 Nervous systems receive sensory input, interpret it, and send out appropriate commands

Nervous systems are the most intricately organized data processing systems on Earth. Your brain, for instance, contains an estimated 100 billion **neurons**, nerve cells that transmit signals from one location in the body to another. A neuron consists of a cell body, containing the nucleus and other cell organelles, and long, thin extensions that convey signals (see Figure 31.2). Each neuron may communicate with thousands of others, forming networks that enable us to learn, remember, perceive our surroundings, and move.

With few exceptions, nervous systems have two main anatomical divisions. The first anatomical division, called the **central nervous system (CNS)**, consists of the brain and, in vertebrates, the spinal cord. The other anatomical division of the nervous system, the **peripheral nervous system (PNS)**, is made up mostly of nerves that carry signals into and out of the CNS. A **nerve** is a communication line consisting of a bundle of neurons tightly wrapped in connective tissue. The PNS also contains several **ganglia** (singular, *ganglion*) where the cell bodies of sensory neurons are clustered.

A nervous system has three interconnected functions (Figure 31.1A). **Sensory input** is the conduction of signals from sensory receptors, such as light-detecting cells of the eye, to the CNS. **Integration** is the analysis and interpretation of the sensory signals and the formulation of appropriate responses. **Motor output** is the conduction of signals from the integration centres to **effector cells**, such as muscle cells or gland cells, which perform the body's responses. The integration of sensory input and motor output is not usually rigid and linear, but involves continuous cyclic activity (symbolized by the circular arrow in Figure 31.1A) to maintain homeostasis.

The relationship between neurons and nervous system structure and function is easiest to see in the relatively simple circuits that produce **reflexes**, or automatic responses to stimuli (Figure 31.1B). The small blue, green, and purple circles in the

▲ **Figure 31.1B** The knee-jerk reflex

figure represent neuron cell bodies; the thin coloured lines represent neuron extensions (these colours are associated with the functions outlined in Figure 31.1A). Three functional types of neurons correspond to a nervous system's three main functions: **Sensory neurons** convey signals from sensory receptors into the CNS. In many animals, **interneurons** are located entirely within the CNS. They integrate data and then relay appropriate signals to other interneurons or to motor neurons. Finally, **motor neurons** convey signals from the CNS to effector cells. (For simplicity, this figure shows only one neuron of each functional type, but nearly every body activity actually involves many neurons of each type.)

When the knee is tapped to elicit the knee-jerk reflex, ❶ a sensory receptor detects a stretch in the muscle, and ❷ a sensory neuron (blue) conveys this information into the spinal cord (part of the CNS). In the CNS, the information goes to ❸ a motor neuron (purple) and to ❹ one or more interneurons (green). One set of muscles (quadriceps) responds to motor signals conveyed by a motor neuron by contracting, jerking the lower leg forward. At the same time, another motor neuron, responding to signals from an interneuron, inhibits the flexor muscles, making them relax and not resist the action of the quadriceps.

As you can see from this example, the nervous system depends on the ability of neurons to receive and convey signals. Next, we will examine how that is done.

❓ If someone tickles the bottom of your foot, your ankle automatically flexes. Arrange the following neurons in the correct sequence for information flow during this reflex: interneuron, sensory neuron, and motor neuron.

▲ **Figure 31.1A** Organization of a nervous system

● Sensory neuron ⟶ interneuron ⟶ motor neuron

31.2 Neurons are the functional units of nervous systems

The ability of neurons to receive and transmit information depends on their structure. **Figure 31.2** depicts a motor neuron, like those that carry command signals from your spinal cord to your skeletal muscles.

Most of a neuron's organelles, including its nucleus, are located in the **cell body**. Arising from the cell body are two types of extensions: numerous dendrites and a single axon. **Dendrites** (from the Greek *dendron*, tree) are highly branched extensions that *receive* signals from stimuli or other neurons and convey this information toward the cell body. Dendrites are often short. In contrast, the **axon**, which originates at the **axon hillock**, is typically a much longer extension that *transmits* signals to other cells, which may be other neurons or effector cells. Some axons, such as the ones that reach from your spinal cord to muscle cells in your feet, can be more than a metre long.

Neurons make up only part of a nervous system. To function normally, neurons of all vertebrates and most invertebrates require supporting cells called **glia**. Depending on the type, glia may nourish neurons, insulate the axons of neurons, or help to maintain homeostasis of the extracellular fluid surrounding neurons. In the mammalian brain, glia outnumber neurons by as many as 50 to 1.

Figure 31.2 also shows one kind of glial cell, called a Schwann cell, which is found in the PNS. (Analogous cells are found in the CNS.) In many vertebrates, axons that convey signals are enclosed along most of their length by a thick insulating material, analogous to the plastic insulation that covers many electrical wires. This insulating material, called the **myelin sheath**, resembles a chain of oblong beads. Each bead is actually a Schwann cell, and the myelin sheath is essentially a chain of Schwann cells, each wrapped many times around the axon. The gaps between Schwann cells are called

nodes of Ranvier, and they are the only points along the axon that require nerve signals to be regenerated, which is a time-consuming process discussed further in Module 31.8. Everywhere else, the myelin sheath insulates the axon, preserving the signal and allowing it to propagate quickly. Thus, when a signal travels along a myelinated axon, it needs to be rejuvenated only at the nodes. The resulting signal is much faster than one that must be regenerated constantly along the length of the axon. In the human nervous system, signals can travel along a myelinated axon about 150 m/s (540 km/h), which means that a command from your brain can make your fingers move in just a few milliseconds. Without myelin sheaths, the signals would be over 10 times slower.

The debilitating autoimmune disease multiple sclerosis (MS) demonstrates the importance of myelin. MS, discussed in the opening essay of Chapter 34, leads to a gradual destruction of myelin sheaths by the individual's own immune system. The result is a progressive loss of signal conduction, muscle control, and brain function.

Notice in Figure 31.2 that the axon ends in a cluster of branches. A typical axon has hundreds or thousands of these branches, each with a **synaptic terminal** at the very end. The junction between a synaptic terminal and another cell is called a synapse. As we will see in Module 31.10, this is where information is passed between neurons. A synapse between a neuron and muscle fibre is called a neuromuscular junction (see Module 33.10). With the basic structure of a neuron in mind, let's take a closer look at how nervous systems are structured in different animals.

? What is the function of the myelin sheath? How does it accomplish this function?

● It speeds up conduction of signals along axons by insulating the axon.

▲ **Figure 31.2** Structure of a myelinated motor neuron

An Overview of Animal Nervous Systems

31.3 The evolution of animal nervous systems reflects changes in body symmetry

There is remarkable uniformity throughout the animal kingdom in the way nerve cells function—a strong indication that the basic architecture of the neuron was an early evolutionary adaptation. But during subsequent animal evolution, great diversity emerged in the organization of nervous systems as a whole.

The ability to sense and react originated billions of years ago with prokaryotes that could detect changes in their environment and respond in ways that enhanced their survival and reproductive success. Later, modification of simple recognition and response processes provided multicellular organisms with a mechanism for communication between cells of the body. By 500 million years ago, systems of neurons allowing animals to sense and move rapidly were present in essentially their current forms.

Animals on the earliest branches of the animal evolutionary tree (see Figure 20.4)—sponges, for instance—lack a nervous system. The first modern phylum to evolve a nervous system was the cnidarians. Hydras, jellies, and other cnidarians have a **nerve net (Figure 31.3A)**, a diffuse, weblike system of interconnected neurons extending throughout the body. Neurons of the nerve net control the contractions of the digestive cavity, movement of the tentacles, and other functions.

Cnidarians and adult echinoderms have radial, uncentralized nervous systems. Sea stars and many other echinoderms have a nerve net in each arm connected by radial nerves to a central nerve ring. This organization is better suited than a diffuse nerve net for controlling complex motion, such as the coordinated movements of hundreds of tube feet that allow a sea star to move in one direction.

The appearance of bilateral symmetry marks a key branch point in the evolution of animals and their nervous systems. Bilaterally symmetric animals tend to move through the environment with the head—usually equipped with sense organs and a brain—first encountering new stimuli. Flatworms are the simplest animals to have evolved two hallmarks of bilateral symmetry: **cephalization**, an evolutionary trend toward

the concentration of the nervous system at the head end, and **centralization**, the presence of a central nervous system distinct from a peripheral nervous system. For example, the planarian worm in **Figure 31.3B** has a small brain composed of ganglia (clusters of neuron cell bodies) and two parallel **nerve cords**, elongated bundles of neurons that control the animal's movements. These elements constitute the simplest clearly defined CNS in the animal kingdom. Nerves that connect the CNS with the rest of the body make up the PNS.

In subsequent animal phyla, the CNS evolved in complexity. For instance, the brains of leeches **(Figure 31.3C)** have a greater concentration of neurons than those of flatworms, and leech ventral nerve cords contain segmentally arranged ganglia. The insect shown in **Figure 31.3D** has a brain composed of several fused ganglia, and its ventral nerve cord also has a ganglion in each body segment. Each of these ganglia directs the activity of muscles in its segment of the body, allowing the animal to control each body segment individually.

Molluscs serve as a good illustration of how natural selection leads to correlation of the structure of a nervous system with an animal's interaction with the environment. Sessile or slow-moving molluscs, such as clams, have little or no cephalization and relatively simple sense organs. In contrast, the relatively large brain of an octopus, as mentioned in the opening essay of this chapter, or of a squid **(Figure 31.3E)**, accompanied by complex eyes and rapid signalling along giant axons, correlates well with the active predatory life of these animals.

In the next several modules, we explore the complex nervous systems that evolved in our own subphylum, the vertebrates.

 Why is it advantageous for the brain of most bilateral animals to be located at the head end?

Cephalization places the brain close to major sense organs, which are concentrated on the end of the animal that leads the way as the animal moves through its environment.

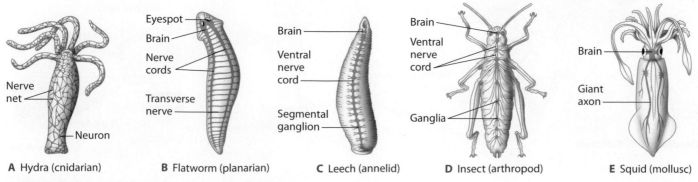

A Hydra (cnidarian) **B** Flatworm (planarian) **C** Leech (annelid) **D** Insect (arthropod) **E** Squid (mollusc)

▲ **Figure 31.3** Invertebrate nervous systems (not to scale)

31.4 Vertebrate nervous systems are highly centralized

Vertebrate nervous systems are diverse in structure and level of sophistication. For instance, those of dolphins and humans are much more complex structurally than those of frogs or fishes; they are also much more powerful integrators. However, all vertebrate nervous systems have fundamental similarities. All have distinct central and peripheral elements and are highly centralized. In all vertebrates, the brain and spinal cord make up the CNS, while the PNS accounts for the rest of the nervous system (**Figure 31.4A**). The **spinal cord**, a jellylike bundle of nerve fibres that runs lengthwise inside the spine, conveys information to and from the brain and integrates simple responses to certain stimuli (such as the knee-jerk reflex). The master control centre of the nervous system, the **brain**, includes homeostatic centres that keep the body functioning smoothly; sensory centres that integrate data from the sense organs; and (in humans, at least) centres of emotion and intellect (the intellect of octopi, discussed in this chapter's opening essay, has evolved independently from that in vertebrates). The brain also sends motor commands to muscles.

▲ **Figure 31.4B** Fluid-filled spaces of the vertebrate CNS

A vast network of blood vessels services the CNS. Brain capillaries are more selective than those elsewhere in the body. They allow essential nutrients and oxygen to pass freely into the brain, but keep out many chemicals, such as metabolic wastes from other parts of the body. This selective mechanism, called the **blood-brain barrier**, maintains a stable chemical environment for the brain.

Fluid-filled spaces in the brain called **ventricles** are continuous with the narrow **central canal** of the spinal cord (**Figure 31.4B**). These cavities are filled with **cerebrospinal fluid**, which is formed within the brain by the filtration of blood. Circulating slowly through the central canal and ventricles (and then draining back into veins), the cerebrospinal fluid cushions the CNS and assists in supplying nutrients and hormones and removing wastes. Also protecting the brain and spinal cord are layers of connective tissue, called **meninges**. If the cerebrospinal fluid becomes infected by bacteria or viruses, the meninges may become inflamed, a condition called meningitis. Viral meningitis is generally not harmful, producing minor symptoms over a short duration, but bacterial meningitis can have serious consequences if not treated with antibiotics. A sample of cerebrospinal fluid can be collected for testing by a spinal tap, a procedure in which a narrow needle is inserted through the spinal column into the central canal. In mammals, cerebrospinal fluid circulates between layers of the meninges, providing an additional protective cushion for the CNS.

As shown on the right side of Figure 31.4B, the CNS has white matter and grey matter. **White matter** is composed mainly of axons (with their whitish myelin sheaths); **grey matter** consists mainly of neuron cell bodies and dendrites.

The ganglia and nerves of the vertebrate PNS are a vast communication network. Cranial nerves originate in the brain and usually end in structures of the head and upper body (your eyes, nose, and ears, for instance). Spinal nerves originate in the spinal cord and extend to parts of the body below the head. All spinal nerves and most cranial nerves contain sensory and

▲ **Figure 31.4A** A vertebrate nervous system (back view)

motor neurons. Thousands of incoming and outgoing signals pass within the same nerves all the time.

In the next module, we look at the impact of spinal cord injuries.

? A vertebrate's central nervous system consists of the _____ and the _____.

● brain; spinal cord

31.5 Spinal cord injuries

Protected inside the bony vertebrae of the spine (your "backbone") is a gelatinous bundle of nervous tissue called the spinal cord. The 2.5 cm thick spinal cord acts as the central communication conduit between the brain and the rest of the body. Millions of nerve fibres carry motor information from the brain to the muscles, while other nerve fibres bring sensory information from the body to the brain. The spinal cord acts like a communication cable packed with fibres, each of which carries high-speed messages between the central nervous system and an outlying area such as a muscle in a finger. These signals control the voluntary and involuntary actions of your body. You will read about the details of these functions in subsequent modules.

If a communications cable is cut, signals cannot get through. In humans, the spinal cord is rarely severed because the bony vertebrae provide rigid protection. But a traumatic blow to the spinal column and subsequent bleeding, swelling, and scarring can crush the delicate nerve bundles and prevent signals from passing. Nervous tissue does not possess the same regenerative capacity as the skin (discussed in the opening essay of Chapter 25). Healing typically occurs very slowly, if at all.

Spinal cord injuries (SCI) most often happen to men, and more than half of those injured are in their teens and twenties. The most common causes are sporting injuries, vehicle accidents, gunshots, and falls. More than 85 000 Canadians are currently living with spinal cord injuries. Many have paraplegia—paralysis of the lower half of the body—while more than half have tetraplegia (quadriplegia)—paralysis from the neck down, which may necessitate permanent breathing assistance from an artificial respirator. SCIs are usually permanent because the complex damage to the spinal cord cannot be repaired.

The medical costs of treating a lifelong SCI ranges from $1.6 million for paraplegia to more than $3 million for tetraplegia. Annual medical costs for treating traumatic SCIs are $1.8 billion in Canada alone. An additional $1.8 billion is spent on indirect costs associated with these injuries. The magnitude of impact is extraordinary not only in the effects it has on humans, but also in economic terms. Each province's publicly funded healthcare system has helped thousands deal with these costs.

Multiple medal–winning paralympian Rick Hansen **(Figure 31.5)** suffered a spinal cord injury in an automobile accident as a teenager. Since then, he has established the Rick Hansen Foundation and devoted his life to assisting people with SCIs. His foundation provides wheelchairs and promotes wheelchair sports, both of which may improve the quality of life for SCI patients. He also established the Rick Hansen Spinal Cord Injury Registry to improve the quality of healthcare by

▲ **Figure 31.5** Rick Hansen, a Canadian icon at the 2010 Vancouver Winter Olympics

facilitating the sharing of knowledge between physicians across Canada. This sharing may lead to better treatments, which will ultimately lead to improved prognoses for new injuries and reduced healthcare costs. The Rick Hansen Foundation also raises funds for research that will ideally find ways to lessen or even repair spinal cord damage. Dr. Freda Miller at the University of Toronto's Hospital for Sick Children is working on ways to stimulate stem cells isolated from the skin to replace damaged nervous tissue. If successful, spinal cord repair may become feasible and help countless people worldwide.

? Why do some spinal cord injuries lead to paraplegia while others cause tetraplegia?

● The site of injury causes the different outcomes. Injuries to the lower spinal cord lead to partial paralysis and those higher up can lead to total paralysis.

31.6 The peripheral nervous system of vertebrates is a functional hierarchy

As shown in **Figure 31.6A**, the PNS can be divided into two functional components: the motor system and the autonomic nervous system. The **motor (somatic) system** carries signals to skeletal muscles, mainly in response to external stimuli. When you read, for instance, these neurons carry commands that make your eye muscles move. The control of skeletal muscles can be voluntary, as when you raise your hand to ask a question, or involuntary, as in a knee-jerk reflex controlled by the spinal cord.

The **autonomic nervous system** regulates the internal environment by controlling smooth and cardiac muscles and the organs and glands of the digestive, cardiovascular, excretory, and endocrine systems. This control is generally involuntary.

As you can see in Figure 31.6A, the autonomic nervous system is composed of three divisions: parasympathetic, sympathetic, and enteric. The parasympathetic and sympathetic divisions have largely antagonistic (opposite) effects on most body organs. The **parasympathetic division** primes the body for activities that gain and conserve energy for the body ("rest and digest"). A sample of the effects of parasympathetic signals appears on the left in **Figure 31.6B**. These include stimulating the digestive organs, such as the salivary glands, stomach, and pancreas; decreasing the heart rate; and increasing glycogen production.

While it is convenient to divide the PNS into motor and autonomic components, it is important to realize that these two divisions cooperate to maintain homeostasis. In response to a drop in body temperature, for example, the brain signals the autonomic nervous system to constrict surface blood vessels, which reduces heat loss. At the same time, the brain also signals the motor nervous system to cause shivering, which increases heat production, an example of negative feedback.

Neurons of the **sympathetic division** tend to have the opposite effect, preparing the body for intense, energy-consuming activities, such as fighting, fleeing, or competing in a strenuous game (the "fight-or-flight" response). You see some of the effects of sympathetic signals on the right side of Figure 31.6B. The digestive organs are inhibited, the bronchi dilate so that more air can pass through them, the heart rate increases, the liver releases the energy compound glucose into the blood, and the adrenal glands secrete the hormones adrenaline and noradrenaline.

Fight-or-flight and relaxation are opposite extremes. Your body usually operates at intermediate levels, with most of your organs receiving both sympathetic and parasympathetic signals. The opposing signals adjust an organ's activity to a suitable level. In regulating some body functions, however, the two divisions complement rather than antagonize each other. For example, in regulating reproduction, erection is promoted by the parasympathetic division while ejaculation is promoted by the sympathetic division.

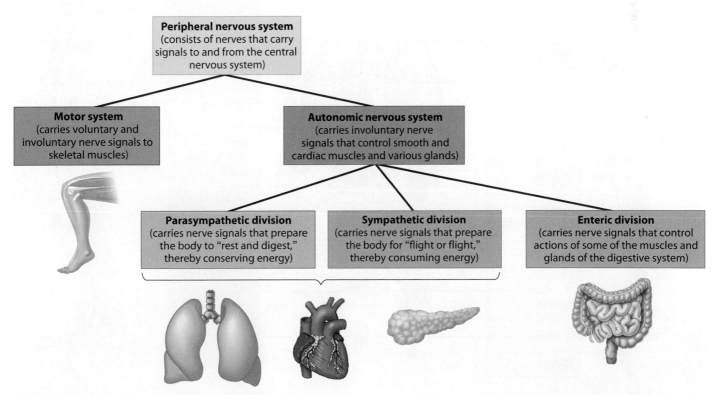

▲ **Figure 31.6A** Functional divisions of the vertebrate PNS

Sympathetic and parasympathetic neurons emerge from different regions of the CNS, represented in Figure 31.6B by black dots, and they use different neurotransmitters. As the dots in the figure indicate, neurons of the parasympathetic system emerge from the brain and the lower part of the spinal cord. Most parasympathetic neurons produce their effects by releasing the neurotransmitter acetylcholine at synapses within target organs. In contrast, neurons of the sympathetic system emerge from the middle regions of the spinal cord. Most sympathetic neurons release the neurotransmitter noradrenaline at target organs.

The **enteric division** (not shown in Figure 31.6B) of the autonomic nervous system consists of networks of neurons in the digestive tract, pancreas, and gallbladder. Within these organs, neurons of the enteric division control secretion as well as activity of the smooth muscles that produce peristalsis. Although the enteric division can function independently, it is normally regulated by the sympathetic and parasympathetic divisions.

In the next several modules, we take a closer look at the signals and how they are transmitted throughout the nervous system.

 How would a drug that inhibits the parasympathetic nervous system affect a person's pulse?

● Since signals from the parasympathetic nervous system slow the heart rate, a drug that inhibits the parasympathetic division would result in an increased pulse.

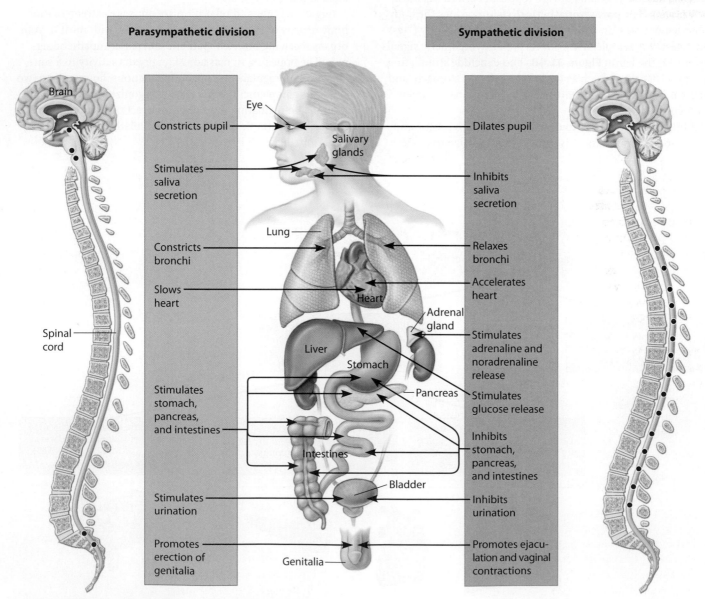

▲ **Figure 31.6B** The parasympathetic and sympathetic divisions of the autonomic nervous system

Nerve Signals and Their Transmission

31.7 Nerve function depends on charge differences across neuron membranes

To understand nerve signals, we must first study a resting neuron, one that is not transmitting a signal. Like all cells, a resting neuron has potential energy (see Module 5.9). In neurons, potential energy can be put to work sending signals from one part of the body to another. This potential energy, called the **membrane potential**, exists as an electrical charge difference across the neuron's plasma membrane: The inside of the cell is negatively charged relative to the outside as a result of unequal distribution of positively and negatively charged ions. Since opposite charges tend to move toward each other, a membrane stores energy by holding opposite charges apart, like a battery. The strength (voltage) of a neuron's stored energy can be measured with microelectrodes connected to a voltmeter. The voltage across the plasma membrane of a resting neuron is called the **resting potential**. A neuron's resting potential is about -70 millivolts (mV)—about 5% of the voltage in a flashlight battery. The minus sign indicates that the inside of the cell is negative relative to the outside.

The resting potential exists because of differences in ionic composition of the fluids inside and outside the neuron **(Figure 31.7)**. The plasma membrane surrounding the neuron has protein channels and pumps that regulate the passage of inorganic ions (see Modules 5.6 and 5.7 for a review of channels and pumps). A resting membrane has many open potassium (K^+) channels but only a few open sodium (Na^+) channels, allowing much more potassium than sodium to diffuse across the membrane. Therefore, Na^+ is more concentrated outside the neuron (150 millimoles per litre, or millimolar [mM]) than inside (15 mM). (Mutations in genes for an Na^+ channel in the brain can cause groups of nerve cells to fire excessively, resulting in epileptic seizures.) But K^+, which is more concentrated inside (140 mM versus 5 mM outside), can flow out through the many open K^+ channels. As the positively charged potassium ions diffuse out, the inside of the neuron becomes less positive—that is, more negative—relative to the outside. Also helping to maintain the resting potential are membrane proteins called **sodium-potassium (Na^+-K^+) pumps**. Using energy from ATP, these pumps actively transport Na^+ out of the neuron and K^+ in, thereby helping to keep the concentration of Na^+ low in the neuron and K^+ high.

▲ **Figure 31.7** How the resting potential is generated

This ionic gradient (high K^+/low Na^+ concentrations inside coupled with low K^+/high Na^+ concentrations outside) produces an electrical potential difference, or voltage, across the membrane—the resting potential. Notice an important point: *The membrane potential can change from its resting value if the membrane's permeability to particular ions changes.* As we will see in the next module, this is the basis of nearly all electrical signals in the nervous system.

 If a neuron's membrane suddenly becomes more permeable to sodium ions, there is a rapid net movement of Na^+ into the cell. What are the two forces that drive the ions inward?

● The greater concentration of Na^+ outside the cell than inside and the membrane potential (negatively charged inside versus outside) favour the inward diffusion of Na^+.

31.8 A nerve signal begins as a change in the membrane potential

Turning on a flashlight uses the potential energy stored in a battery to create light. In a similar way, stimulating a neuron's plasma membrane can trigger the use of the membrane's potential energy to generate a nerve signal. A **stimulus** is any factor that causes a nerve signal to be generated. Examples of stimuli include light, sound, a tap on the knee, or a chemical signal from another neuron.

The discovery of giant axons in squids (up to 1 mm in diameter) gave researchers their first chance to study how stimuli trigger signals in a living neuron. From microelectrode studies with squid neurons, British biologists A. L. Hodgkin and A. F. Huxley worked out the details of nerve signal transmission in the 1940s, earning a Nobel Prize for their findings. The nerve signal transmission process, summarized in

Figure 31.8, applies to neurons in nearly all animals, including humans.

The graph in the middle of the figure traces the electrical changes that make up an **action potential**, a change in membrane voltage that transmits a nerve signal along an axon. The graph records electrical events over time (in milliseconds) at a particular place on the membrane where a stimulus is applied. ❶ The graph at the centre of the figure starts out at the membrane's resting potential (−70 mV). ❷ The stimulus is applied. If it is strong enough, the voltage rises to what is called the **threshold** (−50 mV, in this case). The difference between the threshold and the resting potential is the minimum change in the membrane's voltage that must occur to generate the action potential (+20 mV, in this case). This is an all-or-none response in that an action potential will be generated if threshold is reached, or nothing will happen if it is not. ❸ Once the threshold is reached, the action potential is triggered. The membrane polarity reverses abruptly (called *depolarization*), with the interior of the cell becoming positive with respect to the outside. ❹ The membrane potential rapidly drops back down (called *repolarization*), ❺ passes the resting potential, becomes more negative (called *hyperpolarization*), and ❶ finally returns to the resting potential.

What actually causes the electrical changes of the action potential? The rapid flip-flop of the membrane potential is a result of the rapid movements of ions across the membrane through voltage-gated Na^+ and K^+ channels, so called because they have special gates that open and close, depending on changes in membrane potential. These are a kind of transport protein, as described in Module 5.6. The diagrams surrounding the graph show the ion movements. Starting at lower left, ❶ the resting membrane separates a positively charged outside environment from a negatively charged inside environment. ❷ A stimulus triggers the opening of a few gated Na^+ channels in the membrane, and a tiny amount of Na^+ enters the axon. This makes the inside surface of the membrane slightly less negative. If the stimulus is strong enough, a sufficient number of these Na^+ channels open to raise the voltage to the threshold. ❸ Once the threshold is reached, many voltage-gated Na^+ channels open, allowing even more Na^+ to diffuse into the cell. As more and more Na^+ moves in, the voltage soars to its peak. ❹ The peak voltage triggers closing and inactivation of the voltage-gated Na^+ channels. Meanwhile, the voltage-gated K^+ channels open, allowing K^+ to diffuse out rapidly. These changes produce the downswing on the graph. ❺ A very brief undershoot of the resting potential results because these K^+ channels close slowly. ❶ The membrane then returns to its resting potential. In a typical mammalian neuron, this entire process takes just a few milliseconds, meaning that a neuron can produce hundreds of nerve signals per second.

? **Is the generation of the peak of an action potential an example of positive feedback or negative feedback?**

● The opening of Na^+ gates caused by stimulation of the neuron changes the membrane potential, and this change causes more of the voltage-gated Na^+ channels to open. This is an example of a positive-feedback mechanism.

❸ Additional Na^+ channels open, K^+ channels remain closed; interior of cell becomes more positive.

❷ A stimulus opens some Na^+ channels; if threshold is reached, an action potential is triggered.

❶ Resting state: Voltage-gated Na^+ and K^+ channels are closed; resting potential is maintained by ungated channels (not shown).

Sodium Potassium channel channel
Outside of neuron
Plasma membrane
Inside of neuron

❹ Na^+ channels close and inactivate; K^+ channels open, and K^+ rushes out; interior of cell is more negative than outside.

❺ The K^+ channels close relatively slowly, passing the resting potential.

❶ Return to resting state.

Graph labels: Membrane potential (mV); +50; 0; −50; −100; Action potential; Threshold; Resting potential; Time

▲ **Figure 31.8** The action potential

31.9 The action potential propagates itself along the axon

An action potential is a localized electrical event—a rapid change from the resting potential at a specific place along the neuron. A nerve signal starts out as an action potential generated at the axon hillock, typically where the axon meets the cell body. To function as a long-distance signal, this local event must be passed along the axon from the cell body to the synaptic terminals. It does so by regenerating itself along the axon in a single direction only **(Figure 31.9)**. The effect of this action potential is like tipping the first of a row of standing dominoes: The first domino does not travel along the row, but its fall is relayed to the end of the row, one domino at a time.

The three steps in Figure 31.9 show the changes that occur in an axon segment as a nerve signal passes from left to right. Let's first focus on the axon region on the far left. ❶ When this region of the axon (blue) has its Na⁺ channels open, Na⁺ rushes inward, and an action potential is generated. This corresponds to the upswing of the curve (step 2) in Figure 31.8.

❷ Soon, the K⁺ channels in that same region open, allowing K⁺ to diffuse out of the axon; at this time, its Na⁺ channels are closed and inactivated at that point on the axon, and we would see the downswing of the action potential. ❸ A short time later, we would see no signs of an action potential at this (far-left) spot because the axon membrane here has restored itself and returned to its resting potential.

Now let's see how these events lead to the "domino effect" of a nerve signal. In step 1 of the figure, the blue arrows pointing sideways within the axon indicate local spreading of the electrical changes caused by the inflowing Na⁺ associated with the first action potential. This spreading is caused by the diffusion of Na⁺ ions within the cytoplasm and is large enough to reach threshold in the neighbouring node of Ranvier, triggering the opening of Na⁺ channels. As a result, a second action potential is generated, as indicated by the blue region in step 2. In the same way, a third action potential is generated in step 3, and each action potential generates another all the way down the axon. The net result is the movement of a nerve impulse from the cell body to the synaptic terminals.

So why are action potentials propagated in only one direction along the axon (left to right in the figure)? As the blue arrows indicate, local electrical changes do spread in both directions in the axon. However, these changes cannot open Na⁺ channels and generate an action potential when the Na⁺ channels are inactivated (step 4 in Figure 31.8). Thus, an action potential cannot be generated in the regions where K⁺ is leaving the axon (green in the figure) and Na⁺ channels are still inactivated. Consequently, the inward flow of Na⁺ that depolarizes the axon membrane ahead of the action potential cannot produce another action potential behind it. Once an action potential starts where the cell body and axon meet, it moves along the axon in only one direction: toward the synaptic terminals.

Action potentials are all-or-none events; that is, they are the same no matter how strong or weak the stimulus that triggers them (as long as threshold is reached). How, then, do action potentials relay different intensities of information (such as a loud sound versus a soft sound) to your central nervous system? It is the *frequency* of action potentials that changes with the intensity of stimuli. For example, in the neurons connecting the ear to the brain, loud sounds generate more action potentials per second than quiet sounds.

In the last three modules, we have examined how nerve signals are conducted along a single neuron. In the next three modules, we focus on how signals pass from one neuron to another.

▲ **Figure 31.9** Propagation of the action potential along an unmyelinated portion of an axon

? During an action potential, ions move across the neuron plasma membrane in a direction perpendicular to the direction of the impulse along the neuron. What is it that actually travels along the neuron as the signal?

● The signal is the wavelike change in membrane potential, the self-perpetuated action potential that regenerates sequentially at points farther and farther away from the site of stimulation.

31.10 Neurons communicate at synapses

If an action potential travels in one direction along an axon, what happens when the signal arrives at the end of the neuron? To continue conveying information, the signal must be passed to another cell. This occurs at a **synapse**, or relay point, between a synaptic terminal of a sending neuron and a receiving cell. The receiving cell can be another neuron or an effector cell such as a muscle cell or endocrine cell.

Synapses come in two varieties: electrical and chemical. In an electrical synapse, electrical current flows directly from a neuron to a receiving cell. The receiving cell is stimulated quickly and at the same frequency of action potentials as the sending neuron. Lobsters and many fishes can flip their tails with lightning speed because the neurons that carry signals for these movements communicate by fast electrical synapses. In the human body, electrical synapses are found in the heart and digestive tract, where nerve signals maintain steady, rhythmic muscle contractions.

In contrast, when an action potential reaches a chemical synapse, it stops there. This is because, unlike electrical synapses, chemical synapses have a narrow gap, called the **synaptic cleft**, separating a synaptic terminal of the sending (presynaptic) cell from the receiving (postsynaptic) cell. The cleft is very narrow— only about 50 nm, about 1/1000th the width of a human hair— but it prevents the action potential from spreading directly to the receiving cell. Instead, the action potential (an electrical signal) is first converted to a chemical signal consisting of molecules of **neurotransmitter** (see Module 29.1). The chemical signal may then generate an action potential in the receiving cell.

Let's follow the events that occur at a typical chemical synapse, shown in **Figure 31.10**. Molecules of the neurotransmitter (✸) are in membrane-enclosed sacs called **synaptic vesicles** in the sending neuron's synaptic terminals. ❶ An action potential arrives at the synaptic terminal. ❷ The action potential causes some synaptic vesicles to fuse with the plasma membrane of the sending cell. ❸ The fused vesicles release their neurotransmitter molecules by exocytosis into the synaptic cleft, and the neurotransmitter rapidly diffuses across the cleft.

The subsequent steps in Figure 31.10 show one example of what can happen next at a chemical synapse. ❹ The released neurotransmitter binds to complementary receptors on ion channel proteins in the receiving cell's plasma membrane. ❺ In a typical chemical synapse, the binding of neurotransmitter to receptor opens these chemically gated ion channels in the receiving cell's membrane. With the channels open, ions can diffuse into the receiving cell and trigger new action potentials. ❻ The neurotransmitter is broken down by an enzyme or is transported back into the signalling cell, and the ion channels close. Step 6 ensures that the neurotransmitter's effect is brief and precise.

❺ Ion channel opens   ❻ Ion channel closes

▲ **Figure 31.10** Neuron communication at a typical chemical synapse

You can review what we have covered so far in this chapter by thinking about what is happening right now in your own nervous system. Action potentials carrying information about the words on this page are streaming along sensory neurons from your eyes to your brain. Arriving at synapses with receiving cells (interneurons in the brain), the action potentials are triggering the release of neurotransmitters at the ends of the sensory neurons. The neurotransmitters are diffusing across synaptic clefts and triggering changes in some of your interneurons—changes that lead to integration of the signals and ultimately to what the signals actually mean (in this case, the meaning of words and sentences). Next, motor neurons in your brain will send out action potentials to muscle cells in your eyes, telling them to move to the next section of text.

? How does a synapse ensure that signals pass only in one direction, from a sending neuron to a receiving cell?

● The signal can go only one way at any one synapse because only the sending neuron releases neurotransmitter and only the receiving cell has receptors for the neurotransmitter.

31.11 Chemical synapses enable complex information to be processed

As the drawing and micrograph in **Figure 31.11** indicate, one neuron may interact with many others. In fact, a neuron may receive information via neurotransmitters from hundreds of other neurons connecting at thousands of synaptic terminals (red and green in the drawing). The inputs can be highly varied because each sending neuron may secrete a different quantity or kind of neurotransmitter. The plasma membrane of a neuron resembles a tiny circuit board, receiving and processing bits of information in the form of neurotransmitter molecules. These exceedingly sophisticated living circuit boards account for the nervous system's ability to process data and formulate appropriate responses to stimuli.

What do neurotransmitters actually do to neurons receiving the signal? The binding of a neurotransmitter to a receptor may open ion channels in the receiving cell's plasma membrane, as you saw in Figure 31.10, or trigger a signal transduction pathway that does so. The effect of the neurotransmitter depends on the kind of membrane channel it opens. Neurotransmitters that open Na^+ channels, for instance, may trigger action potentials in the receiving cell. Such effects are referred to as excitatory (green in the drawing). In contrast, many neurotransmitters open membrane channels for ions that *decrease* the tendency to develop action potentials in the receiving cell—such as channels that admit Cl^- or release K^+. These effects are called inhibitory (red). The effects of both excitatory and inhibitory signals can vary in magnitude. In general, the more neurotransmitter molecules that bind to receptors on the receiving cell and the closer the synapse is to the base of the receiving cell's axon, the stronger the effect.

A receiving neuron's plasma membrane may receive signals—both excitatory and inhibitory—from many different sending neurons. If the excitatory signals are collectively strong enough to raise the membrane potential to threshold, an action potential will be generated in the receiving cell. That neuron then passes signals along its axon to other cells at a rate that represents a summation of all the information it has received. Signal frequency is key because action potentials are all-or-none events. Each new receiving cell, in turn, processes this information along with all its other inputs.

Many different types of neurotransmitters can be released at synaptic clefts. However, a single neuron will produce just one neurotransmitter. Small, nitrogen-containing organic neurotransmitters, including **acetylcholine,** are important in the brain and at synapses between motor neurons and muscle cells. Botulinum toxin (Botox), made by the bacteria that cause botulism food poisoning, inhibits the release of acetylcholine. Botox injections disable the synapses that control certain facial muscles, thereby eliminating wrinkles around the eyes or mouth.

Four other neurotransmitters—aspartate, glutamate, glycine, and GABA (gamma aminobutyric acid)—are known to be important in the central nervous system. Aspartate and glutamate act primarily at excitatory synapses, while glycine and GABA act at inhibitory synapses.

Synaptic terminals
Inhibitory Excitatory
Dendrites
Myelin sheath
Axon
Receiving cell body

Synaptic terminals

SEM 5500×

▲ **Figure 31.11** A neuron's multiple synaptic inputs

Still other neurotransmitters, called **biogenic amines,** are derived from amino acids. Some examples are adrenaline, noradrenaline, serotonin, and dopamine, the first two of which also function as hormones (see Chapter 29). Serotonin and dopamine affect sleep, mood, attention, and learning. Imbalances of biogenic amines are associated with various disorders. For example, the degenerative illness Parkinson's disease is associated with a lack of dopamine in the brain.

Many neuropeptides, such as endorphins, are relatively short chains of amino acids and serve as neurotransmitters. Dissolved gases, notably nitric oxide (NO), can also act as chemical signals at a synapse.

? Contrast how excitatory and inhibitory signals change a receiving cell's membrane potential relative to triggering an action potential.

● Neurotransmitters in an excitatory signal open ion channels that move the receiving cell's membrane potential closer to threshold. Neurotransmitters in an inhibitory signal open ion channels that move the cell's membrane potential farther from threshold.

31.12 Many drugs act at chemical synapses

Many psychoactive drugs, even common ones such as caffeine, nicotine, and alcohol, affect the action of neurotransmitters in the brain's billions of synapses (**Figure 31.12**). Caffeine, found in coffee, tea, chocolate, and many soft drinks, keeps us awake by countering the effects of inhibitory neurotransmitters, ones that normally suppress nerve signals. Nicotine acts as a stimulant by binding to and activating acetylcholine receptors. Alcohol is a strong depressant. Its precise effect is not yet known, but it seems to increase the inhibitory effects of the neurotransmitter GABA.

Many prescription drugs used to treat psychological disorders alter the effects of neurotransmitters (see Module 31.19). The most popular class of antidepressant medication works by affecting the action of serotonin. Called selective serotonin reuptake inhibitors (SSRIs), these medications block the removal of serotonin from synapses, increasing the amount of time this mood-altering neurotransmitter is available to receiving cells. Tranquilizers such as diazepam (Valium) and alprazolam (Xanax) activate the receptors for the neurotransmitter GABA, increasing its effect at inhibitory synapses. In other cases, a drug may bind to and block a receptor, reducing

a neurotransmitter's effect. For instance, some drugs used to treat schizophrenia block receptors for the neurotransmitter dopamine. Some drugs used to treat attention deficit hyperactivity disorder (ADHD), such as methylphenidate (Ritalin) and Adderall (a combination drug), block the reuptake of dopamine and noreadrenaline (norepinephrine), which can increase alertness. Some students abuse Adderall as a "study drug," which can be quite dangerous because of significant risk of seizures and cardiac problems. Because the effects of these drugs are poorly understood, a physician should monitor anyone taking them.

What about illegal drugs? Stimulants such as amphetamines and cocaine increase the release and availability of noradrenaline and dopamine at synapses in the pleasure centre of the brain. Abuse of these drugs can cause symptoms resembling schizophrenia. The active ingredient in marijuana (tetrahydrocannabinol [THC]) binds to brain receptors normally used by other neurotransmitters that seem to play a role in pain, depression, appetite, memory, and fertility. Opiates—morphine, codeine, and heroin—bind to endorphin receptors, reducing pain and producing euphoria. Not surprisingly, opiates are used medicinally for pain relief. However, abuse of opiates may permanently change the brain's chemical synapses and reduce normal synthesis of neurotransmitters. As explained in the next module, these drugs are also highly addictive.

The drugs discussed here are used for a variety of purposes, both medicinal and recreational. While they increase alertness and sense of well-being or reduce physical and emotional pain, they may disrupt the brain's finely tuned neural pathways, altering the chemical balances that are the product of millions of years of evolution.

▲ **Figure 31.12** Alcohol, nicotine, and caffeine—drugs that alter the effects of neurotransmitters

 What is the biochemical basis for the pain-relieving properties of morphine?

● Morphine binds to the same receptors as endorphins, the body's natural pain relievers.

The Human Brain

31.13 The structure of a living supercomputer: The human brain

Composed of up to 100 billion intricately organized neurons, with a much larger number of supporting cells, the human brain is more powerful than the most sophisticated computer. **Figure 31.13A** shows three ancestral brain regions in their fully developed adult form. **Table 31.13** summarizes the anatomy and physiology of the major structures of the brain.

Looking first at the lower brain centres, two sections of the hindbrain (blue), the **medulla oblongata** and **pons**, and the midbrain (purple) make up a functional unit called the **brain stem**. Consisting of a stalk with caplike swellings at the anterior end of the spinal cord, the brain stem is, evolutionarily

speaking, one of the older parts of the vertebrate brain. The brain stem coordinates and filters the conduction of information from sensory and motor neurons to the higher brain regions. It also regulates sleep and arousal and helps to coordinate body movements, such as walking. Table 31.13 lists some of the individual functions of the medulla oblongata, pons, and midbrain.

Another part of the hindbrain, the **cerebellum** (light blue), is a planning centre for body movements. It also plays a role in learning, decision making, and remembering motor responses. The cerebellum receives sensory information about the

▲ Figure 31.13A The main parts of the human brain

TABLE 31.13 | **MAJOR STRUCTURES OF THE HUMAN BRAIN**

Brain Structure	Major Functions
Brain stem	Conducts data to and from other brain centres; helps to maintain homeostasis; coordinates body movement
Medulla oblongata	Controls breathing, circulation, swallowing, digestion
Pons	Controls breathing
Midbrain	Receives and integrates auditory data; coordinates visual reflexes; sends sensory data to higher brain centres
Cerebellum	Coordinates body movement; plays role in learning and in remembering motor responses
Thalamus	Serves as input centre for sensory data going to the cerebrum, output centre for motor responses leaving the cerebrum; sorts data
Hypothalamus	Functions as homeostatic control centre; controls pituitary gland; serves as biological clock
Cerebrum	Performs sophisticated integration; plays major role in memory, learning, speech, emotions; formulates complex behavioural responses

position of joints and the length of muscles, as well as information from the auditory and visual systems. It also receives input concerning motor commands issued by the cerebrum. The cerebellum uses this information to coordinate movement and balance. Hand-eye coordination is an example of such control by the cerebellum. If the cerebellum is damaged, the eyes can follow a moving object, but they will not stop at the same place as the object.

The most sophisticated integrating centres are those derived from the forebrain (orange and gold)—the thalamus, the hypothalamus, and the cerebellum. The **thalamus** contains most of the cell bodies of neurons that relay information to the **cerebral cortex**. The thalamus first sorts data into categories (all the touch signals from a hand, for instance). It also suppresses some signals and enhances others. The thalamus then sends on information to the appropriate higher brain centres for further interpretation and integration.

In Module 29.4, we saw that the hypothalamus controls the pituitary gland and the secretion of many hormones. The hypothalamus also regulates body temperature, blood pressure, hunger, thirst, sex drive, and fight-or-flight responses, and it helps us experience emotions such as rage and pleasure. A "pleasure centre" in the hypothalamus could also be called an addiction centre, for it is strongly affected by certain addictive drugs, such as amphetamines and cocaine. As described in the previous module, these drugs increase the effects of noradrenaline and dopamine at synapses in the pleasure centre, producing a short-term high, often followed by depression. Cocaine addiction may involve chemical changes in the pleasure centre and elsewhere in the hypothalamus.

A pair of hypothalmic structures called the suprachiasmatic nuclei function as an internal timekeeper, our **biological clock**. Receiving visual input from the eyes (light–dark cycles, in particular), the clock maintains our **circadian rhythms**—daily cycles of biological activity—such as the sleep–wake cycle. Research with many different species has shown that without environmental cues, biological clocks keep time in a free-running way. For example, when humans are placed in artificial settings that lack environmental cues, our biological clocks and circadian rhythms maintain a cycle of approximately 24 hours 11 minutes, with very little variation among individuals.

The **cerebrum**, the largest and most complex part of our brain, consists of right and left **cerebral hemispheres (Figure 31.13B)**, each responsible for the opposite side of the body. A thick band of nerve fibres called the **corpus callosum** facilitates communication between the hemispheres, enabling them to process information together. Under the corpus callosum, groups of neurons called the **basal nuclei** are important in motor coordination. If they are damaged, a person may be immobilized. Degeneration of the basal nuclei occurs in Parkinson's disease (see Module 31.19). The most extensive area of our cerebrum, the cerebral cortex, is the focus of the next module.

? Choosing from the structures in Table 31.13, identify the brain part most important in solving an algebra problem.

● Cerebrum

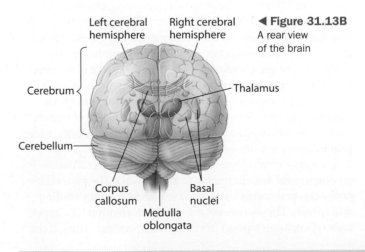

◄ Figure 31.13B A rear view of the brain

31.14 The cerebral cortex is a mosaic of specialized, interactive regions

Although less than 5 mm thick—less than the thickness of a pencil—the highly folded cerebral cortex accounts for about 80% of the total human brain mass. It contains some 10 billion neurons and hundreds of billions of synapses. Its intricate neural circuitry produces our most distinctive human traits: reasoning and mathematical abilities, language skills, imagination, artistic talent, and personality traits. Assembling information it receives from our eyes, ears, nose, taste buds, and touch sensors, the cerebral cortex also creates our sensory perceptions—what we are actually aware of when we see, hear, smell, taste, or touch something. In addition, the cerebral cortex regulates our voluntary movements.

Like the rest of the cerebrum, the cerebral cortex is divided into right and left sides connected by the corpus callosum. Each side of the cerebral cortex has four lobes named for a nearby bone of the skull: the frontal, parietal, temporal, and occipital lobes, which are represented by different colours in **Figure 31.14**. Researchers have identified a number of functional areas within each lobe.

Two areas of known function form the boundary between the frontal and parietal lobes. One area, called the motor cortex, functions mainly in sending commands to skeletal muscles, signalling appropriate responses to sensory stimuli. Next to the motor cortex, the somatosensory cortex receives and partially integrates signals from touch, pain, pressure, and temperature receptors throughout the body. The cerebral cortex also has centres that receive and begin processing sensory information concerned with vision, hearing, taste, and smell.

Making up most of our cerebral cortex are numerous **association areas**, sites of higher mental activities—roughly, what we call thinking. Each sensory-receiving centre of the cerebral cortex and the somatosensory cortex cooperates with an adjacent association area. In humans, a large association area in the frontal lobe uses varied inputs from many other areas of the brain to evaluate consequences, make considered judgments, and also plan for the future. Imaging techniques, such as PET (positron-emission topography) scanning, are beginning to show how a complicated interchange of signals among the sensory-receiving centres and the association areas produces our sensory perceptions.

Language results from extremely complex interactions among several association areas. For instance, the parietal lobe of the cerebral cortex has association areas used for reading and speech. These areas obtain visual information (the appearance of words on a page) from the vision centres. Then, if the

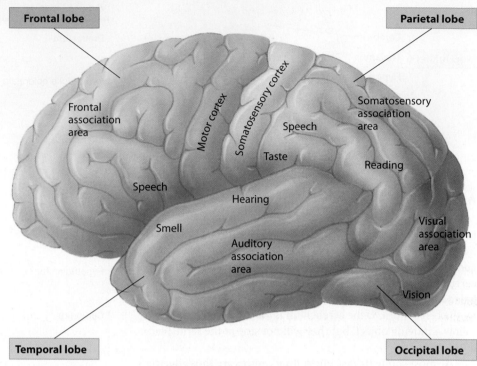

▲ **Figure 31.14** Functional areas of the left cerebral hemisphere

words are to be spoken aloud, they arrange the information into speech patterns and tell another speech centre, in the frontal lobe, how to make the motor cortex move the tongue, lips, and other muscles to form words. When we hear words, the parietal areas perform similar functions by using information from auditory centres of the cerebral cortex.

You may have heard people comment that they are "left-brained" or "right-brained." In a phenomenon known as **lateralization**, areas in the two cerebral hemispheres become specialized for different functions during brain development in infants and children. In most people, the left cerebral hemisphere becomes adept at language, logic, and mathematical operations, as well as detailed skeletal motor control and processing of fine visual and auditory details. The right cerebral hemisphere is stronger at spatial relations, pattern and face recognition, and nonverbal thinking. (In about 10% of us, these roles of the left and right cerebral hemispheres are reversed or the hemispheres are less specialized.)

Research by Canadian psychiatrist and author of the New York Times Bestseller *The Brain That Changes Itself*, Dr. Norman Doidge from the University of Toronto has shown that the human brain is a remarkably plastic organ. That is, the brain can change its structure and function, including these association areas through rigorous training. Doidge has demonstrated that how we use our brains can alter their structure and function. For example, as you read this chapter and learn about nervous systems, new connections are being formed between the cells in your brain. These new connections are reinforced as you practise studying the material. Moreover, if an association area is injured, during a stroke, for example, new connections can be forged and its role can be adopted by another part of the brain.

How have researchers identified the functions of different parts of the brain? We explore this question in the next module.

? A stroke that causes loss of taste and numbness of the right side of the body has probably damaged brain tissue in the _____ lobe of the _____ cerebral hemisphere.

● parietal; left

31.15 Injuries and brain operations provide insight into brain function

The physiology of the human brain is exquisitely complex, making it one of the most difficult structures to study in all of biology. No animal model or computer simulation can accurately predict its complicated functions. New techniques, such as PET scans and fMRIs (see Module 31.17), are allowing researchers to associate specific parts of the brain with various activities. Much of what has been learned about the brain, however, has come from rare individuals whose brains were altered through injury, illness, or surgery. By studying such "broken brains," researchers have gained insight into how healthy brains operate.

The first well-publicized case of this type involved a man named Phineas Gage. In 1848, while working as a railroad construction foreman in Vermont, Gage accidentally exploded a dynamite charge that propelled an almost metre-long spike through his head. The 6 kg steel rod entered his left cheek and travelled upward behind his left eye and out the top of his skull, landing several metres away. Incredibly, Gage walked away from the accident and appeared to have an intact intellect. However, his associates soon noticed drastic changes in his personality, with new propensities toward meanness, vulgarity, irresponsibility, and an inability to control his behaviour.

At the time, Gage's doctor was able to note these changes, but understanding of the brain was insufficient to explain them. Luckily, the doctor preserved Gage's skull and the spike, allowing a group of researchers in 1994 to produce a computer model of the injury (Figure 31.15A). The modern analysis offered an explanation for Gage's bizarre behaviour: The rod had pierced both frontal lobes of his brain. People with these sorts of injuries often exhibit irrational decision making and difficulty processing emotions. As you will learn in Module 31.18, the frontal lobes are part of the limbic system, a group of brain structures involved with emotions.

Beginning with the work of several neurosurgeons in the 1950s, many of the functional areas of the cerebral cortex have been identified during brain surgery. The cortex lacks pain receptors; thus, after anaesthetizing the scalp, a neurosurgeon can operate on the cerebrum with the patient awake. Parts of the cortex can be stimulated with a harmless electrical current. Stimulation of specific areas can cause someone to experience different sensations or recall memories. Researchers can obtain information about the effects simply by questioning the conscious patient.

Neurophysiologists have also gained insight into the interrelatedness of the brain's two cerebral hemispheres. As discussed in Module 31.14, association areas in the left and right sides become specialized for different functions. Much of what we know about this lateralization stems from the work of American neurobiologist Roger Sperry with patients whose corpus callosum (communicating fibres between the two cerebral hemispheres; see Module 31.13) had been surgically cut to treat severe epileptic seizures. In a series of ingenious experiments, Sperry demonstrated that his patients were unable to verbalize sensory information that was received by only the right cerebral hemisphere.

One of the most radical surgical alterations of the brain is a hemispherectomy (Figure 31.15B)— the removal of almost half of the brain, excluding deep structures such as the thalamus, brain stem, and basal nuclei. This procedure is performed to alleviate severe seizure disorders

▲ Figure 31.15B MRI image of hemispherectomy patient after surgery

that originate from one of the cerebral hemispheres as a result of illness, abnormal development, or stroke. Incredibly, with just half a brain, hemispherectomy patients recover

▲ Figure 31.15A Computer model of Phineas Gage's injury

quickly, often leaving the hospital within a few weeks. Their intellectual capacities are undiminished, although the side of the body opposite the surgery remains partially paralyzed. Higher brain functions that previously originated from the missing half of the brain begin to be controlled by the opposite side. Development after hemispherectomy is a striking example of the remarkable plasticity of the

brain and reflects the work of Doidge discussed in the previous module.

 How are researchers able to investigate brain function during brain surgery?

● The cortex lacks pain receptors. Regions of the brain can be stimulated during surgery, and the conscious patient can report sensations or memories.

31.16 Several parts of the brain regulate sleep and arousal

As anyone who has drifted off to sleep during a lecture or while reading a book knows, attentiveness and mental alertness can change rapidly. Arousal is a state of awareness of the outside world. Its counterpart is sleep, a state when external stimuli are received but not consciously perceived.

The brain stem contains several centres for controlling arousal and sleep. One such centre is the reticular formation, a diffuse network of neurons that extends through the core of the brain stem (see Table 31.13). Acting as a sensory filter, the reticular formation receives data from sensory receptors and selects which information reaches the cerebrum. The more information the cerebrum receives, the more alert and aware a person is, although the brain often ignores certain familiar and repetitive stimuli—the feel of your clothes against your skin, for example—while actively processing other inputs. Sleep and wakefulness are also regulated by specific parts of the brain stem: The pons and medulla contain centres that promote sleep when stimulated, and the midbrain has a centre that promotes arousal.

Although we know very little about its function, sleep is essential for survival. Furthermore, sleep is an active state, at

least for the brain. By placing electrodes at multiple sites on the scalp, researchers can record patterns of electrical activity called brain waves in an electroencephalogram, or EEG. These recordings reveal that brain wave frequency changes as the brain progresses through several distinct stages of sleep. During the stage called REM (rapid eye movement) sleep, the brain waves are rapid and irregular, more like those of the awake state. We have most of our dreams during REM sleep, which typically occurs about six times a night for periods of 5–50 minutes each.

Understanding the function of sleeping and dreaming remains a compelling research problem. One hypothesis is that sleep and dreams are involved in the consolidation of learning and memory, and experiments show that regions of the brain activated during a learning task can become active again during sleep.

 What prevents the cerebral cortex from being overwhelmed by all the sensory stimuli arriving from sensory receptors?

● The reticular formation filters out unimportant stimuli.

RUMOUR HAS IT ## 31.17 Do we use only 10% of our brains?

As you have read in the previous two modules, the brain is an incredibly complex organ. Although scientists have learned a great deal about the brain, we are certainly far from understanding it completely. Its complexity has allowed popular media to perpetuate the rumour that we use only 10% of our brains. This belief has survived for decades, perhaps because it provides us with hope for tapping into unused potential. Unfortunately, these are false hopes, as we do in fact use all of our brain, although, not necessarily at the same time.

This rumour is contradicted by several pieces of anecdotal evidence. For example, with an average mass of 1400 g, the brain makes up 2% to 3% of your body weight. Yet, the brain consumes 20% of the body's energy. This disproportionate consumption of energy would be unlikely if only 140 g (10%) of the brain's mass was functional. Also, you should expect that nine out of ten patients with brain injuries (trauma or strokes) would have a complete recovery. Suffering a stroke in an unused region of the brain should have no long-term

consequences. Instead, only 10% of the 50 000 Canadians that will suffer strokes this year will make a full recovery. The remaining survivors have some degree of impairment, potentially severe and lifelong.

Concrete evidence can be obtained using functional magnetic resonance imaging (fMRI), a scanning and imaging technology that highlights metabolically active cells by measuring changes in glucose metabolism. Since the procedure can be performed on a conscious patient, fMRI scans provide significant insights into brain structure and function. This technique uses powerful magnets to align and then locate atoms within living tissue. During fMRI, a subject lies with his or her head in the hole of a large, doughnut-shaped magnet. When the brain is scanned with electromagnetic waves, changes in blood oxygen usage at sites of neuronal activity generate a signal that can be recorded. A computer uses the data to construct a three-dimensional map of the subject's brain activity. Changes in brain function as the patient performs different tasks can be seen in real-time (**Figure 31.17**). Studies using fMRI confirm

▲ **Figure 31.17** fMRI images of a person thinking about words (left) and reading words (right)

hypotheses based on older technologies regarding the roles of specific and separate regions of the brain for intention and movement.

If you examined multiple fMRI scans of a patient performing a wide variety of tasks, you would see each region of the brain highlighted at some point. This indicates that we use nearly all the brain, not just 10%. Though the decisions some people make may perpetuate this rumour, we do use the entirety of our brains.

? How can fMRI be used to learn about the control of different parts of the brain?

● By having patients perform different tasks while in an fMRI machine, physicians can identify what regions of the brain are most active.

31.18 The limbic system is involved in emotions, memory, and learning

Mapping the parts of the brain involved in human emotions, learning, and memory and studying the interactions between these parts are among the great challenges in biology today. Much of human emotion, learning, and memory depends on our **limbic system**. This functional unit includes parts of the thalamus and hypothalamus and two partial rings around them formed by portions of the cerebral cortex **(Figure 31.18)**.

▲ **Figure 31.18** The limbic system (shown in shades of gold)

Two cerebral structures, the amygdala and the hippocampus, play key roles in memory, learning, and emotions.

The limbic system is central to such behaviours as nurturing infants and bonding emotionally to other people. Primary emotions that produce laughing and crying are mediated by the limbic system, and it also attaches emotional "feelings" to basic survival mechanisms of the brain stem, such as feeding, aggression, and sexuality. The intimate relationship between our feelings and our thoughts results from interactions between the limbic system and the prefrontal cortex, which is involved in complex learning, reasoning, and personality.

Memory, which is essential for learning, is the ability to store and retrieve information derived from experience. The **amygdala** is central in recognizing the emotional content of facial expressions and laying down emotional memories. Sensory data converge in the amygdala, which seems to act as a memory filter, somehow labelling information to be remembered by tying it to an event or emotion of the moment. The **hippocampus** is involved in both the formation of memories and their recall. Portions of the frontal lobes are involved in associating primary emotions with different situations. As you read in the opening essay, the ability to recall and use these memories in new situations is indicative of intelligence.

We sense our limbic system's role in both emotion and memory when certain odours bring back "scent memories." Have you ever had a particular smell suddenly make you nostalgic for something that happened when you were a child? As

Thalamus
Cerebrum
Hypothalamus
Prefrontal cortex
Smell
Olfactory bulb
Amygdala
Hippocampus

indicated in Figure 31.18, signals from your nose enter your brain through the olfactory bulb, which connects with the limbic system. Thus, a specific scent can immediately trigger emotional reactions and memories.

Short-term memory, as the name implies, lasts only a short time—usually only a few minutes. It is short-term memory that allows you to dial a phone number just after looking it up. You may, however, be able to recall the number weeks after you originally looked it up, or even longer. This is because you have stored it in **long-term memory**. The transfer of information from short-term to long-term memory is enhanced by rehearsal, positive or negative emotional states mediated by the amygdala, and the association of new data with data previously learned and stored in long-term memory. For example, it's easier to learn a new card game if you already have "card sense" from playing other card games.

Factual memories, involving names, faces, words, and places, are different from skill or procedural memories. Skill memories usually involve motor activities that are learned by repetition without consciously remembering specific information. You perform skills, such as tying your shoes, riding a bicycle, or hitting a baseball, without consciously recalling the individual steps required to do these tasks correctly. Once a skill memory is learned, it is difficult to unlearn. For example,

a person who has played tennis with a self-taught, awkward backhand has a tougher time learning the correct form than a beginner just learning the game. Bad habits, as we all know, are hard to break.

Information processing by the brain generally seems to involve a complex interplay of several integrating centres. By experimenting with animals, by studying amnesia (memory loss) in humans, and by using brain-imaging techniques, scientists have begun to map some of the major brain pathways involved in memory. Their proposed pathway involves the hippocampus and amygdala, which receive sensory information from the cortex and convey it to other parts of the limbic system and to the prefrontal cortex. The storage of a memory is completed when signals return to the area in the cortex where the sensory perception originated.

In the final module of this chapter, we will discuss four major disorders of the nervous system, including their symptoms and treatments.

 Which three factors help to transfer information from short-term to long-term memory?

● Rehearsal, emotional associations, and connection with previously learned data

---

31.19 Changes in brain physiology can produce neurological disorders

Neurological disorders (diseases of the nervous system) take an enormous toll on society. Examples of neurological disorders include schizophrenia, depression, Alzheimer's disease, and Parkinson's disease. While these conditions are not yet curable, there are a number of treatments available.

Schizophrenia   About 1% of the world's population suffers from **schizophrenia**, a severe mental disturbance characterized by psychotic episodes in which patients have a distorted perception of reality. The symptoms of schizophrenia typically include hallucinations (such as "voices" that only the patient can hear); delusions (generally paranoid); blunted emotions; distractibility; lack of initiative; and difficulty with verbal expression. Contrary to commonly held belief, schizophrenics do not necessarily exhibit a "split personality." There seem to be several different forms of schizophrenia, and it is unclear whether they represent different disorders or variations of the same underlying disease.

The physiological causes of schizophrenia are unknown, although the disease has a strong genetic component. Studies of identical twins show that if one twin has schizophrenia, there is a 50% chance that the other twin will have it, too. Since identical twins share identical genes, this indicates that schizophrenia has an equally strong environmental component, the nature of which has not been identified.

There are several treatments for schizophrenia that can usually alleviate the major symptoms, but they often have major side effects. Such treatments focus on brain pathways that use dopamine as a neurotransmitter. Identification of the genetic mutations associated with schizophrenia may yield new

insights about the causes of the disease, which may in turn lead to effective therapies with fewer drawbacks.

Depression   In Canada, 11% of men and 16% of women will experience depression at some point during their lives. Two broad forms of depressive illness are recognized: major depression and bipolar disorder.

People with **major depression** may experience persistent sadness, loss of interest in pleasurable activities, changes in body weight and sleep patterns, loss of energy, and suicidal thoughts. While all of us feel sad from time to time, major depression is extreme and more persistent, leaving a person unable to live a normal life for months at a time. One of the most common forms of mental illness, major depression affects about one in every seven individuals at some point in their adult lives. If left untreated, symptoms may become more frequent and severe over time.

Bipolar disorder, or manic-depressive disorder, is characterized by extreme mood swings and affects about 2.4% of the Canadian population. The manic phase is marked by high self-esteem, increased energy and flow of ideas, extreme talkativeness, inappropriate risk taking, promiscuity, and reckless spending. In its milder forms, this phase is sometimes associated with great creativity, and some well-known artists, musicians, and writers (including Van Gogh, Beethoven, Hemingway, and Winnipeg comic Big Daddy Tazz) had periods of intense creative output during their manic phases. The depressive phase of bipolar disorder is characterized by lowered ability to feel pleasure, loss of motivation, sleep disturbances, and feelings of worthlessness. These symptoms can be so severe that some individuals attempt suicide.

Both bipolar disorder and major depression have a genetic component. As in schizophrenia, there is also a strong environmental influence; stress, especially severe stress in childhood, may be an important factor.

In recent years, researchers have begun to learn how brain physiology is involved in depression. The PET scans shown in **Figure 31.19A** compare the brain of a depressed patient (top) with that of a healthy patient (bottom). The red and yellow colours indicate areas of low brain activity. Note that the PET scan from the depressed patient shows decreased activity in certain areas of the brain.

Several kinds of medication for depression are available and can be quite effective. Many depressed people have an imbalance of neurotransmitters, particularly serotonin. Some medications are intended to correct such imbalances. The most commonly prescribed class of antidepressant drugs are selective serotonin reuptake inhibitors (SSRIs). As mentioned in Module 31.12, these medications increase the amount of time that serotonin is available to stimulate certain neurons in the brain, which appears to relieve some symptoms. In 1987, fluoxetine (best known as Prozac) became the first SSRI approved to treat depression. Other frequently prescribed SSRIs include paroxetine (Paxil) and sertraline (Zoloft). The prescription rate of antidepressants increased at an alarming rate, rising from 9 million prescriptions in 1999 to 15 million prescriptions in 2003. In 2004, Health Canada increased the warnings for the adverse side effects of these drugs. Since then, the prescription rates have stabilized. SSRIs now represent one of the largest classes of medication in Canada, in terms of both dollars spent and number of prescriptions. However, their usefulness in treating depression is being questioned by many doctors.

Alzheimer's Disease   A form of mental deterioration, or dementia, **Alzheimer's disease (AD)** is characterized by confusion and memory loss. Its incidence is usually age related, rising from about 10% at age 65 to about 35% at age 85. Thus, by helping humans live longer, modern medicine is increasing the proportion of AD patients in the population. The disease is progressive; patients gradually become less able to function and eventually need to be dressed, bathed, and fed by others. There are also personality changes, almost always for the worse. Patients often lose their ability to recognize people, even family members, and may treat them with suspicion and hostility.

At present, a firm diagnosis of AD is difficult to make while the patient is alive because there are other causes of dementia. However, AD results in a characteristic pathology of the brain: Neurons die in large numbers, and brain tissue often shrinks. (See Figure 2.4B to view a PET scan of the brain of an Alzheimer's patient.) The shrinkage is visible with brain imaging but is not enough to positively identify AD. What is diagnostic is the postmortem finding of two features—neurofibrillary tangles and senile plaques—in the remaining brain tissue. Neurofibrillary tangles are bundles of a protein called tau, a protein that normally helps to regulate the movement of nutrients along microtubules within neurons. Senile plaques are aggregates of beta-amyloid, an insoluble peptide of 40 to 42 amino acids that is cleaved from a membrane protein normally present in neurons. The plaques appear to trigger the death of surrounding neurons, but whether amyloid plaques cause Alzheimer's or result from it remains unclear.

Parkinson's Disease   Approximately 100 000 Canadians suffer from **Parkinson's disease (Figure 31.19B)**, a motor disorder characterized by difficulty in initiating movements, slowness of movement, and rigidity. Patients often have a masked facial expression, muscle tremors, poor balance, a flexed posture, and a shuffling gait. Like Alzheimer's disease, Parkinson's is progressive, and the risk increases with age. The incidence of Parkinson's disease is about 1% at age 65 and about 5% at age 85.

Much of what we do know about Parkinson's disease comes from chemistry grad student Barry Kidston: not from his

◀ **Figure 31.19A** PET scans showing decreased brain activity (red and yellow areas) in a depressed person (top) compared to a healthy person (bottom)

▲ **Figure 31.19B** Actor Michael J. Fox (right) and boxer Muhammad Ali, both of whom suffer from Parkinson's disease, testifying about funding for the disorder

dedication to science, but from his addiction to illegal drugs. After injecting himself with a homemade batch of synthetic heroin, Kidston quickly developed Parkinson's-like symptoms. A few years later, when Kidston died from a cocaine overdose, doctors conducted an autopsy and identified the specific areas of Kidston's brain that were damaged.

The symptoms of Parkinson's disease result from the death of neurons in the basal nuclei. These neurons normally release dopamine from their synaptic terminals. The disease itself appears to be caused by a combination of environmental and genetic factors. Evidence for a genetic role includes the fact that some families with an increased incidence of Parkinson's disease carry a mutated form of the gene for a protein important in normal brain function.

At present, there is no cure for Parkinson's disease, although various treatments can help to control the symptoms. Treatments include drugs such as L-dopa, a precursor of the neurotransmitter dopamine, and surgery. One potential cure is to develop stem cells into dopamine-secreting neurons in the laboratory and implant them in patients' brains. In laboratory experiments, transplantation of such cells into rats with a Parkinson's-like condition can lead to a recovery of

motor control. Whether this kind of regenerative medicine will also work in humans is one of many important questions on the frontier of modern brain research. Dr. Carles Vilarino-Guell at the University of British Columbia recently discovered the gene responsible for late-onset Parkinson's disease. This important discovery may provide new insight into the disease and potential new therapies, or perhaps even a cure.

Unravelling the biological basis of neurological disorders remains one of the most challenging tasks of modern biology. Recent advances in locating genes that correlate with CNS disorders and creating animal models for these diseases have provided new insights, but many aspects of our nervous system remain mysterious. In the next chapter, we examine another aspect of nervous systems: how sense organs gather information about the environment.

 What do the initials *SSRI* stand for? Relate the name to its mechanism of action.

● SSRIs (selective serotonin reuptake inhibitors) are antidepressant drugs that specifically (*selectively*) prevent (*inhibit*) the reabsorption (*reuptake*) of the neurotransmitter *serotonin* in the brain.

MasteringBiology® **For Practice Quizzes, BioFlix, MP3 Tutors, and Activities, go to masteringbiology.com.**

Reviewing the Concepts

Nervous System Structure and Function (31.1–31.2)

31.1 Nervous systems receive sensory input, interpret it, and send out appropriate commands. The nervous system obtains and processes sensory information and sends commands to effector cells (such as muscle cells) that carry out appropriate responses.

Sensory neurons conduct signals from sensory receptors to the central nervous system (CNS), which consists of the brain and, in vertebrates, the spinal cord. Interneurons in the CNS integrate information and send it to motor neurons. Motor neurons, in turn, convey signals to effector cells. Located outside the CNS, the peripheral nervous system (PNS) consists of nerves (bundles of sensory and motor neurons) and ganglia (clusters of cell bodies of the neurons).

31.2 Neurons are the functional units of nervous systems. Neurons are cells specialized for generating and carrying signals.

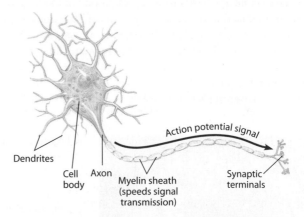

An Overview of Animal Nervous Systems (31.3–31.6)

31.3 The evolution of animal nervous systems reflects changes in body symmetry. Radially symmetric animals have a nervous system arranged in a weblike system of neurons called a nerve net. Among bilaterally symmetric animals, nervous systems evolved to exhibit cephalization, the concentration of the nervous system in the head end, and centralization, the presence of a CNS.

31.4 Vertebrate nervous systems are highly centralized. The brain and spinal cord make up the CNS. Cranial and spinal nerves make up the PNS.

31.5 Spinal cord injuries. Injuries to the spinal cord have a devastating impact on the patient. Medical and ancillary costs are high. The Rick Hansen Foundation strives to improve life for those affected.

31.6 The peripheral nervous system of vertebrates is a functional hierarchy.

Central Nervous System (CNS)		Peripheral Nervous System (PNS)	
Brain	Spinal cord: nerve bundle that communicates with body	Motor system: voluntary control over muscles	Autonomic nervous system: involuntary control over organs • Parasympathetic division: rest and digest • Sympathetic division: fight or flight

Nerve Signals and Their Transmission (31.7–31.12)

31.7 Nerve function depends on charge differences across neuron membranes. At rest, a neuron's plasma membrane has an electrical voltage called the resting potential. The resting potential is caused by the membrane's ability to maintain a relative charge difference across its membrane with the outside being positively and the inside negatively charged.

31.8 A nerve signal begins as a change in the membrane potential. A stimulus alters the permeability of a portion of the membrane, allowing ions to pass through and change the membrane's voltage. A nerve signal, called an action potential, is a change in the membrane voltage from the resting potential to a maximum level and back to the resting potential.

31.9 The action potential propagates itself along the axon. Action potentials are self-propagated in a one-way chain reaction along an axon. An action potential is an all-or-none event. The frequency of action potentials (but not their strength) changes with the strength of the stimulus.

31.10 Neurons communicate at synapses. The transmission of signals between neurons or between neurons and effector cells occurs at junctions called synapses. At electrical synapses, electrical signals pass directly between cells. At chemical synapses, the sending (presynaptic) cell secretes a chemical signal, a neurotransmitter, which crosses the synaptic cleft and binds to a specific receptor on the surface of the receiving (postsynaptic) cell.

31.11 Chemical synapses enable complex information to be processed. Some neurotransmitters excite a receiving cell; others inhibit a receiving cell's activity by decreasing its ability to develop action potentials. A cell may receive differing signals from many neurons; the summation of excitation and inhibition determines whether or not it will transmit a nerve signal.

31.12 Many drugs act at chemical synapses. Many common drugs can affect the brain's delicate chemistry.

The Human Brain (31.13–31.19)

31.13 The structure of a living supercomputer: The human brain. The midbrain and subdivisions of the hindbrain, together with the thalamus and hypothalamus of the forebrain, function mainly in conducting information to and from higher brain centres. They regulate homeostatic functions, keep track of body position, and sort sensory information. The forebrain's cerebrum is the largest and most complex part of the brain. Most of the cerebrum's integrative power resides in the cerebral cortex of the two cerebral hemispheres.

31.14 The cerebral cortex is a mosaic of specialized, interactive regions. Specialized integrative regions of the cerebral cortex include the somatosensory cortex and centres for vision, hearing, taste, and smell. The motor cortex directs responses. Association areas, concerned with higher mental activities such as reasoning and language, make up most of the cerebrum. The right and left cerebral hemispheres tend to specialize in different mental tasks.

31.15 Injuries and brain operations provide insight into brain function. Brain injuries and surgeries have been used to study brain function.

31.16 Several parts of the brain regulate sleep and arousal. Sleep and arousal involve activity by the hypothalamus, medulla oblongata, pons, and neurons of the reticular formation.

31.17 Do we use only 10% of our brains? Different regions of the brain are necessary for all of our day-to-day functions. While we might not use the entire brain at the same time, we do use 100% of it.

31.18 The limbic system is involved in emotions, memory, and learning. The limbic system is a group of integrating centres in the cerebral cortex, thalamus, and hypothalamus. One key function is transfer of information from short-term to long-term memory.

31.19 Changes in brain physiology can produce neurological disorders. Treatment can often improve patients' lives, but cures are elusive.

Connecting the Concepts

1. Test your understanding of the nervous system by matching the following labels with their corresponding letters: CNS, effector cells, interneuron, motor neuron, PNS, sensory neuron, sensory receptor, spinal cord, and synapse.

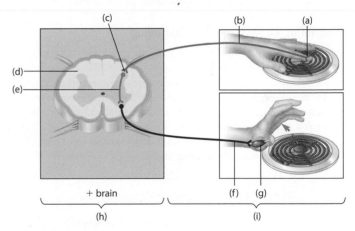

Testing Your Knowledge

Multiple Choice

2. Joe accidentally touched a hot pan. His arm jerked back, and an instant later, he felt a burning pain. How would you explain the fact that his arm moved before he felt the pain?
   a. His limbic system blocked the pain momentarily, but the important pain signals eventually got through.
   b. His response was a spinal cord reflex that occurred before the pain signals got to the brain.
   c. It took a while for his brain to search long-term memory and figure out what was going on.
   d. Motor neurons are myelinated; sensory neurons are not. The signals travelled faster to his muscles.
   e. This scenario is not actually possible. The brain must register pain before a person can react.

3. What is the state of the ion channels during the depolarization stage of an action potential?
   a. Voltage-gated Na^+ channels are open while voltage-gated K^+ channels are closed.
   b. Voltage-gated Na^+ channels are closed while voltage-gated K^+ channels are open.
   c. Both voltage-gated Na^+ and voltage-gated K^+ channels are open.
   d. Both voltage-gated Na^+ and voltage-gated K^+ channels are closed.
   e. Voltage-gated Na^+ channels are closed while Cl^- channels are open.

4. Which of the following mediates sleep and arousal?
   a. the reticular formation, along with the hypothalamus and thalamus
   b. the limbic system, which includes the amygdala and hippocampus
   c. the left hemisphere of the cerebral cortex
   d. the midbrain and cerebellum
   e. the parasympathetic and sympathetic divisions of the nervous system

5. Anaesthetics block pain by blocking the transmission of nerve signals. Which of these three chemicals might work as anaesthetics? *(Circle all that apply and explain your selections.)*
   a. a chemical that prevents the opening of sodium channels in membranes
   b. a chemical that inhibits the enzymes that degrade neurotransmitters
   c. a chemical that blocks neurotransmitter receptors

Describing, Comparing, and Explaining

6. As you hold this book, nerve signals are generated in nerve endings in your fingertips and sent to your brain. Once a touch has caused an action potential at one end of a neuron, what causes the nerve signal to move from that point along the length of the neuron to the other end? What is the nerve signal exactly? Why can't it go backward? How is the nerve signal transmitted from one neuron to the next across a synapse? Write a short paragraph that answers these questions.

Applying the Concepts

7. Using microelectrodes, a researcher recorded nerve signals in four neurons in the brain of a snail. The neurons are called A, B, C, and D in the table below. A, B, and C all can transmit signals to D. In three experiments, the animal was stimulated in different ways. The number of nerve signals transmitted per second by each of the cells is recorded in the table. Write a short paragraph explaining the different results of the three experiments.

	Signals/s			
	A	B	C	D
Experiment 1	50	0	40	30
Experiment 2	50	0	60	45
Experiment 3	50	30	60	0

8. Ouabain is a poison that interferes with the function of the sodium-potassium pumps on cell membranes. How would the action potential of a neuron be affected in the presence of ouabain?

9. Brain injuries tend to be severe because most neurons, once damaged, will not regenerate. The use of embryonic stem cells has been proposed as a potential treatment for many neurological diseases. Neurons developed from such stem cells in laboratory culture might be implanted in the brain of a person with Parkinson's disease, as mentioned in the text, or Alzheimer's. These neurons might be able to replace those damaged by the disease. Do you favour or oppose research along those lines? *(Explain your answer.)*

10. Alcohol's depressant effects on the nervous system cloud judgment and slow reflexes. Alcohol consumption is a factor in most fatal traffic accidents in Canada. What are some other impacts of alcohol abuse on society? What are some of the responses of people and society to alcohol abuse? Do you think this is primarily an individual or societal problem? Do you think our responses to alcohol abuse are appropriate and proportional to the seriousness of the problem?

Answers to all questions can be found in Appendix E.

Sensation

BIG IDEAS

Sensory Reception

(32.1–32.3)

Animal sensations begin as stimuli detected by sensory receptor cells.

Hearing and Balance

(32.4–32.6)

Sound and balance are perceived as vibrations and are detected by mechanoreceptors.

Vision

(32.7–32.10)

Light is detected by photoreceptor cells. Some animals can detect only light and shadow; others can create clear images by using lenses to focus light.

Taste and Smell

(32.11–32.13)

Chemoreceptors detect chemical signals as taste or smell.

The Sensational Star-Nosed Mole

The star-nosed mole (*Condylura cristata*) is a most unusual animal. Living in the moist soils of eastern Canadian boreal wetlands, this mole is well adapted to a semiaquatic life. With 22 fleshy appendages surrounding its nose, this remarkable little animal is aptly named.

Nearly blind, the star-nosed mole relies on its other senses to forage for food. The typical star-nosed mole diet consists of small invertebrates with relatively poor nutritional value. To satisfy its metabolic demand, the star-nosed mole must ingest large amounts. It accomplishes this by eating *very* quickly. Its nose can touch more than 10 different locations every second in search of prey. When a prey item is encountered, the mole recognizes the prey's edibility, ingests it, and resumes searching for more food in an average of only 227 milliseconds. It can eat four prey items in a single second! At this speed, the mole easily meets all of its nutritional requirements.

Covering the surface of the mole's star-shaped nose are more than 25 000 mechanoreceptors that detect tactile (touch) stimuli. These mechanoreceptors are so tightly packed that 600 of them can simultaneously touch a single pinhead. The sensory information from these structures are carried to the brain along 100 000 different neurons. This nickel-sized nose is the most sensitive structure known. By comparison, each of your hands sends information to your brain along 17 000 neurons. With this incredible tactile sensitivity, the mole is able to discern between microscopic textural differences. This clear advantage allows the blind animal to discriminate between the edible and inedible.

This amazing tactile ability to feel for its meals is coupled with olfactory (scent) information. Odourants are molecules that move through the air until they are inhaled. Within the nasopharynx (the innermost part of the nasal cavity), odourants interact with smell receptors that signal the scent to the brain. The mole can follow odour trails to track its prey by using olfaction. Essentially blind, the star-nosed mole relies almost entirely on touch and smell.

In a terrestrial setting, when the tactile receptors detect a potential prey item, the mole will sniff to obtain additional information. If the olfactory and tactile signals are in agreement, the mole quickly ingests the food item. Underwater, however, olfaction typically does not work well. In order for smell receptors to detect odourants in an aqueous medium, water would have to be inhaled. If you have ever had water up your nose accidentally, you would appreciate the mole's desire to avoid this discomfort. Semiaquatic moles, including the star-nosed mole, have developed a different strategy for underwater sniffing.

While foraging underwater, the star-nosed mole feels around with the same exuberance as it does on land. When it detects a potential food item, the mole blows tiny bubbles (about 0.1 mL) out of its nose, against the item. Odourants diffuse into the bubble and then the mole inhales the bubble to receive the olfactory information it requires. This remarkable little mole is equally effective hunting in water and on land.

In this chapter, we focus on four human senses: hearing, vision, taste, and smell. To begin, we look at the general principles of sensory reception that underlie all animal senses. Then we turn our attention to human sensory structures and discuss how they function.

Sensory Reception

32.1 Specialized sensory receptors detect five categories of stimuli

When high school students are asked to name the human senses, they usually come up with a list of five: smell, sight, taste, hearing, and touch. The full gamut of sensation is actually much more complicated. Based on the type of signals to which they respond, we can group sensory receptors into general categories: pain receptors, thermoreceptors (sensors for both heat and cold), mechanoreceptors (sensors for touch and pressure), chemoreceptors, and electromagnetic receptors. These receptor types work in various combinations to produce the five senses typically listed by students, as well as others.

Figure 32.1A, showing a section of mammalian skin, reveals why the surface of our body is sensitive to such a variety of stimuli. Our skin contains pain receptors, thermoreceptors, and mechanoreceptors. Each of these receptors is a modified dendrite of a sensory neuron (see Module 31.2). The neuron recognizes stimuli directly and sends action potentials to the central nervous system (CNS). In other words, each receptor serves as both a receptor cell and a sensory neuron. Most of the dendrites in the dermis (the underlying region of the skin) are wrapped in one or more layers of connective tissue (purple areas in the figure); however, the pain receptors in the epidermis (outer skin layer)

and the touch receptors around the base of hairs are naked dendrites.

Pain Receptors   In most mammals, including humans, the skin has the highest density of **pain receptors** (see pink label in the figure). Pain receptors may respond to excess heat or pressure or to chemicals released from damaged or inflamed tissues. Pain often indicates injury or disease and usually makes an animal withdraw to safety. Chemicals produced in an animal's body sometimes increase pain. For example, damaged tissues produce prostaglandins, which increase pain by increasing the sensitivity of pain receptors. Aspirin and ibuprofen reduce pain by inhibiting prostaglandin synthesis.

Thermoreceptors   **Thermoreceptors** in the skin (blue labels in the figure) detect either heat or cold. Other temperature sensors located deep in the body monitor the temperature of the blood. Receiving action potentials from both surface and deep sensors, the hypothalamus, acting as the body's thermostat, keeps a mammal's or bird's body temperature within a narrow range (see Module 25.15). Interestingly, scientists recently discovered that sensory receptors for high temperatures also respond to capsaicin, the chemical that makes chili peppers taste "spicy hot."

Mechanoreceptors   Different types of **mechanoreceptors** (green labels in the figure) are stimulated by various forms of mechanical energy, such as touch and pressure, stretching, motion, and sound. All of these stimuli produce their effects by bending or stretching the plasma membrane of a receptor cell. When the membrane changes shape, it becomes more permeable to sodium or potassium ions, and the mechanical energy of the stimulus is transduced (converted) into a receptor potential as ions move across the membrane.

At the top of Figure 32.1A, you can see a type of mechanoreceptor that detects light touch. This type of receptor can transduce very slight inputs of mechanical energy into action potentials. For example, these receptors detect the variation of different textures. Another type of pressure sensor, lying deeper in the skin, is stimulated by strong pressure. A third type of mechanoreceptor, the touch receptor around the base of the hair, detects hair movements. These receptors are activated when a small fly walks across your arm. Touch receptors at the base of the stiff whiskers on a cat are extremely sensitive and enable the animal to detect close objects by touch in the dark. Another type of mechanoreceptor (not shown) is found in our skeletal muscles. Sensitive to changes in muscle length, **stretch receptors** monitor the position of body parts.

A variety of mechanoreceptors collectively called **hair cells** detect sound waves and other forms of movement in water. The "hairs" on these sensors are either specialized types of cilia or cellular projections called microvilli. The

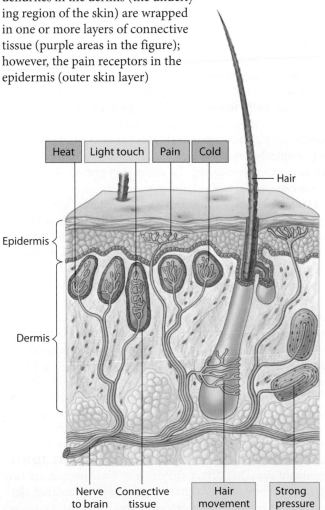

▲ **Figure 32.1A** Sensory receptors in mammalian skin

① Receptor cell at rest

② Fluid moving in one direction

③ Fluid moving in the other direction

▲ **Figure 32.1B** Mechanoreception by a hair cell

sensory hairs project from the surface of a receptor cell into either the external environment, such as the water surrounding a fish, or an internal fluid-filled compartment, such as our inner ear.

Figure 32.1B shows how hair cells work, ① starting with a receptor cell at rest. ② When fluid movement bends the hairs in one direction, the hairs stretch the cell membrane, increasing its permeability to certain ions. This makes the hair cell secrete more neurotransmitter molecules and increases the rate of action potential production by a sensory neuron. ③ When the hairs bend in the opposite direction, ion permeability decreases, the hair cell releases fewer neurotransmitter molecules, and the rate of action potentials decreases. We will see later that hair cells are involved in both hearing and balance.

Chemoreceptors **Chemoreceptors** include the sensory receptors in our nose and taste buds, which are attuned to

▲ **Figure 32.1C** Chemoreceptors on the antennae of a moth

chemicals in the external environment, as well as some receptors that detect chemicals in the body's internal environment. Internal chemoreceptors include sensors in some of our arteries that can detect changes in the amount of O_2 and CO_2 in the blood. Osmoreceptors in the brain detect changes in the total solute concentration of the blood and stimulate thirst when blood osmolarity increases.

One of the most sensitive chemoreceptors in the animal kingdom is on the antennae of the male silkworm moth *Bombyx mori* (**Figure 32.1C**). The antennae are covered with thousands of sensory hairs (visible in the micrograph). The hairs have chemoreceptors that can detect minute quantities of a sex pheromone released by the female.

Electromagnetic Receptors Energy occurring as electricity, magnetism, or various wavelengths of light, may be detected by **electromagnetic receptors**. A platypus, for example, has electroreceptors on its bill that can detect electric fields generated by the muscles of prey, such as crustaceans, frogs, and small fishes.

Many animals appear to use Earth's magnetic field to orient themselves as they migrate. Migratory birds, fishes (such as salmon and trout), turtles, amphibians, and bees are believed to rely on magnetoreception to navigate relative to Earth's magnetic field—although the precise physiological basis for this sense remains to be discovered. Recent evidence suggests that the magnetoreceptor is associated with the retina of the eyes. More specifically, the receptor interacts with *rhodopsin* pigments of the light absorbing *rods* (see Module 32.10). In this orientation, it would seem likely that migrating birds and turtles might actually *see* the Earth's magnetic field.

Photoreceptors, including eyes, are probably the most common type of electromagnetic receptor. Photoreceptors detect the electromagnetic energy of light, which may be in the visible or ultraviolet part of the electromagnetic spectrum (see Module 7.6). The rattlesnake in **Figure 32.1D** has prominent eyes that detect visible light. Near its eyes are two infrared receptor organs. These organs have specialized electromagnetic receptors that detect the body heat of the snake's preferred prey: small mammals and birds. The receptors can

Infrared
receptor

▲ **Figure 32.1D** Electromagnetic receptor organs in a snake

detect the infrared radiation emitted by a mouse a metre away.

A variety of light detectors have evolved in the animal kingdom. Despite their differences, however, all photoreceptors contain similar pigment molecules that absorb light, and evidence indicates that all photoreceptors may be homologous, having a common ancestry. We consider some of the different types of eyes found in animals in Module 32.7. But first, let's consider the senses of hearing and balance.

 For each of the following senses in humans, identify the type of receptor: seeing, tasting, hearing, and smelling.

● Photoreceptor; chemoreceptor; mechanoreceptor; chemoreceptor

32.2 Sensory organs share a common cellular basis

The operation of all animal senses—the ones used by humans as well as the nonhuman senses such as echolocation—originates in **sensory receptors**, specialized neurons or other cells that are tuned to the conditions of the external world or internal organs. Sensory cells detect stimuli: chemical flavourings in your food; light emitted by your TV screen; tension in a muscle as you grasp a computer mouse; sound waves produced by your MP3 player; touch sensations as you hold someone's hand; or other sensations such as electricity, cold, or heat. Once a stimulus is detected, a sensory receptor cell triggers action potentials (electrical signals; see Module 31.8) that send this information to the CNS, the brain and spinal cord.

An example of sensory receptors in action can be observed as a great hammerhead shark (*Sphyrna mokarran*) hunts for prey. It sweeps its wide head back and forth, like a beachcomber scanning the shore with a metal detector **(Figure 32.2)**. As the shark moves, sensory receptor cells in its head can detect prey—perhaps a flounder or a stingray hiding on or just beneath the ocean floor. The shark is hunting with a sense that humans lack: electroreception, the ability to sense electric fields. Certain sensory cells in a hammerhead shark's head are electromagnetic receptors (discussed in the previous module) that can detect the minute electrical activity (action potentials) of muscles or nerves in nearby prey—even if the prey animals are perfectly still—and these same cells can relay reports about this information to the shark's brain. Electroreception is common among fish and is found in some amphibians and the monotremes (egg-laying mammals such as the platypus).

▲ **Figure 32.2** The hammerhead shark hunts using electroreception

Whether electroreception in hammerhead sharks or our own ability to taste or hear, the functioning of every sense starts with the detection of stimuli by sensory receptor cells. Detection leads to sensation, the identification of the particular type of stimulus—the sweet taste of ice cream or the shrill sound of an alarm clock. Sensation depends on the part of the brain that receives the action potential. Before we turn to the details of the various senses, we will next discuss how sensory receptor cells convert stimuli to action potentials.

 How is the signal produced by an electroreceptive cell in a hammerhead shark similar to the signal produced by a cell in your eye?

● Both types of cells produce action potentials that are passed to the CNS.

32.3 Sensory receptors convert stimulus energy to action potentials

Sensory organs, such as your eyes or taste buds, contain sensory receptors that detect stimuli. The sensory receptors in your eyes detect light energy (photons); those in your taste buds detect chemicals, such as salt ions or sugar molecules. The sensory receptor's job is completed when it sends information to the CNS by triggering action potentials.

In stimulus detection, the receptor cell converts one type of signal (the stimulus) to another type, an electrical signal. This conversion, called **sensory transduction**, produces a change in the cell's membrane potential (the potential energy stored by the plasma membrane; see Module 31.7) of the receptor cell. This change results from the opening

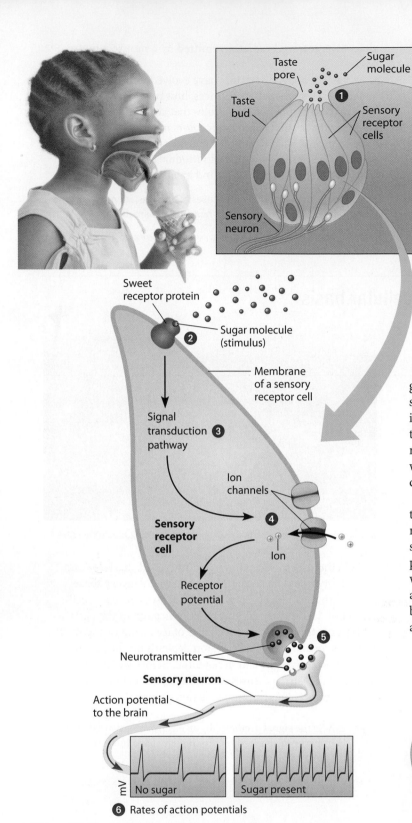

molecules (●●) first arrive at the taste bud, where ❷ they bind to sweet receptor proteins (for simplicity, the figure shows only one). Specific protein molecules embedded in the plasma membrane of a taste receptor cell. The binding triggers ❸ a signal transduction pathway (see Module 11.10) that causes ❹ some ion channels in the membrane to close and other ion channels to open. Changes in the flow of ions create a graded change in membrane potential called a **receptor potential**. Receptor potentials vary; the stronger the stimulus, the greater the receptor potential.

Once a stimulus is converted to a receptor potential, the receptor potential usually results in signals passing into the CNS. In our taste bud example, ❺ each receptor cell forms a synapse with a sensory neuron. In many cases, a receptor cell constantly secretes neurotransmitter (●●) into this synapse at a set rate, triggering a steady stream of action potentials in the sensory neuron. ❻ The graph shows the rate at which the sensory neuron sends action potentials when the taste receptor is not detecting any sugar. The graph also shows what happens when there are enough sugar molecules to trigger a strong receptor potential, causing the receptor cell to release even more neurotransmitter than usual. This additional neurotransmitter increases the rate of action potential generation in the sensory neuron, which in turn signals the brain that the sensory receptor detects a stimulus.

You can see that sensory receptor cells transduce stimuli to receptor potentials at different frequencies. The change in receptor potential frequency can trigger action potentials in sensory neurons, which relay the information to the CNS for processing. Because action potentials are the same no matter where or how they are produced, how do they communicate a sweet taste instead of a salty one? In **Figure 32.3B**, the taste bud on the left has sensory receptors that respond to sugar, and the taste bud on the right responds to salt. The sensory

▲ **Figure 32.3A** Sensory transduction at a taste bud

or closing of ion channels in the sensory receptor's plasma membrane.

Figure 32.3A shows sensory transduction occurring when sensory receptor cells in a taste bud detect sugar molecules, as when you lick an ice cream cone. ❶ The sugar

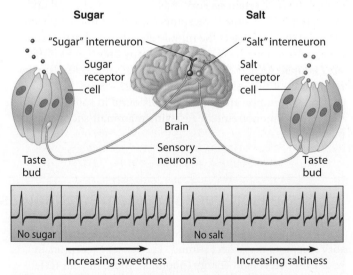

▲ **Figure 32.3B** Action potentials transmitting different taste sensations

neurons from the sugar-detecting taste bud synapse with different interneurons in the brain than those contacted by neurons from the salt-detecting taste bud. The brain distinguishes stimulus types by the particular interneurons that are stimulated.

The graphs in Figure 32.3B also indicate how action potentials communicate information about the intensity of stimuli. In each case, the left part of the graph represents the rate at which the sensory neurons in the taste bud transmit action potentials when the taste receptors are not stimulated. The right side of each graph shows that the rate of transmission depends on the intensity of the stimulus. The stronger the stimulus, the more neurotransmitter released by the receptor cell and the more frequently the sensory neuron transmits action potentials to the brain. Another example of this mechanism of signalling includes the hair cells discussed in Module 32.1 that are used in hearing and balance. The brain interprets the intensity of the stimulus from the rate at which it receives action potentials.

There is an important qualification to what we have just said about stimulus intensity. Have you ever noticed how an odour that is strong at first seems to fade with time, even when you know the odorous substance is still there? Or how the water in a pool may seem shockingly cold when you dive in but not when you get used to it? This effect is called **sensory adaptation**, the tendency of some sensory receptors to become less sensitive when they are stimulated repeatedly. When receptors become less sensitive, they trigger fewer action potentials, and the brain may lose its awareness of stimuli as a result. Sensory adaptation keeps the body from reacting to normal background stimuli, such as the feeling of clothes on your skin.

This overview of sensory transduction, transmission, and adaptation explains how sensory receptors work in general. Now let's look at some different kinds of receptors.

 What is meant by sensory transduction?

● The conversion of a stimulus signal to an electrical signal (a receptor potential) by a sensory receptor cell

Hearing and Balance

32.4 The ear converts air pressure waves to action potentials that are perceived as sound

The vertebrate ear is really two separate organs, one for hearing and the other for maintaining balance. We look at the structure and function of our hearing organ in this module and then turn to our sense of balance in Module 32.5. Both organs operate on the same basic principle: the stimulation of long projections on hair cells (mechanoreceptors) in fluid-filled canals.

Structure   The ear is complex, and it will help you to learn about its structure **(Figure 32.4A)** before studying how it functions. The ear has three regions: the outer ear, the middle ear, and the inner ear. The **outer ear** consists of the flaplike **pinna**—the fleshy structure we commonly refer to as our "ear"—and the **auditory canal**. The pinna and the auditory canal collect sound waves and channel them to the **eardrum**, a sheet of tissue that separates the outer ear from the **middle ear (Figure 32.4B)**. Both the outer ear and middle ear are common sites of childhood infections (called swimmer's ear and otitis media, respectively).

When sound pressure waves strike the eardrum, the eardrum vibrates and passes the vibrations to three small bones of the middle ear (as shown in Figure 32.4B): the hammer (more formally, the malleus), anvil (incus), and stirrup (stapes). The stirrup is connected to the oval window, a membrane-covered hole in the skull bone through which vibrations pass into the inner ear. The middle ear also opens into a passage called the **Eustachian tube**, which connects with the pharynx (back of the throat), allowing air pressure to stay equal on either side of the eardrum. This tube is what enables you to "pop" your ears by swallowing hard or yawning to equalize pressure when changing altitude in an airplane.

The **inner ear** consists of fluid-filled channels in the bones of the skull. Sound vibrations or movements of the head set the fluid in motion. One of the channels, the **cochlea** (Latin for "snail"), is a long, coiled tube. The cross-sectional view of the cochlea in **Figure 32.4C** shows that inside it are three canals, each of which is filled with fluid. Our actual hearing organ, the **organ of Corti**, is located within the middle canal. The organ of Corti consists of an array of hair cells embedded in a **basilar membrane**, the floor of the middle canal. The hair cells are the sensory receptors of the ear. As you can see in the enlargement on the far right, a jellylike projection called the tectorial membrane extends from the wall of the middle canal **(Figure 32.4D)**. Notice that the tips of the hair cells are in contact with the overlying tectorial membrane. Sensory neurons synapse with the base of the hair cells and carry action potentials to the brain via the auditory nerve.

▲ **Figure 32.4A** An overview of the mammalian (human) ear

▲ **Figure 32.4B** The middle ear and the inner ear

Hearing   Now let's see how the parts of the ear function in hearing. Sound waves, which move as pressure waves in the air, are collected by the pinna and auditory canal of the outer ear. These pressure waves make your eardrum vibrate with the same frequency as the sound **(Figure 32.4E)**. The frequency, measured in hertz (Hz), is the number of vibrations per second.

From the eardrum, the vibrations are amplified as they are transferred through the hammer, anvil, and stirrup in the middle ear to the oval window. Vibrations of the oval window then produce pressure waves in the fluid within the cochlea. The vibrations first pass from the oval window into the fluid in the upper canal of the cochlea. Pressure waves travel through the upper canal to the tip of the cochlea, at the coil's centre. The pressure waves then enter the lower canal and gradually fade away.

As a pressure wave passes through the upper canal of the cochlea, it pushes downward on the middle canal, making the basilar membrane vibrate. Vibration of the basilar membrane makes the hairlike projections on the hair cells alternately brush against and draw away from the overlying tectorial membrane. When a hair cell's projections are bent, ion channels in its plasma membrane open, and positive ions enter the cell. As a result, the hair cell develops a receptor potential and releases more neurotransmitter molecules at its synapse with a sensory neuron. In turn, the sensory neuron sends more action potentials to the brain through the auditory nerve.

Volume and Pitch   The brain senses a sound as an increase in the frequency of action potentials from the auditory nerve. But how is the quality of the sound determined? The higher the volume (loudness) of sound, the higher the amplitude (height) of the pressure wave it generates. In the ear, a higher amplitude of pressure waves produces more vigorous vibrations of fluid in the cochlea, more pronounced bending of the

hair cells, and thus more action potentials generated in the sensory neurons.

The pitch of a sound depends on the frequency of the sound waves. High-pitched sounds, such as high notes sung by a soprano, generate high-frequency waves. Low-pitched sounds, like the low notes made by a bass, generate low-frequency waves. How does the cochlea distinguish sounds of different pitch? The key is that the basilar membrane is not uniform along its length. The end near the oval window is relatively narrow and stiff, while the other end, near the tip of the cochlea, is wider and more flexible. As a result, the basilar membrane varies in its sensitivity to particular frequencies of vibration, and the region vibrating most vigorously at any instant sends the most action potentials to auditory centres in the brain. The brain interprets the information and gives us a perception of pitch. Young people with healthy ears can hear pitches in the range of 20–20 000 Hz. We gradually lose the ability to hear the highest tones beginning around age 8, and women generally hear higher tones better than men do. Dogs can hear sounds as high as 40 000 Hz, and bats can emit and hear clicking sounds as high-pitched as 100 000 Hz.

Deafness can be caused by the inability of the ear to conduct sounds, resulting from middle-ear infections, a ruptured eardrum, or stiffening of the middle-ear bones (a common age-related problem). Deafness can also result from damage to sensory receptors or neurons. You may have noticed that a few hours in a very loud environment, such as a rock concert, leaves you with ringing or buzzing sounds in your ears, a condition called tinnitus. Frequent or prolonged exposure to sounds of more than 90 decibels (dB) can damage or destroy hair cells, which are never replaced. Health Canada cautions us that listening to loud music on car stereos or MP3 players can cause permanent hearing loss. Ear plugs can provide protection to both rock musicians and their fans. Because few

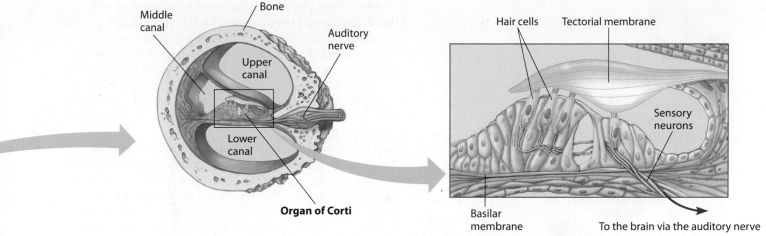

Figure 32.4C label text:

Middle canal

Bone

Upper canal

Auditory nerve

Lower canal

Organ of Corti

▲ **Figure 32.4C** A cross-section through the cochlea

Hair cells

Tectorial membrane

Sensory neurons

Basilar membrane

To the brain via the auditory nerve

▲ **Figure 32.4D** The organ of Corti

parts of our anatomy are more delicate than the organ of Corti, deafness is often progressive and permanent. In recent years, however, many deaf people have received cochlear implants, electronic devices that convert sounds to electrical impulses that stimulate the auditory nerve directly.

? How does the ear convert sound waves in the air to pressure waves of the fluid in the cochlea?

● Sound waves in air cause the eardrum to vibrate. The small bones attached to the inside of the eardrum transmit the movement to the oval window on the wall of the inner ear. Vibrations of the oval window set in motion the fluid in the inner ear, which includes the cochlea.

◀ **Figure 32.4E** The route of sound wave vibrations through the ear

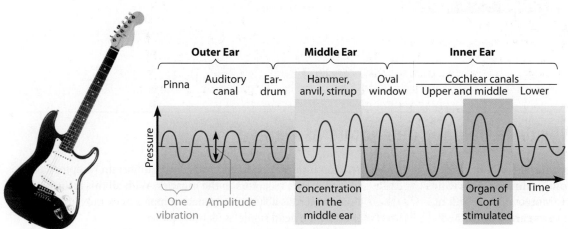

Outer Ear — Pinna, Auditory canal, Ear-drum

Middle Ear — Hammer, anvil, stirrup, Oval window

Inner Ear — Cochlear canals, Upper and middle, Lower

Pressure

One vibration

Amplitude

Concentration in the middle ear

Organ of Corti stimulated

Time

32.5 The inner ear houses our organs of balance

Several organs in the inner ear detect body position and movement. These fluid-filled structures lie next to the cochlea **(Figure 32.5)** and include three semicircular canals and two chambers, the utricle and the saccule. All the equilibrium structures operate on the same principle: the bending of hairs on hair cells.

The ear contains three **semicircular canals** that detect changes in the head's rate of rotation or angular movement. The canals are arranged in three perpendicular planes and can therefore detect movement in all directions. A swelling at the base of each semicircular canal contains a cluster of hair cells with their hairs projecting into a gelatinous mass called a cupula (shown in the enlargements). When you rotate your head in any direction, the thick, sticky fluid in the canals moves more slowly than your head: much the same way as when you rotate a glass and the beverage inside it moves more slowly than the rotating glass. Consequently, the fluid presses against the cupula, bending the hairs. The faster you rotate your head, the greater the pressure and the higher the frequency of action potentials sent to the brain. If you rotate your head at a

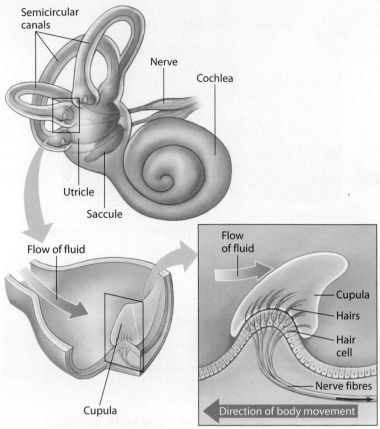

Semicircular canals

Nerve

Cochlea

Utricle

Saccule

Flow of fluid

Cupula

Flow of fluid

Cupula

Hairs

Hair cell

Nerve fibres

Direction of body movement

▲ **Figure 32.5** Equilibrium structures in the inner ear

constant speed, the fluid in the canals begins moving with the head, and the pressure on the cupula is reduced. But if you stop suddenly, the fluid continues to move just as your beverage keeps moving after you stop moving your glass. The swirling fluid continues to stimulate the hair cells, which may make you feel dizzy. This explains why a situation that causes your inner-ear fluid to move—such as a whirling amusement park ride or even just twirling around quickly—makes you dizzy only after you try to stand still.

Clusters of hair cells in the utricle and saccule detect the position of the head with respect to gravity. The hairs of these cells project into a gelatinous material containing many small particles of calcium carbonate. When the position of the head changes, this heavy material bends the hairs in a different direction, causing an increase or decrease in the rate at which action potentials are sent to the brain. The brain determines the new position of the head by interpreting the altered flow of action potentials.

The equilibrium receptors provide data the brain needs to determine the position and movement of the head. Using this information, the brain develops and sends out commands that enable the skeletal muscles to balance the body.

? **What type of receptor cell is common to our senses of hearing and equilibrium?**

Hair cells, which are mechanoreceptors ●

32.6 Why does balance deteriorate as we age?

Falling is a major health concern for older adults. Health Canada states that every year, one in three seniors will fall, sometimes more than once. Moreover, one-fifth of injury-related deaths among seniors can be attributed to a fall.

As you read in the previous module, the inner ear affects balance. The brain also uses information from sensory receptors other than equilibrium receptors. For example, visual cues provide useful information for balance. If your eyes detect a visual cue such as the horizon in motion, the brain may interpret this cue as a head movement. For this information to be useful, however, the brain must discriminate between planned motion and unintentional motion. This distinction is of particular importance when we are learning how to walk or ride a bicycle. The brain interprets unanticipated motion of visual cues as an imbalance that should be corrected. You can experience exactly how important this sensory information is while trying to maintain your balance with your eyes closed.

Some birds, including chickens, have a remarkable ability to keep their head stable, which is an important element of maintaining balance. As the body of the chicken moves, the brain

receives information from visual and equilibrium receptors as well as stretch receptors in the muscles. With all this information, the bird is able to coordinate complex neck movements, keeping the head stable as its body moves.

Although there is no single explanation for the loss of balance in older adults, several risk factors have been identified. As we age, the acuity of our senses tends to decrease. This can be partially explained by the loss of sensory receptors or sensory neurons, cells that cannot be replaced. The attenuation of our vision, hearing, and balance in particular, all have some role in increasing the risk of falling. Leg strengthening exercises are often effective in helping older adults improve their balance.

Motion sickness may result when visual and equilibrium cues conflict. Reading a book while in the car may produce contradictory signals. Your equilibrium receptors tell the brain you are moving while visual cues appear to be stationary. Through an unknown mechanism, these conflicting signals can lead to nausea in some individuals. It is possible that dizziness and a loss of balance in older adults may result from similar sensory disagreements.

Interestingly, research by Dr. Leah Bent at the University of Guelph has indicated that touch receptors in the feet also have a role in balance. Her studies demonstrate an increase in the sensitivity of astronauts' feet to touch. In the microgravity of space, the sensitivity of the inner ear decreases and the brain compensates by relying on other signals to distinguish up from down. While in microgravity, astronauts routinely strap into a treadmill apparatus to keep fit **(Figure 32.6)**. During these activities, the hypersensitivity of the feet is experienced as a tingling. The same sensation is reported upon returning to Earth. The increased sensation in the feet compensates for the lack of equilibrium information. While standing still, pressure is placed on the skin of the feet. Leaning in any direction causes a shift in the pressure, which is detected by as yet unidentified touch receptors.

As with our other senses, the sensitivity of our feet decreases with age and correlates with an increased rate of falls and associated injuries. Understanding what receptors are affected may provide new targets for treatment and rehabilitation in older adults.

? How does the skin on your feet contribute to balance?

● Leaning causes the pressure on the feet to shift slightly and this change is detected by touch receptors in the feet.

▲ **Figure 32.6** Canadian astronaut Chris Hadfield running in space

Vision

EVOLUTION CONNECTION ## 32.7 Several types of eyes have evolved independently among animals

The ability to detect light plays a central role in the lives of nearly all animals. Although there is great diversity in the organs animals use to perceive light (see Module 14.15), comparison across animal species demonstrates unity in the underlying mechanism of light detection. All animal light detectors—from simple clusters of cells that detect only the direction and intensity of light, to complex organs that form images—are based on cells called photoreceptors, which contain pigment molecules that absorb light.

Most invertebrates have some kind of

Dark pigment

Eyecups

▲ **Figure 32.7A** The eyecups of a planarian

light-detecting organ. One of the simplest is the **eyecup**, the visual sensory organ of free-living (nonparasitic) flatworms called planarians **(Figure 32.7A)**. Planarian eyecups contain photoreceptor cells that are partially shielded by darkly pigmented cells. Light can enter the eyecup only where there is no pigment and the openings of the two eyecups face opposite directions. The brain compares the rate of nerve impulses coming from the two eyecups. Although no distinct image is formed, the animal can turn until the sensations are equal and minimal, allowing it to move away from the light source to reach a dark hiding place.

Two major types of image-forming eyes have evolved in invertebrates. Compound eyes are found in insects and crustaceans. A **compound eye** consists of up to several thousand light-detectors called ommatidia (singular, *ommatidium*; **Figure 32.7B**). Every ommatidium has its own light-focusing lens and several photoreceptor cells. Each ommatidium picks up light from a tiny portion of the field of view. The animal's brain then forms a mosaic visual image by assembling the data from all the ommatidia.

Compound eyes are extremely acute motion detectors, providing an important advantage for flying insects and other

▲ **Figure 32.7B** The two compound eyes of a fly, each made up of thousands of ommatidia

small animals often threatened by predators. The compound eyes of most insects also provide excellent colour vision. Some species, such as honeybees, can see ultraviolet light (invisible to humans), which helps them locate certain nectar-bearing flowers.

The second type of image-forming eye to have evolved in invertebrates, such as squid and octopi, is the **single-lens eye**. The single-lens eye also evolved independently in vertebrates. **Figure 32.7C** shows the eye of a vertebrate. (The single-lens eye found in squids and other invertebrates differs in some of the details.) The vertebrate eye has a small opening at the centre of the eye, the **pupil**, through which light enters. Analogous to a camera's shutter, an adjustable doughnut-shaped **iris** changes the diameter of the pupil to let in more or less light. After going through the pupil, light passes through a single disclike **lens**. The lens focuses light onto the **retina**, which consists of many photoreceptor cells (see Module 32.10).

Photoreceptor cells of the retina transduce light energy, and action potentials pass via sensory neurons in the optic nerve to the visual centres of the brain. Photoreceptor cells are highly

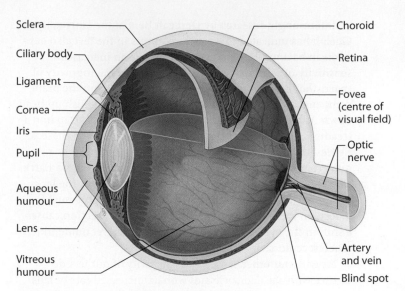

▲ **Figure 32.7C** The single-lens eye of a vertebrate

concentrated at the retina's centre of focus, called the **fovea**. There are no photoreceptor cells in the blind spot, the part of the retina where the optic nerve passes through the back of the eye. We cannot detect light that is focused on the blind spot, but having two eyes with overlapping fields of view enables us to perceive uninterrupted images. In the next module, we examine the human eye's image-forming structures in more detail.

 What key optical feature is found in the eyes of both insects and squids but is not present in planarians?

● Lenses, which focus light onto photoreceptor cells

32.8 Vertebrates have single-lens eyes that focus by changing position or shape

Structure The outer surface of the vertebrate eyeball is a tough, whitish layer of connective tissue called the **sclera** (see Figure 32.7C). At the front of the eye, the sclera becomes the transparent **cornea**, which lets light into the eye and also helps to focus light. The sclera surrounds a pigmented layer called the **choroid**. The anterior choroid forms the iris, which gives the eye its colour. After going through the pupil, the opening at the centre of the iris, light passes through the disclike lens, which is held in position by ligaments. At the back of the eyeball is the retina, a layer just inside the choroid that contains photoreceptor cells.

The lens and ciliary body divide the eye into two fluid-filled chambers. The large chamber behind the lens is filled with jellylike **vitreous humour**. (Humour is the general Latin term for a body fluid.) The much smaller chamber in front of the lens contains the thinner **aqueous humour**. The humours help to maintain the shape of the eyeball. In addition, the aqueous humour circulates through its chamber, supplying nutrients and oxygen to the lens, iris, and cornea and carrying off wastes. Blockage of the ducts that drain this fluid can cause glaucoma,

increased pressure inside the eye that may lead to blindness. If diagnosed early, glaucoma can be treated with medications that increase the circulation of aqueous humour.

A thin mucous membrane helps to keep the outside of the eye moist. This membrane, called the **conjunctiva**, lines the inner surface of the eyelids and folds back over the white of the eye (but not the cornea). An infection or allergic reaction may cause inflammation of the conjunctiva, a condition called conjunctivitis, or "pink eye." Bacterial conjunctivitis usually clears up with antibiotic eye drops. Viral conjunctivitis usually clears up on its own, although it is very contagious, especially among young children. If you are in contact with someone who has conjunctivitis, the best way to avoid spreading the disease is through careful hygiene: Do not touch the affected area, wash your hands frequently and thoroughly, and wash objects that may come into contact with the infection (such as linens and towels) with hot water and bleach.

A gland above the eye secretes tears, a dilute salt solution that is spread across the eyeball by blinking and that drains into ducts that lead into the nasal cavities. This fluid cleanses and moistens the eye surface. Excess secretion in response to eye irritation or strong emotions causes tears to spill over the eyelid and fill the nasal cavities, producing sniffles (also known as post-nasal drip). Some scientists speculate that emotional tears play a role in reducing stress.

Function A lens focuses light onto the retina by bending light rays. Focusing can occur in two ways. The lens may be rigid, as in squids and many fishes. In this case, focusing occurs as muscles move the lens back or forth, as you might focus on an object by using a magnifying glass. Or, as in the mammalian eye, the lens may be flexible, with focusing accomplished by changing the shape of the lens, depending on the distance to the object being viewed. The thicker the lens, the more sharply it bends light.

The shape of the mammalian lens is controlled by the ciliary muscles attached to the choroid and the ligaments that suspend the lens **(Figure 32.8)**. When the eye focuses on a nearby object, these muscles contract, pulling the choroid toward the lens, which actually reduces the tension (indicated by the yellow arrows) on the ligaments and lens. As these ligaments slacken, the elastic lens becomes thick and round, as shown in the top diagram of Figure 32.8. This change allows the diverging light rays from a close object to be bent and focused. The light rays from the object actually cross as they pass through the lens, resulting in an upside-down image striking the retina. (The brain interprets this inverted image so that we perceive it as right side up.)

Light from distant objects approaches in parallel rays that require less bending for proper focusing on the retina. When the eye focuses on a distant object, the ciliary muscles controlling the lens relax, and the choroid moves away from the lens. This puts tension (as indicated by the blue arrows) on the ligaments and flattens the elastic lens, as shown in the bottom diagram.

▲ **Figure 32.8** How vertebrate lenses focus light

Flattening the lens makes it less thick, and so the light is not bent as much. This allows a distant object to be placed into focus. What happens when you focus on an object that is moving toward you? The tension on the lens has to change, a process called accommodation. When the object is far away, the ciliary muscles are relaxed and the lens is flattened under tension. As the object moves toward you, the muscles slowly contract, releasing tension on the lens and allowing it to maintain a focused image. The opposite change occurs if the object is moving away from you. At least, that is how the human eye is *supposed* to work. In the next module, we consider ways that this mechanism can fail and ways to correct such failures.

 Arrange the following eye parts into the correct sequence encountered by photons of light travelling into the eye: pupil, retina, cornea, lens, vitreous humour, and aqueous humour.

● Cornea ⟶ aqueous humour ⟶ pupil ⟶ lens ⟶ vitreous humour ⟶ retina

---

32.9 Artificial lenses or surgery can correct focusing problems

Reading from an eye chart measures your **visual acuity**, the ability of your eyes to distinguish fine detail. When you have your eyes tested, the examiner asks you to read a line of letters sized for legibility at a distance of 20 feet (6 m), using one eye at a time. If you can do this accurately, you have normal (20/20) acuity in each eye. This means that from a distance of 20 feet, each of your eyes can read the chart's line of letters designated for 20 feet.

Visual acuity of 20/10 is better than normal and means that you can read letters from a distance of 20 feet that a

person with 20/20 vision can read only at 10 feet (3 m). On the contrary, visual acuity of 20/50 is worse than normal. In this circumstance, you would have to stand at a distance of 20 feet to read what a person with normal acuity can read at 50 feet (15 m).

Three of the most common vision problems are nearsightedness, farsightedness, and astigmatism. All three are focusing problems, easily corrected with artificial corrective lenses. People with **nearsightedness** cannot focus well on distant objects, although they can see well at short distances (the condition is

▲ **Figure 32.9A** A nearsighted eye (eyeball too long)

▲ **Figure 32.9B** A farsighted eye (eyeball too short)

named for the type of vision that is *unimpaired*). A nearsighted eyeball **(Figure 32.9A)** is longer than normal. The lens cannot flatten enough to compensate, and it focuses distant objects in front of the retina instead of on it. Nearsightedness (also known as myopia) is corrected by glasses or contact lenses that are concave—that is, thinner in the middle than at the outside edge. The lenses make the light rays from distant objects diverge as they enter the eye. The focal point formed by the lens in the eye then falls on the retina.

Farsightedness (also known as hyperopia) is the opposite of nearsightedness. It occurs when the eyeball is shorter than normal, causing the lens to focus images behind the retina **(Figure 32.9B)**. Farsighted people see distant objects normally but cannot focus on close objects. Corrective lenses that are thicker in the middle than at the outside edge (convex) compensate for farsightedness by making light rays from nearby objects converge slightly before they enter the eye. Another type of farsightedness, called presbyopia, develops with age. Beginning around the mid-forties, the lens of the

eye becomes less elastic. As a result, the lens gradually loses its ability to focus on nearby objects, and reading without glasses becomes difficult. Decreased elasticity of the lens also reduces the eye's capacity for accommodation when focusing on a moving object.

Astigmatism is blurred vision caused by a misshapen lens or cornea. This makes light rays converge unevenly and not focus at one point on the retina. Corrective lenses are asymmetric in a way that compensates for the asymmetry in the eye.

Surgical procedures are an option for treating vision disorders. In laser-assisted in situ keratomileusis (LASIK), a laser is used to reshape the cornea and change its focusing ability. More than a million LASIK procedures are performed each year to correct a variety of vision problems.

 Does an individual with 20/100 vision have better than normal vision? Explain your answer.

● No, this individual would have to stand at a distance of 20 feet to see what a person with normal vision can see at a distance of 100 feet (30 m).

32.10 The human retina contains two types of photoreceptors: rods and cones

The human retina contains two types of photoreceptors named for their shapes **(Figure 32.10A)**. **Cones** are stimulated by bright light and can distinguish colour, but they contribute little to night vision. **Rods** are extremely sensitive to light and enable us to see

in dim light, though only in shades of grey. The relative numbers of rods and cones an animal has correlates with whether an animal is most active during the day or night. Each human eye contains about 125 million rod cells and 6 million cone cells.

▲ **Figure 32.10A** Photoreceptor cells

In humans, rods are found in greatest density at the outer edges of the retina and are completely absent from the fovea, the retina's centre of focus. If you look directly toward a dim star in the night sky, the star is hard to see. Looking just to the side, however, makes your lens focus the starlight onto the parts of the retina with the most rods, and you can see the star better. By contrast, you achieve your sharpest day vision by looking straight at the object of interest. This is because cones are densest (about 150 000 per square millimetre) in the fovea.

As Figure 32.10A shows, each rod and cone consists of an array of membranous discs containing light-absorbing visual pigments. Rods contain a visual pigment called **rhodopsin**, which can absorb dim light. (Rhodopsin is derived from vitamin A, which is why vitamin A deficiency can cause "night blindness.") Interestingly, a change in a single amino acid of rhodopsin causes it to react to light in the ultraviolet range; this difference allows many species of birds to see beyond the range of human vision.

Cones contain visual pigments called **photopsins**, which absorb bright, coloured light. We have three types of cones, each containing a different type of photopsin. These cells are called blue cones, green cones, and red cones, referring to the colours of light absorbed best by their photopsin. We can perceive a great number of colours because the light from each particular colour triggers a unique pattern of stimulation among the three types of cones. Colourblindness results from a deficiency in one or more types of cones. The most common type is red-green colourblindness, in which red and green are seen as the same colour—either red or green, depending on which type of cone is deficient.

Figure 32.10B shows the pathway of light into the eye and through the cell layers of the retina. Notice that the tips of the rods and cones are embedded in the back of the retina (light pink cells). Light must pass through several relatively transparent layers of neurons before reaching the pigments in the rods and cones. In squid and octopi, the eye is structured so that light hits the photoreceptors without needing to pass through any cell layer. Because of this anatomic difference, these animals likely have greater visual acuity than we do. Like all sensory receptors, rods and cones are stimulus transducers. When rhodopsin and photopsin absorb light, they change chemically, and the change alters the permeability of the cell's membrane. The resulting receptor potential triggers

▲ **Figure 32.10B** The vision pathway from light source to optic nerve

a change in the release of neurotransmitters from the synaptic terminals (see the left side of the rod and cone in Figure 32.10A). This release initiates a complex integration process in the retina. As shown in Figure 32.10B, visual information transduced by the rods and cones passes from the photoreceptor cells through the network of neurons (red arrows). Notice the numerous synapses between the photoreceptor cells and the neurons and among the neurons themselves. Integration in this maze of synapses helps to sharpen images and increases the contrast between light and dark areas. Action potentials carry the partly integrated information to the brain via the optic nerve. Three-dimensional perceptions (what we actually see) result when visual input coming from the two eyes is integrated further in several processing centres of the cerebral cortex.

? **Explain why our night vision is mostly in shades of grey rather than in colour.**

● Rods are more sensitive than cones to light, and thus low-intensity light stimulates far more rods than cones. Rods do not detect colour.

Taste and Smell

32.11 Taste and odour receptors detect chemicals present in solution or air

Your senses of smell and taste depend on receptor cells that detect chemicals in the environment. Chemoreceptors in your taste buds detect molecules in solution; chemoreceptors in your nose detect airborne molecules.

Olfactory (smell) receptors are sensory neurons that line the upper portion of the nasal cavity and send impulses along their axons directly to the olfactory bulb of the brain (Figure 32.11). Notice the cilia extending from the tips of these chemoreceptors into the mucus that coats the nasal cavity. When an odorous substance () diffuses into this region and dissolves in the mucus, it can bind to specific receptor proteins on the cilia. The binding triggers a membrane depolarization and generates action potentials. As the signals are integrated in the brain, we perceive odour. Humans can distinguish thousands of different odours.

Many animals rely heavily on their sense of smell for survival. Most other mammals have a much more discriminating sense of smell than humans. Odours often provide more information than visual images about food, the presence of mates, or danger. In contrast, humans often pay more attention to sights and sounds than to smells. ("Seeing is believing" is thus a very humanocentric idea!)

Receptor cells for taste in mammals are modified epithelial cells organized into taste buds on the tongue and throughout the oral cavity. In addition to the four familiar taste perceptions—sweet, sour, salty, and bitter—a fifth, called *umami* (Japanese for "delicious") is elicited by glutamate, an amino acid. Umami describes the savory flavour common in meats, cheeses, and other protein-rich foods, as well as the flavour-enhancing chemical monosodium glutamate (MSG). Any region of the mouth with taste buds can detect any of the five types of taste. ("Taste maps" of the tongue can thus

▲ Figure 32.11 Smell in humans

be misleading.) An individual taste cell has a single type of receptor and thus detects only one of the five tastes.

Although the receptors and brain pathways for taste and smell are independent, the two senses do interact. Indeed, much of what we call taste is really smell, as you have probably noticed when a stuffy head cold dulls your perception of taste.

In the next module, we discuss a rumour regarding our pets' sense of smell.

? What is the key structural difference between taste receptors and olfactory receptors in terms of cellular structure? (*Hint*: Review Module 31.3.)

● Taste receptors release neurotransmitters, triggering action potentials carried to the brain by sensory neurons. Olfactory receptors are themselves modified sensory neurons.

RUMOUR HAS IT ## 32.12 Can pets smell human illnesses?

Humans have approximately 5 million chemoreceptors in an area of less than 10 square centimetres (cm²). Compared to our pets, this is a very small amount. Cats have 200 million receptors in 20 cm², and dogs can have up to 300 million chemoreceptors in an area of up to 170 cm². Sensitivity, or detection, limits are about 20 times greater in cats (compared to those of humans) and can be 1000 times greater in dogs.

Cats and dogs also have a second organ for chemoreception, the vomeronasal organ. This organ is primarily devoted to detecting pheromone signals from other members of their species. It is not surprising then that our pets can smell odours that we cannot. But, is it possible that cats or dogs can sense if a human is sick based on smell?

When a person is ill, it is common for their normal biochemical or metabolic pathways to become altered. These changes can lead to the production of novel, volatile molecules and thus a unique chemical signature. The new molecules can travel through the blood to the lungs where they are exhaled, becoming detectable.

In 2006, American physician Michael McCulloch published a study in which dogs were trained to identify cancer patients by the smell of their breath. Labrador retrievers and Portuguese water dogs were trained to identify breast cancer and lung cancer. After only three weeks of training, these dogs could accurately identify these cancers in patients they had never before encountered. The accuracy of identification, confirmed by standard biopsy, was 88% for breast cancer and 97% for lung cancer. Impressively, trained dogs can detect early stages of these cancers. And, early detection significantly improves the prognosis for the patient.

In recent years, similar practices have been used to train dogs to detect ovarian cancer and colon cancer in breath or fecal samples. Using dogs to detect cancers may become an effective method for screening patients for many diseases.

Oscar is a famous cat that lives in a nursing home in Rhode Island in the United States (**Figure 32.12**). At the home, he has predicted the deaths of several residents by entering their rooms and lying with them for a few hours until they passed away. His accuracy is remarkable. During the first two years of his stay at the nursing home, Oscar correctly predicted all 25 deaths that occurred during that time. It is probable that Oscar smells certain chemicals released by dying cells. When Oscar enters the room of a resident, staff members contact the person's family so they can say their goodbyes.

The rumour that our pets can sense when we are sick, or even dying, is one that is well supported in the scientific literature. Although we do not fully understand the exact cues, it appears that well-trained pets can sense illnesses. Future research clearly needs to be performed to identify the olfactory cues that correspond to these diseases.

▲ **Figure 32.12** Oscar, a cat that can predict death

 Compare a dog's and a human's brain and explain how their structure reflects the dog's reliance on smell and our dependence on vision.

● A larger proportion of the dog's brain is devoted to interpreting smell, whereas humans have a large visual cortex.

32.13 Review: The central nervous system couples stimulus with response

In this chapter and the previous one, we focused on information gathering and processing. Sensory receptors provide an animal's nervous system with vital data that enable the animal to avoid danger, find food and mates, and maintain homeostasis—in short, to survive.

A star-nosed mole foraging for food illustrates the sequence of information flow in an animal. When the nasal tentacles contact a possible food item, specific receptors relay information to the brain. Incredibly sensitive touch receptors transduce details about the texture of the item while chemoreceptors transduce the item's composition. Within milliseconds, a vast network of neurons interprets and integrates this information, ultimately deciding the edibility of the item. Coordinating with the motor cortex, commands then travel to muscles along motor neurons, the mole quickly ingests the item and resumes foraging.

In the next chapter, we will see how muscles carry out the commands they receive from the nervous system.

 What three general types of neurons are involved when a star-nosed mole encounters an insect? (*Hint*: Review Module 31.1.)

● Sensory neurons, interneurons, and motor neurons

R E V I E W

MasteringBiology® **For Activity Quizzes, BioFlix, MP3 Tutors, and Activities, go to masteringbiology.com.**

Reviewing the Concepts

Sensory Reception (32.1–32.3)

32.1 Specialized sensory receptors detect five categories of stimuli. Pain receptors sense dangerous stimuli. Thermoreceptors detect heat or cold. Mechanoreceptors respond to mechanical energy (such as touch, pressure, and sound). Chemoreceptors respond to chemicals. Electromagnetic receptors respond to electricity, magnetism, and light (sensed by photoreceptors).

32.2 Sensory organs share a common cellular basis. All animal senses (both human and nonhuman) arise from receptor cells communicating action potentials to the CNS.

32.3 Sensory receptors convert stimulus energy to action potentials. Sensory receptors are specialized cells that detect stimuli. Sensory transduction converts stimulus energy to receptor potentials, which trigger action potentials that are transmitted to the brain. Action potential frequency reflects stimulus strength:

Repeated stimuli may lead to adaptation, a decrease in sensitivity.

Hearing and Balance (32.4–32.6)

32.4 The ear converts air pressure waves to action potentials that are perceived as sound. The human ear channels sound waves through the outer ear to the eardrum to a chain of bones in the middle ear to the fluid in the coiled cochlea in the inner ear. Pressure waves in the fluid bend hair cells of the organ of Corti against a membrane, triggering nerve signals to the brain. Louder sounds generate more action potentials; pitches stimulate different regions of the organ of Corti.

Outer ear   Middle ear   Inner ear

Eardrum   Bones   Organ of Corti (inside the cochlea)

32.5 The inner ear houses our organs of balance. The semicircular canals and utricle and saccule located in the inner ear sense body position and movement.

32.6 Why does balance deteriorate as we age? Maintaining balance involves a number of sensory receptors, equilibrium, vision, and even touch receptors in our feet. Acuity of these senses decline as we get older, making it more difficult to maintain balance.

Vision (32.7–32.10)

32.7 Several types of eyes have evolved independently among animals. Animal eyes range from simple eyecups that sense light intensity and direction to the many-lens compound eyes of insects to the single-lens eyes of squids and vertebrates, including humans.

32.8 Vertebrates have single-lens eyes that focus by changing position or shape. In the mammalian eye, the cornea and flexible lens focus light on photoreceptor cells in the retina:

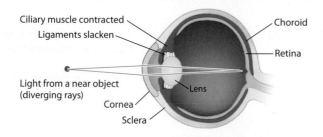

Ciliary muscle contracted
Ligaments slacken
Choroid
Retina
Light from a near object (diverging rays)
Lens
Cornea
Sclera

32.9 Artificial lenses or surgery can correct focusing problems. Focusing involves changing the shape of the lens. Nearsightedness and farsightedness result when the focal point is not on the retina. Corrective lenses bend the light rays to compensate.

32.10 The human retina contains two types of photoreceptors: rods and cones. Rods allow us to see shades of grey in dim light, and cones allow us to see colour in bright light.

Taste and Smell (32.11–32.13)

32.11 Taste and odour receptors detect chemicals present in solution or air. Taste and smell depend on chemoreceptors that bind specific molecules. Taste receptors, located in taste buds on the tongue, produce five taste sensations. Olfactory (smell) sensory neurons line the nasal cavity. Various odours and tastes result from the integration of input from many receptors.

32.12 Can pets smell human illnesses? Many diseases can be associated with unique chemical signatures that trained dogs can recognize. Some animals may use specific cues to predict death.

32.13 Review: The central nervous system couples stimulus with response. The CNS receives sensory information, integrates it, and commands appropriate muscle responses.

Connecting the Concepts

1. Complete this concept map summarizing sensory receptors.

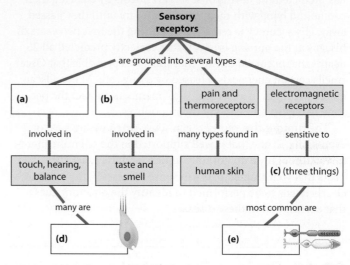

Sensory receptors

are grouped into several types

(a)   (b)   pain and thermoreceptors   electromagnetic receptors

involved in   involved in   many types found in   sensitive to

touch, hearing, balance   taste and smell   human skin   (c) (three things)

many are   most common are

(d)   (e)

Testing Your Knowledge

Multiple Choice

2. Eighty-year-old Mr. Johnson has become slightly deaf. To test Mr. Johnson's hearing, his doctor held a vibrating tuning fork tightly against the back of his skull. This sent vibrations through the bones of the skull, setting the fluid in the cochlea in motion. Mr. Johnson could hear the tuning fork this way, but not when it was held away from his skull several centimetres from his ear. The problem was probably in the _____. *(Explain your choice.)*
   a. auditory centre of Mr. Johnson's brain.
   b. auditory nerve leading to the brain.
   c. hair cells in the cochlea.
   d. bones of the middle ear.
   e. fluid of the cochlea.

3. Which of the following correctly traces the path of light into your eye?
   a. lens, cornea, pupil, retina
   b. cornea, pupil, lens, retina
   c. cornea, lens, pupil, retina
   d. lens, pupil, cornea, retina
   e. pupil, cornea, lens, retina

4. If you look away from this book and focus your eyes on a distant object, the eye muscles _____ and the lenses _____ to focus images on the retinas.
   a. relax; flatten
   b. relax; become more rounded
   c. contract; flatten
   d. contract; become more rounded
   e. contract; relax

5. Which of the following are not present in human skin?
   a. thermoreceptors
   b. electromagnetic receptors
   c. touch receptors
   d. pressure receptors
   e. pain receptors

6. Maintaining balance requires the coordination of many different senses. Which of these receptor types is not known to contribute to the sense of balance?
   a. electromagnetic receptors
   b. stretch receptors
   c. hair cells
   d. chemoreceptors
   e. touch receptors

7. Jim had his eyes tested and found that he has 20/40 vision. This means that
   a. the muscles in his iris accommodate too slowly.
   b. he is farsighted.
   c. the vision in his left eye is normal, but his right eye is defective.
   d. he can see at 40 feet what a person with normal vision can see at 20 feet.
   e. he can see at 20 feet what a person with normal vision can see at 40 feet.

8. What do the mechanoreceptor cells on the skin of a fish and the cochlea of your ear have in common?
   a. They use hair cells to sense sound or pressure waves.
   b. They are organs of equilibrium.
   c. They use electromagnetic receptors to sense pressure waves in fluid.
   d. They use granules that signal a change in position and stimulate their receptor cells.
   e. They are homologous structures that share a common evolutionary origin with all organs of hearing.

9. How could trained dogs possibly be used to detect diseases in humans?
   a. Dogs can see when a patient is sick much better than a physician.
   b. Dogs are very perceptive of human emotions and can detect those associated with diseases.
   c. Dogs have a very keen sense of smell that can detect volatile molecules unique to disease.
   d. As they lick patients, dogs can detect chemical signatures of various diseases by taste.
   e. With their sensitive hearing, dogs can identify changes in cardiac rhythms.

Describing, Comparing, and Explaining

10. How does your brain determine the volume and pitch of sounds?

11. As you read these words, the lenses of your eyes project patterns of light representing the letters onto your retinas. There the photoreceptors respond to the patterns of light and dark and transmit nerve signals to the brain. The brain then interprets the words. In this example, which processes relate to sensation and which to perception?

12. For what purposes do animals use their senses of taste and smell?

Applying the Concepts

13. Sensory organs tend to come in pairs. We have two eyes and two ears. Similarly, a planarian worm has two eyecups, a rattlesnake has two infrared receptors, and a butterfly has two antennae. Propose a testable hypothesis that could explain the advantage of having two ears or eyes instead of one.

14. Sea turtles bury their eggs on the beach above the high-tide line. When the baby turtles hatch, they dig their way to the surface of the sand and quickly head straight for the water. How do you think the turtles know which way to go? Outline an experiment to test your hypothesis.

15. Have you ever felt your ears ringing after listening to loud music from an MP3 player or at a concert? Could this music have been loud enough to permanently impair your hearing? Do you think people are aware of the possible danger of prolonged exposure to loud music? Should anything be done to warn or protect them? If you think so, what action would you suggest? What effect might warnings have?

Answers to all questions can be found in Appendix E.

Animal Locomotion

Movement and Locomotion

(33.1–33.2)

Locomotion requires the collaboration of muscles and skeleton.

The Vertebrate Skeleton

(33.3–33.6)

Vertebrates have similar skeletons, but modifications of the ancestral body plan resulted in structural adaptations for different functions.

Muscle Contraction and Movement

(33.7–33.13)

Muscles work with the skeleton to move the body. Each muscle cell has its own contractile apparatus.

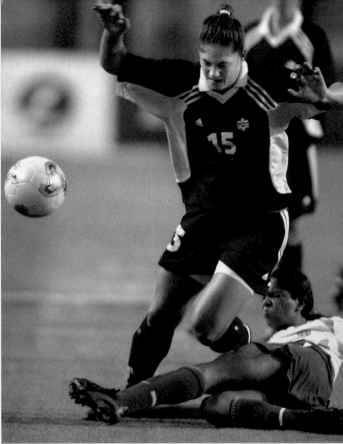

New Hopes for Old Knees

When hominins first stood and walked on two legs, new and exciting possibilities opened up for them. Yet, with the benefits of this new posture came a new vulnerability, the knee. The knee is a typical hinge joint, bending only in one direction. Four small ligaments hold the knee joint together and stabilize its motion through this single plane. Two collateral ligaments, one on either side of the knee, prevent side-to-side movements. Inside the knee, two cruciate ligaments prevent shearing and twisting motions.

Ligaments, bands of fibrous connective tissue, are susceptible to tears or stretching. These injuries typically occur when the knee is forcefully bent in an unnatural direction, most commonly during sport. More than half of all sport-related injuries involve the knee. For professional athletes, including Canadian soccer player Kara Lang, these injuries can be career ending. Quick changes of direction during a sprint or impacts to the side of the knee are two common incidents leading to injury.

Currently, most knee injuries can be repaired using arthroscopic surgery. Damaged tissues can be cleaned up or, in severe cases, removed or replaced. Although surgical techniques have improved with new arthroscopic advances, complications still exist. The chance of developing arthritis within the affected joint increases later in life. Repaired ligaments tend to lose about 20% of their former strength. As damaged ligaments heal, they are replaced with scar tissue. Although scar tissue can hold the joint together, it is very weak, having only

30% the strength of the original ligament. Therefore, repair and healing of an injured ligament can restore function to the knee, but not its original strength. After observing similar outcomes of countless knee surgeries, Dr. Cy Frank at the University of Calgary hopes to find a way to restore full knee strength following an injury.

Frank, a world-leading joint injury specialist, is investigating how to improve the healing process and make post-operative knees stronger. One approach is to actually increase scar tissue formation. Seemingly counterintuitive, if scar tissue is one-third as strong as a normal ligament, then normal strength can be achieved with a scar three times larger. This strategy can work only for ligaments external to the joint. The cruciate ligaments inside the knee, for example, could not be repaired in this fashion. A new experimental approach, gene therapy, may be a better alternative to promote healing. Injecting the appropriate genes into damaged ligaments can stimulate their regrowth, not scar formation. The new ligaments should have no loss of strength. The prognosis for patients with knee injuries may then become complete recovery.

The knee is only one of many joints in our bodies. Locomotion requires the coordinated movement of multiple joints simultaneously. In this chapter, we sample the types of animal movement and the skeletal systems that support it. We also learn about our own muscle and skeletal systems and how we can increase our strength and endurance through athletic training.

Movement and Locomotion

33.1 Locomotion requires energy to overcome friction and gravity

Movement is a distinguishing characteristic of animals. Even animals that are attached to a substrate move their body parts. All types of animal movement have underlying similarities. At the cellular level, every form of movement involves protein strands moving against one another, an energy-consuming process. In muscle cell contraction and amoeboid movement, the cellular system is based on microfilaments. Microtubules are the main components of cilia and flagella (see Module 4.17).

Most animals are fully mobile. **Locomotion**—active travel from place to place—requires energy to overcome two forces that tend to keep an animal stationary: friction and gravity. The relative importance of these two forces varies, depending on the environment. Water is dense and offers considerable resistance to a body moving through it, so an aquatic animal must expend energy overcoming friction. Gravity is not much of a problem, because water supports much or all of the animal's weight. On land, gravity is the main challenge—air provides no support for an animal's body. When a land animal walks, runs, or hops, its leg muscles expend energy both to propel it and to keep it from falling down. However, air offers very little resistance to an animal moving through it, at least at moderate speeds. Friction is limited to the points of contact between the animal's body and the ground. In the remainder of this module, we look at the major modes of animal locomotion.

Swimming   Animals swim in diverse ways. Many insects, for example, swim the way we do, using their legs as oars to push against the water. Squids, scallops, and some jellies are jet-propelled, taking in water and squirting it out in bursts. A fish swims by moving its body and tail from side to side (Figure 33.1A). Whales and other aquatic mammals move by undulating their bodies and tails from top to bottom. A sleek, streamlined shape, like that of seals, porpoises, penguins, and many fishes, is an adaptation that aids rapid swimming.

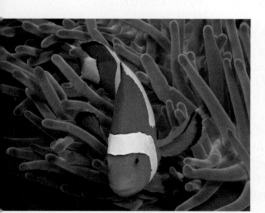
▲ **Figure 33.1A** A fish swimming

Walking and Running   A walking animal moves each leg in turn, overcoming friction between the foot and the ground with each step. To maintain balance, a four-legged animal usually keeps three feet on the ground at all times when walking slowly. Bipedal (two-footed) animals, such as birds and humans, are less stable on land and keep part of at least one foot on the ground when walking. A running four-legged animal may move two or three legs with each stride. At some gaits, all of its feet may

▲ **Figure 33.1B** A dog running at full speed

be off the ground simultaneously (Figure 33.1B). At running speeds, momentum—more than foot contact—stabilizes the body's position, just as it keeps a moving bicycle upright.

Hopping   Some animals—for example, kangaroos—travel mainly by hopping (Figure 33.1C), a specialized mode of locomotion that has also evolved independently in several rodents. Large muscles in the hind legs of kangaroos generate a lot of power. Tendons (which connect muscle to bone) in the legs also momentarily store potential energy when the kangaroo lands—somewhat like the spring on a pogo stick. The higher the jump, the tighter the spring coils when a pogo stick lands and the greater the tension in the tendons when a kangaroo lands. In both cases, the stored energy is available for the next jump. For the kangaroo, the tension in its legs is a cost-free energy boost that reduces the total amount of energy the animal expends to travel. At rest, the kangaroo sits upright with its tail and both hind feet touching the ground. This position stabilizes the animal's body and costs little energy to maintain.

The pogo stick analogy applies to many other land animals as well. The legs of an insect, horse, or human, for instance, retain some spring during walking or running, although less than those of a hopping kangaroo.

Crawling   Animals that have no limbs, or very short limbs, drag their bodies along the ground in a crawling movement. Because much of the animal's body is in contact with the ground, its energy is mainly expended to overcome friction

▲ **Figure 33.1C** Kangaroos hopping

rather than gravity. Many snakes crawl rapidly by undulating the entire body from side to side. Aided by large, movable scales on its underside, a snake's body pushes against the ground, driving the animal forward. Boa constrictors and pythons creep forward in a straight line, driven by muscles that lift belly scales off the ground, tilt them forward, and then push them backward against the ground.

Earthworms crawl by peristalsis, a type of movement produced by rhythmic waves of muscle contractions passing from head to tail. (In Module 26.5, you saw how peristalsis squeezes food through your digestive tract.) To move by peristalsis, an animal needs a set of muscles that elongates the body and another set that shortens it. Also required are a way to anchor its body to the ground and a hydrostatic skeleton, which we discuss further in Module 33.2. As illustrated in **Figure 33.1D**, the contraction of circular muscles, which encircle the circumference of the body, constricts and elongates some regions of the fluid-filled segments of a crawling earthworm. At the same time, longitudinal muscles that run the length of the body shorten and thicken other regions. Stiff bristles on the underside of the body grip the ground and provide traction, like the spikes on track shoes. (If you run your fingers along the belly of an earthworm, the bristles feel like whisker stubble.) In position ❶, segments at the head and tail ends of the worm are short and thick (longitudinal muscles contracted) and anchored to the ground by bristles. Just behind the head, a group of segments is thin and elongated (circular muscles contracted), with bristles held away from the ground. In position ❷, the head has moved forward because circular muscles in the head segments have contracted. Segments just behind the head and near the tail are now thick and anchored by bristles, thus preventing the head from slipping backward. In position ❸, the head segments are thick again and anchored to the ground in their new position, well ahead of their starting point. The rear segments of the worm now release their hold on the ground and are pulled forward.

Flying   Many phyla of animals include species that crawl, walk, or run, and almost all phyla include swimmers. But flying has evolved in only a few animal groups: insects, reptiles (including birds), and, among the mammals, bats. A group of large flying reptiles died out millions of years ago, leaving birds and bats as the only flying vertebrates.

For an animal to become airborne, its wings must develop enough "lift" to completely overcome the pull of gravity. The key to flight is the shape of wings. All types of wings, including those of airplanes, are airfoils—structures whose shape alters air currents in a way that creates lift. As **Figure 33.1E** shows, an airfoil has a leading edge that is thicker than the trailing edge. It also has an upper surface that is somewhat convex and a lower surface that is flattened or concave. This shape makes the air passing over the wing travel farther than the air passing under the wing. As a result, air molecules are spaced farther apart above the wing than below it, and the air pressure underneath the wing is greater. This pressure difference provides the lift for flight.

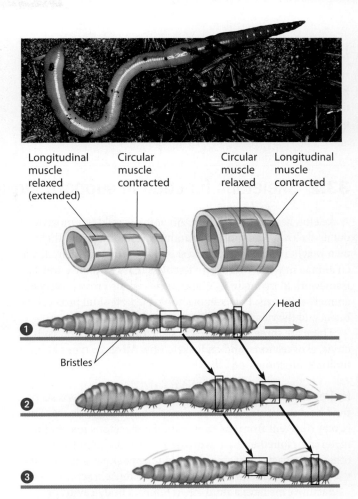

▲ **Figure 33.1D** An earthworm crawling by peristalsis

You may have heard of other vertebrates that are touted as fliers—for example, flying squirrels and flying fish. Although their names suggest flight, these animals simply glide. Using special adaptations such as flaps of skin, flying squirrels slowly glide from branch to branch. They are unable to generate enough lift to overcome gravity and become airborne.

Birds can reach great speeds and cover enormous distances. Swifts, which can fly 170 km/h in level flight, are the fastest. The bird that migrates the farthest is the arctic tern, which flies round trip between the North and South Poles each year.

▼ **Figure 33.1E** A bald eagle flying

An animal's muscle system provides the power to overcome friction and gravity. However, movement and locomotion result from collaboration between muscles and a skeletal system. In the next module, you will learn how skeletal systems are involved in movement. You will also learn about some of the other functions of skeletal systems.

 Contrast swimming with walking in terms of the forces an animal must overcome to move.

● Friction resists an animal moving through water, but gravity has little effect because of the animal's buoyancy; air poses little resistance to an animal walking on land, but the animal must support itself against the force of gravity.

33.2 Skeletons function in support, movement, and protection

A skeleton has many functions. An animal could not move without its skeleton, and most land animals would sag from their own weight if they had no rigid skeleton to support them. Even an animal in water would be a formless mass without a skeletal framework to maintain its shape. Skeletons also may protect an animal's soft parts. For example, the vertebrate skull protects the brain, and the ribs form a cage around the heart and lungs.

There are three main types of skeletons: hydrostatic skeletons, exoskeletons, and endoskeletons. All three types have multiple functions.

Hydrostatic Skeletons A **hydrostatic skeleton** consists of fluid held under pressure in a closed body compartment. This is very different from the more familiar skeletons made of hard materials. Nonetheless, a hydrostatic skeleton helps to protect other body parts by cushioning them from shocks. It also gives the body shape and provides support for muscle action.

Earthworms have a fluid-filled internal body cavity, or coelom (see Module 20.3). As a segmented animal, the earthworm has its coelom divided into separate compartments. The fluid in these segments functions as a hydrostatic skeleton, and the action of circular and longitudinal muscles working against the hydrostatic skeleton produces the peristaltic movement described in Module 33.1.

Cnidarians, such as hydras and jellies, also have a hydrostatic skeleton. A hydra **(Figure 33.2A)**, for example, has contractile cells in its body wall that enable it to alter its body shape by exerting pressure on the water-filled gastrovascular cavity (see Module 20.6). When a hydra closes its mouth and the contractile cells encircling its gastrovascular cavity contract, the body elongates (Figure 33.2A, left) just as the earthworm elongates when its circular muscles contract. The squeezing action also extends the tentacles. A hydra often

▲ **Figure 33.2A** The hydrostatic skeleton of a hydra in two states

sits in this position for hours, waiting for prey such as small worms or crustaceans that it can snare with its tentacles. If the hydra is disturbed, its mouth opens, allowing water to flow out. At the same time, contractile cells arranged longitudinally in the body wall contract, causing the body to shorten (Figure 33.2A, right).

Hydrostatic skeletons work well for many aquatic animals and for terrestrial animals that crawl or burrow by peristalsis. Most animals with hydrostatic skeletons are soft and flexible. In addition to extending its body and tentacles, for example, a hydra can expand its body around ingested prey that are larger than the gastrovascular cavity. An earthworm can burrow through soil because it is flexible and has a hydrostatic skeleton. Similarly, having an expandable body and a hydrostatic skeleton enables tube-dwelling animals such as some polychaete worms (see Figure 20.10B) to extend out of their tubes for feeding and gas exchange and then quickly squeeze back into the tube when threatened. However, a hydrostatic skeleton cannot support the forms of terrestrial locomotion in which an animal's body is held off the ground, such as in walking.

Exoskeletons A variety of aquatic and terrestrial animals have a rigid external skeleton, or **exoskeleton**. Recall from Module 20.11 that the exoskeleton is a characteristic of the phylum Arthropoda, a group that includes insects, spiders, and crustaceans such as crabs. The arthropod exoskeleton is a tough covering composed of layers of protein and the polysaccharide chitin. The muscles are attached to knobs and plates on the inner surfaces of the exoskeleton. At the joints of legs, the exoskeleton is thin and flexible, allowing movement. If you have eaten crab legs, you cracked the exoskeleton to extract the tasty muscle within.

Because the exoskeleton is composed of nonliving material, it does not grow with the animal. It must be shed (moulted) and replaced by a larger exoskeleton at intervals to allow for the animal's growth **(Figure 33.2B)**. Depending on the species, most insects moult from four to eight times before reaching adult size. A few insect species and certain other arthropods, such as lobsters and crabs, moult at intervals throughout life.

An arthropod is never without an exoskeleton of some sort. For instance, a newly moulted crab is covered by a soft, elastic exoskeleton that formed under the old one. Soon after moulting, the crab expands its body by gulping air or water. Its new exoskeleton then hardens in the expanded position, and the animal has room for additional growth. If you have ever eaten soft-shell crab, you took advantage of this brief period when the new exoskeleton is tender enough to chew. As you can imagine, a newly moulted arthropod is very susceptible

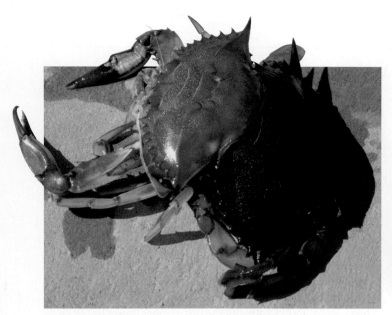

▲ **Figure 33.2B** The exoskeleton of an arthropod: a crab moulting

▼ **Figure 33.2D** A living sea urchin (left) and its endoskeleton (right)

to predation. Besides being weakly armoured, it is usually less mobile, because the soft exoskeleton cannot support the full action of its muscles.

The shells of molluscs such as clams, snails, and cowries **(Figure 33.2C)**—shells you might find on a beach—are also exoskeletons. Unlike the chitinous arthropod exoskeleton, mollusc shells are made of a mineral, calcium carbonate. The mantle, a sheetlike extension of the animal's body wall, secretes the shell. As a mollusc grows, it does not moult; rather, it enlarges the diameter of its shell by adding to its outer edge.

Endoskeletons   An **endoskeleton** consists of hard or leathery supporting elements situated among the soft tissues of an animal. Sponges, for example, are reinforced by a framework of tough protein fibres or by mineral-containing particles. Usually microscopic and sharp-pointed, the particles consist of inorganic material such as calcium salts or silica. Sea stars, sea urchins, and most other echinoderms have an endoskeleton of hard plates beneath their skin (see Module 20.14). In living sea urchins, about all you see are the movable spines, which are attached to the endoskeleton by muscles **(Figure 33.2D)**. A dead

urchin with its spines removed reveals the plates that form a rigid skeletal case (Figure 33.2D, right).

Vertebrates have endoskeletons consisting of cartilage or a combination of cartilage and bone (see Module 25.5). One major lineage of vertebrates, the sharks, have endoskeletons of cartilage reinforced with calcium. **Figure 33.2E** shows the more common condition for vertebrates. Bone makes up most of a frog's skeleton, as it does in bony fishes and land vertebrates. The frog skeleton and the skeletons of most other vertebrates also include some cartilage (blue in the figure), mainly in areas where flexibility is needed. Next, let's take a closer look at endoskeletons.

?   What are the advantages and disadvantages of an exoskeleton as compared to an endoskeleton?

● An exoskeleton tends to offer greater protection to body parts but must usually be moulted for the animal to grow.

Shell (exoskeleton)

Mantle

▲ **Figure 33.2C** The exoskeleton of a mollusc: a cowrie (a marine snail)

◀ **Figure 33.2E** Bone (tan) and cartilage (blue) in the endoskeleton of a vertebrate: a frog

The Vertebrate Skeleton

33.3 Vertebrate skeletons are variations on an ancient theme

As you learned in Module 21.4, the vertebrate skeletal system provided the structural support and means of locomotion that enabled tetrapods to colonize land. Subsequent evolution produced diverse groups of animals: amphibians, reptiles (including birds), and mammals. Each of those groups has diverse body forms whose skeletons are constructed from modified versions of the same parts. Even the skeletons of whales and dolphins, mammals that evolved from land-dwelling ancestors, are variations on the same theme.

All vertebrates have an **axial skeleton** (orange in **Figure 33.3A**) supporting the axis, or trunk, of the body. The axial skeleton

consists of the skull, enclosing and protecting the brain; the vertebral column (backbone), enclosing the spinal cord; and, in most vertebrates, a rib cage around the lungs and heart.

The backbone, the definitive characteristic of vertebrates, consists of a series of individual bones, the vertebrae, joined by pads of tough cartilage known as discs. The number of vertebrae varies among species. Pythons have 400, while an adult human has 24. The size of vertebrae is also highly variable and contributes to prominent morphological differences—for example, consider the giraffe. All vertebrae have the same basic structure, with slight variations that reflect the position of each vertebra in the backbone. Anatomists divide the vertebral column into the regions shown in **Figure 33.3B**: cervical (neck), which support the head; thoracic (chest), which form joints with the ribs; lumbar (lower back); sacral (between the hips); and coccygeal (tail). In humans, the sacral vertebrae fuse into a single bone called the sacrum. Our small coccygeal vertebrae are partially fused into the coccyx, or "tailbone."

Most vertebrates also have an **appendicular skeleton** (tan in Figure 33.3A), which is made up of the bones of the appendages and the bones that anchor the appendages to the axial skeleton. In a land vertebrate, the pectoral (shoulder) girdle and the pelvic girdle provide a base of support for the bones of the forelimbs and hind limbs respectively. Modified versions of the same bones are found in all vertebrate limbs, whether they are arms, legs, fins, or wings (see Figure 13.5A). This variety of limbs equips vertebrates for every form of locomotion.

A few groups of vertebrates, including snakes, lost their limbs during their evolution. How did this happen? The identity of vertebrae is established during embryonic development by the pattern of master control (homeotic) genes expressed in the somites. (Recall from Module 30.6 that somites are the blocks of embryonic tissue that give rise to the vertebral column.) Two of the homeotic genes that direct the differentiation of vertebrae are *Hoxc6* and *Hoxc8*. These genes are associated with the

Skull

Pectoral girdle — **Clavicle**, **Scapula**

Sternum

Ribs

Humerus

Vertebra

Radius

Ulna

Pelvic girdle

Carpals

Phalanges

Metacarpals

Femur

Patella

Tibia

Fibula

Tarsals

Metatarsals

Phalanges

▲ **Figure 33.3A** The human skeleton

7 cervical vertebrae

Intervertebral discs

12 thoracic vertebrae

5 lumbar vertebrae

Hip bone

Sacrum

Coccyx

▲ **Figure 33.3B** The human backbone, showing the groups of vertebrae development of thoracic vertebrae, which support the ribs. **Figure 33.3C** shows the range of vertebrae formed by somites that expressed *Hoxc6* (red), *Hoxc8* (blue), or both (purple) in a chicken and a python.

In the python, both *Hoxc6* and *Hoxc8* are expressed in all somites for nearly the entire length of the vertebral column. As a result, the first rib-bearing thoracic vertebra is located immediately posterior to the head. On the one hand, pythons have no cervical vertebrae. Chickens, on the other hand, have several cervical vertebrae, ending at the point where *Hoxc6* expression—and thoracic vertebrae—begin.

During the evolution of snakes, mutation in the DNA segments that control the expression of *Hoxc6* and *Hoxc8* changed cervical vertebrae to thoracic. In all vertebrates, the forelimbs originate at the boundary between cervical and thoracic vertebrae. Because this position does not exist in snakes, forelimbs do not form.

 What type of vertebrae do chickens and humans both have that snakes do not have? How does this difference affect the appendicular skeleton of snakes?

● Chickens and humans have cervical vertebrae; snakes do not (we did not compare vertebrae posterior to thoracic vertebrae). Because forelimbs form at the boundary between cervical and thoracic vertebrae, snakes lack forelimbs.

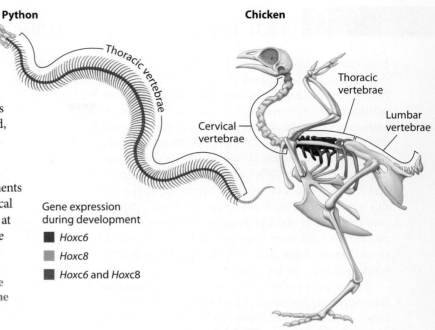

▲ **Figure 33.3C** Expression of two *Hox* genes in a python (left) and a chicken (right)

Gene expression during development
- ■ *Hoxc6*
- ■ *Hoxc8*
- ■ *Hoxc6* and *Hoxc8*

33.4 Bones are complex living organs

The expression "dry as a bone" should not be taken literally. Your bones are actually complex organs consisting of several kinds of moist, living tissues. **Figure 33.4** shows a human humerus (upper arm bone). A sheet of fibrous connective tissue, shown in pink (most visible in the enlargement on the lower right), covers most of the outside surface. This tissue helps to form new bone in the event of a fracture. A thin sheet of cartilage (blue) forms a cushionlike surface for movable joints, protecting the ends of bones as they glide against one another. Bone, a type of connective tissue, contains living cells that secrete a surrounding material, or matrix. Bone matrix consists of flexible fibres of the protein collagen with crystals of a mineral made of calcium and phosphate bonded to them (see Figure 25.5). The collagen keeps the bone flexible and nonbrittle, while the hard mineral matrix resists compression.

The shaft of this long bone is made of compact bone, a term referring to its dense structure. Notice that the compact bone surrounds a central cavity. The central cavity contains **yellow bone marrow**, which is mostly stored fat brought into the bone by the blood. The ends, or heads, of the bone have an outer layer of compact bone and an inner layer of spongy bone, so named because it is honeycombed with small cavities. The cavities contain **red bone marrow** (not shown in the figure), a specialized tissue that produces our blood cells (see Module 34.7).

Like all living tissues, bone cells carry out metabolism. Blood vessels that extend through channels in the bone transport nutrients and regulatory hormones to the bone's cells and remove waste materials. Nerves running parallel to the blood vessels help to regulate the traffic of materials between the bone and the blood.

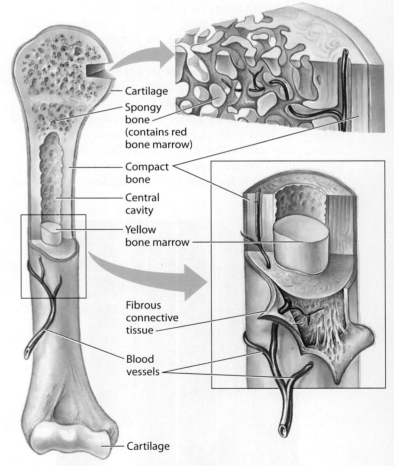

Cartilage
Spongy bone (contains red bone marrow)
Compact bone
Central cavity
Yellow bone marrow
Fibrous connective tissue
Blood vessels
Cartilage

▲ **Figure 33.4** The structure of an arm bone

 What causes the colours of yellow and red bone marrow?

● Stored fat and developing red blood cells, respectively

33.5 Healthy bones resist stress and heal from injuries

Bones are constantly subjected to stress as we go about our daily lives; exercise or physical labour causes additional stress. Excessive bone fatigue can lead to so-called stress fractures, hairline cracks in the bone, just as the accumulation of small amounts of stress on metals can cause a break. For example, when you bend a paper clip repeatedly, the metal fatigues and finally snaps. Unlike metal, however, bone is composed of living, dynamic tissue. Cells continually remove old bone matrix and replace it with new material. Stress fractures occur only if this repair process cannot keep up with the amount of stress placed on a bone. An athlete usually becomes aware of the problem and can allow time for healing, but in a racehorse, stress damage might go unnoticed until the fatigued bone breaks suddenly during a race.

A bone may also break when subjected to an external force that exceeds its resiliency. The average person will break two bones during his or her lifetime, most commonly the forearm or, for people older than age 75, the hip. Usually, this type of fracture occurs from a sudden impact, such as a fall or car accident. Wearing appropriate protective gear, such as seat belts, helmets, or padding, can protect your bones from high-force trauma.

Fortunately for active people, broken bones can heal themselves. A physician assists the process by putting the bone back into its natural alignment and then immobilizing it until the body's normal bone-building cells can repair the break. A splint or cast is used to protect the injured area and prevent movement. In severe cases, a fracture can be repaired surgically by inserting plates, rods, and/or screws that hold the broken pieces together **(Figure 33.5A)**. In certain cases, however, severely injured or diseased bone is beyond repair and must be replaced. Broken hip joints, for example, can be replaced with artificial ones made of titanium or cobalt alloys. Researchers have recently developed new methods of bone replacement, including grafts (from the patient or from a cadaver) and the use of synthetic polymers.

Colourized SEM 55×

Colourized SEM 55×

▲ **Figure 33.5B** Healthy spongy bone tissue (left) and bone damaged by osteoporosis (right)

The risk of bone fracture increases if bones are porous and weak. **Figure 33.5B** contrasts healthy bone tissue (left) and bone eroded by osteoporosis (right). **Osteoporosis** is characterized by low bone mass and structural deterioration of bone tissue. This weakness emerges from an imbalance in the process of bone maintenance—the destruction of bone material exceeds the rate of replacement. On the one hand, because the natural mechanism of bone maintenance responds to bone usage, weight-bearing exercise such as walking or running strengthens bones. On the other hand, disuse causes bones to become thinner. Strong bones also require an adequate intake of dietary calcium and enough vitamin D, which are both essential to bone replacement (see Module 26.16).

Until recently, osteoporosis was mostly considered a problem for women after menopause; estrogen contributes to normal bone maintenance. But while osteoporosis remains a serious health problem for older women, it is also becoming a concern for men and younger people. Doctors have noted a dramatic increase in bone fractures in children and teenagers in recent years. Many scientists believe that this is the result of exercising less and getting less calcium in the diet and less vitamin D from exposure to sunlight. Prevention of osteoporosis in later years begins with exercise and sufficient calcium and vitamin D while bones are still increasing in density (up until about age 30).

Other lifestyle habits, such as smoking, may also contribute to osteoporosis. There is a strong genetic component as well; young women whose mothers or grandmothers suffer from osteoporosis should be especially concerned with maintaining good bone health. Treatments for osteoporosis include calcium and vitamin D supplements and drugs that slow bone loss. But the effectiveness of such supplements may decrease after the onset of disease.

 How do exercise and adequate calcium intake help to prevent osteoporosis?

● Bone tissue responds to the stress of exercise by stepping up the repair process, which builds greater bone density. Calcium is the primary component of the rigid mineral matrix of bone.

▲ **Figure 33.5A** X-rays of a broken leg (left) and the same leg after the bones were set with a plate and screws (right)

33.6 Joints permit different types of movement

Much of the versatility of the vertebrate skeleton comes from its joints. Bands of strong fibrous connective tissue called **ligaments** hold together the bones of movable joints. **Ball-and-socket joints**, such as those found where the humerus joins the pectoral girdle (**Figure 33.6**, left), enable us to rotate our arms and legs and move them in several planes. A ball-and-socket joint also joins the femur to the pelvic girdle. **Hinge joints** permit movement in a single plane, just as the hinge on a door enables it to open and close. Our elbows (shown in Figure 33.6, centre) and knees (the topic of the chapter-opening essay) are hinge joints. Hinge joints are especially vulnerable to injury in sports, such as volleyball, basketball,

and tennis, that demand quick turns, which can twist the joint sideways. A **pivot joint** enables us to rotate the forearm at the elbow (Figure 33.6, right). A pivot joint between the first and second cervical vertebrae allows movement of the head from side to side, for example, the motion you make when you say "no." As you will learn in the next module, muscles supply the force to move the bones of each joint.

 Where we have ball-and-socket joints, horses have hinge joints. How does this affect the movements they can perform?

● Hinge joints restrict the movement of their legs to a single plane, making horses less flexible than humans.

| Ball-and-socket joint | Hinge joint | Pivot joint |

▲ **Figure 33.6** Three kinds of joints

Muscle Contraction and Movement

33.7 The skeleton and muscles interact in movement

Figure 33.7 shows how an animal's muscles interact with its bones to produce movement. Muscles are connected to bones by **tendons**. For example, the upper ends of the biceps and triceps muscles shown in the figure are anchored to bones in the shoulder. The lower ends of these muscles are attached to bones in the forearm. The action of a muscle is always to contract, or shorten. A muscle *pulls* the bone to which it is attached—it can move the bone only in one direction. A different muscle is needed to reverse the action. Thus, back-and-forth movement of body parts involves antagonists, a pair of muscles (or muscle groups) that can pull the same bone in opposite directions. While one antagonist contracts, the other relaxes.

The biceps and triceps muscles are an example of an antagonistic pair. Imagine that you are picking up a glass of water to drink. To raise the glass to your lips, your biceps muscle contracts, pulling the forearm bones toward you as your elbow bends. To put the glass back on the table, you must lower your forearm. Now the triceps muscle contracts, pulling the forearm bones down. The quadriceps, which extend the lower leg, and the hamstring, which flexes the lower leg, are additional examples of an antagonistic pair of muscles.

All animals—very small ones like ants and giant ones like elephants—have antagonistic pairs of muscles that apply

▲ **Figure 33.7** Antagonistic action of muscles to pull bones up or down in the human arm

opposite forces to move parts of their skeletons. Next we see how a muscle's structure explains its ability to contract.

 When exercising to strengthen muscles, why is it important to impose resistance while both flexing and extending the limbs?

● This exercises both muscles of antagonistic pairs, which do work only when they are contracting.

33.8 Each muscle cell has its own contractile apparatus

The skeletal muscle system is a beautiful illustration of the relationship between structure and function. Each muscle in the body is made up of a hierarchy of smaller and smaller parallel strands, from the muscle itself down to the contractile protein molecules that produce body movements.

Figure 33.8 shows the levels of organization of skeletal muscle. As indicated at the top of the figure, a muscle consists of many bundles of **muscle fibres**—roughly 250 000 in a typical human biceps muscle—oriented parallel to one another. Each muscle fibre is a single long, cylindrical cell that has many nuclei. Most of its volume is occupied by hundreds or thousands of **myofibrils**, organelles consisting of discrete bundles of proteins that include the contractile proteins **actin** and **myosin**. Skeletal muscle is also called striated (striped) muscle because the arrangement of the proteins creates a repeating pattern of stripes along the length of a myofibril that is visible under a light microscope. Beneath the drawing of a myofibril in Figure 33.8 is an electron micrograph that shows one unit of the pattern, which is called a **sarcomere**. Structurally, a sarcomere is the region between two dark, narrow lines, called Z lines, in the myofibril. Each myofibril consists of a long series of sarcomeres. Functionally, the sarcomere is the contractile apparatus in a myofibril—the muscle fibre's fundamental unit of action.

The diagram of the sarcomere at the bottom of Figure 33.8 explains the features visible in the micrograph. The pattern of horizontal stripes is the result of the alternating bands of **thin filaments**, composed primarily of actin molecules, and **thick filaments**, which are made up of myosin molecules. The Z lines consist of proteins that connect adjacent thin filaments. The light band surrounding each Z line contains only thin filaments. The dark band centred in the sarcomere is the location of the thick filaments. The actin molecules in the thin filaments are globular proteins arranged in long strands. In addition to actin, thin filaments include proteins called troponin and tropomyosin that play a key role in regulating muscle contraction.

Next we examine the structure of a sarcomere in detail and see how it functions in muscle contraction.

? What are the two most abundant proteins found in a muscle fibre?

● Actin and myosin

► **Figure 33.8** The contractile apparatus of skeletal muscle

Muscle

Several muscle fibres

Single muscle fibre (cell)

Nuclei

Plasma membrane

Myofibril

Light band Dark band Light band

Z line

Sarcomere

TEM 29 000×

Thick filaments (myosin)

Thin filaments (actin)

Z line

Z line

Sarcomere

33.9 A muscle contracts when thin filaments slide along thick filaments

How does the structure of a sarcomere relate to its function? According to the sliding-filament model of muscle contraction, a sarcomere contracts (shortens) when its thin filaments slide along its thick filaments. **Figure 33.9A** is a simplified diagram that shows a sarcomere in a relaxed muscle, in a contracting muscle, and in a fully contracted muscle. Notice in the contracting sarcomere that the Z lines and the thin filaments (blue) have moved closer together. When the muscle is fully contracted, the thin filaments overlap in the middle of the sarcomere. Contraction shortens the sarcomere without changing the lengths of the

thick and thin filaments. A whole muscle can shorten about 35% of its resting length when all sarcomeres contract.

Myosin acts as the engine of movement. Each myosin molecule has a long "tail" region and a globular "head" region. The tails of the myosin molecules in a thick filament lie parallel to each other, with their heads sticking out to the side. Each head has two binding sites. One of the binding sites matches a binding site on the actin molecules (subunits) of the thin filament. ATP binds at the other site, which is also capable of hydrolyzing the ATP to release its energy—the energy that powers muscle contraction.

▲ **Figure 33.9A** The sliding-filament model of muscle contraction

Sarcomere

Dark band

Z   Z

Relaxed muscle

Contracting muscle

Fully contracted muscle

Contracted sarcomere

Each myosin head pivots back and forth in a limited arc as it changes shape from a low-energy configuration to a high-energy configuration and back again. During these changes, the myosin head swings toward the thin filament, binds with an actin molecule, and drags the thin filament through the remainder of its arc. The myosin head then releases the actin molecule and returns to its starting position to repeat the same motion with a different actin molecule.

Let's follow the key events of this process in **Figure 33.9B**. The myosin head binds a molecule of ATP, as shown at **1**. At this point, the myosin head is in its low-energy position. **2** Myosin hydrolyzes the ATP to ADP and phosphate P, both of which remain bound to the myosin molecule. The energy released from ATP extends the myosin head toward the thin filament. **3** The myosin head extends further, and its other binding site latches on to the binding site of an actin. The result is a connection between the two filaments—a cross-bridge. **4** ADP and P are released, and the myosin head pivots back to its low-energy configuration. This action, called the power stroke, pulls the thin filament toward the centre of the sarcomere.

The cross-bridge remains intact until **5** another ATP binds to the myosin head, and the whole process repeats. On the next power stroke, the myosin head attaches to an actin molecule ahead of the previous one on the thin filament (closer to the Z line). This sequence—detach, extend, attach, pull, detach—occurs repeatedly as the muscle contracts. Though we show only one myosin head in the figure, a typical thick filament has about 350 heads, each of which can bind and unbind to a thin filament about five times per second. The combined action of hundreds of myosin heads on each thick filament ratchets the thin filament toward the centre of the sarcomere, much like the people on one side of a tug-of-war. Each person (a myosin head) pulls hand over hand on the rope (the thin filament); the rope moves, the people do not. This mechanism of contraction is referred to as the sliding filament model. As long as sufficient ATP is present, the process continues until the muscle is fully contracted or until the signal to contract stops. Rigor mortis, the rigidity of a corpse, is the result of ATP depletion in the dead muscles. With no ATP to bind the myosin head, the cross-bridges are not broken. Therefore, the muscles, and by extension the body, remain stiff.

▲ **Figure 33.9B** The mechanism of filament sliding

? Which region of a sarcomere becomes shorter during contraction of a muscle?

● The light bands shorten and even disappear as the thin filaments slide (are pulled) toward the centre of the sarcomere.

33.10 Motor neurons stimulate muscle contraction

What prevents muscles from contracting whenever ATP is present? Signals from the central nervous system, conveyed by motor neurons (see Module 31.1), are required to initiate and sustain muscle contraction. When a motor neuron sends out an action potential, its synaptic terminals release the neurotransmitter acetylcholine, which diffuses across the synapse (or neuromuscular junction in this case) to the plasma membrane of the muscle fibre (Figure 33.10A).

The plasma membrane of muscle fibres is unusual in two ways. Like the plasma membrane of neurons, the plasma membrane of a muscle fibre is electrically excitable—it can propagate action potentials. Also, the plasma membrane extends deep into the interior of the muscle fibre via infoldings called transverse (T) tubules. As a result, when a motor neuron triggers an action potential in a muscle fibre, it spreads throughout the entire volume of the cell, rather than only along the surface. The T tubules are in close contact with the endoplasmic reticulum (ER; blue in Figure 33.10A), a network of interconnected tubules within the muscle fibre. The action potential causes channels in the ER to open, releasing calcium ions (Ca^{2+}) into the cytoplasmic fluid. Now let's see why Ca^{2+} is necessary for muscle contraction.

When a muscle fibre is in a resting state, the regulatory proteins tropomyosin and troponin block the myosin binding sites on the actin molecules. As shown in Figure 33.10B, two strands of tropomyosin wrap around the thin filament, blocking access to the binding sites. The muscle fibre cannot contract while these sites are blocked. When Ca^{2+} binds to troponin, the tropomyosin moves away from the myosin-binding sites, allowing contraction to occur. As long as the cytoplasmic fluid is flooded with Ca^{2+}, contraction continues. When motor neurons stop sending action potentials to the muscle fibres, the Ca^{2+} is pumped back into the ER, out of the cytoplasmic fluid; binding sites on the actin molecules are again blocked; the sarcomeres stop contracting; and the muscle relaxes.

A large muscle such as the calf muscle is composed of roughly a million muscle fibres. However, only about

Myosin-binding sites blocked

Actin · Tropomyosin · Ca^{2+}-binding sites · Troponin complex · Blocked myosin-binding site

Ca^{2+} floods the cytoplasmic fluid

Myosin-binding sites exposed

Myosin-binding site

▲ Figure 33.10B Thin filament, showing the interactions among actin, regulatory proteins, and Ca^{2+}

500 motor neurons run to the calf muscle. Each motor neuron has axons that branch out to synapse with many muscle fibres distributed throughout the muscle. Thus, an action potential from a single motor neuron in the calf causes the simultaneous contraction of roughly 2000 muscle fibres. A motor neuron and all the muscle fibres it controls is called a **motor unit**. Figure 33.10C shows two motor units; one controls two muscle fibres (motor unit 1 in the figure), and the other (motor unit 2) controls three.

Motor neuron axon · Action potential · Mitochondrion · Synaptic terminal · T tubule · Endoplasmic reticulum (ER) · Myofibril · Plasma membrane · Sarcomere · Ca^{2+} released from ER

▲ Figure 33.10A How a motor neuron stimulates a muscle fibre

Spinal cord · Motor unit 1 · Motor unit 2 · Nerve · Motor neuron cell body · Motor neuron axon · Synaptic terminals · Muscle · Tendon · Bone · Nuclei · Muscle fibres (cells)

▲ Figure 33.10C Motor units

The organization of individual neurons and muscle cells into motor units is the key to the action of whole muscles. We can vary the amount of force our muscles develop: When you arm wrestle, for example, you might change the amount of force developed by the biceps and triceps several times in the course of a match. The ability to do this depends mainly on the nature of motor units. More forceful contractions result when additional motor units are activated. Thus, depending on how many motor units your brain commands to contract, you can apply a small amount of force to lift a fork or considerably more to lift, say, a textbook. In muscles requiring precise control, such as those controlling eye movements, a motor neuron may control only a single muscle fibre.

 How does the endoplasmic reticulum help to regulate muscle contraction?

● By reversibly taking up and releasing Ca^{2+}, the ER regulates the cytoplasmic concentration of this ion, which is required in the cytoplasmic fluid for the binding of myosin to actin.

33.11 Aerobic respiration supplies most of the energy for exercise

Many people exercise to stay in shape or to lose a few pounds before swimsuit season. Activities such as jogging, swimming, or other aerobic workouts are typical fitness routines (Figure 33.11). Aerobic exercise is an effective method of maintaining or losing weight—the goal is to burn at least as many calories as you consume. The number of calories burned varies with the intensity and duration of the exercise, as you saw in the examples listed in Figure 6.4. Most of the energy expended during exercise is used for muscle movement, specifically, to break the cross-bridges formed during sarcomere contraction. Here we refer to this energy in terms of ATP rather than calories.

Muscles have a very small amount of ATP on hand. ATP can also be obtained using a high-energy molecule called phosphocreatine (PCr; also known as creatine phosphate) that is stored in the muscles. The enzymatic transfer of a phosphate group from PCr to ADP makes ATP almost instantaneously. Together, ATP and PCr can provide enough energy for a 10 to 15 second burst of activity, enough for a 100 m sprint (see Table 33.11).

The bulk of the ATP for aerobic exercise comes from the oxygen-requiring process of aerobic respiration, which

▲ Figure 33.11 Running, a good form of aerobic exercise

derives ATP by the breakdown of the energy-rich sugar glucose (see Module 6.3). Muscles are richly supplied with blood vessels that bring O_2 and glucose and carry away CO_2, the by-product of aerobic respiration. Breathing and heart rate increase during exercise, facilitating the exchange of gases. Muscles can also get oxygen from a hemoglobin-like molecule called myoglobin.

Glucose for ATP production is available from the bloodstream, and muscle tissue stores glycogen (see Module 3.7), which can be broken down to provide more glucose. The liver stores glycogen too and can release glucose into the bloodstream. Although the body can also mobilize fats as a source of fuel, the process of harvesting ATP from fatty acid breakdown is too slow to keep pace with the demands of increasing exercise intensity. Casual athletes are in no danger of running out of metabolic fuel during exercise, though—glycogen stores are typically more than adequate.

When exercise begins, it takes a few minutes for the aerobic "machinery" to start producing enough ATP to meet the increased demand. After exercise, muscles must repay the "oxygen debt" that was incurred during the first few minutes of exercise. For example, after a run, you breathe rapidly, and your heart rate remains elevated for a time as your muscles replenish their supplies of ATP and PCr and restore myoglobin to its oxygenated state. Oxygen is also used to metabolize the lactic acid that was produced by fermentation.

In the next two modules, we consider some of the effects that exercise has on muscles, starting with the soreness you may feel afterward.

TABLE 33.11	SOURCES OF ATP FOR ATHLETIC ACTIVITIES

Athletic Activity	Energy Use	Main Source of ATP
100 m spring; power lifting	10 to 15 second burst of activity	Stored ATP and PCr
200 m or 400 m race	Intense effort sustained over a short period of time	Stored ATP and PCr plus lactic acid fermentation
Jogging; long-distance running	Prolonged, low-level activity	Aerobic respiration
Tennis; squash; soccer	Prolonged, low-level activity with intermittent surges of intense effort	Aerobic respiration and lactic acid fermentation

 Compare the substances required, the ATP output, and the speed of aerobic respiration to lactic acid fermentation in muscles.

● Aerobic respiration requires glucose and O_2; fermentation requires glucose, but not O_2. Aerobic respiration produces many more ATP molecules than fermentation, but fermentation produces ATP molecules faster.

33.12 Does lactic acid buildup cause muscle soreness after exercise?

Have you ever struggled out of bed with aching muscles, regretting attending a new karate or dance class a couple of days earlier? Why do muscles ache for a few days after vigorous use, a condition called delayed-onset muscle soreness (DOMS)? A common explanation implicates the lactic acid that accumulates during a workout. Is there truth behind this rumour?

Muscles are richly supplied with blood vessels that bring O_2 and glucose and carry away CO_2, the by-product of aerobic respiration. Breathing and heart rate increase during exercise, facilitating the exchange of gases. In the previous module, you read that aerobic exercise requires an increase of oxygen. If the demand for ATP outstrips the oxygen supply—as in anaerobic exercises, such as sprinting or power lifting—muscle fibres can carry out the anaerobic process called lactic acid fermentation (see Module 6.13), which also uses glucose as a starting molecule. Fermentation supplies only a fraction of the ATP obtainable through aerobic respiration, but the process works 2½ times faster than respiration. Lactate is produced, but does it cause DOMS?

Lactate production reduces the pH of the muscle fibre cytoplasm. Consequently, enzymes involved in metabolism are not as active and the muscles do not generate as much force. Lactate buildup also produces the burning sensation you feel in active muscles. This important sign signals that you should stop overworking the muscle and enter a recovery period. Within hours of exercise, oxygen levels return to normal and all lactate is converted back into pyruvate. Therefore, when muscle soreness is first felt, a day or two after exercise, lactate levels are typically already low. Many coaches and athletes claim that riding stationary bikes at a moderate pace (a flush ride) after

a game helps to remove lactate. However, unless this method is used immediately post-exercise, there is not much lactate left to be removed from the muscles. If lactate does not cause muscle soreness, what does?

As we exert our muscles, they can become damaged on the cellular and subcellular levels, and muscle fibres become torn. Microscopic muscle tears, like any tissue damage, invariably activate the inflammatory response (see Module 34.2), which is part of the healing process. Inflammation and healing can be painful processes as the damaged tissue swells. The damage incurred during exercise is not necessarily detrimental. During the inflammation and healing, chemical signals are released that stimulate muscle tissue growth. Such stimulation causes the construction of more myofibrils in existing muscle fibres as well as the proliferation of new muscle cells. Combined, these effects increase the overall size and strength of the muscle.

Though lactate does indeed accumulate during anaerobic exercises, it is quickly removed during recovery, long before muscles become sore. Flush rides probably do not help significantly with the removal of lactate, but they may help by maintaining increased blood flow, oxygen delivery, and waste removal. Therefore, the rumour that lactic acid buildup causes muscle soreness is untrue. The pain is caused by inflammation caused by the healing of microscopic injuries sustained during exercise.

? Why does delayed-onset muscle soreness gradually lessen after going to more karate or dance classes on a regular schedule?

● With repeated workouts, muscles become stronger and more resistant to microscopic injuries.

33.13 Characteristics of muscle fibre affect athletic performance

The muscle fibres that make up a typical muscle are all structurally similar, but they do not all function in the same way. "Fast-twitch" fibres produce rapid and powerful contractions, but fatigue quickly. In contrast, "slow-twitch" fibres fatigue much more slowly, but do not generate as much contractile force. The characteristics of slow and fast fibres are summarized in Table 33.13, along with the characteristics of intermediate fibres, which are also abundant in human muscle. Most of the features associated with fibre type reflect the pathway(s) the fibre preferentially uses to generate ATP from energy-rich molecules; the possible pathways are aerobic respiration and fermentation, which is anaerobic.

Each muscle typically has a mixture of fast, slow, and intermediate fibre types, broadly correlated to the type of work it does. Muscles that maintain the body's posture, for example, are constantly active; they have a high proportion of

TABLE 33.13 CHARACTERISTICS OF MUSCLE FIBRES

Characterstic	Slow Fibres	Intermediate Fibres	Fast Fibres
Speed of contraction	Slow	Fast	Fast
Rate of fatigue	Fatigue slowly	Intermediate	Fatigue rapidly
Primary pathway for making ATP	Aerobic respiration	Aerobic (some fermentation)	Anaerobic (fermentation)
Myoglobin content	High	High	Low
Mitochondria and capillaries	Many	Many	Few

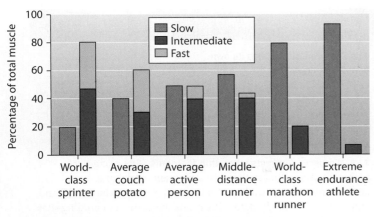

▲ **Figure 33.13** Percentage of slow, intermediate, and fast muscle fibres in quadriceps (thigh) muscles of different individuals

slow, fatigue-resistant fibres. In other muscles, such as those used for walking and running, the proportion of each fibre type varies widely among individuals. Although to some extent training can convert one type of fibre to another, most of this variation appears to be genetic. **Figure 33.13** compares the percentage of the three fibre types that are typical of the quadriceps (thigh) muscles of elite athletes and average adults.

The differences among muscle fibres can be traced to the myosin that makes up the thick filaments. Fast, slow, and intermediate fibres contain different forms of myosin that hydrolyze ATP at different speeds. The faster ATP is consumed during muscle contraction, the faster the metabolic process needed to supply the ATP.

The fastest fibres cycle through cross-bridges rapidly, producing forceful contractions that power brief, explosive movements such as those that occur when hitting a baseball, hoisting a heavy weight, or bursting out of the blocks for a sprint. For such forceful contractions, the fibres use ATP at a breakneck pace. Therefore, the oxygen-independent process of fermentation is the primary mechanism for producing ATP. Few mitochondria and low myoglobin content in fast fibres further reflects their anaerobic nature. The combination of fast fibres with more fatigue-resistant intermediate fibres appears to be ideal for sprinters.

Hydrolysis of ATP occurs much more slowly in the myosin found in slow fibres. The slower pace at which cross-bridges are made and broken results in more sustained but less forceful contractions. Athletes who have a predominance of slow fibres excel at endurance events such as running, cycling, or swimming long distances, events that require copious amounts of oxygen. Slow fibres have numerous mitochondria and high myoglobin concentrations to facilitate aerobic respiration. The

slow fibres that give middle-distance runners aerobic endurance are complemented by intermediate fibres that sustain a higher power output over a longer period.

Exercise can change the composition of muscle fibres to some extent. Indeed, muscles have a remarkable ability to adapt to how they are used. Muscle fibres respond to a variety of signals generated within the cell during exercise, including mechanical stretching, change in calcium concentration, and low oxygen levels. Hormones may also trigger cellular changes. The specific responses of muscle fibres correspond to the stresses placed on them. For example, weightlifting stimulates muscle fibres to produce additional myofibrils. The thick filaments of the new myofibrils are composed of the fast form of myosin, increasing the force that the muscle can generate. Muscles adapt to aerobic exercise by synthesizing more myoglobin, increasing the number of mitochondria, and adding capillaries—changes that result in increased endurance and greater resistance to fatigue. Along with muscle fibres, skeletal muscles have another cell population of stem cells called satellite cells. These cells are normally quiescent, but become activated in response to muscle damage, including the microscopic injuries caused by strenuous exercise discussed in the previous module. When active, satellite cells can fuse with damaged muscle fibres or differentiate into new fibres.

Drs. Michael Rudnicki (University of Ottawa), Fabio Rossi (University of British Columbia), and Jacques Tremblay (Université Laval) are studying a potential use for satellite cells in the treatment of Duchenne muscular dystrophy (DMD). DMD is caused by a defective gene that codes for a nonfunctional dystrophin protein. Without dystrophin, muscle fibres are easily damaged and unable to recover. The patient's satellite cells fuse but fail to restore the fibre. New research demonstrates that satellite cells transplanted from a healthy donor, with a functional dystrophin gene, can fuse with a recipient's muscle fibres. In these cells, dystrophin function is restored, ensuring survival of the affected cell. Though these studies are still in the early stages, the results are very promising and may lead to a treatment or cure for DMD.

As athletes increase their strength and endurance through training, they continue to set new records. The limits of human performance have not yet been reached but improved understanding of how animals move brings us closer to knowing what those limits are.

 According to the graph in Figure 33.13, how does becoming active affect the percentage of muscle fibres that use aerobic respiration?

● The percentages of slow and intermediate fibres, which both use aerobic respiration, increase.

Reviewing the Concepts

Movement and Locomotion (33.1–33.2)

33.1 Locomotion requires energy to overcome friction and gravity. Animals that swim are supported by water but are slowed by friction. Animals that walk, hop, or run on land are less affected by friction but must support themselves against gravity. Burrowing or crawling animals must overcome friction. They may move by side-to-side undulation or by peristalsis. The wings of birds, bats, and flying insects are airfoils, which generate enough lift to overcome gravity.

33.2 Skeletons function in support, movement, and protection. Worms and cnidarians have hydrostatic skeletons—fluid held under pressure in closed body compartments. Exoskeletons are hard external cases, such as the chitinous, jointed skeletons of arthropods. The vertebrate endoskeleton is composed of cartilage and bone.

The Vertebrate Skeleton (33.3–33.6)

33.3 Vertebrate skeletons are variations on an ancient theme. Vertebrate skeletons consist of an axial skeleton (skull, vertebrae, and ribs) and an appendicular skeleton (shoulder girdle, upper limbs, pelvic girdle, and lower limbs). There are many variations on this basic body plan, which may have evolved through changes in gene regulation.

33.4 Bones are complex living organs. Cartilage at the ends of bones cushions the joints. Bone cells, serviced by blood vessels and nerves, reside in a matrix of flexible protein fibres and hard calcium salts. Long bones have a fat-storing central cavity and spongy bone at their ends. Spongy bone contains red marrow, where blood cells are made.

33.5 Healthy bones resist stress and heal from injuries. Bone cells continue to replace and repair bone throughout life. Osteoporosis, a bone disease characterized by weak, porous bones, occurs when bone destruction exceeds replacement.

33.6 Joints permit different types of movement. Rigid skeletons can bend at joints, where ligaments hold bones together. Ball-and-socket joints move in several planes and hinge joints move in only one plane. Pivot joints allow for rotational movements.

Muscle Contraction and Movement (33.7–33.13)

33.7 The skeleton and muscles interact in movement. Antagonistic pairs of muscles produce opposite movements. Muscles perform work only when contracting.

33.8 Each muscle cell has its own contractile apparatus. Muscle fibres, or cells, consist of bundles of myofibrils, which contain bundles of overlapping thick (myosin) and thin (actin) protein filaments. Sarcomeres, repeating groups of thick and thin filaments, are the contractile units.

Sarcomere

Myosin — Actin

33.9 A muscle contracts when thin filaments slide along thick filaments. According to the sliding filament model of muscle contraction, the myosin heads of the thick filaments bind ATP and extend to high-energy states. The heads then attach to binding sites on the actin molecules and pull the thin filaments toward the centre of the sarcomere repeatedly during a muscle contraction.

33.10 Motor neurons stimulate muscle contraction. Motor neurons carry action potentials that initiate muscle contraction. A neuron and the muscle fibres it controls constitute a motor unit. The neurotransmitter acetylcholine released at a synaptic terminal triggers an action potential that passes along T tubules into the centre of the muscle cell. Calcium ions released from the endoplasmic reticulum initiate muscle contraction by allowing the regulatory protein tropomyosin to move away from the myosin-binding sites on actin.

33.11 Aerobic respiration supplies most of the energy for exercise. Aerobic respiration requires a constant supply of glucose and oxygen. The anaerobic process of fermentation can start producing ATP faster than aerobic respiration can, but it produces less.

33.12 Does lactic acid buildup cause muscle soreness after exercise? The muscle pain that follows exercise is caused by an inflammatory response to microscopic injuries within the muscle tissue.

33.13 Characteristics of muscle fibre affect athletic performance. The classification of muscle fibres as slow, intermediate, and fast is based on the pathway(s) they use to generate ATP. Most muscles have a combination of fibre types, which can be affected by exercise. Exercise also affects other aspects of muscle composition.

Connecting the Concepts

1. Complete this concept map on animal movement.

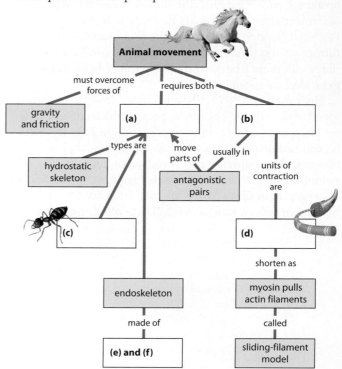

Testing Your Knowledge

Multiple Choice

2. A human's internal organs are protected mainly by the
   a. hydrostatic skeleton.
   b. motor unit.
   c. axial skeleton.
   d. exoskeleton.
   e. appendicular skeleton.

3. Arm muscles and leg muscles are arranged in antagonistic pairs. How does this affect their functioning?
   a. It provides a backup if one of the muscles is injured.
   b. One muscle of the pair pushes while the other pulls.
   c. A single motor neuron can control both of them.
   d. It allows the muscles to produce opposing movements.
   e. It doubles the strength of contraction.

4. Gravity would have the least effect on the movement of which of the following? *(Explain your answer.)*
   a. a salmon
   b. a human
   c. a snake
   d. a sparrow
   e. a grasshopper

5. Which of the following bones in the human arm corresponds to the femur in the leg?
   a. radius
   b. tibia
   c. humerus
   d. metacarpal
   e. ulna

6. Which of the following animals is correctly matched with its type of skeleton?
   a. fly—endoskeleton
   b. earthworm—exoskeleton
   c. dog—exoskeleton
   d. lobster—exoskeleton
   e. bee—hydrostatic skeleton

7. When a horse is running fast, its body position is stabilized by
   a. side-to-side undulation.
   b. energy stored in tendons.
   c. the lift generated by its movement through the air.
   d. foot contact with the ground.
   e. its momentum.

8. What is the role of calcium in muscle contraction?
   a. Its binding to a regulatory protein causes the protein to move, exposing actin binding sites to the myosin heads.
   b. It provides energy for contraction.
   c. It blocks contraction when the muscle relaxes.
   d. It is the neurotransmitter released by a motor neuron, and it initiates an action potential in a muscle fibre.
   e. It forms the heads of the myosin molecules in the thick filaments inside a muscle fibre.

9. Muscle A and muscle B have the same number of fibres, but muscle A is capable of more precise control than muscle B. Which of the following is likely to be true of muscle A? *(Explain your answer.)*
   a. It is controlled by more neurons than muscle B.
   b. It contains fewer motor units than muscle B.
   c. It is controlled by fewer neurons than muscle B.
   d. It has larger sarcomeres than muscle B.
   e. Each of its motor units consists of more cells than the motor units of muscle B.

10. Which of the following statements about skeletons is true?
    a. Hydrostatic skeletons are soft and do not protect body parts.
    b. Chitin is a major component of vertebrate skeletons.
    c. Evolution of bipedalism involved little change in the axial skeleton.
    d. Most cnidarians must shed their skeleton periodically to grow.
    e. Vertebrate bones contain living cells.

Describing, Comparing, and Explaining

11. In terms of both numbers of species and numbers of individuals, insects are the most successful land animals. Write a paragraph explaining how their exoskeletons help them live on land. Are there any disadvantages to having an exoskeleton?

12. A hawk swoops down, seizes a mouse in its talons, and flies back to its perch. Explain how its wings enable it to overcome the downward pull of gravity as it flies upward.

13. The greatest concentration of thoroughbred horse farms is in the bluegrass region of Kentucky. The grass in the limestone-based soil of this area is especially rich in calcium. How does this grass affect the development of championship horses?

14. Describe how you bend your arm, starting with action potentials and ending with the contraction of a muscle. How does a strong contraction differ from a weak one?

15. Using examples, explain this statement: "Vertebrate skeletons are variations on a theme."

Applying the Concepts

16. Drugs are often used to relax muscles during surgery. Which of the following chemicals do you think would make the best muscle relaxant, and why? Chemical A: Blocks acetylcholine receptors on muscle cells. Chemical B: Floods the cytoplasm of muscle cells with calcium ions.

17. An earthworm's body consists of a number of fluid-filled compartments, each with its own set of longitudinal and circular muscles. But in the roundworm, a single fluid-filled cavity occupies the body, and there are only longitudinal muscles that run down its entire length. Predict how the movement of a roundworm would differ from the movement of an earthworm.

18. When a person dies, muscles become rigid and fixed in position—a condition known as rigor. Rigor mortis occurs because muscle cells are no longer supplied with ATP (when breathing stops, ATP synthesis ceases). Calcium also flows freely into dying cells. The rigor eventually disappears because the biological molecules break down. Explain, in terms of the mechanism of contraction described in Modules 33.9 and 33.10, why the presence of calcium and the lack of ATP would cause muscles to become rigid, rather than limp, soon after death.

19. A goal of the *Ontarians with Disabilities Act* (Canada's only disability-related legislation) is to allow people with physical limitations to fully participate in society. Imagine that a neuromuscular disease or injury makes it impossible for you to walk. Think about your activities during the last 24 hours. How would your life be different if you had to get around in a wheelchair? What kinds of barriers or obstacles would you encounter? What kinds of changes would have to be made in your activities and surroundings to accommodate your change in mobility?

Answers to all questions can be found in Appendix E.

34

Animal Immune Systems

Innate Immunity

(34.1–34.3)

All animals have immune defences that are always at the ready.

Adaptive Immunity

(34.4–34.12)

Vertebrates have specific immune responses for specific pathogens.

Inappropriate Immune Responses

(34.13–34.16)

The immune system may respond overzealously to environmental allergens.

Multiple Sclerosis in Canada

The normal, healthy operation of the immune system is the focus of this chapter. However, there are several conditions when the immune system malfunctions. One common malfunction is the initiation of immune responses against normal proteins found within the body (*self-antigens*).

In multiple sclerosis (MS), the body's T cells mount a response against myelin proteins. As a result, the myelin-producing cells within the brain and spinal cord are damaged or destroyed within focal areas called plaques. This impairment leads to the degradation of signals within the unmyelinated neurons, producing a wide range of symptoms that depend on the site of damage.

MS is considered a disease of temperate climates and occurs more frequently in northern countries. Canada has one of the highest rates of MS in the world. Prevalence ranges from 180 cases per 100 000 in Quebec to nearly double that in the prairie provinces. In contrast, Mexico has an incidence rate of only 8 per 100 000.

Why some T cells react against normal human proteins in cases of MS remains a mystery. But many risk factors, including genetic and environmental factors, have been identified. MS has been associated with childhood infection with human herpesvirus-6, the cause of roseola infantum (a common childhood rash). Other studies have implicated that vitamin-D deficiency during adolescence is a risk factor; but, this research also showed that consumption of vitamin-D enriched whole milk actually increases the risk of getting MS. Interestingly, these same studies showed that vitamin-D supplements from sources other than milk did *not* change a person's risk.

Exposure to any environmental factors prior to the age of 15 has the greatest impact on an individual's risk of developing MS later in life. When children younger than 15 migrate to another country, they adopt the risk of their destination. By contrast, individuals who move when they are older than 15 retain the susceptibility of their homeland. The reason for this remains elusive.

As with most autoimmune disorders, MS has no cure. However, our ability to treat this debilitating disease continues to improve. Traditional treatment includes the use of corticosteroids to suppress the immune system. Alternative treatments include daily injections of drugs such as Copaxone; these injections are intended to redirect the inappropriate immune response away from the self-antigens.

Recently, an unconventional surgical treatment has been proposed. Some MS patients have a venous insufficiency, experiencing reduced blood flow from the brain. Associated with this are iron deposits in the nervous tissue that may initiate inflammation. In some patients surgery to enlarge these veins and increase blood flow (called liberation therapy) has reduced the severity of the disease and the frequency of relapse.

Currently this procedure is not available in Canada. Health Canada requires further research and clinical trials before liberation therapy can be approved. The Multiple Sclerosis Society of Canada and the Canadian Institutes of Health Research are currently supporting some of these necessary studies. Unfortunately, the long-term ramifications of this procedure are unknown and unforeseen complications have come to light.

Several Canadians who travelled to receive the treatment have since suffered from blood clots and one Ontario man has died as a result. In light of this new information, liberation therapy may not be approved in Canada.

In this chapter, you will learn about the body's varied defences and how they work to protect the body. Following a discussion of innate immunity, we concentrate on the mechanisms of adaptive immunity and then discuss inappropriate immune responses.

Innate Immunity

34.1 All animals have innate immunity

Nearly everything in the environment teems with **pathogens**, agents that cause disease. Yet we do not constantly become ill, thanks to the **immune system**, the body's system of defences against agents that cause disease. The immune systems of all animals include **innate immunity**, a set of defences that are active immediately upon infection and are the same whether or not the pathogen has been encountered previously (**Figure 34.1A**).

Invertebrate Innate Immunity Invertebrates rely solely on innate immunity. For example, insects have an exoskeleton, which is a tough, dry barrier that keeps out bacteria and viruses. Pathogens that breach these external defences confront a set of internal defences. Additional physical barriers, a low pH, and the secretion of lysozyme, an enzyme that breaks down bacterial cell walls, protect the insect digestive system. Circulating insect immune cells are capable of **phagocytosis**, cellular ingestion and digestion of foreign substances (see Module 5.8). The insect innate immune system also includes recognition proteins that bind to molecules found only on pathogens. Recognition of an invading microbe triggers the production of antimicrobial peptides that bring about the destruction of the invaders.

Vertebrate Innate Immunity In vertebrates, innate immunity coexists with the more recently evolved system of adaptive immunity (discussed later in this chapter). In mammals, innate defences include barriers such as skin and mucous membranes that protect organ systems open to the external environment, such as the

digestive, respiratory, reproductive, and urinary systems. Nostril hairs filter incoming air, and mucus in the respiratory tract traps most microbes and dirt that get past the nasal filter. Cilia on cells lining the respiratory tract then sweep the mucus and any trapped microbes upward and out, helping to prevent lung infections.

Microbes that breach a mammal's external barriers, such as those that enter through a cut in the skin, are confronted by innate immune cells. These are all classified as white blood cells (see Module 28.3), although they are found in interstitial fluid as well as in the blood. Most, such as abundant **neutrophils**, are phagocytes (phagocytic cells). **Macrophages** ("big eaters") are large phagocytic cells that wander through the interstitial fluid, "eating" any bacteria and viruses they encounter. **Natural killer (NK) cells** attack cancer cells and virus-infected cells by releasing chemicals that kill these unhealthy cells.

Other components of vertebrate innate immunity include proteins that either attack microbes directly or impede their reproduction. **Interferons** are proteins, produced by virus-infected cells, that help to limit the cell-to-cell spread of viruses (**Figure 34.1B**). ❶ The virus infects a cell, which causes ❷ interferon genes in the cell's nucleus to be turned on. ❸ The cell synthesizes interferon. The infected cell then dies, but ❹ its interferon molecules may diffuse to neighbouring healthy cells, ❺ stimulating them to produce other proteins that inhibit viral reproduction.

Additional innate immunity in vertebrates is provided by the **complement system**, a group of about 30 different kinds of proteins that circulate in an inactive form in the blood. As you

Innate immunity (34.1–34.3) The response is the same whether or not the pathogen has been previously encountered		Adaptive immunity (34.4–34.12) Found only in vertebrates; previous exposure to the pathogen enhances the immune response
External barriers (34.1)	**Internal defences (34.1–34.2)**	
• Skin/exoskeleton • Acidic environment • Secretions • Mucous membranes • Hairs • Cilia	• Phagocytic cells • NK cells • Defensive proteins • Inflammatory response (34.2)	• Antibodies (34.10–34.11) • Lymphocytes (34.9 and 34.12)
	The lymphatic system (34.3)	

▲ **Figure 34.1A** An overview of animal immune systems, including the modules in which they are discussed

▲ **Figure 34.1B** The interferon mechanism against viral infection

will see later in the chapter, these proteins can act together (in complement) with other defence mechanisms. Substances on the surfaces of many microbes activate the complement system, resulting in a cascade of steps that may lead to the lysis, or bursting, of the invaders. Certain complement proteins also help to trigger the inflammatory response, the subject of the next module.

? Which components of innate immunity described here actually help to prevent infection? Which come into play only after infection has occurred?

● Skin/exoskeleton, secretions, mucous membranes; phagocytic cells (macrophages, neutrophils), NK cells, defensive proteins (interferons, complement system)

34.2 Inflammation mobilizes the innate immune response

The **inflammatory response** is a major component of our innate immunity. Any damage to tissue, whether caused by microorganisms or physical injury—even just a scratch or an insect bite—triggers this response. You may see signs of the inflammatory response when your skin is cut. The area becomes red, warm, and swollen. This reaction is inflammation, which literally means "setting on fire."

Figure 34.2 shows the chain of events when a pin has broken the skin, allowing infection by bacteria. **1** The damaged cells soon release chemical alarm signals, such as **histamine**. **2** The chemicals spark the mobilization of various defences. Histamine, for instance, induces neighbouring blood vessels to dilate and become leaky. Blood flow to the damaged area increases, and blood plasma passes out of the leaky vessels into the interstitial fluid of the affected tissues. Other chemicals, some that are part of the complement system, attract phagocytes to the area. Squeezing between the cells of the blood vessel wall, these phagocytic white blood cells (yellow in the figure) migrate out of the blood into the tissue spaces. The local increase in blood flow, fluid, and cells produces the redness, heat, and swelling characteristic of inflammation.

The major function of the inflammatory response is to disinfect and clean injured tissues. **3** The white blood cells that migrate into the area engulf bacteria and the remains of any body cells killed by them or by the physical injury. Many of the white blood cells die in the process, and

their remains are also engulfed and digested. The pus that often accumulates at the site of an infection consists mainly of dead white blood cells, fluid that has leaked from capillaries, and other tissue debris.

The inflammatory response also helps to prevent the spread of infection to surrounding tissues. Clotting proteins (see Module 28.5) present in blood plasma pass into the interstitial fluid during inflammation. Along with platelets, these substances form local clots that help to seal off the infected region and allow healing to begin.

Inflammation may be localized, as we have just described, or widespread (systemic). Sometimes microorganisms such as bacteria or protozoans get into the blood or release toxins that are carried throughout the body in the bloodstream. The body may react with several inflammatory weapons. For instance, the number of white blood cells circulating in the blood may increase severalfold within just a few hours; an elevated "white cell count" is one way to diagnose the presence of an infection. Another response to systemic infection is fever, an abnormally high body temperature. Toxins themselves may trigger the fever, or macrophages may release compounds that cause the body's thermostat to be set at a higher temperature. A very high fever is dangerous, but a moderate one may stimulate phagocytosis and hasten tissue repair. (Exactly how this happens remains a topic of active debate within

1 Tissue injury; signalling molecules, such as histamine, are released.

2 Dilation and increased leakiness of local blood vessels; phagocytes migrate to the area.

3 Phagocytes (macrophages and neutrophils) consume bacteria and cellular debris; the tissue heals.

▲ **Figure 34.2** The inflammatory response

the medical community.) Anti-inflammatory drugs, such as aspirin and ibuprofen, dampen the normal inflammatory response and thus help to reduce swelling and fever.

Sometimes bacterial infections bring about an overwhelming systemic inflammatory response leading to a condition called septic shock. Characterized by very high fever and dangerously low blood pressure, septic shock is a common cause of death in hospital intensive care units. Clearly, while local

inflammation is an essential step toward healing, widespread inflammation can be devastating.

 Why is the inflammatory response considered a form of *innate* immunity?

● Because the response is the same regardless of whether the invader has been previously encountered

---

34.3 The lymphatic system becomes a crucial battleground during infection

The **lymphatic system**, which is involved in both innate and adaptive immunity, consists of a branching network of vessels, **lymph nodes** (little round organs packed with macrophages and white blood cells called lymphocytes), the bone marrow, and several organs **(Figure 34.3)**. The lymphatic vessels carry a fluid called **lymph**, which is similar to the interstitial fluid that surrounds body cells but contains less oxygen and fewer nutrients.

The lymphatic system is closely associated with the circulatory system. If an infectious agent gets inside the body, it usually winds up in the circulatory system. From there, it is carried into the lymphatic system, which can usually filter it out. The filtered fluid can then be recycled into the circulatory system. The lymphatic system thus has two main functions: to return tissue fluid back to the circulatory system and to fight infection.

As we noted in Module 28.10, a small amount of the fluid that enters the tissue spaces from the blood in a capillary bed does not re-enter the blood capillaries. Instead, this fluid is

returned to the blood via lymphatic vessels. The enlargement in Figure 34.3 (bottom right) shows a branched lymphatic vessel in the process of taking up fluid from tissue spaces in the skin. As shown here, fluid enters the lymphatic system by diffusing into tiny, dead-end lymphatic capillaries that are intermingled among the blood capillaries.

Lymph drains from the lymphatic capillaries into larger and larger lymphatic vessels. Eventually, the fluid re-enters the circulatory system via two large lymphatic vessels that fuse with veins in the chest. As the close-up indicates, the lymphatic vessels resemble veins in having valves that prevent the backflow of fluid toward the capillaries (see Figure 28.7C). Also, like veins, lymphatic vessels depend mainly on the movement of skeletal muscles to squeeze their fluid along. The green arrows in the close-ups indicate the flow of lymph.

When your body is fighting an infection, the organs of the lymphatic system become a major battleground. As lymph

▼ **Figure 34.3** The human lymphatic system

Organs

Adenoid

Tonsils

Lymph nodes

Thymus

Spleen

Large intestine

Appendix

Lymphatic ducts that drain into veins

Lymphatic vessels

Small intestine

Bone marrow

Lymph node

Masses of lymphocytes and macrophages

Valve

Lymphatic vessel

Blood capillary

Tissue cells

Interstitial fluid

Lymphatic capillary

circulates through the lymphatic organs—such as the lymph node shown in Figure 34.3, top right—it carries microbes, parts of microbes, and their toxins picked up from infection sites anywhere in the body. Once inside lymphatic organs, macrophages that reside there permanently may engulf the invaders as part of the innate immune response. Lymph nodes fill with huge numbers of defensive cells, causing the tender "swollen glands" in your neck and armpits that your doctor looks for as a sign of infection. Inside the intestinal tract are countless bacteria and many other potentially harmful substances. As a result, the gut wall is very immunologically active. In fact, there is a continuous, low-grade inflammatory response within the intestinal wall. The intestine also has focal concentrations of immune cells that function like lymph nodes.

In addition to the functioning of macrophages and other components of the innate immune response, cells of the adaptive immune response, called lymphocytes, may be activated against specific invaders. We examine adaptive immunity next.

 What are the two main functions of the lymphatic system?

● To return fluid from interstitial spaces to the circulatory system and to combat infection

Adaptive Immunity

34.4 The adaptive immune response counters specific invaders

All the defences you have learned about so far are called *innate* because you are born with these protective elements and they are always ready to work. Innate defences are always standing by, ready to be used in their current form. When the innate immune response fails to ward off a pathogen, a set of adaptive defences, ones that are "custom-tailored" to each specific invader, provides a second line of defence. **Adaptive immunity**—also called acquired immunity—is a set of defences, found only in vertebrates, that is activated only after exposure to specific pathogens. Thus, unlike innate immunity, adaptive immunity differs from individual to individual, depending on what pathogens they have been previously exposed to. Once activated, the adaptive immune response provides a strong defence against pathogens that is highly specific; that is, it acts against one infectious agent but not another. Moreover, adaptive immunity can amplify certain innate responses, such as inflammation and the complement system.

Any molecule that can potentially elicit an adaptive immune response is called an **antigen**. Antigens may be molecules on the surface of pathogens or other particles, such as viruses, bacteria, mould spores, pollen, house dust, or the cell surfaces of transplanted organs. Antigens may also be substances released into the extracellular fluid, such as toxins secreted by bacteria. When the immune system detects an antigen, it responds with an increase in the number of white blood cells that either attack the invader directly or produce immune proteins called antibodies. An **antibody** is a protein found in blood plasma that attaches to a specific antigen and can prevent its normal function. (The word *antigen* is a contraction of "*anti*body-*gen*erating," a reference to the fact that the foreign agent provokes an adaptive immune response.) The defensive cells and antibodies produced against a particular antigen are usually specific to that antigen; they are ineffective against any other foreign substance.

As molecules that elicit the adaptive immune response, antigens usually do not belong to the host animal. Self-antigens are those found on or in your own cells and are ignored by a healthy immune system. Most antigens are proteins or large polysaccharides that protrude from the surfaces of viruses or foreign cells. Common examples are protein-coat molecules of viruses, parts of the capsules and cell walls of bacteria, and macromolecules on the surface cells of other kinds of organisms, such as protozoans and parasitic worms. (Sometimes a particular microbe is called an antigen, but this usage is misleading because the microbe will almost always have several kinds of antigenic molecules.) Other sources of antigenic molecules include cells of transplanted organs or transfused blood. Antigenic molecules can also be introduced into body fluids; foreign molecules of this type include bacterial toxins and bee venom.

Adaptive immunity has a remarkable "memory"; it can "remember" antigens it has encountered before and react against them more quickly and vigorously on subsequent exposures. For example, if a person is infected by the varicella zoster virus and then contracts chicken pox, the immune system "remembers" certain molecules on the virus. Should the virus enter the body again, the adaptive immune response mounts a quick and decisive attack that usually destroys the virus before symptoms appear. Thus, in the adaptive immune response, unlike innate immunity, exposure to a foreign agent enhances future responses to that same agent.

Adaptive immunity is usually obtained by natural exposure to antigens (that is, by being infected), but it can also be achieved by **vaccination**, also known as immunization. In this procedure, the immune system is confronted with a **vaccine** composed of a harmless variant or part of a disease-causing microbe, such as an inactivated bacterial toxin, a dead or weakened microbe, or a piece of a microbe. The vaccine stimulates the immune system to mount defences against this harmless antigen, defences that will also be effective against the actual pathogen because it has similar antigens. Once you have been successfully vaccinated, your immune system will respond quickly if it is exposed to the actual microbe. Such protection may last for life.

In industrialized nations, routine childhood vaccination has virtually eliminated many viral diseases. In Canada, most children receive a series of shots (starting soon after birth) against 13 serious diseases (Table 34.4). While the schedule varies among provinces, the list of vaccinations typically includes diphtheria, pertussis, and tetanus (DPT, or diptet), polio, hepatitis, chicken pox, and measles, mumps, and rubella (MMR). One of the major success stories of modern vaccination involves smallpox, a potentially fatal viral infection that affected

TABLE 34.4

COMMON VACCINATIONS USED IN CANADA WITH A TYPICAL IMMUNIZATION SCHEDULE (MANITOBA)

Vaccine	Infant Schedule (Age in months)	Child Schedule (Age in years)

DTP
  Diptheria
  Tetanus
  Pertussis
  (whooping cough)
	2, 4, and 6
	18
		4–6
		14–16
		Booster recommended every ten years

Polio	2, 4, and 6 18	4–6
Haemophilus influenza b	2, 4, and 6 18	
Pneumococcal disease	2, 4, and 6 18	

MMR
  Measles
  Mumps
  Rubella
	12	

Varicella (Chicken pox)	12	
Meningitis type C	12	9–10
Hepatitis B		9–10
Human Papillomavirus		11–12 (girls only)

more than 50 million people per year worldwide in the 1950s. A massive vaccination effort has been so effective that there have been no cases of smallpox since 1977.

Whether antigens enter the body naturally (if you catch the flu) or artificially (if you get a flu shot), the resulting immunity is called **active immunity** because the person's own immune system actively produces antibodies. It is also possible to acquire **passive immunity** by receiving premade antibodies. For example, a fetus obtains antibodies from its mother's bloodstream; a baby receives antibodies in breast milk that protect the digestive tract (although these antibodies are broken down there and do not enter the bloodstream); and travellers sometimes get a shot containing antibodies to pathogens they are likely to encounter. In yet another example, the effects of a poisonous snakebite may be counteracted by injecting the victim with antibodies extracted from animals previously immunized against the venom. Passive immunity is temporary because the recipient's immune system is not stimulated by antigens. Immunity lasts only as long as the antibodies do; after a few weeks or months, these proteins break down and are recycled by the body.

We will look at issues surrounding vaccinations in the next two modules.

 Why is protection resulting from a vaccination considered *active* **immunity rather than** *passive* **immunity?**

● **Because the body itself produces the immunity by mounting an immune response and generating antibodies, even though the stimulus consists of artificially introduced antigens**

34.5 Seasonal flu shots

October in Canada is filled with many certainties. The leaves will soon change colour. Colder weather is imminent. We celebrate the harvest at a Thanksgiving feast. And, with flu season just around the corner, the Public Health Agency of Canada and Health Canada will coordinate a national flu vaccination campaign.

The flu is a respiratory infection caused by the influenza virus that affects about 10% to 25% of Canadians annually. Presentation usually starts with headache, coughing, and chills. Symptoms progress to include fever, aches, sneezing, and throat irritation. Contrary to popular belief, there is no such disease as stomach flu. People experiencing acute nausea, vomiting, and diarrhea in the absence of respiratory involvement do not have the flu. More likely, they are suffering from a mild case of food poisoning or rotavirus infection (which is unrelated to influenza).

The flu typically lasts between one and two weeks. However, older adults and immune-compromised individuals may develop serious complications such as pneumonia. Between 4000 and 8000 people die every year from these complications. Vaccination is the best protection against seasonal influenza.

There are many strains of the influenza virus, each with slightly different proteins, hemagglutinin (H) and neuraminidase (N). These proteins facilitate the virus's entry into host cells. Influenza strains are given an alphanumeric designation based on the forms of these two molecules—for example, the avian flu is known as H5N1. Protection from each strain requires a unique vaccine.

Culturing the *virulent* (disease-causing) strains of influenza together with an avirulent (not disease-causing) strain is the first step in vaccine development. Because viruses require a host cell for reproduction, chicken eggs are used to culture these viruses. Chicken eggs are used because they are readily available and the influenza virus grows well within them. Within a single egg, hybridization of the two viruses occurs and *vaccine strains* form. These vaccine strains contain the surface molecules of the virulent strain but lack the genes that cause disease. As a result, they can enter host cells but cannot cause disease. Our primary immune response creates antibodies that can bind to the specific H and N of the vaccine strain (Module 34.8). If we encounter the virulent strain at a later time, memory cells recognize the surface molecules and a secondary immune response quickly destroys the virus, protecting us against disease.

The strains causing flu outbreaks may be different from year to year. The World Health Organization (WHO) surveys the circulating influenza strains annually and recommends three strains for the development of the seasonal flu shot. Each flu shot protects against only the three strains selected. Therefore, annual administration is recommended. In 2012, a team of scientists from the University of British Columbia developed a vaccine that induces protection against a broader range of influenza strains. However, much more research needs to be done before this vaccine will be available for public administration. If it does become available, it may reduce the need for annual flu shots.

While Health Canada recommends immunization to nearly everyone, vaccination is strongly recommended for people who have a higher risk of contracting the flu, such as healthcare workers; people who may develop severe complications (such as pregnant women); children aged 6 to 23 months; and elderly adults. Seasonal flu shots are not recommended for infants under six months and those who have egg allergies.

Occasionally, another vaccine may be recommended in addition to the seasonal flu shot. Throughout history there have been influenza strains that have been extraordinarily devastating. These pandemic strains spread quickly across the globe. The Spanish flu (H1N1) of 1918–1919 killed 20–40 million people worldwide. During this time, no vaccine was available.

In 2009, scientists feared that the swine flu (also called H1N1) might have a similar mortality rate. A massive vaccination effort ensued, and a deadly pandemic was prevented. However, as of 2010, about 20 000 H1N1-related deaths worldwide had been reported. In August 2010, the director-general of WHO announced that the H1N1 influenza has entered the post-pandemic phase and was no longer a major threat.

 Why doesn't getting a flu shot one year give us immunity to the flu in subsequent years?

● Influenza viruses evolve rapidly by frequent mutation; thus, the strains that afflict us in subsequent years are usually different from the ones for which we have been vaccinated.

RUMOUR HAS IT ## 34.6 Do childhood vaccines cause autism?

A number of health organizations, global and national, recommend routine vaccination for protection from serious diseases. Recently, the safety of some vaccines has been placed in doubt. In 1998, a publication in *The Lancet* proclaimed a link between the MMR vaccine and autism. The researchers examined 12 children and 9 were diagnosed with behavioural abnormalities shortly after receiving the MMR vaccine. The article described those behaviours to be consistent with autism spectrum disorders and implicated that the MMR vaccine was the cause.

On first glance, this report was a convincing piece of evidence against the MMR vaccine. Thimerosal, a mercury-containing preservative in some multidose vaccines, was implicated as the causative agent. A multidose vaccine is a single vial that contains enough vaccine to immunize several people. Preservatives are required in these vials to prevent bacteria growth between uses.

A British reporter closely inspected the article about the MMR vaccine–autism connection and revealed the sinister side of the story. Despite the fact that good science must be reproducible, no one could reproduce the original results, not even the authors, who were asked to do so by Britain's General Medical Council. Despite multiple attempts to replicate the study, the initial report has never been validated.

Good science must also be unbiased and accurate. The researchers of the study collected their data with the biased intention of supporting their hypothesis. Even more appalling was the fact that the results of their research were misrepresented. The researchers altered patients' diagnoses and medical histories so that behavioural symptoms "appeared" within two weeks after immunization. In reality, some of the boys participating in the study had symptoms before they were given the MMR vaccine. Moreover, three of the nine children in the study did not even have autism.

One of the researchers also had serious conflicts of interest. He owned a patent for a separate measles vaccine that he hoped would replace the suspect combined MMR vaccine. He knew the results he wanted to show before the study was even completed. This fraudulent and unethical paper has been completely retracted by *The Lancet* (**Figure 34.6**). Currently, no evidence links the MMR vaccine and autism.

Interestingly, thimerosal—the agent that the researchers' identified as suspect—was never used in Canada's MMR vaccine.

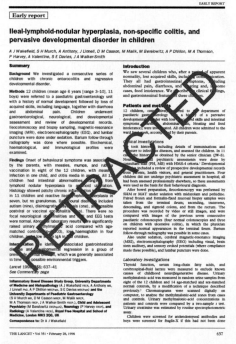

▲ **Figure 34.6** Retracted article from *The Lancet*

Nevertheless, it has been removed from some, but not all, multidose vaccines. Currently, the only vaccines in Canada that still contain thimerosal are for influenza and hepatitis B. It is important to note that the quantity of this preservative in these vaccines is well below the toxic levels set by Health Canada.

Before the fallacy of this article published in *The Lancet* was known, the link between the MMR vaccine and autism became a major headline in the media and was also spread through paid advertisements by various groups. Despite being untrue, some people still propagate this rumour. As a result, many parents stopped vaccinating their children. This choice has led to outbreaks of measles and mumps around the world. These occurrences, though unfortunate, do illustrate the importance and effectiveness of vaccination.

 The rates of autism have not decreased since thimerosal has been removed from most vaccines. What does this evidence suggest?

● This evidence further supports the fact that thimerosal does not cause autism. If it did, the rates of autism should have declined after the removal of thimerosal.

34.7 Lymphocytes mount a dual defence

Lymphocytes, white blood cells that spend most of their time in the tissues and organs of the lymphatic system, are responsible for adaptive immunity. Like all blood cells, lymphocytes originate from stem cells in the bone marrow. As shown in **Figure 34.7A**, some immature lymphocytes continue developing in the bone marrow; these become specialized as B lymphocytes, or **B cells**. Other immature lymphocytes migrate to the thymus, a gland above the heart. There, the lymphocytes become specialized as T lymphocytes, or **T cells**. Both B cells and T cells eventually make their way via the blood to the lymph nodes, spleen, and other lymphatic organs.

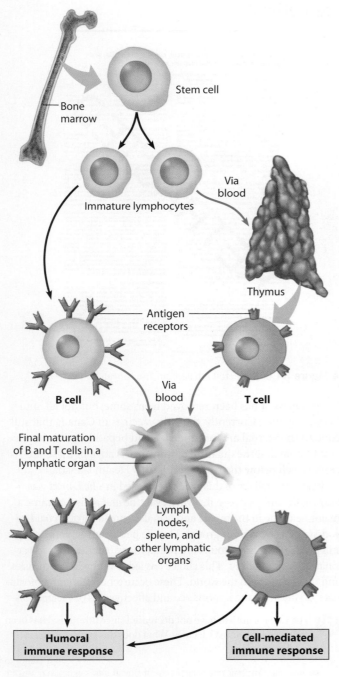

▲ **Figure 34.7A** The development of B cells and T cells

The B cells and T cells of the adaptive immune response together provide a dual defence. The first type of defence is called the **humoral immune response**. The humoral immune response involves the secretion of free-floating antibodies by B cells (**Figure 34.7B**, left) into the blood and lymph. (The humoral response is so named because blood and lymph were long ago called body "humours.") The humoral system defends primarily against bacteria and viruses present in body fluids. As discussed at the end of Module 34.4, the humoral immune response can be passively transferred from an immune individual into a non-immune individual through body fluids such as antibody-containing blood plasma or breast milk. As you will see in Module 34.11, antibodies mark invaders by binding to them. The resulting antigen-antibody complexes are easily recognized for destruction and disposal by phagocytic cells.

The second type of adaptive immunity, produced by T cells (Figure 34.7B, right), is called the **cell-mediated immune response**. As its name implies, this defensive system results from the direct action of defensive cells, in contrast to the action of free-floating defensive antibody proteins of the humoral response. Certain T cells attack unhealthy cells such as cancerous cells and those infected by viruses. Other T cells function indirectly by promoting phagocytosis by other white blood cells and by stimulating B cells to produce antibodies. Thus, T cells play a part in both the cell-mediated and humoral immune responses.

When a B cell develops in bone marrow or a T cell develops in the thymus, certain genes in the cell are turned on. This causes the cell to synthesize molecules of a specific protein, which are then incorporated into the plasma membrane. As indicated in Figure 34.7A, these protein molecules stick out from the cell's surface. The molecules are **antigen receptors**, capable of binding one specific type of antigen. Each B or T cell has about 100 000 antigen receptors, and all the receptors on a single cell are identical—they all recognize the same antigen. In the case of a B cell, the receptors are almost identical to the particular antibody that the B cell will secrete. Once a B cell or T cell has its surface proteins in place, it can recognize a specific antigen and mount an immune response against it. One cell may recognize an antigen on the mumps virus, for instance, while another detects a particular antigen on a tetanus-causing bacterium.

In Figure 34.7A, you can see that after the B cells and T cells have developed their antigen receptors, these lymphocytes leave the bone marrow and thymus and move via the bloodstream to the lymph nodes, spleen, and other parts of the lymphatic system. In these organs, many B and T cells take up residence and encounter infectious agents that have penetrated the body's outer defences. Because lymphatic capillaries extend into virtually all of the body's tissues, bacteria or viruses infecting nearly any part of the body eventually enter the lymph and are carried to the lymphatic organs. As we will describe in Module 34.8, when a B or T cell within a lymphatic organ first confronts the specific antigen that it is programmed to recognize, it differentiates further and becomes a fully mature component of the immune system.

Colourized TEM 4005×

An enormous diversity of B cells and T cells develops in each individual. Researchers estimate that each of us has millions of different kinds—enough to recognize and bind to virtually every possible antigen. A small population of each kind of lymphocyte lies in wait in our body, genetically programmed to recognize and respond to a specific antigen. Only a tiny fraction of the immune system's lymphocytes will ever be used, but they are all available if needed. It is as if the immune system maintains a huge standing army of soldiers, each made to recognize one particular kind of invader. Most of the soldiers never encounter their targets and remain idle. But when an invader does appear, chances are good that some lymphocytes will be able to recognize it, bind to it, and call in reinforcements. We will take a closer look at the different types of T cells in Modules 34.9 and 34.12.

? Contrast the targets of the humoral immune response with those of the cell-mediated immune response.

● The humoral immune response works against pathogens in the body fluids; the cell-mediated immune response attacks infected cells.

34.8 Clonal selection musters defensive forces against specific antigens

The immune system's ability to defend against a wide variety of antigens depends on a process known as **clonal selection**. Once inside the body, an antigen encounters a diverse pool of millions of unique B and T lymphocytes. However, one particular antigen interacts only with the tiny fraction of lymphocytes bearing receptors specific to that antigen. Once activated by the antigen, these few "selected" cells proliferate, forming a clone—a genetically identical population—of thousands of cells all specific for the stimulating antigen. This antigen-driven cloning of lymphocytes—clonal selection—is a vital step in the adaptive immune response against infection.

The Steps of Clonal Selection Figure 34.8A indicates how clonal selection of B cells works in the humoral immune response. (A similar mechanism activates clonal selection for cytotoxic and helper T cells.) **①** The row of three cells at the top of the figure represents a vast repertoire of B cells in a lymph node. Notice that each lymphocyte has its own specific type of antigen receptor embedded in its surface (represented by different colours in the figure). The cells' unique receptors are in place before they ever encounter an antigen.

The first time an antigen enters the body and is swept into a lymph node, **②** specific sites on its surface bind to the few B cells that happen to have complementary receptors. Other lymphocytes, without the appropriate binding sites (in the figure, the ones with the green and blue receptors), are not affected. Primed by the interaction with the antigen, **③** the selected cell is activated: It grows, divides, and differentiates into two genetically identical yet physically distinct types of cells. Both newly produced types of cells are specialized for defending against the very antigen that triggered the response. **④** One group of newly cloned cells is made up of short-lived but fast-acting **effector cells**, which combat the antigen. Because the example in the figure involves B cells, the effector cells produced are **plasma cells**. Each plasma cell secretes antibody molecules into the blood and lymph, all of the same type. Each plasma cell makes as many as 2000 copies of its antibody per second and thus requires large amounts of endoplasmic reticulum, a characteristic of cells actively synthesizing and secreting proteins. The secreted antibodies circulate in the blood and lymphatic fluid, contributing to the humoral immune response. Although highly effective at combating infection, each effector cell lasts only four or five days before dying off.

⑤ A second group of cells produced by the activated B cells is a smaller number of **memory cells**, which differ from effector cells in both appearance and function. In contrast to short-lived effector cells, memory cells may last for decades. They remain in the lymph nodes, poised to be activated by a second exposure to the antigen. In fact, in some cases, memory cells confer lifetime immunity, as they may after vaccination

① Three representative B cells with different antigen receptors

Antigen receptor on the cell surface

② Antigen molecules

③ First exposure to the antigen

Cell activation: growth, division, and differentiation

Antibody molecules

④ First clone ⑤

Endoplasmic reticulum

Plasma (effector) cells secreting antibodies

Memory cells

Antigen molecules

⑥ Second exposure to the same antigen

▲ Figure 34.8A Clonal selection of B cells in the primary and secondary immune responses

against such childhood diseases as mumps and measles. Steps 1–5 show the initial phase of adaptive immunity, called the **primary immune response**. This phase occurs when lymphocytes are exposed to an antigen for the first time.

⑥ When memory cells produced during the primary response are activated by a second exposure to the same antigen—which may occur anytime after the primary immune response—they initiate the **secondary immune response**. This response is much faster and stronger than the first. Another round of clonal selection ensues. The selected memory cells multiply quickly, producing a large second clone of lymphocytes that mount the secondary response. Like the first clone, the second clone includes effector cells that produce antibodies and memory cells capable of responding to future exposures to the antigen. In our example here with B cells, the secondary response produces very high levels of antibodies that, though they are short-lived, are often more effective against the antigen than those produced during the primary response.

The concept of clonal selection is so fundamental to understanding adaptive immunity that it is worth restating: Each antigen, by binding to specific receptors, selectively activates a tiny fraction of lymphocytes; these few selected cells then give rise to a clone of many cells, all specific for and dedicated to eliminating the antigen that started the response. Thus, we see that the versatility of the adaptive immune response depends on a great diversity of pre-existing lymphocytes with different antigen receptors.

Primary Versus Secondary Immune Responses   Now that we have seen how clonal selection works, let's take a look at the two phases of the adaptive immune response in an individual. The blue curve in **Figure 34.8B** illustrates the difference between the two phases, triggered by two exposures to the same antigen. On the far left of the graph, you can see that the primary response does not start right away; it usually takes several days for the lymphocytes to become activated by an antigen (called X here) and form clones of effector cells. When the effector cell clone forms, antibodies start showing up in the blood, as the graph shows. During this delay, the innate immune response is all that is working to combat the infection and a stricken individual may become ill. The antibody level reaches its peak two to three weeks after initial exposure. As the antibody levels in the blood and lymph rise, the symptoms of the illness typically diminish and disappear. The primary response subsides as the effector cells die out.

A subsequent exposure to antigen X (at day 28 in the graph) triggers the secondary immune response. Notice that this secondary response starts faster than the primary response, typically in 2–7 days, versus 10–17 days. As mentioned, the secondary response is also of greater magnitude, producing higher levels of antibodies, and is more prolonged. This is why vaccination is so effective: The vaccine induces a primary immune response that produces memory cells; an encounter with the actual pathogen then elicits a rapid and strong secondary immune response.

Antibody molecules

Clone of plasma (effector) cells secreting antibodies

Second clone

Clone of memory cells

The red curve in Figure 34.8B illustrates the specificity of the immune response. If the body is exposed to a different antigen (Y), even after it has already responded to antigen X, it responds with another primary response, this one directed against antigen Y. The response to Y is not enhanced by the response to X; that is, adaptive immunity is specific.

Second exposure to antigen X, first exposure to antigen Y

Secondary immune response to antigen X

First exposure to antigen X

Primary immune response to antigen X

Primary immune response to antigen Y

Antibodies to X

Antibodies to Y

Antibody concentration

Time (days)

▲ **Figure 34.8B** Primary and secondary adaptive immune responses

Although we have focused on the humoral immune response (produced by B cells) in this module, clonal selection, effector cells, and memory cells are features of the cell-mediated immune response (produced by T cells) as well. In the next several modules, we discuss the humoral immune response further. After that, we focus on how the cell-mediated arm of the immune system helps to defend the body against pathogens.

? What is the immunological basis for referring to certain diseases, such as mumps, as *childhood* diseases?

● One bout with the pathogen, which most often occurs during childhood, is usually enough to confer immunity for the rest of that individual's life.

34.9 Helper T cells stimulate the humoral and cell-mediated immune responses

The antibody-producing B cells of the humoral immune response make up one army of the adaptive immune response network. The humoral defence system identifies and helps to destroy invaders that are in our blood, lymph, or interstitial fluid—in other words, outside our body cells. But many invaders, including all viruses, enter cells and reproduce there. It is the cell-mediated immune response produced by T cells that battles pathogens that have already entered body cells.

Whereas B cells respond to free antigens present in body fluids, T cells respond only to antigens present on the surfaces of the body's own cells. Recall from Module 34.8 that effector cells act quickly against an antigen. There are two main kinds of effector T cells. **Cytotoxic T cells** attack body cells that are infected with pathogens; we will discuss these T cells in Module 34.12. **Helper T cells** play a role in many aspects of immunity. They help to activate cytotoxic T cells and macrophages and even help to stimulate B cells to produce antibodies. Other types of T cells include memory T cells, analogous to memory B cells.

Helper T cells interact with other white blood cells—including macrophages and B cells—that function as **antigen-presenting cells (APCs)**. All of the cell-mediated immune response and much of the humoral immune response depend on the precise interaction of antigen-presenting cells and helper T cells. This interaction activates the helper T cells, which can then go on to activate other cells of the immune system.

As its name implies, an antigen-presenting cell presents a foreign antigen to a helper T cell. Consider a typical antigen-presenting cell, a macrophage. As shown in **Figure 34.9**, ❶ the macrophage ingests a microbe or other foreign particle and breaks it into fragments—foreign antigens (▼). Then molecules of a special protein () belonging to the macrophage, which we will call a **self protein** (because it belongs to the body), ❷ bind the foreign antigens—**nonself molecules**—and ❸ display them on the cell's surface. (Each of us has a unique set of self proteins, which serve as identity markers for our body cells.) ❹ Helper T cells recognize and bind to the combination of a self protein and a foreign antigen—called a self-nonself complex (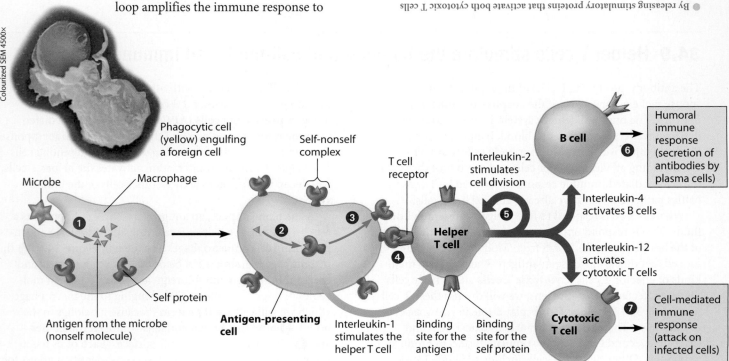)—displayed on an antigen-presenting cell. This double-recognition system is like the system banks use for safety deposit boxes: Opening your box requires the banker's key along with your specific key. Two "keys" are required before a helper T cell will respond.

The ability of a helper T cell to specifically recognize a unique self-nonself complex on an antigen-presenting cell depends on the receptors (purple) embedded in the T cell's plasma membrane. Dr. Tak Wah Mak, director of the Campbell Family Institute for Breast Cancer Research at the University of Toronto, made the remarkable discovery of the T cell receptor. Understanding how T cells recognize individual antigens has been instrumental in increasing our knowledge of many facets of the adaptive immune system. A T cell receptor actually has two binding sites: one for antigen and one for self protein. The two binding sites enable a T cell receptor to recognize the overall shape of a self-nonself complex on an antigen-presenting cell. The immune response is specific because the receptors on each helper T cell bind only one kind of self-nonself complex on an antigen-presenting cell.

The binding of a T cell receptor to a self-nonself complex activates the helper T cell. Several other kinds of signals can enhance this activation. For example, certain proteins secreted by the antigen-presenting cell, such as interleukin-1 (green arrow), diffuse to the helper T cell and stimulate it.

Activated helper T cells promote and direct the adaptive immune response. A major mechanism by which the helper T cells operate is by secreting stimulatory proteins called cytokines. These proteins have effects on many different cells of the immune system. One such cytokine, interleukin-2 (IL-2) ❺, causes the helper T cells to divide, producing both memory cells and additional active helper T cells (effector cells). This positive-feedback loop amplifies the immune response to the antigen at hand. Second, other cytokines released by the helper T cell coordinate either a humoral or cell-mediated immune response. If interleukin-4 is released ❻, B cells become activated and a humoral immune response is initiated. The humoral response will be discussed further in Modules 34.10 and 34.11. Alternatively, if interleukin-12 is released ❼, it will lead to the activation of cytotoxic T cells and a cell-mediated immune response, the topic of Module 34.12.

The humoral or cell-mediated immune responses that may be directed by helper T cells are somewhat mutually exclusive. When one response becomes activated, the other is temporarily downregulated (deactivated). Therefore, cytokines released during a humoral response tend to reduce cell-mediated immunity and the opposite is also true. This dichotomy helps the immune system focus on and respond appropriately to an invasion.

An excessive cell-mediated immune response in the intestinal tract perpetuates some inflammatory bowel diseases. Dr. Derek McKay of the University of Calgary is investigating ways to take advantage of this dichotomy to treat similar intestinal diseases. His experimental probiotic treatment (a therapy that uses live organisms to alleviate disease) uses the tapeworm, *Hymenolepis diminuta*, to lessen the severity of colitis (inflammation of the large intestine or colon caused by an inappropriate cell-mediated response). When a body is infected with this tapeworm, the immune system mounts a strong humoral immune response. This humoral response is robust enough to downregulate the current cell-mediated response, effectively treating the disease. After the intestinal inflammation subsides, the tapeworm infection is easily treated.

? **How can one helper T cell stimulate both humoral and cell-mediated immunity?**

● **By releasing stimulatory proteins that activate both cytotoxic T cells and B cells**

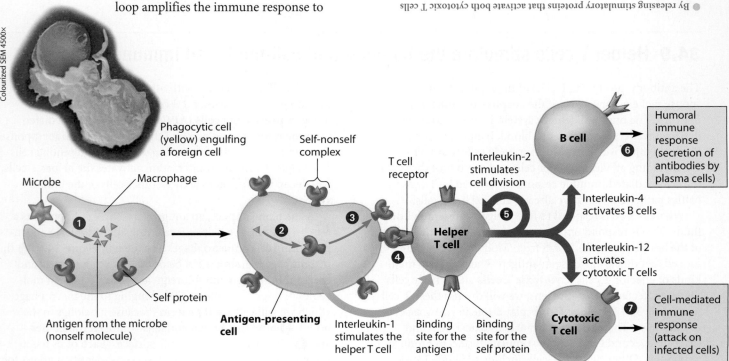

▲ **Figure 34.9** The activation of a helper T cell and its roles in immunity

34.10 Antibodies are the weapons of the humoral immune response

B cells are the "frontline warriors" of the humoral immune response. Plasma cells—the effector cells produced during clonal selection of B cells (as shown in Figure 34.8A)—make and secrete antibodies, proteins that serve as molecular weapons of defence.

We have been using Y-shaped symbols to represent antibodies, and their shape actually does resemble a Y, as the computer-generated three-dimensional rendering of an antibody molecule in **Figure 34.10A** illustrates. **Figure 34.10B** is a simplified diagram explaining antibody structure. Each antibody molecule is made up of four polypeptide chains, two identical "heavy" chains and two identical "light" chains. In both figures, the parts coloured in shades of pink represent the longer heavy chains of amino acids that give the molecule its Y shape. Bonds (the black lines in Figure 34.10B) at the fork of the Y hold these chains together. The two green regions in each figure are shorter chains of amino acids, the light chains. Each of the light chains is bonded to one of the heavy chains. As Figure 34.10A indicates, the bonded chains actually intertwine.

An antibody molecule has two related functions in the humoral immune response: to recognize and bind to a certain antigen and to assist in neutralizing the antigen it recognizes. The structure of an antibody allows it to perform both of these functions. Notice in Figure 34.10B that each of the four chains of the molecule has a C (constant) region, where amino acid sequences vary little among different antibodies, and

▲ **Figure 34.10B** Antibody structure and the binding of an antigen-binding site to its complementary antigen (enlargement)

a V (variable) region, where the amino acid sequence varies extensively among antibodies. At the tip of each arm of the Y, a pair of V regions forms an **antigen-binding site**, a region of the molecule responsible for the antibody's recognition-and-binding function. A huge variety in the three-dimensional shapes of the binding sites of different antibody molecules arises from a similarly large variety in the amino acid sequences in the V regions—hence the term *variable*. The top left of Figure 34.10B illustrates such a fit, with the recognized **antigenic determinant** coloured gold. The great structural variety of antigen-binding sites accounts for the diversity of lymphocytes and gives the humoral immune system the ability to react to virtually any kind of antigen.

The tail of the antibody molecule, formed by the constant regions of the heavy chains, helps to mediate the disposal of the bound antigen. Antibodies with different kinds of heavy-chain C regions are grouped into different classes. Humans and other mammals have five major classes of antibodies, called IgA, IgD, IgE, IgG, and IgM (*Ig* stands for immunoglobulin, another name for antibody). Each of the five classes differs in where it's found in the body and how it works. However, all five classes of antibodies perform the same basic function: They mark invaders for elimination. We take a closer look at this process next.

▲ **Figure 34.10A** A three-dimensional model computer graphic of an antibody molecule

? How is the specificity of an antibody molecule for an antigen analogous to an enzyme's specificity for its substrate?

● Both antibodies and enzymes are proteins with binding sites of specific shape that recognize and bind to other molecules (antigens for antibodies, substrates for enzymes) with complementary shapes.

34.11 Antibodies mark antigens for elimination

As shown in **Figure 34.11A**, an antibody usually recognizes and binds to a small surface-exposed region of an antigen called an antigenic determinant, also known as an epitope. An antigen-binding site, a specific region on the antibody molecule, recognizes an antigenic determinant by the fact that the binding site and antigenic determinant have complementary shapes, like an enzyme and substrate or a lock and key. An antigen usually has several different determinants (there are three in the diagram), so different antibodies (two, in this case) can bind to the same antigen. A single kind of antigen molecule may thus stimulate the immune system to make several distinct antibodies against it. Notice that each antibody molecule has two identical antigen-binding sites.

Antibodies do not kill pathogens. Instead, antibodies mark a pathogen by combining with it to form an antigen-antibody complex. Weak chemical bonds between antigen molecules and the antigen-binding sites on antibody molecules hold the complex together. Once marked in this manner, other immune system components bring about the destruction of the antigen.

As **Figure 34.11B** illustrates, the binding of antibodies to antigens can trigger several mechanisms that disable or destroy an invader. In neutralization, antibodies bind to surface proteins on a virus or bacterium, thereby blocking its ability to infect a host cell and

▲ **Figure 34.11A** The binding of antibodies to antigenic determinants

presenting an easily recognized structure to macrophages. This increases the likelihood that the foreign cell will be engulfed by phagocytosis. Another antibody mechanism is the agglutination (clumping together) of viruses, bacteria, or foreign eukaryotic cells. Because each antibody molecule has at least two binding sites, antibodies can hold a clump of invading cells together. Agglutination makes the cells easy for phagocytes to capture. A third mechanism, precipitation, is similar to agglutination, except that the antibody molecules link dissolved antigen molecules, like toxins, together. This makes the antigen molecules precipitate; that is, they separate, in solid form, from the surrounding liquid.

▲ **Figure 34.11B** Effector mechanisms of the humoral immune response

Precipitation, like the other effector mechanisms discussed so far, enhances engulfment by phagocytes.

One of the most important steps in the humoral immune response is the activation of the complement system (see Module 34.1) by antigen-antibody complexes. Activated complement system proteins (right side of Figure 34.11B) can attach to a foreign cell. Once there, several activated proteins may form a complex that pokes a hole in the plasma membrane of the foreign cell, causing cell lysis, or rupture.

Taken as a whole, this figure illustrates a fundamental concept of adaptive immunity: All antibody mechanisms involve a *specific* recognition-and-attack phase followed by a *nonspecific* destruction phase. Thus, the antibodies of the humoral immune response, which identify and bind to foreign invaders, work with the components of innate immunity, such as phagocytes and complement, to form a complete defence system.

? How does adaptive humoral immunity interact with the body's innate immune system?

● Antibodies mark specific antigens for destruction, but it is usually the complement system, phagocytes, or other components of innate immunity that destroy the antigens.

34.12 Cytotoxic T cells destroy infected body cells

As you learned in Module 34.9, two types of T cells participate in the cell-mediated immune response: helper T cells and cytotoxic T cells. Helper T cells activate many kinds of cells, including cytotoxic T cells, the only T cells that actually kill infected cells.

Once activated, cytotoxic T cells identify infected cells in the same way that helper T cells identify antigen-presenting cells. An infected cell has foreign antigens—molecules belonging to the viruses or bacteria infecting it—attached to self proteins on its surface (Figure 34.12). Like a helper T cell, a cytotoxic T cell carries receptors that can bind with a self-nonself complex on the infected cell.

Cytotoxic T cells also play a role in protecting the body against the spread of some cancers. About 20% of human cancers are caused by viruses. Examples include the hepatitis B virus, which can trigger liver cancer, and the human papillomavirus (HPV), which can trigger cervical cancer. When a human cancer cell harbours such a virus, viral proteins may end up on the surface of the infected cell in a self-nonself complex. If they do, they may be recognized by a cytotoxic T cell, which can then destroy the infected cell, halting the proliferation of that cancerous cell.

The self-nonself complex on an infected body cell is like a red flag to cytotoxic T cells that have complementary receptors. As shown in the figure, ❶ a cytotoxic T cell binds to the infected cell. The binding activates the T cell, which

then synthesizes several toxic proteins that act on the bound cell, including one called perforin (). ❷ Perforin is discharged from the cytotoxic T cell and attaches to the infected cell's plasma membrane, making holes in it. T cell enzymes () then enter the infected cell and promote its death by **apoptosis**, programmed cell death. ❸ The infected cell is destroyed, and the cytotoxic T cell may move on to destroy other cells infected with the same pathogen.

? Compare and contrast the T cell receptor with the antigen receptor on the surface of a B cell.

● Both receptors bind to a specific antigen, but the T cell receptor recognizes that antigen only when it is presented along with a "self" marker on the surface of one of the body's own cells.

❶ A cytotoxic T cell binds to an infected cell.

Self-nonself complex

Foreign antigen

Infected cell

Perforin molecule

Cytotoxic T cell

❷ Perforin makes holes in the infected cell's membrane, and an enzyme that promotes apoptosis enters.

A hole forming

Enzymes that promote apoptosis

❸ The infected cell is destroyed.

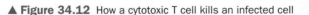

▲ Figure 34.12 How a cytotoxic T cell kills an infected cell

Inappropriate Immune Responses

34.13 The immune system depends on molecular identification

As we have seen, the ability of lymphocytes to recognize the body's own molecules—that is, to distinguish self from nonself—enables our adaptive immune response to battle foreign invaders without harming healthy body cells. The key to this ability is that each person's cells have a unique collection of self proteins on the surface. These specific self proteins provide molecular "identification" that can be recognized by the immune system. As lymphocytes mature, those with receptors that bind the body's own molecules are destroyed or deactivated, leaving only lymphocytes that react to foreign molecules. As a result, our lymphocytes do not attack our own molecules or cells. If this mechanism fails, T cells may leave the thymus and start an immune response against molecules of our bodies. This is the underlying cause of most autoimmune diseases, such as MS, which was discussed in the chapter-opening essay.

The immune system not only distinguishes body cells from microbial cells, but also can tell your cells from those of other people. Genes at multiple chromosomal loci code for **major histocompatibility complex (MHC) molecules**, the main self proteins. (The green self proteins shown in Figures 34.9 and 34.12 are actually MHC molecules.) Because there are hundreds of alleles in the human population for each MHC gene, it is extremely rare for any two people (except identical twins) to have completely matching sets of MHC self proteins.

The immune system's ability to recognize foreign antigens does not always work in our favour. For example, when a person receives an organ transplant or tissue graft, the person's immune system recognizes the MHC markers on the donor's cells as foreign and attacks them. To minimize rejection, doctors look for a donor with self proteins matching the recipient's as closely as possible. The best match is to transplant the patient's own tissue, as when a burn victim receives skin grafts removed from other parts of his or her body. Otherwise, identical twins provide the closest match, followed by nonidentical siblings. Sometimes doctors use drugs to suppress the immune response against the transplant. Unfortunately, these drugs may also reduce the ability to fight infections and cancer.

? In what sense is a cell's set of MHC surface markers analogous to a fingerprint?

● The set of MHC ("self") markers is unique to each individual.

34.14 Allergies are overreactions to certain environmental antigens

Allergies are hypersensitive (exaggerated) responses to otherwise harmless antigens in our surroundings. Antigens that cause allergies are called **allergens**. Common allergens include protein molecules on pollen grains and on the feces of tiny mites that live in house dust. Many people who are allergic to cats and dogs are actually allergic to proteins in the animal's saliva that get deposited on the fur when the animal grooms by licking itself. Allergic reactions typically occur very rapidly and in response to tiny amounts of an allergen. A person allergic to cat or dog saliva, for instance, may react to a few molecules of the allergen in a matter of minutes. Allergic reactions can occur in many parts of the body, including the nasal passages, bronchi, and skin. Symptoms may include sneezing, runny nose, coughing, wheezing, and itching.

The symptoms of an allergy result from the two-stage reaction sequence outlined in **Figure 34.14**. The first stage, called sensitization, occurs when a person is first exposed to an allergen—pollen, for example. ❶ After an allergen enters the bloodstream, it binds to effector B cells (plasma cells) with complementary receptors. ❷ The B cells then proliferate through clonal selection and secrete large amounts of antibodies to this allergen. ❸ Some of these antibodies attach by their base to the surfaces of mast cells, body cells that produce histamine and other chemicals that trigger the inflammatory response (see Module 34.2).

The second stage of an allergic response begins when the person is exposed to the same allergen later. The allergen enters the body and ❹ binds to the antibodies attached to mast cells. ❺ This causes the mast cells to release histamine, which triggers the allergic symptoms. As in inflammation, histamine

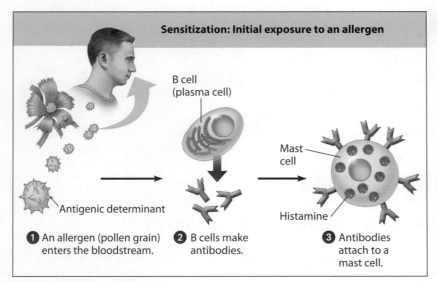

Sensitization: Initial exposure to an allergen

B cell (plasma cell)

Mast cell

Histamine

Antigenic determinant

❶ An allergen (pollen grain) enters the bloodstream.

❷ B cells make antibodies.

❸ Antibodies attach to a mast cell.

Later exposure to the same allergen (the allergic reaction)

❹ The allergen binds to antibodies on a mast cell.

❺ Histamine is released, causing allergy symptoms.

▲ **Figure 34.14** The two stages of an allergic reaction

causes blood vessels to dilate and leak fluid and so causes nasal irritation, itchy skin, and tears. **Antihistamines** are drugs that interfere with histamine's action and give temporary relief from an allergy.

Allergies range from seasonal nuisances to severe, life-threatening responses. Anaphylactic shock is an especially dangerous type of allergic reaction. It may occur in people who are extremely sensitive to certain allergens, such as bee venom, penicillin, or allergens in peanuts or shellfish. Any contact with these allergens makes a large proportion of their mast cells release inflammatory chemicals very suddenly. As a result, their blood vessels dilate abruptly, causing a rapid, potentially fatal drop in blood pressure, a condition called shock. Fortunately, anaphylactic shock can be counteracted with injections of the hormone epinephrine. People with severe allergies often carry EpiPens to protect themselves in case of exposure.

? How do antihistamines relieve allergy symptoms?

● By blocking the action of histamine, which produces the symptoms of the inflammatory response.

34.15 The hygiene hypothesis: Are our kids too clean?

In the opening essay of this chapter, we discussed a potential link between autoimmune disease and childhood infection. Paradoxically, childhood exposure to infectious agents can reduce the chance of developing immune disease later in life. In Canada and other developed countries, the incidence of many infectious diseases, including intestinal worms and bacterial infections, has declined dramatically in recent decades. This improvement has been accompanied by a 3% to 5% annual increase in various diseases, including allergies, autoimmune type I diabetes, and rheumatoid arthritis. The hygiene hypothesis, which proposes a link between frequent childhood infections and a healthy adult immune system, explains this contradiction.

Through the use of antibiotics and vaccines, we have managed to quell many devastating infections. Moreover, improved sanitation and higher standards of hygiene have further reduced our exposure to many harmful pathogens. Our society has a heightened sense of mysophobia, the fear of dirt and contamination (often referred to as germaphobia). Television commercials constantly remind us of the presence of germs in our homes. They suggest that nothing is clean unless you manage to kill 99.9% of germs. As a result, we have developed an excessive standard of hygiene. While this has reduced our exposure to harmful pathogens, it has also prevented our exposure to innocuous environmental microorganisms.

Have we gone too far in our quest for cleanliness? A comparison of the rates of both infectious and immune diseases in Canada to those of developing nations suggests we may have. Typically, developing countries have lower levels of sanitation and hygiene, and limited access to medicine. Under these conditions, children are exposed to more microorganisms, pathogenic and benign alike. As a direct result, the rates of infectious disease are higher. Interestingly, immune diseases are uncommon in adults of developing countries. What is the connection?

At birth, our immune system is not completely developed. Humoral immune responses are usually fully functional within the first few months. Cell-mediated immunity, in contrast, requires practice to develop properly. This practice can only come from repeated exposure to microorganisms and parasites during early childhood. In a healthy individual, these two sides of the adaptive immune system are balanced. Without practice, the cell-mediated immune system may remain weak and humoral responses might overcompensate. Stronger antibody responses may act inappropriately and lead to allergic diseases.

Within Canadian borders, we can find more evidence to support the hygiene hypothesis. Incidence of immune diseases is lower in rural communities than in urban centres. Growing up on a farm offers countless exposures to environmental microorganisms. The cell-mediated immune system of farm children gets a great deal of practice and is well balanced with humoral immunity.

Many questions remain about the best way to deal with this information. Are immune diseases simply a cost of living in a developed and hygienic society? What are the beneficial microorganisms we want to be exposed to? How do we expose our children to these organisms specifically? We know that good hygiene remains an important aspect of disease prevention; however, inhibiting contact with all microorganisms is not a healthy approach either. Targeted hygiene is a practice of eliminating contact with potentially harmful microorganisms in predictable locations. Vigilance in cleaning bathrooms and toilets is beneficial and therefore warranted. But, allowing our children to get dirty **(Figure 34.15)** may also help to prevent serious disease later in life.

? How can keeping our children free of infections during childhood lead to immune diseases in adults?

● If a developing immune system does not get enough practice, it is more likely to respond to germs in an inappropriate fashion, leading to diseases such as asthma and autoimmune disorders.

▲ **Figure 34.15** Childhood exposure to environmental antigens

34.16 Some pathogens have ways to evade our immune system

The presence of an innate immune system in nearly all animals and an adaptive immune system in vertebrates demonstrates the timeless need for defence. The risk of infection has been ever-present because animals and pathogens have always co-existed. This coexistence produces selective pressure on both sides. Animals continue to evolve better methods of protection, and pathogens adapt better methods of infecting their hosts. This relationship will be discussed further in Module 39.14. During this coevolutionary history, pathogens occasionally evolved mechanisms to elude a host's immune responses.

Human cytomegalovirus (CMV) reduces the ability of a cell to present antigens in a self-nonself complex. Without this presentation, T cells are unable to recognize the presence of the virus, and infection persists. This virus can also produce a number of signals, which resemble the cytokines used by immune cells. The interleukins discussed in Module 34.9 are examples of cytokine signals (see Figure 34.9). CMV prevents activation of the host immune system by using several cytokine mimics. As a result, the virus can survive. In fact, 50% to 80% of people are, or have been, infected with CMV, which typically goes unnoticed.

As discussed in Module 34.9, phagocytes typically ingest pathogens, kill them, and present small antigens to helper T cells. Killing is accomplished with digestive enzymes and the production of oxygen radicals such as *superoxide* ($O_2^{\cdot-}$, an oxygen molecule with an extra electron and negative charge denoted by the dot and minus sign) that damage the pathogen. Some intracellular pathogens, such as *Leishmania* (unicellular parasites that infect macrophages), are able to circumvent these killing mechanisms (**Figure 34.16A**). This parasite produces an enzyme, *superoxide dismutase*, which destroys oxygen radicals and, therefore, the macrophage's ability to kill. As a result, *Leishmania* survives very well inside of the macrophage.

Other pathogens take advantage of the specificity of our immune responses. *Trypanosoma* are unicellular parasites that live in the bloodstream of their hosts. The plasma membrane of *Trypanosoma* is completely covered with a single antigen. The host's T cells initiate a humoral response and the production of antibodies that bind to this specific antigen. Once bound, antibodies facilitate the phagocytic removal of the parasite. This is a normal, primary immune response that should result in elimination of the parasite. However, *Trypanosoma*

▲ **Figure 34.16A** A macrophage infected with *Leishmania*

uses a trick called *antigenic variation* (**Figure 34.16B**). As your immune system mounts this primary humoral response (red antibodies in the figure), a few parasites literally change their antigen coat (indicated by the colour change from red to blue). Because the immune system has not seen this new antigen, it must start over with a new primary immune response (blue antibodies). *Trypanosoma* is able to change its surface antigens more than 1000 times. With each change, a new primary immune response is required.

 Why have pathogens evolved various mechanisms of immune evasion?

● Hosts are continually evolving new mechanisms for the removal of pathogens. As a result, there is a strong selective advantage for any mechanism that circumvents the immune system.

▲ **Figure 34.16B** Antigenic variation in *Trypanosoma*

REVIEW

MasteringBiology® **For Practice Quizzes, Bioflix, MP3 Tutors, and Activities, go to masteringbiology.com**

Reviewing the Concepts

Innate Immunity (34.1–34.3)

34.1 All animals have innate immunity. Innate defences include the skin, mucous membranes, phagocytic cells, and antimicrobial proteins such as interferons and the complement system.

34.2 Inflammation mobilizes the innate immune response. Tissue damage triggers the inflammatory response, which can disinfect tissues and limit further infection.

34.3 The lymphatic system becomes a crucial battleground during infection. Lymphatic vessels collect fluid from body tissues and return it as lymph to the blood. Lymph organs, such as the spleen and lymph nodes, are packed with white blood cells that fight infections.

Adaptive Immunity (34.4–34.12)

34.4 The adaptive immune response counters specific invaders. Antigens from infections or vaccinations trigger adaptive immunity.

34.5 Seasonal flu shots. Every year WHO determines three influenza virus strains that pose a threat. Its suggestion directs Canada's development of the seasonal flu vaccine.

34.6 Do childhood vaccines cause autism? A report that linked the MMR vaccine with autism spectrum disorder has been found to be fraudulent and unethical. No link has been shown between vaccination and behavioural disorders.

34.7 Lymphocytes mount a dual defence. Millions of kinds of B cells and T cells, each with different membrane receptors, wait in the lymphatic system, where they may respond to invaders.

The humoral immune response:

B cell — makes → Antibodies — which bind to → Antigens in body fluid

The cell-mediated immune response:

T cell — Infected body cell

Self-nonself complex

34.8 Clonal selection musters defensive forces against specific antigens. When an antigen enters the body, it activates only a small subset of lymphocytes that have complementary receptors. The selected cells multiply into clones of short-lived effector cells specialized for defending against the antigen that triggered the response and also into memory cells, which confer long-term immunity. Activated by subsequent exposure to the antigen, memory cells mount a rapid and strong secondary immune response.

34.9 Helper T cells stimulate the humoral and cell-mediated immune responses. In the cell-mediated immune response, an antigen-presenting cell displays a foreign antigen (a nonself molecule) and one of the body's own self proteins to a helper T cell. The helper T cell's receptors recognize the self-nonself complexes, and the interaction activates the helper T cell. In turn, the helper T cell can activate cytotoxic T cells and B cells.

34.10 Antibodies are the weapons of the humoral immune response. Plasma (effector) B cells secrete antibodies into the blood and lymph. An antibody has antigen-binding sites specific to the antigenic determinants that elicited its secretion.

34.11 Antibodies mark antigens for elimination. Antibodies facilitate the removal of foreign antigens by promoting their ingestion by phagocytes, or through complement causing lysis.

34.12 Cytotoxic T cells destroy infected body cells. Cytotoxic T cells kill our cells that have become altered in some way. An altered cell is one that is either cancerous or infected with a virus.

Inappropriate Immune Responses (34.13–34.16)

34.13 The immune system depends on molecular identification. The immune system normally reacts only against nonself substances, not against self. Transplanted organs may be rejected because these cells lack the unique identity of the recipient's self proteins.

34.14 Allergies are overreactions to certain environmental antigens. An initial sensitization exposure to an environmental antigen or allergen causes the production of antibodies. Subsequent exposure activates mast cells, causing the release of histamine and allergy symptoms.

34.15 The hygiene hypothesis: Are our kids too clean? In Canada, childhood infectious diseases are relatively infrequent. Meanwhile, the frequency of immune disease is high. The hygiene hypothesis proposes a link between frequent childhood infections and a healthy adult immune system.

34.16 Some pathogens have ways to evade our immune system. Our immune system has evolved to protect us against a vast number of pathogens. But, pathogens have been evolving too. Some have developed mechanisms to elude our immune responses and cause serious disease.

Connecting the Concepts

1. Complete this concept map to summarize the key concepts concerning the body's defences.

Testing Your Knowledge

Multiple Choice

2. Foreign molecules that elicit an immune response are called
   - a. pathogens.
   - b. antibodies.
   - c. lymphocytes.
   - d. histamines.
   - e. antigens.

3. Which of the following is *not* part of the vertebrate innate defence system?
   - a. natural killer cells
   - b. antibodies
   - c. interferons
   - d. complement system
   - e. inflammation

4. Which of the following statements about the vaccine strain of an influenza virus is true?
   a. It is an avirulent strain that can protect us against all influenza viruses.
   b. It is a virulent virus for which we should develop a vaccine.
   c. A virulent form of the virus is found within an influenza vaccine.
   d. It is an avirulent strain containing the same hemagglutinin and neuraminidase molecules as a virulent strain.
   e. It is an avirulent strain that has different hemagglutinin and neuraminidase molecules than the virulent strains.

5. Which of the following best describes the difference in the way B cells and cytotoxic T cells deal with invaders?
   a. B cells confer active immunity; T cells confer passive immunity.
   b. B cells send out antibodies to attack; certain T cells can do the attacking themselves.
   c. T cells handle the primary immune response; B cells handle the secondary response.
   d. B cells are responsible for the cell-mediated immune response; T cells are responsible for the humoral immune response.
   e. B cells attack the first time the invader is present; T cells attack subsequent times.

6. The antigen-binding sites of an antibody molecule are formed from the molecule's variable regions. Why are these regions called variable?
   a. They can change their shapes on command to fit different antigens.
   b. They change their shapes when they bind to an antigen.
   c. Their specific shapes are unimportant.
   d. Each antibody has a different shape that can bind to a different antigen.
   e. Their sizes vary considerably from one antibody to another.

7. Which of the following terms describes how antibodies cause multiple pathogens (for example, bacteria) to clump together, enhancing phagocytosis by macrophages?
   a. neutralization
   b. complement activation
   c. precipitation
   d. agglutination
   e. interferon

8. Cytotoxic T cells are able to recognize virally infected body cells because
   a. the infected cells display foreign antigens.
   b. B cells help them.
   c. the infected cells produce antigens.
   d. infected cells release antibodies into the blood.
   e. helper T cells destroy them first.

9. Which of the following statements best describes the hygiene hypothesis?
   a. Higher standards of hygiene can lead to fewer infectious diseases throughout our lives.
   b. Lower standards of hygiene can lead to a person experiencing more infectious diseases as a child and ultimately a higher rate of immune diseases as an adult.
   c. Lower standards of hygiene can lead to a person experiencing fewer infectious diseases as a child and ultimately a lower rate of immune diseases as an adult.
   d. Higher standards of hygiene can lead to a lower rate of immune diseases throughout our lives.
   e. Higher standards of hygiene can reduce the number of infectious diseases a person experiences as a child, ultimately leading to a lower rate of immune diseases as an adult.

10. Which of the following immune responses can still occur during an infection with human cytomegalovirus (CMV)?
    a. Cytotoxic T cells will attack cells infected with the virus.
    b. Helper T cells will release interleukin-4, directing a humoral immune response.
    c. Helper T cells will release interferon-γ and interleukin-12, directing a cell-mediated immune response.
    d. Virus-infected cells will release interferon to make neighbouring cells more resistant to infection.
    e. None of the above. CMV inhibits all facets of the immune system.

Matching

11. Attacks infected body cells	a. lymphocyte
12. Carries out the humoral immune response	b. cytotoxic T cell
13. Causes allergy symptoms	c. helper T cell
14. Phagocytic white blood cell	d. mast cell
15. General name for a B or T cell	e. macrophage
16. Required for initiating the secondary immune response	f. B cell
17. Directs the adaptive immune response	g. memory cell

Describing, Comparing, and Explaining

18. What is inflammation? How does it protect the body? Why is inflammation considered part of the innate immune response?

19. Your roommate is rushed to the hospital after suffering a severe allergic reaction to a bee sting. After she is treated and released, she asks you (the local biology expert!) to explain what happened. She says, "I don't understand how this could have happened. I've been stung by bees before and didn't have a reaction." Suggest a hypothesis to explain what has happened to cause her severe allergic reaction and why she did not have the reaction after previous bee stings.

Applying the Concepts

20. Organ donation saves many lives each year. Even though some transplanted organs are derived from living donors, the majority come from patients who die but still have healthy organs that can be of value to a transplant recipient. Potential organ donors can fill out an organ donation card to specify their wishes. If the donor is in critical condition and dying, the donor's family is usually consulted to discuss the donation process. Generally, the next of kin must approve before donation can occur, regardless of whether the patient has completed an organ donation card. In some cases, the donor's wishes are overridden by a family member. Do you think that family members should be able to deny the stated intentions of the potential donor? Why or why not?

21. Worried about getting influenza and missing class, your friend received a flu shot in October 2011 and remained healthy. Unfortunately, he thought that he would be protected for several years and did not get the flu shot in 2012. During that winter, he came down with the flu and missed two weeks of school. How would you explain the importance of annual flu shots to your friend?

Answers to all questions can be found in Appendix E.

Ecology

The Biosphere: An Introduction to Earth's Diverse Environments

BIG IDEAS

The Biosphere

(35.1–35.5)

The distribution and abundance of life in the biosphere is influenced by living and nonliving components of the environment.

Aquatic Biomes

(35.6–35.8)

In marine biomes, the salt concentration is generally around 3%. In freshwater biomes, the salt concentration is typically less than 1%.

Terrestrial Biomes

(35.9–35.19)

The distribution of terrestrial biomes is primarily determined by temperature and rainfall.

Life on and in the Ice

The Arctic Archipelago is an extensive marine biome that includes the Arctic Ocean and Beaufort Sea. Sea ice is a crucial component to this aquatic biome. Salt water freezes at approximately –1.9°C, forming sea ice. As the temperature drops in autumn, small crystals of ice form and gradually coalesce into massive sheets of ice. These sheets are 2–3 m thick and cover 14 million km² at their maximum extent: an area over 40% larger than Canada! This continuous sheet of ice consists of glaciers over land and sea ice over the oceans. As the temperature rises in the short summer, the ice begins to break. In the southern Arctic, it drifts and melts away completely. However, in the northern reaches, 7 million km² of ice persists throughout the summer.

Sea ice plays an important role for the Arctic community. Several iconic Canadian species depend on the sea ice for their survival. Ocean currents under the ice well up in some localized areas, creating small pockets of open water called polynyas. Marine mammals such as seals and beluga whales take refuge in the polynyas, where they have access to open air. Polar bears obtain the majority of their annual caloric intake by hunting at these holes in the sea ice.

The sea ice is important to more than just the large marine mammals. In fact, within the ice lives a community of micro-organisms (shown in the photograph). Sea ice contains brine networks: small channels and pores filled with briny water (which has a lower salt concentration than sea water). As the ice grows, the microcommunity develops within the brine network as it forms near the bottom of the ice. The brown line in the ice core pictured above is the alga within the brine network. With algae at the base, the food web contains multiple levels of small inverte-brates that have been found nowhere else. This community plays an integral role in the productivity of the Arctic Archipelago, con-tributing up to a quarter of the biome's primary productivity.

Dr. Andrea Niemi at the Freshwater Institute, Fisheries and Oceans Canada, in Winnipeg has been studying this interesting microcommunity and what happens to it during the long dark winter. Winter above the Arctic Circle means the land consis-tently experiences the twilight of polar night. Although it is not completely dark, there is not enough sunlight to power algal photosynthesis. Niemi was the first to examine the microcom-munity during winter. In a 2011 publication, she demonstrated that the assemblage of protists within the sea ice community varies little between winter and spring. However, the winter biomass was significantly lower than in the spring or in the summer. The key algal species of the spring bloom are present during winter, but in a dormant state—much like the larger community members we more often associate with the arctic.

Climate change is severely threatening the Arctic Archi-pelago biome. The extent of the sea ice is diminishing. In 2009, coverage was 23% less than the average between 1979 and 2000. Decreasing amounts of sea ice jeopardize not only the polar bears' hunting grounds, but also the structure of the microcommunity within the ice. Loss of this community would significantly reduce the productivity of the Arctic Archipelago.

From the highest mountain to the deepest ocean, Earth's di-verse environments are bursting with life. Investigating the inter-actions of organisms with their environment offers a context for new discoveries, a means of understanding familiar forms of life, and insight into our own role as inhabitants of Earth. This chap-ter begins our study of ecology with a survey of the diverse array of biomes on Earth, and starts with those found in Canada.

The Biosphere

35.1 Ecologists study how organisms interact with their environment at several levels

Ecology (from the Greek *oikos*, home) is the scientific study of the interactions of organisms with their environment. Ecologists describe the distribution and abundance of organisms—where they live and how many live there. Because the environment is complex, organisms can potentially be affected by many different variables. Ecologists group these variables into two major types, biotic factors and abiotic factors. **Biotic factors**, which include all the organisms in the area, are the living component of the environment. **Abiotic factors** are the environment's nonliving component, the physical and chemical factors such as temperature, forms of energy available, water, and nutrients. An organism's **habitat**, the specific environment it lives in, includes the biotic and abiotic factors present in the organism's surroundings.

As you might expect, field research is fundamental to ecology. But ecologists also test hypotheses by using laboratory experiments, where conditions can be simplified and controlled. Some ecologists take a theoretical approach, devising mathematical and computer models that enable them to simulate large-scale experiments that are impossible to conduct in the field.

Ecologists study environmental interactions at several levels. At the **organism** level, they may examine how one kind of organism meets the challenges and opportunities of its environment through its physiology or behaviour. For example, an ecologist working at this level might study adaptations of the Arctic poppy (*Papaver radicatum*; **Figure 35.1A**) to the freezing temperatures and short days of its abiotic environment.

Another level of study in ecology is the **population**, a group of individuals of the same species living in a particular geographic area. Arctic poppies living in a particular meadow in Nunavut would constitute a population (**Figure 35.1B**). An ecologist studying Arctic poppies might investigate factors that affect the size of the population, such as the availability of chemical nutrients or seed dispersal.

A third level, the **community**, is an assemblage of all the populations of organisms living close enough together for potential interaction—all the biotic factors in the environment. All the organisms in a particular arctic meadow would constitute a community (**Figure 35.1C**). An ecologist working at this level might focus on interspecies interactions, such as the competition between poppies and other plants for soil nutrients or the effect of plant-eaters on poppies.

The fourth level of ecological study, the **ecosystem**, includes both the biotic and abiotic components of the environment (**Figure 35.1D**). Some critical questions at the ecosystem level are concerned with how chemicals cycle and how energy flows between organisms and their surroundings. For an alpine meadow, one ecosystem-level question would be "How rapidly does the decomposition of decaying plants release inorganic molecules?"

Some ecologists take a wider perspective by studying **landscapes**, which are arrays of ecosystems. Landscapes are usually visible from the air as distinctive patches. For example, the Nunavut Arctic meadows are part of a mountain landscape that also includes conifer and broadleaf forests. A landscape

▲ **Figure 35.1A** An organism   ▲ **Figure 35.1B** A population

▲ **Figure 35.1C** A community

▲ **Figure 35.1D** An ecosystem

perspective emphasizes the absence of clearly defined ecosystem boundaries; energy, materials, and organisms may be exchanged by ecosystems within a landscape.

The **biosphere**, which extends from the atmosphere several kilometres above Earth to the depths of the oceans, is all of Earth that is inhabited by life. It is the home of us all, and as you will learn throughout this unit, our actions have consequences for the entire biosphere.

? Of the terms *population*, *ecosystem*, *organism*, and *community*, which level of organization encompasses all the others?

 Ecosystem

35.2 The science of ecology provides insight into environmental problems

In the environmental movement, every time you lose a battle it's for good, but our victories always seem to be temporary and we keep fighting them over and over again.

— David Suzuki

An airplane trip almost anywhere in Canada reveals the extent to which people have changed the landscape **(Figure 35.2A)**. But the cities, farms, and highways visible from the air are only the tip of the vast and largely unseen iceberg of human impact on the environment. Overgrazing, deforestation, and overcultivation of land have caused massive soil erosion. Industrial and agricultural practices have spread chemical pollutants throughout the biosphere. Human-made products have contaminated the groundwater, water that has penetrated the soil and may eventually resurface in the drinking supply. In some areas, groundwater is being depleted by the ever-expanding human population. Hundreds of species of organisms are in danger of joining the growing list of those that we have already driven to extinction. Most worrisome of all, our activities are producing potentially catastrophic changes in the global climate.

Although most of our environmental problems have been many decades in the making, few people were aware of them until the 1960s. Technology had been advancing rapidly, and humankind seemed poised on the brink of freedom from several age-old bonds. New chemical fertilizers and pesticides, for example, showed great promise for increasing agricultural productivity. Massive applications of fertilizer and extensive aerial spraying of pesticides such as DDT brought astonishing increases in crop yields. Pesticides were also used to combat disease-carrying insects, including mosquitoes (which transmit malaria), body lice (typhus), and fleas (plague).

But questions were raised about the long-term effects of widespread DDT use. It became evident that insects were evolving resistance to DDT, rendering this widely used pesticide less effective (see Module 13.3). As DDT lost its killing power, chemical companies introduced ever more potent pesticides. Although harshly criticized by the agriculture and pesticide industries, scientists had begun to document the harmful effects of DDT on predatory birds. Moreover, traces of the pesticide were turning up worldwide, thousands of kilometres from where it had been applied. DDT even showed up in human milk.

▲ **Figure 35.2A** The landscape around Banff, Alberta, which has been changed by humans

▲ **Figure 35.2B** David Suzuki

Public awareness of the problems caused by pesticides quickly developed into a general concern about a host of environmental issues. The 1970s brought a series of legislative acts aimed at curbing pollution and cleaning up the environment. Despite these efforts, serious issues clearly remain. Today, one of Canada's environmental leaders, Dr. David Suzuki, professor emeritus at the University of British Columbia, author, and host of the CBC's *The Nature of Things with David Suzuki* for more than 30 years **(Figure 35.2B)**, is dedicated to raising public awareness about environmental issues. Reaching millions of viewers weekly, Suzuki has greatly increased the average Canadian's understanding about environmentalism and sustainability.

The science of ecology can provide the understanding needed to resolve environmental problems. But these problems cannot be solved by ecologists alone because they require making decisions based on values and ethics. On a personal level, each of us makes daily choices that affect our ecological impact. Legislators and corporations, motivated by environmentally aware voters and consumers, must address questions that have wider implications: How should land use be regulated? Should we try to save all species or just certain ones? What alternatives to environmentally destructive practices can be developed? How can we balance environmental impact with economic needs?

You will learn about some of our environmental problems in Chapter 41. But analyzing environmental issues and planning for better practices begin with an understanding of the basic concepts of ecology, so let's start to explore them now.

 Why can't ecologists alone solve environmental problems?

● The science of ecology can inform the decision-making process, but solving environmental problems involves making ethical, economic, and political judgments that are outside the realm of science.

35.3 Physical and chemical factors influence life in the biosphere

You have learned that life thrives in a wide variety of habitats, from the mountaintops to the seafloor. To be successful, the organisms that live in each place must be adapted to the abiotic factors present in those environments. Let's now consider some important abiotic factors and how they affect the distribution of organisms.

Energy Sources   All organisms require a source of energy to live. Solar energy from sunlight, captured during the process of photosynthesis, powers most ecosystems. Lack of sunlight is seldom the most important factor limiting plant growth for terrestrial ecosystems, although shading by trees does create intense competition for light among plants growing on forest floors. In many aquatic environments, however, light is not uniformly available. Microorganisms and suspended particles, as well as the water itself, absorb light and prevent it from penetrating beyond certain depths. As a result, most photosynthesis occurs near the water's surface.

In dark environments such as caves or hydrothermal vents on the ocean floor, bacteria that extract energy from inorganic chemicals help to power ecosystems. Often, sulphur bacteria perform this function, and many of the animals either feed directly on the sulphur bacteria or derive nutrition from bacteria living inside their bodies. We will discuss these ecosystems more in Module 40.2.

Temperature   Temperature is an important abiotic factor because of its effect on metabolism (see Module 5.13). Few organisms can maintain a sufficiently active metabolism at temperatures close to 0°C, and temperatures above 45°C destroy the enzymes of most organisms. However, extraordinary adaptations enable some species to live outside this temperature range. For example, archaeans living in hot springs have enzymes that function optimally at extremely high temperatures. Mammals and birds, such as the snowy owl in **Figure 35.3**, can remain considerably warmer than their surroundings and can be active at a fairly wide range of temperatures. Amphibians and reptiles, which gain most of their warmth by absorbing heat from their surroundings, have a more limited distribution.

Water   Water is essential to all life. Thus, for terrestrial organisms, drying out in the air is a major danger. As we discussed in Modules 19.1 and 21.6, watertight coverings are key adaptations enabling plants and vertebrates to be successful on land. Aquatic organisms are surrounded by water; their problem is solute concentration. Freshwater organisms live in a hypotonic medium, while the environment of marine organisms is hypertonic. As we saw in Module 25.19, animals maintain fluid balance by a variety of mechanisms.

Inorganic Nutrients   The distribution and abundance of photosynthetic organisms, including plants, algae, and photosynthetic bacteria, depend on the availability of inorganic nutrients such as nitrogen and phosphorus. Plants obtain these

▲ **Figure 35.3** A snowy owl

from the soil. Soil structure, pH, and nutrient content often play major roles in determining the distribution of plants. In many aquatic ecosystems, low levels of nitrogen and phosphorus limit the growth of algae and photosynthetic bacteria. Too many nutrients can have detrimental effects on aquatic ecosystems by fuelling extensive growth of algae (see Module 40.10).

Other Aquatic Factors   Several abiotic factors are important in aquatic, but not terrestrial, ecosystems. While terrestrial organisms have a plentiful supply of oxygen from the air, aquatic organisms must depend on oxygen dissolved in water. This is a critical factor for many species of fish. Trout, for example, require high levels of dissolved oxygen. Cold, fast-moving water has a higher oxygen content than warm or stagnant water. Salinity, current, and tides may also play a role in aquatic ecosystems.

Other Terrestrial Factors   On land, wind and fire are often important abiotic factors. Wind increases an organism's rate of water loss by evaporation. The resulting increase in evaporative cooling (see Module 25.18) can be advantageous on a hot summer day, but it can cause dangerous wind chill in the winter. In some ecosystems, fire occurs frequently enough that many plants have adapted to this disturbance.

Next we examine the interaction between one animal species and the abiotic and biotic factors of its environment.

 Why are birds and mammals, but not amphibians and reptiles other than birds, found in the Nunavut Arctic meadow?

● As ectotherms (see Module 25.16), reptiles and amphibians do not have adaptations that enable them to withstand the cold temperatures of the arctic habitat.

35.4 Organisms adapt to abiotic and biotic factors by means of natural selection

One of the fundamental goals of ecology is to explain the distribution of organisms. The presence of a species in a particular place has two possible explanations: The species may have evolved from ancestors living in that location, or it may have dispersed to that location and been able to survive once it arrived. The magnificent pronghorn "antelope" (*Antilocapra americana*; **Figure 35.4**) is the descendant of ancestors that roamed the open plains and shrub deserts of North America more than a million years ago. The animal is found nowhere else and is only distantly related to the many species of antelope in Africa. What selective factors in the abiotic and biotic environments of its ancestors produced the adaptations we see in the pronghorn that roams North America today?

The pronghorn's present-day habitat, like that of its ancestors, is arid, windswept, and subject to extreme temperature fluctuations both daily and seasonally. Individuals able to survive and reproduce under these conditions left offspring that carried their alleles forward into subsequent generations. Thus, we can infer that many of the adaptations that contribute to the success of present-day pronghorns must also have contributed to the success of their ancestors. For example, the pronghorn has a thick coat made of hollow hairs that trap air, insulating the animal in cold weather. If you drive through southern Saskatchewan or parts of Alberta in the winter, you may see herds of these animals foraging in the open when temperatures are well below 0°C. In hot weather, the pronghorn can raise patches of this stiff hair to release body heat.

The biotic environment, which includes what the animal eats and any predators that threaten it, is also a factor in determining which members of a population survive and reproduce. The pronghorn's main foods are small broadleaf plants, grasses, and woody shrubs. Over time, characteristics that enabled the ancestors of the pronghorn to exploit these food sources more efficiently became established through natural selection. As a result, the teeth of a pronghorn are specialized for biting and chewing tough plant material. Like the stomach of a cow, the pronghorn's stomach contains cellulose-digesting bacteria. As the pronghorn eats plants, the bacteria digest the cellulose, and the animal obtains most of its nutrients from the bacteria.

While many factors in the pronghorn's environment have been fairly consistent throughout its evolutionary history, one aspect has changed significantly. Until around 12 000 years ago, one of the pronghorn's major predators was probably the American cheetah, a fleet-footed feline that bears some similarities to the more familiar African cheetah. The now-extinct American cheetah was one of many ferocious predators of Pleistocene North America, along with lions, jaguars, and sabre-toothed cats with 18 cm canines. Ecologists hypothesize that the selection pressure of the cheetah's pursuit led to the pronghorn's blazing speed, which far exceeds that of its main present-day predator, the wolf. With a top speed of 100 km/h, the pronghorn is easily the fastest mammal on the continent, and an adult pronghorn can keep up a pace of 65 km/h for at least 30 minutes. Unable to match the pronghorn's extravagant speed, wolves typically take adults that have been weakened by age or illness.

Like many large herbivores that live in open grasslands, the pronghorn also derives protection from living in herds. When one pronghorn starts to run, its white rump patch seems to alert other herd members to danger. Other adaptations that help the pronghorn foil predators include its tan and white coat, which provides camouflage, and its keen eyes, which can detect movement at great distances. Thus, the adaptations shaped by natural selection in the distant past still serve as protection from the predators of today's environment.

If the pronghorn's environment changed significantly, the adaptations that contribute to its current success might not be as advantageous. For example, if an increase in rainfall turned the open plains into woodlands, where predators would be more easily hidden by vegetation and could stalk their prey at close range, the pronghorn's adaptations for escaping predators might not be as effective. Thus, in adapting populations to local environmental conditions, natural selection may limit the distribution of organisms.

In the next module, we see how global climatic patterns determine temperature and precipitation, the major abiotic factors that influence the distribution of organisms. We examine the biotic components of the environment more closely in other chapters in this unit.

 What is the role of the environment in adaptive evolution?

▲ **Figure 35.4** A pronghorn (*Antilocapra americana*)

● The individuals whose phenotypes are best suited to the environment (including both abiotic and biotic factors) will pass their alleles to the next generation. But individuals with other phenotypes may not. For example, if the biotic environment includes wolves, a pronghorn that is not able to run for as long as the rest of the herd will probably not survive to reproduce.

35.5 Regional climate influences the distribution of terrestrial communities

When we ask what determines whether a particular organism or community of organisms lives in a certain area, the climate of the region—especially temperature and precipitation—is often a crucial part of the answer. Earth's global climate patterns are largely determined by the input of radiant energy from the sun and the planet's movement in space.

Figure 35.5A shows that because of its curvature, Earth receives an uneven distribution of solar energy. The sun's rays strike equatorial areas most directly (perpendicularly). Away from the equator, the rays strike Earth's surface at a slant. As a result, the same amount of solar energy is spread over a larger area. Thus, any particular area of land or ocean near the equator absorbs more heat than comparable areas in the more northern or southern latitudes.

The seasons of the year result from the permanent tilt of the planet on its axis as it orbits the sun. Contrary to popular belief, the Earth's distance from the sun does not affect seasonality. As **Figure 35.5B** shows, the globe's position relative to the sun changes through the year. The Northern Hemisphere, for instance, is tipped most toward the sun in June. The more direct angle and

increased intensity of the sun result in the long days of summer in that hemisphere. But during this time, days are short and it is winter in the Southern Hemisphere. Conversely, the Southern Hemisphere is tipped farthest toward the sun in December, creating summer there and causing winter in the Northern Hemisphere. On each equinox, the entire globe experiences 12 hours of daylight and 12 hours of dark. The **tropics**, the region surrounding the equator between latitudes 23.5° north (the Tropic of Cancer) and 23.5° south (the Tropic of Capricorn), experience the greatest annual input and the least seasonal variation in solar radiation.

Figure 35.5C shows some of the effects of the intense solar radiation near the equator on global patterns of rainfall and winds. Arrows indicate air movements. High temperatures in the tropics evaporate water from Earth's surface. Heated by the direct rays of the sun, moist air at the equator rises, creating an area of calm or of very light winds known as the **doldrums**. As warm equatorial air rises, it cools and releases much of its water content, creating the abundant precipitation typical of most tropical regions. High temperatures throughout the year and ample rainfall largely explain why rainforests are concentrated near the equator.

After losing their moisture over equatorial zones, high-altitude air masses spread away from the equator until they cool and descend again at latitudes of about 30° north and south. This descending dry air absorbs moisture from the land. Thus, many of the world's great deserts—the Sahara in North Africa and the Arabian on the Arabian Peninsula, for example—are centred at these latitudes. As the dry air descends, some of it spreads back toward the equator. This movement creates the cooling **trade winds**, which dominate the tropics. As the air moves back toward the equator, it warms and picks up moisture until it ascends again.

The latitudes between the tropics and the Arctic Circle in the north and the Antarctic Circle in the south are called **temperate zones**. Generally, these regions have seasonal variations in climate and more moderate temperatures than the tropics or the polar zones. Notice in Figure 35.5C that some of the descending air heads into the latitudes above 30°. At first these air masses pick up moisture, but they tend to drop it as they cool at higher latitudes. This is why the north and south temperate zones, especially latitudes around 60°, tend to be

▲ **Figure 35.5A** How solar radiation varies with latitude

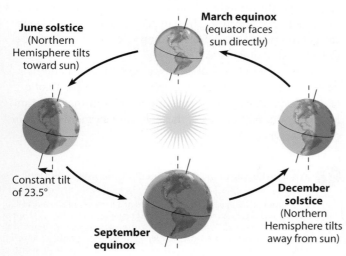

▲ **Figure 35.5B** How Earth's tilt causes the seasons

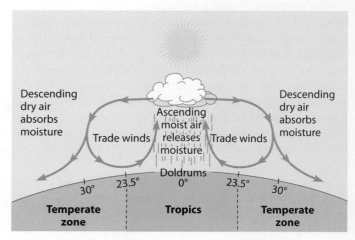

▲ **Figure 35.5C** How uneven heating causes rain and winds

moist. Broad expanses of coniferous forest dominate the landscape at these fairly wet but cool latitudes.

Figure 35.5D shows the major global air movements, called the **prevailing winds**. Prevailing winds (pink arrows) result from the combined effects of the rising and falling of air masses (blue and brown arrows) and Earth's rotation (grey arrows). Because Earth is spherical, its surface moves faster at the equator (where its diameter is greatest) than at other latitudes. In the tropics, Earth's rapidly moving surface deflects vertically circulating air, making the trade winds blow from east to west. In temperate zones, including much of Canada, the slower-moving surface produces the **westerlies**, winds that blow from west to east.

A combination of the prevailing winds, the planet's rotation, unequal heating of surface waters, and the locations and shapes of the continents creates **ocean currents**, riverlike flow patterns in the oceans (Figure 35.5E). Ocean currents have a profound effect on regional climates. For instance, the Gulf Stream circulates warm water northward from the Gulf of Mexico and makes the climate on the west coast of Great Britain warmer during winter than the coast of New England, which is actually farther south but is cooled by a branch of the current flowing south from the coast of Greenland.

Landforms can also affect local climate. Air temperature declines by about 6°C with every 1000 m increase in elevation, an effect you have probably experienced if you have ever hiked up a mountain. Figure 35.5F illustrates the effect of mountains on rainfall. This drawing represents major landforms across British Columbia, but mountain ranges cause similar effects elsewhere. Southern British Columbia is a temperate area in which the prevailing winds are westerlies. As moist air moves in off the Pacific Ocean and encounters the westernmost mountains (the Coast Range), it flows upward, cools at higher altitudes, and drops a large amount of water. The world's tallest trees thrive on the west coast of North America. Farther inland, precipitation increases again as the air moves up and over higher mountains (the Cascade Range). On the eastern side of the Cascades, there is little precipitation, and the dry descending air also absorbs moisture. This effect, called a rain shadow, is responsible for the desert in the southern part of the Okanagan Valley in British Columbia.

The mountains also create other winter weather phenomena, which move across the Prairies. As the air moves up the west side of the Rocky Mountains, it loses heat as well as moisture. When the air moves down the east side of the Rockies, it warms up. However, the air warms up faster as it falls (gaining about 10°C as it falls 1000 m) than it cooled off when it rose (losing 5°C as it rises 1000 m). The resulting phenomenon, known as a chinook, can drastically increase ambient temperature in a very short time. One winter day in 1962, the temperature in Pincher Creek, Alberta, rose from −19°C to 22°C in one hour. When a warm chinook air mass meets cold arctic air in the Prairies, the two may mix and create a winter storm known as an Alberta clipper. Cold temperatures, high wind chills, and frequently heavy snowfalls characterize Alberta clippers. Once formed, these systems move quickly across the Prairies and across the Great Lakes.

Climate and other abiotic factors of the environment control the global distribution of organisms. The influence of these abiotic factors results in **biomes**, expansive geographic areas of land or water with similar climatic conditions and ecological associations. Terrestrial biomes are determined primarily by temperature and precipitation—similar assemblages of plant and animal types are found in areas that have similar climates. Aquatic biomes are defined by different abiotic factors; the primary distinction is based on salinity. Marine biomes, which

▲ **Figure 35.5E** Atlantic Ocean currents (red arrows indicate warming currents; blue arrows indicate cooling currents)

▲ **Figure 35.5D** Prevailing wind patterns

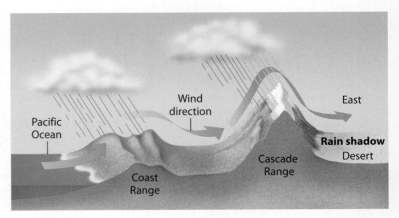

▲ **Figure 35.5F** How mountains affect precipitation (southern British Columbia)

include oceans, intertidal zones, and coral reefs, generally have salt concentrations around 3%, while freshwater biomes (lakes, streams and rivers, and wetlands) typically have salt concentrations that are much lower than 1%. We describe several aquatic biomes in the next Big Idea.

Aquatic Biomes

35.6 Sunlight and substrate are key factors in the distribution of marine organisms

Gazing out over a vast ocean, you might think that it is the most uniform environment on Earth. But marine ecosystems can be as different as night and day. The deepest ocean, where hydrothermal vents are located, is perpetually dark. In contrast, the vivid coral reefs are utterly dependent on sunlight. Habitats near shore are different from those in mid-ocean, and the substrate, which varies with depth and distance from shore, hosts different communities from the open waters.

The seafloor or substrate and the water just above its entire contour are called the **benthic realm**. This realm is home to many benthic organisms, including the oarweed and sea cucumber shown in **Figure 35.6A**. The open water above the benthic realm constitutes the **pelagic realm**. Plankton and whales (Figure 35.6A) are among the vast array of pelagic organisms. These realms can be further divided based on the amount of light they receive. The depth of light penetration, a maximum of 200 m, marks the **photic zone**. In shallow areas such as the submerged parts of continents, called **continental shelves**, the photic zone includes both the pelagic and benthic realms. In these sunlit regions,

photosynthesis by **phytoplankton** (microscopic algae and cyanobacteria) and multicellular algae provides energy and organic carbon for a diverse community of animals. Some sponges, burrowing worms, clams, sea anemones, crabs, and echinoderms inhabit the benthic realm of the photic zone. **Zooplankton** (small, drifting protists and animals), fish, marine mammals, and many other types of animals are abundant in the pelagic photic zone.

Coral reefs, a visually spectacular and biologically diverse biome, are scattered around the globe in the photic zone of warm tropical waters above continental shelves. A reef is built up slowly by successive generations of coral animals—a diverse group of cnidarians that secrete a hard external skeleton—and by multicellular algae encrusted with limestone. Unicellular algae live within the corals, providing the coral with food (see Module 20.6). Coral reefs support a huge variety of invertebrates and fishes. Colder waters are also habitats for corals **(Figure 35.6B)**; however, most corals are solitary and do not form elaborate reefs. Many of the corals in the Canadian Pacific Ocean are being threatened by certain fishing practices. For example, dredging uses a large

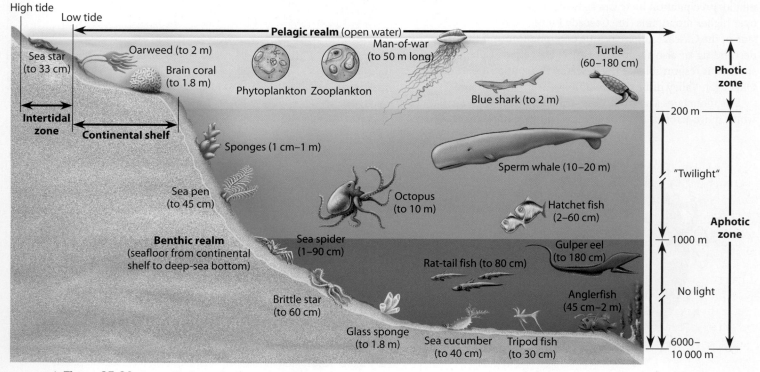

▲ **Figure 35.6A** Ocean life (zone depths and organisms not drawn to scale)

▲ **Figure 35.6B** Corals found off the west coast of British Columbia

▲ **Figure 35.6D** The Musquash Estuary in New Brunswick

scoop net that is dragged along the ocean floor to catch benthos, which are typically bottom-dwelling fishes. Because of the indiscriminate nature of this fishing method, the resulting bycatch (unwanted animals caught accidentally) often includes corals.

Below the photic zone of the ocean lies the **aphotic zone**. Although there is not enough light for photosynthesis between 200 and 1000 m, some light does reach these depths. This dimly lit world, sometimes called the twilight zone, is dominated by a fascinating variety of small fishes and crustaceans. Food sinking from the photic zone provides some sustenance for these animals. In addition, many of them migrate to the surface at night to feed. Some fishes in the twilight zone have enlarged eyes, enabling them to see in the very dim light, and luminescent organs that attract mates and prey.

▲ **Figure 35.6C**
An angler fish

Below 1000 m, the ocean is completely and permanently dark. Adaptation to this environment has produced bizarre-looking creatures, such as the angler fish shown in **Figure 35.6C**. The scarcity of food probably explains the strangely oversized mouths of the angler and other fishes that inhabit this region of the ocean, a feature that allows them to grab any available prey, large or small. Inwardly angled teeth ensure that once caught, prey do not escape. The angler fish improves its chances of encountering prey by dangling a lure lit by bioluminescent bacteria. Most benthic organisms here are deposit feeders, animals that consume detritus on the substrate. Crustaceans, polychaete worms, sea anemones, and echinoderms such as sea cucumbers, sea stars, and sea urchins are common. Because of the scarcity of food, however, the density of animals is low—except at hydrothermal vents, where chemoautotrophic bacteria support an abundance of life.

The marine environment also includes distinctive biomes where the ocean interfaces with land or with fresh water. In the **intertidal zone**, where the ocean meets land, the shore is pounded by waves during high tide and exposed to the sun and drying winds during low tide. The rocky intertidal zone is home to many sedentary organisms, such as algae, barnacles,

and mussels, which attach to rocks and are thus prevented from being washed away when the tide comes in. On sandy beaches, suspension-feeding worms, clams, and predatory crustaceans bury themselves in the ground.

Figure 35.6D shows an **estuary**, a biome that occurs where a freshwater stream or river merges with the ocean. The saltiness of estuaries ranges from nearly that of fresh water to that of the ocean. With their waters enriched by nutrients from the river, estuaries are among the most productive biomes on Earth. Oysters, crabs, and many fishes live in estuaries or reproduce in them. Estuaries are also crucial nesting and feeding areas for waterfowl.

Wetlands constitute a biome that is transitional between an aquatic ecosystem—either marine or freshwater—and a terrestrial one. Covered with water either permanently or periodically, wetlands support the growth of aquatic plants (see Figure 35.8C). Mudflats and salt marshes are coastal wetlands that often border estuaries.

For centuries, people viewed the ocean as a limitless resource, harvesting its bounty and using it as a dumping ground for wastes. The impact of these practices is now being felt in many ways, large and small. From worldwide declines in commercial fish species to dying coral reefs to beaches closed by pollution, danger signs abound. Because of their proximity to land, estuaries and wetlands are especially vulnerable. Many have been completely replaced by development or landfill. Other threats include nutrient pollution, contamination by pathogens or toxic chemicals, alteration of freshwater inflow, and introduction of non-native species. Coral reefs have suffered from many of the same problems. In addition, overfishing has upset the species balance in some reef communities and greatly reduced diversity, and the widespread demise of reef-building corals in some regions has been attributed to climate change.

Freshwater biomes share many characteristics with marine biomes and experience some of the same threats. We introduce freshwater biomes in Module 35.8; but, first, let's discuss a rumour about how marine fish can survive sub-zero temperatures.

 Oil from the 2010 Deepwater Horizon disaster in the Gulf of Mexico has polluted estuaries in Louisiana. Why does this pollution affect other animals in addition to those that live permanently in the estuaries?

● Many species, including fishes and waterfowl, feed or reproduce in estuaries.

35.7 Do arctic fishes have anti-freeze?

Life in the Arctic can be difficult for all organisms. Extreme winter temperatures have driven the evolution of numerous adaptations, which improve an organism's chances of survival. In Module 25.12, we discussed adaptations of polar bears, including the insulative hollow fur that protects them from freezing temperatures. But how do animals without fur prevent themselves from freezing? Some people have suggested that arctic fishes such as the Arctic cod (*Boreogadus saida*; **Figure 35.7A**), actually have antifreeze in their blood. Can this rumour be true? Is antifreeze an evolutionary adaptation to life in the Arctic?

Most fishes are ectotherms and have body temperatures that are the same as their surroundings (see Module 25.16). But if fish are swimming in unfrozen water, do they need to worry about their own tissues freezing? Although the average winter air temperatures in the Canadian Arctic can fall well below –40°C, the temperature of the Arctic Ocean remains warmer because it sits beneath an insulating layer of sea ice. However, because of the water's solute concentration, it does fall below 0°C (the freezing point of pure water). The solutes in a solution lower the solution's freezing point: The higher the solute concentration, the lower the solution's freezing temperature will be. Because of its salinity, the surface water in the Arctic freezes when it reaches –1.9°C. The freezing point of bodily fluids in Arctic fishes is closer to –0.6°C. Therefore, the tissues of a fish can freeze before the water surrounding it freezes. To survive, Arctic fishes must have adaptations that prevent themselves from freezing.

Many cold-tolerant organisms, including Arctic fishes, have proteins in their blood and bodily fluids that inhibit ice formation—so-called antifreeze proteins. While the existence of antifreeze proteins has been known for nearly 50 years, exactly how antifreeze proteins work was only discovered recently. Solutes in a solution lower its freezing point. The antifreeze you add to your car's radiator contains high concentrations of ethylene glycol, which lowers the freezing point of the fluid to –40°C. However, antifreeze proteins do not work in this way. The low concentration of antifreeze proteins does not significantly contribute to the osmolarity (total solute

▲ Figure 35.7B Antifreeze proteins interact with ice

concentration) of the blood plasma. Thus, antifreeze proteins must work by another mechanism.

The highly structured hydrogen bonding that occurs between water molecules in an ice crystal are shown in Figure 2.13. Freezing occurs after nucleation starts the development of ice crystals in solution. Many molecules within an organism can function as *ice nuclei* (not to be confused with the nuclei of cells). When the temperature drops low enough, ice crystals start forming around these molecules in the blood, cytoplasm, and other bodily fluids. If antifreeze proteins are absent, the ice will grow until the entire organism is frozen solid.

How do antifreeze proteins prevent the growth of ice crystals? The answer lies in their structure. Antifreeze proteins from cold-tolerant species are as diverse as the species themselves. However, they all have one surface that can bind to ice. The antifreeze proteins of fish are spiral-shaped proteins, with one side having three amino acids (alanine-alanine-threonine) repeated multiple times (**Figure 35.7B**). The hydroxyl groups of the threonine R groups (red dots) are spaced in a way that allows them to form hydrogen bonds with the oxygen atoms of the ice crystal's water molecules. In this position, antifreeze proteins block new water molecules from joining the ice crystal, causing it to grow. When a small ice crystal becomes covered with antifreeze proteins, it can no longer grow. This allows Arctic fishes to survive temperatures below the freezing point of their bodily fluids.

The rumour that arctic fishes have antifreeze is true. In fact, antifreeze proteins have been found in a wide range of organisms, including plants, fungi, animals, and bacteria. Antifreeze proteins are currently the focus of research because of their practical applications. Dr. Garth Fletcher at Memorial University of Newfoundland has studied antifreeze proteins for much of his career. A primary goal of Fletcher's is to increase the potential of salmon aquaculture on the east coast of Canada. Atlantic salmon do not produce antifreeze proteins and, therefore,

▲ Figure 35.7A The Arctic cod (*Boreogadus saida*)

cannot survive in the frigid waters of the northern Atlantic. By inserting the antifreeze protein gene into salmon eggs and creating transgenic fish (see Module 12.8), Fletcher hopes to create a stock of cold-tolerant salmon, which can be farmed in Canada's northern oceans. Additionally, antifreeze proteins can be collected from the blood of these fish as they are harvested. Adding these proteins to donated platelets at the blood bank

(see Module 28.4) could potentially allow the blood to be stored at lower temperatures, extending its shelf life and usefulness.

 How do antifreeze proteins prevent bodily fluids from freezing?

● Hydroxyl groups on threonine R groups form hydrogen bonds with the water molecule in an ice crystal and prevent the crystal from growing.

35.8 Current, sunlight, and nutrients are important abiotic factors in freshwater biomes

Freshwater biomes cover less than 1% of Earth's surface and contain a mere 0.01% of its water. But they harbour a disproportionate share of biodiversity—an estimated 6% of all described species. Moreover, we depend on freshwater biomes for drinking water, crop irrigation, sanitation, and industry.

Freshwater biomes fall into two broad categories: standing water, which includes lakes and ponds, and flowing water, such as rivers and streams. Because these biomes are embedded in terrestrial landscapes, their characteristics are intimately connected with the soils and organisms of the ecosystems that surround them.

Lakes and Ponds In lakes and large ponds, as in the oceans, the communities of plants, algae, and animals are distributed according to the depth of the water and its distance from shore. Phytoplankton grow in the photic zone, and rooted plants often inhabit shallow waters near shore (**Figure 35.8A**). If a lake or pond is deep enough or murky enough, it has an aphotic zone where light levels are too low to support photosynthesis. In the benthic realm, large populations of microorganisms decompose dead organisms that sink to the bottom. Respiration by microbes removes oxygen from water near the bottom, and in some lakes, benthic areas are unsuitable for any organisms except anaerobic microbes.

Temperature may also have a profound effect on standing water biomes. During the summer, deep lakes have a distinct upper layer of water that has been warmed by the sun and does not mix with underlying, cooler water.

The mineral nutrients nitrogen and phosphorus typically determine the amount of phytoplankton growth in a lake or pond. Many lakes and ponds receive large inputs of nitrogen and phosphorus from sewage and runoff from fertilized lawns and farms. These nutrients may produce a heavy growth ("bloom") of algae, called *eutrophication* (see Module 40.10), which reduces light penetration. When the algae die and decompose, a pond or lake can suffer severe oxygen depletion, killing fish that are adapted to high-oxygen conditions.

Rivers and Streams Rivers and streams generally support communities of organisms quite different from those of lakes and ponds. A river or a stream changes greatly between its source (perhaps a spring or snowmelt) and the point at which it empties into a lake or an ocean. Near the source, the water is usually cold, low in nutrients, and clear (**Figure 35.8B**). The channel is often narrow, with a swift current that does not allow much silt to accumulate on the bottom. The current also inhibits the growth of phytoplankton; most of the organisms found here are supported by the photosynthesis of algae attached to rocks or by organic material, such as leaves, carried into the stream from the surrounding land. The most abundant benthic animals are usually arthropods, such as small crustaceans and insect larvae, that have physical and behavioural adaptations that enable them to resist being swept away. Trout, which locate their insect prey mainly by sight in the clear water, are often the predominant fishes.

Downstream, a river or stream generally widens and slows. The water is usually warmer and may be murkier because of sediments and phytoplankton suspended in it. Worms and insects that burrow into mud are often abundant, as are

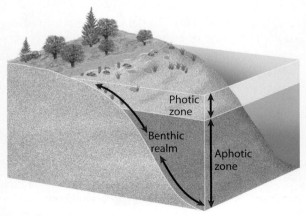

▲ **Figure 35.8A** Zones in a lake

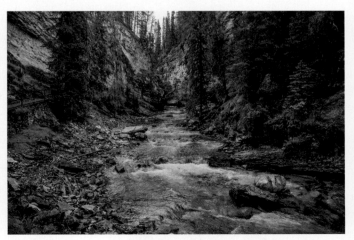

▲ **Figure 35.8B** A stream in Banff National Park, Alberta

waterfowl, frogs, and catfish and other fishes that find food more by scent and taste than by sight.

Wetlands Freshwater wetlands range from marshes, as shown in **Figure 35.8C**, to swamps and bogs. Like marine wetlands, freshwater wetlands are rich in species diversity. They provide water storage areas that reduce flooding and improve water quality by filtering pollutants. Recognition of their ecological and economic value has led to government and private efforts to protect and restore wetlands.

 ? **Why does sewage cause algal blooms in lakes?**

▲ **Figure 35.8C** Oak Hammock Marsh near Stonewall, Manitoba

● The sewage adds nutrients, such as nitrates and phosphates, that stimulate growth of algae.

Terrestrial Biomes

35.9 Terrestrial biomes reflect regional variations in climate

Terrestrial ecosystems are grouped into biomes, which are distinguished primarily by their predominant vegetation. By providing food, shelter, nesting sites, and much of the organic material for decomposers, plants build the foundation for the communities of animals, fungi, and microorganisms that are characteristic of each biome. The geographic distribution of plants, and thus of terrestrial biomes, largely depends on climate, with temperature and precipitation often the key factors determining the kind of biome that exists in a particular region.

Figure 35.9 shows the locations of the major terrestrial biomes. If the climate in two geographically separate

▼ **Figure 35.9** Major terrestrial biomes

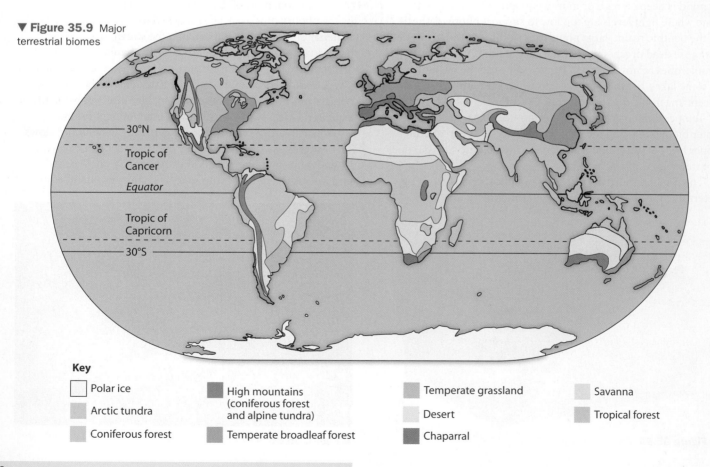

Key

- Polar ice
- Arctic tundra
- Coniferous forest
- High mountains (coniferous forest and alpine tundra)
- Temperate broadleaf forest
- Temperate grassland
- Desert
- Chaparral
- Savanna
- Tropical forest

areas is similar, the same type of biome may occur in both places; notice on the map that each kind of biome occurs on at least two continents. Each biome is characterized by a type of biological community, rather than an assemblage of particular species. For example, the species living in the deserts of the American Southwest and in the Sahara Desert of Africa are different, but all are adapted to desert conditions. Widely separated biomes may look alike because of convergent evolution, the appearance of similar traits in independently evolved species living in similar environments (see Module 15.12).

There is local variation within each biome that gives the vegetation a patchy, rather than a uniform, appearance. For example, in northern coniferous forests, snowfall may break branches and small trees, causing openings where broadleaf trees such as aspen and birch can grow. Local disturbances such as storms and fires also create openings in many biomes. Canada is a large country and there is variation within each biome along a west-to-east direction. Because of different weather patterns, coastal forests in the west are populated by tall trees, whereas forests along the east coast, which experience more severe weather systems, have predominantly shorter shrubs.

The current concern about climate change is generating intense interest in the effect of climate on vegetation patterns. Using powerful new tools such as satellite imagery, scientists are documenting shifts in latitudes of biome borders, changes in snow and ice coverage, and changes in length of the growing season. At the same time, many natural biomes have been fragmented and altered by human activity. As we will discuss in Module 41.2, a high rate of biome alteration by humans is correlated with an unusually high rate of species loss throughout the globe.

Now let's begin our survey of the major terrestrial biomes. We will start with the biomes that are found in Canada, starting with the polar ice and working southward. To help you locate the biomes, an orientation map colour-coded to Figure 35.9 is included with each module. Icons indicate a relative temperate range (in red) and average annual precipitation (in blue) for each biome. Icons also identify biomes in which fire plays a significant role.

> **?** Test your knowledge of world geography: Which biome is most closely associated with a "Mediterranean climate"?

● Chaparral

35.10 Polar ice covers the land at high latitudes

In the Northern Hemisphere, **polar ice** covers land north of the tundra; much of the Arctic Ocean is continuously frozen as well. In the Southern Hemisphere, polar ice covers the continent of Antarctica (**Figure 35.10**), which is surrounded by a ring of sea ice, and numerous islands. Global climate change is having significant impacts on this delicate biome (see Module 41.6).

The temperature in these regions is extremely cold year-round, and precipitation is very low. Only a small portion of these landmasses is free of ice or snow, even during the summer. Nevertheless, small plants, such as mosses, and lichens manage to survive, and invertebrates such as nematodes, mites, and wingless insects called springtails inhabit the frigid soil.

The terrestrial polar biome is closely interconnected with the neighbouring marine biome. Seals and marine birds, such as penguins, gulls, and skuas, feed in the ocean and visit the land or sea ice to rest and to breed. In the Northern Hemisphere, sea ice provides a feeding platform for polar bears (see Figure 41.6B).

> **?** How do small plants, lichens, and invertebrates survive in the polar ice biome?

▲ **Figure 35.10** Polar ice

● These organisms are very tolerant of long, cold winters and can survive in areas that become ice-free in the summer.

35.11 Long, bitter-cold winters characterize the tundra

Tundra (from the Russian word for "marshy plain") covers expansive areas of the Arctic between the boreal forest and polar ice.

Figure 35.11 shows the arctic tundra in the Yukon in the autumn. The climate here is often extremely cold, with little light for much of the autumn and winter. The arctic tundra is characterized by **permafrost**, continuously frozen subsoil.

Only the upper part of the soil thaws in summer. The arctic tundra may receive as little precipitation as some deserts. But poor drainage, because of the permafrost, and slow evaporation keep the soil continually saturated.

Permafrost prevents the roots of plants from penetrating very far into the soil, which is one factor that explains the absence of trees. Extremely cold winter air temperatures and high winds also contribute to the exclusion of trees. Vegetation in the tundra includes dwarf shrubs, grasses and other herbaceous plants, mosses, and lichens. During the brief, warm summers, when there is nearly constant daylight, plants grow quickly and flower in a rapid burst. High winds and cold temperatures create plant communities called alpine tundra on very high mountaintops at all latitudes, including the tropics. Although these communities are similar to arctic tundra, there is no permafrost beneath alpine tundra.

Animals of the tundra withstand the cold by having good insulation that retains heat. Large herbivores include musk ox and caribou. The principal smaller animals are rodents called lemmings and a few predators, such as the Arctic fox and snowy owl. Many animals are migratory, using the tundra as a summer breeding ground. During the brief warm season, the marshy ground supports the aquatic larvae of insects, providing food for migratory waterfowl, and clouds of mosquitoes often fill the tundra air.

? **What three abiotic factors account for the rarity of trees in the arctic tundra?**

▲ **Figure 35.11** Yukon tundra

● Long, very cold winters (short growing season), high winds, and permafrost

35.12 Coniferous forests are often dominated by a few species of trees

Cone-bearing evergreen trees, such as spruce, pine, fir, and hemlock, dominate **coniferous forests**. The northern coniferous forest, referred to as the **boreal forest** or taiga, is the largest terrestrial biome on Earth, stretching in a broad band across North America and Asia south of the Arctic Circle. **Figure 35.12** shows boreal forest in northern Saskatchewan. Boreal forest is also found at cool, high elevations in more temperate latitudes, as in much of the mountainous region of western North America.

The boreal forest is characterized by long, cold winters and short, wet summers, which are sometimes warm. The soil is thin and acidic, and the slow decomposition of conifer needles makes few nutrients available for plant growth. Most of the precipitation is in the form of snow. The conical shape of many conifers prevents too much snow from accumulating on their branches and breaking them. Animals of the boreal forest include moose, elk, hares, bears, wolves, grouse, and migratory birds.

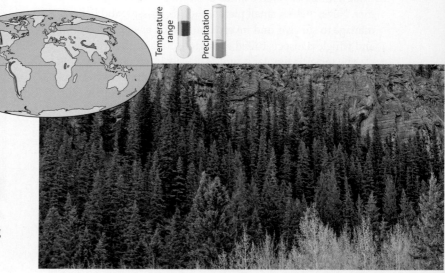

▲ **Figure 35.12** Boreal forest of northern Saskatchewan

The **temperate rainforests** of the Pacific Northwest, along the coastline of British Columbia and the United States, are also coniferous forests. Warm, moist air from the Pacific Ocean supports this unique biome, which, like most coniferous forests, is dominated by a few tree species, such as hemlock, Douglas fir, and cedar. These forests are heavily logged, and the old-growth stands of trees may soon disappear. The mountain pine beetle is also threatening the coniferous forests of British Columbia and Alberta (see the opening essay for Chapter 38).

 How does a boreal forest differ from a temperate rainforest?

● Boreal forests are colder and drier than temperate rainforests.

35.13 Broadleaf trees dominate temperate forests

Temperate broadleaf forests grow throughout midlatitude regions, where there is sufficient moisture to support the growth of large trees. In the Northern Hemisphere, deciduous trees (trees that drop their leaves seasonally) characterize temperate broadleaf forests. Some of the dominant trees include species of maple, poplar, oak, birch, beech, and hickory. The mix of tree species varies widely, depending on such factors as the climate at different latitudes, topography, and local soil conditions. **Figure 35.13** features a photograph taken during the spectacular display of autumn colour in Gatineau Park in Quebec.

Temperatures in temperate broadleaf forests range from very cold in the winter (−30°C) to hot in the summer (30°C). Annual precipitation is relatively high—75–150 cm—and usually evenly distributed throughout the year as either rain or snow. These forests typically have a growing season of five to six months and a distinct annual rhythm. Trees drop their leaves and become dormant in late autumn, preventing the loss of water from the tree at a time when frozen soil makes water less available. The trees produce new leaves in the spring.

The canopy of a temperate broadleaf forest is more open than that of a tropical rainforest, and the trees are not as tall or as diverse. However, their soils are richer in inorganic and organic nutrients. Rates of decomposition are lower in temperate forests than in the tropics, and a thick layer of leaf litter on forest floors conserves many of the biome's nutrients.

Numerous invertebrates live in the soil and leaf litter. Some vertebrates, such as mice, shrews, and ground squirrels, burrow for shelter and food; others, including many species of birds, live in the trees. Predators include bobcats, foxes, black bears, and mountain lions.

▲ **Figure 35.13** Temperate broadleaf forest in Gatineau Park, Quebec

 How does the soil of a temperate broadleaf forest differ from that of a boreal forest?

● The soil in temperate broadleaf forests is rich in inorganic and organic nutrients, while the soil in boreal forests is thin, nutrient-poor, and more acidic.

35.14 Temperate grasslands include the North American prairie

Temperate grasslands are mostly treeless, except along rivers or streams, and are found in regions of relatively cold winter temperatures. Precipitation, averaging between 25 and 75 cm per year, with periodic severe droughts, is too low to support forest growth. Fires and grazing by large mammals also inhibit growth of woody plants but do not harm the belowground grass shoots.

Large grazing mammals, such as the bison and pronghorn of North America and the wild horses and sheep of the Asian steppes, are characteristic of grasslands. Without trees, many birds nest on the ground, and some small mammals dig burrows to escape predators. Enriched by glacial deposits and mulch from decaying plant material, the soil of grasslands supports a great diversity of microorganisms and small animals, including annelids and arthropods.

The amount of annual precipitation influences the height of grassland vegetation. Shortgrass prairie is found in relatively dry regions; tallgrass prairie occurs in wetter areas. **Figure 35.14** shows a mixed-grass prairie in Alberta, Canada. Little remains of North American prairies today. Most of the region is intensively farmed, and it is one of the most productive agricultural regions in the world. The Tall Grass Prairie Preserve in southern Manitoba protects more than 2000 hectares of natural grassland.

 ? What factors inhibit woody plants from growing in temperate grasslands?

Low rainfall, fires, and grazing by large mammals ●

▲ **Figure 35.14** Temperate grassland in Alberta

35.15 Deserts and steppes are defined by their dryness

Deserts are the driest of all terrestrial biomes, characterized by low and unpredictable rainfall (less than 30 cm per year). The large deserts in central Australia and northern Africa have average annual rainfalls of less than 2 cm, and in the Atacama Desert in Chile, the driest place on Earth, there is often no rain at all for decades at a time. But not all desert air is dry. Coastal sections of the Atacama and of the Namib Desert in Africa are often shrouded in fog, although the ground remains extremely dry.

As we discussed in Module 35.5, large tracts of desert occur in two regions of descending dry air centred at the 30° north and 30° south latitudes. At higher latitudes, large deserts may occur in the rain shadows of mountains (see Figure 35.5F); these encompass much of central Asia east of the Caucasus Mountains and in North America, the area east of the Cascade Mountains. The Nk'mip Desert in the Okanagan Valley, British Columbia **(Figure 35.15)**, is in the rain shadow of the Cascades. Although this region is commonly coined Canada's only desert, technically the Nk'mip Desert is a semi-arid biome called a **steppe**, which is an area that receives slightly more precipitation—between 30 and 60 cm annually.

Some deserts, as represented by the temperature icon in Figure 35.15, are very hot, with daytime soil surface temperatures above 60°C and large daily temperature fluctuations. Other deserts, such as those west of the Rocky Mountains, are relatively cold. Air temperatures in cold deserts may fall below –30°C.

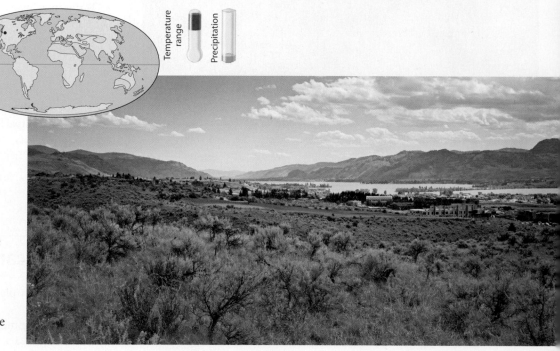

▲ **Figure 35.15** The Nk'mip Desert in British Columbia

The cycles of growth and reproduction in the desert are keyed to rainfall. The driest deserts have no perennial vegetation at all, but less arid regions have scattered deep-rooted shrubs, often interspersed with water-storing succulents such as cacti. To prevent water loss, the leaves of some desert plants have a waxy coating or fine silvery hairs like the sagebrush pictured in Figure 35.15. Desert plants typically produce great numbers of seeds, which may remain dormant until a heavy rain triggers germination. After periods of rainfall (often in late winter), annual plants in deserts may display spectacular blooms.

Like desert plants, desert animals are adapted to drought and extreme temperatures. Many live in burrows and are active only during the cooler nights, and most have special adaptations that conserve water. Seed-eaters such as ants, many birds, and rodents are common in deserts. Lizards, snakes, and hawks eat the seed-eaters.

The process of **desertification**, the conversion of semi-arid steppes to desert, is a significant environmental problem. In northern Africa, for example, a burgeoning human population, overgrazing, and dryland farming are converting large areas of savanna to desert.

 Why isn't "cold desert" an oxymoron?

● Because deserts are defined by low precipitation and dry soil, not by temperature

35.16 Spiny shrubs dominate the chaparral

Chaparral (a Spanish word meaning "place of evergreen scrub oaks") is characterized by dense, spiny shrubs with tough, evergreen leaves. The climate that supports chaparral vegetation results mainly from cool ocean currents circulating offshore, which produce mild, rainy winters and hot, dry summers. As a result, this biome is limited to small coastal areas, including California, where the photograph in **Figure 35.16** was taken. The largest region of chaparral surrounds the Mediterranean Sea; "Mediterranean" is another name for this biome. In addition to the perennial shrubs that dominate chaparral, annual plants are also commonly seen, especially during the wet winter and spring months. Animals characteristic of the chaparral include browsers such as deer, fruit-eating birds, and seed-eating rodents, as well as lizards and snakes.

Chaparral vegetation is adapted to periodic fires, most often caused by lightning. Many plants contain flammable chemicals and burn fiercely, especially where dead brush has accumulated. After a fire, shrubs use food reserves stored in the surviving roots to support rapid shoot regeneration. Some chaparral plant species produce seeds that will germinate only after a hot fire. The ashes of burned vegetation fertilize the soil with mineral nutrients, promoting regrowth of the plant community. Houses do not fare as well, and firestorms that race through the densely populated canyons of Southern California can be devastating.

 What is one way that homeowners in chaparral areas can protect their neighbourhoods from fire?

● They can keep the area clear of dead brush, which is highly flammable.

▲ **Figure 35.16** Chaparral

35.17 Savannas are grasslands with scattered trees

Figure 35.17, a photograph taken in the Serengeti Plain in Tanzania, shows a typical **savanna**, a biome dominated by grasses and scattered trees. The temperature is warm year-round. Rainfall averages 30–50 cm per year, with dramatic seasonal variation. Poor soils and lack of moisture inhibit the establishment of most trees. Grazing animals and frequent fires, caused by lightning or human activity, further inhibit invasion by trees. Grasses survive burning because the growing points of their shoots are below ground. Savanna plants have also been selected for their ability to survive prolonged periods of drought. Many trees and shrubs are deciduous, dropping their leaves during the dry season, an adaptation that helps to conserve water.

Grasses and forbs (small broadleaf plants) grow rapidly during the rainy season, providing a good food source for many animal species. Large grazing mammals must migrate to greener pastures and scattered watering holes during seasonal drought. The dominant herbivores in savannas are actually insects, especially ants and termites. Also common are many burrowing animals, including mice, moles, gophers, snakes, ground squirrels, worms, and numerous arthropods.

Many of the world's large herbivores and their predators inhabit savannas. African savannas are home to giraffes, zebras, and many species of antelope, as well as to lions and cheetahs. Several species of kangaroo are the dominant mammalian herbivores of Australian savannas.

▲ **Figure 35.17** Savanna

? **How do fires help to maintain savannas as grassland ecosystems?**

● By repeatedly preventing the spread of trees and other woody plants; grasses survive because the growing points of their shoots are underground.

35.18 Tropical forests cluster near the equator

Tropical forests occur in equatorial areas where the temperature is warm and days are 11–12 hours long year-round. Rainfall in these areas is quite variable, and this variability, rather than temperature or day length, generally determines the vegetation that grows in a particular tropical forest. In areas where rainfall is scarce or there is a prolonged dry season, tropical dry forests predominate. The plants found there are a mixture of thorny shrubs and deciduous trees and succulents. Tropical rainforests are found in very humid equatorial areas where rainfall is abundant (200–400 cm per year).

Tropical rainforest, such as the lush area on the island of Borneo shown in **Figure 35.18**, is among the most complex

of all biomes, harbouring enormous numbers of different species. Up to 300 species of trees can be found in a single hectare (10 000 m²). The forest structure consists of distinct layers that provide many different habitats: emergent trees growing above a closed upper canopy, one or two layers of lower trees, a shrub understory, and a sparse ground layer of herbaceous plants. Because of the closed canopy, little sunlight reaches the forest floor. Many trees are covered by woody vines growing toward the light. Other plants, including bromeliads and orchids, gain access to sunlight by growing on the branches or the trunks of tall trees. Many of the animals also dwell in trees, where food is abundant. Monkeys, birds, insects, snakes, bats, and frogs find food and shelter many metres above the ground.

The soils of tropical rainforests are typically poor. High temperatures and rainfall lead to rapid decomposition. However, the nutrients released are quickly taken up by the luxuriant vegetation or washed away by the frequent rains.

Human impact on the world's tropical rainforests is an ongoing source of great concern. It is a common practice to clear the forest for lumber or to simply burn it, farm the land for a few years, and then abandon it. Mining has also devastated large tracts of rainforest. Once stripped, the tropical rainforest recovers very slowly because the soil is so nutrient-poor. We will discuss the potential consequences of destroying the tropical forests in Chapter 41, including its impact on world climate.

? **Why are the soils in most tropical rainforests so poor in nutrients that they can support farming only for a few years after the forest is cleared?**

● The conditions favour rapid decomposition of organic litter in the soil and immediate uptake of the resulting nutrients by plants. Thus, most of the ecosystem's nutrients are tied up in the vegetation that is cleared away before farming. Moreover, frequent rain washes nutrients away from soil in cleared areas.

▲ **Figure 35.18** Tropical rainforest

35.19 The global water cycle connects aquatic and terrestrial biomes

Ecological subdivisions such as biomes are not self-contained units. Rather, all parts of the biosphere are linked by the global water cycle, illustrated in **Figure 35.19**, and by nutrient cycles, which you will learn about in Chapter 40. Consequently, events in one biome may reverberate throughout the biosphere.

Recall from Module 35.5 that solar energy helps to drive the movements of water and air in global patterns. In addition, precipitation and evaporation, as well as transpiration from plants (see Module 23.3), continuously move water between the land, oceans, and atmosphere. Over the oceans (left side of Figure 35.19), evaporation exceeds precipitation. The result is a net movement of water vapour to clouds that are carried by winds from the oceans across the land. On land (right side of the figure), precipitation exceeds evaporation and transpiration. Excess precipitation forms systems of surface water (such as lakes and rivers) and groundwater, all of which flow back to the sea, completing the water cycle.

Just as the water draining from your shower carries dead skin cells from your body along with the day's grime, the water washing over and through the ground carries traces of the land and its history. For example, water flowing from land to sea carries with it silt (fine soil particles) and chemicals such as fertilizers and pesticides. The accumulation of silt, aggravated by the development of coastal areas, has muddied the waters of some coral reefs, dimming the light available to the photosynthetic algae that power the reef community. Chemicals in surface water may travel hundreds of kilometres by stream and river to the ocean, where currents then carry them even farther from their point of origin. For instance, in the 1960s, researchers began finding traces of DDT in marine mammals in the Arctic, far from any places DDT had been used (see Module 35.2). Airborne pollutants such as nitrogen oxides and sulphur oxides, which combine with water to form acid precipitation (see Module 2.16), are also distributed by the water cycle.

Human activity also affects the global water cycle itself in a number of important ways. One of the main sources of atmospheric water is transpiration from the dense vegetation making up tropical rainforests. The destruction of these forests changes the amount of water vapour in the air. This, in turn, will likely alter local, and perhaps global, weather patterns. Pumping large amounts of groundwater to the surface for irrigation affects the water cycle, too. This practice can increase the rate of evaporation over land, resulting in higher humidity as well as depleting groundwater supplies. These supplies of surface water and groundwater will also be affected by the melting of glaciers resulting from global climate change (see Module 41.3). As the glaciers melt and disappear, the amount of freshwater they add to the flowing waters will first decrease and then stop completely.

 What is the main way that plants contribute to the water cycle?

Plants move water from the ground to the atmosphere via transpiration.

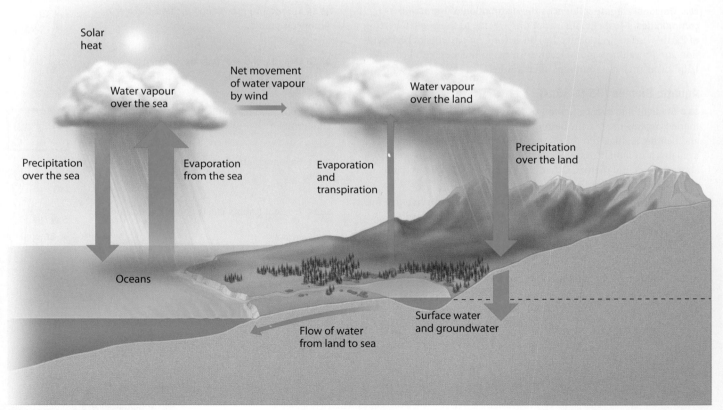

▲ **Figure 35.19** The global water cycle

Reviewing the Concepts

The Biosphere (35.1–35.5)

35.1 Ecologists study how organisms interact with their environment at several levels.

Organismal ecology (individual) — Population ecology (group of individuals of a species) — Community ecology (all organisms in a particular area) — Ecosystem ecology (all organisms and abiotic factors)

35.2 The science of ecology provides insight into environmental problems. Ecologists study all levels from the organism to the ecosystem, and they can identify the impacts that many human activities have on each.

35.3 Physical and chemical factors influence life in the biosphere. Major factors include energy sources, temperature, the presence of water, and inorganic nutrients.

35.4 Organisms adapt to abiotic and biotic factors by means of natural selection. The pronghorn's adaptations show the variety of factors that can affect an organism's fitness.

35.5 Regional climate influences the distribution of terrestrial communities. Most climatic variations are due to the uneven heating of Earth's surface as it orbits the sun, setting up patterns of precipitation and prevailing winds. Ocean currents influence coastal climate. Landforms such as mountains affect rainfall.

Aquatic Biomes (35.6–35.8)

35.6 Sunlight and substrate are key factors in the distribution of marine organisms. Marine biomes are found in both the pelagic and benthic realms, and the biomes are further distinguished by the availability of light. Coral reefs are found in warm, shallow waters above continental shelves. Other marine biomes include wetlands and the intertidal zone.

35.7 Do arctic fishes have anti-freeze? Many fishes survive in water that reaches sub-zero temperatures without their cells freezing by using anti-freeze proteins. The structure of these proteins allows them to bind to small ice crystals, preventing them from growing.

35.8 Current, sunlight, and nutrients are important abiotic factors in freshwater biomes. Standing water biomes (lakes and ponds) differ in structure from flowing water biomes (rivers and streams), and communities vary accordingly. Wetlands include marshes, swamps, and bogs.

Terrestrial Biomes (35.9–35.19)

35.9 Terrestrial biomes reflect regional variations in climate.

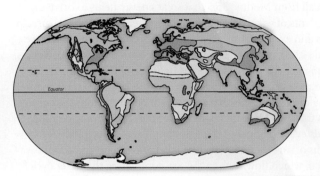

Equator

35.10 Polar ice covers the land at high latitudes.

35.11 Long, bitter-cold winters characterize the tundra.

35.12 Coniferous forests are often dominated by a few species of trees.

35.13 Broadleaf trees dominate temperate forests.

35.14 Temperate grasslands include the North American prairie.

35.15 Deserts and steppes are defined by their dryness.

35.16 Spiny shrubs dominate the chaparral.

35.17 Savannas are grasslands with scattered trees.

35.18 Tropical forests cluster near the equator.

35.19 The global water cycle connects aquatic and terrestrial biomes. All life depends on water. Water is constantly cycling between terrestrial and aquatic ecosystems.

Connecting the Concepts

1. You have seen that Earth's terrestrial biomes reflect regional variations in climate. But what determines these climatic variations? Interpret the following diagrams in reference to global patterns of temperature, rainfall, and winds, as appropriate.

   a. Solar radiation and latitude:

   b. Earth's orbit around the sun:

   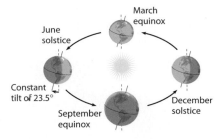

   c. Global patterns of air circulation and rainfall:

2. Aquatic biomes differ in levels of light, nutrients, oxygen, and water movement. These abiotic factors influence the productivity and diversity of freshwater ecosystems.

   a. Productivity, roughly defined as photosynthetic output, is high in estuaries, coral reefs, and shallow ponds. Describe the abiotic factors that contribute to high productivity in these ecosystems.

   b. How does extra input of nitrogen and phosphorus (for instance, by fertilizer runoff) affect the productivity of lakes and ponds? Is this nutrient input beneficial for the ecosystem? Explain.

Testing Your Knowledge

Matching

3. The most complex and diverse biome

4. Ground permanently frozen

5. Deciduous trees such as hickory and birch

6. Mediterranean climate

7. Spruce, fir, pine, and hemlock trees

8. Home of ants, antelopes, and lions

9. North American plains

   a. chaparral
   b. savanna
   c. boreal forest
   d. temperate broadleaf forest
   e. temperate grassland
   f. tropical rainforest
   g. arctic tundra

Multiple Choice

10. Changes in the seasons are caused by
    a. the tilt of Earth's axis toward or away from the sun.
    b. annual cycles of temperature and rainfall.
    c. variation in the distance between Earth and the sun.
    d. an annual cycle in the sun's energy output.
    e. the periodic buildup of heat energy at the equator.

11. What makes the Gobi Desert of Asia a desert?
    a. The growing season there is very short.
    b. Its vegetation is sparse.
    c. It is hot.
    d. Temperatures vary little from summer to winter.
    e. It is dry.

12. Which of the following sea creatures might be described as a pelagic animal of the aphotic zone?
    a. a coral reef fish
    b. a giant clam near a deep-sea hydrothermal vent
    c. an intertidal snail
    d. a deep-sea squid
    e. a harbor seal

13. Why do the tropics and the windward side of mountains receive more rainfall than areas around latitudes 30° north and south and the leeward side of mountains?
    a. Rising warm, moist air cools and drops its moisture as rain.
    b. Descending air condenses, creating clouds and rain.
    c. The tropics and the windward side of mountains are closer to the ocean.
    d. There is more solar radiation in the tropics and on the windward side of mountains.
    e. Earth's rotation creates seasonal differences in rainfall.

14. Phytoplankton are the major photosynthesizers in
    a. the benthic realm of the ocean.
    b. streams.
    c. the ocean photic zone.
    d. the intertidal zone.
    e. the aphotic zone of a lake.

15. An ecologist monitoring the number of gorillas in a wildlife refuge over a five-year period is studying ecology at which level?
    a. organism
    b. population
    c. community
    d. ecosystem
    e. biosphere

16. Many plant species have adaptations for dealing with periodic fires. Such fires are typical of a
    a. chaparral.
    b. savanna.
    c. temperate grassland.
    d. temperate broadleaf forest.
    e. a, b, or c

17. Which of the following statements about the water cycle is correct?
    a. Precipitation is greater than evaporation over the oceans.
    b. Precipitation is greater than evaporation over the land.
    c. Evaporation is greater over land than over the sea.
    d. Precipitation is the only input into surface water and groundwater.
    e. Transpiration is greater over the sea than over the land.

Describing, Comparing, and Explaining

18. Tropical rainforests are the most diverse biomes. What factors contribute to this diversity?

19. What biome do you live in? Describe your climate and the factors that have produced that climate. What plants and animals are typical of this biome? If you live in an urban or agricultural area, how have human interventions changed the natural biome?

Applying the Concepts

20. In the climograph below, biomes are plotted by their range of annual mean temperature and annual mean precipitation. Identify the following biomes: arctic tundra, coniferous forest, desert, grassland, temperate forest, and tropical forest. Explain why there are areas in which biomes overlap on this graph.

21. The North American pronghorn looks and acts like the antelopes of Africa. But the pronghorn is the only survivor of a family of mammals restricted to North America. Propose a hypothesis to explain how these widely separated animals came to be so much alike.

Answers to all questions can be found in Appendix E.

Study on the Go

This QR code leads to Study on the Go—mobile study resources, including practice quizzes, videos, and glossary flashcards for this textbook.

You can access Study on the Go content via your smartphone. Note: Your login information for MasteringBiology is required.

CHAPTER

36

Behavioural Ecology

BIG IDEAS

The Scientific Study of Behaviour

(36.1–36.3)

Behavioural ecologists study behaviour in an evolutionary context, asking both how behaviours are triggered and why behaviours occur.

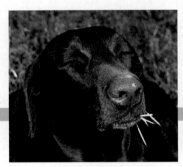

Learning

(36.4–36.11)

Learning, which encompasses a broad range of behaviours, enables animals to change their behaviours in response to changing environmental conditions.

Survival and Reproductive Success

(36.12–36.16)

Many animal behaviours are adaptations that improve the ability to obtain food or increase reproductive success.

Social Behaviour and Sociobiology

(36.17–36.21)

The behaviours of animals that live in groups may include territoriality, conflict resolution, dominance hierarchies, and altruism.

This Is Your Bee on Drugs

Communication is an essential behaviour in social animals, which depend on information from others. One of the most amazing examples of animal communication is found in honeybees (*Apis mellifera*), which have a complex social organization characterized by division of labour. Adult female worker bees leave the hive to forage, bringing back pollen and nectar for the nest. When a forager locates a patch of flowers, she regurgitates some nectar that the others taste and smell, and then communicates the location of the food source by performing a "dance."

Through extensive research, biologists have deciphered the meanings of different honeybee dances. A pattern of movements called the waggle dance communicates the distance and direction of food. The dancer runs a half circle, then turns and runs in a straight line back to her starting point, buzzing her wings and waggling her abdomen as she goes. She then runs a half-circle in the other direction, followed by another waggling run to the starting point. The dance contains all the information other workers need to locate the advertised food source. The length of the straight run and the number of waggles indicate the distance to the food source. The angle of the straight run relative to the vertical surface of the hive is the same as the horizontal angle of the food in relation to the sun. Once the other workers have learned the location of the food source, they leave the hive to forage there.

Australian behavioural scientists studying honeybees discovered that bees do not always dance when they return from foraging. The bees decide whether or not to tell their hive mates about the food source they recently visited based on the quality of the food. Locations of poor quality food will not be advertised, allowing the hive to focus on more rewarding resources. But what if the worker's judgment is impaired by a drug?

Cocaine is a natural compound produced to defend coca plants against insect herbivores. In mammals, high doses of cocaine are extremely toxic, but low doses paradoxically stimulate the reward centre of the brain. It appears that bees also have a reward centre, which can be hijacked by cocaine. The reward centre motivates many behaviours, including food acquisition and reproduction. This connection increases the likelihood that bees will repeat these behaviours.

When low doses of cocaine are given to bees, lower quality food stimulates their reward centre: They think food they find is better than it actually is. When they return to the hive, they are several times more likely to dance than an untreated bee that visited the same resource. The drugged bees do not dance uncontrollably. The dances still contain all the pertinent information for other workers to find the source. If the quality of food is extremely poor, even cocaine-drugged bees will not dance.

Further study of the reward system in the simple brain of the honeybee may help scientists better understand addiction in humans. In this chapter, you will learn how behavioural ecologists explain such strikingly different adaptations for maximizing reproductive success. You will also learn about several other categories of behaviour, including learning.

The Scientific Study of Behaviour

36.1 Behavioural ecologists ask both proximate and ultimate questions

Behaviour encompasses a wide range of activities. At its most basic level, a behaviour is an action carried out by muscles or glands under the control of the nervous system in response to an environmental cue. Collectively, behaviour is the sum of an animal's responses to internal and external environmental cues. Although we commonly think of behaviour in terms of observable actions—for instance, a courtship dance or an aggressive posture—other activities are also considered behaviours. Chemical communication, such as secreting a chemical that attracts mates or marks a territory, is a form of behaviour. Learning is also considered a behavioural process.

The foundation for the scientific study of behaviour was established in the mid-20th century with the work of Karl von Frisch and Konrad Lorenz, of Austria, and Niko Tinbergen, of the Netherlands. These researchers shared a Nobel Prize in 1973 for their discoveries in animal behaviour. Von Frisch, who pioneered the use of experimental methods in behaviour, studied honeybee behaviour in detail. Lorenz, often regarded as the founder of behavioural biology, emphasized the importance of studying and comparing the behaviour of various animals in response to different stimuli. Tinbergen worked closely with Lorenz, concentrating on experimental studies of inborn behaviour and simple forms of learning.

Behavioural ecology is the study of behaviour in an evolutionary context. Behavioural ecologists draw on the knowledge of a variety of disciplines to describe the details of animal behaviours and investigate how they develop, evolve, and contribute to the animal's survival and reproductive success.

The questions investigated by behavioural ecologists fall into two broad categories. **Proximate questions** concern the immediate reason for a behaviour—how it is triggered by **stimuli** (environmental cues that cause a response), what physiological or anatomical mechanisms play a role, and what underlying genetic factors are at work. For example, researchers studying the mating pattern of prairie voles might ask,

"How do voles choose their mates?" or "How does the act of mating cause voles to form lifelong bonds with their partners?" or "How are genetic factors involved in mating behaviour?" Generally, proximate questions help us understand *how* a behaviour occurs. **Proximate causes** are the answers to such questions about the immediate mechanism for a behaviour.

Ultimate questions address *why* a particular behaviour occurs. As a component of the animal's phenotype, behaviours are adaptations that have been shaped by natural selection. The answers to ultimate questions, or **ultimate causes**, are evolutionary explanations—they lie in the adaptive value of the behaviour. For example, researchers think that at some point in their evolutionary history, the ancestors of prairie voles had numerous sexual partners, like the overwhelming majority of mammals. Why did natural selection favour the change in mating behaviour? To explore this ultimate question, researchers test hypotheses on the adaptive value of prairie voles' bonding behaviour. For example, perhaps male prairie voles that form lasting bonds have greater reproductive success because they prevent other males from getting close to their mates. An experiment to determine whether a female vole would have sexual intercourse with other males if she were not constantly accompanied by her mate would shed light on one possible adaptive value of bond formation by males.

In the next module, we look at a type of behaviour that demonstrates the complementary nature of proximate and ultimate questions.

 ? When you touch a hot plate, your arm automatically recoils. What might be the proximate and ultimate causes of this behaviour?

● The proximate cause is a simple reflex, a neural pathway linking stimulation of receptors in your finger to a motor response by muscles of your arm and hand; the ultimate cause is natural selection for a behaviour that minimizes damage to the body, thereby contributing to survival and reproductive success.

36.2 Fixed action patterns are innate behaviours

One important proximate question is how a behaviour develops during an animal's lifespan. Lorenz and Tinbergen were among the first to demonstrate the importance of **innate behaviour**, behaviour that is under strong genetic control and is performed in virtually the same way by all individuals of a species. Many of Lorenz's and Tinbergen's studies were concerned with behavioural sequences called **fixed action patterns (FAPs)**. A FAP is an unchangeable series of actions triggered by a specific **sign stimulus**. Once initiated, the sequence is performed in its entirety, regardless of any changes in circumstances. Consider a coffee vending machine as an analogy. The purchaser feeds money into the machine and presses a button. Having received this stimulus, the machine performs

a series of actions: drops a cup into place; releases a specific volume of coffee; adds cream; adds sugar. Once the stimulus—in this case, the money—triggers the mechanism, it carries out its complete program. Likewise, FAPs are behavioural routines that are completed in full.

Figure 36.2A illustrates one of the FAPs that Lorenz and Tinbergen studied in detail. The bird is the greylag goose, a common European species that nests in shallow depressions on the ground. If the goose happens to bump one of her eggs out of the nest, she always retrieves it in the same manner. As shown in the figure, she stands up, extends her neck, uses a side-to-side head motion to nudge the egg back with her beak, and then sits down on the nest again. If the egg slips away (or is

▲ **Figure 36.2A** A greylag goose retrieving an egg—a FAP

pulled away by an experimenter) while the goose is retrieving it, she continues as though the egg were still there. Only after she sits back down on her eggs does she seem to notice that the egg is still outside the nest. Then she begins another retrieval sequence. If the egg is again pulled away, the goose repeats the retrieval motion without the egg. A goose would even perform the sequence when Lorenz and Tinbergen placed a foreign object, such as a small toy or a ball, near her nest. The goose performs the series of actions regardless of the absence of an egg, just as a coffee vending machine does when the cup dispenser is empty—the coffee, cream, and sugar are poured anyway.

In its simplest form, a FAP is an innate response to a certain stimulus. For the greylag goose, the stimulus for egg retrieval is the presence of an egg (or other object) near the nest. Such relatively simple, innate behaviours seem to occur in all animals. When a baby bird senses that an adult bird is near, it responds with a FAP: It begs for food by raising its head, opening its mouth, and cheeping. In turn, the parent responds with another FAP: It stuffs food into the gaping mouth. Humans perform FAPs, too. Infants grasp strongly with their fingers in response to a touch stimulus on the palm of the hand. They smile in response to a face or even something that vaguely resembles a face, such as two dark spots in a circle.

Although a single FAP is typically a simple behaviour, complex behaviours can result from several FAPs performed sequentially. Many vertebrates engage in courtship rituals that consist of chains of FAPs, as you will learn in Module 36.14. The completion of a single FAP by one partner cues the other partner to begin its next FAP. There is some flexibility in these patterns. For example, a segment of the pattern might be repeated if the partner does not readily respond.

What might be the ultimate causes of FAPs? Automatically performing certain behaviours may maximize fitness to the point that genes that result in variants of that behaviour do not persist in the population. For example, a young animal has to get some things right on the first try if it is to stay alive. Consider kittiwakes, gulls that nest on cliff ledges. Unlike other gull species, kittiwakes show an innate aversion to cliff edges; they turn away from the edge. Chicks in earlier generations that did not show this edge-aversion response would not have lived to pass on the genes for their risk-taking behaviour to the next generation.

FAPs for reproductive behaviours are also under strong selection pressure. One example is the behaviour of mated king penguins. Each member of the pair takes a turn incubating their egg while its mate feeds (**Figure 36.2B**). Standing face-to-face, the pair must execute a delicate series of manoeuvres to pass the egg from the tops of one penguin's feet to the tops of

its partner's feet, where the egg will incubate in a snug fold of the abdominal skin. (You may have seen emperor penguins engage in this behaviour in the film *The March of the Penguins*.) If either partner makes a mistake, the egg may roll onto the ice, where it can freeze in seconds, eliminating the pair's only chance of successful reproduction for the year.

Innate behaviours are under strong genetic control, but the animal's performance of most innate behaviours also improves with experience. And despite the genetic component, input from the environment—an object or sensory stimulus, for example—is required to trigger the behaviour. In the next module, we look at the interaction of genes and environment in producing a behaviour.

? **How would you explain FAPs in the context of proximate and ultimate causes?**

● The proximate cause of a FAP is often a simple environmental cue. The ultimate cause is that natural selection favours behaviours that enable animals to perform tasks essential to survival without any previous experience.

▲ **Figure 36.2B** A pair of king penguins transferring their egg

36.3 Behaviour is the result of both genetic and environmental factors

Evolutionary explanations for behaviour assume that it has a genetic basis. Many scientific studies have corroborated that specific behaviours do indeed have a genetic component. Until recently, though, the heritability of a trait could be estimated only by traditional methods such as constructing pedigrees and performing breeding experiments. With the tools of molecular genetics, scientists have begun to investigate the roles of specific genes in behaviour.

Groundbreaking experiments with fruit flies have led to the discovery of genes that govern learning, memory, internal clocks, and courtship and mating behaviours. For example, a male fruit fly courts a female with an elaborate series of actions that include tapping the female's abdomen with a foreleg and vibrating one of his wings in a courtship "song." Researchers identified a master gene known as *fruitless* (*fru* for short), which in males encodes a protein that switches on a suite of genes responsible for courtship behaviour (Table 36.3). Male fruit flies that possess a mutated version of *fru* attempt to court other male flies. In females, the protein encoded by *fru* is different from the male version of the protein. But when researchers used genetic engineering to produce female flies that made the male *fru* protein, the females behaved like normal males, vigorously courting other females.

Some of the genes governing fruit fly behaviour have counterparts in mice and even in humans. The genetic underpinnings of courtship and mating behaviours in mammals are probably quite different from those of flies, but research on genes implicated in learning and memory has yielded promising results. By studying fruit fly mutants with colourful names

TABLE 36.3

COURTSHIP BEHAVIOUR OF FRUIT FLIES WITH NORMAL OR MUTATED *FRUITLESS* (*FRU*) GENE

	Male	Genetically Altered Female
Normal male *fru*	Courts females	Courts females
Mutated male *fru*	Courts males	—

such as *dunce*, *amnesiac*, and *rutabaga*, scientists have identified key components of memory storage and have even used genetic engineering to produce fruit flies that have exceptionally good memories. Similar genes and their protein products have been identified in mice and humans, sparking a flood of research on memory-enhancing drugs. Such drugs could improve the quality of life for people suffering from Alzheimer's and other neurological diseases that impair memory.

Phenotype depends on the environment as well as genes, as we discussed in Chapter 9. Many environmental factors, including diet and social interactions, can modify how genetic instructions are carried out. In some animals, even an individual's sex can be determined by the environment. For example, sex determination in some reptiles depends on the temperature of the egg during embryonic development.

Let's look at a study that illustrates the influence of environment on behaviour (Figure 36.3). Some female Norway

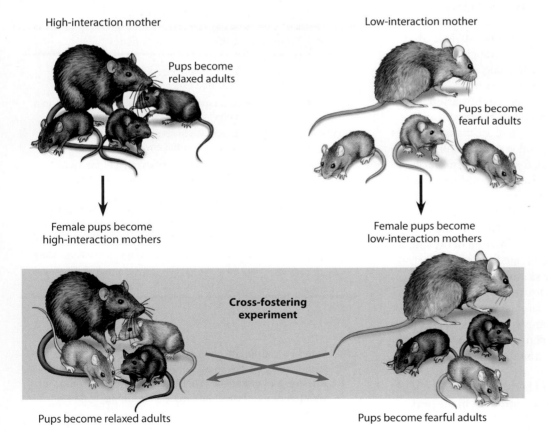

High-interaction mother
Pups become relaxed adults
Female pups become high-interaction mothers

Low-interaction mother
Pups become fearful adults
Female pups become low-interaction mothers

◀ **Figure 36.3** A cross-fostering experiment with rats

Cross-fostering experiment

Pups become relaxed adults
Pups become fearful adults

rats (*Rattus norvegicus*) spend a great deal of time licking and grooming their offspring (called pups), while others have little interaction with their pups. Pups raised by these "low-interaction" mothers tend to be more sensitive as adults to stimuli that trigger the "fight-or-flight" stress response (see Module 29.10) and thus are more fearful and anxious in new situations. Female pups from these litters become low-interaction mothers themselves. On the contrary, pups with "high-interaction" mothers are more relaxed in stressful situations as adults, and the female pups from these litters become high-interaction mothers.

To investigate whether these responses to stress are entirely determined by genetics or are influenced by the interactions with their mothers, researchers performed "cross-fostering" experiments. They placed pups born to high-interaction mothers in nests with low-interaction mothers, and pups born to low-interaction mothers in nests with high-interaction mothers. As adults, the cross-fostered rats responded to stress more like their foster mothers than like their biological mothers. The results showed that the pups' environment—in this case maternal behaviour—was the determining factor in their anxiety level. Remarkably, these experiments also demonstrated that behavioural changes can be passed to future generations, not

through genes, but through the social environment. When the female rats that had been fostered gave birth, they showed the same degree of interaction with their pups as their foster mothers had shown with them. In further studies, researchers learned that interaction with the mother changes the pattern of gene expression in the pups, thus affecting the development of parts of the neuroendocrine system that regulate the fight-or-flight response.

These experiments and others provide evidence that behaviour is the product of both genetic *and* environmental factors. Indeed, the interaction of genes and the environment appears to determine most animal behaviours. One of the most powerful ways that the environment can influence behaviour is through learning, the topic we consider next.

? **Without doing any experiments, how might you distinguish between a behaviour that is mostly controlled by genes and one that is mostly determined by the environment?**

● In many cases, genetically controlled behaviour would not differ much between populations, regardless of the environment, while the environmentally controlled behaviour would differ widely across populations located in different environments.

Learning

36.4 Habituation is a simple type of learning

Learning is modification of behaviour as a result of specific experiences. Learning enables animals to change their behaviours in response to changing environmental conditions. As **Table 36.4** indicates, there are various forms of learning, ranging from a simple behavioural change in response to a single stimulus, to complex problem solving that uses entirely new behaviours.

One of the simplest forms of learning is **habituation**, in which an animal learns not to respond to a repeated stimulus that conveys little or no information. There are many examples of habituation in both invertebrate and vertebrate animals. The cnidarian *Hydra* (see Figure 20.6A), for example, contracts when disturbed by a slight touch; it stops responding, however, if disturbed repeatedly by such a stimulus. Similarly, stimulus from a sound machine mimicking a predator will usually make birds avoid a tree with ripe fruit for a few days. But the birds soon become habituated to the constant location of the sound and return to the orchard. Once habituated to a particular stimulus, an animal still senses the stimulus—its sensory organs detect it—but the animal has learned not to respond to it.

In terms of ultimate causation, habituation may increase fitness by allowing an animal's nervous system to focus on stimuli that signal food, mates, or real danger and not waste time or energy on a vast number of other stimuli that are irrelevant to survival and reproduction.

Proximate and ultimate causes of behaviour are also evident in imprinting, the type of learning we introduce in the next module.

TABLE 36.4 | TYPES OF LEARNING

Learning Type	Defining Characteristics
Habituation	Loss of response to a stimulus after repeated exposure
Imprinting	Learning that is irreversible and limited to a sensitive time period in an animal's life
Spatial learning	Use of landmarks to learn the spatial structure of the environment
Cognitive mapping	An internal representation of the spatial relationships among objects in the environment
Associative learning	Behavioural change based on linking a stimulus or behaviour with a reward or punishment; includes trial-and-error learning
Social learning	Learning by observing and mimicking others
Problem solving	Inventive behaviour that arises in response to a new situation

? **Your new roommate hums continuously while studying. You found this habit extremely annoying at first, but after a while you stopped noticing it. What kind of learning accounts for your tolerance of your roommate's humming?**

● Habituation

36.5 Imprinting requires both innate behaviour and experience

Learning often interacts closely with innate behaviour. Some of the most interesting examples of such an interaction involve the phenomenon known as imprinting. **Imprinting** is learning that is limited to a specific time period in an animal's life and that is generally irreversible. The limited phase in an animal's development when it can learn certain behaviours is called the **sensitive period**.

In classic experiments done in the 1930s, Konrad Lorenz used the greylag goose to demonstrate imprinting. When incubator-hatched goslings spent their first few hours with Lorenz, rather than with their mother, they steadfastly followed Lorenz (**Figure 36.5A**) and showed no recognition of their mother or other adults of their species. Even as adults, the birds continued to prefer the company of Lorenz and other humans to that of geese.

Lorenz demonstrated that the most important imprinting stimulus for greylag geese was movement of an object (normally the parent bird) away from the hatchlings. The effect of movement was increased if the moving object emitted some sound. The sound did not have to be that of a goose, however; Lorenz found that a box with a ticking clock in it was readily and permanently accepted as a "mother."

Just as a young bird requires imprinting to know its parents, the adults must also imprint to recognize their young. For a day or two after their own chicks hatch, adult herring gulls will accept and even defend a strange chick introduced into their nesting territory. However, once imprinted on their offspring, adults will kill any strange chicks that arrive later.

Not all examples of imprinting involve parent-offspring bonding. Newly hatched salmon, for instance, do not receive parental care but seem to imprint on the complex mixture of odours unique to their stream. This imprinting enables adult salmon to find their way back to their home stream to spawn after spending a year or more at sea.

For many kinds of birds, imprinting plays a role in song development. For example, researchers studying song development in white-crowned sparrows found that male birds memorize the song of their species during a sensitive period (the first 50 days of life). They do not sing during this phase, but several months later they begin to practice this song, eventually learning to reproduce it correctly. The birds do not need to hear the adult song during their practice phase; isolated males raised in soundproof chambers learned to sing normally as long as they had heard a recorded song of their species during the sensitive period (**Figure 36.5B**, top sonogram). In contrast, isolated males that did not hear their species' song until they were more than 50 days old sang an abnormal song (Figure 36.5B, bottom). Researchers also discovered a purely genetic component of white-crowned sparrow song development: Isolated males exposed to recorded songs of *other* species during the sensitive period did not adopt these foreign songs. When they later learned to sing, these birds sang an abnormal song similar to that of the isolated males of their own species that had heard no recorded bird songs.

The ability of parents and offspring to keep track of each other and the ability of male songbirds to attract mates are examples of behaviours that have direct and immediate effects on survival and reproduction. Imprinting provides a way for such behaviour to become more or less fixed in an animal's nervous system.

? Explain why we say that imprinting has both innate and learned components.

● Its innate component is the tendency to imprint on a stimulus during a sensitive period. The imprinting itself is a form of learning.

▲ **Figure 36.5B** The songs of male white-crowned sparrows that heard an adult sing during the sensitive period (top) and after the sensitive period (bottom)

▲ **Figure 36.5A** Konrad Lorenz with geese imprinted on him

36.6 Imprinting poses problems and opportunities for conservation programs

In attempting to save species that are at the edge of extinction, biologists sometimes try to increase the species' numbers in captivity. Generally, the strategy of a captive breeding program is to provide a safe environment for infants and juveniles, the stages at which many animals are most vulnerable to predation and other risks. In some programs, adult animals are caught and kept in conditions that are conducive to breeding. Offspring are usually raised by the parents and may be kept for breeding or released back to the wild. In other programs, parents are absent, as when eggs are removed from a nest. Artificial incubation is often successful, but without parents available as models for imprinting, the offspring may not learn appropriate behaviours. The effort to save the whooping crane is one example of a program that has successfully used surrogate parents, though they are a bit unusual.

The whooping crane (*Grus americana*) is a migratory waterfowl that reaches a height of about 1.5 m and has a white body with black-tipped wings that spread out over 2 m. Its name comes from its distinctive call. Once common in North American skies during their north-south migrations, whooping cranes were almost killed off by habitat loss and hunting. By the 1940s, only 16 wild birds returned from their summer breeding ground in Wood Buffalo National Park in Alberta and the Northwest Territories to one of their wintering areas on the Texas coast. Because a whooping crane does not reach sexual maturity until it is four years old, new generations of birds are not produced quickly. And although whooping cranes often lay two eggs, parents usually successfully rear only one chick. Protections for whooping cranes were established, and in 1967, Canadian and U.S. wildlife officials launched long-term recovery and captive breeding efforts.

At first, biologists used sandhill cranes as surrogate parents for whooping crane chicks. All went well until the whooping cranes reached maturity. Having imprinted on the sandhill cranes, the whooping cranes showed no interest in breeding with their own kind. Biologists realized that they needed another approach. With plans to set up a separate breeding colony of whooping cranes in Wisconsin, they turned to Operation Migration to help get the birds to a winter nesting site in Florida. This bird advocacy group, based in Ontario, had developed ways to hatch geese and sandhill cranes, to teach the birds to recognize a small, lightweight plane as a parent figure, and to train them to follow the plane along migratory routes.

In 2001, Operation Migration applied its techniques to whooping cranes. Incubating crane eggs were serenaded with recorded sounds of a plane's engine. When the chicks emerged from their shells, the first thing they saw was a hand puppet, shaped and painted in the form of an adult whooping crane. As the chicks grew, the same type of puppet guided them through exercise and training (**Figure 36.6A**). But now the puppet was attached to a plane that rolled along the ground, coaxing the chicks to follow it. To make sure the birds bonded with the puppet and plane and not humans, pilots and other members of Operation

▲ **Figure 36.6A** A whooping crane chick interacting with a puppet "parent"

Migration were cloaked in hooded suits. Eventually, the birds started following the plane on short flights (**Figure 36.6B**).

October 2001 brought the real test. Would the young whooping cranes follow the plane from their protected grounds in Wisconsin along a migratory route to Florida? The trip took 48 days but ultimately proved successful. Each flight day, the young cranes lined up eagerly behind the plane, wings raised, ready to follow their "parent" to the next stop. And the next spring, five of the eight young cranes retraced the route to Wisconsin on their own. Operation Migration has since taught several more generations of whooping cranes to migrate, boosting the species' chances of survival. At the end of 2012, there were about 437 whooping cranes in the wild.

 What features of whooping cranes have made their recovery difficult?

● They do not breed until four years of age and usually raise only one chick each breeding season. As migratory birds, they require resources and protection in two habitats.

▲ **Figure 36.6B** Whooping cranes following a surrogate parent

36.7 Animal movement may be a simple response to stimuli or require spatial learning

Moving in a directed way enables animals to avoid predators, migrate to a more favourable environment, obtain food, and find mates and nest sites. The simplest kinds of movement do not involve learning. A random movement in response to a stimulus is called a **kinesis** (plural, *kineses*; from the Greek word for "movement"). A kinesis may be merely starting or stopping, changing speed, or turning more or less frequently. Sow bugs **(Figure 36.7A)**, which are small terrestrial crustaceans, are not as well protected from drying out as their insect cousins. Consequently, they typically live in moist habitats, such as the underside of rocks or logs. In a dry area, sow bugs exhibit kinesis, becoming more active and moving about randomly. The more they move, the greater their chance of finding a moist area. Once they are in a more favourable environment, their decreased activity tends to keep them there.

▲ **Figure 36.7A** A sow bug (also known as a roly-poly or a woodlouse)

In contrast to kineses, a **taxis** (plural, *taxes*; from the Greek *tasso*, put in order) is a response directed toward (positive taxis) or away from (negative taxis) a stimulus. For example, many stream fish, such as salmon, exhibit positive taxis in the current; they automatically swim or orient in an upstream direction **(Figure 36.7B)**. This orientation keeps them from being swept away by the current and keeps them facing in the direction food is likely to come from.

In **spatial learning**, animals establish memories of landmarks in their environment that indicate the locations of food, nest sites, prospective mates, and potential hazards. **Figure 36.7C** illustrates a classic experiment Tinbergen performed to investigate spatial learning in an insect called the digger wasp. The female digger wasp builds its nest in a small burrow in the ground. She will often excavate four or five separate nests and fly to each one daily, cleaning them and bringing food to the larvae in the nests. Before leaving each nest, she hides the entrance. To test his hypothesis that the digger wasp uses landmarks to keep track of her nests, ❶ Tinbergen placed a circle of pinecones around a nest opening and waited for the mother wasp to return and tend the nest. After the wasp flew away, ❷ Tinbergen moved the pinecones about a metre to one side of the nest opening. The next time the wasp returned, she flew to the centre of the pinecone circle instead of to the actual nest opening.

This experiment indicated that the wasp did use landmarks and that she could learn new ones to keep track of her nests. Next, to test whether the wasp was responding to the pinecones themselves or to their circular arrangement, ❸ Tinbergen arranged the pinecones in a triangle around the nest and made a circle of small stones to one side of the nest opening. This time, the wasp flew to the stones, indicating that her cue was the *arrangement* of the landmarks rather than their appearance.

While many animals find their way by learning the particular set of landmarks in their area, others appear to use more sophisticated navigation mechanisms, as we see next.

? Planarians (see Figure 20.7A) move directly away from light into dark places. What type of movement is this?

● Negative taxis (directed movement away from light)

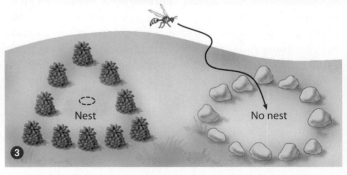

▲ **Figure 36.7C** The nest-locating behaviour of the digger wasp

▲ **Figure 36.7B** Salmon exhibiting positive taxis to a current as they swim upstream to spawn

Direction of river current

36.8 Movements of animals may depend on cognitive maps

An animal can move around its environment by using landmarks alone. Honeybees, for instance, might learn 10 or so landmarks and locate their hive and flowers in relation to those features. An even more powerful mechanism is a **cognitive map**, an internal representation, or code, of the spatial relationships among objects in an animal's surroundings.

It is actually very difficult to distinguish experimentally between an animal that is simply using landmarks and one that is using a true cognitive map. The best evidence for cognitive maps comes from research on the family of birds that includes jays, crows, and nutcrackers. Many of these birds hide food in caches. A single bird may store nuts in thousands of caches that may be widely dispersed. The bird not only finds each cache, but also keeps track of food quality, bypassing caches in which the food was relatively perishable and would have decayed. It would seem that these birds use cognitive maps to memorize the locations of their food stores.

The most extensive studies of cognitive maps have involved animals that exhibit **migration**, the regular back-and-forth movement of animals between two geographic areas. Migration enables many species, such as the whooping cranes discussed in Module 36.6, to access food resources throughout the year and to breed or winter in areas that favour survival.

A notable long-distance traveller is the grey whale. During the summer, these giant mammals feast on small, bottom-dwelling invertebrates that abound in northern oceans. In the autumn, they leave their feeding grounds north of Alaska and begin the long trip south along the North American coastline to winter in the warm lagoons of Baja California (Mexico). Females give birth there before migrating back north with their young. The yearly round trip, some 20 000 km, is the longest made by any mammal.

Researchers have found that migrating animals stay on course by using a variety of cues. Grey whales seem to use the coastline to pilot their way north and south. Whale watchers sometimes see grey whales stick their heads straight up out of the water, perhaps to obtain a visual reference point on land. Grey whales may also use the topography of the ocean floor, cues from the temperature and chemistry of the water, and magnetic sensing to guide their journey.

Many birds migrate at night, navigating by the stars the way early sailors did. Navigating by the sun or stars requires an internal timing device to compensate for the continuous daily movement of celestial objects. Consider what would happen if you started walking one day, orienting yourself by keeping the sun on your left. In the morning, you would be heading south, but by evening you would be heading back north, having made a circle and gotten nowhere. A calibration mechanism must also allow for the apparent change in position of celestial objects as the animal moves over its migration route.

At least one night-migrating bird, the indigo bunting, seems to avoid the need for a timing mechanism by fixing on the North Star, the one bright star in northern skies that appears almost stationary. **Figure 36.8** illustrates an experimental setup that was used to study the bunting's navigational mechanism.

During the migratory season, wild and laboratory-reared buntings were placed in funnel-shaped cages in a planetarium. Each funnel had an ink pad at its base and was lined with blotting paper. When a bird stepped on the ink pad and then tried to fly in a certain direction, it tracked ink on the paper. The researchers found that wild buntings tracked ink in the direction of the North Star, as did those raised in the lab and introduced to the northern sky in a planetarium. Furthermore, researchers found that buntings raised under a planetarium sky with a different fixed-location star oriented to that star. Apparently, buntings learn to construct a star map and guide on a stationary star.

Some animals appear to migrate using only innate responses to environmental cues. For example, each fall, a new generation of monarch butterflies flies about 4000 km over a route they have never flown before to specific wintering sites. Studies of other animals, including some songbirds, show the interaction of genes and experience in migration. Research efforts continue to reveal the complex mechanisms by which animals traverse Earth.

? Why is a timekeeping mechanism essential for navigating by the stars?

● Because the positions of the stars change with time of night and season

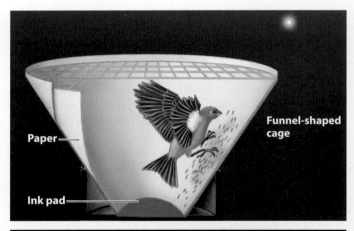

Paper

Funnel-shaped cage

Ink pad

▲ **Figure 36.8** An indigo bunting in an experimental funnel (top); a researcher setting up funnels in the planetarium (bottom)

36.9 Animals may learn to associate a stimulus or behaviour with a response

Associative learning is the ability to associate one environmental feature with another. In one type of associative learning, an animal learns to link a particular stimulus to a particular outcome. If you keep a pet, you have probably observed this type of associative learning firsthand. A dog or cat will learn to associate a particular sound, word, or gesture (stimulus) with a specific punishment or reward (outcome). For example, the sound of a can being opened may bring a cat running for food.

In the other type of associative learning, called **trial-and-error learning**, an animal learns to associate one of its own behaviours with a positive or negative effect. The animal then tends to repeat the response if it is rewarded or avoid the response if it is harmed. For example, predators quickly learn to associate certain kinds of prey with painful experiences. A porcupine's sharp quills and ability to roll into a quill-covered ball are strong deterrents against many predators. Coyotes, mountain lions, and domestic dogs often learn the hard way to avoid attacking porcupines nose-first (**Figure 36.9**).

Memory is the key to all associative learning. The prairie vole, where the female becomes sexually receptive from the scent of a partner, provides insight into the mechanisms involved. During mating, three neurochemical events occur simultaneously: Neural reward circuits are activated; olfactory signals identify the partner; and hormones are released in the brain. The brain of the monogamous prairie vole has dense clusters of hormone receptors in the area associated with social memory. As a result, the brain forms a memory that connects

▲ **Figure 36.9** Trial-and-error learning by a dog

the reward to the current partner's scent. Other species of vole are promiscuous—they mate with multiple partners and form no lasting bonds. Promiscuous voles experience the same biochemical reward during the act of mating but have very few hormone receptors in the area of the brain associated with social memory. Thus, the brain fails to forge a link between the partner and the reward.

? **How might the fact that many bad-tasting or stinging insect species have similar colour patterns benefit both the insects and the animals that may prey on them?**

● Potential predators associate insects displaying that coloration with a negative effect, and consequently, all these insects are less likely to be preyed on.

36.10 Social learning employs observation and imitation of others

Another form of learning is **social learning**—learning by observing the behaviour of others. Many predators, including cats, coyotes, and wolves, seem to learn some of their basic hunting tactics by observing and imitating their mothers.

Studies of the alarm calls of vervet monkeys in Amboseli National Park, in Kenya, provide an interesting example of how performance of a behaviour can improve through social learning. Vervet monkeys (*Cercopithecus aethiops*) are about the size of a domestic cat. They give distinct alarm calls when they see leopards, eagles, or snakes, all of which prey on vervets. When a vervet sees a leopard, it gives a loud barking sound; when it sees an eagle, it gives a short two-syllable cough; and the snake alarm call is a "chutter." Upon hearing a particular alarm call, other vervets in the group behave in an appropriate way: They run up a tree on hearing the alarm for a leopard (vervets are nimbler than leopards in trees); look up on hearing the alarm for an eagle; and look down on hearing the alarm for a snake (**Figure 36.10**).

Infant vervet monkeys give alarm calls, but in a relatively undiscriminating way. For example, they give the "eagle" alarm on seeing any bird, including harmless birds such as bee-eaters. With age, the monkeys improve their accuracy. In fact, adult

▲ **Figure 36.10** On seeing a python (foreground), a vervet monkey gives a distinct "snake" alarm call (inset)

vervet monkeys give the eagle alarm only on seeing an eagle belonging to either of the two species that eat vervets. Infants probably learn how to give the right call by observing other members of the group and by receiving social confirmation. For instance, if the infant gives the call on the right occasion—an eagle alarm when there is an eagle overhead—another member of the group will also give the eagle call. But if the infant gives the call when a bee-eater flies by, the adults in the group are silent. Thus, vervet monkeys have an initial, unlearned tendency to give calls on seeing potentially threatening objects in the environment. Learning fine-tunes the calls so that by adulthood, vervets give calls only in response to genuine danger and are prepared to fine-tune the alarm calls of the next generation.

Dr. James Hare at the University of Manitoba has documented similar social learning in a species closer to home, the Richardson's ground squirrel (*Urocitellus richardsonii*). Calls by these squirrels also relay information about types of threat. Untrustworthy individuals, those who "cry wolf" when there is no threat, are eventually ignored. However, neither vervets, ground squirrels, nor any other species comes close to matching the social learning and cultural transmission that occurs among humans, a topic we will explore later in the chapter.

? **What type of learning in humans is exemplified by identification with a role model?**

● Social learning (observation and imitation)

36.11 Problem-solving behaviour relies on cognition

A broad definition of **cognition** is the process carried out by an animal's nervous system to perceive, store, integrate, and use information gathered by the senses. One area of research in the study of animal cognition is how an animal's brain represents physical objects in the environment. For instance, some researchers have discovered that many animals, including insects, are capable of categorizing objects in their environment according to concepts such as "same" and "different." One research team has trained honeybees to match colours and black-and-white patterns. Other researchers have developed innovative experiments, in the tradition of Lorenz and Tinbergen, for demonstrating pattern recognition in birds called nuthatches. These studies suggest that nuthatches apply simple geometric rules to locate their many seed caches.

Some animals have complex cognitive abilities that include **problem solving**—the process of applying past experience to overcome obstacles in novel situations. Problem-solving behaviour is highly developed in some mammals, especially dolphins, elephants, and primates. If a chimpanzee is placed in a room with a banana hung high above its head and several boxes on the floor, the chimp will assess the situation and then stack the boxes in order to reach the food. One way many animals learn to solve problems is by observing the behaviour of other individuals. For example, young chimpanzees can learn how to crack oil palm nuts by using two stones as a hammer and anvil from watching their elders (**Figure 36.11A**).

Problem-solving behaviour has also been observed in some bird species. For example, researchers placed ravens in situations in which they had to obtain food hanging from a string. Interestingly, the researchers observed a great deal of variation in the ravens' solutions. The raven in **Figure 36.11B** used one foot to pull up the string incrementally and the other foot to secure the string so the food did not drop. An excellent test of human cognition and problem-solving behaviour is in the construction of experiments that allow us to explore the cognition and problem-solving behaviour of other animals!

? **Besides problem solving, what other type of learning is illustrated in Figure 36.11A?**

● Social learning (observation)

▲ **Figure 36.11A** A chimpanzee solving a problem

▲ **Figure 36.11B** A raven solving a problem

Survival and Reproductive Success

36.12 Behavioural ecologists use cost-benefit analysis to study foraging

Because adequate nutrition is essential to an animal's survival and reproductive success, we should expect natural selection to refine behaviours that enhance the efficiency of feeding. Food-obtaining behaviour, or **foraging**, includes not only eating, but also any mechanism an animal uses to search for, recognize, and capture food items.

Animals forage in a great many ways. Some animals are "generalists," whereas others are "specialists." Crows, for instance, are extreme generalists; they will eat just about anything that is readily available—plant or animal, alive or dead. In sharp contrast, the koala of Australia, an extreme feeding specialist, eats only the leaves of a few species of eucalyptus trees. As a result, the koala is restricted to certain areas and is extremely vulnerable to habitat loss. Most animals are somewhere in between crows and koalas in the range of their diet. The pronghorn, for example (see Module 35.4), eats a variety of plants, including forbs, grasses, and woody shrubs.

Often, even a generalist will concentrate on a particular item of food when it is readily available. The mechanism that enables an animal to find particular foods efficiently is called a **search image**. If the favoured food item becomes scarce, the animal may develop a search image for a different food item. (People often use search images; for example, when you look for something on a kitchen shelf, you probably scan rapidly to find a package of a certain size and colour rather than reading all the labels you see.)

Whenever an animal has food choices, trade-offs are involved in selection. The amount of energy required to locate, capture, subdue, and prepare prey for consumption may vary considerably among the items available. Some behavioural ecologists use an approach known as cost-benefit analysis, comparing the positive and negative aspects of the alternative choices, to evaluate the efficiency of foraging behaviours. According to the predictions of **optimal foraging theory**, an animal's feeding behaviour should provide maximal energy gain with minimal energy expense and minimal risk of being eaten while foraging. A researcher tested part of this theory by studying insectivorous birds called wagtails (**Figure 36.12A**).

In England, wagtails are commonly seen in cow pastures foraging for dung flies (**Figure 36.12B**). The researcher collected data on the time required for a wagtail to catch and consume dung flies of different sizes (**Figure 36.12C**). He then calculated the number of calories the

◀ **Figure 36.12B** A dung fly

bird gained per second of "handling" time for the different sizes of flies. The smallest flies were easily handled but yielded few calories, while the caloric value of large flies was offset by the energy required to catch and consume them. An optimal forager would be expected to choose medium-sized flies most often. The researcher tested this prediction by observing wagtails as they foraged for dung flies in a cow pasture. As **Figure 36.12D** shows, he found that wagtails did select medium-sized flies most often, even though they were not the most abundant size class.

Predation is one of the most significant potential costs of foraging. Studies have shown that foraging in groups, as done by herds of antelopes, flocks of birds, or schools of fish, reduces the individual's risk of predation. And for some predators, such as wolves and spotted hyenas, hunting in groups improves their success. Thus, group behaviour may increase foraging efficiency by both reducing the costs and increasing the benefits of foraging.

In the following modules, we will consider other strategies that promote survival and reproductive success: communication, mating behaviour, and mating systems.

? Early humans were hunter-gatherers, but evidence suggests that they obtained more nutrition from gathering than hunting. How does this finding relate to optimal foraging theory?

● Meat is very nutritious, but hunting poses relatively high costs in effort and risk compared with the gathering of plant products and dead animals.

▶ **Figure 36.12A**
A wagtail

◀ **Figure 36.12C**
The relationship between the calories gained by the wagtail and the size of its prey (the dung fly)

X-axis: Dung fly body length (mm) — 5, 6, 7, 8, 9, 10
Y-axis: Wagtail calorie intake per second of handling time — 0, 10, 12, 14, 16

◀ **Figure 36.12D**
The prey sizes selected by wagtails compared with the prey sizes available

Legend: Dung flies available (Total = 460); Dung flies eaten (Total = 252)
X-axis: Dung fly body length (mm) — 5, 6, 7, 8, 9, 10
Y-axis: Percentage of total — 0, 10, 20, 30, 40, 50

36.13 Communication is an essential element of interactions between animals

Interactions between animals depend on some form of signalling between the participating individuals. In behavioural ecology, a **signal** is a stimulus transmitted by one animal to another animal. The sending of, reception of, and response to signals constitute animal **communication**, an essential element of interactions between individuals. In general, the more complex the social organization of a species, the more complex the signalling required to sustain it.

What determines the type of signal animals use to communicate? Most terrestrial mammals are nocturnal (active at night), which makes visual displays relatively ineffective. Many nocturnal mammals use odour and auditory (sound) signals, which work well in the dark. Birds, by contrast, are mostly diurnal (active in daytime) and use visual and auditory signals. Humans are also diurnal and likewise use mainly visual and auditory signals. Therefore, we can detect the bright colours and songs birds use to communicate. If we had the well-developed olfactory abilities of most mammals and could detect the rich world of odour cues, mammal-sniffing might be as popular with us as birdwatching.

What types of signals are effective in aquatic environments? Marine mammals use sound for courtship, territoriality, and maintaining contact with their group. A common visual signal used by territorial fishes is to erect their fins, which is generally enough to drive off intruders. Electrical signals produced by certain fishes communicate hierarchy or status. Fish may also use sound to communicate. For example, the males of some species make noises to attract mates. Communication among Pacific herring is an unusual example of how fish use sounds. Dr. Ben Wilson at the Bamfield Marine Sciences Centre on Vancouver Island has recorded high-frequency ticking sounds made by the fish during the dark hours of the night. These sounds, produced by releasing air bubbles from the anus, are called fast repetitive ticks (FRTs). The FRTs released by the fish help them group together for protection in dense

shoals at times when vision is limited. The air released in a FRT is not actually flatulence; it originates from the fish's swim bladder, an air-filled sac that maintains buoyancy.

Animals often use more than one type of signal simultaneously. **Figure 36.13A** shows a Kermode spirit bear, also featured on the book's cover, posturing with another black bear. When bears encounter one another, they establish a hierarchy between them. Submissive animals give way to the dominant alpha, or top-ranked, bear. The standing display shown in the figure is a clear demonstration of size. Often, the smaller bear submits to the larger, dominant bear. However, smaller bears with a more aggressive attitude can dominate larger individuals. During these contests, bears also use auditory signals. Grunts and loud blows are also used to intimidate opponents into submission. Bears also mark their territories with urine and other secretions. These chemical signals inform passing individuals about the presence of a dominant bear without an encounter.

One of the most amazing examples of animal communication is found in honeybees, as described in the chapter-opening essay. Adult worker bees leave the hive to forage, bringing back pollen and nectar for the nest. When a forager locates a patch of flowers, she regurgitates some nectar that the others taste and smell, and then communicates the location of the food source by performing a waggle dance **(Figure 36.13B)**. Once the other workers have learned the location of the food source, they leave the hive to forage there.

? **What types of signals do honeybees use?**

Visual and chemical ●

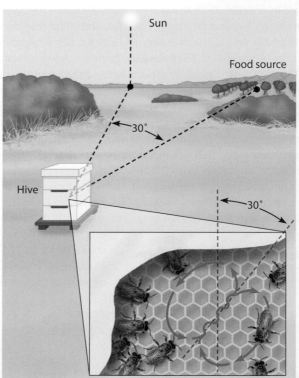

▲ **Figure 36.13B** A returning honeybee forager performing the waggle dance inside the hive

▲ **Figure 36.13A** Bears communicating through posturing

36.14 Mating behaviour often includes elaborate courtship rituals

Animals of many species tend to view members of their own species as competitors to be driven away. Even animals that forage and travel in groups often maintain a distance from their companions. Thus, careful communication is an essential prerequisite for mating. In many species, prospective mates must perform an elaborate courtship ritual, which confirms that individuals are of the same species, of the opposite sex, physically primed for mating, and not threats to each other. Courtship rituals are common among vertebrates as well as some groups of invertebrates, such as insects and cephalopods. The male cuttlefish in **Figure 36.14A**, for instance, is using part of his enormous repertoire of colour changes to signal a female.

Figure 36.14B shows the courtship behaviour of the common loon, which breeds on secluded lakes throughout Canada. The courting male and female swim side by side, performing a series of displays, ❶ frequently turning their heads away from each other. (In contrast, a male loon defending his territory charges at an intruder with his beak pointed straight ahead.) ❷ The birds then dip their beaks in the water and submerge their heads. ❸ The male invites the female onto land by turning his head backward with his beak down. There, they copulate. Each movement in this complex behaviour is a FAP (see Module 36.2). When a FAP is executed successfully by one partner, it triggers the next FAP in the other partner. Thus, the entire routine is a chain of FAPs that must be performed flawlessly if mating is to occur.

In some species, courtship is a group activity in which members of one or both sexes choose mates from a group of candidates. (See Module 14.8 to review mate choice and sexual selection.) For example, consider the sage grouse, a chickenlike bird whose range includes southern Alberta and Saskatchewan. Every day in early spring, 50 or more males congregate in an open area, where they strut about, erecting their tail feathers in a bright, fanlike display **(Figure 36.14C)**. A booming sound produced in the male's inflated air sac accompanies the show. Dominant males usually defend a prime territory near the centre of the area. Females arrive several weeks after the males. After watching the males perform, a female selects

❶

❷

❸

▲ **Figure 36.14B** Courtship of the common loon

one, and the pair copulates. Usually, all the females choose dominant males, so only about 10% of the males actually mate. In choosing a dominant male, a female sage grouse may be

▲ **Figure 36.14A** A male cuttlefish displaying courtship colours

▲ **Figure 36.14C** A courtship display by a male sage grouse

giving her offspring, and thus her own genes, the best chance for survival. Research on several species of animals has shown a connection between a male's physical characteristics and the quality of his genes.

? What categories of signals do the cuttlefish, loon, and sage grouse use to communicate with potential mates?

● All three use visual signals. The sage grouse also uses an auditory signal.

36.15 Mating systems and parental care enhance reproductive success

Courtship and mating are not the only elements of reproductive success. In order for genes to be passed on to successive generations, the offspring produced by the union must themselves survive and reproduce. Therefore, the needs of the young are an important factor in the evolution of mating systems. Animal mating systems fall into three major categories: **promiscuous** (no strong pair-bonds or lasting relationships between males and females), **monogamous** (a bond between one male and one female, with shared parental care), and **polygamous** (an individual of one sex mating with several of the other). Polygamous relationships most often involve a single male and many females, although in some species this is reversed, and a single female mates with several males.

Most newly hatched birds cannot care for themselves and require a large, continuous food supply that a single parent may not be able to provide. A male may leave more viable offspring by helping a single mate than by seeking multiple mates. This may explain why most birds are monogamous, though often with a new partner each breeding season. (And in many species of birds, one or both members of the pair also seek other sexual partners.) On the contrary, birds whose young can feed and care for themselves almost immediately after hatching, such as pheasants and quail, gain less benefit from monogamy—a polygamous or promiscuous mating system may maximize their reproductive success.

In the case of mammals, the lactating female is often the only food source for the young, and males usually play no role in caring for their offspring.

Parental care involves significant costs, including energy expenditure and the loss of other mating opportunities. For females, the investment almost always pays off in terms of reproductive success—young born or eggs laid definitely contain the mother's genes. But even in the case of a normally monogamous relationship, the young may have been fathered by a male other than the female's usual mate. As a result, certainty of paternity may be a factor in the evolution of male mating behaviour and parental care.

The certainty of paternity is relatively low in most species with internal fertilization because the acts of mating and birth (or mating and egg laying) are separated over time. This may help to explain why species in which males are the sole parental caregiver are rare in birds and mammals. However, the males of many species with internal fertilization do engage in behaviours that appear to increase their certainty of paternity, such as guarding females from other males. In species such as lions, where males protect the females and young, a male or small group of males typically guard many females at once in a harem. The aggression that the male prairie vole displays toward intruders is another example of this mate-guarding behaviour.

Certainty of paternity is much higher when egg laying and mating occur together, as happens when fertilization is external. This connection may explain why parental care in aquatic invertebrates, fishes, and amphibians, when care occurs at all, is at least as likely to be by males as by females. **Figure 36.15** shows a male jawfish exhibiting paternal care of eggs. Jawfish, which are found in tropical marine habitats, hold the eggs they have fertilized in their mouths, keeping them aerated (by spitting them out and sucking them back in) and protected from predators until they hatch. Seahorses have the most extreme method of ensuring paternity. Females lay their eggs in a brood pouch in the male's abdomen, where they are fertilized by his sperm. When the eggs hatch a few weeks later, the pouch opens and the male pushes them out with pumping movements.

Keep in mind that when behavioural ecologists use the phrase *certainty of paternity*, they do not mean that animals are aware of paternity when they behave a certain way. Parental behaviours associated with certainty of paternity exist because they have been reinforced over generations by natural selection. Individuals with genes for such behaviours reproduced more successfully and passed on those genes to the next generation.

? Based on what you know of the sage grouse's mating behaviour, what would you predict about the need to care for young?

● Sage grouse are promiscuous, and the male does not contribute to caring for the offspring. It is likely that their young can feed and care for themselves immediately after hatching, like those of pheasants and quail.

▲ **Figure 36.15** A male jawfish with his mouth full of eggs

36.16 Do birth control pills alter animal behaviour?

Many organic compounds that we release into the environment are resistant to degradation processes. As such, these persistent organic pollutants (POPs) may accumulate in living tissues or become concentrated as they move throughout food chains. Recently, the idea that POPs found in birth control pills are contaminating our water systems has been gaining support. Some people are also worried that birth control POPs are affecting the behaviour of exposed wildlife. But is there truth behind this story, or is it just a rumour?

Appropriate behaviour is the cornerstone of reproductive success in the animal world. So, something is amiss when fish are lackadaisical about territorial defence, salamanders ignore mating cues, birds exhibit sloppy nest-building techniques, and mice take inexplicable risks. Scientists have linked observations of these abnormal behaviours, as well as many others, to endocrine-disrupting chemicals. Endocrine disruptors are a diverse group of substances that affect the vertebrate endocrine system by mimicking a hormone or by enhancing or inhibiting hormone activity. Endocrine disruptors are especially worrisome pollutants because they persist in the environment for decades and become concentrated in the food chain (see Figure 41.2E).

The estrogen compounds in birth control pills, both natural and synthetic, are potent endocrine disruptors in aquatic systems. But how are animals exposed to these disruptors? Millions of Canadian women use birth control pills. These estrogen hormones are excreted in their urine. Sewage treatment practices are unable to remove the estrogens and they are released in wastewater. Environmental estrogen accumulates in the food chain, and can reach higher concentrations in fish blood than in a woman taking the pill.

Hundreds of studies have demonstrated the effects of endocrine disruptors on vertebrate reproduction and development.

For example, triclosan, an additive in some cleaning products (see Module 17.10), acts as a thyroid hormone mimic in North American bullfrogs, inhibiting the normal production of thyroid hormone. Like hormones, some endocrine disruptors also affect behaviour. For example, some male fish attract females during the breeding season by defending territories. These males have high levels of androgens (male hormones) during this time. Researchers showed that the intensity of nest-guarding behaviour in male sticklebacks (a type of fish) dropped after the fish were exposed to environmental estrogens. Male sticklebacks' performance of courtship rituals was also impaired.

It is not only fish that are affected by environmental estrogens. The reproductive behaviour of frogs may also change. Biologists have shown that male frogs exposed to low levels of estrogen voice fewer mating calls. Estrogen also decreases their attractiveness to females. In these ways, environmental concentrations of estrogen can significantly reduce the frogs' reproductive success.

Could endocrine disruptors in drinking water or food affect humans, too? Answers are not yet clear. But, the *Canadian Environmental Protection Act, 1999* proclaims that research on endocrine disruptors is a duty of both Health Canada and Environment Canada. So, the rumour that birth control pills can alter animal behaviour is true. By increasing environmental estrogen concentrations, the reproductive and courting behaviours of some male fish and frogs are altered.

 How can ineffective courtship behaviour affect the fitness of a male fish?

● A male whose courtship display is perceived by females as inferior will not be successful in attracting mates and will thus be less likely to produce offspring. Therefore, the male's fitness would be reduced.

Social Behaviour and Sociobiology

36.17 Sociobiology places social behaviour in an evolutionary context

Biologists define **social behaviour** as any kind of interaction between two or more animals, usually of the same species. The courtship behaviours of loons and sage grouse are examples of social behaviour. Other social behaviours observed in animals are aggression and cooperation.

Many animals migrate and feed in large groups (flocks, packs, herds, or schools). Pronghorns, for example, derive protection from feeding in herds. Many watchful eyes increase the chance that a predator will be spotted before it can strike. When alarmed, a pronghorn flares out the white hairs on its rump, sending a danger signal to other members of its herd. Predators, too, may benefit from travelling in a group. Wolves usually hunt in a pack consisting of a tightly knit group of

family members. Hunting in packs enables them to kill large animals, such as moose or elk, that would be unattainable by an individual wolf.

The discipline of **sociobiology** applies evolutionary theory to the study and interpretation of social behaviour—the study of how social behaviours are adaptive and how they could have evolved by natural selection. We discuss several aspects of social behaviour in the next several modules.

 Why is communication essential to social behaviour?

● Group members must be able to transfer information—for example, to signal danger or to cooperate in obtaining food.

36.18 Territorial behaviour parcels out space and resources

Many animals exhibit territorial behaviour. A **territory** is an area, usually fixed in location, that individuals defend and from which other members of the same species are usually excluded. The size of the territory varies with the species, the function of the territory, and the resources available. Territories are typically used for feeding, mating, rearing young, or combinations of these activities.

Figure 36.18A shows a nesting colony of gannets in l'Île-Bonaventure-et-du-Rocher-Percé National Park, Quebec. Space is at a premium, and the birds defend territories just large enough for their nests by calling out and pecking at other birds. As you can see, each gannet is literally only a peck away from its closest neighbours. Such small nesting territories are characteristic of many colonial seabirds. In contrast, most cats, including jaguars, leopards, cheetahs, and even domestic cats, defend much larger territories, which they use for foraging as well as breeding.

Individuals that have established a territory usually proclaim their territorial rights continually; this is the function of most bird songs, the noisy bellowing of sea lions, and the chattering of squirrels. Wolves use visual signals to mark the perimeter of their territories. Rubbing against trees leaves tufts of fur behind and informs others of the boundary. Scent markers are frequently used to signal a territory's boundaries. The male cheetah in **Figure 36.18B**, a resident of Africa's Serengeti National Park, is spraying urine on a tree. The odour will serve as a chemical "No Trespassing" sign. Other males that approach the area will sniff the marked tree and recognize that the urine is not their own. Usually, the intruder will avoid the marked territory and a potentially deadly confrontation with its proprietor.

Not all species are territorial. However, for those that are, the territory can provide exclusive access to food supplies, breeding areas, and places to raise young. Familiarity with a specific area may help individuals avoid predators or forage more efficiently. In a territorial species, such benefits increase fitness and outweigh the energy costs of defending a territory.

 Why is the territory of a gannet so much smaller than the territory of a cheetah?

● The gannet uses its territory only for raising young, not for foraging. Cheetahs use their territories for foraging as well as for breeding.

▲ **Figure 36.18A** Gannet territories

▲ **Figure 36.18B** A cheetah marking its territory

36.19 Agonistic behaviour often resolves confrontations between competitors

In many species, conflicts that arise over limited resources, such as food, mates, or territories, are settled by **agonistic behaviour** (from the Greek *agon*, struggle), including threats, rituals, and sometimes combat that determine which competitor gains access to the resource. An agonistic encounter may involve a test of strength, such as when male moose lower their heads, lock antlers, and push against each other. More commonly, animals engage in exaggerated posturing and other symbolic displays that make the individual look large or aggressive. For example, the colourful Siamese fighting fish (*Betta splendens*) spreads its fins dramatically when it encounters a rival, thus appearing much bigger than it actually is. Eventually, one individual stops threatening and becomes submissive, exhibiting some type of appeasement display—in effect, surrendering.

Because violent combat may injure the victor as well as the vanquished in a way that reduces reproductive fitness, we would predict that natural selection would favour ritualized contests. And, in fact, this is what usually happens in nature. The rattlesnakes pictured in **Figure 36.19**, for example, are rival males wrestling over access to a mate. If they bit each other, both would die from the toxin in their fangs, but they are engaged in a pushing, rather than a biting, match. One snake usually tires before the other, and the winner pins the loser's head to the ground. In a way, the snakes are like two people who settle an argument by arm wrestling instead of resorting to fists or guns. In a typical case, the agonistic ritual inhibits further aggressive activity. Once two individuals have settled a dispute by agonistic behaviour, future encounters between them usually involve less conflict, with the original loser giving way to the original victor. Often the victor of an agonistic ritual gains first or exclusive access to mates, and so this form of social behaviour can directly affect an individual's evolutionary fitness.

? Why is "fighting to the death" an unusual form of agonistic behaviour among animals?

● Because ritualized posturing or nonlethal combat can usually produce a winner without injuries that would lower reproductive fitness for the winner and eliminate it altogether for the loser.

▲ **Figure 36.19** Ritual wrestling by rattlesnakes

36.20 Dominance hierarchies are maintained by agonistic behaviour

Many animals live in social groups maintained by agonistic behaviour. Chickens are an example. If several hens unfamiliar with one another are put together, they respond by chasing and pecking each other. Eventually, they establish a clear "pecking order." The alpha hen in the pecking order (the one on the right in **Figure 36.20**) is dominant; she is not pecked by any other hens and can usually drive off all the others by threats rather than actual pecking. The alpha hen also has first access to resources such as food, water, and roosting sites. The beta, or second-ranked, hen similarly subdues all others except the alpha, and so on down the line to the omega, or lowest, animal.

Pecking order in chickens is an example of a **dominance hierarchy**, a ranking of individuals based on social interactions. Once a hierarchy is established, each animal's status in the group is fixed, often for several months or even years. Dominance hierarchies are common, especially in vertebrate populations. In a wolf pack, for example, there is a dominance hierarchy among the females, and this hierarchy may control the pack's size. When food is abundant, the alpha female mates and also allows others to do so. When food is scarce, she usually monopolizes the males for herself and keeps other females from mating. In other species, such as savanna baboons and red deer, the dominant male monopolizes fertile females. As a result, his reproductive success is much greater than that of lower-ranking males.

As you will learn in the next module, however, not all social behaviours pit one individual against another.

▲ **Figure 36.20** Chickens exhibiting pecking order

? Dog trainers such as Cesar Millan, TV's "Dog Whisperer," advise dog owners to be sure the dog understands that the owner is the alpha. How might this facilitate obedience?

● Like wolves, dogs are pack animals. They are more likely to respond to commands from a higher-ranking individual.

36.21 Jane Goodall revolutionized our understanding of chimpanzee behaviour

People are fascinated by the humanlike qualities of primates, especially chimpanzees. With their expressive faces and playful behaviour, chimpanzees have long been stars in the entertainment industry. For example, a chimpanzee named Cheeta appeared in dozens of Tarzan movies from the 1930s through the 1960s. In the early days of television, NBC's *Today Show* attracted few viewers until a chimpanzee joined the show as the host's sidekick. Like their human counterparts, however, these chimpanzees were only playing a role. No one knew how they behaved in the wild, without the influence of trainers or zookeepers. A young Englishwoman named Jane Goodall changed that.

In 1960, paleoanthropologist Louis Leakey, who discovered *Homo habilis* and its stone tools (see Module 21.14), thought that studying the behaviour of our closest relatives might provide insight into the behaviour of early humans. Jane Goodall had no scientific background—she did not even have a college

▲ **Figure 36.21A** Jane Goodall observing interactions between two chimpanzees (*Pan troglodytes*)

▲ **Figure 36.21B** A female chimpanzee foraging with an infant

degree, though she later earned a Ph.D. from Cambridge—when Leakey hired her to observe chimpanzees in the wild.

Through countless hours of carefully recorded observations in an area that was later designated the Gombe Stream Research Center, near Lake Tanganyika, Africa, Goodall documented the social organization and behaviour of chimpanzees (**Figure 36.21A**). Most astonishingly, she reported that chimpanzees make and use tools by fashioning plant stems into probes for extracting termites from their mounds. Until that time, scientists thought that toolmaking defined humans, setting them apart from other animals.

Goodall discovered other important aspects of chimpanzee life, too. She learned that chimpanzees eat meat as well as plants. She described the close bond between chimpanzee mothers and their offspring, who are constantly together for several years after birth. She also recorded the daily foraging activities undertaken by small groups consisting of a mother and her offspring, sometimes with one or two males (**Figure 36.21B**).

In areas of abundant food, where these separate groups often came together, Goodall observed the establishment of a male dominance hierarchy through agonistic displays. The alpha periodically reasserted his status with an intimidating charging display, during which, in Goodall's words, he "races across the ground, hurls rocks, drags branches, leaps up, and shakes the vegetation." Goodall witnessed several dramatic episodes in which a subordinate male overthrew the reigning alpha, as well as numerous unsuccessful challenges. These clashes, which cause tension among the group members, were

usually followed by some kind of reconciliation behaviour. After a conflict, a chimpanzee would make peace through gestures such as embracing or grooming a defeated rival. Grooming—picking through the fur and removing debris or parasites—is the social glue of a chimpanzee community. As Goodall put it, "It improves bad relationships and maintains good ones."

Goodall's pioneering research added immeasurably to our scientific knowledge of primate behaviour. She has also spent half a century communicating another aspect of what she learned during her decades in Gombe: "The most important spin-off of the chimp research is probably the humbling effect it has on us who do the research. We are not, after all, the only aware, reasoning beings on this planet." Through her many books, lecture tours, and television appearances, Goodall has educated the public about our closest relatives. For more than 30 years, the Jane Goodall Institute has promoted issues related to the conservation of primates and their habitats, an increasing concern as deforestation, war, and the "bushmeat" trade (the practice of hunting wild animals, including primates, for food) take a rising toll on Africa's great apes. In addition, Goodall has been at the forefront of efforts to ban the use of invasive research methods on chimpanzees and to ensure the humane and ethical treatment of captive chimpanzees in research facilities and zoos.

 Why is the study of chimpanzee behaviour relevant to understanding the origins of certain human behaviours?

Because chimpanzees and humans share a common ancestor.

Reviewing the Concepts

The Scientific Study of Behaviour (36.1–36.3)

36.1 Behavioural ecologists ask both proximate and ultimate questions. Behavioural ecology is the study of behaviour in an evolutionary context, considering both proximate (immediate) and ultimate (evolutionary) causes of an animal's actions. Natural selection preserves behaviours that enhance fitness.

36.2 Fixed action patterns are innate behaviours. Innate behaviour is performed the same way by all members of a species. A fixed action pattern (FAP) is an unchangeable series of actions triggered by a specific stimulus. FAPs ensure that activities essential to survival are performed correctly without practice.

36.3 Behaviour is the result of both genetic and environmental factors. Genetic engineering has been used to investigate genes that influence behaviour. Cross-fostering experiments are useful for studying environmental factors that affect behaviour.

Learning (36.4–36.11)

36.4 Habituation is a simple type of learning. Learning is a change in behaviour resulting from experience. Habituation is learning to ignore a repeated, unimportant stimulus.

36.5 Imprinting requires both innate behaviour and experience. Imprinting is irreversible learning limited to a sensitive period in the animal's life.

36.6 Imprinting poses problems and opportunities for conservation programs. If organisms intended to be released into the wild imprint on humans, they may not interact with their own kind.

36.7 Animal movement may be a simple response to stimuli or require spatial learning. Kineses and taxes are simple movements in response to a stimulus. Spatial learning involves using landmarks to move through the environment.

36.8 Movements of animals may depend on cognitive maps. Cognitive maps are internal representations of spatial relationships of objects in the surroundings. Migratory animals may move between areas by using the sun, stars, landmarks, or other cues.

36.9 Animals may learn to associate a stimulus or behaviour with a response. In associative learning, animals learn by associating external stimuli or their own behaviour with positive or negative effects.

36.10 Social learning employs observation and imitation of others. By imitating others, younger individuals learn how to act around others.

36.11 Problem-solving behaviour relies on cognition. Cognition is the process of perceiving, storing, integrating, and using information. Problem-solving behaviour involves complex cognitive processes.

Survival and Reproductive Success (36.12–36.16)

36.12 Behavioural ecologists use cost-benefit analysis to study foraging. Foraging includes identifying, obtaining, and eating food. Optimal foraging theory predicts that feeding behaviour will maximize energy gain and minimize energy expenditure and risk.

36.13 Communication is an essential element of interactions between animals. Signalling in the form of sounds, scents, displays, or touches provides means of communication.

36.14 Mating behaviour often includes elaborate courtship rituals. Courtship rituals advertise the species, sex, and physical condition of potential mates.

36.15 Mating systems and parental care enhance reproductive success. Mating systems may be promiscuous, monogamous, or polygamous. The needs of offspring and certainty of paternity help to explain differences in mating systems and parental care by males.

36.16 Do birth control pills alter animal behaviour? Endocrine disruptors, including estrogens from birth control pills, are chemicals in the environment that may cause abnormal behaviour as well as reproductive abnormalities in animals.

Social Behaviour and Sociobiology (36.17–36.21)

36.17 Sociobiology places social behaviour in an evolutionary context. Social behaviour is any kind of interaction between two or more animals.

36.18 Territorial behaviour parcels out space and resources. Animals exhibiting this behaviour defend their territories.

36.19 Agonistic behaviour often resolves confrontations between competitors. Agonistic behaviour includes threats, rituals, and sometimes combat.

36.20 Dominance hierarchies are maintained by agonistic behaviour. Dominance hierarchies determine each individual's position within a social group. Aspiring juveniles often have to fight their way to the top.

36.21 Jane Goodall revolutionized our understanding of chimpanzee behaviour. In decades of fieldwork, Goodall described many aspects of chimpanzee social behaviour. She also discovered that chimpanzees make and use tools.

Connecting the Concepts

1. Complete this map, which reviews the genetic and environmental components of animal behaviour and their relationship to learning.

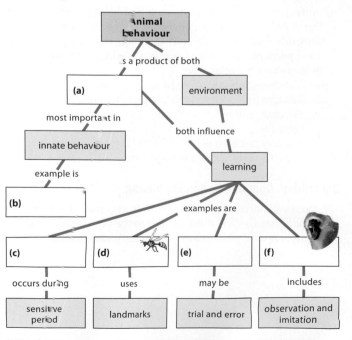

Testing Your Knowledge

Multiple Choice

2. Although many chimpanzee populations live in environments containing oil palm nuts, members of only a few populations use stones to crack open the nuts. The most likely explanation for this behavioural difference between populations is that
   a. members of different populations differ in manual dexterity.
   b. members of different populations have different nutritional requirements.
   c. members of different populations differ in learning ability.
   d. the use of stones to crack nuts has arisen and spread through social learning in only some populations.
   e. the behavioural difference is caused by genetic differences between populations.

3. Pheasants do not feed their chicks. Immediately after hatching, a pheasant chick starts pecking at seeds and insects on the ground. How might a behavioural ecologist explain the ultimate cause of this behaviour?
   a. Pecking is a fixed action pattern.
   b. Pheasants learned to peck, and their offspring inherited this behaviour.
   c. Pheasants that pecked survived and reproduced best.
   d. Pecking is a result of imprinting during a sensitive period.
   e. Pecking is an example of habituation.

4. If you see another person yawn, you often find yourself yawning as well, which you cannot stop. Therefore another person yawning is considered
   a. a learned response.
   b. an imprint.
   c. a sign stimulus.
   d. an agonistic behaviour.
   e. a coincidence.

5. Sow bugs become more active in dry areas, moving randomly, and less active in humid areas. This is an example of
   a. taxis.
   b. tropism.
   c. conditioning.
   d. kinesis.
   e. cognition.

6. Ants carry dead ants out of the anthill and dump them on a "trash pile." If a live ant is painted with a chemical from dead ants, other ants repeatedly carry it, kicking and struggling, to the trash pile, until the substance wears off. Which of the following best explains this behaviour?
   a. The chemical triggers a fixed action pattern.
   b. The ants have become imprinted on the chemical.
   c. The ants continue the behaviour until they become habituated.
   d. The ants can learn only by trial and error.
   e. The chemical triggers a negative taxis.

Describing, Comparing, and Explaining

7. Almost all the behaviours of a housefly are innate. What are some advantages and disadvantages to the fly of innate behaviours compared with behaviours that are mainly learned?

8. In Module 36.3, you learned that Norway rat offspring whose mothers do not interact with them much grow up to be fearful and anxious in new situations. Suggest a possible ultimate cause for this link between maternal behaviour and stress response of offspring. (*Hint:* Under what circumstances might high reactivity to stress be more adaptive than being relaxed?)

9. A chorus of frogs fills the air on a spring evening. The frog calls are courtship signals. What are the functions of courtship behaviours? How might a behavioural ecologist explain the proximate cause of this behaviour? The ultimate cause?

Applying the Concepts

10. Crows break the shells of certain molluscs before eating them by dropping them onto rocks. Hypothesizing that crows drop the molluscs from a height that gives the most food for the least effort (optimal foraging), a researcher dropped shells from different heights and counted the drops it took to break them.

Height of Drop (m)	Average Number of Drops Required to Break Shell	Total Flight Height (Number of Drops × Height per Drop)
2	55	110
3	13	39
5	6	30
7	5	35
15	4	60

   a. The researcher measured the average drop height for crows and found that it was 5.23 m. Does this support the researcher's hypothesis? Explain.
   b. Describe an experiment that would determine whether this feeding behaviour of crows is learned or innate.

11. Researchers are very interested in studying identical twins who were raised apart. Among other things, they hope to answer questions about the roles of inheritance and upbringing in human behaviour. Why do identical twins make such good subjects for this kind of research? What are the potential pitfalls of this research? What abuses might occur in the use of these data if the studies are not evaluated critically?

12. Do animals think and feel the same kinds of things we do? These questions bear on animal rights, a subject much in the news. Many important biological discoveries have come from experiments performed on animals, yet some animal rights activists believe that all animal experimentation is cruel and should be stopped. They have harassed researchers, vandalized laboratories, and set animals free. Why are animals used in experiments? Are there uses of animals that should be discontinued? What kinds of guidelines should researchers follow in using animals in experiments, and who should establish and enforce the guidelines?

Answers to all questions can be found in Appendix E.

CHAPTER

37

Population Ecology

BIG IDEAS

Population Structure and Dynamics

(37.1–37.9)

Population ecology is concerned with
characteristics that describe populations,
changes in population size, and factors that
regulate populations over time.

The Human Population

(37.10–37.12)

The principles of population ecology can
be used to describe the growth of the
human population and its limits.

Sable Island Horse Play

Sable Island, Canada's newest national park, is a small crescent-shaped island 290 km east of Halifax, Nova Scotia. Coined the "Graveyard of the Atlantic," this famous island has been the site of more than 350 shipwrecks. The entire island is made of sand held together by beach grass and other small plants. No trees live on the island. A lone, stunted pine stands about 1 m tall, the only survivor of thousands of tree-planting attempts. The island is home to six endemic species of invertebrates and the world's largest population of grey seals, and is a breeding site for numerous species of birds—some of which nest nowhere else. But Sable Island is also famous for its sole terrestrial mammal population, wild horses (*Equus ferus caballus*).

The Sable Island horses are the descendants of about 60 horses confiscated from the Acadians during their deportation in 1760. The horses were brought to the island to help residents assist shipwreck victims. Once domesticated, the now feral horses have adapted well to island life. Today, the population numbers approximately 450 horses. Upon returning to their feral state, the Sable Island horses readopted a social system of small bands common among horses. There are currently about 70 bands on Sable Island, which typically consist of a dominant stallion, his harem composed of a few mares, and their offspring. Males without bands live in roaming bachelor groups or tag along with the bands of established stallions before competing to establish their own harem.

This small, isolated population in a unique location is ideal for ecological research. In 2007, Dr. Philip McLoughlin at the University of Saskatchewan began a study of the Sable Island horses to understand how individuals contribute to population dynamics. The researchers began by identifying and uniquely naming the horses. They plan to follow the life experiences of the horses for at least 30 years. The horse in the photograph is named Rocky, the stallion of a band of eight individuals on the west side of the island.

Despite the island's small size, the environment is not homogenous. The west side of the island has more fresh water and many resources, and can support twice as many animals as the east side. A horse with access to more resources may have higher reproductive success and contribute more to population growth. The sex ratio is also different on the two sides of the island, affecting the gender composition of the bands and reproductive behaviours of the individuals. A western stallion will defend a larger harem and sire more offspring than his eastern counterpart. Eastern bands can have multiple males, each of which may sire offspring. With different degrees of competition, sexual selection pressures are also different between the two sides.

By studying how individuals (as units of natural selection) behave, make use of resources, and contribute to population growth and the gene pool over successive generations, McLoughlin hopes to gain insight into how behavioural ecology is directly linked to microevolution and population ecology.

In this chapter, you will learn about the structure and dynamics of populations and the factors that regulate populations over time. As ecologists gain greater insight into natural populations, we become better equipped to develop sustainable food sources, assess the impact of human activities, and balance human needs with the conservation of biodiversity and resources.

Population Structure and Dynamics

37.1 Population ecology is the study of how and why populations change

Ecologists usually define a **population** as a group of individuals of a single species that occupy the same general area. These individuals rely on the same resources, are influenced by the same environmental factors, and are likely to interact and breed with one another. For example, the emperor penguins living near Dumont d'Urville Station, where *March of the Penguins* was filmed, are a population. When a researcher chooses a population to study, he or she defines it by boundaries appropriate to the species being studied and to the purposes of the investigation.

Population ecology is concerned with changes in population size and the factors that regulate populations over time. A population ecologist might use statistics such as the number and distribution of individuals to describe a population. Population ecologists also examine population dynamics, the interactions between biotic and abiotic factors that cause variation in population sizes. One important aspect of population dynamics—and a major topic for this chapter—is population growth. The penguin population at Dumont d'Urville Station increases through births and the immigration of penguins from nearby colonies. Deaths and the emigration of individuals away from Dumont d'Urville Station decrease the population. Population ecologists might investigate how various environmental factors, such as availability of food, predation by killer whales, or the extent of sea ice, affect the size, distribution, or dynamics of the population.

Population ecology plays a key role in applied research. For example, population ecology provides critical information for identifying and saving endangered species. Population ecology is being used to manage wildlife populations and to develop sustainable fisheries throughout the world. The population ecology of pests and pathogens provides insight into controlling their spread. Population ecologists also study human population growth, one of the most critical environmental issues of our time.

? What is the relationship between a population and a species?

● A population is a localized group of individuals of a single species.

37.2 Density and distribution patterns are important population variables

Two important aspects of population structure are population density and distribution pattern. **Population density** is the number of individuals of a species per unit area or volume—the number of oak trees per square kilometre (km^2) in a forest, for instance, or the number of earthworms per cubic metre (m^3) in forest soil. Because it is impractical or impossible to count all individuals in a population in most cases, ecologists use a variety of sampling techniques to estimate population densities. For example, they might base an estimate of the density of poplars in a forest on a count of individuals in a few sample plots of 1 h (100 m × 100 m) each. The larger the number and size of sample plots, the more accurate the estimates. In some cases, population densities are estimated not by counts of organisms but by indirect indicators, such as number of bird nests or rodent burrows.

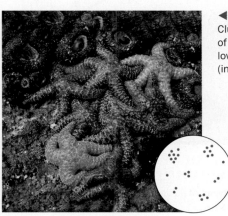

◀ **Figure 37.2A**
Clumped distribution of ochre sea stars at low tide and schematic (inset)

Within a population's geographic range, local densities may vary greatly. The **distribution pattern** of a population refers to the way individuals are spaced within their area. A **clumped distribution pattern**, in which individuals are grouped in patches, is the most common in nature. Clumping often results from an unequal distribution of resources in the environment. For instance, plants or fungi may be clumped in areas where soil conditions and other factors favour germination and growth. Clumping of animals often results from uneven food distribution. For example, the sea stars shown in **Figure 37.2A** group together where food is abundant. Clumping may also reduce the risk of predation, or be associated with social behaviour.

A **uniform distribution pattern** is one in which all individuals are distributed evenly and each has approximately the same amount of space. This pattern often results from interactions between the individuals of a population. For instance, some plants secrete chemicals that inhibit the germination and growth of nearby plants that could compete for resources. Animals may exhibit uniform distribution as a result of territorial behaviour. **Figure 37.2B** shows the uniform distribution of penguins in the Falkland Islands.

In a **random distribution pattern**, individuals in a population are spaced in an unpredictable way, without a pattern. Plants, such as dandelions (**Figure 37.2C**), that grow from windblown seeds might be randomly dispersed. However, varying habitat conditions and social interactions make random distribution rare.

Estimates of population density and distribution patterns enable researchers to monitor changes in a population and to

▲ **Figure 37.2B** Uniform distribution of penguins in the Falkland Islands and schematic (inset)

compare and contrast the growth and stability of populations in different areas. The next module describes another tool that ecologists use to study populations.

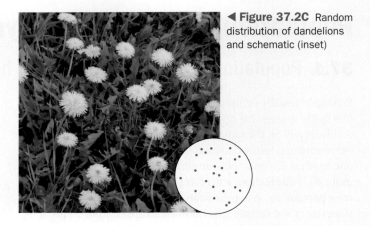

◄ **Figure 37.2C** Random distribution of dandelions and schematic (inset)

? What distribution pattern would you predict in a forest population of termites, which live in damp, rotting wood?

Clumped (in fallen logs or dead trees) ●

37.3 Life tables track survivorship in populations

Life tables track survivorship, the chance of an individual in a given population surviving to various ages. Starting with a population of 100 000 people, Table 37.3 shows the number who are expected to be alive at the beginning of each age interval, based on death rates in 2009. For example, 97 619 out of 100 000 people (that is, 97.6%) are expected to live to age 50. The chance of surviving to age 60, shown in the last column of the table, is 0.953. The chance of surviving to age 90, however, is only 0.407. The life insurance industry uses life tables to predict how long, on average, a person will live. Population ecologists have adopted this technique and constructed life tables for various other species. By identifying the most vulnerable stages of an organism's life, life table data help conservationists develop effective measures for maintaining a viable population.

Life tables can be used to construct **survivorship curves**, which plot survivorship as the proportion of individuals from an initial population that are alive at each age (Figure 37.3). By using a percentage scale instead of actual ages on the *x*-axis, we can compare species with widely varying lifespans on the same graph. The curve for the human population shows that most people survive to the older age intervals, as we saw in the life table. Ecologists refer to the shape of this curve as Type I survivorship. Species that exhibit a Type I curve—humans and many other large mammals—usually produce few offspring but give them good care, increasing the likelihood that they will survive to maturity.

In contrast, a Type III curve indicates low survivorship for the very young, followed by a period when survivorship is high for those few individuals who live to a certain age. Species with this type of survivorship curve usually produce very large numbers of offspring but provide little or no care for them.

TABLE 37.3 | LIFE TABLE FOR THE CANADIAN POPULATION IN 2009

Age Interval	Number Living at Start of Age Interval (*N*)	Number Dying During Age Interval (*D*)	Chance of surviving Interval 1-(*D/N*)
0–10	100 000	654	0.993
11–20	99 346	335	0.997
21–30	99 011	573	0.994
31–40	98 438	819	0.992
41–50	97 619	1889	0.981
51–60	95 730	4527	0.953
61–70	91 203	10 080	0.889
71–80	81 123	21 259	0.738
81–90	59 864	35 523	0.407
91+	24 341	24 341	0.000

▲ **Figure 37.3** Three types of survivorship curves in humans (I), squirrels (II), and oysters (III)

Some fishes, for example, can produce millions of eggs at a time, but most offspring die as larvae from predation or other causes. Many invertebrates, such as oysters, also have Type III survivorship curves.

A Type II curve (shown for squirrels in Figure 37.3) is intermediate, with survivorship constant over the lifespan. That is, individuals are no more vulnerable at one stage of the life cycle than at another. This type of survivorship has been observed in some invertebrates, lizards, and rodents.

? How does the chance of survival change with age in organisms with a Type III survivorship curve?

● The chance of survival is initially low but increases after an individual reaches a certain age.

37.4 Idealized models predict patterns of population growth

Population size fluctuates as new individuals are born or immigrate into an area and others die or emigrate. Some populations—for example, trees in a mature forest—are relatively constant over time. Other populations change rapidly, even explosively. Consider a single bacterium that divides every 20 minutes. There would be two bacteria after 20 minutes, four after 40 minutes, eight after 60 minutes, and so on. In just 12 hours, the population would approach 70 billion cells. If reproduction continued at this rate for a day and a half—a mere 36 hours—there would be enough bacteria to form a layer 30 cm deep over Earth's entire surface. Using idealized models, population ecologists can predict how the size of a particular population will change over time under different conditions.

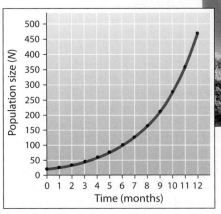

▲ **Figure 37.4A** Exponential growth of rabbits

The Exponential Growth Model The rate of population increase under ideal conditions, called exponential growth, can be calculated using the simple equation $G = rN$. The G stands for the growth rate of the population (the number of *new* individuals added per time interval); N is the population size (the number of individuals in the population at a particular time); and r stands for the **per capita rate of increase** (the average contribution of each individual to population growth; per capita means "per person").

How do we estimate the per capita rate of increase? Population growth reflects the number of births minus the number of deaths (the model assumes that immigration and emigration are equal). Suppose a population of rabbits has 100 individuals, and there are 50 births and 20 deaths in one month. The net increase (G) is $50 - 20$, or 30 rabbits. The per capita increase in the population ($r = G/N$) is 30/100, or 0.3.

In a population growing in an ideal environment with unlimited space and resources, r is the maximum capacity of members of that population to reproduce. Thus, the value of r depends on the kind of organism. For example, rabbits have a higher r than elephants, and bacteria have a higher r than rabbits.

When a population is expanding without limits, r remains constant and the rate of population growth depends on the number of individuals already in the population (N). In **Table 37.4A**, a population begins with 20 rabbits. The growth rate (G) for this population, using $r = 0.3$, is shown in the right-hand column. Notice that the larger the population size, the more new individuals are added during each time interval.

Graphing these data in **Figure 37.4A** produces a J-shaped curve, which is typical of exponential growth. The lower part of the J, where the slope of the line is almost flat, results from the relatively slow growth when N is small. As the population increases, the slope becomes steeper.

The **exponential growth model** gives an idealized picture of unlimited population growth. There is no restriction on the abilities of the organisms to live, grow, and reproduce. Even elephants, the slowest breeders on the planet, would increase exponentially if enough resources were available. Although elephants typically produce only six young in a 100-year

TABLE 37.4A	EXPONENTIAL GROWTH OF RABBITS, $r = 0.3$	
Time (months)	**N**	**G = rN**
0	20	6
1	26	8
2	34	10
3	44	13
4	57	17
5	74	22
6	96	29
7	125	38
8	163	49
9	212	64
10	276	83
11	359	108
12	467	140

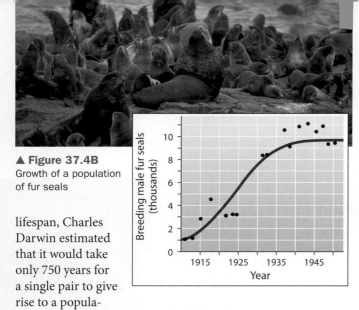

▲ Figure 37.4B
Growth of a population of fur seals

lifespan, Charles Darwin estimated that it would take only 750 years for a single pair to give rise to a population of 19 million. But any population—bacteria, rabbits, or elephants—will eventually be limited by the resources available. This is why we are not walking around in 30 cm of bacteria.

Limiting Factors and the Logistic Growth Model

In nature, a population that is introduced to a new environment or is rebounding from a catastrophic decline in numbers may grow exponentially for a while. Eventually, however, one or more environmental factors will limit its growth rate as the population reaches its maximum sustainable size. Environmental factors that restrict population growth are called **limiting factors**.

You can see the effect of population-limiting factors in the graph in **Figure 37.4B**, which illustrates the growth of a population of fur seals on St. Paul Island, off the coast of Alaska. (For simplicity, only the mated bulls were counted. Each has a harem of a number of females, as shown in the photograph.) Before 1925, the seal population on the island remained low because of uncontrolled hunting, although it changed from year to year. After hunting was controlled, the population increased rapidly until about 1935, when it began to level off and started fluctuating around a population size of about 10 000 bull seals. At this point, a number of limiting factors, including some hunting and the amount of space suitable for breeding, restricted population growth.

The fur seal growth curve fits the **logistic growth model**, a description of idealized population growth that is slowed by limiting factors as the population size increases. **Figure 37.4C** compares the logistic growth model (red) with the exponential growth model (blue). As you can see, the logistic curve is J-shaped at first, but gradually levels off to form an S-shaped curve.

To model logistic growth, the formula for exponential growth, rN, is multiplied by an expression that describes the effect of limiting factors on an increasing population size:

$$G = rN \frac{(K - N)}{K}$$

This equation is actually simpler than it looks. The only new symbol in the equation is K, which stands for carrying capacity. **Carrying capacity** is the maximum population size that a particular environment can sustain ("carry"). For the fur seal population on St. Paul Island, for instance, K is about 10 000 mated males. The value of K varies, depending on the species

▲ Figure 37.4C Logistic growth and exponential growth compared

and the resources available in the habitat. K might be considerably less than 10 000 for a fur seal population on a smaller island with fewer breeding sites. Even in one location, K is not a fixed number. Organisms interact with other organisms in their communities, including predators, parasites, and food sources, that may affect K. Changes in abiotic factors may also increase or decrease carrying capacity. In any case, the concept of carrying capacity expresses an essential fact of nature: Resources are finite.

Table 37.4B demonstrates how the expression $(K - N)/K$ in the logistic growth model produces the S-shaped curve. At the outset, N (the population size) is very small compared to K (the carrying capacity). Thus, $(K - N)/K$ nearly equals K/K, or 1, and population growth (G) is close to rN—that is, exponential growth. As the population increases and N gets closer to carrying capacity, $(K - N)/K$ becomes an increasingly smaller fraction. The growth rate slows as rN is multiplied by that fraction. At carrying capacity, the population is as large as it can theoretically get in its environment; at this point, $N = K$, and $(K - N)/K = 0$. The population growth rate (G) becomes zero. If the population size should exceed the carrying capacity, $(K - N)/K$ becomes a negative fraction and the population will start to shrink.

What does the logistic growth model suggest to us about real populations in nature? The model predicts that a population's growth rate will be small when the population size is *either* small or large, and highest when the population is at an intermediate level relative to the carrying capacity. At a low population

TABLE 37.4B — EFFECT OF K ON GROWTH RATE AS N APPROACHES K, $K = 1000$, $r = 0.1$

N	rN	$(K - N)/K$	$G = rN(K - N)/K$
10	1	0.99	0.99
100	10	0.9	9.00
400	40	0.6	24.00
500	50	0.5	25.00
600	60	0.4	24.00
700	70	0.3	21.00
900	95	0.05	0.25
1000	100	0.00	0.00

level, resources are abundant, and the population is able to grow nearly exponentially. At this point, however, the increase is small because N is small. In contrast, at a high population level, limiting factors strongly oppose the population's potential to increase. There might be less food available per individual or fewer breeding territories, nest sites, or shelters. These limiting factors cause the birth rate to decrease, the death rate to increase, or both. Eventually, when the birth rate equals the death rate, the population stabilizes at the carrying capacity (K).

It is important to realize that the logistic growth model presents a mathematical ideal that is a useful starting point for studying population growth and for constructing more complex models. Like any good starting hypothesis, the logistic model has stimulated research, leading to a better understanding of the factors affecting population growth. We take a closer look at some of these factors next.

 In logistic growth, at what population size (in terms of K) is the population increasing most rapidly? Explain why.

● When N is 1/2 K. At this population size, there are more reproducing individuals than at lower population sizes and still lots of space or other resources available for growth.

37.5 Multiple factors may limit population growth

The logistic growth model predicts that population growth will slow and eventually stop as population density increases. That is, at higher population densities, the birth rate decreases, the death rate increases, or both. What are the possible causes of these density-dependent changes in birth and death rates?

Several **density-dependent factors**—limiting factors whose intensity is related to population density—appear to limit growth in natural populations. The most obvious is **intraspecific competition**—competition between individuals of the same species for limited resources. (The prefix *intra* means "within.") As a limited food supply is divided among more and more individuals, birth rates may decline as individuals have less energy available for reproduction. In **Figure 37.5A**, clutch size (the number of eggs a female bird lays in a "litter") declines as the population density, and therefore the number of competitors, increases.

Density-dependent factors often depress a population's growth by increasing the death rate. In a laboratory experiment with flour beetles, for example, survivorship declined with increasing population density **(Figure 37.5B)**. In a natural setting, plants that grow close together may experience increased mortality as competition for resources increases. And those that survive will likely produce fewer flowers, fruits, and seeds than uncrowded individuals. In an animal population, the

▲ **Figure 37.5B** Decreasing survival rates with increasing density in a population of flour beetles

death rate may climb as a result of increased disease transmission under crowded conditions or the accumulation of toxic waste products. Predation may also be an important cause of density-dependent mortality. A predator may concentrate on a particular kind of prey as that prey becomes abundant.

A limiting factor may be something other than food or nutrients. In many vertebrates that defend a territory, the availability of space may limit reproduction. For instance, the number of nesting sites on rocky islands in Newfoundland and Labrador may limit the population size of seabirds such as gannets. Or, like a game of musical chairs, the number of safe hiding places may limit a prey population by exposing some individuals to a greater risk of predation.

For some animal species, physiological factors may regulate population size. White-footed mice in a small field enclosure will multiply from a few to a colony of 30 to 40 individuals, but reproduction then declines until the population ceases to grow. This drop in reproduction occurs even when additional food and shelter are provided. High population densities in mice appear to induce a stress syndrome in which hormonal changes can delay sexual maturation, cause reproductive organs to shrink, and depress the immune system. In this case, high densities cause both a decrease in birth rate and an increase in

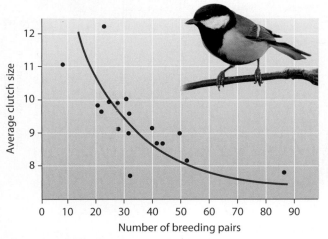

▲ **Figure 37.5A** Decreasing birth rate with increasing density in a population of great tits

death rate. Similar effects of crowding have been observed in wild populations of other rodents.

In many natural populations, abiotic factors such as weather may affect population size well before density-dependent factors become important. A population-limiting factor whose intensity is unrelated to population density is called a **density-independent factor**. If we look at the growth curve of such a population, we see something like exponential growth followed by a rapid decline, rather than a levelling off. **Figure 37.5C** shows this effect for a population of aphids, insects that feed on the sugary phloem sap of plants. These and many other insects undergo virtually exponential growth in the spring and then rapidly die off when the weather turns hot and dry in the summer. A few individuals may survive, and these may allow population growth to resume if favourable conditions return. In some populations of insects—many mosquitoes and grasshoppers, for instance—adults die off entirely, leaving only eggs, which initiate population growth the following year. In addition to seasonal changes in the weather, disturbances—such as fire, storms, and habitat disruption by human activity—can affect a population's size regardless of its density.

Over the long term, most populations are probably regulated by a mixture of factors. Some populations remain fairly stable in size and are presumably close to a carrying capacity that is determined by biotic factors such as competition or predation. Most populations for which we have long-term data, however, show fluctuations in numbers. Thus, the dynamics

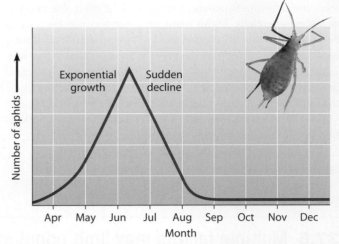

▲ **Figure 37.5C** Weather change as a density-independent factor limiting aphid population growth

of many populations result from a complex interaction of both density-dependent factors and density-independent abiotic factors such as climate and disturbances.

 List some of the factors that may reduce birth rate or increase death rate as population density increases.

● Food and nutrient limitations, insufficient territories, increase in disease and predation, accumulation of toxins

---

37.6 Some populations have "boom-and-bust" cycles

Some populations of insects, birds, and mammals undergo dramatic fluctuations in density with remarkable regularity. "Booms" characterized by rapid exponential growth are followed by "busts," during which the population falls back to a minimal level. A striking example is the boom-and-bust growth cycles of lemming populations that occur every three to four years. You will learn more about lemming population dynamics in the next module.

Figure 37.6 illustrates another well-known example—the cycles of snowshoe hare and lynx. The sizes of these populations have been well documented over the last 150 years, in part because of the collections by Hudson's Bay Company trappers. The lynx is one of the main predators of the snowshoe hare in the far northern forests of Canada and Alaska. About every 10 years, both hare and lynx populations show a rapid increase followed by a sharp decline.

What causes these boom-and-bust cycles? Since ups and downs in the two populations seem to almost match each other on the graph, does this mean that changes in one directly affect

▲ **Figure 37.6** Population cycles of the snowshoe hare and the lynx

the other? For the hare cycles, there are three main hypotheses. First, cycles may be caused by winter food shortages that result from overgrazing. Second, cycles may be due to predator–prey interactions. Many predators other than lynx, such as coyotes, foxes, and great horned owls, eat hares, and the combination of predators might overexploit their prey. Third, cycles could be affected by a combination of limited food resources and excessive predation. Recent field experiments support the hypothesis that the 10-year cycles of the snowshoe hare are largely driven by excessive predation, but are also influenced by fluctuations in the hare's food supplies.

For the lynx and many other predators that depend heavily on a single species of prey, the availability of prey can have a strong influence on population size. Thus, the 10-year cycles in the lynx population probably do result at least in part from the 10-year cycles in the hare population. As the lynx population declines, the prey population—released from predator pressure—rebounds. Long-term studies are the key to unravelling the complex causes of such population cycles.

? **In one experiment, providing more food to hares increased their population density, but the population continued to show cyclic collapses. What might you conclude from these results?**

● Hare population cycles are not primarily caused by food shortages.

RUMOUR HAS IT **37.7 Do lemmings commit mass suicide by jumping over cliffs?**

If you have heard about lemmings **(Figure 37.7)**, small rodents that live in Canada's tundra, you have likely heard the rumour that lemmings periodically commit suicide in large numbers. It is not uncommon to find dead lemmings washed up on riverbanks and shorelines. The frequency of these findings led to the idea that lemmings must choose to kill themselves by drowning. This story has been told for centuries and was promulgated by the 1958 Academy Award–winning Disney documentary *White Wilderness*. The lemming metaphor, which describes people who go along with popular opinion without question, has even crept into popular culture, appearing in television shows, songs, and video games.

Lemming populations have regular boom-and-bust cycles, similar to many other rodents. Population booms occur every three to four years and are followed shortly after by a bust. It is commonly thought that the bust is caused by mass suicide in response to high population density. Although we do not fully understand the dynamics of lemming populations, biologists believe that food supply and predation are the real causes behind the population bust.

Resources become scarce as the lemming population booms. To avoid increased competition for food, large numbers of lemmings disperse in search of greener pastures. The search for food frequently takes them across rivers or lakes. Although lemmings may be seen jumping into water, they do so to swim across the water to find new sources of food. Lemmings are adept swimmers, but if large numbers are trying to cross a passage simultaneously, often some individuals drown because they are pushed under the water. If the lemmings migrate into unfamiliar territory, accidental drownings can occur as they swim to a distant shore. Any drowning, however, is not a conscious choice on the lemming's part. These deaths, unintentional though they are, do alleviate the pressures of competition within the population. In fact, under the stress caused by high population density, lemmings are more likely to kill each other than themselves.

But if this behaviour was captured on film in *White Wilderness*, how can we be sure this rumour is false? Because the movie's footage was completely staged near Calgary, Alberta, a region where there are no lemmings or ocean. The film's producers' purchased lemmings from children in Churchill, Manitoba, and flew them to the filming location. What was not shown in this film was the crew forcing the lemmings off a precipice with the help of a turntable. The CBC's 1982 documentary *Cruel Camera* uncovered the truth behind the Disney footage. Although many nature documentaries stage shots to explain real biological phenomena, creating a fictional event is an entirely different issue.

The rumour of lemming suicide is untrue and past documentation of this event was staged. Some lemmings may drown during migration, but not intentionally. In the next module, we will discuss how evolution can shape life histories.

? **What factor prompts the migration of large numbers of lemmings?**

● Increased competition for food and resources

▲ **Figure 37.7** A northern collared lemming (*Dicrostonyx groenlandicus*)

37.8 Evolution shapes life histories

Now that we have looked at patterns of population growth, we turn our attention to the differences in reproductive patterns of populations and how they are shaped by natural selection.

The traits that affect an organism's schedule of reproduction and death make up its **life history**. Some key life history traits are the age of first reproduction, the frequency of reproduction, the number of offspring, and the amount of parental care given. Natural selection cannot optimize all these traits simultaneously because an organism has limited time, energy, and nutrients. For example, an organism that gives birth to a large number of offspring will not be able to provide a great deal of parental care. Consequently, the combination of life history traits in a population represents trade-offs that balance the demands of reproduction and survival. Because selective pressures vary, life histories are very diverse. Nevertheless, ecologists have observed some patterns that are useful for understanding how life history characteristics have been shaped by natural selection.

One life history pattern is typified by small-bodied, short-lived animals (for example, insects and small rodents) that develop and reach sexual maturity rapidly, have a large number of offspring, and offer little or no parental care. A similar pattern is seen in small, nonwoody plants such as dandelions that produce thousands of tiny seeds. Ecologists hypothesize that selection for this set of life history traits occurs in environments where resources are abundant, permitting exponential growth. It is sometimes called *r-selection* because *r* (the per capita rate of increase) is maximized. Most *r*-selected species have an advantage in habitats that experience unpredictable disturbances, such as fire, floods, hurricanes, drought, or cold weather, which create new opportunities by suddenly reducing a population to low levels. Human activity is a major cause of disturbance, producing road cuts, freshly cleared fields and woodlots, and poorly maintained lawns that are commonly colonized by *r*-selected plants and animals.

In contrast, large-bodied, long-lived animals (such as bears and elephants) develop slowly and produce few, but well-cared-for, offspring. Plants with comparable life history traits include coconut palms, which produce relatively few seeds that are well stocked with nutrient-rich material—the plant's version of parental care. Ecologists hypothesize that selection for this set of life history traits occurs in environments where the population size is near carrying capacity (*K*), so it is sometimes called *K*-selection. Population growth in these situations is limited by density-dependent factors. Because competition for resources is keen, *K*-selected organisms gain an advantage by allocating energy to their own survival and to the survival of their descendants. Thus, *K*-selected organisms are adapted to environments that typically have a stable climate and little opportunity for rapid population growth.

The hypothesis of *r*- and *K*-selection has been criticized as an oversimplification, and most organisms fall somewhere between the extremes. However, this hypothesis has stimulated a vigorous subfield of ecological research on the evolution of life histories.

A long-term project in Trinidad has provided direct evidence that life history traits can be shaped by natural selection. For years, researchers have been studying guppy populations living in small, relatively isolated pools. As shown in **Figure 37.8**, some guppy populations live in pools with predators called killifish, which eat mainly small, immature guppies (Pool 1). Other guppy populations live where larger fish, called pike-cichlids, eat mostly mature, large-bodied guppies (Pool 2). Guppies in populations exposed to these pike-cichlids tend to be smaller, mature earlier, and produce more offspring at a time than those in areas

▲ **Figure 37.8** The effect of predation on the life history traits of guppies

with killifish. Thus, guppy populations differ in certain life history traits, depending on the kind of predator in their environment. In these guppies, the age of maturation is both variable and heritable and, therefore, can change in response to pressure (predation) by means of natural selection.

To test whether the feeding preferences of different predators caused these differences in life histories by natural selection, researchers introduced guppies from a pike-cichlid habitat into a guppy-free pool inhabited by killifish (Pool 3). The scientists tracked the weight and age at sexual maturity in the experimental guppy populations for 11 years, comparing these guppies with control guppies that remained in the pike-cichlid pools. The average weight and age at sexual maturity of the transplanted populations increased significantly as compared with the control populations. These studies demonstrate not only that life history traits are heritable and shaped by natural selection, but also that questions about evolution can be tested by field experiments.

As we have seen, population ecology involves theoretical model building as well as observations and experiments in the field. Next we look at how the principles of population ecology can be applied to conservation and management.

 Refer to Module 37.3. Which type of survivorship curve would you expect to find in a population experiencing *r*-selection? *K*-selection?

● Type III for a population experiencing *r*-selection; Type I for *K*-selection

---

BIOLOGY AND SOCIETY

37.9 Principles of population ecology may help to save the Atlantic cod

Principles of population ecology can help to guide us toward resource management goals, such as increasing populations we wish to harvest or save from extinction. Wildlife managers, fishery biologists, and foresters try to use **sustainable resource management**: harvesting crops without damaging the resource. In terms of population growth, this means maintaining a high population growth rate to replenish the population. According to the logistic growth model, the fastest growth rate occurs when the population size is at roughly half the carrying capacity of the habitat. Theoretically, a resource manager should achieve the best results by harvesting the populations down to this level. However, the logistic model assumes that growth rate and carrying capacity are stable over time. Calculations based on these assumptions, which are not realistic for some populations, may lead to unsustainably high harvest levels that ultimately deplete the resource. In addition, economic and political pressures often outweigh ecological concerns, and the amount of scientific information is frequently insufficient.

Fishes, the only wild animals still hunted on a large scale, are particularly vulnerable to overharvesting. Overfishing in the Atlantic cod fishery off eastern Canada, for example, has nearly decimated the population. Between 1950 and 1990, the population of Atlantic cod was reduced by 99% and declared endangered.

What led to the near extinction of this fish? The advent of factory freezer trawlers allowed fish to be processed at sea. With fewer trips between the fishing grounds and port, more fish could be caught more efficiently. Moreover, estimates of cod population sizes were too high, and the practice of discarding young cod (fish below the legal size limit) at sea caused a higher mortality rate than predicted.

The Canadian government intervened in an attempt to save the species from extinction. In 1992, it imposed a two-year moratorium (complete ban) on the fishing of Atlantic cod. **Figure 37.9** shows the rapid reduction in yield to zero tonnes at this time. By eliminating the harvest, hopes were that the population would recover. By 1994, there were no signs of recovery and the moratorium was extended for another five years. Twenty years after the initial moratorium, the population remains small and the moratorium is still in effect. However, Dr. Ken Frank of the Bedford

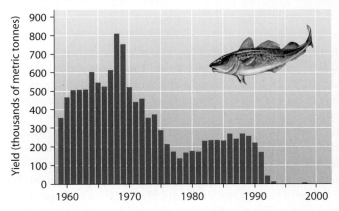

▲ **Figure 37.9** Collapse of the Atlantic cod fishery off Newfoundland

Institute of Oceanography in Dartmouth, Nova Scotia, has shown that the Atlantic cod is now in its initial stages of recovery. The population of Atlantic cod near the Grand Banks area increased by nearly 70% between 2007 and 2010. Despite this promising percentage, the stock is still only 10% of the size it was 50 years ago. Although optimistic, Frank still suggests caution to ensure the past is not repeated.

Following the decline of many other populations, including other fish and whales, resource managers are trying to minimize the risk of resource collapse by setting minimum population sizes or imposing protected, harvest-free areas. For species that are in decline or facing extinction, resource managers may try to provide additional habitat or improve the quality of existing habitat to raise the carrying capacity and thus increase population growth.

As you have learned, many factors influence a population's size. To effectively manage any population, we must identify those variables, account for the unpredictability of the environment, consider interactions with other species, and weigh the economic, political, and conservation issues. These same issues apply to the growth of the human population, which we explore next.

 Explain why managers often try to maintain populations of fish and game species at about half their carrying capacity.

● To protect wildlife from overharvesting yet maintain lower population levels so that growth rate is high and mortality from resource limitation is reduced

CHAPTER 37 | Population Ecology **799**

The Human Population

37.10 The human population continues to increase, but the growth rate is slowing

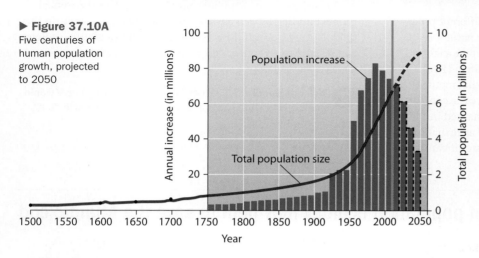

▶ **Figure 37.10A**
Five centuries of human population growth, projected to 2050

As the world population skyrocketed from 2 billion in 1927 to 3 billion just 33 years later, some scientists became alarmed. They feared that Earth's carrying capacity would be reached and that density-dependent factors (see Module 37.5) would maintain that population size through human suffering and death. But the overall growth rate peaked in 1962. In the more developed nations, advanced medical care continued to improve survivorship, but effective contraceptives held down the birth rate. As a result, the overall growth rate of the world's population began a downward trend.

In the few seconds it takes you to read this sentence, 21 babies will be born somewhere in the world and 9 people will die. The statistics may have changed a bit since this book was printed, but births will still far outnumber deaths. An imbalance between births and deaths is the cause of population growth (or decline), and as the red curve in **Figure 37.10A** shows, the human population is expected to continue increasing for at least the next several decades. The United Nations marked October 31, 2011, as the day that the global population reached 7 billion. The bar graph in Figure 37.10A tells a different part of the story. The number of people added to the population each year has been declining since the 1980s. How do we explain these patterns of human population growth?

Let's begin with the rise in population from 480 million people in 1500 to the current population. In our simplest model (see Module 37.4), population growth depends on r (per capita rate of increase) and N (population size). Because the value of r was assumed to be constant in a given environment, the growth rate in the examples we used in Module 37.4 depended wholly on the population size. Throughout most of human history, the same was true of people. Although parents had many children, mortality was also high, so r (birth rate − death rate) was only slightly higher than zero. As a result, population growth was very slow. (If we extended the x-axis of Figure 37.10A back in time to year 1, when the population was roughly 300 million, the line would be almost flat for 1500 years.) The 1 billion mark was not reached until the early 19th century.

As economic development in Europe and North America led to advances in nutrition and sanitation and later, medical care, people took control of their population's rate of increase (r). At first, the death rate decreased, while the birth rate remained the same. The net rate of increase rose, and population growth began to pick up steam as the 20th century began. By mid-century, improvements in nutrition, sanitation, and healthcare had spread to the developing world, spurring growth at a breakneck pace as birth rates far outstripped death rates.

Demographic Transition The world population is undergoing a change known as a **demographic transition**, a shift from zero population growth in which birth rates and death rates are high but roughly equal, to zero population growth characterized by low but roughly equal birth and death rates. **Figure 37.10B** shows the demographic transition of Mexico, which is projected to approach zero population growth with low birth and death rates in the next few decades. Notice that the death rate dropped sharply from 1925 to 1975 (the spike corresponds to the worldwide flu epidemic of 1918–1919), while the birth rate remained high until the 1960s. This pattern is typical for demographic transitions.

Because economic development has occurred at different times in different regions, worldwide demographic transition is a mosaic of the changes occurring in different countries. The most developed nations have completed or are nearing completion of their demographic transitions. In these countries collectively, the rate of increase per 1000 individuals was estimated at 0.4 in 2011 (Table 37.10). In the developing world, death rates have dropped, but high birth rates persist. As a result, these populations are growing rapidly. Of the more than 74 million people added to the world in 2011, more than 71 million were in developing nations.

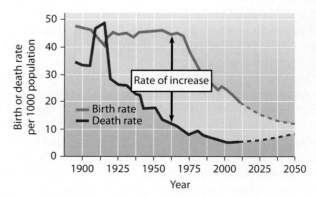

▲ **Figure 37.10B** Demographic transition in Mexico

TABLE 37.10

TABLE 37.10 | POPULATION CHANGES IN 2011 (ESTIMATED)

Population	Birth Rate (per 1000)	Death Rate (per 1000)	Rate of Increase (per 1000)
World	19.14	7.99	11.15
More developed nations	11.33	9.83	1.50
Less developed nations	21.84	7.73	14.11

Reduced family size is the key to the demographic transition. As women's status and education increase, they delay reproduction and choose to have fewer children. This phenomenon has been observed in both developed and developing countries, wherever the lives of women have improved. Given access to affordable contraceptive methods, women generally practice birth control, and many countries now subsidize family planning services and have official population policies. In many other countries, however, issues of family planning remain socially and politically charged, with heated disagreement over how much support should be provided for family planning.

Age Structures A demographic tool called an age-structure diagram is helpful for predicting a population's future growth. The **age structure** of a population is the number of individuals in different age groups. **Figure 37.10C** shows the age structure of Mexico's population in 1985 and 2010 and its projected age structure in 2035. In these diagrams, green represents the portion of the population in their prereproductive years (0–14), pink indicates the part of the population in prime reproductive years (15–44), and blue is the proportion in postreproductive years (45 and older). Within each of these broader groups,

each horizontal bar represents the population in a five-year age group. The area to the left of each vertical centre line represents the number of males in each age group; females are represented on the right side of the line.

An age structure with a broad base, such as Mexico's in 1985, reflects a population that has a high proportion of children and a high birth rate. On average, each woman is substantially exceeding the replacement rate of two children per couple. As Figure 37.10B shows, the birth rate and the rate of increase have dropped 25 years later, but the population continues to be affected by its earlier expansion. This situation, which results from the increased proportion of women of child-bearing age in the population, is known as **population momentum**. Girls aged 0–14 in the 1985 age structure (outlined in yellow) are in their reproductive years in 2010, and girls who are aged 0–14 in 2010 (outlined in purple) will carry the legacy of rapid growth forward to 2035. Putting the brakes on a rapidly expanding population is like stopping a freight train—the end result takes place long after the decision to do it was made. Even when fertility is reduced to replacement rate, the total population will continue to increase for several decades. The percentage of individuals under the age of 15 gives a rough idea of future growth. In the developing countries, about 29% of the population is in this age group. In contrast, roughly 16% of the population of developed nations is under the age of 15. Population momentum also explains why the population size in Figure 37.10A continues to increase even though fewer people are added to the population each year.

In the next module, we examine the age structure of Canada.

? During the demographic transition from high birth and death rates to low birth and death rates, countries usually undergo rapid population growth. Explain why.

● The death rate declines before the birth rate declines, creating a period when births greatly outnumber deaths. This also sets up population momentum.

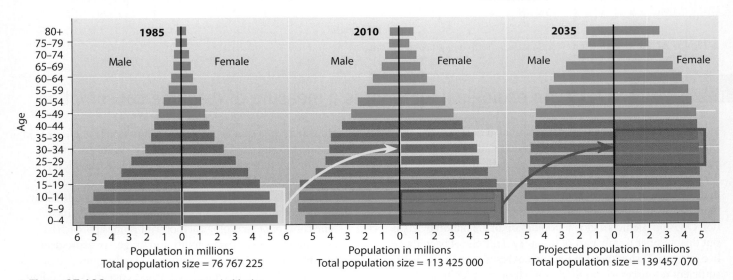

▲ **Figure 37.10C** Population momentum in Mexico

1985 — Population in millions — Total population size = 76 767 225

2010 — Population in millions — Total population size = 113 425 000

2035 — Projected population in millions — Total population size = 139 457 070

37.11 Age structures reveal social and economic trends

Age-structure diagrams not only reveal a population's growth trends, but also indicate social conditions. For instance, an expanding population has an increasing need for schools, employment, and infrastructure. A large elderly population requires that extensive resources be allotted to healthcare. Let's look at trends in the age structure of Canada from 2009 to 2036 (**Figure 37.11**).

The large bulge in the 2009 age structure corresponds to the "baby boom" that lasted for about two decades after World War II ended in 1945. The large number of children swelled school enrolments, prompting construction of new schools and creating a demand for teachers. However, graduates who were born near the end of the boom faced stiff competition for jobs. Because they make up such a large segment of the population, boomers have had an enormous influence on social and economic trends.

Where are the baby boomers now? The leading edge has reached retirement age, which will place increasing pressure on programs such as Medicare, Old Age Security, and Canada Pension Plan. The **demographic dependency ratio (DDR)** is the ratio of youths (aged 0 to 14) and seniors (aged 65 and older) to the number of individuals in the workforce between the ages of 15 and 64. Changes in the DDR are indicative of changes in the population age structure. A lower DDR means that there are more workers paying into social programs and fewer collecting from these programs. As the DDR increases, greater social and/or economic demands are placed on working Canadians. In 2009, the DDR was 0.44. That is, there were 44 dependents for every 100 individuals in the workforce. Projections for 2036 suggest this number may rise to a staggering 0.65, with the majority of dependents being seniors. The percentage of the population over the age of 80, which was 3.5% in 2009, is projected to rise to nearly 6.8%—more than 3 million people—in 2036.

 During the baby boom after World War II, the DDR was high (around 0.8) because of an increased birth rate. What social and economic costs were associated with this large youth population?

● A greater demand for schools and teachers was paid for by the taxpaying workforce.

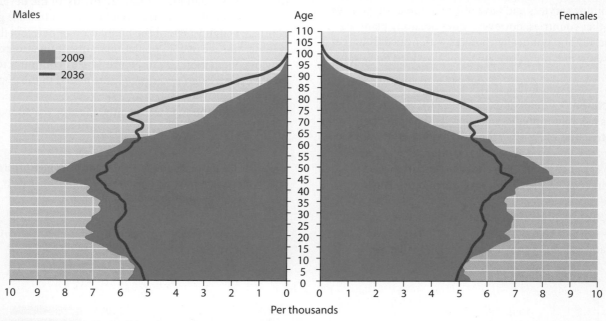

▲ **Figure 37.11** Age structures for Canada in 2009 and 2036 (projected)

37.12 An ecological footprint is a measure of resource consumption

How large a population of humans can Earth hold? In Module 37.10, we saw that the world's population is growing exponentially, though at a slower rate than it did in the last century. The rate of increase, as well as population momentum, predict that the populations of most developing nations will continue to increase for the foreseeable future. The United Nations Population Division predicts a global population of 9.2 billion by 2050. But this number is only part of the story. Trillions of bacteria can live in a petri dish *if* they have sufficient resources. Do we have sufficient resources to sustain 8 or 9 billion people? To accommodate all the people expected to live on our planet by 2050, the world will have to double food production (see Module 23.11). Water use has risen sixfold over the past 70 years, causing rivers to run dry, water for irrigation to be depleted, and levels of groundwater to drop. And because so much open space will be needed to support the expanding human population, many thousands of other species are expected to become extinct.

The concept of an ecological footprint is one approach to understanding resource availability and usage. An **ecological footprint** is an estimate of the amount of land required to provide the raw materials an individual or a nation consumes, including food, fuel, water, housing, and waste disposal. When the total area

▲ **Figure 37.12A** Families in India (left) and North America (right) display their possessions

of ecologically productive land on Earth is divided by the global population, we each have a share of about 1.8 global hectares per capita (1 hectare, or ha, = 10 000 m²; a *global hectare* [gha] is a hectare with world-average ability to produce resources and absorb wastes). According to the Global Footprint Network, in 2009 (the most recent year for which data are available), the average ecological footprint for the world's population was 2.6 gha—we have already overshot the planet's capacity to sustain us.

On average, at 6.5 gha per person, Canadians have a much higher ecological footprint than the global average,

making Canada, the ninth highest in the world. Looking at **Figure 37.12A**, it is not difficult to understand why. Compared with a family in rural India, Canadians have an abundance of possessions. Canadians also consume a disproportionate amount of food and fuel. By this measure, the ecological impact of affluent nations such as Canada is potentially as damaging as unrestrained population growth in the developing world. So the problem is not just overpopulation but overconsumption. **Figure 37.12B** shows the ecological footprint of each country. The world's richest countries, with

The Ecological Footprint of Nations

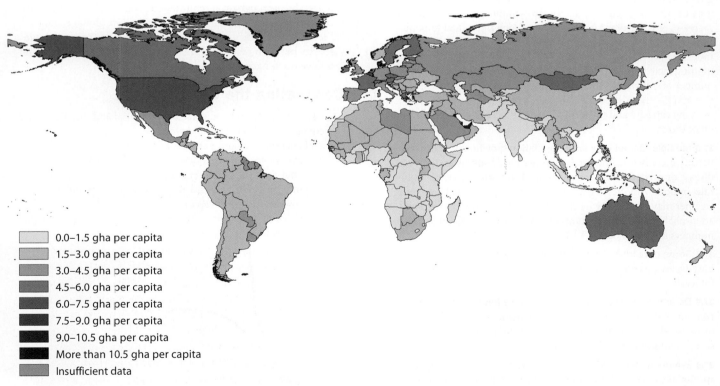

- 0.0–1.5 gha per capita
- 1.5–3.0 gha per capita
- 3.0–4.5 gha per capita
- 4.5–6.0 gha per capita
- 6.0–7.5 gha per capita
- 7.5–9.0 gha per capita
- 9.0–10.5 gha per capita
- More than 10.5 gha per capita
- Insufficient data

Global Footprint Network, 2013. Data 2009 from National Footprint Accounts 2012 Edition

▲ **Figure 37.12B** Ecological footprints around the world

15% of the global population, account for 36% of humanity's total footprint. Global Footprint Network estimates that providing everyone with the same standard of living as Canada would require the resources of more than 3.5 planet Earths.

? What is your ecological footprint? Do an online search to find a site that calculates personal resource consumption.

REVIEW

MasteringBiology® **For Practice Quizzes, BioFlix, MP3 Tutors, and Activities, go to masteringbiology.com.**

Reviewing the Concepts

Population Structure and Dynamics (37.1–37.9)

37.1 Population ecology is the study of how and why populations change. Populations are dynamic and their structure changes over time.

37.2 Density and distribution patterns are important population variables. Population density is the number of individuals in a given area or volume. Environmental and social factors influence the spacing of individuals in various distribution patterns: clumped (most common), uniform, or random.

37.3 Life tables track survivorship in populations. Life tables and survivorship curves predict an individual's statistical chance of dying or surviving during each interval in its life. The three types of survivorship curves reflect species' differences in reproduction and mortality.

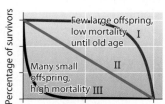

37.4 Idealized models predict patterns of population growth. Exponential growth is the accelerating increase that occurs when growth is unlimited. The equation $G = rN$ describes this J-shaped growth curve; G = the population growth rate; r = per capita rate of increase, or the average contribution of each individual to population growth; and N = the population size. Logistic growth is the model that represents the slowing of population growth as a result of limiting factors and the levelling off at carrying capacity, which is the number of individuals the environment can support. The equation $G = rN(K - N)/K$ describes a logistic growth curve, where K = carrying capacity and the term $(K - N)/K$ accounts for the levelling off of the curve.

37.5 Multiple factors may limit population growth. As a population's density increases, factors such as limited food supply and increased disease or predation may increase the death rate, decrease the birth rate, or both. Abiotic, density-independent factors such as severe weather may limit many natural populations. Most populations are probably regulated by a mixture of factors, and fluctuations in numbers are common.

37.6 Some populations have "boom-and-bust" cycles. Boom-and-bust cycles alternate population growth and decline at regular intervals.

37.7 Do lemmings commit mass suicide by jumping over cliffs? The rumour that lemmings commit mass suicide is untrue. Lemmings disperse when the population gets large and resources become scarce, and some may die accidentally.

37.8 Evolution shapes life histories. Natural selection shapes a species' life history, the series of events from birth through repro- duction to death. Populations with so-called r-selected life history traits produce many offspring and grow rapidly in unpredictable environments. Populations with K-selected traits raise few offspring and maintain relatively stable populations. Most species fall between these extremes.

37.9 Principles of population ecology may help to save the Atlantic cod. The principles of population ecology have practical implications. They strongly suggested that the only way to save the Atlantic cod was to institute a total ban on that fishery.

The Human Population (37.10–37.12)

37.10 The human population continues to increase, but the growth rate is slowing. The human population grew rapidly during the 20th century and currently stands at above 7 billion. Demographic transition, the shift from high birth and death rates to low birth and death rates, has lowered the rate of growth in developed countries. In developing nations, death rates have dropped, but birth rates are still high. The age structure of a population—the proportion of individuals in different age groups—affects its future growth. Population momentum is the continued growth that occurs despite reduced fertility and is a result of girls in the 0–14 age group of a previously expanding population reaching their child-bearing years.

37.11 Age structures reveal social and economic trends. The large number of baby boomers may put strains on Canadian social programs in the future.

37.12 An ecological footprint is a measure of resource consumption. An ecological footprint estimates the amount of land required by each person or country to produce all the resources it consumes and to absorb all of its wastes. The global ecological footprint already exceeds a sustainable level. There is a huge disparity between resource consumption in more developed and less developed nations.

Connecting the Concepts

1. Use this graph of the idealized exponential and logistic growth curves to complete the following.
   a. Label the axes and curves on the graph.
   b. Give the formula that describes the blue curve.
   c. What does the dotted line represent?
   d. For each curve, indicate and explain where population growth is the most rapid.
   e. Which of these curves best represents global human population growth?

2. This graph shows the demographic transition for a hypothetical country. Many developed countries that have achieved a stable population size have undergone a transition similar to this. Answer the following questions concerning this graph.
   a. What does the blue line represent? The red line?
   b. This diagram has been divided into four sections. Describe what is happening in each section.
   c. In which section(s) is the population size stable?
   d. In which section is the population growth rate the highest?

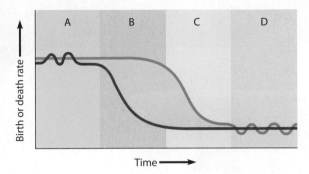

Testing Your Knowledge

Multiple Choice

3. After seeds have sprouted, gardeners often pull up some of the seedlings so that only a few grow to maturity. How does this practice help to produce the best yield?
   a. by increasing K
   b. by decreasing r
   c. by changing the population's age structure
   d. by reducing intraspecific competition
   e. by adding a density-independent factor to the environment

4. To figure out the human population density of your community, you would need to know the number of people living there and
   a. the land area in which they live.
   b. the birth rate of the population.
   c. whether population growth is logistic or exponential.
   d. the distribution pattern of the population.
   e. the carrying capacity.

5. The term $(K - N)/K$
   a. is the carrying capacity for a population.
   b. is greatest when K is very large.
   c. is zero when population size equals carrying capacity.
   d. increases in value as N approaches K.
   e. accounts for the population growing larger than the carrying capacity.

6. With regard to its rate of growth, a population that is growing logistically
   a. grows fastest when density is lowest.
   b. grows at a constant rate.
   c. grows fastest at an intermediate population density.
   d. grows fastest as it approaches carrying capacity.
   e. is always slowed by abiotic factors.

7. Which of the following represents a demographic transition?
   a. A population switches from exponential to logistic growth.
   b. A population reaches zero population growth when the birth rate drops to zero.
   c. There are equal numbers of individuals in all age groups.
   d. A population exhibits boom-and-bust cycles.
   e. A population switches from high birth and death rates to low birth and death rates.

8. Skyrocketing growth of the human population appears to be mainly a result of
   a. migration to thinly settled regions of the globe.
   b. a drop in death rate because of sanitation and healthcare.
   c. better nutrition boosting the birth rate.
   d. the concentration of humans in cities.
   e. social changes that make it desirable to have more children.

9. According to data on ecological footprints,
   a. the carrying capacity of the world is 10 billion.
   b. the carrying capacity of the world would increase if all people ate more meat.
   c. the current demand on global resources by developed countries is less than the resources available in those countries.
   d. an increase in consumerism increases the size of the ecological footprint.
   e. nations with the largest ecological footprints have the fastest population growth rates.

Describing, Comparing, and Explaining

10. What are some factors that might have a density-dependent limiting effect on population growth?

11. What is survivorship? What does a survivorship curve show? Explain what the three survivorship curves tell us about humans, squirrels, and oysters.

12. Describe the factors that might produce the following three types of distribution patterns in populations.

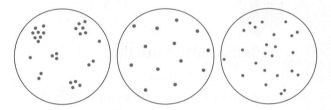

Applying the Concepts

13. The mountain gorilla, spotted owl, giant panda, snow leopard, and grizzly bear are all endangered by human encroachment on their environments. Another thing these animals have in common is that they all have K-selected life history traits. Why might they be more easily endangered than animals with r-selected life history traits? What general type of survivorship curve would you expect these species to exhibit? Explain your answer.

14. How will Canada's changing age structure affect such social programs as the Canadian Pension Plan and Medicare if left unchanged?

15. Many people regard the rapid population growth of developing countries as our most serious environmental problem. Others think that the growth of developed countries, though slower, is actually a greater threat to the environment. What kinds of environmental problems result from population growth in (a) developing countries and (b) developed countries? Which do you think is the greater threat? Why?

Answers to all questions can be found in Appendix E.

Community Ecology

BIG IDEAS

Community Structure

(38.1–38.6)

Community ecologists examine factors that influence the species composition and distribution of communities and factors that affect community stability.

Community Dynamics

(38.7–38.13)

Community structure can change over time, especially after a disturbance.

Landscape Ecology

(38.14–38.15)

Landscape ecologists study the pattern and interaction of adjacent communities.

Help! A Plague of Pine Beetles

Generally unknown prior to the 1980s, the mountain pine beetle (*Dendroctonus ponderosae*), a native of British Columbia, is now infamous. After the pine beetle's decimation of vast tracts of pine forest in British Columbia's interior, its infamy is well deserved. It is estimated that by the time you read this book, the mountain pine beetle will have destroyed nearly 58% of British Columbia's pine forests. In a relatively short time, the dynamics of this mountain community have been dramatically altered.

How can a tiny beetle kill a massive pine tree, let alone an entire forest? First, a female beetle searches for mature (80 years or older) trees, typically lodgepole pines (*Pinus contorta*), and then she bores through and tunnels underneath the bark. Next, she attracts males to the tree through the release of pheromones (volatile chemical reproductive signals). The males arrive and, in turn, attract more females, and a crowd of beetles gathers. Mating occurs and the females lay eggs within the network of excavated tunnels. To defend itself, the tree produces a sticky, toxic resin (often and mistakenly referred to as sap), which may trap and kill a few beetles. Unfortunately for the tree, the beetles do not come alone. They bring the spores of a blue-stained fungus (*Grosmannia clavigera*) with them. (The mycelium of this fungus stains the wood a bluish colour, hence the name.) Insect feeding introduces the spores under the tree's bark. The spores quickly germinate and the fungus grows through the tunnels dug by the beetles. Fungal growth inhibits the release of resin and negates the major defence mechanism of the tree. And together, the sinister symbiosis between beetle and fungus kills the tree.

Thirty-five years ago, beetle numbers were relatively low. Only a few beetles gathered at any infected tree. The low level of infection meant that the death rate of infected trees was low. But in recent years, something changed. Now, instead of a few scattered trees being infected, entire mountainsides of forest succumb to infestation. Two major factors aided the spread of the mountain pine beetle: forestry management practices and climate change.

Forest fires interfere with the spread of the mountain pine beetle. However, forest fires destroy timber valuable to the forestry industry. Therefore, foresters benefit by suppressing forest fires. This practice allows for the accumulation of mature pines—a favoured target of the pine beetle. Fewer fires mean more habitat for the mountain pine beetle.

Exacerbating the problem are the less severe winters associated with global climate change. Pine beetles lay eggs in midsummer and larvae hatch about two weeks later. The larvae feed as they burrow under the bark in the fall. Protected from the cold by the bark, larvae can overwinter. In areas with extremely cold winters, the bark is not protective enough and the larvae die. Until recently, this weakness limited the range of the mountain pine beetle. But with extreme cold becoming less common across Canada, more larvae are surviving through the winter, and the range of the pine beetle is expanding as a result. Once a problem only in British Columbia, the mountain pine beetle has already started to invade forests in Alberta and Saskatchewan.

The mountain pine beetle infestation has now peaked in B.C. The government is no longer trying to control the spread, but is instead focused on managing the environmental and economic effects of the infestation. The havoc wreaked by pine beetles clearly demonstrates how the populations within a community interact in a fine balance. When the balance is disturbed, dire consequences can occur. In this chapter, you will examine the ecology of communities, which includes interactions between organisms and populations. You will read how community structure can change and how different communities form mosaics in the larger ecosystem.

Community Structure

38.1 A community includes all the organisms inhabiting a particular area

In the preceding chapter, we saw that a population is a group of interacting individuals of a particular species. We now move one step up the hierarchy of nature to the level of the community. A biological **community** is an assemblage of all the populations of organisms living close enough together for potential interaction. Ecologists define the boundaries of the community according to the research questions they want to investigate. For example, one ecologist interested in wetland communities might study the shoreline plants and animals of a particular marsh, while another might investigate only the benthic (bottom-dwelling) microbes.

A community can be described by its species composition. You will learn more about species composition, or biodiversity, in the next module. Community ecologists seek to understand how abiotic factors and interactions between populations affect the composition and distribution of communities. For example, a community ecologist might compare the benthic microbes of a marsh located in the temperate zone with those

of a tundra marsh. Community ecologists also investigate community dynamics, the variability or stability in the species composition of a community caused by biotic and abiotic factors. For example, a community ecologist might study changes in the species composition of a saltwater marsh in Nova Scotia after a hurricane.

Community ecology is necessary for the conservation of endangered species and the management of wildlife, game, and fisheries. It is vital for controlling diseases that animals carry, such as malaria, bird flu, and Lyme disease. Community ecology also has applications in agriculture, where people attempt to control the species composition of communities they have established.

? What is the relationship between a community and a population?

A community is a group of populations that interact with each other.

38.2 Biodiversity includes relative abundance and species richness

A community's **biological diversity**, or **biodiversity**, is defined by two components: *species richness*, or the number of different species in a community, and *relative abundance*, the proportional representation of a species in a community. A species' relative abundance is calculated by dividing its population size (number of individuals) by the total number of individuals in the community and then multiplying this result by 100%. For example, if a woodlot community totalling 200 individuals contains 40 poplar trees, the relative abundance of the poplars = 40/200 × 100%, or 20%. To understand why both components are important for describing biodiversity, imagine walking through woodlot A on the path shown in **Figure 38.2A**. You would pass by four different species of trees, but most of the trees you encounter would be the same species. Now imagine walking on the path through woodlot B in **Figure 38.2B**. You would see the same four

species of trees that you saw in woodlot A—the species richness of the two woodlots is the same. However, woodlot B would probably seem more diverse to you, because no single species predominates. As **Table 38.2** shows, the relative abundance of one species in woodlot A is much higher than the relative abundances of the other three species. In woodlot B, all four species are equally abundant. As a result, biodiversity is greater in woodlot B.

Plant biodiversity in a community often has consequences for the biodiversity of animals in the community. For example, suppose a species of caterpillar eats only the leaves of a tree that makes up just 5% of woodlot A. If the caterpillar is present at all, its population may be small and scattered. Birds that depend on those caterpillars to feed their young may be absent. But the caterpillars would easily be able to locate their food source in woodlot B, and their abundance would attract birds

▲ **Figure 38.2A** Species composition of woodlot A

▲ **Figure 38.2B** Species composition of woodlot B

TABLE 38.2 RELATIVE ABUNDANCE OF TREE SPECIES IN WOODLOTS A AND B

Species	Relative Abundance in Woodlot A (%)	Relative Abundance in Woodlot B (%)
	80	25
	10	25
	5	25
	5	25

as well. By providing a broader range of habitats, a diverse tree community promotes animal diversity.

Biodiversity also has consequences for pathogens. Most pathogens infect a limited range of host species or may even be restricted to a single host species. When many potential hosts are living close together, it is easy for a pathogen to spread from one to another. On the one hand, in woodlot A, for example, a pathogen that infects the most abundant tree would rapidly be transmitted through the entire forest. On the other hand,

the more isolated trees in woodlot B are more likely to escape infection.

Low biodiversity is characteristic of most modern agricultural ecosystems. For efficiency, crops and trees are often planted in monoculture—a single species grown over a wide area (see Module 23.10). Monocultures are especially vulnerable to attack by pathogens and herbivorous insects. Also, plants grown in monoculture have been bred for certain desirable characteristics, so their genetic variation is typically low, too. As a result, a pathogen can potentially devastate an entire field or more. Between 1845 and 1849, a pathogen wiped out a monoculture of genetically uniform potatoes throughout Ireland. As a result, thousands of people died of starvation, and thousands more left the country.

To combat potential losses, many farmers and forest managers rely heavily on chemical methods of controlling pests. Modern crop scientists have bred varieties of plants that are genetically resistant to common pathogens, but these varieties can suddenly become vulnerable, too. In 1970, pathogen evolution led to an epidemic of a disease called corn leaf blight that resulted in a billion dollars of crop damage in North America. Some researchers are now investigating the use of more diverse agricultural ecosystems—polyculture—as an alternative to monoculture.

? **Which would you expect to have higher biodiversity, a well-maintained lawn or one that is poorly maintained? Explain.**

● A lawn that is poorly maintained would have higher biodiversity. A well-maintained lawn should have low biodiversity. While a lawn that is cared for may not be a perfect monoculture, any weeds that are present would have low relative abundance. The opposite is true if the lawn is not cared for.

38.3 Interspecific interactions are fundamental to community structure

In Chapters 36 and 37, we discussed interactions between members of the same species. Organisms also engage in **interspecific interactions**—relationships with individuals of other species in the community—that greatly affect population structure and dynamics. In **Table 38.3**, interspecific interactions are classified according to the effect on the populations concerned, which may be helpful (**+**) or harmful (**—**).

TABLE 38.3 INTERSPECIFIC INTERACTIONS

Interspecific Interaction	Effect on Species 1	Effect on Species 2	Example
Competition	—	—	Squirrels/black bears
Predation	+	—	Crocodiles/fish
Herbivory	+	—	Caterpillars/leaves

Recall from Module 37.5 that individuals may compete for limited resources such as food or space. **Interspecific competition** occurs when populations of two different species compete for the same limited resource. For example, desert plants compete for water, while plants in a tropical rainforest compete for light. Squirrels and black bears are among the animals that feed on acorns in a temperate broadleaf forest in autumn. When acorn production is low, the nut is a limited resource for which squirrels and bears compete. In general, the effect of interspecific competition is negative for both populations (**—/—**). However, it may be far more harmful for one population than the other. Interspecific competition is responsible for some of the disastrous effects of introducing nonnative species into a community, a topic we will explore further in Module 38.12. Competition can also occur between members of the same species. This intraspecific competition can occur among squirrels that are scavenging for acorns during a season with low production.

There are three categories of interactions in which one species exploits another species (**+/—**). In **predation**, one species (the predator) kills and eats another species (the prey). **Herbivory** is consumption of plant parts or algae by an animal. Both plants and animals may be victimized by **parasites** (see Chapter 39) or bacterial pathogens (see Module 17.1). Thus, parasite-host and pathogen-host interactions are also +/−.

Sometimes individuals within a community foster more intimate, symbiotic relationships. In mutualism, both populations benefit (+/+). Herbivores and the cellulose-digesting microbes that inhabit their digestive tracts as well as flowers and their pollinators are examples of mutualism between symbiotic species (see Module 39.4). Symbiotic relationships are the focus of the next chapter.

In the next several modules, you will learn more about these interspecific interactions and how they affect communities. You will also discover how interspecific interactions can act as powerful agents of natural selection. In the next chapter, you will learn about more intimate symbiotic interspecific relationships.

? **Populations of eastern bluebirds declined after the introduction of non-native house sparrows and European starlings. All three species nest in tree cavities. Suggest how an interspecific interaction could explain the bluebird's decline.**

● Based on the information given, interspecific competition for nest sites is a plausible explanation.

38.4 Competition may occur when a shared resource is limited

Each species in a community has an **ecological niche**, defined as the sum of its use of the biotic and abiotic resources in its environment. An organism's niche also describes how it evolved to best meet its needs. For example, the ecological niche of the Arctic fox (*Vulpes lagopus*; **Figure 38.4A**) includes its breeding sites, the rodents or eggs it eats, and climatic conditions such as snowfall and temperature that enable it to survive. In other words, the ecological niche encompasses everything the Arctic fox needs to survive. The behavioural and physical adaptations that allow the Arctic fox to exist where it does are also a part of its niche.

Interspecific competition occurs when the niches of two populations overlap and both populations require a common resource that is in limited supply. Competition may be minimized if the two species have evolved distinct mechanisms to obtain the resource in question. Ecologists can study the effects of competition by physically removing all the members of one species from a study site and then observing the effects on the other species. Alternatively, they can study the effects of one population expanding its range and encroaching on the niche of another species. For example, the range of the red fox (*Vulpes vulpes*; **Figure 38.4B**) is constrained by the same resource requirements as the range of the Arctic fox, but the red fox cannot tolerate the harsh environment of Canada's Arctic. Because of a changing climate, however, the range of the red fox has been expanding northward, intruding on the southern limits of the Arctic fox's niche. In this overlapping terrain that can potentially support either species, the red fox is a superior competitor for resources. As a result, the Arctic fox must either move out or die.

In this example, the northern limit of the red fox range is highly dependent on climate and resource availability. In contrast, the southern limit of the Arctic fox is determined, primarily, by competition with the red fox. The process whereby one species outcompetes another and ultimately eliminates that species from its niche is called **competitive exclusion**.

In general, competition lowers the carrying capacity (see Module 37.4) for competing populations because the resources used by one population are not available to the other population. In 1934, Russian ecologist G. F. Gause demonstrated the effects of interspecific competition by using three closely related species of ciliates (see Module 18.3): *Paramecium caudatum*, *P. aurelia*, and *P. bursaria*. He first determined the carrying capacity for each species under laboratory conditions. Then he grew cultures of two species together. In a mixed culture of *P. caudatum* and *P. bursaria*, population sizes stabilized at lower numbers than each achieved in the absence of a

−/−

▲ **Figure 38.4A** An Arctic fox (*Vulpes lagopus*)

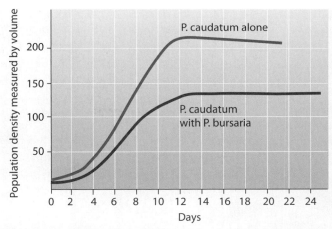

▲ **Figure 38.4C** Population size of *Paramecium caudatum* grown alone (blue line) and with *P. bursaria* (red line)

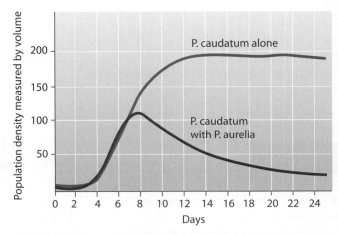

▲ **Figure 38.4D** Population size of *Paramecium caudatum* grown alone (blue line) and with *P. aurelia* (red line)

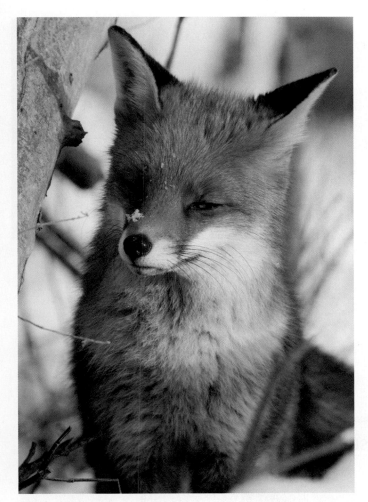

▲ **Figure 38.4B** A red fox (*Vulpes vulpes*)

competing species—that is, competition lowered the carrying capacity of the environment **(Figure 38.4C)**. On the contrary, in a mixed culture of *P. caudatum* and *P. aurelia*, only *P. aurelia* survived **(Figure 38.4D)**. Gause concluded that the requirements of these two species were so similar that they could not coexist under those conditions; *P. aurelia* outcompeted *P. caudatum* for essential resources.

? Which do you think has more severe effects, competition between members of the same species or competition between members of different species? Explain why.

● Competition between members of the same species is more severe because members of the same species have exactly the same niche. Thus, they compete for exactly the same resources.

38.5 Predation leads to diverse adaptations in prey species

Predation benefits the predator but kills the prey. Because predation has such a negative impact on reproductive success, numerous adaptations for predator avoidance have evolved in prey populations through natural selection.

In Module 20.12, you learned how insect colour patterns, including camouflage, provide protection against predators. Camouflage is also common in other animals. As **Figure 38.5A** shows, the grey treefrog (*Hyla versicolor*), found in southeastern Canada, becomes almost invisible on a grey tree trunk.

Other protective devices include mechanical defences, such as the sharp quills of a porcupine (see Figure 36.9) or the hard shells of clams and oysters. Chemical defences are also widespread. Animals with effective chemical defences usually have bright colour patterns, often yellow, orange, or red in combination with black. Predators learn to associate these colour patterns with undesirable consequences, such as noxious taste or a painful sting, and avoid potential prey with similar markings. The vivid orange and black pattern of monarch butterflies **(Figure 38.5B)** warns potential predators of a nasty taste. Monarchs acquire and store the unpalatable chemicals

▲ **Figure 38.5A** Camouflage: a grey treefrog on bark

▲ **Figure 38.5B** Chemical defences: the monarch butterfly

during the larval stage, when the caterpillars feed on milkweed plants. We will discuss this further in the next module. And, in Chapter 39, we will discuss how another species takes advantage of this and mimics the monarch butterfly.

? Explain why predation is a powerful factor in the adaptive evolution of prey species.

● The prey that avoid being eaten will most likely survive and reproduce, passing on alleles for antipredator adaptations to their offspring.

38.6 Herbivory leads to diverse adaptations in plants

In contrast to predation, herbivory is not usually fatal. Nevertheless, a plant whose body parts have been eaten by an animal must expend energy to replace the loss. Consequently, numerous defences against herbivores have evolved in plants. For example, thorns and spines are obvious anti-herbivore devices, as anyone who has plucked a rose from a thorny rosebush or brushed against a spiky cactus knows.

Chemical toxins are also very common in plants. Like the chemical defences of animals, toxins in plants tend to be distasteful, and herbivores learn to avoid them. Among such chemical weapons are the poison strychnine, produced by a tropical vine called *Strychnos nux-vomica*; morphine, from the opium poppy; nicotine, produced by the tobacco plant; mescaline, from peyote cactus; and tannins, from a variety of plant species. A variety of sulphur compounds, including those that give Brussels sprouts and cabbage (both are varieties of *Brassica oleracea*) their distinctive taste, are also toxic to herbivorous insects and mammals such as cattle. (The vegetables we eat are not toxic because the amount of chemicals in them has been reduced by crop breeders.) Milkweed (*Asclepias syriaca*; **Figure 38.6A**) is native to central and eastern Canada and produces compounds called cardiac glycosides, which can cause heart problems and death in many herbivores, including livestock. However, not all animals are affected negatively by these compounds. The monarch butterfly mentioned in the previous module feeds on milkweed and stores the cardiac glycosides in its tissues as a defence mechanism to avoid its own

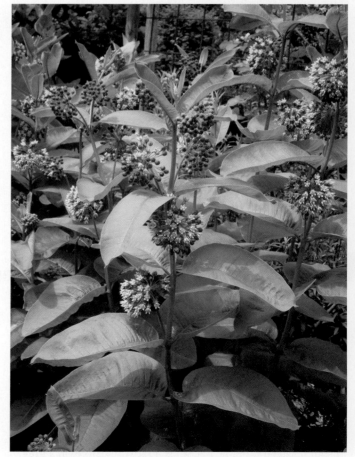

▲ **Figure 38.6A** Chemical defences: milkweed

predators. Some plants even produce chemicals that cause abnormal development in insects that eat them. Chemical companies have taken advantage of the poisonous properties of certain plants to produce the pesticides called pyrethrin and rotenone (see Module 6.11). Nicotine is also used as an insecticide.

Some herbivore-plant interactions illustrate the concept of **co-evolution**, a series of reciprocal evolutionary adaptations in two species. Co-evolution occurs when a change in one species acts as a new selective force on another species, and the resulting adaptations of the second species in turn affect the selection of individuals in the first species. **Figure 38.6B** illustrates an example of co-evolution between an herbivorous insect (the caterpillar of the butterfly *Heliconius*, top) and a plant (the passionflower, *Passiflora*, a tropical vine). *Passiflora* produces toxic chemicals that protect its leaves from most insects, but *Heliconius* caterpillars have digestive enzymes that break down the toxins. As a result, *Heliconius* gains access to a food source that few other insects can eat.

These poison-resistant caterpillars seem to be a strong selective force for *Passiflora* plants, and defences have evolved in some species. For instance, the leaves of some *Passiflora* species produce yellow sugar deposits that look like *Heliconius* eggs. You can see an egg in the centre photograph of Figure 38.6B and egg-like sugar deposits in the bottom photo. Female butterflies avoid laying their eggs on leaves that already have eggs, presumably ensuring that only a few caterpillars will hatch and feed on any one leaf. Because the butterfly often mistakes the yellow sugar deposits for eggs, *Passiflora* species with the yellow deposits are less likely to be eaten.

The story of *Passiflora* is even more complicated, however. The egglike sugar deposits attract ants and wasps that prey on *Heliconius* eggs and larvae. Thus, adaptations that appear to be co-evolutionary responses between just two species may in fact involve interactions among many species in a community.

? People find most bitter-tasting foods objectionable. Why do you suppose we have taste receptors for bitter-tasting chemicals?

● Individuals having bitter taste receptors presumably survived better because they could identify potentially toxic food when they foraged.

▲ **Figure 38.6B** Co-evolution: *Heliconius* and the passionflower vine (*Passiflora*)

Community Dynamics

38.7 Trophic structure is a key factor in community dynamics

Every community has a trophic structure, a pattern of feeding relationships consisting of several different levels. The sequence of food transfer up the trophic levels is known as a **food chain**. This transfer of food moves chemical nutrients and energy from organism to organism up through the trophic levels in a community. The flow of nutrients and energy in Figure 1.4 occurs through food chains.

Figure 38.7 compares a terrestrial food chain and an aquatic food chain. In this figure, the trophic levels are arranged vertically, and the names of the levels appear in coloured boxes. The arrows connecting the organisms point from the food to the consumer. Starting at the bottom, the trophic level that supports all others consists of autotrophs ("self-feeders"), which ecologists call **producers**. Photosynthetic producers use light energy to power the synthesis of organic compounds. Plants are the main producers on land. In water, the producers are mainly photosynthetic unicellular protists and cyanobacteria, collectively called phytoplankton. Multicellular algae and aquatic plants are also important producers in shallow waters.

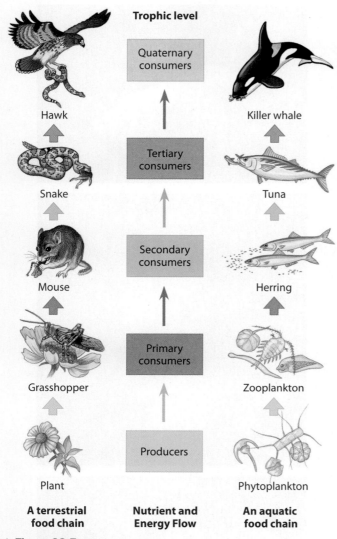

Trophic level

Hawk

Quaternary consumers

Killer whale

Snake

Tertiary consumers

Tuna

Mouse

Secondary consumers

Herring

Grasshopper

Primary consumers

Zooplankton

Plant

Producers

Phytoplankton

A terrestrial food chain

Nutrient and Energy Flow

An aquatic food chain

▲ **Figure 38.7** Two food chains

In a few communities, such as deep-sea hydrothermal vents (see Module 40.2), the producers are chemosynthetic prokaryotes.

All organisms in trophic levels above the producers are heterotrophs ("other-feeders"), or consumers, and all consumers are directly or indirectly dependent on the output of producers. Herbivores, which eat plants, algae, or phytoplankton, are **primary consumers**. Primary consumers on land include grasshoppers and many other insects, snails, and certain vertebrates, such as grazing mammals and birds that eat seeds and

fruits. In aquatic environments, primary consumers include a variety of zooplankton (mainly protists and microscopic animals such as small shrimps) that eat phytoplankton.

Above primary consumers, the trophic levels are made up of carnivores, which eat the consumers from the level below. On land, **secondary consumers** include many small mammals, such as the mouse shown here eating a herbivorous insect, and a great variety of birds, frogs, and spiders, as well as lions and other large carnivores that eat grazers. In aquatic ecosystems, secondary consumers are mainly small fishes, such as herring, that eat zooplankton.

Higher trophic levels include **tertiary** (third-level) **consumers**, such as snakes that eat mice and other secondary consumers. Most ecosystems have secondary and tertiary consumers. As the figure indicates, some also have higher level, **quaternary** (fourth-level) **consumers**. These include hawks in terrestrial ecosystems and killer whales in the marine environment.

Not shown in Figure 38.7 is another trophic level—consumers that derive their energy from **detritus**, the dead material produced at all the trophic levels. Detritus includes animal wastes, plant litter, and the bodies of dead organisms. Different organisms consume detritus in different stages of decay. **Scavengers**, which are large animals, such as crows and vultures, feast on carcasses left behind by predators or speeding cars. The diet of **detritivores** is made up primarily of decaying organic material. Examples of detritivores include earthworms and millipedes. **Decomposers**, mainly prokaryotes and fungi, secrete enzymes that digest dead organic material. Some decomposers break down large organic molecules into smaller organic units, while other decomposers convert organic material to inorganic material. Enormous numbers of microscopic decomposers in the soil and in the mud at the bottom of lakes and oceans break down most of the community's organic materials to inorganic compounds that plants or phytoplankton can use. The breakdown of organic materials to inorganic ones is called **decomposition**. By breaking down detritus, decomposers link all trophic levels. Their role is essential for all communities and, indeed, for the continuation of life on Earth.

? Even consumers at the highest level of a food chain eventually become food for _____ and _____.

● detritivores; decomposers

38.8 Food chains interconnect, forming food webs

A more realistic view of the trophic structure of a community is a **food web**, a network of interconnecting food chains. **Figure 38.8** shows a simplified example of a food web for a kelp forest community in British Columbia. As in the food chains of Figure 38.7, the arrows indicate the direction of nutrient transfer ("who is eaten by whom") and are colour-coded by trophic level.

Notice that a consumer may eat more than one type of producer, and several species of primary consumers may feed

on the same species of producer. Some animals weave into the web at more than one trophic level. The sea urchin and abalone are primary consumers, eating kelp and algae. The larger crab, however, is a primary consumer when it eats algae off of rocks, a secondary consumer when it eats an abalone, and a tertiary consumer when it feeds on a sea star. The sea otter at the top of the web is a secondary, tertiary, or quaternary consumer, depending on its prey. Food webs, like food

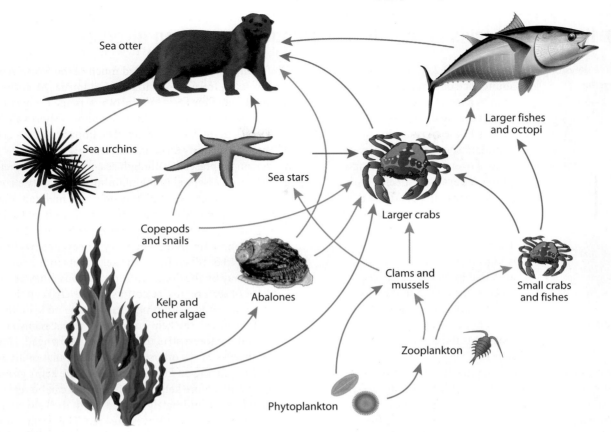

▲ **Figure 38.8** A BC kelp forest food web

chains, do not typically show detritivores and decomposers, which obtain energy from dead organic material from all trophic levels.

 I'm eating a cheese pizza. At which trophic level(s) am I feeding?

● Primary consumer (flour and tomato sauce) and secondary consumer (cheese, a product from cows, which are primary consumers)

38.9 Organisms that perform a similar ecological role can be grouped together in a guild

After reading Module 38.8, you can now appreciate that assigning a trophic level to an organism is not a simple task. In fact, it is often easier to group organisms within a community not by what they eat, but by how they contribute to the structure and function of the community. Organisms that perform a similar function or use a common resource are grouped together in a function group or **guild**. For example, all animals that feed on nectar can be grouped together in a guild based on the common role they play in the community. Although the member species of this guild could all be considered primary consumers, not all primary consumers would be included. For instance, those that ate fruit would be in a separate guild.

In different communities, particular functions may be carried out by different organisms. Organizing communities into functional groups based on these roles simplifies the study of the complex interactions that exist within a single community. Identifying guilds also facilitates easier comparison of different communities. For example, every community must have primary producers, because they harvest energy and fix carbon for the other species. In the kelp forest shown in Figure 38.8,

the phytoplankton, kelp, and other algae perform this task. The same role in the tallgrass prairie is performed by various land plants such as grasses and forbs. Similarly, dead organic material must be recycled in every community. The scavengers, detritivores, and decomposers discussed in Module 38.7, regardless of what species are involved, are functional groups of organisms that can be found in any community.

In the kelp forest community, sea urchins, abalones, and crabs all feed on kelp. Ecologists studying this community structure may group these unrelated organisms into a guild because they have a similar role in the community structure. If, for any reason, these populations were able to expand significantly, there could be serious consequences for the kelp. We will explore these consequences further in the next module.

 What other organisms from Figure 38.8, could be placed with zooplankton in the same guild based on feeding? Explain your answer.

● Bivalves including clams and mussels also feed on phytoplankton and therefore belong to the same guild.

38.10 Keystone species have a disproportionate impact on diversity

Keystone

Keystone absent

▲ **Figure 38.10A** Arch collapse with removal of keystone

In Module 38.2, you saw that the abundance of dominant species such as a forest tree can have an impact on the diversity of other species in the community. But less abundant species may also exert control over community composition. A **keystone species** is a species whose impact on its community is much larger than its biomass or abundance would indicate. The word *keystone* comes from the wedge-shaped stone at the top of an arch that locks the other pieces in place. If the keystone is removed, the arch collapses **(Figure 38.10A)**. A keystone species occupies a niche that holds the rest of its community in place.

To investigate the role of a potential keystone species in a community, ecologists compare diversity when the species is present and when it is absent. Experiments by American ecologist Robert Paine in the 1960s were among the first to provide evidence of the keystone species effect. Paine manually removed a predator, a sea star of the genus *Pisaster*, from experimental areas within the intertidal zone of the Washington coast. The result was that *Pisaster*'s main prey, a mussel of the genus *Mytilus*, outcompeted many of the other shoreline organisms (algae, barnacles, and snails, for instance) for the important resource of space on the rocks. The number of different organisms present in experimental areas dropped from more than 15 species to fewer than 5 species.

Within a kelp forest community **(Figure 38.10B)**, a wide variety of species are dependent on the towering giant kelp for sustenance and shelter. Figure 38.8 shows the food web for such a community when sea otters, a keystone species, are present.

The keystone concept has practical application in efforts to restore or rehabilitate damaged ecosystems. The sea otter

(*Enhydra lutris*) once inhabited much of the North American Pacific coast, from Alaska to Baja California. After they were heavily hunted for their fur, the otters' range is now limited to the Alaskan and central British Columbian shores and a few focal areas in the United States. The impact that sea otters have on their community structure is readily apparent now that they are no longer present. Although sea otters feed a variety of species, they are essential in maintaining community structure by feeding on sea urchins. But how does this maintain the community structure? Sea urchins are herbivores that feed on algae and giant kelp. As they graze, they quickly chew through the kelp's attachments, in the same way a beaver chews through the trunk of a tree. When freed, the kelp floats to the surface and is washed away by the ocean currents. Because they are a major predator of sea urchins, sea otters effectively keep the urchin population low, thus limiting their grazing on kelp. In the presence of sea otters, the kelp growth rate replaces any kelp that is lost and the forest structure remains unchanged. However, in the absence of sea otters, the urchin population booms, and the rate of grazing on kelp far surpasses the kelp's growth rate. Consequently, more kelp is removed than can be replaced and the kelp forest is ultimately cleared. With the kelp gone, any species dependent on it leaves the area. The result is an entirely different community called an urchin barren **(Figure 38.10C)**.

In the 1970s, efforts to reintroduce sea otters throughout their original range were successful. Twenty years after the release of 89 otters on Vancouver Island, the population had grown to more than 1500 animals. Today, the urchin population is once again under control and the kelp forest community is slowly being re-established.

 ? Removing kelp from the coastal community we described in Module 38.8 would have a drastic impact, and yet kelp is not considered a keystone species. Why not?

● Kelp is abundant and makes up a large part of the community. Keystone species have a large effect relative to their representation in the community just as a keystone is a small but vital piece of an arch.

▲ **Figure 38.10B** A kelp forest community

▲ **Figure 38.10C** A sea urchin barren community

38.11 Disturbance is a prominent feature of most communities

Early ecologists viewed biological communities as more or less stable in structure and species composition. But like many university campuses, where some construction or renovation project is always under way, many communities are frequently disrupted by sudden change. **Disturbances** are events such as storms, fires, floods, droughts, or human activities that damage biological communities and alter the availability of resources. The types of disturbances and their frequency and severity vary from community to community.

Communities change drastically following a severe disturbance that strips away vegetation and even soil. The disturbed area may be colonized by a variety of species, which are gradually replaced by a succession of other species, in a process called **ecological succession**. When ecological succession begins in a virtually lifeless area with no soil, it is called **primary succession**. Examples of such areas are the rubble left by a retreating glacier or fresh volcanic lava flows (**Figure 38.11A**). The events that occurred across nearly all of Canada when the glaciers of the last ice age retreated 10 000 to 12 000 years ago is an example of primary succession. Often the only life forms initially present are autotrophic bacteria. Lichens (see Module 39.4) and mosses, which grow from windblown spores, are commonly the first large photosynthesizers to colonize the area. Soil develops gradually as rocks break down and organic matter accumulates from the decomposed remains of the early colonizers. Lichens and mosses are gradually overgrown by larger plants that sprout from seeds blown in from nearby areas or carried in by animals. Eventually, the area is colonized by plants that become the community's prevalent form of vegetation. Primary succession can take hundreds or thousands of years.

Secondary succession occurs where a disturbance has cleared away an existing community but left the soil intact. For example, secondary succession occurs as areas recover from fires or floods. Some disturbances that lead to secondary succession are caused by human activities. Even before colonial times, people were clearing the forests of eastern North America for agriculture and settlements. Some of this land was later abandoned as the soil was depleted of its chemical nutrients or the residents moved west to new territories. Whenever human intervention stops, secondary succession begins.

Numerous studies have documented the stages by which an abandoned farm field (a large-scale disturbance) returns to forest (**Figure 38.11B**). A recently disturbed site provides an environment that is favourable to *r*-selected species (see Module 37.8)—plants and animals that reach reproductive age rapidly, produce huge numbers of offspring, and provide little or no parental care. Interspecific competition is not a major factor during the very early stages of succession, when biodiversity is low and the community is dominated by relatively few species of weedy annual plants such as crabgrass and ragweed. Biodiversity increases as different plant species return to the field. Perennial grasses, small broadleaf plants, and softwood trees, especially pines, begin to invade within five years. (An annual plant completes its life cycle in a single year. Perennial plants live for many years.) The area develops into a diverse pine forest in roughly 10 to 15 years. But as the trees grow, fewer plants can survive in the shadows of the understory and biodiversity starts to decline. Even pine seedlings, which need high levels of light to grow, do not do well in the understory. The seedlings of many hardwood species are more shade tolerant, and thus trees such as oak and maple begin to replace pine as competition becomes a significant force in determining the composition of the community. As species are outcompeted and eliminated from the area, biodiversity is reduced. The final mixture of species depends on local abiotic factors such as soil and topography. Because animals depend on plants for food and shelter, the animal community undergoes similar successional changes. The diversity of bird species, for example, increases dramatically as trees replace herbaceous plants. Birds that are dependent on pine, however, will leave the area as the hardwood trees take over.

▲ **Figure 38.11A** Primary succession on a lava flow

Figure 38.11C shows a common trend that can be seen in the changes in biodiversity during succession after large-scale disturbances. Initially, biodiversity is low, but it gradually increases as new species are recruited to the site. In the late stages, biodiversity actually decreases as a few species become dominant and replace or eliminate others. For example, an old-growth forest may be dominated by a few species of hardwood trees. Many

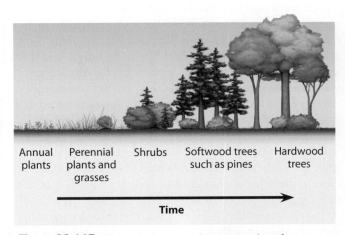

| Annual plants | Perennial plants and grasses | Shrubs | Softwood trees such as pines | Hardwood trees |

Time

▲ **Figure 38.11B** Stages in the secondary succession of an abandoned farm field

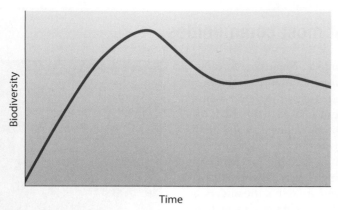

▲ **Figure 38.11C** Changes in biodiversity during succession

smaller plants, which grew before the trees, cannot compete for sunlight and disappear from the community, decreasing biodiversity. Then, the number of species becomes relatively stable.

Understanding the effects of disturbance in communities is especially important today. As we discuss in Chapter 41, people are the most widespread and significant agents of disturbance. Disturbances may also create opportunities for plants and animals that people transport to new habitats, which is the topic of the next module.

 What is the main abiotic factor that distinguishes primary from secondary succession?

● Absence (primary) versus presence (secondary) of soil at the onset of succession.

38.12 Invasive species can devastate communities

For as long as people have travelled from one region to another, they have carried organisms along, sometimes intentionally and sometimes by accident. Many of these non-native species have established themselves firmly in their new locations. Furthermore, many have become **invasive species**, spreading far beyond the original point of introduction and causing environmental or economic damage by colonizing and dominating wherever they find a suitable habitat. In Canada alone, there are hundreds of invasive species, including plants, mammals, birds, fishes, arthropods, and molluscs. Worldwide, there are thousands more. Invasive species are a leading cause of local extinctions, a topic we will return to in Chapter 41. The economic costs of invasive species are enormous—causing an estimated $20 billion of lost revenue every year in Canada. Regardless of where you live, an invasive plant or animal is probably living nearby.

▲ **Figure 38.12A** Purple loosestrife (*Lythrum salicaria*) distribution in Ontario (black dots)

Not every organism that is introduced to a new habitat is successful, and not every species that is able to survive in its new habitat becomes invasive. For example, 20% of the plant species in Canada were introduced here, but only half of them are invasive. There is no single explanation for why any nonnative species turns into a destructive pest, but community ecology offers some insight. Interspecific interactions act as a system of checks and balances on the populations in a community. Every population is subject to multiple negative effects, whether from competitors, predators, herbivores, or pathogens, that curb its growth rate. Without biotic factors such as these to check population growth, a population will continue to expand until limited by abiotic factors.

Purple loosestrife (*Lythrum salicaria*) is now a common sight in Canadian wetlands. However, this was not always the case. The seeds of purple loosestrife were brought to North America in the soil-filled ballasts of European ships in the 19th century. Upon germination, young seedlings grow rapidly into plants that have several 1–2 m tall stems. Each plant can produce more than 2.5 million seeds in a single year, allowing for far-reaching dissemination by water, wind, animals, and humans. Once established, purple loosestrife is extremely difficult to eradicate and spreads quickly. Often referred to as the purple plague, purple loosestrife has invaded wetland habitats in Ontario (**Figure 38.12A**) and all other provinces. These beautiful killers grow and spread so quickly that they outcompete native plants for sunlight, nutrients, and space. The natural plant communities are crowded out and ultimately replaced by dense, brushlike stands of purple loosestrife. In less than 15 years, purple loosestrife can increase from 5% to 90% of the total biomass in a community. With the eradication of the native plant community, dependent animal species, including fish, amphibians, birds, and mammals, are also eradicated. The end result is a significant reduction in biodiversity.

After many fruitless attempts to control the loosestrife population, research into **biological control** (the intentional release of natural enemies to attack the invasive population) began in 1992. Two loosestrife leaf-eating beetles (*Galerucella pusilla* and *G. calmariensis*) and one root-mining weevil (*Hylobius transversovittatus*) were imported from Europe and released. The beetles defoliate the plants and reduce their seed production. The weevils burrow through the vascular tissue of the roots, reducing flow of nutrients and stored carbohydrates. These insects have highly specific diets: They eat only purple loosestrife. Together, these insects have proven effective in greatly reducing the loosestrife population (**Figure 38.12B**). In areas where these natural enemies have been released, native plants and animals have returned to the wetland communities. Canada will likely never be rid of purple loosestrife. But with biological control, we can manage the problem.

Another example of invasive species concerns the introduction of rabbits into Australia. In Module 37.4, we illustrated exponential population growth with rabbits, which are notoriously prolific breeders. In 1859, a European who wanted to hunt familiar game released 12 pairs of European rabbits (*Oryctolagus cuniculus*) on a ranch in southern Australia. In 1865, 20 000 rabbits were killed on the ranch. By 1900, several hundred million rabbits were distributed over much of the continent. Their activities destroyed farm and grazing land because they ate vegetation down to, and sometimes including, the roots (**Figure 38.12C**). Especially in arid regions, the loss of plant cover led to soil erosion. In 1950 the Australian government turned to biological control. A virus lethal to rabbits was introduced into the environment. The rabbits and virus then underwent several co-evolutionary cycles as the rabbits became more resistant to the disease and the virus became less lethal. The government managed to stave off a complete resurgence of the rabbit population by introducing new viral strains; but, in 1995, they had to switch to a different pathogen to maintain control.

Co-evolution is just one potential pitfall of biological control. The imported enemy may not be as successful in the new environment as the target species. It may not disperse widely enough, or its population growth rate may not be high enough to overtake a rapidly expanding population. Caution is especially warranted because the control agent may turn out to be as invasive as its target. For example, cane toads imported to

▲ **Figure 38.12B** Before and after biological control of purple loosestrife

▲ **Figure 38.12C** A familiar sight in early 20th-century Australia

control an agricultural pest in Australia became a widespread threat to native wildlife.

 What is the ecological basis for biological control of pests?

● By having a negative effect on population growth rate, a natural enemy keeps the target population in check.

38.13 Are disturbances always detrimental?

The term *disturbance* has a negative connotation because of its literal meaning. As a result, there is a common misconception that all disturbances are bad for a community. Previous modules have illustrated specific examples of disturbances and their negative impacts. However, not all disturbances are detrimental to a community. In fact, certain communities exist only because of disturbances.

Disturbances can have direct effects on biodiversity, which is often used as a measure of community health. The

impact a disturbance has on biodiversity and health of a community depends largely on its intensity. A large-scale disturbance, such as the clearing of a forest for agriculture, greatly reduces the biodiversity of a community by removing massive stands of plant life and forcing animal inhabitants to relocate. A single tree falling in a forest is a small-scale disturbance, which may cause little or no change in biodiversity.

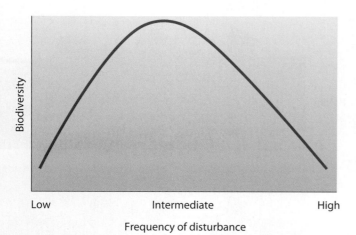

▲ **Figure 38.13** Effects of disturbance regime on biodiversity

to become dominant. As the **intermediate disturbance hypothesis** describes, biodiversity is greatest in communities with this disturbance regime.

Livestock grazing, especially along riverbanks, is a practical example of the effects of intermediate disturbance. Under heavy grazing, few plants persist in these areas, and the loss of diversity and topsoil because of erosion become serious concerns. In the absence of grazing, the riverbanks become dominated by one or a few species of plants. For example, the reed canarygrass outcompetes shrubs and displaces them as it becomes a dominant species. The shallow root systems of the reeds are unable to stabilize the soil, and it may erode during seasonal flooding of the river systems. However, when the riverbanks are under intermediate grazing, enough reed canarygrass is consumed that its dominance is prevented. Under these conditions, the shrubs are not displaced and their deep roots are better able to retain the soil during the seasonal flooding of the river system. To protect the riverbanks, many cattle ranchers control grazing intensities by routinely moving their herds from pasture to pasture.

As mentioned above, some communities exist only because of disturbances. Grass fires are a common occurrence in prairie communities that prevent trees from becoming established. As the fire burns, the aboveground shoot systems of all plants are burned, leaving a blackened swath of land. Primary growth in trees occurs from meristems at the tips of each branch (see Module 22.7). These structures are destroyed in the fire and the tree cannot regrow. The meristems of grasses, on the other hand, are belowground, protected from the fire above. Within days of the fire, the grasses resume their growth. Because grasslands are held in an intermediate state of succession, they are referred to as **disclimax communities**.

Occasionally, disturbances can have unforeseen consequences. In Prince Edward County in southeastern Ontario, for example, several large sand dunes were removed for the manufacturing of cement. The end result of this disturbance was the formation of *pannes*, seasonally flooded, flat, sandy plains, which are now home to many diverse and endangered species, including many migratory birds. The Prince Edward County pannes were declared a National Wildlife Area in 1980.

Although we tend to think of disturbances in negative terms, small-scale disturbances often have positive effects. Using biodiversity as a measure, the rumour that all disturbances have negative impacts is not true. Disturbances of moderate size or intermediate frequency actually increase biodiversity.

However, moderate-sized disturbances can actually increase biodiversity within a community. A windstorm knocking down several (but not all) large trees in a stand is an example of a moderate-sized disturbance. Because their populations are much larger than other community members, dominant species are affected to a greater extent. When dominance is reduced, biodiversity increases. In this scenario, space is opened up and allows for colonization by smaller plants, which otherwise could not compete with dominant species. Biodiversity is further increased as these new species move into the area. If biodiversity is your measure of community health, a moderate disturbance would appear beneficial rather than detrimental.

Along with the size of a disturbance, the frequency of disturbances, or **disturbance regime**, also has a big impact on a community's biodiversity. Succession follows every disturbance event, as described in Module 38.11. And, each disturbance in the regime resets the succession process.

Frequent disturbances will have short intervals of succession between events. As a result only a few species of weedy pioneer plants will be able to colonize the area. However, before more species can be recruited, another disturbance event can reset the process. Therefore, biodiversity is maintained at a low level **(Figure 38.13)**. Communities with infrequent disturbances have long periods of time for succession to occur between events. In these old-growth communities, a few species have time to become dominant and biodiversity is low, as shown in the figure. Just as moderate-sized disturbances increase biodiversity, so can an intermediate disturbance regime (Figure 38.13). Enough time passes between events to allow colonization by many different species, not just the pioneers. However, not enough time elapses to allow for any one species

 Why do small disturbances have little impact on biodiversity?

Landscape Ecology

38.14 Communities change structure across the landscape

Communities represent groups of plants and animals that inhabit a specific area. On a larger scale, an ecological **landscape** is a regional assemblage of interacting communities, such as a

forest, adjacent fields, wetlands, streams, and streamside habitats. **Landscape ecology** is the application of ecological principles to the study of the structure and dynamics of a collection of ecosystems.

▲ **Figure 38.14A** A mosaic of communities on the North Saskatchewan River

▲ **Figure 38.14B** Satellite image of King Mountain in Gatineau Park, Quebec (bar = 200 m)

Figure 38.14A shows a mosaic pattern of the landscape surrounding the North Saskatchewan River near Fielding, Saskatchewan. As you can see, the landscape consists of **patches** of different communities embedded within the surrounding community called the **matrix**. In the figure, you can see patches of forest communities and the river community surrounded by the grassland matrix. Landscape ecology is the study of the patterns and consequences of community mosaics.

Why do communities exist in patches and not cover the entire area? Within a given geographic area, the physical environment can be quite variable. Weather patterns may be similar across an expanse of land; however, there is often variability in smaller, localized areas called **microclimates**. Differences in localized rock formations, hills and valleys, or soil structure all have an impact on what type of community can develop. An outcropping of granite can change the depth and quality of the soil in a small area. These areas may also have poor drainage, keeping the soil wet. Variation in soil has a big impact on what plant species can grow in an area.

Topography, the physical features including hills and valleys, also has a large affect on the environment conditions within an area. In the Northern Hemisphere, the southern aspects of hills or valleys receive more direct sunlight than those facing north. Thus, their temperature tends to be higher and humidity lower because of increased evaporation. Therefore,

plants that prefer a cool, humid climate will tend to grow on northern aspects of the land (see Module 19.5).

A walk around King Mountain in Gatineau Park near Gatineau, Quebec, clearly demonstrates how aspect affects community structure. A short trail (the red line in **Figure 38.14B**) circumnavigates the tallest point in the park, named for Prime Minister William Lyon Mackenzie King, and takes you through several distinct communities. Starting on the northern aspect, the slope is covered by a dark forest of hemlock trees, which prefer moist, cool, and shady climates. As you round the mountain to the southern aspect, the forest community changes to one that is dominated by red and white oaks. Oak trees prefer drier, warmer climates.

We will take a closer look at the interactions of adjacent communities in the next module.

? How does a northern aspect slope differ in its microclimate from a southern aspect slope?

● Northern aspect slopes tend to be cooler and more humid than southern aspect slopes.

38.15 Transition zones occur between community patches in the landscape

Edges, or boundaries between communities, are prominent features of landscapes. The photograph in Figure 38.14A shows a landscape area near Fielding, Saskatchewan, that includes grassland and forest communities. A **border** is where the edges of two patches are connected. The structure of the border is usually distinct from either adjoining community. For example, a distinct hybrid community, which is neither grassland nor forest, exists where these two communities meet **(Figure 38.15A)**.

Some borders are very narrow and one community abruptly changes to the next. The borders between terrestrial and

aquatic communities—a riverbank, for example—are characterized by a sharp change in structure. In contrast, **ecotones**, or **transition zones**, are wide borders between patches where the community structure changes gradually from one to the other **(Figure 38.15B)**. Species that cannot survive well in either patch may be able to thrive in an ecotone. Ecotones at the edges of forests receive more light and are less humid than the forest communities. Plants that are tolerant of drier conditions and intolerant to shade may suffer in the undergrowth of a forest but grow very well in the sunnier, drier border shared with grassland. Animals that require different plant communities

▲ **Figure 38.15A** The border between forest and grassland communities

often do well in the ecotone between them. For instance, the brown-headed cowbird (*Molothrus ater*), an edge-adapted species that lays its eggs in the nests of other birds, is currently expanding in many areas of North America (see Module 39.6). Cowbirds forage in open fields on insects disturbed by or attracted to cattle and other large herbivores; the cowbirds also need forests where they can parasitize the nests of other birds. Species that depend on and may be restricted to ecotones are called **edge species**.

Although some animals depend on the edge communities, others shy away from border regions. These **interior species** are adapted to the structure of one parent community. The ovenbird (*Seiurus aurocapilla*) feeds on ground-dwelling insects and therefore prefers the old-growth forest community, which has deep leaf litter and little undergrowth. The edges of a forest receive more light than its interior, and the undergrowth becomes too dense for this bird.

The distinctiveness of border communities is apparent in their biodiversity. Ecotones are able to support many species from either bordering community, as well as a variety of edge species. Thus, ecotones tend to have high biodiversity, known as the edge effect. The wider the ecotone, the more pronounced the edge effect is.

Human activities, such as logging and road building, often create edges that are more abrupt than those delineating natural landscapes. Such edges have their own sets of physical conditions and thus their own communities of organisms. Some organisms thrive in edges because they require resources from the two adjacent areas. For instance, white-tailed deer browse on woody shrubs found in edge areas between woods and fields, and their populations often expand when forests are logged or interrupted with housing developments.

? **Why is the biodiversity of an ecotone higher than either of its adjacent communities?**

● An ecotone can often support species from both communities as well as novel edge species.

Oven bird
Interior species

Cowbird
Edge species

Transition zone or Ecotone

▲ **Figure 38.15B** The ecotone between a forest and a grassland community

Reviewing the Concepts

Community Structure (38.1–38.6)

38.1 A community includes all the organisms inhabiting a particular area. Community ecology is concerned with factors that influence the species composition and distribution of communities and with factors that affect community stability.

38.2 Biodiversity includes relative abundance and species richness. Thus, diversity takes into account both the number of species in a community and the proportion of the community that each species represents.

38.3 Interspecific interactions are fundamental to community structure. Interspecific interactions can be categorized according to their effect on the interacting populations.

38.4 Competition may occur when a shared resource is limited. When resources are low, competition (−/−) between individuals of different species or the same species ensues.

38.5 Predation leads to diverse adaptations in prey species. Natural selection favours traits in a prey species, which minimize predation (+/−). Camouflage or physical defences are common adaptations.

38.6 Herbivory leads to diverse adaptations in plants. Some herbivore-plant interactions (+/−) illustrate co-evolution or reciprocal evolutionary adaptations.

Community Dynamics (38.7–38.13)

38.7 Trophic structure is a key factor in community dynamics. Trophic structure can be represented by a food chain.

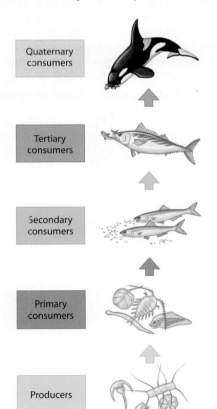

38.8 Food chains interconnect, forming food webs. Energy and nutrient flow within a community are often much more complex than a single linear food chain.

38.9 Organisms that perform a similar ecological role can be grouped together in a guild. A guild is a functional grouping of organisms. Members of a guild may not be related but perform a common task in the community.

38.10 Keystone species have a disproportionate impact on diversity. Although a keystone species has low biomass or relative abundance, its removal from a community results in lower biodiversity.

38.11 Disturbance is a prominent feature of most communities. Ecological succession is a transition in species composition of a community. Primary succession is the gradual colonization of barren rocks. Secondary succession occurs after a disturbance has destroyed a community but left the soil intact.

38.12 Invasive species can devastate communities. Organisms that have been introduced to non-native habitats by human actions and have established themselves at the expense of native communities are considered invasive. The absence of natural enemies often allows rapid population growth of invasive species.

38.13 Are disturbances always detrimental? Disturbances are not always detrimental to a community. Those of moderate size and intermediate frequency can increase biodiversity.

Landscape Ecology (38.14–38.15)

38.14 Communities change structure across the landscape. A landscape is a diverse mosaic of community patches within a matrix community.

38.15 Transition zones occur between community patches in the landscape. The edges of communities meet at a border, which can be narrow or broad. When this area is broad, community structure gradually changes from one community to the other; this is called a transition zone, or ecotone. Ecotones may also support novel edge species that depend on multiple community types.

Connecting the Concepts

1. Fill in the blanks of this concept map to help you tie together many of the key concepts of community ecology.

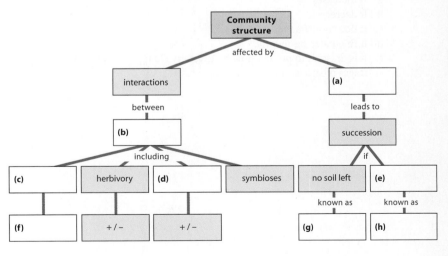

Testing Your Knowledge

Multiple Choice

2. Which of the following describes the total number of species present within a community?
   a. biodiversity
   b. ecological niche
   c. species richness
   d. abundance
   e. food web

3. Food webs are organized into _____ based on where organisms obtain their nutrients.
   a. niches
   b. trophic levels
   c. guilds
   d. symbioses
   e. food chains

4. A keystone species
   a. is the most abundant in the community.
   b. takes up a large amount of space within a community.
   c. has less of an impact within the community than would be expected.
   d. has more of an impact within the community than would be expected.
   e. occupies all trophic levels within the food web of a community.

5. Which of the following organisms is mismatched with its trophic level?
   a. algae—producer
   b. fungi—decomposer
   c. phytoplankton—primary consumer
   d. carnivorous fish larvae—secondary consumer
   e. otter—tertiary or quaternary consumer

6. Which of the following best illustrates ecological succession?
   a. A mouse eats seeds, and an owl eats the mouse.
   b. Decomposition in soil releases nitrogen that plants can use.
   c. Overgrazing causes a loss of nutrients from soil.
   d. Imported pheasants increase in numbers, while local quail disappear.
   e. Grasses grow on a beach, followed by shrubs and then trees.

7. What happens to biodiversity in the earlier stages of succession?
   a. It increases.
   b. It decreases.
   c. It does not change.
   d. It fluctuates frequently.
   e. It is difficult to predict how biodiversity changes in the early stages of succession.

8. Plants that are adapted to forest edge environments tend to be
   a. tolerant of shade and dry conditions.
   b. tolerant of shade and to prefer damp environments.
   c. intolerant of shade and to prefer damp environments.
   d. intolerant of shade and to prefer dry conditions.
   e. the same as those found in a forest community.

Describing, Comparing, and Explaining

9. Using the kelp forest example, explain how an animal can occupy more than one trophic level. Is it possible for a plant to occupy multiple trophic levels?

10. Describe what happens to a community after a disturbance. How does biodiversity change during succession?

11. Compare an edge species with an interior species. Provide an example of each.

Applying the Concepts

12. An ecologist studying plants in the desert performed the following experiment. She staked out two identical plots, which included a few sagebrush plants and numerous small, annual wildflowers. She found the same five wildflower species in roughly equal numbers on both plots. She then enclosed one of the plots with a fence to keep out kangaroo rats, the most common grain-eaters of the area. After two years, to her surprise, four of the wildflower species were no longer present in the fenced plot, but one species had increased dramatically. The control plot had not changed. Using the principles of ecology, propose a hypothesis to explain the ecologist's results. What additional evidence would support your hypothesis?

13. Sometime in 1986, near Detroit, a freighter pumped out water ballast containing larvae of European zebra mussels. The molluscs multiplied wildly, spreading through Lake Erie and entering Lake Ontario. In some places, they have become so numerous that they have blocked the intake pipes of power plants and water treatment plants, fouled boat hulls, and sunk buoys. What makes this kind of population explosion occur? What might happen to native organisms that suddenly must share the Great Lakes ecosystem with zebra mussels? How would you suggest trying to solve the mussel population problem?

Answers to all questions can be found in Appendix E.

Symbioses

Organisms Live Together

(39.1–39.3)

Organisms can live together and have long-term, intimate relationships.

Relationships Affect the Fitness of the Partners

(39.4–39.12)

Individuals in a symbiotic relationship may be affected in a positive, negative, or neutral fashion.

Relationships Form Through Co-Evolution

(39.13–39.14)

Relationships form as a result of special adaptations and are under selective pressure.

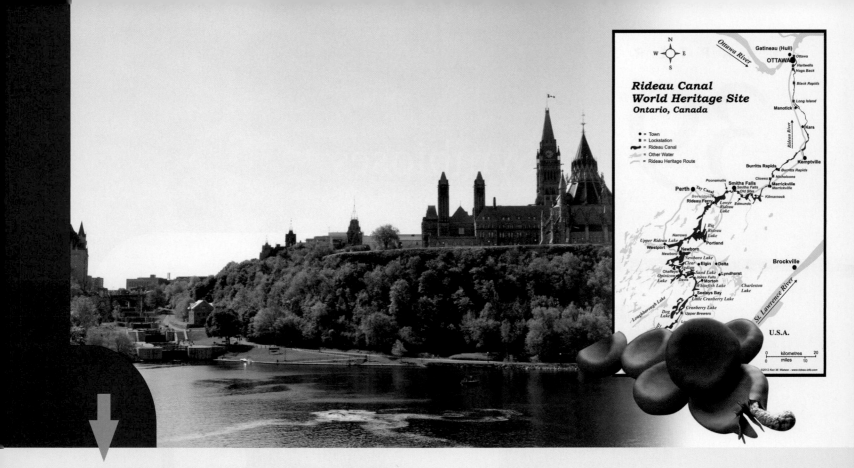

A Tropical Disease in the Great White North

Almost every Canadian is familiar with the lingering itch of a mosquito bite. Aside from the ritual application of insect repellents, we seldom pay additional thought to these pests. If you visit a tropical country, however, a mosquito bite may carry deadly consequences. In many tropical regions (including Central Africa, India, and to a lesser extent Central and South America) mosquitoes may be a host to *Plasmodium*, the causative agent of malaria. Your school may have participated in the Canadian Spread the Net campaign to help fight this disease. The goal of this campaign is to help prevent malarial infections by purchasing mosquito bed nets for impoverished people living in areas of Africa where malaria is endemic.

Worldwide, 250 million new cases of malaria cause nearly a million deaths every year. People cannot pass malaria directly to one another. Infected mosquitoes transmit all infections. Symptoms include recurring episodes of anemia, fever, and shivering every 48 or 72 hours. A significant loss of red blood cells, which are destroyed by the replication and release of thousands of parasites every cycle, leads to these symptoms. Depending on the species of *Plasmodium*, the infection may last upward of 50 years. Travellers to endemic regions are encouraged to take antimalarial drugs to help prevent infection.

The Rideau Canal in Ontario, linking Ottawa and Kingston, was built during the years 1826–1832 (after the War of 1812) to protect Canadian trade routes from American attack. Many of the workers were British soldiers who had recently returned from India with malarial infections. During the summer months of construction, malaria was rampant, and infection spread to 60% of the labourers, killing many of them.

Many people attributed these outbreaks to a foreign *Plasmodium*. However, a temperate species is indigenous to Canada. In 1997, a Toronto hospital diagnosed a patient who had never travelled outside of Canada with malaria. The only plausible source of infection could have been a Canadian mosquito and parasite. Likewise, during the construction of the Rideau Canal, there were many new infections that could have been transmitted only by local mosquitoes.

Outbreaks of malaria can occur if four risk factors are present. The factors include the presence of (1) the *Anopheles* mosquito, (2) standing water, (3) average daily temperatures above 20°C, and (4) a large pool of infected individuals. All four were present during the construction of the Rideau Canal.

Plasmodium can infect only the *Anopheles* mosquito. Therefore, malaria is limited to the range of this mosquito, which includes southeastern Canada and southwest British Columbia. Furthermore, *Anopheles* reproduction requires semi-permanent bodies of standing water in which the females lay eggs. The uncovered rain barrels and storm sewer collection ponds that are present in many residential areas meet this requirement.

Temperature greatly affects the rate of development of the parasite inside the gut of a mosquito. If temperatures are not consistently warm for at least three weeks or so, the time required for *Plasmodium* development becomes longer than the mosquito's lifespan. This time requirement generally restricts outbreaks to the tropics; however, a particularly warm Canadian summer can suffice.

With only a few infected people in one area, the chances a mosquito will pick up the parasite are relatively small.

Subsequently, the transmission rate will also be very low. As the number of human infections increases, so does the rate of transmission because more mosquitoes become infected by biting infected humans. This situation can result in an outbreak. In Canada today, there are only an estimated 2000 cases annually (about 400 of which are reported). This incidence (rate of infection) of 0.006% is far too low to cause alarm. While malaria is no longer endemic to southern Ontario, it is possible that the threat will return. If trends in climate change continue and if the incidence were to increase, an outbreak would become more likely.

This chapter will look at parasitism and other symbioses that occur between different species. We will see that many of these relationships occur directly between closely interacting individuals, while others occur indirectly between organisms that may never physically interact. First, let's define what a symbiosis is.

Organisms Live Together

39.1 Organisms do not live in isolation

In earlier chapters (Units IV through VI) we explored the diversity, form, and function of living things. There, we focused on the level of the individual. But when we examine organisms in their natural habitats, we quickly see that they do not live alone. All populations living and interacting in a given area are collectively called a **community** (see Chapter 38). In this chapter, we will focus on some specific types of relationships that species within a community may have with one another.

Many relationships between species are centred on the acquisition of food. Predation, herbivory, and competition were introduced in Module 38.3. A wolf killing and eating a deer is an example of predation. A deer feeding on the leaves of a willow tree is an example of herbivory. While these are important relationships for the survival of the organisms, they are relatively brief. After feeding, the deer moves on. Competition, another form of interaction, occurs when two species use a common resource. The diets of black bears (*Ursus americanus*) and red squirrels (*Tamiasciurus hudsonicus*) overlap partially, creating competition.

In contrast to competition, predation, and herbivory, sometimes much stronger, longer term relationships form between two organisms that last all or a significant portion of the organisms' lifespans. A symbiotic relationship, or symbioses (singular, **symbiosis**), is defined as the long-term association, either direct or indirect, of two different species within a community. Organisms can physically interact in a direct relationship. Relationships can also be indirect, where one species may benefit or harm another without having physical contact. The individuals involved in a symbiosis are called **symbionts**. (Although many biologists use the term *symbiont* to refer to an organism that gains benefit by living inside of another, in this book we will adopt the more general meaning of this term to refer to any organism in a symbiosis.)

Table 39.1 summarizes the interactions between symbionts in a symbiotic relationship. Within these relationships, one partner always benefits, while the other can be affected positively (*mutualism*, +/+), negatively (*parasitism*, +/−), or not at all (*commensalism*, +/0). There may be costs on both sides associated with maintaining these relationships. The net difference between all costs and all gains will determine the ultimate effect on each individual. Whether the relationships of *altruism* and *mimicry* are considered symbiotic is debatable, as they do not involve partners in the usual sense (that is, two distinct species that interact directly). Altruism typically occurs between two individuals of the same species where one organism sacrifices to benefit another (−/+). In mimicry, there may be no direct interaction between the partners (+/0). However, when one organism copies the appearance of another, an indirect relationship is forged. We will discuss all of these relationships in this chapter.

? Why are some relationships, but not others, considered symbiotic?

● For a relationship to be truly symbiotic, the relationship must be very strong and long term.

TABLE 39.1	INTERACTIONS IN SYMBIOTIC RELATIONSHIPS		
Symbiosis	**Effects on Symbiont 1**	**Effects on Symbiont 2**	**Example**
Mutualism	+	+	Plants/ Mycorrhizae
Parasitism	+	−	Meningeal worm/Whitetail deer
Commensalism	+	0	Anemonefish/ Sea anenome
Altruism	−	+	Richardson's ground squirrel (kin selection)
Mimicry	+	0	Milk snake/ Coral snake

39.2 One organism may live inside of another

With many symbiotic relationships, both the symbionts and their interactions can be easily observed in the environment. North American badgers (*Taxidea taxus*) and coyotes (*Canis latrans*) can be seen hunting cooperatively for ground-dwelling prey. Cowbirds (*Molothrus ater*) can easily be seen moving from one bison (*Bison bison*) to another, eating insects off of their backs. Winter ticks (*Dermacentor albipictus*) can be seen attached to the skin of a moose (*Alces alces*).

In the case of **endosymbiosis**, however, only one of the partners is observable. The second partner (the **endosymbiont**) is hidden from sight, living inside the other (the **host**). On the one hand, endosymbionts usually benefit from the stable environment inside of their hosts. Hosts, on the other hand, may be affected positively, negatively, or not at all.

Termites typically ingest wood as the primary (or sole) constituent of their diets. Wood is composed of mostly xylem—the cellulose-containing cell walls of dead cells (see Module 22.8). At one time it was thought that animals could not produce *cellulase*, the enzyme that breaks down cellulose into usable energy. Therefore, animals that ingest cellulose were thought to depend entirely on cellulose-producing microorganisms living in their digestive tracts, including certain bacteria and protists. In fact, termites do play host to protist endosymbionts that digest their wood meals. However, recent discoveries have shown that some species of termites actually produce their own cellulase. These species still form beneficial symbioses with protists, but are not entirely dependent on them.

The relationships between endosymbiotic algae and corals have been known for some time. The algae receive essential nitrogen, a waste product of the coral. In return, the corals benefit by having access to increased oxygen concentrations and sugars, the end products of photosynthesis. Embryos of the spotted salamander (*Ambystoma maculatum*) have a similar relationship with the alga *Oophila amblystomatis* **(Figure 39.2)**. While this association has been known for more than 120 years, it was originally thought that the algae lived alongside, not inside, of the embryos. Recently, the endosymbiotic nature of this relationship was discovered by Dr. Ryan Kerney, a post-doctoral fellow at Dalhousie University in Halifax, Nova Scotia. This discovery is the first of its kind involving a vertebrate host.

The human colon contains approximately 100 trillion bacteria representing about 600 species. (In general, we have about 10 times as many bacteria as cells in our body.) Many of these bacteria are believed to be *commensal*, having no consequences on healthy human hosts. They benefit from the stable and hospitable environment of our large intestine. However, their presence may be beneficial in that they prevent colonization by harmful bacteria.

An understanding of endosymbiosis affects how we view certain aspects of biology. For example, when dealing with issues of biodiversity or conservation, we should identify possible endosymbionts. And when studying how organisms function in their environment, physiologists should take into account the implications of endosymbiotic relationships.

▲ **Figure 39.2** A relationship between algae and salamander embryos

 How do bacterial endosymbionts get into human hosts?

● Colonization usually occurs early in infancy, when humans inadvertently ingest the bacteria.

39.3 A rare case of organism-organelle symbiosis

Photosynthesis is a process that should conjure up images of plants, algae, or cyanobacteria, but certainly not animals. The green sea slug (*Elysia chlorotica*) found in eastern Canadian salt marshes, however, forces us to stretch our notions of this process **(Figure 39.3A)**. This curious little animal is photosynthetic.

Green sea slugs do not start life with this ability. During its first few weeks of life, these sea slugs feed on the green alga *Vaucheria litoria*. The algal chloroplasts (products of another symbiosis discussed in Module 4.15) are not digested with the rest of the cellular contents. Instead, they are collected and internalized by cells lining the intestinal tract, as indicated in **Figure 39.3B**. They stay there for the remainder of the 12-month lifespan of these animals and synthesize glucose. During this prolonged period, the sea slug no longer feeds, depending solely on the chloroplasts for its nutrients. In essence, this is an endosymbiotic relationship between the sea slug and a single organelle of the alga. Many sea slugs have the ability to take structures from other organisms. For example, several species are able to collect cnidocytes (specialized stinging cells) from ingested cnidarian polyps and incorporate them into their skin. How they do this without discharging the cnidocytes remains a mystery.

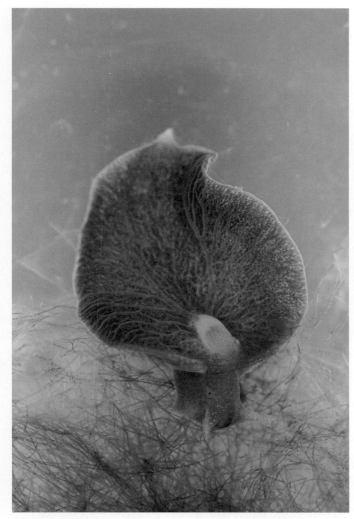

▲ **Figure 39.3A** A green sea slug (*Elysia chlorotica*) on a bed of algae (*Vaucheria litoria*)

▲ **Figure 39.3B** Chloroplasts within the lining of a sea slug's digestive tract

In plants and algae, approximately 90% of the gene products required for chloroplast function come from the organelle's chromosome. The remaining 10% come from the cell nucleus. Intriguingly, algal nuclear genes can also be found within the nuclei of a green sea slug's intestinal cells. How can genes that evolved within plants and algae suddenly appear within the nuclei of animal cells?

Genes that support chloroplast function have moved from the alga to the sea slug. The mechanism of gene transfer from the algal genome to that of a green sea slug is still unknown. One theory is that marine viruses have carried the pertinent genes from the alga to the slug in a form of horizontal gene transfer (see Module 17.7). The process would be similar to transduction in bacteria. However, genome analysis published in May 2013 failed to support this hypothesis. This unusual example may force us to rethink our current definition of symbiosis. In the other examples discussed in this chapter, the relationship occurs between whole organisms. With the green sea slug, the relationship is between an organism and only a single organelle.

 What is the evolutionary significance of the transfer of genes from one organism to another?

● Horizontal gene transfer means there is a way of acquiring genes that differs from Mendelian inheritance.

Relationships Affect the Fitness of the Partners

39.4 Both partners benefit in mutualism

Mutualism is a symbiotic relationship that is beneficial to both parties. Mutualism can be seen in many different forms, both direct and indirect, throughout the natural world. The organisms involved can benefit in different ways, such as by having a nutritional or resource requirement fulfilled or by being provided a necessary service. For example, pollinators gain a nutritional benefit as they feed on nectar provided by many flowering plants (see Module 19.13). The plants receive a service benefit by having their sperm-carrying pollen carried to other flowers. This sort of relationship, in which one species sees an increase in its reproductive fitness by having its pollen or seeds scattered, is called **dispersive mutualism**. Another example is the dissemination of embryo-containing seeds in fruit that are eaten by animals. (This example is discussed further in Module 39.13.)

Symbioses often occur between two specific species. But in **diffuse mutualism**, one species forms a mutually beneficial relationship with multiple species. For example, a flowering plant may be pollinated by a wide variety of insect species.

Trophic mutualism describes those relationships in which both partners gain a resource or nutritional benefit. The term

▲ Figure 39.4 Ants protect colonies of aphids in exchange for honeydew

trophic used in this context refers to the acquisition of nutrients and does not directly relate to the concept of trophic levels (discussed in Module 38.7). Lichens are an example of a mutualistic relationship between a fungus and a green or blue-green alga. The endosymbiotic alga produces glucose via photosynthesis. The fungus is provided with some of this glucose in return for nitrogen compounds it derives from the substrate. Another example concerns cattle (and other ruminants),

which have a digestive chamber called a rumen. Within this structure live billions of bacteria that possess cellulase. Similar to the diet of termites, the grass and leaf diet of cattle is high in cellulose. Ingested plant material enters the rumen where the bacterial cellulase digests it. Without the bacteria, the animal would be unable to digest cellulose. In these trophic mutualisms, both partners gain access to more resources than they would have alone.

In **defensive mutualism**, one organism provides food or shelter and in return protects its partner from predation or parasitism. For example, consider aphids (*Aphis*). They feed on the phloem sap of many different plants. This sap contains a high concentration of sugar and relatively little protein. Therefore, aphids must ingest large quantities to acquire enough essential amino acids. Any unused sugars are excreted as honeydew. Some ants (*Lasius flavus*, for example) milk the aphids and feed on this sugary excretion **(Figure 39.4)**. In return, they defend large colonies of aphids from predators such as ladybird beetles (ladybugs; *Coccinella*).

 Why don't humans need endosymbionts to help digest the plant material in our diets?

● The plant material common to the human diet consists primarily of fruits and starchy vegetables. Cellulose in fruit is broken down during the ripening process, and most starch is easy for humans to digest.

39.5 Plants benefit from several mutualistic relationships

Reliance on the soil for nutrients that may be in short supply makes it imperative that the roots of plants have a large surface area for absorption. As we saw in Module 23.2, root hairs add a great deal of surface to plant roots. About 80% of living plant species gain even more absorptive surface by teaming up with fungi.

The micrograph in **Figure 39.5A** shows a root of a eucalyptus tree. The root is covered with a twisted mat of fungal filaments. Together, the roots and the fungus form a mutually beneficial relationship called a mycorrhiza (meaning "fungus root"). The fungus benefits from a steady supply of sugar supplied by the host plant. In return, the fungus increases the surface area for water uptake and selectively absorbs phosphate and other minerals from the soil and supplies them to the plant **(Figure 39.5B)**. The fungi of mycorrhizae also secrete growth factors that stimulate roots to grow and branch, as well as antibiotics that may protect the plant from pathogens in the soil.

Evolution of mutually beneficial symbiotic associations between roots and fungi was a critical step in the successful colonization of land by plants. Evidence for this is found in the fact that fossilized roots from some of the earliest plants show that they already contained mycorrhizae. When terrestrial ecosystems were young, the soil was probably not very rich in nutrients. The fungi of mycorrhizae, which are more efficient at absorbing minerals than the roots, would have helped to nourish the pioneering plants. Even today, the plants that first become established on nutrient-poor soils, such as abandoned farmland or eroded hillsides, are usually heavily colonized with mycorrhizal fungi.

Roots can be transformed into mycorrhizae only if they are exposed to the appropriate species of fungus. For example, if seeds are collected in one environment and planted in foreign soil, the plants may show signs of malnutrition resulting from

▲ Figure 39.5A Mycorrhizae, an interaction between a fungus mycelium and a eucalyptus plant root

▲ Figure 39.5B The impact on the early growth of spruce trees with (left) and without (right) mycorrhizae

▲ Figure 39.5C Root nodules on a soybean plant, a legume with bacteria-filled cytoplasmic vesicles (inset)

the absence of the plants' natural mycorrhizal partners. Farmers can avoid this problem by inoculating seeds with spores of appropriate mycorrhizal fungi.

Plants also form mutually beneficial symbiotic relationships with other organisms besides fungi. Some plant species maintain close associations with nitrogen-fixing bacteria. For example, the roots of plants in the legume family—including peas, beans, peanuts, alfalfa, and many other plants that produce their seeds in pods—have swellings called nodules (Figure 39.5C). Within these nodules, nitrogen-fixing bacteria of the genus *Rhizobium*, which means "root living," have colonized the plant cells. *Rhizobium* bacteria reside in cytoplasmic vesicles formed by the root cell (the red spots in the inset micrograph). Each legume is associated with a particular strain of *Rhizobium*. Other nitrogen-fixing bacteria are found in the root nodules of some plants that are not legumes, such as alders.

The relationship between a plant and its nitrogen-fixing bacteria is mutually beneficial. The plant provides the bacteria with carbohydrates and other organic compounds. The bacteria have enzymes that catalyze the conversion of atmospheric N_2 to ammonium ions (NH_4^+), a form readily used by the plant. When conditions are favourable, root nodule bacteria fix so much nitrogen that the nodules secrete excess NH_4^+, which increases the fertility of the soil. This is one reason why farmers practise crop rotation, one year planting a non-legume, such as corn, and the next year planting a legume, such as alfalfa. The legume crop may be plowed under so that it will decompose as "green manure," reducing the need for fertilizer.

 ? How do the nitrogen-fixing bacteria of root nodules benefit from their symbiotic relationship with plants?

● The bacteria receive organic nutrients produced by the plant.

39.6 In parasitism, one partner benefits at the cost of the other

Relationships between predators and their prey are relatively simple. A predator must kill its prey before it can consume it to obtain nutrients. **Parasites**, on the contrary, obtain some or all of their nutrients from another organism (their host) but they very rarely kill the host organism. The loss of nutrients can be a major burden for the host. This loss ultimately leads to a lower reproductive rate because the host has less energy available for the production of offspring. It is important to note that not all parasites are endosymbionts (**endoparasites**). Many, called **ectoparasites**, live outside of their hosts. The next few modules will provide examples illustrating both endoparasites and ectoparasites.

To prevent the death of their host, some endoparasites have adapted to limit their numbers (known as the parasite load) within the host. This reduces the damage to internal organs and ensures that all essential nutrients are not stolen from the host. For example, **Figure 39.6A** shows the meningeal worm (*Parelaphostrongylus tenuis*) within the cranium of a white-tailed deer (*Odocoileus virginianus*). Only a few worms are normally found in the cranium of any infected deer. In turn, the deer suffers only benign symptoms, if any at all. This balance of parasite number is the direct result of the co-evolution between the worm and the deer. Because it is not advantageous for the worm to kill its host, it has adapted to small parasite loads within deer. When organisms do not have a finely tuned relationship, parasite loads can become very high. For example, the moose is an **aberrant host** of the meningeal worm, which means they have little or no co-evolutionary history. As a result, infected moose suffer significant damage to brain tissue, leading to severe disease and often death.

The meningeal worm is an example of a **host-specialist** that is well adapted to infect a single host species. In contrast,

▲ **Figure 39.6A** Cranium of a deer infected with two meningeal worms

host-generalists have adapted to infect multiple species. The brown-headed cowbird (*Molothrus ater*) is a brood parasite of southern Canada and the United States. Cowbirds lay their eggs in the unattended nests of more than 200 different species of host birds. In this relationship, it is the cowbird chicks that are parasitic. When the cowbird chicks hatch, the unknowing foster parents will spend time and energy feeding the foreign chicks. As they outgrow and outcompete their foster siblings, the cowbird chicks may even oust the other chicks from the nest. This assures they get even more food from their host parents.

Parasites can be found in nearly all groups of eukaryotic organisms. While there are countless examples of animal parasites, several plants and fungi have also evolved parasitic lifestyles. **Figure 39.6B** shows dodder (*Cuscuta*), a leafless, parasitic vine that grows in Manitoba eastward through to the Maritime provinces as well as many parts of the United States. It has no roots, no leaves, and little to no chlorophyll. This gives it the appearance of yellow string with small white flowers. With no chlorophyll, this plant is unable to harvest light or synthesize glucose. The dodder must steal the sugars it requires by tapping into its host plant's vascular tissue.

Of the 100 000 known species of fungi, about 30% are parasitic. Fungi are a serious problem as agricultural pests. Crop fields typically contain genetically identical individuals of a single species planted close together—ideal conditions for the spread of disease. About 80% of plant diseases are caused by fungi, causing tremendous economic losses each year. Between 10% and 50% of the world's fruit harvest is lost each year to fungal attack. A variety of fungi, including smuts and rusts, are common on grain crops. The ear of corn shown in **Figure 39.6C** is infected with a club fungus called corn smut. The greyish growths, known as galls, are made up of heterokaryotic hyphae that invade a developing corn kernel and eventually displace it. When a gall matures, it breaks open and releases thousands of blackish spores. In parts of Central America, the smutted ears are cooked and eaten as a delicacy, but generally corn smut is regarded as a scourge.

The yeast, a single-celled fungus, that causes vaginal infections (*Candida albicans*) is an example of an opportunistic pathogen—a normal inhabitant of the body that becomes parasitic only when some change in the body's microbiology, chemistry, or immunology allows the yeast to grow unchecked.

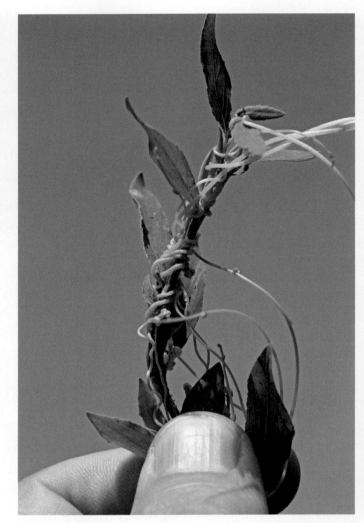

▲ **Figure 39.6B** The leafless dodder growing on nettle

A similar relationship to **parasitism** occurs between a **parasitoid** and its host. Unlike most parasites, the parasitoid always kills its host. In this regard, parasitoids are similar to predators. But parasitoids generally do not kill their host until their young are almost fully developed, while predators tend to kill their prey before consuming it. The jewel wasp (*Nasonia vitripennis*) is common in North America and lays its eggs on the pupa (a developmental stage) of the blowfly (*Calliphoridae*). The developing wasp larvae kill the pupa and then ingest its tissue before they themselves pupate and mature into adults.

▲ **Figure 39.6C** Corn smut

? Why don't parasites tend to kill their host?

 They are dependent on their host for nutrients. The main reason they would cause the death of one host would be to facilitate the infection of another.

39.7 Parasites must get from one host to another

It is crucial for a parasite to encounter and infect new hosts in order to complete its life cycle or ensure the survival of its offspring. This process of *transmission* is a major challenge and requires a diverse array of parasite adaptations. **Passive transmission** describes the strategies some parasites use when they rely on hosts to infect themselves by ingestion of contaminated material. The protist *Giardia duodenalis* is the causative agent of giardiasis (commonly known as beaver fever), the most common waterborne disease in North America. Resilient, dormant cysts contaminate water systems from the feces of infected individuals. Infection of a new host is passive, and *Giardia* relies on potential hosts to drink cyst-contaminated water. Once ingested, the cysts release single-celled parasites that live and reproduce asexually in the small intestine. There, they complete their life cycle by producing new cysts that then pass in the feces.

Another form of passive transmission is through the exploitation of a **vector organism**. Numerous parasites are transmitted to their next host by insects that feed on blood. For example, as we saw in the chapter-opening essay, female *Anopheles* mosquitoes play host to the malaria parasite (*Plasmodium*). They also act as a vector, carrying the unicellular parasite to the next mammalian host in the life cycle. When an infected mosquito takes a blood meal, the parasite is introduced through the saliva directly into the new host's bloodstream.

In contrast to passive transmission, **active transmission** occurs when the parasite infects its host under its own power. For example, the Schistosomatidae are a family of blood flukes (including *Schistosoma*) that actively burrow into the skin of their hosts. The itchy, red welts experienced during swimmer's itch are caused by immune responses to the larvae of a *Schistosoma* species that infects waterfowl. These parasites, however, are not adapted to humans and our immune system is able to destroy the infection **(Figure 39.7A)**.

To guarantee transmission, some parasites have evolved elaborate techniques that control or change the behaviour of their host. For instance, the lancet fluke (*Dicrocoelium dendriticum*) infects the livers of ruminants such as sheep and cattle. While grazing on grasses, these herbivores inadvertently ingest infected ants. The sinister side of this story is that when the parasite infects the ant, it modifies the ant's behaviour. Within the ant, a few flukes migrate to the brain where they control some of its actions. During the heat of the afternoon, healthy ants usually take refuge under low-lying vegetation. However, infected ants climb to the tips of vegetation, where they grab on and do not let go **(Figure 39.7B)**. There, they are more likely to be consumed by grazing cattle or sheep. In this way, the lancet fluke is transmitted to its next host.

Parasites must evolve methods of transmission for every host in their life cycle. Those with **direct life cycles** are completed within a single host organism. Therefore, only one method is required. *Giardia* (discussed at the beginning of this module) is an example of such a parasite. By contrast, parasites with **indirect life cycles** are more complicated, requiring two or even three different host species. Here, the parasite uses one or more species as an *intermediate host*

▲ **Figure 39.7A** Swimmer's itch

▲ **Figure 39.7B** An ant under the control of *Dicrocoelium*

for growth and development only. Then the parasite uses another species as the *definitive host* for maturation and reproduction. *Schistosoma* infect the bloodstream of their definitive host, usually a mammal such as a human. Eggs are then produced and shed in either the urine or feces. In the water system, eggs hatch into free-swimming larvae and will infect a snail, the intermediate host. There, only growth and development occur. Larvae that are released from the snail

then actively seek out a new definitive host in which they will mature and reproduce.

 Why don't parasites generally have more than a few hosts in a life cycle?

● With every additional host, the likelihood of transmission and successful completion of the life cycle becomes lower. Therefore, having too many hosts in a life cycle would be a selective disadvantage.

EVERYDAY BIOLOGY

39.8 Don't let a parasite break your dog's heart

Canine heartworm (*Dirofilaria immitis*) is a potentially fatal, nematode parasite. Adult worms live in the pulmonary arteries and heart of their host, typically a dog. Parasite load may reach levels where the worms physically interfere with blood circulation through the heart **(Figure 39.8A)**. Live offspring (called microfilariae) are produced and shed into the bloodstream **(Figure 39.8B)**. As with *Plasmodium*, a feeding mosquito vector transmits heartworm to new hosts. Initially restricted to southern North America, heartworm is now common in central and eastern Canada and throughout the United States. Hosts are typically domestic and wild canines, although cats and ferrets are also at risk. However, the incidence of feline infection is significantly lower, about 5% of that for dogs.

Routine screening is recommended by veterinarians because it can take up to six months for animals to show signs of heartworm infection. Active dogs may develop

▲ **Figure 39.8B** Microfilaria of heartworm in a blood smear

▲ **Figure 39.8A** A dog heart infested by canine heartworm (*Dirofilaria immitis*)

early signs, such as coughing and early exhaustion, as adult worms amass in their pulmonary arteries. Later signs of infection include blood in the sputum (saliva), weight loss, and fainting.

If left untreated, infection generally leads to fatal congestive heart failure. Treatment requires several injections of antihelminths (drugs that kill worms), but it has its own concerns. One problem is that dead worms remain in the circulatory system until they are slowly eliminated by the host immune system. Another problem is that exercise can dislodge and move dead worms throughout the circulatory system. Therefore, dog owners should try to keep their dogs calm and inactive during the treatment—not always an easy task.

By all accounts, prevention is the best medicine. If you live in or visit an endemic area, prophylactic (that is, preventative) treatment is strongly recommended. During the mosquito season, monthly treatments (pill or topical) are enough to prevent infection. These drugs are effective in killing any larvae introduced by an infected mosquito. Domestic dogs will always be at risk of contracting canine heartworm. Choosing not to treat is a risky gamble: a bet that an infected mosquito will not bite your dog. The minor cost of the prophylactic drugs is far offset by happy, healthy dogs (**Figure 39.8C**).

? **Could heartworm be eradicated if every domestic dog was treated to prevent infection? Why or why not?**

● Heartworm can infect wild canines such as coyotes and wolves. It would be impossible to treat all potential hosts, making eradication unfeasible.

▲ **Figure 39.8C** Heartworm-free mini Australian shepherds, Blue and Cobber

---

39.9 Can tapeworms help you lose weight?

People struggling with weight issues have been the unfortunate target of many schemes and fad diets. Obesity has been associated with many human health problems, including heart disease and some cancers. A wide range of weight-loss plans can be found on the Internet, and many go so far as to claim "weight loss with no exercise required." In a dark corner of the

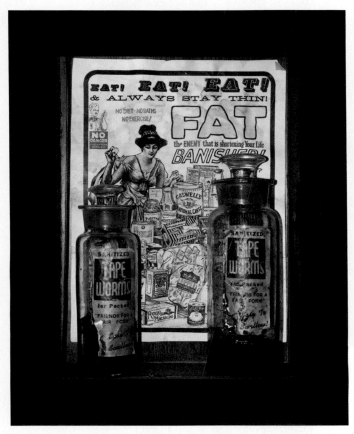

▲ **Figure 39.9A** Old advertisement for a tapeworm diet

World Wide Web, you may even come across articles claiming that tapeworms can be used to produce significant weight loss (**Figure 39.9A**). Sites state that this treatment is not approved by Canadian or American governments and is only available in Mexico at the bargain price of $1500.

The beef tapeworm (*Taenia saginata*) is so named because it is normally acquired through the ingestion of infected beef. Its life cycle is shown in **Figure 39.9B**. *Taenia*, like most tapeworms, takes advantage of the predator-prey relationships of their hosts. Infected hosts pass eggs in their feces and contaminate the environment **1**. Cattle (a prey species) may become infected when they ingest contaminated grass **2**. Larval tapeworms, called cystercercoids, develop in the tissues of this host **3** and infect a predator when eaten **4** (that is, when a human eats undercooked beef). Adult tapeworms live in the small intestine of their definitive host and release eggs into the feces **5** continuing the cycle. The beef tapeworm used in this diet can grow to lengths of 4 m and produce dangerous symptoms in its host.

As discussed in Module 20.7, tapeworms lack a digestive tract of their own. Instead, they absorb nutrients across their body surface, thereby competing with their host for the nutritional content of its meals. Numerous studies have shown that intestinal infection with tapeworm species causes significant weight loss in the host animal. A full-length tapeworm can steal a large proportion of the daily caloric intake, which ultimately leads to weight loss. These findings are the basis of using tapeworms to promote weight loss. There are, however, significant costs to the host that have been overlooked.

Unfortunately, infections do not end with the plundering of unwanted *calories*. Typical symptoms of tapeworm infections include abdominal pain, diarrhea, and nausea. Additionally, research has reported that humans infected with tapeworms showed signs of pernicious anemia caused by vitamin B_{12} deficiency, both of which are also risk factors for heart disease.

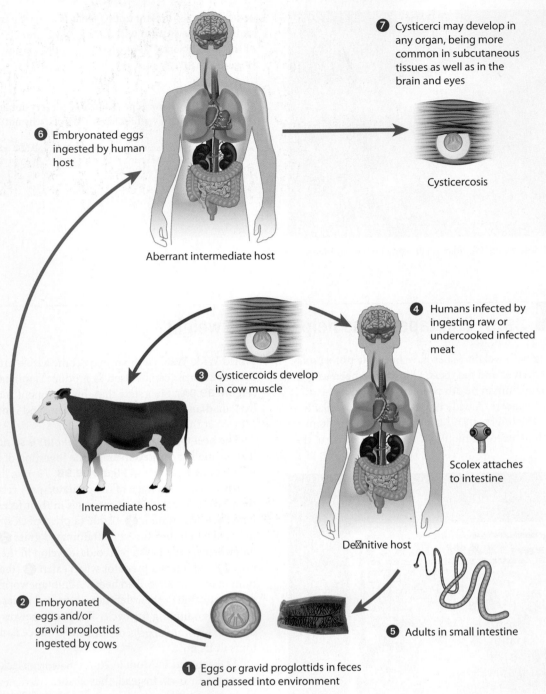

⑦ Cysticerci may develop in any organ, being more common in subcutaneous tissues as well as in the brain and eyes

Cysticercosis

⑥ Embryonated eggs ingested by human host

Aberrant intermediate host

④ Humans infected by ingesting raw or undercooked infected meat

❸ Cysticercoids develop in cow muscle

Scolex attaches to intestine

Intermediate host

Definitive host

❷ Embryonated eggs and/or gravid proglottids ingested by cows

❺ Adults in small intestine

❶ Eggs or gravid proglottids in feces and passed into environment

▲ **Figure 39.9B** The beef tapeworm life cycle

Another major problem concerns the stage of the tapeworm life cycle at which it is ingested. If larval forms are swallowed, they will develop into adults that will absorb nutrients across their body surface. However, if eggs are ingested **⑥**, a very dangerous cysticercoid develops **⑦**. A cysticercoid is a developmental stage of a tapeworm that can form anywhere in the body, including the lungs, liver, and brain. The growth of these cysticercoids can lead to extensive tissue destruction **(Figure 39.9C)**, severe symptoms, and may even result in death.

Internet rumours state that model Claudia Schiffer and the late opera singer Maria Callas used tapeworms to maintain their weight. While the allegations about Claudia Schiffer are unsubstantiated, Callas's autopsy did reveal a tapeworm infection. This information was mistakenly used to support the benefits of a tapeworm diet. However, Callas's appetite for raw beef was a more likely cause of infection than the intentional consumption of tapeworms as a diet aid.

The scientific evidence supporting the use of tapeworms for human weight control is extremely limited. While it is plausible

▲ Figure 39.9C Human brain with tapeworm cysticercoids (holes)

that tapeworms may help an individual lose weight, the side effects clearly outweigh the health benefits. Figure 39.9A refers to obesity as "the ENEMY that is shortening Your Life;" but, a tapeworm diet only replaces one risk factor for heart disease with two more. The simple truth is nothing works as well as a healthy diet and exercise. If you burn more calories than you ingest, you will lose weight.

? Many fish, such as salmon, are potential sources of tapeworm infections but cooking them thoroughly kills the parasites. How do sushi chefs avoid infecting their patrons when they serve raw salmon?

● Sushi-grade salmon is frozen at −20°C for at least 48 hours. This treatment is also effective in killing the infective stages of the tapeworm.

39.10 One partner benefits while the other is unaffected in commensalism

We have already discussed mutualism and parasitism. Now let us consider commensalism, the third main category of symbiotic relationships. In **commensalism**, one partner derives benefit from the relationship while the other is unaffected. Quite often, the distinction between commensalism and other types of symbioses is difficult to make. The benefit to one species is usually obvious. However, the other partner may experience a subtle effect that is far less obvious and often overlooked. The examples provided below illustrate the concept of commensalism. However, subsequent critical examination may reveal subtle positive or negative effects on the supposedly neutral symbiont, thus making true commensalism rare.

Anemonefish (also known as clownfish) take refuge in the tentacles of sea anemones, their cnidarian counterpart (Figure 39.10). The skin of these fish secretes mucus to protect them from the anemone's stinging cnidocytes. Predators that lack protective mucus avoid the dangerous tentacles and therefore the anemonefish they protect. This is clearly beneficial to the anemonefish. At first look, it seems that the anemone gets nothing from the interaction. Upon further consideration, it is possible that the anemonefish may lure predators close to the anemone, causing them to become paralyzed by the anemone, becoming its prey. Seen in this light, the relationship is somewhat mutualistic.

For different plants in a community, competition for light is a major issue. Growing taller reduces competition and increases access to light. For plants growing in the undergrowth, there is considerable competition for the penetrating light. *Epiphytes*, plants that grow anchored to other plants, escape the competition by growing high on the trunks of trees (see Module 23.12). For example, the staghorn fern grows on the trunks of trees. The higher growth site gives the plant a competitive edge over the remaining undergrowth. Because their roots do not penetrate the soil, epiphytes usually have adaptations to collect and store rainwater. They acquire other essential nutrients from debris that falls and decomposes near their base. With these adaptations, the trees they grow on are seemingly unaffected.

Burdock (*Arctium*) has been introduced throughout North America. Its flowers grow on prickly heads and produce hooked seeds called burrs. Burrs grab onto the fur (or clothing) of passing animals and are subsequently carried away. Thus, burdock has a commensal relationship with its seed disseminators. It clearly benefits by having the unsuspecting animals carry the burrs away from the parent plant. Aside from the annoyance, there is no evidence that the animals are significantly affected. Close examination of the hook structures of this plant gave George de Mestral the idea to invent Velcro.

? Why is true commensalism difficult to confirm?

● The member that is thought to be neutral may experience subtle benefits or costs that are not readily apparent.

▲ Figure 39.10 An anemonefish with its cnidarian partner

39.11 In altruism, one organism reduces its fitness to benefit another

The existence of **altruism**, the selfless giving by one organism to another with no gain, is a highly debated issue because a natural example of this has yet to be confirmed. Many claims of altruistic relationships have been disproven upon closer look.

Most descriptions of altruism involve two individuals of the same species. Moreover, the two individuals are often related to one another. Richardson's ground squirrels (*Urocitellus richardsonii*; commonly referred to as gophers throughout the Prairies) have been used as an example of an altruistic species. Ground squirrels are social animals, living in colonies of many individuals based on maternal relationships. A matriarch will tolerate related females (such as daughters and nieces), but not unrelated females, in their colony. Members of the colony keep a constant vigil for the threat of a predator (see **Figure 39.11**). When a threat is perceived, vigilant members give audible and ultrasonic alarm calls. Other ground squirrels benefit by quickly retreating to their burrows after hearing the call. Alarm calls do impart a cost to the caller by drawing the attention of the would-be predator to itself.

▲ **Figure 39.11** Vigilant Richardson's ground squirrel (*Urocitellus richardsonii*) watching for threats

Superficially, this relationship does indeed appear to be altruistic. The caller seems to be selflessly drawing predator attention to itself, giving others time to escape. The fallacy of this claim becomes clear when we consider the genes of those protected. As mentioned, the colonies of ground squirrels consist of groups of related individuals. On average, siblings share half of their genes, while cousins share one-quarter. As discussed in previous chapters, the main underlying drive of living organisms is the perpetuation of their genes in the population. The caller, by saving its siblings and cousins, is saving its own genes.

The concept of **inclusive fitness** describes an individual's success at perpetuating its genes by producing its own offspring and by helping close relatives, who likely share many of those genes, to produce offspring. The correct scientific term for this type of relationship is **kin selection**, not altruism. The concept of kin selection is currently under debate. One opponent of kin selection is E. O. Wilson, the biologist who first proposed the idea 40 years ago.

Let's consider the example of vampire bats. They roost in colonies during the day and come out to feed at night. They bite the skin of mammalian hosts and feed on the pooling blood. Not every individual feeds successfully every night. A bat that fails to feed more than two nights in a row is at serious risk of starvation. If nearby bats recognize the predicament of their comrade, they regurgitate a small amount of their blood meal. Eating this can sustain the hungry bat for another night. Again, on first inspection, the sharing behaviour seems to be altruistic. However, by enabling another bat to survive longer, bats that give some of their food are more likely to receive a similar donation should they find themselves starving. This possible future reciprocity makes this relationship more mutualistic than altruistic and can more accurately be considered an example of *reciprocal altruism*. If the two bats are related, this would also be another example of kin selection.

Similar reasoning might explain many if not all claims of altruism reported to date.

 ? **Why are examples of altruism so rare in nature, if they exist at all?**

● Relationships where one organism freely sacrifices to benefit another are not evolutionarily sound.

39.12 Many organisms acquire indirect benefits through mimicry

Whether or not *mimicry* should be considered a type of symbiosis is currently under debate. We will include a discussion here and let you decide for yourself. The reason for the debate is that there is no *direct* relationship between the two individuals. However, one species (the **mimic**) does indeed benefit by copying another (the **model**). As with other forms of symbioses, mimicry strategies vary greatly. Several forms of mimicry are seen in nature; only a few prominent examples will be discussed in this module. The variations are typically named after the biologist who first described them.

Defence is a common strategy for mimics. Many animals use toxins and venoms to protect themselves from would-be predators. Harmful organisms often advertise their toxicity by using bright, highly contrasting colours. Predators quickly learn to associate the colour pattern with danger and avoid preying on these animals. Occasionally, a harmless species evolves colour patterns similar to those of a distasteful model. Predators see the mimic as potentially harmful and leave them be. The eastern coral snake (*Micrurus tener*; Figure 1.9B) is a highly venomous snake that warrants extreme caution. The harmless scarlet king snake (*Lampropeltis elapsoides*; Figure 1.9C) has evolved a similar banding pattern that predators also avoid (see Module 1.9). This relationship is called **Batesian mimicry**. Batesian mimicry tends to break down if the population of mimics is larger than the models. With such numbers, it is more probable that predators will eat a tasty mimic than a distasteful model. Therefore,

▲ **Figure 39.12A** A monarch butterfly (*Danaus plexippus*)

predators will fail to form the association between the colour pattern and distastefulness.

The orange and black coloration shared by the monarch butterfly (*Danaus plexippus*; **Figure 39.12A**) and the viceroy butterfly (*Limenitis archippus*; **Figure 39.12B**) demonstrates **Müllerian mimicry**. In Module 38.5, you learned how the monarch butterfly defends against predation by collecting distasteful chemicals. Viceroy butterflies are also distasteful and avoided by predators. Regardless of which prey item a naive host first ingests, an association between coloration and toxicity forms. Therefore, both species benefit from this indirect relationship. It is often a challenge to identify which species is the mimic and which is the model in Müllerian mimicry. The two are often referred to as co-mimics.

An **aggressive mimic** is a harmful species that has evolved a similar appearance to that of a harmless model. By doing so, the mimic can approach prey without raising alarm. This increases its access to prey and enhances its foraging success. The cleaner wrasse (*Labroides dimidiatus*) is a small, mutualistic reef fish. Larger fish benefit by allowing the wrasse to access their gills to eat any parasites and dead skin. The sabre-toothed blenny (*Aspidontus taeniatus*) takes advantage of this association by mimicking the coloration and behaviours of the wrasse. When the large fish grants access, the blenny takes bites out of its gills or fins.

Flowering plants and pollinators have co-evolved in mutualistic relationships. But not all plants are as generous in producing nectar for their ally. Some plants use trickery called

▲ **Figure 39.12B** A viceroy butterfly (*Limenitis archippus*)

Pouyannian mimicry. Many orchids employ this strategy to attract pollinators such as bees and wasps. The flower structure of these orchids has evolved to resemble the female bees or wasps. When an unsuspecting male attempts to mate with the mimic (pseudocopulation), pollen is transferred to his body. Frustrated, the male flies away and may attempt mating with another flower. In doing so, the pollen he is carrying is deposited.

 ? **What type of symbiosis occurs with orchids that trick their pollinators?**

● Providing the males do not waste a significant amount of energy in pseudocopulation, the relationship would be commensal. But if the males do waste a great deal of energy, the relationship would be parasitic.

Relationships Form Through Co-Evolution

39.13 Symbiotic relationships do not form overnight

Interactions between species can improve their fitness and hence are subject to natural selection. But two organisms cannot just decide that they should work together. The interaction must first be facilitated by special adaptations (as we will discuss in Module 39.14). Initially, interactions may be nothing more than brief encounters, offering a minor advantage to one or both species. Through natural selection, these encounters may become longer and stronger, providing greater benefit to at least one of the partners. The strongest symbiotic relationship can be seen in all known eukaryotic cells. Mitochondria are the products of a two-billion-year-old symbiotic relationship (see Module 4.15). Over time, the collaboration was fortified to the point where two different types of cells eventually became one. Chloroplasts share a similar evolutionary history, albeit a marginally shorter one.

Most other symbioses have not evolved to a point where the two species are indistinguishable. However, we do see great variation in the strength of relationships and how dependent the organisms are on each other. In many well-established relationships, the individuals are completely dependent on each other. Without its counterpart, one organism cannot survive or complete its life cycle. Such relationships are called **obligate symbioses**. For example, lichens are a composite organism formed by the obligate mutualistic relationship between a fungus and an alga. The alga synthesizes sugars for itself and the fungus. Meanwhile, the fungus provides a hospitable environment for the alga to survive. Attempts to culture either symbiont independently in a laboratory setting have proven to be unsuccessful. Each species is completely dependent on the other.

By contrast, symbionts in **facultative symbioses** are still able to survive without their partners. For instance, many plants produce seed-containing fruit that are eaten by animals. The animals assist in dissemination as they carry the seeds away in their digestive tract. Undigested seeds are later deposited in their feces, where they germinate away from the parent plant. While the plants benefit through a reduction in competition with their offspring, they can survive without animals eating their fruit. Un-eaten fruit may fall and the seeds germinate near the parent plant.

Interactions can provide new abilities that individual species may not possess alone. These beneficial associations may have selective value under natural selection. Furthermore, this adaptation can occur much more rapidly than that of a favour-able trait in a single population. Mycorrhizae, a mutualistic relationship between plants and soil-dwelling fungi discussed in Module 39.5, demonstrate this phenomenon. In plants, the abil-ity to absorb nutrients from the soil is directly related to the sur-face area of the root system. Increasing the absorptive surface area will increase access to nutrients, and subsequently growth. The evolution of a large root system would be a very slow, gradual change by means of natural selection. Adaptations that facilitate symbiotic interactions with soil-dwelling fungi would, very rapidly, increase the nutrient availability to the plant. In return, the plant would provide glucose to the fungus as an en-ergy source. Figure 39.5B shows the effect of this relationship on the growth of plant seedlings. A single fungus can forge re-lationships with different species of plants simultaneously. Each plant gains the benefits described above. Drs. Melanie Jones and Daniel Durall of the University of British Columbia Okanagan have demonstrated a new benefit that arises from these mul-tispecies associations in the field. Plants that share a common mycorrhizal fungus are able to transfer carbon between them. This potential cooperation between plant species may mean that competition for sunlight is not as important for a plant's success as we once thought. The ecological ramifications of this resource sharing are under investigation.

The evolution of a symbiosis does not necessarily stop once the relationship is formed. In fact, the dynamics of the relationship can continue to evolve over time, especially as the cost or benefit to the individuals change. Consider parasites, which place a selective pressure on their host species. Adap-tations to reduce the cost of infection (that is, the immune response) would be favourable to the host. A less robust host immune response would benefit the parasite. It is plausible that a host adapts so that the cost of the infection is negated. In this instance, a relationship that started as parasitism evolves into commensalism. Moreover, if the host adapts so that it too profits, the relationship becomes mutualistic. For example, the eyelash mite *Demodex brevis* **(Figure 39.13A)**, lives in the hair follicles of our eyebrows and eyelashes. This mite is commen-sal, feeding on our oily secretions and eliciting no response from us. However, several species of *Demodex* cause severe skin irritation and hair loss, a disease known as mange. It is likely that the commensal nature of our symbiosis with the eyelash mite has evolved from one that was formerly parasitic, similar to our relationship with other *Demodex*.

Relationships can also change in the opposite direction. A few parasitic species have evolved from mutualistic ancestors.

Colourized SEM

▲ **Figure 39.13A** The eyelash mite (*Demodex brevis*) within a hair follicle

In general, yucca moths (*Tegeticula*) have a mutualistic re-lationship with the yucca plant (*Yucca*). They pollinate the yucca flowers and in return their larvae feed on yucca fruit and seeds **(Figure 39.13B)**. Dr. John Addicott at the University of Calgary demonstrated that a couple of species of cheaters exist within the yucca moth genus. Acting like parasites, the cheaters do not pollinate the flowers, but their larvae still eat the seeds. In this case, a parasitic relationship has evolved from what was likely a mutualistic ancestor.

? **What evolutionary factor might cause a relationship to become obligate rather than facultative?**

● Relationships that have been evolving for a longer period of time may become so strong that the two symbionts become completely dependent on each other.

▲ **Figure 39.13B** Yucca flower (*Yucca*) with its pollinator, the yucca moth (*Tegeticula*)

39.14 Relationships are fostered by special adaptations

The condition of two organisms living and interacting within the same environment is simply not enough reason for a symbiotic relationship to evolve. At least one member species must also possess special traits, or adaptations, that allow a more intimate relationship to develop. These adaptations, like any other heritable characteristic, evolve by means of natural selection. As beneficial adaptations continue to evolve within one (or both) species, the symbiosis is strengthened. Evolution of one species often places selective pressure on the other. As a result, both populations are said to co-evolve. Although two examples are discussed below, the assortment of special adaptations is as diverse as the symbioses they foster.

At one point in Lewis Carroll's *Through the Looking Glass* (1872), Alice tries to approach the Red Queen. When Alice advances, the Red Queen quickly moves away. As Alice speeds up, so does the Red Queen, with the result that the distance between them is unchanged. When questioned, the Red Queen replies, "Now, HERE, you see, it takes all the running YOU can do to keep in the same place" **(Figure 39.14A)**. If we consider the evolution of relationships between parasites and their hosts, we see a similar situation. Parasites continue to evolve new and better ways to take advantage of their host more efficiently. In response, hosts continue to evolve new adaptations to better protect themselves from infection. **Co-evolution** of the host and the parasite maintain the symbiotic status quo. Evolutionary biologists describe this arms race as the Red Queen hypothesis.

One does not need to go far to see beautiful examples of adaptations that foster mutualistic relationships. In fact, gardens are full of them. Most flowering plants have co-evolved with animal pollinators. Being stationary, the transfer of pollen from male to female reproductive structures is difficult for plants to accomplish alone. Having animals carry pollen from one flower to another is a distinct advantage. To attract pollinators, plants use colour and smell, and may even produce sugary nectar. For example, western columbine (*Aquilegia formosa*) produces energy-rich nectar for its pollinators, including the Calliope hummingbird (*Stelluta calliope*; **Figure 39.14B**). Animals inadvertently pick up and transfer pollen from flower to

▲ **Figure 39.14B** A calliope hummingbird (*Stelluta calliope*) feeding on western columbine (*Aquilegia formosa*)

flower as they feed on the nectar. Some of these mutually beneficial relationships have co-evolved to such an extent that the plant depends on only one species of pollinator.

The common remora (*Remora remora*) is a marine fish that has a commensal relationship with sharks and other large vertebrates. Remoras attach themselves to the bodies of sharks by using an adapted dorsal fin **(Figure 39.14C)**. This fin has been highly modified into a large suction cup on the top of the fish's head. While attached, the remora benefits by travelling with the shark and eating scraps when it feeds. The attachment does not harm or benefit the shark. However, as with other commensal relationships, the neutral effects on the sharks are difficult to confirm.

While symbiotic relationships require certain special adaptations, it is also possible to see the reduction or loss of other structures. This **degeneracy** is common in many parasites as they evolve different mechanisms to acquire their nutrients from their hosts. As new adaptations provide alternative means for meeting requirements, other structures may become redundant and no longer be valuable to the parasite. For example, tapeworms (Cestoda) evolved from

▲ **Figure 39.14A** Alice in pursuit of the Red Queen from *Through the Looking Glass*

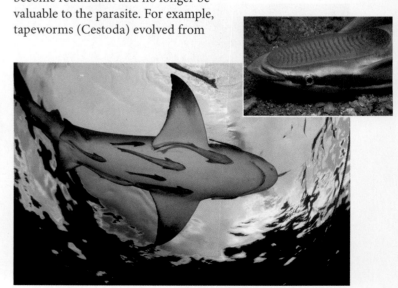

▲ **Figure 39.14C** Remora hitching a ride with a lemon shark

an ancestor that originally had a gastrovascular cavity. These worms have established parasitic relationships, living within the intestinal tract of their hosts. In this nutrient-rich environment, their integuments became adapted for absorption. Rather than spending energy ingesting and producing digestive enzymes, it became advantageous to depend solely on the host's digestive ability. As more and more nutrients were absorbed across their body surface, the role of the gut became redundant and the structure was eventually lost.

 What special adaptation allows the mosquito to feed on blood?

Mosquitoes have sharp, hollow mouthparts that penetrate skin and anticoagulants that prevent blood clotting at the point of contact.

R E V I E W

MasteringBiology® **For Practice Quizzes, BioFlix, MP3 Tutors, and Activities, go to masteringbiology.com.**

Reviewing the Concepts

Organisms Live Together (39.1–39.3)

39.1 Organisms do not live in isolation. Species in a community often interact with one another. When these relationships are intimate and long term, they are referred to as symbioses. Members of a symbiosis are called symbionts, and they may be affected positively, negatively, or not at all.

39.2 One organism may live inside of another. In many symbiotic relationships, one organism will live within the body of the other. Some bacterial endosymbionts flourish inside human hosts.

39.3 A rare case of organism-organelle symbiosis. The photosynthetic sea slug is a rare example of an animal that is photosynthetic. This animal forms a symbiotic relationship with a single organelle, a chloroplast, from its partner.

Relationships Affect the Fitness of the Partners (39.4–39.12)

39.4 Both partners benefit in mutualism. In mutualistic relationships, both symbionts benefit. Mutualisms are classified according to the benefits the organisms receive. Dissemination of an organism's gametes is the gain involved in dispersive mutualism. Nutritional benefits are realized in trophic mutualisms. Protection is the gain in defensive mutualisms.

39.5 Plants benefit from several mutualistic relationships. Many plants form mycorrhizae, mutually beneficial associations between roots and fungi. A network of fungal threads increases a plant's absorption of nutrients and water, and the fungus receives some nutrients from the plant. Legumes and certain other plants have nodules in their roots that house nitrogen-fixing bacteria.

39.6 In parasitism, one partner benefits at the cost of the other. Parasitism describes a relationship where one organism (a parasite) benefits at the cost of the other (the host). While the host experiences a cost, it is usually not killed. Host-generalists are parasites that have adapted to infect many different species, whereas host-specialists are parasites that can infect only one species.

39.7 Parasites must get from one host to another. Parasite life cycles may be direct (where the parasite completes its life cycle using a single host organism) or indirect (where the parasite requires two or more host species to complete its life cycle). Transmission is the movement of a parasite from one host to the next in its life cycle. This can be accomplished by active or passive mechanisms. Some parasites use a vector organism to infect the next host in their life cycle.

39.8 Don't let a parasite break your dog's heart. Canine heartworm is a parasite that infects dogs and cats. Mosquito vectors transmit this disease. If left untreated, this parasite can lead to congestive heart failure. Infection can be prevented by special drugs administered monthly.

39.9 Can tapeworms help you lose weight? Ingesting tapeworms is a very dangerous way to try to lose weight. The parasite causes anemia and vitamin B_{12} deficiency. And, if the eggs of the tapeworm are ingested, death can result.

39.10 One partner benefits while the other is unaffected in commensalism. Commensal relationships, in which one organism benefits while the other is unaffected, are not always easy to identify. In-depth examination often reveals some small positive or negative effect on the supposedly "neutral" partner.

39.11 In altruism, one organism reduces its fitness to benefit another. Altruism may or may not exist in nature. Relationships where one organism freely sacrifices to benefit another are not evolutionarily sound unless kin selection or reciprocal altruism are involved.

39.12 Many organisms acquire indirect benefits through mimicry. Mimicry is a debatable form of indirect symbiosis. One organism (the mimic) copies the colour pattern or behaviours of another (the model). Batesian mimics are a harmless species that copy a harmful species to deter predation. In Müllerian mimicry, both the mimic and the model are harmful to predators. Aggressive mimics are a harmful species that copy a harmless species to gain access to more prey. Some flowers use reproductive mimicry, called Pouyannian mimicry, in which they copy females and dupe males into pseudocopulation.

Relationships Form Through Co-Evolution (39.13–39.14)

39.13 Symbiotic relationships do not form overnight. Symbiotic relationships are under the same evolutionary pressures as any heritable characteristic. As a result, these relationships form and are strengthened over long periods of time. Facultative relationships benefit organisms but are not essential to their survival. In contrast, obligate symbionts cannot survive without their partners.

39.14 Relationships are fostered by special adaptations. Organisms have special adaptations that facilitate symbiotic relationships. Environmental pressures and natural selection drives the evolution of these structures. The Red Queen hypothesis describes the evolutionary arms race between a parasite and its host. Loss of unused characters (degeneracy) is common with parasites and occurs through selection processes.

Connecting the Concepts

1. Complete the blank cells in the table below to summarize the types of interspecies relationships. In columns 2 and 3, a plus sign stands for benefit, a minus sign stands for cost, and a zero stands for no cost and no benefit.

Interspecies Relationships	Effects on Species 1	Effects on Species 2	Symbiotic (Yes or No)	Example
Predation		−		
	−	−	No	
Mutualism	+			
	+	0		
Parasitoid	+			
Mimicry			Yes	

2. For each example you used above, discuss how the reproductive fitness of each partner is affected by the relationship.

Testing Your Knowledge

Multiple Choice

3. Which of the following is an example of an endosymbiont?
   a. mosquito
   b. epiphyte
   c. cellulose-digesting protist
   d. cowbird chick
   e. scarlet king snake

4. The photosynthetic sea slug is a partner in a novel form of symbiosis. What makes this relationship so different from other symbioses?
   a. It is a relationship between an animal and a plant.
   b. It is a relationship between an animal and a single-celled alga.
   c. It is a relationship between an animal and a single organelle from an algal cell.
   d. It is a relationship where the sea slug mimics the coloration of distasteful leaves.
   e. It is a relationship in which an algal cell parasitizes an animal.

5. What type of relationship occurs between a flowering plant and a specific hummingbird pollinator?
   a. trophic mutualism
   b. diffuse mutualism
   c. reproductive mimicry
   d. dispersive mutualism
   e. parasitism

6. *Giardia lamblia* is able to infect many different host species. Which of the following terms best describes this ability?
   a. host-specialist
   b. host-generalist
   c. parasitoid
   d. endosymbiosis
   e. kin selection

7. In which of the following direct symbiotic relationships does one symbiont benefit while the other experiences no effects?
   a. parasitism
   b. altruism
   c. mutualism
   d. commensalism
   e. mimicry

8. Which of the following best describes the canine heartworm (*Dirofilaria immitis*) life cycle?
   a. The mosquito is an intermediate host and the dog is the definitive host.
   b. The mosquito is a definitive host and the dog is the intermediate host.
   c. The dog is both the definitive host and a vector for *Dirofilaria*.
   d. The mosquito is both the definitive host and a vector for *Dirofilaria*.
   e. *Dirofilaria* has a direct life cycle.

9. Which of the following best describes a parasitoid?
   a. It ultimately kills its host before its development is complete.
   b. A vector organism transmits it from host to host.
   c. It infects plants but not animals.
   d. It is an endosymbiont that can have either positive or negative effects on its host.
   e. It rarely kills its host as it develops.

10. What type of mimicry describes a situation when both the model and mimic are distasteful?
   a. Batesian mimicry
   b. Pouyannian mimicry
   c. Müllerian mimicry
   d. aggressive mimicry
   e. reproductive mimicry

11. Which of the following hypothetical evolutionary changes could transform a parasitic relationship into one that is mutualistic?
    a. The parasite adapts methods to get more resources from its host, thus increasing its benefit.
    b. The host adapts better ways to limit parasite load, reducing the cost of infection.
    c. The parasite decreases its load to reduce the nutrients it takes away, reducing its burden on the host.
    d. The host evolves so that the parasite no longer has any effect on it.
    e. The host adapts to a method to acquire an essential amino acid from the parasite in return for the loss of carbohydrates.

Describing, Comparing, and Explaining

12. Compare and contrast predation with parasitism. Make sure to discuss the costs and benefits to each organism in the relationship.

13. Describe the types of symbioses you may have with any of the 600 species of bacteria living in your large intestine.

14. Explain in your own words why examples of true altruism do not likely exist.

15. Batesian mimicry breaks down when there are more mimics than models. Under aggressive mimicry, what effects could too many aggressive mimics have on the model species as well as on the prey? Use the relationship between the cleaner wrasse and the sabre-toothed blenny as an example.

Applying the Concepts

16. While walking around your school campus, you discover a small plant growing on the trunk of a large tree. You correctly interpret the two species to be in a long-term, intimate relationship. Describe how you would determine the type of symbiotic relationship between these two species. What adaptations could you expect to find if the relationship was parasitic? If it was commensal? If it was mutualistic?

Answers to all questions can be found in Appendix E.

Ecosystem Structure

40.1 Ecosystem ecology emphasizes energy flow and chemical cycling

An **ecosystem** consists of all the organisms in a community as well as the abiotic environment with which the organisms interact. Ecosystem ecologists are especially interested in **energy flow**, the passage of energy *through* the components of the ecosystem, and **chemical cycling**, the transfer of materials *within* the ecosystem.

The terrarium in **Figure 40.1** represents a familiar type of ecosystem and illustrates the fundamentals of energy flow. Energy enters the terrarium in the form of sunlight ( ). Plants (producers) convert light energy to chemical energy ( ) through the process of photosynthesis. Animals (consumers) take in some of this chemical energy in the form of organic compounds when they eat the plants. Decomposers, such as bacteria and fungi in the soil, obtain chemical energy when they decompose the dead remains of plants and animals. Every use of chemical energy by organisms involves a loss of some

energy to the surroundings in the form of heat (; see Module 6.1). Because so much of the energy captured by photosynthesis is lost as heat, the ecosystem would run out of energy if it were not powered by a continuous inflow of energy from the sun. Figure 40.1 shows light energy fuelling the example ecosystem. We will explore the common belief that this is always the case in the next module.

In contrast to energy flow, chemical cycling ( ) involves the transfer of materials *within* the ecosystem. While most ecosystems have a constant input of energy from sunlight, the supply of the chemical elements used to construct molecules is limited. Chemical elements such as carbon and nitrogen are cycled between the abiotic component of the ecosystem, including air, water, and soil, and the biotic component of the ecosystem (the community). Plants acquire these chemical elements in inorganic form from the air and the soil and use them to build organic molecules. Animals, such as the snail in Figure 40.1, consume some of these organic molecules. When the plants and animals become detritus, decomposers return most of the elements to the soil and air in inorganic form. Some elements are also returned to the soil as the by-products of plant and animal metabolism.

In summary, both energy flow and chemical cycling involve the transfer of substances through the trophic levels of the ecosystem. However, energy flows through, and ultimately out of, ecosystems, whereas chemicals are recycled within ecosystems. We explore these fundamental ecosystem dynamics in the rest of the chapter.

? **How do chemical cycles in an ecosystem directly relate to food chains in a community?**

Energy flow ▶

Light energy

Chemical cycling

Chemical energy

Heat energy

Chemical elements

Bacteria, protists, and fungi

▲ **Figure 40.1** A terrarium ecosystem

● Chemicals pass through one or more abiotic components of an ecosystem as well as passing through the biotic components (food chain).

40.2 Do all ecosystems get their energy from the sun?

All ecosystems require a constant flow of energy. The primary producers convert the energy into chemical energy, typically glucose. There is a commonly held belief that the sun is the source of energy for all ecosystems. For example, Figure 40.1 shows a schematic of a terrarium ecosystem with the sun supplying the required energy to the producers. Is it safe to make such a generalization? Do all ecosystems obtain energy from the sun? In short, the answer to these questions is no.

As you dive deeper into the oceans, light becomes more faint and is mostly attenuated at a depth of 200 m. In the abyss

at the bottom of Earth's oceans, more than 2500 m below the surface, there is absolutely no light left. And if sunlight powered all of Earth's ecosystems, there should be little life present. However, in 1977, biologists discovered an amazing density of life surrounding a hydrothermal vent at a great depth **(Figure 40.2A)**. The biodiversity at the vents is roughly four to five orders of magnitude higher than the surrounding seafloor.

If the energy does not come from the sun, from where is it coming? In Module 17.2, you read about the nutritional diversity found among bacteria. The water spewing out of the

▲ **Figure 40.2A** A community surrounding a hydrothermal vent

▲ **Figure 40.2B** Tube worms at a cold seep

vents contains high concentrations of sulphur compounds. Chemoautotrophic bacteria harness the energy within these compounds and environmental CO_2 to produce glucose. Small crustaceans feed on the bacteria and the energy travels through the food web to the top predators: fishes.

The giant tubeworms in Figure 40.2A, cover the vents and provide the matrix for the community. These worms have a symbiotic relationship with the bacteria. The worms have no mouth or digestive tract. The red tip extending from the hardened casing is a respiratory surface that acquires oxygen and sulphur compounds from the water. Bacteria living in a specialized organ in the worm's body get energy from the sulphur—a lot of energy, which they share with the worm. These worms are among the fastest growing invertebrates known and can grow to be more than 2 m long.

Later, in 1990, scientists discovered another community in the abyss of the Gulf of Mexico, which thrives in the complete absence of sunlight. Cold seeps are areas surrounding salty pools on the seafloor. Similar to a hydrothermal vent, cold seep communities are based on chemoautotrophic bacteria. Bacteria that feed on hydrogen sulphide sustain a large number of species, including another species of tubeworm that also grows near cold seeps **(Figure 40.2B)**. However, in addition

to sulphur compounds, some cold seep bacteria can get their energy from the methane gas that bubbles up through cracks in the seafloor.

Although the vast majority of ecosystems are based on energy from the sun, we have described above two known exceptions. In both instances, bacteria harness chemical energy to sustain the community. We have explored only about 1% of the oceans. It is possible that we may find other communities that dwell in the dark. In biology, blanket statements (such as "All ecosystems get their energy from the sun.") are risky to make. With the vast diversity of life on Earth, and our limited (but growing) understanding of it, one should not be surprised that exceptions to "rules" exist.

 Where do chemoautotrophic bacteria get their energy and carbon?

● Energy comes from the sulphur compounds and carbon from CO_2.

40.3 Primary production sets the energy budget for ecosystems

Each day, Earth receives about 1019 kcal of solar energy, the energy equivalent of about 100 million atomic bombs. Most of this energy is absorbed, scattered, or reflected by the atmosphere or by Earth's surface. Of the visible light that reaches plants, algae, and cyanobacteria, only about 1% is converted to chemical energy by photosynthesis.

Ecologists call the amount, or mass, of living organic material in an ecosystem the **biomass**. The amount of solar energy converted to chemical energy (in organic compounds) by an ecosystem's producers for a given area and during a given time period is called **primary production**. It can be expressed in

units of energy or units of mass. The primary production of the entire biosphere is roughly 150 billion tonnes of biomass per year.

Different ecosystems vary considerably in their primary production as well as in their contribution to the total production of the biosphere. **Figure 40.3** contrasts the net primary production of a number of different ecosystems. (Net primary production refers to the amount of biomass produced minus the amount used by producers as fuel for their own cellular respiration.) Tropical rainforests are among the most productive terrestrial ecosystems and contribute a large portion of

▲ **Figure 40.3** Net primary production of various ecosystems

the planet's overall production of biomass. Coral reefs also have very high production, but their contribution to global production is small because they cover such a small area. Interestingly, even though the open ocean has very low production, it contributes the most to Earth's total net primary production because of its huge size—it covers about 70% of Earth's surface area.

? Deserts and semidesert scrub cover about the same amount of surface area as tropical forests but contribute less than 1% of Earth's net primary production, while rainforests contribute 22%. Explain this difference.

● The primary production of tropical rainforests is more than 20 times greater than that of desert and semidesert scrub ecosystems.

Ecosystem Dynamics

40.4 Energy supply limits the length of food chains

When energy flows as organic matter through the trophic levels of an ecosystem, much of it is lost at each link in a food chain. Consider the transfer of organic matter from a producer to a primary consumer, such as the caterpillar shown in **Figure 40.4A**. The caterpillar might digest and absorb only about half the organic material it eats, passing the indigestible wastes as feces. Of the organic compounds it does absorb, the caterpillar typically uses two-thirds as fuel for cellular respiration. Only the chemical energy left over after respiration—15% of the organic material the caterpillar consumed—can be converted to caterpillar biomass. Thus, a secondary consumer that eats the caterpillar gets only 15% of the biomass (and the energy it contains) that was in the leaves the caterpillar ate.

Figure 40.4B, called a *pyramid of production*, illustrates the cumulative loss of energy with each transfer in a food chain. Each tier of the pyramid represents the chemical energy present in all the organisms at one trophic level of a food chain.

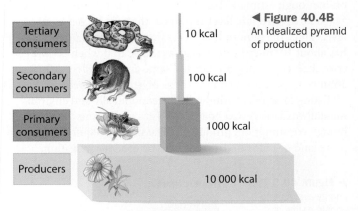

◀ **Figure 40.4B** An idealized pyramid of production

The width of each tier indicates how much of the chemical energy of the tier below is actually incorporated into the organic matter of that trophic level. Pyramids of production can represent the number of individuals in a trophic level or its total biomass. Note that producers convert only about 1% of the energy in the sunlight available to them to primary production. In this idealized pyramid, 10% of the energy available at each trophic level becomes incorporated into the next higher level. The efficiencies of energy transfer as one organism eats another usually range from 5% to 20%. In other words, 80%–95% of the energy at one trophic level never transfers to the next.

An important implication of this stepwise decline of energy in a trophic structure is that the amount of energy converted from the sun by producers that is available to top-level consumers is small compared with that available to lower-level consumers. Only a tiny fraction of the energy stored by photosynthesis flows through a food chain all the way to a tertiary consumer. This explains why top-level consumers such as lions and hawks require so much geographic territory; it takes a lot of vegetation to support trophic levels so many steps removed

▲ **Figure 40.4A** The fate of leaf biomass consumed by a caterpillar

from photosynthetic production. Pyramids of production help us understand why most food chains are limited to three to five levels; there is simply not enough energy at the very top of an ecological pyramid to support another trophic level.

? **Approximately what proportion of the energy produced by photosynthesis makes it to the snake in Figure 40.4B?**

● 1/1000 of the 10 000 kcal produced by photosynthesis
[0.1 × 0.1 × 0.1) (10 000 kcal) = 10 kcal]

40.5 A pyramid of production explains the ecological cost of meat

The dynamics of energy flow apply to the human population as much as to other organisms. As omnivores, people eat both plant material and meat. When we eat grain or fruit, we are primary consumers; when we eat beef or other meat from herbivores, we are secondary consumers. When we eat fish such as trout and salmon (which eat insects and other small animals), we are tertiary or quaternary consumers.

The pyramid of production on the left in **Figure 40.5** indicates energy flow from producers to vegetarians (primary consumers). The energy in the producer trophic level comes from a corn crop. The pyramid on the right illustrates energy flow from the same corn crop, with people as secondary consumers, eating beef. These two pyramids are generalized models, based on the rough estimate that about 10% of the chemical energy available in a trophic level appears at the next higher trophic level. Thus, the pyramids indicate that the human population has about 10 times more energy available to it when people eat corn than when they process the same amount of corn through another trophic level and eat corn- or grain-fed beef.

Eating meat of any kind is both economically and environmentally expensive. Compared with growing plants for direct human consumption, producing meat usually requires that more land be cultivated, more water be used for irrigation,

more fossil fuels be burned, and more chemical fertilizers and pesticides be applied to croplands used for growing grain. In many countries, people cannot afford to buy much meat and are vegetarians by necessity. Sometimes religion also plays a role in the decision. In India, for example, about 80% of the population practises Hinduism, a religion that discourages meat-eating. India's meat consumption was roughly 3.3 kg per person annually in 2010 (the most recent year for which statistics are available). In Mexico, where many people are too poor to eat meat daily, per capita consumption of meat in 2010 was 63.3 kg per year. That is a large amount compared with India, but it is about two-thirds of that of Canada, where only 4% of the population are vegetarians and the per capita rate was 98.8 kg in 2010.

We turn next to the subject of chemical nutrients. Unlike energy, which is ultimately lost from an ecosystem, all chemical nutrients cycle within ecosystems.

? **Why does demand for meat also tend to drive up prices of fruits, vegetables, and grains such as wheat and rice?**

● The potential supply of plants for direct consumption as food for humans is diminished by the use of agricultural land to grow feed for cattle, chickens, and other meat sources.

▶ **Figure 40.5** Food energy available to people eating at different trophic levels

Trophic level

Secondary consumers

Primary consumers

Producers

Vegetarians

Corn

Meat-eaters

Cattle

Corn

40.6 Chemicals are cycled between organic matter and abiotic reservoirs

The sun (or in some cases Earth's interior, as we saw in Module 40.2) supplies ecosystems with a continual influx of energy; but, aside from an occasional meteorite, there are no extraterrestrial sources of chemical elements. Life, therefore, depends on the recycling of chemicals. While an organism is alive, much of its chemical stock changes continuously as nutrients are acquired and waste products are released. Atoms

present in the complex molecules of an organism at the time of its death are returned to the environment by the action of decomposers, replenishing the pool of inorganic nutrients that plants and other producers use to build new organic matter.

Because chemical cycles in an ecosystem include both biotic and abiotic (geologic and atmospheric) components, they are called **biogeochemical cycles**. **Figure 40.6** is a general scheme

▲ **Figure 40.6** A general model of the biogeochemical cycling of nutrients

for the cycling of a nutrient within an ecosystem. Note that the cycle has **abiotic reservoirs**, where chemicals accumulate or are stockpiled outside of living organisms. The atmosphere, for example, is an abiotic reservoir for carbon and nitrogen. Phosphorus, on the other hand, is available only from the soil.

Let's trace the general biogeochemical cycle in Figure 40.6. ❶ Producers incorporate chemicals from the abiotic reservoirs into organic compounds. ❷ Consumers feed on the producers, incorporating some of the chemicals into their own bodies. ❸ Both producers and consumers release some chemicals back to the environment in waste products (CO_2 and nitrogenous wastes of animals). ❹ Decomposers play a central role by breaking down the complex organic molecules in detritus such as plant litter, animal wastes, and dead organisms. The products of this metabolism are inorganic compounds such as nitrates (NO_3^-), phosphates (PO_43^-), and CO_2, which replenish the abiotic reservoirs. Geologic processes such as erosion and the weathering of rock also contribute to the abiotic reservoirs. Producers use the inorganic molecules from abiotic reservoirs as raw materials for synthesizing new organic molecules (carbohydrates and proteins, for example), and the cycle continues.

Biogeochemical cycles can be local or global. Soil is the main reservoir for nutrients in a local cycle, such as in the phosphorus cycle. In contrast, for those chemicals that exist primarily in gaseous form—carbon and nitrogen are examples—the cycling is essentially global. For instance, some of the carbon a plant acquires from the air may have been released into the atmosphere by the respiration of an organism on another continent.

In the next three modules, we look at the cyclic movements of carbon, nitrogen, and phosphorous. As you study the cycles, look for the four basic steps we have cited, as well as the geologic processes that may move chemicals around and between ecosystems. For example, as water erodes the surface of a rock, minerals become dissolved and accessible to living organisms. In the diagrams, the main abiotic reservoirs are highlighted in white boxes.

? Which boxes in Figure 40.6 represent biotic components of an ecosystem?

● Consumers, producers, and decomposers

40.7 The carbon cycle depends on photosynthesis and respiration

Carbon, the major ingredient of all organic molecules, has an atmospheric reservoir and cycles globally. Carbon also resides in fossil fuels and sedimentary rocks, such as limestone ($CaCO_3$), and as dissolved carbon compounds in the oceans.

As shown in **Figure 40.7**, the reciprocal metabolic processes of photosynthesis and cellular respiration are mainly responsible for the cycling of carbon between the biotic and abiotic worlds. ❶ Photosynthesis removes CO_2 from the atmosphere and incorporates it into organic molecules, which are ❷ passed along the food chain by consumers. ❸ Cellular respiration by producers and consumers returns CO_2 to the atmosphere. ❹ Decomposers break down the carbon compounds in detritus; that carbon, too, is eventually released as CO_2.

On a global scale, the return of CO_2 to the atmosphere by cellular respiration closely balances its removal by photosynthesis. However,

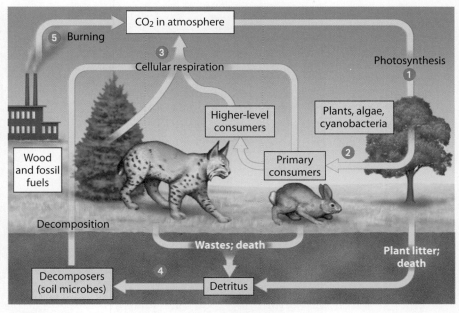

▲ **Figure 40.7** The carbon cycle

⑤ human influence, such as the increased burning of wood and fossil fuels (coal and petroleum), is raising the level of CO_2 in the atmosphere. As we will discuss in Module 41.6, this increase in CO_2 is leading to significant global climate change.

? **What would happen to the carbon cycle if all the decomposers suddenly went on "strike" and stopped working?**

● Carbon would accumulate in organic mass, the atmospheric reservoir of carbon would decline, and plants would eventually be starved for CO_2.

40.8 The nitrogen cycle depends on bacteria

As an ingredient of proteins and nucleic acids, nitrogen is essential to the structure and functioning of all organisms. In particular, it is a crucial and often limiting plant nutrient. Nitrogen has two abiotic reservoirs, the atmosphere and the soil. The atmospheric reservoir is huge; almost 80% of the atmosphere is nitrogen gas (N_2). However, plants cannot absorb nitrogen in the form of N_2. The process of **nitrogen fixation**, which is performed by some bacteria, converts N_2 to compounds of nitrogen that can be used by plants. Without these organisms, the natural reservoir of usable soil nitrogen would be extremely limited.

Figure 40.8 illustrates the actions of two types of nitrogen-fixing bacteria, both free-living and bacteria that live within the root nodules of certain plants. Starting at the far right in the figure, ❶ some bacteria live symbiotically in the roots of certain species of plants, supplying their hosts with a direct source of usable nitrogen. The largest group of plants with this mutualistic relationship is the legumes, a family that includes peanuts, soybeans, and alfalfa (see Module 39.5). A number of non-legume plants that live in nitrogen-poor soils have a similar relationship with bacteria. ❷ Free-living nitrogen-fixing bacteria in soil or water convert N_2 to ammonia (NH_3), which then picks up another H^+ to become ammonium (NH_4^+) (see Module 23.9).

❸ After nitrogen is "fixed," some of the NH_4^+ is taken up and used by plants. ❹ Nitrifying bacteria in the soil convert some of the NH_4^+ to nitrate (NO_3^-), which is more readily ❺ absorbed by plants. Plants use the nitrogen they assimilate to synthesize molecules such as amino acids, which are then incorporated into proteins.

❻ When an herbivore (represented by the rabbit in Figure 40.8) eats a plant, it digests the proteins into amino acids, and then uses the amino acids to build the proteins it needs. Higher-order consumers gain nitrogen from their prey. Recall from Module 28.15 that nitrogen-containing waste products are formed during protein metabolism; consumers excrete some nitrogen as well as incorporate some into their body tissues. Mammals, such as the rabbit, excrete nitrogen as urea, a substance that is widely used as an agricultural fertilizer.

Organisms that are not consumed eventually die and become detritus, which is decomposed by bacteria and fungi. ❼ Decomposition releases NH_4^+ from organic compounds

▶ **Figure 40.8**
The nitrogen cycle

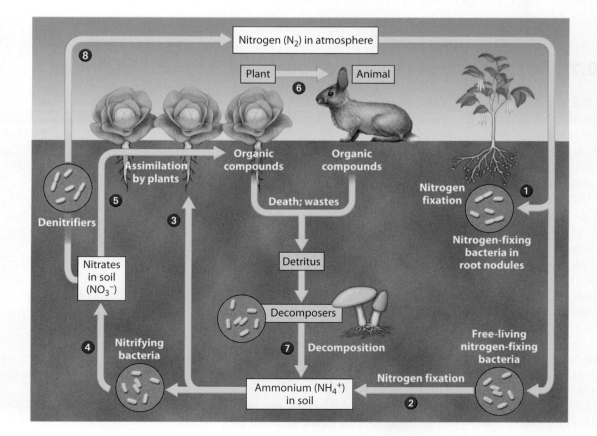

back into the soil, replenishing the soil reservoir of NH_4^+ and, with the help of nitrifying bacteria (step 4), NO_3^-. Under low-oxygen conditions, however, ❽ soil bacteria known as denitrifiers strip the oxygens from NO_3^-, releasing N_2 back into the atmosphere and depleting the soil reservoir of usable nitrogen.

Although not shown in the figure, some NH_4^+ and NO_3^- are made in the atmosphere by chemical reactions involving N_2 and ammonia gas (NH_3). The ions produced by these chemical reactions reach the soil in precipitation and dust, which are crucial sources of nitrogen for plants in some ecosystems.

Human activities are disrupting the nitrogen cycle by adding more nitrogen to the biosphere each year than natural processes. Combustion of fossil fuels in motor vehicles and coal-fired power plants produces nitrogen oxides (NO and NO_2). Nitrogen oxides react with other gases in the lower atmosphere to increase the production of ozone. Unlike the protective ozone layer in the upper atmosphere (see Module 7.14), ground-level ozone is a health hazard. Exposure to ozone, which irritates the respiratory system, can cause coughing and breathing difficulties. It is especially dangerous for people with respiratory problems such as asthma. In many regions, ozone

alerts are common during hot, dry summer weather. Nitrogen oxides also combine with water in the atmosphere to become nitric acid. The Canada–United States Air Quality Agreement Amendments of 1991 diminished acid precipitation from sulphur emissions (see Module 2.16), but environmental damage from nitric acid precipitation is causing new concern.

Modern agricultural practices are another major source of nitrogen. Animal wastes from intensive livestock production release ammonia into the atmosphere. Farmers use enormous amounts of nitrogen fertilizer to supplement natural nitrogen fixation by bacteria. Worldwide, the application of synthetic nitrogen fertilizer has increased a hundredfold since the late 1950s. However, less than half the fertilizer is taken up by the crop plants. Some nitrogen escapes to the atmosphere, where it forms NO_2 or nitrous oxide (N_2O), an inert gas that lingers in the atmosphere and contributes to climate change (see Module 41.4). As you will learn in Module 40.10, nitrogen fertilizers also pollute aquatic systems.

? What are the abiotic reservoirs of nitrogen? In what form does nitrogen occur in each reservoir?

● Atmosphere: N_2; soil: NH_4^+ and NO_3^-

40.9 The phosphorus cycle depends on the weathering of rock

Organisms require phosphorus—usually in the form of the phosphate ion (PO_43^-)—as an ingredient of nucleic acids, phospholipids, and ATP and (in vertebrates) as a mineral component of bones and teeth. In contrast to the carbon cycle and the other major biogeochemical cycles, the phosphorus cycle does not have an atmospheric component. Rocks are the only source of phosphorus for terrestrial ecosystems; in fact, rocks that have high phosphorus content are mined for agricultural fertilizer.

At the centre of **Figure 40.9**, ❶ the weathering (breakdown) of rock gradually adds inorganic phosphate (PO_43^-) to the soil. ❷ Plants assimilate the dissolved phosphate ions in the soil and build them into organic compounds. ❸ Consumers obtain phosphorus in organic form by eating plants. ❹ Phosphates are returned to the soil by the action of decomposers on animal waste and the remains of dead plants and animals. ❺ Some phosphate drains from terrestrial ecosystems into the sea, where it may settle and eventually become part of new rocks. This phosphorus will not cycle back into living organisms until ❻ geologic processes uplift the rocks and expose them to weathering, a process that takes millions of years.

Because phosphates are transferred from terrestrial to aquatic ecosystems much more rapidly than they are replaced, the amount in terrestrial ecosystems gradually diminishes over time. Furthermore, much of the soluble phosphate released by weathering quickly binds to soil particles, rendering it inaccessible to plants. As a result, the phosphate availability is often quite low and commonly a limiting factor. Mycorrhizal fungi (see Module 18.10) that facilitate phosphorus uptake are essential to many plants, especially those living in older, highly weathered soils. Soil erosion from

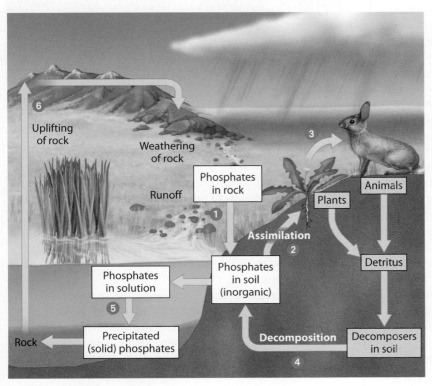

▲ **Figure 40.9** The phosphorus cycle

land cleared for agriculture or development accelerates the loss of phosphates.

Farmers and gardeners often use crushed phosphate rock, bone meal (finely ground bones from slaughtered livestock), or guano to add phosphorus to the soil. Guano, the droppings of seabirds and bats, is mined from densely populated colonies or caves, where metres-deep deposits have accumulated. As you

will learn in the next module, however, runoff of large amounts of phosphate fertilizer pollutes aquatic ecosystems.

 Over the short term, why does phosphorus cycling tend to be more localized than either carbon or nitrogen cycling?

● Because phosphorus is cycled almost entirely within the soil rather than transferred over long distances via the atmosphere

---

40.10 Too many nutrients are killing Lake Winnipeg

Low levels of nutrients, especially phosphorus and nitrogen, often limit the growth of algae and cyanobacteria—and thus primary production—in aquatic ecosystems. Standing-water ecosystems (lakes and ponds) gradually accumulate nutrients from the decomposition of organic matter and fresh influx from the watershed (the surrounding land that drains into the lake). As a result, primary production increases naturally over time in a process known as **eutrophication**. Human activities that add nutrients to aquatic ecosystems accelerate this process and also cause eutrophication in rivers, estuaries, coastal waters, and coral reefs. Rapid eutrophication is currently threatening numerous aquatic ecosystems in Canada, including Lake Winnipeg: the tenth largest lake in the world is now touted as Canada's sickest lake.

You might think that an increase in primary production would be beneficial to a biological community. After all, Figure 40.3 shows that coral reefs and tropical rainforests, ecosystems renowned for spectacular biodiversity, have the greatest net primary production. But rapid eutrophication actually lowers biodiversity. In some ecosystems, cyanobacteria replace green algae as primary producers. These bacteria, which are often encased in a slimy coating, form extensive mats on the surface of the water that prevent light from penetrating the water. Cyanobacteria also produce toxins that have serious implications for the health of the ecosystem and the people using it. These heavy growths, or "blooms," of either cyanobacteria or algae (or both) can be so massive that they can be seen in satellite images. The blue-green mat shown in **Figure 40.10A** covered most of the lake's 24 500 km² surface in 2006. Blooms of unicellular diatoms, toxin-producing dinoflagellates (see Figure 18.3B), or multicellular algae overrun other ecosystems. At night, when the photosynthesizers respire, the oxygen levels in the lake are greatly reduced. As the cyanobacteria and algae die, microbes consume a great deal of oxygen as they decompose the extra biomass. Thus, rapid nutrient enrichment results in oxygen depletion of the water. Oxygen depletion disrupts benthic communities and creates "dead zones," displacing fishes and invertebrates and killing organisms that are attached to the substrate.

Major sources of excess nutrients include sewage treatment facilities and agriculture. Sewage treatment facilities may discharge large amounts of dissolved inorganic nutrients, including phosphorus and nitrogen into rivers or streams when extreme conditions (such as unusually high rainfall) overwhelm their capacity. Agricultural sources of phosphorus and nitrogen include feedlots (where hundreds of animals are

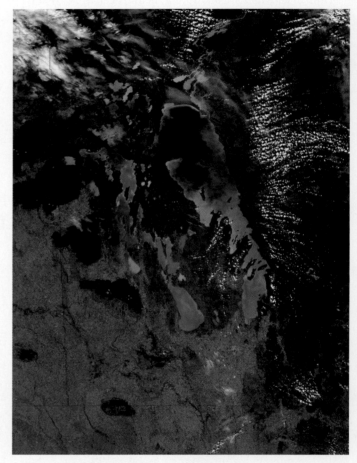

▲ **Figure 40.10A** Satellite image of an algal bloom in Lake Winnipeg

penned together), improperly treated sewage from livestock, and the large amounts of inorganic fertilizers that are routinely applied to crops, lawns, and golf courses. Within the area of a watershed, plants take up some of the nutrients in fertilizer and soil bacteria use a fraction, but unused nutrients are easily washed out of the soil by rain or irrigation and ultimately enter lakes or oceans.

The watershed for Lake Winnipeg is the second largest in Canada, covering nearly 1 million km² of land **(Figure 40.10B)**. Within this area live more than 6 million people and 17 million livestock producing sewage, and fertilizer is applied to over 55 million ha of agricultural land. Excess nutrient load from these sources is a huge burden on Lake Winnipeg. Levels of phosphorus in this lake are three times

▲ Figure 40.10B The Lake Winnipeg watershed

Dr. Peter Leavitt, Canada Research Chair in Environmental Change and Society at the University of Regina, studies the impact of human activities on lakes. Recommendations by Leavitt, which include a recommended 50% reduction of phosphorus in the lake, would require extensive efforts throughout the entire watershed. A similar response was imperative in the recovery of Lake Erie. To reduce the amount of phosphorus entering Lake Winnipeg, the Government of Manitoba introduced legislation in 2011 that changed hog farming practices and the standards for municipal waste treatment. To be effective, similar legislation or changes must occur throughout the watershed, which would require the cooperation of several governments. Reaching agreements between the governments of two countries, four provinces, four states, dozens of municipalities, and several First Nations peoples is a daunting but necessary task.

higher than the levels that were in Lake Erie when it was declared "dead" in 1970. Although, Lake Winnipeg is not dead, it is at a tipping point. If nothing is done to prevent further eutrophication, it soon will be.

 How does the excessive addition of mineral nutrients to a lake eventually lead to the loss of many fish species?

● The nutrients initially cause population explosions of algae and cyanobacteria. Their respiration and that of the decomposers of all the detritus as the algae and cyanobacteria die consume most of the lake's oxygen, which the fish require.

BIOLOGY AND SOCIETY

40.11 Ecosystem services are essential to human well-being

As you will learn in Chapter 41, people rely on numerous services that natural ecosystems provide. In addition to supplying fresh water and some foods, healthy ecosystems recycle nutrients, decompose wastes, and regulate climate and air quality. Wetlands buffer coastal populations against tidal waves and hurricanes, reduce the impact of flooding rivers, and filter pollutants. Natural vegetation helps to retain fertile soil and prevent landslides and mudslides.

Ecosystems that we create are also essential to our well-being. For example, agricultural ecosystems supply most of our food and fibres. Although we manage these ecosystems, they are modifications of natural ecosystems and make use of ecosystem services, such as control of agricultural pests by natural predators and pollination of crops. Soil fertility, the foundation for crop growth, depends on nutrient cycling, another ecosystem service. But conventional, large-scale agricultural practices introduced over the past several decades have pushed croplands beyond their natural capacity to produce food. Large inputs of chemical fertilizers are needed to supplement soil nutrients. Synthetic pesticides are used to control the population growth of crop-eating insects and pathogens that take advantage of vast monocultures of crop species. Herbicides are applied to kill weeds that would compete with crop plants for water and nutrients. And, in many areas, crops require additional water supplied by irrigation. The Canadian Prairies is one of the few areas in the world where irrigation is not common practice. In particular, many grain farmers in Alberta, Saskatchewan, and Manitoba use dryland farming practices.

Conventional, large-scale agricultural practices have resulted in enormous increases in food production, but at the expense of natural ecosystems and the services they provide.

The detrimental effects of nutrient runoff, discussed in the previous module, are affecting both freshwater and marine ecosystems as fertilizer use increases. Pesticides may kill beneficial organisms as well as pests, and as you learned previously, chemicals that persist in the environment can be carried far from their point of origin (see Modules 35.2, 35.19, and 36.16). Perhaps most worrisome is the deterioration of fertile soil. Clearing and cultivation expose land to wind and water that erode the rich topsoil. Erosion and soil degradation are especially severe in grassland, savanna, and some forest ecosystems where low amounts of precipitation and high rates of evaporation result in low levels of soil moisture. In recent years, dust storms sweeping across over-cultivated areas have removed millions of tonnes of topsoil from these stressed ecosystems. In China, for example, overgrazing and other poor agricultural practices are turning 2,330 km² of land—an area slightly smaller than Metro Vancouver—into desert each year (Figure 40.11A). Irrigation of arid land enables farmers to grow crops but leaves a

▲ Figure 40.11A A dust storm in Changling, China

salty residue that eventually prevents plant growth. In addition, population growth in these regions places increasing demands on the already scarce water supply.

Human activities also threaten many forest ecosystems and the services they provide. Every year, more and more land is cleared for agriculture. Some of this land is needed to feed the growing human population, but replacing worn-out cropland accounts for much of the deforestation occurring today. Forests are also cut down to provide timber and fuel wood; many people in non-industrialized countries use wood for heating and cooking (Figure 40.11B). The most immediate impact of deforestation is soil erosion. In Haiti, for example, where less than 2% of the original tree cover remains, heavy rains inevitably bring flooding and mudslides that damage crops. During recent hurricanes, floodwaters surging down stripped hillsides caused thousands of deaths. With much of the soil destabilized by the devastating earthquake in 2010, massive landslides are likely to cause further ecological and economic destruction during storms.

The growing demand of the human population for food, fibres, and water has largely been satisfied at the expense of other ecosystem services, but these practices cannot continue indefinitely. **Sustainability** is the goal of developing, managing, and conserving Earth's resources in ways that meet the needs of people today without compromising the ability of future generations to meet theirs. In the next chapter, you will learn how scientists are applying their knowledge of

▶ Figure 40.11B A woman in Haiti gathering wood to process into charcoal

population, community, and ecosystem ecology to conserve natural ecosystems and even to repair some of the ecological damage that we have done.

 How can clear-cutting a forest (removing all trees) damage the water quality of nearby aquatic ecosystems?

● Without the growing trees to assimilate minerals from the soil, more of the minerals run off and end up polluting water resources.

R E V I E W

Reviewing the Concepts

Ecosystem Structure (40.1–40.3)

40.1 Ecosystem ecology emphasizes energy flow and chemical cycling. An ecosystem includes a community and the abiotic factors with which it interacts.

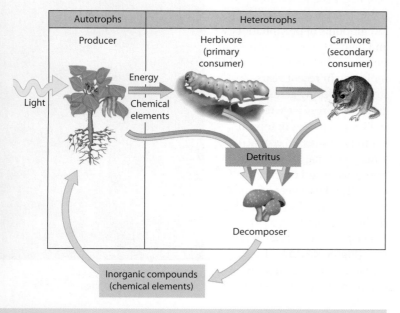

40.2 Do all ecosystems get their energy from the sun? Although the sun powers most ecosystems, we know of two abyssal communities that thrive in complete darkness. The primary producers in these ecosystems are chemoautotrophic bacteria.

40.3 Primary production sets the energy budget for ecosystems. The amount of biomass that an ecosystem can support is determined by the production of the primary producers.

Ecosystem Dynamics (40.4–40.11)

40.4 Energy supply limits the length of food chains. A pyramid of production shows the flow of energy from producers to primary consumers and to higher trophic levels. Only about 10% of the energy stored at each trophic level is available to the next level.

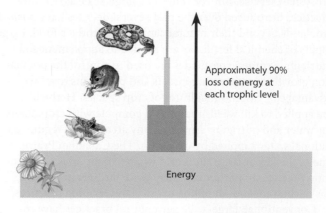

Approximately 90% loss of energy at each trophic level

Energy

40.5 A pyramid of production explains the ecological cost of meat. A field of corn can support many more human vegetarians than meat-eaters.

40.6 Chemicals are cycled between organic matter and abiotic reservoirs. Producers incorporate chemicals from abiotic sources. Consumers feed on the producers and incorporate some of the chemicals. Chemicals are released back to the abiotic pools by all organisms as waste products or during decomposition.

40.7 The carbon cycle depends on photosynthesis and respiration. Photosynthesis fixes atmospheric CO_2 into sugars, which move throughout the food web. Cellular respiration consumes sugar to produce ATP energy and releases carbon as CO_2.

40.8 The nitrogen cycle depends on bacteria. Various bacteria in soil (and root nodules of some plants) convert gaseous N_2 to compounds that plants can use, such as ammonium (NH_4^+) and nitrate (NO_3^-).

40.9 The phosphorus cycle depends on the weathering of rock. There is no atmospheric pool for phosphorous. The cycle is therefore very slow and depends largely on geological processes.

40.10 Too many nutrients are killing Lake Winnipeg. Nutrient input from fertilizer and other sources causes rapid eutrophication, resulting in decreased species diversity and oxygen depletion of lakes, rivers, and coastal waters. Eutrophication has made Lake Winnipeg Canada's sickest lake.

40.11 Ecosystem services are essential to human well-being. Although agricultural and other managed ecosystems are necessary to supply our needs, we also depend on services provided by natural ecosystems.

Connecting the Concepts

1. Fill in the blanks in the table below summarizing terrestrial nutrient cycles.

	Carbon	Nitrogen	Phosphorus
Main abiotic reservoir(s)			
Form in abiotic reservoir			
Form used by producers			
Human activities that alter cycle			
Effects of altering cycle			

Testing Your Knowledge

Multiple Choice

2. Which of the following groups is absolutely essential to the functioning of an ecosystem?
   a. producers
   b. producers and herbivores
   c. producers, herbivores, and carnivores
   d. detritivores
   e. producers and decomposers

3. The open ocean and tropical rainforests contribute the most to Earth's net primary production because
   a. both have high rates of net primary production.
   b. both cover huge surface areas of Earth.
   c. nutrients cycle fastest in these two ecosystems.
   d. the ocean covers a huge surface area and the tropical rainforest has a high rate of production.
   e. both have high rates of net primary production and cover a huge surface of Earth.

4. Which of the following types of organisms is not considered a primary producer?
   a. photosynthetic bacteria in a pond
   b. sulphur-fixing bacteria at a hydrothermal vent
   c. nitrogen-fixing bacteria in the soil
   d. methane-fixing bacteria in a cold seep
   e. photosynthetic algae in the intertidal regions

5. Which of the following nutrients is most closely linked to the energy flow through ecosystems?
   a. phosphorous
   b. nitrogen
   c. oxygen
   d. carbon
   e. potassium

6. To ensure adequate nitrogen for a crop, a farmer would want to decrease _____ by soil bacteria.
   a. cellular respiration
   b. nitrification
   c. denitrification
   d. nitrogen fixation
   e. decomposition

Describing, Comparing, and Explaining

7. What is rapid eutrophication? What steps might be taken to slow this process?

8. Local conditions, such as heavy rainfall or the removal of plants, may limit the amount of nitrogen, phosphorus, or calcium available, but the amount of carbon available in an ecosystem is seldom a problem. Explain.

9. In Southeast Asia, there's an old saying: "There is only one tiger to a hill." In terms of energy flow in ecosystems, explain why big predatory animals such as tigers and sharks are relatively rare.

10. For which chemicals do biogeochemical cycles move nutrients throughout the entire globe? *Explain your answer.*

11. What roles do bacteria play in the nitrogen cycle?

Applying the Concepts

12. What would happen to the nutrient cycles if all decomposers were removed from the ecosystem?

13. Clear-cutting tropical rainforests for agricultural purposes is a significant concern in South America. How does deforestation in the tropical rainforest alter the carbon cycle within the newly cultivated land?

Answers to all questions can be found in Appendix E.

Conservation and Sustainability

The Loss of Biodiversity

(41.1–41.7)

Biodiversity is declining rapidly worldwide as a result of human activities.

Conservation Biology and Sustainability

(41.8–41.14)

Biologists are applying their knowledge of ecology to slow the loss of biodiversity and to help define a sustainable future.

A Fine Balance

As the human population has expanded, we have changed natural ecosystems to serve our needs. Only about one-quarter of Earth's land surfaces remain untouched by human alterations. Our activities have also had an enormous impact on aquatic biomes.

What is the value of natural ecosystems? Most people appreciate the direct benefits provided by certain ecosystems. For example, some of the resources we use, including water and food such as fish and shellfish, come from natural or near-natural ecosystems. Many people enjoy outdoor recreation such as hiking or whitewater rafting in pristine ecosystems, while others appreciate nature in less strenuous ways.

But human well-being also depends on less obvious services that healthy ecosystems provide. The coastal wetlands affected by the 2010 oil spill in the Gulf of Mexico normally act as a buffer against hurricanes, reduce the impact of flooding, and filter pollutants. The wetlands also furnish nesting sites for birds and marine turtles, and provide breeding areas and nurseries for a wide variety of fish and shellfish. Other services provided by natural ecosystems include recycling nutrients, preventing erosion and mudslides, and controlling agricultural pests and pollinating crops.

Maintaining ecosystems is of utmost importance to their future as well as our own. Ecosystem management is a constantly evolving philosophy that strives to balance the exploitation and protection of all resources. This sustainable approach aims to protect our natural world for future generations. It is essential to note that we are a part of the ecosystem and the human species cannot survive without it.

Ecosystem management requires a holistic view of both natural and social systems. This requires fundamental changes to the policies of government agencies—federal, provincial, and municipal—and current practices of natural resource businesses. Ecosystems also have social and cultural facets in addition to their biological and physical characteristics. Maintaining the integrity of ecosystems needs to be managed within ecological boundaries—those governed by the environment—rather than administrative boundaries set by policy-makers. Successful management depends on the relationship between humans and the environment. For example, Natural Resources Canada has established sustainable forest management strategies that meet the needs of the environment, society, and the timber industry. Strategies must evolve in response to changes in the ecosystem and their inherent natural variation. Ecosystem management is a hands-on process. We need to repeat our successes and learn from our mistakes.

Fisheries and Oceans Canada, Environment Canada, and Parks Canada use a coordinated approach to protect and conserve all natural environments. For example, the Ecosystem Management Branch of Fisheries and Oceans Canada is charged with the management and stewardship of Canada's marine ecosystems. Our oceans are deeply integrated into the social and economic aspects of the Maritimes, as shown in the photograph. Through several federal acts, including the *Oceans Act*, *Species at Risk Act*, and the *Fisheries Act*, Fisheries and Oceans Canada works to maintain the sustainable use of our waters.

In this final chapter, you will learn about one of the major ecological challenges of our time—the rapid loss of biodiversity that is a result of our dominance over the environment. As you learn about the fight to save our biological heritage, you will see that conservation biology touches all levels of ecology, from a single bear to the forest it roams.

The Loss of Biodiversity

41.1 Loss of biodiversity includes the loss of ecosystems, species, and genes

Why should we care about the extinction of species and loss of biodiversity? One reason is what Harvard biologist E. O. Wilson calls biophilia: our sense of connection to nature and other forms of life. Also, many people share a moral belief that other species have an inherent right to life. But, as you learned in Module 40.11, our dependence on vital ecosystem services also gives us practical reasons for preserving biodiversity.

Biodiversity encompasses more than individual species—it includes ecosystem diversity, species diversity, and genetic diversity. Let's examine each level of diversity to see what we stand to lose if the decline is not stopped.

Ecosystem Diversity The world's natural ecosystems are rapidly disappearing. Nearly half of Earth's forests are gone, and thousands more square kilometres disappear every year. Grassland ecosystems in North America (see Figure 35.14), where millions of bison roamed as recently as the 19th century, have overwhelmingly been lost to agriculture and development.

Vancouver Island, off the west coast of British Columbia, has the most diverse range of ecosystems in Canada (**Figure 41.1A**). Different habitats include offshore kelp forests, intertidal zones and estuaries, alpine meadows, the towering stands of trees in the Cathedral Grove, and temperate rainforests. The island's vast array of ecosystems is at risk because of human activities. These habitats are fragmented by roads and logging and are displaced by urban and agricultural development. For example, human encroachment has placed the Garry oak ecosystem under immediate threat—95% of it has been destroyed.

Aquatic ecosystems are also threatened. For example, an estimated 20% of the world's coral reefs, ecosystems known for their species richness and productivity (see Figure 35.6B), have been destroyed by human activities, and 15% are in danger of collapse

within the next two decades. The deteriorating state of freshwater ecosystems is particularly worrisome (see Module 40.10). Tens of thousands of species live in lakes and rivers, and these ecosystems supply food and water for many terrestrial species as well—including us.

As natural ecosystems are lost, so are essential services. Water purification is one of the services provided free of charge by healthy ecosystems. As water moves slowly through forests, streams, and wetlands, pollutants and sediments are filtered out. Whether taken from surface waters such as lakes or subsurface sources (groundwater), the drinking water supplied by public water systems typically has passed through this natural filtration process. When natural filtration is lost because of ecosystem destruction, the human need to treat municipal water sources increases. Higher concentrations of chlorine, which is harmful to aquatic ecosystems, may be required to effectively kill microorganisms. We need to construct filtration plants to remove particulates. Such plants are costly to build and operate. We should strive to design them in a way that minimizes environmental damage.

Species Diversity When ecosystems are lost, populations of the species that make up their biological communities are also lost. A species may disappear from a local ecosystem but remain in others; for example, a population of tigers may be lost from one region of India while other populations survive elsewhere. Ecologists refer to the loss of a single population of a species as **extirpation**. Although extirpation and declining population sizes are strong signals that a species is in trouble, it may still be possible to save it. **Extinction** means that all populations of a species have disappeared, an irreversible situation.

How rapidly are species being lost? Because biologists are uncertain of the total number of species that exist, it is difficult to determine the actual rate of species loss. Some scientists estimate that current extinction rates are around 100 times greater than the natural rate of extinction. The International Union for Conservation of Nature (IUCN) is a global environmental network that keeps track of the status of species worldwide. **Figure 41.1B** shows the 2011 IUCN assessment of five major groups of animals and flowering plants. Notice the large proportions of amphibians and fishes that are considered threatened; this is a further indication of the declining health of freshwater ecosystems.

Because of the network of community interactions among populations of different species within an ecosystem, the loss of one species can have a negative impact on the overall species richness of the ecosystem. Keystone species illustrate this effect (see Module 38.10). Other species modify their habitat in ways that encourage species diversity. In prairie ecosystems, for instance, plant and arthropod diversity is greatest near prairie

▲ **Figure 41.1A** The Vancouver Island wilderness, home to a wide variety of ecosystems

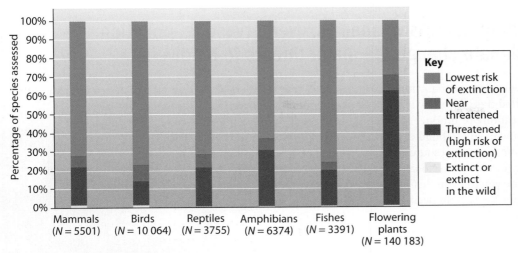

▲ **Figure 41.1B** Results of the 2011 IUCN assessment of species at risk for extinction (*N* = the number of species assessed)

Key
- Lowest risk of extinction
- Near threatened
- Threatened (high risk of extinction)
- Extinct or extinct in the wild

dog burrows, where the soil has been altered by the animal's digging **(Figure 41.1C)**. Abandoned burrows provide homes for cottontail rabbits, burrowing owls, and other animals. Thus, extirpation of prairie dogs results in lower species diversity in prairie communities.

In Canada, the *Species at Risk Act*, *Canadian Environmental Protection Act*, and the Committee on the Status of Endangered Wildlife in Canada (COSEWIC) protect species and the ecosystems on which they depend. Many other nations have also enacted laws to protect biodiversity, and an international agreement, the Convention on International Trade in Endangered Species (CITES), protects over 33 000 species of wild animals and plants from trade that would threaten their survival.

Species loss also has practical consequences for human well-being. Many drugs have been developed from substances found in the natural world, including penicillin, aspirin, antimalarial agents, and anticancer drugs. Dozens more potentially

▼ **Figure 41.1C** A group of young black-tailed prairie dogs (*Cynomys ludovicianus*) near their burrow

useful chemicals from a variety of organisms are currently being investigated. For example, researchers are testing possible new antibiotics produced by microbial symbionts of marine sponges; painkillers extracted from a species of poison dart frog; and anti-HIV and anticancer drugs derived from compounds in rainforest plants.

Genetic Diversity The genetic diversity within and between populations of a species is the raw material that makes microevolution and adaptation to the environment possible—a hedge against future environmental changes (see Module 14.5). If local populations are lost and the total number of individuals of a species declines, so, too, do the genetic resources for that species. Severe reduction in genetic variation threatens the survival of a species.

The enormous genetic diversity of all the organisms on Earth has great potential benefit for people, too. As you learned in Module 19.14, breeding programs have narrowed the genetic diversity of crop plants to a handful of varieties, leaving them vulnerable to pathogens. For example, researchers are currently scrambling to stop the spread of a deadly new strain of wheat stem rust, a fungal pathogen that has devastated harvests in Africa and central Asia. Resistance genes found in the wild relatives of wheat **(Figure 41.1D)** may hold the key to the world's future food supply. Many researchers and biotechnology leaders are enthusiastic about the possibilities that "bioprospecting" for potentially useful genes in other organisms holds for the development of new medicines, industrial chemicals, and other products.

▲ **Figure 41.1D** Einkorn wheat, a wild relative of modern cultivated varieties

Now that you have some insight into the nature and value of biodiversity, let's examine in more detail the causes for its decline.

? **What are two reasons to be concerned about the impact of the biodiversity crisis on human welfare?**

● The environmental degradation threatening other species may also harm us. We are dependent on biodiversity, both directly through use of organisms and their products and indirectly through ecosystem services.

41.2 Habitat loss, invasive species, overharvesting, pollution, and climate change are major threats to biodiversity

The human population has been growing exponentially for more than 100 years. We have supported this growth by using increasingly effective technologies to capture or produce food, to extract resources from the environment, and to build cities. In industrialized countries, we consume far more resources than are required to meet our basic requirements for food and shelter. Thus, it should not surprise you to learn that human activities are largely responsible for the current decline of biodiversity. In this section, we examine the major factors that threaten biodiversity.

Habitat Loss   Human alteration of habitats poses the single greatest threat to biodiversity throughout the biosphere. Agriculture, urban development, forestry, mining, and environmental pollution have brought about massive destruction and fragmentation of habitats. Deforestation continues at a blistering pace in tropical and coniferous forests (**Figure 41.2A**).

The amount of human-altered land surface is approaching 50%, and we use over half of all accessible surface fresh water. The natural course of most of the world's major rivers has been changed. Worldwide, tens of thousands of dams constructed for flood control, hydroelectric power, drinking water, and irrigation have damaged river and wetland ecosystems. Some of the most productive aquatic habitats in estuaries and intertidal wetlands have been overrun by commercial and residential development. The loss of marine habitat is severe, especially in coastal areas and coral reefs.

Invasive Species   Ranking second behind habitat loss as a threat to biodiversity are invasive species, which disrupt communities by competing with, preying on, or parasitizing native species. The lack of interspecific interactions that keeps the newcomer populations in check is often a key factor in a nonnative species becoming invasive (see Module 38.12). Meanwhile, a newly arrived species is an unfamiliar biotic factor in the environment of native species. Natives are especially vulnerable when a new species poses an unprecedented threat. In the absence of an evolutionary history with predators, for example,

animals may lack defence mechanisms or even a fundamental recognition of danger. Once introduced, invasive species can be very difficult to remove (as discussed in Module 38.12). The Pacific island of Guam was home to 13 species of forest birds—but no native snakes—when brown tree snakes (*Boiga irregularis*; **Figure 41.2B**) arrived as stowaways on a cargo plane. With no competitors, predators, or parasites to hinder them, the snakes

▲ **Figure 41.2B** A brown tree snake (*Boiga irregularis*)

proliferated rapidly on a diet of unwary birds. Four of the native species of birds were extirpated, although they survive on nearby islands. Three species of birds that lived nowhere else but Guam are now extinct. As the populations of two other species of birds became perilously low, officials took the remaining individuals into protective custody; they now exist only in zoos. The brown tree snake also eliminated species of seabirds and lizards.

Overharvesting   The third major threat to biodiversity is overexploitation of wildlife by harvesting at rates that exceed the ability of populations to rebound. Such overharvesting has threatened some rare trees that produce valuable wood, such as mahogany and rosewood. Animal species whose numbers have been drastically reduced by excessive commercial harvest, poaching, or sport hunting include whales, rhinoceroses, Galápagos tortoises, and numerous fishes. In parts of Africa, Asia, and South America, wild animals are heavily hunted for food, and the African term *bushmeat* is now used to refer generally to such meat. As once-impenetrable forests are opened to exploitation, the commercial bushmeat trade has become one of the greatest threats to primates, including gorillas, chimpanzees, and many species of monkeys, as well as other mammals and birds (**Figure 41.2C**). No longer hunted only for local use, large quantities of bushmeat are sold at urban markets or exported worldwide, including illegally to Canada.

Aquatic species are suffering overexploitation, too. Many edible marine fish and seafood species are in a precarious state (see Module 37.9). Worldwide, fishing fleets are working farther offshore and harvesting fish from greater depths to obtain hauls comparable to those of previous decades.

▲ **Figure 41.2A** Clear-cut areas in British Columbia's Great Bear Rainforest

▲ **Figure 41.2C** Lemurs killed by poachers for sale in a bushmeat market

Pollution Pollutants released by human activities can have local, regional, and global effects. Some pollutants, such as oil spills, contaminate local areas **(Figure 41.2D)**. Recall from Module 35.19 that the global water cycle can transport pollutants—for instance, pesticides used on land—from terrestrial to aquatic ecosystems hundreds of kilometres away. Pollutants that are emitted into the atmosphere, such as nitrogen oxides from the burning of fossil fuels, may be carried aloft for a great distance before falling to earth in the form of acid precipitation.

Ozone depletion in the upper atmosphere is another example of the global impact of pollution. As you learned in Module 7.14, the **ozone layer** protects Earth from the harmful ultraviolet rays in sunlight. Beginning in the mid-1970s, scientists realized that the ozone layer was gradually thinning. The consequences of ozone depletion for life on Earth could be quite severe, not only increasing skin cancers, but harming crops and natural communities, especially the phytoplankton that are responsible for a large proportion of Earth's primary production. International agreements to phase out the production of chemicals implicated in ozone destruction have been effective in slowing the rate of ozone depletion. Even so, complete ozone recovery is probably decades away.

In addition to being transported to areas far from where they originate, many toxins produced by industrial wastes or applied as pesticides become concentrated as they pass through the food chain. This concentration, or **biomagnification**, occurs because the biomass at any given trophic level is produced from a much larger toxin-containing biomass ingested from the level below (see Module 40.4). Thus, top-level predators are usually the organisms most severely damaged by toxic compounds in the environment. In the Great Lakes food chain shown in **Figure 41.2E**, the concentration of industrial chemicals called PCBs increased at each successive trophic level. The PCB concentration measured in the eggs of herring gulls, top-level consumers, was almost 5000 times higher than that measured in phytoplankton. Many other synthetic chemicals that cannot be degraded by microorganisms also become concentrated through biomagnification, including DDT and mercury. Mercury, a by-product of plastic production and coal-fired power plants, enters the food chain after being converted to

▲ **Figure 41.2E** Biomagnification of PCBs in a food web, measured in parts per million (ppm)

highly toxic methylmercury by benthic bacteria. Since people are top-level predators, too, eating fish from contaminated waters can be dangerous.

Recently, scientists have recognized a new type of aquatic pollutant: plastic particles that are small enough to be eaten by zooplankton. Many body washes and facial cleansers include plastic "microbeads" to boost scrubbing power. (To see if your shower products contain plastic, check the list of ingredients for polyethylene.) Too small to be captured by wastewater treatment plants, these microparticles enter the watershed and eventually wash out to sea. Larger particles called preproduction pellets, or "nurdles," used in making plastic products, are also common marine pollutants. Nurdles may be broken down to microbead size in the ocean. Toxins such as PCBs and DDT adhere to these plastic spheres. Thus, toxins may be concentrated first on microparticles and then again by biomagnification.

Global Climate Change According to many scientists, the changes in global climate (see Module 7.13) are likely to become a leading cause of biodiversity loss. In the next five modules, you will learn about some of the causes and consequences of global climate change.

▲ **Figure 41.2D** A brown pelican on the Louisiana coast suffering the effects of the 2010 Deepwater Horizon oil rig explosion

 List four threats to biodiversity and give an example of each.

Habitat loss—deforestation; invasive species—brown tree snake; overharvesting—bushmeat; pollution—biomagnification of PCBs, DDT, and mercury. (Other examples could be used.)

41.3 Rapid warming is changing the global climate

The scientific debate about climate change is over. The vast majority of scientists now agree that rising concentrations of greenhouse gases in the atmosphere (see Module 7.13), such as carbon dioxide (CO_2), methane (CH_4), and nitrous oxide (N_2O), are changing global climate patterns. This was the overarching conclusion of the assessment report released by the Intergovernmental Panel on Climate Change (IPCC) in 2007. Thousands of scientists and policy-makers from more than 100 countries participated in producing the report, which is based on data published in hundreds of scientific papers.

The signature effect of increasing greenhouse gases is the steady increase in the average global temperature, which has risen 0.8°C over the last 100 years, with 0.6°C of that increase occurring over the last three decades. Further increases of 2–4.5°C are likely by the end of the 21st century, depending on the rate of future greenhouse gas emissions. Ocean temperatures are also rising, in deeper layers as well as at the surface. But the temperature increases are not distributed evenly around the globe. Warming is greater over land than sea, and the largest increases are in the northernmost regions of the Northern Hemisphere. In **Figure 41.3A**, red areas indicate the greatest temperature increases. In parts of Alaska and Canada, for example, the temperature has risen 1.4°C just since 1961. Some of the consequences of the climate change trend are already clear from rising temperatures, unusual precipitation patterns, and melting ice.

Many of the world's glaciers are receding rapidly, including mountain glaciers in the Himalayas, the Alps, the Andes, and the Rocky Mountains. For example, the Athabasca Glacier, part of the Columbia Icefield (**Figure 41.3B**), has lost over half of its volume and retreated 1.5 km since the beginning of the 20th century. The permafrost that characterizes the tundra biome is also melting.

Permanent Arctic sea ice is shrinking; each summer brings increased melting and thinner ice. The massive ice sheets of Greenland and Antarctica are thinning and collapsing. If this melting trend accelerates, rising sea levels would cause catastrophic flooding of coastal areas worldwide.

▲ **Figure 41.3B** Athabasca Glacier in Jasper National Park in 1919 and 2005

Warm weather is beginning earlier each year. Cold days and nights and frosts have become less frequent; hot days and nights have become more frequent. Deadly heat waves are increasing in frequency and duration.

Precipitation patterns are changing, bringing longer and more intense drought to some areas. In other regions, a greater proportion of the total precipitation is falling in torrential downpours that cause flooding. Hurricane intensity is increasing, fuelled by higher sea surface temperatures.

Many of these changes will have a profound impact on biodiversity, as we explore in Modules 41.6 and 41.7. In the next module, we examine the causes of rising greenhouse gas emissions.

? From the map in Figure 41.3A, which biomes are likely to be most affected by climate change, and why?

The high-latitude biomes of the Northern Hemisphere, tundra and taiga, and the polar ice biomes will be most affected. Those biomes are experiencing the greatest temperature change. Also, the organisms that live there are adapted to cold weather and a short growing season, so their survival is on the line.

:4.1   :4   :2   :1   :0.5   :0.2   0.2   0.5   1   2   4   4.1

▲ **Figure 41.3A** Differences in temperature during 2000–2009 relative to temperatures during 1951–1980 (in °C)

41.4 Human activities are responsible for rising concentrations of greenhouse gases

Without its blanket of natural greenhouse gases such as CO_2 and water vapour to trap heat, Earth would be too cold to support most life. However, increasing the insulation that the blanket provides is making the planet uncomfortably warm, and that increase is occurring rapidly. For 650 000 years, the atmospheric concentration of CO_2 did not exceed 300 parts per million (ppm); the preindustrial concentration was 280 ppm. Today, atmospheric CO_2 is approximately 385 ppm. The levels of nitrous oxide (N_2O) and methane (CH_4), which also trap heat in the atmosphere, have increased dramatically, too **(Figure 41.4A)**. CO_2 and N_2O are released when fossil fuels—oil, coal, and natural gas—are burned. N_2O is also released when nitrogen fertilizers are used in agriculture. Landfills are a factor responsible for increases of atmospheric CH_4. The consensus of scientists, as reported by the IPCC, is that rising concentrations of greenhouse gases—and thus, climate change—are the result of human activities.

Let's take a closer look at CO_2, the dominant greenhouse gas. Recall from Module 40.7 that atmospheric CO_2 is a major reservoir for carbon. (CH_4 is also part of that reservoir.) CO_2 is removed from the atmosphere by the process of photosynthesis and stored in organic molecules such as carbohydrates **(Figure 41.4B)**. Thus, biomass, the organic molecules in an ecosystem, is a biotic carbon reservoir. The carbon-containing molecules in living organisms may be used in the process of cellular respiration, which releases carbon in the form of CO_2. Nonliving biomass may be decomposed by microorganisms or fungi that also release CO_2. Overall, uptake of CO_2 by photosynthesis roughly equals the release of CO_2 by cellular respiration. CO_2 is also exchanged between the atmosphere and the surface waters of the oceans.

Fossil fuels consist of biomass that was buried under sediments without being completely decomposed (see Module 19.7). The burning of fossil fuels and wood, which is also an organic material, can be thought of as a rapid form of decomposition. While cellular respiration releases energy from organic molecules slowly and harnesses it to make ATP, combustion liberates the energy rapidly as heat and light. In both processes, the carbon atoms that make up the organic fuel are released in CO_2.

The CO_2 flooding into the atmosphere from combustion of fossil fuels may be absorbed by photosynthetic organisms and incorporated into biomass. But deforestation has significantly decreased the number of CO_2 molecules that can be accommodated by this pathway. CO_2 may also be absorbed into the ocean. For decades, the oceans have been absorbing considerably more CO_2 than they have released, and they will continue to do so; but, the excess CO_2 is beginning to affect ocean chemistry. When CO_2 dissolves in water, it becomes carbonic acid. Recently, measurable decreases in ocean pH have raised concern among biologists. Organisms that construct shells or exoskeletons out of calcium carbonate ($CaCO_3$), including corals and many plankton, are most likely to be affected as decreasing pH reduces the concentration of the carbonate ions (see Module 2.16).

Greenhouse gas emissions are accelerating. From 2000 to 2005, global CO_2 emissions increased four times faster than in the preceding 10-year span. At this rate, further climate change is inevitable.

In the next module, we will take a closer look at the rumour about the impact bovine flatulence has on the climate.

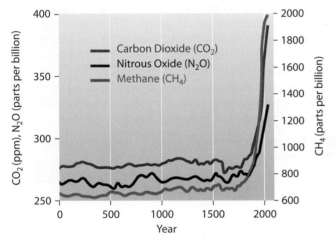

▲ **Figure 41.4A** Atmospheric concentrations of CO_2 and N_2O (y-axis, left), and CH_4 (y-axis, right), as of 2009

▲ **Figure 41.4B** Carbon cycling

❓ The amount of CO_2 you are responsible for releasing every year is called your *carbon footprint*. Search for an online calculator that estimates your carbon footprint. What are the primary sources of the CO_2 you generate?

● Transportation and home energy use are the two major categories contributing to carbon footprint.

41.5 Does bovine flatulence contribute to climate change?

In the previous module, you read about how human activities contribute to climate change by producing greenhouse gases. According to a common rumour, yet another human activity—raising livestock—contributes to greenhouse gases in the form of bovine flatulence. But do cattle emissions really contribute to climate change?

A United Nations report states that cattle actually generate more greenhouse gases than forms of transportation, including planes, trains, and automobiles. Thus, the rumour has credibility. However, cattle release the vast majority of gases in belches rather than flatulence. These belches contain a high percentage of methane. Although some methane can be detected in feces, approximately 90% is released from the mouth. Methane is an extremely potent greenhouse gas: It has 21 times the warming effect of CO_2.

In Canada, bovine belches account for 72% of methane emissions. Worldwide, cattle emissions account for 37% of total methane. Each animal can release up to 600 L of methane every day. With more than 15 million head of cattle in Canada, nearly 9 billion L of bovine methane are entering the atmosphere daily. The amount is staggering on a global scale because more than 1.3 billion head of cattle exist around the world. Over the next 50 years, 15% to 17% of the changes in climate will be attributed to bovine methane.

Where does the methane in bovine belches come from? Cattle and most other animals cannot digest the cellulose in the cell walls of the plants they ingest. To gain access to this valuable energy source, cattle rely on symbiotic bacteria within their first stomach, or rumen (see Module 39.4). The animal's resident bacteria break down cellulose in a fermentation reaction. The by-products of one bacterial species (*Methanobrevibacter ruminantium*) include copious amounts of methane. This methane escapes when the animal belches.

Dr. Stephen Moore, at the University of Alberta, and scientists throughout the world are looking for ways to decrease bovine emissions. By identifying contributing factors, such as genetics and diet, Moore hopes to reduce the impact of cattle farming on the environment.

The amount of methane produced increases with food intake. All cattle need to eat a certain amount of food for body maintenance and production of either beef or milk. Most animals eat more than this requirement. The extra food does not increase production further but does contribute to methane production. Moore has found that the degree of extra eating is both variable and heritable. Selective breeding of cattle, which eat only a small extra amount, may reduce methane production by 25%, without sacrificing production.

Changing the diets of cattle can further reduce methane emissions. Adding alfalfa and flax to the diets of dairy cows has decreased methane production by 12% without affecting milk production. By combining breeding strategies to produce more efficient cattle and changing diets, a significant source of greenhouse gases could be greatly reduced.

The rumour that cattle are a significant source of greenhouse gases, methane in particular, is true—but the methane is released in belches rather than by flatulence.

 ? Why are methane emissions such a concern for climate scientists?

● Methane has 21 times the warming capacity of CO_2.

41.6 Global climate change affects biomes, ecosystems, communities, and populations

The distribution of terrestrial biomes, which is primarily determined by temperature and rainfall, is changing as a consequence of warming associated with climate change. Climate change has implications for all organisms at all levels. Melting permafrost is shifting the boundary of the tundra as shrubs and conifers are able to stretch their ranges to previously frozen ground. Prolonged droughts will increasingly extend the boundaries of deserts. Great expanses of the Amazonian tropical rainforest will gradually become savanna as increased temperatures dry out the soil.

The combined effects of climate change on components of forest ecosystems in western North America have spawned catastrophic wildfire seasons (Figure 41.6A). In these mountainous regions, spring snowmelt releases water into streams that sustain forest moisture levels over the summer dry season. With the earlier arrival of spring, snowmelt begins earlier and dwindles away before the dry season ends. As a result, the fire season has been getting longer since the 1980s. In addition, drought conditions have made trees more vulnerable to insect and pathogen attack (see the opening essay for Chapter 38); vast numbers of dead trees add fuel to the flames. Fires burn longer, and the number of hectares burned has increased dramatically. As dry conditions persist and snowpacks diminish, the problem will worsen.

The earlier arrival of warm weather in the spring is disturbing ecological communities in other ways. In many animal and plant species, certain annual spring events are triggered by temperature increases. With temperatures rising earlier in the year, a variety of species, including some birds and frogs, have begun their breeding season earlier. Satellite images show earlier greening of the landscape, and flowering occurs sooner. For other species, day length is the

▲ **Figure 41.6A** A wildfire raging in northern Alberta

environmental cue that spring has arrived. Because global climate change affects temperature but not day length, interactions between species may become out of sync. For example, plants may bloom before pollinators have emerged, or eggs may hatch before a dependable food source for the young is available. Because the magnitude of seasonal shifts increases from the tropics to the poles, migratory birds may also experience timing mismatches. For instance, birds arriving in the Arctic to breed may find that the period of peak food availability has already passed.

Warming oceans threaten tropical coral reef communities. When stressed by high temperatures, corals expel their symbiotic algae and become light in colour in a phenomenon called bleaching. Corals can recover if temperatures return to normal, but they cannot survive prolonged temperature increases. When corals die, the community is overrun by large algae, and species diversity plummets.

The distributions of populations and species are also changing in response to climate change. Recall from Module 35.4 that the distribution of a species may be determined by its adaptations to the abiotic conditions in its environment. With rising temperatures, the ranges of many species have already shifted toward the poles or to higher elevations. For example, researchers have reported that the ranges of more than two dozen species of butterflies have moved north by as much as 280 km. Shifts in the ranges of many bird species have also been reported; Inuit living north of the Arctic Circle have sighted birds such as robins in the region for the first time.

In comparison, species that live on mountaintops or in polar regions have nowhere to go. Researchers in Costa Rica have reported the disappearance of 20 species of frogs and toads as warmer Pacific Ocean temperatures reduce the dry-season mists in their mountain habitats. In the Arctic, polar bears **(Figure 41.6B)**, which stalk their prey on ice and need to store up body fat for the warmer months, are showing signs of starvation as their hunting grounds melt away. Similarly, in the Antarctic, the disappearance of sea ice is blamed for recent decreases in populations of Emperor and Adélie penguins.

Global climate change has been a boon to some organisms, but so far the beneficiaries have been species that have a negative impact on humans. For example, in mountainous regions of Africa, Southeast Asia, and Central and South America, the ranges of mosquitoes that carry diseases such as malaria, yellow fever, and dengue are restricted to lower elevations by frost. With rising temperatures and fewer days of frost, these mosquitoes—and the diseases they carry—are appearing at higher elevations and northern latitudes. The return of malaria to Canada is a possibility because of climate change (see the opening essay for Chapter 39). In another example, longer summers in western North America have enabled bark beetles to complete their life cycle in one year instead of two, promoting beetle outbreaks that have destroyed millions of hectares of conifers (see the opening essay for Chapter 38). Undesirable plants such as poison ivy and kudzu have also benefited from rising temperatures.

Environmental change has always been a part of life; in fact, it is a key ingredient of evolutionary change. In the next module, we consider the evidence of evolutionary adaptation to climate change.

? **How might timing mismatches caused by climate change affect an individual's reproductive fitness?**

● Any factor that reduces the number of offspring an organism produces may affect fitness. Examples: flowers emerging too soon or too late for pollinators; birds that arrive too late in the season to find food for offspring

▲ **Figure 41.6B** A polar bear (*Ursus maritimus*) on melting pack ice

41.7 Climate change is an agent of natural selection

Global climate change is already affecting habitats throughout the world. Why do some species appear to be adapting to these changes while others, like the polar bear, are endangered by them?

In the previous module, we described several ways in which organisms have responded to global climate change. For the most part, those examples can be attributed to **phenotypic plasticity**, the ability to change phenotype in response to local environmental conditions. Differences resulting from phenotypic plasticity are within the normal range of expression for an individual's genotype. Phenotypic plasticity allows organisms to cope with short-term environmental changes. Then again, phenotypic plasticity is itself a trait that has a genetic basis and can evolve. Researchers studying the effects of climate change on populations have detected microevolutionary changes in phenotypic plasticity.

A common bird in Europe, the great tit **(Figure 41.7A)** is the third link in a food chain that has been altered by climate change. As warm weather arrives earlier in the spring, tree leaves emerge earlier and caterpillars, which use the swelling buds and unfolding leaves as their food source, hatch sooner. The reproductive success of great tits depends on having an ample supply of these nutritious caterpillars to feed their offspring. Like many other birds, great tits have some phenotypic plasticity in the timing of their breeding, which helps them synchronize their reproduction with the availability of caterpillars. The range and degree of plasticity vary among great tits, and this variation has a genetic basis. Researchers have found evidence of directional selection (see Module 14.7) favouring individuals that have the greatest phenotypic plasticity and lay their eggs earlier, when the abundance of food gives their offspring a better chance of survival.

In another example, scientists studied reproduction in a population of red squirrels (*Tamiasciurus hudsonicus*; **Figure 41.7B**) in the Yukon Territory, where spring temperatures have increased by approximately 2°C in the last three

▶ **Figure 41.7B** A red squirrel (*Tamiasciurus hudsonicus*) eating the seeds from a spruce cone

▲ **Figure 41.7A**
A great tit (*Parus major*)

decades. These researchers also found earlier breeding times in the spring. Over a period of 10 years, the date on which female squirrels gave birth advanced by 18 days, a change of about 6 days per generation. Using statistical analysis, the scientists determined that phenotypic plasticity was responsible for most of the shift in breeding times. However, a small but significant portion of the change (roughly 15%) could be attributed to microevolution, directional selection for earlier breeding. The researchers hypothesize that red squirrels born earlier in the year are larger and more capable of gathering and storing food in the autumn and thus have a better chance of successful reproduction the following spring.

From the scant evidence available at this time, it appears that some populations, especially those with high genetic variability and short lifespans, may adapt quickly enough to avoid extinction. In addition to the studies on phenotypic plasticity in great tits and red squirrels, researchers have documented microevolutionary changes in traits such as dispersal ability and timing of life cycle events in insect populations. However, evolutionary adaptation is unlikely to save long-lived species such as polar bears and penguins that are experiencing rapid habitat loss. The rate of climate change is incredibly fast compared with major climate shifts in evolutionary history, and if it continues on its present course, thousands of species—the IPCC estimates as many as 30% of plants and animals—will likely become extinct.

 How does a short generation time hasten the process of evolutionary adaptation?

● Each generation has the potential for testing new phenotypes in the environment, allowing natural selection to proceed rapidly.

Conservation Biology and Sustainability

41.8 Protecting endangered populations is one goal of conservation biology

As we have seen in this unit, many of the environmental problems facing us today are consequences of human enterprises. But the science of ecology is not just useful for telling us how things have gone wrong. Ecological research is the foundation for finding solutions to these problems and for reversing the

negative consequences of ecosystem alteration. Thus, we end the ecology unit with a section that highlights some of these applications of ecological research.

Conservation biology is a goal-oriented science that seeks to understand and counter the loss of biodiversity. Some

▲ **Figure 41.8A** A black-footed ferret (*Mustela nigripes*)

▲ **Figure 41.8B** The Oregon spotted frog (*Rana pretiosa*)

conservation biologists focus on protecting populations of threatened species. This approach requires an understanding of the behaviour and ecological niche of the target species, including its key habitat requirements and interactions with other members of its community. Threats posed by human activities are also assessed. With this knowledge, scientists can design a plan to expand or protect the resources needed. For example, the territory size required to support a tiger varies with the abundance of prey. Consequently, preserves set aside for Siberian tigers in Russia, where prey are scarce, must be 10 times as large as those provided for Bengal tigers in India.

How do scientists determine which species require protection? In Module 41.1, we saw that the IUCN assesses the status of species worldwide and ranks them according to their risk level. COSEWIC focuses on the status of Canadian wildlife by using guidelines similar to those outlined by IUCN.

The case of the black-footed ferret (*Mustela nigripes*; **Figure 41.8A**) provides an example of the population approach to conservation. Little was known about this elusive nocturnal predator until the mid-20th century, and by then it was almost too late—population decline was already under way. Black-footed ferrets, one of three ferret species worldwide and the only one found in North America, feed almost exclusively on prairie dogs (see Figure 41.1C). Over the past century, prairie dogs have been extirpated from most of their former range by land-use changes and by poisoning or shooting. Epidemics of sylvatic plague, the animal version of bubonic plague (see Module 17.15), have devastated populations of black-footed ferrets as well as their prey. Listed as extirpated from Canada in 1978 by COSEWIC, only a few small populations survived in the United States. When an outbreak threatened to wipe out the last known population of black-footed ferrets, conservation biologists captured 18 remaining individuals and began breeding them in captivity. The Toronto Zoo has been part of the efforts to rebuild population numbers since 1992. Genetic variation, a prerequisite for adaptive evolutionary responses to environmental change, is a concern, given the bottleneck effect of near-extinction (see Module 14.5). Matings in the captive breeding facilities are carefully arranged to maintain as much genetic diversity as possible in the ferret populations.

In 2009, biologists reintroduced 34 captive-bred black-footed ferrets in Grasslands National Park in Saskatchewan.

Research carried out during these efforts has improved the success rate of reintroductions. For example, scientists found that the predatory behaviour of ferrets has both innate and learned components. This discovery led to more effective methods of preparing captive-bred animals to survive in the wild. Today, about 800 adult ferrets are living in the wild at sites scattered from Canada to Mexico. Despite the successes achieved thus far, however, the future of the black-footed ferret is far from secure. Biologists continue to monitor and manage the populations and their habitats.

Captive breeding programs are being used for numerous other species whose population numbers are perilously low. For example, you learned about efforts to save the whooping crane in Module 36.6. **Figure 41.8B** shows an Oregon spotted frog (*Rana pretiosa*; mentioned in the opening essay of Chapter 30). This species, found in a small area of southwestern British Columbia, is at extreme risk of extinction because of habitat loss, environmental contamination, and climate change. In 1999, the Oregon Spotted Frog Recovery Team was established in an effort to protect the species. Captive breeding programs, Dr. Vance Trudeau's love potion, and reintroduction into the wild are at the centre of the conservation efforts.

By using a variety of methods, biologists have improved the conservation status of some endangered species, reintroduced many species to areas where they had been extirpated, and reversed declining population trends for others. However, we will not be able to save every threatened species. Unfortunately, many species we know to be endangered are beyond recovery. Furthermore, countless unidentified species are also endangered, which we cannot protect. One way to select worthwhile targets is to identify and protect keystone species that may help to preserve entire communities. And in many situations, conservation biologists must look beyond individual species to ecosystems.

 What do you think is the first priority for conservation biologists when they select a site for ferret reintroduction?

The presence of a sufficiently large population of prairie dogs

41.9 Sustaining ecosystems and landscapes is a conservation priority

One of the most harmful effects of habitat loss is population fragmentation, the splitting and consequent isolation of portions of populations. As you saw in Figure 41.2A, for example, logging carves a large patch of once-continuous forest into several smaller disconnected patches. For many species, the world instantly shrinks to a fraction of its former size. Populations are reduced, and so are resources such as food and shelter. To counteract the effects of fragmentation, conservation biology often aims to sustain the biodiversity of landscapes and entire ecosystems.

Fragmentation drastically increases the proportion of edges relative to the interior communities (**Figure 41.9A**). The increased area of edges and the communities they support can put extra pressures on interior species. For instance, fragmentation of a forest would increase the relative amount of edges and number of edge species, such as the brown-headed cowbird (*Molothrus ater*; see Module 38.15). Increasing cowbird parasitism and loss of habitats are correlated with declining populations of several songbird species.

Where habitats have been severely fragmented, a **movement corridor**, a narrow strip or series of small clumps of high-quality habitat connecting otherwise isolated patches, can be a deciding factor in conserving biodiversity. In areas of heavy human use, artificial corridors are sometimes constructed. In many areas, bridges or tunnels have reduced the number of animals killed as they try to cross highways. **Figure 41.9B** shows a wildlife bridge over the Trans-Canada Highway in Banff National Park, Alberta. Several bridges, similar to the one in the photograph, have now been constructed.

Corridors can also promote dispersal and reduce inbreeding in declining populations. Corridors are especially important to

▲ Figure 41.9B A wildlife bridge in Banff National Park, Alberta

species that migrate between different habitats seasonally. In some European countries, amphibian tunnels have been constructed to help frogs, toads, and salamanders cross roads to access their breeding territories.

Nevertheless, a corridor can be harmful—as, for example, in the spread of diseases, especially among small subpopulations in closely situated habitat patches. The effects of movement corridors between habitats in a landscape are not completely understood, and researchers continue to study them.

? How can "living on the edge" be a good thing for some species, such as cowbirds?

■ Interior
■ Edge

▲ **Figure 41.9A** Fragmentation changes community structure

● Such animals use a combination of resources from the two ecosystems on either side of the edge.

41.10 Establishing protected areas slows the loss of biodiversity

Conservation biologists are applying their understanding of population, community, ecosystem, and landscape dynamics in establishing parks, wilderness areas, and other legally protected nature reserves. Choosing locations for protection often focuses on **biodiversity hot spots**. These relatively small areas have a large number of endangered and threatened species and an exceptional concentration of **endemic species**, those that are found nowhere else. Together, the "hottest" of Earth's biodiversity hot spots, shown in **Figure 41.10A**, total less than 1.5% of Earth's land but are home to one-third of all species of plants and vertebrates. For example, lemurs are endemic to

Madagascar, which is home to more than 100 species. In fact, almost all the mammals, reptiles, amphibians, and plants that inhabit Madagascar are endemic. There are also hot spots in aquatic ecosystems, such as certain river systems and coral reefs.

Because endemic species are limited to specific areas, they are highly sensitive to habitat degradation. Thus, biodiversity hot spots can also be hot spots of extinction. They rank high on the list of areas demanding strong global conservation efforts.

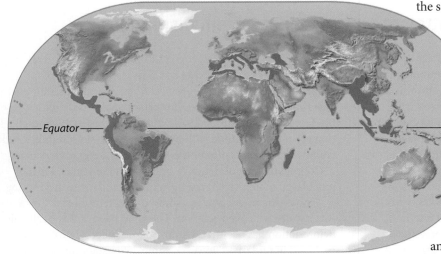

▲ **Figure 41.10A** Earth's terrestrial biodiversity hot spots (pink)

Concentrations of species provide an opportunity to protect many species in very limited areas. However, the "hot spot" designation tends to favour the most noticeable organisms, especially vertebrates and plants. Invertebrates and microorganisms are often overlooked. Furthermore, species endangerment is a truly global problem, and it is important that a focus on hot spots not detract from efforts to conserve habitats and species diversity in other areas.

Migratory species pose a special problem for conservationists. For example, monarch butterflies occupy much of Canada and the United States during the summer months, but migrate in the autumn to specific sites in Mexico and California, where they congregate in huge numbers. Overwintering populations are particularly susceptible to habitat disturbances because they are concentrated in small areas. Thus, habitat preservation must extend across all the sites that monarchs inhabit in order to protect them. The situation is similar for many species of migratory birds, waterfowl, marine mammals, and sea turtles.

The Bay of Fundy, located between New Brunswick and Nova Scotia, boasts the highest tides in the world (17 m above low tide). When the tide is out, approximately 3000 ha of intertidal pools and mudflats become exposed. These areas are prime feeding grounds for many animals, including

the semipalmated sandpipers (*Calidris pusilla*; **Figure 41.10B**). During their southward migration in July and August, upward of 2.5 million sandpipers (nearly 75% of the world's population) stop in the bay, making it an important area to preserve. The Western Hemisphere Shorebird Reserve Network, in conjunction with the Provinces of New Brunswick and Nova Scotia, and the Canadian Wildlife Service, has established an ecological reserve that encompasses 62 000 ha.

Sea turtles, such as the loggerhead sea turtle (*Caretta caretta*; **Figure 41.10C**), are threatened both in their ocean feeding grounds and on land. Loggerheads take about 20 years to reach sexual maturity, and great numbers of juveniles and adults are drowned at sea when caught in fishing nets. The adults mate at sea, and the females migrate to specific sites on sandy beaches to lay their eggs. Buried in shallow depressions, the eggs are susceptible to predators, especially raccoons. And many egg-laying sites have become housing developments and beachside resorts. An ongoing international effort to conserve sea turtles focuses on protecting egg-laying sites and minimizing the death rates of adults and juveniles at sea.

Currently, governments have set aside about 7% of the world's land in various forms of reserves. In Canada, the amount of protected land has been increasing since 1992; in 2012, it totalled 10% of the country. One major conservation question is whether it is better to create one large reserve or a group of smaller ones. Far-ranging animals with low-density populations, such as grey wolves, require extensive habitats. As conservation biologists learn more about the requirements for achieving minimum population sizes to sustain endangered species, it is becoming clear that most national parks and other reserves are far too small. Given political and economic realities, it is unlikely that many existing parks will be enlarged, and most new reserves will also be too small. In the next two modules, we look at two approaches to this problem.

? What is a biodiversity hot spot?

● A relatively small area with a disproportionate number of endangered and threatened species, many of which are endemic

▲ **Figure 41.10B** A semipalmated sandpiper (*Calidris pusilla*)

▲ **Figure 41.10C** An adult loggerhead sea turtle (*Caretta caretta*) swimming off the coast of Belize

41.11 Zoned reserves are an attempt to reverse ecosystem disruption

Conservation of Earth's natural resources is not purely a scientific issue. The causes of declining biodiversity are rooted in complex social and economic issues, and the solutions must take these factors into account. Let's look at how the small Central American nation of Costa Rica is managing its biodiversity.

Despite its small size (about 51 000 km², slightly smaller than Nova Scotia), Costa Rica is a treasure trove of biodiversity. Its varied ecosystems, which extend over mountains and two coasts, are home to at least half a million species. As Figure 41.10A shows, the entire country is a biodiversity hot spot. Since the 1970s, the Costa Rican government and international agencies have worked together to preserve these unique assets. Approximately 25% of Costa Rica's territory is currently protected in some way **(Figure 41.11A)**.

One type of protection is called a **zoned reserve**, an extensive region of land that includes one or more areas undisturbed by humans. The lands surrounding these areas continue to be used to support the human population, but they are protected from extensive alteration. As a result, they serve as a buffer zone, or shield, against further intrusion into the undisturbed areas. A primary goal of the zoned reserve approach is to develop a social and economic climate in the buffer zone that is compatible with the long-term viability of the protected area.

Costa Rica is making progress in managing its reserves so that the buffer zones provide a steady, lasting supply of forest products, water, and hydroelectric power and also support **sustainable agriculture**. An important goal is providing a stable economic base for people living there. Destructive practices that are not compatible with long-term ecosystem stability and from which there is often little local profit are gradually being discouraged. Such destructive practices include massive logging, large-scale single-crop agriculture, and extensive mining.

However, a recent analysis showed mixed results for Costa Rica's system of zoned reserves. The good news is that negligible deforestation has occurred within and just beyond protected parkland boundaries. However, some deforestation has occurred in the buffer zones, with plantations of cash crops such as banana and palm replacing the natural vegetation. Conservationists fear that continuing these practices will isolate protected areas, restricting gene flow and decreasing species and genetic diversity.

Costa Rica's commitment to conservation has resulted in a new source of income for the country—**ecotourism**, travel to natural areas for tourism and recreation **(Figure 41.11B)**. People from all over the world come to experience Costa Rica's spectacular range of biodiversity, generating thousands of jobs and a significant chunk of the country's revenue. Worldwide, ecotourism has grown into a multibillion-dollar industry as tourists flock to the world's remaining natural areas. Whether ecotourism dollars ultimately help to conserve Earth's biodiversity, however, remains to be seen.

? **Why is it important for zoned reserves to prevent large-scale alterations of habitat in the buffer zones? Why is it also important to support sustainable development for the people living there?**

● Large-scale disruptions could affect the nearby undisturbed areas. Preservation is a realistic goal only if it is compatible with an acceptable standard of living for the local people.

▲ **Figure 41.11A** Costa Rica

■ National Parks and Reserves

NORTH AMERICA

SOUTH AMERICA

NICARAGUA

COSTA RICA

PANAMA

▲ **Figure 41.11B** Ecotourism: seeing the tropical rainforest by boat in Costa Rica's Tortuguero National Park

41.12 The Yellowstone to Yukon Conservation Initiative seeks to preserve biodiversity by connecting protected areas

If many existing reserves are too small to sustain a large number of threatened species, how can biologists include the land and water around reserves in conservation efforts? In North America, one ambitious biodiversity plan is creating innovative ways to give wild creatures more room. The plan builds on lessons from research on a howling predator that once roamed a vast stretch of the northern Rocky Mountains.

This predator was a single individual, a grey wolf dubbed Pluie that was captured by scientists in Alberta's Peter Lougheed Provincial Park in 1991. The biologists fitted the five-year-old female with a radio tracking collar and released her—routine work in studies of threatened animals. But the scientists were stunned by what they learned from Pluie. Over the next two years, this wolf roamed an area of more than 100 000 km², crossing between Canada and the United States and travelling between protected reserves and lands where she was fair game for killing. In 1995, her story came to a bloody end. While moving through lands outside the boundary of a nearby national park, Pluie, her mate, and one of her pups were shot (legally) by a hunter.

Biologists who had studied Pluie realized that the wolf's life captured all the promise—and all the pitfalls—of efforts to protect her. She had thrived for years within the sporadic shelter of parks and other protected territory. But such lands were never big enough to hold her. Like others of her species (*Canis lupus*), Pluie needed more room. Reserves could shield animals briefly, the scientists realized. True protection would have to include paths of safe passage between reserves.

This conclusion inspired Calgarian Harvey Locke, a lawyer and environmentalist, to create the Yellowstone to Yukon Conservation Initiative (Y2Y), one of the world's most ambitious conservation biology efforts. The initiative aims to preserve the web of life that has long defined the Rocky Mountains of Canada and the northern United States. This area is dotted with famous parks—Alberta's Banff National Park and Wyoming's Yellowstone National Park among them—but scientists behind Y2Y now say that those areas alone cannot protect native species from human threats.

Y2Y seeks to knit together a string of parks and reserves, creating a vast 3200 km wildlife corridor stretching from the Yukon Territory to northern Wyoming (**Figure 41.12A**). The idea is not to create one giant park, but rather to connect parks with protected corridors where wildlife can travel safely.

Many of the signature species that live in this vast region, such as grizzly bears (**Figure 41.12B**), lynx, moose, and elk, do not confine themselves to human boundaries. But few have as great a range as the wolf. If Y2Y can provide safe passage for grey wolves, it will have also created secure zones for other animals in the Rockies.

Grey wolves (**Figure 41.12C**) once roamed all of North America. These carnivorous hunters live in packs that protect pups and search cooperatively for food. A pack may have a territory of about 130 km² or range much farther to find prey.

The wolf's hunting prowess kept it the top predator of North American ecosystems as long as the human population was small. Things changed when large numbers of people migrated from Europe and pushed into the continent.

Deeming wolves a dangerous predator and competitor that threatened people and livestock, settlers in North America launched widespread campaigns to wipe out wolves. By the early 20th century, grey wolves were nearly extinct in the lower 48 states, with only a few hundred surviving in northern Minnesota. More managed to stay alive in the wilds of less populated western Canada and Alaska.

Scientists gradually realized that widespread damage rippled through habitats after wolves had been removed. Without a predator to control their numbers, populations of elk and deer grew unchecked. As these increasing numbers of herbivores

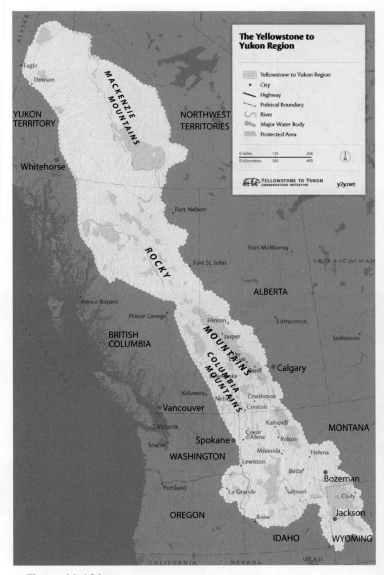

▲ **Figure 41.12A** A map of the Yellowstone to Yukon Conservation Initiative region, with protected areas shown in green

foraged for food, vegetation that sheltered smaller animals was damaged. Other animals, such as ravens and foxes, had once fed on the carcasses of wildlife killed by wolves and were now left without an important source of food. Grey wolves, biologists determined, were a keystone species (see Module 38.10).

That understanding led to one of the most important and controversial conservation biology efforts in the Yellowstone to Yukon area. After a 50-year hiatus from sheltering the animals, Yellowstone National Park received 60 wolves from Jasper National Park in 1995 and 1996. After careful planning, the U.S. government established a compensation fund to cover any losses of livestock by local ranchers.

As wolf howls once again echoed through the Wyoming darkness, the wolf quickly became a hopeful symbol for Y2Y backers. Yellowstone's wolves formed new packs and raised pups. By 2004, scientists counted 12 wolf packs inside the park, totalling about 300 wolves. And the wolf's return has brought more than howling. Park officials noted significant environmental improvements as wolves once again roamed Yellowstone. As wolves killed elk, moose, and deer, streambeds and other lands near waterways started to shelter a greater variety of plants and animals. Fewer hoofed animals meant more grasses and taller trees. Those plants brought more birds, along with more water-dwelling beaver. In all, park biologists report that the wolf's return has affected at least 25 different species.

True to their nature, Yellowstone's wolves have not adhered to human borders; six packs have been found just outside Yellowstone. As wolves are roaming throughout the Y2Y region more frequently, the need to protect this corridor is more apparent.

Such successes also bring risks—and reminders from scientists that wolves need safe corridors. A Yellowstone wolf found in Colorado was discovered dead by the side of a highway, most likely the victim of a car. Its appearance sparked

angry protests from ranchers in the state, who said that any new wolves that appear should either be shot or shipped back to Yellowstone. Meanwhile, wildlife advocates maintain that wolves should be allowed to migrate naturally.

The biologists involved in Y2Y are studying wildlife population dynamics on a landscape scale to help support regional conservation planning. The initiative is backing a range of research projects to determine the requirements for maintaining terrestrial and aquatic ecosystems in the Y2Y region. Their efforts to connect habitats include wildlife bridges, such as the one in Banff National Park (see Figure 41.9B). This cross-border initiative is also providing broader lessons for global conservation. In Southeast Asia, for example, plans for a tiger reserve in Myanmar (Burma) include proposals to link the Myanmar reserve with others in neighbouring countries.

In addition to creating reserves to protect species and their habitats from human disruptions, conservation efforts also attempt to restore ecosystems degraded by human activities. We look at the field of restoration ecology next.

? For what reasons are grey wolves considered a keystone species?

● Wolves impact the community to a greater extent than the abundance of individuals would indicate by regulating the populations of their prey, preventing these herbivores from damaging vegetation and degrading habitat for other members of the community. Wolf kills also provide food for other animals.

▶ **Figure 41.12C**
A grey wolf

▼ **Figure 41.12B** A grizzly bear with cubs in Yellowstone National Park

41.13 The study of how to restore degraded habitats is an evolving science

For centuries, humans have altered and degraded natural areas without considering the consequences. But as people have gradually come to realize the severity of some of the consequences of ecosystem alteration, they have sought ways to return degraded areas to their natural state. The expanding field of **restoration ecology** uses ecological principles to develop methods of achieving this goal.

One of the major strategies in restoration ecology is **bioremediation**, the use of living organisms to detoxify polluted ecosystems. For example, the fescue plants discussed in the opening essay of Chapter 19, as well as bacteria, have been used to clean up oil spills and old mining sites. Bacteria are also employed to metabolize toxins in dump sites. Plants have successfully extracted potentially toxic metals such as zinc, nickel, lead, and cadmium from contaminated soil. Researchers are using trees and lichens to clean up soil polluted with uranium.

Some restoration projects have the broader goal of returning ecosystems to their natural state. This may involve replanting vegetation, fencing out non-native animals, or removing dams that restrict water flow. Hundreds of restoration projects are currently under way in Canada. The *Principles and Guidelines for Ecological Restoration in Canada's Protected Natural Areas* is a set of national guidelines that provides a framework for consistent practices across the country. Its three guiding principles suggest that restoration efforts should be effective, efficient, and engaging.

The six-year restoration of the aquatic ecosystems of La Mauricie National Park, in the Canadian Shield ecosystem, 190 km west of Quebec City, was completed in 2010. Past human activity in the park had severely disrupted its water systems. Logging within the area started around 1850 and continued until the park was established in 1970. By that time, however, nearly half of the area's forests were logged. Removal of these trees had a significant impact on the area's water system. Dams and logjams (floating logs that collect and prevent outflow from the lake) sealed off lakes. Thousands of water-soaked logs were scattered across the bottoms and shorelines of lakes and streams **(Figure 41.13A)**.

The aquatic communities were also disrupted by the addition of invasive fish species. Between 1940 and 1950, several fish and game clubs (associations of wealthy sport fishers and hunters) dotted the area. To increase the draw for sport fishers, lakes were stocked with 19 species of non-native fish. These species were a major threat to the native brook trout (*Salvelinus fontinalis*), which was extirpated from several lakes in the area.

Removing dams in six lakes started the restoration of natural water levels in the aquatic systems. More than 13 000 logs, 4 m in length, were removed from the lakes, streams, and adjacent riparian zones. A combination of these efforts has greatly improved the health of the shorelines. The effectiveness of the restoration efforts is obvious in **Figure 41.13B**. Where Figure 41.13A shows the national park's Lac Isaïe before the restoration, Figure 41.13B shows the same lake in pristine condition afterwards. Natural fish communities were restocked after the removal of invasive species from lakes. Care was taken to maintain the genetic diversity of the area by restocking with genetic strains of brook trout present in the area.

An advisory committee continually assessed the project's efficiency through vigilant monitoring and scientific studies. To further increase efficiency, salvaged timber was used in the construction of an interpretive outreach structure at another of the park's lakes. The community has also been engaged throughout the entire restoration project. Such engagement is imperative to raise awareness of ecological processes and the importance of conservation across Canada. Parks Canada has several success stories and implementations of the *Principles and Guidelines for Ecological Restoration in Canada's Protected Natural Areas* on its website.

 ? Why was it important to use brook trout stocks of local strains in the restoration of La Mauricie National Park?

● Using random strains of fish would alter the genetic diversity within the region.

▲ **Figure 41.13A** Lac Isaïe, located in La Mauricie National Park, before restoration efforts

▲ **Figure 41.13B** Lac Isaïe after restoration efforts

41.14 Sustainable development is an ultimate goal

The demand for the "provisioning" services of ecosystems, such as food, fibres, and water, is increasing as the world's population grows and many communities become more affluent. Although these demands are currently being met, they are satisfied at the expense of other critical ecosystem services, such as climate regulation and protection against natural disasters. Clearly, we have set the biosphere and ourselves on a precarious path into the future. How can we best manage Earth's resources to ensure that all generations inherit an adequate supply of natural and economic resources and a relatively stable environment?

Many nations, scientific societies, and private foundations have embraced the concept of sustainable development. The Ecological Society of America, the world's largest organization of ecologists, endorses a research agenda called the Sustainable Biosphere Initiative. The goal of this initiative is to acquire the basic ecological information necessary for the intelligent and responsible development, management, and conservation of Earth's resources. The research agenda includes devising ways to sustain the productivity of natural and artificial ecosystems and studying the relationship between biological diversity, global climate change, and ecological processes. The Canadian Environmental Grantmakers' Network, made up of public, private, and corporate foundations, has provided more than $50 million in grants in support of environmental research in Canada.

Sustainable development does not depend only on continued research and application of ecological knowledge. It also requires us to connect the life sciences with the social sciences, economics, and humanities. Conservation and restoration of biodiversity is only one side of sustainable development; the other key facet is improving the human condition. Public education and the political commitment and cooperation of nations, especially Canada and the United States, are essential to the success of this endeavour.

The image of the Kermode spirit bear on the book's cover serves as a reminder of what we stand to lose if we fail to recognize and solve the ecological crisis at hand. Luckily for the spirit bear, the Kitasoo Spirit Bear Conservancy protects the natural habitat of these bears. Unfortunately, not all species are given the same level of protection. Nearly all of Madagascar's 103 species of lemurs, including the ring-tailed lemur (*Lemur catta*) in **Figure 41.14**, are threatened with extinction, as are dozens of other species endemic to the island. Unlike the flora on Vancouver Island, less than 20% of the original vegetation of Madagascar remains, and deforestation for agriculture, logging, and fuel wood continue. The country's steadily growing human population is beset by political and economic woes. Consequently, the future of Madagascar's splendid biodiversity

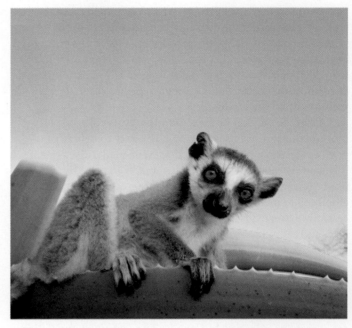

▲ **Figure 41.14** The ring-tailed lemur (*Lemur catta*)

may be bleak. Nevertheless, national and international initiatives in sustainable agriculture, ecotourism, conservation, and ecosystem restoration could turn the tide and save this showcase of biodiversity.

Biology is the scientific expression of the human desire to know nature. We are most likely to save what we appreciate, and we are most likely to appreciate what we understand. By learning about the processes and diversity of life, we also become more aware of our dependence on healthy ecosystems. An awareness of our unique ability to alter the biosphere and jeopardize the existence of other species, as well as our own, may help us choose a path toward a sustainable future.

The risk of a world without adequate natural resources for all of its people is not a vision of the distant future. It is a prospect for your children's lifetimes, or perhaps even your own. But although the current state of the biosphere is grim, the situation is far from hopeless. Now is the time to aggressively pursue more knowledge about life and to work toward long-term sustainability.

 Why is a concern for the well-being of future generations essential for progress toward sustainable development?

● Sustainable development is a long-term goal—longer than a human lifetime. Preoccupation with the here and now is an obstacle to sustainable development because it discourages behaviour that benefits future generations.

MasteringBiology® For Practice Quizzes, BioFlix, MP3 Tutors, and Activities, go to masteringbiology.com.

Reviewing the Concepts

The Loss of Biodiversity (41.1–41.7)

41.1 Loss of biodiversity includes the loss of ecosystems, species, and genes. While valuable for its own sake, biodiversity also provides food, fibres, medicines, and ecosystem services.

Ecosystem diversity

Species diversity

Genetic diversity

41.2 Habitat loss, invasive species, overharvesting, pollution, and climate change are major threats to biodiversity. Human alteration of habitats is the single greatest threat to biodiversity. Invasive species disrupt communities by competing with, preying on, or parasitizing native species. Harvesting at rates that exceed a population's ability to rebound is a threat to many species. Human activities produce diverse pollutants that may affect ecosystems far from their source. Biomagnification concentrates synthetic toxins that cannot be degraded by organisms.

41.3 Rapid warming is changing the global climate. Increased global temperature caused by rising concentrations of greenhouse gases is changing climatic patterns, with grave consequences.

41.4 Human activities are responsible for rising concentrations of greenhouse gases. Much of the increase is the result of burning fossil fuels.

41.5 Does bovine flatulence contribute to climate change? Methane released in bovine belches, not flatulence, is a significant contributor to climate change.

41.6 Global climate change affects biomes, ecosystems, communities, and populations. Organisms that live at high latitudes and high elevations are experiencing the greatest impact.

41.7 Climate change is an agent of natural selection. Phenotypic plasticity has minimized the impact on some species, and a few cases of microevolutionary change have been observed. However, the rapidity of the environmental changes makes it unlikely that evolutionary processes will save many species from extinction.

Conservation Biology and Sustainability (41.8–41.14)

41.8 Protecting endangered populations is one goal of conservation biology. Conservation biology is a goal-driven science that seeks to understand and counter the rapid loss of biodiversity. Some conservation biologists direct their efforts at increasing the size of endangered populations.

41.9 Sustaining ecosystems and landscapes is a conservation priority. Conservation efforts are increasingly aimed at sustaining ecosystems and landscapes. Edges between ecosystems have distinct sets of features and species. The increased frequency and abruptness of edges caused by human activities can increase species loss. Movement corridors connecting isolated habitats may be helpful to fragmented populations.

41.10 Establishing protected areas slows the loss of biodiversity. Biodiversity hot spots have high concentrations of endemic species.

41.11 Zoned reserves are an attempt to reverse ecosystem disruption. Zoned reserves are undisturbed wildlands surrounded by buffer zones of compatible economic development. Costa Rica has established many zoned reserves. Ecotourism has become an important source of revenue for conservation efforts.

41.12 The Yellowstone to Yukon Conservation Initiative seeks to preserve biodiversity by connecting protected areas. The success of this innovative international research and conservation effort hinged on the reintroduction of grey wolves.

41.13 The study of how to restore degraded habitats is an evolving science. Restoration ecology uses ecological principles to return degraded areas to their natural state, a process that may include detoxifying polluted ecosystems, replanting native vegetation, and returning waterways to their natural courses.

41.14 Sustainable development is an ultimate goal. Sustainable development seeks to improve the human condition while conserving biodiversity. It depends on increasing and applying ecological knowledge as well as valuing our links to the biosphere.

Connecting the Concepts

1. Complete the following concept map, which organizes some of the key concepts of conservation biology.

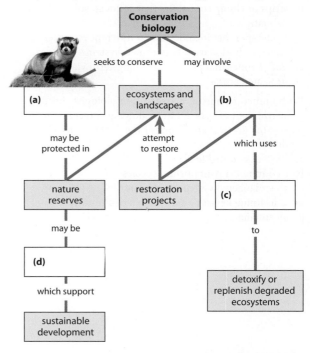

Testing Your Knowledge

Multiple Choice

2. Which of these statements best describes what conservation biologists mean by the "the rapid loss of biodiversity"?
    a. Introduced species, such as starlings and zebra mussels, have rapidly expanded their ranges.
    b. Harvests of marine fishes, such as cod and bluefin tuna, are declining.
    c. The current species extinction rate is as much as 1000 times greater than at any time in the last 100 000 years.
    d. Many potential medicines are being lost as plant species become extinct.
    e. The number of hot spots worldwide is rapidly declining.

3. Which of the following poses the single greatest threat to biodiversity?
    a. invasive species
    b. overhunting
    c. movement corridors
    d. habitat loss
    e. pollution

4. Which of the following is characteristic of endemic species?
    a. They are often found in biodiversity hot spots.
    b. They are distributed widely in the biosphere.
    c. They require edges between ecosystems.
    d. Their trophic position makes them very susceptible to the effects of biomagnification.
    e. They are often keystone species whose presence helps to structure a community.

5. Ospreys and other top predators are most severely affected by pesticides such as PCBs because they
    a. are especially sensitive to chemicals.
    b. have rapid reproductive rates.
    c. have very long lifespans.
    d. store the pesticides in their tissues.
    e. consume prey in which pesticides are concentrated.

6. Movement corridors are
    a. the routes taken by migratory animals.
    b. strips or clumps of habitat that connect isolated fragments of habitat.
    c. landscapes that include several different ecosystems.
    d. edges, or boundaries, between ecosystems.
    e. buffer zones that promote the long-term viability of protected areas.

7. With limited resources, conservation biologists need to prioritize their efforts. Of the following choices, which should receive the greatest attention for the goal of conserving biodiversity?
    a. the black-footed ferret
    b. a commercially important species
    c. all endangered vertebrate species
    d. a declining keystone species in a community
    e. all endangered species

8. Which of the following statements about protected areas is *not* correct?
    a. We now protect 25% of the land areas of the planet.
    b. National parks are only one type of protected area.
    c. Most reserves are smaller in size than the ranges of some of the species they are meant to protect.
    d. Management of protected areas must coordinate with the management of lands outside the protected zone.
    e. Biodiversity hot spots are important areas to protect.

Describing, Comparing, and Explaining

9. What are the three levels of biological diversity? Explain how human activities threaten each of these levels.

10. What are the so-called greenhouse gases? How are they important to life on Earth?

11. What are the causes and possible consequences of climate change? Why is international cooperation necessary if we are to solve this problem?

Applying the Concepts

12. Biologists are concerned that populations of many migratory songbirds are declining. Evidence suggests that some of these birds might be victims of pesticides. Most of the pesticides implicated in songbird mortality have not been used since the 1970s. Suggest a hypothesis to explain the current decline in songbird numbers.

13. You may have heard that human activities cause the extinction of one species every hour. Such estimates vary widely because we do not know how many species exist or how fast their habitats are being destroyed. You can make your own estimate of the rate of extinction. Start with the number of species that have been identified. To keep things simple, ignore extinction in the temperate latitudes and focus on the 80% of plants and animals that live in the tropical rainforest. Assume that destruction of the forest continues at a rate of 1% per year, so the forest will be gone in 100 years. Assume (optimistically) that half the rainforest species will survive in preserves, forest remnants, and zoos. How many species will disappear in the next century? How many species is that per year? Per day? Recent studies of the rainforest canopy have led some experts to predict that there may be as many as 30 million species on Earth. How does starting with this figure change your estimates?

14. The price of energy does not reflect its real costs. What kinds of hidden environmental costs are not reflected in the price of fossil fuels? How are these costs paid, and by whom? Do you think these costs could or should be figured into the price of oil? How might that be done?

15. Research your country's per capita carbon emissions. Compare your carbon footprint with the average for your country. (See the question at the end of Module 41.4). How can individuals reduce the carbon emissions for which they are directly responsible? Make a list of actions that you are willing to take to reduce your carbon footprint.

16. Until recently, response to environmental problems has been fragmented—an antipollution law here, incentives for recycling there. Meanwhile, the problems of the gap between the rich and poor nations, diminishing resources, and pollution continue to grow. Now people and governments are starting to envision a sustainable society. The Worldwatch Institute, a respected environmental monitoring organization, estimates that we must reach sustainability by the year 2030 to avoid economic and environmental disaster. To get there, we must begin shaping a sustainable society during this decade. In what ways is our present system not sustainable? What might a sustainable society be like? Do you think a sustainable society is an achievable goal? Why or why not? What is the alternative? What might we do to work toward sustainability? What are the major roadblocks to achieving sustainability? How would your life be different in a sustainable society?

Answers to all questions can be found in Appendix E.

The Periodic Table

Name (Symbol)	Atomic Number	Name (Symbol)	Atomic Number	Name (Symbol)	Atomic Number	Name (Symbol)	Atomic Number	Name (Symbol)	Atomic Number
Actinium (Ac)	89	Copernicium (Cn)	112	Iridium (Ir)	77	Palladium (Pd)	46	Sodium (Na)	11
Aluminum (Al)	13	Copper (Cu)	29	Iron (Fe)	26	Phosphorus (P)	15	Strontium (Sr)	38
Americium (Am)	95	Curium (Cm)	96	Krypton (Kr)	36	Platinum (Pt)	78	Sulphur (S)	16
Antimony (Sb)	51	Darmstadtium (Ds)	110	Lanthanum (La)	57	Plutonium (Pu)	94	Tantalum (Ta)	73
Argon (Ar)	18	Dubnium (Db)	105	Lawrencium (Lr)	103	Polonium (Po)	84	Technetium (Tc)	43
Arsenic (As)	33	Dysprosium (Dy)	66	Lead (Pb)	82	Potassium (K)	19	Tellurium (Te)	52
Astatine (At)	85	Einsteinium (Es)	99	Lithium (Li)	3	Praseodymium (Pr)	59	Terbium (Tb)	65
Barium (Ba)	56	Erbium (Er)	68	Lutetium (Lu)	71	Promethium (Pm)	61	Thallium (Tl)	81
Berkelium (Bk)	97	Europium (Eu)	63	Magnesium (Mg)	12	Protactinium (Pa)	91	Thorium (Th)	90
Beryllium (Be)	4	Fermium (Fm)	100	Manganese (Mn)	25	Radium (Ra)	88	Thulium (Tm)	69
Bismuth (Bi)	83	Fluorine (F)	9	Meitnerium (Mt)	109	Radon (Rn)	86	Tin (Sn)	50
Bohrium (Bh)	107	Francium (Fr)	87	Mendelevium (Md)	101	Rhenium (Re)	75	Titanium (Ti)	22
Boron (B)	5	Gadolinium (Gd)	64	Mercury (Hg)	80	Rhodium (Rh)	45	Tungsten (W)	74
Bromine (Br)	35	Gallium (Ga)	31	Molybdenum (Mo)	42	Roentgenium (Rg)	111	Uranium (U)	92
Cadmium (Cd)	48	Germanium (Ge)	32	Neodymium (Nd)	60	Rubidium (Rb)	37	Vanadium (V)	23
Calcium (Ca)	20	Gold (Au)	79	Neon (Ne)	10	Ruthenium (Ru)	44	Xenon (Xe)	54
Californium (Cf)	98	Hafnium (Hf)	72	Neptunium (Np)	93	Rutherfordium (Rf)	104	Ytterbium (Yb)	70
Carbon (C)	6	Hassium (Hs)	108	Nickel (Ni)	28	Samarium (Sm)	62	Yttrium (Y)	39
Cerium (Ce)	58	Helium (He)	2	Niobium (Nb)	41	Scandium (Sc)	21	Zinc (Zn)	30
Cesium (Cs)	55	Holmium (Ho)	67	Nitrogen (N)	7	Seaborgium (Sg)	106	Zirconium (Zr)	40
Chlorine (Cl)	17	Hydrogen (H)	1	Nobelium (No)	102	Selenium (Se)	34		
Chromium (Cr)	24	Indium (In)	49	Osmium (Os)	76	Silicon (Si)	14		
Cobalt (Co)	27	Iodine (I)	53	Oxygen (O)	8	Silver (Ag)	47		

APPENDIX B # The Amino Acids of Proteins

APPENDIX C Some Organic Functional Groups and

CHEMICAL GROUP	Hydroxyl	Carbonyl	Carboxyl
STRUCTURE	—OH (may be written HO—) In a **hydroxyl group** (—OH), a hydrogen atom is bonded to an oxygen atom, which in turn is bonded to the carbon skeleton of the organic molecule. (Do not confuse this functional group with the hydroxide ion, OH⁻.)	The **carbonyl group** ($>$CO) consists of a carbon atom joined to an oxygen atom by a double bond.	When an oxygen atom is double-bonded to a carbon atom that is also bonded to an —OH group, the entire assembly of atoms is called a **carboxyl group** (—COOH).
NAME OF COMPOUND	**Alcohols** (Their specific names usually end in -*ol*.)	**Ketones** if the carbonyl group is within a carbon skeleton **Aldehydes** if the carbonyl group is at the end of the carbon skeleton	**Carboxylic acids**, or organic acids
EXAMPLE	**Ethanol**, the alcohol present in alcoholic beverages	**Acetone**, the simplest ketone **Propanal**, an aldehyde	**Acetic acid**, which gives vinegar its sour taste
FUNCTIONAL PROPERTIES	• Is polar as a result of the electrons spending more time near the electronegative oxygen atom. • Can form hydrogen bonds with water molecules, helping to dissolve organic compounds such as sugars.	• A ketone and an aldehyde may be structural isomers with different properties, as is the case for acetone and propanal. • Ketone and aldehyde groups are also found in sugars, giving rise to two major groups of sugars: ketoses (containing ketone groups) and aldoses (containing aldehyde groups).	• Acts as an acid; can donate an H⁺ because the covalent bond between oxygen and hydrogen is so polar: Non-ionized ⇌ Ionized + H⁺ • Found in cells in the ionized form with a charge of 1− and called a carboxylate ion.

Their Properties

Amino	Sulfhydryl	Phosphate	Methyl

Amino	Sulfhydryl	Phosphate	Methyl
The **amino group** (—NH₂) consists of a nitrogen atom bonded to two hydrogen atoms and to the carbon skeleton.	The **sulfhydryl group** (—SH) consists of a sulphur atom bonded to an atom of hydrogen; it resembles a hydroxyl group in shape.	In the **phosphate group** shown here, a phosphorus atom is bonded to four oxygen atoms; one oxygen is bonded to the carbon skeleton; two oxygens carry negative charges (—OPO₃²⁻). In this text, (P) represents an attached phosphate group.	A **methyl group** (—CH₃) consists of a carbon bonded to three hydrogen atoms. The carbon of a methyl group may be attached to a carbon or to a different atom.

Amines	Thiols	Organic phosphates	Methylated compounds
Glycine, a compound that is both an amine and a carboxylic acid because it has both an amino group and a carboxyl group; compounds with both groups are called **amino acids**	**Cysteine**, an important sulphur-containing amino acid	**Glycerol phosphate**, which takes part in many important chemical reactions in cells; glycerol phosphate also provides the backbone for phospholipids, the most prevalent molecules in cell membranes	**5-Methyl cytidine**, a component of DNA that has been modified by addition of a methyl group

Amino	Sulfhydryl	Phosphate	Methyl
• Acts as a base; can pick up an H⁺ from the surrounding solution (water, in living organisms): H⁺ + —N(H)(H) ⇌ —⁺N(H)(H)(H) Non-ionized Ionized • Found in cells in the ionized form with a charge of 1+.	• Two sulfhydryl groups can react, forming a covalent bond. This "cross-linking" helps to stabilize protein structure. • Cross-linking of cysteines in hair proteins maintains the curliness or straightness of hair. Straight hair can be "permanently" curled by shaping it around curlers and then breaking and re-forming the cross-linking bonds.	• Contributes negative charge to the molecule of which it is a part (2− when at the end of a molecule, as above; 1− when located internally in a chain of phosphates). • Molecules containing phosphate groups have the potential to react with water, releasing energy.	• Addition of a methyl group to DNA, or to molecules bound to DNA, affects the expression of genes. • Arrangement of methyl groups in male and female sex hormones affects their shape and function.

Their Properties

APPENDIX C

A-4

APPENDIX D The Language of Biology

Prefix	Root	Suffix	Meaning	Example
a-, ab-, abs-			from, away from	Nutrients that are **ab**sorbed by a plant are taken away from the soil.
	aberr-		to go astray	An **aberr**ant host is an incorrect host for a parasite.
	acr-		summit, extremity	The **acr**osome is at the tip (summit) of the sperm.
ad-			above	The **ad**renal gland sits above the kidney.
	adip-		animal fat	In animals, **adip**ose tissue stores fat.
	agon-		contest	Competitors in a contest display **agon**istic behaviour.
	ali-		to nourish	The **ali**mentary canal is another name for the intestine.
allo-			different, other	**Allo**patric speciation can occur when part of a population is relocated to another region.
	altru-		give to others	**Altru**ism is when one organism freely gives to another.
	alveol-		hollow	The hollow air sacs in a lung are called **alveol**i.
	amni-		membrane around a fetus	The **amni**on is a membrane that surrounds a developing fetus.
	amphi-		both, of both kinds	**Amphi**bians depend on land and water for survival.
	amygd-		almond	Its almond shape gives the **amygd**ala its name.
a-, an-			not, without	**A**sexual reproduction occurs without the fusion of gametes.
ana-			again, anew	The origin of two new nuclei starts during **ana**phase.
	andro-		male, masculine	Hormones that promote male characteristics are called **andro**gens.
	angi-		vessel, container	A gamet**angi**um is a container in which gametes are produced.
	ann-		year	**Ann**ual plants complete their life cycles in a single year.
	ann-, annul-		ring	The **ann**elids are named for the appearance of rings along their bodies.
ant-			against, opposite	The **ant**icodons of tRNA are the opposite of (complementary to) the codons on mRNA.
ante-			before	An animal's head is at its **ante**rior end.
	anth-		flower	The **anth**er is the male part of the flower.
	anthr-		man, male	The **anthr**opoid apes resemble humans.
apic-			tip, summit, apex	An **apic**al meristem is at the tip of each branch.
	append-		something attached	The **append**ix is attached to the large intestine.
	aps-, apt-		to join	Neurons meet other cells at syn**aps**es.
	apt-		fitted	Organisms become fitted to their environments through ad**apt**ations.
	aqu-		water	Water-based solutions are called **aqu**eous.
	arachn-		spider, spider web	**Arachn**ophobia is the fear of spiders.
	archae-		old, ancient	The **Archae**an era of Earth is the oldest.
	arthr-		joint	**Arthr**opods are animals with jointed legs.
		-ary	pertaining to	Structures near the armpit are in an axill**ary** position.
	asc-		sac	Sac fungi are also called **asc**ocarps.
		-ase	enzyme	Lig**ase** is an enzyme that joins nucleotides together.
	ather-		porridge	A symptom of **ather**osclerosis is the buildup of cholesterol in the arteries, which resembles porridge.
		-ation	the process of	A gastrula develops during the process of gastrul**ation**.
	atri-		entrance hall or foyer	The first chamber of the heart that blood enters is the **atri**um.
	aud-, audit-		hearing	The **audit**ory nerve relays the sense of hearing to the brain.

APPENDIX D

Prefix	Root	Suffix	Meaning	Example
auto-			self	**Auto**trophs are organisms that can make their own organic carbon molecules.
	aux-		to increase	In plants, **aux**in stimulates shoot growth.
	ax-		axis	The axis of the cranium and spine constitute the **ax**ial skeleton.
	axill-		armpit, upper arm, nook	A branch joins a stem, or an arm joins the body at the **axill**ary region.
	bac-		rod shape	**Bac**illi are rod-shaped bacteria.
	bas-		bottom or base	At the base of a eukaryotic flagellum is the **bas**al body.
	basidi-		club, little pedestal	The club fungi are also called **basidi**ocarps.
	benth-		depth of the sea	The seafloor and the water just above it make up the **benth**ic region.
bi-			two	Every species is given two names in **bi**nomial nomenclature.
	bio-		life	**Bio**logy is the study of living things.
	blast-		bud, embryonic cell, sprout, germ	**Blast**ulas are small balls of embryonic cells.
	bronch-		air tube	**Bronch**ioles are small airways in a lung.
	bry-		moss	Mosses are also called **bry**ophytes.
	calor-		heat	A **Calor**ie is the amount of heat required to warm 1 L of water 1°C.
	camb-		exchange	Plant tissues exchange nutrients and water with the vascular **camb**ium.
	capill-		hair	**Capill**aries are fine, hair-like blood vessels.
	caps-		box	The **caps**id is the box that enclosed a virus's genetic material.
	cardi-		heart	**Cardi**ac muscle is found only in the vertebrate heart.
	carn-		flesh	**Carn**ivores eat the flesh of animals.
	carp-		body	The fruiting body of a club fungus is a basidio**carp**.
	cat-		down	**Cat**alysis is the process of breaking something down.
	cav-		hollowed out, to hollow	Ex**cav**ates are protists with a hollowed out body shape.
	cec-, caec-		blind, hidden	A **cec**um is a blind-ended pouch off of the intestines.
cent-			hundredth, hundred	**Cent**ipedes are said (incorrectly) to have 100 legs.
	centr-		centre	The **centr**omere is the centre part of a chromosome.
	cephal-		head	**Cephal**ization describes the evolutionary process of forming a head.
	cess-		come after	Suc**cess**ion describes the series of organisms that come one after another following a disturbance.
	chaet-		bristle	Poly**chaet**e worms have elaborate bristles.
	chel-		claw	**Chel**icerates are arthropods with large claws.
	chem-		chemical	**Chem**oreceptors detect chemical signals.
	chiasm-		cross	The optic nerves cross at the optic **chiasm**a.
	chit-		tunic or frock	Insects are covered in a **chit**inous exoskeleton, which is likened to a tunic.
	chloro-		green	**Chloro**phyll is a green-coloured pigment.
	choano-		collar	**Choano**cytes have a collar of microvilli surrounding their flagellum.
	chole-		bile	**Chole**sterol was originally identified in gallstones in the gallbladder where bile is stored.
	chondr-		cartilage, granule	**Chondr**ichthes are fish with cartilaginous skeletons.
	chor-, chori-		tunic of the eyeball	The **chor**oid is the outer covering of the eyeball.
	chord-		structure resembling a string	The noto**chord** is a long, skinny supporting rod found among the chordates.
	chrom-		colour	Different phyto**chrom**es detect specific colours of light.
		-cide	to kill	Spermi**cide**s are contraceptives that kill sperm.

Prefix	Root	Suffix	Meaning	Example
	cili-		eyelash	**Cili**a on a cell were thought to resemble eyelashes.
	circ-		circle	Blood moves in a complete circle as it travels through the **circ**ulatory system.
	clad-		young branch	A **clad**e is a branch of a phylogenetic tree that includes a common ancestor and all of its descendants.
	clim-		region or slope of the earth	**Clim**ate changes with varying light intensity because of the angle (slope) of Earth's rotation.
	cnid-		nettle (stinging)	**Cnid**arians are animals with specialized stinging cells.
co-			together	**Co**valent bonds hold atoms together.
	cocc-		berry-shaped organism	**Cocc**i are berry-shaped bacteria.
	cochl-		spiral shell	The **cochl**ea of the inner ear resembles the shell of a snail.
	coel-		cavity	A cavity between the body wall and digestive tract is called a **coel**om.
	cogn-, cognosc-		to get to know	**Cogn**ition is ability to understand.
	coll-		glue	**Coll**agen fibres help to hold cells together in a tissue.
	comp-		to put together	De**comp**osers break down large organic molecules.
con-			to bring together	**Con**traction of a muscle brings its ends closer together.
contra-			opposite, against	**Contra**ceptive techniques are intended to prevent the conceiving of a child.
	copul-		to join together	Male and female are joined together during **copul**ation.
	corn-		horny web or sheath	The tough, horny layer covering in front of the iris of the eye is the **corn**ea.
	cort-, cortic-		outer layer, bark	The outer layer of parenchyma tissue in a plant root is the **cort**ex.
	cot-, cotyl-		seed leaf	**Cotyl**edons are embryonic leaves that develop within the seed.
	counter-		opposite	In **counter**current exchangers, blood flows in opposite directions.
	crani-		cranium, skull	**Crani**ates are animals with skulls.
	crin-		to secrete	The endo**crin**e system involves a number of secreted hormones.
	crist-		crest	The **crist**ae with a mitochondrion resemble the crests of waves.
	crust-		rind, hard shell, bark	**Crust**aceans have hardened exoskeletons.
	cut-		skin	A sub**cut**aneous injection is given under the skin.
	cyan-		blue	**Cyan**obacteria have a blue-green colour.
	cyt-		cell	The **cyt**oskeleton supports the shape of a cell.
de-			down, away, off	In the **de**hydration reaction, water is taken away as a bond between two monomers is formed.
	demo-		people	**Demo**graphy records the characteristics of populations of people.
	dendr-		tree	The **dendr**ites of a neuron resemble the branches of a tree.
	derm-		skin	Ecto**derm** is the outermost tissue layer (skin) of an embryo.
	desmo-		to bind	**Desmo**somes are sites where adjacent cells are bound together.
	detrit-		wear away	**Detrit**ivores break down (or wear away) dead organic material.
deuter-			second	The mouth develops from the second opening that forms in the **deuter**ostomes.
di-			two	A **di**saccharide is a sugar consisting of two monomers.
	didym-		twin, testicle	The epi**didym**is sits on top of the testis.
	diff-		to pour out or away in every direction	When a substance **diff**uses, it drifts away in all directions.
	digest-		to separate, to divide	**Digest**ion involved the separation of larger macromolecules.
dis-			apart, in different directions	You cut structures apart during a **dis**section.

Prefix	Root	Suffix	Meaning	Example
	dist-		to be apart	In terms of urine flow, the **dist**al tubules are at the far end of the nephron.
	dors-		back	An animal's back is its **dors**al surface.
	duct-		tube, passageway	The ovi**duct** is the tube through which eggs travel.
	duoden-		12	The **duoden**um is approximately the width of 12 fingers.
ec-, ex-			out, outside of	An **ec**topic pregnancy occurs outside of the uterus.
	echino-		spine	The skin of most **echino**derms is covered with spines.
	eco-		house or habitation	**Eco**logy is the study of interactions between organisms and their environments (dwellings).
ecto-			outside	An **ecto**therm obtains its heat from outside of its body (its environment).
	electr-		electrical	**Electr**olytes are ions with single positive or negative (electrical) charges.
	embry-		young one, that which grows within	The **embry**o is a common developmental stage.
	enchym-		tissue	Par**enchym**a is a type of ground tissue in plants.
endo-			inside or within	**Endo**skeletons are located inside the body, underneath soft tissue.
	enter-		intestine	The **enter**ic division of the autonomic nervous system regulates gut function.
epi-			top, upon	The **epi**dermis is the uppermost layer of the skin.
	erg-		energy, activity	The activity of an all**erg**en initiates an immune response.
	erythr-		red	**Erythr**ocytes are red blood cells.
eu-			well, true, normal	**Eu**karyotes have a true nucleus.
ex-			out, from, removal	**Ex**ergonic reactions release energy.
	excr-		to discharge	**Excr**etion is the process of discharging or eliminating waste.
exo-			outside, external	In **exo**cytosis, cells expel the contents of some vacuoles.
	extirp-		root out or eliminate	**Extirp**ation is the elimination of a population from one of its habitats.
extra-			outside	The **extra**cellular matrix is a network of proteins outside of the cell.
		-fer	to bear	A coni**fer** is a cone-bearing tree.
	fertil-		bearing in abundance, productive	**Fertil**ization is an early step in reproduction.
	fet-		offspring	After nine weeks of gestation, a developing human is called a **fet**us.
	fibr-		filament, fibre	**Fibr**ous connective tissue contains numerous extracellular filaments.
	fil-		thread	A **fil**ament is a long, thread-like protein.
	fimbr-		fringe, border	Under a microscope, bacterial **fimbr**iae look like a fringe around the edge of the cell.
	fiss-		to split	One bacterium divides into two through binary **fiss**ion.
	flagell-		whip	**Flagell**a move with a whipping motion.
	flex-, flect-		to bend	Bending your arm is a movement called **flex**ing.
	foll-		bag	Ovarian **foll**icles resemble little bags, which hold oocytes.
	foram-		pore, hole	**Foram**iniferans are protists with porous shells.
	fove-		small pit	The **fove**a is a small pit in the retina where the optic nerve exits the eye.
	fus-		to pour	Molecules move (pour) away from areas of high concentration during dif**fus**ion.
	gam-		marriage	Poly**gam**ous animals have multiple mates.
	gamet-		gamete	A **gamet**ophyte is a plant that produces gametes.
	gangli-		mass of nervous tissue	A **gangli**on is a cluster of nerve cells.

Prefix	Root	Suffix	Meaning	Example
	gastr-		stomach	**Gastr**itis is inflammation of the stomach.
	ge-		earth	**Ge**ological processes have shaped Earth's continents.
		-gen	to create	A patho**gen** is any organism that causes disease.
	gen-, genit-		to produce	**Gen**es are expressed to produce proteins.
	germ-		seed	Young seedlings emerge from their seeds during **germ**ination.
	gest-		to carry, to bear	Female mammals carry their developing young during **gest**ation.
	glan-		acorn	The **glan**s of the penis was originally described as having an acorn-like shape.
	glia-		glue	**Glia**l cells help to maintain the structure of the central nervous system.
	glob-		globe, globular	Hemo**glob**in consists of four globular-shaped subunits.
	glomer-		ball of yarn	The **glomer**ulus capillaries associated with the nephron resemble a ball of yarn.
	gluc-, glyc-		sweet	Animals store excess sugar as **glyc**ogen.
	gon-,		act of generation	The **gon**ads are reproductive organs.
	grad-		to step, to walk	Molecules move down a concentration **grad**ient.
	graph-		to write, to record	A micro**graph** is a record of what was seen through a microscope.
	grav-		gravity	Plant roots grow downward because of **grav**itropism.
	greg-		flock, herd	Many birds ag**greg**ate together in large flocks.
	gymn-		naked	**Gymn**osperms are plants that produce naked seeds.
	habit-		to live, to dwell	An animal's **habit**at is the region in which it lives.
	hapl-		single	A **hapl**oid cell has a single set of chromosomes.
hemi-			half	The brain is divided into left and right **hemi**spheres.
	hemo-		blood	**Hemo**globin carries oxygen in the blood.
	hepat-		liver	Liver cells are called **hepat**ocytes.
	herb-		plants (herbs)	Animals that eat only plants are called **herb**ivores.
	hes-		to stick	Molecules stick together by means of co**hes**ion.
heter-			different	Being **heter**ozygous means having two different alleles for a gene.
	hist-		tissue	Donated organs are rejected if their tissues are not **hist**ocompatible.
hom-			same	The chromosomes of a **hom**ologous pair contain the same genes at the same loci.
	hormon-		to set in motion	**Hormon**es are chemical messages that elicit (set in motion) effects in their targets.
	hum-		on the ground	The **hum**us layer is made of the organic debris lying on the ground.
	humor, humour		body fluid	The aqueous **humour** is the fluid between the cornea and lens of the eye.
	hydr-		water	**Hydr**olysis is the breaking of a covalent bond through the addition of water.
hyper-			above	A **hyper**tonic solution has more solutions than another solution.
hyp-			below	The **hyp**othalamus is situated below the thalamus in the brain.
	hyph-		web	The **hyph**ae of fungi have a web-like appearance.
		-ic	pertaining to	Synapt**ic** refers to the synapse.
in-			within, into, on	**In**breeding is mating between relatives within a family unit.
in-			not	Alleles that are **in**completely dominant do not mask other alleles.
	inflamm-		to set on fire	A burning feeling is often associated with **inflamm**ation.
inter-			between	**Inter**neurons relay information between other neurons.
intra-			within	**Intra**specific competition occurs within a species, between its members.
iso-			same	Two **iso**mers have the same chemical composition.

Prefix	Root	Suffix	Meaning	Example
		-itis	inflammation	Gastritis is inflammation of the stomach.
		-ium	part or region	The gametangium is the region where plant gametes are produced.
	jacul-		to throw	Semen is "thrown" out of the body during ejaculation.
	junct-		to join	When present, gap junctions join the cytoplasm of adjacent cells.
	kary-		nut, nucleus	Eukaryotic organisms have true nuclei.
kilo-			thousand	One kilogram is 1000 grams.
	kin-		movement	Motion is a form of kinetic energy.
	kont-		flagella	Unikonta are organisms with one flagellum.
	labi-, labr-		lip, fold of skin	The labia minor and labia majora are the skin folds of human female genitalia.
	lact-		milk	Lactose is the sugar found in milk.
	later-		side	Bilateral animals have mirror-image left and right sides.
	leuk-		white	Collectively, white blood cells are leukocytes.
	lig-		to bind, to tie	DNA ligase joins two pieces of DNA by sealing the nick between them.
	ligni-		wood	The compound lignin contributes to the hardness of wood.
	lim-, limb-		small branch of a tree	Tetrapod limbs come off of the trunk like branches of a tree.
	lip-		fat	Lipids include fats.
	lite-		stone	Stromatolites are fossilized prokaryotes.
	loc-		place	A specific place on a chromosome containing a gene is called a locus.
	lymph-		water, lymph (body fluid)	In animals with closed circulatory systems, the interstitial fluid is called lymph.
	lys-		to break	Hydrolysis is the breaking of covalent bonds by the addition of water.
macro-			large	Macromolecules are large molecules consisting of many monomers.
	magnif-			Microscopes magnify cells so they can be visualized.
mal-			badly, wrongly	An improper diet leads to malnutrition.
	mamm-		breast	Mammary glands are located within the breasts of human females.
	marsup-		pouch, bag	Marsupials are mammals that raise their young in pouches.
	matr-, matern-		mother	Maternal behaviours include nursing and grooming offspring.
	me-, moe-		to change	Amoebas frequently change their shape.
	mea(r)-		to pass	Solutes can pass through a membrane that is permeable to them.
	mechan-		mechanics	Mechanoreceptors detect physical/mechanical distortions.
	med-		middle, core	The central region of the kidney is the medulla.
	meio-		to lessen	Meiosis decreases the number of chromosomes in the daughter cells.
	menstr-		monthly	Menstrual cycles occur roughly every month.
		-ment	result of, act of, means of	Bones are attached by means of ligaments.
	mer-		part	The centromere is the centre part of a chromosome.
meso-			middle	The middle of the leaf is called the mesophyll.
meta-			change	Animals that change form in their life cycle undergo metamorphosis.
	metr-		uterus	The endometrium is the inner layer of the uterus.
		-metry	the science of measuring	The amount of radioisotopes in a sample can be measured by radiometry.
micro-			small, one-millionth	A micrometre is one-millionth of a metre.
	migr-		to move from place to place	Migratory birds travel long distances.

Prefix	Root	Suffix	Meaning	Example
mil-, mill			thousandth, thousand	One one-thousandth of a litre is a **milli**litre.
	mim-		to imitate	For defence, many **mim**ics imitate the coloration of other organisms.
	misc-		to mix	Pro**misc**uous females mate with many (a mix) of males.
	mit-		thread	Thread-like chromosomes separate during **mit**osis.
	molt-, moult-		to shed	To grow, insects must shed their exoskeleton, or **moult**.
mon-			one	A single unit of a macromolecule is a **mon**omer.
	morph-		form, shape	**Morph**ology is the study of an organism's form.
multi-			many	**Multi**potent cells can become one of many possibilities.
	mut-		to change	A **mut**ation is a change in DNA sequence.
	mutu-		reciprocal	In **mutu**alism, both partners have reciprocal benefits.
	myc-		fungus	The body of a fungus is the **myc**elium.
	myel-		spinal cord, marrow	**Myel**oid stem cells in bone marrow give rise to all blood cells.
	myo-		muscle	**Myo**sin is an important protein for muscle contraction.
nano-			one-billionth	One **nano**metre is one-billionth of a metre.
	nemat-		thread	**Nemat**odes have a thread-like appearance.
	nephr-		kidney	**Nephr**ons are the functional units of the kidney.
	neur-		nerve, nervous system, tendon	**Neur**ons conduct impulses throughout the nervous system.
	neutr-		neutral (as in charge)	**Neutr**ophils bind to dyes without electrical charges.
	nom-		name	Bi**nom**ial **nom**enclature uses two names for every organism.
non-			not	A **non**-native species does not originate in the area in which it is found.
	not-		back, buttock	The **not**ochord is the supporting rod under the dorsal surface of a chordate.
	nutri-, nutrit-		nourish	A nourishing diet contains many **nutri**ents.
	oblig-		to bind, to connect	**Oblig**ate anaerobes can grow only in the absence of oxygen.
		-oid	in the form of	Parasit**oid**s function like parasites, except that they ultimately kill their hosts.
		-ole	little	Arteri**ole**s are small arteries.
		-ology	the scientific study of	Bi**ology** is the study of living organisms.
	-oma		tumour	Melan**oma** is a tumour containing cancerous melanocytes.
omni-			all, of every kind	**Omni**vores eat all kinds of food.
	onc-		cancer	**Onc**ogenes are turned on to make a cell cancerous.
	oo-		pertaining to the egg	**Oo**genesis is the process of producing eggs.
	ops-, opt-		vision	The **opt**ic nerve relays the sense of vision to the brain.
	or-		of the mouth	The mouth is an **or**al cavity.
		-ory	having to do with, place for	An animal's territ**ory** is the land it defends.
		-osis	the process of	Cells ingest solid particles in the process of phagocyt**osis**.
	osmo-		thrusting, pushing	A concentration gradient of impermeable molecules pushes water across the membrane by **osmo**sis.
	ost-, oste-		bone	**Oste**ocytes are bone cells.
		-ous	having to do with	Structures that are associated with the membrane are membran**ous**.

Prefix	Root	Suffix	Meaning	Example
	ov-		egg, female gamete	An egg is also called an **ov**um.
	ox-, oxy-		oxygen	Oxygen is consumed in **ox**idative phosphorylation.
	paed-		child	**Paedo**morphosis is the retention of child-like characteristics in an adult.
	pale-, palae-		old, ancient	**Pale**ontologists study ancient fossils.
para-			beside	**Para**sites were thought to feed beside their host.
	path-		disease	A **path**ogen creates disease.
	patr-		homeland	Sym**patr**ic speciation occurs within the same area.
	ped-		foot	A milli**ped**e is (erroneously) described as having 1000 legs.
	pelag-		open sea, high sea	The open ocean is the **pelag**ic region.
	pept-		cooked, digested	A **pept**ic ulcer occurs when part of the stomach is eroded or digested away.
	peptid-		protein	Proteins can also be called poly**peptid**es.
per-			through	**Per**istalsis moves food through the intestinal tract.
	phag-		to eat	**Phag**ocytes ingest debris and foreign cells.
	pharyn-		throat	The throat region is referred to as the **pharyn**x.
	phen-		to bring to light, apparent	The **phen**otype is the outward appearance of the genotype.
	pher-		to bear, to carry, to go	A **pher**omone carries a signal from one organism to another.
	phil-		love, friendship	Polar hydro**phil**ic molecules are those that are soluble in water.
	phlo-		bark	**Phlo**em transports photosynthates within the bark of a tree.
	phob-		fearing	Nonpolar hydro**phob**ic molecules are not soluble in water.
	phot-		light	**Phot**osynthesis uses light energy to produce sugars.
	phrag-		to block, to wall up	The dia**phrag**m forms a wall between the chest and the abdomen.
	phyl-		race	**Phyl**ogeny is the evolutionary history of species (races).
	phyll-		leaf	The middle of a leaf is called the meso**phyll**.
	phys-		natural or medical science	**Phys**iology is the study of how organisms work naturally.
	phyt-		plant	A sporo**phyt**e is a plant that produces spores.
	pin-		wing	The **pin**na is the exterior portion of the ear, which in some species resembles a wing.
	pino-		to drink	Cells consume liquids during **pino**cytosis.
	plac-, plat-		flat	The **plac**enta is a flat disc of tissue where exchanges occur between mother and fetus.
	plankt-		wandering, drifting	**Plankt**on are organisms that drift with water currents.
	plas-, plasm-, plast-		something moulded or created	The cyto**plasm** is moulded to the form of the cell membrane.
	pleio-		more	A substance that is **pleio**tropic has more than one function.
pluri-			plus, more	A **pluri**potent cell can become more than one type of mature cell.
	pod-		foot	Deca**pod**s are arthro**pod**s with 10 feet.
	poie-		to make	Erythro**poie**tin is a hormone that stimulates the production of red blood cells.
	poll-		dust	**Poll**en has a dust-like texture.
poly-			many	**Poly**mers are made up of many pieces or monomers.
	por-		passage, pore	**Por**iferans have highly porous bodies.
	pos-		position	A trans**pos**able genetic element can change locations within the genome.
post-			after	**Post**zygotic barriers prevent hybrid organisms from developing into sexually mature adults.

Prefix	Root	Suffix	Meaning	Example
	pot-		to be powerful, to have ability	A multi**pot**ent stem cell has the ability to become a number of possible mature cells.
pre-, pro-			before	In mammals, the **pre**molars are situated in front of the molars.
proto-			first	Mouths of **proto**stomes develop from the first opening.
	prox-		to be near	The **prox**imal tubule in the kidney is closest to the glomerulus.
pseudo-			false	A **pseudo**podia is a foot-like projection used for cellular locomotion.
	pulmon-		lung	The **pulmon**ary circulations move blood from the heart to the lungs and back.
quat-			four, fourth	A protein's **quat**ernary structure is the fourth level of structure.
	rad-		to scrape	The **rad**ula of gastropods is used to scrape algae off of rocks.
	radi-		spoke of a wheel	The skeleton of the **radi**olarians has numerous projections that resemble the spokes of a wheel.
re-			again, back	**Re**spiration involves repeated inhalations and exhalations.
	rect-		straight	The **rect**um of some animals (for example, horses) is a very straight tube.
	ren-		kidney	The **ren**al vein carries blood from the kidney toward the heart.
	ret-		net, network	The endoplasmic **ret**iculum is a network of membranes within the cell.
	rhiz-, rrhiz-		root	Myco**rrhiz**ae are symbioses between fungi and plant roots.
	rumin-		to chew cud	**Rumin**ants such as cattle chew their cud to enhance digestion.
	sacch-		sugar	A mono**sacch**aride is a single sugar monomer.
	saliv-		spittle	**Saliv**ary glands produce saliva.
	sarc-		muscle	The **sarc**omere is the functional unit of muscle contraction.
	scis-		to cut	Ab**scis**ic acid is a plant hormone that prevents cell division, or the "cutting" of a mother cell into two daughter cells.
	scler-		hard	**Scler**enchyma cells have hardened cell walls.
	scop-		to view	Micro**scop**es allow biologists to see very small objects.
	scrib-, script-		to write	Tran**script**ion is essentially rewriting DNA as RNA.
	scrot-		shroud or garment	The **scrot**um enshrouds the testes of many mammals.
se-			aside, away	The law of **se**gregation describes how homologous chromosomes are moved away from each other during meiosis.
	secr-		to separate, to set apart	Cells can release products through **secr**etion.
	sem-, semin-		seed	**Sem**en is sperm-containing fluid, which is sometimes referred to as seed.
	sens-, sent-		to feel	**Sens**ation is the perception of information from the external environment.
	serv-		to keep safe	Con**serv**ation is the act of protecting wildlife.
	sess-		to sit	**Sess**ile organisms sit in one place and do not move.
	sin-		sinus, cavity	The human skull has six pairs of cavities, or **sin**uses.
	sit-		to feed	Para**sit**es were originally described as organisms that feed beside their host.
	skel-		dried up	The **skel**eton remains long after a dead organism has dried up or decayed.
	soci-		society, social	**Soci**al behaviour involves the interaction of two or more individuals.
	sol-, solv-		to loosen	A **solv**ent such as water can dissolve or loosen crystals of salt.
	som-		body	A lyso**som**e is a vacuole (or body) within a cell that is involved in the digestion of foreign particles.
	sorb-, sorp-		to suck in	When the intestine ab**sorb**s nutrients, it brings them into the body.

Prefix	Root	Suffix	Meaning	Example
	spat-		space	**Spat**ial learning modifies behaviour based on experiences in the three-dimensional environment.
	spec-		kind, sort	A **spec**ies is a specific kind of organism.
	sperm-		seed or semen, male gamete	Gymno**sperm**s are plants that produce naked seeds.
	spers-		to scatter	Many trees di**spers**e their seeds by having them scatter on the wind.
	spir-		to breathe	Re**spir**ation is the action of breathing.
	spir-		coil	**Spir**ochaetes are coil-shaped bacteria.
	spor-		seed, spore	In fungi, **spor**es germinate into new hyphae.
	stal-		to send, to contract	Peri**stal**sis sends food through the intestinal tract.
	stat-		to stand, to stop, to fix	An animal's hydro**stat**ic skeleton helps to maintain its shape.
	stear-, ster-		fat	**Ster**oids are a type of lipid molecule.
	stig-		pricking, mark, point	The **stig**ma is at the point of the flower's carpel.
	stol-		to contract	The contraction of the heart produces the sy**stol**ic blood pressure.
	stom-		mouth, opening	**Stom**ata are small openings in the dermis of leaves.
	strat-		layer	**Strat**a are layers of rock formed by sedimentation.
	strom-		covering	The **strom**a is the fluid that surrounds the thylakoids within a chloroplast.
sub-			below	The surface that an organism lives on is its **sub**strate.
	suspen-		to hang	Water molecules **suspen**d solutes in a solution.
sym-, syn-, sys-			together	In most **sym**biotic relationships, organisms live together.
	system-		organized whole, body	**System**s biology aims to understand the whole based on the interactions of the parts.
	tax-		arrangement	**Tax**onomists work to arrange species into related family groups.
	teg-		to cover over	The in**teg**umentary system includes the skin and its derivatives, which cover underlying tissues.
telo-			far off, occurring exceptionally	**Telo**meres are repetitive segments of DNA at the ends of chromosomes.
	tend-		to stretch	**Tend**ons, which attach muscles to bones, can stretch and store potential energy during running.
	terr-		earth, land	An animal's **terr**itory is the land in which it lives.
tert-			three, third	Interactions between R groups establish its third level or **tert**iary structure.
tetr-			four	**Tetr**apods are vertebrates with four legs.
	thel-		teat, nipple	The epi**thel**ium is the tissue that covers the body (breast) and lines internal surfaces.
	ther-		wild beast	Mammals with true placenta were considered proper beasts, or eu**ther**ians.
	therm-		heat	Endo**therm**ic animals generate body heat through metabolic reactions.
	thigm-		pressure or touch	**Thigm**otropism is a plant's directional growth in response to touch.
	tom-		to cut	The study of ana**tom**y involves dissection.
	ton-		stretching, tension	The **ton**icity of the extracellular solution can put tension on the cell if water is moved in or out.
	top-		place	Ec**top**ic pregnancies occur in places other than the uterus.
toti-			whole, total	A **toti**potent stem cell can become any other cell type.
	tox-		poison	Some bacteria produce **tox**ins, which can cause severe symptoms.
	trach-		neck	The airway through the neck is the **trach**ea.
trans-			across	Ions can be moved across a membrane by active or passive **trans**port.

Prefix	Root	Suffix	Meaning	Example
	trem-		hole	Parasitic **trem**atodes pierce holes through tissue as they feed and migrate.
	trop-		to turn in response to stimulus	Plant stems are photo**trop**ic and grow toward light.
	troph-		to eat	Auto**troph**s can feed themselves through photosynthesis.
		-type	kind	A karyo**type** displays a cell's chromosomes and can be used to determine the kind of cell.
		-ula, -ule	little	A ven**ule** is a small vein.
uni-			one	The **Uni**konta are organisms grouped by the presence of a single flagellum.
	ur-		urine, urinary system	The **ur**eter and **ur**ethra are ducts of the urinary system.
	uter-		womb	The **uter**us is often referred to as the womb.
	vacc-		cow	The original **vacc**ine was discovered when cow pox protected milkmaids from small pox.
	vacu-		empty	**Vacu**oles were once thought to be empty spaces within cells.
	vad-, vas-		to go, to walk	An in**vas**ive species is introduced (moves in) to another community.
	vagin-		sheath	The **vagin**a sheathes the penis during copulation.
	val-		to be strong, to be well	Atoms are bound strongly in a co**val**ent bond.
	valv-		fold, hinged shell	The shell of a bi**valv**e is in two hinged halves.
	vap-		steam, heat	Water e**vap**orates when heated.
	vas-		vessel	The cardio**vas**cular system includes the heart and a series of blood vessels.
	vect-		to carry, to convey	**Vect**ors can carry parasites from one host to another.
	vel-		veil, covering	The nuclear en**vel**ope surrounds the nucleus.
	ven-		vein	**Ven**ous blood is that which is flowing within the veins.
	ventr-		belly	An animal's belly is its **ventr**al surface.
	vers-		to turn	In**vers**ions are DNA mutations that involve a segment of a chromosome turning around.
	vertebr-		spine, joint of spine	**Vertebr**ates include all chordates with a spine.
	vesic-		bladder	A **vesic**le is a small bladder-like organelle within a cell.
	vill-		tuft, shaggy	Small intestinal **vill**i resemble shag carpet.
	vir-		poison	A **vir**ulent microorganism is able to cause disease in an organism.
	viscer-		entrails	The organs within the abdominal cavity of an animal are referred to as **viscer**a.
	vitr-		glass	In **vitr**o fertilization occurs in glass (in a laboratory).
	vor-		to eat	Herbi**vor**es eat only plant material.
	xyl-		wood	**Xyl**em is the major component of wood.
	zo-		animal	**Zo**oplankton has animal-like qualities.
	zyg-		yolk	A **zyg**ote is a diploid cell (a fertilized egg) containing yolk.

Answers to Chapter Review Questions

Chapter 1

1. The vertical scale of biology refers to the hierarchy of biological organization: from molecules to organelles, cells, tissues, organs, organ systems, organisms, populations, communities, ecosystems, and the biosphere. At each level, emergent properties arise from the interaction and organization of component parts. The horizontal scale of biology refers to the incredible diversity of living organisms, past and present, including the 1.8 million species that have been named so far. Biologists divide these species into three domains—Bacteria, Archaea, and Eukarya— and organize them into kingdoms and other groups that attempt to reflect evolutionary relationships.

2. a. life; b. evolution; c. natural selection; d. unity of life; e. three domains (or numerous kingdoms; 1.8 million species)

3. d 4. c 5. e (You may have been tempted to choose b, the molecular level. However, protists may have chemical communication or interactions with other protists. No protists, however, have organs.) 6. d 7. c 8. b 9. d

10. Both energy and chemical nutrients are passed through an ecosystem from producers to consumers to decomposers. But energy enters an ecosystem as sunlight and leaves as heat. Chemical nutrients are recycled from the soil or atmosphere through plants, consumers, and decomposers and returned to the air, soil, and water.

11. Darwin described how natural selection operates in populations whose individuals have varied traits that are inherited. When natural selection favours the reproductive success of certain individuals in a population more than others, the proportions of heritable variations change over the generations, gradually adapting a population to its environment.

12. In pursuit of answers to questions about nature, a scientist uses a logical thought process involving these key elements: observations about natural phenomena, questions derived from observations, hypotheses posed as tentative explanations of observations, logical predictions of the outcome of tests if the hypotheses are correct, and actual tests of hypotheses. The scientific method is not rigid because a scientist must adapt these processes to the set of conditions particular to each study. Intuition, chance, and luck are also part of science.

13. Technology is the application of scientific knowledge. For example, the use of solar power to run a calculator or heat a home is an application of our knowledge, derived by the scientific method, of the nature of light as a type of energy and how light energy can be converted to other forms of energy. Another example is the use of DNA to insert new genes into crop plants. This process, often called genetic engineering, stems from decades of scientific research on the structure and function of DNA from many kinds of organisms.

14. Natural selection screens (edits) heritable variations by favouring the reproductive success of some individuals over others. It can select only from the variations that are present in the population; it does not create new genes or variations.

15. a. *Hypothesis:* Giving rewards to mice will improve their learning. *Prediction:* If mice are rewarded with food, they will learn to run a maze faster.
    b. The control group was the mice that were not rewarded. The experimental group was made up of the mice that did receive a reward. Without the control group, it would be impossible to know if the mice that were rewarded decreased their time running the maze only because of practice.
    c. Both groups of mice should not have run the maze before and should be about the same age. Both experiments should be run at the same time of day and under the same conditions.
    d. Yes, the results fail to falsify the hypothesis because data show that the rewarded mice began to run the maze faster by day 3 and improved their performance (ran faster than the control mice) each day thereafter.

16. No, the conclusion is not justified. The researcher needed to compare the number of attacks on artificial king snakes with attacks on artificial brown snakes. It may be that there were simply more predators in the coral snake areas or that the predators were hungrier than the predators in the other areas. The experiment needed a control and proper data analysis.

17. If cell division control genes are involved in producing larger tomatoes, they may have similar effects if transferred to other fruits and vegetables. Cancer is a result of uncontrolled cell division. One could see if there are similarities between the tomato genes and any human genes that could be related to human development or disease. The control of cell division is a fundamental process in growth, repair, and asexual reproduction—all important topics in biology.

18. Virtually any news report or magazine contains stories that are mainly about biology or at least have biological connections. How about biological connections in advertisements?

Chapter 2

1. a. protons; b. neutrons; c. electrons; d. different isotopes; e. covalent bonds; f. ionic bonds; g. polar covalent bonds; h. hydrogen bonding

2.

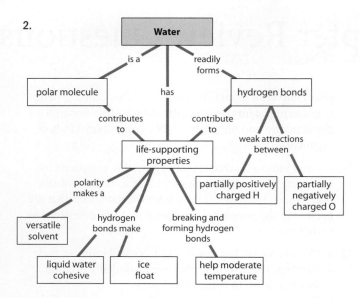

3. c 4. b 5. c 6. e 7. a (It needs to share 2 more electrons for a full outer shell of 8.) 8. a 9. c 10. d

11. F (Only salt and water are compounds; carbon is an element.)

12. F (The smallest unit of an element is an atom.) 13. T 14. T

15. F (Water molecules in ice are farther apart.)

16. T 17. F (Most acid precipitation results from burning fossil fuels.) 18. T

19. For a diagram, see Figure 2.8. Water molecules form hydrogen bonds because their slightly negative O atoms are attracted to the slightly positive H atoms of neighbouring molecules. The unique properties of water that result from hydrogen bonding are cohesion, adhesion, surface tension, the ability to absorb and store large amounts of heat and to release heat as water cools, a solid form (ice) that is less dense than liquid water, and solvent properties.

20. First: Because increasing the temperature of water (the average speed of its molecules) requires breaking hydrogen bonds, a process that absorbs heat, a large amount of heat can be added to water before the water's temperature starts to rise. Conversely, when the surrounding temperature falls, new hydrogen bonds form in water, with the release of heat that slows the cooling process. Second: When the body becomes overheated, water evaporating from its surface decreases the body's temperature (evaporative cooling) because the hotter water molecules leave.

21. A covalent bond forms when atoms complete their outer shells by sharing electrons. Atoms can also complete their outer shells by gaining or losing electrons. This leaves the atoms as ions, with + or − charges. The oppositely charged ions are attracted to each other, forming an ionic bond.

22. An acid is a compound that donates hydrogen ions (H^+) to a solution. A base is a compound that accepts hydrogen ions and removes them from a solution. Acidity is described by the pH scale, which measures H^+ concentration on a scale of 0 (most acidic) to 14 (most basic).

23. Fluorine needs 1 electron for a full outer shell of 8, and if potassium loses 1 electron, its outer shell will have 8. Potassium will lose an electron (becoming a + ion), and fluorine will pick it up (becoming a − ion). The ions can form an ionic bond.

24. The elements in a row all have the same number of electron shells. In a column, all the elements have the same number of electrons in their outer shell.

25. These extreme environments may be similar to those found on other planets. The fact that life may have evolved and continues to flourish in such extreme environments here on Earth suggests that some form of life may have evolved on other planets. Astrobiologists would want to study these extreme habitats and the adaptations to such challenging conditions that have evolved in extremophiles. In addition to seeking evidence for the past or current presence of water on Mars or other planets, scientists now know to search in environments that previously would have been thought incapable of supporting life.

Chapter 3

1. Carbon forms four covalent bonds, either with other carbon atoms, producing chains or rings of various lengths and shapes, or with other atoms, such as characteristic chemical groups that confer specific properties on a molecule. This is the basis for the incredible diversity of organic compounds. Organisms can link a small number of monomers into different arrangements to produce a huge variety of polymers.

2. a. glucose; b. energy storage; c. cellulose; d. fats; e. cell membrane component; f. steroids; g. amino group; h. carboxyl group; i. R group; j. enzyme; k. structural protein; l. movement; m. hemoglobin; n. defence; o. phosphate group; p. nitrogenous base; q. ribose or deoxyribose; r. DNA; s. code for proteins

3. d (The second kind of molecule is a polymer of the first.)

4. c 5. d 6. c 7. a 8. b 9. e 10. d

11. Fats (triglycerides)—energy storage. Phospholipids—major components of membranes. Steroids—cholesterol is a component of animal cell membranes; other steroids function as hormones.

12. Weak bonds that stabilize the three-dimensional structure of a protein are disrupted, and the protein unfolds. Function depends on shape, so if the protein is the wrong shape, it won't function properly.

13. Proteins are made of 20 amino acids arranged in many different sequences into chains of many different lengths. Genes, defined stretches of DNA, dictate the amino acid sequences of proteins in the cell.

14. Proteins function as enzymes, which catalyze chemical reactions. They also function in structure, movement, transport, defence, signalling, signal reception, and storage of amino acids (see Module 3.9).

15. The sequence of nucleotides in DNA is transcribed into a sequence of nucleotides in RNA, which determines the sequence of amino acids that will be used to build a polypeptide. Proteins mediate all the activities of a cell; thus, by coding for proteins, DNA controls the functions of a cell.

16. This is a hydrolysis reaction, which consumes water. It is essentially the reverse of the diagram in Figure 3.5, except that fructose has a different shape than glucose.

17. Circle NH$_2$, an amino group; COOH, a carboxyl group; and OH, a hydroxyl group on the R group. This is an amino acid, a monomer of proteins. The OH group makes it a polar amino acid.

18. a. A: at about 37°C; B: at about 78°C. b. A: from humans (human body temperature is about 37°C); B: from thermophilic bacteria. c. Above 40°C, the human enzyme denatures and loses its shape and thus its function. The increased thermal energy disrupts the weak bonds that maintain secondary and tertiary structure in an enzyme.

19. The atomic number represents the number of protons. Atoms without charge also have the same number of electrons within their electron shells. The first electron shell holds two electrons and the second and third each hold eight. With 14 electrons, silicon has four in its outer electron shell, as does carbon (with six electrons). One would predict that silicon could thus form complex molecules by binding with four partners. The 10 electrons of neon completely fill both of its electron shells, making neon nonreactive. Sulphur can form only two covalent bonds and thus would not have the versatility of carbon or silicon.

Chapter 4

1. a. nucleus; b. nucleolus; c. ribosomes; d. Golgi apparatus; e. plasma membrane; f. mitochondrion; g. cytoskeleton; h. peroxisome; i. centriole; j. lysosome; k. rough endoplasmic reticulum; l. smooth endoplasmic reticulum. For functions, see Table 4.22.

2. flagellum or cilia (some plant sperm cells have flagella), lysosome, centriole (involved with microtubule formation)

3. chloroplast, central vacuole, cell wall   4. d

5. c (Small cells have a greater ratio of surface area to volume.)   6. b   7. d   8. e   9. a   10. c   11. b   12. d   13. c

14. DNA as genetic material, ribosomes, plasma membrane, and cytoplasm

15. Tight junctions form leak-proof sheets of cells. Anchoring junctions link cells to each other; they form strong sheets of cells. Gap junctions are channels through which small molecules can move from cell to cell.

16. Both process energy. A chloroplast converts light energy to chemical energy (sugar molecules). A mitochondrion converts chemical energy (food molecules) to another form of chemical energy (ATP).

17. Different conditions and conflicting processes can occur simultaneously within separate, membrane-enclosed compartments. Also, there is increased area for membrane-attached enzymes that carry out metabolic processes.

18. Cilia may propel a cell through its environment or sweep a fluid environment past the cell.

19. A protein inside the ER is packaged inside transport vesicles that bud off the ER and then join to the Golgi apparatus. A transport vesicle containing the finished protein product then buds off the Golgi and travels to and joins with the plasma membrane, expelling the protein from the cell.

20. Part true, part false. All animal and plant cells have mitochondria; plant cells but not animal cells have chloroplasts.

21. The plasma membrane is a phospholipid bilayer with the hydrophilic heads facing the aqueous environment on both sides and the hydrophobic fatty acid tails mingling in the centre of the membrane. Proteins are embedded in and attached to this membrane. Microfilaments form a three-dimensional network just inside the plasma membrane. The extracellular matrix outside the membrane is composed largely of glycoproteins, which may be attached to membrane proteins called integrins. Integrins can transmit information from the ECM to microfilaments on the other side of the membrane.

22. Cell 1: S = 1,256 μm^2; V = 4187 μm^3; S/V = 0.3. Cell 2: S = 5,024 μm^2; V = 33,493 μm^3; S/V = 0.15. The smaller cell has a larger surface area relative to volume for absorbing food and oxygen and excreting waste. Small cells thus perform these activities more efficiently.

23. Individuals with PCD have nonfunctional cilia and flagella because of a lack of dynein motor proteins. This defect would also mean that the cilia involved in left-right pattern formation in the embryo would not be able to set up the fluid flow that initiates the normal arrangement of organs.

24. A single layer of phospholipids surrounding the oil droplet would have their hydrophobic fatty acid tails associated with the hydrophobic oil and their hydrophilic heads facing the aqueous environment of the cell outside the droplet.

Hydrophobic tails

Oil droplet

Hydrophilic head of phospholipid

Chapter 5

1. a. active transport; b. concentration gradient; c. small nonpolar molecules; d. facilitated diffusion; e. transport proteins

2. a. enzyme; b. active site of enzyme; c. substrate; d. substrate in active site—induced fit strains substrate bonds; e. substrate converted to products; f. product molecules released—enzyme is ready for next catalytic cycle

3. b **4.** d **5.** e **6.** c (Only active transport can move solute against a concentration gradient.) **7.** d **8.** b **9.** d **10.** b

11. Aquaporins are water transport channels that allow for very rapid diffusion of water through a cell membrane. They are found in cells that have high water transport needs, such as blood cells, kidney cells, and plant cells.

12. Energy is neither created nor destroyed but can be transferred and transformed. Plants transform the energy of sunlight into chemical energy stored in organic molecules. Almost all organisms rely on the products of photosynthesis for the source of their energy. In every energy transfer or transformation, disorder increases as some energy is lost to the random motion of heat. For example, we become warm when we exercise, as our muscles convert chemical energy to kinetic energy.

13. The work of cells falls into three main categories: mechanical, chemical, and transport. ATP provides the energy for cellular work by transferring a phosphate group to a protein (movement and transport) or to a substrate (chemical).

14. Energy is stored in the chemical bonds of organic molecules. The barrier of E_A prevents these molecules from spontaneously breaking down and releasing that energy. When a substrate fits into an enzyme's active site with an induced fit, its bonds may be strained and thus easier to break, or the active site may orient two substrates in such a way as to facilitate the reaction.

15. Cell membranes are composed of a phospholipid bilayer with embedded proteins. The bilayer creates the hydrophobic boundary between cells and their surroundings (or between organelles and the cytoplasm). The proteins perform the many functions of membranes, such as enzyme action, transport, attachment, and signalling.

16. Inhibitors that are toxins or poisons irreversibly inhibit key cellular enzymes. Inhibitors that are designed as drugs are beneficial, such as when they interfere with the enzymes of bacterial or viral invaders or cancer cells. Cells use feedback inhibition of enzymes in metabolic pathways as important mechanisms that conserve resources.

17. Heating, pickling, and salting denature enzymes, changing their shapes so they do not fit substrates. Freezing decreases the kinetic energy of molecules, so enzymes are less likely to interact with their substrates.

18. a. The more enzyme present, the faster the rate of reaction, because it is more likely that the enzyme and substrate molecules will meet.

b. The more substrate present, the faster the reaction—for the same reason as that given for answer a—but only up to a point. An enzyme molecule can work only so fast; once it is saturated (working at top speed), more substrate does not increase the rate.

19. The black curve on the left would correspond to the stomach enzyme pepsin, which has a lower optimal pH, as is found in the stomach; the red curve on the right would correspond to trypsin, which has a higher optimal pH. The curve for a lysosomal enzyme should have an optimal pH at 4.5.

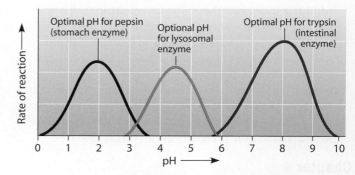

20. Some issues and questions to consider: Is improving crop yields of paramount importance in a world where many people can't get enough food? Does the fact that these compounds rapidly break down indicate that the risk to humans is low? How about the risks to people who work in agriculture or to other organisms, such as bees and other pollinating insects, birds, and small mammals? Might there be negative effects on ecosystems that are impossible to predict?

Chapter 6

1. a. glycolysis; b. citric acid cycle; c. oxidative phosphorylation; d. oxygen; e. electron transport chain; f. CO_2; g. H_2O

2. e **3.** c (NAD^+ and FAD, which are recycled by electron transport, are in limited supply in a cell.)

4. e **5.** d **6.** c **7.** b (at the same time NADH is oxidized to NAD^+) **8.** a

9. Glycolysis is considered the most ancient because it occurs in all living cells and doesn't require oxygen or membrane-enclosed organelles.

10. Oxygen picks up electrons from the oxidation of glucose at the end of the electron transport chain. Carbon dioxide results from the oxidation of glucose. It is released in the oxidation of pyruvate and in the citric acid cycle.

11. In lactic acid fermentation (in muscle cells), pyruvate is reduced by NADH to form lactate, and NAD^+ is recycled. In alcohol fermentation, pyruvate is broken down to CO_2 and ethanol as NADH is oxidized to NAD^+. Both types of fermentation allow glycolysis to continue to produce 2 ATP per glucose by recycling NAD^+.

12. As carbohydrates are broken down in glycolysis and the oxidation of pyruvate, glycerol can be made from G3P and fatty acids can be made from acetyl CoA. Amino groups, containing nitrogen atoms, must be supplied to various intermediates of glycolysis and the citric acid cycle to produce amino acids.

13. *After glycolysis:*

    4 glucose + 8 NAD^+ + 8 ADP + Ⓟ → 8 pyruvate + 8 NADH + 8 ATP (SLP)

    Acetyl CoA production:

    8 pyruvate + 8 CoA + 8 NAD^+ → 8 Acetyl CoA + 8 CO_2 + 8 NADH

    Citric acid cycle (8 rounds):

    8 Acetyl CoA + 24 NAD^+ + 8 FAD → 16 CO_2 + 24 NADH + 8 $FADH_2$ + 8 ATP (SLP)

    Electron transport chain:

    40 NADH + 8 $FADH_2$ + 112 ADP + 112 Ⓟ → 40 NAD^+ + 8 FAD + about 112 ATP (OP)

14. 100 kcal per day is 700 kcal per week. On the basis of Figure 6.4, walking 4.8 km/h would require 700/245 = about 2.9 h; walking 6.4 km/h, 2.1 h; swimming, 1.7 h; running, 0.7 h.

15. NAD^+ and FAD are coenzymes that are not used up during the oxidation of glucose. NAD^+ and FAD are recycled when NADH and $FADH_2$ pass the electrons they are carrying to the electron transport chain. We need a small additional supply to replace those that are damaged.

16. a. No, this graph shows the blue colour getting more intense. The reaction decolorizes the blue dye.
    b. No, this graph shows the dye being decolorized, but it also shows the three mixtures with different initial colour intensities. The intensities should have started out the same, since all mixtures used the same concentration of dye.
    c. Correct. The mixtures all start out the same, and then the ones with more succinate (reactant) decolorize faster.

17. The presence of ATP synthase enzymes in prokaryotic plasma membranes and the inner membrane of mitochondria provides support for the theory of endosymbiosis—that mitochondria evolved from an engulfed prokaryote that used aerobic respiration (see Module 4.15).

18. Some issues and questions to consider: Is your customer aware of the danger? Do you have an obligation to protect the customer, even against her wishes? Does your employer have the right to dismiss you for informing the customer? For refusing to serve the customer? Could you or the restaurant later be held liable for injury to the fetus? Or is the mother responsible for willfully disregarding warnings about drinking?

Chapter 7

1. a. electron transport chain; b. ATP synthase; c. thylakoid space; d. stroma; e. ATP. The higher H^+ concentration is found in the intermembrane space of the mitochondrion and in the thylakoid space of the chloroplast.

2. *In mitochondria:* a. Electrons come from food molecules. b. Electrons have high potential energy in the bonds in organic molecules. c. Electrons are passed to oxygen, which picks up H^+ and forms water; d. See below. *In chloroplasts:* a. Electrons come from splitting of water. b. Light energy excites the electrons to a higher energy level. c. Electrons flow from water to the reaction-centre chlorophyll in photosystem II to the reaction-centre chlorophyll in photosystem I to $NADP^+$, reducing it to NADPH. *In both processes:* d. Energy released by redox reactions in the electron transport chain is used to transport H^+ across a membrane. The flow of H^+ down its concentration gradient back through ATP synthase drives the phosphorylation of ADP to make ATP.

3. a. light energy; b. light reactions; c. Calvin cycle; d. O_2 released; e. the electron transport chain; f. NADPH; g. ATP; h. 3-PGA is reduced. **4.** c **5.** c **6.** a

7. c (NADPH and ATP from the light reactions are required by the Calvin cycle.) **8.** d **9.** e **10.** b **11.** c

12. Light reactions: Light and water are inputs; ATP, NADPH, and O_2 are outputs. Calvin cycle: CO_2, ATP, and NADPH are inputs; G3P is the output. Also, ADP and $NADP^+$ are inputs to the light reactions and outputs of the Calvin cycle.

13. The light reactions require ADP and $NADP^+$, which are not recycled from ATP and NADPH when the Calvin cycle stops.

14. Plants can break down the sugar for energy in cellular respiration or use the sugar as a raw material for making other organic molecules. Excess sugar is stored as starch.

15. Some issues and questions to consider: What are the risks that we take and costs we must pay if global warming continues? How certain do we have to be that warming is caused by human activities before we act? What can we do to reduce CO_2 emissions? Is it possible that the costs and sacrifices of reducing CO_2 emissions might actually improve our lifestyle?

16. Some issues and questions to consider: How much land would be required for large-scale conversion to biofuel production, and would that detract from land needed to produce food? Are there fertilizer needs and waste disposal issues with biofuel production? Is there a difference in net input and output of CO_2 between production and use of fossil fuels and production and use of biofuels? Which one offers a more long-term solution to energy needs? How do other alternative energy sources compare in costs, potential problems and pollution, and benefits?

Chapter 8

1.

	Mitosis	Meiosis
Number of chromosomal replications	1	1
Number of cell divisions	1	2
Number of daughter cells produced	2	4
Number of chromosomes in the daughter cells	Diploid (2n)	Haploid (n)
How the chromosomes line up during metaphase	Singly	In tetrads (metaphase I), and then singly (metaphase II)
Genetic relationship of the daughter cells to the parent cell	Genetically identical	Genetically unique
Function performed in the human body	Growth, development, and repair	Production of gametes

2. c 3. a 4. b 5. c

6. e (A diploid cell would have an even number of chromosomes; the odd number suggests that meiosis I has been completed. Sister chromatids are together only in prophase and metaphase of meiosis II.) 7. c 8. b 9. c 10. b 11. d

12. Mitosis without cytokinesis would result in a single cell with two nuclei. Multiple rounds of cell division like this could produce such a "megacell."

13. Various orientations of chromosomes at metaphase I of meiosis lead to different combinations of chromosomes in gametes. Crossing over during prophase I results in an exchange of chromosome segments and new combinations of genes. Random fertilization of eggs by sperm further increases possibilities for variation in offspring.

14. In culture, normal cells usually divide only when they are in contact with a surface but not touching other cells on all sides (the cells usually grow to form only a single layer). The density-dependent inhibition of cell division apparently results from local depletion of substances called growth factors. Growth factors are proteins secreted by certain cells that stimulate other cells to divide; they act via signal transduction pathways to signal the cell cycle control system of the affected cell to proceed past its checkpoints. The cell cycle control systems of cancer cells do not function properly. Cancer cells generally do not stop growing after making contact with neighbouring cells, nor do they require externally supplied growth factors to complete the cell cycle, and they divide indefinitely (in contrast to normal mammalian cells, which stop dividing after 20 to 50 generations)—two reasons why they are relatively easy to grow in the lab. Furthermore, cancer cells can often grow without contacting a solid surface, making it possible to culture them in suspension in a liquid medium.

15. *Interphase* (for example, third column from left in micrograph, third cell from top): Growth; metabolic activity; DNA synthesis. *Prophase* (for example, second column, cell at bottom): Chromosomes shorten and thicken; mitotic spindle forms. *Metaphase* (for example, first column, middle cell): Chromosomes line up at the metaphase plate. *Anaphase* (for example, third column, second cell from top): Sister chromatids separate and move to the poles of the cell. *Telophase* (for example, fourth column, fourth complete cell from top): Daughter nuclei form around chromosomes; cytokinesis usually occurs.

16. In both plant and animal cells, cytokinesis divides the cytoplasm and produces two daughter cells. A ring of microfilaments pinches an animal cell in two, a process called cleavage. In a plant cell, membranous vesicles form a disc called the cell plate at the midline of the parent cell, cell plate membranes fuse with the plasma membrane, and a cell wall grows in the space, separating the daughter cells.

17. See Figures 8.21A and 8.21B.

18. a. No. For this to happen, the chromosomes of the two gametes that fused would have to represent, together, a complete set of the donor's maternal chromosomes (the ones that originally came from the donor's mother) and a complete set of the donor's paternal chromosomes (from the donor's father). It is much more likely that the zygote would be missing one or more maternal chromosomes and would have an excess of paternal chromosomes, or vice versa. b. Correct. Consider what would have to happen to produce a zygote genetically identical to the gamete donor: The zygote would have to have a complete set of the donor's maternal chromosomes and a complete set of the donor's paternal chromosomes. The first gamete in this union could contain any mixture of maternal and paternal chromosomes, but once that first gamete was "chosen," the second one would have to have one particular combination of chromosomes—the combination that supplies whatever the first gamete did not supply. So, for example, if the first three chromosomes of the first gamete were maternal, maternal, and paternal, the first three of the second gamete would have to be paternal, paternal, and maternal. The chance that all 23 chromosome pairs would be complementary in this way is only 1 in 2^{23} (that is, one in 8,388,608). Because of independent assortment, it is much more likely that the zygote would have an unpredictable combination of chromosomes from the donor's father and mother. c. No. First, the zygote could be genetically identical to the gamete donor (see answer b). Second, the zygote could not be identical to either of the gamete donor's parents because the donor has only half the genetic material of each of his or her parents. For example, even if the zygote were formed by two gametes containing only paternal chromosomes, the combined set of chromosomes could not be identical to that of the donor's father because it would still be missing half of the father's chromosomes. d. No. See answer c.

19. Some possible hypotheses: The replication of the DNA of the bacterial chromosome takes less time than the replication of the DNA in a eukaryotic cell. The time required for a growing bacterium to roughly double its

cytoplasm is much less than for a eukaryotic cell. Bacteria have a cell cycle control system much simpler than that of eukaryotes.

20. $1 \text{ cm}^3 = 1000 \text{ mm}^3$, so 5000 cm^3 of blood contains $5000 \times 1000 \times 5\,000\,000 = 25\,000\,000\,000\,000$, or 2.5×10^{13}, red blood cells. The number of cells replaced each day $= 2.5 \times 10^{13}/120 = 2.1 \times 10^{11}$ cells. There are $24 \times 60 \times 60 = 86\,400$ seconds in a day. Therefore, the number of cells replaced each second $= 2.1 \times 10^{11}/86\,400 =$ about 2×10^6, or 2 million. Thus, about 2 million cell divisions must occur each second to replace red blood cells that are lost.

21. Each chromosome is on its own in mitosis; chromosome replication and the separation of sister chromatids occur independently for each horse or donkey chromosome. Therefore, mitotic divisions, starting with the zygote, are not impaired. In meiosis, however, homologous chromosomes must pair in prophase I. This process of synapsis cannot occur properly because horse and donkey chromosomes do not match in number or content.

Chapter 9

1. a. alleles; b. loci; c. homozygous; d. dominant; e. recessive; f. incomplete dominance

2. c 3. d 4. d (Neither parent is ruby-eyed, but some offspring are, so the allele is recessive. Different ratios among male and female offspring show that the trait is sex-linked.) 5. e

6. Genes on the single X chromosome in males are always expressed because there are no corresponding genes on the Y chromosome to mask them. A male needs only one recessive colourblindness allele (from his mother) to show the trait; a female must inherit the allele from both parents, which is less likely.

7. The parental gametes are WS and ws. Recombinant gametes are Ws and wS, produced by crossing over.

8. Height appears to be a quantitative trait resulting from polygenic inheritance, like human skin colour. See Module 9.13.

9.

	F	F
F	FF—Freckles	fF—Freckles
f	Ff—Freckles	ff—No freckles

The trait of freckles is dominant, so Tim and Jan must both be heterozygous. There is a ¾ chance that they will produce a child with freckles and a ¼ chance that they will produce a child without freckles. The probability that the next two children will have freckles is $¾ \times ¾ = \tfrac{9}{16}$.

10. As in question 9, both Tim and Jan are heterozygous, and Mike is homozygous recessive. The probability of the next child having freckles is ¾. The probability of the next child having a straight hairline is ¼. The probability that the next child will have freckles and a straight hairline is $¾ \times ¼ = \tfrac{3}{16}$.

11. The genotype of the black short-haired parent rabbit is BBSS. The genotype of the brown long-haired parent rabbit is bbss. The F₁ rabbits will all be black and short-haired, BbSs. Assuming the genes are not linked, the F₂ rabbits will be $\tfrac{9}{16}$ black short-haired, $\tfrac{3}{16}$ black long-haired, $\tfrac{3}{16}$ brown short-haired, and $\tfrac{1}{16}$ brown long-haired.

12. If the genes are not linked, the proportions among the offspring will be 25% grey red, 25% grey purple, 25% black red, and 25% black purple. The actual percentages show that the genes are linked. The recombination frequency is 6%.

13. The recombination frequencies are black dumpy 36%, purple dumpy 41%, and black purple 6% (see question 12). Since these recombination frequencies reflect distances between the genes, the sequence must be purple-black dumpy (or dumpy black-purple).

14. Of the couple's children, ¼ will be boys suffering from hemophilia, and ¼ will be female carriers. (The mother is a heterozygous carrier, and the father is normal.)

15. For a woman to be colourblind, she must inherit X chromosomes bearing the colourblindness allele from both parents. Her father has only one X chromosome, which he passes on to all his daughters, so he must be colourblind. A male need only inherit the colourblindness allele from a carrier mother; both his parents are usually phenotypically normal.

16. Start out by breeding the cat to get a population to work with. If the curl allele is recessive, two curl cats can have only curl kittens. If the allele is dominant, curl cats can have "normal" kittens. If the curl allele is sex-linked, ratios will differ in male and female offspring of some crosses. If the curl allele is autosomal, the same ratios will be seen among males and females. Once you have established that the curl allele is dominant and autosomal, you can determine if a particular curl cat is true-breeding (homozygous) by doing a testcross with a normal cat. If the curl cat is homozygous, all offspring of the testcross will be curl; if heterozygous, half of the offspring will be curl and half normal.

17. The hypothetical trait in the pedigree cannot be autosomal dominant because of the children of couples 3 and 4. Neither parent from this couple is affected, but the couple has an affected child. If the trait was autosomal dominant, at least one of the parents would be affected. Every instance of an affected person could be explained if the trait was autosomal recessive. If individuals 3 and 4 were carriers, they could produce an affected child. We do not know about individual 3, but individual 4 must have inherited a recessive allele from her mother. The trait could not be X-linked recessive because individual 5 would have inherited a copy of the recessive allele from his mother and therefore be affected.

Chapter 10

1. a. nucleotides; b. transcription; c. RNA polymerase; d. mRNA; e. rRNA; f. tRNA; g. translation; h. ribosomes; i. amino acids 2. d 3. a 4. e 5. b 6. c

7. *Ingredients:* Original DNA, nucleotides, several enzymes and other proteins, including DNA polymerase and DNA ligase. *Steps:* Original DNA strands separate at a specific

site (origin of replication), free nucleotides hydrogen-bond to each strand according to base-pairing rules, and DNA polymerase covalently bonds the nucleotides to form new strands. New nucleotides are added only to the 3′ end of a growing strand. One new strand is made in one continuous piece; the other new strand is made in a series of short pieces that are then joined by DNA ligase. *Final product:* Two identical DNA molecules, each with one old strand and one new strand.

8. A gene is the polynucleotide sequence with information for making one polypeptide. Each codon—a triplet of bases in DNA or RNA—codes for one amino acid. Transcription occurs when RNA polymerase produces RNA by using one strand of DNA as a template. In prokaryotic cells, the RNA transcript may immediately serve as mRNA. In eukaryotic cells, the RNA is processed: A cap and tail are added, and RNA splicing removes introns and links exons together to form a continuous coding sequence. A ribosome is the site of translation, or polypeptide synthesis, and tRNA molecules serve as interpreters of the genetic code. Each folded tRNA molecule has an amino acid attached at one end and a three-base anticodon at the other end. Beginning at the start codon, mRNA is moved relative to the ribosome a codon at a time. A tRNA with a complementary anticodon pairs with each codon, adding its amino acid to the polypeptide chain. The amino acids are linked by peptide bonds. Translation stops at a stop codon, and the finished polypeptide is released. The polypeptide folds to form a functional protein, sometimes in combination with other polypeptides.

9.

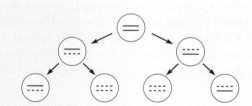

10. *mRNA:* GAUGCGAUCCGCUAACUGA. *Amino acids:* Met-Arg-Ser-Ala-Asn.

11. Some issues and questions to consider: Is it fair to issue a patent for a gene or gene product that occurs naturally in every human being? Or should a patent be issued only for something new that is invented rather than found? Suppose another scientist slightly modifies the gene or protein. How different does the gene or protein have to be to avoid patent infringement? Might patents encourage secrecy and interfere with the free flow of scientific information? What are the benefits to the holder of a patent? When research discoveries cannot be patented, what are the scientists' incentives for doing the research? What are the incentives for the institution or company that is providing financial support?

Chapter 11

1. a. proto-oncogene; b. repressor (or activator); c. cancer; d. operator; e. X inactivation; f. transcription factors; g. alternative RNA splicing

2. b (Different genes are active in different kinds of cells.)

3. c 4. b 5. b 6. e 7. b

8. A mutation in a single gene can influence the actions of many other genes if the mutated gene is a control gene, such as a homeotic gene. A single control gene may encode a protein that affects (activates or represses) the expression of a number of other genes. In addition, some of the affected genes may themselves be control genes that in turn affect other batteries of genes. Cascades of gene expression are common in embryonic development.

9. Black, because the DNA of the cell was obtained from a black mouse.

10. a. If the mutated repressor could still bind to the operator on the DNA, it would continuously repress the operon; enzymes for lactose utilization would not be made, whether or not lactose was present. b. The *lac* genes would continue to be transcribed and the enzymes made, whether or not lactose was present. c. Same predicted result as for answer b. d. RNA polymerase would not be able to transcribe the genes; no proteins would be made, whether or not lactose was present.

11. The protein to which dioxin binds in the cell is probably a transcription factor that regulates multiple genes (see Module 11.4). If the binding of dioxin influences the activity of this transcription factor—either activating or inactivating it—dioxin could thereby affect multiple genes and thus have a variety of effects on the body. The differing effects in different animals might be explained by differing genetic details in the different species.

Chapter 12

1. a. PCR; b. a restriction enzyme; c. gel electrophoresis; d. nucleic acid probe; e. cloning 2. d 3. c 4. b

5. c (Bacteria lack the RNA-splicing machinery needed to delete eukaryotic introns.) 6. b 7. d

8. Because it would be too expensive and time-consuming to compare whole genomes. By choosing STR sites that vary considerably from person to person, investigators can get the necessary degree of specificity without sequencing DNA.

9. Isolate plasmids from a culture of *E. coli.* Cut the plasmids and the human DNA containing the HGH gene with the restriction enzyme to produce molecules with sticky ends. Join the plasmids and the fragments of human DNA with ligase. Allow *E. coli* to take up recombinant plasmids. Bacteria will then replicate plasmids and multiply, producing clones of bacterial cells. Identify a clone carrying and expressing the HGH gene by using a nucleic acid probe. Grow large amounts of the bacteria and extract and purify HGH from the culture.

10. *Medicine:* Genes can be used to produce transgenic lab animals for AIDS research or for research related to human gene therapy. Proteins can be hormones, enzymes, blood-clotting factor, or the active ingredient of vaccines. *Agriculture:* Foreign genes can be inserted into plant cells

or animal eggs to produce transgenic crop plants or farm animals. Animal growth hormones are examples of agriculturally useful proteins that can be made using recombinant DNA technology.

11. She could start with DNA isolated from liver cells (the entire genome) and carry out the procedure outlined in Module 12.1 to produce a collection of recombinant bacterial clones, each carrying a small piece of liver cell DNA. To find the clone with the desired gene, she could then make a probe of radioactive RNA with a nucleotide sequence complementary to part of the gene: GACCUGACUGU. This probe would bind to the gene, labelling it and identifying the clone that carries it. Alternatively, the biochemist could start with mRNA isolated from liver cells and use it as a template to make cDNA (by using reverse transcriptase). Cloning this DNA rather than the entire genome would yield a smaller library of genes to be screened—only those active in liver cells. Furthermore, the genes would lack introns, making the desired gene easier to manipulate after isolation.

12. Determining the nucleotide sequences is just the first step. Once researchers have written out the DNA "book," they will have to try to figure out what it means—what the nucleotide sequences code for and how they work.

13. Some issues and questions to consider: What are some of the unknowns in recombinant DNA experiments? Do we know enough to anticipate and deal with possible unforeseen and negative consequences? Do we want this kind of power over evolution? Who should make these decisions? If scientists doing the research were to make the decisions about guidelines, what factors might shape their judgment? What might shape the judgment of business executives in the decision-making process? Does the public have a right to a voice in the direction of scientific research? Does the public know enough about biology to get involved in this decision-making process? Who represents "the public," anyway?

14. Some issues and questions to consider: What kinds of impact will gene therapy have on the individuals who are treated? On society? Who will decide what patients and diseases will be treated? What costs will be involved, and who will pay them? How do we draw the line between treating disorders and "improving" the human species?

15. Some issues and questions to consider: Should genetic testing be mandatory or voluntary? Under what circumstances? Why might employers and insurance companies be interested in genetic data? Since genetic characteristics differ among ethnic groups and between the sexes, might such information be used to discriminate? Which of these questions do you think is most important? Which issues are likely to be the most serious in the future?

Chapter 13

1. According to Darwin's theory of descent with modification, all life has descended from a common ancestral form as a result of natural selection. Individuals in a population have hereditary variations. The overproduction of offspring in the face of limited resources leads to a struggle for existence. Individuals that are well suited to their environment tend to leave more offspring than other individuals, leading to the gradual accumulation of adaptations to the local environment in the population.

2. a. Abiotic synthesis of important molecules from simpler chemicals in atmosphere, with lightning or UV radiation as energy source; b. Polymerization of monomers, perhaps on hot rocks; c. Enclosure within a lipid membrane, which maintained a distinct internal environment; d. Beginnings of heredity as RNA molecules replicated themselves. Natural selection could have acted on protocells that enclosed self-replicating RNA.

3. e 4. b (The birds are the lineage of dinosaurs that survived past the Cretaceous period.) 5. c

6. b (Among the choices, DNA sequences represent the closest link to the hereditary background and relationship to a common ancestor.) 7. c 8. c 9. b 10. d 11. b

12. Some evidence to include: fossils and the fossil record, biogeography, comparative anatomy, comparative embryology, DNA and protein comparisons, artificial selection, and examples of natural selection.

13. The latter are more likely to be closely related, because even small genetic changes can produce divergent physical appearances. But if genes have diverged greatly, it implies that lineages have been separate for some time, and the similar appearances may be have evolved independently and are not homologous.

14. Some issues and questions to consider: Who should decide curriculum, scientific experts in a field or members of the community? Are these alternative versions scientific ideas? Who judges what is scientific? Are the scientific theories presented testable? If it is fairer to consider alternatives, should the door be open to all alternatives? Are Charter issues (freedom of religion) involved here? Can teachers be compelled to teach an idea they disagree with? Should students be required to learn an idea they think is wrong?

15. 22 920 years old, a result of four half-life reductions

Chapter 14

1. Microevolution is the change in the gene pool of a population from one generation to the next. Macroevolution involves the pattern of evolutionary changes over large time spans and includes the origin of new groups and evolutionary novelties as well as mass extinctions.

2. a. genetic drift; b. gene flow; c. natural selection; d. small population; e. founder effect; f. bottleneck effect; g. unequal reproductive success 3. b 4. e 5. d 6. e

7. b (Erratic rainfall and unequal reproductive success would ensure that a mixture of both forms remained in the population.) 8. e 9. c 10. e

11. If $q^2 = 0.0025$, $q = 0.05$. Since $p \times q = 1$, $p = 1 - q = 0.95$. The proportion of heterozygotes is $2pq = 2 \times 0.95 \times 0.05 = 0.095$. About 9.5% of African-Canadians are carriers.

12. Genetic variation is retained in a population by diploidy and balancing selection. Recessive alleles are hidden from selection when in the heterozygote; thus, less adaptive or even harmful alleles are maintained in the gene pool and are available should environmental conditions change. Both heterozygote advantage and frequency-dependent selection tend to maintain alternative alleles in a population.

13. Complex structures can evolve by the gradual refinement of earlier versions of those structures, all of which served a useful function in each ancestor.

14. Where and when key developmental genes are expressed in a developing embryo can greatly affect the final form and arrangement of body parts. The regulation of gene expression allows these genes to continue to be expressed in some areas, turned off in other areas, and/or expressed at different times during development.

15. The unstriped snails appear to be better adapted. Striped snails make up 47.1% of the living population but 56.3% of the broken shells. Assuming that all the broken shells result from the meals of birds, we would predict that bird predation would reduce the frequency of striped snails and the frequency of unstriped individuals would increase.

16. A broad hypothesis would be that cultivated American cotton arose from a sequence of hybridization, mistakes in cell division, and self-fertilization. We can divide this broad statement into at least three hypotheses. *Hypothesis 1:* The first step in the origin of cultivated American cotton was hybridization between a wild American cotton plant (with 13 pairs of small chromosomes) and an Old World cotton plant (with 13 pairs of large chromosomes). If this hypothesis is correct, we would predict that the hybrid offspring would have had 13 small chromosomes and 13 large chromosomes. *Hypothesis 2:* The second step in the origin of cultivated American cotton was a failure of cell division in the hybrid offspring, such that all chromosomes were duplicated (now 26 small and 26 large). If this hypothesis is true, we would expect the resulting gametes to each have had 13 large chromosomes and 13 small chromosomes. *Hypothesis 3:* The third step in the origin of cultivated American cotton was self-fertilization of these gametes. If this hypothesis is true, we would expect the outcome of self-fertilization to be a hybrid plant with 52 chromosomes: 13 pairs of large ones and 13 pairs of small ones. Indeed, this is the genetic makeup of cultivated American cotton.

17. Some issues and questions to consider: One could look at this question in two ways: On the one hand, if the biological species concept is followed strictly, one could argue that red wolves and coyotes are the same species, since they can interbreed. Because coyotes are not rare, this line of argument would suggest that red wolves should not be protected. On the other hand, because red wolves and coyotes differ in many ways, they can be viewed as distinct species by other species concepts. Protecting the remaining red wolves from hybridizing with coyotes can preserve their distinct species status. The rationale behind protecting all endangered groups is the desire to preserve genetic diversity. Questions for society in general are as follows: What is the value of any particular species and its genetically distinct subgroups? And how far are we willing to go to preserve a rare and distinct group of organisms? How should the costs of preserving genetic diversity compare with the costs of other public projects?

Chapter 15

1. a. Allopatric speciation: Reproductive barriers may evolve between these two geographically separated populations as a by-product of the genetic changes associated with each population's adaptation to its own environment or as a result of genetic drift or mutation. b. Sympatric speciation: Some change, perhaps in resource use or female mate choice, may lead to a reproductive barrier that isolates the gene pools of these two populations, which are not separated geographically. Once the gene pools are separated, each species may go down its own evolutionary path. If speciation occurs by polyploidy—which is common in plants but unusual in animals—then the new species is instantly isolated from the parent species.

2. a. phylogeny; b. homologies; c. morphology; d. analogies; e. phylogenetic tree; f. outgroup; g. shared derived characters

3. b   4. c   5. b   6. a   7. d   8. c   9. c   10. a   11. d   12. e

13. Different physical appearances may indicate that organisms belong in different species; but, they may just be physical differences within a species. Isolated populations may or may not be able to interbreed; breeding experiments would need to be performed to determine this. Organisms that reproduce only asexually and fossil organisms do not have the potential to interbreed and produce fertile offspring; therefore, the biological species concept cannot apply to them.

14. There is more chance for gene flow between populations on a mainland and nearby island. This interbreeding would make it more difficult for reproductive isolation to develop and separate the two populations.

15. The ribosomal RNA genes, which specify the RNA parts of ribosomes, have evolved so slowly that homologies between even distantly related organisms can still be detected. Analysis of other homologous genes is also used.

16. Yes. Factors such as polyploidy, sexual selection, and habitat specialization can lead to reproductive barriers that would separate the gene pools of allopatric as well as sympatric populations.

17. If two species are actually breeding and producing hybrids, the reproductive barrier must be a postzygotic one. If the hybrids are sterile, reduced hybrid fertility is the reproductive barrier. However, if the hybrids can mate and produce offspring, which are feeble or sterile, then the barrier is hybrid breakdown. In the case of the Dall's-harbour porpoise hybrid, evidence that hybrids can

become pregnant indicates that the reproductive barrier is hybrid breakdown.

18. By decreasing the ability of females to distinguish males of their own species, the polluted turbid waters of Lake Victoria have increased the frequency of mating between members of species that had been reproductively isolated from one another. As the number of hybrid fish increase, the parent species' gene pools may fuse, resulting in a loss of the two separate parent species and the formation of a new hybrid species. Future speciation events in Lake Victoria cichlids are less likely to occur in turbid water because females are less able to base mate choice on male breeding colour. Reducing the pollution in the lake may help to reverse this trend.

19.

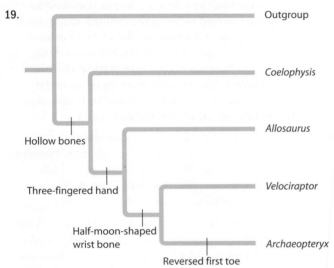

20. Some issues and questions to consider: Whereas previous mass extinctions have resulted from catastrophic events, such as asteroid collisions or volcanism, a sixth mass extinction would be caused by a single species—the result of human-caused environmental alteration. Mass extinctions can reduce complex ecological communities to much simpler ones. It can take millions of years for diversity to recover from a mass extinction. Do we have an ethical responsibility to preserve other species? By disrupting ecological communities throughout the world, a sixth mass extinction would have great consequences for all species alive today—including humans.

Chapter 16

1. a. binding; b. entry; c. viral nucleic acid; d. nucleic acid replication; e. viral RNA; f. translation; g. viral proteins (capsomeres); h. assembly; i. release

2. a. double stranded; b. reverse transcriptase; c. minus-strand; d. RNA replicase; e. RNA polymerase; f. plus-strand; g. minus-strand; h. ribosomes; i. new viral dsRNA

3. e (Only the phage DNA enters a host cell; lambda DNA determines both DNA and protein.)

4. a 5. b 6. e 7. b 8. c 9. d 10. a

11. The two replicative cycles of the lambda phage are the lytic and lysogenic cycles. During the lysogenic cycle, the virus DNA becomes a prophage as it enters the host chromosome. As a prophage, the virus remains dormant and is replicated along with the bacterial chromosome during binary fission. Harsh environmental conditions typically trigger the switch to the lytic cycle. First, the prophage leaves the host chromosome and is copied several hundred times. Synthesis of viral proteins begins and new viruses are assembled. Production of lysozymes weakens the cell wall and the bacterium lyses, releasing new viruses.

12. The three hypotheses for viral origin are the reduction, escape, and co-evolution hypotheses. The reduction and escape hypotheses are similar in that they both assume that cells were present before the first viruses, but the co-evolution hypothesis does not assume this. The reduction hypothesis suggests that viruses evolved from cellular pathogens and that natural selection favoured the extreme reduction into the form of a virus. The escape hypothesis states that genetic elements escaped from the host genome and became the first viruses. The co-evolution hypothesis suggests that viruses are even more ancient than the first cells, evolving from the primordial RNA gene pool.

13. When certain insects feed on an infected plant, they may ingest viruses. These viruses can persist for a period of time on or in the insect. During this time, the plant viruses are not replicating. Some viruses adhere to the insect's biting mouthparts for a short time. If the insect feeds within a few hours, viruses may dislodge and enter the new plant. Other plant viruses are ingested but penetrate the intestinal wall of the insect. After migrating to the salivary glands, they can be injected into a new plant host several weeks after being swallowed.

14. Air travel allows people to fly halfway around the world in less than a day. This means someone can become infected in an endemic area and, unknowingly carrying a virus, travel to any other city on the planet before exhibiting signs of infection. Airports are crowded places, increasing the odds of transmission from person to person. Taken together, these situations mean that viruses can spread globally in a very short time.

15. Viruses are simply nucleic acids surrounded by a protein capsid or, in some cases, by an envelope. After viruses are released into the environment from a cell or host, they are metabolically inert. They do not contain enzymes that cells use for any metabolic process. Therefore, antibiotics that block these cellular processes would have no effect on the viruses.

Chapter 17

1. *Cell wall:* maintains cell shape; provides physical protection; prevents cell from bursting in a hypotonic environment; *Capsule:* enables cell to stick to substrate or to other individuals in a colony; shields pathogens from host's defensive cells; *Flagella:* provide motility, enabling cell to respond to chemical or physical signals in the environment that lead to nutrients or other members of their species and away from toxic substances; *Fimbriae:* allow cells to attach to surfaces, including host cells, or to each other; *Endospores:* withstand harsh conditions.

2. Bacteria and Archaea have many significant differences, which clearly place them in different domains. Each domain has unique rRNA sequences, but the archaea and eukaryotes have some that match. Bacteria have one kind of RNA polymerase, whereas archaea and eukaryotes have several. Introns are rare in bacteria, present in most eukaryotic genes, and found in some genes of archaea. Bacteria have peptidoglycan in their cell walls, archaea have a related molecule, and the eukarya can have cellulose or chitin. Histones are associated with eukaryotic DNA but not bacterial DNA; some species of Archaea have histones.

3. b 4. b 5. e 6. c 7. d 8. a 9. b

10. Rapid rate of reproduction enables bacteria to colonize favourable habitats quickly. The production of large numbers of cells by binary fission results in a great deal of genetic variation, making it more likely that some individuals will survive—and be able to recolonize the habitat—if the environment changes again.

11. The scientist would test the hypothesis by using Koch's postulates. First, the bacterium must be present in all cases of the disease. Secondly, the bacterium must be isolated from an individual with the disease and grown in pure culture. Then, when the bacterium is given to a healthy subject, they should develop the disease. Finally, the bacterium must be isolated from the experimentally infected subject. If all four postulates are fulfilled, the hypothesis is supported.

12. Biofilms can form on solid substrates or the surface of stagnant water. First, bacteria release signalling molecules that attract other bacteria, which clump together. As the cluster starts to grow, an extracellular matrix made of polysaccharides and a complex three-dimensional structure is produced. Biofilms affect human life in many ways. Dental plaque is a biofilm that causes tooth decay. Patients with cystic fibrosis may suffer from hard to treat biofilms growing in their lungs. They can grow on surgical implants and are not sensitive to antibiotic treatments. Biofilms grow in pipelines where they increase drag and the cost of piping liquids such as water and oil. Killing biofilms requires higher concentrations of chlorine, increasing the cost of water treatment.

13. This is not a good idea; all life depends on bacteria. You could predict that eliminating all bacteria from an environment would result in a buildup of toxic wastes and dead organisms (both of which bacteria decompose), a shutdown of all chemical cycling, and the consequent death of all organisms.

14. Farmers could stop adding antibiotics to livestock feed. This would remove needless exposure to antibiotics and prolonged exposure increases the risk. Doctors could take cultures from patients to verify bacterial infection before prescribing antibiotics. Antibiotics do not affect viruses and prescribing them for a viral infection is needless exposure. Patients should not stop taking antibiotics partway through their prescriptions. Even though they may feel better, bacteria are still present and stopping the dose

prematurely may cause the remaining bacteria to acquire resistance. One could avoid using products containing triclosan, which has been attributed to producing resistance in bacteria, even to antibiotics they haven't been exposed to.

Chapter 18

1. a. archaeplastids; b. charophytes; c. unikonts; d. fungi; e. choanoflagellates; f. animals

2. a. fusion of cytoplasm; b. heterokaryotic stage $(n + n)$; c. fusion of nuclei; d. zygote ($2n$); e. meiosis; f. spores (n); g. mycelium (n); h. spores (n); i. germination

3. c 4. b 5. d 6. d 7. b 8. e 9. a 10. b

11. Small, free-living prokaryotes were probably engulfed by a larger cell and took up residence inside. A symbiotic relationship developed between the host cell and engulfed cells, which became mitochondria. By a similar process, heterotrophic eukaryotic cells engulfed cyanobacteria, which became chloroplasts. Lineages of these autotrophic cells diverged into red and green algae. Secondary endosymbiosis of eukaryotic cells by red and green algae gave rise to diverse lineages of protists.

12. *Chlamydomonas* is a eukaryotic cell containing membrane-bound organelles, and is much more complex than a prokaryotic bacterium. It is autotrophic, while amoebas are heterotrophic. It is unicellular, unlike multicellular sea lettuce.

13. In the haploid (n) stage of a fungal life cycle, each cell has only one set of chromosomes within its nucleus. In a diploid ($2n$) cell, each nucleus has two sets of chromosomes; one set from each parent. The heterokaryotic ($n + n$) stage occurs after membrane fusion and is distinct in that each cell has two distinct haploid nuclei. Eventually, the nuclear fusion produces the diploid nucleus of the zygote.

14. Some issues and questions to consider: Could we determine beforehand whether the iron would really have the desired effect? How? Would the "fertilization" need to be repeated? Could it be a cure for the problem, or would it merely treat the symptoms? Might the iron treatment have side effects? What might they be?

15. Antibiotics probably kill off bacteria that compete with fungi for food. Similarly, bad tastes and odours deter animals that eat or compete with fungi. Those fungi that produce antibiotics or bad-smelling and bad-tasting chemicals would survive and reproduce more successfully than fungi unable to inhibit competitors. Animals that could recognize the smells and tastes as being detrimental to their health and avoid them would also survive and reproduce better than their competitors. Thus, natural selection would favour fungi that produce the chemicals and, to some extent, the competitors deterred by them.

Chapter 19

1. a. bryophytes (nonvascular plants); b. seedless vascular plants (ferns and relatives); c. gymnosperms; d. angiosperms; 1. apical meristems and embryos retained in the

parent plant; 2. lignin-hardened vascular tissue; 3. seeds that protect and disperse embryos

2. a. sporophyte plant (*2n*); b. meiosis; c. haploid (*n*); d. gametophyte plant; e. mitosis; f. haploid (*n*); g. egg; h. fertilization; i. mitosis 3. b

4. c (It is the only gametophyte among the possible answers.)

5. a 6. e 7. a 8. a (The zucchini develops from the ovary in a flower; all the other choices do not come from flowers.)

9. c 10. d

11. The alga is surrounded and supported by water, and it has no supporting tissues, vascular system, or special adaptations for obtaining or conserving water. Its whole body is photosynthetic, and its gametes and embryos are dispersed into the water. The seed plant has lignified vascular tissues that support it against gravity and carry food and water. The seed plant also has specialized organs that absorb water and minerals (roots), provide support (stems and roots), and photosynthesize (leaves and stems). It is covered by a waterproof cuticle and has stomata for gas exchange. Its sperm are carried by pollen grains, and embryos develop on the parent plant and are then protected and provided for by seeds.

12. Gymnosperm pollen is generally carried to the ovule by the wind, whereas the pollen of angiosperms may be carried to the stigma by the wind or by animals, and then extend a pollen tube to the ovule. Gymnosperm seeds develop within ovules located in the female cones and angiosperm seeds develop in ovules within the ovary of a flower. In both gymnosperms and angiosperms, the ovule wall becomes the seed coat and the embryo forms after fertilization of the egg by the sperm. Mature gymnosperm seeds are dispersed by the wind. Angiosperm seeds may be dispersed by wind or by animals, either through their digestive tracts or by clinging to their bodies.

13. Animals carry pollen from flower to flower and thus help to fertilize the plants' eggs. They also disperse seeds by consuming fruit or carrying fruit that clings to their fur. In return, they get food (nectar, pollen, fruit).

14. Plants are autotrophs; they have chlorophyll and make their own food by photosynthesis. Fungi are heterotrophs that digest food externally and absorb nutrient molecules. There are also many structural differences; for example, the threadlike fungal mycelium is different from the plant body, and their cell walls are made of different substances. Plants evolved from green algae, which belong to the protist supergroup Archaeplastida; the ancestor of fungi was in the protist supergroup Unikonta. Molecular evidence indicates that fungi are more closely related to animals than to plants.

15. Moss gametophytes, the dominant stage in the moss life cycle, are haploid plants. The diploid (sporophyte) generation is dominant in most other plants. Recessive mutations are not expressed in a diploid organism unless both homologous chromosomes carry the mutation. In haploid organisms, recessive mutations are apparent in the phenotype of the organism because haploid organisms have only one set of chromosomes. Some factors to consider in designing your experiment: What are the advantages/disadvantages of performing the experiment in the laboratory? In the field? What variables would be important to control? How many potted plants should you use? At what distances from the radiation source should you place them? What would serve as a control group for the experiment? What age of plants should you use?

Chapter 20

1.

Phylum	Characteristics	Representatives
Sponges	Sessile, saclike body with pores, suspension feeder	Sponges
Cnidarians	Radial symmetry, gastrovascular cavity, cnidocytes, polyp or medusa body form	Hydras, sea anemones, jellies, corals
Flatworms	Bilateral symmetry, gastrovascular cavity, no body cavity	Free-living planarians, flukes, tapeworms
Nematodes	Pseudocoelom, covered with cuticle, complete digestive tract, ubiquitous, free-living and parasitic	Roundworms, heartworms, hookworms, trichinosis worms
Molluscs	Muscular foot, mantle, visceral mass, circulatory system, many with shells, radula in some	Snails and slugs, bivalves, cephalopods (squids and octopi)
Annelids	Segmented worms, closed circulatory system, many organs repeated in each segment	Earthworms, polychaetes, leeches
Arthropods	Exoskeleton, jointed appendages, segmentation, open circulatory system	Chelicerates (spiders), crustaceans (lobsters, crabs), millipedes and centipedes, insects
Echinoderms	Radial symmetry as adult, water vascular system with tube feet, endoskeleton, spiny skin	Sea stars, sea urchins
Chordates	Notochord; dorsal, hollow nerve cord; pharyngeal slits; post-anal tail	Tunicates, lancelets, hagfish, and all the vertebrates (lampreys, sharks, ray-finned fishes, lobe-fins, amphibians, reptiles (including birds), mammals)

2. c 3. d 4. a (The invertebrates include all animals except the vertebrates.) 5. d 6. c 7. i 8. f 9. e 10. c 11. a 12. d 13. h 14. b 15. g

16. The gastrovascular cavity of a flatworm is an incomplete digestive tract; the worm takes in food and expels waste through the same opening. An earthworm has a complete digestive tract; food travels one way, and different areas are specialized for different functions. The flatworm's body is solid and unsegmented. The earthworm has a true coelom, allowing its internal organs to grow and move independently of its outer body wall. Fluid in the coelom cushions internal organs, acts as a skeleton, and aids circulation. Segmentation of the earthworm, including its coelom, allows for greater flexibility and mobility.

17. Cnidarians and most adult echinoderms are radially symmetric, while most other animals, such as arthropods and chordates, are bilaterally symmetric. Most radially symmetric animals stay in one spot or float passively. Most bilateral animals are more active and move headfirst through their environment.

18. For example, the legs of a horseshoe crab are used for walking, while the antennae of a grasshopper have a sensory function. Some appendages on the abdomen of a lobster are used for swimming, while the scorpion catches prey with its pincers. (Note that the scorpion stinger and insect wings are not considered jointed appendages.)

19. Both trees agree on the early branching of eumetazoans into two groups based on body symmetry and the number of cell layers formed in gastrulation. Both trees recognize deuterostomes as a clade of bilaterians. In the morphological tree, protostomes are a second clade of bilaterians. The molecular tree distinguishes two clades within the protostomes, lophotrochozoans and ecdysozoans.

20. Important characteristics include symmetry, the presence and type of body cavity, segmentation, type of digestive tract, type of skeleton, and appendages.

21. The three phyla of worms discussed in this book are Platyhelminthes (the flatworms), Nematoda (the roundworms), and Annelida (the segmented worms). To determine which of these three phyla the unknown worm belongs to, you should ask about its body shape. Nematodes and most annelids are round in cross-section, whereas platyhelminthes are flattened. You should also ask if rings can be seen along the worm's body length. Annelids have rings (indicative of segmentation), but nematodes and platyhelminthes do not. A third question you should ask is whether the worm has a cuticle. Nematodes have a tough cuticle, but the other worms do not.

Chapter 21

1. a. Old World monkeys; b. gibbons; c. orangutans; d. gorillas; e. chimpanzees. All are anthropoids; gibbons, orangutans, gorillas, chimpanzees, and humans are apes.

2. a. brain; b. head; c. vertebral column; d. jaws; e. lungs or lung derivatives; f. lobed fins; g. legs; h. amniotic egg; i. milk

3. c 4. c 5. b 6. b 7. c 8. c 9. a

10. Amphibians have four limbs adapted for locomotion on land, a skeletal structure that supports the body in a nonbuoyant medium, and lungs. However, most amphibians are tied to water because they obtain some of their oxygen through thin, moist skin and they require water for fertilization and development. Reptiles are completely adapted to life on land. They have amniotic eggs that contain food and water for the developing embryo and a shell to protect it from dehydration. Reptiles are covered by waterproof scales that enable them to resist dehydration (more efficient lungs eliminate the need for gas exchange through the skin).

11. Fossil evidence supports the evolution of birds from a small, bipedal, feathered dinosaur, which was probably endothermic. The last common ancestor that birds and mammals shared was the ancestral amniote. The four-chambered hearts of birds and mammals must have evolved independently.

12. Several primate characteristics make it easy for us to make and use tools—mobile digits, opposable fingers and thumb, and great sensitivity of touch. Primates also have forward-facing eyes, which enhances depth perception and eye-hand coordination, and a relatively large brain.

13. The paleontologists who discovered *Tiktaalik* hypothesized the existence of transitional forms between fishlike tetrapods such as *Panderichthys* and tetrapod-like fish such as *Acanthostega*. From the available evidence, they knew the time periods when fishlike tetrapods and tetrapod-like fish lived. From the rocks in which the fossils had been found, they knew the geographic region and the type of habitat these creatures occupied. With this knowledge, they predicted the type of rock formation where transitional fossils might be found.

14. Our intelligence and culture—accumulated and transmitted knowledge, beliefs, arts, and products—have enabled us to overcome our physical limitations and alter the environment to fit our needs and desires.

15. Most anthropologists think that humans and chimpanzees diverged from a common ancestor 6–7 million years ago. Primate fossils 4–8 million years old might help us understand how the human lineage first evolved.

If, however, the ice water cooled the blood vessel that supplies the thermostat in your brain so that it sensed a decrease in temperature, this control centre would respond by inhibiting sweating and constricting blood vessels in the skin, thereby slowing the cooling of your body.

21. People who cannot sweat will not be able to use evaporative cooling to help maintain their body temperature on a hot summer day. Although they may still lose some heat from dilated capillaries in their skin, this method of cooling is far less efficient without sweat. They could spray water on their skin to regain the benefits of this cooling technique. Otherwise, they should stay in the shade as much as possible.

Chapter 26

1. a. oral cavity—ingests and chews food; b. salivary glands—produce saliva; c. liver—produces bile and processes nutrient-laden blood from intestines; d. gallbladder—stores bile; e. pancreas—produces digestive enzymes and bicarbonate; f. rectum—stores feces before elimination; g. pharynx—site of openings into esophagus and trachea; h. esophagus—transports bolus to stomach by peristalsis; i. stomach—stores food, mixes food with acid, begins digestion of proteins; j. small intestine—digestion and absorption; k. large intestine—compacts feces; l. anus—eliminates feces

2. a. fuel, chemical energy; b. raw materials, monomers; c. essential nutrients; d. overnutrition or obesity; e. vitamins and minerals; f. essential amino acids; g. malnutrition

3. e 4. e 5. c 6. c 7. b 8. d 9. e

10. You ingest the sandwich one bite at a time. In the oral cavity, chewing begins mechanical digestion, and salivary amylase action on starch begins chemical digestion. When you swallow, food passes through the pharynx and esophagus to the stomach. Mechanical and chemical digestion continues in the stomach, where HCl in gastric juice breaks apart food cells and pepsin begins protein digestion. In the small intestine, enzymes from the pancreas and intestinal wall break down starch, protein, and nucleic acids to monomers. Bile from the liver and gallbladder emulsifies fat droplets for attack by enzymes. Most nutrients are absorbed into the bloodstream through the villi of the small intestine. Fats travel through lymph vessels. In the large intestine, absorption of water is completed, and undigested material and intestinal bacteria are compacted into feces, which are eliminated through the anus.

11. Our craving for fatty foods may have evolved from the feast-and-famine existence of our ancestors. Natural selection may have favoured individuals who gorged on and stored high energy molecules, as they were more likely to survive famines.

12. There are multiple advantages to eating fresh fruits and vegetables. First, they are nutrient dense, providing substantial amounts of vitamins, minerals, and other nutrients and relatively few calories. Fruit and vegetables are

typically low in cholesterol and many will lower your blood LDLs (bad cholesterol) and raise HDLs (good cholesterol). Many fruits and vegetables contain antioxidants that help to lower the risk of certain cancers.

13. Some issues and questions to consider: What are the roles of family, school, advertising, media, and government in providing nutritional information? How might the available information be improved? What types of scientific studies form the foundation of various nutritional claims?

14. Some issues and questions to consider: In wealthy countries, what are the factors that make it difficult for some people to get enough food? In your community, what types of help exist to feed hungry people? Think of two recent food crises in other countries and what caused them. Did other countries or international organizations provide aid? Which ones, and how did they help? Did that aid address the underlying causes of malnutrition and starvation in the stricken area or provide only temporary relief? How might that aid be changed to offer more permanent solutions to food shortages?

Chapter 27

1. a. respiratory surface; b. circulatory system; c. lungs; d. hemoglobin; e. cellular respiration; f. negative pressure breathing; g. O_2

2. a. nasal cavity; b. pharynx; c. larynx; d. trachea; e. right lung; f. bronchus; g. bronchiole; h. diaphragm

3. c 4. b 5. d 6. a 7. e 8. d 9. c

10. An advantage of breathing air is that air has a higher concentration of O_2 than water and is easier to move over the respiratory surface. A disadvantage is that living cells on the respiratory surface must remain moist, but breathing air dries out this surface.

11. Nasal cavity, pharynx, larynx, trachea, bronchus, bronchiole, alveolus, through wall of alveolus into blood vessel, blood plasma, into red blood cell, attaches to hemoglobin, carried by blood through heart, blood vessel in muscle, dropped off by hemoglobin, out of red blood cell, into blood plasma, through capillary wall, through interstitial fluid, and into muscle cell

12. Several key adaptations must have occurred in the evolution of cloacal gill respiration. Structurally, the ancestral bursae would have become much larger structures present in the Fitzroy River turtle. Also, adaptation of the bursa lining would have included structures to greatly increase its surface area. Combined, these two adaptations create a large surface area for gas exchange. The capillary beds, already present in the digestive tract, may have become more extensive in parallel. Behaviourally, the action of bringing water through the cloaca, into the lower digestive tract, would be necessary for ventilation.

13. Both these effects of CO interfere with cellular respiration and the production of ATP. By binding more tightly to hemoglobin, CO would decrease the amount of O_2 picked up in the lungs and delivered to body cells. Without

sufficient O_2 to act as the final electron acceptor, cellular respiration would slow. And by blocking electron flow in the electron transport chain, cellular respiration and ATP production would cease. Without ATP, cellular work stops and cells and organisms die.

14. Llama hemoglobin has a higher affinity for O_2 than does human hemoglobin. The dissociation curve shows that its hemoglobin becomes saturated with O_2 at the lower PO_2 of the high altitudes to which llamas are adapted. At this PO_2, of high altitudes, human hemoglobin is only 80% saturated.

15. The athlete's body would respond to training at high altitudes or sleeping in an artificial atmosphere with lower PO_2 by producing more red blood cells. Thus, the athlete's blood would carry more O_2, and this increase in aerobic capacity may improve endurance and performance.

16. Insects have a tracheal system for gas exchange. To provide O_2 to all the body cells in such a huge moth, the tracheal tubes would have to be wider (to provide enough ventilation across longer distances) and very extensive (to service large flight muscles and other tissues), thus presenting problems of water loss and increased weight. Both the tracheal system and the weight of the exoskeleton limit the size of insects.

Chapter 28

1. a. capillaries of head, chest, and arms; b. aorta; c. pulmonary artery; d. capillaries of left lung; e. pulmonary vein; f. left atrium; g. left ventricle; h. aorta; i. capillaries of abdominal region and legs; j. inferior vena cava; k. right ventricle; l. right atrium; m. pulmonary vein; n. capillaries of right lung; o. pulmonary artery; p. superior vena cava. See Figure 28.11A for numbers and red vessels that carry oxygen-rich blood.

2. a. filtration: water; NaCl, HCO_3^-, H^+, urea, glucose, amino acids, some drugs; b. reabsorption: nutrients, NaCl, water, HCO_3^-, urea; c. secretion: some drugs and toxins, H^+, K^+; d. excretion: urine containing water, urea, and excess ions

3. b 4. d (The second sound is the closing of the semilunar valves as the ventricles relax.) 5. c 6. c 7. a 8. b 9. a 10. d 11. a 12. e

13. Pulmonary vein, left atrium, left ventricle, aorta, artery, arteriole, body tissue capillary bed, venule, vein, vena cava, right atrium, right ventricle, pulmonary artery, capillary bed in lung, pulmonary vein

14. a. Plasma (the straw-coloured fluid) would contain water, inorganic salts (ions such as sodium, potassium, calcium, magnesium, chloride, and bicarbonate), plasma proteins such as fibrinogen and immunoglobulins (antibodies), and substances transported by blood, such as nutrients (for example, glucose, amino acids, vitamins), waste products of metabolism, a small amount of respiratory gases (O_2 and CO_2), and hormones.
    b. The red portion would contain erythrocytes (red blood cells), leukocytes (white blood cells—basophils, eosinophils, neutrophils, lymphocytes, and monocytes), and platelets.

15. Oxygen content is reduced as oxygen-poor blood returning to the right ventricle from the systemic circuit mixes with oxygen-rich blood of the left ventricle.

16. Proteins are important solutes in blood, accounting for much of the osmotic pressure that counters the flow of fluid out of a capillary. If protein concentration is reduced, the inward pull of osmotic pressure will fail to balance the outward push of blood pressure, and more fluid will leave the capillary and accumulate in the tissues.

17. Some issues and questions to consider: Is it ethical to have a child to save the life of another? Is it right to conceive a child as a means to an end—to produce a tissue or organ? Is this a less acceptable reason than most reasons parents have for bearing children? Do parents even need a reason for conceiving a child? Do parents have the right to make a donation decision for their young children? How will the donor (and recipient) feel about this when the donor is old enough to know what happened?

18. With a three-chambered heart, there is some mixing of oxygen-rich blood returning from the lungs with oxygen-poor blood returning from the systemic circulation. Thus, the blood of a dinosaur might not have supplied enough O_2 to support the higher metabolism and strong cardiac muscle contractions needed to generate such a high systolic blood pressure. Also, with a single ventricle pumping simultaneously to both pulmonary and systemic circuits, the blood pumped to the lungs would be at such a high pressure that it would damage the lungs.

19. Some issues and questions to consider: Could drug use endanger the safety of the employee or others? Is drug testing relevant to jobs where safety is not a factor? Is drug testing an invasion of privacy, interfering in the private life of an employee? Is an employer justified in banning drug use off the job if it does not affect safety or ability to do the job? Do the same criteria apply to employers requiring the test? Could an employer use a drug test to regulate other employee behaviour that is legal, such as smoking?

20. Some issues and questions to consider: Should human organs be sold? If the donor is poor, he or she may also not be in the best of health. What are the health risks to the donor? Will the recipient be assured of buying a healthy organ? How much does the organ broker make from this transaction? Both parties in such a transaction are extremely desperate. Should regulations be in place when people may not be able to make reasoned decisions? Or do people have a right to sell parts of their bodies, just as they can now sell other possessions or their labour?

Chapter 29

1. Thyroid gland: e
2. Adrenal medulla: c
3. Testes: d
4. Pancreas: a
5. Pineal gland: f
6. Anterior pituitary: b

7. Parathyroid gland: g

8. Hypothalamus: h **9.** d **10.** e **11.** a

12. b (Negative feedback: When thyroxine increases, it inhibits TSH, which reduces thyroxine secretion.) **13.** d

14. The hypothalamus secretes releasing hormones and inhibiting hormones, which are carried by the blood to the anterior pituitary. In response to these signals from the hypothalamus, the anterior pituitary increases or decreases its secretion of a variety of hormones that directly affect body activities or influence other glands. Neurosecretory cells that extend from the hypothalamus into the posterior pituitary secrete hormones that are stored in the posterior pituitary until they are released into the blood.

15. Only cells with the proper receptors will respond to a hormone. For a steroid hormone, the presence (or absence) and types of receptor proteins inside the cell determine the hormone's effect. For a nonsteroid hormone, the types of receptors on the cell's plasma membrane are key, and the proteins of the signal transduction pathway may have different effects inside different cells.

16. a. No. Blood sugar level goes too low. Diabetes would tend to make the blood sugar level go too high after a meal.
    b. No. Insulin is working, as seen by the homeostatic blood sugar response to feeding.
    c. Correct. Without glucagon, exercise and fasting lower blood sugar, the cells cannot mobilize any sugar reserves, and blood sugar level drops. Insulin (which lowers blood sugar) has no effect.
    d. No. If this were true, blood sugar level would increase too much after a meal.

17. If cells within a male embryo do not secrete testosterone at the proper time during development, the embryo will develop into a female despite being genetically male.

Chapter 30

1. A. FSH; B. estrogen; C. LH; D. progesterone; P. menstruation; Q. growth of follicle; R. ovulation; S. development of corpus luteum. If pregnancy occurs, the embryo produces human chorionic gonadotropin (hCG), which maintains the corpus luteum, keeping levels of estrogen and progesterone high.

2. c **3.** c (The outer layer in a gastrula is the ectoderm; of the choices given, only the brain develops from ectoderm.)

4. a **5.** d **6.** e **7.** g **8.** d **9.** h **10.** f **11.** a **12.** b **13.** c

14. Both produce haploid gametes. Spermatogenesis produces four small sperm; oogenesis produces one large egg. In humans, the ovary contains all the primary oocytes at birth, while testes can keep making primary spermatocytes throughout life. Oogenesis is not complete until fertilization, but sperm mature without eggs.

15. The extraembryonic membranes provide a moist environment for the embryos of terrestrial vertebrates and enable the embryos to absorb food and oxygen and dispose of wastes. Such membranes are not needed when an embryo is surrounded by water, as are those of fishes and amphibians.

16. Some questions to consider: Does the technique have any long-term effects? How long is the recovery? (Some people who use the method may eventually want to conceive and recovery would be essential.) What is the minimum effective dose? (Knowing this will allow someone to maintain effectiveness while using the shortest possible treatment.) Are there any complications? (If risks outweigh benefits, this method will not be useful.)

17. The researcher might find out whether chemicals from the notochord stimulate the nearby ectoderm to become the neural tube, a process called induction. Transplanted notochord tissue might cause ectoderm anywhere in the embryo to become neural tissue. Control: Transplant non-notochord tissue under the ectoderm of the belly area.

18. Some issues and questions to consider: What characteristics might parents like to select for? If parents had the right to choose embryos based on these characteristics, what are some of the possible benefits? What are potential pitfalls? Could an imbalance of the population result?

Chapter 31

1. a. sensory receptor; b. sensory neuron; c. synapse; d. spinal cord; e. interneuron; f. motor neuron; g. effector cells; h. CNS; i. PNS

2. b **3.** a **4.** a

5. Both a and c would prevent action potentials from occurring; b could actually increase the generation of action potentials.

6. At the point where the action potential is triggered, sodium ions rush into the neuron. They diffuse laterally and cause sodium gates to open in the adjacent part of the membrane, triggering another action potential. The moving wave of action potentials, each triggering the next, is a moving nerve signal. Behind the action potential, sodium gates are temporarily inactivated, so the action potential can go only forward. At a synapse, the transmitting cell releases a chemical neurotransmitter, which binds to receptors on the receiving cell and may trigger a nerve signal in the receiving cell.

7. The results show the cumulative effect of all incoming signals on neuron D. Comparing experiments 1 and 2, we see that the more nerve signals D receives from C, the more it sends; C is excitatory. Because neuron A is not varied here, its action is unknown; it may be either excitatory or mildly inhibitory. Comparing experiments 2 and 3, we see that neuron B must release a strongly inhibitory neurotransmitter, because when B is transmitting, D stops.

8. Ouabain binds to and blocks the actions of the Na^+–K^+ pump, which is responsible for establishing and maintaining the sodium and potassium gradients across a neuron's cell membrane. In a resting neuron, the concentration of sodium is much higher outside of the cell and that of potassium is higher in the cytoplasm. Without the Na^+–K^+ pump, these gradients would disappear, and the resting membrane potential would reach equilibrium at 0 mV. In this state, no action potential can be generated, as there

could be no net movement of ions across the membrane if the channels were to open.

9. Some issues and questions to consider: Some people might be against the use of embryonic stem cells for any disorder. This may be related to religious or moral beliefs. Potentially, some people may not be aware of the source of these stem cells and may be against their use because they believe that the cells come from elective abortions. Other people may agree with the use of stem cell research because of the potential to cure diseases that are currently fatal. Some people who may have a neutral opinion on the issue might be swayed by the thought of a loved one who might be helped by stem cell therapy.

10. Some issues and questions to consider: What is the role of alcohol in crime? What are its effects on families and in the workplace? In what ways is the individual responsible for alcohol abuse? The family? Society? Who is affected by alcohol abuse? How effective are treatment and punishment in curbing alcohol abuse? Who pays for alcohol abuse and consequent treatment or punishment? Is it possible to enjoy alcohol without abusing it?

Chapter 32

1. a. mechanoreceptors; b. chemoreceptors; c. electricity, magnetism, light; d. hair cells; e. photoreceptors

2. d (He could hear the tuning fork against his skull, so the cochlea, nerve, and brain are functioning properly. However, sounds are not being transmitted to the cochlea; therefore, the bones are the problem.)

3. b 4. a 5. b 6. d 7. e 8. a 9. c

10. Louder sounds create pressure waves with greater amplitude, moving hair cells more and generating a greater frequency of action potentials. Different pitches affect different parts of the basilar membrane; different hair cells stimulate different sensory neurons that transmit action potentials to different parts of the brain.

11. Sensation is the detection of stimuli (light) by the photoreceptors of the retina and transmission of action potentials to the brain. Perception is the interpretation of these nerve signals—that is, sorting out the patterns of light and dark and determining their meaning.

12. Taste is used to sample food and determine its quality. Smell is used for many functions—communicating territories (scent marking), navigating (salmon), locating mates (moths), sensing danger (predators, fires), and finding food.

13. Some possible hypotheses: Paired sensory receptors enable an animal to determine the direction from which stimuli come. Paired receptors enable comparison of the intensity of stimuli on either side. Paired receptors enable comparison of slightly different images seen by the eyes or sounds heard by the ears (thus enabling the brain to perceive depth and distance).

14. Some possible research questions and experiment plans: Do the turtles hear the surf? Plug the ears of some turtles and not others. If turtles without earplugs head for the water and turtles with earplugs get lost, they probably hear the ocean. Or, do turtles smell the water? Plug the nostrils of only some turtles and follow the same process mentioned above.

15. Some questions to consider: Assuming that the sound is loud enough to impair hearing, how long an exposure is necessary for this to occur? Does exposure have to occur all at once or is damage cumulative? Who is responsible, concert promoters or listeners? Should there be regulations regarding sound exposure at concerts (as there are for job-related noise)? Are young people sufficiently mature to heed such warnings?

Chapter 33

1. a. skeleton; b. muscles; c. exoskeleton; d. sarcomeres; e. bone; f. cartilage

2. c 3. d 4. a (Water supports aquatic animals, reducing the effects of gravity.) 5. c 6. d 7. e 8. a

9. a (Each neuron controls a smaller number of muscle fibres.) 10. e

11. Advantages of an insect exoskeleton include strength, good protection for the body, flexibility at joints, and protection from water loss. The major disadvantage is that the exoskeleton must be shed periodically as the insect grows, leaving the insect temporarily weak and vulnerable.

12. The bird's wings are airfoils, with convex upper surfaces and flat or concave lower surfaces. As the wings beat, air passing over them travels farther than air beneath. Air molecules above the wings are more spread out, lowering pressure. Higher pressure beneath the wings pushes them up.

13. Calcium is needed for healthy bone development. It strengthens the horses' bones and makes them less susceptible to stress fractures.

14. Action potentials from the brain travel down the spinal cord and along a motor neuron to the muscle. The neuron releases a neurotransmitter, which triggers action potentials in a muscle fibre membrane. These action potentials initiate the release of calcium ions from the endoplasmic reticulum of the cell. Calcium enables myosin heads of the thick filaments to bind with the actin of the thin filaments. ATP provides energy for the movement of myosin heads, which causes the thick and thin filaments to slide along one another, shortening the muscle fibre. The shortening of muscle fibres pulls on bones, bending the arm. If more motor units are activated, the contraction is stronger.

15. The fundamental vertebrate body plan includes an axial skeleton (skull, backbone, and rib cage) and an appendicular skeleton (bones of the appendages). Species vary in the numbers of vertebrae and the numbers of different types of vertebrae they possess. For example, pythons have no cervical vertebrae. Almost all mammals have seven cervical vertebrae but may have different numbers of other types. For example, human coccygeal vertebrae are small and fused together, but horses and other animals with long

tails have many coccygeal vertebrae. Limb bones have been modified into a variety of appendages, such as wings, fins, and limbs. Snakes have no appendages.

16. Chemical A would work better, because acetylcholine triggers contraction. Blocking it would prevent contraction. Chemical B would actually increase contraction, because Ca^{2+} allows contraction to occur.

17. Circular muscles in the earthworm body wall decrease the diameter of each segment, squeezing internal fluid and lengthening the segment. Longitudinal muscles shorten and thicken each segment. Different parts of the earthworm can lengthen while others shorten, producing a crawling motion. The whole roundworm body moves at once because of a lack of segmentation. The body can only shorten or bend, not lengthen, because of a lack of circular muscles. Roundworms simply thrash from side to side.

18. The binding of calcium ions causes the regulatory protein tropomyosin to move out of the way, enabling myosin heads to bind to actin. ATP causes the myosin heads of the thick filaments to detach from the thin filaments (Figure 33.9B). This results in muscle contraction. If there is no ATP present, the myosin heads remain attached to the thin filaments, and the muscle fibre remains fixed in position.

19. Some issues and questions to consider: Are the places where you live, work, or attend class accessible to a person in a wheelchair? If you did use a wheelchair, would you have trouble with doors, stairs, drinking fountains, toilet facilities, and eating facilities? What kinds of transportation would be available to you, and how convenient would they be? What activities would you have to forgo? How might your disability alter your relationships with your friends and family? How well would you manage on your own?

Chapter 34

1. a. innate immunity; b. adaptive immunity; c. B cells; d. T cells; e. antibodies; f. helper T cells

2. e 3. b 4. a 5. b 6. d 7. d 8. a 9. c 10. d 11. b 12. f 13. d 14. e 15. a 16. g 17. c

18. Inflammation is triggered by tissue injury. Damaged cells release histamine and other chemicals, which cause nearby blood vessels to dilate and become leakier. Blood plasma leaves vessels, and phagocytes are attracted to the site of injury. An increase in blood flow, fluid accumulation, and increased cell population cause redness, heat, and swelling. Inflammation disinfects and cleans the area and curtails the spread of infection from the injured area. Inflammation is considered part of the innate immune response because similar defences are presented in response to any infection.

19. One hypothesis is that your roommate's previous bee stings caused her to become sensitized to the allergens in bee venom. During sensitization, antibodies to allergens attach to receptor proteins on mast cells. During this sensitization stage, she would not have experienced allergy symptoms. When she was exposed to the bee venom again

at a later time, the bee venom allergens bound to the mast cells, which triggered her allergic reaction.

20. There is no correct answer to this question. Some issues to consider: Possible directions include the idea that if the donor felt strongly about the process, then his or her wishes should be respected. The opposite direction would be that the next of kin should be able to approve or deny the procedure. Other considerations may be appropriate, including religious beliefs.

21. You should start by explaining how the flu shot immunizes against only three different strains of influenza. Each strain has a different combination of surface proteins called hemagglutinin and neuraminidase. Scientists and physicians at the World Health Organization predict which influenza strains will be circulating each flu season. The circulating strains change frequently, so a previous flu shot is not likely to protect you against influenza in subsequent years. Therefore, it is advised to receive annual flu shots to minimize your risk of getting the flu.

Chapter 35

1. a. The shape of Earth results in uneven heating, such that the tropics are warm and polar regions are cold.
   b. The seasonal differences of winter and summer in temperate and polar regions are produced as Earth tips toward or away from the sun during its orbit around the sun.
   c. Intense solar radiation in the tropics evaporates moisture; warm air rises, cools, and drops its moisture as rain; air circulates, cools, and drops around 30° north and south, warming as it descends and absorbing moisture from land, which creates arid regions.

2. a. All three areas have plenty of sunlight and nutrients.
   b. The addition of excess nitrogen or phosphorus "fertilizes" the algae living in ponds and lakes, leading to explosive population growth—a process known as eutrophication. (These nutrients are typically in short supply in aquatic ecosystems.) The effects are harmful to the ecosystem. Algae cover the surface, reducing light penetration. When the algae die, bacterial decomposition of the large amount of biomass can deplete the oxygen available in the pond or the lake, which may adversely affect the animal community.

3. f 4. g 5. d 6. a 7. c 8. b 9. e 10. a 11. e 12. d 13. a 14. c 15. b 16. e 17. b

18. Tropical rainforests have a warm, moist climate, with favourable growing conditions year-round. The diverse plant growth provides various habitats for other organisms.

19. After identifying your biome by looking at the map in Figure 35.9, review Module 35.5 on climate and the module that describes your biome (Modules 35.10–35.18).

20. a. desert; b. grassland; c. tropical forest; d. temperate forest; e. coniferous forest; f. arctic tundra. Areas of overlap have to do with seasonal variations in temperature and precipitation.

21. Through convergent evolution, these unrelated animals adapted in similar ways to similar environments—temperate grasslands and savanna.

Chapter 36

1. a. genes; b. fixed action pattern (FAP); c. imprinting; d. spatial learning; e. associative learning; f. social learning

2. d 3. c 4. c 5. d 6. a

7. Main advantage: Flies do not live long. Innate behaviours can be performed the first time without learning, enabling flies to find food, mates, and so on without practice. Main disadvantage: Innate behaviours are rigid; flies cannot learn to adapt to specific situations.

8. In a stressful environment, for example, where predators are abundant, rats that behave cautiously are more likely to survive long enough to reproduce.

9. Courtship behaviours reduce aggression between potential mates and confirm their species, sex, and physical condition. Environmental changes such as rainfall, temperature, and day length probably lead frogs to start calling, so these would be the proximate causes. The ultimate cause relates to evolution. Fitness (reproductive success) is enhanced for frogs that engage in courtship behaviours.

10. a. Yes. The experimenter found that 5 m provided the most food for the least energy because the total flight height (number of drops × height per drop) was the lowest. Crows appear to be using an optimal foraging strategy.
    b. An experiment could measure the average drop height for juvenile and adult birds, or it could trace individual birds during a time span from juvenile to adult and see if their drop height changed.

11. Identical twins are genetically the same, so any differences between them are due to environment. Thus, the study of identical twins enables researchers to sort out the effects of "nature" and "nurture" on human behaviour. Some people find these studies disturbing because they seem to leave less room for free will and self-improvement than we would like. Results of such studies may be carelessly cited in support of a particular social agenda.

12. Animals are used in experiments for various reasons. A particular species of animal may have features that make it well suited to answer an important biological question. Squids, for example, have a giant nerve fibre that made possible the discovery of how all nerve cells function. Animal experiments play a major role in medical research. Many vaccines that protect humans against deadly diseases, as well as drugs that can cure diseases, have been developed using animal experiments. Animals also benefit, as vaccines and drugs are developed for combating their own pathogens. Some researchers point out that the number of animals used in research is a small fraction of those killed as strays by animal shelters and a minuscule fraction of those killed for human food. They also maintain that modern research facilities are models of responsible and considerate treatment of animals. Whether or not this is true, the possibility that at least some kinds of animals used in research suffer physical pain as a result, and perhaps mental anguish as well, raises serious ethical issues. Some questions to consider: What are some medical treatments or products that have undergone testing in animals? Have you benefited from any of them? Are there alternatives to using animals in experiments? Would alternatives put humans at risk? Are all kinds of animal experiments equally valuable? In your opinion, what kinds of experiments are acceptable, and what kinds are unnecessary? What kinds of treatment are humane, and what kinds are inhumane?

Chapter 37

1. a. The x-axis is time; the y-axis is the number of individuals (N). The blue curve represents exponential growth; red is logistic growth.
    b. $G = rN$
    c. The carrying capacity of the environment (K).
    d. In exponential growth, population growth continues to increase as the population size increases. In logistic growth, the population grows fastest when the population is about half of the carrying capacity—when N is large enough so that rN produces a large increase, but the expression $(K - N)/K$ has not yet slowed growth as much as it will as N gets closer to K.
    e. The exponential growth curve, although the worldwide growth rate is slowing.

2. a. The blue line is the birth rate; the red line is the death rate.
    b. A. Both birth and death rates are high. B. Birth rate remains high. Death rate decreases, perhaps as a result of increased sanitation and healthcare. C. Birth rate declines, often coupled with increased opportunities for women and access to birth control. Death rates are low. D. Both birth and death rates are low.
    c. I and IV
    d. II, when death rate has fallen but birth rate remains high

3. d 4. a 5. c 6. c 7. e 8. b 9. d

10. Food and resource limitation, such as food or nesting sites; accumulation of toxic wastes; disease; increase in predation; stress responses, such as those seen in some rodents.

11. Survivorship is the fraction of individuals in a given age interval that survive to the next interval. It is a measure of the probability of surviving at any given age. A survivorship curve shows the fraction of individuals in a population surviving at each age interval during the lifespan. Oysters produce large numbers of offspring, most of which die young, with a few living a full lifespan. Few humans die young; most live out a full lifespan and die of old age. Squirrels have approximately constant mortality and about an equal chance of surviving at all ages.

12. Clumped is the most common dispersion pattern, usually associated with unevenly distributed resources or social grouping. Uniform dispersion may be related to territories or inhibitory interactions between plants. A random dispersion is least common and may occur when other factors do not influence the distribution of organisms.

13. Populations with *K*-selected life history traits tend to live in fairly stable environments held near carrying capacity by density-dependent limiting factors. They reproduce later and have fewer offspring than species with *r*-selected traits. Their lower reproductive rate makes it hard for them to recover from human-caused disruption of their habitat. We would expect species with *K*-selected life histories to have a Type I survivorship curve (see Module 37.3).

14. The largest population segment, the baby boomers, is currently in the workforce in their peak earning years, paying into the Canada Pension Plan and Medicare premiums. However, they are approaching the end of their contributing years, and there will be fewer working Canadians to replace them. Therefore, more people will be withdrawing from these social programs while fewer are contributing to them. This imbalance will undoubtedly put stress on these essential programs.

15. Some issues and questions to consider: How does population growth in developing countries relate to food supply, pollution, and the use of natural resources such as fossil fuels? How are these things affected by population growth in developed countries? Which of these factors are most critical to our survival? Are they affected more by the growth of developing or developed countries? What will happen as developing countries become more developed? Will it be possible for everyone to live at the level of the developed world?

Chapter 38

1. a. disturbances; b. organisms; c. competition; d. predation; e. soil present; f. $+/-$; g. primary succession; h. secondary succession

2. c 3. b 4. d 5. c 6. e 7. a 8. d

9. The sea otters are an excellent example of how an animal can occupy multiple trophic levels. When the otter consumes sea urchins (primary consumers), it is a secondary consumer. But sea otters also eat sea stars (secondary consumers) and fish (tertiary consumers). When it does, the otter is acting as a tertiary and quaternary consumer, respectively. The only plants that can occupy multiple trophic levels would be carnivorous plants such as those discussed in the opening essay of Chapter 23. They are primary producers, and when they ingest insects, they are acting as secondary consumers.

10. After a disturbance, biodiversity is initially very low. A few species of weedy plants colonize the site and gradually more species follow in a predictable order. Small perennial plants and grasses follow the weedy annual plants. Then, shrubs, softwood trees, and hardwood trees follow in order. Initially biodiversity increases, but it decreases as the hardwood trees become dominant within the community.

11. Cowbirds are an edge species, which depend on two separate communities. Cowbirds feed on insects attracted to large herbivores of grassland communities. They also require forest communities that attract nest-building birds because the cowbirds use their nests for reproduction. Cowbirds thrive in edges where both communities are readily accessible. An interior species, such as the ovenbird, is one that requires a homogenous community structure. To forage on ground-dwelling insects, ovenbirds need the tall canopy that keeps the undergrowth thin and open. More light penetrates around a forest's edges and the undergrowth there is too dense for the ovenbird.

12. *Hypothesis:* The kangaroo rat is a keystone species in the desert. (Apparently, herbivory by the rats kept the one plant from outcompeting the others; removing the rats reduced plant diversity.) *Additional supporting evidence:* Observations of the rats preferentially eating dominant plants; finding that the dominant plant recovers from herbivore damage faster.

13. Some issues and questions to consider: What relationships (predators, competitors, parasites) might exist in the mussels' native habitat that are altered in the Great Lakes? How might the mussels compete with Great Lakes organisms? Might the Great Lakes species adapt in some way? Might the mussels adapt? Could possible solutions present problems of their own?

Chapter 39

1.

Interspecies Relationship	Effects on Species 1	Effects on Species 2	Symbiotic (Yes or No)	Example
Predation	+	−	No	Wolf/deer
Competition	−	−	No	Black bear/ red squirrel
Mutualism	+	+	Yes	Plant/ mycorrhiza
Commensalism	+	0	Yes	Anemonefish/ anenome
Parasitoid	+	−	No	Jewel wasp/ blowfly
Mimicry	+	0	Yes	Milk snake/ coral snake

2. The following answers correspond with the examples used in question 1. *Wolf/deer:* The wolf benefits from the meal while the deer pays with its life. The wolf may use some of the energy in its meal to support reproduction. The fitness of the deer ends. *Black bear/red squirrel:* As the bear and squirrel compete for nuts, they each have fewer nuts to eat. With less food, each species has less energy available for reproduction. *Plant/mycorrhiza:* The plant gains access to more nutrients, which it can use for growth and reproduction. The fungus receives sugar energy that it wouldn't otherwise have access to. *Anemonefish/anemone:* The anemone deters predators

of the anemonefish. A longer life can translate to more opportunities to reproduce and a higher fitness. There may be no effect on fitness of the anemone. *Jewel wasp/blowfly:* The jewel wasp increases its reproductive fitness by enabling its larvae to develop and mature by ingesting the pupa of the blowfly. The fitness of the blowfly ends with its death at the pupa stage. *Milk snake/coral snake:* Predators leave the milk snake alone as they fear it is harmful. Living longer increases the milk snake's probability of reproduction. The coral snake is unaffected unless the population of the milk snake becomes too high, in which case the colours of the coral snake would no longer deter predators.

3. c 4. c 5. d 6. b 7. d 8. a 9. a 10. c 11. e

12. Predation and parasitism are similar in that they are both +/− relationships where one individual gains a benefit at the cost of the other. They are different in that a predator must kill its prey before eating it. By contrast, a parasite rarely kills its host; it does so only to facilitate transmission to its next host.

13. All 600 species of bacteria that live in the human intestine benefit from the stable environment of the intestinal tract. The human host may be affected in different ways by different bacteria. Some species form commensal relationships, producing no effect on the human host. Many species are in a mutually beneficial relationship as they aid in the processing of essential vitamins or prevent colonization by harmful bacteria. Others may have detrimental effects on the host. For example, certain strains of *Escherichia coli* can cause debilitating diseases of the large intestine and would be considered parasites.

14. Altruisum does not likely exist because a voluntary reduction in overall fitness is not a viable strategy according to natural selection. Traits that increase fitness have selective value and thus are likely to be passed on in a population. On the contrary, altruism is a selective disadvantage and thus is less likely to be passed on.

15. If there were more sabre-toothed blennies than cleaner wrasses in a community, there would probably be detrimental effects on both species as well as on the larger fishes with which they interact. Larger fishes would become reluctant to open their gills to small fishes if too many of them were to bite them. This reluctance would affect the mutualism between the cleaner wrasse and these larger fishes. Moreover, the large number of sabre-tooth blennies would negatively affect their fitness because they would lose access to a valuable food source.

16. To answer these questions, you would need to examine the relationship's effect on the fitness of each symbiont. You could try to grow each plant separately and measure growth rates and reproductive success to determine if fitness is altered. This experiment would indicate whether the relationship was mutualistic, commensal, or parasitic. For example, a parasitic relationship would be fostered if the small plant developed a root system that invaded the vascular tissues of the tree. With this adaptation, the shrub would be able to collect nutrients as they flow through the tree. A commensal relationship would be fostered if the root system attached to, but did not harm, the tree trunk. In this case, the shrub would have to evolve a mechanism to acquire nutrients and water from sources other than the soil or the tree. A mutualistic relationship might be either trophic or defensive. A trophic mutualistic relationship might have developed if the tree and shrub had adaptations that facilitated the exchange of nutrients. A defensive mutualistic relationship might be occurring if the shrub offered the tree protection from herbivores (by releasing chemical deterrents) in exchange for nutrients.

Chapter 40

1.

	Carbon	Nitrogen	Phosphorus
Main abiotic reservoir(s)	Atmosphere	Atmosphere, Soil	Rocks
Form in abiotic reservoir	Carbon dioxide (CO_2)	N_2 in atmosphere; ammonium (NH_4^+) or nitrate (NO_3^-) in soil	Phosphate (PO_4^-) bound with other minerals in rock
Form used by producers	Carbon dioxide (CO_2)	NH_4^+ or NO_3^-	Phospate (PO_4^{3-})
Human activities that alter cycle	Burning wood and fossil fuels	Agriculture (fertilizers, feedlots, soil erosion); combustion of fossil fuels; manufacture of nitrogen fertilizer	Agriculture (fertilizers, feedlots, pesticides, soil erosion)
Effects of altering cycle	Global warming	Eutrophication of aquatic ecosystems; nutrient-depleted soils; global warming; smog; depletion of ozone layer; acid precipitation	Eutrophication of aquatic ecosystem; nutrient-depleted soils

2. e 3. d 4. c 5. d 6. c

7. Rapid eutrophication occurs when bodies of water receive nutrient pollution (for example, from agricultural runoff) that results in blooms of cyanobacteria and algae. Respiration from these organisms and their decomposers depletes oxygen levels, leading to the death of fish. Reducing this type of pollution will require controlling the sources of excess inorganic nutrients, for example, runoff from feedlots and fertilizers.

8. The abiotic reservoir of the first three nutrients is the soil. Carbon is available as carbon dioxide in the atmosphere.

9. These animals are secondary or tertiary consumers, at the top of the production pyramid. Stepwise energy loss means not much energy is left for them; thus, they are rare and require large territories in which to hunt.

10. Chemicals with a gaseous form in the atmosphere, such as carbon and nitrogen, have a global biogeochemical cycle.

11. Nitrogen fixation of atmospheric N_2 into ammonium; decomposition of detritus into ammonium; nitrification of ammonium into nitrate; denitrification (by denitrifiers) of nitrates into N_2.

12. Decomposers play a key role in nutrient cycles by breaking down the complex organic molecules of the detritus. Without the decomposers, all essential nutrients would be locked away in the accumulating organic material. The part of the cycles that moves the nutrients from the biotic to the abiotic pools would be missing. Eventually, the cycles could no longer continue.

13. The majority of biomass in a tropical rainforest is stored in the vegetation. Additionally, removing this vegetation—by logging or burning—removes a significant amount of carbon. Replacing tropical rainforest with cultivated land severely decreases the amount of primary production (from about 2200 to 600 g/m^2 per year. This change reduces the amount of carbon entering the biotic community by almost 75%. Such a change would mean that fewer nutrients and less energy would be available for the consumers; many would have to leave or die.

Chapter 41

1. a. species at risk of extinction; b. restoration ecology; c. bioremediation; d. zoned reserves

2. c 3. d 4. a 5. e 6. b 7. d 8. a

9. The three levels are genetic, species, and ecosystem diversity. As populations become smaller, genetic diversity is usually reduced. Genetic diversity is also threatened when local populations of a species are extirpated owing to habitat destruction or other assaults or when entire species are lost. Many human activities have led to the extinction of species. The greatest threats include habitat loss, invasive species, and overharvesting. Species extinction or population extirpation may alter the structure of whole communities. Pollution and other widespread disruptions may lead to the loss of entire ecosystems.

10. Greenhouse gases in the atmosphere, including carbon dioxide, methane, and nitrous oxide, absorb infrared radiation and thus slow the escape of heat from Earth. This is called the greenhouse effect (see Module 7.13). Without greenhouse gases in the atmosphere, the temperature at Earth's surface would be much colder and less hospitable for life.

11. Fossil fuel consumption, industry, and agriculture are increasing the quantity of greenhouse gases—such as carbon dioxide (CO_2), methane, and nitrous oxide—in the atmosphere. These gases are trapping more heat and raising atmospheric temperatures. Increases of 2–5°C are projected over the next century. Logging and the clearing of forests for farming contribute to climate change by reducing the uptake of CO_2 by plants (and adding CO_2 to the air when trees are burned). Climate change is having numerous effects already, including melting polar ice, permafrost, and glaciers, shifting patterns of precipitation, causing spring temperatures to arrive earlier, and reducing the number of cold days and nights. Future consequences include rising sea levels and the extinction of many plants and animals. Climate change is an international problem; air and climate do not recognize international boundaries. Greenhouse gases are primarily produced by industrialized nations. Cooperation and commitment to reduce use of fossil fuels and to reduce deforestation will be necessary if the problem of climate change is to be solved.

12. These birds might be affected by pesticides while in their wintering grounds in Central and South America, where such chemicals may still be in use. The birds are also affected by deforestation throughout their range.

13. About 1.8 million species have been named and described. Assume that 80% of all living things (not just plants and animals) live in tropical rainforests. This means that they contain 1.44 million species. If half the species survive, this means that 0.72 million species will be extinct in 100 years, or 7400 per year. This means that more than 19 species will disappear per day, or almost 1 per hour. If there are 30 million species on Earth, 24 million live in the tropics, and 12 million will disappear in the next century. This is 120 000 per year, 329 per day, or 14 per hour.

14. Some issues and questions to consider: How does the use of fossil fuels affect the environment? What about oil spills? Disruption of wildlife habitat for construction of oil fields and pipelines? Burning of fossil fuels and possible climate change and flooding from global warming? Pollution of lakes and destruction of property by acid precipitation? Health effects of polluted air on humans? How are we paying for these "side effects" of fossil fuel use? In taxes? In health insurance premiums? Do we pay a nonfinancial price in terms of poorer health and quality of life? Could oil companies be required to pick up the tab for environmental effects of fossil fuel use? Could these costs be covered by an oil tax? How would this change the price of oil? How would a change in the price of oil change our pattern of energy use, our lifestyle, and our environment?

15. Data on carbon emissions can be found at a number of websites, including the United Nations Statistics Division (http://unstats.un.org/unsd/default.htm) and the World

Resources Institute (www.wri.org/climate/). The per capita rankings of Canada and the United States are generally very high, along with other developed nations. Transportation and energy use are the major contributors to the carbon footprint. Any actions you can take to reduce these will help. For example, if you have a car, you can try to minimize the number of kilometres you drive by consolidating errands into fewer trips and by using an alternative means of transportation (public transportation, walking, biking) whenever possible. To reduce energy consumption, be aware of the energy you use: Turn off lights, disconnect electronics that draw power when on standby, do laundry in cold water, for example. Websites such as www.ucsusa.org (Union of Concerned Scientists) and http://climatecrisis.net offer simple suggestions such as changing to energy-efficient light bulbs. An online search will turn up plenty of sites.

16. Some issues and questions to consider: How do population growth, resource consumption, pollution, and reduction in biodiversity relate to sustainability? How do poverty, economic growth and development, and political issues relate to sustainability? Why might developed and developing nations take different views of a sustainable society? What would life be like in a sustainable society? Have any steps toward sustainability been taken in your community? What are the obstacles to sustainability in your community? What steps have you taken toward a sustainable lifestyle? How old will you be in 2030? What do you think life will be like then?

Glossary

A

A site One of two of a ribosome's binding sites for tRNA during translation. The A site holds the tRNA that carries the next amino acid in the polypeptide chain. (*A* stands for aminoacyl tRNA.)

aberrant host A host that is not part of the natural life cycle of a parasite and is mistakenly infected.

abiotic factor (ā′-bī-ot′-ik) A nonliving component of an ecosystem, such as air, water, or temperature.

abiotic reservoir The part of an ecosystem where a chemical, such as carbon or nitrogen, accumulates or is stockpiled outside of living organisms.

ABO blood groups Genetically determined classes of human blood that are based on the presence or absence of carbohydrates A and B on the surface of red blood cells. The ABO blood group phenotypes, also called blood types, are A, B, AB, and O.

abscisic acid (ABA) (ab-sis′-ik) A plant hormone that inhibits cell division, promotes dormancy, and interacts with gibberellins in regulating seed germination.

absorption The uptake of small nutrient molecules by an organism's own body; the third main stage of food processing, following digestion.

acetyl CoA (a-sē′til -kō′a′) (acetyl coenzyme A) The entry compound for the citric acid cycle in cellular respiration; formed from a fragment of pyruvate attached to a coenzyme.

acetylcholine (a-sē′-til-kō′lēn) A nitrogen-containing neurotransmitter. Among other effects, it slows the heart rate and makes skeletal muscles contract.

achondroplasia (uh-kon′-druh-plā′-zhuh) A form of human dwarfism caused by a single dominant allele; the homozygous condition is lethal.

acid A substance that increases the hydrogen ion (H^+) concentration in a solution.

acid precipitation Rain, snow, or fog that is more acidic than pH 5.2.

acrosome (ak′-ruh-som) A membrane-enclosed sac at the tip of a sperm; contains enzymes that help the sperm penetrate an egg.

actin A globular protein that links into chains, two of which twist helically around each other, forming microfilaments in muscle cells.

action potential A change in membrane voltage that transmits a nerve signal along an axon.

activation energy The amount of energy that reactants must absorb before a chemical reaction will start.

activator A protein that switches on a gene or group of genes.

active immunity Immunity conferred by recovering from an infectious disease or by receiving a vaccine.

active site The part of an enzyme molecule where a substrate molecule attaches (by means of weak chemical bonds); typically, a pocket or groove on the enzyme's surface.

active transmission The movement of a parasite from one host to another that occurs under the parasite's own power.

active transport The movement of a substance across a biological membrane against its concentration gradient, aided by specific transport proteins and requiring an input of energy (often as ATP).

adaptation An inherited characteristic that enhances an organism's ability to survive and reproduce in a particular environment.

adaptive immunity A vertebrate-specific defence that is activated only after exposure to an antigen and is mediated by lymphocytes; exhibits specificity, memory, and self–nonself recognition; also called acquired immunity.

adaptive radiation Period of evolutionary change in which groups of organisms form many new species whose adaptations allow them to fill new or vacant ecological roles in their communities.

adenine (A) (ad′-uh-nēn) A double-ring nitrogenous base found in DNA and RNA.

adhesion The attraction between different kinds of molecules.

adipose tissue A type of connective tissue whose cells contain fat.

adrenal cortex (uh-drē′-nul) The outer portion of an adrenal gland; controlled by ACTH from the anterior pituitary; secretes hormones called glucocorticoids and mineralocorticoids.

adrenal gland One of a pair of endocrine glands; located atop each kidney in mammals; composed of an outer cortex and a central medulla.

adrenal medulla (uh-drē′-nul muh-dul′-uh) The central portion of an adrenal gland; controlled by nerve signals; secretes the fight-or-flight hormones adrenalin and noradrenalin.

adrenaline (uh-dre-nuh-lin) An amine hormone secreted by the adrenal medulla that prepares body organs for action (fight or flight); serves as a neurotransmitter; also called epinephrine.

adrenocorticotropic hormone (ACTH) (uh-drē′-nō-cōr′-ti-kō-trop′-ik) A protein hormone secreted by the anterior pituitary that stimulates the adrenal cortex to secrete corticosteroids.

adult stem cell A cell present in adult tissues that generates replacements for nondividing differentiated cells; is capable of differentiating into multiple cell types but is not as developmentally flexible as an embryonic stem cell.

age structure The relative number of individuals of each age in a population.

aggressive mimicry A type of mimicry in which the mimic has evolved similar coloration to a passive species, increasing its foraging success.

agonistic behaviour (a′-gō-nis′-tik) Confrontational behaviour involving a contest waged by threats, displays, or actual combat that settles disputes over limited resources, such as food or mates.

alcohol fermentation Glycolysis followed by the reduction of pyruvate to ethyl alcohol, regenerating NAD^+ and releasing carbon dioxide.

alga (al′-guh) (plural, **algae**) A protist that produces its food by photosynthesis.

alimentary canal (al′-uh-men′-tuh-rē) A complete digestive tract consisting of a tube running between a mouth and an anus.

allantois (al′-an-tō′-is) In animals, an extraembryonic membrane that develops from the yolk sac; helps to dispose of the embryo's nitrogenous wastes and forms part of the umbilical cord in mammals.

allele (uh-lē′-ul) An alternative version of a gene.

allergen (al′-er-jen) An antigen that causes an allergy.

allergy A disorder of the immune system caused by an abnormally high sensitivity to an antigen. Symptoms are triggered by histamines released from mast cells.

allopatric speciation The formation of new species in populations that are geographically isolated from one another.

alternation of generations A life cycle in which there is both a multicellular diploid form, the sporophyte, and a multicellular haploid form, the gametophyte; a characteristic of plants and multicellular green algae.

alternative RNA splicing A type of regulation at the RNA-processing level in which different mRNA molecules are produced from the same primary transcript, depending on which RNA segments are treated as exons and which as introns.

altruism (al′-trū-iz-um) Behaviour that reduces an individual's fitness while increasing the fitness of another individual.

alveolus (al-vē′-oh-lus) (plural, **alveoli**) One of the dead-end air sacs within the mammalian lung where gas exchange occurs.

Alzheimer's disease (AD) An age-related dementia (mental deterioration) characterized by confusion, memory loss, and other symptoms.

amino acid (uh-mēn′-ō) An organic molecule containing a carboxyl group and an amino group; serves as the monomer of proteins.

amino-acid-derived hormone A regulatory chemical consisting of a protein, peptide (a short polypeptide), or amine (modified amino acids); is water soluble (but not lipid soluble).

amino group A chemical group consisting of a nitrogen atom bonded to two hydrogen atoms.

ammonia NH_3; A small and very toxic nitrogenous waste produced by metabolism.

amniocentesis (am′-nē-ō-sen-tē′-sis) A technique for diagnosing genetic defects while a fetus is in the uterus. A sample of amniotic fluid, obtained by a needle inserted into the uterus, is analyzed for telltale chemicals and defective fetal cells.

amnion (am′-nē-on) In vertebrate animals, the extraembryonic membrane that encloses the fluid-filled amniotic sac containing the embryo.

amniote Member of a clade of tetrapods that have an amniotic egg containing specialized membranes that protect the embryo. Amniotes include mammals and birds and other reptiles.

amniotic egg (am′-nē-ot′-ik) A shelled egg in which an embryo develops within a fluid-filled amniotic sac and is nourished by yolk. Produced by reptiles (including birds) and egg-laying mammals, the amniotic egg enables them to complete their life cycles on dry land.

amoeba (uh-mē′-buh) A general term for a protist that moves and feeds by means of pseudopodia.

amoebocyte (uh-mē′-buh-sīt) An amoeba-like cell that moves by pseudopodia and is found in most animals; depending on the species, may digest and distribute food, dispose of wastes, form skeletal fibres, fight infections, and change into other cell types.

amoebozoan A member of a clade of protists in the supergroup Unikonta that includes amoebas and slime moulds and is characterized by lobe-shaped pseudopodia.

amphibian Member of a clade of tetrapods that includes frogs, toads, salamanders, and caecilians.

amygdala (uh-mig′-duh-la) An integrative centre of the cerebrum; functionally, the part of the limbic system that seems central in recognizing the emotional content of facial expressions and laying down emotional memories.

analogy The similarity between two species that is due to convergent evolution rather than to descent from a common ancestor with the same trait.

anaphase The fourth stage of mitosis, beginning when sister chromatids separate from each other and ending when a complete set of daughter chromosomes arrives at each of the two poles of the cell.

anatomy The study of the structures of an organism.

anchorage dependence The requirement that a cell must be attached to a solid surface to divide.

androgen (an′-drō-jen) A steroid sex hormone secreted by the gonads that promotes the development and maintenance of the male reproductive system and male body features.

anemia (uh-nē′-me-ah) A condition in which an abnormally low amount of hemoglobin or a low number of red blood cells results in the body cells receiving too little oxygen.

angiosperm (an′-jē-ō-sperm) A flowering plant, which forms seeds inside a protective chamber called an ovary.

annelid (uh-nel′-id) A segmented worm. Annelids include earthworms, polychaetes, and leeches.

annual A plant that completes its life cycle in a single year or growing season.

antagonistic hormones Two hormones that have opposite effects.

anterior Pertaining to the front, or head, of a bilaterally symmetric animal.

anterior pituitary (puh-tū′-uh-tār-ē) An endocrine gland, adjacent to the hypothalamus and the posterior pituitary, that synthesizes several hormones, including some that control the activity of other endocrine glands.

anther A sac located at the tip of a flower's stamen; contains male sporangia in which meiosis occurs to produce spores that form the male gametophytes, or pollen grains.

anthropoid (an′-thruh-poyd) A member of a primate group made up of the apes (gibbons, orangutans, gorillas, chimpanzees, bonobos, and humans) and monkeys.

antibody (an′-tih-bod′-ē) A protein dissolved in blood plasma that attaches to a specific kind of antigen and helps to counter its effects.

anticodon (an′-tī-kō′-don) On a tRNA molecule, a specific sequence of three nucleotides that is complementary to a codon triplet on mRNA.

antidiuretic hormone (ADH) (an′-tē-dī′-yū-ret′-ik) A hormone made by the hypothalamus and secreted by the posterior pituitary that promotes water retention by the kidneys.

antigen (an′-tuh-jen) A foreign (nonself) molecule that elicits an adaptive immune response.

antigen receptor A transmembrane version of an antibody molecule that B cells and T cells use to recognize specific antigens; also called a membrane antibody.

antigen-binding site A region of the antibody molecule responsible for the antibody's recognition and binding function.

antigen-presenting cell (APC) One of a family of white blood cells (for example, a macrophage) that ingests a foreign substance or a microbe and attaches antigenic portions of the ingested material to its own surface, thereby displaying the antigens to a helper T cell.

antigenic determinant A region on the surface of an antigen molecule to which an antibody binds.

antihistamine (an′-tē-his′-tuh-mēn) A drug that interferes with the action of histamine, providing temporary relief from an allergic reaction.

anus The opening through which undigested materials are expelled.

aorta (ā-or′-tuh) A large artery that conveys blood directly from the left ventricle of the heart to other arteries.

aphotic zone (ā-fō′-tik) The region of an aquatic ecosystem beneath the photic zone, where light does not penetrate enough for photosynthesis to take place.

apical dominance (ā′-pik-ul) In a plant, the hormonal inhibition of axillary buds by a terminal bud.

apical meristem (ā′-pik-ul mer′-uh-stem) Plant tissue made up of undifferentiated cells located at the tip of a plant root or in the terminal or axillary bud of a shoot; enables roots and shoots to grow in length.

apoptosis (ā-puh-tō′-sus) The timely and tidy suicide of cells; also called programmed cell death.

aposematism (ā-pō-sem-at-ism) A high contrast, bright colour pattern in some animals that is often a warning sign of toxicity.

appendicular skeleton (ap′-en-dik′-yū-ler) Components of the skeletal system that support the fins of a fish or the arms and legs of a land vertebrate; in land vertebrates, the cartilage and bones of the shoulder girdle, pelvic girdle, forelimbs, and hind limbs. *See also* axial skeleton.

appendix (uh-pen′-dix) A small, fingerlike extension of the vertebrate cecum; contains a mass of white blood cells that contribute to immunity.

aquaporin A transport protein in the plasma membrane of some plant or animal cells that facilitates the diffusion of water across the membrane (osmosis).

aqueous humour (ā′-kwē-us hyū′-mer) Plasma-like liquid in the space between the lens and the cornea in the vertebrate eye; helps to maintain the shape of the eye, supplies nutrients and oxygen to its tissues, and disposes of its wastes.

aqueous solution (ā′-kwā-us) A solution in which water is the solvent.

arachnid A member of a major arthropod group (chelicerates) that includes spiders, scorpions, ticks, and mites.

Archaea (ar′-kē-uh) One of two prokaryotic domains of life, the other being Bacteria.

Archaeplastida One of five supergroups proposed in a current hypothesis of the evolutionary history of eukaryotes. The other four supergroups are Chromalveolata, Rhizaria, Excavata, and Unikonta.

arteriole (ar-ter′-ē-ōl) A vessel that conveys blood between an artery and a capillary bed.

artery A vessel that carries blood away from the heart to other parts of the body.

arthropod (ar′-thrō-pod) A member of the most diverse phylum in the animal kingdom. Arthropods include the horseshoe crab, arachnids (for example, spiders, ticks, scorpions, and mites), crustaceans (for example, crayfish, lobsters, crabs, and barnacles), millipedes, centipedes, and insects. Arthropods are characterized by a chitinous exoskeleton, moulting, jointed appendages, and a body formed of distinct groups of segments.

artificial selection The selective breeding of domesticated plants and animals to promote the occurrence of desirable traits.

ascomycete Member of a group of fungi characterized by saclike structures called asci that produce spores in sexual reproduction.

asexual reproduction The creation of genetically identical offspring by a single parent, without the participation of sperm and egg.

assisted reproductive technology Procedure that involves surgically removing eggs from a woman's ovaries, fertilizing them, and then returning them to the woman's body. *See also* in vitro fertilization.

association areas Sites of higher mental activities making up most of the cerebral cortex.

associative learning Learning that a particular stimulus or response is linked to a reward or a punishment; includes classical conditioning and trial-and-error learning.

astigmatism (uh-stig′-muh-tizm) Blurred vision caused by a misshapen lens or cornea.

atherosclerosis (ath′-uh-rō′-skluh-rō′-sis) A cardiovascular disease in which fatty deposits called plaques develop on the inner walls of the arteries, narrowing their inner diameters.

atom The smallest unit of matter that retains the properties of an element.

atomic mass The total mass of an atom; also called atomic weight. Given as a whole number, the atomic mass approximately equals the mass number.

atomic number The number of protons in each atom of a particular element.

ATP Adenosine triphosphate, the main energy source for cells.

ATP synthase A cluster of several membrane proteins that function in chemiosmosis with adjacent electron transport chains, using the energy of a hydrogen ion concentration gradient to make ATP.

atrium (ā′-trē-um) (plural, **atria**) A heart chamber that receives blood from the veins.

auditory canal Part of the vertebrate outer ear that channels sound waves from the pinna or outer body surface to the eardrum.

autonomic nervous system (ot′-ō-nom′-ik) The component of the vertebrate peripheral nervous system that regulates the internal environment; made up of sympathetic and parasympathetic subdivisions. Most actions of the autonomic nervous system are involuntary.

autosome A chromosome not directly involved in determining the sex of an organism; in mammals, for example, any chromosome other than X or Y.

autotroph (ot′-ō-trōf) An organism that makes its own food (often by photosynthesis), thereby sustaining itself without eating other organisms or their molecules. Plants, algae, and numerous bacteria are autotrophs.

auxin (ok′-sin) A plant hormone (indoleacetic acid or a related compound) whose chief effect is to promote seedling elongation.

AV (atrioventricular) node A region of specialized heart muscle tissue between the left and right atria where electrical impulses are delayed for about 0.1 second before spreading to both ventricles and causing them to contract.

axial skeleton (ak′-sē-ul) Components of the skeletal system that support the central trunk of the body: the skull, backbone, and rib cage in a vertebrate. *See also* appendicular skeleton.

axillary bud (ak′-sil-ār-ē) An embryonic shoot present in the angle formed by a leaf and stem.

axon (ak′-son) A neuron extension that conducts signals to another neuron or to an effector cell. A neuron has one long axon.

B

B cell A type of lymphocyte that matures in the bone marrow and later produces antibodies; is responsible for the humoral immune response.

bacillus (buh-sil′-us) (plural, **bacilli**) A rod-shaped prokaryotic cell.

Bacteria One of two prokaryotic domains of life, the other being Archaea.

bacteriophage (bak-tēr′-ē-ō-fāj) A virus that infects bacteria; also called a phage.

balancing selection Natural selection that maintains stable frequencies of two or more phenotypic forms in a population.

ball-and-socket joint A joint that allows rotation and movement in several planes. Examples in humans are the hip and shoulder joints.

bark All the tissues external to the vascular cambium in a plant that is growing in thickness; made up of secondary phloem, cork cambium, and cork.

Barr body A dense body formed from a deactivated X chromosome found in the nuclei of female mammalian cells.

basal metabolic rate (BMR) The number of kilocalories a resting animal requires to fuel its essential body processes for a given time.

basal nuclei (bā′-sul nū′-klē-ī) Clusters of nerve cell bodies located deep within the cerebrum that are important in motor coordination.

base A substance that decreases the hydrogen ion (H^+) concentration in a solution.

basidiomycete (buh-sid′-ē-ō-mī′sēt) Member of a group of fungi characterized by club-shaped, spore-producing structures called basidia.

basilar membrane The floor of the middle canal of the inner ear.

Batesian mimicry A type of mimicry in which the mimic has evolved similar coloration to a distasteful species, dissuading would-be predators.

behaviour Individually, an action carried out by the muscles or glands under control of the nervous system in response to a stimulus; collectively, the sum of an animal's responses to external and internal stimuli.

behavioural ecology The study of behaviour in an evolutionary context.

benign tumour An abnormal mass of cells that remains at its original site in the body.

benthic realm A seafloor, or the bottom of a freshwater lake, pond, river, or stream.

β-lactam antibiotic An antibiotic that contains a β-lactam ring made of three carbon atoms and one nitrogen atom.

biennial A plant that completes its life cycle in two years.

bilateral symmetry An arrangement of body parts such that an organism can be divided equally by a single cut passing longitudinally through it. A bilaterally symmetric organism has mirror-image right and left sides.

bilaterian Member of the clade Bilateria, animals exhibiting bilateral symmetry.

bile A mixture of substances that is produced by the liver and stored in the gallbladder; emulsifies fats and aids in their digestion.

binary fission A means of asexual reproduction in which a parent organism, often a single cell, divides into two genetically identical individuals of about equal size.

binomial A two-part, Latinized name of a species; for example, *Homo sapiens*.

biodiversity The composition of a species; also known as biological diversity and species diversity.

biodiversity hot spot A small geographic area with an exceptional concentration of endangered and threatened species, especially endemic species (those found nowhere else).

biofilm A surface-coating colony of prokaryotes that engage in metabolic cooperation.

biogenic amine A neurotransmitter derived from an amino acid. Examples of biogenic amines are epinephrine and dopamine.

biogeochemical cycle Any of the various chemical circuits that involve both biotic and abiotic components of an ecosystem.

biogeography The study of the past and present distribution of organisms.

biological clock An internal timekeeper that controls an organism's biological rhythms, marking time with or without environmental cues but often requiring signals from the environment to remain tuned to an appropriate period. *See also* circadian rhythm.

biological control The intentional release of a natural enemy to attack a pest population.

biological diversity *See* biodiversity.

biological species concept Definition of a species as a group of populations whose members have the potential to interbreed in nature and produce viable, fertile offspring, but do not produce viable, fertile offspring with members of other such populations.

biology The scientific study of life.

biomagnification The accumulation of harmful chemicals that are retained in the living tissues of consumers in food chains.

biomass The amount, or mass, of organic material in an ecosystem.

biome (bī'-ōm) A major type of ecological association that occupies a broad geographic region of land or water and is characterized by organisms adapted to the particular environment.

bioremediation The use of living organisms to detoxify and restore polluted and degraded ecosystems.

biosphere The entire portion of Earth inhabited by life; the sum of all the planet's ecosystems.

biotechnology The manipulation of living organisms or their components to make useful products.

biotic factor (bī-o'-tik) A living component of a biological community; an organism, or a factor pertaining to one or more organisms.

bipolar disorder Depressive mental illness characterized by extreme mood swings; also called manic-depressive disorder.

birds Members of a clade of reptiles that have feathers and adaptations for flight.

birth control pill A chemical contraceptive that contains synthetic estrogen and/or progesterone (or a synthetic progesterone-like hormone called progestin) and prevents the release of eggs.

bivalve A member of a group of molluscs that includes clams, mussels, scallops, and oysters.

blastocoel (blas'-tuh-sēl) In a developing animal, a central, fluid-filled cavity in a blastula.

blastocyst (blas'-tō-sist) A mammalian embryo (equivalent to an amphibian blastula) made up of a hollow ball of cells that results from cleavage and that implants in the mother's endometrium.

blastula (blas'-tyū-luh) An embryonic stage that marks the end of cleavage during animal development; a hollow ball of cells in many species.

blinded experiment An experiment that controls for researcher bias by having the investigators measure samples without knowing which group they belong to; only after the data is collected do the researchers find out.

blood A type of connective tissue with a fluid matrix called plasma in which red blood cells, white blood cells, and platelets are suspended.

blood pressure The force that blood exerts against the walls of blood vessels.

blood-brain barrier A system of capillaries in the brain that restricts passage of most substances into the brain, thereby preventing large fluctuations in the brain's environment.

body cavity A fluid-containing space between the digestive tract and the body wall.

bolus A lubricated ball of chewed food.

bone A type of connective tissue consisting of living cells held in a rigid matrix of collagen fibres embedded in calcium salts.

boreal forest The northern coniferous forest, characterized by long, snowy winters and short, wet summers, extending across North America and Eurasia to the southern border of the arctic tundra; also found just below alpine tundra on mountainsides in temperate zones.

bottleneck effect Genetic drift resulting from a drastic reduction in population size. Typically, the surviving population is no longer genetically representative of the original population.

Bowman's capsule A cup-shaped swelling at the receiving end of a nephron in the vertebrate kidney; collects the filtrate from the blood.

brain The master control centre of the nervous system, involved in regulating and controlling body activity and interpreting information from the senses transmitted through the nervous system.

brain stem A functional unit of the vertebrate brain, composed of the midbrain, the medulla oblongata, and the pons; serves mainly as a sensory filter, selecting which information reaches higher brain centres.

breathing Ventilation of the lungs through alternating inhalation and exhalation.

breathing control centre The part of the medulla in the brain that directs the activity of organs involved in breathing.

bronchiole (bron'-kē-ōl) A fine branch of the bronchi that transports air to alveoli.

bronchus (bron'-kus) (plural, **bronchi**) One of a pair of breathing tubes that branch from the trachea into the lungs.

brown alga One of a group of marine, multicellular, autotrophic protists belonging to the supergroup Chromalveolata; the most common and largest type of seaweed. Brown algae include the kelps.

bryophyte (brī'-uh-fīt) A plant that lacks xylem and phloem; a seedless nonvascular plant. Bryophytes include mosses, liverworts, and hornworts.

budding A means of asexual reproduction whereby a new individual develops from an outgrowth of a parent. The new individual eventually splits off and lives independently.

buffer A chemical substance that resists changes in pH by accepting hydrogen ions from or donating hydrogen ions to solutions.

bulbourethral gland (bul'-bō-yū-rē'-thrul) One of a pair of glands near the base of the penis in the human male that secrete a clear alkaline mucus.

bulk feeder An animal that eats relatively large pieces of food.

C

C$_3$ plant A plant that uses the Calvin cycle for the initial steps that incorporate CO_2 into organic material, forming a three-carbon compound as the first stable intermediate.

C$_4$ plant A plant that prefaces the Calvin cycle with reactions that incorporate CO_2 into four-carbon compounds, the end product of which supplies CO_2 for the Calvin cycle.

calcitonin (kal'-sih-tōn'-in) A peptide hormone secreted by the thyroid gland that lowers the blood calcium level.

Calvin cycle The second of two stages of photosynthesis; a cyclic series of chemical reactions that occur in the stroma of a chloroplast by using the carbon in CO_2 and the ATP and NADPH produced by the light reactions to make the energy-rich sugar molecule G3P.

CAM plant A plant that uses an adaptation for photosynthesis in arid conditions in which carbon dioxide entering open stomata during the night is converted to organic acids, which release CO_2 for the Calvin cycle during the day, when stomata are closed.

cancer A disease characterized by the presence of malignant tumours (rapidly growing and spreading masses of abnormal body cells) in the body.

capillary (kap'-il-er-ē) A microscopic blood vessel that conveys blood between an arteriole and a venule; enables the exchange of nutrients and dissolved gases between the blood and interstitial fluid.

capillary bed A network of capillaries in a tissue or organ.

capsid The protein shell that encloses a viral genome.

capsomere A protein subunit of a viral protein coat.

carbohydrate (kar'-bō-hi'-drāt) Member of the class of biological molecules consisting of single-monomer sugars (monosaccharides), two-monomer sugars (disaccharides), and polymers (polysaccharides).

carbon fixation The incorporation of carbon from atmospheric CO_2 into the carbon in organic compounds. During photosynthesis in a C_3 plant, carbon is fixed into a three-carbon sugar as it enters the Calvin cycle. In C_4 and CAM plants, carbon is fixed into a four-carbon sugar.

carbon skeleton The chain of carbon atoms that forms the structural backbone of an organic molecule.

carbonyl group (kar´-buh-nēl´) A chemical group consisting of a carbon atom linked by a double bond to an oxygen atom.

carboxyl group (kar´-bok-sil) A chemical group consisting of a carbon atom double-bonded to an oxygen atom and also bonded to a hydroxyl group.

carcinogen (kar-sin´-uh-jin) A cancer-causing agent, either high-energy radiation (such as X-rays or UV light) or a chemical.

carcinoma (kar´-sih-nō´-muh) Cancer that originates in the coverings of the body, such as skin or the lining of the intestinal tract.

cardiac cycle (kar´-dē-ak) The alternating contractions and relaxations of the heart.

cardiac muscle A type of striated muscle that forms the contractile wall of the heart.

cardiac output The volume of blood pumped per minute by each ventricle of the heart.

cardiovascular disease (kar´-dē-ō-vas´-kyū-ler) Disorders of the heart and blood vessels.

cardiovascular system A closed circulatory system with a heart and a branching network of arteries, capillaries, and veins.

carnivore An animal that mainly eats other animals.

carpel (kar´-pul) The female part of a flower, consisting of a stalk with an ovary at the base and a stigma, which traps pollen, at the tip.

carrier An individual who is heterozygous for a recessively inherited disorder and who therefore does not show symptoms of that disorder but who may pass on the recessive allele to offspring.

carrying capacity In a population, the number of individuals that an environment can sustain.

cartilage (kar´-ti-lij) A flexible connective tissue consisting of living cells and collagenous fibres embedded in a rubbery matrix.

Casparian strip (kas-par´-ē-un) A waxy barrier in the walls of endodermal cells in a plant root that prevents water and ions from entering the xylem without crossing one or more cell membranes.

cation exchange A process in which positively charged minerals are made available to a plant when hydrogen ions in the soil displace mineral ions from the clay particles.

cecum (sē´-kum) (plural, **ceca**) A blind outpocket at the beginning of the large intestine.

cell A basic unit of living matter separated from its environment by a plasma membrane; the fundamental structural unit of life.

cell body The part of a cell, such as a neuron, that houses the nucleus.

cell cycle An ordered sequence of events (including interphase and the mitotic phase) that extends from the time a eukaryotic cell is first formed from a dividing parent cell until its own division into two cells.

cell cycle control system A cyclically operating set of proteins that triggers and coordinates events in the eukaryotic cell cycle.

cell division The reproduction of a cell through duplication of the genome and division of the cytoplasm.

cell plate A double membrane across the midline of a dividing plant cell, between which the new cell wall forms during cytokinesis.

cell theory The theory that all living things are composed of cells and that all cells come from other cells.

cell wall A protective layer external to the plasma membrane in plant cells, bacteria, fungi, and some protists; protects the cell and helps to maintain its shape.

cell-mediated immune response The type of specific immunity brought about by T cells. The cell-mediated immune response fights body cells infected with pathogens. *See also* humoral immune response.

cellular metabolism (muh-tab´-uh-lizm) All the chemical activities of a cell.

cellular respiration The aerobic harvesting of energy from food molecules; the energy-releasing chemical breakdown of food molecules, such as glucose, and the storage of potential energy in a form that cells can use to perform work; involves glycolysis, the citric acid cycle, and oxidative phosphorylation (the electron transport chain and chemiosmosis).

cellular slime mould A type of protist that has unicellular amoeboid cells and aggregated reproductive bodies in its life cycle; a member of the amoebozoan clade.

cellulose (sel´-yū-lōs) A structural polysaccharide of plant cell walls composed of glucose monomers. Cellulose molecules are linked into cablelike fibrils.

centipede A carnivorous terrestrial arthropod that has one pair of long legs for each of its numerous body segments, with the front pair modified as poison claws.

central canal The narrow cavity in the centre of the spinal cord that is continuous with the fluid-filled ventricles of the brain.

central nervous system (CNS) The integration and command centre of the nervous system; the brain and, in vertebrates, the spinal cord.

central vacuole In a plant cell, a large membranous sac with diverse roles in growth and the storage of chemicals and wastes.

centralization The presence of a central nervous system distinct from a peripheral nervous system.

centriole (sen´-trē-ōl) A structure in an animal cell composed of cylinders of microtubule triplets arranged in a 9 + 0 pattern. An animal usually has a centrosome with a pair of centrioles involved in cell division.

centromere (sen´-trō-mēr) The region of a duplicated chromosome where two sister chromatids are joined (often appearing as a narrow "waist") and where spindle microtubules attach during mitosis and meiosis. The centromere divides at the onset of anaphase during mitosis and anaphase II during meiosis.

centrosome (sen´-trō-sōm) Material in the cytoplasm of a eukaryotic cell that gives rise to microtubules; important in mitosis and meiosis; also called the microtubule-organizing centre.

cephalization (sef´-uh-luh-zā´-shun) An evolutionary trend toward concentration of the nervous system at the head end.

cephalopod A member of a group of molluscs that includes squids, cuttlefish, octopi, and nautiluses.

cerebellum (sār´-ruh-bel´-um) Part of the vertebrate hindbrain; mainly a planning centre that interacts closely with the cerebrum in coordinating body movement.

cerebral cortex (suh-rē´-brul kor´-teks) A folded sheet of grey matter forming the surface of the cerebrum. In humans, it contains integrating centres for higher brain functions such as reasoning, speech, language, and imagination.

cerebral hemisphere The right or left half of the vertebrate cerebrum.

cerebrospinal fluid (suh-rē´-brō-spī´-nul) Blood-derived fluid that surrounds, nourishes, and cushions the brain and spinal cord.

cerebrum (suh-rē´-brum) The largest, most sophisticated, and most dominant part of the vertebrate forebrain, made up of right and left cerebral hemispheres.

cervix (ser´-viks) The neck of the uterus, which opens into the vagina.

chaparral (shap´-uh-ral´) A biome dominated by spiny evergreen shrubs adapted to periodic drought and fires; found where cold ocean currents circulate offshore, creating mild, rainy winters and long, hot, dry summers.

character A heritable feature that varies among individuals within a population, such as flower colour in pea plants or eye colour in humans.

chelicerate (kē-lih-suh´-rāte) A lineage of arthropods that includes horseshoe crabs, scorpions, ticks, and spiders.

chemical bond An attraction between two atoms resulting from a sharing of outer-shell electrons or the presence of opposite charges on the atoms. The bonded atoms gain complete outer electron shells.

chemical cycling The use and reuse of a chemical element, such as carbon, within an ecosystem.

chemical energy Energy available in molecules for release in a chemical reaction; a form of potential energy.

chemical reaction The making and breaking of chemical bonds, leading to changes in the composition of matter.

chemiosmosis (kem′-ē-oz-mō′-sis) Energy-coupling mechanism that uses the energy of hydrogen ion (H^+) gradients across membranes to drive cellular work, such as the phosphorylation of ADP; powers most ATP synthesis in cells.

chemoautotroph An organism that obtains both energy and carbon from inorganic chemicals. A chemoautotroph makes its own organic compounds from CO_2 without using light energy.

chemoheterotroph An organism that obtains both energy and carbon from organic compounds.

chemoreceptor (kē′-mō-rē-sep′-ter) A sensory receptor that detects chemical changes within the body or a specific kind of molecule in the external environment.

chiasma (kī-az′-muh) (plural, **chiasmata**) The microscopically visible site where crossing over has occurred between chromatids of homologous chromosomes during prophase I of meiosis.

chitin (kī-tin) A structural polysaccharide found in many fungal cell walls and in the exoskeletons of arthropods.

chlamydia (plural, **chlamydiae**) A member of a group of bacteria that live inside eukaryotic host cells. Chlamydiae include human pathogens that cause blindness and nongonococcal urethritis, a common sexually transmitted disease.

chlorophyll (klō-ruh-fil) A green pigment located within the chloroplasts of plants, algae, and certain prokaryotes. Chlorophyll *a* can participate directly in the light reactions that convert solar energy to chemical energy.

chlorophyll *a* The central pigment within the reaction centres of photosystems I and II.

chloroplast (klō′-rō-plast) An organelle found in plants and photosynthetic protists that absorbs sunlight and uses it to drive the synthesis of organic molecules (sugars) from carbon dioxide and water.

choanocyte (kō-an′-uh-sīt) A flagellated feeding cell found in sponges. Also called a collar cell, it has a collarlike ring that traps food particles around the base of its flagellum.

cholesterol (kō-les′-tuh-rol) A steroid that is an important component of animal cell membranes and that acts as a precursor molecule for the synthesis of other steroids, such as hormones.

chondrichthyan (kon-drik′-thē-an) Cartilaginous fish; member of a clade of jawed vertebrates with skeletons made mostly of cartilage, such as sharks and rays.

chorion (kōr′-ē-on) In animals, the outermost extraembryonic membrane, which becomes the mammalian embryo's part of the placenta.

chorionic villi (kōr′-ē-on′-ik vil-ī) Outgrowths of the chorion, containing embryonic blood vessels. As part of the placenta, chorionic villi absorb nutrients and oxygen from, and pass wastes into, the mother's bloodstream.

chorionic villus sampling (CVS) A technique for diagnosing genetic defects while the fetus is in an early development stage within the uterus. A small sample of the fetal portion of the placenta is removed and analyzed.

choroid (kōr′-oyd) A thin, pigmented layer in the vertebrate eye, surrounded by the sclera. The iris is part of the choroid.

Chromalveolata (krō-mal-vē-ō-la-ta) One of five supergroups proposed in a current hypothesis of the evolutionary history of eukaryotes. The other four supergroups are Rhizaria, Excavata, Unikonta, and Archaeplastida.

chromatin (krō′-muh-tin) The combination of DNA and proteins that constitutes eukaryotic chromosomes; often used to refer to the diffuse, very extended form taken by chromosomes when a cell is not dividing.

chromosome (krō′-muh-sōm) A threadlike, gene-carrying structure found in the nucleus of a eukaryotic cell and most visible during mitosis and meiosis; also, the main gene-carrying structure of a prokaryotic cell; consists of one very long piece of chromatin, a combination of DNA and protein.

chromosome theory of inheritance A basic principle in biology stating that genes are located on chromosomes and that the behaviour of chromosomes during meiosis accounts for inheritance patterns.

chyme (kīm) The mixture of partially digested food and digestive juices formed in the stomach.

chytrid (kī-trid) Member of a group of fungi that are mostly aquatic and have flagellated spores. They probably represent the most primitive fungal lineage.

ciliate (sil′-ē-it) A type of protist that moves and feeds by means of cilia. Ciliates belong to the supergroup Chromalveolata.

cilium (plural, **cilia**) A short cellular appendage specialized for locomotion, formed from a core of nine outer doublet microtubules and two single microtubules (the 9 + 2 pattern) covered by the cell's plasma membrane.

circadian rhythm (ser-kā′-dē-un) In an organism, a biological cycle of about 24 hours that is controlled by a biological clock, usually under the influence of environmental cues; a pattern of activity that is repeated daily. *See also* biological clock.

circulatory system The organ system that transports materials such as nutrients, O_2, and hormones to body cells and transports CO_2 and other wastes from body cells.

citric acid cycle The chemical cycle that completes the metabolic breakdown of glucose molecules begun in glycolysis by oxidizing acetyl CoA (derived from pyruvate) to carbon dioxide. The cycle occurs in the matrix of mitochondria and supplies most of the NADH molecules that carry energy to the electron transport chains. Together with pyruvate oxidation, the second major stage of cellular respiration.

clade A group of species that includes an ancestral species and all of its descendants.

cladistics (kluh-dis′-tiks) An approach to systematics in which common descent is the primary criterion used to classify organisms by placing them into groups called clades.

class In Linnaean classification, the taxonomic category above order.

cleavage (klē′-vij) (1) Cytokinesis in animal cells and in some protists, characterized by pinching in of the plasma membrane. (2) In animal development, the first major phase of embryonic development, in which rapid cell divisions without cell growth transforms the animal zygote into a ball of cells.

cleavage furrow The first sign of cytokinesis during cell division in an animal cell; a shallow groove in the cell surface near the old metaphase plate.

clitoris An organ in the female that engorges with blood and becomes erect during sexual arousal.

cloaca (klō-ā-ka) A single opening that services multiple organ systems such as the reproductive and digestive systems.

clonal selection (klōn′-ul) The production of a lineage of genetically identical cells that recognize and attack the specific antigen that stimulated their proliferation; is the mechanism that underlies the immune system's specificity and memory of antigens.

clone As a verb, to produce genetically identical copies of a cell, organism, or DNA molecule. As a noun, the collection of cells, organisms, or molecules resulting from cloning; colloquially, a single organism that is genetically identical to another because it arose from the cloning of a somatic cell.

closed circulatory system A circulatory system in which blood is confined to vessels and is kept separate from the interstitial fluid.

club fungus *See* basidiomycete.

clumped distribution pattern A pattern in which the individuals of a population are aggregated in patches.

cnidarian (nī-dār′-ē-un) An animal characterized by cnidocytes, radial symmetry, a gastrovascular cavity, and a polyp and medusa body form. Cnidarians include the hydras, jellies, sea anemones, corals, and related animals.

cnidocyte (nī′-duh-sīt) A specialized cell for which the phylum Cnidaria is named; consists of a capsule containing a fine coiled thread, which, when discharged, functions in defence and prey capture.

coccus (kok´-us) (plural, **cocci**) A spherical prokaryotic cell.

cochlea (kok´-lē-uh) A coiled tube in the inner ear of birds and mammals that contains the hearing organ, the organ of Corti.

codominant Inheritance pattern in which a heterozygote expresses the distinct trait of both alleles.

codon (kō´-don) A three-nucleotide sequence in mRNA that specifies a particular amino acid or polypeptide termination signal; the basic unit of the genetic code.

coelom (sē´-lom) A body cavity completely lined with mesoderm.

coenzyme An organic molecule serving as a cofactor. Most vitamins function as coenzymes in important metabolic reactions.

co-evolution Evolutionary change in which adaptations in one species act as a selective force on a second species, inducing adaptations that in turn act as a selective force on the first species; mutual influence on the evolution of two different interacting species.

cofactor A nonprotein molecule or ion that is required for the proper functioning of an enzyme. *See also* coenzyme.

cognition The process carried out by an animal's nervous system that includes perceiving, storing, integrating, and using the information obtained by the animal's sensory receptors.

cognitive map A representation, within an animal's nervous system, of spatial relations among objects in the animal's environment.

cohesion (kō-hē´-zhun) The sticking together of molecules of the same kind, often by hydrogen bonds.

collecting duct A tube in the vertebrate kidney that concentrates urine while conveying it to the renal pelvis.

collenchyma cell (kō-len´-kim-uh) In plants, a cell with a thick primary wall and no secondary wall, functioning mainly in supporting growing parts.

colon (kō´-lun) Large intestine; the portion of the vertebrate alimentary canal between the small intestine and the anus; functions mainly in water absorption and the formation of feces.

commensalism A symbiosis in which one partner benefits while the other is not affected.

communication Animal behaviour including transmission of, reception of, and response to signals.

community An assemblage of all the organisms living together and potentially interacting in a particular area.

companion cell In a plant, a cell connected to a sieve-tube element whose nucleus and ribosomes provide proteins for the sieve-tube element.

competitive exclusion A type of exclusion where one species outcompetes another and ultimately eliminates it from the area.

competitive inhibitor A substance that reduces the activity of an enzyme by binding to the enzyme's active site in place of the substrate; structure mimics that of the enzyme's substrate.

complement system A family of innate defensive blood proteins that cooperate with other components of the vertebrate defence system to protect against microbes; can enhance phagocytosis, directly lyse pathogens, and amplify the inflammatory response.

complementary DNA (cDNA) A DNA molecule made in vitro by using mRNA as a template and the enzyme reverse transcriptase. A cDNA molecule therefore corresponds to a gene but lacks the introns present in the DNA of the genome.

complete digestive tract A digestive tube with two openings, a mouth and an anus.

complete dominance A type of inheritance in which the phenotypes of the heterozygote and dominant homozygote are indistinguishable.

complete metamorphosis (met´-uh-mōr´-fuh-sis) A type of development in certain insects in which development from larva to adult is achieved by multiple moults that are followed by a pupal stage. While encased in its pupa, the body rebuilds from clusters of embryonic cells that have been held in reserve. The adult emerges from the pupa.

compost Decomposing organic material that can be used to add nutrients to soil.

compound A substance containing two or more elements in a fixed ratio. For example, table salt (NaCl) consists of one atom of the element sodium (Na) for every atom of chlorine (Cl).

compound eye The photoreceptor in many invertebrates; made up of many tiny light detectors, each of which detects light from a tiny portion of the field of view.

concentration gradient A region along which the density of a chemical substance increases or decreases. Cells often maintain concentration gradients of ions across their membranes. When a gradient exists, substances tend to move from where they are more concentrated to where they are less concentrated.

conception The fertilization of the egg by a sperm cell in humans.

cone (1) In vertebrates, a photoreceptor cell in the retina stimulated by bright light and enabling colour vision. (2) In conifers, a reproductive structure bearing pollen or ovules.

coniferous forest A biome characterized by conifers, cone-bearing evergreen trees.

conjugation The union (mating) of two bacterial cells or protist cells and the transfer of DNA between the two cells.

conjunctiva A thin mucous membrane that lines the inner surface of vertebrate eyelids.

connective tissue Animal tissue that functions mainly to bind and support other tissues, having a sparse population of cells scattered through an extracellular matrix, which they produce.

conservation biology A goal-oriented science that endeavours to sustain biological diversity.

continental shelf The submerged part of a continent.

contraception The deliberate prevention of pregnancy.

controlled experiment An experiment in which an experimental group is compared with a control group that varies only in the factor being tested.

convergent evolution The evolution of similar features in different evolutionary lineages, which can result from living in very similar environments.

copulation Sexual intercourse, usually necessary for internal fertilization to occur.

cork The outermost protective layer of a plant's bark, produced by the cork cambium.

cork cambium Meristematic tissue that produces cork cells during secondary growth of a plant.

cornea (kor´-nē-uh) The transparent frontal portion of the sclera, which admits light into the vertebrate eye.

corpus callosum (kor´-pus kuh-lō´-sum) The thick band of nerve fibres that connect the right and left cerebral hemispheres in placental mammals, enabling the hemispheres to process information together.

corpus luteum (kor´-pus lū´-tē-um) A small body of endocrine tissue that develops from an ovarian follicle after ovulation and secretes progesterone and estrogen during pregnancy.

cortex In plants, the ground tissue system of a root, made up mostly of parenchyma cells, which store food and absorb minerals that have passed through the epidermis.

corticosteroid A hormone synthesized and secreted by the adrenal cortex. The corticosteroids include the mineralocorticoids and glucocorticoids.

cotyledon (kot´-uh-lē´-don) The first leaf that appears on an embryo of a flowering plant; a seed leaf. Monocot embryos have one cotyledon; dicot embryos have two.

countercurrent exchange The transfer of a substance or heat between two fluids flowing in opposite directions.

countercurrent heat exchange A circulatory adaptation in which parallel blood vessels convey warm and cold blood in opposite directions, maximizing heat transfer to the cold blood.

covalent bond (ko-vā´-lent) A strong chemical bond in which two atoms share one or more pairs of outer-shell electrons.

craniate A chordate with a head.

crista (kris´tuh) (plural, **cristae**) An infolding of the inner mitochondrial membrane.

crop A pouchlike organ in a digestive tract where food is softened and may be stored temporarily.

cross A mating of two sexually reproducing individuals; often used to describe a genetics experiment involving a controlled mating (a "genetic cross").

cross-fertilization The fusion of sperm and egg derived from two different individuals.

crossing over The exchange of segments between chromatids of homologous chromosomes during synapsis in prophase I of meiosis; also, the exchange of segments between DNA molecules in prokaryotes.

crustacean A member of a major arthropod group that includes lobsters, crayfish, crabs, shrimps, and barnacles.

cuticle (kyū′-tuh-kul) (1) In animals, a tough, nonliving outer layer of the skin. (2) In plants, a waxy coating on the surface of stems and leaves that helps to retain water.

cyanobacteria (sī-an′-ō-bak-tēr′-ē-uh) Photoautotrophic prokaryotes with plantlike, oxygen-generating photosynthesis.

cystic fibrosis (sis′-tik fī-brō′-sis) A genetic disease that occurs in people with two copies of a certain recessive allele; characterized by an excessive secretion of mucus and vulnerability to infection; fatal if untreated.

cytokinesis (sī′-tō-kuh-nē′-sis) The division of the cytoplasm to form two separate daughter cells. Cytokinesis usually occurs in conjunction with telophase of mitosis. Mitosis and cytokinesis make up the mitotic (M) phase of the cell cycle.

cytokinin (sī′-tō-kī′-nin) One of a family of plant hormones that promotes cell division, retards aging in flowers and fruits, and may interact antagonistically with auxins in regulating plant growth and development.

cytoplasm (si′-tō-plaz′-um) The contents of a eukaryotic cell between the plasma membrane and the nucleus; consists of a semi-fluid medium and organelles; can also refer to the interior of a prokaryotic cell.

cytosine (C) (sī′-tuh-sin) A single-ring nitrogenous base found in DNA and RNA.

cytoskeleton A network of protein fibres in the cytoplasm of a eukaryotic cell; includes microfilaments, intermediate filaments, and microtubules.

cytotoxic T cell (sī′-tō-tok′-sik) A type of lymphocyte that attacks body cells infected with pathogens.

D

decomposer Prokaryotes and fungi that secrete enzymes that digest nutrients from organic material and convert them to inorganic forms.

decomposition The breakdown of organic materials into inorganic ones.

dedifferentiate When a mature cell reverts back to an immature cell type with some degree of potency.

deductive reasoning A type of logic in which specific results are predicted from a general premise.

defensive mutualism When one symbiont receives a defensive benefit from a mutualistic relationship.

degeneracy In evolution, the loss of structures that become redundant or unnecessary.

dehydration reaction (dē-hī-drā′-shun) A chemical reaction in which two molecules become covalently bonded to each other with the removal of a water molecule.

deletion The loss of one or more nucleotides from a gene by mutation; the loss of a fragment of a chromosome.

demographic dependency ratio (DDR) The ratio of youths (aged 0 to 14) and seniors (aged 65 and older) to the number of individuals in the workforce between the ages of 15 and 64.

demographic transition A shift from zero population growth in which birth rates and death rates are high to zero population growth characterized by low birth and death rates.

denaturation (dē-nā′-chur-ā′-shun) A process in which a protein unravels, losing its specific structure and hence function; can be caused by changes in pH or salt concentration or by high temperature; also refers to the separation of the two strands of the DNA double helix, caused by similar factors.

dendrite (den′-drīt) A neuron fibre that conveys signals from its tip inward, toward the rest of the neuron. A neuron typically has many short dendrites.

density-dependent factor A population-limiting factor whose intensity is linked to population density. For example, there may be a decline in birth rates or a rise in death rates in response to an increase in the number of individuals living in a designated area.

density-dependent inhibition The ceasing of cell division that occurs when cells touch one another.

density-independent factor A population-limiting factor whose intensity is unrelated to population density.

deoxyribonucleic acid (DNA) (dē-ok′-sē-rī′-bō-nū-klā′-ik) A double-stranded helical nucleic acid molecule consisting of nucleotide monomers with deoxyribose sugar and the nitrogenous bases adenine (A), cytosine (C), guanine (G), and thymine (T). Capable of replicating, DNA is an organism's genetic material. *See also* gene.

dermal tissue system The outer protective covering of plants.

desert A biome characterized by organisms adapted to sparse rainfall (less than 30 cm per year) and rapid evaporation.

desertification The conversion of semi-arid regions to desert.

determinate growth Termination of growth after reaching a certain size, as in most animals. *See also* indeterminate growth.

detritivore (duh-trī′-tuh-vor) An organism that consumes organic wastes and dead organisms.

detritus (duh-trī′-tus) Dead organic matter.

deuterostome (dū-ter′-ō-stōm) A mode of animal development in which the opening formed during gastrulation becomes the anus. Animals with the deuterostome pattern of development include the echinoderms and the chordates.

diabetes mellitus (dī′-uh-bē′-tis me-lī′-tis) A human hormonal disease in which body cells cannot absorb enough glucose from the blood and become energy starved; body fats and proteins are then consumed for their energy. Type 1 (insulin-dependent) diabetes results when the pancreas does not produce insulin; type 2 (non-insulin-dependent) diabetes results when body cells fail to respond to insulin.

dialysis (dī-al′-uh-sis) Separation and disposal of metabolic wastes from the blood by mechanical means; an artificial method of performing the functions of the kidneys that can be life sustaining in the event of kidney failure.

diaphragm (dī′-uh-fram) The sheet of muscle separating the chest cavity from the abdominal cavity in mammals. Its contraction expands the chest cavity, and its relaxation reduces it.

diastole (d′-as′-tō-lē) The stage of the heart cycle in which the heart muscle is relaxed, allowing the chambers to fill with blood. *See also* systole.

diatom (dī′-uh-tom) A unicellular, autotrophic protist that belongs to the supergroup Chromalveolata; possesses a unique glassy cell wall containing silica.

dicot (dī′-kot) A term traditionally used to refer to flowering plants that have two embryonic seed leaves, or cotyledons.

differentiation The specialization in the structure and function of cells that occurs during the development of an organism; results from selective activation and deactivation of the cells' genes.

diffuse mutualism When one symbiont can form similar mutualistic relationships with many different species.

diffusion The spontaneous movement of a substance down its concentration gradient from where it is more concentrated to where it is less concentrated.

digestion The mechanical and chemical breakdown of food into molecules small enough for the body to absorb; the second stage of food processing in animals.

digestive system The organ system involved in ingestion and digestion of food, absorption of nutrients, and elimination of wastes.

dihybrid An individual that is heterozygous for two genes of interest.

dihybrid cross (dī′-hī′-brid) An experimental mating of individuals differing in two characters.

dinoflagellate (dī′-nō-flaj′-uh-let) A member of a group of protists belonging to the supergroup Chromalveolata. Dinoflagellates are common components of marine and freshwater phytoplankton.

diploid In an organism that reproduces sexually, a cell containing two homologous sets of chromosomes, one set inherited from each parent; a 2n cell.

direct life cycle A life cycle of a parasite in which only a single host is required.

directional selection Natural selection in which individuals at one end of the phenotypic range survive and reproduce more successfully than do other individuals.

disaccharide (dī-sak′-uh-rīd) A sugar molecule consisting of two monosaccharides linked by a dehydration reaction.

disclimax community A community that is held in an intermediate state of succession by its disturbance regime.

dispersive mutualism When one symbiont benefits from a mutualistic relationship by having its gametes or offspring dispersed.

disruptive selection Natural selection in which individuals on both extremes of a phenotypic range are favoured over intermediate phenotypes.

distal tubule In the vertebrate kidney, the portion of a nephron that helps to refine filtrate and empties it into a collecting duct.

distribution pattern The manner in which individuals in a population are spaced within their area. Three types of dispersion patterns are clumped (individuals are aggregated in patches), uniform (individuals are evenly distributed), and random (unpredictable distribution).

disturbance In ecology, a force that changes a biological community and usually removes organisms from it.

disturbance regime The pattern of disturbances within a community described by frequency and intensity of events.

dizygotic twins (dī-zī-gah-tic) A multiple birth when each twin develops from a separate egg that was fertilized by a separate sperm; also called fraternal twins.

DNA *See* deoxyribonucleic acid (DNA).

DNA ligase (lī′-gās) An enzyme, essential for DNA replication, that catalyzes the covalent bonding of adjacent DNA polynucleotide strands; used in genetic engineering to paste a specific piece of DNA containing a gene of interest into a bacterial plasmid or other vector.

DNA polymerase (puh-lim′-er-ās) A large molecular complex that assembles DNA nucleotides into polynucleotides by using a pre-existing strand of DNA as a template.

DNA profiling A procedure that analyzes DNA samples to determine if they came from the same individual.

DNA technology Methods used to study and/or manipulate DNA, including recombinant DNA technology.

doldrums (dol′-drums) An area of calm or very light winds near the equator, caused by rising warm air.

domain A taxonomic category above the kingdom level. The three domains of life are Archaea, Bacteria, and Eukarya.

dominance hierarchy The ranking of individuals within a group, based on social interactions and usually maintained by agonistic behaviour.

dominant allele The allele that determines the phenotype of a gene when the individual is heterozygous for that gene.

dorsal Pertaining to the back of a bilaterally symmetric animal.

dorsal, hollow nerve cord One of the four hallmarks of chordates, a tube that forms on the dorsal side of the body, above the notochord.

double circulation A circulatory system with separate pulmonary and systemic circuits, in which blood passes through the heart after completing each circuit; ensures vigorous blood flow to all organs.

double fertilization In flowering plants, the formation of both a zygote and a cell with a triploid nucleus, which develops into the endosperm.

double helix The form of native DNA, referring to its two adjacent polynucleotide strands intertwined into a spiral shape.

Down syndrome A human genetic disorder resulting from the presence of an extra chromosome 21; characterized by heart and respiratory defects and varying degrees of intellectual deficiencies.

Duchenne muscular dystrophy (duh-shen′ dis′-truh-fē) A human genetic disease caused by a sex-linked recessive allele; characterized by progressive weakening and a loss of muscle tissue.

duodenum (dū-ō-dē′-num) The first portion of the vertebrate small intestine after the stomach, where chyme from the stomach mixes with bile and digestive enzymes.

duplication Repetition of part of a chromosome resulting from fusion with a fragment from a homologous chromosome; can result from an error in meiosis or from mutagenesis.

E

eardrum A sheet of connective tissue separating the outer ear from the middle ear that vibrates when stimulated by sound waves and passes the waves to the middle ear.

early genes The first genes expressed after viral entry into a host and whose products are used to take over.

echinoderm (uh-kī′-nō-derm) Member of a phylum of slow-moving or sessile marine animals characterized by a rough or spiny skin, a water vascular system, an endoskeleton, and radial symmetry in adults. Echinoderms include sea stars, sea urchins, and sand dollars.

ecological footprint An estimate of the amount of land required to provide the raw materials an individual or nation consumes, including food, fuel, water, housing, and waste disposal.

ecological niche (nich) The role of a species in its community; the sum total of the use of the biotic and abiotic resources by a species in its environment.

ecological species concept A definition of species in terms of ecological niche, the sum of how members of the species interact with the nonliving and living parts of their environment.

ecological succession The process of biological community change resulting from disturbance; transition in the species composition of a biological community, often following a flood, fire, or volcanic eruption. *See also* primary succession; secondary succession.

ecology The scientific study of how organisms interact with their environment.

ecosystem (ē′-kō-sis-tem) All the organisms in a given area, along with the nonliving (abiotic) factors with which they interact; a biological community and its physical environment.

ecotone The gradual transition between two adjacent communities across a wider border. *See also* transition zone.

ecotourism Travel to natural areas for tourism and recreation.

ectoderm (ek′-tō-derm) The outer layer of three embryonic cell layers in a gastrula. The ectoderm forms the skin of the gastrula and gives rise to the epidermis and nervous system in the adult.

ectoparasite A parasitic organism that lives attached to the exterior of its host.

ectopic pregnancy (ek-top′-ik) The implantation and development of an embryo outside the uterus.

ectotherm (ek′-tō-therm) An animal that warms itself mainly by absorbing heat from its surroundings. Examples include most amphibians, lizards, and invertebrates.

ectothermic Referring to organisms that do not produce enough metabolic heat to have much effect on body temperature. *See also* ectotherm.

edge species A species that depends on two adjacent communities for its survival and usually lives within or near transition zones.

effector cell (1) A muscle cell or gland cell that performs the body's response to stimuli, responding to signals from the brain or other processing centre of the nervous system. (2) A lymphocyte that has undergone clonal selection and is capable of mediating an acquired immune response.

egg A female gamete.

ejaculation (ih-jak′-yū-lā′-shun) Expulsion of semen from the penis.

ejaculatory duct The short section of the ejaculatory route in mammals formed by the convergence of the vas deferens and a duct from the seminal vesicle. The ejaculatory duct transports sperm from the vas deferens to the urethra.

electromagnetic receptor A sensory receptor that detects energy of different wavelengths, such as electricity, magnetism, and light.

electromagnetic spectrum The entire spectrum of radiation ranging in wavelength from less than a nanometre to more than a kilometre.

electron A subatomic particle with a single negative electrical charge. One or more electrons move around the nucleus of an atom.

electron microscope (EM) A microscope that uses magnets to focus an electron beam through, or onto the surface of, a specimen; achieves a hundredfold greater resolution than a light microscope.

electron shell An energy level representing the distance of an electron from the nucleus of an atom.

electron transport chain A series of electron carrier molecules that shuttle electrons during the redox reactions that release energy used to make ATP; located in the inner membrane of mitochondria, the thylakoid membranes of chloroplasts, and the plasma membranes of prokaryotes.

electronegativity The attraction of a given atom for the electrons of a covalent bond.

element A substance that cannot be broken down to other substances by chemical means.

elimination The passing of undigested material out of the digestive compartment; the fourth and final stage of food processing in animals.

embryo (em'-brē-ō) A developing stage of a multicellular organism. In humans, the stage in the development of offspring from the first division of the zygote until body structures begin to appear, about the ninth week of gestation.

embryo sac The female gametophyte contained in the ovule of a flowering plant.

embryonic stem cell (ES cell) Cell in the early animal embryo that differentiates during development to give rise to all the different kinds of specialized cells in the body.

embryophyte Another name for land plants, recognizing that land plants share the common derived trait of multicellular, dependent embryos.

emergent properties New properties that arise with each step upward in the hierarchy of life, owing to the arrangement and interactions of parts as complexity increases.

emerging virus A virus that has appeared suddenly or has recently come to the attention of medical scientists.

endemic species A species whose distribution is limited to a specific geographic area.

endergonic reaction (en'-der-gon'-ik) An energy-requiring chemical reaction that yields products with more potential energy than the reactants. The amount of energy stored in the products equals the difference between the potential energy in the reactants and that in the products.

endocrine gland (en'-dō-krin) A ductless gland that synthesizes hormone molecules and secretes them directly into the bloodstream.

endocrine system (en'-dō-krin) The organ system consisting of ductless glands that secrete hormones and the molecular receptors on or in target cells that respond to the hormones; cooperates with the nervous system in regulating body functions and maintaining homeostasis.

endocytosis (en'-dō-sī-tō'-sis) Cellular uptake of molecules or particles via formation of new vesicles from the plasma membrane.

endoderm (en'-dō-derm) The innermost of three embryonic cell layers in a gastrula; forms the archenteron in the gastrula and gives rise to the innermost linings of the digestive tract and other hollow organs in the adult.

endodermis The innermost layer (a one-cell-thick cylinder) of the cortex of a plant root; forms a selective barrier determining which substances pass from the cortex into the vascular tissue.

endomembrane system A network of membranes inside and around a eukaryotic cell, related either through direct physical contact or by the transfer of membranous vesicles.

endometrium (en'-dō-mē'-trē-um) The inner lining of the uterus in mammals, richly supplied with blood vessels that provide the maternal part of the placenta and nourish the developing embryo.

endoparasite A parasitic organism that lives within the body or tissue of its host.

endoplasmic reticulum (ER) An extensive membranous network in a eukaryotic cell, continuous with the outer nuclear membrane and composed of ribosome-studded (rough) and ribosome-free (smooth) regions. *See also* rough endoplasmic reticulum; smooth endoplasmic reticulum.

endorphin (en-dōr'-fin) A pain-inhibiting hormone produced by the brain and anterior pituitary; also serves as a neurotransmitter.

endoskeleton A hard skeleton located within the soft tissues of an animal; includes spicules of sponges, the hard plates of echinoderms, and the cartilage and bony skeletons of vertebrates.

endosperm In flowering plants, a nutrient-rich mass formed by the union of a sperm cell with two polar nuclei during double fertilization; provides nourishment to the developing embryo in the seed.

endospore A thick-coated, protective cell produced within a bacterial cell; becomes dormant and is able to survive harsh environmental conditions.

endosymbiont A symbiont that lives within the body of its partner. *See* host.

endosymbiont theory (en'-dō-sim'-bī-ont) A theory that mitochondria and chloroplasts originated as prokaryotic cells engulfed by an ancestral eukaryotic cell. The engulfed cell and its host cell then evolved into a single organism.

endosymbiosis A symbiotic relationship in which one partner lives within the body of the other.

endotherm An animal that derives most of its body heat from its own metabolism. Examples include most mammals and birds.

endothermic Referring to animals that use heat generated by metabolism to maintain a warm, steady body temperature. *See also* endotherm.

endotoxin A poisonous component of the outer membrane of gram-negative bacteria that is released only when the bacteria die.

energy The capacity to cause change, especially to perform work.

energy coupling In cellular metabolism, the use of energy released from an exergonic reaction to drive an endergonic reaction.

energy flow The passage of energy through the components of an ecosystem.

enhancer A eukaryotic DNA sequence that helps to stimulate the transcription of a gene at some distance from it. An enhancer functions by means of a transcription factor called an activator, which binds to it and then to the rest of the transcription apparatus. *See also* silencer.

enteric division Part of the autonomic nervous system consisting of complex networks of neurons in the digestive tract, pancreas, and gallbladder.

entropy (en'-truh-pē) A measure of disorder. One form of disorder is heat, which is random molecular motion.

envelope In some viruses, the phospholipid bilayer that surrounds the protein coat, which arises from the host cell membrane.

enzyme (en'-zīm) A macromolecule, usually a protein, that serves as a biological catalyst, changing the rate of a chemical reaction without being consumed by the reaction.

epidermis (ep'-uh-der'-mis) (1) In animals, one or more living layers of cells forming the protective covering, or outer skin. (2) In plants, the tissue system forming the protective outer covering of leaves, young stems, and young roots.

epididymis (ep'-uh-did'-uh-mus) A long coiled tube into which sperm pass from the testis and where they are stored until mature and ejaculated.

epigenetic inheritance The inheritance of traits transmitted by mechanisms not directly involving the nucleotide sequence of a genome, such as the chemical modification of histone proteins or DNA bases.

epigenetics The modification of the genome without alterations to its nucleotide sequence.

epithelial tissue (ep'-uh-thē'-lē-ul) A sheet of tightly packed cells lining organs, body cavities, and external surfaces; also called epithelium.

erythrocyte (eh-rith'-rō-sīt) A blood cell containing hemoglobin, which transports oxygen; also called a red blood cell.

erythropoietin (EPO) (eh-rith'-rō-poy'-uh-tin) A hormone that stimulates the production of erythrocytes; secreted by the kidney when tissues of the body do not receive enough oxygen.

GLOSSARY

esophagus (eh-sof´-uh-gus) A muscular tube that conducts food by peristalsis, usually from the pharynx to the stomach.

essential amino acid An amino acid that an animal cannot synthesize itself and must obtain from food. Eight amino acids are essential for the human adult.

essential element In plants, a chemical element required for the plant to complete its life cycle (to grow from a seed and to produce another generation of seeds).

essential fatty acid An unsaturated fatty acid that an animal needs but cannot make.

essential nutrient A substance that an organism must absorb in preassembled form because it cannot synthesize it from any other material. In humans, there are essential vitamins, minerals, amino acids, and fatty acids.

estrogen (es´-trō-jen) One of several chemically similar steroid hormones secreted by the gonads; maintains the female reproductive system and promotes the development of female body features.

estuary (es´-chū-ār-ē) The area where a freshwater stream or river merges with the ocean.

ethylene A gas that functions as a hormone in plants, triggering aging responses such as fruit ripening and leaf drop.

eudicot (yū-dē-kot) Member of a group that consists of the vast majority of flowering plants that have two embryonic seed leaves, or cotyledons.

Eukarya (yū-kar´-ē-uh) Domain of life that includes all eukaryotes.

eukaryotic cell (yū-kar-ē-ot´-ik) A type of cell that has a membrane-enclosed nucleus and other membrane-enclosed organelles. All organisms except bacteria and archaea are composed of eukaryotic cells.

eumetazoan (yū-met-uh-zō´-un) Member of the clade of "true animals," the animals with true tissues (all animals except sponges).

Eustachian tube (yū-stā´-shun) An air passage between the middle ear and throat of vertebrates that equalizes air pressure on either side of the eardrum.

eutherian (yū-thēr´-ē-un) Placental mammal; mammal whose young complete their embryonic development within the uterus, joined to the mother by the placenta.

eutrophication The increase in productivity of an aquatic system, usually a lake, causing massive algae blooms and oxygen depletion during their decomposition after they die.

evaporative cooling The process in which the surface of an object becomes cooler during evaporation.

evo-devo Evolutionary developmental biology; the field of biology that combines evolutionary biology with developmental biology.

evolution Descent with modification; the idea that living species are descendants of ancestral species that were different from present-day ones; also, the genetic changes in a population from generation to generation.

evolutionary tree A branching diagram that reflects a hypothesis about evolutionary relationships among groups of organisms.

Excavata One of five supergroups proposed in a current hypothesis of the evolutionary history of eukaryotes. The other four supergroups are Chromalveolata, Rhizaria, Unikonta, and Archaeplastida.

excretion (ek-skrē´-shun) The disposal of nitrogen-containing metabolic wastes.

exergonic reaction (ek´-ser-gon´-ik) An energy-releasing chemical reaction in which the reactants contain more potential energy than the products. The reaction releases an amount of energy equal to the difference in potential energy between the reactants and the products.

exocytosis (ek´-sō-sī-tō´-sis) The movement of materials out of the cytoplasm of a cell by the fusion of vesicles with the plasma membrane.

exons The coding regions of a gene; can be interrupted by introns.

exoskeleton A hard external skeleton that protects an animal and provides points of attachment for muscles.

exotoxin A poisonous protein secreted by certain bacteria.

exponential growth model A mathematical description of idealized, unregulated population growth.

external fertilization The fusion of gametes that parents have discharged into the environment.

extinction The irrevocable loss of a species.

extirpation The loss of a single population of a species.

extracellular matrix (ECM) The meshwork surrounding animal cells; consists of glycoproteins and polysaccharides.

extraembryonic membranes Four membranes (the yolk sac, amnion, chorion, and allantois) that form a life-support system for the developing embryo of a reptile, bird, or mammal.

extreme halophile A microorganism that lives in a highly saline environment, such as the Great Salt Lake or the Dead Sea.

extreme thermophile A microorganism that thrives in a hot environment (often 60–80°C).

eyecup The simplest type of photoreceptor, a cluster of photoreceptor cells shaded by a cuplike cluster of pigmented cells; detects light intensity and direction.

F

F factor A piece of DNA that can exist as a bacterial plasmid; carries genes for making sex pili and other structures needed for conjugation, as well as a site where DNA replication can start. F stands for fertility.

F_1 generation The offspring of two parental (P generation) individuals; F_1 stands for first filial.

F_2 generation The offspring of the F_1 generation; F_2 stands for second filial.

facilitated diffusion The passage of a substance through a specific transport protein across a biological membrane down its concentration gradient.

facultative symbiosis A symbiotic relationship in which the symbionts benefit from the relationship but can survive without it.

family In Linnaean classification, the taxonomic category above genus.

farsightedness An inability to focus on close objects; occurs when the eyeball is shorter than normal and the focal point of the lens is behind the retina; also called hyperopia.

fat A lipid composed of three fatty acids linked to one glycerol molecule; a triglyceride. Most fats function as energy-storage molecules.

feedback inhibition A method of metabolic control in which a product of a metabolic pathway acts as an inhibitor of an enzyme within that pathway.

fertilization The union of the nucleus of a sperm cell with the nucleus of an egg cell, producing a zygote.

fertilizer A compound given to plants to promote their growth.

fetus (fē´-tus) A developing human from the ninth week of gestation until birth; has all the major structures of an adult.

fibre (1) In animals, an elongate, supportive thread in the matrix of connective tissue; an extension of a neuron; a muscle cell. (2) In plants, a long, slender sclerenchyma cell that usually occurs in a bundle.

fibrin (fi´-brin) The activated form of the blood-clotting protein fibrinogen, which aggregates into threads that form the fabric of a blood clot.

fibrinogen (fi-brin´-uh-jen) The plasma protein that is activated to form a clot when a blood vessel is injured.

fibrous connective tissue A dense tissue with large numbers of collagenous fibres organized into parallel bundles; the dominant tissue in tendons and ligaments.

filtrate Fluid extracted by the excretory system from the blood or body cavity. The excretory system produces urine from the filtrate after removing valuable solutes from it and concentrating it.

filtration In the vertebrate kidney, the extraction of water and small solutes, including metabolic wastes, from the blood by the nephrons.

fimbria (plural, **fimbriae**) One of the short, hairlike projections on some prokaryotic cells that help to attach the cells to their substrate or to other cells.

first law of thermodynamics The principle of conservation of energy: Energy can be transferred and transformed, but it cannot be created or destroyed.

fission A means of asexual reproduction whereby a parent separates into two or more genetically identical individuals of about equal size.

fixed action pattern (FAP) A genetically programmed, virtually unchangeable behavioural sequence performed in response to a certain stimulus.

flagellum (fluh-jel′-um) (plural, **flagella**) A long cellular appendage specialized for locomotion. The flagella of prokaryotes and eukaryotes differ in both structure and function. Like cilia, eukaryotic flagella have a 9 + 2 arrangement of microtubules covered by the cell's plasma membrane.

flatworm A member of the phylum Platyhelminthes.

fluid feeder An animal that lives by sucking nutrient-rich fluids from another living organism.

fluid mosaic A description of membrane structure, depicting a cellular membrane as a mosaic of diverse protein molecules embedded in a fluid bilayer of phospholipid molecules.

fluke One of a group of parasitic flatworms.

follicle (fol′-uh-kul) A cluster of cells that surround, protect, and nourish a developing egg cell in the ovary. Follicles secrete the hormone estrogen.

food chain A sequence of food transfers from producers through one to four levels of consumers in an ecosystem.

food web A network of interconnecting food chains.

foot In an invertebrate animal, a structure used for locomotion or attachment, such as the muscular organ extending from the ventral side of a mollusc.

foraging Behaviour used in recognizing, searching for, capturing, and consuming food.

foraminiferan A protist that moves and feeds by means of threadlike pseudopodia and has porous shells composed of calcium carbonate.

forebrain One of three ancestral and embryonic regions of the vertebrate brain; develops into the thalamus, hypothalamus, and cerebrum.

forensics The scientific analysis of evidence for crime scene and other legal proceedings. Also referred to as forensic science.

fossil A preserved remnant or impression of an organism that lived in the past.

fossil fuel An energy-containing deposit of organic material formed from the remains of ancient organisms.

fossil record The chronicle of evolution over millions of years of geologic time engraved in the order in which fossils appear in rock strata.

founder effect Genetic drift that occurs when a few individuals become isolated from a larger population and form a new population whose gene pool is not reflective of that of the original population.

fovea (fō′-vē-uh) An eye's centre of focus and the place on the retina where photoreceptors are highly concentrated.

fragmentation A means of asexual reproduction whereby a single parent breaks into parts that regenerate into whole new individuals.

fraternal twins Twins that arise from two separate eggs that are fertilized by two separate sperm.

free-living flatworm A nonparasitic flatworm.

frequency-dependent selection Selection in which the fitness of a phenotype depends on how common the phenotype is in a population.

fruit A ripened, thickened ovary of a flower, which protects developing seeds and aids in their dispersal.

functional group A specific configuration of atoms commonly attached to the carbon skeletons of organic molecules and involved in chemical reactions.

Fungi (fun′-ji) The kingdom that contains the fungi.

G

gallbladder An organ that stores bile and releases it as needed into the small intestine.

gametangium (gam′-uh-tan′-jē-um) (plural, **gametangia**) A reproductive organ that houses and protects the gametes of a plant.

gamete (gam′-ēt) A sex cell; a haploid egg or sperm. The union of two gametes of opposite sex (fertilization) produces a zygote.

gametogenesis The creation of gametes within the gonads.

gametophyte (guh-mē′-tō-fīt) The multicellular haploid form in the life cycle of organisms undergoing alternation of generations; mitotically produces haploid gametes that unite and grow into the sporophyte generation.

ganglion (gang′-glē-un) (plural, **ganglia**) A cluster of neuron cell bodies in a peripheral nervous system.

gas exchange The exchange of O_2 and CO_2 between an organism and its environment.

gastric juice The collection of fluids (mucus, enzymes, and acid) secreted by the stomach.

gastrin A digestive hormone that stimulates the secretion of gastric juice.

gastropod A member of the largest group of molluscs, including snails and slugs.

gastrovascular cavity A central compartment with a single opening, the mouth; functions in both digestion and nutrient distribution and may also function in circulation, body support, waste disposal, and gas exchange.

gastrula (gas′-trū-luh) The embryonic stage resulting from gastrulation in animal development. Most animals have a gastrula made up of three layers of cells: ectoderm, endoderm, and mesoderm.

gastrulation (gas′-trū-lā′-shun) The second major phase of embryonic development, which transforms the blastula into a gastrula; adds more cells to the embryo and sorts the cells into distinct cell layers.

gel electrophoresis (jel′ ē-lek′-trō-fōr-ē′-sis) A technique for separating and purifying macromolecules, either DNAs or proteins. A mixture of the macromolecules is placed on a gel between a positively charged electrode and a negatively charged one. Negative charges on the molecules are attracted to the positive electrode, and the molecules migrate toward that electrode. The molecules separate in the gel according to their rates of migration, which is mostly determined by their size: Smaller molecules generally move faster through the gel, while larger molecules generally move more slowly.

gene A discrete unit of hereditary information consisting of a specific nucleotide sequence in DNA (or RNA, in some viruses). Most of the genes of a eukaryote are located in its chromosomal DNA; a few are carried by the DNA of mitochondria and chloroplasts.

gene cloning The production of multiple copies of a gene.

gene expression The process whereby genetic information flows from genes to proteins; the flow of genetic information from the genotype to the phenotype.

gene flow The transfer of alleles from one population to another as a result of the movement of individuals or their gametes.

gene pool All the alleles for all the genes in a population.

gene regulation The turning on and off of genes within a cell in response to environmental stimuli or other factors (such as developmental stage).

gene therapy A treatment for a disease in which the patient's defective gene is supplemented or altered.

generative cell The cell within a pollen grain (male gametophyte) that divides to form two sperm.

genetic code The set of rules that dictates the correspondence between RNA codons in an mRNA molecule and amino acids in protein.

genetic drift A change in the gene pool of a population because of chance. Effects of genetic drift are most pronounced in small populations.

genetic engineering The direct manipulation of genes for practical purposes.

genetic recombination The production, by crossing over and/or independent assortment of chromosomes during meiosis, of offspring with allele combinations different from those in the parents. The term may also be used more specifically to mean the production by crossing over of eukaryotic or prokaryotic chromosomes with gene combinations different from those in the original chromosomes.

genetically modified (GM) organism An organism that has acquired one or more genes by artificial means. If the gene is from another species, the organism is also known as a transgenic organism.

genetics The scientific study of heredity. Modern genetics began with the work of Gregor Mendel in the 19th century.

genomic library (juh-nō′-mik) A set of DNA fragments representing an organism's entire genome. Each segment is usually carried by a plasmid or phage.

genomics The study of whole sets of genes and their interactions.

genotype (jē′-nō-tīp) The genetic makeup of an organism.

genus (jē′-nus) (plural, **genera**) In classification, the taxonomic category above species; the first part of the binomial of a species; for example, *Homo*.

geologic record A time scale established by geologists that divides Earth's history into three eons—Archaean, Proterozoic, and Phanerozoic—and further subdivides it into eras, periods, and epochs.

germinate To start developing or growing.

gestation (jes-tā′-shun) Pregnancy; the state of carrying developing young within the female reproductive tract.

gibberellin (jib′-uh-rel′-in) One of a family of plant hormones that triggers the germination of seeds and interacts with auxins in regulating growth and fruit development.

gill An extension of the body surface of an aquatic animal, specialized for gas exchange and/or suspension feeding.

gizzard A pouchlike organ in a digestive tract where food is mechanically ground.

glans The rounded, highly sensitive head of the clitoris in females and the penis in males.

glia A network of supporting cells that is essential for the structural integrity and normal functioning of the nervous system.

global climate change Increase in temperature and change in weather patterns all around the planet, mostly because of increasing atmospheric CO_2 levels from the burning of fossil fuels.

glomeromycete Member of a group of fungi characterized by a distinct branching form of mycorrhizae (symbiotic relationships with plant roots) called arbuscules.

glomerulus (glō-mer′-ū-lus) (plural, **glomeruli**) In the vertebrate kidney, the part of a nephron consisting of the capillaries that are surrounded by Bowman's capsule; together, a glomerulus and Bowman's capsule produce the filtrate from the blood.

glucagon (glū′-kuh-gon) A peptide hormone, secreted by the islets of Langerhans in the pancreas, that raises the level of glucose in the blood; is antagonistic with insulin.

glucocorticoid (glū′-kuh-kor′-tih-koyd) A corticosteroid hormone secreted by the adrenal cortex that increases the blood glucose level and helps to maintain the body's response to long-term stress.

glycogen (glī′-kō-jen) An extensively branched glucose storage polysaccharide found in liver and muscle cells; the animal equivalent of starch.

glycolysis (glī-kol′-uh-sis) The multistep chemical breakdown of a molecule of glucose into two molecules of pyruvate; the first stage of cellular respiration in all organisms; occurs in the cytoplasmic fluid.

glycoprotein (glī′-kō-prō′-tēn) A protein with one or more short chains of sugars attached to it.

goiter An enlargement of the thyroid gland resulting from a dietary iodine deficiency.

Golgi apparatus (gol′-jē) An organelle in eukaryotic cells consisting of stacks of membranous sacs that modify, store, and ship products of the endoplasmic reticulum.

gonad A sex organ in an animal; an ovary or testis.

Gram stain Microbiological technique to identify the cell wall composition of bacteria. Results categorize bacteria as gram-positive or gram-negative.

gram-positive bacteria Diverse group of bacteria with a cell wall that is structurally less complex and contains more peptidoglycan than that of gram-negative bacteria; usually less toxic than gram-negative bacteria.

granum (gran′-um) (plural, **grana**) A stack of membrane-bounded thylakoids in a chloroplast. Grana are the sites where light energy is trapped by chlorophyll and converted to chemical energy during the light reactions of photosynthesis.

gravitropism (grav′-uh-trō′-pizm) A plant's directional growth in response to gravity.

green alga A member of a group of photosynthetic protists that includes chlorophytes and charophyceans, the closest living relatives of land plants. Green algae include unicellular, colonial, and multicellular species and belong to the supergroup Archaeplastida.

greenhouse effect The warming of Earth on account of the atmospheric accumulation of CO_2 and certain other gases that absorb infrared radiation and reradiate some of it back toward Earth.

grey matter Regions within the central nervous system composed mainly of nerve cell bodies and dendrites.

ground tissue system A tissue of mostly parenchyma cells that makes up the bulk of a young plant and is continuous throughout its body. The ground tissue system fills the space between the epidermis and the vascular tissue system.

growth factor A protein secreted by certain body cells that stimulates other cells to divide.

growth hormone (GH) A protein hormone secreted by the anterior pituitary that promotes development and growth and stimulates metabolism.

guanine (G) (gwa′-nēn) A double-ring nitrogenous base found in DNA and RNA.

guard cell A specialized epidermal cell in plants that regulates the size of a stoma, allowing gas exchange between the surrounding air and the photosynthetic cells in the leaf.

guild Organisms that perform a similar function or use a common resource are grouped together in a function group.

gymnosperm (jim′-nō-sperm) A naked-seed plant—that is, a plant whose seed is not enclosed in an ovary.

H

habitat A place where an organism lives; the environment in which an organism lives.

habituation Learning not to respond to a repeated stimulus that conveys little or no information.

hair cell A type of mechanoreceptor that detects sound waves and other forms of movement in air or water.

haploid In the life cycle of an organism that reproduces sexually, a cell containing a single set of chromosomes; an *n* cell.

Hardy-Weinberg principle The principle that frequencies of alleles and genotypes in a population remain constant from generation to generation provided that only Mendelian segregation and recombination of alleles are at work.

heart A muscular pump that propels a circulatory fluid (blood) through vessels to the body.

heart attack The damage or death of cardiac muscle cells and the resulting failure of the heart to deliver enough blood to the body.

heart murmur A hissing sound that most often results from blood squirting backward through a leaky valve in the heart.

heart rate The frequency of heart contraction, usually expressed in number of beats per minute.

heartwood In the centre of trees, the darkened, older layers of secondary xylem made up of cells that no longer transport water and are clogged with resins. *See also* sapwood.

heat Thermal energy; the amount of energy associated with the movement of the atoms and molecules in a body of matter; energy in its most random form.

helper T cell A type of lymphocyte that helps to activate other types of T cells and may help to stimulate B cells to produce antibodies.

hemoglobin (hē′-mō-glō-bin) An iron-containing protein in red blood cells that reversibly binds O_2.

hemolymph The circulatory fluid of animals with open circulatory systems having the combined functions of blood and lymph.

hemophilia (hē′-mō-fil′-ē-uh) A human genetic disease caused by a sex-linked recessive allele; characterized by excessive bleeding following injury.

hepatic portal vein A blood vessel that conveys nutrient-laden blood from capillaries surrounding the intestine directly to the liver.

herbivore An animal that mainly eats plants or algae. *See also* carnivore; omnivore.

herbivory Consumption of plant parts or algae by an animal.

heredity The transmission of traits (inherited features) from one generation to the next.

hermaphroditism (her-maf′-rō-dī-tizm) A condition in which an individual has both female and male gonads and functions as both a male and a female in sexual reproduction by producing both sperm and eggs.

heterokaryotic stage (het′-er-ō-ker-ē-ot′-ik) A fungal life cycle stage that contains two genetically different haploid nuclei in the same cell.

heterotroph (het′-er-ō-trōf) An organism that cannot make its own organic food molecules and must obtain them by consuming other organisms or their organic products; a consumer or a decomposer in a food chain.

heterozygote advantage Greater reproductive success of heterozygous individuals compared to homozygotes; tends to preserve variation in gene pools.

heterozygous (het′-er-ō-zī′-gus) Having two different alleles for a given gene.

high-density lipoprotein (HDL) A cholesterol-carrying particle in the blood, made up of thousands of cholesterol molecules and other lipids bound to a protein; scavenges excess cholesterol.

hinge joint A joint that allows movement in only one plane. In humans, examples include the elbow and knee.

hippocampus (hip′-uh-kam′-pus) An integrative centre of the cerebrum; functionally, the part of the limbic system that plays a central role in the formation of memories and their recall.

histamine (his′-tuh-mēn) A chemical alarm signal released by injured cells of vertebrates that causes blood vessels to dilate during an inflammatory response.

histone (his′-tōn) A small protein molecule associated with DNA and important in DNA packing in the eukaryotic chromosome. Eukaryotic chromatin consists of roughly equal parts of DNA and histone protein.

homeobox (hō′-mē-ō-boks′) A 180-nucleotide sequence within a homeotic gene and some other developmental genes.

homeostasis (hō′-mē-ō-stā′-sis) The steady state of body functioning; a state of equilibrium characterized by a dynamic interplay between outside forces that tend to change an organism's internal environment and the internal control mechanisms that oppose such changes.

homeotic gene (hō′-mē-ot′-ik) A master control gene that determines the identity of a body structure of a developing organism, presumably by controlling the developmental fate of groups of cells.

hominin (hah′-mi-nid) Member of a species on the human branch of the evolutionary tree; a species more closely related to humans than to chimpanzees.

homologous chromosomes (hō-mol′-uh-gus) The two chromosomes that make up a matched pair in a diploid cell. Homologous chromosomes are of the same length, centromere position, and staining pattern and possess genes for the same characteristics at corresponding loci. One homologous chromosome is inherited from the organism's father, the other from the mother.

homologous structures Structures in different species that are similar because of common ancestry.

homology Similarity in characteristics resulting from a shared ancestry.

homozygous (hō′-mō-zī′-gus) Having two identical alleles for a given gene.

horizontal gene transfer The transfer of genes from one genome to another through mechanisms such as transposable elements, plasmid exchange, viral activity, and perhaps fusions of different organisms.

hormone (1) In animals, a regulatory chemical that travels in the blood from its production site, usually an endocrine gland, to other sites, where target cells respond to the regulatory signal. (2) In plants, a chemical that is produced in one part of the plant and travels to another part, where it acts on target cells to change their functioning.

horseshoe crab A bottom-dwelling marine chelicerate; a member of the phylum Arthropoda.

host A symbiont that has its partner living inside of its body. *See* endosymbiont.

host-generalist A parasite that is able to infect a wide range of host species.

host-specialist A parasite that is able to infect only one or a few related host species.

human chorionic gonadotropin (hCG) (kōr′-ē-on′-ik gon′-uh-dō-trō′-pin) A hormone secreted by the chorion that maintains the production of estrogen and progesterone by the corpus luteum of the ovary during the first few months of pregnancy. hCG secreted in the urine is the target of many home pregnancy tests.

Human Genome Project (HGP) An international collaborative effort to map and sequence the DNA of the entire human genome. The project was begun in 1990 and completed in 2004.

humoral immune response The type of specific immunity brought about by antibody-producing B cells. The humoral immune response fights bacteria and viruses in body fluids. *See also* cell-mediated immune response.

humus (hyū′-mus) Decomposing organic material found in topsoil.

Huntington's disease A human genetic disease caused by a single dominant allele; characterized by uncontrollable body movements and degeneration of the nervous system; usually fatal 10 to 20 years after the onset of symptoms.

hybrid An offspring of parents of two different species or of two different varieties of one species; an offspring of two parents that differ in one or more inherited traits; an individual that is heterozygous for one or more pairs of genes.

hybrid zone A geographic region in which members of different species meet and mate, producing at least some hybrid offspring.

hydrocarbon An organic compound composed only of the elements carbon and hydrogen.

hydrogen bond A type of weak chemical bond formed when the partially positive hydrogen atom participating in a polar covalent bond in one molecule is attracted to the partially negative atom participating in a polar covalent bond in another molecule (or in another region of the same molecule).

hydrolysis (hī-drol′-uh-sis) A chemical reaction that breaks bonds between two molecules by the addition of water; process by which polymers are broken down and an essential part of digestion.

hydrophilic (hī′-drō-fil′-ik) "Water-loving"; pertaining to polar or charged molecules (or parts of molecules) that are soluble in water.

hydrophobic (hī′-drō-fō′-bik) "Water-fearing"; pertaining to nonpolar molecules (or parts of molecules) that do not dissolve in water.

hydrostatic skeleton A skeletal system composed of fluid held under pressure in a closed body compartment; the main skeleton of most cnidarians, flatworms, nematodes, and annelids.

hydroxyl group (hī-drok′-sil) A chemical group consisting of an oxygen atom bonded to a hydrogen atom.

hypertension A disorder in which blood pressure remains abnormally high.

hypertonic Referring to a solution that, when surrounding a cell, will cause the cell to lose water.

hypha (hī′-fuh) (plural, **hyphae**) One of many filaments making up the body of a fungus.

hypothalamus (hī-pō-thal′-uh-mus) The master control centre of the endocrine system located in the ventral portion of the vertebrate forebrain; functions in maintaining homeostasis, especially in coordinating the endocrine and nervous systems; secretes hormones of the posterior pituitary and releases hormones that regulate the anterior pituitary.

hypothesis (hī-poth′-uh-sis) (plural, **hypotheses**) A testable explanation for a set of observations based on the available data and guided by inductive reasoning.

hypotonic Referring to a solution that, when surrounding a cell, will cause the cell to take up water.

I

identical twins *See* monozygotic twins.

immune system An animal body's system of defences against agents that cause disease.

imperfect fungus A fungus with no known sexual stage.

impotence The inability to maintain an erection; also called erectile dysfunction.

imprinting Learning that is limited to a specific critical period in an animal's life and that is generally irreversible.

in vitro fertilization (IVF) (vē′-tro) Uniting sperm and egg in a laboratory container, followed by the placement of a resulting early embryo in the mother's uterus.

inbreeding Mating between close blood relatives.

inclusive fitness An individual's success at perpetuating its genes by producing its own offspring and by helping close relatives to produce offspring.

incomplete dominance A type of inheritance in which the phenotype of a heterozygote (*Aa*) is intermediate between the phenotypes of the two types of homozygotes (*AA* and *aa*).

incomplete metamorphosis A type of development in certain insects in which development from larva to adult is achieved by multiple moults, but without forming a pupa.

indeterminate growth Growth that continues throughout life, as in most plants. *See also* determinate growth.

indirect life cycle A parasitic life cycle that requires multiple hosts for completion.

induced fit The change in shape of the active site of an enzyme, caused by entry of the substrate, so that it binds more snugly to the substrate.

induction During embryonic development, the influence of one group of cells on an adjacent group of cells.

inductive reasoning A type of logic in which generalizations are based on a large number of specific observations.

inferior vena cava (vē′-nuh kā′-vuh) A large vein that returns oxygen-poor blood to the heart from the lower, or posterior, part of the body. *See also* superior vena cava.

infertility The inability to conceive after one year of regular, unprotected intercourse.

inflammatory response An innate body defence in vertebrates caused by a release of histamine and other chemical alarm signals that trigger increased blood flow, a local increase in white blood cells, and fluid leakage from the blood. The resulting inflammatory response includes redness, heat, and swelling in the affected tissues.

ingestion The act of eating; the first main stage of food processing in animals.

ingroup In a cladistic study of evolutionary relationships, the group of taxa whose evolutionary relationships are being determined. *See also* outgroup.

inhibiting hormone A kind of hormone released from the hypothalamus that prompts the anterior pituitary to stop secreting hormone.

innate behaviour Behaviour that is under strong genetic control and is performed in virtually the same way by all members of a species.

innate immunity The kind of immunity that is present in an animal before exposure to pathogens and is effective from birth. Innate immune defences include barriers, phagocytic cells, antimicrobial proteins, the inflammatory response, and natural killer cells.

inner ear One of three main regions of the vertebrate ear; includes the cochlea, organ of Corti, and semicircular canals.

insulin A protein hormone, secreted by the islets of Langerhans in the pancreas, that lowers the level of glucose in the blood; is antagonistic with glucagon.

integration The analysis and interpretation of sensory signals within neural processing centres of the central nervous system.

integrins A transmembrane protein that interconnects the extracellular matrix and the cytoskeleton.

integumentary system (in-teg′-yū-ment-ter-ē) The organ system consisting of the skin and its derivatives, such as hair and nails in mammals; helps to protect the body from drying out, mechanical injury, and infection.

interferon (in′-ter-fer′-on) An innate defensive protein produced by virus-infected vertebrate cells that is capable of helping other cells resist viruses.

interior species A species that depends on only one community for its survival and shies away from transition zones.

intermediate One of the compounds that form between the initial reactant and the final product in a metabolic pathway, such as between glucose and pyruvate in glycolysis.

intermediate disturbance hypothesis An ecological theory that suggests a regime of moderate disturbances (both their intensity and frequency) maximizes the biodiversity within a community.

intermediate filament An intermediate-sized protein fibre that is one of the three main kinds of fibres making up the cytoskeleton of eukaryotic cells. Intermediate filaments are ropelike, made of fibrous proteins.

internal fertilization Reproduction in which sperm are typically deposited in or near the female reproductive tract and fertilization occurs within the tract.

interneuron (in′-ter-nūr′-on) A nerve cell, located entirely within the central nervous system, that integrates sensory signals and relays signals to other interneurons and to motor neurons.

internode The portion of a plant stem between two nodes.

interphase The period in the eukaryotic cell cycle when the cell is not actually dividing. Interphase constitutes the majority of the time spent in the cell cycle. *See also* mitotic phase (M phase).

interspecific competition Competition between individuals or populations of two or more species requiring a limited resource.

interspecific interactions Relationships between individuals of different species in a community.

interstitial fluid (in′-ter-stish′-ul) An aqueous solution that surrounds body cells and through which materials pass back and forth between the blood and the body tissues.

intertidal zone (in′-ter-tīd′-ul) A shallow zone where the waters of an estuary or ocean meet land.

intestine The region of a digestive tract located between the gizzard or stomach and the anus and where chemical digestion and nutrient absorption usually occur.

intraspecific competition Competition between members of a population for a limited resource.

introns An intervening sequence of non-coding DNA within a gene that must be removed from the RNA transcript during post-translational modification.

invasive species A non-native species that spreads beyond its original point of introduction and causes environmental or economic damage.

inversion A change in a chromosome resulting from reattachment of a chromosome fragment to the original chromosome but in a reverse direction. Mutagens and errors during meiosis can cause inversions.

invertebrate An animal that lacks a backbone.

ion (ī-on) An atom or group of atoms that has gained or lost one or more electrons, thus acquiring a charge.

ionic bond (ī-on′-ik) A chemical bond resulting from the attraction between oppositely charged ions.

iris The coloured part of the vertebrate eye, formed by the anterior portion of the choroid.

isomers (ī′-sō-mers) Organic compounds with the same molecular formula but different structures and, therefore, different properties.

isotonic (ī-sō-ton′-ik) Referring to a solution that, when surrounding a cell, has no effect on the passage of water into or out of the cell.

isotope (ī′-sō-tōp) One of several atomic forms of an element, each with the same number of protons but a different number of neutrons.

K

karyotype (kār′-ē-ō-tīp) A display of micrographs of the metaphase chromosomes of a cell, arranged by size and centromere position; may be used to identify certain chromosomal abnormalities.

kelp Large, multicellular brown algae that form undersea "forests."

keystone species A species that is not usually abundant in a community yet exerts strong control on community structure by the nature of its ecological role, or niche.

kilocalorie (kcal) A quantity of heat equal to 1000 calories. Used to measure the energy content of food, it is usually called a "Calorie."

kin selection The natural selection that favours altruistic behaviour by enhancing reproductive success of relatives.

kinesis (kuh-nē′-sis) (plural, **kineses**) Random movement in response to a stimulus.

kinetic energy (kuh-net′-ik) The energy of motion; the energy of a mass of matter that is moving. Moving matter does work by imparting motion to other matter.

kingdom In classification, the broad taxonomic category above phylum.

***K*-selection** The concept that in certain (*K*-selected) populations, life history is centred on producing relatively few offspring that have a good chance of survival.

L

labia majora (lā′-bē-uh muh-jor′-uh) A pair of outer thickened folds of skin that protect the female genital region.

labia minora (lā′-bē-uh mi-nor′-uh) A pair of inner folds of skin, bordering and protecting the female genital region.

labour The series of events that expel the infant from the uterus.

lactic acid fermentation Glycolysis followed by the reduction of pyruvate to lactate, regenerating NAD^+.

lancelet One of a group of small, bladelike, invertebrate chordates.

landscape Several different ecosystems linked by exchanges of energy, materials, and organisms.

landscape ecology The application of ecological principles to the study of the structure and dynamics of a collection of ecosystems; the scientific study of the biodiversity of interacting ecosystems.

large intestine *See* colon.

larva (lar′-vuh) (plural, **larvae**) A free-living, sexually immature form in some animal life cycles that may differ from the adult in morphology, nutrition, and habitat.

larynx (lār′-inks) The upper portion of the respiratory tract containing the vocal cords; also called the voice box.

late genes Genes expressed later in a viral infection and whose products are important for viral replication and release.

lateral line system A row of sensory organs along each side of a fish's body that is sensitive to changes in water pressure; enables a fish to detect minor vibrations in the water.

lateral meristem Plant tissue made up of undifferentiated cells that enable roots and shoots of woody plants to thicken. The vascular cambium and cork cambium are lateral meristems.

lateralization The phenomenon in which the two hemispheres of the brain become specialized for different functions during infant and child brain development.

law of independent assortment A general rule in inheritance (originally formulated by Gregor Mendel) that when gametes form during meiosis, each pair of alleles for a particular characteristic segregate independently of other pairs; also called Mendel's second law of inheritance.

law of segregation A general rule in inheritance (originally formulated by Gregor Mendel) that individuals have two alleles for each gene and that when gametes form by meiosis, the two alleles separate, each resulting gamete ending up with only one allele of each gene; also called Mendel's first law of inheritance.

leaf The main site of photosynthesis in a plant; typically consists of a flattened blade and a stalk (petiole) that joins the leaf to the stem.

learning Modification of behaviour as a result of specific experiences.

leech A member of one of the three large groups of annelids, known for its bloodsucking ability. *See* annelid.

lens The structure in an eye that focuses light rays onto the retina.

leukemia (lū-kē′-mē-ah) A type of cancer of the blood-forming tissues, characterized by an excessive production of white blood cells and an abnormally high number of them in the blood; cancer of the bone marrow cells that produce leukocytes.

leukocyte (lū′-kō-sīt) A blood cell that functions in fighting infections; also called a white blood cell.

lichen (lī′-ken) A close association between a fungus and an alga or between a fungus and a cyanobacterium, some of which are known to be beneficial to both partners.

life cycle The entire sequence of stages in the life of an organism, from the adults of one generation to the adults of the next.

life history The series of events from birth through reproduction to death.

life table A listing of survivals and deaths in a population in a particular time period and predictions of how long, on average, an individual of a given age will live.

ligament A type of fibrous connective tissue that joins bones together at joints.

light microscope (LM) An optical instrument with lenses that refract (bend) visible light to magnify images and project them into a viewer's eye or onto photographic film.

light-dependent reactions The first of two stages in photosynthesis; the steps in which solar energy is absorbed and converted to chemical energy in the form of ATP and NADPH. The light reactions power the sugar-producing Calvin cycle but produce no sugar themselves.

lignin A chemical that hardens the cell walls of plants.

limbic system (lim′-bik) A functional unit of several integrating and relay centres located deep in the human forebrain; interacts with the cerebral cortex in creating emotions and storing memories.

limiting factor An environmental factor that restricts population growth.

linkage map A listing of the relative locations of genes along a chromosome, as determined by recombination frequencies.

linked genes Genes located near each other on the same chromosome that tend to be inherited together.

lipid An organic compound consisting mainly of carbon and hydrogen atoms linked by nonpolar covalent bonds, making the compound mostly hydrophobic. Lipids include fats, phospholipids, and steroids and are insoluble in water.

lipoprotein A large molecule that is made up of lipids and proteins that are covalently bound together.

liver The largest gland in the vertebrate body. The liver performs diverse functions, such as producing bile, preparing nitrogenous wastes for disposal, and detoxifying poisonous chemicals in the blood.

lobe-fin A bony fish with strong, muscular limbs supported by bones.

locomotion Active movement from place to place.

locus (plural, **loci**) The particular site where a gene is found on a chromosome. Homologous chromosomes have corresponding gene loci.

logistic growth model A mathematical description of idealized population growth that is restricted by limiting factors.

long-day plant A plant that flowers in late spring or early summer, when day length is long; actually flowers in response to short nights.

long-term memory The ability to hold, associate, and recall information over one's lifetime.

loop of Henle (hen′-lē) In the vertebrate kidney, the portion of a nephron that helps to concentrate the filtrate while conveying it between a proximal tubule and a distal tubule.

loose connective tissue The most widespread connective tissue in the vertebrate body; binds epithelia to underlying tissues and functions as packing material, holding organs in place.

low-density lipoprotein (LDL) A cholesterol-carrying particle in the blood, made up of thousands of cholesterol molecules and other lipids bound to a protein. An LDL particle transports cholesterol from the liver for incorporation into cell membranes.

lung An infolded respiratory surface of terrestrial vertebrates that connects to the atmosphere by narrow tubes.

lymph A colourless fluid, derived from interstitial fluid, that circulates in the lymphatic system.

lymph node An organ of the immune system located along a lymph vessel; filters lymph and contains cells that attack viruses and bacteria.

lymphatic system (lim-fat′-ik) The vertebrate organ system through which lymph circulates; includes lymph vessels, lymph nodes, and the spleen; helps to remove toxins and pathogens from the blood and interstitial fluid and returns fluid and solutes from the interstitial fluid to the circulatory system.

lymphocyte (lim′-fuh-sīt) A type of white blood cell that is chiefly responsible for the acquired immune response and is found mostly in the lymphatic system. *See also* B cell; T cell.

lymphoma (lim-fō′-muh) Cancer of the tissues that form white blood cells.

lysogenic cycle (lī′-sō-jen′-ik) A type of bacteriophage replication cycle in which the viral genome is incorporated into the bacterial host chromosome as a prophage. New phages are not produced, and the host cell is not killed or lysed unless the viral genome leaves the host chromosome.

lysosome (lī-sō-sōm) A digestive organelle in eukaryotic cells; contains hydrolytic enzymes that digest engulfed food or damaged organelles.

lysozyme An enzyme that digests peptidoglycan in bacterial cell walls.

lytic cycle (lit′-ik) A type of viral replication cycle resulting in the release of new viruses by lysis (breaking open) of the host cell.

M

macroevolution Evolutionary change above the species level, encompassing the origin of new taxonomic groups, adaptive radiation, and mass extinction.

macromolecule A giant molecule formed by the joining of smaller molecules, usually by a dehydration reaction: a protein, carbohydrate, or nucleic acid.

macronutrient A chemical substance that an organism must obtain in relatively large amounts. *See also* micronutrient.

macrophage (mak′-rō-fāj) A large, amoeboid, phagocytic white blood cell that functions in innate immunity by destroying microbes and in acquired immunity as an antigen-presenting cell.

major depression Depressive mental illness characterized by a low mood most of the time.

major histocompatibility complex (MHC) molecule *See* self protein.

malignant tumour An abnormal tissue mass that can spread into neighbouring tissue and to other parts of the body; a cancerous tumour.

malnutrition A failure to obtain adequate nutrition.

mammal Member of a clade of amniotes that possess mammary glands and hair.

mantle In a mollusc, the outgrowth of the body surface that drapes over the animal. The mantle produces the shell and forms the mantle cavity.

marsupial (mar-sū′-pē-ul) A pouched mammal, such as a kangaroo, opossum, or koala; gives birth to embryonic offspring that complete development while housed in a pouch and attached to nipples on the mother's abdomen.

mass number The sum of the number of protons and neutrons in an atom's nucleus.

matrix The predominant community within an ecological landscape that contains patches of distinct communities within. *See also* patch.

matter Anything that occupies space and has mass.

mechanoreceptor (mek′-uh-nō-ri-sep′-ter) A sensory receptor that detects changes in the environment associated with pressure, touch, stretch, motion, or sound.

medulla oblongata (meh-duh′-luh ob′-long-got′-uh) Part of the vertebrate hindbrain, continuous with the spinal cord; passes data between the spinal cord and forebrain and controls autonomic, homeostatic functions, including breathing, heart rate, swallowing, and digestion.

medusa (med-ū′-suh) (plural, **medusae**) One of two types of cnidarian body forms; an umbrella-like body form.

meiosis (mī-ō′-sis) In a sexually reproducing organism, the division of a single diploid nucleus into four haploid daughter nuclei. Meiosis and cytokinesis produce haploid gametes or spores from diploid cells in the reproductive organs of the parents.

melanin A dark pigment that contributes to the colour or tone of hair and skin.

melanocyte (mel-an-ō-sīt) A pigmented cell that contains granules of melanin.

membrane potential The charge difference between a cell's cytoplasm and extracellular fluid because of the differential distribution of ions.

memory The ability to store and retrieve information. *See also* long-term memory; short-term memory.

memory cell A clone of long-lived lymphocytes formed during the primary immune response. Memory cells remain in lymph nodes until activated by exposure to the same antigen that triggered their formation. When activated, memory cells form a large clone that mounts the secondary immune response.

meninges (muh-nin′-jēz) Layers of connective tissue that wrap and protect the brain and spinal cord.

menstrual cycle (men′-strū-ul) The hormonally synchronized cyclic buildup and breakdown of the endometrium of some primates, including humans.

menstruation (men′-strū-ā′-shun) Uterine bleeding resulting from shedding of the endometrium during a menstrual cycle.

meristem (mer′-eh-stem) Plant tissue consisting of undifferentiated cells that divide and generate new cells and tissues.

mesoderm (mez′-ō-derm) The middle layer of the three embryonic cell layers in a gastrula; gives rise to muscles, bones, the dermis of the skin, and most other organs in the adult.

mesophyll (mes′-ō-fil) The green tissue in the interior of a leaf; a leaf's ground tissue system; the main site of photosynthesis.

messenger RNA (mRNA) The type of ribonucleic acid that encodes genetic information from DNA and conveys it to ribosomes, where the information is translated into amino acid sequences.

metabolic pathway A series of chemical reactions that either builds a complex molecule or breaks down a complex molecule into simpler compounds.

metabolic rate The total amount of energy an animal uses in a unit of time.

metabolism The totality of an organism's chemical reactions.

metamorphosis (met′-uh-mōr′-fuh-sis) The transformation of a larva into an adult. *See* complete metamorphosis; incomplete metamorphosis.

metaphase (met′-eh-fāz) The third stage of mitosis, during which all of the cell's duplicated chromosomes are lined up at an imaginary plane equidistant between the poles of the mitotic spindle.

metastasis (muh-tas′-tuh-sis) The spread of cancer cells beyond their original site.

methanogen (meth-an′-ō-jen) An archaean that produces methane as a metabolic waste product.

methyl group A chemical group consisting of a carbon atom bonded to three hydrogen atoms.

microclimate A focal region with environmental conditions that differ from the general climate of the area.

microevolution A change in a population's gene pool over generations.

microfilament The thinnest of the three main kinds of protein fibres making up the cytoskeleton of a eukaryotic cell; a solid, helical rod composed of the globular protein actin.

micrograph A photograph taken through a microscope.

micronutrient An element that an organism needs in very small amounts and that functions as a component or cofactor of enzymes. *See also* macronutrient.

microRNA (miRNA) A small, single-stranded RNA molecule that associates with one or more proteins in a complex that can degrade or prevent translation of an mRNA with a complementary sequence.

microtubule The thickest of the three main kinds of fibres making up the cytoskeleton of a eukaryotic cell; a hollow tube made of globular proteins called tubulins; found in cilia and flagella.

microvillus (plural, **microvilli**) One of many microscopic projections on the epithelial cells in the lumen of the small intestine. Microvilli increase the surface area of the small intestine.

middle ear One of three main regions of the vertebrate ear; a chamber containing three small bones (the hammer, anvil, and stirrup) that convey vibrations from the eardrum to the oval window.

migration The regular back-and-forth movement of animals between two geographic areas at particular times of the year.

millipede A terrestrial arthropod that has two pairs of short legs for each of its numerous body segments and that eats decaying plant matter.

mimic An organism that has evolved similar morphology to a model in a mimicry relationship. *See also* model.

mineral In nutrition, a simple inorganic nutrient that an organism requires in small amounts for proper body functioning.

mineralocorticoid (min′-er-uh-lō-kort′-uh-koyd) A corticosteroid hormone secreted by the adrenal cortex that helps to maintain salt and water homeostasis and may increase blood pressure in response to long-term stress.

missense mutation A change in the nucleotide sequence of a gene that alters the amino acid sequence of the resulting polypeptide. In a missense mutation, a codon is changed from encoding one amino acid to encoding a different amino acid.

mitochondrial matrix The compartment of the mitochondrion enclosed by the inner membrane and containing enzymes and substrates for the citric acid cycle.

mitochondrion (mī′-tō-kon′-drē-on) (plural, **mitochondria**) An organelle in eukaryotic cells where cellular respiration occurs. Enclosed by two membranes, it is where most of the cell's ATP is made.

mitosis (mī′-tō-sis) The division of a single nucleus into two genetically identical nuclei. Mitosis and cytokinesis make up the mitotic (M) phase of the cell cycle.

mitotic phase (M phase) The part of the cell cycle when the nucleus divides (via mitosis), its chromosomes are distributed to the daughter nuclei, and the cytoplasm divides (via cytokinesis), producing two daughter cells.

mitotic spindle A football-shaped structure formed of microtubules and associated proteins that is involved in the movement of chromosomes during mitosis and meiosis.

mixotroph A protist that is capable of both autotrophy and heterotrophy.

model An organism that a mimic has evolved to resemble in a mimicry relationship. *See also* mimic.

molecular biology The study of the molecular basis of genes and gene expression; molecular genetics.

molecular clock Evolutionary timing method based on the observation that at least some regions of genomes evolve at constant rates.

molecular systematics A scientific discipline that uses nucleic acids or other molecules in different species to infer evolutionary relationships.

molecule Two or more atoms held together by covalent bonds.

mollusc (mol′-lusk) A soft-bodied animal characterized by a muscular foot, mantle, mantle cavity, and visceral mass. Molluscs include gastropods (snails and slugs), bivalves (clams, oysters, and scallops), and cephalopods (squids and octopi).

monocot (mon′-ō-kot) A flowering plant whose embryos have a single seed leaf, or cotyledon.

monogamous Referring to a type of relationship in which one male mates with just one female, and both parents care for the children.

monohybrid cross An experimental mating of individuals differing in a single character.

monomer (mon′-uh-mer) The subunit that serves as a building block of a polymer.

monophyletic (mon′-ō-fī-let′-ik) Pertaining to a group of taxa that consists of a common ancestor and all of its descendants, equivalent to a clade.

monosaccharide (mon′-ō-sak′-uh-rīd) The simplest carbohydrate; a simple sugar with a molecular formula that is generally some multiple of CH_2O; the monomer of a disaccharide and polysaccharide.

monotreme (mon′-uh-trēm) An egg-laying mammal, such as the platypus.

monozygotic twins *See* identical twins.

morning after pill (MAP) A birth control pill taken within three days of unprotected intercourse to prevent fertilization or implantation of an egg.

morphological species concept A definition of species in terms of measurable anatomical criteria.

motor neuron A nerve cell that conveys command signals from the central nervous system to effector cells, such as muscle cells or gland cells.

motor output The conduction of signals from a processing centre in the central nervous system to effector cells.

motor system The component of the vertebrate peripheral nervous system that carries signals to and from skeletal muscles, mainly in response to external stimuli. Most actions of the motor system are voluntary.

motor unit A motor neuron and all the muscle fibres it controls.

mould A rapidly growing fungus that reproduces asexually by producing spores.

moulting The process of shedding an old exoskeleton or cuticle and secreting a new, larger one.

mouth An opening through which food is taken into an animal's body; synonymous with oral cavity.

movement corridor A series of small clumps or a narrow strip of quality habitat (usable by organisms) that connects otherwise isolated patches of quality habitat.

Müllerian mimicry A type of mimicry in which both mimic and model are distasteful, reinforcing this mechanism of defence.

multipotent stem cell An unspecialized cell that can divide to produce one identical daughter cell and a more specialized daughter cell, which undergoes differentiation; can form multiple types of cells but not all types of cells in the body.

muscle fibre Muscle cell.

muscle tissue Tissue consisting of long muscle cells that can contract, either on its own or when stimulated by nerve impulses; the most abundant tissue in a typical animal. *See also* skeletal muscle; cardiac muscle; smooth muscle.

muscular system The organ system that includes all the skeletal muscles in the body. (Cardiac muscle and smooth muscle are components of other organ systems.)

mutagen (myū′-tuh-jen) A chemical or physical agent that interacts with DNA and causes a mutation.

mutagenesis (myū′-tuh-jen′-uh-sis) The creation of a change in the nucleotide sequence of an organism's DNA.

mutation A change in the nucleotide sequence of an organism's DNA; the ultimate source of genetic diversity; can also occur in the DNA or RNA of a virus.

mutualism An interspecific relationship in which both partners benefit.

mycelium (mī-sē′-lē-um) (plural, **mycelia**) The densely branched network of hyphae in a fungus.

mycorrhiza (mī′-kō-rī′-zuh) (plural, **mycorrhizae**) A close association of plant roots and fungi that is beneficial to both partners.

myelin sheath (mī′-uh-lin) A series of cells, each wound around, and thus insulating, the axon of a nerve cell in vertebrates. Each pair of cells in the sheath is separated by a space called a node of Ranvier.

myofibril (mī′-ō-fī′-bril) A contractile strand in a muscle cell (fibre), made up of many sarcomeres. Longitudinal bundles of myofibrils make up a muscle fibre.

myosin A type of protein filament that interacts with actin filaments to cause cell contraction.

N

NAD⁺ Nicotinamide adenine dinucleotide, a coenzyme that can accept electrons during the redox reactions of cellular metabolism. The plus sign indicates that the molecule is oxidized and ready to pick up hydrogens; the reduced, hydrogen (electron)-carrying form is NADH.

NADP⁺ Nicotinamide adenine dinucleotide phosphate, an electron acceptor that, as NADPH, temporarily stores energized electrons produced during the light reactions.

natural family planning A form of contraception that relies on refraining from sexual intercourse when conception is most likely to occur; also called the rhythm method.

natural killer (NK) cell A cell type that provides an innate immune response by attacking cancer cells and infected body cells, especially those harbouring viruses.

natural selection A process in which individuals with certain inherited traits are more likely to survive and reproduce than are individuals that do not have those traits.

nearsightedness An inability to focus on distant objects; occurs when the eyeball is longer than normal and the lens focuses distant objects in front of the retina; also called myopia.

negative feedback A primary mechanism of homeostasis, whereby a change in a physiological variable triggers a response that counteracts the initial change. Negative feedback is a common control mechanism in which a chemical reaction, metabolic pathway, or hormone-secreting gland is inhibited by the products of the reaction, pathway, or gland. As the concentration of the products builds up, the product molecules themselves inhibit the process that produced them.

negative pressure breathing A breathing system in which air is pulled into the lungs.

nematode (nem′-uh-tōd) A roundworm, characterized by a pseudocoelom, a cylindrical, wormlike body form, and a tough cuticle that is moulted to permit growth.

nephron The tubular excretory unit and associated blood vessels of the vertebrate kidney; extracts filtrate from the blood and refines it into urine. The nephron is the functional unit of the urinary system.

nerve A cablelike bundle of neurons tightly wrapped in connective tissue.

nerve cord An elongated bundle of neurons, usually extending longitudinally from the brain or anterior ganglia. One or more nerve cords and the brain make up the central nervous system in many animals.

nerve net A weblike system of interconnected neurons, characteristic of radially symmetric animals such as a hydra.

nervous system The organ system that forms a communication and coordination network between all parts of an animal's body.

nervous tissue Tissue made up of neurons and supportive cells.

neural tube (nyūr′-ul) An embryonic cylinder that develops from the ectoderm after gastrulation and gives rise to the brain and spinal cord.

neuron (nyūr′-on) A nerve cell; the fundamental structural and functional unit of the nervous system, specialized for carrying signals from one location in the body to another.

neurosecretory cell A nerve cell that synthesizes hormones and secretes them into the blood and also conducts nerve signals.

neurotransmitter A chemical messenger that carries information from a transmitting neuron to a receiving cell, either another neuron or an effector cell.

neutron A subatomic particle having no electrical charge, found in the nucleus of an atom.

neutrophil (nyū′-truh-fil) An innate, defensive, phagocytic white blood cell that can engulf bacteria and viruses in infected tissue.

nitrogen fixation The conversion of atmospheric nitrogen (N_2) to nitrogen compounds (NH_4^+, NO_3^-) that plants can absorb and use.

node of Ranvier (ron′-vē-ā) An unmyelinated region on a myelinated axon of a nerve cell, where nerve signals are regenerated.

node The point of attachment of a leaf on a stem.

noncoding DNA Regions of the genome that do not code for genes.

noncompetitive inhibitor A substance that reduces the activity of an enzyme without entering an active site. By binding elsewhere on the enzyme, a noncompetitive inhibitor changes the shape of the enzyme so that the active site no longer effectively catalyzes the conversion of substrate to product.

nondisjunction An accident of meiosis or mitosis in which a pair of homologous chromosomes or a pair of sister chromatids fail to separate at anaphase.

nonpolar covalent bond A covalent bond in which electrons are shared equally between two atoms of similar electronegativity.

nonself molecule A foreign antigen; a protein or other macromolecule that is not part of an organism's body. *See also* self protein.

nonsense mutation A change in the nucleotide sequence of a gene that converts an amino-acid-encoding codon to a stop codon; results in a shortened polypeptide.

noradrenaline An amine hormone secreted by the adrenal medulla that prepares body organs for action (fight or flight); serves as a neurotransmitter; also called norepinephrine.

notochord (nō′-tuh-kord) A flexible, cartilage-like, longitudinal rod located between the digestive tract and nerve cord in chordate animals; present only in embryos in many species.

nuclear envelope A double membrane that encloses the nucleus, perforated with pores that regulate traffic with the cytoplasm.

nuclear transplantation A technique in which the nucleus of one cell is placed into another cell that already has a nucleus or in which the nucleus has been previously destroyed.

nucleic acid (nū-klā′-ik) A polymer consisting of many nucleotide monomers; serves as a blueprint for proteins and, through the actions of proteins, for all cellular structures and activities. The two types of nucleic acids are DNA and RNA.

nucleic acid probe In DNA technology, a radioactively or fluorescently labelled single-stranded nucleic acid molecule used to find a specific gene or other nucleotide sequence within a mass of DNA. The probe hydrogen-bonds to the complementary sequence in the targeted DNA.

nucleoid (nū′-klē-oyd) A dense region of DNA in a prokaryotic cell.

nucleolus (nū-klē′-ō-lus) A structure within the nucleus where ribosomal RNA is made and assembled with proteins imported from the cytoplasm to make ribosomal subunits.

nucleosome (nū′-klē-ō-sōm) The beadlike unit of DNA packing in a eukaryotic cell; consists of DNA wound around a protein core made up of eight histone molecules.

nucleotide (nū′-klē-ō-tīd) A building block of nucleic acids consisting of a five-carbon sugar covalently bonded to a nitrogenous base and one or more phosphate groups.

nucleus (plural, **nuclei**) (1) An atom's central core, containing protons and neutrons. (2) The genetic control centre of a eukaryotic cell.

O

obesity The excessive accumulation of fat in the body.

obligate symbiosis A symbiotic relationship in which at least one symbiont cannot survive without the other.

ocean acidification Decreasing pH of ocean waters because of the absorption of excess atmospheric CO_2 from the burning of fossil fuels.

ocean current One of the riverlike flow patterns in the oceans.

omnivore An animal that eats animals as well as plants or algae.

oncogene (on′-kō-jēn) A cancer-causing gene; usually contributes to malignancy by abnormally enhancing the amount or activity of a growth factor made by the cell.

oogenesis (ō′-uh-jen′-uh-sis) The development of mature egg cells.

open circulatory system A circulatory system in which blood is pumped through open-ended vessels and bathes the tissues and organs directly. In an animal with an open circulatory system, blood and interstitial fluid are one and the same.

operator In prokaryotic DNA, a sequence of nucleotides near the start of an operon to which an active repressor protein can attach. The binding of a repressor prevents RNA polymerase from attaching to the promoter and transcribing the genes of the operon. The operator sequence thereby acts as a "genetic switch" that can turn all the genes in an operon on or off as a single functional unit.

operculum (ō-per′-kyuh-lum) (plural, **opercula**) A protective flap on each side of a fish's head that covers a chamber housing the gills. Movement of the operculum increases the flow of oxygen-bearing water over the gills.

operon (op′-er-on) A unit of genetic regulation common in prokaryotes; a cluster of genes with related functions, along with the promoter and operator that control their transcription.

opposable thumb An arrangement of the fingers such that the thumb can touch the ventral surface of the fingertips of all four fingers.

optimal foraging theory The basis for analyzing behaviour as a compromise between feeding costs and feeding benefits.

oral cavity The mouth of an animal.

oral contraceptive See birth control pill.

order In Linnaean classification, the taxonomic category above family.

organ A specialized structure composed of several different types of tissues that together perform specific functions.

organ of Corti (kor′-tē) The hearing organ in birds and mammals, located within the cochlea.

organ system A group of organs that work together in performing vital body functions.

organelle (ōr-guh-nel′) A membrane-enclosed structure with a specialized function within a cell.

organic compound A chemical compound containing the element carbon and usually the element hydrogen.

organism An individual living thing, such as a bacterium, fungus, protist, plant, or animal.

orgasm A series of rhythmic, involuntary contractions of the reproductive structures.

osmoconformer (oz′-mō-con-form′-er) An organism whose body fluids have a solute concentration equal to that of its surroundings. Osmoconformers do not have a net gain or loss of water by osmosis. Examples include most marine invertebrates.

osmoregulation The homeostatic maintenance of solute concentrations and the balance of water gain and loss.

osmoregulator An organism whose body fluids have a solute concentration different from that of its environment and that must use energy in controlling water loss or gain. Examples include most land-dwelling and freshwater animals.

osmosis (oz-mō′-sis) The diffusion of water across a selectively permeable membrane.

osteoporosis (os′-tē-ō-puh-rō′-sis) A skeletal disorder characterized by thinning, porous, and easily broken bones.

outer ear One of three main regions of the ear in reptiles (including birds) and mammals; made up of the auditory canal and, in many birds and mammals, the pinna.

outgroup In a cladistic study, a taxon or group of taxa known to have diverged before the lineage that contains the group of species being studied. See also ingroup.

ovarian cycle (ō-vār′-ē-un) Hormonally synchronized cyclic events in the mammalian ovary, culminating in ovulation.

ovary (1) In animals, the female gonad, which produces egg cells and reproductive hormones. (2) In flowering plants, the basal portion of a carpel in which the egg-containing ovules develop.

oviduct (ō′-vuh-dukt) The tube that conveys egg cells away from an ovary; also called a fallopian tube. In humans, the oviduct is the normal site of fertilization.

ovulation (ah′-vyū-lā′-shun) The release of an egg cell from an ovarian follicle.

ovule (ō-vyūl) In plants, a structure that develops within the ovary of a seed plant and contains the female gametophyte.

oxidation The loss of electrons from a substance involved in a redox reaction; always accompanies reduction.

oxidative phosphorylation (fos′-fōr-uh-lā′-shun) The production of ATP by using energy derived from the redox reactions of an electron transport chain; the third major stage of cellular respiration.

ozone layer The layer of ozone (O_3) in the upper atmosphere that protects life on Earth from the harmful ultraviolet rays in sunlight.

P

P generation The parent individuals from which offspring are derived in studies of inheritance; *P* stands for parental.

P site One of two of a ribosome's binding sites for tRNA during translation; holds the tRNA carrying the growing polypeptide chain. *P* stands for peptidyl tRNA.

paedomorphosis (pē′-duh-mōr′-fuh-sis) The retention in an adult of juvenile features of its evolutionary ancestors.

pain receptor A sensory receptor that detects pain.

paleoanthropology (pā′-lē-ō-an′-thruh-pol′-uh-jē) The study of human origins and evolution.

paleontologist (pa′-lē-on-tol′-uh-jist) A scientist who studies fossils.

pancreas (pan′-krē-us) A gland with dual functions: The digestive portion secretes digestive enzymes and an alkaline solution into the small intestine via a duct. The endocrine portion secretes the hormones insulin and glucagon into the blood.

Pangaea (pan-jē′-uh) The supercontinent that formed near the end of the Paleozoic era, when plate movements brought all the land masses of Earth together.

parasite Organism that derives its nutrition from a living host, which is harmed by the interaction.

parasitism A symbiosis in which one partner benefits at the cost of the other.

parasitoid A relationship similar to parasitism except the parasitoid always kills its host.

parasympathetic division The component of the autonomic nervous system that generally promotes body activities that gain and conserve energy, such as digestion and reduced heart rate. *See also* sympathetic division.

parathyroid gland (pār′-uh-thī′-royd) One of four endocrine glands that are embedded in the surface of the thyroid gland and that secrete parathyroid hormone.

parathyroid hormone (PTH) A peptide hormone secreted by the parathyroid glands that raises blood calcium level.

parenchyma cell (puh-ren′-kim-uh) In plants, a relatively unspecialized cell with a thin primary wall and no secondary wall; functions in photosynthesis, food storage, and aerobic respiration and may differentiate into other cell types.

Parkinson's disease A motor disorder caused by a progressive brain disease and characterized by difficulty in initiating movements, slowness of movement, and rigidity.

parsimony (par′-suh-mō′-nē) In scientific studies, the search for the least complex explanation for an observed phenomenon.

partial pressure The pressure exerted by a particular gas in a mixture of gases; a measure of the relative amount of a gas.

passive immunity Temporary immunity obtained by acquiring ready-made antibodies; lasts only a few weeks or months.

passive transmission The movement of a parasite from one host to another, which relies on the host to infect itself or a vector.

passive transport The diffusion of a substance across a biological membrane, with no expenditure of energy.

patch A localized community that is distinct from its surroundings. *See also* matrix.

pathogen An agent, such as a virus, bacteria, or fungus, that causes disease.

pattern formation During embryonic development, the emergence of a body form with specialized organs and tissues in the right places.

PCR *See* polymerase chain reaction (PCR).

pedigree A family genetic tree representing the occurrence of heritable traits in parents and offspring across a number of generations; can be used to determine genotypes of matings that have already occurred.

pelagic realm (puh-laj´-ik) The region of an ocean occupied by seawater.

penis The copulatory structure of male mammals.

peptide bond The covalent bond between two amino acid units in a polypeptide, formed by a dehydration reaction.

peptidoglycan (pep´-tid-ō-glī´-kan) A polymer of complex sugars cross-linked by short polypeptides; a material unique to bacterial cell walls.

per capita rate of increase The average contribution of each individual in a population to population growth.

perennial (puh-ren´-ē-ul) A plant that lives for many years.

peripheral nervous system (PNS) The network of nerves and ganglia carrying signals into and out of the central nervous system.

peristalsis (per´-uh-stal´-sis) Rhythmic waves of contraction of smooth muscles; propels food through a digestive tract and also enables many animals, such as earthworms, to crawl.

permafrost Continuously frozen ground found in the tundra.

peroxisome An organelle containing enzymes that transfer hydrogen atoms from various substrates to oxygen, producing and then degrading hydrogen peroxide.

petal A modified leaf of a flowering plant; often the colourful part of a flower that advertises it to pollinators.

pH scale A measure of the relative acidity of a solution, ranging in value from 0 (most acidic) to 14 (most basic). The letters *pH* stand for potential hydrogen and refer to the concentration of hydrogen ions (H^+).

phage (fāj) *See* bacteriophage.

phagocyte (fag´-ō-sīt) A white blood cell (for example, a neutrophil or monocyte) that engulfs bacteria, foreign proteins, and the remains of dead body cells.

phagocytosis (fag´-ō-sī-tō´-sis) Cellular "eating"; a type of endocytosis in which a cell engulfs macromolecules, other cells, or particles into its cytoplasm.

pharyngeal slit (fā-rin´-jē-ul) A gill structure in the pharynx; found in chordate embryos and some adult chordates.

pharynx (fār´-inks) The organ in a digestive tract that receives food from the oral cavity; in terrestrial vertebrates, the throat region where the air and food passages cross.

phenotype (fē´-nō-tīp) The expressed traits of an organism.

phenotypic plasticity An individual's ability to change phenotype in response to local environmental conditions.

phloem (flō´-um) The portion of a plant's vascular tissue system that transports sugars and other organic nutrients from leaves or storage tissues to other parts of the plant.

phloem sap The solution of sugars, other nutrients, and hormones conveyed throughout a plant via phloem tissue.

phosphate group (fos´-fāt) A chemical group consisting of a phosphorus atom bonded to four oxygen atoms.

phospholipid (fos´-fō-lip´-id) A lipid made up of glycerol joined to two fatty acids and a phosphate group, giving the molecule two nonpolar hydrophobic tails and a polar hydrophilic head. Phospholipids form bilayers that function as biological membranes.

phosphorylation (fos´-fōr-uh-lā´-shun) The transfer of a phosphate group, usually from ATP, to a molecule. Nearly all cellular work depends on ATP energizing other molecules by phosphorylation.

photic zone (fō´-tik) The region of an aquatic ecosystem into which light penetrates and where photosynthesis occurs.

photoautotroph An organism that obtains energy from sunlight and carbon from CO_2 by photosynthesis.

photoheterotroph An organism that obtains energy from sunlight and carbon from organic sources.

photon (fō´-ton) A fixed quantity of light energy: the shorter the wavelength of light, the greater the energy of a photon.

photoperiod The relative lengths of day and night; an environmental stimulus that plants use to detect the time of year.

photophosphorylation (fō´-tō-fos´-fōr-uh-lā´-shun) The production of ATP by chemiosmosis during the light reactions of photosynthesis.

photopsin (fō-top´-sin) One of a family of visual pigments in the cones of the vertebrate eye that absorb bright, coloured light.

photoreceptor A type of electromagnetic sensory receptor that detects light.

photorespiration In a plant cell, a metabolic pathway that consumes O_2, releases CO_2, and decreases photosynthetic output. Photorespiration generally occurs on hot, dry days; when stomata close, O_2 accumulates in the leaf, and rubisco fixes O_2 rather than CO_2. Photorespiration produces no sugar molecules or ATP.

photosynthesis (fō´-tō-sin´-thuh-sis) The process by which plants, autotrophic protists, and some bacteria use light energy to make sugars and other organic food molecules from carbon dioxide and water.

photosystem A light-capturing unit of a chloroplast's thylakoid membrane, consisting of a reaction-centre complex surrounded by numerous light-harvesting complexes.

phototropism (fō´-tō-trō´-pizm) The growth of a plant shoot toward light (positive phototropism) or away from light (negative phototropism).

phylogenetic species concept A definition of species as the smallest group of individuals that shares a common ancestor, forming one branch on the tree of life.

phylogenetic tree (fī´-lō-juh-net´-ik) A branching diagram that represents a hypothesis about the evolutionary history of a group of organisms.

phylogeny (fī-loj´-uh-nē) The evolutionary history of a species or group of related species.

phylum (fī´-lum) (plural, **phyla**) In Linnaean classification, the taxonomic category above class.

physiology (fī´-zē-ol´-uh-ji) The study of the functions of an organism's structures.

phytochrome (fī´-tuh-krōm) A plant protein that has a light-absorbing component.

phytoplankton (fī´-tō-plank´-ton) Algae and photosynthetic bacteria that drift passively in aquatic environments.

phytoremediation The use of plants to clean up environmental contaminants.

pigment A molecule that can absorb a specific wavelength of light.

pineal gland (pin´-ē-ul) An outgrowth of the vertebrate brain that secretes the hormone melatonin, which coordinates daily and seasonal body activities such as the sleep–wake circadian rhythm with environmental light conditions.

pinna (pin´-uh) The flaplike part of the outer ear, projecting from the body surface of many birds and mammals; collects sound waves and channels them to the auditory canal.

pinocytosis (pē´-nō-sī-tō´-sis) Cellular "drinking"; a type of endocytosis in which the cell takes fluid and dissolved solutes into small membranous vesicles.

pistil Part of the reproductive organ of an angiosperm, a single carpel or a group of fused carpels.

pith Part of the ground tissue system of a dicot plant; fills the centre of a stem and may store food.

pituitary gland An endocrine gland at the base of the hypothalamus; consists of a posterior lobe, which stores and releases two hormones produced by the hypothalamus, and an anterior lobe, which produces and secretes many hormones that regulate diverse body functions.

pivot joint A joint that allows precise rotations in multiple planes. An example in humans is the joint that rotates the forearm at the elbow.

placenta (pluh-sen′-tuh) In most mammals, the organ that provides nutrients and oxygen to the embryo and helps to dispose of its metabolic wastes; formed of the embryo's chorion and the mother's endometrial blood vessels.

placental mammal (pluh-sen′-tul) Mammal whose young complete their embryonic development in the uterus, nourished via the mother's blood vessels in the placenta; also called a eutherian.

plasma The liquid matrix of the blood in which the blood cells are suspended.

plasma cell An antibody-secreting B cell.

plasma membrane The membrane at the boundary of every cell that acts as a selective barrier to the passage of ions and molecules into and out of the cell; consists of a phospholipid bilayer with embedded proteins.

plasmid A small ring of independently replicating DNA separate from the main chromosome(s). Plasmids are found in prokaryotes and yeasts.

plasmodesma (plaz′-mō-dez′-muh) (plural, **plasmodesmata**) An open channel in a plant cell wall through which strands of cytoplasm connect from adjacent cells.

plasmodial slime mould (plaz-mō′-dē-ul) A type of protist that has amoeboid cells, flagellated cells, and an amoeboid plasmodial feeding stage in its life cycle.

plasmodium (1) A single mass of cytoplasm containing many nuclei. (2) The amoeboid feeding stage in the life cycle of a plasmodial slime mould.

plate tectonics (tek-tän′-iks) The theory that the continents are part of great plates of Earth's crust that float on the hot, underlying portion of the mantle. Movements in the mantle cause the continents to move slowly over time.

platelet A pinched-off cytoplasmic fragment of a bone marrow cell. Platelets circulate in the blood and are important in blood clotting.

pleiotropy (plī′-uh-trō-pē) The control of more than one phenotypic characteristic by a single gene.

pluripotent stem cell A stem cell that can give rise to most but not all cell types within the body.

polar covalent bond A covalent bond between atoms that differ in electronegativity. The shared electrons are pulled closer to the more electronegative atom, making it slightly negative and the other atom slightly positive.

polar ice A terrestrial biome that includes regions of extremely cold temperature and low precipitation located at high latitudes north of the arctic tundra and in Antarctica.

polar molecule A molecule containing polar covalent bonds and having an unequal distribution of charges.

pollen grain The structure that will produce the sperm in seed plants; the male gametophyte.

pollination In seed plants, the delivery by wind or animals of pollen from the pollen-producing parts of a plant to the stigma of a carpel.

polychaete (pol′-ē-kēt) A member of the largest group of annelids. *See* annelid.

polygamous Referring to a type of relationship in which an individual of one sex mates with several of the other.

polygenic inheritance (pol′-ē-jen′-ik) The additive effects of two or more gene loci on a single phenotypic characteristic.

polymer (pol′-uh-mer) A large molecule consisting of many identical or similar monomers linked together by covalent bonds.

polymerase chain reaction (PCR) (puh-lim′-uh-rās) A technique used to obtain many copies of a DNA molecule or a specific part of a DNA molecule. In the procedure, the starting DNA is mixed with a heat-resistant DNA polymerase, DNA nucleotides, and a few other ingredients. Specific nucleotide primers flanking the region to be copied ensure that it, and not other regions of the DNA, is replicated during the PCR procedure.

polynucleotide (pol′-ē-nū′-klē-ō-tīd) A polymer made up of many nucleotide monomers covalently bonded together.

polyp (pol′-ip) One of two types of cnidarian body forms; a columnar, hydra-like body.

polypeptide A polymer (chain) of amino acids linked by peptide bonds.

polyploid An organism that has more than two complete sets of chromosomes as a result of an accident of cell division.

polysaccharide (pol′-ē-sak′-uh-rīd) A carbohydrate polymer of many monosaccharides (sugars) linked by dehydration reactions.

pons (pahnz) Part of the vertebrate hindbrain that functions with the medulla oblongata in passing data between the spinal cord and forebrain and in controlling autonomic, homeostatic functions.

population A group of individuals belonging to one species and living in the same geographic area.

population density The number of individuals of a species per unit area or volume.

population ecology The study of how members of a population interact with their environment, focusing on factors that influence population density and growth.

population momentum In a population in which $r = 0$, the continuation of population growth as girls in the prereproductive age group reach their reproductive years.

positive feedback A type of control in which a change triggers mechanisms that amplify that change.

post-anal tail A tail posterior to the anus; found in chordate embryos and most adult chordates.

posterior Pertaining to the rear, or tail, of a bilaterally symmetric animal.

posterior pituitary An extension of the hypothalamus composed of nervous tissue that secretes hormones made in the hypothalamus; a temporary storage site for hypothalamic hormones.

postzygotic barrier A reproductive barrier that prevents hybrid zygotes produced by two different species from developing into viable, fertile adults; includes reduced hybrid viability, reduced hybrid fertility, and hybrid breakdown.

potency The ability of a cell to change or differentiate into another cell type.

potential energy The energy that matter possesses because of its location or arrangement. Water behind a dam possesses potential energy, and so do chemical bonds.

Pouyannian mimicry A form of mimicry in which plants have evolved flowers that resemble potential mates to attract unsuspecting insects to carry their pollen.

predation An interaction between species in which one species, the predator, eats the other, the prey.

prepuce (prē′-pyūs) A fold of skin covering the head of the clitoris or penis.

pressure flow mechanism The method by which phloem sap is transported through a plant from a sugar source, where sugars are produced, to a sugar sink, where sugars are used.

prevailing winds Winds that result from the combined effects of Earth's rotation and the rising and falling of air masses.

prezygotic barrier A reproductive barrier that impedes mating between species or hinders fertilization if mating between two species is attempted; includes temporal, habitat, behavioural, mechanical, and gametic isolation.

primary consumer In the trophic structure of an ecosystem, an organism that eats plants or algae.

primary growth Growth in the length of a plant root or shoot, produced by an apical meristem.

primary immune response The initial immune response to an antigen, which appears after a lag of several days.

primary oocyte (ō′-uh-sīt) A diploid cell, in prophase I of meiosis, that can be hormonally triggered to develop into an egg.

primary phloem *See* phloem.

primary production The amount of solar energy converted to chemical energy (in organic compounds) by autotrophs in an ecosystem during a given time period.

primary spermatocyte (sper-mat′-eh-sīt′) A diploid cell in the testis that undergoes meiosis I.

primary structure The first level of protein structure; the specific sequence of amino acids making up a polypeptide chain.

primary succession A type of ecological succession in which a biological community arises in an area without soil. *See also* secondary succession.

primary xylem *See* xylem.

primers Short, artificially created, single-stranded DNA molecules that bind to each end of a target sequence during a PCR procedure.

prion An infectious form of protein that may multiply by converting related proteins to more prions. Prions cause several related diseases in different animals, including scrapie in sheep and mad cow disease.

problem solving Applying past experiences to overcome obstacles in novel situations.

producer An organism that makes organic food molecules from CO_2, H_2O, and other inorganic raw materials: a plant, alga, or autotrophic prokaryote.

product An ending material in a chemical reaction.

proenzyme An enzyme in an inactive state.

progestin (prō-jes′-tin) One of a family of steroid hormones, including progesterone, produced by the mammalian ovary; prepares the uterus for pregnancy.

programmed cell death The timely and tidy suicide (and disposal of the remains) of certain cells, triggered by certain genes; an essential process in normal development; also called apoptosis.

prokaryotic cell (prō-kār′-ē-ot′-ik) A type of cell lacking a membrane-enclosed nucleus and other membrane-enclosed organelles; found only in the domains Bacteria and Archaea.

prolactin (PRL) (prō-lak′-tin) A protein hormone secreted by the anterior pituitary that stimulates human mammary glands to produce and release milk and produces other responses in different animals.

prometaphase The second stage of mitosis, during which the nuclear envelope fragments and the spindle microtubules attach to the kinetochores of the sister chromatids.

promiscuous Referring to a type of relationship in which mating occurs with no strong pair-bonds or lasting relationships.

promoter A specific nucleotide sequence in DNA located near the start of a gene that is the binding site for RNA polymerase and the place where transcription begins.

prophage (prō′-fāj) Phage DNA that was inserted by genetic recombination into the DNA of a bacterial chromosome.

prophase The first stage of mitosis, during which the chromatin condenses to form structures (sister chromatids) visible with a light microscope and the mitotic spindle begins to form, but the nucleus is still intact.

prostate gland (pros′-tāt) A gland in human males that secretes a thin fluid that nourishes the sperm.

protein A functional biological molecule consisting of one or more polypeptides folded into a specific three-dimensional structure.

proteobacteria A clade of gram-negative bacteria that encompasses enormous diversity, including all four modes of nutrition.

proteomics The study of whole sets of proteins and their interactions.

protist A member of the kingdom Protista. Most protists are unicellular, though some are colonial or multicellular.

proton A subatomic particle with a single positive electrical charge, found in the nucleus of an atom.

proto-oncogene (prō′-tō-on′-kō-jēn) A normal gene that, through mutation, can be converted to a cancer-causing gene.

protostome A mode of animal development in which the opening formed during gastrulation becomes the mouth. Animals with the protostome pattern of development include the flatworms, molluscs, annelids, nematodes, and arthropods.

proximal tubule In the vertebrate kidney, the portion of a nephron immediately downstream from Bowman's capsule that conveys and helps to refine filtrate.

proximate cause In animal behaviour, a condition in an animal's internal or external environment that is the immediate reason or mechanism for a behaviour.

proximate question In animal behaviour, a question that concerns the immediate reason for a behaviour.

pseudocoelom (sū′-dō-sē′-lōm) A body cavity that is not lined with mesoderm and is in direct contact with the wall of the digestive tract.

pseudopodium (sū′-dō-pō′-dē-um) (plural, **pseudopodia**) A temporary extension of an amoeboid cell; functions in moving cells and engulfing food.

pulmonary artery A large blood vessel that conveys blood from the heart to a lung.

pulmonary circuit The branch of the circulatory system that supplies the lungs. *See also* systemic circuit.

pulmonary vein A blood vessel that conveys blood from a lung to the heart.

pulse The rhythmic stretching of the arteries caused by the pressure of blood during contraction of ventricles in systole.

punctuated equilibria In the fossil record, long periods of apparent stasis, in which a species undergoes little or no morphological change, interrupted by relatively brief periods of sudden change.

Punnett square A diagram used in the study of inheritance to show the results of random fertilization.

pupil The opening in the iris that admits light into the interior of the vertebrate eye. Muscles in the iris regulate the pupil's size.

Q

quaternary consumer (kwot′-er-ner-ē) An organism that eats tertiary consumers.

quaternary structure The fourth level of protein structure; the shape resulting from the association of two or more polypeptide subunits.

R

R plasmid A bacterial plasmid that carries genes for enzymes that destroy particular antibiotics, thus making the bacterium resistant to the antibiotics.

radial symmetry An arrangement of the body parts of an organism like pieces of a pie around an imaginary central axis. Any slice passing longitudinally through a radially symmetric organism's central axis divides it into mirror-image halves.

radioactive isotope *See* radioisotope.

radioisotope An isotope whose nucleus decays spontaneously, giving off particles and energy.

radiolarian A protist that moves and feeds by means of threadlike pseudopodia and has a mineralized support structure composed of silica.

radiometric dating A method for determining the absolute ages of fossils and rocks, based on the half-life of radioactive isotopes.

radula (rad′-yū-luh) A toothed, rasping organ used to scrape up or shred food; found in many molluscs.

random distribution pattern A pattern in which the individuals of a population are spaced in an unpredictable way.

randomized experiment An experiment in which specimens are assigned to groups without bias.

ray-finned fish Bony fish; member of a clade of jawed vertebrates having fins supported by thin, flexible skeletal rays.

reabsorption In the vertebrate kidney, the reclaiming of water and valuable solutes from the filtrate.

reactant A starting material in a chemical reaction.

reading frame The way a cell's mRNA-translating machinery groups the mRNA nucleotides into codons.

receptor potential The electrical signal produced by sensory transduction.

receptor-mediated endocytosis (en′-dō-sī-tō′-sis) The movement of specific molecules into a cell by the inward budding of membranous vesicles, which contain proteins with receptor sites specific to the molecules being taken in.

recessive allele An allele that has no noticeable effect on the phenotype of a gene when the individual is heterozygous for that gene.

recombinant DNA A DNA molecule carrying nucleotide sequences derived from two or more sources.

recombination frequency With respect to two given genes, the number of recombinant progeny from a mating divided by the total number of progeny. Recombinant progeny carry combinations of alleles different from those in either of the parents as a result of crossing over during meiosis.

Recommended Dietary Allowance (RDA) A recommendation for daily nutrient intake established by a national scientific panel.

rectum The terminal portion of the large intestine where the feces are stored until they are eliminated.

red alga A member of a group of marine, mostly multicellular, autotrophic protists, which includes the reef-building coralline algae. Red algae belong to the supergroup Archaeplastida.

red blood cell *See* erythrocyte.

red bone marrow A specialized tissue that is found in the cavities at the ends of bones and that produces blood cells.

red-green colourblindness A category of common, sex-linked human disorders involving several genes on the X chromosome; characterized by a malfunction of light-sensitive cells in the eyes; affects mostly males but also homozygous females.

redox reaction Short for **red**uction-**ox**idation reaction; a chemical reaction in which electrons are lost from one substance (oxidation) and added to another (reduction).

reduction The gain of electrons by a substance involved in a redox reaction; always accompanies oxidation.

reflex An automatic reaction to a stimulus, mediated by the spinal cord or lower brain.

regeneration The regrowth of body parts from pieces of an organism.

regulatory gene A gene that codes for a protein, such as a repressor, that controls the transcription of another gene or group of genes.

relative fitness The contribution an individual makes to the gene pool of the next generation, relative to the contributions of other individuals in the population.

releasing hormone A kind of hormone secreted by the hypothalamus that promotes the release of hormones from the anterior pituitary.

renal cortex The outer portion of the vertebrate kidney, above the renal medulla.

renal medulla The inner portion of the vertebrate kidney, beneath the renal cortex.

repetitive DNA Nucleotide sequences that are present in many copies in the DNA of a genome. The repeated sequences may be long or short and may be located next to each other (in tandom) or dispersed in the DNA.

repressor A protein that blocks the transcription of a gene or operon.

reproduction The creation of new individuals from existing ones.

reproductive cloning Using a somatic cell from a multicellular organism to make one or more genetically identical individuals.

reproductive cycle A recurring sequence of events that produces eggs, makes them available for fertilization, and prepares the female body for pregnancy.

reproductive isolation The existence of biological factors (barriers) that impede members of two species from producing viable, fertile hybrids.

reproductive mimicry A form of mimicry that increases the reproductive success of the mimic.

reproductive system The organ system responsible for reproduction.

reptile Member of the clade of amniotes that includes snakes, lizards, turtles, crocodilians, and birds, along with a number of extinct groups, such as dinosaurs.

respiratory system The organ system that functions in exchanging gases with the environment; supplies the blood with O_2 and disposes of CO_2.

resting potential The voltage across the plasma membrane of a resting neuron. The resting potential in a vertebrate neuron is typically around –70 millivolts, with the inside of the cell negatively charged relative to the outside.

restoration ecology The use of ecological principles to develop ways to return degraded ecosystems to conditions as similar as possible to their natural, predegraded state.

restriction enzyme A bacterial enzyme that cuts up foreign DNA (at specific DNA sequences called restriction sites), thus protecting bacteria against intruding DNA from phages and other organisms. Restriction enzymes are used in DNA technology to cut DNA molecules in reproducible ways. The pieces of cut DNA are called restriction fragments.

restriction fragment length polymorphism (RFLP) (rif′-lip) Variation in the length of a restriction fragment; produced when homologous DNA sequences containing SNPs are cut up with restriction enzymes.

restriction fragments Molecules of DNA produced from a longer DNA molecule cut up by a restriction enzyme; used in genome mapping and other applications.

restriction site A specific sequence on a DNA strand that is recognized as a "cut site" by a restriction enzyme.

retina (ret′-uh-nuh) The light-sensitive layer in an eye, made up of photoreceptor cells and sensory neurons.

retrovirus An RNA virus that reproduces by means of a DNA molecule. It reverse-transcribes its RNA into DNA, inserts the DNA into a cellular chromosome, and then transcribes more copies of the RNA from the viral DNA. HIV and a number of cancer-causing viruses are retroviruses.

reverse transcriptase (tran-skrip′-tās) An enzyme used by retroviruses that catalyzes the synthesis of DNA on an RNA template.

RFLP *See* restriction fragment length polymorphism (RFLP).

Rhizaria One of five supergroups proposed in a current hypothesis of the evolutionary history of eukaryotes. The other four supergroups are Chromalveolata, Excavata, Unikonta, and Archaeplastida.

rhizome (rī′-zōm) A horizontal stem that grows below the ground.

rhodopsin (ro-dop′-sin) A visual pigment that is located in the rods of the vertebrate eye and that absorbs dim light.

rhythm method A form of contraception that relies on refraining from sexual intercourse when conception is most likely to occur; also called natural family planning.

ribonucleic acid (RNA) (rī-bō-nū-klā′-ik) A type of nucleic acid consisting of nucleotide monomers with a ribose sugar and the nitrogenous bases adenine (A), cytosine (C), guanine (G), and uracil (U); usually single-stranded; functions in protein synthesis, gene regulation, and as the genome of some viruses.

ribosomal RNA (rRNA) (rī′-buh-sōm′-ul) The type of ribonucleic acid that, together with proteins, makes up ribosomes; the most abundant type of RNA in most cells.

ribosome (rī′-buh-sōm) A cell structure consisting of RNA and protein organized into two subunits and functioning as the site of protein synthesis in the cytoplasm. In eukaryotic cells, the ribosomal subunits are constructed in the nucleolus.

ribozyme (rī′-bō-zīm) An RNA molecule that functions as an enzyme.

RNA interference (RNAi) A biotechnology technique used to silence the expression of specific genes. Synthetic RNA molecules with sequences that correspond to particular genes trigger the breakdown of the gene's mRNA.

RNA polymerase (puh-lim′-uh-rās) A large molecular complex that links together the growing chain of RNA nucleotides during transcription by using a DNA strand as a template.

RNA replicase A viral enzyme that synthesizes RNA from an RNA template.

RNA splicing The removal of introns and joining of exons in eukaryotic RNA, forming an mRNA molecule with a continuous coding sequence; occurs before mRNA leaves the nucleus.

rod A photoreceptor cell in the vertebrate retina enabling vision in dim light.

root cap A cone of cells at the tip of a plant root that protects the root's apical meristem.

root hair An outgrowth of an epidermal cell on a root, which increases the root's absorptive surface area.

root pressure The upward push of xylem sap in a vascular plant caused by the active pumping of minerals into the xylem by root cells.

root system All of a plant's roots, which anchor it in the soil, absorb and transport minerals and water, and store food.

rough endoplasmic reticulum (reh-tik′-yuh-lum) That portion of the endoplasmic reticulum with ribosomes attached that make membrane proteins and secretory proteins.

r-selection The concept that in certain (r-selected) populations, a high reproductive rate is the chief determinant of life history.

rule of addition A rule stating that the probability that an event can occur in two or more alternative ways is the sum of the separate probabilities of the different ways.

rule of multiplication A rule stating that the probability of a compound event is the product of the separate probabilities of the independent events.

ruminant (rū′-min-ent) An animal, such as a cow or sheep, with multiple stomach compartments housing microorganisms that can digest cellulose.

S

SA (sinoatrial) node (sī-nō′-ā-trē-ul) The pacemaker of the heart, located in the wall of the right atrium, that sets the rate and timing at which all cardiac muscle cells contract.

sac fungus *See* ascomycete.

salivary glands Glands associated with the oral cavity that secrete substances to lubricate food and begin the process of chemical digestion.

salt A compound resulting from the formation of ionic bonds; also called an ionic compound.

sapwood Light-coloured, water-conducting secondary xylem in a tree. *See also* heartwood.

sarcoma (sar-kō′-muh) Cancer of the supportive tissues, such as bone, cartilage, and muscle.

sarcomere (sar′-kō-mēr) The fundamental unit of muscle contraction, composed of thin filaments of actin and thick filaments of myosin; in electron micrographs, the region between two narrow, dark lines, called Z lines, in a myofibril.

saturated fatty acid A fatty acid in which all carbons in the hydrocarbon tail are connected by single bonds and the maximum number of hydrogen atoms are attached to the carbon skeleton. Saturated fats and fatty acids solidify at room temperature.

savanna A biome dominated by grasses and scattered trees.

scanning electron microscope (SEM) A microscope that uses an electron beam to study the fine details of cell surfaces or other specimens.

scavenger An animal that feeds on the carcasses of dead animals.

schizophrenia Severe mental disturbance characterized by psychotic episodes in which patients have a distorted perception of reality.

sclera (sklār′-uh) A layer of connective tissue forming the outer surface of the vertebrate eye. The cornea is the frontal part of the sclera.

sclereid (sklār′-ē-id) In plants, a very hard sclerenchyma cell found in nutshells and seed coats.

sclerenchyma cell (skluh-ren′-kē-muh) In plants, a supportive cell with rigid secondary walls hardened with lignin.

scrotum A pouch of skin outside the abdomen that houses the testes and functions in cooling sperm, keeping them viable.

search image The mechanism that enables an animal to find a particular kind of food efficiently.

second law of thermodynamics The principle stating that every energy conversion reduces the order of the universe, increasing its entropy. Ordered forms of energy are at least partly converted to heat.

secondary consumer An organism that eats primary consumers.

secondary endosymbiosis A theory that explains the evolution of protist diversity as the product of a symbiotic association that arose when an autotrophic eukaryotic protist (a product of primary endosymbiosis) was engulfed by a heterotrophic eukaryotic protist.

secondary growth An increase in a plant's diameter, involving cell division in the vascular cambium and cork cambium.

secondary immune response The immune response elicited when an animal encounters the same antigen at some later time; is more rapid, of greater magnitude, and of longer duration than the primary immune response.

secondary oocyte (ō′-uh-sīt′) A haploid cell resulting from meiosis I in oogenesis, which will become an egg after meiosis II.

secondary phloem *See* phloem.

secondary spermatocyte (sper-mat′-uh-sīt′) A haploid cell that results from meiosis I in spermatogenesis and becomes a sperm cell after meiosis II.

secondary structure The second level of protein structure; the regular local patterns of coils or folds of a polypeptide chain.

secondary succession A type of ecological succession that occurs where a disturbance has destroyed an existing biological community but left the soil intact. *See also* primary succession.

secondary xylem *See* xylem.

secretion (1) The discharge of molecules synthesized by a cell. (2) In the vertebrate kidney, the discharge of wastes from the blood into the filtrate from the nephron tubules.

seed A plant embryo packaged with a food supply within a protective covering.

seed coat A tough outer covering of a seed, formed from the outer coat (integuments) of an ovule. In a flowering plant, the seed coat encloses and protects the embryo and endosperm.

seedless vascular plants The informal collective name for lycophytes (club mosses and their relatives) and pterophytes (ferns and their relatives).

segmentation Subdivision along the length of an animal body into a series of repeated parts called segments; allows for greater flexibility and mobility.

selective permeability (per′-mē-uh-bil′-uh-tē) A property of biological membranes that allows some substances to cross more easily than others and blocks the passage of other substances altogether.

self protein A protein on the surface of an antigen-presenting cell that can hold a foreign antigen and display it to helper T cells. Each individual has a unique set of self proteins that serve as molecular markers for the body. Lymphocytes do not attack self proteins unless the proteins are displaying foreign antigens; therefore, self proteins mark normal body cells as off limits to the immune system. The technical name for self proteins is major histocompatibility complex (MHC) proteins. *See also* nonself molecule.

self-fertilize A form of reproduction that involves fusion of sperm and egg produced by the same individual organism.

semen (sē′-mun) The sperm-containing fluid that is ejaculated by the male during orgasm.

semicircular canals Fluid-filled channels in the inner ear that detect changes in the head's rate of rotation or angular movement.

semiconservative model Type of DNA replication in which the replicated double helix consists of one old strand, derived from the old molecule, and one newly made strand.

seminal vesicle (sem′-uh-nul ves′-uh-kul) A gland in males that secretes a thick fluid that contains fructose, which provides most of the sperm's energy.

seminiferous tubule (sem′-uh-nif′-uh-rus) A coiled sperm-producing tube in a testis.

sensitive period A limited phase in an individual animal's development when learning of particular behaviours can take place.

sensory adaptation The tendency of sensory neurons to become less sensitive when they are stimulated repeatedly. For example, a prominent smell becomes unnoticeable over time.

sensory input The conduction of signals from sensory receptors to processing centres in the central nervous system.

sensory neuron A nerve cell that receives information from sensory receptors and conveys signals into the central nervous system.

sensory receptor A specialized cell or neuron that detects stimuli and sends information to the central nervous system.

sensory transduction The conversion of a stimulus signal to an electrical signal by a sensory receptor.

sepal (sē′-pul) A modified leaf of a flowering plant. A whorl of sepals encloses and protects the flower bud before it opens.

sessile An organism that is anchored to its substrate.

sex chromosome A chromosome that determines whether an individual is male or female.

sex-linked gene A gene located on a sex chromosome. In humans, the vast majority of sex-linked genes are located on the X chromosome.

sexual dimorphism (dī-môr′-fizm) Marked differences between the secondary sex characteristics of males and females.

sexual reproduction The creation of genetically unique offspring by the fusion of two haploid sex cells (gametes) forming a diploid zygote.

sexual selection A form of natural selection in which individuals with certain inherited traits are more likely than other individuals to obtain mates.

shared ancestral characters A character shared by members of a particular clade that originated in an ancestor that is not a member of that clade.

shared derived characters An evolutionary novelty that is unique to a particular clade.

shoot system All of a plant's stems, leaves, and reproductive structures.

short tandem repeat (STR) A series of short DNA sequences that are repeated many times in a row in the genome.

short-day plant A plant that flowers in late summer, fall, or winter, when day length is short. Short-day plants actually flower in response to long nights.

short-term memory The ability to hold information, anticipations, or goals for a time and then release them if they become irrelevant.

sickle-cell disease A genetic condition caused by a mutation in the gene for hemoglobin. The mutation causes the protein to crystallize, which deforms red blood cells into a curved shape. Such blood cells produce a cascade of symptoms that can be life-threatening.

sieve plate An end wall in a sieve-tube element that facilitates the flow of phloem sap.

sieve-tube element A food-conducting cell in a plant; also called a sieve-tube member. Chains of sieve-tube elements make up phloem tissue.

sign stimulus A stimulus that produces a fixed action pattern when perceived.

signal In behavioural ecology, a stimulus transmitted by one animal to another animal.

signal transduction pathway In cell biology, a series of molecular changes that converts a signal on a target cell's surface to a specific response inside the cell.

silencer A eukaryotic DNA sequence that functions to inhibit the start of gene transcription; may act analogously to an enhancer by binding a repressor. *See also* enhancer.

silent mutation A mutation in a gene that changes a codon to one that encodes for the same amino acid as the original codon. The amino acid sequence of the resulting polypeptide is thus unchanged.

single circulation A circulatory system with a single pump and circuit, in which blood passes from the sites of gas exchange to the rest of the body before returning to the heart.

single nucleotide polymorphism (SNP) A one-nucleotide variation in DNA sequence found within the genomes of at least 1% of a population.

single-lens eye The camera-like eye found in some jellies, polychaetes, spiders, many molluscs, and vertebrates.

sister chromatid (krō′-muh-tid) One of the two identical parts of a duplicated chromosome in a eukaryotic cell. Prior to mitosis, sister chromatids remain attached to each another at the centromere.

skeletal muscle A type of striated muscle attached to the skeleton; generally responsible for voluntary movements of the body.

skeletal system The organ system that provides body support and protects body organs, such as the brain, heart, and lungs.

small intestine The longest section of the alimentary canal; the principal site of the enzymatic hydrolysis of food macromolecules and the absorption of nutrients.

smooth endoplasmic reticulum That portion of the endoplasmic reticulum that lacks ribosomes.

smooth muscle A type of muscle lacking striations; responsible for involuntary body activities.

SNP *See* single nucleotide polymorphism (SNP).

social behaviour Any kind of interaction between two or more animals, usually of the same species.

social learning Modification of behaviour through the observation of other individuals.

sociobiology The study of the evolutionary basis of social behaviour.

sodium-potassium (Na$^+$-K$^+$) pump A membrane protein that transports sodium ions out of, and potassium ions into, a cell against their concentration gradients. The process is powered by ATP.

solute (sol′-yūt) A substance that is dissolved in a solution.

solution A liquid that is a homogeneous mixture of two or more substances.

solvent The dissolving agent of a solution. Water is the most versatile solvent known.

somatic cell (sō-mat′-ik) Any cell in a multicellular organism except a sperm or egg cell or a cell that develops into a sperm or egg.

somite Repeating bands of mesodermal tissue within the embryos of chordates.

spatial learning Modification of behaviour based on experience of the spatial structure of the environment.

speciation The evolution of a new species.

species A group whose members possess similar anatomical characteristics and have the ability to interbreed and produce viable, fertile offspring. *See also* biological species concept.

species diversity *See* biodiversity.

sperm A male gamete.

sperm count The number of sperm in the ejaculate; used as a measure of fertility.

sperm mobility The ability of sperm to swim; used as a measure of fertility.

sperm morphology The overall shape of sperm used as a measure of fertility

spermatogenesis (sper-mat′-ō-jen′-uh-sis) The formation of sperm cells.

spermicide A sperm-killing chemical (cream, jelly, or foam) that works with a barrier device as a method of contraception.

sphincter (sfink′-ter) A ringlike band of muscle fibres that regulates passage between some compartments of the alimentary canal.

spinal cord A jellylike bundle of nerve fibres that runs lengthwise inside the spine in vertebrates and integrates simple responses to certain stimuli.

spirochete A member of a group of helical bacteria that spiral through the environment by means of rotating, internal filaments.

sponge An aquatic animal characterized by a highly porous body.

sporangium (spuh-ranj′-ē-um′) (plural, **sporangia**) A structure in fungi and plants in which meiosis occurs and haploid spores develop.

spore (1) In plants and algae, a haploid cell that can develop into a multicellular individual without fusing with another cell. (2) In prokaryotes, protists, and fungi, any of a variety of thick-walled life cycle stages capable of surviving unfavourable environmental conditions.

sporophyte (spōr′-uh-fīt) The multicellular diploid form in the life cycle of organisms undergoing alternation of generations; results from a union of gametes and meiotically produces haploid spores that grow into the gametophyte generation.

stabilizing selection Natural selection that favours intermediate variants by acting against extreme phenotypes.

stamen (stā′-men) A pollen-producing male reproductive part of a flower, consisting of a filament and an anther.

starch A storage polysaccharide in plants; a polymer of glucose.

start codon (kō′-don) On mRNA, the specific three-nucleotide sequence (AUG) to which an initiator tRNA molecule binds, starting translation of genetic information.

stem The part of a plant's shoot system that supports the leaves and reproductive structures.

stem cell An unspecialized cell that can divide to produce an identical daughter cell and a more specialized daughter cell, which undergoes differentiation.

steroid (ster′-oyd) A type of lipid whose carbon skeleton is in the form of four fused rings with various chemical groups attached. Examples are cholesterol, testosterone, and estrogen.

steroid hormone A lipid made from cholesterol that acts as a regulatory chemical, entering a target cell and activating the transcription of specific genes.

stigma (stig′-muh) (plural, **stigmata**) The sticky tip of a flower's carpel that traps pollen grains.

stimulus (plural, **stimuli**) (1) In the context of a nervous system, any factor that causes a nerve signal to be generated. (2) In behavioural biology, an environmental cue that triggers a specific response.

stoma (stō′-muh) (plural, **stomata**) A pore surrounded by guard cells in the epidermis of a leaf. When stomata are open, CO_2 enters a leaf, and water and O_2 exit. A plant conserves water when its stomata are closed.

stomach An organ in a digestive tract that stores food and performs preliminary steps of digestion.

stop codon In mRNA, one of three triplets (UAG, UAA, UGA) that signal gene translation to stop.

STR See short tandem repeat (STR).

STR analysis Short tandem repeat analysis; a method of DNA profiling that compares the lengths of short tandem repeats (STRs) selected from specific sites within the genome.

strata (singular, **stratum**) Rock layers formed when new layers of sediment cover older ones and compress them.

stretch receptor A type of mechanoreceptor sensitive to changes in muscle length; detects the position of body parts.

stroke The death of nervous tissue in the brain, usually resulting from rupture or blockage of arteries in the head.

stroma (strō′-muh) The dense fluid within the chloroplast that surrounds the thylakoid membrane and is involved in the synthesis of organic molecules from carbon dioxide and water. Sugars are made in the stroma by the enzymes of the Calvin cycle.

stromatolite (strō-mat′-uh-līt) Layered rock that results from the activities of prokaryotes that bind thin films of sediment together.

substrate (1) A specific substance (reactant) on which an enzyme acts. Each enzyme recognizes only the specific substrate or substrates of the reaction it catalyzes. (2) A surface in or on which an organism lives.

substrate feeder An organism that lives in or on its food source, eating its way through the food.

substrate-level phosphorylation The formation of ATP by an enzyme directly transferring a phosphate group to ADP from an organic molecule (for example, one of the intermediates in glycolysis or the citric acid cycle).

sugar sink A plant organ that is a net consumer or storer of sugar. Growing roots, shoot tips, stems, and fruits are sugar sinks supplied by phloem.

sugar source A plant organ in which sugar is being produced by either photosynthesis or the breakdown of starch. Mature leaves are the primary sugar sources of plants.

sugar-phosphate backbone In a polynucleotide (DNA or RNA strand), the alternating chain of sugar and phosphate to which nitrogenous bases are attached.

superior vena cava (vē′-nuh kā′-vuh) A large vein that returns oxygen-poor blood to the heart from the upper body and head. See also inferior vena cava.

surface tension A measure of how difficult it is to stretch or break the surface of a liquid. Water has a high surface tension because of the hydrogen bonding of surface molecules.

surfactant A substance secreted by alveoli that decreases surface tension in the fluid that coats the alveoli.

survivorship curve A plot of the number of members of a cohort that are still alive at each age; one way to represent age-specific mortality.

suspension feeder An aquatic animal that sifts small food particles from the water; sometimes called a filter feeder.

sustainability The goal of developing, managing, and conserving Earth's resources in ways that meet the needs of people today without compromising the ability of future generations to meet theirs.

sustainable agriculture Long-term productive farming methods that are environmentally safe.

sustainable resource management Management of a natural resource so as not to damage the resource.

swim bladder A gas-filled internal sac that helps bony fishes maintain buoyancy.

symbiont An individual in a symbiotic relationship.

symbiosis (sim′-bē-ō-sis) (plural, **symbioses**) A physically close association between organisms of two or more species.

sympathetic division A set of neurons in the autonomic nervous system that generally prepares the body for energy-consuming activities, such as fleeing or fighting. See also parasympathetic division.

sympatric speciation The formation of new species in populations that live in the same geographic area.

synapse (sin′-aps) A junction between two neurons, or between a neuron and an effector cell. Electrical or chemical signals are relayed from one cell to another at a synapse.

synaptic cleft (sin-ap′-tik) In a chemical synapse, a narrow gap separating the synaptic terminal of a transmitting neuron from a receiving neuron or an effector cell.

synaptic terminal The tip of a transmitting neuron's axon, where signals are sent to another neuron or to an effector cell.

synaptic vesicle A membrane-enclosed sac containing neurotransmitter molecules at the tip of the presynaptic axon.

syncytium (sin′-si-shē-um) A large, multinucleated cell that arose from repeated nuclear divisions (karyokinesis) but not cytokinesis.

systematics A scientific discipline focused on classifying organisms and determining their evolutionary relationships.

systemic acquired resistance A defensive response in plants infected with a pathogenic microbe; helps to protect healthy tissue from the microbe.

systemic circuit The branch of the circulatory system that supplies oxygen-rich blood to, and carries oxygen-poor blood away from, organs and tissues in the body. See also pulmonary circuit.

systems biology An approach to studying biology that aims to model the dynamic behaviour of whole biological systems based on a study of the interactions among the system's parts.

systole (sis′-tō-lē) The contraction stage of the heart cycle, when the heart chambers actively pump blood. See also diastole.

T

T cell A type of lymphocyte that matures in the thymus and is responsible for the cell-mediated immune response; involved in humoral immunity.

tapeworm A parasitic flatworm characterized by the absence of a digestive tract.

target cell A cell that responds to a regulatory signal, such as a hormone.

taxis (tak′-sis) (plural, **taxes**) Virtually automatic orientation toward or away from a stimulus.

taxon A named taxonomic unit at any given level of classification.

taxonomy The scientific discipline concerned with naming and classifying the diverse forms of life.

technology The application of scientific knowledge for a specific purpose, often involving industry or commerce but also including uses in basic research.

telomere (tel′-uh-mēr) The repetitive DNA at each end of a eukaryotic chromosome.

telophase The fifth and final stage of mitosis, during which daughter nuclei form at the two poles of a cell; usually occurs together with cytokinesis.

temperate broadleaf forest A biome located throughout midlatitude regions where sufficient moisture supports the growth of large, broadleaf deciduous trees.

temperate grassland A grassland region maintained by seasonal drought, occasional fires, and grazing by large mammals.

temperate rainforest Coniferous forests of coastal North America (from Alaska to Oregon) supported by warm, moist air from the Pacific Ocean.

temperate zones Latitudes between the tropics and the Arctic Circle in the north and the Antarctic Circle in the south; regions with milder climates than the tropics or polar regions.

temperature A measure of the intensity of heat in degrees, reflecting the average kinetic energy or speed of molecules.

template strand The strand of the DNA double helix that is read by RNA polymerase and used to produce an RNA molecule.

tendon Fibrous connective tissue connecting a muscle to a bone.

tendril A modified leaf used by some plants to climb around a fixed structure.

terminal bud Embryonic tissue at the tip of a shoot, made up of developing leaves and a compact series of nodes and internodes.

terminator A special sequence of nucleotides in DNA that marks the end of a gene; signals RNA polymerase to release the newly made RNA molecule and then to depart from the gene.

territory An area that one or more individuals defend and from which other members of the same species are usually excluded.

tertiary consumer (ter′-shē-ār-ē) An organism that eats secondary consumers.

tertiary structure The third level of protein structure; the overall three-dimensional shape of a polypeptide because of interactions of the R groups of the amino acids making up the chain.

testcross The mating between an individual of unknown genotype for a particular characteristic and an individual that is homozygous recessive for that same characteristic; can be used to determine the unknown genotype (homozygous dominant versus heterozygous).

testicle A testis and scrotum together.

testis (plural, **testes**) The male gonad in an animal; produces sperm and, in many species, reproductive hormones.

testosterone (tes-tos′-tuh-rōn) An androgen hormone that stimulates an embryo to develop into a male and promotes male body features.

tetrad A paired set of homologous chromosomes, each composed of two sister chromatids; forms during prophase I of meiosis, when crossing over may occur.

tetrapod A vertebrate with two pairs of limbs. Tetrapods include mammals, amphibians, and birds and other reptiles.

thalamus (thal′-uh-mus) An integrating and relay centre of the vertebrate forebrain; sorts and relays selected information to specific areas in the cerebral cortex.

theory A widely accepted explanatory idea that is broader in scope than a hypothesis, generates new hypotheses, and is supported by a large body of evidence.

therapeutic cloning The cloning of human cells by nuclear transplantation for therapeutic purposes, such as the generation of embryonic stem cells. *See* nuclear transplantation; reproductive cloning.

thermodynamics The study of energy transformation that occurs in a collection of matter. *See* first law of thermodynamics; second law of thermodynamics.

thermoreceptor A sensory receptor that detects heat or cold.

thermoregulation The homeostatic maintenance of internal temperature within a range that allows cells to function efficiently.

thick filament The thicker of the two protein filaments in muscle fibres, consisting of staggered arrays of myosin molecules.

thigmotropism (thig′-mō-trō′-pizm) A plant's directional growth movement in response to touch.

thin filament The thinner of the two protein filaments in muscle fibres, consisting of two strands of actin and two strands of regulatory protein coiled around each other.

three-domain system A system of taxonomic classification based on three basic groups: Bacteria, Archaea, and Eukarya.

threshold The minimum change in a membrane's voltage that must occur to generate an action potential (nerve signal).

thylakoid (thī′-luh-koyd) A flattened membranous sac inside a chloroplast. Thylakoid membranes contain chlorophyll and the molecular complexes of the light reactions of photosynthesis. A stack of thylakoids is called a granum.

thymine (T) (thī′-min) A single-ring nitrogenous base found in DNA.

thymine dimer The covalent linkage of adjacent thymine bases within the DNA double helix, usually caused by ultraviolet light.

thymus gland (thī′-mus) An endocrine gland in the neck region of mammals that is active in establishing the immune system; secretes several hormones that promote the development and differentiation of T cells.

thyroid gland (thī′-royd) An endocrine gland located in the neck that secretes thyroxine (T_4), triiodothyronine (T_3), and calcitonin.

thyroid-stimulating hormone (TSH) A protein hormone secreted by the anterior pituitary that stimulates the thyroid gland to secrete its hormones.

thyroxine (T_4) (thī-rok′-sin) An amine hormone secreted by the thyroid gland that stimulates metabolism in virtually all body tissues. Each molecule of this hormone contains four atoms of iodine.

Ti plasmid A bacterial plasmid that induces tumours in plant cells that the bacterium infects. Ti plasmids are often used as vectors to introduce new genes into plant cells. *Ti* stands for tumour inducing.

tidal volume The volume of air moved in and out during a normal breath.

tissue An integrated group of cells with a common function, structure, or both.

tissue system One or more tissues organized into a functional unit within a plant or an animal.

tonicity The ability of a solution surrounding a cell to cause that cell to gain or lose water.

topsoil The uppermost soil layer, consisting of a mixture of particles derived from rock, living organisms, and humus.

totipotent stem cell (to′-tē-pō-tent) A cell that can differentiate into any other cell type. A zygote will ultimately give rise to all cells in the body.

trace element An element that is essential for life but required in extremely minute amounts.

trachea (trā′-kē-uh) (plural, **tracheae**) The windpipe; the portion of the respiratory tube that passes from the larynx to the two bronchi.

tracheal system A system of branched, air-filled tubes in insects that extends throughout the body and carries oxygen directly to cells.

tracheid (trā′-kē-id) A tapered, porous, water-conducting and supportive cell in plants. Chains of tracheids or vessel elements make up the water-conducting, supportive tubes in xylem.

trade winds The movement of air in the tropics (those regions that lie between 23.5° north latitude and 23.5° south latitude).

trait A variant of a character found within a population, such as purple or white flowers in pea plants.

transcript Any product of transcription.

transcription factor In the eukaryotic cell, a protein that functions in initiating or regulating transcription; binds to DNA or to another protein that binds to DNA.

transcription The synthesis of RNA on a DNA template.

transduction (1) The transfer of bacterial genes from one bacterial cell to another by a phage. (2) *See* sensory transduction. (3) *See* signal transduction pathway.

transfer RNA (tRNA) A type of ribonucleic acid that functions as an interpreter in translation. Each tRNA molecule has a specific anticodon, picks up a specific amino acid, and conveys the amino acid to the appropriate codon on mRNA.

transformation The incorporation of new genes into a cell from DNA that the cell takes up from the surrounding environment.

transgenic organism An organism that contains genes from another species.

transition zone The area between two adjacent communities where one gradually transitions into the other. *See also* ecotone.

translation The synthesis of a polypeptide using the genetic information encoded in an mRNA molecule. There is a change of "language" from nucleotides to amino acids.

translocation (1) During protein synthesis, the movement of a tRNA molecule carrying a growing polypeptide chain from the A site to the P site on a ribosome. (The mRNA travels with it.) (2) A change in a chromosome resulting from a chromosomal fragment attaching to a nonhomologous chromosome; can occur as a result of an error in meiosis or from mutagenesis.

transmission electron microscope (TEM) A microscope that uses an electron beam to study the internal structure of thinly sectioned specimens.

transpiration The evaporative loss of water from a plant.

transpiration-cohesion-adhesion mechanism A transport mechanism that drives the upward movement of water in plants. Transpiration exerts a pull that is relayed downward along a string of molecules held together by cohesion and helped upward by adhesion.

transport vesicle A small membranous sac in a eukaryotic cell's cytoplasm carrying molecules produced by the cell. The vesicle buds from the endoplasmic reticulum or Golgi and eventually fuses with another organelle or the plasma membrane, releasing its contents.

transposable element A transposable genetic element, or "jumping gene"; a segment of DNA that can move from one site to another within a cell and serve as an agent of genetic change.

TRH (TSH-releasing hormone) A peptide hormone that triggers the release of TSH (thyroid-stimulating hormone), which in turn stimulates the thyroid gland.

trial-and-error learning Learning to associate a particular behaviour with a positive or negative effect.

triiodothyronine (T₃) (trī-ī-ō-dō-thī'-rō-nīn) An amine hormone secreted by the thyroid gland that stimulates metabolism in virtually all body tissues. Each molecule of this hormone contains four atoms of iodine.

trimester In human development, one of three 3-month-long periods of pregnancy.

triplet code A set of three-nucleotide-long "words" that specify the amino acids for polypeptide chains. *See* genetic code.

trisomy 21 *See* Down syndrome.

trophic mutualism A mutualistic relationship in which both partners benefit by having increased access to resources.

trophoblast (trōf'-ō-blast) In mammalian development, the outer portion of a blastocyst. Cells of the trophoblast secrete enzymes that enable the blastocyst to implant in the endometrium of the mother's uterus.

tropical forest A terrestrial biome characterized by high levels of precipitation and warm temperatures year-round.

tropics Latitudes between 23.5° north and south.

tropism (trō'-pizm) A growth response that makes a plant grow toward or away from a stimulus.

true coelom A body cavity completely lined with tissue derived from mesoderm.

true-breeding Referring to organisms for which sexual reproduction produces offspring with inherited traits identical to those of the parents. The organisms are homozygous for the characteristics under consideration.

tubal ligation A means of sterilization in which a segment of each of a woman's two oviducts (fallopian tubes) is removed. The ends of the tubes are then tied closed to prevent eggs from reaching the uterus (commonly referred to as having the "tubes tied").

tube cell The cell within a pollen grain (male gametophyte) that extends toward the ovule within the female gametophyte, forming the pollen tube.

tuber An enlargement at the end of a rhizome in which food is stored.

tumour An abnormal mass of rapidly growing cells that forms within otherwise normal tissue.

tumour-suppressor gene A gene whose product inhibits cell division, thereby preventing uncontrolled cell growth. A mutation that deactivates a tumour-suppressor gene may lead to cancer.

tundra A biome at the northernmost limits of plant growth and at high altitudes, characterized by dwarf woody shrubs, grasses, mosses, and lichens.

tunicate One of a group of invertebrate chordates; also called sea squirts.

U

ultimate cause In animal behaviour, the evolutionary reason for a behaviour.

ultimate question In animal behaviour, a question that addresses the evolutionary basis for behaviour.

ultrasound imaging A technique for examining a fetus in the uterus. High-frequency sound waves echoing off the fetus are used to produce an image of the fetus.

uniform distribution pattern A pattern in which the individuals of a population are evenly distributed over an area.

Unikonta One of five supergroups proposed in a current hypothesis of the evolutionary history of eukaryotes. The other four supergroups are Chromalveolata, Rhizaria, Excavata, and Archaeplastida.

unsaturated fatty acid A fatty acid that has one or more double bonds between carbons in the hydrocarbon tail and thus lacks the maximum number of hydrogen atoms. Unsaturated fats and fatty acids do not solidify at room temperature.

uracil (U) (yū'-ruh-sil) A single-ring nitrogenous base found in RNA.

urea (yū-rē'-ah) A soluble form of nitrogenous waste excreted by mammals and most adult amphibians.

ureter (yū-rē'-ter or yū'-reh-ter) A duct that conveys urine from the kidney to the urinary bladder.

urethra (yū-rē'-thruh) A duct that conveys urine from the urinary bladder to the outside. In the male, the urethra also conveys semen out of the body during ejaculation.

uric acid (yū'-rik) An insoluble precipitate of nitrogenous waste excreted by land snails, insects, birds, and some reptiles.

urinary bladder The pouch where urine is stored prior to elimination.

urinary system The organ system that forms and excretes urine while regulating the amount of water and ions in the body fluids.

urine Concentrated filtrate produced by the kidneys and excreted by the bladder.

uterus (yū'-ter-us) In the reproductive system of a mammalian female, the organ where the development of young occurs; the womb.

V

vaccination (vak'-suh-nā'-shun) A procedure that presents the immune system with a harmless variant or derivative of a pathogen, thereby stimulating the immune system to mount a long-term defence against the pathogen.

vaccine (vak-sēn') A harmless variant or derivative of a pathogen used to stimulate a host organism's immune system to mount a long-term defence against the pathogen.

vacuole (vak'-ū-ōl) A membrane-enclosed sac that is part of the endomembrane system of a eukaryotic cell and has diverse functions.

vagina (vuh-jī'-nuh) Part of the female reproductive system between the uterus and the outside opening; the birth canal in mammals; also accommodates the male's penis and receives sperm during copulation.

valence shell The outermost electron shell of an atom; contains electrons that may be available for chemical bonding.

vas deferens (vas def'-er-enz) (plural, **vasa deferentia**) Part of the male reproductive system that conveys sperm away from the testis;

the sperm duct; in humans, the tube that conveys sperm between the epididymis and the common duct that leads to the urethra.

vascular bundle (vas′-kyū-ler) A strand of vascular tissues (both xylem and phloem) in a plant stem.

vascular cambium (vas′-kyū-ler kam′-bē-um) During secondary growth of a plant, the cylinder of meristematic cells, surrounding the xylem and pith, that produces secondary xylem and phloem.

vascular cylinder The central cylinder of vascular tissue in a plant root.

vascular plant A plant with xylem and phloem, including club mosses, ferns, gymnosperms, and angiosperms.

vascular tissue Plant tissue consisting of cells joined into tubes that transport water and nutrients throughout the plant body.

vascular tissue system A transport system formed by xylem and phloem throughout the plant. Xylem transports water and minerals, while phloem transports sugars and other organic nutrients.

vasectomy (vuh-sek′-tuh-mē) Surgical removal of a section of the two sperm ducts (vasa deferentia) to prevent sperm from reaching the urethra; a means of sterilization in males.

vector In molecular biology, a piece of DNA, usually a plasmid or a viral genome, that is used to move genes from one cell to another.

vector organism An organism that transmits infection by carrying parasites from one host to another.

vein (1) In animals, a vessel that returns blood to the heart. (2) In plants, a vascular bundle in a leaf, composed of xylem and phloem.

ventilation A mechanism that provides for the flow of air or water over a respiratory surface.

ventral Pertaining to the underside, or bottom, of a bilaterally symmetric animal.

ventricle (ven′-truh-kul) (1) A heart chamber that pumps blood out of the heart. (2) A space in the vertebrate brain filled with cerebrospinal fluid.

venule (ven′-yūl) A vessel that conveys blood between a capillary bed and a vein.

vertebra (ver′-tuh-bruh) (plural, **vertebrae**) One of a series of segmented skeletal units that enclose the nerve cord, making up the backbone of a vertebrate animal.

vertebral column Backbone, composed of a series of segmented units called vertebrae.

vertebrate (ver′-tuh-brāt) A chordate animal with a backbone. Vertebrates include lampreys, chondrichthyans, ray-finned fishes, lobe-finned fishes, amphibians, reptiles (including birds), and mammals.

vertical gene transfer The transfer of genetic information from one generation to the next through reproductive means.

vesicle (ves′-i-kul) A sac made of membrane in the cytoplasm of a eukaryotic cell.

vessel element A short, open-ended, water-conducting and supportive cell in plants. Chains of vessel elements or tracheids make up the water-conducting, supportive tubes in xylem.

vestigial structure (ve′-sti-jē-ul) A feature of an organism that is a historical remnant of a structure that served a function in the organism's ancestors.

villus (vil′-us) (plural, **villi**) (1) A fingerlike projection of the inner surface of the small intestine. (2) A fingerlike projection of the chorion of the mammalian placenta. Large numbers of villi increase the surface areas of these organs.

viroid (vī′-royd) A plant pathogen composed of molecules of naked, circular RNA several hundred nucleotides long.

virus A microscopic particle capable of infecting cells of living organisms and inserting its genetic material. Viruses are generally not considered to be alive because they do not display all the characteristics associated with life.

visceral mass (vis′-uh-rul) One of the three main parts of a mollusc, containing most of the internal organs.

visual acuity The ability of the eyes to distinguish fine detail. Normal visual acuity in humans is usually reported as "20/20 vision."

vital capacity The maximum volume of air that a mammal can inhale and exhale with each breath.

vitamin An organic nutrient that an organism requires in very small quantities. Many vitamins serve as coenzymes or parts of coenzymes.

vitreous humour (vit′-rē-us hyū′-mer) A jellylike substance filling the space behind the lens in the vertebrate eye; helps to maintain the shape of the eye.

vocal cord One of a pair of bands of elastic tissue in the larynx. Air rushing past the tensed vocal cords makes them vibrate, producing sounds.

vulva The collective term for the external female genitalia.

W

water mould A funguslike protist in the supergroup Chromalveolata.

water vascular system In echinoderms, a radially arranged system of water-filled canals that branch into extensions called tube feet. The system provides movement and circulates water, facilitating gas exchange and waste disposal.

wavelength The distance between crests of adjacent waves, such as those of the electromagnetic spectrum.

westerlies Winds that blow from west to east.

wetland An ecosystem intermediate between an aquatic ecosystem and a terrestrial ecosystem. Wetland soil is saturated with water permanently or periodically.

white blood cell *See* leukocyte.

white matter Regions within the central nervous system composed mainly of axons, with their whitish myelin sheaths.

whole-genome shotgun method A method for determining the DNA sequence of an entire genome. After a genome is cut into small fragments, each fragment is sequenced and then placed in the proper order.

wild-type trait The version of a character that most commonly occurs in nature.

wood Secondary xylem of a plant. *See also* heartwood; sapwood.

wood ray A column of parenchyma cells that radiates from the centre of a log and transports water to its outer living tissues.

X

X chromosome inactivation In female mammals, the inactivation of one X chromosome in each somatic cell.

xylem (zī′-lum) The nonliving portion of a plant's vascular system that provides support and conveys xylem sap from the roots to the rest of the plant. Xylem is made up of vessel elements and/or tracheids, water-conducting cells. Primary xylem is derived from the procambium. Secondary xylem is derived from the vascular cambium in plants exhibiting secondary growth.

xylem sap The solution of inorganic nutrients conveyed in xylem tissue from a plant's roots to its shoots.

Y

yeast A single-celled fungus that inhabits liquid or moist habitats and reproduces asexually by simple cell division or by the pinching of small buds off a parent cell.

yellow bone marrow A tissue found within the central cavities of long bones, consisting mostly of stored fat.

yolk sac An extraembryonic membrane that develops from the endoderm; produces the embryo's first blood cells and germ cells and gives rise to the allantois.

Z

zoned reserve An extensive region of land that includes one or more areas that are undisturbed by humans. The undisturbed areas are surrounded by lands that have been altered by human activity.

zooplankton (zō′-ō-plank′-tun) Animals that drift in aquatic environments.

zygomycete (zī′-guh-mī-sēt) Member of a group of fungi characterized by a sturdy structure called a zygosporangium, in which meiosis produces haploid spores.

zygote (zī′-gōt) The diploid fertilized egg, which results from the union of a sperm cell nucleus and an egg cell nucleus.

zygote fungus *See* zygomycete.

Credits

Photo Credits

Cover: © Breene Yuen.

Unit Openers: **Unit 1** David Becker/Photo Researchers. **Unit 2** © Suravid/Shutterstock. **Unit 3** Vaughan Fleming/Photo Researchers. **Unit 4** © Wild Wonders of Europe/Lundgren/naturepl.com. **Unit 5** Kevin Scott. **Unit 6** © Martin Harvey/Gallo Images/Corbis. **Unit 7** © Barrett & MacKay/All Canada Photos.

Chapter 1: **p.1 top left to right** © Frans Lanting/Corbis, Neg./Transparency no. 326668. Courtesy Dept. of Library Services, American Museum of Natural History. **bottom left to right** © Jason Ondreicka/Alamy, Courtesy of The Pipedreams Project, www.thepipedreamsproject.org. **Chapter Opener left** Reprinted from Figure 1 in *Current Biology*. Volume 11(18), Ritland K, Newton C, Marshall HD. 2001. Inheritance and population structure of the white-phased "Kermode" black bear, pp.1468–1472. Copyright 2001, with permission from Elsevier. DOI: 10.1016/S0960-9822(01)00448-1, **right** Kevin Scott. **1.1.1** Image State Media Partners Limited. **1.1.2** © Frans Lanting/Corbis. **1.1.3** © Frans Lanting/Corbis. **1.1.4** © Imagebroker/Alamy. **1.1.5** Kim Taylor and Jane Burton © Dorling Kindersley. **1.1.6** Chris Mattison/Photolibrary. **1.1.7** © Frans Lanting/DanitaDelimont.com. **1.2 top to bottom** © Anton Balazh/Fotolia, © Steven J. Kazlowski/Alamy/Getstock, © Eric Baccega/AGE/First Light. **1.3 left** Steve Gschmeissner/Photo Researchers, **right** S. C. Holt/Biological Photo Service. **1.4** © Morales/AGE/First Light. **1.6 top** Oliver Meckes/Nicole Ottawa/Photo Researchers, **centre** Eye of Science/Photo Researchers, **centre left** D. P. Wilson/Photo Researchers, **centre right** © Florapix/Alamy, **bottom left** © Frank Young/Papilio/Corbis, **bottom right** © Michael and Patricia Fogden/Corbis. **1.7A** Maureen Spuhler. **1.7B** Neg./Transparency no. 326668. Courtesy Dept. of Library Services, American Museum of Natural History. **1.7D top** © Photoshot Holdings Ltd/Alamy, **bottom** Fred Felleman/Stone/Getty Images. **1.8** Colin Radford. **1.9B** © Jason Ondreicka/Alamy. **1.9C** Steve Kaufman/Photolibrary. **1.9D** David Pfennig. **1.10** Courtesy of The Pipedreams Project, www.thepipedreams project.org. **1.11** © Philip Date/Fotolia. **p.16** © Morales/AGE/First Light.

Chapter 2: **Chapter Opener left** © Armando Frazao/Shutterstock, **right** © Aksenova Natalya/Shutterstock. **2.1 left to right** Chip Clark/Fundamental Photographs, NYC, Pearson Education/Pearson Science, Pearson Education/Pearson Science. **2.2A** Alison Wright/Photo Researchers. **2.2B** © Anton Prado/Alamy. **2.2C** © Lansera/Fotolia. **2.4A** Will & Deni McIntyre/Photo Researchers. **2.4B** W. E. Klunk and C. A. Mathis, University of Pittsburgh. **2.7B** Pearson Education/Pearson Science. **2.10A** © Kreutzer/Imagebroker/First Light. **2.10B** Courtesy of Joanne Long, IO Rodeo Inc. **2.11** Herman Eisenbeiss/Photo Researchers. **2.12** Novastock/Photolibrary. **2.13** thp73/iStockphoto. **2.15** © VR Photos/Shutterstock, © VBeth Van Trees/Shutterstock. **2.16** © Shutterstock. **2.17** NASA/JPL-Caltech/University of Arizona/Texas A&M University.

Chapter 3: **p.38** Fotosearch/AGE Fotostock. **Chapter Opener left** © Markus Mainka/Fotolia, **right** © uckyo/Fotolia. **3.2 left** © Miki Verebes/Shutterstock, **right** © Herbert Kratky/iStockphoto. **3.4A** © Alexandru Magurean/iStockphoto. **3.6A** Kevin Scott. **3.7 clockwise from top left** Dougal Waters/Digital Vision/Getty Images; Biophoto Associates/Photo Researchers; Courtesy of Dr. L. M. Beidler; Biophoto Associates/Photo Researchers. **3.9A** Fotosearch/AGE Fotostock. **p.50** © Peter Zaharov/iStockphoto. **3.13** Serge de Sazo/Photo Researchers. **3.14A** © Tony Hamblin/Frank Lane Picture Agency/Corbis.

Chapter 4: **p.58 top left to right** Andrew Syred/Photo Researchers, Dr. Gopal Murti/Science Photo Library, **bottom left to right** Don W. Fawcett/Photo Researchers, Dr. Jeremy Burgess/Science Source, Mark Ladinsky. **Chapter Opener left to right** Michael Abbey/Photo Researchers, Eye of Science/Photo Researchers, Herve Conge, ISM/Science Photo Library. **4.1A** Michael Abbey/Photo Researchers. **4.1C** Andrew Syred/Photo Researchers. **4.1D** Dr. Klaus Boller/Photo Researchers. **4.1E** M. I. Walker/Photo Researchers. **4.3** S. C. Holt, University of Texas Health Center/Biological Photo Service. **4.5** Dr. Gopal Murti/Science Photo Library. **4.6** D. W. Fawcett/Photo Researchers. **4.8A** R. Bolender, D. Fawcett/Photo Researchers. **4.9** Don W. Fawcett/Photo Researchers. **4.11A** Roland Birke/Peter Arnold/Getty Images. **4.11B** Biophoto Associates/Photo Researchers. **4.13** Nicolae Simionescu. **4.14** Dr. Jeremy Burgess/Science Source. **4.16 left to right** Dr. Frank Solomon; Mark S. Ladinsky and J. Richard McIntosh, University of Colorado; Dr. Mary Osborn. **4.17A** Science Photo Library/Photo Researchers. **4.17B** Eye of Science/Photo Researchers. **4.17C** Dr. Gopal Murti/Science Photo Library. **4.18** Bjorn Afzelius.

Chapter 5: **Chapter Opener** Dante Fenolio/Photo Researchers. **5.2** Peter B. Armstrong. **5.6B** This water permeation through aquaporin was made by Drs. Emad Tajkhorshid and Klaus Schulten using VMD and is owned by the Theoretical and Computational Biophysics Group, NIH Resource for Macromolecular Modeling and Bioinformatics, at the Beckman Institute, University of Illinois at Urbana-Champaign. **5.8 top to bottom** Oxford Scientific/Photolibrary; D.W. Fawcett/Science Source/Photo Researchers; M.M. Perry. **5.15** © Africa Studio/Fotolia. **5.16** Krista Kennell/Newscom.

Chapter 6: **p.100 left** © StockLite/Shutterstock, **right** Paul Nicklen/National Geographic Creative. **Chapter Opener left** Courtesy of Sarah Olmstead, **right** © Image Asset Management/AGE/MaXximages.com. **6.1** © Morales/AGE/First Light. **6.2** Quinn Rooney/Getty Images. **6.4** Fuse/Getty Images. **6.13C top** © StockLite/Shutterstock, **bottom** Sean Lower/Marty Taylor. **6.14** Green marula fruits by Rotational, Wikimedia Commons http://commons.wikimedia.org/wiki/File:Marula01.jpg. **6.16** Simon Smith © Dorling Kindersley. **6.17** Paul Nicklen/National Geographic Creative.

Chapter 7: **p.119** © Martin Shields/Alamy. **Chapter Opener left** Bernd Settnik/DPA/Landov, **right** Photo taken by Jake Eaton (1958–2013), who contributed greatly to the adoption of Populus spp. as a short-rotation woody crop that is being grown commercially on a large scale for a variety of end uses (e.g., fiber for papermaking, dimensional lumber, and biofuel feedstock). Because of his involvement with projects in North and South America, Asia, and Europe, Jake's influence was felt worldwide. **7.1A** Theresa de Salis/Peter Arnold/Photolibrary, Inc./Photo Library. **7.1B** M. I. Walker/Photo Researchers. **7.1C** © Jeff Rotman/naturepl.com. **7.1D** Susan M. Barns, Ph.D. **7.2 top to bottom** © rodho/Shutterstock, Graham Kent/Pearson Education/Pearson Science, Dr. Jeremy Burgess/Science Source. **7.3** © Martin Shields/Alamy. **7.6B** © loriklaszlo/Shutterstock. **7.7A** Christine Case. **7.11 left** © Dinodia/Pixtal/AGE Fotostock, **right** ImageDJ/Jupiter Images/Getty Images. **7.13A** © Kevin Day/Shutterstock. **7.14A** Robert Simmon/NASA GSFC.

Chapter 8: **p.124 top left to right** London School of Hygiene & Tropical Medicine/Science Source/Photo Researchers, Conly L. Rieder, Ph.D., **bottom left to right** Mark Petronczki, © Michelle Gilders/Alamy. **Chapter Opener left** © frankonline/Fotolia, **right** Cyanea kuhihewa by David H. Lorence, National Tropical Botanical Garden. **8.1A** London School of Hygiene & Tropical Medicine/Photo Researchers. **8.1B** Roger Steene/imagequestmarine.com. **8.1C** Eric J. Simon. **8.1D** Bob Thomas/Photographers Choice/Getty Images. **8.1E** Dr. Yorgos Nikas/Photo

© Bruce Coleman/Alamy, **right** Purestock/Getty Images. **20.13** George Grall/National Geographic Creative. **20.14B** © Marevision/AGE/First Light. **20.14C** © Louise Murray/Robert Harding Picture Library/AGE Fotostock. **20.15A** Michael Neumann/Science Source. **20.15B** Oxford Scientific/Photolibrary. **20.17A** Michael Fogden/Oxford Scientific/Photolibrary. **20.17B** Steve Paddock, Ph.D.

Chapter 21: p.440 © Anup Shah/naturepl.com. **Chapter Opener** *Beringia Winter Scene* © Government of Yukon/Artist George "Rinaldinao" Teichmann, 1996. **21.2A** Tom McHugh/Photo Researchers, inset Photo by Andra Zommers, SPARK, Comparative Biomaterials Lab, University of Guelph. Used with permission. **21.2B** © Marevision/AGE Fotostock, insets Gary Meszaros/Photo Researchers and © A Hartl/AGE/First Light. **21.3B** George Grall/National Geographic Creative. **21.3C** Wolfgang Poelzer/Peter Arnold/Photolibrary. **21.3D** Tom and Pat Leeson/Photo Researchers. **21.3E top to bottom** © Marevision/AGE Fotostock, Stephen Frink/Digital Vision/Getty Images, Jeff Rotman/Image Bank/Getty Images. **19.3F** RudieKuiter/OceanwideImages.com. **21.4C** Publiphoto/Photo Researchers. **21.5A** © Melinda Fawver/Shutterstock. **21.5B** A. Noellert/Peter Arnold/Photolibrary. **21.5C** © Photoshot/Michael P. Fogden. **21.5D** © Oceans-Image/Photoshot/Stephen Dalton. **21.5E** Hans Pfletschinger/Peter Arnold/Photolibrary. **21.6A** Sylvain Cordier/Peter Arnold/Getty Images. **21.6C** © Steven David Miller/naturepl.com. **21.7A top to bottom** © infografick/Shutterstock, © Eric Isselee/Shutterstock, © Eric Isselee/Shutterstock. **21.8A** Sodapix/Photolibrary Royalty Free. **21.8B** © Frans Lanting/Corbis. **21.9A** Jean-Philippe Varin/Photo Researchers. **21.9B** © Mark Higgins/Shutterstock. **21.9C** Mitch Reardon/Photo Researchers. **21.10A** E. H. Rao/Photo Researchers. **21.10C** Bilda-gentur/Photolibrary Royalty Free. **21.10D** © David Tipling/naturepl.com. **21.10E left** Kevin Schafer/Corbis, **right** © Arco Images GmbH/Alamy. **21.10F** Digital Vision/Getty Images. **21.11 bottom left** Gerry Ellis/Digital Vision/Getty Images, **top left** © Steve Bloom/Alamy, **top right** © Anup Shah/naturepl.com, **bottom right** © Image Source/Alamy. **21.13B** John Reader/SPL/Photo Researchers. **21.16** © Beawiharta/Reuters/Corbis. **21.18A** AFP Photo/Newscom. **21.18B** Tim Laman/National Geographic Creative. **21.18C** Tim Laman/National Geographic Creative.

Chapter 22: p.466 top © Don Mason/Corbis, **bottom** © Zhuda/Shutterstock. **Chapter Opener** © Christian Kober 1/Alamy. **22.1** © O Diez/ARCO/AGE Fotostock. **22.3** Adam Hart-Davis/SPL/Photo Researchers. **22.4A** Eric J. Simon. **22.4B left** Rosemary Mayer/FLPA, **top right** Donald Gregory Clever, **bottom right** © FhF Greenmedia/AGE Fotostock. **22.4C left** Scott Camazine/Photo Researchers, **right** © Raul Gonzalez/http://www.flowerphotos.com/EyeUbiquitous/Corbis. **22.6B** Ed Reschke/Peter Arnold/Photolibrary. **22.6C** Graham Kent/Pearson Education/Pearson Science. **22.6D** Graham Kent/Pearson Education/Pearson Science. **22.6E** N.C. Brown Center for Ultrastructure Studies, SUNY-Environmental Science& Forestry, Syracuse, NY. **22.6F** Graham Kent/Pearson Education/Pearson Science. **22.7B top** © Viktor Kitaykin/iStockphoto.com, **bottom** Ed Reschke/Peter Arnold/Photolibrary. **22.7C** Ed Reschke. **22.8B** © Don Mason/Corbis. **22.8C** California Historical Society Collection (CHS-1177), University of Southern California on behalf of the USC Specialized Libraries and Archival Collections. **22.9A:** Dr. Morley Read/Science Photo Library. **22.10A clockwise from top left** © Ostanina Ekaterina/Shutterstock; © alohaspirit/iStockphoto; © Alex James Bramwell/Shutterstock; © Zhuda/Shutterstock. **22.13A** Walter H. Hodge/Peter Arnold/Photolibrary. **22.13C top** © © Bryan Busovicki/Shutterstock, **centre left** © Corbis RF, **centre right** © Rolf Klebsattel/Shutterstock, **bottom** © Elena Schweitzer/Shutterstock. **22.15A** © Tim Hill/Alamy. **22.15B** © Edmund Lowe/Alamy. **22.15C** Dan Suzio/SPL/Photo Researchers. **22.15D** © Dennis Frates/Alamy. **31.15E** Rosenfeld Images Ltd/Photo Researchers.

Chapter 23: p.489 Brian Capon. **Chapter Opener** © Caroline Brinkmann/Imagebroker/First Light. **23.1B** Mario Verin/Photolibrary. **23.2A** Brian Capon. **23.4 left** Frank Greenaway © Dorling Kindersley, **centre and right** Power and Syred/Science Photo Library. **23.5A** Professor Ray F. Evert. **23.5B** © Lezh/iStockphoto. **23.5C top left** Nigel Cattlin/FLPA, **centre and right** P. B. Tomlinson. **23.7B** Paul Rapson/Photo Researchers. **23.8A** USDA/ARS/Agricultural Research Service. **23.9B** Eye of Science/Science Photo Library. **23.10** Dean Bicknell/

The Calgary Herald. Reprinted with permission of The Calgary Herald. **23.11** Take 27 Ltd./Science Photo Library. **23.12A** Oxford Scientific/Photolibrary. **23.12B** © H Reinhard/ARCO/AGE Fotostock. **23.12C** Jean-Philippe Delobelle/Peter Arnold/Photolibrary.

Chapter 24: p.506 left Fred Jensen, **right** Martin Shields/Photo Researchers. **Chapter Opener** © Blickwinkel/Alamy. **24.1A** Matthew Ward © Dorling Kindersley. **24.3A** William M. Gray. **24.4** © Nigel Cattlin/Alamy. **24.5A** Alan Crozier. **24.5B** Kristin Piljay. **24.5C** Fred Jensen. **24.6** © Johner Images/Alamy. **24.7A** Kristin Piljay. **24.7B left** © Yuri Shirokov/Stockphoto.com, **right** Ed Reschke. **24.8A** © John T. Fowler/Alamy. **24.8B** Courtesy of Liisa Wihman, intercontinentalgardener .com. **p.517 centre** © Rudolf Madár/Shutterstock. **24.9** Stockbyte/Getty Images. **24.10A** Michael Evans. **24.10B** Martin Shields/Photo Researchers. **24.11 both** © Martin Shields/Alamy. **24.14A** USDA/Nature Source/Photo Researchers.

Chapter 25: p.526 Nina Zanetti/Pearson Education/Pearson Science. **Chapter Opener left** © Nature Production/naturepl.com, **top right** Courtesy of David M. Gardiner, University of California, Irvine, **bottom right** © Melinda Fawver/Shutterstock, **25.1** © Eric Baccega/AGE/First Light. **25.2 left to right** Frank Greenaway © Dorling Kindersley, Courtesy of the Hunstanton Sea Life Centre, Hunstanton, Norfolk, Corbis RF, kp Wolf/Peter Arnold/Photolibrary. **25.4** Image Source/Getty Images. **25.5** Image Source/Getty Images. **25.5A** Nina Zanetti. **25.5B** Ed Reschke/Peter Arnold/Photolibrary. **25.5C** Nina Zanetti. **25.5D** Chuck Brown/Photo Researchers. **25.5E** Nina Zanetti. **25.5F** Dr. Gopal Murti/SPL/Photo Researchers. **25.6** © Paul Burns/Blend Images/Alamy. **25.6A** Nina Zanetti. **25.6B** Manfred Kage/Peter Arnold/Photolibrary. **25.6C** Ed Reschke/Peter Arnold/Photolibrary. **25.7** Ulrich Gartner. **25.8** © Paul Burns/Blend Images/Alamy. **25.9** AP Photo/Brian Walker. **25.10A** © Image Source/Corbis. **25.10B** © Hiroshi Yagi/MIXA/Alamy. **25.10C–D** © Douglas Pulsipher/Alamy. **25.10E** Hiroshi Yagi/MIXA/Alamy. **25.10F** © Rolf Bruderer/Blend Images/Corbis. **25.10G** Jeremy Woodhouse/Blend Images/Getty Images. **25.10H** © moodboard/Corbis. **25.10I** Rubberball/Getty Images. **25.10J** Andy Crawford © Dorling Kindersley. **25.10K** Ryan McVay/Photodisc/Getty Images. **25.12A** © andreanita/Fotolia. **25.12B** Power and Syred/Science Photo Library. **25.13B** SPL/PhotoResearchers. **p.539 left** Cre8tive Images/Shutterstock. **25.14** Mvaresvuo/Peter Arnold/Photolibrary. **25.17** © Mike Wilkes/naturepl.com. **25.18** © Cherkas/Shutterstock. **25.18A** © Four Oaks/Shutterstock. **25.18B left** Jeffrey Lepore/Photo Researchers, **right** © O. Alamany & E. Vicens/Corbis. **25.19A left** © George Peters/iStockphoto.com, **right** © Holbox/Shutterstock. **p.543 right** Zigmund Leszczynski/Oxford Scientific/Photolibrary.

Chapter 26: p.546 top © Shutterstock, **bottom** © Geo Martinez/Shutterstock. **Chapter Opener left** © Craig R. Smith, Department of Oceanography, University of Hawaii at Manoa, **right** Courtesy of Stephen R. Wing, Department of Marine Science, University of Otago, New Zealand. **26.1A** Pete Atkinson/Taxi/Getty Images. **26.1B** Thomas Eisner, Cornell University. **26.1C** Roger Eritja/Peter Arnold/Photolibrary. **26.1D** Jennette van Dyk/Getty Images. **26.2A** © Shutterstock. **26.4 left** Kristin Piljay/Pearson Science, **right** Tom Brakefield/Photodisc/Getty Images. **26.5** © Geo Martinez/Shutterstock. **25.8** Eye of Science/Photo Researchers. **26.12A** Sonny Tubelaka/AFP/Getty Images. **26.12B** © Scenics & Science/Alamy/Getstock. **26.15 top to bottom** © iStockphoto.com, Corbis RF, Debbie Hardin/Pearson Education. **Table 26.16A top to bottom** Steve Gorton © Dorling Kindersley, © iStockphoto.com, © Magnet Creative/iStockphoto.com, © Motorolka/Shutterstock, © NatUlrick/Shutterstock. **26.17B** Courtesy of The Jackson Laboratory, Bar Harbor, Maine. **26.18** Steve Allen/Brand X Pictures/Jupiter Images. **p.567** © Geo Martinez/Shutterstock.

Chapter 27: p.569 © Douglas Pulsipher/Alamy. **Chapter Opener left** Andrew Nelmerm © Dorling Kindersley, Courtesy of the Royal British Columbia Museum, Victoria, Canada, **right** Used with permission of Jeremy Tame, Yokohama City University, Japan. **27.1** © Corbis RF/AGE Fotostock. **27.3A** Thomas Eisner. **27.3B** Paulo De Oliveira/Oxford Scientific/Photolibrary. **27.5** Ted Daeschler/VIREO/The Academy of Natural Sciences. **27.6** © Angus McNab. **27.7A** © Douglas Pulsipher/Alamy.

Data found at the National Heart, Lung, and Blood Institute: http://www
.nhlbi.nih.gov/guidelines/obesity/bmi_tbl.htm.

Chapter 27: p.569 and 27.12A Illustration, Irving Geis. Image from the Irving Geis Collection, Howard Hughes Medical Institute. Rights owned by HHMI. Used with permission. **27.11:** Adapted from Fig. 22.17, p.856, in MARIEB, ELAINE N.; HOEHN, KATJA, HUMAN ANATOMY AND PHYSIOLOGY, 7th, © 2007. Printed and Electronically reproduced by permission of Pearson Education, Inc., Upper Saddle River, New Jersey. **27.13:** Adapted from Fig. 28.7e, p.1073, in MARIEB, ELAINE N.; HOEHN, KATJA, HUMAN ANATOMY & PHYSIOLOGY, 9th ed., © 2013. Printed and Electronically reproduced by permission of Pearson Education, Inc., Upper Saddle River, New Jersey.

Chapter 28: 28.15: Based on Fig 7.6 in Lawrence G. Mitchell, John A. Mutchmor, and Warren D. Dolphin, *Zoology,* p.153. © 1988 Pearson Education, Inc., publishing as Pearson Benjamin Cummings. **28.18:** Adapted from Fig. 25.15, p.973, in MARIEB, ELAINE N.; HOEHN, KATJA, HUMAN ANATOMY & PHYSIOLOGY, 9th ed., © 2013. Printed and Electronically reproduced by permission of Pearson Education, Inc., Upper Saddle River, New Jersey.

Chapter 29: 29.9A: Data from C. J. Bryne, D. F. Saxton, et al., *Laboratory Tests: Implications for Nursing Care,* 2nd ed. Copyright © 1986 Pearson Education, Inc., publishing as Pearson Benjamin Cummings.

Chapter 30: 30.8B: Adapted from an illustration by William McGinnis in Peter Radetsky, "The homeobox: Something very precious that we share with flies, from egg to adult." Bethesda, MD: Howard Hughes Medical Institute, 1992, p.92. Reprinted by permission of William McGinnis. **30.9A:** Adapted from Fig. 27.14, p.1037, in MARIEB, ELAINE N.; HOEHN, KATJA, HUMAN ANATOMY & PHYSIOLOGY, 9th ed., © 2013. Printed and Electronically reproduced by permission of Pearson Education, Inc., Upper Saddle River, New Jersey. **30.9C:** Adapted from Fig. 27.12, p.1035, in MARIEB, ELAINE N.; HOEHN, KATJA, HUMAN ANATOMY & PHYSIOLOGY, 9th ed., © 2013. Printed and Electronically reproduced by permission of Pearson Education, Inc., Upper Saddle River, New Jersey. **30.10B:** Adapted from Fig. 27.1, p.1019, in MARIEB, ELAINE N.; HOEHN, KATJA, HUMAN ANATOMY & PHYSIOLOGY, 9th ed., © 2013. Printed and Electronically reproduced by permission of Pearson Education, Inc., Upper Saddle River, New Jersey. **30.10C:** Adapted from Figure 5.6, p.140, from Crooks/Baur. *Our Sexuality,* 2nd ed. © 1983 Wadsworth, a part of Cengage Learning, Inc. Reproduced with permission. www.cengage.com/permissions. **Table 30.14** Data from R. Hatcher et al., Contraceptive Technology: 1990–1992, p.134 (New York: Irvington, 1990). **30.17B:** Adapted from Fig. 28.18(c–d), p.1086, in MARIEB, ELAINE N.; HOEHN, KATJA, HUMAN ANATOMY & PHYSIOLOGY, 9th ed., © 2013. Printed and Electronically reproduced by permission of Pearson Education, Inc., Upper Saddle River, New Jersey.

Chapter 31: 31.8: Adapted from G. Matthews, 2003. *Cellular Physiology of Nerve and Muscle,* 4th edition, fig. 6-2d, p.61. Cambridge, MA: Blackwell Scientific Publications. Reproduced with permission of John Wiley & Sons Ltd. **31.10:** Adapted from Fig. 13-28, p.384, in HARDIN, JEFF; BERTONI, GREGORY PAUL; KLEINSMITH, LEWIS J.; BECKER'S WORLD OF THE CELL, 8th ed., ©2012. Printed and Electronically reproduced by permission of Pearson Education, Inc., Upper Saddle River, New Jersey.

Chapter 32: 32.5: Adapted from Fig. 5.35(a&c), p.582, in MARIEB, ELAINE N.; HOEHN, KATJA, HUMAN ANATOMY & PHYSIOLOGY, 9th ed., © 2013. Printed and Electronically reproduced by permission of Pearson Education, Inc., Upper Saddle River, New Jersey. **32.9A:** Adapted from Fig. 15.14, p. 557, in MARIEB, ELAINE N.; HOEHN, KATJA, HUMAN ANATOMY & PHYSIOLOGY, 9th ed., © 2013. Printed and Electronically reproduced by permission of Pearson Education, Inc., Upper Saddle River, New Jersey. **32.9B:** Adapted from Fig. 15.14, p.557, in MARIEB, ELAINE N.; HOEHN, KATJA, HUMAN ANATOMY & PHYSIOLOGY, 9th ed., © 2013. Printed and Electronically reproduced by permission of Pearson Education, Inc., Upper Saddle River, New Jersey.

Chapter 33: p.704 and 33.2E: Based on Fig 30.5 in Lawrence G. Mitchell, John A. Mutchmor, and Warren D. Dolphin, *Zoology,* p.734. © 1988

Pearson Education, Inc., publishing as Pearson Benjamin Cummings. **33.4:** Adapted from Fig. 6.4(a–c), p.178, in MARIEB, ELAINE N.; HOEHN, KATJA, HUMAN ANATOMY & PHYSIOLOGY, 9th ed., © 2013. Printed and Electronically reproduced by permission of Pearson Education, Inc., Upper Saddle River, New Jersey. **33.10C:** Adapted from Fig. 9.13A, p.294, in MARIEB, ELAINE N.; HOEHN, KATJA, HUMAN ANATOMY & PHYSIOLOGY, 9th ed., © 2013. Printed and Electronically reproduced by permission of Pearson Education, Inc., Upper Saddle River, New Jersey. **33.13:** Adapted from J. L. Andersen, et al. 2000. Muscles, genes, and athletic performance, illustrated by Jennifer Johansen. *Scientific American,* September, 2000, p.49. Reprinted by permission of Jennifer Johansen Hutton.

Chapter 34: 34.4: Source: Vaccines Prevent Diseases http://www
.phac-aspc.gc.ca/im/iyc-vve/prevention-eng.php, Health Canada, 2011. Reproduced with the permission of the Minister of Public Works and Government Services Canada, 2013. **34.10B:** Adapted from Fig. 17.3a–b, p.506, in TORTORA, GERARD J.; FUNKE, BERDELL R.; CASE, CHRISTINE L., MICROBIOLOGY: AN INTRODUCTION, 9th ed., © 2007. Printed and Electronically reproduced by permission of Pearson Education, Inc., Upper Saddle River, New Jersey. **34.16B:** Courtesy of the Gloria Rudenko Laboratory.

Chapter 35: 35.7B: Adapted from Zongchao Jia, Peter L Davies, 2002. Antifreeze proteins: an unusual receptor–ligand interaction. *Trends in BioChem Sciences* Volume 27, Issue 2, 1 February 2002, Pages 101–106, Fig 5. Trends in Biochemical Sciences by ELSEVIER LTD. Reproduced with permission of ELSEVIER LTD. in the format reuse in a book/textbook via Copyright Clearance Center. DOI: 10.1016/S0968-0004(01)02028-X.

Chapter 36: 36.5B: Courtesy of Masakazu Konishi. **36.7C:** Based on Fig 13.4 in Lawrence G. Mitchell, John A. Mutchmor, and Warren D. Dolphin, *Zoology,* p.304. © 1988 Pearson Education, Inc., publishing as Pearson Benjamin Cummings. **36.12C:** Graph from N. B. Davies. 1977. Prey selection and social behaviour in wagtails (Aves: Motacillidae). *Journal of Animal Ecology* 46(1): 37–57, fig. 9. Reproduced with permission of John Wiley & Sons Ltd. **36.12D:** Graph adapted from N. B. Davies. 1977. Prey selection and social behaviour in wagtails (Aves: Motacillidae). *Journal of Animal Ecology* 46(1): 37–57, fig. 8. Reproduced with permission of John Wiley & Sons Ltd. **36.14B:** From *The Common Loon: Spirit of Northern Lakes* by Judith W. McIntyre, drawings by Anne Olson, p.97. (Minneapolis, MN: University Minnesota Press, 1988). Copyright © 1988 by University of Minnesota Press. Used by permission of the publisher. **Module 36.21:** Adapted from an interview in Neil Campbell, *Biology,* 3rd ed. Copyright © 1993 Pearson Education, Inc., publishing as Pearson Benjamin Cummings.

Chapter 37: Table 37.3: Life table from the Canadian Human Mortality Database, available at www.bdlc.umontreal.ca (data downloaded on 02/26/2013), under the direction of Robert Bourbeau (Département de démographie, Université de Montréal) and Nadine Ouellette (Department of Demography, University of California, Berkeley). **37.10C:** 2010 population pyramid based on data obtained from Mexican National Institute of Statistics, Geography and Informatics (INEGI), Population and Housing Census, 2010, http://cuentame.inegi.org.mx/poblacion/habitantes
.aspx?tema=P. **37.11:** Statistics Canada, Demography Division, Chart 3.12: Age pyramids (in relative value) of the Canadian population, 2009 and 2036 (scenario M1), Date Modified: 2010-06-18. **37.12B:** Source: Global Footprint Network, 2013. Data 2009 from National Footprint Accounts 2012 Edition, www.footprintnetwork.org.

Chapter 38: 38.4C–D: Based on Gause, G.F., *The struggle for existence,* Baltimore: Williams and Wilkins, 1934. **38.12A:** Courtesy of the Ontario Federation of Anglers & Hunters, www.invadingspecies.com. Data provided by: EDDMapS Ontario. 2013. Early Detection and Distribution Mapping System for Ontario. The University of Georgia – Center for Invasive Species and Ecosystem Health. Available online at http://www
.eddmaps.org/ontario/; last accessed July 8, 2013. Projection: Lambert Conformal Conic. Datum: North American Datum 1983. Map Designed and Produced by: Karen Shier, Invasive Species GIS Technologist, Invading Species Awareness Program, Fish and Wildlife Services Department,

Ontario Federation of Angler and Hunters, Peterborough, Ontario, July 12, 2013. Note: The map point data is based on records contained in the Invasive Species Database, compiled from various sources–July 8, 2013. This map is illustrative only. Do not rely on this map as a definitive distribution as it is subject to change based on additional confirmed invasive species sites. This map may contain cartographic errors or omissions.

Chapter 39: 39.9B: Based on The Beef Tapeworm Life Cycle from Centers for Disease Control & Prevention Center for Global Health, CDC-DPDx.

Chapter 40: 40.10B: Courtesy of Richard E. Grosshans, International Institute for Sustainable Development (IISD), www.iisd.org.

Chapter 41: 41.1B: Data from IUCN Global Species Programme Red List Unit; *The IUCN Red List of Threatened Species,* Table 3a: Status category summary by major taxonomic group (animals); http://www.iucnredlist .org/documents/summarystatistics/2012_2_RL_Stats_Table_3a.pdf. **41.3A:** From J. Hansen et al. 2006. Global temperature change. *PNAS* 103(39): 14288–14293, fig. 1B. Copyright 2006 National Academy of Sciences, U.S.A. Used with permission. **41.4A:** From *Climate Change 2007: The Physical Science Basis.* Working Group I Contribution to the Fourth Assessment Report of the Intergovernmental Panel on Climate Change, FAQ 2.1, Figure 1. Cambridge University Press. Reprinted by permission of IPCC, c/o World Meteorological Organization. **41.10A:** Reprinted by permission from Macmillan Publishers Ltd.: *Nature.* From N. Myers et al. 2000. Biodiversity hotspots for conservation priorities. Vol. 403: 853–858, figure 1, copyright 2000. DOI: 10.1038/35002501. **41.11A** Adapted from http://disc.sci.gsfc.nasa.gov/education-and-outreach/additional/science-focus/ocean-color/papagayo.shtml. **41.12A:** Used with permission of Yellowstone to Yukon Conservation Initiative, Canmore, Alberta (www.y2y.net) © 2013.

Index

Note: The letter *f* indicates a figure appears on the page. The letter *t* indicates a table. Bold format indicates key term appears on the page.

INDEX

INDEX

INDEX

INDEX

INDEX

INDEX

INDEX